A History of Icelandic Literature

Histories of Scandinavian Literature

Sven H. Rossel, General Editor

VOLUME 5

A History of Icelandic Literature

Edited by Daisy Neijmann

Published by
the University of
Nebraska Press,
Lincoln & London,
in cooperation
with The American-
Scandinavian Foundation

Publication of this book was
assisted by grants from the
National Endowment for
the Humanities, the
National Endowment for
the Arts, and from the Fund
for the Promotion of
Icelandic Literature.

Library of Congress
Cataloging-in-
Publication Data
A history of Icelandic
literature / edited by
Daisy Neijmann.
p. cm. — (Histories of
Scandinavian literature ;
v. 5)
Includes bibliographical
references and index.
ISBN-13: 978-0-8032-3346-1
(cloth : alk. paper)
ISBN-10: 0-8032-3346-9
(cloth : alk. paper)
1. Icelandic literature —
History and criticism. I.
Neijmann, Daisy L., 1963–
II. American-Scandinavian
Foundation.
PT7154.H57 2006
839′.6909 — dc22
2006021625

Contents

Acknowledgments /vii

Introduction /ix

Maps /xiii

1. The Middle Ages /1
Vésteinn Ólason and Sverrir Tómasson

Old Icelandic Poetry (*Ólason*) /1

Old Icelandic Prose (*Tómasson*) /64

2. From Reformation to Enlightenment /174
Margrét Eggertsdóttir

3. From Romanticism to Realism /251
Þórir Óskarsson

4. From Realism to Neoromanticism /308
Guðni Elísson

5. Realism and Revolt: Between the
World Wars /357
Jón Yngvi Jóhannsson

6. Icelandic Prose Literature, 1940–2000 /404
Ástráður Eysteinsson and Úlfhildur Dagsdóttir
Icelandic Prose Literature, 1940–1980 (*Eysteinsson*) /404
Icelandic Prose Literature, 1980–2000 (*Eysteinsson and Dagsdóttir*) /438

7. Icelandic Poetry since 1940 /471
Eysteinn Þorvaldsson

8. Searching for Herself: Female Experience and
Female Tradition in Icelandic Literature /503
Helga Kress

9. Icelandic Theater /552
Árni Ibsen and Hávar Sigurjónsson
Icelandic Theater, 1790–1975 (*Ibsen*) /552
Icelandic Theater since 1975 (*Sigurjónsson*) /571

10. Icelandic Children's Literature, 1780–2000
/586
Silja Aðalsteinsdóttir

11. Icelandic Canadian Literature /608
Daisy Neijmann

Bibliography /643
Contributors /699
Index /703

Acknowledgments

This project has been realized against all odds. It was started a long time ago and then abandoned for many years, until Helga Kress from the University of Iceland made me aware of it and suggested that I explore the possibility of taking it on. I am very grateful to her for her suggestion and her encouragement. I am also very grateful to the Fund for the Promotion of Icelandic Literature for its financial support in the form of a grant.

It is never easy to revive a project, neither for the editor nor for the contributors, especially a project that lay dormant for so long and that has involved so many people. I extend my sincere thanks to all those who have granted me their cooperation, goodwill, and trust. Ástráður Eysteinsson has been particularly helpful and supportive throughout the editorial process, for which I owe him a debt of gratitude. I am also very grateful to the staff at the University of Nebraska Press for their friendly assistance and their patience as well as to Dan Ross and Sven Rossel, both of whom have been exceptionally supportive, helpful, and kind. The press's freelance copyeditor Joe Brown did a fine job editing the text, and I am also grateful for his good work.

Expertise in the various areas of Icelandic literature, particularly after the Middle Ages, remains largely located in Iceland as yet, and this in some cases necessitated the assistance of translators. Translating academic prose is by no means an easy task. I extend thanks to Joe Allard from the University of Essex and Alison Tartt from WordWorks for their efforts as well as to Rory McTurk for his poetry translations in chapter 4. Special thanks must go to Gunnþórunn Guðmundsdóttir at the University of Iceland, who took on the remaining bulk of the translations when no one else would, and whose comments, constructive criticism, and moral support throughout have been invaluable.

I am grateful to Catherine D'Alton from the Department of Geography at University College London for the maps of Iceland included in this book.

Finally, I would like to express my heartfelt gratitude to Alison Finlay, Richard Perkins, Matthew Driscoll, Richard North, Rory McTurk, and Mark Berge, who were all generous enough to donate some of their very valuable time to read individual chapters and provide important information and suggestions for improvement.

Introduction

Literary histories of the Icelandic Middle Ages have been fairly readily and consistently available in the English language. The same cannot be said for histories of Icelandic literature that include the postmedieval period. Stefán Einarsson's 1957 *History of Icelandic Literature* has been virtually the sole resource in this respect, and, despite its undisputed value for everyone interested in learning more about Icelandic literature beyond the sagas and the Eddas, it has long been both out of date and out of print. This fact is revealing of what has shaped the position and study of Icelandic literature, no less than the literature itself, to a considerable extent. Postmedieval Icelandic literature has had to live and develop "in the shadow of the sagas," as the contemporary author Thor Vilhjálmsson once called it in an article for the *Times Literary Supplement* (10 September 1971, 1093). Whereas Old Icelandic prose and poetry have enjoyed both scholarly and general interest and recognition, there long remained a perception that what happened afterward was of little consequence. Situated on the periphery of Europe, and with a population of less than 300,000, Iceland has traditionally occupied a position even more marginal than that of the other Scandinavian countries in the European cultural consciousness, where it remained stuck in the Middle Ages. Nor was this perception entirely without foundation: socially and economically, Iceland was long out of sync with the rest of Europe as its society remained resolutely rural and virtually untouched by modernity. While this created unusual conditions that importantly shaped the nature, development, and dissemination of Icelandic culture, it should be emphasized that, culturally, Iceland has, throughout its history, neither been isolated nor remained untouched by currents and ideas holding sway elsewhere in Europe. Iceland was part of the Danish realm from the end of the fourteenth century until 1944, when full independence was achieved, and Copenhagen was the cultural center for Icelanders during those centuries. Those with the social status and financial support would go to study at the University of Copenhagen, bringing back new ideas and fashions.

Like the cultures of other countries, that of Iceland has been both inward and outward looking, adapting new ideas and perspectives to its own situation. Not until recently, however, has this fact translated into changed scholarly approaches and perceptions. During Iceland's long struggle for independence during the nineteenth and early twentieth century, its literary heritage, which had remained a living tradition in part thanks to the fact that the language spoken by the common people had remained largely unchanged, became a powerful weapon, testimony to Iceland's cultural distinctiveness. Nationalist scholars emphasized Iceland's uniqueness, playing down, if not ignoring altogether, the links with and influences from other cultures. During the last several decades, however, a sea change has taken place. Following its rather sudden and drastic "leap" into the modern world, Iceland has recently called attention to itself as a nation and a culture fully abreast of current developments — and not infrequently ahead of them. Halldór Laxness, Iceland's twentieth-century Nobel Prize–winning author, has fully secured his place in world literature, his works now widely and generally available in translation, while younger authors like Einar Már Guðmundsson and Hallgrímur Helgason are also commanding attention in the international literary arena. At the same time, new generations of Icelandic scholars are reassessing traditional views of Icelandic literature, subjecting it to new approaches, and examining aspects that had previously been ignored.

Such profound changes clearly called for a new history of Icelandic literature, and the five-volume work on the histories of the Scandinavian literatures undertaken by the University of Nebraska Press provided the perfect opportunity. Although the project had to be put on hold for several years and incurred a long delay, the initial efforts of the previous editor, Patricia Conroy, were the inspiration for a new history of Icelandic literature in Icelandic — the five-volume *Íslensk bókmenntasaga* (1992–2006) — while the current volume aims to fill the gap for those unable to read Icelandic. The authors, all experts and fully versed in contemporary ideas, are in many cases representative of the changed and diverse views of Icelandic literature, including much that was previously excluded, and bringing a fresh, international perspective to their area of discussion. Readers may, nevertheless, detect a remaining thread of cultural nationalism, at least in some cases.

Like many "small" countries producing literature in "small" languages across our globalized world, Iceland finds itself in a defensive, if not threatened, position with regard to the preservation of its language and culture. This concern is both general and real in contemporary Iceland and affects author and scholar alike.

The editorial policy for this volume has been the same as that for the series in general and has allowed for methodological and stylistic pluralism to reflect the diversity of current Icelandic scholarship. Authors were, nevertheless, strongly encouraged to view authors and works in a larger sociocultural and ideological context, both national and international, and always to keep the general reader's interest in mind and make their chapters above all clear and informative. The international status of Old Icelandic literature posed certain problems in this respect, however. Whereas postmedieval Icelandic literature is largely unknown and the main thrust of its presentation can, thus, be informative, Old Icelandic literature has its own scholarly tradition within the English-speaking world, which means that a reader may be looking for different kinds of information, such as the history of different critical approaches or a history of the reception of certain works. While a literary history such as this could never hope to provide a survey of that scope, the discussion of Old Icelandic literature in this volume does reflect this.

In the present volume, Icelandic orthography has been retained, and the spelling of Icelandic names has not been Anglicized, except in those cases (confined to Old Icelandic) where a name has a tradition in English. For reasons of user-friendliness, however, the Icelandic convention of using first names has been abandoned, and authors are listed by their last name in references and in the bibliography, with the exception of medieval authors, where the general convention of going by first name has been followed.

Literary histories cannot avoid the problems and shortcomings inherent in the process of selection and exclusion or those of the ultimate artificiality of labeling and periodization, but they can, and should, foreground them. Authors were given the freedom to make their own selections based, first, on the needs of the reader and, second, on their own expertise in the field and choice of methodology. Most contributors display a keen awareness of these issues and address them in their discussions. Literature is a living and fluid entity, and one movement seldom "ends" conveniently where another is perceived to have its inception. Similarly, certain authors are discussed in several chapters because their careers span more than one period, because their work was (re)discovered at a later time, or because they contributed to more than one genre or movement. To facilitate usage, internal references have been included throughout the volume. Authors may also reappear in one of the four chapters that have been included to introduce the reader to areas of Icelandic literature that traditionally have often been overlooked: women's literature; theater; children's literature; and emigrant literature. Rather than emphazing their exclusivity and/or precluding their inclusion in the mainstream literary tradition, their discussion in separate chapters is meant to allow the opportunity to view authors, works, and ideas on their own terms, from a different critical perspective, and from within the framework of their own individual tradition instead of from canonical margins.

The size of this final volume in the series may seem incongruous in relation to the size of the country, as compared to that of the other Scandinavian countries. It should not, however, surprise anybody even slightly familiar with Icelandic literature. Quite aside from Iceland's medieval contribution, on which subject alone many volumes larger than the current one have been written, literature has constituted the country's main, and for part of its history virtually the only, form of cultural expression. As has often been pointed out, Iceland lacks the museums filled with works of art from previous centuries and the imposing buildings and castles from times past that are found in most other Western capitals. Until the twentieth century, a musical or visual arts tradition in the general European sense was almost entirely absent. Iceland's monuments are its literature, its cultural heritage is the written word.

Recently, there has been a remarkable upsurge in the interest in things Icelandic, not least in its literature. Most of Halldór Laxness's major works are, again, in print and available in English translation, and increasingly so are those of other contemporary authors. I feel safe in saying that it is the hope of all who have contributed to this volume that it will help promote this interest and the knowledge of Icelandic literature outside Iceland as well as assisting the inclusion of the various aspects of Icelandic literature in the increasingly numerous comparative studies of literatures across national and linguistic boundaries.

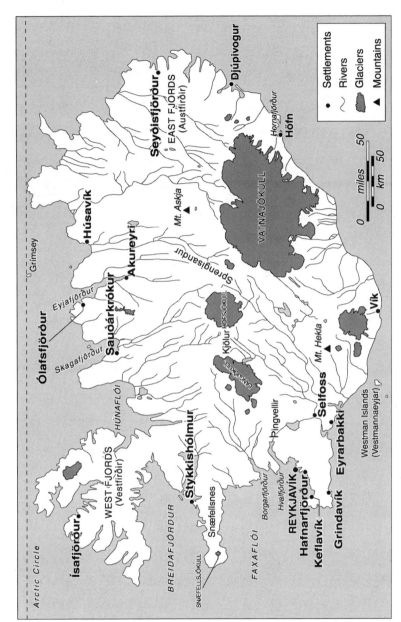

Map 1. Iceland

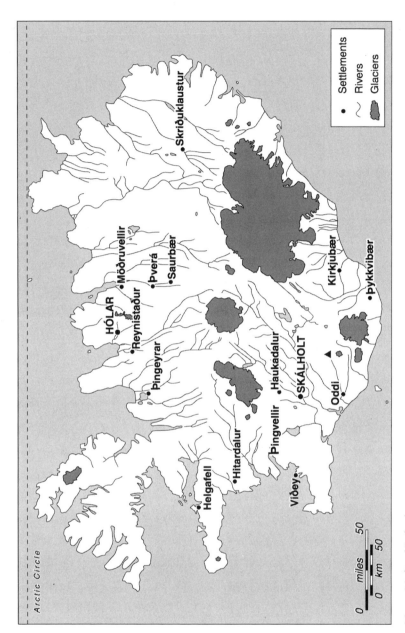

Map 2. Medieval Iceland

A History of Icelandic Literature

The Middle Ages

Vésteinn Ólason
and Sverrir Tómasson

1

Old Icelandic Poetry: *Vésteinn Ólason*

HISTORICAL BACKGROUND

Iceland was settled between ca. AD 870 and ca. AD 930 by people predominantly of Norwegian origin. Many of the settlers had come to Iceland after living for a time in the Scandinavian colonies of the British Isles, and Celtic influence is evident in personal names and place-names. Although there is historical as well as genetic evidence that a substantial percentage of the original settlers were of Celtic origin, the dominant social elite was Norse in language and culture. While they obviously had to take along some cattle and rudimentary equipment for the kind of farming they expected to do in the new country, no less important were the ideas and ideologies dominant in the places of origin at the time of settlement. The most important ideas were those that were embedded in their traditions, in their religion and customs, and in their poetry and tales.

The Scandinavian countries and the Scandinavian settlements in the British Isles were converted to Christianity during the tenth and eleventh centuries, with the Icelanders formally accepting the Christian faith at the

Note on the text: This text was originally drafted in English by the author, but it was thoroughly edited by Patricia Conroy, for which he owes her a debt of gratitude, in particular for the translations of quotations, which are hers, excepting the quotations from Eddic poetry. James E. Knirk read the text in an early version and Gísli Sigurðsson in a late one, and both made valuable suggestions toward its improvement. Direct quotations from Old Icelandic poetry are from the standard editions listed in the bibliography and appear here with normalized Icelandic spelling and Modern Icelandic orthography; thus, ö stands for ø and ǫ, while æ stands both for æ and for œ.

General Assembly or Althing in the year 1000. The new religion was to have a revolutionary effect on Icelandic secular society as well as on religious beliefs and institutions. Despite the decision at the Althing, people did not empty their minds of pagan ideas all at once: the understanding and reception of Christianity was, no doubt, conditioned by previous habits of mind; and, in society at large, some pagan ideas and institutions were eradicated completely, while others were only modified.

The earliest extant documents written in Iceland in the vernacular date from the second half of the twelfth century. After Iceland's adoption of Christianity, some of the most important chieftains in the country had sent their sons to England or the Continent to be educated in clerical institutions. Once the first Icelandic bishop had been appointed in 1056 and the church began to organize itself in the country, the education of clerics was quickly established on the basis of the learning introduced by the church.

Iceland differed from its neighboring countries in that it had no king or any other centralized authority or public executive power; it was, instead, an unstable federation of chieftaincies accepting a common law and a common system of courts. The status of the church in Iceland was different as well. Since Icelandic literature, too, was unlike any other European literature of the High Middle Ages, it is only natural to assume that there was a connection between the particular social and religious aspects of society and the unique character of the literature that it produced.

The old social and ethical order that obtained in Iceland between the time of settlement and the Norwegian hegemony, established in 1262, held freemen to a stringent code of heroic conduct. In the absence of public executive power, men of all social ranks had to be responsible for their own safety and might often have to risk their lives when their family's interests and honor, or those of the family of their chieftain, were at stake. The heroic tenor of Icelandic society coexisted with a literary culture brought about by the church. The flowering of that literary culture was the product of a fortunate cooperation of a national church, which brought learning to the country, and a ruling class that accepted the church and its learning eagerly without giving up its respect and love for traditional culture, even if much of it was pagan in origin. The result of this cooperation can best be evaluated by taking a closer look at the literature itself.

It is impossible to know how much of the literature of medieval Iceland was actually based on traditions brought by the settlers. By the time these traditions were written down, they had been adapted and re-created by Icelanders for over two centuries, under the influence, not only of the social structure, history, and natural surroundings of Iceland itself, but also of the poetry and legends that reached the country through its foreign trade and through the church and its clergy. Comparative historical analysis has revealed that Iceland's literature has numerous links with the Germanic past — not only with the early Viking Age (beginning about 800), but also with the Migration Period (ca. 400–600). In this remote island with its harsh natural conditions, a remarkable amount of poetry was preserved orally; and, owing to an unusual alliance between the church and a native ruling class, much of oral tradition came to be recorded.

Old Icelandic poetry is by far the richest source preserving the pre-Christian mythology of the Germanic peoples as well as their heroic legends. Obviously, the information that these poems yield bears most directly on the mythology and religion of the Icelanders and other Norsemen, but comparative studies show that Norse religion shares its roots with the pre-Christian mythology of other Germanic peoples and is similar even to the religions of more remotely related cultures of Indo-European descent in several ways. The heroic lays of the *Poetic Edda* — a collection of poetry preserved in an Old Icelandic manuscript that scholars in the seventeenth century named *Sæmundar Edda* (Sæmundur's Edda), incorrectly attributing it to Sæmundur the Wise (see p. 60) — record more fully than any other source the characteristics of a relatively homogeneous Germanic poetic culture that is also evident in such works as the Old English *Beowulf*, the Old High German *Hildebrandslied*, and the Middle High German *Nibelungenlied*. Legendary rulers from the Migration Period, such as Ermanaric, king of the Ostrogoths (d. 375), Attila, king of the Huns (d. 453), and Theoderic, king of the Ostrogoths (d. 526), presented as contemporaries in a remote past, work out their disastrous conflicts of pride and ambition, love and jealousy, in the sturdy verse lines of Eddic poetry, where the same metrical principles apply as in the poetry of other Germanic peoples. In addition to heroic legends, the *Poetic Edda* contains poems based on mythological lore and gnomic wisdom and composed in the same meters as the heroic lays.

POETIC FORM

The metrical form of narrative poetry about gods and heroes, as well as of didactic poetry, seems to have been the same all over the Germanic world: a line in which there are four strong beats and in which certain stressed syllables alliterate with each other. It should be noted that, apart from stress, syllable quantity plays a role in the structure of the verse. The alliterative four-stress line is divided by a medial caesura into two half lines or short lines. The alliteration falls on the third stressed syllable (i.e., the first stressed syllable in the second half line), called the *head stave* (*höfuðstafr*), which alliterates with one or both of the stressed syllables of the first half line, thus creating one or two *stuðlar* ("props" or "supports"). Another, related meter where the stanza is only four lines (six short lines) and lines 2 and 4 have only two props but no head stave and no caesura (see below) is known only from Old Norse. Old Icelandic poetry in these two meters is referred to as *Eddic poetry*.

Eddic poems differ from *Beowulf* and the *Hildebrandslied* by being stanzaic. The most common Eddic meter is called *fornyrðislag* (old epic meter), in which the stanzas have eight short lines (for practical reasons, each pair of lines is here presented as a long line with a caesura), that is, four alliterating pairs, which can be divided into two half stanzas (*vísuhelmingar*):

Ár var alda, || þar er Ymir byggði:
vara sandr né sær || né svalar unnir.
Jörð fannsk æva || né upphiminn:
gap var ginnunga || en gras hvergi.
("Völuspá," st. 3)

Young were the years when Ymir made his settlement,
there was no sand nor sea nor cool waves;
earth was nowhere nor the sky above,
chaos yawned, grass was there nowhere.
(*Poetic Edda*, trans. Larrington, 4)

In this example, the first head stave is the *y* in *Ymir*, showing that the first stress in a line need not fall on the first word, and the prop alliteration is carried by the initial vowels in *Ár* and *alda*. The next pair of half lines is linked by alliteration on *s*, the head stave being *svalar* and the props *sandr* and *sær*. There are no strict rules governing the number and distribution of unstressed syllables, although they commonly number two or three in a short line, depending on the quantity of the stressed syllables; however, the occasional practice of regularly adding one or two unstressed syllables to the *fornyrðislag* line is called *málaháttur* (speech meter).

Another common Eddic meter is *ljóðaháttur* (chant meter), most frequently used in dialogue or gnomic poetry. Each stanza is divided into two halves, each half consisting of one pair of half lines linked by alliteration as in *fornyrðislag*, plus a somewhat longer line with three (occasionally only two) stressed syllables and its own internal alliteration:

Ungr var ek forðum || fór ek einn saman;
þá varð ek villr vega;
auðigr þóttumk || er ek annan fann;
maðr er manns gaman.
("Hávamál," st. 47)

I was young once, I travelled alone,
then I found myself going astray;
rich I thought myself when I found someone else,
for man is the joy of man.
(*Poetic Edda*, trans. Larrington, 47)

In the first half stanza, the pair of half lines is marked by alliteration on vowels, *u* and *ei*, while, in the third line, the alliteration is on *v*. In the second half stanza, the half lines alliterate on vowels again, *auðigr* and *annan*. The alliteration in the long line is on *m*.

Although the typical *fornyrðislag* stanza consists of eight half lines, stanzas may vary in length from four to twelve lines. The free distribution of stressed syllables coupled with the alliteration of important words makes the lines of Eddic poetry very different from those of modern verse: instead of modifying and regularizing the rhythm of the spoken language, as most verse of later times does, the Eddic meters exaggerate it and make it more staccato.

Not all Old Icelandic literature concerned itself with mythological or legendary figures or themes; the poets and storytellers of Iceland followed events in the rest of Scandinavia with keen interest, composing new works about contemporary matters. Icelandic professional poets, called *skalds*, traveled among the courts of Scandinavian kings and noblemen, composing and performing verse in praise of their hosts. This type of praise poetry had been composed in Norway before the settlement of Iceland, but, in time, Icelandic skalds came to monopolize the function of court poet in Scandinavia, and the sagas also tell of their visits to the courts of kings and earls in the British Isles. Skaldic verse demands of its practitioners the skillful use of an intricate metrics and a highly conventionalized style, and it also assumes the poet's familiarity with a vast amount of traditional lore — mythological, heroic, and historical. The existence of this class of Icelandic professional court poets may be one of the reasons why traditional poetry was preserved in Iceland longer than in other places, and the perseverance of traditional poetry may also have influenced the development of uniquely Icelandic forms of oral narrative in prose. In contrast to the narrative mode of Eddic poetry, skaldic poetry is mainly in a lyric mode. The skalds do not link the events they describe; rather, they dwell on isolated moments or phenomena, in an attempt to render a subjective response, strong emotions such as admiration of bravery or splendor, the terror of battles and birds of prey, and also, in the case of more personal poetry, feelings of love or hate, joy or sorrow.

The more intricate forms of line and stanza used in skaldic poetry seem to have been an indigenous Norse development, although the possibility of Irish influence cannot be excluded. Whatever their origins, the skaldic verse forms depart radically from earlier Eddic traditions, being much more bound by rules with regard to rhythm, number and quantity of syllables per line, alliteration, and rhyme. The heavy internal rhyming and alliteration within the six-syllable, three-stressed line of the common skaldic meter called *dróttkvætt* (court meter) make it much more ponderous and difficult to enjoy than the Eddic meters and nigh impossible to translate metrically:

> Fullöflug lét fjalla
> framm haf-Sleipni þramma
> Hildr; en Hropts of gildar
> hjalmelda mar felldu.

> The very strong valkyrie of the mountains [giantess] made Odin's horse
> of the sea [ship] lumber forth; and Hroptr's [Odin's] players of
> helmet fires [warriors] felled her steed.

In this half stanza from Úlfur Uggason's "Húsdrápa" (House lay), describing a scene from Baldur's funeral, two out of three stressed syllables in the first line alliterate on *f*, and the second line is linked to the first by the head stave in *framm*. In the odd lines of an entire *dróttkvætt* stanza (1, 3, 5, 7) there is assonant rhyme on consonants (e.g., *full-* and *fjall-* in the first line), while in the even lines (2, 4, 6, 8) there are full rhymes (e.g., *framm* and *þramm-* in the second). In its use of disharmonious and even cacophonous effects, skaldic verse at times resembles modernist poetry.

Eddic and skaldic verse differ, not only in meter, but also in style. Eddic word order and sentence structure are relatively straightforward. Eddic diction is marked by the use of *heiti*, nouns used only in verse. *Heiti* may be archaic words that survive only in poetic use (e.g., the English *swain* for "young man"); they may be metonyms (e.g., words like *surf*, *wave*, or *tide* used to mean "ocean"); or they may be common words that have different meanings in poetry (e.g., English *maid*). Eddic verse also uses special names for the gods: Odin may be called Sigföður (father of victory), Valföður (father of those slain in battle), Grímnir (masked or helmeted one) or Gangleri (traveler). Usually more concrete than abstract, Eddic verse also makes limited but effective use of metaphoric language. Its most striking characteristic is the economy of language. In an Eddic poem a long journey or fierce battle may be treated effectively in one stanza. The one Eddic technique that appears to modern readers to be generous or even wasteful of words is the series of varied appositives, a technique found throughout Germanic epic verse and used texturally to sharpen focus or, indeed, to freeze the flow of events for a moment. The four-beat alliterative meter allows the Eddic poet easily to emphasize important words and concepts, and it imparts to the poetry an unmistakable dignity that coexists with simplicity of sentence structure and laconism of style.

Skaldic verse, on the other hand, is characterized by the interweaving of sentences and by complicated and often obscure imagery. It is marked by the use of a paraphrastic device, the kenning, or compound poetic name (e.g., *baugbroti*, "breaker of rings," to refer to a leader or chieftain who is assumed to demonstrate generosity by distributing gold among his followers). Originally, the kennings were permeated by allusions to pagan mythology, and, although such allusions never disappeared, the advent of Christianity changed the style considerably. The main skaldic forms later on became the vehicle of Christian religious themes, and it was not until the late Middle Ages that Icelandic religious poetry adopted meters with end rhyme and easy rhythms common in Christian poetry throughout Europe.

EDDIC POETRY

Most of the Eddic poetry that has come down to us is preserved in a small, unpretentious vellum manuscript, the Codex Regius (King's book), so-called because, after its discovery in seventeenth-century Iceland, then a part of the kingdom of Denmark, it was donated to the king and remained for three centuries one of the jewels of the manuscript collection in the Royal Library in Copenhagen. In 1971, when Iceland had been an independent republic for a quarter of a century, the Danish government restored the Codex Regius to Iceland as part of the first shipment of approximately eighteen hundred Icelandic manuscripts from Danish collections to be handed over to the University of Iceland. The manuscript was produced in Iceland in the second half of the thirteenth century, copied from older manuscripts from the period 1200–1240 that have since been lost. These lost manuscripts are commonly considered to have been Icelandic too, although the oral origins of some of the poems may lie elsewhere. A few of the poems and individual stanzas are found in other Icelandic manuscripts. In the seventeenth century the collection was given the name *Edda* by scholars who connected it with the Edda of Snorri Sturluson (1178–1241), a work also known in English as the *Prose Edda* (see also pp. 151–58). While the expression *Poetic Edda* refers to the collection of poetry in the Codex Regius, scholars also apply the label *Eddic* to several poems in Eddic meters found only in manuscripts produced somewhat later than the Codex Regius.

There is no doubt that most of the Eddic poems were recorded from oral tradition. With the exception of "Völuspá" (The seeress's prophecy), which has come down to us in three seemingly independent versions, we have only one manuscript version of each poem, and, thus, we lack sufficient evidence from which to construct a notion of the character and history of the oral tradition behind the manuscript texts. Theories about the nature of oral transmission that have been formulated in the study of other oral cultures can be consulted for what they may have to tell us about the prehistory of Eddic poetry. The Eddic lays are relatively short, and, although they contain a considerable number of formulaic expressions, there is also great variation in structure and style from one poem or group of poems to another. Moreover, there are numerous expressions that seem to be unique to the places where they are found. Consequently, it is not very likely that the Eddic lays were composed in performance at the time of their recording in the same way as Parry and Lord propose for the Homeric and South Slavic epic poems (on Parry and Lord, see, e.g., Foley).

On the other hand, skepticism about the relevance of a radical "oral theory" to Eddic poetry should not lead to the uncritical acceptance of a literary model for its origin and transmission. The idea that each poem was composed by a certain poet at a particular time and subsequently transmitted with only small, accidental changes down to the time of recording is untenable. Not only must a practicable theory of the prehistory of Eddic poetry do justice to the variety within the corpus and to the unmistakable individuality of many poems, but it must also take into account the creativity within the conventions of a culture that preserved great amounts of anonymous traditional material. Here, the position will be taken that the narrative structure and verbal expression of an individual poem must in principle be dated to the thirteenth century, when it was written down, although the myths and legends on which it is based are clearly much older. It must, however, be considered very likely that some Eddic poems have been preserved so well from the time of composition, which happened long before they were written down, that the thirteenth-century texts give a tolerably good impression of the conceptions and style of composition of poets of the Viking Age.

With regard to those epic poems, or lays, considered to have originated in the Viking Age (ca. 800–1066), it is difficult, if not impossible, to find criteria for whether they may have led a previous existence as verbally constructed unities, not in Iceland, where they were recorded, but in Norway, the British Isles, or elsewhere. When scholars have surmised, for example, that "Völuspá" was composed in Iceland and "Hávamál" (Sayings of the High One) in Norway, they have often based their arguments on the descriptions of natural and social phenomena found in the poems. But these arguments are superficial and unconvincing, for both poems were without doubt composed by people whose knowledge of the world extended beyond their own native places. The traditional wisdom cataloged in "Hávamál" cannot have been the product of one individual mind or generation. When a poem is considered late and even literary, as is "Alvíssmál" (All-wise's sayings), for instance, the likelihood of Icelandic composition is overwhelming. In the discussion that follows, however, the likely place of a poem's composition is not of importance. What makes Eddic poetry part of Icelandic literary history is the fact that it was a living part of the cultural heritage of the Icelanders during the first centuries they lived in the country.

Because Eddic poetry is anonymous and most of it is relatively easy to understand, it may reasonably be considered popular poetry. But some of the poems, not least some of the heroic lays, seem to be inscribed with the worldview of the ruling class in Viking Age society. There are close ties between skaldic and Eddic poetry because in their kennings skalds often refer to myths and legends told in Eddic poetry and the same code of heroic conduct informs both heroic lays and court verse. Within the corpus of Eddic poetry itself tastes and attitudes vary, and in some cases this variation is most clearly explained with reference to social setting. The mythological lays have their roots in religion, but in their preserved form they are not likely to have been ritual songs, although performance in a ritual context in pagan times should not be excluded. The narrative is comic as often as it is tragic, and the poems were probably used for entertainment as well as instruction at all levels of society.

Dialogue is a prominent feature in most of the Eddic lays, and some poems consist exclusively of direct speech, sometimes connected with short narrative passages or commentary in prose. In dialogue poems it is not always easy to decide who speaks, and the scribe of the Codex Regius has sometimes systematically added marginal notes indicating who speaks in each stanza in the same way that contemporary Continental scribes marked the texts of works intended for dramatic performance. It has been proposed that such poems were presented as drama by people impersonating the various characters.

Mythological Poetry

The Codex Regius contains ten mythological lays, while three others are preserved elsewhere. These poems vary greatly in structure. "Þrymskviða" (Þrymur's poem) and "Rígsþula" (List of Ríg) use a mixture of dialogue and objective narrative to tell a single coherent tale. "Skírnismál" (Skírnir's journey) also tells a single tale, but presents it through dialogue only, apart from a short prose introduction and brief explanatory comments in prose. Some of the poems make use of frame stories that provide an occasion for question-and-answer contests concerning mythological lore, including "Vafþrúðnismál" (Vafþrúðnir's sayings), "Grímnismál" (Grímnir's sayings), and "Alvíssmál." Other poems stage dramatic encounters that illustrate the nature of individual gods or other mythological figures who refer to various myths in their dialogues: "Hárbarðsljóð" (Hárbarður's song) and "Lokasenna" (Loki's flyting). "Völuspá" stands apart because it encompasses cosmology, creation, and eschatology. Many of these lays have a didactic element, while didacticism dominates "Hávamál," which is probably a late compilation of various wisdom poems of different ages and origins.

Elements of pagan Scandinavian mythology are found in a variety of sources, but the idea we have of it as a coherent view of the world is mainly based on three poems, "Völuspá," "Vafþrúðnismál," and "Grímnismál," that were also among the sources for Snorri Sturluson's systematic presentation of the mythology in his *Prose Edda* (see p. 155).

"Völuspá" is a poem of great contrasts in style and theme. It presents a vision of the beginning and the end of the world in the form of a monologue in which the seeress addresses an audience of humans and gods, including Odin, and describes her knowledge of the past and a vision of the future of the gods and the cosmos. She tells how Odin and his brothers create the world, making a cosmos out of chaos, and how Odin and his kin go to live in Ásgarður. Ásgarður is threatened by giants from without and by the moral shortcomings of the gods within. The one who seems to possess moral as well as physical perfection, Baldur, is killed by his brother through the scheming of Odin's evil foster brother, Loki. Though Loki is caught and bound, nothing can stop the apocalyptic battle of Ragnarök. The destruction of the world in Ragnarök is described in a dramatic sequence of stanzas (sts. 50–58). The gods are attacked by giants and monsters, and toward the end destruction seems to be complete:

Sól tér sortna, || sígr fold í mar,
hverfa af himni || heiðar stjörnur;
geisar eimi || við aldrnara,
leikr hár hiti || við himin sjalfan.
(st. 57)

The Sun turns black, earth sinks into the sea,
the bright stars vanish from the sky;
steam rises up in the conflagration,
a high flame plays against heaven itself.
(*Poetic Edda*, trans. Larrington, 11)

This is not the end of the universe, however. In a beautiful, almost lyric final movement, it is described how the earth is seen to rise cleansed from the sea; Baldur and a new generation of gods return to begin a happy life in a world populated by good people. The final stanza is obscure and has been interpreted variously. It may be a return to the frame situation, the seeress's speech, or simply a reminder that the new world, too, contains evil:

Þá kömr hinn dimmi || dreki fljúgandi,
naðr fránn neðan || frá Niðafjöllum;
berr sér í fjöðrum || —flýgr völl yfir—
Níðhöggr nái. || Nú mun hún sökkvask.
(st. 66)

There comes the dark dragon flying,
the shining serpent, up from the Dark-of-moon Hills;
Nidhogg flies over the plain, in his wings
he carries corpses; now she must sink down.
(*Poetic Edda*, trans. Larrington, 13)

In part, the dramatic effect of "Völuspá" stems from its subject matter, but it is also a result of the magnificent language and memorable images in which the seeress expresses her visions. She variously refers to herself in the first or third person, and this feature, as well as the use of refrains reminiscent of skaldic praise poems, enhances the strong feeling of presence evoked by the poem; it is neither a tale from a far past nor a vision of a distant future; it all takes place in a moment of performance and participation. Yggdrasill, the tree that mysteriously unites all parts of the universe and reflects the state of all things, shows us that, in the place created in the empty gap between ice and fire, human life is entwined with the existence of the gods and man and god share the same fate. Although the poem is tragic, it contains passages that express pure joy of life. There is no doubt that the point of departure for the "Völuspá" poet is ancient pagan myth, and some of the phraseology probably goes back to old Germanic poetry about the creation of the world. Most scholars, however, are agreed that "Völuspá" also reveals a knowledge of Christian ideas.

The influence of Christianity might account for some of the moralistic elements in the poem as well as for the strong sense of drama and the persuasive contrast between the doomed present world and its cleansed successor. But are we to believe that the poet was a devout pagan, fighting Christianity with the full power of imagination and verbal skill, or a Christian who composed a moral fable or allegory out of old material? There seems to be very little reason to accept the latter explanation. A medieval Christian is unlikely to have composed such an allegory without providing any direct clues to its correct interpretation. That said, however, no precise conclusion about the poet's knowledge of or attitude toward Christianity seems possible, especially in view of the probability that in its preserved form the poem has been modified by generations of Christians and that some elements are late additions. While it is obvious that by itself the poem is not a reliable source of knowledge about the pagan worldview, the main constituents of its cosmology and world history are, nevertheless, corroborated by other sources. "Vafþrúðnismál" knows of the return of life after Ragnarök, and Ragnarök itself is mentioned on numerous occasions in various sources. Although "Völuspá" was not composed as a Christian allegory, it may have survived and found its way onto vellum precisely because Christians could interpret it as a symbolic drama about the contest of good against evil, the end of the world, and the resurrection of man.

Two other poems take up themes from the divine tragedy narrated in "Völuspá." A short lay not found in the Codex Regius, "Baldrs draumar" (Baldur's dreams), makes use of a frame similar to that employed in "Völuspá" — here Odin awakens a dead seeress and forces her to tell him about the future death of Baldur. The other poem, "Lokasenna," also evokes a world shadowed by the approach of Ragnarök, but its tone is satiric, even farcical. Each of the gods is mocked in this lay, which is entirely made up of dialogue in *ljóðaháttur*. Loki addresses each of the gods, accusing them of promiscuity, incest, and cowardice, among other things, and reminding them of past humiliations and situations that have made them more vulnerable as Ragnarök draws near. Many of the accusations find confirmation in other lays and myths. The poem ends with Thor's driving Loki away with threats.

"Lokasenna" has frequently been understood as a Christian diatribe against the pagan gods, and classical models have been suggested. It is tempting, however, to see the poem, or the myth behind it, as connected with some kind of cathartic ritual. The Menippean satires might be a parallel rather than a model. In many heroic poems a *senna*, or flyting, belongs to the preparatory stages of a battle, and many of the accusations made by Loki point toward Ragnarök, where he is on the side of the forces who, at terrible cost to the gods, suffer defeat.

The mythological lays, with their abundance of names of places and phenomena in the worlds of gods and men, provide a poetic topography of the mythical universe. "Grímnismál" and "Vafþrúðnismál" are good examples of the poetry of names, and both are most likely based on ancient material. "Alvíssmál," on the other hand, which makes a system of name giving, is probably literary and late (twelfth or early thirteenth century) since many of its names seem to have been especially created for it. The poem demonstrates a vivid feeling for the poetic qualities of names as well as a splendid command of the *ljóðaháttur* measure.

The god Thor plays a major role in many of the Eddic poems. In "Alvíssmál" he is quite out of character, using guile instead of the enormous strength that characterizes him in a number of lays. Although he perishes in Ragnarök, he is not as closely connected with the fate of the world as Odin. In "Hárbarðsljóð" the two are engaged in a flyting and presented as opposites. Odin is more intelligent but dangerously amoral, while Thor seems to be more like an innocent and good-natured farmer. The dialogue is farcical, and it has even been suggested that it parodies flyting poetry. In any case it is a comedy, as is another lay about Thor, "Þrymskviða," in which a giant steals Thor's hammer and the strongest and most masculine of gods must dress up as a bride to retrieve it. Some scholars think that "Þrymskviða" was composed in the thirteenth century, while others believe it to have originated in the pagan past. Although solid arguments for either position are hard to find, comparative study indicates that the comic treatment of a god need not in itself rule out the possibility of a work's pagan origin. Still another humorous poem about Thor, "Hymiskviða" (Hymir's poem), combines elements from several myths, but the climax is Thor's attempt to catch Miðgarðsormur, the World Serpent. The poem is probably rather late in its present form, but there is no doubt about the authenticity of the mythological elements; the catching of the serpent is treated by a number of skalds from Bragi the Old (Bragi Boddason; early ninth century) on and depicted on stones in both Denmark and Sweden and possibly also England.

The family of Norse gods consisted of two groups that had originally been enemies. The Vanir are less prominent than the Æsir (Odin, Thor, etc.) in our sources, but there is no doubt that their cult was strong in many areas of Scandinavia. Foremost among them are the sea god Njörður and his children Freyr, the god of fertility, and Freyja, the goddess of love, war, and magic. "Skírnismál" tells how Freyr fell in love with a giant maiden who refused both offers of gold and threats of violence but was at last won over by the curses and threats that magic would be used against her. At the end of the poem Freyr is impatiently awaiting his union with the maiden, which is to take place in a grove named Barri. The poem has been interpreted as a fertility myth, as a social myth dealing with the problems of exogamy, and most recently as part of a myth explaining the origin of the Swedish-Norwegian dynasty. These interpretations are not mutually exclusive, but they do not account for the emotional power of the poem. The maiden is described with images of shining light, and the god is possessed by his love. The maiden resists threats of torture and gives in only when threatened with the most extreme sexual humiliation. Although the poem may have been less mysterious to the people of the Viking Age, the terrible force and cruelty of divine desire must have stricken them with awe.

"Rígsþula" may also be connected to the Vanir. It tells the tale of a god (Heimdallur, according to an introductory prose passage, although he acts more like Odin) wandering around among humans, going to bed with couples, and laying the foundations of a class-divided society with slaves, farmers, and aristocrats. It is found in a fourteenth-century manuscript of Snorri Sturluson's *Prose Edda*, although there is no clear indication that Snorri knew the poem, and some scholars have suggested that it is a learned construction from the thirteenth century. The poem is repetitive and for-mulaic, but the descriptions of the supposed forefathers are vivid and the differences between the classes clearly marked. The poet shows great inven-tiveness in his name giving. Several elements in the poem have been consid-ered to be of Celtic origin, which would support its claim to a background in the early oral tradition.

Didactic Poetry

There is a didactic element in many of the mythological lays, but nowhere is it as prominent as in "Hávamál," spoken by Odin, the "High One." As preserved, the poem is a written compilation based on older oral poetry. Until recently scholars thought that in large the poem was composed in pagan Norway, but its origins are probably mixed, and the learned Chris-tian compiler of the version that has come down to us may have been a poet in his own right. It has been maintained that the lonely wanderer who speaks reflects the rootlessness created by the Viking Age, but there is nothing about warfare in the poem, and, although there is much common wisdom of the kind also found in writings in medieval Latin, the emphasis in the poem is on practical and secular issues. The main moral message is that everyone must take care of himself first: there is nothing about loving your neighbor, let alone God.

The 164 stanzas of "Hávamál," mainly in *ljóðaháttur*, can be divided into several parts that differ in content and style. As it exists today, "Hávamál" seems to have been made up of several shorter poems, but it is not always easy to tell where one of these shorter pieces ends and the next one begins. The first seventy-seven or perhaps eighty stanzas constitute a gnomic or proverbial poem supposedly spoken by Odin but without any narrative or dramatic frame. The speaker reveals no divine wisdom but appears as a wise wanderer who has seen much of the world and whose theme is human relations and human happiness. He advocates caution and moderation in all situations. Loyalty to friends is essential, but one should also know one's enemies and be their enemy in turn. Wisdom is necessary, but too much wisdom does not make anyone happy. Although good health and a good life are the highest values, they are transitory; it is only fame that is immortal:

Deyr fé, ‖ deyja frændr,
deyr sjálfr it sama;
en orðstírr ‖ deyr aldregi
hveim er sér góðan getr.
(st. 77)

Cattle die, kinsmen die,
the self must also die;
but glory never dies
for the man who is able to achieve it.
(*Poetic Edda*, trans. Larrington, 24)

Although the ethics of the poem are self-centered and egotistical, humility is also in evidence, along with a genuine respect for life, even the life of the very poor.

The second and third poems of the compilation tell tales about Odin's erotic adventures; they are surrounded by loosely connected verse, often with an antifeminine bias. The first tale, in which Odin is cheated by a woman, may be late and literary in origin, but the story about his dealings with Gunnlöð, a giant's daughter with whom he slept and from whom he stole the "precious mead" (identified by Snorri Sturluson as the "mead of poetry"), is no doubt based on genuine myth.

Stanza 111 marks a break in the poem, indicating that, henceforth, it will deal with Odin's special knowledge. However, what immediately follows is another gnomic poem, of poorer quality than the first one.

Stanzas 138–41 are among the most interesting in the poem. Here, Odin describes how he acquired wisdom, runes, and magic through a symbolic sacrifice of himself to himself by hanging, wounding, and fasting. During his hanging for nine nights (and days), he visited the world of the dead. The pagan and shamanistic origin of this poetry can hardly be doubted. The description of the god's sudden intellectual growth as a result of the ordeals is poignantly phrased:

Þá nam ek fræðask || ok fróðr vera
ok vaxa ok vel hafask;
orð mér af orði || orðs leitaði,
verk mér af verki || verks leitaði.
(st. 141)

Then I began to quicken and be wise,
and to grow and to prosper;
one word found another word for me,
one deed found another deed for me.
(*Poetic Edda*, trans. Larrington, 34)

The poem ends with an enumeration of the magical chants known to Odin and with a declaration by him that his last poem will never be taught to anybody.

"Hávamál" contains some of the most frequently quoted stanzas in Old Norse poetry and is a unique source of information about the mentality of the Icelanders and the Norwegians in the Viking Age and the following centuries.

Legends with Mythological Overtones

There are a few Eddic poems that tell tales neither about gods nor about the usual type of human hero and seem to be based on legends rather than myths. The only one preserved in the Codex Regius is "Völundarkviða" (The lay of Völundur), and there it is placed among the mythological poems, although scholarship has defined it as heroic. It combines the fairy tale motif of the swan maiden and a Germanic version of an ancient legend about a fabulous smith, Wayland or Welent, known also from Old English and Old German sources. In a prose introduction, Völundur is said to be the king of the Lapps, while he and his brothers are described as hunters and craftsmen living in the forest with their swan maidens, who eventually leave them. Völundur is maimed and imprisoned on an island by an enemy king, but, after killing the king's two sons and getting his daughter pregnant, he flies away, presumably by means of a device of his own making. Although the poem as we have it is probably incomplete, it is strongly unified, and the poet's careful diction yields individual stanzas of striking beauty.

Völundur seems more akin to the shamans found in the *Kalevala* than to Germanic heroes. His craft, which enables him to fly in defiance of the laws of nature, makes him somewhat of a magician. Like Daedalus, he belongs to a category of famous smiths appearing in myths and legends that probably express the wonder aroused by early metallurgy in the cultures it was changing. The Old English poem "Deor" refers to the main events related in the second half of "Völundarkviða," and there seems to be some verbal correspondence between the two poems. An English casket from the eighth century or earlier, the Franks Casket, is engraved with pictures from the tale.

Also from the border area between heroic and mythological poetry is "Grottasöngr" (The song of Grotti), preserved only in two manuscripts of the *Prose Edda*. It tells of two giant maidens who are enslaved and forced to grind gold for the legendary Danish king Frodi. The maidens tell their story and describe their plight in picturesque stanzas and predict the fall of the king. The poem seems to be based on an old myth relating how the greed for gold causes the end of an early golden age of peace. The mill, as well as the smithy, is a powerful symbol of early means of cultivating natural products.

Another poem in Eddic meter that is not included in the Codex Regius and may, indeed, be of later date is "Svipdagsmál" (Svipdagur's poem) — itself made up of two parts, "Grógaldr" (The magic of Gró) and "Fjölsvinnsmál" (Fjolsvinnur's sayings). Found only in paper copies from the seventeenth century, the poem can, on the evidence of its style and language, hardly be later than the thirteenth century or possibly the early fourteenth. The first part of the poem tells of a young man under a spell from his stepmother who seeks advice from his dead mother and gets charms from her that protect him on his journey to the maiden he is to marry. The second part deals with a contest of question and answer in which the young man must prove himself before he is accepted by the maiden. This story, also told in the Danish ballad "Ungen Svejdal" (Young Svejdal), contains so many Celtic elements that it must have been brought from that quarter to the North, where it was re-created by an Icelandic poet drawing heavily on

Eddic tradition. The poem or its motifs may be connected in some way with initiation rites, and the maiden, Menglöð, is reminiscent of a goddess. However, Svipdagur himself is a typical fairy tale hero who succeeds through a woman's assistance and his own verbal skills. The union of the lovers in the end is beautifully described, and the poem would have been excellent entertainment at weddings.

Heroic Poetry

The drama and tragedy of what is left to us of the heroic poetry and legends of the Germanic peoples rise from the inhuman demands made on the heroes by their code of conduct. The only objective of a hero is honor, and the heroic quality of a man or a woman can be measured only in the face of death. Strength of will and integrity of character are the essential characteristics of a hero, and, thus, the poetry pays minimal attention to physical superiority, which is taken for granted. Strong female characters arouse admiration and awe no less than do male heroes.

Much of the subject matter of the heroic lays preserved in Iceland deals with characters from the Migration Period and evidently reached the North from more southern locations, primarily Germany. There is material that originated in mainland Scandinavia too, however, making clear references to the Viking Age, and often exhibiting supernatural motifs. The Icelandic tradition brought these separate strains together by making family and in-laws of all the major figures in the heroic lays. The heroic poems in the Codex Regius have been linked together with prose passages in an effort to organize the material and make it cohere. As far as can be judged, however, the "editor" of the Codex Regius recorded his sources faithfully and allowed the old poems to retain many of the repetitions and inconsistencies that arise when they are grouped together. The final phase of this merger was achieved in the thirteenth-century *Völsunga saga* (The saga of the Völsungar), a prose narrative that may be based on a collection of lays slightly older than the Codex Regius but closely related to it (see p. 147).

The heroes of "Helga kviða Hundingsbana" (The lay of Helgi Hunding's killer) I and II and "Helga kviða Hjörvarðssonar" (The lay of Helgi Hjörvarðsson) are not, as in the other heroic lays, Hunnish, Burgundian, or Gothic but Nordic. The common theme of the Helgi lays is the love between a warrior prince and a young woman who is a valkyrie. The story is tragic because the prince falls in battle and his beloved cannot go on living after his death. In all three lays, high points in the conflict are preceded by a coarse flyting, which serves as comic relief and a warming up for battle. "Helga kviða Hundingsbana" I, the best preserved of the Helgi lays, comes to an end before the prince's fall in battle. It is an eloquent and lofty poem whose emphasis is on the victorious prince and his happy love. Because its style is often reminiscent of skaldic praise poetry, it has been tentatively attributed to an eleventh-century skald. The two other Helgi lays are made up of a mixture of prose narration and dialogue in verse form. "Helga kviða Hjörvarðssonar" does not fully develop the tragic potential of its story, but the economy and pointed phrasing of some of the stanzas are noteworthy. The vulgarity of a flyting scene between a warrior and a giantess seems inconsistent with the rest of the poem. "Helga kviða Hundingsbana" II is the most uneven of the Helgi lays, but it contains some of the most memorable stanzas and scenes in Eddic poetry. Before he can marry his beloved Sigrún, Helgi must fight her family and ends up killing her father and all but one of her brothers. Sigrún persists in her love for Helgi in spite of this, and she fiercely curses her surviving brother after he kills Helgi in revenge. When Helgi appears to her after his death, she spends a night with him in his burial mound. Her praise of him after his death is expressed in exquisite epic similes:

"Svá bar Helgi ‖ af hildingum
sem ítrskapaðr ‖ askr af þyrni,
eða sá dýrkálfr ‖ döggu slunginn,
er öfri ferr öllum dýrum
ok horn glóa við himin sjalfan!"
(st. 38)

"So was Helgi beside the chieftains
like the bright-growing ash beside the thorn-bush
and the young stag, drenched in dew,
who surpasses all animals
and whose horns glow against the sky itself!"
(*Poetic Edda*, trans. Larrington, 139)

As is the case with "Helga kviða Hjörvarðssonar," parts of "Helga kviða Hundingsbana" II are mediocre and in dubious poetic taste. There is reason to believe that what has been edited under this title in the Codex Regius are, in fact, the remains of more than one poem.

According to the Codex Regius, Helgi Hunding's killer is the half brother of Sigurd the Dragon-slayer (see also p. 147), and poems about Sigurd follow the Helgi lays. The first of the Sigurd poems, "Grípisspá" (The prophecy of Grípir), is a prophecy in *fornyrðislag* about Sigurd's life. It is late, based on other Sigurd poems, and probably originally composed, not orally, but in writing. After "Grípisspá," a long section of the manuscript contains prose mixed with poetry, just as in two of the Helgi lays. It can be read as a kind of Legendary Saga with only the dialogue in verse, and editors have separated it into three lays named after Sigurd's speech partners — "Reginsmál" (The lay of Reginn), "Fáfnismál" (The lay of Fáfnir), and "Sigrdrífumál" (The lay of Sigrdrífa). These poems tell the story of how Sigurd avenges his father; kills the dragon Fáfnir and takes his treasure; kills Reginn, who intended to betray him; and then meets a valkyrie, Sigrdrífa, who, in a long final monologue, teaches him magic. Its supernatural themes and many didactic passages bring this section of the Edda closer to mythological poetry than do other heroic lays. Although there are some beautiful stanzas — particularly noteworthy is the tenderness expressed in the passage where Sigurd and Sigrdrífa meet-the verses overall do not give the impression of being part of a single composition, and they may, indeed, be relatively late or of differing ages and origins. Although a legend about Sigurd as a dragon killer and the owner of a treasure existed as part of an old Germanic heritage, this poetry does not indicate that the legend had a fixed form in the Norse tradition.

Not only do the Helgi lays and the poetry about Sigurd's youth contain mythological elements, but they also explore the interpenetrability of mythical and human realms. Valkyries are both semimythical beings and human princesses, humanized, in fact, by their love for their young men. In turn, because of the valkyries' love, young heroes are enabled to reach higher levels of potentiality and individuality. Thus, Helgi Hunding's killer is protected in battle, Helgi Hjörvarðsson receives his proper name, and Sigurd learns hidden wisdom. The extraordinary nature of this love is underlined by the extreme reaction of the valkyries to the deaths of their lovers. The poetic portrayal of love as a civilizing influence superseding family ties may be a Viking Age phenomenon. It may also be connected with the feminine point of view that is prominent in much of the Eddic heroic poetry (see pp. 509–10).

After "Sigrdrífumál," several leaves (eight of the original fifty-three) are missing from the Codex Regius, and what they might have contained can be reconstructed only with the help of *Völsunga saga*. The poems after the lacuna deal with the death of Sigurd and subsequent events. It is characteristic of this poetry that great events are mentioned only in passing and that the main emphasis is on the emotional reactions of the people involved, especially the women. An important feature of these poems, sometimes the structuring principle of a whole piece, is the flashback, usually in the form of a monologue by a suffering woman.

The first poem after the lacuna, "Brot af Sigurðarkviðu" (Fragment of a Sigurd lay), lacks its beginning, probably no more than a few stanzas. It has a few relatively archaic features and shows considerable economy of expression in its mixture of narration and direct speech. It does not give the impression of being old, however. The focus is domestic: Brynhildur, who has been duped by Sigurd into marrying Gunnar, the brother of Guðrún and Högni, forces her husband to attack Sigurd. The murder takes place offstage, and Högni, who has helped Gunnar, breaks the news to Guðrún, who is Sigurd's wife:

"Sundr höfum Sigurð || sverði högginn,
gnapir æ grár jór || yfir gram dauðum."
(st. 7)

"Sigurd we hacked into pieces with a sword,
the grey horse droops his head over the dead prince."
(*Poetic Edda*, trans. Larrington, 175)

Guðrún's sorrow and Brynhildur's gloating are effectively portrayed, whereupon the focus moves to a rather pathetic Gunnar. The poem ends with Brynhildur's revelation in a monologue of several stanzas that she lied to Gunnar in order to bring about revenge for her deception and hurt pride. Interest in the psychology of the characters is even more pronounced in "Sigurðarkviða skamma" (The short lay of Sigurd), which, at more than seventy stanzas, is, in fact, one of the longest lays. The poem tells the story from the moment Sigurd arrives at the court of Guðrún's father, but the main theme is Brynhildur's passion and conflicts. Brynhildur's initial youth and purity are emphasized, until Sigurd's betrayal transforms her; in the last half of the poem, Brynhildur dominates the stage and ends by having herself burned on Sigurd's pyre. The poem mixes narration and direct speech, and it ends with a long monologue in which Brynhildur predicts the fate of the other characters and prescribes the arrangements surrounding her own death. The text of the poem is well preserved and shows no clear signs of oral composition. It may well be a literary composition of the early thirteenth century.

The origins of seven short lays centered on the experience of female characters from the heroic legends have been a matter of much scholarly dispute. These lays have often been called *elegies* because many of them thematize the sorrow of bereft women and their main structural device is the flashback in monologue. They are, however, too structurally different from each other to qualify as a specific subgenre. Andreas Heusler (*Die altger-

manische Dichtung) considered these poems — "Helreið Brynhildar" (Brynhildur's ride to hell), "Guðrúnarkviða" (The lay of Guðrún) I, II, and III, "Oddrúnargrátr" (Oddrún's lament), and "Guðrúnarhvöt" (Guðrún's inciting) — to be of late origin, like "Sigurðarkviða skamma" and "Atlamál in grænlensku" (The Greenland lay of Atli), all products of an indigenous Icelandic development under the influence of oral sagas that had, Heusler thought, flourished in the eleventh century. Other scholars have pointed out similarities between these elegiac lays and the ballad genre, similarities that might in both cases be the result of influence from chivalric and religious literature, and such influence is, indeed, possible in Iceland from ca. 1200 on. Although the emotional and elegiac features of these seven poems may be taken as indicative of late composition, it should be kept in mind that elegy and exploration of emotion are prominent features in the other rich tradition of Germanic poetry that has come down to us, the Old English one.

"Guðrúnarkviða" II, structurally the most complex of these poems, the richest in narrative material, and probably the oldest, seems to be an attempt to reconcile different traditions about the life of the heroine. A striking feature of the poem is its description of ladies sitting and making tapestries, a scene common in both chivalric literature and ballads. In "Guðrúnarkviða" I, which is tightly constructed and literary in flavor, a number of women tell of their sorrows, but the climax is Guðrún's weeping and her final monologue, in which she laments Sigurd. The poem takes Guðrún's part against Brynhildur, who is portrayed as monstrous. In "Helreið Brynhildar," Brynhildur gets a chance to defend herself. "Guðrúnarkviða" III and "Oddrúnargrátr" are more balladic and more novelistic than the other elegiac poems. Heroines play an important role in most Eddic heroic lays, and it is likely that this poetry was popular among women. But in this group the feminine point of view is exceptionally strong, so it is possible that these works originated as women's poetry. None of them bears traces of a long life in oral tradition, and influence from chivalric literature is, indeed, most likely to have taken place about or after 1200. In the Legendary Sagas (*fornaldarsögur*; see pp. 145–51), there are a few poems in monologue spoken by men, but these are different in style and content from the so-called women's elegies: a hero looks back on his life at the hour of his death, and the resulting elegy tends to become a catalog of battles and ordeals.

The oldest of the ancient tragedies dealt with in Eddic poetry are the death of the Ostrogothic king Ermanaric, or Jörmunrek (d. AD 375), and the conflict between the Huns, whose most famous leader was Attila, or Atli (d. AD 474), and the Burgundian dynasty, whose most famous king was Gundaharius, son of Gibicha, or Gunnar Gjúkason, killed in a battle with the Huns in AD 437. The death of Ermanaric is referred to in very old skaldic poetry and dealt with at greater length in "Hamðismál" (The lay of Hamðir), a poem with many archaic features. The defeat of the Burgundians, a prominent theme in old Germanic poetry, is the subject of "Atlakviða" (The lay of Atli) and "Atlamál in grænlensku." In "Hlöðskviða" (The lay of Hlöð), a large number of names point back to the ancient history of the Goths and their battles in Central and Eastern Europe. These names, along with archaic stylistic features, have tempted scholars to search for historical events at the root of the narrative, but the results are highly speculative. Although the historical basis of the legends treated in these poems is slender indeed, they all embody a form of the Germanic heroic spirit so extreme that it has been suggested that one of them, "Hamðismál," may be a parody, a demonstration of the absurdity of the uncompromising demand for blood vengeance at any cost.

According to "Atlakviða," Guðrún, daughter of Gjúki, was married to King Atli after the death of her first husband, Sigurd. Her new husband invites her brothers, Gunnar and Högni, to a feast, captures them, and tries to force them to give him the Nibelungen treasure. When they refuse, he has them tortured and killed. In revenge, Guðrún kills her two sons by Atli, makes him eat their flesh and drink their blood, and afterward kills him and sets fire to his hall. "Atlakviða" is an aristocratic poem, honoring the dignity of kings and heroes in descriptions of magnificent halls, weapons, gold, and jewelry. Gunnar's sense of his own heroic stature is such that, despite a warning from his sister, he does not hesitate to risk his life, kingdom, and possessions by accepting Atli's invitation. One of the puzzling features of "Atlakviða" is that, in the narration of the brothers' fight to defend themselves, Högni kills eight people while Gunnar's feats are not mentioned. Gunnar ends his life playing a harp in a snake pit, having first ensured that his brother is killed before him. The greatest achievement of the poem is to deal with Guðrún's revenge in such a way that she appears, not as a monster, but as an impressive tragic figure. Nothing is done to reduce the horror of her deed, but the final stanza expresses a mixture of admiration and awe:

Fullrætt er um þetta; || ferr engi svá síðan
brúðr í brynju || bróðr at hefna.
Hún hefir þriggja || þjóðkonunga
banorð borit, || björt, áðr sylti.
(st. 44)

Now this story is all told; never since has a bride
in a byrnie acted so to avenge her brothers;
she brought death to three great kings,
that bright woman, before she died.
(*Poetic Edda*, trans. Larrington, 216)

"Atlakviða" is characterized by passionate concentration and speed. The characters are stylized in the extreme, delineated only through action and speech. For instance, we hear nothing about Guðrún's feelings when she kills her children, yet her address to Atli describing the deed leaves no doubt of her awareness of the dimensions of what she has done. The poem's narrative economy is such that images emphasizing the splendor and passion of its subject do not interfere with the speed at which the action unfolds. There is more variation in the length of the verse lines than in any other Eddic poem; the effects of the variation are often striking, although it is hard to tell when they may be the result of a deliberate artistic plan. It has been suggested that "Atlakviða" was composed by one of the poets of Haraldur Fairhair (d. ca. 930), and it does, indeed, seem a poem more likely than any other to have been the product of the cultural milieu that produced early skaldic praise poetry, the court of a Viking king. However, theories of such a great age for this poem have recently been contested (see Wolf's "Mythisch-heroische Überlieferungen").

"Atlamál in grænlensku," the longest of the heroic lays of the Edda, tells the same story as "Atlakviða," but it expresses a totally different worldview and artistic aspiration. The setting is rural and narrow, and the heroes are peasants. Ursula Dronke has pointed out that the treatment can be compared to many modern works in its attempt "not to render the legend mundane, but invest the everyday world with drama" (*The Poetic Edda*, 1:99). On the other hand, the amount of detail in the narration has been viewed by W. P. Ker in *Epic and Romance* as evidence that "Atlamál" was beginning to develop along the lines of an epic. The realistic, occasionally pedantic narration in no way mitigates the horror of the story, as, for instance, a scene in which Guðrún describes her plans to her sons before she kills them. Although "Atlamál" tells a coherent story in regular *málaháttur* meter and the poet shows a knowledge of older Eddic poems such as "Atlakviða," the rather prosaic style and peasant-like world of the poem makes it tempting to assume that the poet was familiar with prose sagas, in which case the poem must be very late and have been written down at the same time as or soon after it was composed. The issue is complicated by the fact that, in the Codex Regius, both "Atlakviða" and "Atlamál" are said to be "Greenlandic." As far as "Atlakviða" is concerned, most scholars have disregarded this, while it is not unlikely that the tradition on which these poems are based, if not the poems themselves, actually came to Iceland via Greenland.

One of the lays about the Gjúkungar family is "Hamðismál." Not so well preserved as "Atlakviða," it is more difficult to interpret because of its fragmentary state. Although the historical Ermanaric died approximately sixty years earlier than Gundaharius, son of Gibicha, the Edda makes him a son-in-law of Guðrún, daughter of Gjúki, and he is killed by her sons, Sörli and Hamðir, in revenge for their sister Svanhildur. Svanhildur was Ermanaric's wife, and he had her cruelly killed because he suspected her of infidelity. According to "Hamðismál," which differs from "Atlakviða" in this, Guðrún marries for the third time after killing Atli and in this marriage produces the two sons who are the protagonists of "Hamðismál." She eggs them on to avenge their sister, knowing that they will not come back. Although they blame her for sending them to certain death, they go and are killed. We find Guðrún's egging speech again at the beginning of another related poem, "Guðrúnarhvöt," an elegy in which Guðrún looks back on her tragic life at the hour of death.

An account by the medieval historian Jordanes on the origins and deeds of the Goths and the Huns shows that a legend about the death of Ermanaric containing many of the names and events found in "Hamðismál" was known by Germanic peoples as early as the sixth century. The legend is referred to in Bragi Boddason's "Ragnarsdrápa" (A poetic tribute to Ragnar), and it is, therefore, likely that it was well known in Norway in the ninth century. Most scholars believe that "Hamðismál" dates from that time, but recently it has been argued that the poem is very late and is to be interpreted as criticizing the ideology of revenge. It is most likely that the extant text is a mixture of very old and somewhat later elements.

"Hamðismál" has some fine stanzas that can compare with the best in "Atlakviða" and "Völundarkviða," although the text is corrupt. Its comments on the consequences of revenge at any cost do show an awareness of the absurdity of the blood feud when carried to extremes, and it is not unlikely that they are influenced by Christian ethics. The penultimate stanza, however, seems to confirm the fact that, in the milieu of the poem, the heroes, however far removed they are from everyday life, evoke admiration:

Vel höfum vit vegit, ‖ stöndum á val Gotna,
ofan eggmóðum ‖ sem ernir á kvisti,
Góðs höfum tírar fengit ‖ þótt skylim nú eða í gær deyja.
Kveld lifir maðr ekki ‖ eptir kvið norna.
(st. 30)

We have fought well, we stand on Goth corpses,
weary from the sword-edge like eagles on a branch;
we have won great glory if we die now or yesterday,
after the norns have given their verdict, no man outlasts the evening.
(*Poetic Edda*, trans. Larrington, 242)

With "Hamðismál" the Codex Regius comes to an end; all heroes and heroines are dead, and one-third of the last page is blank. Although this collection forms an impressive whole that has been composed by an editor in the thirteenth century, a few poems that are not part of the collection have been discussed here in accordance with scholarly tradition. Some poems and fragments incorporated into the Legendary Sagas also show so many affinities with the poems in the Codex Regius that it is natural to discuss them in the same context.

Eddic Verse in the Legendary Sagas

The mythic-heroic Legendary Sagas contain a considerable amount of Eddic verse in addition to the previously mentioned men's elegies. The heroic poem "Hlöðskviða" is found in a thirteenth-century Legendary Saga, *Heiðreks saga* (The saga of King Heiðrek). The poem is incomplete, the connections between the stanzas that are preserved being supplied in a prose commentary by the saga writer. The poem is full of ancient lore, and individual stanzas have the same kind of suggestive power as is found in other archaic Eddic lays. More epic in scope than the lays of the Codex Regius, "Hlöðskviða" describes a battle between two nations, the Goths and the Huns, in which thousands are killed, but the basic conflict is interpreted in ethical and personal, not political, terms. It is seen as stemming from the individual pride of the leaders of each army, and, because these leaders are half brothers, the poem conveys a powerful sense of tragedy.

There are in the Legendary Sagas a number of poetic fragments that, like "Hlöðskviða," must be older than the sagas in which they are preserved. "Bjarkamál" (The lay of Bjarki), which is preserved among legends about Danish kings, was translated into Latin by Saxo Grammaticus around 1200, and a few stanzas of the poem are preserved in Snorri's *Prose Edda*. "Dánaróðr Hildibrands" (Hildibrand's death song) in *Ásmundar saga kappabana* (The saga of Asmund the champion slayer) refers to persons and events described in the Old High German *Hildebrandslied*, and the early Legendary Sagas can, indeed, be seen as a continuation of the Germanic heroic tradition. The harshness of the old lays rapidly softened after their inclusion in prose literature, and the resulting poetry is often beautiful and even sentimental, as, for instance, in a poem called "Dánaróðr Hjálmars" (Hjálmar's death song), preserved in *Örvar-Odds saga* (The saga of Arrow-Oddur; see p. 148) and *Heiðreks saga*, both probably composed in the thirteenth century.

Although Eddic poetry shares two important characteristics with folk poetry — anonymity and origins in oral tradition — much of it was undoubtedly composed among a social and intellectual elite, as mentioned above. This applies particularly to the heroic lays as well as to poems like "Völuspá" and "Hávamál." There are, however, a few examples of poetry of a more popular kind, such as the comic stanzas referring to an ancient phallic cult that are found in *Völsaþáttr* (The tale of Völsi). The riddles collected in "Gátur Gestumblinda" (The riddles of Gestumblindi) in *Heiðreks saga* contain miniature pictures from nature and the daily life of common people. Some of these are genuine folk riddles, although they have been given poetic form by a practiced poet; some have parallels in the riddles of other countries; and a number have been found in the later Icelandic folk tradition.

The impossibility of making a clear separation between Eddic poetry, often accompanied by short prose passages in the Codex Regius, and the *prosimetrum* (mixture of prose and verse) of the early Legendary Saga is the kind of difficulty that comes about whenever we consider the birth of a literary tradition from its parent oral culture. The dialectics of oral versus written are at work in the entire corpus of early Icelandic poetry.

SKALDIC POETRY

Court Poetry

There are many kinds of secular skaldic poetry, but for the sake of convenience I shall here divide them into two main categories, court poetry and personal poetry. Court poetry was composed for princes and other rulers and includes, in addition to laudatory verse, genealogical and mythological poetry. Personal poetry consists mainly of single stanzas, *lausavísur* (sg. *-vísa*; "loose verse"), but does include several longer poems or fragments of such poems. It treats such themes as fights and travels, love and grief, and ranges in tone from the mocking of an enemy to the celebration of the art of poetry. The preservation of skaldic poetry is to a large extent accidental; that is, it has been preserved because it was either quoted as source material or incorporated for other reasons in sagas more or less historical in nature or because it was used as an example in treatises on poetics. A large proportion is ascribed to named poets, but this information is often unreliable. The arrangement of stanzas into poems is frequently the work of modern editors and should in such cases be accepted only as hypothetical. The normalized texts found in most editions are established usually by a conflation of texts from more than one manuscript and sometimes even by conjecture based on emendation of the manuscript record.

In one of the manuscripts of the *Prose Edda*, and in one manuscript of *Heimskringla* (see p. 101), there is preserved a catalog of skalds or court poets, *Skáldatal*, that is arranged chronologically according to the kings and other magnates praised by the poets. First mentioned is Ragnar Loðbrók (Hairy-Leg), the legendary ninth-century Danish Viking king; his skald is Bragi Boddason, often called Bragi the Old. More than twenty stanzas or half stanzas are ascribed to Bragi in the *Prose Edda*; one of them is explicitly said to be from his "Ragnarsdrápa," although most of these stanzas are generally thought to belong to this poem. Scholars agree that, while "Ragnarsdrápa" is most likely very old, it is doubtful that the Ragnar addressed there is, in fact, Ragnar Loðbrók. Several other early Danish or Swedish kings, along with their skalds, are mentioned in *Skáldatal*, but no other poetry has been preserved that praises either Danish or Swedish kings before the Golden Age of Icelandic court poetry, about AD 1000. There is much stronger evidence for the practice of praise poetry in the skaldic style at the courts of Norwegian kings from the time of Haraldur Fairhair on. Haraldur's skalds were Norwegian, but after his rule the only Norwegian court skald we know of is Eyvindur skáldaspillir (the plagiarist), who praised King Hákon the Good (d. 960) and Earl Hákon of Hlaðir (d. 995) in the last decades of the tenth century. It may be that there was a great quantity of work by Norwegian skalds that has simply not survived, but, according to what has come down to us, Icelanders dominated court poetry from the late tenth century on.

The skald or "scop" had his place among Germanic peoples long before the Viking Age, either as a visitor or as a retainer at the royal court. The skalds were respected for their art, and, although lavish praise was well received by kings, there were some skalds who dared to criticize their king or praise his enemies. Skalds retained their importance into the twelfth century, but by then complaints of an ungenerous reception and competition from "low" entertainers like jugglers and clowns begin to appear. Norwegian kings accepted praise poems from Icelandic nobles throughout the thirteenth century, but perhaps for reasons of diplomacy rather than any appreciation of the art of the skald. By that time skalds such as Snorri Sturluson and Sturla Þórðarson (1214–84) were also historiographers and wrote sagas about the kings (see pp. 84, 101, 120). Praise poetry had a function in these sagas as the testimony of contemporary witnesses to events.

Since secular skaldic poetry is preserved almost exclusively in the form of quotations in prose works, the context should always be taken into consideration. Most court poetry is preserved in the Kings' Sagas (*konungasögur*), while numerous examples of both court poetry and personal poetry are preserved in the *Prose Edda* and in a treatise on rhetoric, *Málskrúðsfræði*, written by Snorri's nephew Ólafur Þórðarson (d. 1259), himself a court poet. A considerable amount of personal poetry is quoted in the Sagas of Icelanders (*Íslendingasögur*) and other sagas with Icelandic themes, such as the Bishops' Sagas (*biskupasögur*) and contemporary sagas (see part two of this chapter). It is usually difficult to establish a good text for skaldic verse. Not only is there always the possibility that the verse was already corrupt when it was first recorded, but scribes of later centuries often misunderstood and rearranged what was already a difficult text. Manuscript sources usually ascribe certain poems to named poets and occasions. In the nineteenth century and the early twentieth, these datings were usually accepted by scholars. A more critical attitude has since been taken. There is no doubt that the style and diction of skaldic verse began their development in pagan times, and a good deal of the poetry ascribed to the early skalds shows its pagan origins sufficiently clearly to rule out composition by Christian skalds of later times. Scholars are willing to accept that the mythological poetry and much of the praise poetry in the Kings' Sagas is traditional and that what the sagas tell us about the context of composition can be used to date the poems correctly. Much of the skaldic verse in the Sagas of Icelanders — some of it court poetry, but most of it personal poetry — is more commonly thought to have been composed later than reported, even by the saga writers themselves. Sometimes linguistic criteria can be applied, and in some cases Christian influence is obvious. There are, however, no clear lines between what scholars can agree to be old and authentic and what they suspect to be falsely ascribed to skalds of the tenth and eleventh centuries.

A combination of intricate meter and complicated style characterizes skaldic verse from its earliest extant examples. Although there are a few anomalies in the rhyme schemes of Bragi Boddason's *dróttkvætt* when it is compared to the norm followed by later poets, the forms as well as the diction are fully developed in verse ascribed to the poets of Haraldur Fairhair around 900, and it is, thus, most likely that the development of the form took place at the courts of Norwegian petty kings in the ninth century. As pointed out by Hallvard Lie in the 1950s (see the essays reprinted in his *Om sagakunst og skaldskap*), there are definite affinities with the ornate style of visual art during the period, which distorts and defamiliarizes traditional motifs, although it is not easy to say exactly how these arts could have influenced each other or what habits of mind could have informed them.

There are several points of likeness to Irish verse from this period, and the question of Celtic influence has occupied scholars for more than a century. It would be tempting to connect the rise of court poetry with the growth of the dynasty of the kings of Viken in eastern Norway, who eventually conquered the whole country. The wealth and culture of this dynasty before the days of Haraldur Fairhair is witnessed by archaeological evidence, such as the magnificent finds from Vestfold, including the Oseberg and Gokstad ships. It is, therefore, remarkable that the settlers of Iceland, who usually came from western and southwestern Norway, sometimes actually fleeing the usurpation of their rights by ambitious kings, were so well versed in the art of the skald that their descendants became leading court poets. Southwestern Norway had early contacts with the British Isles, and an origin of skaldic poetry in that part of Norway, as well as its strong position in Iceland, would harmonize well with the Celtic theory.

There were two types of praise poem, the *drápa* (pl. *drápur*) and the *flokkur* (pl. *flokkar*). The word *drápa* must be derived from *drepa*, "to strike." A *drápa* had three sections, the middle one divided into subsections with a refrain (*stef*), and was considered more prestigious than the *flokkur*; it eventually became the only form used for the praise of kings. Although skalds used several stanza forms, the "court measure," *dróttkvætt*, was by far the most common for *drápa* and *flokkur* alike. The word *flokkur* means "group"; the name implies that there are no formal rules of composition above the stanza level. It is revealing in another sense too: praise poetry is usually rather incoherent. Although full of narrative material, skaldic poetry treats events in a lyric manner as a sequence of isolated incidents, more often than not connected only by one main actor, the recipient of the poem.

A particularized setting is rare. Instead, the skalds usually operate with stock settings. One of these is the battlefield with fighting men, showers of arrows and ringing weapons, masses of corpses and animals of prey (with slight modifications, the battlefield theme can also be used for encounters at sea). Another stock setting is the prince's banquet hall with drinking, the giving of gifts, and the reciting of poetry. These contrasting scenes have parallels in the world of the gods, where the *einherjar* (champions) in Odin's retinue go out and fight every day and come back to Valhalla for feasting and drinking in the evening, rising from the dead if they have fallen in battle during the day. These parallels are constantly reinforced by imagery alluding to martial gods, to goddesses and valkyries carrying drinks to the warriors, to the elements of the battle scene, and, last but not least, to the divine origin of poetry.

Compared with the poetics of the Eddic tradition and the Germanic tradition as a whole, skaldic poetics is distinguished by four unique features: (1) The lines of the most frequently used meters are longer than the short lines of Eddic verse, and they have a fixed number of syllables. (2) Each line has internal rhyme, and very early on it becomes the rule that lines 2, 4, 6, and 8 have full rhymes and the odd lines consonantal rhymes only. (3) The poets avoid using common words for the most frequently mentioned subjects, using instead words meant only for poetry, *heiti*, or paraphrases with at least two components, the kennings, frequently with mythological allusions. (4) Word order is extremely free, and the familiar features of spoken language are avoided through inversions and convolutions involving two or more sentences.

Of all the striking features of skaldic poetry, the kenning is the most complex. Many kennings, but not all, have a metaphoric component, for example, *unda gjalfr* ("sea of wounds," or "blood"). Because each component of a kenning can itself be replaced by a whole kenning, the resulting extended figures must be translated in order to make any sense within the sentence, for example, *unda gjalfrs eldi* ("fire of the sea of wounds," or "sword"). The effect often seems deliberately chaotic; in any case, it creates a remarkable contrast to the strict regularity of meter. Mythological allusions add a special dimension to this poetry and create the feeling that the worlds of gods and men are parallel: "the goddess of the goblet" is woman, "the Thor of the ship" is man. With Christianity this way of thinking became obsolete, if not heretical, and mythological kennings gradually developed into "dead," or arbitrary, signs, while some poets avoided them altogether.

Modern students of skaldic poetry have often been astonished by its complexity and asked whether the audience in a prince's hall could possibly have understood the poems while they were being recited. Here, the words of the great modern poet T. S. Eliot apply: "Genuine poetry can communicate before it is understood" (*Selected Essays*, 200). The sound and fury of battle poetry, for instance, must have got through to the audience even when not every detail was immediately put in its right place for the decoding of the message. Skaldic poetry is made difficult by a special use of language, and one must assume that one of its pleasures for its audience was the satisfaction of cracking the code, even the feeling that one belonged to an exclusive group with access to sacred and secret messages. There is a curious contrast between the monotony of the content of skaldic poetry once the message has been decoded and the endless variety of its expression, a variety that obviously generates messages around and above the primary one. This contrast is natural: a sign system dealing with an infinitely varied world must be economical, but the sign system of skaldic poetry deals with a maximally stylized, simplified, and closed world and can, therefore, afford an almost unparalleled amount of variety and redundancy.

The creation of kennings is also based on systems; thus, the idea of gold as a fire or light that is not extinguished in water provides the basis for innumerable kennings with fire as one component and liquid as the other, for example, "bonfire of the Rhine" or "river fire." And gold (either the word itself or as a kenning) is, in turn, a frequent component of kennings; a woman is a goddess of gold (because of her gold rings or bracelets), whereas a king or a chieftain is a breaker or squanderer of gold (because of his generosity). The audience, experienced in skaldic poetry, knows basically what to expect, and the purpose of the skald's artistry is at the same time to satisfy their expectations and to surprise them with new combinations. Moreover, the distortions of syntax, extreme as they may seem, also follow certain patterns and rules. A qualified audience may, therefore, have understood much of a skaldic poem on first hearing. Additional pleasure was derived from learning poems by heart and thinking them over detail by detail until their complex messages had been decoded and the artistry of the skald revealed.

Among the oldest extant examples of skaldic poetry that have come down to us, we find descriptions of pictures of shield ornaments or other decorations that depict mythological beings or scenes. Two early shield poems from the ninth century, "Ragnarsdrápa" by Bragi Boddason and "Haustlöng" (Autumn-long) by Þjóðólfur from Hvinir-both preserved in the *Prose Edda*—contain mythological as well as heroic motifs, such as Thor's fishing expedition to catch the World Serpent, the rape of the goddess Iðunn, and the slaying of Ermanaric. Both poets make use of an archaic and complicated manner of creating kennings with great distortions of syntax. Bragi's images can strike one as wooden, but their disjointed stiffness nevertheless makes a strong impression. "Haustlöng" is somewhat more relaxed, and this allows for the play of humor. Its most impressive stanzas, however — those describing Thor's ride in his wagon to meet the giant Hrungnir — are unsurpassed in forceful aural and visual imagery and seem to express religious awe.

Mythological poems by two Icelandic skalds of the tenth century have also come down to us. In the *Prose Edda*, one whole stanza and eleven half stanzas, attributed to one Úlfur Uggason, all seem to be from his "Hússdrápa," a poem that is reported to have been composed about pictures decorating the hall of Ólafur pá (Peacock), whose story is told in *Laxdæla saga* (The saga of the Laxdælir). Someone named Ólafur is addressed, whatever his identity, and there can be no doubt of the pagan origin of this fragment. In imagery basically similar to Bragi's but more metaphoric in style, Thor is portrayed as he catches the World Serpent. There is also a glimpse of a fight between Loki and Heimdallur about which little else is known and a detailed description of Baldur's funeral that is the basis for Snorri's description of this event.

Somewhat unlike other mythological poems, and with no indications that it is ekphrastic in nature, is "Þórsdrápa" (A poetic tribute to Thor; late tenth century) by Eilífur Guðrúnarson, which is considered one of the most difficult skaldic poems. It is as if the skald is stretching to its limits the creation of far-fetched, even ridiculous, kennings, especially about Thor himself. At the same time the poet often plays consciously on the connotations — not least the sexual connotations — of the individual elements of his kennings and succeeds in conveying a complex message. The poem tells the story of Thor's journey to the giant Geirröð, a myth with many components that has been interpreted as the young god's initiation ordeal. In addition to the main conflict with the giant, the poem exhibits a great preoccupation with female forces. Because "Þórsdrápa" has a comic touch, the suggestion has been made that it is a parody, but there are no convincing arguments for this theory.

Constituting a distinct subgenre of skaldic poetry are the genealogical poems in *kviðuháttur* meter. The stanza consists of eight short lines of, alternately, three and four syllables, and enjambment across strophes is not uncommon. Þjóðólfur's "Ynglingatal" (List of the Ynglingar dynasty), supposedly from the late ninth century and tracing the genealogy of the kin of Haraldur Fairhair from the gods down through the Swedish dynasty of the Ynglingar, is the most archaic and interesting of these poems. Its descriptions of the deaths of individual kings often verge on the grotesque. "Ynglingatal" may not be as old as sources maintain, but attempts to date it to the twelfth century are not convincing. It was used by Snorri Sturluson as a source for *Ynglinga saga* (see pp. 105–7). "Háleygjatal" (List of the chieftains of Hálogaland) is traditionally dated to the tenth century and seen as an imitation of "Ynglingatal," connecting the earls of Hlaðir in Norway with Odin. In the Icelandic "Noregskonungatal" (List of the kings of Norway) from ca. 1200, which forms a continuation of "Ynglingatal," the dynasty of Haraldur Fairhair is traced down from his father to King Sverrir (d. 1202), concluding with a final section connecting the Icelandic Oddaverjar family and its great chieftain, Jón Loftsson, Snorri Sturluson's foster father, to this kin.

While the composition of praise poetry about princes may have begun earlier, the oldest extant fragments are from works composed by the poets of the court of Haraldur Fairhair. Indeed, "Glymdrápa" ([The] clangor poem), attributed to Þorbjörn hornklofi (Horn-cleaver), sets the standard for this poetry in content as well as diction for the duration of its practice. Only a fragment is preserved, and, therefore, we cannot know whether the poem was a regular *drápa*, although this seems likely.

Drápur by Icelandic court poets of the tenth century are only fragmentarily preserved, with the exception of "Höfuðlausn" (Head-ransom) by Egill Skallagrímsson (ca. 910–990), the authenticity of which has been called into question. This *drápa* — composed, according to *Egils saga*, in one night — devotes twenty stanzas in the end-rhymed meter *runhent* to a freely flowing, pleasant-sounding encomium of King Eirik Blood-ax (d. 954), who was holding Egill captive in York at the time. With a variety of simple kennings it praises Eirik in the most general of terms. For several reasons it has been suggested that the poem is a twelfth-century composition: it is absent from one of the most important manuscripts of *Egils saga*; its end-rhymed meter is unlikely to have been developed as early as the tenth century; and it presents some post-tenth-century linguistic traits.

The most impressive and genuinely pagan praise poetry by Icelandic skalds that has come down to us was composed by Einar skálaglamm (Goblet-ringer) and Hallfreður Óttarsson vandræðaskáld (the troublesome poet) about Earl Hákon of Hlaðir. Considerable sections of Einar's "Vellekla" (Lack of gold) are preserved. In the introduction the skald addresses the king and his court and asks them to listen to his poetry. Through the kennings expressing this message, images of the harsh viking life at sea are evoked, and the nature of poetry as a divine gift is emphasized. As the poem continues, Hákon's victories in battle and his struggle to uphold the cult of the Æsir are eulogized, and the kennings reveal a belief in the divine nature of kingship. Hákon is described as the representative and defender of the gods and is seen in especially close relationship to Thor.

The identification of Earl Hákon with divine powers is taken a step further by Hallfreður. Nine *dróttkvætt* half stanzas of his "Hákonardrápa" (A poetic tribute to Hákon) are preserved in the *Prose Edda*, and four of them are devoted to an extended metaphor: the basic statement is that Hákon has conquered Norway and become its ruler, but the conquest is described in terms of a love affair. The kennings refer to Odin's union with Jörð (Earth), from which, according to one myth, Thor was born, and they also emphasize the special relation between sacral kingship and the forces of nature:

Sannyrðum spenr sverða
snarr þiggjandi viggjar
barrhaddaða byrjar
biðkván und sik Þriðja.

With true words of swords, the keen owner of the horses of the breeze
[ships] clasps under him the barley-haired waiting wife of Thridi
[wife of Odin, i.e., Earth].

It can hardly be doubted that such imagery must have pleased the earl, who
was a notorious womanizer and a fervent worshipper of the Æsir. The
coordination of the kennings to form two or more parallel strata of reference through an extended metaphor in which several kennings and verbs
work together is a method that, absent in other examples of the oldest
Norwegian court poetry, can be found in *kviðuháttur* poems. It became
popular among the best Icelandic poets, and, according to Snorri Sturluson, it is called a *nýgerving* (novelty), although it never ousted the apparently older style of creating kennings with totally different connotations,
which Snorri calls *nykrat* (monstrous, mixed).

The advent of Christianity necessarily posed a threat to skalds like Hallfreður who believed in the mythical origin of their art and based the most
important element of their diction on references to myths. The survival of
Icelandic court poetry at the courts of the militant missionaries Ólafur
Tryggvason (d. 1000) and Ólafur Haraldsson (Saint Olaf; d. 1030) is a
testament to the strength of the institution of court poetry and the profes-
sional skill of its great craftsmen. Hallfreður himself is a prime example.
Only a few years after he composed his inspired heathen *drápa* about
Hákon, he was converted to Christianity and became the court poet of
Ólafur Tryggvason. A considerable amount of his praise poetry about
Ólafur is preserved in the form of occasional stanzas and the fragments of
two *drápur*.

Hallfreður's stanzas show that his conversion was not easy. Hallfreður
says that it is hard to begin to hate Frigg's husband (Odin) and that he has
been forced to pray to God instead of to Freyja's kin. Although his rejection
of mythological kennings meant that he never again attained the brilliant
metaphoric style of "Hákonardrápa," he succeeds in forging his own imagery, and his poetry becomes much more personal, beautifully expressing his
devotion to King Ólafur. In "Erfidrápa" (Memorial poem), composed after
Ólafur's death, he uses hyperbole effectively to articulate his grief: "All the
countries of the North lie waste after the death of the king; all peace is
disturbed after the fall of the brave son of Tryggvi." Along with Egill

Skallagrímsson, Hallfreður is unique among skaldic poets in expressing personal grief and revealing personal religious conflict.

If Hallfreður cleared the way for a new kind of court poetry acceptable to Christian princes, the position of the Christian skalds was strengthened by Sighvatur Þórðarson (ca. 995–1045), the skald of Saint Olaf and his son Magnús the Good (d. 1047). Sighvatur seems to have left Iceland as a young man to join Olaf and soon became an honored member of his court. When Olaf was killed, Sighvatur was on a pilgrimage to Rome, but he later joined Olaf's son Magnús and became his teacher in the art of government.

Sighvatur avoids mythological references; his kennings are generally simple and easily understood, but he is a master of the art of intertwining sentences and has absolute command of his meters. Most of his poetry is in *dróttkvætt*, but in "Knúts drápa," which he composed in praise of the Danish-English King Canute (d. 1035), he uses *töglag*, a meter with only four syllables in each short line that nonetheless incorporates the same demands of alliteration and rhyme as does *dróttkvætt*. A great deal of Sighvatur's poetry consists of conventional enumerations of battles and conquests, at some of which he was probably not even present. But, in addition to several elegant occasional stanzas, his travelogue "Austrfararvísur" (Verses about an Eastern journey) and the admonitory poem "Bersöglisvísur" (Outspoken verses) substantiate his claim to excellence. "Austrfararvísur" is a loosely connected sequence of stanzas describing in a humorous vein the adventures of Sighvatur and his companions on a diplomatic mission to Götland in Sweden on behalf of Saint Olaf. The *drótt* (king's retinue) is addressed in the opening lines, and no doubt the poem was composed to entertain the king and his men. The poet describes the Swedish peasants with a mixture of humor and condescension, but he is capable of taking a humorous look at himself too. At the same time, his self-confidence and pride are well expressed in a stanza in which he responds to a woman who has noted his black eyes. Incidentally, this stanza marks the first appearance of the adjective *íslenzkr*, "Icelandic":

Oss hafa augun þessi
íslenzk, konan, vísat
brattan stíg at baugi
björtum langt en svörtu;
sjá hefr, mjöð-Nannan, manni
mínn ókunnar þínum
fótr á fornar brautir
fulldrengila gengit.

These black Icelandic eyes, woman, have shown us far along the steep
    path to the shining ring; this foot of mine, Mead-Goddess, has
    walked quite boldly on ancient roads, unknown to your man.

After the death of Saint Olaf, Norway was ruled by Danes until the
Norwegian chieftains rebelled and summoned Magnús, Olaf's young son,
to ascend the throne. Some of these particular chieftains had also taken part
in the rebellion against Saint Olaf, and Magnús, still in his teens, began to
think of revenge on them, despite the fact that they had become his own
supporters. Sighvatur then took it on himself to speak openly to the king
about the dangers involved. In "Bersöglisvísur" he analyzes the political
situation in which King Magnús finds himself and advises him to be moderate in the use of power and to keep up good relations with his chieftains. At
the end of the poem Sighvatur explains that, although he prefers to stay
with Magnús, he will leave him if he does not mend his ways. This poem is a
refreshing contrast to all the flattery of conventional court poetry.

Sighvatur's best stanza, composed after he had heard about the death of
his beloved Olaf, closely connects the king with his country, and the skald
uses natural imagery to express his state of mind in a way that has more in
common with modern poetry than with the poetry of his pagan predecessors:

Há þótti mér hlæja
höll of Noreg allan,
fyrr vark kenndr á knörrum,
klif meðan Ólafr lifði;
nú þykkir mér miklu,
mitt stríð er svá, hlíðir,
jöfrs hylli varðk alla,
óblíðari síðan.

The high inclined cliffs seemed to me to be laughing throughout all of
    Norway — I was formerly known on ships — while Olaf was alive;
    now the slopes seem to me — such is my grief — much less blithe; I
    got all the favor of the prince.

There is no space here to discuss the court poetry of the great number of
skalds who were Sighvatur's contemporaries and successors. Remarkable
for his brilliant, if somewhat superficial, style and for the introduction of the
hrynhent meter into court poetry was Arnór Þórðarson jarlaskáld (Earl-
poet; eleventh century). He composed poems about the earls of Orkney
and the Norwegian kings Magnús the Good and Haraldur Sigurðarson
Hard-ruler (d. 1066). Best known is his *hrynhent drápa* on Magnús that,

with its eight-syllable lines and trochaic rhythm (probably modeled on rhythms frequent in Latin hymns while at the same time retaining the conventional use of internal rhyme and alliteration), marks a departure from the sturdy *dróttkvætt* style. Although the poem is reported to have been a success with his contemporaries, Arnór continued to use *dróttkvætt* in most of his work. Perhaps he found *hrynhent*'s easy rhythms somehow undignified or insufficiently expressive of his expertise.

Icelanders continued to praise and no doubt exaggerate killings and burnings and other deeds or misdeeds of kings and their warriors as long as the kings were prepared to lend an ear. In the twelfth century, however, interest seems to have started dwindling in Denmark and even in Norway, although the craft of the skald enjoyed popularity in Orkney during the reign of Earl Rögnvaldur kali (d. 1158), who was born in Norway and was himself an excellent skald. Around 1200, Icelanders seem to have sent written poems to kings and other nobles in Norway, and, in the thirteenth century, Sturla Þórðarson composed poems to adorn the sagas that he was commissioned to write about the Norwegian kings Hákon Hákonarson (d. 1263) and Magnús Law-mender (d. 1280; see p. 120).

During the twelfth and thirteenth centuries skaldic poetry increasingly became a learned activity dealing with heroes of the past such as the legendary Danish Viking fraternity called Jómsvíkingar, whose adventures are described in *Jómsvíkinga saga* (see p. 114), or famous kings like Ólafur Tryggvason. A skald about whom we know little, Haukur Valdísarson (probably late twelfth century), composed an "Íslendingadrápa" enumerating among Icelandic champions the protagonists of certain sagas. This native lore was combined with a broader type of learning when the Icelander Hallur Þorarinsson (twelfth century) and Earl Rögnvaldur kali composed their *Háttalykill*, a *clavis metrica* (catalog of meters) demonstrating examples of a great number of meters and stanza forms and employing themes from heroic legend. The *clavis metrica* form was later used for *Háttatal* (List of verse forms), composed by Snorri Sturluson in praise of King Hákon of Norway and Earl (later Duke) Skúli, and later included with commentary in the *Prose Edda* (see pp. 152–57). The tendency to treat legendary themes as well as the systematic interest in metrics and style that characterize twelfth- and thirteenth-century skaldic poetry are a result of more widespread literacy and an increased knowledge of medieval poetics and rhetoric. There is reason to believe that the systematic study of traditional poetry and its stylistic and metrical devices forms the background for the court poetry of the thirteenth century, especially as practiced by the Sturlungar — Snorri Sturluson, Sturla Þórðarson, and Ólafur Þórðarson. The difficult art of skaldic poetry was, indeed, a discipline that must always have called for the training and guidance of aspiring poets by older, experienced ones. *Egils saga* describes how the young poet Einar skálaglamm sought the company of Egill Skallagrímsson to discuss poetry with him; Snorri Sturluson and Ólafur Þórðarson also taught young poets the traditional art of poetry, although their teaching methods and the discipline that they passed on were deeply influenced by medieval learning. The increasingly learned quality of skaldic poetry coincides with the development of saga writing. In time, sagas superseded skaldic verse as historical evidence, but, by incorporating court poetry into their work, the saga writers saved much of it for posterity.

Personal Poetry

Personal poetry often treats the same themes as court poetry — fights and sea voyages — but centers on the personal situation of the poet. The most celebrated practitioner of this genre, Egill Skallagrímsson, lived in the tenth century and, according to his saga, was the son of settlers from Norway. Egill was a great viking and traveler, getting involved in conflicts with the royal family of Norway, but surviving to die of old age in Iceland. Although we will never be sure how much of the poetry ascribed to him in his saga he really composed, it is now generally, although not unanimously, accepted that two of the three poems attributed to him are his, along with a number of occasional *lausavísur*. Early or late, much of the verse ascribed to Egill is among the most forceful and personal poetry preserved in Old Icelandic.

Firmly anchored in the tradition of the oldest Norwegian court poetry, Egill's verse nevertheless strikes a new note with its individualism in content and style. The poet we meet is a traveler and fighter with a fierce temperament, but he is also a sensitive man who highly values ties to kin and friends. He is capable of deep feelings; his sorrow over the death of his sons makes him question the gods he has believed in, and only after a hard mental struggle can he be reconciled with them. The kind of stylistic experimentation that Egill practiced is illustrated in one of his best-known stanzas, which describes a journey by sea:

> Þél höggr stórt fyr stáli
> stafnkvígs á veg jafnan
> út með éla meitli
> andærr jötunn vandar,
> en svalbúinn selju
> sverfr eirar vanr þeiri
> Gestils ölpt með gustum
> gandr of stál fyr brandi.

The furiously opposing enemy of the mast [headwind] is chopping out
with the chisel of storms a file on the even path of the steel-prowed
bull [sea]; with it the cool-clad wolf of willows [wind] mercilessly
grinds away at the swan of Gestil [ship] with gusts over the
bowsprit before the prow.

In the first half of the stanza, archaic kennings transform the storm and the
ship into living beings, a bull and a giant. These creatures are brought
together when the effect of the storm on the sea is pictured as a giant in his
smithy forging a file with rugged teeth. Here is a poet who has the strength
and the originality to attempt a combination of *nykrat* and *nýgerving*, as if
the *dróttkvætt* meter were no more of an obstacle than the relatively permis-
sive *kviðuháttur*. The poet does not abandon the old style for the metaphor,
however, and in the second half the ship has turned into a swan and the
wind into a wolf, who is putting the already forged file to the swan's breast.
The metaphoric layers are by no means reconciled, as in a *nýgerving*, but
allowed to fight each other as fiercely as the subjects of the stanza—the
storm, the sea, and the ship. The heavy rhythm and the tight clusters of
consonants further emphasize the conflict of adverse elements.

Sorrow and generosity are central themes in Egill's poems "Sonatorrek"
and "Arinbjarnarkviða." "Sonatorrek" (A lament for sons) is undoubtedly
one of the greatest works of Old Icelandic literature, although bad preservation makes it difficult to interpret. Egill lost two sons, one to sickness, the
other to the sea. In the poem he is beside himself with grief and describes
how difficult it is to move his tongue, to carry the timber of poetry, grown
with leaves of speech, out of the temple of words. At first the poem is loaded
with heavy, complicated kennings. Gradually, however, powerful images
begin to appear, and Egill's attention turns to the importance of the family,
which the poet sees as both a wall around the individual and a rope of which
he is one strand. The loss of a loved one (called in the poem *ástvinur*, "love-
friend") is the breaking of a strand in the family rope. Having expressed the
importance of family and kin in general, Egill turns to his own particular
reaction to his loss, directing his anger at Ægir, the giant who personifies
the sea and against whom he wishes he could take revenge. Egill's memories
of his favorite son, who was always obedient, lead him to contemplate his
own relationship with Odin, to whom he pledged his loyalty in youth but
who now has betrayed this loyalty. The poet must admit, however, that
Odin has given him some compensation, the gift of poetry, and in the final
stanza Egill achieves reconciliation with his fate.

"Arinbjarnarkviða" (The lay of Arinbjörn) is a less complex poem, demonstrating the dimensions of Egill's self-esteem no less vividly than it shows his love for his Norwegian friend and cousin Arinbjörn. The poem is incomplete, but it is characterized by brilliant imagery and skillful variation. It contains an excellent example of a *nýgerving* in which Egill describes his confrontation with an angry Eirik Blood-ax, the ruler for whom he composed "Höfuðlausn" and from whom he succeeded in escaping with his life with the assistance of Arinbjörn:

Vara þat tunglskin || tryggt at líta
né ógnlaust || Eiríks bráa,
þás ormfránn || ennimáni
skein allvalds || ægigeislum.

It was not safe or without menace to look at the shining of the moon of
    Eirik's brow when the serpent-shining moon of the prince's
    forehead glittered with rays of terror.

The poem is a gold mine of original kennings that demonstrate the same strange and original poetic vision that characterizes Egill's *lausavísur*.

The art of the single stanza, the *lausavísa*, in *dróttkvætt* meter was practiced by Icelanders for centuries after Egill's time, and, although no one surpassed him, there have come down to us striking examples of poetic skill from other skalds. The Sagas of Icelanders preserve a great number of stanzas about fighting; much of this verse is doggerel, but some of the best of it expresses the feelings of men who are facing death. Þormóður Kolbrúnarskáld, who fell with Saint Olaf in 1030, describes for a woman who wondered why he is so pale how an arrow has pierced him and given him a fatal wound. Our appreciation of the stanza's exact images and carefully measured rhythms is little affected by whether we choose to see it as an example of Þormóður's bravery in the face of death or as the result of the skald's poetic imagination. This stanza and similar ones express a feeling, deeply rooted in the peoples of the North, that death should be met with equanimity.

Equanimity in the face of danger was, no doubt, also frequently demanded of Viking Age Icelanders on their journeys at sea. Many of the most effective *lausavísur*, such as the example by Egill already discussed, take up this theme. Although she was not involved in the incident herself, the poet Steinunn Refsdóttir (late tenth century) describes how Thor took the ship of a missionary and dashed it against the shore. Her verse is picturesque, reminiscent of the way Bragi and other early poets depicted Thor's struggle against the World Serpent. Steinunn's son, Hofgarða-Refur (eleventh century), describes dangers at sea in some wonderfully concrete and evocative stanzas. Although a Christian and the court poet of Christian kings, Hofgarða-Refur was not afraid of using kennings with mythological references. He may have forsaken his mother's belief in Thor, but he certainly remained loyal to the poetic traditions that she revered.

Love is a major theme of the *lausavísa*, as we might expect. The authenticity of the love poetry preserved in the sagas has been the subject of a controversy that takes in the possibility of influence from poetry in Latin and the poetry of the troubadours. The stanzas preserved in *Kormáks saga* (The saga of Kormákur), ascribed to its eponymous hero, are full of mythological kennings and convoluted syntax, but at the same time they express a sensibility so strikingly modern that the term *alienation* springs to mind. With outrageous hyperbole Kormákur describes the woman he loves, enumerating the countries of his world that, put together, are less valuable than she, and declaring that the mountains will be swallowed by the sea before another woman so beautiful is born. Through all skaldic love poetry there rings a note of tragedy: love is the mother of pain, and the sight of his beloved immediately evokes in the poet the certainty of sorrows to come. "The moon of the eyelashes of the woman [the ale-valkyrie] beautifully dressed in linen shone sharply on me, but that ray shining from the goddess of bracelets will cause sorrow for me and that goddess of rings," says Kormákur in one of his stanzas. Or perhaps it was Gunnlaugur ormstunga (Serpent-tongue) who said it since the stanza is also ascribed to him in his own saga (see also p. 137). In *Eyrbyggja saga* (The saga of the people of Eyri) we read of the doomed love between the famous hero Björn the Breiðavík-champion and the married sister of an important chieftain. When he must take leave of his mistress for good, Björn composes a stanza expressing a wish that the time from dawn to dusk might last forever because, when night falls, he is going to attend the funeral of his happiness. The stanza exemplifies a tendency in erotic *lausavísur* to express feelings through natural imagery while their mythological kennings seem largely mechanical.

The *lausavísa* was the most persistent of skaldic forms, and many of the skaldic verses that retain aesthetic appeal are *lausavísur*. This is not surprising when we remember that the art of the skald is primarily to express a reaction to a moment of experience. Because of this, many skaldic poems could as well be described as series of single stanzas. A superimposed principle of composition, like the insertion of a refrain in the *drápa*, is needed to connect the stanzas to each other. There are exceptions, of course, above all the long poems ascribed to Egill Skallagrímsson.

One of the most plausible etymologies suggested for the word *skald* is the one that connects it with verbs like English *scold* and German *schelten*. Originally, personal invective, not praise, may have been the main subject of skaldic poetry. The use of poetry for this purpose was long lasting among the Icelanders, and it was not considered harmless fun by any means because people believed that the word had the power to affect people's lives and that this power was enhanced by difficult and intricate versification. Versified invective and love poetry addressed to a woman were equally punishable by law. The pagan Icelanders considered the craft of poetry a gift from the gods, an effective weapon, and, when put to legitimate use, a "blameless accomplishment." Fortunately, the respect for this accomplishment proved stronger than the contempt for the old religion after Christianization.

CHRISTIAN RELIGIOUS POETRY

The Roman Catholic Church brought new kinds of music and versification to Iceland, but Latin hymns had no immediate effect on the ancestral poetic tradition, apart from the *hrynhent* meter mentioned above. It must have been a natural reaction of the converts to try to put together in skaldic style words of praise for their new king of kings, Christ. One thing the skalds knew how to do was to adapt to the tastes and preferences of different kings. A new type of kenning was introduced, one based on the idea of a "king of heaven." Since *king* could be traditionally expressed, especially with *heiti*, and there were many ways of paraphrasing *heaven* in natural terms, such as "hall of the winds," great possibilities for variation lay open to the religious skalds and were much used for over three centuries. When mentioning secular subjects, the poets made free use of old kenning types; while they avoided mentioning the most important gods, such as Odin, Thor, Freyja, or Freyr, they continued to use mythological elements, although with diminishing frequency, until about the beginning of the fourteenth century.

The oldest half stanza that we have in praise of Christ is probably by the same Eilífur Guðrúnarson who composed "Þórsdrápa." The poet praises Christ as a victorious southern king, but his references are pagan. Other poets who converted at an early age, such as the influential lawspeaker (*lögsögumaður*) Skafti Þóroddsson (d. 1030), praised Christ as a king more powerful than any other and as the creator of the world. Although their diction bears no obvious witness to paganism, their worldview seems only superficially affected by Christianity.

The earliest extant poem to include Christian references is a praise poem by Þórarinn loftunga (Praise-tongue) from the 1030s that mentions Saint Olaf and some of his miracles. From about the mid-twelfth century on entire religious poems were composed in skaldic meters. Most of them appear in manuscripts from later periods, but, because these poems were composed in writing to begin with and did not go through a period of oral transmission, they are well preserved.

Among the oldest Christian poems is "Plácítusdrápa" (The poem of Placitus), preserved in a manuscript from around 1200, and probably composed no later than ca. 1150. It tells the story of *Plácítus saga*, a translation of the Latin life (vita) of Saint Eustace. Composed in *dróttkvætt* meter and in a genuine and rather complex skaldic style, the poem has as its most striking feature the attempt to construct a coherent narrative with dialogue. This was an innovation in skaldic poetry, and the attempt was not repeated by following generations of poets.

Einar Skúlason (twelfth century), a priest and one of the many skalds descended from Egill Skallagrímsson, was a well-known court poet, and splendid secular *lausavísur* by him are preserved. Einar's career reached a high point in 1152, when he was called on to deliver a poem in the new cathedral of Saint Olaf in Nidaros (Trondheim) before an audience including three kings and an archbishop. His "Geisli" (Beam of light), a *drápa*, brilliantly unites skaldic traditions with theological learning and Christian symbolism. The saint is described as a beam of light shining from Christ, the true sun. After an introduction expressing basic Christian truths and an address to the dignitaries present, the poet turns to his main subject, Olaf's death and his miracles, and in a final section the saint is praised in general terms. The poem has much of the official and somewhat distant quality of court poetry. It initiated an era in skaldic poetry that saw conventional symbols of medieval Christianity adapted to skaldic style and the mythological element of the kennings gradually reduced.

The twelfth-century "Leiðarvísan" (Guidance) employs a theme widely known in the Middle Ages: the letter about the Sabbath sent from heaven by Christ himself. "Harmsól" (Sorrow-sun) by Gamli, a canon of the Augustinian monastery at Þykkvibær in southern Iceland, is an impressive poem characterized by humility and deep religious feeling clearly relating to the congregation that the poet addresses: "my brothers and sisters." Christ the Conqueror has been replaced here by the suffering Redeemer on the cross, and the poet stresses the need for human repentance. Paradoxically, the poem is in strict *drápa* form, and Gamli uses pagan kennings freely. By this time the pagan references must have been accepted as purely conventional, as poetic, not religious, language. The poem reaches its climax in the description of Judgment Day, in which mastery of skaldic style and echoes of the apocalyptic vision of "Völuspá" are harnessed to express the profound drama of Christianity.

In "Líknarbraut" (The road to grace), a beautiful *drápa* of the thirteenth century or the early fourteenth, the use of kennings has been reduced, and mythological elements have been largely supplanted by conventional Christian symbolism. Nevertheless, the poem stays within the skaldic tradition, the word order becoming occasionally quite complicated. "Líknarbraut" focuses on the cross and the Passion, anticipating thematically and in some of its imagery the seventeenth-century *Passíusálmar* (Passion hymns) by Hallgrímur Pétursson (see pp. 215–17).

It was only natural that Icelanders who wanted to praise the Lord should make use of the well-established form for the praise poem that they had inherited in the *drápa*. It may seem more paradoxical that deeply religious men, such as the poets who wrote "Harmsól," "Leiðarvísan," and "Líknarbraut," whose piety kept them far from the flamboyant self-aggrandizement of the earlier skalds, should have remained so faithful to skaldic meter and style instead of trying to imitate the Latin hymns with which they most certainly were familiar. The power of the poetic tradition is seen in "Heilags anda vísur" (Verses of the Holy Spirit), probably from the thirteenth century and in genuine skaldic style, a substantial part of which is a free translation of the well-known ninth-century hymn "Veni creator spiritus." Nor did religious poetry in simpler meters and style seek models in Latin poetry either. Three stanzas in the end-rhymed *runhent* by the secular chieftain Kolbeinn Tumason (1173–1208), a contemporary of Gamli's, address the Lord humbly and in simple words:

Heyr, himna smiðr
hvers skáldit biðr:
komi mjúk til mín
miskunnin þín.
Því heitk á þik
þú hefr skaptan mik.
Ek em þrællinn þinn,
þú ert dróttinn minn.

Hark, maker of heaven,
to what the poet prays:
May your mercy mild
make its way to me.

I call to you,
for you gave me life.
I am your servant,
you are my Lord.

The form of these stanzas is skaldic, the meter is the same as in Egill's "Höfuðlausn," but the simplicity is far from conventional *drápa* style.

The most original religious poet of Iceland in the Middle Ages also chose a native model but turned to Eddic meter and style—to "Hávamál," as a matter of fact. His "Sólarljóð" (Song of the sun) is preserved only in paper manuscripts from the seventeenth and eighteenth centuries. The text is, no doubt, corrupt in places, but there is no reason to believe that anything important is missing or that the order of stanzas is incorrect. The poem's eighty-two stanzas in *ljóðaháttur* can be divided into three main sections.

The first section (sts. 1–32) is didactic, opening with five brief exempla, short narratives exemplifying different types of human actions and their consequences, and ending with seven pieces of advice. There is an obvious parallel here to the opening part of "Hávamál," although the message is, of course, totally different; the exempla have a transcendental reference to spiritual truth alien to pre-Christian thought. The second section (sts. 33–52) is a first-person narrative. It begins with a contemplation of man's sinful nature, which had bound the speaker to this life, and continues with a description of the experience of death: sickness and fear torment body and mind, and at death the body stiffens and is gradually absorbed into nature. Death itself is described from the point of view of the dying individual in a sequence of seven highly poetic stanzas all beginning with the line "Sól ek sá" (I saw the sun): what is seen is clearly the natural sun, but it is at the same time a symbol of human life in this world and of the glory and grace of God, who gives life to man. The section ends with a stanza describing how the soul, "star of hope," flies from the body, and then the "I" of the poem is born a second time. The sun stanzas stand at the very center of the poem and mark a turning point in its content as well as a high point in its verbal art.

The third section of "Sólarljóð" deals with the otherworld that awaits the soul after death. It is influenced by the medieval tradition of dream visions of the otherworld, but it stands apart from them in that the narrator has not been led to the otherworld in a dream, like Dante or other visionaries known from other Icelandic works (see pp. 171–72), but has died and is appearing in his son's dream. In the first part of the vision, the soul has left the not-yet-buried body but is still tied to the material world and cannot find a place in the otherworld. The continuation describes punishment and reward in visual terms and goes on to speak of mysterious beings symbolizing otherworldly powers. Many of these figures are enigmatic and difficult to interpret, but the Revelation of Saint John is, without doubt, the main source of the very effective imagery.

In the last two stanzas the speaker addresses his son, telling him to recite the poem to those who are still alive, and bidding him farewell with the following stanza:

Hér við skiljumsk
ok hittask munum
á feginsdegi fira;
drottinn minn
gefi dauðum ró
en hinum líkn sem lifa.

Here we must part
and will meet again
on the *dies laetitiae*;
may my lord
grant peace to the dead
and grace to the living.

The poet of "Sólarljóð" has full command of Eddic style, and the most expressive of his stanzas match the best of "Hávamál." There can be no doubt about his strong faith and sound knowledge of Scripture as well as his thorough familiarity with the native tradition. But the result is no simple sum of these parts. A powerfully poetic mind has expressed a deeply original vision of man's destiny. The traditional economy and concreteness of expression combined with apocalyptic imagery in the style of the Book of Revelation has created a unique poem that continues to fascinate because of the way it confronts its reader with the mysteries of life and death.

Although scholars have variously dated "Sólarljóð" to ca. 1200, to ca. 1300, and even to the fourteenth century, its firm command of Eddic style would seem to indicate that the poem was composed earlier than 1300. Its combination of artistry and apocalyptic vision could well have been the product of a late thirteenth-century worldview, one that expressed itself in the tragic terms of a work like *Njáls saga* and grew out of the turbulent Age of the Sturlungar (see also part two of this chapter).

The composition of religious *drápur* continued into the fourteenth century. Several *drápur* praise the Icelandic bishop Guðmundur Arason, and poems were also composed about Saint Nicholas, Saint Catherine, and the apostles John, Peter, and Andrew; there is a quantity of poetry about the Blessed Virgin, some of it as early as the thirteenth century, but most of it is from the late Middle Ages.

In the fourteenth century and after, there are two dominant styles of religious poetry. The *drápa* form survives, but only in *hrynhent* meter, and generally avoiding such old poetic diction as kennings and *heiti*; and a new kind of song appears, making use of a simple style and end-rhymed stanza forms probably connected with melodies and a mode of singing imported from abroad.

"Lilja" (The lily), composed just before the middle of the fourteenth century, was recognized as a masterpiece of religious verse almost immediately, and it became an important influence on subsequent poetry. The "Brother Eysteinn" to whom it is attributed in one late manuscript may be the rebellious monk from the Augustinian monastery at Þykkvibær mentioned in an annal of 1343 or the Eysteinn Ásgrímsson of the monastery of Helgisetr in Norway who in the years 1349–61 was involved in Icelandic church affairs as a representative of the bishop of Skálholt and the archbishop of Nidaros; the two may also be the same person. In any event, the language of the poem shows beyond any doubt that the poet was an Icelander who had full command of the learning of his time, rhetoric as well as theology, and was well acquainted with older Icelandic poetry.

Eysteinn saw the architectural potential of the *drápa* form and made more efficient use of it than any poet before him. Although he also realized that, with its long lines and even rhythms, the *hrynhent* meter was eminently suitable for his purposes, he explicitly denounced traditional poetic diction: "It is most important that each word should be correctly understood" (st. 97). He also states: "The custom of introducing innumerable obscure archaisms in a poem obstructs the understanding" (st. 98), echoing Geoffrey of Vinsauf's *Poetria nova*. Eysteinn is, thus, the first Icelandic poet to accept the full consequences of the generally accepted Christian attitude that poetic expression should serve only the purpose of revealing the message of the church. As his practice shows, this does not entail any aversion to metrical or stylistic elegance; but to classify his poetry, and the poetry that later was modeled on his, as skaldic, as most editions and reference works do, is to ignore his own statements.

"Lilja" is one hundred stanzas long. The introductory section (*upphaf*) of twenty-five stanzas is followed by a main part (*stefjabálkar*) of fifty stanzas evenly divided in two parts, each with its separate refrain, while the final twenty-five stanzas form the closing (*slæmur*). The first and last quarters have no refrain. The poet praises the Holy Trinity and asks the help of God and Mary in composing the poem. Then the story of Creation is told, the fall of Lucifer, the creation of Adam and Eve, their temptation and fall, and the consequences. At the end of the introduction the poet describes how the archangel Gabriel is commissioned to make the Annunciation to Mary. The two central sections tell the story of Christ's incarnation and his work as the Redeemer. The first part takes the story from conception to the Crucifixion. Stanza 49 tells of Christ nailed to the cross, and stanza 50 is a prayer and praise, including the last appearance of the refrain that has linked the first group of stanzas together. In stanza 51, the second refrain, which will knit the next twenty-five stanzas together, is introduced. The story continues with a moving description of Christ on the cross and Mary's sorrow, and it goes on to tell of Christ's Harrowing of Hell, the Resurrection, the Ascension, the descent of the Holy Ghost at Pentecost, and the Day of Judgment. The closing is concerned with prayer and worship: the poet confesses his sins to God the Father and to Christ the Son. In stanzas 86–95 Mary is praised with great eloquence; at the end the poet turns to Christ and his mother together, telling them why he composed the poem, and giving it the name "Lilja." Stanza 100 repeats the first stanza:

Almáttigr guð allra stétta,
yfirbjóðandi engla og þjóða,
ei þurfandi stað né stunda,
stað haldandi í kyrrleiks valdi,
senn verandi úti og inni,
uppi og niðri og þar í miðju!
Lof sé þér um aldr og ævi,
Eining sönn í þrennum greinum.

Almighty God of all places,
ruler of angels and peoples,
independent of time and space,
standing firm in the power of peace,
at once inside and outside
above and below and in between!
Praise be to you for all ages and time,
three in one and one in three.

Eysteinn's attempt to define God at the same time as he addresses him is impressive and displays the clarity and consistency of his worldview. In Eysteinn's poetry can be found a range of tones and subjects, from the theological to the comic. Satan, who up to this time had led a rather shadowy existence in Icelandic religious poetry, becomes in "Lilja" a lively figure, at once comic and contemptible, his defeat by Christ described with great relish by the poet. The descriptions of the suffering Christ and Mary are vivid and moving; the figure of Mary in particular seems to call forth Eysteinn's best poetry. The poet is a dramatic and effective storyteller, although sometimes rather too enthusiastic when hammering home the moral of his story. The art of "Lilja" reaches its highest achievement in the lyric final section, where the poet's humility and faith are expressed by a variety of stylistic means, from the most simple and low-key to a virtuoso display of rhetorical devices that climaxes in his praise of Mary:

> María, ertu móðir skærust,
> María, lifir þú sæmd í hári,
> María, ertu af miskunn kærust,
> María, léttu synda fári,
> María, lít þú mein þau er vóru,
> María, lít þú klökk á tárin,
> María, græð þú meinin stóru,
> María, ber þú smyrsl á sárin.

> Mary, thou art the brightest of mothers;
> Mary, thou livest honored on high;
> Mary, thou art adored for thy mercy;
> Mary, relieve the plague of sins;
> Mary, behold the evil that was;
> Mary, behold our tears with compassion;
> Mary, heal the great injury;
> Mary, rub ointment on wounds.

The anaphoric apostrophe has made it easy for the poet to add end rhyme to the internal rhymes. Although such eloquence may seem artificial to the modern reader, the individual sentences are, in fact, simple and straightforward.

A more ornate style with imagery fundamentally different from the traditional kenning is found in another stanza praising Mary:

> Þú ert hreinlífis dyggðuð dúfa,
> dóttir guðs og lækning sótta,
> giftu vegr og geisli lofta,
> gimsteinn brúða og drottning himna,
> guðs herbergi og gleyming sorga,

gleðinnar past og eyðing lasta,
líknar æðr og lífgan þjóða;
loflig mær, þú ert englum hæri.

Thou art the virtuous dove of purity,
daughter of God and healing of sickness,
road of happiness and sunbeam of the air,
jewel among brides and queen of heavens,
God's abode and forgetting of sorrows,
place of joy and remover of vices,
vein of grace and life-giver of peoples;
excellent virgin, thou art higher than angels.

These images are based on conventional Christian symbolism, but what distinguishes many of them formally from kennings is the fact that the basic meaning is revealed in the defining component, "road of happiness," "place of joy," "vein of grace," etc. This is a florid style that became popular in late medieval Icelandic poetry.

"Lilja" is not an original vision in the same sense as "Sólarljóð" is, but, through its command of theology and poetic expression, it overshadows everything else in medieval Icelandic Christian art. Icelandic poetry was not to be the same after "Lilja." "All poets wish that they had composed 'Lilja,'" as the old Icelandic saying goes, and later the *hrynhent* meter was often called *Liljulag*, "'Lilja's measure." Echoes of "Lilja" are frequently to be found in later poems of the fourteenth, fifteenth, and sixteenth centuries, and, by breaking with the skaldic tradition, the poem cleared the way for the direct influence of meters and styles practiced in European religious poetry.

The influence of "Lilja" is apparent in "Guðmundardrápa," a poem composed in 1345, soon after "Lilja." Around 1500, "Rósa," a *drápa* in *hrynhent* by Sigurður the Blind of Fagradalur in eastern Iceland, openly imitates "Lilja." Here, however, the narrative material is greatly increased with added tales (e.g., about Saint Ann, the mother of Mary) and with greater detail in the treatment of the Passion, while the lyric component is much less prominent. The poet, who was a layman, demonstrates a good command of meter and style. The same applies to his contemporary Hallur Ögmundsson, a priest from the northwest corner of Iceland. Hallur was a prolific writer of religious poetry and made frequent use of *hrynhent* meter, for instance, in "Náð" (Grace), his long *drápa* about Mary and Saint Ann and the history of redemption.

The most interesting poem about this subject matter is "Ljómur" (The bright poem). "Ljómur" has the same metrical structure as a canzone, with the rhyme scheme *abcabcdddd*. It was sung to a melody that has been preserved to this day on the Faroe Islands. Here, the main emphasis is on the Last Judgment, and what awaits the damned is picturesquely described; Mary and John intercede with Christ, asking him to redeem all mankind, both good and evil, and he grants their request. On the evidence of seventeenth-century manuscripts, "Ljómur" has been attributed to Jón Arason (1484–1550), a well-known poet and the last Roman Catholic bishop of Iceland, who was decapitated in 1550 for his resistance to the Reformation and the king. The credibility of this attribution is undermined by the fact that the oldest manuscript containing the poem, one produced during the bishop's lifetime, does not mention him as the author. "Davíðsdiktur" (Poem for David), a free translation of Psalm 51 in the same meter as "Ljómur," can on more solid grounds be attributed to Bishop Jón.

Numerous poems about Christ and the cross, based on the Bible and on medieval legends, were composed in the late Middle Ages. In "Náð," Hallur Ögmundsson's detailed descriptions of the torturing of Christ have a sadistic flavor reminiscent of much German poetry of this time and point toward the Protestant poetry of the seventeenth century. One of the most memorable poems about Christ from around 1500 is "Niðurstigningarvísur" (Verses on the Harrowing of Hell), tentatively attributed to Bishop Jón Arason. The poem forcefully narrates the fighting in hell, and there is real joy in the description of the breaking down of Satan's fortresses and the extinguishing of his fires when the King of Heaven crushes the devils under his feet. The stanzas are in a simple canzone form.

The most popular theme of the religious poets of the late Middle Ages is the Virgin Mary. Either the poems on this subject are primarily narrative, drawing on *Maríu saga* (The life of the Virgin Mary), and dealing with Mary's life and miracles, but including a lyric component of praise and prayer, especially if they depict Mary at the cross; or they are pure lyric poems of worship. Although a few poems about miracles are in skaldic meters, most of the narrative Marian poems are in end-rhymed meters, which sometimes give them a balladic quality. Mary's kindness and influence are frequently illustrated by showing how she helps even the most undeserving because they have shown her some devotion. We meet here the same lenient attitude as in "Ljómur": Mary is too kind to accept any human being's suffering in eternal damnation. The lyric poems to Mary are heavily rhymed and simple in syntax and vocabulary, although making abundant use of Latin words and phrases. As a group they seldom rise high as poetry, but they do impress the reader as both sincere and charming.

A great number of late medieval poems are devoted to saints and apostles. Among the most interesting are poems about Saint Olaf, particularly "Ólafs vísur" (Verses of Olaf), composed about 1500 by a layman, Gunni Hallsson. Based on Snorri Sturluson's *Ólafs saga helga* (The saga of Saint Olaf; see also p. 103), it is a reverent poem composed in intricate meter and a style often picturesque.

Although "Lilja" was never surpassed, the religious poetry from the early sixteenth century is rich in forms and themes. By this time skaldic style had been rejected, but the language remained free of the flow of Low German and Scandinavian words and forms that came with the Reformation and had cropped up earlier in secular poetry. Sigurður the Blind, Hallur Ögmundsson, the poets of "Ljómur" and "Niðurstigningarvísur," and other poets of the period are comparable with the best poets of other ages.

Christian religious poets of the Middle Ages did not strive for originality. Their ambition was to join the angelic choir singing the praises of the Lord and to repeat the eternal truths in appropriate language. It took a long time for the Icelandic poets to break their ties with skaldic poetry and to adopt conventions used by their colleagues in other parts of Europe. Even after this step was definitively taken by Brother Eysteinn, the poetry of Iceland retained its own distinct characteristics: the poetic tradition was renewed but never broken.

SECULAR POETRY OF THE LATE MIDDLE AGES

Although the main stanza forms survived in religious poetry and in the *lausavísa*, court poetry came to an end during the thirteenth century. Secular poets also gradually adopted foreign forms and modes of poetry, incorporating them into native traditions of metrics and style. The alliterative system was retained, as were many of the traditional *heiti* and a somewhat simplified system of kennings.

After Iceland had come under the rule of Norway in 1262–64, communication between the two countries was strengthened, and the king of Norway kept representatives in the country. Until the Reformation, Iceland was always considered part of the Norwegian state and partly governed through Norway, even after Norway came under the Danish crown in 1387. During the late Middle Ages, with Iceland being part of the archbishopric of Nidaros in Norway, the church controlled increasing amounts of Icelandic property and power.

In the late thirteenth century and the early fourteenth, Norway had strong commercial and diplomatic ties to the rest of the European continent as well as to Britain, and, in the course of their travels to Norway and more distant countries, the Icelanders came into contact with European culture. Around 1400, the English began fishing off the coast of Iceland and trading with the Icelanders, and, while British influence was strong throughout the fifteenth century, from about 1475 German Hanseatic merchants were an increasing presence. Although communication with English and German traders and fishermen would have introduced Icelanders only to popular culture, such relations opened the way for broader cultural contacts. English bishops were appointed to Icelandic bishoprics, and Icelanders went to England to seek education. Cultural contact with Germany is amply documented from the late fifteenth and early sixteenth centuries. Links with Norway, however, were not yet broken. Some of the trade with Germany was conducted through Bergen in Norway, and the rulers of Denmark and Norway made efforts, both diplomatic and military, to ensure that Iceland remained part of the state. The Danish monarchy took control of religious and secular affairs in stages during the years 1530–50; from then on Iceland was ruled directly from Denmark, and communications with Norway came to a halt.

No less than elsewhere in Europe, the late Middle Ages in Iceland were a time of weak administration and arbitrary justice. There were economic fluctuations, but exploitation of the fishing grounds surrounding the country brought in riches. Unevenly distributed, this wealth brought to prominence several rich families, some of whom considered themselves aristocratic, and it also formed the basis of ecclesiastical power. The literary culture of the country depended on the strong economic position of the church and the gentry, but its survival was also due to the relatively high rate of literacy among the laity.

Lyric and Satiric Poetry

Most of the secular Icelandic poetry of the late Middle Ages is anonymous, and much of it is preserved only in manuscripts compiled long after the poems themselves were composed. We assume that much has been lost, especially from the fifteenth century, about which our knowledge is limited. One of the richest men in Iceland and a *hirðstjóri* (the king's highest representative) in the first half of the century was Loftur Guttormsson (d. 1433). An interesting *háttalykill* is attributed to him. Loftur's meters are basically the old skaldic ones, although several innovations and changes in preference can be seen, and his diction is also skaldic. However, his themes are chivalric, consisting largely of declarations of love and melancholy complaints about obstacles to the union of lovers, and similar to the themes of courtly love in contemporary and earlier European lyrics.

With the beginning of the sixteenth century, our knowledge about poets increases. Bishop Jón Arason, for example, did not limit himself to religious themes but wrote a lively poem about his dealings with Danish emissaries sent to enforce Protestantism in Iceland. The bishop boasts of his effective armed attack on the Danes, whom he mocks. He is obviously proud that, in his old age, he is capable of such feats. Paradoxically, a lay contemporary of the bishop's, Jón Hallson, seems much more pious. In "Ellikvæði" (Poem about old age), he complains of the ailments of old age — infirmity, loss of influence, and lack of attention — but concludes with reflections on the necessity of preparing for death. The stanza form is that of the simple canzone, and the main theme is treated in a spirit similar to that of European poetry on the same subject. Although earlier poets occasionally complain about old age, this is the first example of this genre in Icelandic, and many such poems were to follow.

Another poet who probably lived around 1500 was Skáld-Sveinn, about whom nothing is known but his name, which is mentioned in connection with one of the most remarkable poems of the period, the satiric "Heimsósómi" (The wicked ways of the world). This is an eloquent poem in the same meter as "Ljómur" and "Davíðsdiktur." Its biting satire is directed primarily against the lawlessness of the times and the corruption of the upper class: bribes and naked force rule the courts; the rich man lives in luxury and oppresses the poor; and his greed is limitless. The poet goes on to describe with passionate anger and contempt how, at death, the rich man will be thrown into the grave as food for worms and how his soul will enjoy in hell an everlasting "merciless party." The poem ends on a more conciliatory note, with admonitions to the rich to mend their ways and prepare for death. Icelandic annals show that there was ample occasion for such angry sermons around 1500, but both style and rhetoric are, evidently, inspired by the poetry of other countries: there are numerous parallels in English, German, and even Danish poetry from the fifteenth century, although few equal the eloquence and passion of Skáld-Sveinn.

Most of the anonymous secular lyric poetry that has been preserved from the Middle Ages concerns erotic themes and is in the form of individual stanzas or short poems, *brunakvæði* (passionate poems) or *afmorskvæði* (poems of love; from the French *amour*). This poetry is usually in end-rhymed meters and an unpretentious style, although the presence of *heiti* and simple kennings shows that the ties to the skaldic tradition have not been broken entirely. Those ties, however, are much stronger in narrative poetry.

Narrative Poetry: Rímur
Narrative prose on native themes in Icelandic had come to an end by 1400, although the composition of fictional sagas on romance themes continued

(see pp. 139, 151). By that time an entirely new narrative genre had appeared, one that was to hold a prominent place in Icelandic literature for half a millennium: the *rímur* (sg. *ríma*; "rhymes").

At the beginning of the 1390s, a poem consisting of sixty-five stanzas was recorded in the *Flateyjarbók* manuscript under the heading *Ólafs ríma Haraldssonar er Einar Gilsson kvað* (*Ríma* about Ólafur Haraldsson composed by Einar Gilsson). The poet was a lawman (*lögmaður*), a high office at the time, and is known to us also as the composer of a religious *drápa* about Bishop Guðmundur Arason. The reason for the inclusion of *Ólafs ríma* in this manuscript — mainly a compilation of Kings' Sagas — is, of course, its protagonist, Saint Olaf. Other medieval *rímur* or cycles of *rímur* are preserved in collections from the end of the fifteenth century and later. Although this version of *Ólafs ríma* is found in a manuscript that was compiled a hundred years earlier than any other *rímur* text was recorded, it displays a meter, a style, and a narrative technique that were fully developed when the poem was composed, probably about 1350. The genre must, therefore, predate the mid-fourteenth century; a few of the extant *rímur* cycles were probably composed in the fourteenth century, and we have a considerable number from the fifteenth century. Most of the medieval *rímur* are anonymous and, therefore, difficult to date, but, after the middle of the sixteenth century, the names of their authors are almost always recorded, making dating easier.

Rímur are long rhymed narratives, similar to the metrical romances of England and Germany in the High and late Middle Ages. The *rímur* poets did not make up their own stories but almost always versified prose sagas, most frequently the Legendary Sagas or prose romances known as the Knights' Sagas (*riddarasögur*). The diction of the *rímur* is skaldic, but the syntax is simpler and better suited for narrative. The basic metrical forms are well-known from European narrative and lyric poetry: the *septenar* or the *vagant* strophe with four plus three stresses in each half stanza, which is the model used in the most frequently employed meter, *ferskeytt* (rhymed *abab*). Another frequently used stanza form is the *stafhent*, based on the octosyllabic couplet with four plus four stresses, and rhymed *aabb*; more rarely the half stanza has four plus two stresses with *abab* rhymes, a form known mainly from lyric poetry outside Iceland.

These meters are also known in Scandinavian ballads, and many scholars have assumed that the *rímur* poets borrowed them from that source. Very little is known, however, about the Scandinavian ballad so early, and, more important, *rímur* meters are much more heavily laden with rhyme and have more fixed rhythms than the ballads. All the oldest stanza forms actually have closer counterparts in English and German metrical romances and lyric poetry than in the ballad. The Icelanders who created this genre seem to have been inspired by foreign poetry of various kinds, which they may have encountered through minstrels or other entertainers in Bergen or farther away from home.

The Icelandic *rímur* poets were most interested in the invention of new and complicated rhyme schemes and stanza forms. In the fourteenth-century *rímur*, *ferskeytt* and other basic stanza forms are most commonly used, but later more variation was preferred, and it became usual to change meter with each new *ríma*.

The fact that poets took the trouble to versify already available prose narratives indicates that this new form of narrative was popular. Sung or chanted, *rímur* could be performed for groups of any size and, easier to memorize than prose sagas, were less dependent on books — an expensive medium at this time — for circulation and preservation. In later centuries *rímur* were a popular evening's entertainment, and it is natural to assume that this was the case in the Middle Ages as well. There is also some evidence that *rímur* were occasionally sung to be danced to. Despite their widespread popularity, which indicates oral transmission, all extant *rímur* show clear signs of having been composed in writing.

A *ríma*, or a cycle of *rímur*, tells a story, beginning by introducing the characters, then developing the action through narration and dialogue to a well-motivated conclusion. When the narrative is fairly long, as is most often the case, it is divided into sections or songs, each of which is a *ríma*. As a rule, the beginning and end of each *ríma* are signaled by a direct address to the audience. Although such passages of direct address were not obligatory in the oldest *rímur*, it gradually became a fixed convention to extend the beginning address through several stanzas of a lyric nature called the *mansöngur* (love song) and directed toward the women in the audience, who were told of the poet's adventures — often unhappy — in love. The *mansöngur* has parallels in both German and English narrative verse, but it has most in common, including its clichés, with the subjective and sentimental European love lyric. The nature imagery that marks the troubadours and minnesingers, however, is not found in the Icelandic *mansöngur*.

Skaldic diction — *heiti* and kennings — characterizes *rímur* throughout their long history. Their kennings are simple, and as a rule there is no attempt to make them the basis of a metaphoric style. Mythological kennings are used without any hesitation, but limited knowledge of mythology, insufficient understanding of older poetry, and the influence of a florid style often yield corrupt kennings or paraphrases different in nature from true kennings. In contrast to epic singers making use of formulas, the *rímur* poets avoid word-for-word repetition of lines or stanzas; but the systematic variations in the style of kennings offer the possibility of expressing identical ideas in various ways according to the demands of meter and stanza form, and to this extent the kennings of *rímur* function in a way similar to formulas in epic songs. In spite of the kennings, *rímur* style is simple and easy to follow because word order and sentence structure are always straightforward.

The Kings' Sagas and the Sagas of Icelanders furnished the stories on which a few *rímur* cycles are based. Snorri Sturluson's version of *Ólafs saga helga* is the source for *Ólafs ríma*, although the poet emphasizes the king's saintliness more heavily than is done in the saga (see pp. 103–5). Although the *ríma* is pious in tone at the beginning and end, it is devoted to a description of the battle of Stiklarstaðir (Stiklestad), and Olaf's miracles are only briefly referred to. The most interesting of the *rímur* based on the Sagas of Icelanders is *Skáld-Helga rímur* (*Rímur* of Skáld-Helgi), a cycle dated to the fifteenth century. It is based on a lost, very late saga with a romantic theme: lovers kept apart by fate and evil people.

Three *rímur* cycles are based on heroic and Eddic sources. *Völsungs rímur*, based on *Völsunga saga*, has been dated to the fourteenth century; its meter is plain *ferskeytt*, and it has no *mansöngur*. The poet calls himself *vitulus vates*, "Calf the Poet," and is probably the same Calf (Kálfur) who composed a *drápa* on Saint Catherine early in the century. *Þrymlur* (*Rímur* of Þrymur) is loosely based on "Þrymskviða," and the differences between them are interesting. The *rímur* poet has added material from other sources to flesh out his characters. Compared to the Eddic poem the story has been vulgarized, but much of the fun survives. *Lokrur* (*Rímur* of Loki) is based on the *Prose Edda*. It shares with other "Eddic" cycles a tendency to treat its source more freely than do *rímur* based on Legendary Sagas or romances.

Most medieval *rímur* are based on prose romances, some on translations of European sources, such as *Karlamagnús saga* (The saga of Charlemagne) and *Þiðriks saga* (The saga of Þiðrek), but many more on Legendary Sagas and Icelandic Knights' Sagas (see pp. 139–51). The majority of these *rímur* are concerned with the superb courage, physical strength, and warrior skill of their heroes, but, unlike the old Germanic heroic poetry, the *rímur* are comic. Usually, the hero prevails over his enemies, obtaining a bride (beautiful and virtuous, usually waiting passively for the hero to come and get her) and, if he does not already have one, a throne. His adversaries are cruel Vikings, sorcerers or sorceresses (the evil women are hideous and no less dangerous than their male counterparts), giants and dwarves—although dwarves may, on occasion, come to the aid of heroes. The descriptions of heroic deeds in *rímur*, especially when the source is a Legendary Saga, are reminiscent of skaldic poetry, in which princes were praised for their Viking activities, killing and looting in enemy territory, no less than for fighting worthy enemies. The diction of the *rímur* may be stale compared to skaldic practice, but they offer lively narratives with a great deal of humor.

Modern readers of *rímur* often delight in the *mansöngur* because its subject, feelings rather than battles, leads the poet to create lively images and metaphors and because, while it may contain clichés, the *mansöngur* does not paraphrase a preexisting prose text. In the narrative sections of *rímur*, the poets are most creative in their descriptions of nature; like the skalds, they are often inspired by sailing and seafaring.

The diction developed by *rímur* poets influenced other kinds of secular poetry, both lyric and narrative, during the late Middle Ages and after. In *Skíðaríma* (*Ríma* of Skíði), the form is parodied in a travesty of legends and myths. This remarkable poem, longer than any other single *ríma* (two hundred stanzas) and first found in manuscripts from the eighteenth century, can hardly be younger than the beginning of the sixteenth century. The hero, Skíði, is a tramp who falls asleep after heavy eating and, in a dream, is led by Thor into Valhalla, where he becomes the cause of a fight among the gods and heroes. The introductory description of the tramp is lively and comic, and, although exaggerated, it contains realistic details. The appearance of such a figure in the company of Odin, Thor, and Freyja, to say nothing of Sigurd the Dragon-slayer and other legendary figures, creates a comic situation that the poet puts to effective use. The poem is a parody, not only of *rímur*, but also of the visions of the otherworld so popular in medieval literature.

Skíðaríma has been attributed to more than one lay poet living in the west of Iceland in the fifteenth century. There is no doubt that the *ríma* comes from that region, but the identity of its author remains in doubt. Another humorous poem from this time, *Skaufhalabálkur* (Verses about Big Tail), has been attributed to one of the poets who has been credited with *Skíðaríma*; not a *ríma* but in Eddic meter, the poem has as its hero a fox, Skaufhali. The fox is humanized as an old outlaw who is mortally wounded on his last hunt, and the portrait of the old "hero" is drawn with humor and compassion. Despite a thematic relation with poems about Reynard the fox, this Icelandic poem has its own peculiar characteristics.

Popular Poetry with Medieval Roots: Ballads

In the seventeenth and eighteenth centuries, and increasingly in the nineteenth, a great deal of popular poetry was recorded in Iceland. Much of it is likely to have its roots in the Middle Ages, either in the sense that ideas, forms, and formulas can be traced back to that time, or in the sense that the actual texts have survived without radical alterations from that period. Although such poetry is usually discussed in the context of the time when it was recorded, there are good reasons for making an exception for popular traditional ballads (*sagnadansar*), which in most cases portray the world in distinctly medieval terms. By the time they began to be recorded in the 1660s, they were already called *fornkvæði* (old poems). Comparative studies have substantiated the conventional belief that the Scandinavian ballad flowered during the Middle Ages and was introduced into Iceland at that time.

The recording of popular ballads in written form began in the second half of the sixteenth century in Denmark and Sweden but only somewhat later in the rest of the Nordic area. Closely related to the ballads of other areas, particularly those of Great Britain, the Scandinavian ballads are in either couplets or quatrains and almost always carry a refrain. It is likely that they were sung for dancing during the Middle Ages, just as they are to this day on the Faroe Islands. The typical ballad tells a story, objectively and with copious use of dialogue, and carries a lyric refrain that has little or no direct bearing on the story. Dancing is referred to in Icelandic texts as having been practiced in the twelfth century. A couple of lyric stanzas or fragments called *danzar* (dances) have been preserved from the thirteenth century, but there is no evidence that narrative poems were sung to accompany dancing at that time. Individual ballads may well have been known in Iceland as early as the fourteenth century, and, among those preserved, a considerable number show every sign of belonging to a western Nordic tradition that almost certainly was brought to Iceland no later than ca. 1500. A somewhat smaller group is likely to have been brought to Iceland directly from Denmark, probably during the sixteenth and seventeenth centuries, when there was the most direct communication between the two countries. Although most of the ballads found in Iceland originated elsewhere in Scandinavia, a certain number have come down to us that were composed in Iceland itself.

Scandinavian ballads are of two main kinds, chivalric and heroic. Like *rímur*, heroic ballads are often comic, optimistic, and celebratory of physical strength; also like *rímur*, they are usually based on literary works, especially Legendary Sagas and romances or related tales from oral tradition.

Heroic ballads were rare in Iceland, possibly because the Icelanders were already treating the themes that are most popular in such ballads in sagas and *rímur*. Everywhere else in Scandinavia heroic ballads were well-known, flourishing to a remarkable degree in the Faroe Islands. The chivalric type of ballad — usually with a more concentrated and dramatic, often tragic, plot — is generally held to be of eastern Nordic origin, although a Norwegian origin has recently been postulated; be that as it may, the genre seems to have flourished in Norway quite early and come to Iceland in all its subtypes: ballads of the supernatural; (Christian) legendary ballads; historical ballads; and ballads of chivalry. Most of the hundred-odd ballads found in Iceland belong to these subtypes, although none can strictly be considered historical, that is, dealing with historical figures and events. Our acquaintance with the ballad genre is based mainly on seventeenth-century collections that contain most types of ballads and usually the longest and, from a literary point of view, the most satisfactory versions. The only important post–seventeenth century addition to the corpus is the jocular ballad, which had been considered too unimportant or too immoral to be worthy of recording by those who began collecting ballads in the seventeenth century.

Ballads distinguish themselves from almost all kinds of Icelandic poetry previous to the twentieth century in that they do not follow the traditional rules for alliteration in line pairs. Alliteration does appear, as in all popular poetry, but it is occasional, ornamental rather than structural, or a feature of a stock phrase. The rhythm of ballads is looser than that of *rímur*, the number of unstressed syllables varying greatly, and even the number of stressed syllables in a line may be subject to change. The most characteristic features of ballad style are formulaic diction (including commonplace stanzas), various kinds of repetition, and hyperbole. Fixed elements of a story, such as the summons to a meeting, the sending of a messenger, departure and return, the breaking into a young woman's bower, and the like, are as a rule expressed through formulaic stanzas or stock sequences of stanzas. Important moments are emphasized through incremental repetition, and heights of feeling and action are expressed through hyperbole: the heart of a hero receiving bad news may break into many parts or burst with a noise loud enough to be heard for nine miles. To modern readers, ballad narrative may seem staccato or disjointed. Ballads center on emotional conflicts that climax in scenes with dialogue: scenes are loosely connected, and silent action is summarily presented. Details that are foregrounded by way of repetition do not always seem salient enough to merit being dwelt on.

Ballads deal with exotic people — kings and queens, knights and their ladies — and take place, appropriately, in castles and halls or in the greenwood. The ballad register makes use of foreign words and irregular grammatical features eminently suited to the evocation of a world remote from the daily experience of the audience. The stories told in the ballads also have the appeal of the unusual: although the basic themes are the universal ones of love, jealousy and hate, ballad characters, unlike everyday people, respond to their passions with immediate and heedless action, the result of which is more likely to be a daring elopement, a rape, a murder, or an illegitimate birth than it is to be the blissful union of lovers, although this also occurs. In this overwrought atmosphere the supernatural is ubiquitous, not only in the elves and monsters and magic powers in the secular stories, but also in the intervention of saints in the ones with Christian motifs. The jocular ballads involve common people in the action and demonstrate how human frailty and stupidity make high and low equally ridiculous.

The reception of ballads in Iceland has not been very creative. Seldom is anything of significance added in transmission; more often something is simplified or lost. There are no rules or trends: a Christian moral may be added in one case and omitted in another. There are many examples of ballads that have been so simplified as to have lost any status as art, but there are other examples, such as the beautiful "Kvæði af Knúti í Borg" (The ballad of Knútur of Borg), that are markedly more pleasing and effective in the Icelandic version than in any of the parallel versions found in the other Scandinavian countries. There is no tendency in the Icelandic ballads to make the world familiar to the audience or give it local color. The fascination of the ballads lay in their strangeness. In one way Icelandic ballads are distinctive: a majority were recorded from the songs of women. In view of this fact it is interesting to note that, in at least two Icelandic ballads dealing with the theme of rape, "Kvæði af kóng Símoni" (The ballad of King Simon) and "Ebbadætra kvæði" (The ballad of Ebbi's daughters), rapists are treated with a powerful antipathy absent from these poems' Danish parallels.

The ballads, or ballad types, recorded from oral tradition in Iceland number about one hundred, but there may be multiple recordings of a single ballad. In the dozen of whose Icelandic origin we are sure, the influence of *rímur* style is often found, but to so slight a degree that we cannot talk of anything like a hybrid genre. The one truly heroic ballad that we know to have been composed in Iceland is called *Þorgeirs rímur* (*Rímur* of Þorgeir); it does contain a few stanzas in pure *rímur* style, but they do not fit into the poem very well and must be considered additions. Even a ballad about Saint Olaf is typically balladic in style and theme, telling the story of the conception and birth of Olaf's illegitimate son, Magnús, and showing the influence of religious poetry only at the end.

Among the most beautiful ballads of Scandinavia is "Tristrams kvæði" (The ballad of Tristram), which is based on a Norse prose translation of a French romance. "Tristrams kvæði" is at once purely balladic and purely Icelandic in diction and style. Tristram is wounded in his last battle and sends for Ísodd bjarta (Isolde the Bright) to heal him. His heart bursts when his wife, Ísodd svarta (Isolde the Black), lies to him, saying that Ísodd bjarta is not on the ships that are coming. Ísodd bjarta comes ashore and walks to the church as the bells are ringing. When she comes to Tristram's body, she kisses him and dies. The queen buries them on either side of the church, and the trees that grow from their graves intertwine above the roof. The ballad is moderately formulaic, but repetitions skillfully enhance the tragic feeling. We have several variants of this poem, with two different refrains, both beautiful and well chosen.

The refrains of the Icelandic ballads are often lyrically evocative, making effective use of nature imagery. They seem to have lived a life of their own, the same refrain appearing with different ballads and even in poems of other kinds, especially the *vikivakakvæði* (carols or dance poems). A refrain might be part of the larger stanza that sometimes stood as the introduction to a ballad; occasionally the refrain appeared in full only in other poems. Under these circumstances it is often impossible to know whether the refrain proper is a fragment or whether the larger stanza is a secondary augmentation. Aside from their refrains, the ballads seem to have had little influence on other kinds of poetry in Iceland.

CONCLUSION

This first part of chapter 1 has treated the history of Icelandic verse through six centuries—and even longer if we take into account the early roots of Eddic and skaldic poetry as well as the afterlife of popular poetry in the postmedieval tradition. Although the traditions of meter and diction were exceptionally conservative—preserving features lost elsewhere, such as the old Germanic type of alliteration, archaic poetic diction, and the kenning— great changes took place during these centuries: end rhyme, possibly introduced as early as the Viking Age, grew increasingly popular, becoming by about 1500 a dominant feature of Icelandic verse; the uneven sentence-based rhythms of the early poetry were, from the fourteenth century on, replaced by more even rhythms, most commonly iambic or dactylic. Changes in subject matter and attitude were more radical. The first Icelandic poetry on record was deeply influenced by the tastes and ideologies of the small courts of the petty kings of Norway during the Viking Age, and Icelandic poets made use of poetic forms developed for the praise of princes. The equally ancient lays of the *Poetic Edda* contain legendary and mythological motifs and are to a great extent shaped by the oral culture of Viking Age society, its attitudes, and its needs. With Christianity there came new kinds of poetry and poetics. Above all, the need to convey a clear message was in direct opposition to the native traditions of enigmatic style, and, with the fourteenth-century Christian poem "Lilja," this new clarity won the day. The new end-rhymed poetry that arose in the fourteenth century, especially religious verse and the narrative *rímur*, was clearly influenced by poetry in Latin and even the vernacular narrative poetry of England and France. In popular poetry recorded later from oral tradition, the same influences are felt.

As a whole, the verse preserved from medieval Iceland is no less impressive in its amount than in its quality. The balance preserved between continuity and change is also remarkable. The thread of tradition was never broken, as Icelandic verse continued far beyond the six centuries here discussed to offer entertainment in a variety of ways at the same time as it remained an efficient tool to give expression to the most deeply felt convictions of the people.

Old Icelandic Prose: *Sverrir Tómasson*

THE DAWN OF THE WRITTEN ERA

The origins of Icelandic prose writing have traditionally been traced back to the first half of the twelfth century. Only one work has been preserved from that period: *Íslendingabók* (The book of Icelanders), written by the priest

This chapter is mainly summarized from my literary history in *Íslensk bókmenntasaga*, ed. Ólason, where I discuss Old Norse–Icelandic prose. I have taken new studies into consideration in only a few instances—and no work published after 2003. Dr. Gunnþórunn Guðmundsdóttir translated the first draft, which I revised with the assistance of Dr. Alison Finlay and Dr. Richard North. I wish to express my warmest thanks for their fine work. I am responsible for all translations from the Old Norse that are attributed to non-English-language sources. Finally, I wish to thank the publisher's copyeditor, Joseph Brown, for his helpful comments and for scrutinizing the text and, last but not least, Dr. Daisy L. Neijmann, the volume editor, for her patience and enthusiasm for the work.

Ari Þorgilsson the Wise (d. 1148) sometime during the 1120s. This work is similar in structure to Latin chronicles and is our first evidence of law codes being recorded, in this case during the winter of 1117–18. The recording of these laws is considered to mark a turning point in Icelandic cultural history. It is the first mention of any vernacular material being put down in writing. One must assume, however, that Icelanders were familiar with writing and book production as it existed elsewhere in Europe. Priests and bishops had access to books in Latin, and Latin script must have reached Iceland at the start of the eleventh century, when people gradually began to convert to Christianity. Nevertheless, books were undoubtedly a great novelty for most Icelanders. The oldest preserved Icelandic manuscripts are fragments from the second half of the twelfth century.

The Latin alphabet could not represent every phoneme in Old Norse; it lacked a number of symbols that could adequately signify recognized Norse sounds. At the time, runes — an ancient form of Germanic writing influenced by Greek script — were to be found across Scandinavia. They had been used for inscriptions for many centuries, but they were less suited than Latin script to symbolize the sounds of the language, as may be deduced from the fact that the younger runic alphabet consisted of only sixteen letters. Neither type of alphabet was, thus, capable of representing all the sounds of the language.

The difficulty of writing in the vernacular is the subject of a small monograph from the middle of the twelfth century. The author's main aim was to create for Icelanders as accurate an alphabet as was possible in Latin script, one that would eliminate all doubt as to how a word should be pronounced and written, thereby reducing the risk of ambiguity. As the author himself says, the book was meant to make it "easier to write and read as is customary in this country both laws and genealogies or religious interpretations as well as the wise lore which Ari Þorgilsson has composed with a reasoned conception" (*The First Grammatical Treatise*, 208). While the book is titled *Fyrsta málfræðiritgerðin*, that is, "The First Grammatical Treatise," it is almost exclusively concerned with spelling. The author offers only a few innovations, but his work is an important record of the language spoken in twelfth-century Iceland.

It has been maintained that the author of the *Treatise* was mostly concerned with law codes. These had to be written in as clear a language as possible so that the meaning of the words would never be in doubt. Law codes were, after all, written down so that leaders could assert their authority with reference to them. The same was also true of genealogy, the family trees that traced people's ancestry, sometimes even to Odin or Noah. A noble lineage in the male line of descent could mean the right to rule over men and land. Law codes and lineages were of equal importance in that they could be used to demonstrate the superiority of the clergy and the secular aristocracy.

Society

There are few reliable sources on Icelandic society at the beginning of the twelfth century. This period, from the start of settlement (ca. 870) to 1262–64, has been called *þjóðveldið* (the Commonwealth). This label is misleading, however, for it was not the public (*þjóð*, "people") that held power (*veldi*) but designated chieftains called *goðar* (sg. *goði*). *Goðar* are thought originally to have had spiritual authority as well, to have been priests in pagan times and presided over pagan sacrifices and other religious rituals. The word *goði* probably signified "one who has his authority from the gods." But, little over a generation after Christianity was accepted by law in the year 1000, control of the church had passed completely into the hands of native Icelandic bishops, as was the custom elsewhere, and, until the thirteenth century, most of the bishops came from famous noble families, which, thus, exercised considerable influence in ecclesiastical affairs. National legislative and judicial power rested with two assemblies: the *vorþing* or Spring Assembly, which was a kind of district assembly, and the *alþing* or Althing, which was the General Assembly. As well as being responsible for the adoption of laws, the Althing was also the highest court in the country and passed verdicts. It is uncertain to what extent the judiciary and the legislature remained separate.

Each *goði* had a certain authority to which sources refer as a *goðorð* (chieftancy). This should be understood to mean that a *goði* was trusted by certain people, his "thing men" or assembly men, to guard their rights as established by law and to determine their duties. People did not need to live in the same area to serve under a *goði*; his authority was not tied to a certain district. There was neither a public executive power nor one overarching ruler, such as an earl or a king.

The laws as recorded in *Grágás* — the common name for the law codes preserved in manuscripts and manuscript fragments from the latter half of the thirteenth century — reflect a legal system that is described in some detail in several Sagas of Icelanders (see pp. 122–39), some of which are thought to have been composed in the last decades of the thirteenth century and the first decades of the fourteenth. It is, however, by no means certain that the laws as recorded in *Grágás* were ever in force — and, if so, which ones. It should also be noted that most of the Sagas of Icelanders are stylized narratives about a society of which, at a three- to four-hundred-year remove, little was actually known. The social setting as it appears in one particular literary genre cannot be seen as a direct reflection of Icelandic society during the period 870–1030. The laws of *Grágás* can hardly be considered the collected laws of one society; they should, instead, be regarded as the private collections of individuals. Other law books may have been in existence as well.

As early as the twelfth century, social changes began to emerge that were to have far-reaching consequences. Power became concentrated among ever fewer chieftains, which meant that one man held many *goðorð* and, thereby, ruled many districts. Leaders thus arrived on the scene who controlled large regions of the country. This meant that Icelandic society increasingly resembled other European societies and would, unavoidably, become overwhelmingly similar to them, although this happened only in 1262–64, when the Icelandic people became subjects of the Norwegian king.

Icelandic books and booklets from the twelfth century and later, such as the genealogies that have been preserved, clearly reflect a stratified society. Not everyone is equal before the law, as is apparent from compensations paid out after killings. The church and its institutions spurred on even stricter class divisions. The leaders of the Icelandic church were almost all from the country's most noble families, and the interests of the church and those of the secular authorities coincided well into the thirteenth century.

During the latter half of the twelfth century, and up to the last decades of the thirteenth, the power of Icelandic leaders can to some extent be compared to that which was wielded by nobility elsewhere in Europe, even though the Icelandic power system is not wholly parallel to the European feudal system. Members of the Sturlungar family in the west of Iceland, the Ásbirningar family in the north, the Svínfellingar family in the east, and the Oddaverjar and Haukdælir families in the south all considered themselves born to rule and consolidated and further increased their power through intermarriage.

Education and Foreign Influences

It is a well-known topos in Old Icelandic writing to describe the country as a remote island and Icelanders as living on the edge of the known world, outside civilization. This view is far from the truth. For Icelanders, traveling abroad was not unusual, and communication with other nations was as common as it was elsewhere in Europe. As early as the mid-eleventh century, the first bishop of Iceland, Ísleifur Gissurarson, and his son Gissur presumably studied at a monastery in Herford, Germany, and undoubtedly brought home with them foreign material that they remodeled to suit Icelandic methods.

Ísleifur and his son were of the Haukdælir family, which then, and for nearly the whole of the thirteenth century, was one of the most powerful families in the country. There was some sort of educational institution at Haukadalur in the late eleventh century and the early twelfth where Ari the Wise was taught. The Haukdælir family, or chieftains related to them, virtually controlled Skálholt until well into the twelfth century. The Oddaverjar family was also famous for its learning and knowledge. Originally the family's leader was Sæmundur Sigfússon the Wise (d. 1133), who, according to Ari Þorgilsson in *Íslendingabók*, had studied in France. For a considerable period, the country's most important center of learning was at Oddi: Saint Þorlákur Þórhallsson, his nephew Páll Jónsson (later bishop), and, last but not least, Snorri Sturluson were taught there. Two of these scholars went abroad to study: Þorlákur Þórhallsson went first to France, to study in Paris, and then to England; Páll Jónsson followed in his footsteps. Thus, cultural influences from both the Continent and England reached Iceland in the twelfth century. Unfortunately, no mention is made of the importation of the books and other cultural artifacts that must have helped convey these influences.

From its establishment in 1056, the Icelandic bishopric at Skálholt belonged to the diocese of the archbishopric of Bremen in Germany and, from 1103, to its counterpart the diocese of the archbishopric of Lund. Another see was established in Iceland at Hólar in the north in 1106. Lund was part of Denmark at the time. From 1152 until the Reformation in 1550, the whole of Iceland was part of the archbishopric of Nidaros (Trondheim). Icelandic bishops received their teaching mostly from these sees.

Eleventh-century Icelandic bishops may well have heard of one of the greatest German authors of the time: Adam of Bremen. Icelandic church leaders who traveled to Norway at the end of the twelfth century probably also knew of the monk Theodoricus, who composed a history of the Norwegian kings. Saint Þorlákur is very likely to have been introduced to the ideas of the Victorines in Paris during his years of study and may have brought them back to Iceland with him. From the middle of the century there also exists an almost complete itinerary by Abbot Nikulás Bergsson of Munka-Þverá (d. 1159), who went to the Holy Land and no doubt brought back some news in the spring of 1153.

Not much is known about educational institutions in twelfth-century Iceland; indeed, sources about Icelandic education are very limited up to the sixteenth century. Originally, teaching was probably in the hands of the bishops and a few learned men, but from 1200 on it is certain that regular cathedral schools were run at both bishoprics.

The old laws in *Grágás* state that a priest's education should last for at least four years, sponsored by a church franklin. Hardly anything is known about the education of children, although it is thought to have been similar to the existing European norm: they learned to read from the Psalter and practiced writing. The curriculum for priests seems also to have been largely comparable to what their colleagues in Europe studied: the seven liberal arts, especially grammar, rhetoric, logic, and music. It has been maintained that scholars at Haukadalur and at Oddi, where such famous learned men as Sæmundur the Wise and his son Eyjólfur (d. 1158) taught, mainly concentrated on Icelandic secular studies, but it would be more accurate to say that these were also included, as is clear from the life of Saint Þorlákur.

All teaching was, no doubt, originally designed to enable priests to perform their congregational duties, although many of those who studied with the learned men at Oddi, at Haukadalur, or at the cathredal schools were never ordained. Priests and the lower clergy in Iceland seem to have been expected to know Latin sufficiently well to be able to explain *þýðingar helgar* (religious interpretations). This is confirmed by other reliable sources: many translations from Latin demonstrate a solid knowledge of the language.

It can be estimated that, yearly during the Middle Ages, there were around four hundred learned men in Iceland who, naturally, made use of their education and learning. Their writings in Latin are, for the most part, lost to us, but foreign learning can be detected in the many extant works in the vernacular. Icelanders were, however, selective in what they appropriated. The country already had an indigenous lyric and narrative tradition, into which scholars and writers gradually tried to incorporate foreign learning. As a result of their efforts, certain rhetorical devices gained a foothold in narrative art and poetry.

The clearest proof of this activity is found in Iceland's three treatises on grammar, preserved in a fourteenth-century manuscript, but for the most part composed in the thirteenth century. The treatises are concerned with various aspects of sounds, their quantity and quality, as well as with the description and application of rhetorical devices, and they are clearly based on Donatus, Priscian, and, later, Alexander Villa-Dei and Eberhard of Bethune. Last but not least, there is, of course, the Edda of Snorri Sturluson (1178–1241) — a work also known in English as the *Prose Edda* — which, while it incidentally explains ancient myths, was first and foremost a handbook of poetics (see p. 151). It is also an invaluable record of a living mythological tradition that often manifests itself in the literature of the period.

The twelfth century has sometimes been called the *medieval* or *First Renaissance*. This label is appropriate as the beginning of the century saw a cultural awakening in Europe, along with an increase in scholarly interest in classical learning. It is not known exactly which books were kept by Icelandic educational establishments in the twelfth and thirteenth centuries, but, judging from the books listed in inventories from the following centuries, one may assume that, like their fellows abroad, Icelandic schoolboys were acquainted with ancient Roman culture and were made to imitate the style of the great writers in Latin (*imitatio*). It is likely that they had more than a nodding acquaintance with the *Ilias Latina*, Sallust's *Bellum Catilinae* or *Bellum Jugurthinum*, and Lucan's *Pharsalia*. In addition, they probably sampled some of Ovid's erotic poetry. Alongside this classical literature they read ordinary textbooks, such as Donatus's work on Latin grammar for beginners, as well as part of Priscian's grammar.

Other works that the priests studied also influenced medieval Icelandic literature, for instance, the *Physiologus*, *Prosper's Epigrams*, and, finally, the *Elucidarius* of Honorius Augustodunensis. These works survive in translation, either in their entirety or in fragments, from the end of the twelfth century and the beginning of the thirteenth. The translators appear to have made an effort to explain theological concepts; Norse audiences thus became familiar with the ideas contained in these works, and Icelandic writers could refer to religious matters in their own work and even employ exegetical interpretations and still be understood by most.

For Icelandic narrative art the translations of the *Ilias Latina* and Sallust's and Lucan's works mentioned above were, however, probably more important than Christian educational books. Sources refer to Sallust and Lucan by the one collective name *Rómverja saga* (The saga of the Romans), which clearly demonstrates that the works of Latin writers existed in the country, and it has been proved that Sallust and Lucan were translated into the vernacular as early as the second half of the twelfth century.

Sources do not mention any classroom manuals of rhetoric. The Viðey monastery, however, owned the *De doctrina christiana* of Augustine of Hippo late in the fourteenth century, and it is likely that the work was around in Iceland much earlier. In it Augustine laid down some guidelines for the use of oratory in sermons, guidelines based on the works of Cicero. Through this work, priests and other scholars who studied under the aegis of the church, had direct knowledge of classical rhetoric.

Cultural Centers

There is no surviving evidence that individual heads of families encouraged indigenous writing. However, it is more than likely that a powerful family like the Oddaverjar, who traced their lineage back to the kings of ancient times and the principle kings of Norway, wished to enhance their reputation in their locality. The same is true of other noble families in the twelfth century, especially the Haukdælir. In the thirteenth century, the Sturlungar doubtless sponsored the writing of their own family history, and Sturla Þórðarson (d. 1284) became, in effect, a royal scribe of Norway. This will be discussed in more detail later.

In the twelfth century, the main centers of learning were located in the monasteries at Þingeyrar and Munka-Þverá as well as at Haukadalur and Oddi. While they were not cultural centers in the modern sense, village-type communities presumably formed around the bishoprics at Hólar and Skálholt, and a kind of town culture may have existed in those places that included theatrical performances. As far as one can tell, no chapter was ever active at either of the two cathedrals. In the thirteenth century leaders moved their residences more often than they had done before, with the result that secular learning seldom got the chance to flourish in the same place for any length of time. It seems, however, that composition and copying took place at Reykholt while Snorri Sturluson lived there, and his nephew Ólafur hvítaskáld Þórðarson (see p. 29) appears to have taught privately at Stafholt. A school was run at Vellir in the north at the end of the thirteenth century, but that institution might have been an annex of the cathedral school at Hólar.

Monks and nuns were, above all, representatives of their own institutions: their sphere was a spiritual one, and the secular world need not concern them. But, fortunately, at times it did, as most Icelanders in holy orders came from chieftains' families. Indeed, this is one of the reasons why Icelanders have such a remarkable secular literature composed by monks such as Abbot Karl Jónsson (d. 1213) at Þingeyrar. This fact has been of great importance to Icelandic literature: those who entered the monasteries knew the world outside their walls and could write on everyday matters without interpreting them in religious terms. During the twelfth century and the first part of the thirteenth, the writings of the Icelandic clergy on domestic subjects are first and foremost characterized by a secular view of the world and are mostly composed in a clear prose without imagery or emotional fervor. In addition, the monasteries served as the publishers of their time: Helgafell, Þingeyrar, and Munka-Þverá had scriptoria, and their books, not all religious texts, reached many parts of the country as well as Norway.

Not much is known about the influence of foreign thinkers on the secular prose writing of the time. Many of the most famous medieval texts were well-known, such as the *Etymologiae* of Isidore of Seville (ca. 560–636) and the *De virtutibus et vitiis* of Alcuin. In addition to the earlier-mentioned *Elucidarius*, the *Imago mundi* was widely known and referred to, as were the works of Hugh of Saint Victor in Paris, one of which, the *Soliloquium de arrha animae*, was translated, along with a section from his *Didascalicon*. Hugh's theory of epistemology and pedagogy may have informed the opinions of the clergy, although this has not yet been studied in detail. Hugh's disciples, Richard of Saint Victor (d. 1173) and Peter Comestor (d. 1179), were especially influential because the latter's *Historia scholastica* was used as a textbook in Iceland and is widely cited, for instance, in the compilation of Old Testament history known as *Stjórn* I and III from the latter half of the thirteenth century and the beginning of the fourteenth. The Victorines seem to have been more influential in Norway, as may be seen, for instance, in the Latin history of Norwegian kings *De antiquitate regum Norwagiensium*, by Theodoricus the Monk.

Methods and Outlook

Icelandic historiographers appear to have been familiar with the rhetorical difference between *historia*, *argumentum*, and *fabula*. The word *saga* (pl. *sögur*) is often used in medieval Icelandic sources to mean *historia* (history). From the start, the meaning of the word in Icelandic is "that which is told or has been told in prose," and *saga* can, therefore, refer to both written and oral narrative; further, no distinction is made between fact and fiction. The word still carries the same meaning in modern Icelandic, where it is also used to denote "history." The bulk of medieval Icelandic prose literature is referred to as *sögur*, and it is evident that the word itself does not differentiate between historical texts and fiction. In the titles of the sagas there is some categorization with respect to the subject of the narrative: *Rómverja saga* (The saga of the Romans); *Íslendinga saga* (The saga of the Icelanders); *Ragnars saga loðbrókar* (The saga of Ragnar Hairy-leg). But no other differentiation is made.

If medieval writers had obeyed in every respect the rules of rhetoric on what should be included in *historia*, their narratives would have been little more than chronological lists of events — chronicles and annals, which were well-known in Iceland. Fortunately for readers today, they added their own contributions, interpreting events, and composing dialogues and speeches for their characters. Growing knowledge in Iceland in the twelfth century of the works of school authors such as Sallust was to increase their confidence, and the imitation of the speeches of ancient heroes and the re-creation of events from ancient times probably inspired them to do the same with their own histories. Historiographers became aware of the individual, and, as a result, characterization in historical works became more important. At the same time ideas on an inner life were forming: inner lives became the topic of discussion and speculation, and the soul (*anima*) was personified and entered into long dialogues with the body. Philosophers began increasingly to mull over the nature and emotions of humankind. We can see evidence of this in Icelandic texts, especially religious ones.

The Welsh writer Geoffrey of Monmouth (d. 1154) seems to have been known in Iceland by 1200 (see also below). His influence there was similar to what it was elsewhere in Europe. His works appear to have made Norsemen aware of the relevance of the distant past to contemporary history: kings traced their lineage to ancient heroes or to the gods of the Trojans and the Jews, divine origin proving their nobility and, at the same time, their ability to control the populace. Icelandic writers also learned typological thought from foreign writers and the Bible, regarding the new as a reflection of the old. This view is apparent in many medieval Icelandic texts.

Medieval Icelandic historiographers employed methods that were similar to those of their counterparts abroad. They gathered sources in a similar fashion, relying on eyewitness and hearsay accounts as well as on written sources. They evaluated their sources in a similar fashion, invariably describing them as knowledgeable, wise, and truthful. The use of verse is a distinctive feature of Icelandic historical works. Snorri Sturluson often cites poetry as the testimony of eyewitnesses: the poets tell the truth of battles and other events. Authors of other works that are now no longer considered historiographic also employed methods similar to those of the medieval historians. The writers of the saints' lives, for instance, claimed to work in the same fashion, although their outlook is different, and this influences their writing. In the Sagas of Icelanders, the Legendary Sagas, and the Knights' Sagas, a different tradition took shape, as we will see later. Here, the narrative relies on other methods, the authorial consciousness is different, and the authors seem to have been aware that they were interpreting the past and re-creating it without relying on anything except the facts of the imagination. It is self-evident that the use of poetry in prose works of this kind marks them as being in a different mode than standard historical narratives.

Storytelling as Entertainment

The sagas written in the vernacular were chiefly meant for reading out loud at large gatherings, during either work or festivities. The presence of the audience is most apparent in the Knights' Sagas and the saints' lives, where it is evident that people were expected to be listening to the reading. Although it seems to have been most common that these works were read to many people — and evidence of this is to be found in prefaces to some of the sagas — we also find mention of a work being read to only one listener, and not always for entertainment, as is clear in *Hákonar saga Hákonarsonar* (The saga of Hákon Hákonarson), where the king is being read to on his sickbed.

The son of Hákon, Magnús Lawmender, and his queen were, according to *Sturlu þáttur* (The tale of Sturla), fond of the tales told by Sturla Þórðarson, at a time when books were not available. Indeed, as well as the reading aloud of books, there was also oral storytelling in Iceland, as we know from several accounts. The most famous account is that in *Þorgils saga og Haflíða* (The saga of Þorgils and Haflíði; *Sturlunga saga*, Thorsson et al., eds., 1:22) of the entertainment at a wedding in Reykhólar in 1119. There, people enjoyed themselves with games, dancing, and wrestling, and the story explains:

> Something is told, though it is of small importance, of who the entertainers were and what their entertainment was. What is related is now contradicted by many, who maintain that they have never accepted it, for many are blind to the truth and think what is false to be true and what is true to be a lie. Hrólf from Skálmarnes told a story about Hröngvið the viking and Óláf liðmannakonung and the mound-breaking of Þráin the berserk and Hrómund Gripsson, with many verses in it. This story was used to entertain King Sverrir and he declared such "lying sagas" were most amusing; men can however trace their genealogies to Hrómund Gripsson. Hrólf himself had composed this saga. Ingimund the priest told the story of Orm Barreyjarskáld, including many verses and with good *flokkr* [a poem without a refrain], which Ingimund had composed, at the end of the saga. Nevertheless, many learned men regard this story as true. (trans. Peter Foote in his *Aurvandilstá*, 65n1)

It has been claimed that the anecdote in *Þorgils saga og Haflíða* is evidence that sagas were read aloud from a written text rather than told. This view is based on the fact that the verb *segja* can mean both "to tell" and "to read out loud." It has, however, also been pointed out that the evidentiary value of *Þorgils saga og Haflíða* with regard to twelfth-century oral storytelling is doubtful as it was composed at least a hundred years after the feast, by which time it had become much more common for stories to be read aloud. Nevertheless, the truth of the anecdote is supported by comments in the preface to *Þiðriks saga af Bern* (The saga of Þidrek of Bern), although it is not clearly stated there whether the stories are read aloud or recited from memory.

The statement in *Þiðriks saga* probably dates from the fourteenth century, and it supports the idea, as does the anecdote from *Þorgils saga og Hafliða*, that the teller of the sagas differentiated between sagas according to type. From the preface of *Þiðriks saga*, it is clear that the description of sagas in a different narrative mode refers to the *modus fictivus* (fictional mode). Nevertheless, all the sources referred to here clearly show that, whether it involved reading aloud or reciting from memory, storytelling was highly respected, both among the Icelandic elite and at the Norwegian court.

Literary Genres

Scholars of medieval Icelandic literature base their discussions on genre categories that date back to research from the nineteenth century and earlier, research in which the sagas are grouped according to theme or subject matter. The main categories were five: (1) the Kings' Sagas, which included both biographies of contemporary rulers (like the kings Sverrir Sigurðarson [d. 1202] and Hákon Hákonarson, Sverrir's grandson) and histories or pseudohistories of ancient and even mythical, saintly kings of the remote past (like Snorri Sturluson's *Heimskringla* [The world's orb]); (2) national histories and pseudohistories of Iceland, past and present, to which group belonged *Íslendingabók* by Ari Þorgilsson, *Landnámabók* (The book of settlements), *Kristni saga* (The book of Christianity), the compilation *Sturlunga saga* (The saga of the Sturlungar), and biographies of both secular and ecclesiastical leaders, among them all the versions of the lives of the three Icelandic saints; (3) the Sagas of Icelanders, including works like *Njáls saga* (The saga of Njal) and *Laxdæla saga* (The saga of the Laxdælir); (4) the sagas of knights or chevaliers, the so-called *riddarasögur*, or Knights' Sagas; and (5) the Legendary Sagas, sagas of Scandinavian and German heroes of the distant past, the so-called *fornaldarsögur*. To these categories some scholars added both translated and indigenous lives of the saints. This categorization is not satisfactory, as it does not take into account the form, the structure, or the object and aim of the individual sagas. The Kings' Sagas, for instance, originate in medieval historiography, and most of them are structured like biographies or national histories. Some of the Sagas of Icelanders may originally have been intended as historiography, while others are clearly an interpretation of the past, and it is not at all clear whether they should be classified as history or fiction. Where it is possible to determine their origins, this information still tells us very little about them as a genre. Furthermore, the Sagas of Icelanders include such a wide variety of individual saga types that it becomes difficult to define them generically.

This matter has, unfortunately, never been investigated from a literary perspective. In the absence of definitive research in this field, I partly adhere to the traditional categories here, discussing the Kings' Sagas and the national histories and pseudohistories in a section of historical and pseudo-historical literature, leaving out the hagiographic biographies of kings, earls, and bishops. The Sagas of Icelanders are discussed in a separate section, but the Knights' Sagas and the Legendary Sagas are combined and dealt with as romances. To these I add the category of saints' lives, both indigenous and translated, preceded by a discussion of related religious matters, Old Norse mythology, and the use of that mythology in poetry according to the *Prose Edda* of Snorri Sturluson.

HISTORICAL AND PSEUDOHISTORICAL LITERATURE

National Histories: The Works of Ari the Wise
It is not clear from sources how many books Ari Þorgilsson the Wise actually wrote, and, of his works, only *Íslendingabók* has been preserved, although other works have been attributed to him. Scholars have based their assertions in this matter on Ari's own comments in the preface to *Íslendingabók* and on Snorri Sturluson's comments in the preamble to *Heimskringla*, a history of the kings of Norway (see below). From Ari's comments it can be concluded that he wrote two versions of *Íslendingabók* and that the text that has been preserved is the later version. Not much is known about the earlier version, and it is very likely that it was simply the author's draft, which he never passed on. Scholars have, nevertheless, reckoned that evidence of Norse authors using this early version as a source — for instance, on kings — can be detected.

It is very likely that Ari wrote more than one book during his lifetime; the *áttartala* (genealogy) and *konunga ævi* (biographies of kings), which are mentioned in the preface to *Íslendingabók*, may well have been preserved separately for a long time. At the back of *Íslendingabók* are lineages, and scholars have presumed this section to be a fragment of the *áttartala*. It is, however, unclear how much larger that particular work was. Of other works by Ari very little is known for certain. It is, however, likely that he had a part in writing one of the books of the settlement of Iceland.

Even though *Íslendingabók* is clearly a national history, not much is said in it of ordinary people. Ari does not trace the origin of the Icelandic people to ancient times, as was the custom in comparable works. He starts the book with a preface, as was common in Latin chronicles during the period. But his preamble is different from foreign ones in that it does not mention the occasion or the aim of the work. Ari does, however, explain that he initially wrote the book for the bishops at Skálholt and Hólar. Admittedly, neither of them is addressed, and neither is the priest Sæmundur the Wise. All three are said to have read the work at an early stage. It would be highly surprising if they had passed this early version on to others; as representatives of the religious and secular authorities in Iceland, they would more likely have acted as censors. Indeed, from Ari's words it is obvious that they had a hand in the composition of the book and even selected some of the material.

Íslendingabók was, in all likelihood, written sometime before 1133. It starts with an account of the settlement of Iceland and where the settlers came from. Ari locates the settlement in time, basing his account on two types of sources:

> Iceland was first settled in the reign of Haraldur Fairhair, son of Halfdan the Black, at the time — according to the opinion and reckoning of my tutor Teitur, son of Bishop Ísleifur, the wisest of men, and of my father's brother, Þorkell Gellisson, whose memory reached far back, and of Þuríður Snorradóttir, the daughter of the chieftain Snorri [Snorri godi], who was very wise and trustworthy — when Ivar son of Ragnar Hairy-leg had the English king, Saint Edmund, slain, and this was 870 years after the birth of Christ according to what is written in his Life. (*Íslendingabók*, ed. Benediktsson, 4)

This paragraph neatly and concisely demonstrates the methodology of *Íslendingabók*. Ari is preoccupied with the chronology of events and firmly establishes dates in two ways: both relatively, by relating them to the life of a known individual, and absolutely, by relating them to the birth of Christ. He is also careful with his sources and straightaway names noble witnesses to events: in this case Teitur of the Haukdælir family and two descendants of Snorri the Chieftain. Then comes a short description of the settlement of a country that was "covered with forest" (*Íslendingabók*, ed. Benediktsson, 5). The narrative follows chronological order and is concerned chiefly with major events in the history of the country up to Ari's own time. First four main settler families are mentioned: the Mosfellingar, the Breiðfirðingar, the Eyfirðingar, and the Síðumenn. Then come short chapters on the Althing and the law, the calendar and the seasons, and the discovery of Greenland and Vinland. The central focus of the work is the conversion to Christianity at the Althing in the year 1000. After that there are brief descriptions of the first bishops, Ísleifur and his son Gissur, interspersed with anecdotes about law speakers and significant events abroad.

Ari's narrative is usually concise, the style is dry, and sometimes it seems as if the narrative had originally been conceived in Latin. Nevertheless, there are some personal comments that give the reader a surprising insight into the historiographer Ari Þorgilsson. He evaluates people, saying, for example, about his contemporary Bishop Gissur that he had been better loved "by all of his countrymen than any other man" (*Íslendingabók*, ed. Benediktsson, 22).

The narrative of *Íslendingabók* has all the hallmarks of objectivity as far as it goes. Ari clearly adheres to the belief that people should learn from history; history should be a series of good examples, like some of the saints' lives. He appears to have learned a great deal from foreign historiographers. No typological understanding is, however, brought to bear on Icelandic history, although it is possible that portions of his account are modeled after the Bible. For instance, the story of how Úlfljótur brought law to the Icelandic people is written in a hagiographic vein and has been compared to the Old Testament tale of Moses and the law of the Jews. These stories do share some similarities. Indeed, according to the religious ideas of many different peoples, laws are received from the highest authority by the intervention of an earthly representative, although precisely such a reference is lacking in Ari's account: Úlfljótur fetches the law from Norway, and there is no mention of divine intervention. Nevertheless, Ari clearly writes his country's history in the spirit of Christian historiography: it matters that, before pagans settled the country, Christians were already to be found there. When Ingólfur and his people reached Iceland's shores, Irish monks were there and left behind "Irish books, bells, and croziers" (*Íslendingabók*, ed. Benediktsson, 15) when they departed.

The chapter on the conversion to Christianity at the Althing is one of the best written in the book. Here, one sees the author's involvement in the course of events. Ari first explains in detail the antecedents: the missionary work and how it has failed to convert people to the Christian faith. One of those who preach Christ's words is Gissur the White, the very ancestor of the Haukdælir. With him is Hjalti Skeggjason. Ari first quotes Hjalti's verse on the goddess Freyja: "I do not want to bark at the gods [i.e., mock them], / yet I consider Freyja to be a bitch" (*Íslendingabók*, ed. Benediktsson, 15).

These lines serve as an introduction to Gissur and Hjalti riding to the Althing at Þingvellir. The account of this event is fluent; it is carefully structured and shows that Ari has worked from oral sources: "Teitur told us this event, how Christianity was brought to Iceland." At the end of the chapter, Ari recounts the main points of Þorgeir Ljósvetningagoði's speech in support of Christianity and concludes with a direct quotation from it: "And let us all have one law and one faith. It will become true that, if we tear up the law, we will also tear apart the peace" (*Íslendingabók*, ed. Benediktsson, 17). He does not make as much of the speeches of the Christians.

Historiographers of the following generations in the twelfth and thirteenth centuries might have been tempted to make more of Teitur's story; they might have brought together two arguing sections of pagan and Christian men and let the leaders utter speeches. Ari refrains from this. It is clear, however, that he considered the event to be a miracle. The events leading up to the conversion to Christianity are similar to what took place elsewhere in Europe: behind the missionary work there is at least one secular leader, a king who promises peace if the people convert. The narrative pattern plotted around those events has many equivalents in foreign works; indeed, there may have been similar circumstances elsewhere where the conversion to Christianity was agreed on, and there is, therefore, no reason to doubt that Þorgeir Ljósvetningagoði negotiated a settlement as this was a political necessity.

Around the time Ari wrote *Íslendingabók*, or a little earlier, feuds between the chieftains Þorgils Oddason and Hafliði Másson flared up, marking the beginning of a period of unrest in Iceland that lasted into the thirteenth century. The view held by Svend Ellehøj and other scholars — that *Íslendingabók* was intended to encourage the Icelandic people to live in peace at a time when the country was so close to war — is persuasive. The book supposedly shows that the country prospered in times of peace, when people obeyed the law. In short, it focuses on peacekeeping. Peace is guaranteed when leaders, both secular and religious, work together and, with the help of God, agree on one law. Ari's preoccupation corresponds to the ideas on governance that were dominant up to the time when church leaders started demanding independence in their own affairs and their interests no longer matched those of secular leaders.

Íslendingabók bears witness to the fact that Ari the Wise possessed a solid knowledge of foreign historiography. He refers, for instance, to *Játmundar saga* (*Passio Sancti Eadmundi*, The life and passion of Saint Edmund) by Abbo of Fleury (d. 1004). He probably knew the Venerable Bede's church history (*Historia ecclesiastica gentis Anglorum*), although it is unclear whether he also knew the works of Adam of Bremen. *Íslendingabók* is, in part, a public ecclesiastical history; most of the work is taken up by the history of the church in Iceland. And although his work has been most influential as church history, to this day Ari is the most reliable source on the general history of Iceland in the first centuries of settlement.

Books of Settlement

Narratives of the settlement of Iceland were, in all probability, copied many times during the thirteenth and fourteenth centuries. Of these works, three versions have been preserved in whole or in part: *Sturlubók*; *Hauksbók*; and *Melabók*. Also extant are two seventeenth-century copies, *Skarðsárbók* and *Þórðarbók*, which are of independent value. Their relation is clear, even though scholars do not agree on the details, and, indeed, they are often referred to simply as *Landnámabók*. *Hauksbók* is named after its owner and chief scribe, Haukur Erlendsson (d. 1334), and it includes the following epilogue:

> Now the settlements in Iceland have been described according to what wise men have written, first Ari the Wise and Kolskeggur the Wise. This book, however, I, Haukur Erlendsson, have written after the book that that very learned man Sir Sturla Þórðarson the Lawman composed and also according to another book by Styrmir the Wise. I have taken whatever was related more fully, but in the main things both books agreed. It is therefore not surprising that this book of settlements is longer than any other. (*Landnámabók*, ed. Benediktsson, 395, 397)

If Haukur Erlendsson is right, there can be no doubt that Ari Þorgilsson also wrote about the settlement of Iceland. Scholars have, however, disagreed as to how large a part Ari had in the writing of such a history. The available sources make it impossible to ascertain whether Ari wrote on the settlement with others or wrote *Landnámabók* on his own. It must, however, be considered very likely that, in the first half of the twelfth century, some among the learned had started collecting information on the first settlers, and *Íslendingabók* bears witness to Ari's considerable knowledge of families and places of residence.

As to books of settlement, two were committed to writing probably in the thirteenth century: *Sturlubók* and *Melabók*. Scholars believe Sturla Þórðarson the Lawman to have written *Sturlubók* sometime during the period 1275–80. *Melabók*, of which only two pieces of parchment survive, was written by a descendant of the Melamenn ca. 1300, while the genealogies at the end are attributed to Snorri Markússon (d. 1313) of Melar in Borgarfjörður. *Þórðarbók* was copied by Þórður Jónsson (d. 1670) from *Skarðsárbók* with part of the text of *Melabók*. It is thought to be based on a book of settlement by Styrmir Kárason (d. 1245), *Styrmisbók*, now lost, which was probably written at the beginning of the thirteenth century. *Hauksbók*, on the other hand, was probably written for the most part in the first decade of the fourteenth century, and Haukur's comments in the epilogue give us an idea of how he went about his work.

If the text of *Melabók* is an indication of what the oldest versions of the books of settlement were like, there was little to be found in them beside lineages. Nevertheless, it does also include some personal opinions, expressing the author's perspective on individual leaders, and explaining to what end the book was written.

In *Þórðarbók* there is a remarkable epilogue—which scholars think was originally in *Melabók*—that states the author's opinion in a clear and concise manner:

> Many men maintain that writing about the settlements is unrelated learning but we are of the opinion that we can better answer foreigners when they accuse us of being descended from slaves or rogues, if we know for certain the truth about our ancestry. And those who want to know how to trace genealogies, it is better to depart from the beginning than in the middle. All reasonable peoples want to know about their origins and the development of their settlements or beginnings of their own ancestry. (*Landnámabók*, ed. Benediktsson, 336)

Jón Jóhannesson reckoned that this epilogue originated from *Styrmisbók*, and most scholars have agreed with him. The view voiced here on writing about a people's origin becomes a topos in twelfth-century texts and may well have been known to Styrmir Kárason. The significance of this idea is twofold: on the one hand, the demonstration of the settlers' noble origins and, on the other, the assumption that many related and even unrelated families together form a gens.

All the Icelandic settlement books follow a similar pattern. They start with information about the people concerned, relating the settler's name, his genealogy, his wife's genealogy, and the names of their descendants. The size of the settlement is usually mentioned, and in some instances other pieces of information are given. Settlement narratives generally began their accounts in southern Iceland and moved clockwise, district by district, to the west and north, concluding in the east. But some authors restructured their narratives and started in the part of the country they considered to be of most importance. Both Sturla Þórðarson and Haukur Erlendsson added information from other sources to their texts; their works are not simply copies of older books of settlement. Sturla, for instance, adds a long introductory chapter on the first journeys to Iceland and the discovery of the country, and he organizes his material differently from that in *Melabók*. Rather than starting by listing settlers in the south, as happens in *Melabók*, Sturla continues with settlers in the west and north after he has recounted the settlement of Ingólfur Arnarson and Hjörleifur Hróðmarsson (who settled in the southwest).

Sturla makes use of foreign works; for instance, he cites the Venerable Bede's *Aldarfarsbók*, probably referring to his *De temporum ratione* (On the reckoning of time). Among native sources, *Styrmisbók* seems to have been of most use to him. He does not, however, copy straight from it; rather, he improves and adjusts, especially where he also has other sources to rely on, as scholars have deduced from his account of the settlement of Skallagrímur Kveldúlfsson in Mýrar, for instance. According to philologists, Sturla also made use of the Sagas of Icelanders, in some cases versions earlier than those that have been preserved.

Haukur Erlendsson is more dependent on his sources than Sturla is. He should not, however, be considered a mere copyist. Sometimes he shortens the text, and sometimes he adds to it, especially where he has more reliable sources. It seems that he wants to preserve as much material as possible, but in brief. As can be seen from his epilogue, he is familiar with Sturla's works and had access to *Styrmisbók*. It is interesting to note his interest in the Irish and all that came from Ireland. He seems also to have relied on sources now unknown, possibly oral.

Sturlubók and *Hauksbók* mention approximately thirty-five hundred personal names and fifteen hundred place-names. The *Landnámabók* is, however, not just a dry listing of names and genealogies. Also included are short stories and tales that rival the best anecdotes in the Sagas of Icelanders or *Sturlunga saga*.

Much has been written on the historical value of *Landnámabók*. It is obvious that it is a unique source for personal names and place-names, but how reliable it is with regard to other facts is unclear. Some of the people mentioned in it have, in all probability, been made up; their origins can sometimes be traced to explanations of place-names. Possibly, the original intention was to defend old rights or to list landownership. In the thirteenth century, however, the work's original function must have altered. If we can rely on the opinion expressed in the epilogue to *Þórðarbók*, the origin of the Icelanders was what mattered most, although those who expressed such concerns were more often defending the rights of the nobility and clergy while concealing their partisanship. With *Sturlubók*, times have clearly changed, and *Landnámabók* has become a work, not only of genealogy, but also of independent historiography, and the same is true of

Hauksbók. This, however, does not change the fact that lineage has always been a matter of importance to the nobility, and Sturla Þórðarson, Haukur Erlendsson, and the Melamenn are no exceptions to this.

Scholars have emphasized the use made by Sturla Þórðarson and Haukur Erlendsson of the Sagas of Icelanders. One cannot, however, infer from this that the sagas were intended as histories or that, by using parts of them, Sturla and Haukur considered them to be so. The attitude of the authors of the Sagas of Icelanders to a work such as *Landnámabók* must have been similar to Chrétien de Troyes's view of the Anglo-Norman historical writers Wace or Geoffrey of Monmouth: he made liberal use of these sources, all the while adapting the past to contemporary chivalric ideals.

Sturla Þórðarson writes history in the same spirit as his uncle, Snorri Sturluson: he brings the past closer to his own generation with tales of living persons, and, like his uncle, introduces characters that he believes to have expressed their views at some point. The difference between the methods of Snorri and Sturla, on the one hand, and Chrétien, on the other, is that Snorri and Sturla never entertain a noble ideal that commands belief because it is good and beautiful. Readers must decide for themselves whether a story that they relate is historical truth or fiction, something that has, in fact, continued to confuse readers up to the present day.

Kristni Saga

Kristni saga is a little longer than *Íslendingabók* and is concerned with only one part of Icelandic history: the missionary work and the conversion to Christianity. Its author is not a representative of a public institution, as Ari was with his *Íslendingabók*, and he approaches his subject matter in a different way. The narrative is lively, and it is clear that the author had access to written sources or storytellers who knew and were willing to tell more of past events than Ari — and not afraid to do so.

According to *Kristni saga*, the nobles of northwest Iceland were among the first to be christened. Þorvaldur Koðráðsson, the son of a local farmer, is converted to Christianity in Saxony, follows a bishop named Friðrekur, and interprets for him, as "the bishop understood not the Norse tongue" (*Biskupa sögur*, ed. Steingrímsson et al., 1:6). The story tells in detail of Þorvaldur's missionary work and what becomes of him and then, after his death, traces subsequent missionary work up to the national conversion at the Althing. It covers the period 980–1118, the same period Ari focuses on. The narrative is much more thorough than in other sources and is interspersed with verses, among them libelous (*níð*) ones in which Þorvaldur and Bishop Friðrekur are accused of homosexuality.

Kristni saga is thought to have been written in the thirteenth century. It has all the hallmarks of historiography that characterize the works of Snorri Sturluson and his nephew Sturla Þórðarson (see also pp. 84, 101, 120). The author includes verses both to serve as the testimony of witnesses and to enliven the prose. The work also contains fragments of dialogue, and people's responses are often noted.

The author made use of *Íslendingabók* and also clearly had access to sources now lost. He is a skilled narrator who knows how minor events can be used to reveal character and behavior. It is not because of this, however, that scholars have attributed the work to Sturla Þórðarson but rather because of how it was preserved. In his introduction to his and Eiríkur Jónsson's edition of *Hauksbók*, Finnur Jónsson agreed with Brenner (in *Über die Kristni-Saga*) and found it likely that Sturla Þórðarson had written the work, meaning to place it after his settlement account, but before *Þorgils saga og Hafliða*; the first sentence in *Kristni saga*, "Here begins how Christianity came to Iceland," was directly linked to the end of *Sturlubók*. In addition, *Kristni saga* has been preserved only in *Hauksbók* and is placed there directly after the book of settlement by Haukur, who had access to Sturla's book of settlements. The methodology of *Kristni saga* and other works that are definitely known to be the works of Sturla has, however, never been subjected to close comparative analysis.

Sturlunga Saga

Sturlunga saga is a large compilation preserved in two manuscripts, *Króksfjarðarbók* and *Reykjarfjarðarbók*. Both these manuscripts were written in the latter half of the fourteenth century, and there are lacunae in them that have been filled with material from seventeenth-century paper copies of the manuscripts made when they were still complete.

It is clear that the stories contained in the compilation were meant to form one whole, telling the story of individual families from the settlement up to the end of the thirteenth century. The compilation begins with *Geirmundar þáttur* (The story of Geirmundur), followed by (in chronological order of the events narrated) *Þorgils saga og Hafliða* (1117–21), *Ættartölur* (Genealogies), *Sturlu saga* (1148–83; The saga of Sturla), *Prestssaga Guðmundar góða Arasonar* (1161–1202; The saga of the priest Guðmundur Arason the Good [included in part in *Íslendinga saga*]), and *Guðmundar saga dýra* (1186–1200; The saga of Guðmundur dýri). The main part of the work, however, is *Íslendinga saga* by Sturla Þórðarson. In it have been interwoven *Haukdæla þáttur* (The story of the Haukdælir), *Hrafns saga Sveinbjarnarsonar* (The saga of Hrafn Sveinbjarnarson), *Þórðar saga kakala* (The saga of Þórður kakali), and *Svínfellinga saga* (The saga of the Svínfellingar). Here, the narrative moves from the story of one clan to the story of the nation as a whole and the men in authority over it. *Reykjarfjarðarbók* also includes *Þorgils saga skarða* (The saga of Þorgils Hare-lip), *Sturlu páttur*, *Jarteinabók Guðmundar Arasonar* (The miracles of Guðmundur Arason the Good), and *Árna saga biskups* (The saga of Bishop Árni), the last two of which are not found in *Króksfjarðarbók*.

For a long time scholars agreed that the compiler included the above-mentioned sagas — which had existed independently — unchanged. Research has revealed, however, that he rearranged his subject matter in order to shape it as one complete history. In addition, there is a considerable difference in interpretation between the two main manuscripts. *Reykjarfjarðarbók* is more concerned with ecclesiastical affairs, as its additional material, *Jarteinabók Guðmundar Arasonar* and *Árna saga biskups*, clearly shows.

We cannot be entirely sure of the original chronological range of Sturla Þórðarson's *Íslendinga saga*, but scholars have presumed that it begins where *Sturlu saga* ends, in 1183. Determining the end point of *Íslendinga saga* is problematic, mainly because many of the sagas in the compilation, especially those written after the middle of the thirteenth century, are very carefully woven together by the compiler.

In the compiler's commentary it says that some of what is related in *Íslendinga saga* had been witnessed by Sturla himself and that some relied on the knowledge of learned men as well as on short relations (*bréf*). Seeing how close Sturla was to the events described, his story has been considered reliable and, for the most part, objective. He observes chronology carefully, the narrative moves rapidly season by season, and mention is often made of the mass day on which events took place. Those who followed chieftains on their missions are listed, as are those who fell in battle with them and those of their opponents who were spared and under what conditions. In this way the story resembles Kings' Sagas such as *Sverris saga Sigurðarsonar* (The saga of King Sverrir). Particularly noteworthy is the degree of detail used to describe men's wounds; indeed, it has been claimed that these descriptions are based on eyewitness accounts that had the express purpose of evaluation for compensation, in accordance with the Commonwealth laws contained in *Grágás*. It is clear that Sturla also relied on annals, one of which he is thought to have written himself (see p. 95). The narrative at times resembles annalistic writing, but it is in many places richer and more reminiscent of a diary.

When it comes to descriptions of individuals, whether they are Sturla's relatives or chieftains from other families, images spring from the page that can hardly be considered historically objective. Sturla's uncle, Snorri

Sturluson, for instance, does not appear in his traditional guise of omniscient and moderate chieftain. Instead, the author makes fun of his domineering habits and implies that he was cowardly, self-serving, and tightfisted with his closest relatives. Sturla's relative and namesake Sturla Sighvatsson is presented as a haughty and vengeful aggressor who does not respond well to the sarcastic humor of his father, Sighvatur. Gissur Þorvaldsson does not always receive flattering treatment either; he seems to be well-spoken, but no one knows whether to consider him friend or foe. One of the most chilling descriptions of him is at the battle of Örlygsstaðir, where he takes the life of Sturla Sighvatsson as he lies exhausted and bleeding.

While Sturla Þórðarson was himself present at Örlygsstaðir and would have seen and heard what went on, it is worth noting that the description of Sturla Sighvatsson in the battle is structured according to traditional narrative conventions. In fact, the author stages the event in a way similar to that found in the Sagas of Icelanders: the battle takes place at dawn in the autumn; the narrator's sympathy lies with the hero, Sturla Sighvatsson, who defends himself heroically but is overpowered; and the hero is treated maliciously by his enemies, in this case Gissur and his men. Sturla Sighvatsson wears a black robe, his father, Sighvatur, a black cape. Where the battle descriptions in *Sturlunga saga* and those in the Sagas of Icelanders differ is that the weapons are often not sharp enough in *Sturlunga saga* (with the result that usually heads do not fly off torsos) and men are slain even though they ask to be spared. Sturla also often uses verse to voice his own opinion or that of his family, the Sturlungar, a device well-known from the Sagas of Icelanders.

Premonitions play a part in setting the scene. Sturla has a bad dream the night before the battle; rubbing his cheek hard he says: "Take no notice of dreams." And, indeed, the first wounds that Sturla receives are to his cheeks: he is speared first in the right cheek and then in the left, "and the spear cut out a piece of the tongue, and the wound reached the bone" (*Sturlunga saga*, Thorsson et al., eds., 1:416, 421). The narrative technique here is not different from that of the Sagas of Icelanders and their use of verses and dreams to reveal feelings or opinions.

Sturla Þórðarson's narrative art becomes even more apparent in the account of another event that, like the battle of Örlygsstaðir, took place in Skagafjörður. It is made clear in *Íslendinga saga* that there is animosity between Sturla Þórðarson and Gissur Þorvaldsson, but, as they grow older, they are reconciled and seal the reconciliation when Sturla gives Hallur, son of Gissur, the hand of his daughter, Ingibjörg, in marriage. The wedding is held at Flugumýri in Skagafjörður, where Gissur resided. Gissur's opponents pledge to pursue him after the wedding. This they do, burning the farm, and killing many people. Gissur in his linen gown escapes by hiding in a tub of sour whey that is buried in the ground. Sturla says that at first it was cold in the sour whey and that Gissur's enemies had come into the pantry in the cellar and thrust spears into the tub. Then, he says: "Gissur gently put his palms in front of his belly so that they would not notice anything in the tub. He was scratched on his palms as well as on his legs, receiving many slight wounds. Gissur has himself told that before they entered the pantry he had been shivering so much that the whey rippled in the tub, but as they arrived he did not shake at all." After the fire, attention is first drawn to Gissur's losses, and then we are told: "Ísleifur was carried out on his shield, and nothing was left of him except the roasted torso inside his coat of arms. The breasts of Gróa were also found and their remains brought to Gissur on a shield. Then Gissur said: 'My cousin, Páll, here you can see my son Ísleifur and my wife Gróa.'" Then Páll saw Gissur turn away, and something jumped from his face similar to hailstones." The description of Gissur's reaction is traditional: it is intended to show his manliness. And there is no sentimentality when the attention is turned to the writer's own children. His daughter, Ingibjörg, gets out of the fire alive, and he says of her: "She was quite worn out, still just a child" (*Sturlunga saga*, Thorsson et al., eds., 2:641–42).

Íslendinga saga is without a doubt the most remarkable piece of historiography of the thirteenth century. Not much is known about its author. Sturla Þórðarson was Snorri Sturluson's nephew and lived at Reykholt for a while. It is entirely possible that he became interested in historical literature there, just as his brother, Ólafur hvítaskáld, became interested in poetics and grammar. He seems to have taken the side of his relatives, first Sturla Sighvatsson, and later, after the death of Snorri, Óraekja Snorrason. He appears, however, to have been critical of their deeds, and at times a notable sarcasm infuses his narrative. Somehow he managed to stay alive in this war among the various families and their chieftains. After he was reconciled with Gissur Þorvaldsson, he became a baron, and in the 1260s he gained the favor of the king of Norway, Magnús Hákonarson Lawmender, and was commissioned to write a code of law for Iceland. He also wrote *Magnúsar saga lagabætis* (The saga of Magnús Lawmender) as well as *Hákonar saga*. Sturla was a clever politician in his day; he shows both slyness and fidelity. It is very probable that he favored the monarchy, as he would hardly have been involved in drafting the law code had he not been a supporter of Hákon and his son Magnús Lawmender. It is, however, hardly possible to detect any sense of a peace-loving king in his descriptions of the bloody thirteenth century. Indeed, it is not at all clear what exactly Sturla's aim was in writing this saga.

The narrative mode of the sagas included in the *Sturlunga saga* compilation is uneven from one saga to another, and each may originally have served different purposes.

Biographies of Bishops

The Bishops' Sagas have traditionally been viewed as one group, without generic distinctions. But, in fact, the lives of Saint Jón and Saint Þorlákur, along with three versions (the B-, C, and D-redactions) of *Guðmundar saga* (The life of Bishop Guðmundur), should be considered hagiography; these three bishops are confessors, and their lives (vitae) are discussed later in this chapter. The biographies of other Icelandic bishops conform to other, if related, narrative models, even though at times they seem more akin to the magnanimous lives of saints than to realistic biography. Bishops' Sagas were probably first written down in the first part of the thirteenth century, *Hungurvaka* (The appetizer) being the oldest. *Páls saga* (The saga of Bishop Páll) was written at around the same time, but then a century passed until other Bishops' Sagas were again composed: *Árna saga Þorlákssonar* (The saga of Bishop Árni Þorláksson) at the start of the fourteenth century; the A-redaction of *Guðmundar saga*, probably during the first half of the same century; and, finally, *Laurentius saga* (The saga of Bishop Laurentius), which Einar Hafliðason, the chancellor at Hólar, wrote around the middle of the century. Included among the Bishops' Sagas are two *þættir* (tales; sg. *þáttur*): *Ísleifs þáttur Gissurarsonar* (The tale of Bishop Ísleifur Gissurarson; thirteenth century) and *Jóns þáttur Halldórssonar* (The tale of Bishop Jón Halldórsson; fourteenth century). The former is closely related to the *Íslendingaþættir* (Tales of Icelanders) found in the Kings' Sagas, while the latter is a kind of introduction to a collection of exempla. Neither *þáttur* can be considered to be a biography as they are structured like exempla and aim to educate their readers.

Medieval biographies were rigidly structured. They would start off by introducing the subject's parents and family and then cover periods in the subject's life the author considered it imperative to preserve for posterity. Usually the narrative is in chronological order. The authors often used annals to determine dates and referred especially to occurrences that coincided with events in the subject's life.

Latin rhetoric exercised a considerable influence on biographical writing because it taught how to praise a man and describe his talents. Lives of saints and the biographies of ordinary men have in common the detailed description of the subject's merits. And such praise is also much in evidence in the Bishops' Sagas. As a result, character flaws are generally missing from the narrative, and not much attention is paid to emotional life, with the result that the descriptions become very monotonous. There are exceptions to this, for instance, in *Páls saga* and *Laurentius saga*, where the narrative style is mostly realistic, without much use of florid or elevated style.

Southern Bishops' Sagas
In the preface to the synoptic history of the bishops of Skálholt up to Saint Þorlákur, the author begins by giving the work a title—he calls it *Hungurvaka*—and refers appropriately to it as a pamphlet: it tells briefly of the first five bishops of Skálholt. While the work's preface is long and learned and includes many well-known topoi from medieval Latin literature, the biographies themselves are short and seldom describe anything beyond the subject's merit: the author expects the reader to learn from the work how Christianity increased in strength and power at Skálholt.

In *Hungurvaka* the work of Ari the Wise is continued. The structure of the work is similar, relative dating is used in relation to the lives of the bishops, and important events from abroad and in Iceland are referred to, but the Christian calendar according to Gerlandus's chronology is also used. *Hungurvaka* can be considered a public church history, probably written at Skálholt shortly after 1200. The biographies it contains can be viewed as examples of Christian conduct. The final part includes a comment hinting that the work was supposed to have been longer, but in its surviving form *Hungurvaka* straddles a boundary, being in large part a church history like *Íslendingabók*, and at the same time one of the first attempts at writing continuous biographical chapters.

The narrative of *Hungurvaka* reveals that the author had studied Latin. While the style is, for the most part, simple and without flourishes, the preface illuminates the evidence of the writer's knowledge of rhetoric. In places there are, however, naive comments that reveal something of the life of the clerics at Skálholt during the twelfth century. One could well imagine that the author had been a teacher there and had studied with Gissur Hallsson (d. 1206), a well-known, learned member of the Haukdælir family who is most sincerely thanked in the preface for the knowledge that he imparted to the author.

Páls saga is a biography that attempts to justify Páll's actions and deeds during his rule in every way. If we believe the saga, Páll ruled to the satisfaction of both chieftains and clergy. The author of the story is sympathetic to the ecclesiastical administration that was in force until Saint Þorlákur: chieftains who knew how to take care of financial matters, yet still live generously, should reside at Skálholt. *Páls saga* is well written, and the author is relatively familiar with the historiographic methods of his day.

Historiography of this kind then seems to have been discontinued in Skálholt until the writing of *Árna saga Þorlákssonar*. Of course it is possible that southern writers recorded historical matter, but no examples of such work survive today.

Árna saga Þorlákssonar was written in defense of the deeds of a controversial servant of God who did all he could to protect the autonomy of the church and insisted that all benefices should be under its rule. Árni had great disputes with secular leaders, disputes that eventually resulted in the agreement of Ögvaldsnes in Norway in 1297. He did not live to see the agreement being put into practice, as he died a year later.

The nineteenth-century scholar Guðbrandur Vigfússon was of the opinion that the saga was written by Bishop Árni Helgason at the beginning of the fourteenth century (see *Biskupa sögur*, ed. Vigfússon and Sigurðsson, 1:lxxix). This opinion has since been refuted, but all scholars now agree that the saga was written during the bishopric of Árni Helgason and under the auspices of Skálholt. *Árna saga Þorlákssonar* is an important historical document because the author had access to the charters of the bishopric and often cites their contents briefly. Otherwise the narrative is mostly dry, a simple report full of Latin loanwords. The author relied on annals, especially *Konungsannáll* (King's annal), which he uses for chronological reference. The style occasionally resembles that of fourteenth-century religious texts, and the author clearly knows his rhetoric. The overall tone is serious but at times shows flashes of sympathetic humor. The saga in its preserved form seems to be an author's draft.

Northern Bishop's Sagas
In addition to the chapters on the life of Bishop Guðmundur Arason the Good (1161–1237) included in the *Sturlunga saga* compilation, a biography of him — the A-redaction of *Guðmundar saga* — exists separately. It was composed during the first half of the fourteenth century.

The A-redaction of *Guðmundar saga* is a compilation. Its editor has made use of the so-called *Prestssaga* (The priest's saga), an unfinished part of the life of Bishop Guðmundur also used in the *Sturlunga saga* compilation, *Hrafns saga Sveinbjarnarsonar*, Sturla Þórðarson's *Íslendinga saga*, *Áróns saga* (The saga of Árón), and annals. He rarely ventures his own opinion; he is a compiler first and foremost, and it is not possible to assess today what his objective was. He is, on the other hand, representative of a style in biographical writing that first became apparent in *Árna saga biskups*, a style that is concerned with collecting as many facts from a person's life as possible in one book, following a strict chronology, and grounding that chronology with the help of annals. This type of biography also tells of the main events in Iceland and abroad and becomes a type of chronicle. This method had a permanent influence on Icelandic hagiographic compositions during the fourteenth century.

Laurentius Kálfsson was bishop of Hólar from 1324 to 1331. He was probably born in 1267 and was of a noble but poor family. Laurentius was ordained as a priest and later became a monk at Þingeyrar for a while. *Laurentius saga* claims that he soon outshone the other students in learning and knowledge. He was considered quite a domineering bishop, and the saga makes it clear that he did not get on well with the inhabitants of the north.

Laurentius saga is one of the best biographies written in Iceland before the Reformation. However, like all sagas of this genre, it has been shaped by a rhetorical structure and a Christian outlook. Laurentius's virtues are, for instance, described in detail as in a saint's life; his authoritarianism in all matters is described as entirely in line with the administrative practices of other officials of his class. But the author has the advantage of having had access to Laurentius and perhaps even followed his own account of many events in his life, especially relating to his childhood and upbringing and other personal matters.

The Icelandic bishop Finnur Jónsson (1704–89) was the first to claim Einar Hafliðason (1307–93), a close colleague of Laurentius's, as the author (*Lárentíus saga biskups*, ed. Grímsdóttir, ixv). Other scholars have since agreed with him. Einar was ten years old when his father placed him for study with Laurentius, who was then at Þingeyrar. Later Einar served as a deacon with Bishop Laurentius, whom "he loved best of all his clerics and kept as his true confidant" (*Laurentius saga biskups*, ed. Árni Björnsson, 98). It is evident from the story that Einar was the bishop's confidant as he became his cellarer, read saints' lives to him, and took care of him on his deathbed. Einar Hafliðason is also thought to have written *Lögmannsannáll* (The lawman's annal), which is in many places identical to the saga.

It is nowhere stated in the story what the occasion or purpose of its writing was. Einar was clearly grateful to Laurentius and wanted to reward him for his mentorship. But *Laurentius saga* is also political; at the end of the story Laurentius is said to have written a letter to the archbishop in which he emphasizes that, from then on, Icelanders should be ordained as bishops as this would be best for the church.

The saga's ending is missing from manuscripts. It is possible that *Laurentius saga* was meant to promote the autonomy of the national church, for, according to the annals, it is exactly at the middle of the century that the dominance of foreign bishops became overwhelming. One must bear in mind, however, that bishops' biographies were partly intended to be reports on their official duties and governance. This is also true of *Laurentius saga*, which stands out as the best of its kind and shows an accomplished writer at work, one who knows how to maintain the reader's attention and enlivens his material with comic anecdotes. *Laurentius saga* is also the most informative source on teaching and education available from the fourteenth century.

Biographies of Icelandic Leaders

Hrafn Sveinbjarnarson (d. 1213) was a well-known leader from western Iceland who appears in many places in *Sturlunga saga*. There is also a separate saga of him in two versions, both of which scholars believe to be based on one original story, of which *Sturlunga saga* also made use. The saga was supposed to show a fair leader, one pure of mind and Christian. At times Hrafn is described almost as a holy man, while his opponent, Þorvaldur of Vatnsfjörður, reminds us of the infamous stereotypical opponents of Christianity. The author of the saga has learned many things from the saints' lives: his description of Hrafn's medical work resembles famous miracles as described there. Hrafn does not, however, work any wonders; his cures are all brought about by his knowledge, not by divine powers. The description of Hrafn conforms to that of a character in the biographies of national governors to the extent that it is supposed to show a secular leader who is fair and just and rules over others because of his virtues. In this respect the saga is a political apologia: it sets out to describe its subject's leadership and shed light on his image as a leader. As far as style and narration are concerned, *Hrafns saga* is similar to the sagas in the *Sturlunga saga* compilation; it includes realistic descriptions and makes use of colloquial idioms. Guðrún P. Helgadóttir, who has edited and researched the saga, believes that it can be dated to the decades between 1230 and 1260 (*Hrafns saga Sveinbjarnarsonar*, ed. Helgadóttir, lxxxvii–xci) and that, of the possible authors suggested by scholars, the priest Tómas Þórarinsson is most likely to have written it.

Árons saga is one of the most peculiar medieval biographies. It tells of Árón Hjörleifsson, one of Bishop Guðmundur Arason's most warlike men, his battles alongside Guðmundur, and, finally, his exile in Norway, where he becomes a courtier of King Hákon Hákonarson's. Árón's life ends shortly after a trip to Iceland, when he has been reconciled with those of his countrymen who have had scores to settle with him. The author of the saga based his story on a poem by Ólafur hvítaskáld Þórðarson and on the priest Þormóður Ólafsson's verses on Árón. *Áróns saga* is thought to have been written around the middle of the fourteenth century. It covers the same period as Sturla Þórðarson's *Íslendinga saga* and is, therefore, often printed with *Sturlunga saga*. It is the biography of a hero and carries all the hall-marks of a heroic tale, in which courage and chivalry are cherished above all else.

The A-redaction of *Guðmundar saga* and *Áróns saga* are the last medieval biographies of Icelanders. Biographical writing spanned two centuries and can be divided into three periods. In the oldest sagas, only a few life events are narrated, and it is, therefore, possible that *Ævi Snorra goða* (The life of Snorri the Chieftain), a small piece of biographical data concerning the main protagonist of *Eyrbyggja saga* (The saga of the people of Eyri; see pp. 132, 136), is one of the earliest. *Hungurvaka* and *Páls saga* belong to the next period, which is characterized by the inclusion of descriptions of daily life, in addition to simple life events, as well as some praise and criticism of the subject. The last period starts with *Árna saga biskups*, the A-redaction of *Guðmundar saga*, and *Laurentius saga*, by which time biographies have become detailed reports and are largely concerned with significant periods in the country's history, even though they mostly cover ecclesiastical matters. *Hrafns saga* and *Áróns saga* also belong to this last group of sagas, even though their focus is on secular leaders. And, strange as it may seem, it is, in fact, these two works that contain the most apparent hagiographic influences.

Pseudohistorical Works: Universal Histories and Annals
From the early Middle Ages well into the sixteenth century, people were introduced to the history of the world either through the Bible or through the so-called universal histories (*veraldarsögur*). In Old Icelandic texts they were referred to as *heimsaldrar* (sg. *heimsaldur*) or *aldartala*, that is, *aetates mundi*, the word *öld* (gen. *aldar*, pl. *aldir*) in Old Norse denoting both a specific period and mankind itself.

The categorization of history into *aetates mundi* was well known in Iceland from very early on and was used in historical works. Universal histories are also among the first literature written in the country. At least five such works exist, whole and in fragments, differing in size and age. The most complete is a text that was named *Veraldar saga* (The world's history) by Konráð Gíslason (d. 1891) in the nineteenth century. History is there divided into six ages: the first age of the world starts with God's work, while the sixth and last reaches the twelfth century. Toward the end of the story Fredericus barbarossa, the emperor of Germany, who died in 1190, is mentioned as being alive, which means that *Veraldar saga* must have been written before that time.

Veraldar saga has been preserved in two redactions. The difference between *Veraldar saga* A and *Veraldar saga* B is that the latter adds some exegetical commentary on each world age. The work is far from being a dry list of historical facts. The author is a capable writer, and the narrative is light and fluent. For a long time *Veraldar saga* was thought to be a translation, but, as it has not been possible to identify a model for it, it is most likely that it was written by an Icelander who was familiar with foreign texts on the subject. Some scholars have attributed the saga to Gissur Hallsson, but it is more likely that it was written in an educational institution, where it was important for students at the start of their studies to obtain an overview of the calendar from creation on, covering the most important events in world history and their interpretation. Skálholt is, therefore, the most likely place. This likelihood is supported by the view that *Veraldar saga* would hardly have been written in a place where there would have been available neither foreign texts on biblical interpretation, nor a calendar, nor even any instructive texts such as Sallust's *Bellum Jugurthinum*, the works of Dares Phrygius, or the *Ilias Latina*.

Universal histories laid the groundwork for the historiographic methods of the medieval period and at the same time opened people's eyes to the possibility of linking national and foreign events, of writing a continuous history of man in chronological order. Such work in its most primitive form is found in annalistic writing, and it is believed that in Iceland annalistic writing began in the twelfth century, although we do not have examples to prove this conclusively.

Late in the nineteenth century the Norwegian scholar Gustav Storm published ten medieval Icelandic annals, giving them the titles that they have carried since: *Resensannáll*; *Forni annáll*; *Høyersannáll*; *Konungsannáll*; *Skálholtsannáll*; *Annálsbrot úr Skálholti*; *Lögmannsannáll*; *Gottskálksannáll*; *Flateyjarbókarannáll*; and *Oddaverjaannáll*. Storm reached the conclusion that Icelandic annal writing began in the late thirteenth century and that the Icelandic annals traced their origins back to one original annal written in the latter half of the thirteenth century. The arguments that Storm presented to support his theory were that large parts of all the annals were identical, that they had been based on similar sources, and that they used the same computus (a method of keeping track of time). In *Den oldnorske og oldislandske litteraturs historie*, his literary history, Finnur Jónsson expressed largely the same opinion.

Shortly after Storm's edition (*Islandske Annaler indtil 1578*) was published, however, Natanael Beckman pointed out (in his and Klund's edition *Alfræði íslenzk*) that a description of a solar eclipse must indicate that annal writing started much earlier than Storm and Finnur Jónsson had assumed—since a solar eclipse could have been seen in Iceland only in the twelfth century, not the thirteenth. Hermann Pálsson (*Eftir þjóðveldið*, 50–51; also *Tólfta öldin*, 32–43) drew attention to the fact that much of the material that *Konungsannáll* contains, over and above *Resensannáll*, *Høyersannáll*, and *Forni annáll*, must have come from a lost annal based in the monastery at Þingeyrar. It must also be considered likely that annal writing began in the early twelfth century and was continued in monasteries and chieftains' residences, where people wanted to commemorate important events. The writing of universal histories in the twelfth century supports this view because these two kinds of historical literature very often run parallel.

Annal writing elsewhere in Europe is usually not tied to single authors; rather, each generation writes on contemporary events. This does not preclude the possibility that such writing could be influenced by a monastery or a family. *Resensannáll* is a clear example of this. In it are listed important events and the hour of death of the Sturlungar family members. Finnur Jónsson first pointed to this in his literary history (*Den oldnorske og oldislandske litteraturs historie*, 3:71), and Jón Jóhannesson thought it almost certain that some member of the Sturlungar family wrote the annal (see his *Gerðir Landnámabókar*). Recently Stefán Karlsson has also argued that the last person to write in the annal was Sturla Þórðarson himself (see his *Stafkrókar*, 279–302). If this is correct, it increases the value of the annal for the insights it might provide into *Íslendinga saga*. The same can be said of *Lögmannsannáll* and *Laurentius saga*. By comparing these sources one can see more clearly how these historical writers worked.

It has often been claimed that the Icelandic annals were based on historical texts. This is hard to prove. It is more natural to assume that the medieval historians based their works on annals, rather than the other way round, and then fleshed out the details.

Icelandic annals are different from other native literary genres in that they often contain long chapters in Latin. Their writers constantly referred to foreign textbooks such as the *Historia scholastica* by Peter Comestor and the *Speculum historiale* by Vincent of Beauvais (d. 1264) and relied on Danish and Swedish annals as well as on Anglo-Saxon royal lineages.

Translated Pseudohistorical Works

The Latin textbook *Ilias Latina*, known in translation as *Trójumanna saga* (The saga of the Trojans), Sallust's work on the Jugurthine War, and Lucan's *Pharsalia* exist in translations and retellings of various ages and are known collectively in Icelandic as *Rómverja saga*. On the heels of these textbooks followed translations of other works written in the twelfth century, such as Geoffrey of Monmouth's *Historia regum Britanniae*, known as *Breta sögur* (The sagas of the Britons), and the *Alexandreis* by Walter of Châtillon (d. after 1185) (written, evidently, for students), known as *Alexanders saga* (The saga of Alexander the Great).

Scholars have not been able to determine the age of these translations with any degree of certainty. In all likelihood the oldest is the compilation *Rómverja saga*, preserved in two redactions. The older of these redactions has been preserved in two manuscripts from the fourteenth century, the younger in several manuscripts, the oldest of which dates from the fourteenth century. The translations are varied in quality and, as is generally the case with medieval translations, are more appropriately considered retellings or renderings.

The value of *Rómverja saga* for Icelandic historiography lies not least in its demonstration of how Roman authors wrote about the past, for instance, giving ancient leaders speeches that obeyed the rhetorical rules that Icelandic students had to study during this time; the re-creation of the past with the help of rhetorical devices brought history to life for the audience, which included students who later were to write their own works. The saga of King Sverrir and the works of Snorri Sturluson immediately spring to mind.

The title *Trójumanna saga* has been given to the compilations that have their roots in the work of Dares Phrygius: *De excidio Troiae*, on the one hand, and *Ilias Latina*, on the other. *Trójumanna saga* exists in three redactions that are preserved in *Hauksbók* and in other manuscripts from the fourteenth century and later. It is clear, however, that a cycle either in prose or in verse about the Trojans had been known much earlier; Snorri Sturluson was familiar with Trojan stories, and they are referred to in *Veraldar saga*.

The versions of *Trójumanna saga* that have been preserved to this day bear witness to literary activity during the thirteenth century and later. It is possible that they influenced secular historiography, as the Latin narratives did earlier, but in this case their influence was mainly on the narrative style of prose romances (the Knights' Sagas, the Legendary Sagas) and the Sagas of Icelanders: the magnificent descriptions of ancient heroes encouraged exaggerated descriptions of country lads from Iceland. Apart from this work and Geoffrey of Monmouth's *Historia regum Britanniae*, *Gyðinga saga* (The saga of the Jewish people) and *Alexanders saga* formed an important part of the great compilations of the fourteenth century where the compilers tried to combine native and universal history.

The *Historia regum Britanniae* followed the versions of *Trójumanna saga* found in the *Hauksbók*: "Here follows a story of Aeneas and those who settled in Britain" (*Trójumanna saga*, Louis-Jensen, ed., 226). Such preservation shows how medieval people viewed the sagas: to them they represented one continuous history. The *Historia regum Britanniae* also exists in another redaction that probably also followed *Trójumanna saga* in manuscripts. Nothing is known about the age of these translations, but Brother Gunnlaugur Leifsson (d. 1218), a monk at Þingeyrar, had the *Historia regum Britanniae* at hand in Latin and translated one part of it into verse: the *Prophetiae Merlini*, or *Merlínus spá*. Gunnlaugur's comments on the prehistory of the prophecy show that he knew all of Geoffrey of Monmouth's work. Gunnlaugur's translation has been included in the correct place in the text of *Hauksbók*, but it has been omitted from the other redaction. In both places he is, however, said to be the translator of the poem.

The fact that Geoffrey of Monmouth's work was known in Iceland at the start of the thirteenth century is very significant. Geoffrey was an innovator in many respects. He divorces historiography from its conventional theological framework: events take place, not because of divine intervention, but because of the actions of individuals; people create the past. This viewpoint opens new historical horizons; events are interpreted in light of the behavior of individuals. The author of *Skjöldunga saga*, and, later, Snorri Sturluson, adopted similar methods, opening the door to historical fictional narrative.

In style and method the *Historia regum Britanniae* resembles chivalric romances. The language is, at times, flowery, and the translation is, in some places, more wordy than the original text, although there are some omissions in *Hauksbók*.

During the latter half of the thirteenth century, Abbot Brandur Jónsson (d. 1264) of the monastery at Þykkvibær is among the most famous clerical writers. As well as *Alexanders saga* and *Gyðinga saga*, part of a Bible translation known as *Stjórn* III has been attributed to him.

It has been doubted whether Brandur Jónsson translated both *Gyðinga saga* and *Alexanders saga* as they are so different in style and form. It should not be forgotten, however, that the original works themselves are very different. The *Alexandreis* is written in a verbose style, and its author is very fond of rhetorical flourishes. *Gyðinga saga*, on the other hand, was collated from many sources, for instance, the apocryphal Maccabees books in the Old Testament, the *Historia scholastica*, and the so-called *Historia apocrypha*, which is thought to have been used by Jacobus de Voragine (d. 1298) in the *Legenda aurea*. These texts are for the most part in *sermo humilis* (low style), which is naturally reflected in the translation.

Gyðinga saga is not a very innovative work and has exerted little influence. *Alexanders saga* is a different matter. It is without a doubt among the best translations to be produced in medieval Iceland. Walter of Châtillon composed the *Alexandreis* in hexameters, but Brandur adapted the narrative form to the established conventions of Icelandic historiography. He omits, for instance, Walter's introduction to each individual book of the poem, although he occasionally manages to include Walter's ethical message and his authorial asides by referring to the original work. He has also tried to convey most of the stylistic traits of the original, even though he sometimes has to explain the text where the Icelandic audience did not know the prehistory. It is also characteristic of the translation that Brandur often shortens the rhetorical digressions, and, for instance, narrative devices like retardations are not used in the same way as in the original. However, Brandur often allows Walter's personifications to stand. While *Alexanders saga* did not have a marked influence on the narrative style of historical texts, it did so all the more on the Sagas of Icelanders and the prose romances.

KINGS' SAGAS

Beginnings
The Kings' Sagas have traditionally been considered a separate genre in scholarly texts on Icelandic literature, but, after careful consideration, it becomes clear that such a categorization is not justified. These sagas are mostly concerned, not with Icelanders, but with kings in Sweden, Norway, and Denmark, and they take place abroad. Their handling of material is, on the other hand, based on the same historiographic methodology described above. Either narratives on kings are biographies of individual leaders alive or dead, or they span a longer period and trace the origins of Norse peoples and their leaders back to ancient times and, as such, are national histories. The narration of both types is realistic, and the writers' use of sources is similar, even though their execution and aims are, in many ways, different.

Scholars have long debated the origins of the Kings' Sagas, and the writers Ari Þorgilsson the Wise and his contemporary Sæmundur Sigfússon are often mentioned in this connection. In the fortieth stanza of "Noregskonungatal" (List of the kings of Norway), a poem that Jón Loftsson (d. 1197) of Oddi commissioned about his ancestors, Sæmundur, Jón's grandfather, is mentioned as a source. Snorri Sturluson, on the other hand, considers Ari the Wise to be the father of Icelandic historiography. With the authority of this verse and Snorri's comments, scholars have assumed that, at the start of the twelfth century, there existed two histories of the kings of Norway: one written in Latin by Sæmundur Sigfússon, the other written in the vernacular by Ari the Wise.

The settlers of Iceland traced their origins for the most part to Norway. It was, therefore, self-evident that part of the Icelandic national histories would be devoted to Norway. It is, however, not quite clear why historiographers were so preoccupied with the history of the Norwegian kings if they considered themselves a separate people, as is suggested in the *Þórðarbók* version of *Landnámabók*. One should note, however, that both the Haukdælir and the Oddaverjar families considered themselves descendants of Norwegian kings. Their story of origin was important to them, not only because of connections and relations, but also because such a noble origin could constitute a claim for secular power during the period of writing. Sæmundur died in 1133, and it was not until the time of his grandson, Jón, that the Oddaverjar started to brag about their royal ancestry. The poem "Noregskonungatal" clearly shows that Jón considered himself to be a leader of men, but, from preserved sources, it is not possible to conclude that the political concept of one state with one king had any adherents in twelfth-century Iceland.

Eiríkur Oddsson's *Hryggjarstykki* (Backbone piece), cited in *Heimskringla*, is the first historical work that covers, in part, contemporary events. This work is now lost, but the author of *Morkinskinna* (The rotten vellum), so named by Þormóður Torfason, and Snorri Sturluson relied on it. It is unclear just how much of *Hryggjarstykki* they made use of, but, from their quotations of Eiríkur, it becomes clear that his work made use of the eyewitness accounts of people who told of events soon after they took place. Other biographies follow: *Sverris saga*, *Böglunga sögur* (The sagas of the Baglar), *Hákonar saga*, and *Magnúsar saga lagabætis*.

With the exception of the references to *Hryggjarstykki*, not much is known about the writing of the Kings' Sagas in the twelfth century. The first lives of Ólafur Tryggason and Saint Ólafur Haraldsson (Saint Olaf) in prose were probably written ca. 1200, but these works are not comparable to secular biographies in most respects. Snorri and later compilers borrowed some material from these works, as we will see below. However, the writers who put the stories of kings down in writing and have been considered simply compilers in fact often adjusted the narrative: the hand was controlled by a creative mind. The compilations *Fagurskinna* (Fair parchment), *Heimskringla* and, later, *Morkinskinna*, all considered national histories, have unmistakable authorial voices.

Norwegian National Histories

It is thought that Norwegians began to write their own national histories during the latter half of the twelfth century. Of these works, two have been preserved in Old Norse and two in Latin. One of the Latin sagas, called *Historia de antiquitate regum Norwagiensium*, was written by Theodoricus the Monk, probably in the 1180s or 1190s, and dedicated to one Archbishop Augustine, who is thought to have been Archbishop Eysteinn of Nidaros (Trondheim).

Opinions are divided on the age and origins of the other Latin saga of Norwegian kings, *Historia Norwegiæ*. Its manuscript was found in Scotland around the middle of the nineteenth century. It is generally thought to have been written around the middle of the fifteenth century and to have originated in Orkney. The dispute about the age of the manuscript and its origins has not, however, been resolved; the original work could be from the latter half of the twelfth century, but nothing rules out a more recent dating, say, from the start of the thirteenth century. The author made use of the same sources on the Ynglingar dynasty as Ari the Wise and Snorri Sturluson. The work starts with a description of Norway and its neighboring countries, which are populated by pagans. Next, the countries colonized by Norway are described — the Orkneys, the Shetlands, the Faeroes, Iceland, and Greenland.

The oldest Norwegian book on kings in the vernacular, probably written in the last decades of the twelfth century, has since the nineteenth century been called *Ágrip* (A compendium). This name is appropriate in the sense that the narrative spans a long period in the history of Norway and covers some important events only briefly, although it also covers in detail some events that to modern eyes do not seem so vital, for instance, the first meeting of Haraldur harðráði (Hard-ruler) and Magnús the Good. *Ágrip* probably started with the life of Hálfdan the Black, the father of Haraldur Fairhair, but that story is now missing as the first part of the manuscript is lost. The kings' lives are recounted in chronological order.

In *Ágrip* we do not meet some of the innovations that were beginning to appear in historical writing elsewhere in Europe during the first half of the twelfth century. The same can be said about the fourth Norwegian historical text from this period, *Fagurskinna*. It covers the same period as *Ágrip*, from King Hálfdan the Black up to the battle of Ré in Norway in 1177, and was probably written ca. 1220. Its author has made use of *Ágrip*, and he knows the life of Saint Olaf and the sagas of the earls of Hlaðir.

Fagurskinna is uneven in quality. The character flaws of the various kings are hardly mentioned, and other matters are glossed over as well. The author is loyal to the Birkibeinar, King Sverrir Sigurðarson's group of rebels in Norway, and he emphasizes the right of the descendants of Haraldur Fairhair to the throne.

Fagurskinna's style is at times plodding, but in many places pointed, if simple, stylistic devices such as antithesis are used to good effect. Most remarkable is probably the use of verse in the work. It has, for instance, preserved the historical poem "Hrafnsmál" (The lay of the raven), also known as "Haraldskvæði" (The poem of Haraldur), and it is thought to be quite old as its handling of material corresponds to ancient Germanic traditions. This poem can be considered the first of its kind in staging historical events in dramatic fashion.

Fagurskinna's author uses poets' verses as eyewitness accounts but explains nowhere in any detail the way in which he uses them, and any comparison with Snorri Sturluson's use of the same sources is to his detriment. He is certainly not as critical as Snorri regarding the value of historical verses.

Scholars have long debated the relation between *Fagurskinna* and Snorri's *Heimskringla*. Nowadays, most are agreed that *Fagurskinna*'s author did not make use of Snorri's work, but there is less agreement as to whether Snorri made use of *Fagurskinna* or whether both authors relied on the same source. Long chapters in the histories of Haraldur Fairhair and Hálfdan the Black are identical, but it is interesting to note how many of the stories in *Heimskringla* are not found in *Fagurskinna*. Philologists maintain that Snorri knew *Fagurskinna* and in some places made use of it but that he also relied on other sources, which he treated in his individual, independent way.

Snorri Sturluson's National Histories

In no medieval source is Snorri Sturluson named as the author of either *Heimskringla* or *Ólafs saga helga hin sérstaka* (The separate saga of Saint Olaf). It is not until the sixteenth century that he is so named — and then in a Norwegian translation by the king's landholder Laurents Hanssøn, from Skough near Bergen. Snorri is, nonetheless, frequently mentioned in medieval sources, but only rarely can one deduce from these quotations that he wrote other books than the *Prose Edda*, attributed to him in a manuscript from the first quarter of the fourteenth century. There, Snorri is also said to be a poet and to have composed a long eulogy, *Háttatal* (List of verse forms; see also pp. 38 and 152), honoring King Hákon Hákonarson and Duke Skúli Bárðarson. Among the quotations that refer to Snorri's historical works, the most significant are to be found in *Ólafs saga Tryggvasonar hin mesta* (The longest saga of Ólafur Tryggvason).

There are, however, other sources on the historian Snorri Sturluson. Sturla Þórðarson explains clearly in his *Íslendinga saga* that Snorri worked at his writing in Reykholt. His account runs thus: "This summer [that of 1230] was quiet, and there was a good peace in Iceland; few rode to the Althing. Snorri did not go to the Althing but ordered that the priest Styrmir the Wise should ride with his jurisdiction as law speaker. Now the relationship between Snorri and Sturla [Sighvatsson] improved, and Sturla spent a long time in Reykjaholt [now Reykholt] and intended to copy the books Snorri had composed" (*Sturlunga saga*, 1:328–29, Thorsson et al., eds.).

Unfortunately, Sturla Þórðarson does not mention which books these were; he undoubtedly assumed that all his listeners would be familiar with his uncle's work. From examples quoted in *Ólafs saga Tryggvasonar hin mesta*, we may deduce that they dealt with Norwegian kings, and in all likelihood *Heimskringla* is meant. While few sources on Snorri's writing are known to us today, there seems to be no reason to doubt these testimonies.

Snorri Sturluson was the son of Sturla Þórðarson, a chieftain, and Guðný Böðvarsdóttir. Sturla Þórðarson was an unruly man and made most events in the district his business. With him, the rise of the Sturlungar family begins as his disputes with his neighbors almost always resulted in more power for him. His intervention in the feuds between the priest Páll Sölvason and his father-in-law, Böðvar Þórðarson, led Jón Loftsson to offer to foster and teach Snorri, an offer that reconciled the disputing parties. Jón took Snorri into his home and then invited Sturla himself to the anniversary of the Saint Nicholas church at Oddi in the south, and Sturla accepted "fine gifts from Jón" (*Sturlunga saga*, 1:99, Thorsson et al., eds.). Snorri is said to have been born in either 1178 or 1179. He was, thus, hardly more than three years old when in 1181 he came under the guidance of the Oddaverjar family.

On Snorri's childhood and education at Oddi nothing is known, but his stay there was surely fruitful in many ways. We do not know for certain what he studied with Jón Loftsson or the other scholars there, who had read at centers of learning in France and England. From the *Prose Edda* it is clear that he knew the *Elucidarius* of Honorius Augustodunensis well and probably some other clerical works. A few scholars — among them Peter and

Ursula Dronke ("The Prologue of the Prose Edda"), Anthony Faulkes ("Pagan Sympathy"), and, recently, Margaret Clunies Ross (*Skáldskaparmál*) — have also pointed to evidence of the influence of the twelfth-century French Neoplatonic thinkers in the *Prose Edda*. While the evidence of foreign influences is, admittedly, clear, it should not be made too much of; Snorri mainly works with Norse material and rarely transgresses native conventions. In the last part of *Heimskringla*, some accounts can be traced to Jón Loftsson himself, who stayed in Norway for a while.

It is not impossible that Snorri's views of the Norwegian kings were formed during his years with Jón at Oddi. Snorri went abroad only after his studies had been completed, so he must have learned his scholarship in Iceland, most probably at Oddi. He married Herdís, a rich woman from Borg, where he resided for a few winters. He moved to Reykholt in 1206 and took over many *goðorð*. He went abroad for the first time in 1218, to Norway, where he soon became a favorite of Duke Skúli Bárðarson, then the most powerful man in Norway. It seems that Snorri was awarded the rank of baron by Duke Skúli and King Hákon Hákonarson.

Scholars have long thought that Snorri drafted his Kings' Sagas during his first travels abroad and that *Ólafs saga helga hin sérstaka* was written first, followed by *Heimskringla*. The lucid descriptions of Norway and especially Sweden, in which he refers to Swedish accounts, could support this. Scholars have considered it likely that Snorri had heard these tales on his travels in Sweden.

It is natural to assume that Snorri became interested in this material, especially the verses on kings, while working on the *Prose Edda*. The *Prose Edda* must have been written shortly after Snorri finished *Háttatal*, which forms the last part of the *Prose Edda* and was, possibly, composed in the winter of 1221–22. After completing the *Prose Edda*, he turned to *Ólafs saga helga hin sérstaka* and then, finally, to *Heimskringla*. There is not much difference between *Ólafs saga helga* (The saga of Saint Olaf), which forms the middle part of *Heimskringla*, and *Ólafs saga helga hin sérstaka*. *Ólafs saga helga hin sérstaka* starts off with an account of the Norwegian kings, beginning with Haraldur Fairhair, a topic covered in much more detail in the first third of *Heimskringla*. *Ólafs saga helga* also recounts individual events differently, and the miracles collected at the end of *Ólafs saga helga hin sérstaka* are scattered over the last third of *Heimskringla*. Because the same events are treated in more detail in *Heimskringla* than in *Ólafs saga helga hin sérstaka*, scholars have assumed that Snorri thought the material deserved more discussion and, therefore, added to it at the beginning and at the end, the eventual result being the development of a national history from a biography, with the saint representing in both instances the bearer of new political ideas. There are prefaces to all Snorri's works, and they provide important information on his methodology and opinions, even though it is impossible not to wonder whether some parts of the two prefaces to *Ólafs saga helga hin sérstaka* originated in the workshop at Reykholt.

In his historical works Snorri has ever in mind to illustrate both the good and the bad sides of monarchical government. For this purpose a life of a saintly king could serve as a good example. It also shows Snorri's courage and reason that he chose Saint Olaf's life to interpret the political and royal duties of his contemporaries. Snorri is obviously conscious of the fact that Saint Olaf's life is considered to contain nothing but the truth, just like other saints' lives. He does not deny that Saint Olaf is a special friend of God and faithfully records his virtues and miracles, but he also does not conceal Saint Olaf's misdeeds and evil acts.

In *Ólafs saga helga*, Snorri emphasizes time and again that Saint Olaf got his power from God. For example, he reports that this dispensation is revealed to Saint Olaf in two symbolic dreams. In the first, which occurs when he is outlawed, a nobleman in expensive costume, whom he believes to be his predecessor, Ólafur Tryggvason, stands by his bed. In the second he views the whole of Norway when he arrives west of Kjölur (Kjølen):

> A while ago I saw strange sights. Looking westward from the mountains, I saw all of Norway. It struck me that many a day I had been happy in that land; and then I had a vision: I saw the entire district of Trondheim, and then all of Norway, and the longer it lasted, the more I saw, until I saw the whole world, both land and sea. I clearly recognized the places I had been to before and seen. And with the same clarity I saw places I had not seen before, some I had heard of, some I had not heard of, both inhabited and uninhabited, as far as the world extends. (*Heimskringla*, ed. Kristjánsdóttir et al., 2:351)

This vision proclaims Saint Olaf's eternal kingdom and, at the same time, his eternal power over the minds of his countrymen. The kings who followed on the throne thus took their power symbolically from him.

Although Snorri omits few of Saint Olaf's miracles from his saga, he is careful when it comes to such supernatural events. It is, however, quite clear that the hagiography frames what is, in fact, a political history. The accounts of Saint Olaf's life paint a traditional picture of the struggle of a holy man — the opposing worlds represented by Christianity and paganism clash — who dies a martyr. Snorri keeps all these details together, and motifs from the life of Christ are all given their place, just as in the stories of martyrs. But in

Snorri's hands the events are turned into a political battleground. The battle is over power and autonomy, with the battle over religion subordinated to the ideal that leaders should have autonomy in all matters that concern them. The martyr himself dies an absolute monarch after a coup. Snorri is, however, careful never actually to say directly that Saint Olaf was an unfair king or even a tyrant. Instead, he uses *the Stout*, Olaf's old sobriquet, right at the beginning of the story, which may be viewed as an indication of what is to come. Snorri describes the rule and governance of Saint Olaf first and foremost with examples, especially in *Ásbjarnar þáttur Selsbana* (The tale of Ásbjörn the Seal-slayer).

The image of the saint is consistent in the main, both in *Ólafs saga helga hin sérstaka* and in *Heimskringla*. This image reflects the kernel of Snorri's ideas on the monarchy. He appears to believe in the individual's autonomy, although he accepts the authority of rulers in some matters. And, although both sagas tells of his downfall as a secular king, Saint Olaf lives on after death: the religious hero conquers both peasants and chieftains despite the odds. They acknowledge his power by worshipping him as a saint. When his son, Magnús, is fetched from Russia and crowned king, a corner has been turned in Norwegian history: monarchs of the same dynasty should rule the state of Norway. Therefore, their national history had to be continued. Snorri told the story right up to the Birkibeinar uprising. He did not need to go any further.

The third part of *Heimskringla* is much more detailed than the other parts of the work, but it is a little more uneven as well as the interpretation of events becomes more careful. In its descriptions of people, especially of Haraldur Hard-ruler, however, the narrative equals the best of the first two parts. There is also evidence of typological thinking and ethical interpretation in *Heimskringla*: Haraldur Fairhair's womanizing hurts his descendants, and the fratricides in *Ynglinga saga* are repeated in the saga of the sons of Haraldur Fairhair and again in the fights of the sons of Haraldur Gilchrist. While it is quite possible that the killings in fact happened as Snorri relates and that he may have relied on ancient sources, he also often improves on older stories and puts them in new contexts. This is very clear in *Ólafs saga Tryggvasonar* (The life of King Ólafur Tryggvason), in the first part of *Heimskringla*, for instance, where the king is walking along a street in the early spring and a man approaches him in the market

with many sticks of angelica, amazingly big at that time of the spring. The king took one stick in his hand and walked to Queen Þyri's chambers. Þyri sat in her room weeping as the king entered.

The king said: "Look at this great angelica stick I am going to give you." She struck it away with her hand and answered: "Greater were Haraldur Gormsson's presents, and he was not afraid to leave the country to fetch his property as you are, as became clear when he arrived here in Norway and destroyed most of this country and got everything, tributes and taxes, but you do not dare to travel through the realm of the Danes because of my brother, Sveinn." King Ólafur jumped up when she had spoken and answered loudly: "Never shall I retreat for fear of your brother Sveinn, and if we meet, he shall retreat." (*Heimskringla*, ed. Kristjánsdóttir et al., 1:343)

Snorri relies for the most part on Oddur Snorrason's account (see p. 163) for the life story of Ólafur Tryggvason. In Oddur's version, the queen's answers are polite and without rancor; Þyri mentions only that she was given *tannfé*, "tooth gift" (a present as the first tooth appears), in Denmark while taking a bite of angelica, which was probably used as a toothbrush in those days. Snorri, on the other hand, lets Ólafur Tryggvason become angry, Þyri's words inciting him because — as Snorri and his audience probably well knew — angelica was also a symbol of love and fertility. In Snorri's version, the king thus accuses the queen of being frigid by handing her the plant, and she immediately retorts and accuses him of cowardice. In this way Snorri enhances the story and hones the lines of the portrayal: the missionary king becomes human and is angered by the queen's challenge.

Snorri also uses other parts of Oddur's hagiographic account: Ólafur Tryggvason, Saint Olaf's predecessor, dies in battle, as does Saint Olaf, and the battle of Stiklarstaðir (Stiklestad) is, in part, a repetition on land of the naval battle at Svöldur (Svold). Snorri does not, however, describe the light that, according to Oddur's version, follows the saint's fall at the battle of Svöldur. He cites other sources claiming that Ólafur Tryggvason escaped and gives Hallfreður vandræðaskáld (the troublesome skald) the last word on the matter: "I do not care for gossip" (*Heimskringla*, ed. Kristjánsdóttir et al., 1:370 [verse 169]). In this way Snorri re-creates past events and gives them new meaning while moving away from Oddur Snorrason's hagiographic interpretation.

Ólafs saga helga hin sérstaka, and, in fact, every saga in *Heimskringla*, follows a biographical pattern. The narrative flows in chronological order, even though dates are seldom mentioned and the chronology is relative, as in *Íslendingabók* by Ari the Wise. In his prefaces Snorri explains his views on saga writing and his use of sources, but, unfortunately, he does not mention the purpose of the work. From the preface to *Heimskringla* it is clear that he considers poets' verses to be equal in value to eyewitness accounts, a principle that he also applies to events in ancient times that other writers, such as Theodoricus, omitted owing to a lack of reliable source material. Snorri seems to be of the opinion that poems like "Háleygjatal" (List of the chieftains of Hálogaland) and "Ynglingatal" (List of the Ynglingar dynasty) are truthful sources (see p. 33). The largest part of his discussion in the preface to *Heimskringla* is, in fact, devoted to defending these opinions because his contemporaries had begun to doubt the historical value of verses. Snorri's point of view in this regard seems to be similar to that of Geoffrey of Monmouth in his *Historia regum Britanniae*. The emphasis is on the interpretation; each tale may contain truth, as may a line composed by a poet whose talent and inspiration were a gift from the gods.

In his 1920 book *Snorri Sturluson*, Sigurður Nordal suggested that, in Snorri's work, the two brooks of learning and entertainment formed one and the same river: Snorri imbued dry historical knowledge with life, without ever relaxing the demand for truth in his narrative. Nordal compared Snorri to Ari the Wise and his *Íslendingabók* and suggested that, in *Heimskringla*, Icelandic history had become narrative art. Nordal had a point, but, like many other scholars, he overlooked the fact that, rather than combining two methods, in his historiography Snorri employed a method altogether different from that of Ari; his attitude toward history was different from that of his forerunners. Snorri was also not burdened by having to adhere to an official view of history, in that neither bishops nor secular leaders censored his work. Instead, he sought to interpret the past in a way similar to that of historiographers elsewhere in Europe at the time, and he seems to have taken Geoffrey of Monmouth as his model, tracing his story back to the divine origin of the kings' ancestors. Yet, for all this, he is very much reliant on his sources, and it is not easy to catch him spinning tall tales of ancient times. He cedes to the poets Þjóðólfur of Hvinir and Eyvindur skáldaspillir responsibility for the narrative of their time, but, as he comes closer to his own time, he gives the verses of individual poets a scholarly function similar to footnotes in modern academic texts.

The idea of linking the genesis of the Norsemen to a divine origin in Asia Minor and the belief that the Norwegian kings were descended from gods and the heroes of Troy were almost certainly influenced by foreign scholarly and historical texts. There is hardly any doubt that Snorri knew a version of the history of the Trojans and that he was familiar with the content of the *Historia regum Britanniae*; certainly the *Prophetiae Merlini* must have been well-known to him. Snorri is not the first to trace the kings' lineage back to the Ynglingar dynasty; Ari does the same, as does the author of *Historia*

Norwegiæ. Snorri, however, places these origins in an ideological context: the Norwegian kings are descended from gods, and this is supported irrefutably by the etymology of the time. He relates the root form of *Ásíá* (Asia) to the plural form, *æsir*, of *ás*, "god." This is hardly the first time that a justification for power has been sought in linguistics. When the time comes, kings of the Ynglingar dynasty are ready to take over divine power. A similar symbolic tracing of lineage is evident in the opening chapters of the *Orkneyinga saga* (The saga of the Orkney Islanders), which Snorri is said to have known in an older version than now exists.

Snorri's work has often been interpreted as an effective way for the author, the chieftain Snorri, to elucidate his own attitude toward the monarchy. Two chapters in *Heimskringla* in particular have occasioned this interpretation. One is in the so-called *friðgerðarsaga* (the saga of the pact) in *Ólafs saga helga*, where the Icelandic chieftain Hjalti Skeggjason mediates between King Ólafur the Swede and King Ólafur of Norway. Into this dispute are mixed the marriage plans of the Norwegian king. Earl Rögnvaldur Úlfsson of West Gotland and the lawman Þorgnýr Þorgnýsson of Uppland, whom Snorri calls the wisest man in Sweden, also try to reconcile the kings. Here, Þorgnýr delivers the speech that is thought to describe the views of Snorri himself. Þorgnýr says, for instance:

> Now it is our yeomen's will that you and King Ólafur the Stout should be reconciled and you should give him your daughter Ingigerður's hand. And if you want to conquer again the countries in the East [i.e., the Baltic] that your ancestors and relatives ruled in former times, we will support you to do so. If on the other hand you do not do as we now tell you, we will attack and kill you, and we will not endure any warfare from you or lawlessness. Our forefathers did so before. At the assembly at Múli they pitched into a morass those five kings who had been too arrogant, just as you are now toward us. Tell us at once which option you choose.

Snorri reports that Ólafur the Swede responds to the speech by saying that he wants "what the yeomen want" and that "it has been so with all kings of Sweden, to let yeomen decide whatever they want" (*Heimskringla*, ed. Kristjánsdóttir et al., 2:116).

From this speech it is clear that Þorgnýr chooses a form of monarchy in which chieftains share power with the king. No king should be an absolute ruler, and, should any sign of absolute rule come to light, the king should be removed from the throne, for such is the country's old custom. Snorri includes this speech as an example, and one cannot automatically assume that it therefore reflects his own views on the monarchy. The disparagement of royal power is, however, clear from the lawman's speech, and Ólafur the Swede appears to agree to the power structure upheld by his ancestors.

The other chapter in *Heimskringla* thought to reflect Snorri's opinions is Einar Þveræingur's speech when King Ólafur's messenger, Þórarinn Nefjólfsson, introduces to the Althing the king's wish to "ask in friendship of the Northerners that they give him the island or skerry that lies before Eyjafjörður and is named Grímsey." Einar's answer in a nutshell is that people should not accept being "taxed by King Ólafur or accept any such burden he has put on his subjects in Norway." Einar also mentions the lack of freedom involved and the fact that kings vary: "Some are good, others bad." The end of Einar's speech is its most famous part: "Anyhow, speaking of Grímsey, if nothing that can be considered as food is brought from the island, an army can be fed there. If a foreign army stayed on the island and sailed from there to the continent, I would think that many a peasant would feel their doors being thronged about" (*Heimskringla*, ed. Kristjánsdóttir et al., 2:215–16).

The opinion represented here corresponds to the ideas on monarchy elsewhere in *Heimskringla*. Although Einar speaks of a foreign army on Icelandic soil, there is no hint of nationalism in his words. This is first and foremost a matter of survival and of quality of life. In this respect the account resembles *Ásbjarnar þáttur Selsbana*, where the king himself wants to enjoy the country's natural wealth.

Nothing is known about Snorri's own opinion of King Hákon. Sturla Þórðarson's opinion of Snorri as a baron is, however, beyond question: Snorri did not bring the country under the king, as Sturla says he should have done, and he left Norway in 1239 and sailed to Iceland without the king's permission. The king therefore considered him to have committed treason, which is why he had him killed on 23 September 1241. Consequently, it is quite possible that *Heimskringla* expresses Snorri's doubts about absolute monarchy, that he was, indeed, opposed to the idea of power sharing between king and barons that made its appearance in the days of King Sverrir and was perfected with the absolute monarchy of King Hákon Hákonarson in 1240, after he had Duke Skúli Bárðarson killed. Einar Þveræingur is not Snorri's mouthpiece; his speech on Grímsey is a parable, just as Þorgnýr's speech is. That the medieval audience might well have interpreted what is only hinted at in the text is another matter. Indeed, this particular aspect of Einar Þveræingur's speech motivated its use to support Icelandic nationalism during the nineteenth and twentieth centuries.

Snorri describes the character traits and habits of the various kings in an innovative fashion, one that places the individual at the center of historical events. But *Heimskringla* also contains other innovations. It lets characters deliver speeches at assemblies and before battles, and it delights in dialogue. Most scholars in fact believe the speeches and dialogues to be Snorri's most personal contribution to his work. In them Snorri is careful to balance opposing views and usually compares the past with the present. The speech form itself is not completely in the manner of classical rhetoric, but Snorri was obviously familiar with some of its methods.

Snorri's style is, at first sight, very simple and similar to *sermo humilis*, but, on closer inspection, some stylistic traits become apparent that greatly enhance the story. This is most apparent in speeches and responses. One example is as follows: "King Ólafur went again to the first room of the ship and saw what Erlingur did. The King spoke to him and said: 'You stand with your face [*öndverður*] toward me, Erlingur?' He answered: 'Face to face [*öndverðir*] shall the eagles fight'" (*Heimskringla*, ed. Kristjánsdóttir et al., 2:31). This response is almost identical to the one given in *Ólafs saga helga*, but Snorri adds one adjective, *öndurður* (facing), to the king's question, and Erlingur's response is the more effective for starting with the same word. Otherwise Snorri's most common stylistic trait is the use of antithesis, which he employs with great acumen.

As mentioned above, the structure of *Heimskringla* does not differ much from that of other large medieval historical works. At the end of his preface, Snorri provides a traditional description of the country, one similar to the beginning of the Venerable Bede's *Historia ecclesiastica gentis Anglorum*. He also knows how to tell two stories simultaneously, and the digressions that take place in Iceland, in Orkney, and in the Faeroe Islands are remarkable. Ólafur's missionary work reached all these countries, and, while Snorri might have been dependent on his sources, this narrative must, nevertheless, have appealed to an Icelandic audience. Indeed, in the preface to *Ólafs saga helga hin sérstaka* he apologizes for the fact that Icelanders feature so prominently in the saga: "If this narrative should reach foreign shores, I know that people will think that I have recorded too many things to do with Icelanders, but the reason is that they saw or heard of those events and brought their knowledge to this country, and from them people have since learned about these things" (*Heimskringla*, ed. Kristjánsdóttir et al., 2:422).

It is quite possible that *Heimskringla* and *Ólafs saga helga hin sérstaka* had, in fact, been written predominantly for an Icelandic audience because the ideology expressed in them could hardly have been agreeable to the descendants of King Sverrir in Norway during the latter half of the thirteenth century and into the fourteenth. And, looking at the structure of

Ólafs saga helga hin sérstaka, it is clear that it follows the traditional form of a saint's life—childhood, upbringing, mature years, suffering. On the other hand, it is possible to view the fall of Erlingur Skjálgsson as the climax of the work and the vengeance taken for him that leads to Saint Olaf's fall as the aftermath. Viewed in this way, the pattern is very similar to the structure of some Sagas of Icelanders from the thirteenth century, which is a possible indication that both narratives were aimed at the same audience.

Snorri Sturluson had access to the main works on Norwegian kings written around 1200, but, compared to Snorri's, the ones that have been preserved are like drafts. His achievement was to write a continuous narrative of the Norwegian kings and to follow a particular view of history acceptable to the demands of the time. He does not, however, diverge much from conventional methods; his work is written largely in accordance with the European historiographic tradition. He recites remarkable examples and leaves the audience to interpret them. With *Heimskringla*, Snorri intended to write the story of the Norsemen, placing their national history into the frame of *aetates mundi* (universal histories), and, certainly as far as artistry is concerned, no Icelandic historian of the Middle Ages has bettered him.

Morkinskinna *and Later Surveys*

Norse national histories do not end with *Heimskringla*. The manuscript *Morkinskinna*, written in the latter half of the thirteenth century, contains tales of Norwegian kings, although the manuscript is not whole and there are many gaps in the narrative. It starts with the saga of Magnús Ólafsson the Good and concludes with the saga of Ingi and his brothers, the sons of Haraldur Gilchrist. The main part of the manuscript is thought to have been copied from a manuscript from the first decades of the thirteenth century dealing with the same sources Snorri knew and used. There are some philological arguments for this, but that does not change the fact that *Morkinskinna* must be considered a work from the latter half of the thirteenth century and that its so-called *þættir* are innovations, probably composed by the author.

Morkinskinna's narrative is highly variable in quality: there are quite a few repetitions and even contradictions. It seems that the structure was not well thought-out. The story follows a certain chronology, but, in many places, the narrative is broken up with material of different sorts, chapters obviously meant to serve as exempla, describing and analyzing the kings' temperaments, either singing their praises or pointing out their faults. These chapters have been called *þættir*. The word *þáttur* (sg.) in Old Norse means "a string" or "a thread," and the *þættir* in a work should, thus, be woven together to form one strand. It has been maintained that *Morkin-skinna*'s *þættir* were originally independent tales and only later included in the work, but there are no literary arguments to support this. Short stories as we know them today are hardly known elsewhere until the fourteenth century; Giovanni Boccaccio (1313–75) is considered by some scholars to be their originator. However, from ca. 1200 until well into the fourteenth century, the fabliau and exemplum traditions in Europe flourished, and their influence is to some extent apparent in the Icelandic *þættir*.

Many of the *þættir* in *Morkinskinna* follow a pattern common to folk- and fairy tales, while others follow the rules of exempla. One of their characteristics is that most of them are concerned with Icelanders and their relationship with the king, and some of the motifs are well-known from the Sagas of Icelanders. This is the case, for instance, in the *þáttur* of Oddur Ófeigsson, which tells of Oddur's trip to Finnmark and how he tricks Haraldur Hard-ruler and hides the taxes collected from the Lapps (Finnar) from him. Oddur's hiding places are identical to the ones that Þráinn Sigfússon uses in *Njáls saga*, in which he hides Hrappur and speedily sails to Iceland. The most famous of *Morkinskinna*'s *þættir* are *Auðunar þáttur* (The tale of Auðun), *Brands þáttur örva* (The tale of Brandur the Generous), *Hreiðars þáttur heimska* (The tale of Hreiðar the Foolish), and *Ívars þáttur Ingimundarsonar* (The tale of Ívar Ingimundarson). The first three highlight Haraldur Hard-ruler's temperament and are clearly supposed to show the virtues that every king should possess: generosity; mercy; and wisdom. *Auðunar þáttur* shows King Haraldur's wisdom and his good deeds toward pilgrims to Rome. *Brands þáttur örva* could be an analysis of friendship, one based on a moral message from the Bible: "Let the man with two coats give to him who has none" (Luke 3:11). It could also be based on the explanation of courtly duties found in *Konungs skuggsjá* (The king's mirror): "If a rich man is asked to do something [for someone] and the favour is described for him, he should then bear in mind whether he can by the favour be hurt or honoured" (*Konungs skuggsiá*, ed. Holm-Olsen, 122). *Ívars þáttur Ingimundarsonar*, on the other hand, is centered around the retainers' sorrow (*amour heroes*) and shows King Eysteinn Magnússon's concern for his courtiers and the rest of his people. It also holds some good advice for a common human complaint: depression.

A few *þættir* in *Saga Haralds harðráða* (The saga of Haraldur Hard-ruler) give a different and bleaker picture of King Haraldur Hard-ruler. Before *Brands þáttur örva* there is the so-called *Úlfs þáttur* (The tale of Úlfur), which tells of a feast that Úlfur the Rich hosts for the king. Haraldur decides to entertain the guests by telling them about Úlfur's ancestor, the slave

Álfsteinn, and, at the end of the story, the king wants to dress Úlfur in a gray slave's cloak. The thought behind the story is that each man belongs in the class he is born into; Úlfur is descended from a slave and can, therefore, never be counted as a person of rank. At the same time Haraldur's cruelty is revealed; he can, at times, be a malevolent ruler and treat his people harshly. *Brands þáttur örva* is, therefore, thought to counterbalance the story of Úlfur. But the author also knows the art of revealing Haraldur's faults even more clearly. This is most apparent in *Hreiðars þáttur heimska*, where the related kings Magnús Ólafsson and Haraldur both appear. Hreiðar kills one of Haraldur's courtiers in a game, and Haraldur asks Magnús for compensation, but Magnús thinks that the man has fallen without the right to compensation. Hreiðar is then placed with Eyvindur, one of Magnús's barons. There he settles down and fashions an excellent silver object that he gives to Haraldur when the courtiers apprehend him and he is at the king's mercy:

> "See, here is an object I want to give you," and he puts it on the table in front of him. It was a swine, made of silver, and gilded. The king looked at the swine and said: "You are so good a craftsman that I have hardly seen a thing as well made as this one." Then it was handed on to his men. The king says that he wants to be reconciled with him, and "it is my opinion that it will be good to send you on great errands because you are strong and fearless." The swine is now passed back to the king, and he tossed it and looked at it with more care than before and noticed teats on it — it was a sow — and he threw it down, and realized that it was made to mock him, and said: "May the devils take you, men shall rise and kill him." (*Morkinskinna*, ed. Jónsson, 135)

Hreiðar has made the object, not only to mock Haraldur, but also to hint subtly at Haraldur's origin as the son of Sigurður Sow, accusing him of animal behavior; it is even likely that the audience thought that Hreiðar was accusing him of deviant sexual behavior or homosexuality.

Morkinskinna's *þættir* are an inseparable part of the narrative; they serve to keep the narrative balanced, the good in the kings' natures being explained along with the bad, so that the audience will get a clear picture of its leaders while also being entertained with stories of comic events from their lives. The writing of the Kings' Sagas continues in the same spirit. *Hulda* (The secret vellum) and *Hrokkinskinna* (The wrinkled vellum), which are compiled both from *Heimskringla* and from *Morkinskinna* in the late fourteenth century and the fifteenth, are in a similar vein. They have, unfortunately, been published only in imperfect editions, so it is not possible to detect the work of the compilers of the collections. Literary research on the compilation *Flateyjarbók* (The book of Flatey), which also contains national histories similar to those in *Morkinskinna*, is also lacking.

Danish National Histories and Earls' Sagas

Skjöldunga saga (The saga of the Skjöldungar [an ancient Danish dynasty]), referred to in Snorri's *Ynglinga saga*, once existed on vellum but has survived only in the retelling of Arngrímur Jónsson the Learned (see p. 188). *Skjöldunga saga* is supposed to have been written before *Heimskringla*, ca. 1200 according to Bjarni Guðnason, who has thoroughly investigated the sources for this lost story (see Guðnason's *Um Skjöldungasögu*, iv–cxiv). Guðnason also believes that a longer version of the saga once existed, one written around the middle of the thirteenth century, the remains of which now form the text that has been called *Sögubrot af fornkonungum* (Fragmentary saga of ancient kings).

Scholars have assumed that, orginally, *Skjöldunga saga* must have told of Odin's son Skjöldur's descendants and, like *Ynglinga saga*, related the origins of the Danish royal family, thus forming a national history of the Danish people. Its narrative of kings probably resembled other contemporary historical writing, tracing the divine origin of the royal family back to the Trojans. *Skjöldunga saga* was the first example of learned European historiography in Iceland and paved the way for Snorri Sturluson.

It has been suggested that other stories existed about Danish kings, but reliable sources for this are lacking. *Knýtlinga saga* (The saga of the Knýtlingar) does still exist, but *Jómsvíkinga saga* (The saga of the Jómsvíkingar), which some scholars have considered to belong to the stories of Danish kings, is, in fact, not a Kings' Saga. It is, however, possible that, in its present form, it shows how the first step from history to fiction was taken.

Knýtlinga saga begins with the reign of Haraldur Gormsson the Old and then works in chronological order up through all the Danish kings to Knútur Valdimarsson (d. 1202). It is often divided into three parts: (1) the lives of Haraldur Gormsson Bluetooth and the kings who came after him down to Sveinn Úlfsson; (2) the life of Saint Knútur (Canute), which forms the largest part (almost two-fifths of the saga), even though Canute reigned for only six years; and (3) the period from Ólafur Sveinsson to Knútur Valdimarsson.

The author of *Knýtlinga saga* relied on many sources, but the most useful one was obviously *Heimskringla*. Bjarni Guðnason believes that *Knýtlinga saga* was started in Denmark and that the author used local sources that he later took with him to Iceland, where he completed the saga (see *Dana-*

konunga sögur, ed. Guðnason, clxxviii–clxxix). *Heimskringla* clearly serves as a model for the author as far as structure and method are concerned: he uses written sources as Snorri does, and he knows how to cite poets' verses as sources. The aim must have been to write a continuous national history of Denmark down to the author's time.

Knýtlinga saga is thought to have been written sometime between 1235 and 1300. It marks the end of the writing of independent national histories centered on the lives of native kings. Similar in fashion and roughly contemporary were the Earls' Sagas, or the sagas of the Earls of Orkney, to which I now turn.

In *Ólafs saga helga hin sérstaka*, Snorri Sturluson refers to a work that he calls *Jarla saga* or *Jarla sögur* (Earls' saga[s]), which Finnur Jónsson and Sigurður Nordal believed to have been written ca. 1200. It is clear from the context that this refers to stories that now form part of *Orkneyinga saga*. *Orkneyinga saga* has been preserved almost in its entirety in *Flateyjarbók*. It was included there as part of the sagas of Saint Olaf and Ólafur Tryggvason, but parts of the saga exist on vellum fragments from ca. 1300. From these leaves it is clear that the saga existed independently.

Orkneyinga saga is considered by most scholars to have been written in the thirteenth century. In its existing form, it must have been written after Snorri completed his works because it refers to them. It is unclear whether *Orkneyinga saga* echoes the *Jarla saga* Snorri refers to; it is more likely that it represents the kind of historical writing that became common after Snorri blazed the trail for Norse national histories.

Orkneyinga saga tells of the Orkney Islands' earls from around 900 down to the thirteenth century. Preceding the story proper is an account of the origins of the earls of Orkney that shows how well Norse historiographers had assimilated the approaches of their learned predecessors: the earls are of royal blood, and they are descended from a man named Fornjótur who ruled Kvenland and Finnland and had three sons: "One was named Hlér, whom we call Ægir [Sea], the second Logi [Fire], and the third Kári [Wind] — he was the father of Frosti [Frost], the father of Snær [Snow] the Old. His son was Þorri [the name of a winter month]. He had two sons, one was called Nór, the other Gór; his daughter was called Gói [the name of another winter month]" (*Orkneyinga saga*, ed. Guðmundsson, 3).

Genealogy of this kind is, of course, symbolic: natural forces are intended to show ancestral heroism. The ancestors were used to cold and snow; they were men of the North. The author of *Orkneyinga saga* had some help from poets' verses, especially from Arnór jarlaskáld's "Þorfinns-drápa." He also used eyewitness accounts and included tales of Saint Magnus's miracles. Worth a mention is the author's tale of the crusades (1151–53) of Earl Rögnvaldur kali, which is quite detailed and probably originally based on eyewitness accounts.

The author of *Orkneyinga saga* searched widely for sources and was familiar with historical places. The saga does, at times, side with Hákon Pálsson, who had Saint Magnus killed. Nothing is known about the author of the saga. Finnbogi Guðmundson, its most recent editor, believes that the saga in its present form originated in Snorri Sturluson's study. It is, however, more likely that the author is his follower and shaped the work in accordance with existing thirteenth-century national histories.

Kings' Biographies
As was briefly mentioned earlier, it seems that Eiríkur Oddsson was the first Norse author to write a history (now lost) based directly on the accounts of those who had themselves taken part in the events described. It has not been possible definitively to ascertain the meaning of that work's title, *Hryggjarstykki*, which translates as "Backbone Piece" but probably refers to the simile of the body as society, thereby suggesting that some leaders should be considered the backbone of the social body.

We may infer from *Heimskringla* that *Hryggjarstykki* covered at least the period between 1130 and 1139. Some scholars believe it to have continued down to the year 1161, when Ingi Haraldsson died. On the basis of Snorri's account in *Heimskringla* it is possible to establish only that the work was concerned with Haraldur Gilchrist and his sons, who were all called *kings*, and with the rebel Sigurður Slembir, who claimed to be of royal blood. *Hryggjarstykki* was probably a saga of noble rulers, their progress related in chronological order, their life story told, and their deeds justified, in other words, a kind of contemporary political history.

Nothing is known about Eiríkur Oddsson. From quotations from his work it is clear that he was encouraged to write the story, which was commissioned by the rulers themselves. His role can be viewed as a variation on that of the court poet; instead of composing poetry about events, as Saint Olaf demanded of his poets before the battle of Stiklarstaðir, Eiríkur was to write a prose account of barons and princes. This same function is fulfilled by at least two named Icelandic authors, Abbot Karl Jónsson, who wrote the first draft of *Sverris saga*, and Sturla Þórðarson, who wrote *Hákonar saga* and *Magnúsar saga lagabætis*. These authors admittedly had different methods, but they did have the same aim: to write satisfactory political biographies for Norwegian kings and their followers.

Sverris saga has traditionally been considered one of the oldest Icelandic biographies. The most significant support for this claim comes from the preface to the preserved manuscripts, where Abbot Karl Jónsson is said to be the author: "[The book] will start telling of events that occurred a while ago and have been in the memory of those men who related them for this book, that is, to tell of King Sverrir, the son of King Sigurður Haraldsson — and that is the beginning of the book that is written after the one that Abbot Karl Jónsson first wrote after the dictation of King Sverrir himself, who decided what to write. That account does not reach far" (*Sverris saga*, ed. Indrebø, 1). If interpreted literally, this means that this particular work was copied from the book that Karl Jónsson wrote based on Sverrir's own account. In other words, one version of *Sverris saga* predates the present work. The preface also makes clear that the structure of the preserved *Sverris saga* is more recent and based on two parts. Finally, the preface bears witness to the fact that the existing saga was not written at King Sverrir's instigation; there is no indication that the work was a commission, nor is there an address to the king, and in the preface the word *Karl* is used instead of *eg* (I) or *vér* (we), as one would expect had the king himself commissioned it.

There is no reason to doubt the veracity of this source. The chronology used in *Sverris saga* is, for instance, according to the Gerlandus calendar, known from several Icelandic texts composed in the first decades of the thirteenth century. The author had a wealth of material to choose from; the original sources were accounts of contemporaries and the king himself.

The oldest manuscript fragment of the saga is from the last quarter of the thirteenth century, but most of its manuscripts are from ca. 1300 and later. We must consider it likely that the preserved *Sverris saga* was put together not later than the middle of the thirteenth century and after Sverrir's grandson Hákon Hákonarson the Old had strengthened his position.

Scholars have, of course, been curious to find out how a twelfth-century Icelandic abbot came to write a king's biography. To this end, many scholars have tried to determine exactly how long a period is covered by the part of the story in the preface called *Grýla*. If truth be told, such attempts have not yielded much in the way of results, especially since there are few characteristics in the first part that are sufficiently obvious to point to a clear authorial voice. The saga as a whole is very well put together and bears witness to editorial skill.

The name *Grýla* (which translates as "something causing fright or terror") has also raised questions: Why is it used, and does it have a religious reference? In the preface the word is used in the following manner: "As the book advances his [i.e., Sverrir's] strength grows, and the same strength foreshadows greater things; because of this they named that part of the book Grýla" (*Sverris saga*, ed. Indrebø, 1). As it happens, the preface also exists in another version in *Flateyjarbók*, composed in the last two decades of the fourteenth century. The account there of the editorial process is slightly different, and two editors, Prior Styrmir Kárason and the priest Magnús Þórhallsson, are said to have finished the work. *Flateyjarbók*'s text of the preface includes additions that must be theirs, although it is impossible to distinguish between the two. In this version of the preface the latter half of the book is given a title, *perfecta fortitudo*. It is unlikely that Styrmir and Magnús created this title; the Latin *fortitudo* means strength, and this force arouses fear, is *Grýla*. The work's bipartite structure is common in medieval texts, especially saints' lives and biographies. This structure emphasized that Sverrir Sigurðarson was a king through divine right, and the absolute strength (*perfecta fortitudo*) obtained after the fall of Magnús Erlingsson enabled him to show better that his rule was divine. This theological reading, which is invoked in the interpretation of the virtue strength (*fortitudo*), is supported by legendary motifs from the beginning of the saga, with wonders in a dream that Sverrir's mother, Gunnhildur, has before he is born; those wonders must be viewed as divine symbols of the coming strength of the son.

So why did a leader in Norway choose an Icelandic cleric to write his biography? One possible reason that has been suggested is that, in doing so, King Sverrir was choosing a neutral yet Norse person to put his story down in writing, but this is not a very satisfactory explanation. It is more likely that the king would have wanted to have his story told from a sympathetic political viewpoint from the start, and Norwegian clerics were no special friends of his. Icelanders, on the other hand, were well-known at the time for their scholarship and narrative skill, at least according to Saxo Grammaticus's history of Denmark, written ca. 1200. Exactly which parts of the existing *Sverris saga* can be traced back to the twelfth century is another matter.

Sverris saga relates in some detail the career of this unique leader. The Birkibeinar, who in the latter half of the twelfth century were much like a group of rioters, chose this priest from the Faeroe Islands as their leader. The story is confident that Sverrir is the son of King Sigurður Haraldsson Mouth and that he himself is in no doubt about his paternity. However, the portion of the narrative proving that paternity is undeniably brief: only Sverrir's mother's admission in the confessional is cited. On the other hand, Sverrir later lets his half brother, Eiríkur, undergo the ordeal of bearing hot iron as proof of his paternity. It was clearly important for Sverrir to be able to show that he was born to rule. Saint Olaf appears to Sverrir in a dream, washes by a table in the upper rooms, calls Sverrir *magnus*, and asks him "to wash in the same water" (*Sverris saga*, ed. Indrebø, 4). Sverrir's dream refers to both his main opponent, Magnús, and the well-known idea of the *vir magnus*, the great man who becomes a national leader. The main purpose of *Sverris saga* is to create the image of such a leader, one who has the virtues required in a great man, indeed, those of a king. The ideas expressed here could well be seen to correspond to the thought that begins to appear among twelfth-century political thinkers: that noble parentage by itself was not enough for leadership, that virtues and good qualities were, in fact, more important.

Sverrir's leadership talents crystallize in his skill in encouraging other people to great feats, even when all avenues look closed. This particular talent is expressed for the most part through the medium of motivational speeches. Indeed, Sverrir's speeches are the high point of the saga. They are so well composed that it has been assumed that they must have come directly from the king himself. Closer inspection, however, reveals many literary qualities that unmistakably point to a knowledge of rhetoric. While Sverrir himself had received a clerical education and would, thus, have been familiar with the discipline, he is unlikely to have had the detailed knowledge evinced in the speeches, in which the author of the saga must have had a hand beyond simple transcription. The saga's speeches are also used to express contrasting points of view. In fact, the most famous speeches are those given by Sverrir and Magnús Erlingsson before the battle at Fimreiti in Sogn.

Sverris saga is among the most remarkable biographies written in medieval Iceland. The saga is admittedly traditional in style, but, despite the pervasive use of classical motifs and the monotonous character descriptions, the author manages to paint a memorable picture of King Sverrir as a man who rises to the highest power through his own fortitude, an islander who becomes the leader of a large country. Styrmir Kárason's part in writing the story was mentioned above, but nothing can be attributed to him with any certainty. By the time Magnús Þórhallsson wrote down the saga in *Flateyjarbók*, things had changed: according to the preface there, the saga had lost its political value and was aimed more at entertaining the audience.

Böglunga sögur can be viewed as a direct continuation of *Sverris saga* as they focus on the period from Sverrir's death, in 1202, to the year 1217. The sagas tell of three Birkibeinar kings, Hákon Sverrisson, Guttormur Sigurðarson, and Ingi Bárðarson, as well as the kings of the Baglar, the enemies of the Birkibeinar, Ingi Magnússon, Erlingur Steinveggur, and

Philippús Símonarson. They relate the division of power in Norway and its results: the supposed reconciliation in 1208 of the tribes of the Baglar and the Birkibeinar. *Böglunga sögur* exist in two redactions: the longer one covers the entire period, while the shorter one ends in 1210.

Although *Böglunga sögur* cannot be compared to *Sverris saga* as far as artistry is concerned, the speeches, although few, are memorable, for instance, Marshal Loðinn's speech before the Baglar's attack on the Birkibeinar in Nidaros in 1206, and some of the sagas' dialogues are fairly well written.

The last Icelander who is known to have written a king's biography commissioned by the ruler himself is Sturla Þórðarson, who composed *Hákonar saga* and *Magnúsar saga lagabætis*. In *Sturlu þáttur* it says, for instance: "Sturla soon became the king's greatest friend, and the king often sought his advice and asked him to be responsible for composing the biography of King Hákon his father under his auspices and the guidance of the wisest men" (*Sturlunga saga*, Thorsson et al., eds., 2:767).

In all probability Sturla resided with his wife, Helga, in Norway for nearly eight years during the period 1263–71. Their son, Þórður, became the court cleric of King Magnús Lawmender, and it is likely that Sturla collected material for the saga sometime during the years 1264–65. *Hákonar saga* contains a repetition of the material dealt with in *Sverris saga*, which Sturla clearly knew, as well as in *Böglunga sögur*. Sturla emphasizes strongly to his audience that Hákon Hákonarson was the rightful heir to the Norwegian crown and cites proof that he is a king by divine right. What is noteworthy is that Sturla does not gloss over the fact that the Icelanders Snorri Sturluson, Þórður kakali, and Gissur Þorvaldsson did not fully carry out the king's errands in Iceland.

The opinion has been voiced that Sturla disliked writing this saga but felt that he needed to win the king's favor as he could have been facing a death sentence for his failed attack on the king's retainer Hrafn Oddsson in Stafholt in 1263. It is impossible to confirm this, but there is no doubt that *Hákonar saga* is a much drier read than *Íslendinga saga*. The liveliness and humor are missing from the few dialogues that it contains. Sturla used court decisions, legal texts, letters, and other documents in order carefully to trace the king's life in chronological order, as was the norm in biographies of the period. The most important of Sturla's contributions to the saga are his own verses, which, it seems, he wrote in order to comment on and interpret his own prose narrative.

Sturlu þáttur also relates that Sturla had based *Magnúsar saga lagabætis* on "letters and his own advice" (*Sturlunga saga*, Thorsson et al., eds.,

2:767). This saga has been preserved only in fragments, but Arngrímur the Learned knew its fuller version when he wrote *Crymogæa* in the seventeenth century (see p. 190). From its fragments it can be ascertained that it resembled *Hákonar saga* in style and form. Sturla also composed a poem on Magnús that partly follows the conventions of the old court poetry.

The Decline of the Kings' Sagas

In literary histories it has usually been claimed that, with Sturla Þórðarson's historical writing on father and son, Hákon and Magnús, the writing of Icelandic Kings' Sagas comes to an end. This claim is correct as far as it goes: biographical writing on contemporary kings ends, but this means discounting the efforts of fourteenth-century writers. During this period large compilations on Norwegian kings see the light of day. To some extent these are only collections, bringing together all available materials concerning the kings in question. It is, however, undeniable that, in some of these manuscripts, one can see flashes of independent creation, with material added to appeal to new audiences. In this respect *Ólafs saga Tryggvasonar hin mesta*, which has been attributed to Abbott Bergur Sokkason (fourteenth century), is unique. It contains a collection of most of the material known about King Ólafur Tryggvason, and it looks as if the author intended to write, not a saint's life, but rather a biography that is at the same time a history of Christianity in Norway and Iceland.

But for whom were thirteenth- and fourteenth-century Kings' Sagas written? The early Kings' Sagas, by Sæmundur Sigfússon, Ari the Wise, and Snorri Sturluson, were probably written for an Icelandic audience — and the first two specifically for noble and powerful family leaders, probably the Oddaverjar or the Haukdælir. The emphasis of Snorri Sturluson's work may well have suited Norwegian leaders other than the kings themselves, and it is likely that these sagas, along with other Kings' Sagas manuscripts, were written for export to Norway. There are also examples of Icelandic manuscripts intended for Norwegian readers. It should be emphasized, however, that most of the Kings' Sagas were written after the Icelanders had come under Norwegian rule and the country had become part of the Norwegian realm. It must have been important to leaders that the islanders be acquainted with correct political ideas about the monarchy and get a "truthful" picture of the ancestors of the then rulers of Norway. *Flateyjarbók*, which contains more than Kings' Sagas alone, represents probably the last example of sagas intended for Norwegian governors. Ólafur Halldórsson has speculated that it was intended for King Ólafur Hákonarson (d. 1387) (see his *Grettisfærsla*, 427–31). But by 1400 there was such a difference between the languages of Iceland and Norway that only a small number of Norwegians would have been able to understand the narrative. Those able to buy expensive books, townsmen and the aristocracy, spoke a related but distinct language removed from Old Norse — and had other interests besides. Thus, the market disappeared, and the independent writing of Kings' Sagas ended.

SAGAS OF ICELANDERS

Icelandic literature is best known internationally for the Sagas of Icelanders. These sagas focus largely on Icelandic men and women, and, while they are usually set in the Icelandic countryside, some are also set in Greenland, the Faeroe Islands, and the old homelands in Norway. Because of their subject matter they have traditionally been considered one genre, but determining what distinguishes them from works in other genres is by no means a straightforward task. Many of the sagas are structured like chronicles with a strict outer time frame and are in that way no different from the Norse national histories classified above as medieval historiography. The narrative world of the Icelandic sagas is often different from that of historiographies, however, because of the constant interaction with the reality of the audience, their imagination and emotions. While the descriptions of Icelandic places and society are realistic, this sense of reality often diminishes once the narrator moves out of the country, at which point the narrative becomes more fantastic, more like heroic tales and adventures. The same often happens when characters express their emotions in verse, using metaphors and imagery from mythology, or their consciousness is revealed through symbol-laden dream visions.

It has been thought that, at the time when the Sagas of Icelanders began to be written down, many types of saga writing were established in Iceland: the Kings' Sagas were well on their way, and there already existed a long tradition of saints' lives, among them such translated sagas as *Klemens saga páfa* (The life of Clement the Pope), which borrowed themes from Greek literature. Scholars have even suggested that Icelanders started writing about their ancestors only when all material from their Scandinavian past had been used up: first they wrote the stories of Norse kings and heroes and only then realized that the people who moved to Iceland from Norway were just as remarkable. The story of the settlers was the story of their own origin, their descent from kings and earls. Iceland also had a rich indigenous poetic tradition consisting of Eddic and skaldic (*dróttkvætt*) poetry, in which heroic ancestral deeds were praised and the past was distant and golden (see the first part of this chapter). Indeed, a direct influence from Eddic heroic poetry can be seen at work in the Sagas of Icelanders, even though more often one can discern prose transformations of certain Eddic motifs: of heroism, moral duties, and ideals. Such transformations might have been conscious: the saga authors had a certain reference point when they put together their narratives of heroes and kings. It is just as plausible, however, that a deep structure of old narrative motifs from verse and oral tales reappears here in changed form. Where the Sagas of Icelanders differ from epics is that the main characters are not consistently heroic.

The Sagas of Icelanders take place for the most part in a period spanning two centuries: their outer historical time is continuous from the settlement of Iceland late in the ninth century into the eleventh century. The picture they paint of society during this entire period is consistent and largely unchanging. The subject matter, the descriptions of Icelandic chieftains and their business, is at first sight monotonous and homogeneous. A famous eighteenth-century Icelander, Jón Ólafsson of Grunnavík (d. 1779), secretary to the manuscript collector Árni Magnússon (d. 1730; see p. 198), summarized it in one brief sentence: "Farmers fighting." But, despite this uniformity of subject matter, there is a considerable variation in style and treatment among the sagas that is independent of their age and the result rather of the work of individual saga authors and their own approach toward the material and intended audience.

During nearly all the nineteenth century and well into the twentieth, the Sagas of Icelanders were believed by most — especially Icelanders — to be historical works, describing events that had taken place, and close to a truthful account of Icelandic chieftains at home and abroad, their feuds and battles, loves and fates. Nowadays, most scholars are agreed that the sagas are for the most part fiction, interpretations of a few veracious written sources and more or less trustworthy oral narratives that had been passed down through the centuries. Some of these sagas were probably meant as historiography. But when did Icelanders start to interpret the past, re-creating it as novelists do nowadays? It has often been claimed that medieval people did not differentiate between history and fiction, which come together in the Sagas of Icelanders. This is admittedly a simplification of a much more complex issue, but it is true that, as early as the first decades of the thirteenth century, pseudohistorical works appear in which the distant past is re-created, gaps are filled, and ancient poetry is interpreted freely. A new avenue then opens up for writers: from narrow historical chronicle they were now only a step away from story as narratives of the past became fiction, interpretation. This much certainly seems to have been clear to those who wrote down the Sagas of Icelanders. It has also been claimed that Snorri himself is the originator of the genre and that *Egils saga* (The saga of Egill), of which he is believed to be the author, was the first work of this kind, but there is no strong argument for this. It is more plausible that Snorri's *Ynglinga saga* could to a certain extent have served as a model for those who wrote Sagas of Icelanders, and Snorri's views on ancient historical verse may have caused a reevaluation of the role of verse as a source for the past. This does not mean, however, that Sagas of Icelanders are the descendants of Kings' Sagas or the Norse national histories.

At the start of the twentieth century Andreas Heusler (d. 1940) put forward the theory that the Sagas of Icelanders had been preserved nearly unchanged in oral tradition, from generation to generation, until they were eventually written down on vellum. Rudolf Keyser (d. 1864) had previously also maintained this. This view came to be known as *sagnfesta* (free prose). Late in the nineteenth century, on the other hand, Konrad Maurer (d. 1902) suggested that the Sagas of Icelanders were composed in the thirteenth century, the result of individual creation attributable to authors who had based their work on written sources that they treated freely. This view has since been referred to as *bókfesta* (book prose). Well into the twentieth century scholars were divided into two groups, depending on which opinion they endorsed. As yet there has not been a widely accepted explanation of the origins of the Sagas of Icelanders. It has, however, become clearer, especially with the research of Theodore M. Andersson (e.g., *The Problem of Icelandic Saga Origins*), that most sagas exhibit a certain narrative pattern that can be traced to oral tradition.

Taken together, the Sagas of Icelanders number just over forty, discounting the fifty-two *þættir*, which are mostly embedded in *Morkinskinna* or later compilations, but including *Færeyinga saga* (The saga of the Faeroe Islanders) and the so-called Vinland Sagas. But the Sagas of Icelanders are so varied in nature that it is inappropriate to speak of only one genre, even though this is done here for practical reasons. The sagas tell of events taking place in all districts across the country, except Skagafjörður. Abroad, the setting is mostly Greenland and Norway, but other areas, such as the Faeroe Islands, Sweden, and "Vínland" (in North America), also appear. Despite their different handling of material, the Sagas of Icelanders can be considered to form one *sagnabálkur* (cycle) as the same characters appear in many sagas and knowledge of one of the sagas can be crucial for the understanding of another.

Opinion is divided on the age of the Sagas of Icelanders, even though most scholars agree that they rose to prominence in the thirteenth century.

But no markers have yet been found that would allow the dating of individual sagas. The oldest manuscripts, a fragment of *Egils saga* and another of *Laxdæla saga*, have been dated to the middle of the thirteenth century, while most of the other manuscripts are from the end of the thirteenth century and the fourteenth and fifteenth centuries. Around the middle of the twentieth century some distinguished scholars, Sigurður Nordal prominent among them, attempted to categorize the sagas according to their maturity. Nordal considered certain sagas to be more primitive than others and assumed a certain development within the cycle just as in the natural sciences, from the primitive (*Heiðarvíga saga* [The saga of the moor killings) to the most accomplished (*Njáls saga* and *Hrafnkels saga* [The saga of Hrafnkell]), followed by a period of decline (see his "Sagalitteraturen," 235–69). Such categorization says more about the views of the scholars in question than it does about the actual age of the sagas. Another way to determine the time of writing is a comparison with other works that can be dated with some certainty, finding evidence of textual relationship. This method has served well in some instances, especially when it is possible to point to references to laws in forms identifiable from law codes known to have been accepted in Iceland in 1271 and 1280, thus allowing us to determine the *terminus post quem*. The influence of one work on another is harder to ascertain as it is often difficult to see which work borrowed material from the other. But sometimes a reference in one saga to another saga can give us a clue to their relative age.

There are no reliable sources on the Sagas of Icelanders before 1250, but certainly stories about Icelanders existed. Those tales need not, however, have been written down, as genealogical and biographical, historical lore can, of course, be preserved in memory. Those who put together the Sagas of Icelanders did not work like scholars, and written sources do not form the basis of all the narratives. Books of settlement could give some idea, and they might have served as a guide to or inspiration for the material without being a direct source. Genealogies in the Sagas of Icelanders cannot be traced exclusively to written sources, and, in any case, it must have been easy for the writer to make such things up, as becomes obvious where some names of genealogies reflect certain place-names in the neighborhood where the action is said to have taken place. If the audience was aware of such fabrication, then there must have been a certain purpose to the interpretation of the material in this way, for instance, allowing the tracing of lineage back to gods or natural spirits. Scholars have also noted that traditional storytelling motifs and topoi are most apparent where events deviate the most from historical sources.

No individual work among the Sagas of Icelanders has been linked to any named narrator, and no author or narrator is named in medieval sources. There is only one reference to the storyteller: "Helga lived on at Arnheiðarstaðir after Ingjaldur's death, as did Þorkell, the son of her and Grímur. Þorvaldur had a son whose name was Ingjaldur. It was his son, named Þorvaldur, who told this story. It was one year after Þangbrandur the priest came to Iceland that Helgi Droplaugarson fell" (trans. Rory McTurk in *Complete Sagas of Icelanders*, ed. Hreinsson, 4:367). Scholars have not been satisfied with this, and quite a few suggestions as to possible authors have been put forward. *Egils saga* has since the nineteenth century been attributed to Snorri Sturluson, and *Laxdæla saga* has also been considered to be either his work or that of his nephew, Ólafur hvítaskáld Þórðarson. This matter will never be resolved, although research in this area has resulted in the clarification of the cultural circumstances of certain sagas, as in Richard Perkins's examination of *Flóamanna saga* (The saga of the people of Flói).

Many attempts have also been made to divide the sagas into categories, but no one method has gained widespread acceptance. If one were to think in large categories, one might distinguish two main groups. In the first group we have district and family feud sagas, by far the largest group, including *Eyrbyggja saga*, *Vatnsdæla saga* (The saga of the people of Vatnsdalur), *Vopnfirðinga saga* (The saga of the people of Vopnafjörður), *Reykdæla saga* (The saga of the people of Reykjadalur), *Svarfdæla saga* (The saga of the people of Svarfaðardalur), *Laxdæla saga* and *Njáls saga*. From a literary point of view these sagas are varied, and scholars have tried to divide them into subgroups. In the second group we have sagas of individuals with a biographical structure, the best known of which are *Hrafnkels saga*, the so-called poets' sagas (*Kormáks saga* [The saga of Kormákur], *Hallfreðar saga* [The saga of Hallfreður], *Gunnlaugs saga ormstungu* [The saga of Gunnlaugur the Serpent-tongue], and *Egils saga*), and the outlaw sagas (*Gísla saga* [The saga of Gísli], *Grettis saga* [The saga of Grettir], and *Harðar saga* [The saga of Hörður]). In the second group a few stand out: *Finnboga saga* (The saga of Finnbogi), *Króka-Refs saga* (The saga of Refur the Wily), *Hávarðar saga Ísfirðings* (The saga of Hávarður of Ísafjörður), *Fóstbræðra saga* (The saga of the sworn brothers), *Bandamanna saga* (The saga of the confederates), *Bárðar saga* (The saga of Bárður), and *Víglundar saga* (The saga of Víglundur), in which a different image of the hero appears. The last two are, in fact, on the very borders of the genre as they are very different in their handling of the subject matter and are more reminiscent of romances.

In truth this categorization of the Sagas of Icelanders is far from clear as the two main groups overlap in many ways and it is not easy to find literary markers to distinguish them or give the genre a well-defined status within medieval Icelandic literature. *Eiríks saga rauða* (The saga of Eirik the Red) springs to mind in this connection. It has been noted that this saga is, in fact, about Guðríður Þorbjarnardóttir rather than Eirik the Red and that the narrative is not tied to one district, the heroes instead traveling between countries. Indeed, a main concern in the saga is the search for a better world, a paradise that the saga calls "Vínland" (Wineland). In this respect *Eiríks saga rauða* resembles medieval travel accounts and is, for instance, more closely related to *Yngvars saga víðförla* (The saga of Yngvar the Distant Traveler), the navigation of Saint Brendan, and secular visions (*visiones*) such as *Eiríks saga víðförla* (The saga of Eirik the Distant Traveler).

Some of the Sagas of Icelanders exist in more than one redaction; there are, for instance, two versions of *Bandamanna saga*, *Gísla saga*, *Njáls saga*, and *Flóamanna saga* and three of *Egils saga*. These redactions show us that, at times, the material was adapted for different audiences, adaptations that can be traced to changing times and tastes. The clearest example of this is *Bandamanna saga*, where the textual changes in the K-redaction (a fifteenth-century manuscript) show clearly that it is aimed at a late fourteenth-century and later audience, making the saga's polemic more obvious to them. Some of the sagas feature the ancestors of famous thirteenth-century chieftains, but, in the main, it is impossible to point to any specific audience, although this has been attempted. *Laxdæla saga*, *Egils saga*, and *Eyrbyggja saga* have, for instance, been connected with the Sturlungar and *Njáls saga* with the Svínfellingar, a powerful family in the east of Iceland. Vésteinn Ólason has recently argued that the Sturlungar, the youngest but most powerful family in thirteenth-century Iceland, must have been inclined to praise their ancestors and make them equal to ancient foreign kings, as is obvious in the above-mentioned works (see his *Dialogues with the Viking Age*). No manuscripts commissioned by the nobility in the thirteenth century have, however, survived; only large compilations like *Möðruvallabók* (The book of Möðruvellir) from the middle of the fourteenth century are still preserved. The problem is that we do not know for whom these manuscripts were written.

It has often been noted that the Sagas of Icelanders mirror occurrences related in the *Sturlunga saga* and other historical accounts of thirteenth-century events. The burning of Njal in the saga named after him has been compared to a famous fire at Flugumýri, one set by Gissur Þorvaldsson's enemies, who tried to kill him by burning his residence (see p. 87). The outlaw Gísli Súrsson is thought to be modeled on Árón Hjörleifsson, one of Bishop Guðmundur Arason's followers (see pp. 169–71). Such comparison is, of course, one strand of modern literary analysis, and, with careful consideration, it is possible to see various similarities, although it is often hard to believe that the saga authors had contemporary events as their model. Reference to contemporary life can take other forms than a direct reference to certain events. It is more likely that each saga involves a message to the audience, for instance, an encouragement to keep the peace and honor the law through the juxtaposition of two worlds, a world of killings and a world of peace and prosperity. And it is undeniable that feuds in the sagas must to some extent have mirrored the domestic conflicts that prevailed before the country was ruled by one king. As there was no executive power, families kept together to guard their interests. Killings are, thus, one strand in the battle of interests between families or within a family, as one can see in *Laxdæla saga*, where the dominant theme is fratricide, and this power struggle is continued until the descendants of the chieftain's oldest son hold sole power.

In the fourteenth and fifteenth centuries, most of the old chieftain families merged with lesser-known families, and a new nobility came to the fore, a group that often had close ties with the Norwegian monarchy. The ancient society of *goðar* and the old legislative rule of the Althing had vanished; the social superstructure had taken on a different form, while the Althing had become simply a court of law. After such social change, the image of society depicted in the fourteenth-century sagas became even further removed from reality than before, and this could, of course, open avenues for various interpretations of the past. Admittedly many of the ruling classes were still descended from the old chieftains, and the natural conditions of the land had changed little: Iceland remained a farming and fishing economy well into the fourteenth century, although fishing did not become a profitable trade until the late fourteenth century. In other words, the setting and the external reality of the sagas hardly changed until the twentieth century. This explains, in part, the popularity of the sagas in Iceland and the way they have been read by Icelanders down to the present day.

Narrative Mode

It has often been maintained that the narrative style used in the Sagas of Icelanders is very simple and plain and close to spoken language, that it is unusually objective, and that not many learned rhetorical devices are used. This is correct as far as it goes. A simple style does not necessarily signify a common, oral narration; it is just as likely that the saga authors had assimilated a low style, also widely found, for instance, in religious texts where the *sermo humilis* was supposed to appeal to the commoners so that they could understand better the message of the Word.

The vocabulary used in the sagas is usually concerned with actions, describing everyday objects, such as tools and clothing. Paragraphs are generally short, with main clauses and paratactic clauses predominant. Long sentences with subordinate clauses are rare as little in the way of logical analysis occurs. Present tense and past tense often appear in the same sentence, and indirect speech changes into direct speech without any markers. People, their actions, and events are usually described in very much the same fashion. Wording is often formulaic, which is indicative of both an oral storytelling tradition and a literary tradition. The following may serve as an example of this kind of wording: 146 men in the sagas are described as *miklir* (great) and *sterkir* (strong), while in descriptions of women there are 22 instances of the word *ofláti* (haughty), just under half of these referring to women also described as *vænar* (well built, fine).

Some words are linked to particular descriptions, for instance, the adverbs *drengiliga* (honorably) and *alldrengiliga* (very honorably), which are almost without exception used in combination with the verb *verjask* (to defend oneself): in the sagas men fight *djarfliga* (courageously) but defend themselves *drengiliga*.

Similes, metaphors, and rhetorical devices such as alliteration, homoeoteleutons, and antitheses are known but not common. These devices are used so subtly that the reader is hardly aware of them. Famous examples, which are, in fact, influenced by poetry, are found in *Fóstbræðra saga*:

> The daughters of the sea-goddess, Rán, tried to embrace them. . . .
> The wind, like wild cur, howled constantly and with relentless force
> the whole night long, and gnawled at the ground with its cold savage
> jaws. (trans. Martin S. Regal in *Complete Sagas of Icelanders*, ed.
> Hreinsson, 2:337)

One of the most common stylistic devices in the Sagas of Icelanders is understatement (litotes). It has been claimed that this is characteristic of oral narrative, but the device is well-known in rhetoric. Hyperboles are rare, but sayings or proverbs are quite numerous, both in dialogues and outside them. Proverbs are, for instance, very common in *Grettis saga*, and it is not quite clear whether they were intended to serve a certain stylistic or ideological purpose within each narrative unit. The narrator very seldom makes himself present in the narrative, and, when he does, he uses the first-person plural.

Dialogues make up an important part of the Sagas of Icelanders. They are mostly incisive, no word is superfluous, and the only talkative characters are itinerant women and those charged, implicitly or explicitly, with stupidity. Information is provided by way of clear main clauses, sometimes using metaphoric language, for instance, Skarphéðinn's reply in *Njáls saga* when his father, Njal, asks him where he is going fully armed: "'To look for your sheep', he said. Njal said, 'You wouldn't be armed if you planned that, so it must be something else.' 'We're going salmon-fishing, father, if we don't find the sheep', said Skarphéðinn" (trans. Robert Cook in *Complete Sagas of Icelanders*, ed. Hreinsson, 3:53). Incisiveness appears perhaps most famously in characters' dying words. "Broad spears are the fashion these days," says Atli Ásmundarson, Grettir's brother, in *Grettis saga* when he has been speared (trans. Bernard Scudder in *Complete Sagas of Icelanders*, ed. Hreinsson, 2:119). Another characteristic of the dialogue in the sagas is the absence of sociolects. Whether the person in question is a slave, a priest, or a chieftain, class does not appear in his or her language. One could say that the dialogue in the sagas is more reminiscent of refined spoken language in realistic plays from the beginning of the twentieth century than colloquial language. It has even been claimed that, in fact, people never spoke this incisively, but it should be noted that there are no sources for medieval spoken Icelandic, which means that it is difficult to investigate the social basis of speech in the sagas. Only in rare cases do spoken exchanges turn into whole speeches, as they do, for instance, in *Heiðarvíga saga*.

One characteristic of the narrative style of the Sagas of Icelanders is that verses are intermingled with the prose. They are tools for the expression of emotions and can, then, replace inner monologues, or they become part of the narrative itself and serve a purpose similar to that of dialogue. Some versions of certain sagas contain more verses than others. Egill Skallagrímsson's famous poem "Höfuðlausn" (Head ransom) occurs, for instance, in only one version of *Egils saga*. In the *Reykjabók* (The book of Reykir) version of *Njáls saga* Skarphéðinn composes verses where in the other version there is only prose. Consequently, a different picture of him emerges from the version usually printed now, which is mainly based on *Möðruvallabók*.

Some verses also appear to have been intended as riddles, inviting the audience to interpret the narrative and even to envision the outcome. A good example of this is when Unnur Marðardóttir composes verses in the *Reykjabók* version of *Njáls saga*, telling of her marriage to Hrútur. Another and better-known example is the verse spoken by Gísli Súrsson to his sister Þórdís after the ball game at Hóll suggesting who killed Þorgrímur. Such use of verse also shows that the scribes of the manuscripts had different audiences in mind. In the former example verse is used to mask sexual problems, while in the latter it is intended to give an educated audience a clue as to the progress of the story. Last but not least, one should not forget the role often played by verses to indicate to the audience the presence of supernatural powers behind the related events.

Point of View and Structure

No one who reads the Sagas of Icelanders is in any doubt that those who composed them made use of a certain pattern that may possibly have its origins in an oral narrative tradition. This pattern, which scholars have related to either feud or revenge, is ordered in a similar fashion in one saga after another, although it is absent from the occasional saga, such as, for instance, *Eyrbyggja saga*. The pattern is made up of six narrative parts: introduction; conflict; climax; revenge; reconciliation; and aftermath. It does not, however, determine the actual structure of the sagas, which are quite obviously constructed carefully and according to principles common to many other medieval literary genres.

Few medieval authors plot their narratives the way modern novelists do. One can, however, detect a hint of plotting and the careful placing of narrative devices to maintain the audience's interest. Characters are introduced immediately at the start of each saga, often with lengthy lineages, where both names and sobriquets can be significant. One can view these genealogies as a sort of preamble, although they do not serve the same purpose as prologues; prefaces are unknown in the Sagas of Icelanders. These preambles often demarcate the outer time frames of the sagas.

Prolepsis, or foreshadowing, is a very common narrative strategy, applied with the most artistry in *Njáls saga* and *Laxdæla saga*. The beginning of *Njáls saga* suggests the plot's later development: as the young girl Hallgerður is playing on the floor, Hrútur says to his brother, Höskuldur: "The girl is very beautiful and many will pay for that" (trans. Robert Cook in *Complete Sagas of Icelanders*, ed. Hreinsson, 3:2). Most commonly, however, it is dreams that are used to foreshadow future events, the most famous in this respect being Þorsteinn of Borg's dream in *Gunnlaugs saga* and Guðrún Ósvífursdóttir's dreams in *Laxdæla saga*. Dreams in the Sagas of Icelanders are more commonly narrative devices (prolepsis, analepsis) than tools to express emotions.

The sagas are narrated mostly in chronological order. The outer time frame is established at the start, but many years can pass between events covered in two consecutive chapters, while the inner time frame can cover the biographies of many generations. Thus, *Laxdæla saga*, for instance, takes place over a period that spans the lives of four generations, but the audience and readers are hardly aware of the aging of the main characters. The narrators knew the art of making time disappear; after the saga has been allocated a time in years at the start, it is hardly ever mentioned when events take place. A common narrative device to link events is the formula: "Now things were quiet for a while." Sometimes a character's age is indicated; for instance, it is said of Grettir that he was outlawed for nineteen years, but chronology as it is employed in histories of the period is of no consequence in the Sagas of Icelanders. Admittedly, however, both genres do share certain narrative techniques, for instance, the staging of two stories simultaneously.

One of the most impressive narrative techniques in the Sagas of Icelanders is the restraint shown in giving information and the concomitantly limited point of view. Although prophecies may be mentioned at the beginning, narrators follow their own story and do not stray from their time frame. They tell the story as if they were completely unaware of their characters' plans or what has been said in conversations between two people. Vésteinn Ólason ("Nokkrar athugasemdir," 13) notes in this connection the conversation between Styr and Snorri the Chieftain at Helgafell in chapter 28 of *Eyrbyggja saga*, when Snorri advises Styr on how he should get rid of the berserks. At times the point of view is focused on emotions, as is clear in the description in *Egils saga* of Egill at King Athelstan's court. But the best-known example of a limited point of view is the account in chapters 13 and 16 of *Gísla saga* of the killing of Vésteinn and Þorgrímur. During the first killing, the point of view is with Gísli's men, and the events are interpreted by them. But, when Gísli kills Þorgrímur, the reader follows him, focusing entirely on Gísli's actions: "Then he noticed that not everyone was asleep. He saw the hand of a young man reach for the third light, take down the lamp-holder and snuff the flame." The reader stays with Gísli until the point where we get the reactions of the people at Sæból. The narrator does, however, stray ever so slightly from Gísli's point of view when he tells of Þórdís's and Þorgrímur's reactions:

> He walked farther into the house and up to the bed closet where his sister, Þórdís, and Þorgrímur slept. The door was pulled to, and they were both in bed. He went to the bed, groped about inside and touched his sister's breast. She was sleeping on the near side. Then Þórdís said, "Why is your hand so cold, Þorgrímur?" and thereby woke him up. Þorgrímur replied, "Do you want me to turn towards

you?" She thought it had been his hand that touched her. Gísli waited a little longer, warming his hand inside his tunic. (trans. Martin S. Regal in *Complete Sagas of Icelanders*, ed. Hreinsson, 2:19)

A common feature in the structure of the Sagas of Icelanders is the slowing down of the narrative with frequent changes of scene in order to delay the climax of the saga. One of the best examples of this type of retardation is found in *Laxdæla saga*: the attack on Helgi Harðbeinsson, where Bolli Þorleiksson is avenged. There is a long description in dialogue form of the equipment and clothing of Bolli Bollason and his men before the narrator finally lets them approach the farm and start the battle. Another famous example is the account of the events leading up to the killings on the moor in *Heiðarvíga saga*.

Even though dreams, prophecies, and other narrative devices play an important role, it is obvious that the writers relied on an overall structure common to medieval texts. *Njáls saga*, for instance, is divided into two parts of similar length (with a preamble at the beginning and an epilogue at the end); the first part tells of the fall of Gunnar, the latter of the fall of Njal. This division is no coincidence, and it is certainly not the case either that these are two separate sagas, as scholars at the start of the twentieth century claimed. Events that occur in Gunnar's life, the killings in his saga, are reflected in slightly different form, enlarged, in the latter half. A similar repetition is evident in shorter chapters of the saga: the three killings of farmworkers by Bergþóra and Hallgerður represent a gradual escalation in the same narrative element.

The clearest example of a bipartite structure is, however, in *Hrafnkels saga*. The narrative starts with an introduction of the characters, Hallfreður's settlement, and the chieftain Hrafnkell's move to Aðalból. The story lingers here for a while and describes Hrafnkell's love of Freyr and Freyfaxi and his power in the district. The next part deals with the feuds, the killing of Einar the shepherd, and the pursuing of the case by Einar's father, old Þorbjörn; it concludes with Hrafnkell being outlawed at the Althing. The third movement of the first part forms, then, the high point of the story, when Sámur humiliates Hrafnkell and settles at Aðalból. After this climax, the story tells of Hrafnkell moving across the river, of his revenge and the killing of Eyvindur, the reconciliation, and Hrafnkell's seizing of power; it relates how the sons of Þjóstar, Sámur's supporters, deny Sámur their following, and, finally, it tells of the death of Hrafnkell and of his descendants. The high point of the saga is unusual: instead of Hrafnkell being executed, he is thrown upside down on a rack like a leg of mutton; in other words, he is tortured like a martyr. And, just as in passions (*passiones*) generally, a new life after death begins for the martyr at Aðalból: he settles in Fljótsdalur and gets back on top. This structure of the saga broadens its meaning from both an ethical and a political point of view by satirizing well-known hagiographic motifs and by using at the same time their structural techniques: life in this world, Hrafnkelsdalur; life in the next world, Fljótsdalur. The saga thus becomes a diptych.

A similar approach is also apparent in sagas where events in one part of the work are repeated in another, strengthening and expanding the narrative plot. This kind of structure is apparent, for instance, in *Gísla saga* (the longer redaction), where most of the events that take place in Iceland echo events in Norway, before Gísli's family moves to Iceland. The events that occur in Norway form only a small part of the whole, but the same motifs are amplified when the narrator tells of similar events in Iceland. A similar structure is found in *Egils saga*. It is perfectly plausible that the saga author planned a typological narrative, one in which Þórólfur Kveldúlfsson was supposed to be a forerunner of Þórólfur Skallagrímsson. Kveldúlfur's feud with King Haraldur Fairhair and, later, Skallagrímur's feud with the king are repeated in the narrative of Egill's dealings with Eirik Blood-axe, Haraldur's son. It should not be forgotten in this respect that the art of rhetoric was practiced in medieval Iceland from the inception of the era of written texts and that *amplificatio* was a known stylistic device, used to broaden the text and augment it.

Character Descriptions and Roles
At first glance the way characters are introduced in the Sagas of Icelanders might seem to be unique to the genre, but on closer inspection such descriptions were also common in European literature. Parts of the descriptions are, however, homegrown. These introductions, either at the start of the saga or when a new character is brought into the narrative, often give important clues to the character's personality. The description of Skarphéðinn in *Njáls saga* may serve as an example:

> Skarphéðinn was the eldest, a big and strong man and a good fighter. He swam like a seal and was swift of foot, quick to make up his mind and sure of himself; he spoke to the point and was quick to do so, though mostly he restrained himself. His hair was reddish-brown and curled and he had fine eyes; his face was pale and sharp-featured with a bent nose and a broad row of upper teeth. His mouth was ugly, and yet he was very like a warrior. (trans. Robert Cook in *Complete Sagas of Icelanders*, ed. Hreinsson, 3:30–31)

Portraits of this kind are very common. The characters' thoughts, on the other hand, are hardly ever described. Instead, characters are seen from the outside and their thoughts revealed only in the course of actions and events. There is no character development; characters appear fully formed and remain the same throughout the saga. They have a designated role from the start and can be categorized according to this role. Women, for instance, can be divided into two groups: those who are formidable and strong and those who are good and loyal wives. Any given categorization is, however, only an indication as a change of role can occur in the course of a saga. Hallgerður Long-leg in *Njáls saga* is hard on Þorvaldur Ósvífursson, her first husband — in fact, she kills him — but she is good and loyal to Glúmur, her second husband. Nevertheless, she plays a part in the deaths of all her husbands: she controls what she wants and usually appears as a battle-ax. Examples of the good, loyal wife are the two Auðurs, one in *Eyrbyggja saga*, the other in *Gísla saga*. They stand by their husbands through thick and thin — the couple will not be torn apart. Another loyal wife is Þorlaug in *Ljósvetninga saga* (The saga of the Ljósavatn family), who advises Guðmundur the Powerful well on many occasions. Of course the social situation of women has molded these roles. The housewife, the married woman, stands generally outside the feuds and battles and has no influence on their outcome. The exception is Bergþóra Skarphéðinsdóttir in *Njáls saga*, a strong-tempered woman and a loyal wife, and, while the saga never intimates that she goes against the will of her husband, Njal, she often has her own way and exercises incredible power over the turn of events. Anonymous itinerant women and servants can also greatly influence the turn of events, for instance, the traveling women's slander in *Njáls saga*. And it is the washerwoman in *Hrafnkels saga* who incites the apparently cowardly chieftain Hrafnkell to revenge and, in so doing, upsets the balance of power: each man must be what he is born to be, so the rightful inheritor and chieftain takes over his homestead again, while a chieftain of lower birth who does not make the right decisions at the right time eventually must yield. Similarly, magicians and seers often influence the course of events.

It is rare to find a saga that is wholly devoted to women, and *Laxdæla saga* and *Eiríks saga rauða* are unusual in this respect. The main character in *Laxdæla saga*, Guðrún Ósvífursdóttir, is above all a leader, a queen, and she exhibits certain characteristics of the female heroes of Eddic poetry, the valkyries Brynhildur and Guðrún Gjúkadóttir. Such heroic characteristics are, however, more common in descriptions of men. Like the female characters, the male characters have been divided into types. There are noble leaders such as Ólafur Peacock, wise thinkers like Gestur Oddleifsson, those whose wisdom is flawed like Njal, dark heroes like Skarphéðinn Njálsson, and fair ones like Gunnar Hámundarson and Kjartan Ólafsson. Scholars have claimed that the latter group is modeled on legendary heroes such as Sigurður Fáfnisbani (Sigurd the Dragon-slayer) and Helgi Hundingsbani (Helgi Slayer-of-Hunding), but the descriptions of these fair heroes are complex. Kjartan's, for instance, resembles that of a king; certain traits from his collection of virtues are those commonly associated with princes, and even the life of Christ is, in part, reflected in that of Kjartan, most notably at his hour of death. The behavior of Mörður Valgarðsson in *Njáls saga* has reminded scholars of Loki, the originator of deceit in Norse mythology, while Njal has more than once been compared to Odin himself. While it is true that certain mythological traits can often be detected in character descriptions, it is often forgotten that each saga character is composed of many parts, and dissecting a description can mar a character's overall image in the saga. Last but not least, some characters are given animal traits, either through a name, like Refur (which translates as "fox"), or through reference to animal and grotesque characteristics, like, most famously, Egill Skallagrímsson, who oscillates between two poles, the sensitive poet and the vicious wolf who rips out people's throats.

In the same way as certain events in the sagas have been thought to refer to particular contemporary events, certain characters have been compared with real-life individuals who lived at the time the sagas were written. Snorri the Chieftain in *Eyrbyggja saga* has often been compared to his wise descendant Snorri Sturluson. Much more fruitful, however, is the comparison of characters between sagas, revealing different interpretations. Guðmundur "the Powerful" Eyjólfsson, for instance, is mentioned in quite a few sagas. He appears in a rather more positive light in *Njáls saga* and *Vopnfirðinga saga* than he does in *Ljósvetninga saga*, where he is the main character, but he always appears as an important chieftain as well as an adviser and reconciler of men. Hrútur Herjólfsson also appears very differently in *Laxdæla saga* than he does in *Njáls saga*. Such differences can point to different audiences for the sagas.

Minor characters in sagas often have names that refer to their role. The workman who initiates the quarrel between Hallgerður and Bergþóra in *Njáls saga* is called Kolur (Dark): "He had been with her a long time, and was the worst sort of person" (trans. Robert Cook in *Complete Sagas of Icelanders*, ed. Hreinsson, 3:41). It is he who kills Svartur (Black). Glaumur is the sobriquet of Grettir's servant in Drangey—the name is etymologically related to the verb *gleyma* (forget) and indicates that the character is careless, perhaps forgetful: he sleeps while on guard, allowing Grettir's enemies to attack. Very rarely is the name of a main character symbolic of his or her role, but it does occasionally happen; for instance, in *Króka-Refs saga* Refur the Wily knows how to deceive his enemies, and in *Hávarðar saga* it is Bjargey (*bjarga*, "save") who saves her husband.

The range of characterization in the Sagas of Icelanders is not particularly rich compared to that in modern novels. Mature individual characters rarely appear. The wolf-like poet Egill Skallagrímsson is, however, an exception. The author of *Egils saga* has, despite the use of traditional motifs, successfully brought to life a very peculiar character, one whose complex emotions the reader comes to understand, a process that is rare in the Sagas of Icelanders.

Worldview and Outlook on Life
The medieval Icelandic worldview did not differ much from that in other European countries at the time. However, Icelanders may have traveled more widely and acquainted themselves with different cultures; they explored countries in the West and the East and sailed to Jerusalem, at the time the center of the known world. The sagas include all these places in their settings, even though they take place for the most part in their home district in Iceland. While the horizon thus appears to be quite wide, when it comes to the outlook on life and work, it narrows considerably. At first glance it seems marked by the struggle to survive, which determines the way people in the sagas view their existence, themselves, and their families.

One of the main subjects in the Sagas of Icelanders is the individual who has to take power, establish himself as the family chieftain, and try to control his brothers and sisters. Usually the saga starts when the individual goes abroad in order to visit the old home country, Norway, and returns a more experienced man. Abroad he gets to know earls and kings, whose traits he tries to emulate to some extent once he is back home. *Gunnlaugs saga* provides an excellent portrait of one such country lad. Gunnlaugur is an unusually mature teenager who wants to marry before he is man enough to handle the responsibility. The saga's main concern here is whether the young son of a leader is capable of taking over the family chieftaincy. The saga intimates clearly that Gunnlaugur is not: he breaks all the rules that society has laid down for him, which is why things turn out as they do. Accounts of travels in the Sagas of Icelanders as well as those in the *Íslendingaþættir* (both those that are known separately and those that are embedded in Kings' Sagas) are intended to show that the main character has been able to deal with the trials that he has faced abroad and that he is ready, on his return home, to become a worthy member of society.

Another common subject that reflects the outlook on life in the sagas is the idea of honor, which is tied, not to a single individual, but to an entire family. Family honor can never be slighted. Battles and killings usually start when a freeborn man is dishonored; men must defend their honor, and it is not uncommon that they die in the process. Their kinsmen must, then, avenge them. This usually marks the start of a long string of killings.

The ideas of luck and happiness in the sagas — those who do the right thing are usually saved — owe something to the Christian outlook, but, at the same time, it often seems that fortune follows one family and misfortune another. Among the luckless are a number of characters related to Grettir, such as Óspakur in *Bandamanna saga*. People's looks often bear witness to their misfortune, as is clear from *Njáls saga*'s description of Skarphéðinn Njálsson at the Althing after the killing of Höskuldur Hvítanesgoði.

Ancient knowledge of all kinds plays a substantial role in the Sagas of Icelanders. Magicians and sorcerers figure prominently, and the old pagan heritage is alive in memory at the time of writing. Sometimes these features seem to be literary motifs, but more often they represent the remnants of much older narratives, for instance, the beliefs of Þórólfur Mostraskegg related in *Eyrbyggja saga*. The adoption of Christianity in the year 1000 became a fruitful topic for many authors, and a Christian outlook is apparent in many places in the sagas. Whoever composed *Njáls saga*, for instance, wondered why evil existed since God was good and his people were in his hands. Usually the moral message of the sagas is nowhere clearly stated, residing, instead, under the surface of the narrative. Philosophical thought is, perhaps, most apparent in those sagas describing loneliness and the exclusion of individuals from society. The outlaw Grettir in Drangey shows us the alienation of those who cannot fit into society. The solitude of Grettir is, in some ways, comparable to that of Gregorius peccator tied to the rock in the epic poem of Hartmann von Aue (d. 1210–20): both are suffering for unbearable sins or evil deeds.

Conclusion

The latest vellum manuscripts of the Sagas of Icelanders date from the sixteenth century. After the end of the Middle Ages paper copies were made, a practice that continued mainly in the sixteenth and seventeenth centuries and even grew as paper became more widely available, with the result that copies of the sagas can number in the hundreds. Scholars are divided on how long Sagas of Icelanders continued to be composed, but their "golden age" is surely the latter half of the thirteenth century and into the fourteenth. Perhaps the genre reached its peak when antiheroes who mocked the old ideals and values started to appear. This is most clear in

Hávarðar saga and the *Flateyjarbók* version of *Fóstbræðra saga*: in the former a layabout becomes a hero and a fighter, while in the latter the killings committed by Þorgeir Hávarsson become a grotesque farce. In sagas that were probably written in the fourteenth century, such as *Grettis saga*, one can also see the influence of European fabliaux. After the fourteenth century some sagas may still have been composed, but it is more common for older sagas to be copied, sometimes with additions in which earlier scholars could find no merit. Even later, during the seventeenth century and well into the nineteenth, Sagas of Icelanders were still being written: the old sagas were imitated and new narratives added that took place in districts where no earlier sagas had been set.

ROMANCES: THE KNIGHTS' SAGAS AND THE LEGENDARY SAGAS

With Snorri's account of the Ynglingar dynasty, new story worlds had opened up where the past was interpreted freely, without the interpreter feeling too dependent on contemporary reality and its facts. Instead, the imagination roamed freely, and storytellers got to tell of mythical events or *örskipti* (wonders), to use the word from the preface to *Þiðriks saga*. The so-called *annar frásagnarháttur* (*modus fictivus*) had arrived on the scene. This literary tradition possibly had its roots in an oral storytelling tradition and first appeared in written form during the first half of the thirteenth century. This type of literature, however, has dual origins: on the one hand, stories translated from Old French and Middle High and Low German and indigenous imitations of these, collectively called Knights' Sagas (*riddarasögur*) in Icelandic sources; on the other hand, Icelandic narratives often closely related to Germanic and Old Norse poetry on mythical heroes that existed long before the settlement of Iceland, or, to translate the words of C. C. Rafn, from "before the period that reliable stories come from" (*Fornaldar sögur Nordrlanda*, 1:v). These sagas are commonly known as the Northern Sagas of Antiquity (*fornaldarsögur Norðurlanda*), or the Legendary Sagas. Common to both story worlds is that they are far removed from audiences in time and place: the main protagonists are, at times, hardly human in their behavior, they have supernatural powers or virtues, and they have various relations with beings from other worlds, such as dwarfs, trolls, monsters in the woods, fire-breathing dragons, and long-headed vultures. And, last but not least, Odin himself appears on the scene in these Norse heroic tales and intervenes in events, as he does in Eddic poetry.

The setting of both story worlds is known, and the narratives are, at times, based on real geographic knowledge, for instance, *Mírmanns saga*

(The saga of Mírmann), which clearly uses an itinerary, such as the travel account of Nikulás Bergsson. The Legendary Sagas take place for the most part in the Scandinavian countries, even though the heroes often travel widely: from Russia, to France, to Jerusalem. The titles given to these sagas have their roots in the setting. The other category of sagas, the Knights' Sagas, whose settings reach as far as Southern Europe, Istanbul, North Africa, and Ethiopia, has accordingly also been called the Southern Sagas of Antiquity (*fornsögur Suðurlanda*). These two types of sagas are, for the most part, structured identically.

Despite the similar narrative mode, however, these two types of sagas often display different ideas, but such divergences have not prevented them from being considered to belong to one genre, as, indeed, they were by their writers. Around the middle of *Samsons saga fagra* (The saga of Samson the Fair), there is a turning point where, suddenly, Britain and its knights are left behind and the story turns, instead, to giants and to a character well-known from the Legendary Sagas. The narrator intervenes and introduces Guðmundur of Glæsisvellir as follows: "The second part of the story begins here and tells of a king who was named Guðmundur. His reign was on Glæsisvellir in the East. That is, east of Giantland, which lies to the east and north of the Baltic countries, and from there, far into the North, is the country that is called Jötunheimar [Home of Giants], where ogres and monsters live" (Wilson, ed., *Samsons saga fagra*, 31).

It is, thus, clear that the author of *Samsons saga* thought it appropriate to switch settings without changing the subject matter. He clearly assumes the audience to be familiar with the Northern story world, and the hero can, thus, play his role both in the North and in the South, as long as the difference between these two worlds is emphasized. In other words, story-tellers thought of the Legendary Sagas and the Knights' Sagas as belonging to the same group of stories. This categorization is, in fact, old, dating back to medieval manuscripts in which the two types of sagas are grouped together. However, medieval writers seem, at times, to have divided them into separate groups, as is apparent, for instance, in *Flóres saga og sona hans* (The saga of King Flóres and his sons), which differentiates between stories "of powerful kings" that mention "polite behavior at court or how to serve great leaders" and other stories of kings who "are placed in danger" (Lager-holm, ed., *Drei Lygisögur*, 121). This division into subgenres will be maintained here, and I will discuss the Knights' Sagas first and then the Legendary Sagas even though, ultimately, both groups are considered to belong to one genre: that of the romance.

The Knights' Sagas constitute one of the largest groups of Icelandic and

Norwegian prose texts. In her bibliography (with P. M. Mitchell) of Old Norse Icelandic romances, Marianne Kalinke has counted 45 such stories, while Stefán Einarsson (*History of Icelandic Literature*, 165) believes them to number no fewer than 265 altogether, including stories written after the Reformation (i.e., after 1550). Icelanders continued to write Knights' Sagas for centuries, and the most recent date from the nineteenth and twentieth centuries.

Chivalric ideals of love (*amor*), chivalry (*chevalerie*), and education (*clergie*) as they appear in twelfth-century French literature are believed to have gained popularity in Northern European countries beginning in the latter half of the twelfth century. They appealed especially to the aristocracy, educated men and women who had read classical literature, especially the poetry of Ovid.

In Norway at that time a power struggle was in progress, and it was not until 1240 that King Hákon Hákonarson, thought to have reigned from 1217 but sharing power with Duke Skúli Bárðarson until 1240, managed to establish a hereditary monarchy. Still, the civil war that had been waging in Iceland throughout the first half of the thirteenth century ended only when Icelanders accepted the rule of the Norwegian king in 1262–64.

There are no reliable sources for a courtly tradition in Norway and Iceland such as existed in France. Sturla Þórðarson's *Hákonar saga* does not say much about the king's court and courtesy, only that he had saints' lives and histories read to him on his deathbed, rather than Christian chivalric tales (see p. 74). King Hákon seems to have been an educated man, and the thirteenth-century English chronicler Matthew Paris calls him *bene litteratus*. Sturla Þórðarson related to Magnús Lawmender's queen and courtiers *Huldar saga* (The saga of Huld), probably a type of Legendary Saga. *Hirðskrá* (The retainers' scroll), which was put together at Magnús's behest, is a rule book on how courtiers should behave, and *Konungs skuggsjá*, which was very likely written on royal initiative, partly deals with chivalric behavior. In *Hákonar saga* it is made clear that Hákon tried to adopt the manners of kings elsewhere in Europe, and he kept in contact with the English king Henry III. Hákon brings peace to Norway and also to Iceland, establishes a central government in Norway, and appoints earls and governors.

Literary histories have always stated with certainty that the first chivalric narratives were translated early in Hákon's reign, perhaps even as early as 1226. The reasoning behind this date is derived from *Tristrams saga og Isöndar* (The saga of Tristram and Isond), where at the beginning of the saga it is said that Brother Robert had translated it on the order of the honorable King Hákon (see Tómasson, "Hvenær"). This passage has been preserved only in a seventeenth-century Icelandic manuscript and resembles book titles from that century. In some other Knights' Sagas' colophons Hákon the Old and his son are said to be behind the translation of other French literature. Apart from *Tristrams saga* (from Thomas's *Tristran*), *Elís saga og Rosamundu* (The saga of Elis and Rosamunda; from the Old French *Elie de Saint Gille*), the *Strengleikar* (from the *Lais* of Marie de France), *Ívens saga* (The saga of Iven; from the *Yvain* of Chrétien de Troyes), and *Möttuls saga* (from the fabliau *Le lai du cort mantel* [The lay of the short mantle]) are mentioned. The problem is, however, that only small portions of these works have been preserved in Norwegian manuscripts; they are mostly contained in Icelandic manuscripts from the fourteenth to the seventeenth centuries.

Strengleikar and *Elís saga* are preserved in a Norwegian manuscript, De la Gardie 4–7, written ca. 1270, but one of the *Strengleikar*, *Guiamar* (from *Guigemar*), has also been preserved in a later Icelandic manuscript, and the text of this is at times closer to the French text. This indicates that there was an original Norse text, but it is hard to say whether it was Norwegian or Icelandic. De la Gardie 4–7 bears admirable witness to the interests of learned Norwegian leaders in the latter half of the thirteenth century. It also includes a fragmentary prose translation of *Pamphilus de amore*, probably translated around the middle of the century or a little earlier. This comic love poem is appropriate to the ideals that noblemen played with during the latter half of the twelfth century. The work was taught in schools and derives part of its message from the Latin poet Ovid. The translation reveals that learned men in Norway knew how to appreciate such play and possibly also the same amours told by Thomas and Chrétien de Troyes.

This background indicates that chivalric literature was available at court or at chieftains' feasts during the latter half of the thirteenth century and possibly even earlier. It is doubtful that the stories were simply meant for entertainment, as has been claimed; courtly humor usually reflects lessons in behavior and ideology. Analysis of the audience as it appears in the stories themselves — in the form of the narrators' references to that audience — seems to indicate a constant interaction between audience and performers. The subject matter itself — where the opposites Christian knight and heathen foe are brought together — supports the belief that the stories found favor mainly with those who belonged to the upper stratum of society (courtiers and the aristocracy) and knights, whom they spurred on to imitation. Concerning knights, either Norwegian or Icelandic, however, there are few reliable historical sources until the fourteenth and fifteenth centuries.

Critics have believed most of the Knights' Sagas to be Norwegian. But this fails to take into account that most of the texts have been preserved in Icelandic manuscripts and address Icelandic audiences, among them, probably, some of the king's retainers. As early as the end of the twelfth century there were in Iceland educated leaders who had become acquainted with learning in France (see pp. 67–69), and it is certain that some of the ideas that were a prerequisite for the survival of chivalric literature were well-known in Iceland.

It is noteworthy how varied the translations from the French were. Beside verse romances by Thomas (*Tristran*) and Chrétien de Troyes (*Erec, Yvain, Parceval*), Marie de France's *Lais* are translated into prose, a fabliau (or a *lai*) is translated in *Möttuls saga*, and chansons de geste on Charlemagne's men and heroic deeds (*Chanson d'Otinel, Le pèlerinage de Charlemagne, Chanson de Roland, Chanson d'Aspremont*) were also rendered into prose. *Bevers saga* (The saga of Boeve de Haumtone) was translated from Anglo-Norman, while *Þiðriks saga* has its roots in Low German poetry based on the same material as Eddic heroic poetry. These translations are of varying ages and are embedded in compilations known in more than one redaction. This is the case, for example, with *Karlamagnús saga* (The saga of Charlemagne), which also includes material from the *Pseudo-Turpin Chronicle*, and *Þiðriks saga*, which has been preserved in two redactions.

It has been suggested that, owing to the differing lengths of syllables and the different forms of rhyme, the meter of French narrative poetry was too difficult for the translators to reproduce, that they did not believe themselves capable of doing the material justice in Norse as poetry and, therefore, chose to bring it to the audience as prose. On more careful consideration it becomes evident that there was, in fact, no obstacle to metrical translation; *Prophetiae Merlini*, an insertion in the prose *Breta sögur* based on Geoffrey of Monmouth's *Historia regum Britanniae*, was translated into the old Eddic meter *fornyrðislag*, for instance. What must have guided the choice is the fact that Iceland and Norway already had a strong narrative tradition in prose. Whether minstrels performed Marie de France's poetry in French at the Norwegian court is another matter, but certainly the *Strengleikar* were translated into prose for those who did not know French.

The documentary value of the sur- and subtitles in manuscripts from later centuries is subject to doubt. It seems clear, however, that the romances reviewed above were translated for a learned aristocracy in Iceland and Norway during the thirteenth century. For audiences of the fourteenth and fifteenth centuries and later, they might have had a different value; Chrétien de Troyes's stories of the knights Erec and Yvain are, for instance, preserved in abridged translations in manuscripts from these centuries. It is not clear whether the translations were abridged in the copying or based on French models that were themselves abridged, but the abridgment seems clearly to have served an ideological purpose. Noteworthy here, for instance, is that detailed poetic descriptions of love and of psychological observations on character have been lost, that the dialogue has been cut, and that inner monologues are only a shadow of the original. If these copies are faithful to a thirteenth-century original, it is likely that they reflect the views of the ruling classes at the time as well as the prevailing narrative tradition, which contained little in the way of inner monologue and descriptions of emotional life, unless veiled in euphemistic language in verse. On the other hand, they might also have been adapted for an audience of the fourteenth or fifteenth century or later, when Old Norse literature thrived almost exclusively in Iceland.

The value of the translations lies first and foremost in the fact that they taught Norsemen new methods of character description and style. Their influence can clearly be detected in the Sagas of Icelanders: *Spesar þáttur* (The tale of Spes) at the end of *Grettis saga* was influenced by *Tristrams saga*, while the duel between Gunnlaugur and Hrafn in *Gunnlaugs saga* shows that the saga author knew chivalric literature, and the behavioral pattern of the court in that saga is not unlike the descriptions in chivalric tales. The ideology and imagery of chivalric tales are also evident in both *Laxdæla saga* and *Njáls saga*, although pseudohistorical works such as *Breta sögur*, *Trójumanna saga*, and, last but not least, *Alexanders saga* have also influenced descriptions in the Sagas of Icelanders. Opinions are divided whether the bipartite structure of some Icelandic sagas is due to influences from French romances.

The world of French knights was, perhaps, a little distant from an Icelandic audience in space, but certainly not in time. While feasts and celebrations were rather more refined in Southern Europe than in Northern, the main plot — in which the knight/protagonist leaves the human world in search of himself or of happiness, whether in the form of a bridal quest or a religious transformation — was common to both, and the conclusion was always the same: the hero returns to the world or ideals he left behind and seems finally content with his lot. And an Icelandic audience could probably well appreciate the knight's independence in the romances of Chrétien de Troyes, where the knight was the king's faithful servant but not a slave.

When scholars maintain that most of the indigenous and translated Knights' Sagas were written to entertain Icelandic audiences in the fourteenth and fifteenth centuries, they tend to overlook the fact that entertainment also involved edification and that the message is, more often than not, religious: the knight fights for the true religion, Christianity and moral behavior go hand in hand, and good conquers evil in the end. *Mírmanns saga* is a good example of a narrative of this kind and could be considered a hagiographic romance. Characteristic of the original sagas are the names of the protagonists. The knight usually has a foreign name, such as Bæringur, Dámusti, Dínus, Clarus, Hektor, or Viktor. The female characters, however, are usually given names expressive of their role, although one needs some learning to understand them: in *Adónías saga* (The saga of Adonias), for instance, Remedia is she who gives help, and another woman is called Sedantia, the name referring to her becoming pregnant at the right moment. Both the original stories and the translations form one story world. In *Samsons saga* it is presumed that the audience knows *Möttuls saga* (called *Skikkju saga* in *Samsons saga*); well-known motifs from fabliaux appear, for instance, in *Sigurðar saga turnara* (The saga of Sigurður the Tournament-fighter), where it is obvious that the saga author uses a famous fabliau about a crucified priest (*Du prestre crucifié*). *Nítída saga* (The saga of Nitida) is about a maiden king and was very popular, the text stating that it was meant for "youngsters."

Even though the indigenous Knights' Sagas were very traditional, each topos following another, as Astrid van Nahl has shown, and their structure conforming to traditional adventures, as demonstrated by Jürg Glauser, at times the sagas were also intended to serve a political purpose. *Adónías saga* may serve as an example. One of its manuscripts includes a preface that first discusses *translatio studii* and then mentions *amplicatio*; it is noted that the saga is a *fræðisaga*, which means that it was meant for edification. Then the author of the preface interprets two well-known animal fables, those of the fox and the raven and of the wolf and the lamb. The saga's main plot is concerned with treason and how a powerful and cunning leader, Konstantínus, appropriates the state and power. The state, according to the rules of the society, is meant for another, Adonias. He then conquers the state that is his by right. The saga's outlook reflects the ideal of a fair feudal lord, and the preface's criticism is that leaders should take only what is theirs by right and use neither deceit nor violence. *Adónías saga* was, thus, intended to serve as an exemplum, and it is possible that the preface's wolf and fox are intended to be symbolic, to refer to families or leaders in the community the saga was meant for, that of the late medieval Icelandic aristocracy.

Legendary Sagas
At the wedding in Reykhólar mentioned in *Þorgils saga og Haflíða* (see p. 74), sagas of legendary heroes were told, and, if the date 1119 is reliable,

then this is the first time such sagas are mentioned. King Sverrir, as we have seen, called them "lying sagas" (*lygisögur*; see p. 74); in his *Jóns saga baptista* (The life of John the Baptist) Grímur Hólmsteinsson (d. 1298) described similar accounts using the word *víkingasögur* (viking sagas); and, finally, in the introduction to *Bósa saga og Herrauðs* (The saga of Bosi and Herrauður) the saga is called an *ævintýr* (adventure). Oddur Snorrason's *Ólafs saga Tryggvasonar* (The life of King Ólafur Tryggvason) mentions *stjúpmæðrasögur* (stepmothers' tales), which may or may not have been Legendary Sagas. Saxo Grammaticus is thought to have used quite a few Legendary Sagas, some of which are now lost, when writing his *Gesta Danorum* (ca. 1200). He refers to Icelandic sources, and his comments are evidence that, around the time he was composing his work, it was common to tell sagas dealing with past events similar to Legendary Sagas.

The oldest manuscripts of Legendary Sagas are from the early fourteenth century. Most of the Legendary Sagas were composed during the roughly 250-year period that lasted from the mid-fourteenth century into the early years of the seventeenth — and even beyond that. Some versions may have roots that are even older. Whether the original versions of the Legendary sagas were oral or written will not be discussed here.

The Legendary Sagas are mostly set in the eight and ninth centuries — and some even earlier. Icelanders are, of course, not mentioned in them, but their famous ancestors are. For a long time these sagas were classified into three groups — heroic, viking, and adventure sagas — but this demarcation is vague. Most closely related in terms of material are the two last groups, the heroic sagas differing from the viking and adventure sagas in that they have closer ties to Norse and Germanic heroic verse (even if the others occasionally add some verse in Eddic meter). The heroic sagas can be viewed as a direct continuation of the heroic verses in the Edda and are characterized by the fact that the hero dies at the end. The viking and adventure sagas usually end happily: the protagonists have gained power, fame, and fortune as well as a noble bride and, as often as not, land and a kingdom along with her. They share these characteristics with the Knights' Sagas, which is why the viking and adventure sagas are considered to belong to the same genre.

The four best-known heroic sagas are *Hervarar saga og Heiðreks* (The saga of Hervör and King Heiðrek), *Völsunga saga* (The saga of the Völsungar), *Hrólfs saga kraka* (The saga of Hrólfur and his champions), and *Hálfs saga og Hálfsrekka* (The saga of Hálfur and his champions), the latter being not unlike the so-called viking sagas. To this group is sometimes also added the *Norna-Gests þáttur* (The tale of Norna-Gestur), which is embedded in the *Flateyjarbók* version of *Ólafs saga Tryggvasonar hin mesta*, as it tells of how Norna-Gestur entertained King Ólafur Tryggvason with tales of the hero Sigurður Fáfnisbani. The sources for the heroic sagas are often either verses that now are mostly lost or older sagas based on verses in manuscripts that now are lost but had close parallels in the Codex Regius of the *Poetic Edda* (see p. 151). This is the case with *Norna-Gests þáttur* and also with the most famous saga of this type, *Völsunga saga*. In the manuscript the latter precedes *Ragnars saga loðbrókar*, so scholars have assumed it to be a prehistory of sorts, designed to prove that Ragnar was of noble descent, his ancestor being Odin himself.

Völsunga saga is thought to have been written around the middle of the thirteenth century. Its characters are all known. Some of them can be traced to Germanic or Hun leaders from the Great Migration, as, for instance, Attila, king of the Huns, who is in all probability the model for Atli, the second husband of Guðrún Gjúkadóttir. It is Odin who controls events in *Völsunga saga*, just as Zeus did in Homer's epics; he hands out triumph to some characters and failure to others.

Völsunga saga must be considered above all else to be the story of the hero Sigurd the Dragon-slayer. His origin is explained, he is given divine intellect, but the saga's main concern is whether he has kept the oaths laid on this divine hero or failed them. The story is told in short sentences and in a concise style, interspersed with verses. One part is influenced by *Þiðriks saga*, which is also concerned with the same families.

Völsunga saga is structurally divided into two parts. The first part deals with the Völsungar family and the hero Sigurd, while the second half focuses on the Gjúkungar, with Guðrún Gjúkadóttir as the main protagonist. This structure is highly appropriate to the prevailing narrative tradition. Critics have admittedly claimed that oral tradition determined the way in which the individual narrative units are structured: the narrative flows in short, demarcated parts governed by common rules of oral narrative art, such as three repetitions of the same motif. These characteristics could, however, also be traced to the fact that the story is probably based on very incisive poems.

In 1979 Carola L. Gottzman proposed that it was not sufficient to consider *Völsunga saga* to be simply a kind of rewriting of heroic poetry. She believed that the saga and *Ragnars saga loðbrókar* should be considered parables on royal power; if leaders do the right thing and show good judgment, then they stay in power; otherwise a different kind of power intervenes, and they are ousted. The symbolic wielder of this punitive force is Odin himself. It is possible to interpret *Hrólfs saga kraka* in the same way.

That saga survives in a more recent version; the older version is thought to have traced its material back to "Bjarkamál hin fornu" (The ancient lay of Bjarki). In its present form *Hrólfs saga kraka* serves an ideological purpose: to point out the faults and virtues of the king and at the same time to satirize life at court.

One of the most peculiar Legendary Sagas is *Örvar-Odds saga* (The saga of Arrow-Oddur). It has long been grouped with the viking sagas and exists in short and long versions. The short one is considered the older. Scholars long believed that many Legendary Sagas contained a historical kernel that once existed in oral form. It is difficult to prove whether such predecessors ever existed, and it is not at all certain that the stories of these champions were always based on verses or that they formed the inspiration for the prose sagas. What is clear, however, is that the verses in *Örvar-Odds saga* serve a distinct purpose. Apart from reflecting on the fellowship of storyteller and audience, who may be sitting together drinking, they usually consist of hostile verbal matches, or flytings, supposed to shed light on the image of the viking. In addition, the *flokkur* or biographical poem at the end of the sagas, for example, that in *Örvar-Odds saga*, may well have served as a reminder that the storyteller was faithful to the story.

The structure of both versions of *Örvar-Odds saga* follows a distinct biographical pattern: childhood at home; multiple perils far away from home or in another world; and, finally, death in the hero's native region. This basic structure is, however, greatly elaborated, and the longer version contains material that at first sight seems only loosely tied to the plot, included as if by coincidence: Oddur is torn away by a big vulture that drops him into its nest, from which he is saved by a giant. This chapter can be called the giant episode. It is woven into the story and is not intended for entertainment alone. Oddur is famous for his travels to Bjarmaland, a trip that is mentioned time and again throughout the story, and in almost all his adventures he triumphs. In the giant episode and the battles with Ögmundur Eyþjófsbani, however, another picture of the viking hero Oddur emerges. The giant who saved Oddur from the nest gives him to his daughter — beside whom Oddur is the size of a child — for a plaything. As she cuddles him, however, Oddur responds to her endearments and gets her pregnant. It is clear that the author of this version had some knowledge of fabliaux and intended to show that Oddur has a soft side and is, after all, as small as other men, even though he is twelve *álnir* (eighteen feet) tall and lives to the age of three hundred. The episode is intended to be an example of *mésure* and has a similar function as in the romances.

Oddur is finally defeated in a battle with Ögmundur; he cannot triumph over evil. This battle has been described as Oddur's acknowledgment that "in the end, after a hopeless battle with the force of Ögmundur, and with the limits of human life and human character, he is able to die" (Bandle, *Schriften*, 294). This is an apt observation, but Oddur's battle with Ögmundur can also be viewed as a duel with his alter ego, one that he cannot win despite all his heroism. Just like other heroes, he must succumb to the fate the seeress prophesied for him at the start of the story: that he would be killed by a horse's head. This may seem an ignominious death, but, in the end, it is actually a snake that gets him, its poison killing him when the wound becomes gangrenous. This tale of Ögmundur and Oddur's repeated duels with him reminds us of Grettir's battle with Glámur, who can be seen as Grettir's alter ego; even though Grettir gets the better of him, he is haunted by him for the rest of his life. It cannot be a coincidence that both sagas deal with the question of whether man can triumph over evil and master his own fear. They show that the Legendary Sagas and the Sagas of Icelanders were not told for entertainment alone, even if they were mainly told at feasts.

Each of Oddur's new adventures represents an amplification of his former feats, his final battle with Ögmundur forming the climax of the series. His search for himself is now at an end. The handling of the adventure material in *Örvar-Odds saga* points to a strong literary tradition; sagas of this type would hardly be composed unless there existed a knowledge of how to construct them and for whom. Such literary consciousness is very apparent in another viking saga, *Göngu-Hrólfs saga* (The saga of Göngu-Hrólfur). There is an introduction to the saga that also serves as the introduction to *Sigurðar saga þögla* (The saga of Sigurður the Silent) and that, despite its formulaic nature, contains an excellent justification for exaggerated tales of this kind:

> Of the many stories written for people's entertainment, a number come down to us from ancient manuscripts or from learned men. Some of these tales from old books must have been set down very briefly at first and expanded afterwards, since most of what they contain took place later than is told. Now not everyone shares the same knowledge, and even when two men happen to be present at the same event, one of them will often hear or see something which the other doesn't. Moreover there are plenty of people so foolish that they believe nothing but what they have seen with their own eyes or heard with their own ears—never anything unfamiliar to them, such as counsels of the wise.

An even better example of the saga author's view of his material follows later in the work: "Then there are wise men who have written figuratively — men such as Master Gualterus in *Alexanders saga* and the poet Homer in *Trójumanna saga*. Masters who have come after these have vouched for truth of what was written, and not denied that things might have happened that way" (*Göngu-Hrolfs Saga*, trans. Pálsson and Edwards, 27, 84). In other words, even though the material is exaggerated and narrated figuratively, it can, it is clear, be proved true once the story had been glossed and the veil of exaggeration lifted.

The meaning of most Legendary Sagas is not so hidden that it needs to be unveiled, however. One of the best-known among them is *Bósa saga*. Like *Örvar-Odds saga*, *Göngu-Hrólfs saga*, and *Hrólfs saga kraka*, *Bósa saga* has its roots in fourteenth-century literary tradition. The author of the saga is, in fact, so well versed in tradition that he flies in its face. In its outer form, *Bósa saga* appears to conform to existing generic conventions: the protagonist, the farmer's son Bósi, is asked to perform a deed considered to be beyond human capacity. He has become the enemy of King Hringur and kills his older son, Sjóður. His friendship with Herrauður, Hringur's younger son, does not save his life, but the magical power of his foster mother, old Busla, does. Bósi is outlawed and saves life and limb only by bringing the king a treasure, a kind of vulture's egg "inscribed all over with golden letters," from the temple of the heathen god Jómali in Bjarmaland. The egg admittedly constitutes a break in motif convention; treasures in temples are usually not eggs, and it has been maintained that the narrator is making fun of traditional treasure hunts. To get his hands on this hoard, Bósi must acquire certain knowledge, which he obtains by sleeping with farmers' daughters. Thus, the Legendary Saga tradition is broken, and myth takes over as Bósi follows in Odin's footsteps.

The chapters on Bósi's sexual exploits are unusual in Icelandic prose literature. For the first time, physical pleasure is described for the audience's enjoyment, which is not the norm in the Knights' Sagas or Icelandic histories, where the nocturnal escapades of characters were only ever hinted at. The language of *Bósa saga* is rich in imagery that has no parallel in Icelandic literature. A good example is when Bósi wants to satisfy his lust with one of the girls: "'I want to water my foal in your fountain.' 'Do you think you are able to,' she said, 'he is hardly used to such a well as mine'" (Tómasson, ed., *Bósa saga og Herrauðs*, 29–31). Metaphoric language of this kind is found only in the verses in *Grettis saga*, although, as mentioned earlier, influences from fabliaux are apparent in other Legendary Sagas as well. In fact, these descriptions are reminiscent of a famous French fabliau entitled *La da-*

moisele qui ne pooit oir parler de foutre. Although it is by no means certain that this fabliau was known in Iceland, such imagery is common to the genre, and there is no doubt that similar French fabliaux were known.

Bósa saga is very well composed. The narrator at times pokes fun at its hero. The exaggerations are so broad that, at times, they turn into parody. And it is hardly a coincidence that Bósi solves problems with the help of women, just as Odin did, and finally marries a princess called Edda. With this the author sealed the story, marked it with a knowledge he could be sure his audience possessed, that of fiction itself, while at the same time playing with mythological motifs.

For the medieval Icelandic saga tradition, the main value of the Legendary Sagas lies in the variety of innovations that they bring to it. The narrator is closer to the audience than in the objective narratives of the Sagas of Icelanders and national Norse histories; he intervenes at times and addresses the audience. The characters are admittedly very traditional and represent stereotyped roles, as in fairy tales. The narrative is also usually in *sermo humilis*, even in passages of exaggeration, but at times we detect influences from chivalric literature in attempts at refinement. As in the translated romances, inner monologue appears but is not common.

Legendary Sagas form one group of sagas, but their authors seem to have been familiar with other sagas as well. Intertextuality occurs. Where most of the Sagas of Icelanders begin with either the Great Migration or settlement, this is where the Legendary Sagas end. Only occasional, passing references to settlers are found in them.

The French and German verse romances and chansons de geste that may originally have been translated in Norway are, in the fourteenth century, part of Icelandic literary tradition. This is the case, for instance, with the large compilations on Charlemagne and his men and with *Þiðriks saga*. This tradition continues unbroken into the nineteenth and twentieth centuries, with the copying of individual sagas, the reworking of others, and the composing of new ones. Last but not least, the sagas are revived as poetry in the *rímur* and to some extent also in *danskvæði* (ballads).

MYTHOLOGY AND POETICS

Snorri Sturluson's Prose Edda
The *Prose Edda*, attributed to Snorri Sturluson, has been preserved in eight medieval manuscripts and fragments, although nowhere in its entirety. The main manuscripts, the Codex Regius, the Codex Uppsaliensis, and the Codex Wormianus, are from ca. 1300–1350, and scholars are divided on

their relation to each other because of the differences between them. The material in the *Prose Edda* is also organized differently in the manuscripts. In the title of the Codex Uppsaliensis it is stated: "This book is called Edda. It was compiled by Snorri Sturluson in the manner in which it is arranged here. There is told first about the Æsir and Ymir, then *Skáldskaparmál* and terms for many things, finally *Háttatal* which Snorri has composed about King Hákon and Duke Skúli" (*Edda*, trans. Faulkes, vi). This order does not agree with the manuscript itself, for there the text of *Skáldskaparmál* (The language of poetry) is broken up, first with *Skáldatal* (The list of poets), then with *Lögsögumannatal* (The list of lawspeakers), which goes up to Snorri Sturluson, while *Skáldskaparmál* is followed by the *Second Grammatical Treatise* and by *Háttatal*, which is also rather loosely related to the other material in the *Edda* of the Codex Wormianus, where *Háttatal* comes after four grammatical treatises. In the Codex Regius, on the other hand, the order is almost identical to the description given in the Codex Uppsaliensis.

In most editions of the work, the material is ordered according to the passage in the Codex Uppsaliensis, but it remains uncertain whether this, rather than what appears in the other manuscripts, represents the original structure of the work. The organization of material could point to the fact that some parts of the *Prose Edda* had been preserved separately; the material, especially in *Skáldskaparmál*, is of such a nature that interpreters in later centuries could easily have added their own comments. And, because of the great differences in some parts between individual manuscripts, one may also assume that, as early as the thirteenth century, the *Prose Edda* existed in many versions. For the most part the texts of the preserved manuscripts are Snorri's work, but they were probably augmented with comments from thirteenth-century scholars, as was common in the works of school authors and scholars everywhere in Europe.

The Codex Uppsaliensis probably belonged to descendants of the Sturlungar family. This could be taken as evidence that the work is correctly attributed to Snorri. In AM 748 I 4to, one of the main manuscripts of the *Third Grammatical Treatise*, Snorri is said to have compiled the poetics, while according to its surtitle, *Háttatal* is the work of Snorri Sturluson.

Thirteenth-century opinion was evidently not agreed on the merits of Snorri as a poet, as becomes apparent in Sturla Þórðarson's sarcastic account of the southern Icelanders' criticism of Snorri and his *Háttatal*. However, elsewhere in *Íslendinga saga* Sturla claims that Snorri was an accomplished poet, and Ólafur hvítaskáld Þórðarson is of the same opinion; he would hardly have referred to *Háttatal* if he did not think much of it. Ólafur also quotes Snorri's verse on Bishop Guðmundur Arason the Good as well as a verse on the Norwegian Gautur Jónsson of Mel, who is mentioned in *Hákonar saga*. Sources thus seem to indicate that Snorri was considered a good poet, and poetics (*ars poetica*) could have been a subject close to his heart, although no sources survive that indicate why he was more fond of it than other contemporary poets were, indeed, so fond that he wrote a book on it.

It has been suggested that, at the beginning of the thirteenth century, interest in ancient poetry was diminishing as new fashions in meter had taken over. Snorri had, therefore, thought it expedient to compose his treatise on poetics to draw attention to the poetical skills of his ancestors. It is justly observed that new poetic styles always invite resistance, and, indeed, the audience's conservatism shows in various ways, but it is worth noting that we do not know for certain when a new style of poetry first arrived in Iceland. *Jóns saga helga* (The life of Saint Jón of Hólar) mentions ballads (see pp. 60–63), but it is doubtful that either their meter or their rhyme influenced Icelandic poetry that early. Skaldic poems (*dróttkvæði*; see pp. 5–6, 27–43) were most often composed for well-educated noble families, and this art does not seem to suffer in the thirteenth century. A story in one manuscript of *Sverris saga*, the tale of Máni the Poet, complains that poetry has had to compete with the performance of minstrels and the silliness of clowns, but it is uncertain whether this tale is older than this version of *Sverris saga*, which is from the middle of the thirteenth century. It must be considered unlikely that a new poetic fashion alone caused Snorri to write the *Prose Edda*; other causes must have contributed to it.

The name of the work, *Edda*, has caused some confusion. The word *edda* appears in "Rígsþula" and there denotes a great-grandmother. Even though the book preserved ancient learning, Snorri hardly intended it simply as a monument to ancient times, however, so this explanation of the name is not satisfactory. The name has also been linked to Oddi, where Snorri stayed during his formative years, doubtless learning much from the scholars there. The third explanation is that the name was constructed from the word *óður* (ode) and a suffix, *ido-*, resulting in *edda* (as *stedda* [young mare] is derived from *stóð*), meaning "ode theory" or poetics (*ars poetica*). This explanation, however, does not comply with phonological rules. The fourth explanation is that the name is derived from the Latin verb *edo* (I publish, I edit, I compose), which became *edda* in Icelandic, just as *credo* became *kredda*. Magnús Ólafsson (d. 1636) from Laufás (see p. 181) first made this link early in the seventeenth century, but Árni Magnússon and other rationalists were not impressed with this explanation. This is not the place to evaluate these various explanations, but it seems very plausible that the name should refer to the purpose of the work, as was common in the Middle Ages. This purpose is also explained at the end of the introductory chapter of *Skáldskaparmál*:

But these things have now to be told to young poets who desire to learn the language of poetry and to furnish themselves with a wide vocabulary using traditional terms; or else they desire to be able to understand what is expressed obscurely. Then let such a one as that take this book as scholarly inquiry and entertainment. These stories are not to be consigned to oblivion or demonstrated to be false, and as a result deprive poetry of ancient kennings which major poets have been happy to use. At the same time Christian people must not believe in heathen gods, nor in the truth of this account in any other way than that in which it is presented at the beginning of this book. (*Edda*, trans. Faulkes, 64–65)

With these words in mind, one might agree with Magnús Ólafsson's explanation: Snorri obviously intended to tell of ancient events, publish the narratives, and at the same time shed light on obscure poetry. While this interpretation would turn Snorri into a philologist, it is also true that it links his works more closely to the works of other twelfth-century European scholars and writers on one particular function served by *ars poetica*: to lead the way into the essence of poetry and lift the veil from its hidden truths.

The *Prose Edda* is divided into four parts: *Prologus*; *Gylfaginning* (The tricking of Gylfi); *Skáldskaparmál*; and, finally, *Háttatal*. As we have seen, it is assumed that Snorri first composed *Háttatal* in 1221–22 and then added the rest of the *Prose Edda* before it.

Few parts of the *Prose Edda* have been as much debated as its prologue. Using concise language, it tells of the creation of man, the four natural forces, and, finally, the origin of the Æsir, the gods. When compared to the material that follows, that is, *Gylfaginning* and *Skáldskaparmál*, the prologue can be seen to contain a few paradoxes that have proved difficult to explain, and scholars have pondered the reasons for this. On the basis of this it has, for instance, been maintained that the prologue was not the work of Snorri at all. It has, however, been preserved in all the manuscripts of the work (although admittedly incompletely in the Codex Regius), and it must be considered a philosophical introduction to the entire work: it is intended to show the Norse people's understanding of existence before they adopted the Christian faith. This opinion echoes the worldview of *Gylfaginning*, and it is possible that Snorri was here influenced by twelfth-century philosophy, especially the views of William of Conches (d. 1154) and Thierry of

Chartres (d. after 1149), although the material that Snorri includes on the four natural forces and the earth as a body can also be traced to the teachings of church fathers such as Martin of Braga (sixth century), Hrabanus Maurus (d. 856), and Isidore of Seville. After this introductory chapter Snorri turns to more familiar exposition: where the Æsir came from and how they were related to the kings of Sweden. Here he puts forward well-known medieval ideas on the origin of the divine power of kings (*euhemerismus*).

The prologue was probably originally divided into two parts: a *prologus praeter rem* and a *prologus ante rem*, where the first half was intended for audiences while the second introduced the material. To medieval minds, this part of the work employed a different style from that in the main body of the work, although the surtitle from the Codex Uppsaliensis could be a reworking of a lost *prologus praeter rem*.

Gylfaginning is a framed narrative. King Gylfi has problems with the Æsir and has suffered from their cunning. It was, therefore, "natural to let him be the second party in the story that he was now creating," says Sigurður Nordal (*Snorri Sturluson*, 111). Gylfi, who is here called Gangleri (one of Odin's names), arriving from trackless ways, "requested that he might have a night's lodging." He has a look round, and recites a stanza from "Hávamál," and "saw three thrones, one above the other, and there were three men, one sitting in each" (*Edda*, trans. Faulkes, 2). Then the game begins.

Gangleri asks and the kings answer. A question-and-answer session of this kind was well-known from the Eddic poem "Vafþrúðnismál" (see p. 10), and the play with illusions was common in medieval literature. Snorri probably based the structure of the narrative on textbooks: the *Elucidarius* and Gregory's *Dialogues* spring to mind, where the disciple asks the master a number of questions. Edifying books of this kind existed already in Snorri's youth in Old Norse translations. His organization of the material resembles that in encyclopedias such as the *De natura rerum* by the Venerable Bede and the *Imago mundi* by Honorius Augustodunensis, which first tell of the creation of the world, its division, the stars, the ocean, and then other natural phenomena. The end of *Gylfaginning* relates the end of the world and the people saved in Hoddmímisholt:

> And in a place called Hoddmímir's holt two people will lie hid during Surt's fire called Life and Leifthrasir, and their food will be the dews of morning. And from these people there will be descended such a great progeny that all the world will be inhabited. As it says here: "Life and Leifthrasir, and they shall lie hid in Hoddmímir's holt.

Dews of morning they shall have as their food, and from them shall grow mankind." (*Edda*, trans. Faulkes, 57)

Even though the narrative framework is derived from foreign texts and the organization of the material is based on contemporary encyclopedias, Snorri's narrative stands out from foreign contemporary works dealing with similar subject matter. This is not only because he tells of the old pagan religion, the ancient gods and their lives in Ásgarður, explaining their virtues and faults, but also because one would be hard-pressed to find elsewhere such an aesthetic style and disciplined narrative, one where each example could stand on its own. The narrative is interspersed with Eddic verses, where Snorri has sometimes relied on other redactions than are known from the Codex Regius of Eddic poetry.

Gylfaginning, along with *Skáldskaparmál*, is our main source on pagan Norse tradition. The narrative has, however, been subject to doubt, and Snorri has been accused of spinning tales. There is no way to prove this, however, and it is certain that, in the main, Snorri's account is accurate. The comparative studies of Georges Dumézil and other historians of religion have demonstrated that Snorri's narrative cannot be much exaggerated. But it is also obvious that Snorri was influenced by Christian thought and works, and it is possible that he concludes in some cases with what he knows from Christian tradition. He still had quite a few ancient sources available to him, however, especially in poetry, and he knew how to use them with moderation and humor. It is, in fact, not least Snorri's humor that has caused some to doubt his accuracy. The gods are never spared mockery, and some of Snorri's tales are equal to the best medieval fabliaux, for instance, those of the horse Sleipnir and of the giantess Gjálp (see *Edda*, trans. Faulkes, 34–35, 81–82). Snorri's descriptions of pagan religion are never opposed to the Christian worldview; indeed, many themes are common to both the *Prose Edda* and Christian literature. The most obvious comparison is the golden age of the Æsir and Christian ideas of paradise. Another ideological connection is between the Holy Trinity and the three leaders: Hár (High); Jafnhár (Equally High); and Þriðji (Third). Some scholars have also thought that they could detect influences from Augustine in the *Prose Edda*. But Christians, too, often played with tales of Greek and Roman pagan gods, as Theodolus's famous poem *Ecloga* shows. It is, in fact, quite possible that Snorri got the idea from exactly such educational poetry, the works of Fulgentius or the so-called Third Vatican mythograph. It is Snorri's own genius, however, that combines a mythological system with *ars poetica* in order to show how knowledge of both is necessary for the understanding of ancient poetry. And, with the help of examples, he shows how one can use mythological knowledge in living poetry. This Snorri makes even clearer in *Skáldskaparmál*, which continues where *Gylfaginning* leaves off.

Snorri abandons the dialogue form in *Skáldskaparmál*, where the narrative is in the third-person singular, as if he meant to frame the narrative originally but then changed his mind. *Skáldskaparmál* is not as well put together as *Gylfaginning*; it contains more general comments on literature and includes many tales for which no room could be found in *Gylfaginning*. Snorri frequently mentions his sources in *Skáldskaparmál*, which can often be compared to well-known narratives such as *Hrólfs saga kraka*, *Völsunga saga*, and *Ynglinga saga*. In *Skáldskaparmál* Snorri quotes the verse of over sixty poets. He divides *Skáldskaparmál* into two sections: one on kennings and one on *heiti* (see pp. 6, 31). He mostly adheres to this division, but there are exceptions, as the narratives of this part of the work do not form as strong a whole as do those in *Gylfaginning*: they explain individual kennings but do not form a part of a larger, collective picture. Snorri's interpretation of individual components of *ars poetica* is sometimes at odds with those of later commentators as he is not as dependent on Latin models as they are.

The last part of the *Prose Edda* is *Háttatal*, where Snorri composes on King Hákon Hákonarson and Duke Skúli Bárðarson. *Háttatal* consists of 102 verses, each illustrating a different kind of meter, and is divided into three sections: 1–30 on Hákon; 31–66 on Skúli; and 67–102 on both Hákon and Skúli. Snorri's praise of these leaders is excessive in places, and the material has to fit the demands of the meter. Snorri clearly considers *dróttkvætt* to be the original meter and orders things accordingly — *dróttkvætt* verses first and the last stanzas in *fornyrðislag* and its variations. Between the stanzas are comments in rather a textbook fashion.

Háttatal seems to have had little influence on Icelandic poetry. The *Prose Edda* itself was, however, read well into later centuries, as a result of which concepts such as *eddulist* (Eddic art) and *edduborinn kveðskapur* (poetry in Eddic style) came to refer to the kennings and *heiti* in skaldic poetry and *rímur* (see pp. 56–58) and not to Eddic poetry. The *Prose Edda* was often copied as well. The *þulur*, or long lists of names arranged in alliterative meter, which have been preserved separately, can be viewed as additions to the *Prose Edda*.

The *Prose Edda* continued for centuries to be the young poet's textbook. It has even been claimed that it prevented poetic innovation. This is not really the case, even though one could say that the innovations did not have much resonance in readers' minds. New directions in poetics seem to have appeared as early as the fourteenth century — if the remarks of the editor of the Codex Wormianus (AM 242 fol.) in his preface to the four grammatical treatises are to be believed. Another instruction on how to write poetry is to be found in the poem "Lilja" (see p. 48), where it says that one should write using "clear words." Peter Foote has shown that its poet, Brother Eysteinn, relied on parts of the *Poetria nova* by Geoffrey of Vinsauf, and presumably he read other parts of it as well (*Aurvandilstá*, 249–70). This shows that the *Prose Edda* was not the only handbook for fourteenth-century poets. It does, however, seem that it was the most widely used, and it is not until the translation of the rhetorical handbook by Friedrich Riederer, *Spiegel der waren Rhetoric*, by Magnús Jónsson (d. 1591) in the sixteenth century that works on rhetoric and poetics are mentioned (see p. 188); no *ars poetica* in the vernacular other than the *Prose Edda* seems to have been known.

Snorri's work increased in value in the seventeenth century when it was first published in printed form. Up to then there probably existed many types of Eddas or compilations of the *Prose Edda*, and poets, especially *rímur* poets, often used kennings incorrectly, at least according to the *Prose Edda*, but that is another story.

The origins of religious writing in Iceland are very clear: translations, beginning in the twelfth century, from the Latin of works that were brought to the country from continental Europe or England. Probably by the late twelfth century and the early thirteenth, indigenous works like Saint Þorlákur's life began to appear, their authors looking to the New Testament as well as classical literature for models. Christian religious literature is often divided into three main groups: saints' lives (lives, passions, and visions); sermons; and panegyrics.

All types of saints' lives are known in Iceland from the Catholic era. Only a small number of them were originally written in Iceland, and these are on Icelandic and Norwegian Christian missionary kings, earls, and bishops. At first saints' lives were mostly written in Latin and then translated into Old Norse. Among these lives are narratives on the bishops Saint Guðmundur Arason, Saint Jón Ögmundarson, and Saint Þorlákur Þórhallsson, the Norwegian kings Ólafur Tryggvason and Ólafur Haraldsson (Saint Olaf), and, finally, Saint Magnus Erlendsson, Earl of the Orkneys.

The oldest preserved translations of saints' lives originated in the twelfth century, and translation activity continues nearly without a break for four centuries until the Catholic writing of saints' lives stops at the start of the sixteenth century with *Reykjahólabók* (Stock. Perg. fol. nr. 3), which is a compilation of saints' lives, mostly translated and retold from Low German.

Norse passions (*píslarsögur*) and lives were either translated straight from the Latin by Icelandic editors or reworked from a variety of foreign sources. In this way many of the best-known works of medieval Europe exist in Icelandic translations. *Marteins saga biskups* is, for instance, a translation of one version of the *Life of Saint Martin* by Sulpicius Severus, one of the best-known early medieval hagiographers. The first part of the collection of exempla on hermits, the *Vitae patrum*, usually called the *Historia eremitica* or the *Historia monachorum in Ægypto* and thought to be by the Italian monk Rufinus (d. ca. 410), was probably translated at the end of the thirteenth century. Some saints' lives were also translated or rendered from the *Legenda aurea* by Jacobus de Voragine, and selections from the *Speculum historiale*, which is one part of the large encyclopedia *Speculum maius* by Vincent of Beauvais, are embedded in several legendary compilations of the fourteenth century.

Translated saints' lives exercised a considerable influence on secular writing, which in turn influenced the saints' lives. The effect of these reciprocal influences on Icelandic literature has not been fully investigated. Exactly which Latin sources the Icelandic translations are based on also remains to be better explored.

The oldest relatively complete translations are contained in the manuscript AM 645 4to, from the beginning of the thirteenth century. This manuscript includes the lives of the apostles Peter, James, Bartholomew, Matthew, Andrew, and Paul. Also to be found in this manuscript are the oldest preserved miracles of Saint Þorlákur, *Niðurstigningar saga* (The Harrowing of Hell), and *Klemens saga páfa*, which is often considered one of the Apostles' Sagas (*postulasögur*). Another manuscript containing an Apostles' Saga collection from the mid-thirteenth century is AM 652 4to. The manuscript AM 623 4to, which includes, among other things, *Alexíus saga* (The life of Saint Alexis), *Jóns saga postula* (The saga of John the Apostle), and a fragment of *Niðurstigningar saga*, is also believed to have been written in the thirteenth century, although this remains uncertain.

At the end of the twelfth century and at the start of the thirteenth, the Þingeyrar monks Gunnlaugur Leifsson and Oddur Snorrason composed the lives of Saint Jón Ögmundarson and King Ólafur Tryggvason in Latin, which are now lost. Perhaps there also existed a Latin version of the life of

Saint Þorlákur, but only fragments and *lectiones* now survive. Icelandic writing of saints' lives is continued into the thirteenth century with the lives of Saint Þorlákur and later three versions of the life of Saint Guðmundur Arason, but their composition is not concluded until the latter half of the fourteenth century. At the same time *Jóns saga helga* was reworked. It is not certain where the Icelandic saints' lives were written, but most likely this happened in the scriptoria of the monasteries at Þingeyrar, Helgafell, Munka-Þverá, and Möðruvellir.

It is not known for certain when saints' lives were first translated into Icelandic, but both *Marteins saga biskups* and the oldest version of *Nikulás saga erkibiskups* (The life of Saint Nicholas) were translated in the twelfth century. The oldest seem to be the lives of Blasius, Erasmus, and Silvester, manuscript fragments of which have been preserved from the decades before and after 1200. The style of the oldest narratives seems to have been adapted to spoken language: it is simple and mostly without ornament. This is in accordance with the guidelines of the model for writers of saints' lives, Sulpicius Severus, outlined in his introduction to the life of Saint Martin: a writer should bring a worthy and beautiful errand in a simple form, be like a priest, and mediate the Christian message. Sulpicius's views echo the Apostle Paul in 1 Cor. 2:4. The role of writers of saints' lives was, in Sulpicius's view, to preach religion in simple words so that fishermen and peasants could understand it, for the Bible was written for them. The writers were, however, so well versed in oratory that their style was often laden with rhetorical devices. Their declarations on preaching Christianity in simple words could, therefore, be in direct opposition to the style of their works. And the words of Sulpicius and Paul seem to refer, not only to saints' lives in Latin, but also to those in the vernacular, and it might well be that the style of the oldest Icelandic confessors' lives was shaped by these views.

Lives of over forty confessors were translated into Icelandic from the twelfth century until well into the sixteenth, not including several short accounts found among the large collections of Marian miracles or unpublished texts. Many legends have also been preserved in later manuscripts that are either copies of older manuscripts or new translations. This material has so far hardly been examined.

As mentioned above, *Fyrsta málfræðiritgerðin* talks of *þýðingar helgar* (sacred interpretations), and this is our first source on the explanation of religious matter. Both the Icelandic and the Norwegian books of homilies reflect traditional biblical exegesis. The Bible in its entirety was not translated into the vernacular until after the Reformation in 1550, but parts of the Old Testament exist in translations of varying ages from the thirteenth and fourteenth centuries under the collective name *Stjórn*. The oldest part, *Stjórn* II, is almost entirely without exegetical interpretation, but, in *Stjórn* I, as well as in *Stjórn* III, the text is often explained, although mostly according to the historical sense (*sensus historicus*). The biblical interpretation in *Stjórn* seems to go hand in hand with new views on the composition of saints' lives, views that are most apparent in the compilation *Maríu saga* (The life of the Virgin Mary), which was probably written in the latter half of the thirteenth century, and in the work of Grímur Hólmsteinsson on John the Baptist, compiled around the same time. One can say that Grímur is an innovator in the composition of saints' lives, a form that reaches its high point in the fourteenth century.

Passions of Kings and Earls

Pagan nations made up Northern Europe in the tenth century, and, at the start of the eleventh century, missionary work was at its height there. Two of the most famous missionaries in Norway and Iceland were the namesakes and kings Ólafur Tryggvason and Ólafur Haraldsson. There exist many accounts of them, among them three lives/passions. *Ólafs saga Tryggvasonar* by the monk Oddur Snorrason is probably the oldest; it was written in Latin ca. 1190 at Þingeyrar, where Oddur was a monk, and is thought to have been translated into Icelandic ca. 1200. The life of Saint Olaf, *Helgisagan um Ólaf digra Haraldsson* (The legendary saga of Saint Olaf), is more recent, probably written in the first quarter of the thirteenth century, but it is based on older material. The most recent saga in this group is *Magnús saga Eyjajarls* (The life of Saint Magnus), which has been preserved in two Icelandic versions and a Latin one.

The sagas of the two missionary kings have commonly been considered to form part of another literary genre, the Kings' Sagas. It is, however, clear that both belong more appropriately with the saints' lives. One is largely concerned with missionary work. Both kings die for their religion, and after the death of King Ólafur Haraldsson miracles occur. The structure of the sagas is similar to that of the lives of the apostles; the missionary is on a never-ending journey, and, at the end of the story, before the death of the protagonist, the king speaks to his enemies in a way that resembles a judge's interrogation of a martyr. This retardation delays the high point of the narrative: the martyrdom. The main aspects of the lives of both kings are recounted and based on many sources, both annals and biographies. Tue Gad has suggested that this type of saint's life has been influenced by English hagiography and mentions in this respect the legends of Saint Edward.

Lives of Saint Olaf

The so-called *Helgisaga* (i.e., *Helgisagan um Ólaf digra Haraldsson*) has been preserved only in a Norwegian manuscript. It is clear that its author relied on older texts, but today we cannot know with any certainty which ones, except in a few cases. On the sainthood of Ólafur Haraldsson the Stout there are a few old Norse sources, the oldest of which are verses by famous poets. Þórarinn loftunga (Praise-tongue) mentions miracles at the king's grave in "Glælognskviða" (Calm sea poem; see also p. 44), and Sighvatur Þórðarson mentions some of them in his "Erfidrápa" (Memorial poem). Most noteworthy is Einar Skúlason's poem "Geisli" (Beam of light), which the poet himself recited in the cathedral in Nidaros in 1152 (see p. 44). One English manuscript includes a Latin office (*officium*) of Saint Olaf and his passion, and miracles also exist in Latin in two versions, a shorter version and a longer one (*Passio et miracula Sancti Olavi*). The monk Theodoricus mentions the exhumation of Saint Olaf's relics, and it is possible that he is here referring to a separate text. In the Norwegian book of homilies one sermon tells of Saint Olaf's death and miracles at his grave, and scholars believe these miracles as well as the narratives of other wonders to be derived from the shorter Latin version of his passion. In 1893 the Norwegian scholar Gustav Storm published eight fragments of the saga of Ólafur Haraldsson, known in English as the *Oldest Saga of Saint Olaf*. Since then it has been shown that two of these fragments are from another source: one fragment is on Saint Olaf's miracles, and the other is a text related to *Morkinskinna*. It remains uncertain to which genre the other six belonged.

Even though sources on Saint Olaf were not abundant, they could be useful to a writer composing a passion. Some of this source material also appears in *Helgisaga*, but material has also been added, for instance, single verses and more extended poems. But for the miracles at the end of the saga, there is little here that resembles a conventional martyr narrative. The saint's youth is not presented in gilded terms: he is an unruly teenager, and the testing of his manhood occurs on viking raids rather than in prayer or during the course of a hermit's life. Some motifs, however, allude to his piety: he does not fight on a holy day, he escapes great danger three times over because of his powers, and, most remarkably, he feeds his people by Skerfsurð when they are on the run in the East. His Christian message is of a rather brutal nature, and he plays many tricks on rich landowners such as Dala-Guðbrandur. Sometimes it is hard to see whether the author wants to show him as a warrior king or as a missionary. The description of his virtues and his looks is, however, in the spirit of traditional saints' lives.

The *Helgisaga* is in parts wooden, and the structure is loose; narratives are repeated without obvious purpose, and the manuscript includes the same paragraph twice in the same chapter. Some of these faults can no doubt be blamed on a scribe, but others can be attributed to the author. The manuscript is clearly written by a Norwegian, but opinions are divided on the nationality of the text itself. In its present form it is the oldest example of a king's passion, a tradition that greatly influenced secular historiography and indigenous hagiography.

Lífssaga Ólafs helga (The life of Saint Olaf) by Styrmir Kárason, prior in Viðey, presumably also belonged to this literary genre. It was probably written at the start of the thirteenth century, and it has been preserved only in a few chapters added to *Ólafs saga helga hin sérstaka* by Snorri Sturluson in *Flateyjarbók*. From these chapters one may conclude that Styrmir's work resembled the *Helgisaga* and that its material was collected in a similar fashion.

Yngsta píslarsaga Ólafs (The youngest passion of Saint Olaf) exists in a manuscript from ca. 1400. It has, however, been thought to be much older and is well put together; the style is simple and the narrative free of exegetical interpretations. Saint Olaf's viking expeditions are not dwelled on, and his missionary work is not described in any detail. The story does not begin until his escape across Skerfsurð, and verses are not included. The emphasis is on the saint's martyrdom at the battle of Stiklarstaðir and on the miracles that take place during the moving of his body and at his grave in the cathedral in Nidaros. Either Snorri Sturluson's *Ólafs saga helga hin sérstaka* or his *Ólafs saga* in *Heimskringla* seems to be the source for this text.

Ólafs saga Tryggvasonar

Ólafs saga Tryggvasonar by Oddur Snorrason now exists in three versions translated from Latin into Icelandic and has been preserved in three defective manuscripts from the latter half of the thirteenth century. The initial translation must date back to the first decades of that century since Snorri Sturluson made use of it in *Heimskringla*. However, the *Ólafs saga Tryggvasonar* by Gunnlaugur Leifsson is lost.

When scholars group Oddur's *Ólafs saga Tryggvasonar* with the Kings' Sagas, their focus is clearly more on the subject matter than on the author's handling of it. Oddur has written a prologue where he states his intention to praise the king. On the face of things he seems to want to praise him for his mercy and justice, as was common in royal panegyrics. But it turns out that he means for his audience to praise him with "human praise uplifted by God to holy praise" (*Saga Óláfs Tryggvasonar*, ed. Jónsson, 2), which indicates that his intention is, rather, to praise Ólafur the miracle worker.

It seems that Oddur intended right from the start to write the life of

Ólafur Tryggvason. He tells of Ólafur's childhood in Russia and his marriage, although the main narrative is concerned with his feats in Norway and the North Atlantic islands, his missionary work. Up to the moment when he loses his life (or disappears) in the battle of Svöldur, his life is one long journey. This structure reveals the story type: the pattern is the same as that in the Apostles' Sagas; indeed, Ólafur is referred to as "the apostle of the Northern countries" in the subtitle of the saga. One of the most famous episodes in *Ólafs saga Tryggvasonar* — the scene in which King Ólafur's ships sail one by one before his assembled enemies — represents a break in the narrative comparable to the retardation made when an apostle is cast into a dungeon before his martyrdom. The battle of Svöldur is Ólafur's martyrdom. Yet at the end of the saga there are no miracles. Oddur excuses this in the prologue: "It is known to everyone that after his death Saint Olaf Haraldsson shone in his miracles. The most famous King Ólafur Tryggvason is not known to have performed any miracles after his death. We believe, however, that he was a glorious and a noble man and God's friend" (*Saga Óláfs Tryggvasonar*, ed. Jónsson, 1).

As in the *Helgisaga*, two opposing elements battle it out in the description of Ólafur Tryggvason. The king is described either as a murderous viking or as a missionary who can be ruthless at times. His cruelty does not befit a Christian man. At the end of one version it seems that he must suffer punishment for a killing; he must go on a pilgrimage and then become a hermit. The use of verses in the narrative, especially as the battle at Svöldur draws closer, is reminiscent of the *Helgisaga*, where the poets praise the king's courage and fighting prowess; writers of saints' lives normally ignore such witnesses as verses and poems in their works are songs of praise or hymns on the virtues of the holy man.

It has been pointed out that few sources existed on King Ólafur Tryggvason when Oddur started his work. He relied, however, on all that was available: poets' verses; parts of the works of Ari Þorgilsson, Sæmundur the Wise, and Theodoricus; and saints' lives from Selja (*Acta sanctorum in Selio*). The description of Ólafur's fleet before the battle of Svöldur has been thought to have been influenced by narratives about Charlemagne. Lars Lönnroth ("Studier," 54–94) has also shown that some of the feats that Oddur attributes to Ólafur Tryggvason are in more reliable sources attributed to Saint Olaf. Lönnroth surmised that behind this lay nationalism: the monks at Þingeyrar wanted to rectify the role of Ólafur Tryggvason, the king who first preached the Christian message in Iceland. It is admittedly hard to pinpoint the role of nationalism in this matter, but it is correct that some deeds of Saint Olaf are here transferred to his namesake.

Oddur clearly understood Ólafur Tryggvason to be the forerunner of

Saint Olaf, who, according to Icelandic tradition, had, like John the Baptist, baptized his namesake; hence the following line from the New Testament is appropriate to the kings: "He must increase but I must decrease" (John 3:30). Oddur here introduces a comparison that justifies the transferral of subject matter from one king to the other: in Oddur's version, Ólafur Tryggvason fulfills the same role as John the Baptist does in the gospel: what Christ did, John the Baptist had done before him, and the kings Ólafur Tryggvason and Saint Olaf Haraldsson confirm their relationship: "like everyone should with holy strength and glorious works" (*Saga Óláfs Tryggvasonar*, ed. Jónsson, 1). At the same time it becomes clear why no miracles follow the text. John the Baptist was like Ólafur Tryggvason: "His strength was hidden . . . but clear to God's eyes" (Unger, ed., *Postola sögur*, 842).

The Lives of Saint Magnus of Orkney

Two independent Icelandic lives exist on Saint Magnus Erlendsson, Earl of the Orkneys. The longer one is from the fourteenth century and has been attributed to Abbot Bergur Sokkason, but its main source is a twelfth-century Latin life by Robert of Cricklade, prior of the monastery of Saint Fridewide in Oxford. The shorter version has been preserved in a manuscript from ca. 1400 but could be older, possibly a thirteenth-century work.

Magnús saga is unlike foreign passions in that Magnus's martyrdom is not of a religious nature and the structure of the work does not follow the principles of a passion. Magnus is said to be a fair leader who loses his life in a political power struggle. His life is described to some extent; he is the son of a nobleman who takes part in neither the games of youth nor, later, when he has become a courtier of King Magnús Bare-leg, battles. In this way the pattern resembles an ordinary life.

In the longer version there are long chapters that appear to be translations of the work of Robert of Cricklade, frequently used by the author instead of his own exposition. The style is florid and resembles other fourteenth-century Icelandic saints' lives.

Icelandic Confessors: The Lives of Saint Þorlákur and Saint Jón

The word *lífssaga* (biography) is used in old Icelandic sources as a translation for the Latin word *vita*, "a life." It is always used about saints' lives. At times sources use the terms *upplitningarlíf* (*vita contemplativa*) for texts that describe hermits or ascetics and *sýslulíf* (*vita activa*) for lives of those confessors who served the sick, consoled the sad, and concerned themselves with worldly matters. Texts on the Icelandic bishops Jón Ögmundarson, Þorlákur Þórhallsson, and Guðmundur Arason belong to the last-named group.

At the end of the twelfth century Icelanders got their first saint, the bishop Þorlákur Þórhallsson. His remains were exhumed in 1198, and a year later his feast, held on 23 December, was lawfully adopted at the Althing. In the same year the feast of Jón Ögmundarson was also adopted by law, and thereby the number of Icelandic saints had become two, both originating from the southern part of the country, even though Bishop Jón served the church in the north, at Hólar. It was not until the fourteenth century that Guðmundur Arason was added to the list of Icelandic saints.

The sagas of Jón and Þorlákur both exist in three redactions, and there are also three saints' lives on Guðmundur. All these texts have most often been classified as biographies and placed with *Hungurvaka*, *Páls saga*, *Laurentius saga*, *Árna saga Þorlákssonar*, and even *Sturlunga saga*.

The named author of *Jóns saga helga* is Gunnlaugur Leifsson the monk. According to the annals Gunnlaugur died in 1218, so *Jóns saga helga* was written before that, probably shortly after the exhumation of the saint's relics in 1198. The three redactions of the saga are, however, different in style and vocabulary. Scholars were long divided on which was the oldest, but nowadays most believe the A-redaction to be the oldest and the B- and C-redactions not to have been written until the end of the thirteenth century or the start of the fourteenth. The C-redaction is a compilation of the other two. The B-redaction is one of the sagas also attributed to Bergur Sokkason. *Jóns saga helga* was first written in Latin, but that redaction is now lost. It is uncertain how faithful the Icelandic translations were to the Latin original; this is particularly true of the A-redaction as the B- and C-redactions were reworked and rewritten in the style of fourteenth-century saints' lives. What follows here on *Jóns saga helga* refers almost exclusively to the A-redaction of the saga.

Not much is known for certain about who wrote the first *Þorláks saga* (The life of Saint Þorlákur), but, like *Jóns saga helga*, the saga exists in three redactions of varying ages: the A-, B-, and C-redactions. A few of Þorlákur's miracles have also been preserved in a very old manuscript from the first decades of the thirteenth century (AM 645 4to), and fragments of the Latin life of Þorlákur exist from ca. 1200, as do a few Latin *lectiones*. The oldest Icelandic redaction of the saga, the A-redaction, is thought to have been written before the death of Páll Jónsson in 1211 and probably a little after the remains of Þorlákur were exhumed, also the time from which the oldest miracles date. It is believed that the author had a close connection with Skálholt. He had access to many good sources on Þorlákur and traces the main events: Þorlákur's education in Paris and in Lincoln; his service as canon of the Þykkvibær monastery; and, finally, his bishopric. On these events his tale seems reliable. The B- and C-redactions differ here from the A-redaction as they include a long chapter on Þorlákur's feud with Jón Loftsson: *Oddaverja þáttur* (The tale of the Oddaverjar). The B-redaction is thought to have been written after 1222 because Sæmundur Jónsson is mentioned there as if he had died some time ago. The C-redaction ends with a miracle said to have taken place in 1325. *Þorláks saga* is a typical saint's life: each stage of the saint is recounted and his imitation of Christ confirmed with biblical citations. It is incredible how well the author of the A-redaction is able to give the narrative an objective tone and to raise up Þorlákur like a lifeless statue on a pedestal. Particularly because of these authorial tendencies, the saga is a very unreliable source as far as historical events during the reign of Þorlákur are concerned. Only in one place does the author mention Þorlákur's quarrels with the chieftains regarding church property, and the language used here is as objective as that of a report designed to please all and offend none.

In *Oddaverja þáttur* Þorlákur appears primarily as a powerful chieftain of the church. Despite relying on very traditional themes, the author does manage to highlight some personality traits, and the dialogues between the saint and Jón Loftsson are memorable. Those dialogues are obviously structured like arguments, the right opinion against the wrong, and resemble verbal contests in other religious texts. It is possible to view the story in *Oddaverja þáttur* as a series of six exempla: three narratives on church quarrels with laymen and three on matrimonial matters. And any reader can see the resemblance between the tricks that Jón Loftsson plays on Bishop Þorlákur and famous events from the Sagas of Icelanders and *Sturlunga saga*; the motifs are the same and might be true, but primarily they serve an exemplary purpose. In *Oddaverja þáttur*, Þorlákur appears as an ambitious church leader who uses the logic of learned men instead of weapons, a very different holy man from the Þorlákur in *Sturlu saga*, who advises the priest Páll Sölvason to carry weapons.

Northerners, and especially the bishops Brandur Sæmundarson and Guðmundur Arason, encouraged Bishop Páll Jónsson to exhume Þorlákur's remains. But it was not long before they had their own saint. Bishop Brandur had the relics of two bishops exhumed, those of Jón Ögmundarson and Bjarni Gilsson, in 1198. It turned out that Jón was the better choice politically for the northerners, so his coffin was moved to the cathedral's choir on 3 March 1200. Miracles that took place by his coffin must have been witnessed and written down as soon as they happened or a little later, but there would hardly have been a large variety of sources on his life. Jón's family was well-known; he was of noble southern and eastern stock, born in

Breiðabólsstaður in the south and a descendent of Síðu-Hallur, the first Icelander to be baptized. The men at Hólar must have known about some of Jón's clerical activities, including the fact that he taught priests. It was also known that he had married twice, something that the author of the saga, Gunnlaugur Leifsson, was not able to conceal. Considering the sparse sources available it must be said that Gunnlaugur did a very good job and made the best of what was available, adding much that enlivens the saga. *Jóns saga helga* is not, like *Þorláks saga*, a report on a flawless life; the author is not always affirming the life of the saint with the help of biblical citations on the imitation of Christ. He chooses more often to tell stories that could pertain to any holy man, thus succeeding in giving international, traditional motifs an Icelandic flavor.

Gunnlaugur's model nevertheless seems to have been *Þorláks saga*. The narrative technique of *Jóns saga helga* is similar to that of *Þorláks saga* in its use of motifs and the description of the saint's virtues. However, where *Þorláks saga* shows us a learned hagiographer at work, *Jóns saga helga* — admittedly learned — makes use of knowledge differently, Gunnlaugur letting his clerical fancy soar. It is possible that Guðmundur Arason encouraged Gunnlaugur to write *Jóns saga helga*.

The cult of Saint Jón seems to have been very limited in the thirteenth century, and it is not until Auðun Þorbergsson the Red becomes a bishop in 1315 that Saint Jón's *translatio* day is declared a major feast. The B-redaction of *Jóns saga helga*, which undeniably has most of the characteristics of a saint's life from the fourteenth century, must have been published to take advantage of that opportunity.

The Northern Benedictine School and the Lives of Guðmundur Arason

With *Jóns saga baptista* and *Maríu saga* a turning point is reached in medieval Icelandic hagiography. The most important fourteenth-century authors wrote sagas in the same spirit: they edit lives from various sources, foreign and native, and sometimes add exegetical interpretations as well. The most important representatives of this style are the abbots and Benedictine monks Bergur Sokkason and Arngrímur Brandsson and the monk Árni Laurentiusson, all of whom edit their work from varied sources about holy men and express themselves with more weight than was known before. Their style is florid and considerably influenced by rhetoric.

Bergur was elected abbot in Munka-Þverá in 1325. This indicates that he was born not later than 1300. He is believed to have started writing around 1320. Peter Hallberg has attributed various works to Bergur (see his *Stilsignalement och författarskap i norrön sagalitteratur*): *Tveggja postula saga Jóns og*

Jakobs (The lives of Saint John and Saint James); *Jóns saga postula* IV (The life of Saint John the Evangelist); *Tómas saga erkibiskups* II (The life of Saint Thomas Becket); the D-redaction of *Guðmundar saga*; the B-redaction of *Jóns saga helga*; and the longer redaction of *Magnús saga*; as well as parts of the *Maríujarteinir* (Marian miracles) in a fifteenth-century manuscript. In addition, Hallberg attributed to Bergur two parts of *Karlamagnús saga*, *Drauma-Jóns saga* (The saga of Jon the Dream-interpreter), a few exempla in the *Disciplina clericalis*, and, finally, *Klári saga* (The saga of Clarus). All these works show similar usage of certain words and set phrases and seem certain to have been written in a similar cultural environment during the first half of the fourteenth century. *Tómas saga* II and the D-redaction of *Guðmundar saga* should, however, instead be attributed to Arngrímur Brandsson, but the C-redaction of *Guðmundar saga* should be added to Bergur's works. All these sagas are so similar in style and treatment of subject matter that they can be attributed to one school, the Northern Benedictine school.

In two works from the fourteenth century, *Nikulás saga erkibiskups* and *Mikjáls saga* (The life of the archangel Michael), Bergur is mentioned as a compiler. These two works clearly manifest his methodology. Bergur collects all available sources, retells, for instance, an earlier story of Saint Nicholas, and quotes Gregory's *Dialogues*, Isidore of Seville, and Augustine. It is not clear whether he had many of these works available to him, but it is likely that he used florilegia (anthologies); his aims, as well as the school's, were to educate and edify. What differentiates his works from older saints' lives is that the chronology of events is followed more closely; the narrative is ordered by district or by the chieftains who lived when the events took place. In every way he tries to give the narrative a realistic tone, and reliable sources, such as church fathers and their explications, are used to confirm the narrative and explain it; the story happened, and people should believe it. It is possible that such a frame is modeled on foreign examples. Árni Laurentiusson uses, for instance, English sources on Saint Dunstan in which the hagiographers emphasized the correctness of dates. The life therefore becomes more of a biography, with attempts to link a saint's career to the present day in order to reflect the current mood. In the attempt those narrative genres that a large part of the audience was most used to — biography and chronicle — emerge.

Three lives of Saint Guðmundur Arason were written in the fourteenth century. Guðmundur was already well-known during his lifetime for various miracles. The public had strong faith in him, as is clear from references to him in the oldest Icelandic Marian miracles. His behavior was not, however, to the liking of the leaders of the country. Bishop Guðmundur seems to have been influenced by the ideal of poverty of the Franciscans or other mendicant movements at the start of the thirteenth century, but he also wanted to lift the status of the church as high as possible and wanted it to exercise control over all church matters.

It is not known for certain when Saint Guðmundur Arason's miracles were first collected into one book. It is clear from the *Íslendinga saga* that Sturla Þórðarson knew of the wonders that had occurred on Guðmundur's journeys through the country, but Sturla states that those events will not be recounted there. In one of the main manuscripts of *Sturlunga saga*, *Reykjarfjarðarbók*, miracles have been added (although some scholars believe that they were there originally). One must consider it possible that Saint Guðmundur Arason's miracles existed in a book before Bishop Auðun the Red had his relics exhumed in 1315, but at the same time Auðun must have collected witnessed miracles of the saint. These miracles survive incomplete in the B-redaction of *Guðmundar saga*. The other lives are the C- and D-redactions of *Guðmundar saga*. The fourth account of Saint Guðmundur, the A-redaction of *Guðmundar saga*, is a secular biography. The C-redaction has as yet not been published.

The B-redaction was the first attempt to write a saint's life of this imposing bishop. It was not very successful: it did not manage to increase the fame of the saint, and neither was it suitable to help promote Guðmundur's canonization. The friends and relatives of Guðmundur Arason who backed the writing of it were not up to the task. It is probable that this led to the writing of the C-redaction. Stefán Karlsson has worked on the sagas on Guðmundur and believes the author of the C-redaction to be Bergur Sokkason (see Karlsson, *Stafkrókar*, 153–71).

The author of the C-redaction relied in part on the B-redaction, but he also had access to the original sources of that version. He organized his material much better than did the author of the B-redaction and ordered events chronologically, so the miracles that occurred during Guðmundur Arason's lifetime are placed in their correct order in the narrative. The C-redaction also contains some important material on Guðmundur's life that had not appeared before. The narration of the saga resembles that of Bergur Sokkason's *Nikulás saga erkibiskups*. The author is interested in the monastery at Munka-Þverá, which might also point to it being Bergur's work.

The most ambitious fourteenth-century Icelandic saint's life is the life of Guðmundur by Arngrímur Brandsson, the D-redaction of *Guðmundar saga*. His work seems to be the final attempt to have Guðmundur canonized. Arngrímur was a close associate of the bishop, Ormur Ásláksson, who in 1344 had Guðmundur's remains transferred for the second time. In one place in the work Arngrímur lists himself as a source.

The work bears witness to the author's intimate knowledge of his subject and what is appropriate for a holy man. Arngrímur skims over Guðmundur's youth, avoids mentioning that Guðmundur was an illegitimate child, and omits any stories on Guðmundur's father and his stay in Norway, which had taken up so much space in the earlier works. Instead of using biblical citations to confirm Guðmundur's imitation of Christ, he uses comparisons with other holy men, especially Saint Thomas of Canterbury.

The main subject of Arngrímur's narrative seems to be the construction of a picture of Guðmundur Arason reminiscent of Thomas of Canterbury: Arngrímur wants to recount "his sorrows and the trials of his patience" (*Biskupa sögur*, eds. Vigfússon and Sigurðsson, 2:4). This comparison with the English martyr is illustrated by many examples given throughout the work. Arngrímur also glosses over Guðmundur's participation in battles; in this work it is the fighter by means of the Word who features and who must eventually yield to secular authority. The wording has so much in common with that used in *Tómas saga* II that the author must have known that work well; the narrative technique is also very similar in places.

Tómas saga II is from the same time as Arngrímur's life of Guðmundur. It was put together from earlier works on Thomas, and it interprets and explains material in a fashion similar to that employed in Arngrímur's life. Because of these similarities Stefán Karlsson has claimed that the same author composed both (*Stafkrókar*, 135–71). This is not unlikely, and, although no one has, as yet, been able to point out clear authorial characteristics in these works, it is possible to maintain that both originated in the same cultural environment.

Visionary Literature

It is not known when visionary literature first reached the ears of Icelanders; *Niðurstigningar saga*, the story of Christ's descent into hell, exists in two fragmented translations and was probably first translated in the twelfth century. *Niðurstigningar saga* is, admittedly, not a vision but describes a journey to another world. *Visio Pauli*, or *Pálsleiðsla*, was also translated into Icelandic, but it survives in fragments in a manuscript from ca. 1500. Mattias Tveitane, who published an edition of the work, maintained that the translation was Norwegian and originated in the twelfth century, but there is no evidence to support this.

Drychthelm's Vision, originally from the Venerable Bede's church history, was translated from the Latin in the fourteenth century and can probably be traced to the *Speculum ecclesie* by Honorius Augustodunensis. More influential, however, were Gregory's examples in the fourth book of his *Dialogues*, translated in the twelfth century. Those descriptions of hell are well-known and have probably influenced Icelandic narratives of journeys to the nether regions. *Rannveigarleiðsla* (The vision of Rannveig), included in the D-redaction of *Guðmundar saga*, resembles Gregory's examples: the audience is not taken through many stages; rather, the journey leads straight to where secular leaders are suffering torment. The soul is then shown into blooming fields, even and beautiful, where holy people — Mary, Saint Þorlákur, and others who have behaved according to the teachings of the church — wander. Arngrímur Brandsson handles this material skillfully and also includes the famous vision of Elisabeth of Schönau in his narrative, but it is unclear whether this vision was known in a separate translation in his day.

At the start of the fourteenth century *Visio Tnugdali*, or *Duggalsleiðsla*, was probably translated on the initiative of King Hákon High-leg Magnússon (d. 1319). Although the translation is handled well in part, there are some lacunae and misunderstandings.

The influence of visionary literature is also obvious in "Sólarljóð" (Song of the sun), and it is possible that the authors of "Völuspá" (The seeress's prophecy), *Skíðaríma* (*Ríma* of Skíði), and "Kötludraumur" (Katla's dream) were aware of them as well (see also the first part of this chapter). But most original is the use of themes from this literary genre in *Eiríks saga víðförla*, probably composed in the fourteenth century. According to the saga, Eiríkur Þrándarson is a farmer's son from Trondheim. He goes on a search for the Ódáinsakur (pasture of immortality) and finds out that it is east of Constantinople. He is christened in Constantinople and continues his journey with his companions. Finally, he reaches the river Phison, which originates in paradise. There is a stone arch over the river, and in the middle of it is a dragon that "with a gaping mouth threatened them and wanted to bite them," but, on the other side of the river, they see a country "all covered with flowers and grasses and dripping honey," and they detect "a sweet fragrance" (Jensen, ed., *Eiríks saga víðförla*, 74). It is clear that the author was well versed in Christian literature and knew Icelandic as well as foreign visions. He intended to interpret the journey of an earthly man to paradise, not a soul's journey; in other words, he allowed himself to imbue the vision with an earthly understanding.

THE END OF ICELANDIC HAGIOGRAPHY

In the fourteenth century foreign bishops brought with them quite a few exempla from famous medieval collections, among them the *Disciplina cleri-*

calis. Exempla were translated and recorded in separate collections but also included into other works, and medieval Icelandic authors seem to have known how to use them, even though they do not occur in sermons. A few of these exempla were translated from Middle English.

Not much is known about literary activity in the fifteenth century. From the beginning of the sixteenth century, however, a substantial manuscript called *Reykjahólabók* exists. It contains twenty-five saints' lives that Björn Þorleifsson — probably born sometime between 1471 and 1474 — in Reykhólar put together and in part translated. Björn based the text of *Reykjahólabók* on Low German sources, but he also relied on earlier Icelandic texts. The book contains a few saints' lives that are not known from earlier sources. Its language and style are considered peculiar, greatly influenced by Danish and German, and it has been suggested that Björn wanted to adapt Icelandic to the other Scandinavian languages. This could be the explanation, but perhaps too much has been made of Björn's use of foreign words. The language of the narratives is not so different from that of other sixteenth-century Icelandic theological texts. With Björn's work, the writing of saints' lives in Iceland ends.

Saints' lives are the first Christian literature written in Iceland. There is no doubt that the influence of these narratives on other literary forms is marked, especially in the twelfth and thirteenth centuries. They are written in robust language and not translated word for word from Latin texts. They have been a significant influence on the understanding of life span, origin, and virtues of character in Icelandic narrative art, although it is going too far to say that Icelanders derived their own literary language entirely from them.

CONCLUSION

For almost four centuries Icelandic prose writers showed a remarkable obstinacy in that they never fully adopted European Latin narrative modes. During the medieval period in Iceland there seem to be constant conflicts between two cultures: the native oral traditions and the learned rhetorical way of thought. From these conflicts rise indigenous masterpieces, such as *Njáls saga*, that used the best from both these cultures: native artistic skill alongside a critical attitude toward foreign learning.

Translated by Gunnþórunn Guðmundsdóttir

From Reformation to Enlightenment

Margrét Eggertsdóttir

2

The period covered in the present chapter begins with the Lutheran Reformation, complete in Iceland by 1550, which, as elsewhere in Northern
Europe, had a wide-ranging effect, not only on religious practice, but also
on the social, political, and intellectual life of the country. The two centuries
following the Reformation are traditionally referred to as the Age of Learning (Lærdómsöld). This is appropriate in that the Renaissance humanism
that made its way to Iceland in the wake of the Reformation (rather than
the other way around, as was the case in many other countries) brought
with it, not just a renewed interest in antiquarian sources (Greek and Roman antiquity) as elsewhere in Europe, but particularly a resurgent interest
in the country's own ancient texts and manuscripts as well as its present
topography and natural and cultural phenomena, reflecting contemporary
scientific developments and the study of man and his environment.

At the same time the epithet reflects the fact that, during this period, the
majority of Icelandic poets were members of the educated official classes
(clergymen, magistrates, etc.) and representative of an attitude toward
poetry itself: that a degree of learning was necessary in order to write it. Ideas
of an individual creative genius and originality of expression were not to
appear until much later. The large majority of poets read Latin verse and
introduced aspects of classical Greco-Roman literature into the native poetic
tradition. Some composed Latin poetry as well. In Iceland and the other
Scandinavian countries, however, many poets also looked to Old Icelandic
literature, its poetics and mythology, as a model, whereas elsewhere on the
European continent poets showed little interest in their vernacular past and
modeled their work primarily on that from ancient Greece and Rome.

The change in religion was to play an essential role in the areas of education and learning in exclusively rural Iceland, which had neither universities, urban centers, nor a middle class to implement the Reformation. It soon embarked on the literary education of the people, using the newly introduced technique of printing. As on the Protestant mainland, all children had to learn Luther's catechism by heart, but, while in countries like Denmark this was done through primary schools, in Iceland it was parents who were responsible for teaching their children and pastors for supervising their reading and progress. As a result, primary schools were largely absent from Iceland until the nineteenth century. The sons of officials, the Icelandic upper class, on the other hand, left home to learn Latin and prepare themselves for further study at the cathedral schools of Skálholt or Hólar.

The period from 1550 to 1627 can be viewed as a distinct whole, marked by the upheaval that followed in the wake of religious and political change, beginning with the execution of Jón Arason, the last Catholic bishop of Iceland, and extending to the death of Bishop Guðbrandur Þorláksson. The latter had worked harder than most to promote the new faith, and, by the time of his death in 1627, Lutheranism was firmly established in Iceland.

Elsewhere in Europe the literature of the seventeenth century is associated primarily with the baroque; in England it is the age of the metaphysical poets, and the Icelandic literature of the period reveals many of the same themes and ideas that were prominent in neighboring countries. Not much new happened on the literary front in Iceland during the early eighteenth century until around 1750, by which point Enlightenment ideas had begun to make themselves felt; as a result, instead of speaking of the seventeenth century, it would be more accurate to talk about the period 1627–1750. Period divisions always remain arbitrary to a certain degree, and overlaps will inevitably occur. Many poets of the period contributed to a variety of genres, foreign and native, religious and secular, learned and popular.

Although the literacy rate was comparatively high, few people had access to printed material beyond the required religious works, nor were there many who were able to write. Although formal schooling was, thus, inaccessible to most, in nearly every household evening religious services made up the final part of the so-called *kvöldvaka* (lit. "evening wake"). The *kvöldvaka* constituted the main literary arena where literary and linguistic tastes were practiced and formed in a largely democratic setting. It also allowed for the continuation of a secular and popular literary tradition, where sagas and *rímur* (lit. "rhymes," metrical romances; see pp. 55–59) were recited and copied and stories were told that were not part of the literature sanctioned by the church.

Icelandic literature after the Reformation comprises not only works that were "published" in the conventional modern sense, that is, printed, but also works that circulated in manuscript copies as well as a significant body of literature that was neither printed nor written down. From the Reformation until the middle of the eighteenth century there was only a single printing press in Iceland, one that was in the hands of the church, and during this period almost nothing was printed other than works which the church considered necessary or suitable reading matter for the people, predominately works of a religious nature. A far greater number of literary works from this period were never printed, however. Romances, both in verse and in prose, constituted the overwhelmingly favorite literary genre for the large majority of Icelanders, and they were copied extensively. The introduction of paper to Iceland, which occurred at about the same time as the introduction of the printing press (around 1530), was in many ways of greater consequence for literary production and dissemination, as paper was much less expensive than vellum.

Other material preserved in manuscripts from this period—often paper copies of medieval vellums—included the ancient saga literature, which may be said to have had a semiofficial status; it was generally highly regarded, but no attempt was made to print it until much later. In addition there were poems and tales that circulated only orally and that no one appears to have considered writing down. A flourishing literature thus existed in Iceland that, although widely and consistently popular and influential, never found its way into print and was written down only in manuscripts. When discussing the history of Icelandic literature during this period it is essential to take into account works that were never printed as well as those that were. Doing so is not without its difficulties, however, particularly as much primary research remains to be done in this area, although the situation has improved significantly in recent years. Nevertheless, a history of Icelandic literature in the seventeenth and eighteenth centuries that looked only at printed works would not be telling even half the story.

THE REFORMATION: 1550–1627

In the sixteenth century radical new ideas concerning Christianity and the church led to confrontation and change in Iceland, as elsewhere in Europe. Iceland was at this time part of the Danish realm. With the ascension of Christian III to the throne in 1536 the success of Lutheran Protestantism in Denmark was assured. The king seized property belonging to the church both in Denmark and in Norway (also part of the Danish realm), imprisoned bishops, and took away the church's political power. The Roman Catholic Church was to be dismantled and a state church established in its place; as head of the church, the king himself decided who was to be made a bishop. In Iceland the bishoprics of Skálholt and Hólar were not abolished, and all subsequent bishops were Icelandic, recommended by the Icelandic clergy to the king, who in nearly all cases ratified their choice.

German merchants from Hamburg, where Protestantism had been embraced in 1528, were particularly influential in Iceland at this time. A lively German-Iceland trade in stockfish had been run from this Hanseatic city, and, from the early 1500s, Hamburgers settled in Iceland, making the town of Hafnarfjörður their main base in the country. It was here that they built a Protestant church, served by German ministers. It is clear that by that point a few Icelanders were already favorably disposed toward the Reformation: Bishop Ögmundur Pálsson (ca. 1475–1541) wrote in a letter from 1534 that there was no shortage of men in the country willing to embrace the new faith. Ögmundur Pálsson had been consecrated bishop of Skálholt in 1521 and immediately entered into a series of bitter clashes with Jón Arason (1484–1550), the bishop-elect of Hólar. These clashes had little to do with ideology but were, rather, concerned with the division of property and power between the two episcopal sees. Bishop Ögmundur excommunicated Jón Arason, who managed to escape to Denmark, where he was, nevertheless, consecrated bishop in 1523. For the next thirteen years the two bishops sat reasonably securely in their sees and were able to increase both their own wealth and that of the church.

Although as far as we know there was no popular Protestant movement among Icelanders, there were four students among Bishop Ögmundur's men at Skálholt who had been influenced by the ideas of the Reformation, which they had encountered while studying abroad, although they kept this largely secret. Foremost among them were Gissur Einarsson (ca. 1512–48), Bishop Ögmundur's right-hand man and subsequently his successor, Oddur Gottskálksson (ca. 1515–56), later a lawman (*lögmaður*, the highest legal office in the land), and Gísli Jónsson (1513–87), dean of Skálholt and later bishop.

Oddur Gottskálksson translated the New Testament into Icelandic. His translation (based in part on an older translation by Jón Arason) was published in Roskilde in Denmark in 1540 and is the oldest printed book preserved in Icelandic. With this publication the status of Icelandic as a language separate from Danish within the Danish church was recognized, and this was of great importance for the subsequent history of the Icelandic language. It is said, although how truthfully is unclear, that Oddur Gotts-kálksson went about his translating activities somewhat clandestinely while Bishop Ögmundur lived.

It may be said that the Reformation was largely complete in the diocese of Skálholt with the consecration of Gissur Einarsson in 1542. Jón Arason continued to serve as bishop of Hólar, a powerful churchman and fine poet (see p. 52). With his concubine, Helga Sigurðardóttir, he had nine children, and he and his sons fought hard against the new order. They were finally seized by their enemies and taken as prisoners to Skálholt, where they were executed in November 1550. Lutheranism had been victorious, but Jón Arason became a national hero in the eyes of many, a symbol of resistance to foreign power, as the many poems composed about him testify.

The Reformation had a profound effect on Icelandic society. Religious power and secular power were now combined, one result of which was that one-sixth of all the landed property in Iceland became crown property, and all tithes, fines, and taxes fell similarly to the king. Valuable artifacts that had belonged to churches and monasteries in Iceland were sent to Denmark.

With the Reformation a new chapter in Icelandic cultural history began. From abroad came new ideas, new concepts, for which new words had to be found or coined. The most obvious comparison is with the fundamental cultural changes that took place after the acceptance of Christianity in the year 1000. New literary genres emerged, while others, such as saints' lives (*heilagramannasögur*) and Catholic religious poems, disappear. To familiarize the Icelandic population with the new faith, religious and moral tracts were translated in large numbers, along with hymns and other kinds of religious poetry, and the Bible was translated and printed in Icelandic. But the innovations were not restricted to religious literature alone. New types of secular poetry were also introduced, including commemorative verse of various kinds, lyric poetry, and epic poetry with a basis in folklore and written in Eddic meters (see pp. 3–5). The writing of sagas continued, but with new forms and emphases, and learned histories of medieval Icelandic literature appeared. Some literary genres continued to flourish after the Reformation, in particular *rímur* and ballads (*sagnadansar*; see pp. 60–63) and other popular literature. From the *rímur* the tradition of the *lausavísa* (pl. *lausavísur*), a single stanza or epigram in *rímur* meters (see pp. 27, 42), developed. The *lausavísa* has a very long history in Icelandic and is found in the earliest manuscripts. It deals with a wide variety of subjects; there are, for instance, love poems and satiric and defamatory verses as well as poems in praise of horses, tobacco, and other pleasures in life.

Literature in the Service of the Reformed Church

According to Martin Luther, hymns were to play a crucial role in religious instruction, so it should come as no surprise that they were among the first and most important literary innovations that followed in the wake of the Reformation. The first Icelandic hymnal, entitled *Lítið sálmakver* (A small book of hymns), was published in 1555 and contained only translated hymns, some Danish, but most German, about half of which were by Luther; the translations were by Marteinn Einarsson (ca. 1500–1576). Three years later another hymnal was published by Gísli Jónsson, bishop of Skálholt, again containing only translated material. These translations, particularly those by Gísli Jónsson, were rather poor, extremely literal, and, in their lack of alliteration, at odds with the Icelandic poetic tradition. It was not until the publication of Bishop Guðbrandur Þorláksson's hymnal in 1589 that Icelanders finally obtained acceptable Lutheran hymns that incorporated native poetic conventions.

It was Guðbrandur Þorláksson (ca. 1541–1627), bishop of Hólar for half a century, who contributed most to the establishment of Lutheranism in Iceland. He was the first Icelander known to have studied at the university in Copenhagen, the chief intellectual and cultural center for Icelanders from soon after the Reformation until well into the twentieth century. Bishop Guðbrandur was a man of great energy and many talents who accomplished much; he worked out Iceland's geographic position and produced a map of Iceland that was far more accurate than previous maps had been. Under his auspices around ninety books were printed, including the Bible. The country's sole printing press, which Jón Arason had brought to Skálholt in about 1530 and Guðbrandur Þorláksson had moved to Hólar, was of great importance for the intellectual life of the population.

The so-called *Guðbrandsbiblía* (Guðbrandur's Bible) was printed in an edition of five hundred copies at Hólar in 1584. It contains twenty-seven woodcuts and many ornamental initials and is a fine example of early Icelandic book production. Bishop Guðbrandur did much of the translation himself, although he made use of the older translation of the New Testament by Oddur Gottskálksson and translations of some of the books of the Old Testament by Gissur Einarsson. The text of Guðbrandur's Bible was extremely good, as can be seen from the fact that relatively few changes were made in subsequent translations. It has often been said that the publication of the Bible in Icelandic so soon after the Reformation and with very little in the way of influence from other languages was of great importance for the survival of Icelandic as a language in the subsequent centuries under Danish rule.

Bishop Guðbrandur's hymnal, *Ein ný sálmabók* (1589; A new hymnbook), contained three hundred hymns. Most of these were translated from German, Danish, or Latin, but around twenty were original Icelandic compositions. Guðbrandur's *Graduale* (often referred to in Icelandic as *Grallarinn*, which, amusingly enough for Icelanders, also means "the wag") — published in 1594 — contained the liturgy, hymns, and hymn melodies. The preface to the hymnal contains the first discussion of literature to be published in Icelandic, from which a number of interesting things emerge. For one thing it is clear that the bishop was extremely unhappy with the literary taste of his countrymen and keen to do what he could to change it: "Men might be able to put away unprofitable songs of Ogres and of the Heathen of old, Rímur, naughty love-songs, amorous verses, sonnets of lust, verses of mockery and malice, and other foul and evil poesy, ribaldry, wantonness, and lampoonery and satire, such as are loved and used by the commonalty of this land" (quoted in Driscoll, 14). But there is more of interest in the bishop's preface. Guðbrandur also stresses that hymns should be in the vernacular and writes of the importance of music, the excellence of Icelandic, and the value of eloquence. He argues against those who claim that the outward form of poetry is unimportant, recognizing that carefully crafted poetry and good melodies are more likely to have an effect on people. He is also aware of the uniqueness of Icelandic — which he refers to as *norræna* (Norse) — which had preserved a unique poetic tradition that, with its distinct metrical forms, alliteration, and diction, deserved to be nurtured.

The Vísnabók: *An Attempt at Reconciliation*
Bishop Guðbrandur began his publishing activities in about 1575. Despite his great vigor he fell short of the mark he had set himself. It is clear from the preface to the *Vísnabók* (Book of verses), which he published in 1612, that he did not feel his previous endeavors had borne fruit to the extent that he had wished but that he hoped to meet his public halfway with this publication. From the poems brought together in *Vísnabók* it is obvious that the bishop had attempted to collect poetry that he thought would appeal to a wide audience while at the same time serving to spread the message of the church. One important innovation was the inclusion of *rímur* based on books of the Bible (and other religious material) and poems on religious subjects in the secular *vikivaki* or carol meter (see also below). The book contains some two hundred poems, both sacred and profane, most by contemporary poets. The bishop got the Reverend Ólafur

Guðmundsson of Sauðanes (ca. 1537–ca. 1609), who knew both Latin and German, to revise older hymns and add new ones, both translated and original. Many of the poems in the *Vísnabók* are by the Reverend Einar Sigurðsson of Eydalir (1538–1626); others who feature prominently are the Reverend Sigfús Guðmundsson (d. 1597), Magnús Jónsson (ca. 1531–91; known to his contemporaries as Magnús Jónsson prúði, "the courteous"), and Ólafur Einarsson of Kirkjubær (ca. 1573–1651), all of whom will be discussed later. Particularly noteworthy is the fact that a number of Catholic religious poems were included, such as "Lilja" (The lily) by the monk Eysteinn Ásgrímsson (d. 1361 or 1366; see p. 48), and even two poems by Jón Arason: "Píslargrátur" (Lament of the Passion) and "Davíðsdiktur" (Poem for David; see p. 52).

In Bishop Guðbrandur's *Vísnabók* there are also a number of poems by the clergyman and poet Magnús Ólafsson of Laufás (1573–1636), who is best known for his *Laufás-Edda* — a version of Snorri Sturluson's *Prose Edda* (see pp. 151–58) — in which the kennings and other poetic figures were listed in alphabetical order, making it more accessible and easier for poets to use. Magnús Ólafsson was himself in many ways a remarkable poet. His hymns are simple and unpretentious, but in his occasional verses he makes use of complex kennings and learned stylistic elements. The dedicatory poem of the *Vísnabók* is by him, and there is also printed the poem "Klögun af þremur sálaróvinum, holdi, heimi og djöfli" (Complaint on the soul's three enemies: The flesh, the world, and the devil). Magnús was well versed in Latin and in Old Icelandic literature and composed poems both in Latin and in the vernacular. He was close friends with Arngrímur Jónsson the Learned (see p. 188), and his correspondence with him and with the Danish antiquarian Ole Worm (see p. 191) is a valuable source of information on the interest in and study of Old Icelandic at the time.

Another prolific poet who has many poems in the *Vísnabók* is the clergyman Jón Bjarnason (ca. 1560–1634?), who composed the biblical *Rímur af Tobías* (*Rímur* of Tobiah) and *Síraksrímur* (*Rímur* of Jesus Sirach). His poetry in the *Vísnabók* displays an interest in proverbs. His Icelandic translation of the Latin poem *Disticha Catonis*, in *rímur* meter, was printed at Hólar in 1620 along with Arngrímur the Learned's *Spakmæli sjö Grikklands spekinga*, a translation of the *Aphorisms of Seven Greek Philosophers*.

Sigfús Guðmundsson, another prominent contributor to the *Vísnabók*, was a poor clergyman with a large family. There is a humorous poem composed by him on the occasion of his being presented to a living: the ceilings in the new vicarage are so low that he doubts that he and his family will be able to enter without knocking their heads. In his sacred poems he discusses the transitory and inequitable world and contrasts the material rewards of this life with the eternal spiritual reward of the life to come. At the same time there are occasional descriptions of nature, fair days seen as manifestations of "divine delight." He talks about how different men's lots can be and paints a number of memorable pictures, for example, of people who are unable to have children who survive even a single night while others have so many that it is a constant struggle to provide for them.

Three Hymnists
There is much to indicate that Ólafur Jónsson of Sandar (1560–1627) was a highly esteemed and popular poet during his lifetime. While the works of most of the poets of the period are preserved here and there in miscellanies, Jónsson's poems are preserved as a single collection, the original of which is admittedly lost, but many copies of which survive. The collection is divided into two parts, a division that is the poet's own: the first part contains poems that deal with various aspects of Christian doctrine, while in the second part there are occasional poems, elegies, and poems on "one thing and another about which I wished to write a poem" (NKS 139b 4to, IV).

Ólafur Jónsson of Sandar was the first to paraphrase the new doctrine in true poetic form. He principally wrote poems on religious subjects and was highly regarded by his contemporaries for his poetic, and particularly his lyric, skills, although his reputation has subsequently been overshadowed by that of Hallgrímur Pétursson. Jónsson was also well versed in music and set some of his poems to music, possibly in some cases music he himself had composed.

Jónsson was a pastor in the West Fjords and related to important people there, most notably, the lawman Eggert Hannesson and Eggert's daughter Ragnheiður. He was chaplain in the household of Ragnheiður and her husband, Magnús Jónsson. This family had relations with Hamburg, and it is known that Ólafur Jónsson knew German well and translated some of his poems from German.

Jónsson also composed a single set of *rímur*, which dealt with the destruction of Jerusalem. In the first *mansöngur* (pl. *mansöngvar*; a lyric introduction to a new chapter in a *rímur* cycle), he mentions the changes that have taken place in the spiritual life and literary practice of the country, clearly referring to the effects of the Reformation. Previously people had read and enjoyed accounts of "jousting and battles, slayings and destruction," but now poets do everything they can to ensure that their poems are "the pure word of God" and compose works based on Holy Scripture (see *Rímur um foreyðslu borgarinnar Jerúsalem*, preserved in JS 264 4to, AM 146a

8vo, and Rask 42). It emerges that there are still some who are interested in these unchristian stories, but Jónsson says that he will not judge such people and that there is no reason to be against stories that have some knowledge to convey.

Einar Sigurðsson of Eydalir was born in the Catholic period but became one of the greatest poets of the new religion. He attended the newly established cathedral school at Hólar from 1552, along with Guðbrandur Þorláksson, later a bishop. He took orders at a young age and had many children; twice married, he had eight children with his first wife, only three of whom survived childhood, and ten children with his second wife. There is a poem by him called "Þakklætisbæn fyrir barnaheill" (Poem of thanks for children's good fortune) in which he thanks God for his thirteen children and expresses his hope that they will be happy. It was fortunate for the poor pastor with so many children that he was a good friend of Bishop Guðbrandur's. His own firstborn son, Oddur Einarsson, later became the bishop of Skálholt and saw to it that his father was presented to a better living than he had previously had, at Eydalir in eastern Iceland, after which his situation began to improve.

Einar Sigurðsson's poetry represents the first instance of the secular carol meter for religious subject matter, an innovation indicating that the church was not always averse to using forms that were popular among the general public. Among his best-known works is the beautiful Christmas hymn "Nóttin var sú ágæt ein" (One fine night), which is still sung today, to a melody by the Icelandic composer Sigvaldi Kaldalóns (1881–1946). In the refrain the poet says that with his song he would like to rock Jesus' cradle gently, which shows an affinity with Luther's hymn "Vom Himmel hoch, da komm' ich her."

Sigurðsson's contribution to Bishop Guðbrandur's *Vísnabók* was greater than that of any other poet of the time. Sigurðsson says himself that he had written poetry from an early age, and there is an autobiographical poem (*ævikvæði*) in which he tells his own story. In the poem "Hugbót" (Vision) he says that it became clear to him at the age of thirty that he should use his poetic gift to honor God. This he certainly did, composing among other things verses on the Gospels, *rímur* on biblical themes, and didactic poems on Christian subjects for children. He also wrote a beautiful poem on the Virgin Mary, printed in the *Vísnabók*, that represents a kind of settling of accounts with the Catholic tradition of Marian praise poetry; while rejecting the veneration of the Virgin, he wishes to retain Mary as the model of piety.

One of the most prolific hymnists during Bishop Guðbrandur's term of office was Jón Þorsteinsson (ca. 1570–1627). He wrote a lengthy cycle of hymns called *Genesissálmar*, based on the Book of Genesis. Later, he undertook the ambitious task of translating the Psalms of David into Icelandic verse, at about the same time as the Danish baroque poet Anders Arrebo (1587–1637) was doing his translations in Denmark. Jón Þorsteinsson was a pastor in the Vestmannaeyjar (Westman Islands, south of the mainland) when North African pirates attacked the islands in 1627 (see also below); he was killed in the skirmish and, thereafter, long regarded as a martyr.

Disaffection with the New Religion

Not everyone seemed convinced that the religious changes had all been for the better. A nostalgic longing for the old faith and criticism of the new is evident in the poem "Aldasöngur" (Song of ages) by Bjarni Jónsson, known as Borgfirðingaskáld (Borgarfjörður-poet) or Bjarni skáldi. He is believed to have been born around 1560 and to have died around 1640, but little is known about his life. He knew the poet Hallgrímur Pétursson (see below); they lived in the same area, and there are poems that the two are thought to have composed together. In addition there is a set of *rímur* based on the history *Florent et Lyon* (1534), begun by Bjarni skáldi, who composed the first fifteen fits, and completed by Hallgrímur Pétursson, who added another nine. Bjarni's poems and hymns are found widely distributed in poetic miscellanies, as is frequently the case with poets from this period.

In the poem "Aldasöngur" the poet says he is about seventy years old. He looks back to the time before the Reformation, after which everything declined and deteriorated, from the state of Icelandic industry and people's livelihoods to the weather. He describes the rites of the Catholic Church as beautiful and cultured, whereas now the churches have been stripped of their holy objects and have fallen into disrepair, in addition to which the standard of living of the common people has declined. The following strophe is often cited and provides a graphic description of the brutality with which the agents of the Reformation dealt with books and works of art that were, in their view, "papist":

All writing and ornamentation
is now torn up and burnt,
Christ's image broken,
pages and statues decayed,
bells left without their tongues,
but the doctrine's beauty remains.
(*Íslenskt ljóðasafn*, 362)

Bjarni skáldi composed many other beautiful religious poems. Among his secular works most worthy of mention are his *öfugmælavísur*, paradoxes or topsy-turvy poems (see also below), many of which are still known today, for example:

Into fire it's best to ladle snow
that way the flame increases
it is good to wear shoes made of glass
when walking on cliffs.
(*Íslenskt ljóðasafn*, 356)

Bjarni also wrote "Ekkjuríma" (Widow's rhyme), a short humorous poem in *rímur* meter about a widow who uses various means to rid herself of overly persistent suitors, and a poem in carol meter about his kinsmen on the farm Kalmanstunga in Borgarfjörður, in which he describes vividly the farm and the home life of the couple, their hospitality and generosity. It is clear, however, that the heyday that he describes is gone and that times have changed for the worse.

SECULAR LITERATURE IN THE SIXTEENTH CENTURY

Occasional and Topographical Poetry
Not all post-Reformation poetry is devoted to religious topics. In the course of the sixteenth century a new genre, occasional poetry, became popular in Iceland. The model for such poetry in the vernacular, here as elsewhere, was classical Latin poetry and the poetics that lay behind it. The most common function of this genre was to honor king, church, or another authority, but it was also frequently used to commemorate less elevated occasions such as inaugurations, addresses, celebrations, the welcoming of guests, a new acquisition, and other notable events. One of the first to try his hand at occasional verse in Icelandic was Magnús Ólafsson, who wrote in Latin as well and was well versed in the classics. However, in his occasional poems Ólafsson does not rely exclusively on classical literature but makes frequent use of skaldic meters (*dróttkvætt*; see p. 6), thus showing that Old Icelandic poetry could also serve as a model, as, for example, in his forty-eight verses in skaldic style in honor of Chancellor Christian Friis. He composed funeral odes on Bishop Guðbrandur and on Einar Sigurðsson of Eydalir, discussed earlier. Magnús Ólafsson in all likelihood also wrote the poem "Sumargjöf á Hólum 1621" (Summer gift at Hólar 1621), which is clearly addressed to a woman. The poem bears witness to the tradition of giving gifts on the first day of summer, practiced to this day. Other occa-

sional poems by Ólafsson include "cushion and drapery ditties," poems on new bed curtains and on chess.

Ólafur Jónsson of Sandar, who was mentioned earlier, and Ólafur Einarsson of Kirkjubær wrote occasional poems of a kind more generally associated with the genre, such as elegies. Einar Sigurðsson of Eydalir wrote a eulogy on Bishop Guðbrandur Þorláksson and another one on the king of Iceland and Denmark of which only a fragment has survived.

One notable branch of occasional poetry is topographical poetry. In the spirit of the European Renaissance, with its renewed interest in man and his environment, there were great developments in cartography, geography, and ethnography. As a result, topographical literature and travel descriptions flourished and became very popular throughout sixteenth-century Europe. Iceland was to play an important role in these developments. While its isolated location on the northern periphery of Europe overstimulated the imagination of some European writers, its dramatic natural landscape inspired descriptions of the land and its regions at home, often dedicated to a person of importance.

Probably one of the earliest topographical poems written in Icelandic is "Íslands gæði" (Iceland's blessings), composed by Einar Sigurðsson of Eydalir around 1600, which contains both historical material and a description of Iceland. The historical material deals mostly with the new Lutheran faith and the Danish kings who were involved in the process of introducing the new religion. It has been pointed out that there are some verbal similarities that would indicate that this poem was composed as an answer to Ólafur Tómasson's poem "Minningarkvæði um Jón Arason og sonu hans" (Memorial poem about Bishop Jón Arason and sons). Tómasson, who was Jón Arason's foster son, was only eighteen years old when the bishop was executed. The poem is thought to have been written much later, however, in 1594, the year before Tómasson's death. Even if the title is "memorial," this is not an elegy in the strictest sense of that word but rather a historical poem. It describes Jón Arason, his rule as bishop, and the events leading up to the Reformation and the course it took in Iceland. There is no doubt that the author's sympathies lie with the bishop and his supporters, and the poem contains harsh criticism of the forces behind the Reformation, both its Icelandic supporters and foreign royal power.

The poem "Um hrörnun Íslands" (On the decay of Iceland) by Ólafur Jónsson of Sandar is also a kind of topographical poem, but it is unusual in that the emphasis is on the negative. The refrain is as follows:

Fair Iceland fades
the country's flowers flag

Towards heaven I long
for there live God's good children
Fair Iceland fades.
(*Íslenskt ljóðasafn*, 343)

In the poem, which is written in carol meter, the poet describes the cold winters and long, dark nights, the infrequent visits of·merchants, failed harvests, the lack of employment, the untimely deaths of good people, and how there are many whose only thought is of worldly matters. The picture is not entirely bleak, however; there are people in the country who trust in God and are keen to live according to his word, and it is these people who are Iceland's greatest asset. Iceland is then compared to other countries, and reference is made to those who had traveled widely and returned full of praise for other nations. The poet says that, in the place of ordinary sunlight, Icelanders benefit from the holy sunlight—referring to the new Lutheranism—that bathes the land in light and makes up for all the other things that are lacking. Ólafur of Sandar tells his countrymen to pay no heed to negative reports about Iceland. He goes on to say that he has not composed the poem in order to dishonor or discredit Iceland. Iceland will thrive again, he says, on Judgment Day. By comparison he mentions that, in the most prosperous part of the world, the people are heathen; these lands are held in high regard by some, but what value have they, he asks, if they lack the Christian faith? The poem ends with a prayer to God on behalf of the nation.

Ólafur of Sandar also wrote a poem on a contemporary event, the so-called Spanish Killings (Spánverjavíg), a conflict between local residents and "Spanish" (Basque) fishermen in the West Fjords in 1615 that resulted in the deaths of the latter (see also p. 199). The poet takes the side of the locals, not surprisingly, perhaps, as one of the leaders was his friend and benefactor.

Foreign Influences
Páll Jónsson of Staðarhóll (ca. 1530–98), known as Staðarhóls Páll, is in many ways an exceptional figure among sixteenth-century poets. He was a magistrate (*sýslumaður*) and from a good family, but throughout his life he was involved in all sorts of disputes, and there are many stories of his involvements with women. It is possible that he suffered from some sort of mental disorder; at the very least he had an impetuous and emotional nature. It appears that he was not accounted a poet by his contemporaries: he is not included in older lists of poets or in early literary histories. A letter from him to Bishop Guðbrandur has been preserved, however, that reveals

that he sent the bishop and his daughters a collection of his poems. Nothing by him has survived that belongs to the most common poetic genres in Iceland at the time: *rímur* and hymns. He did, however, pursue another popular form of poetry in Iceland: epigrams.

His poems and verses are included here and there in various manuscripts from the seventeenth and eighteenth centuries. Two highly unusual poems by him have been preserved, of great lyric beauty, and clearly influenced by foreign models: "Eikarlundurinn" (The oak grove) and "Blómið í garðinum" (The flower in the garden). The former is a description of nature, an allegory on the transitory nature of man's existence. The latter describes a beautiful flower that is, it emerges, a young woman. Páll Jónsson's poetry is in some ways reminiscent of Icelandic folk poetry, creating an otherworldly, mystical atmosphere where events are presented with little elaboration, background, or explanation. At the same time the influence of the popular poetry of contemporary Europe, in particular Germany and Denmark, is clearly discernible, particularly in terms of diction, meter, and general structure. At the time it was common to liken the life of man to a flower or a tree and to describe feminine beauty with metaphors from nature.

Páll Jónsson's brother was Magnús Jónsson the Courteous, whom we encountered earlier, and who deserves mention here for his *Pontus rímur*, which were composed in 1564–66 on the model of the German chapbook *Pontus und Sidonia*, first printed in Germany in 1483 (see also below). These *rímur* are the earliest evidence in Iceland of familiarity with the German *Volksbücher* or chapbooks, adaptations of medieval romances that enjoyed great popularity on the European continent. The bulk of this form of light literary entertainment came from Danish sources, but some also from German and Latin, and circulated in Iceland almost exclusively in manuscript form. The presence of such material in Iceland provides an interesting example of how literary influences could, and did, reach the country in a variety of ways, including those not sanctioned by the church. At the same time it is clear from *Pontus rímur* that Magnús Jónsson was well versed in the classical literary tradition and knew how to use rhetorical devices, not surprisingly, perhaps, as he had also translated Riederer's 1493 rhetorical work the *Spiegel der waren Rhetoric* (as *Spegill þeirrar sönnu rhetorica*).

The Image of Iceland Abroad
Arngrímur Jónsson (1568–1648), known as "the Learned," was one of the most remarkable scholars and writers of his day. Encouraged by Bishop Guðbrandur, he wrote a short work in Latin on Iceland (*Brevis commentarius de Islandia*) that was intended to refute the misrepresentations and

calumnies that had appeared in a description of Iceland published in 1561 by Gories Peerse (or Gregorius Peerson), a merchant from Hamburg who had made several trips to Iceland in the mid-sixteenth century. By the time Arngrímur Jónsson's book was published (in Copenhagen) in 1593, Peerse's book had been reprinted three times. Its popularity, clearly attributable to the contemporary interest in utopias and sensationalist descriptions of foreign peoples, had greatly galled the Icelanders, not least because of the strong economic ties to Hamburg at the time. Bishop Guðbrandur said in his preface to the *Brevis*: "And this was done with impunity in a city which for many years has conducted its business in Iceland with great profit. The printer's name is Joachim Leo, and it would be truly fitting if he were to be devoured by lions" (*Arngrimi Jonae*, 6–7).

It became quickly apparent, however, that the book had not succeeded in refuting malicious reports of Iceland. In Holland in 1607 a work on Iceland was published, also in Latin, by one Dithmar Blefken. Arngrímur Jónsson replied with the work *Anatome Blefkeniana*, published at Hólar in 1612. Despite Icelandic attempts to set the record straight, however, Blefken's book became very popular: translations of it into Dutch and other languages were published time and again, in addition to chapters from it appearing in foreign learned journals. Yet another work by Arngrímur Jónsson in the same vein is the *Epistula pro patria defensoria*, printed in Hamburg in 1618.

Arngrímur Jónsson's contribution was, however, to be more, and more important, than polemics. While his writings did not have the desired effect of correcting the Icelandic image abroad, they did serve to bring him to the attention of Danish historiographers, who soon realized that important sources of the history of the Nordic countries had been uniquely preserved in Iceland. Humanism had sparked a great interest in antiquities, including Nordic antiquity. Arngrímur Jónsson was asked to write a survey of the history of the Nordic countries, a work that was to be a kind of source collection for Danish historians who were working under the auspices of the Danish king. The king, eager to trace the origins of the royal family of Denmark just as those of the royal family of Sweden recently had been, sent an open letter to Icelanders instructing them to provide Arngrímur Jónsson with the necessary written sources for this endeavor. The author and scholar happily undertook to do this, at the same time using the opportunity to gather sources on the histories of Iceland and Greenland. Around the turn of the seventeenth century he wrote *Crymogæa*, a history of Iceland in three volumes. In addition he wrote a work called *Gronlandia*, a kind of appendix to *Crymogæa*.

A New Historiography
Crymogæa was published in Hamburg in 1609. *Gronlandia*, on the other hand, remained unpublished until Arngrímur Jónsson's collected works were published in the twentieth century. The title *Crymogæa* is a Greek translation of the name "Ice-land." Such an affectation was common in contemporary learned circles, meant to give a work a learned appearance and bear witness to its author's scholarship. *Crymogæa* was written in Latin, aimed at a foreign audience. This work, along with his other writings, made Arngrímur Jónsson the most widely known Icelander in European learned circles of the seventeenth century. There is no doubt, however, that, in the long run, its influence was most marked in Iceland. The first part of *Crymogæa* traces the main events in the history of Iceland from the settlement to the end of the Commonwealth. The second part describes Icelandic heroes of the tenth and eleventh centuries and their deeds, while the third part describes Icelandic history under foreign rule down to the latter half of the sixteenth century. Arngrímur Jónsson viewed the past, and the Commonwealth period in particular, as a lost golden age and described the ancient Icelanders as great heroes of noble birth. He also introduced the idea that the postmedieval period in Iceland was one of degeneration, caused by a concentration of domestic power and foreign rule. This idea proved to be extremely long-lived and gained particular prominence during the nineteenth and early twentieth centuries under the influence of the nationalist movement.

It must have been a revelation to those in Iceland who knew Latin and could read the work that one could depict Icelandic history in the way the author did, stressing its former glory and worth. Not only had he described the prehistory of Iceland, but he had shown how in the Commonwealth period there had been Icelandic heroes on a par with foreign dignitaries and had placed the history of Iceland on an equal footing with that of important foreign lands. With *Crymogæa* Arngrímur the Learned introduced into Iceland humanist ideas with which he had come in contact through his association with Danish historians during his stay in Copenhagen from 1592 to 1593. The effect was that Icelanders began to look at their own past, and the sources pertaining to it, with new eyes and renewed interest, as a result of which scholarship flourished in Iceland during the seventeenth century. Arngrímur Jónsson thus had a deep impact on the Icelanders' self-image and their sense of history.

At about the same time as Arngrímur Jónsson was writing his defense of Iceland, another book in Latin on Iceland was being written: *Qualiscunque descriptio Islandiæ*, believed to be the work of Oddur Einarsson, son of the poet Einar Sigurðsson of Eydalir. Oddur Einarsson studied in Copenhagen, returned to Iceland in 1586, and subsequently became the bishop of Skálholt (1589–1630). It is likely that *Qualiscunque descriptio Islandiæ* was written for the same reasons as Arngrímur Jónsson's works, although it is considerably more objective. The author systematically describes Iceland's geography, climate, and plant and animal life and gives a brief history of the nation. Following this is a description of contemporary Iceland, with sections on customs and beliefs, manner of dress, housing, and diet. Finally, there is a discussion of the Icelandic language and Icelandic poetry. *Qualiscunque descriptio Islandiæ* is one of the best sources of information on Iceland from this period.

Another example of this new type of historiography is the *Bishops' Annals*, which were compiled by the Reverend Jón Egilsson (1548–ca. 1636) on the suggestion of Bishop Oddur Einarsson. These annals contain accounts of the bishops of Skálholt from the beginning, ending with Gísli Jónsson, Oddur Einarsson's predecessor. They are well put together and extremely valuable as a historical source.

Also of great importance was the work of Björn Jónsson of Skarðsá (1574–1655). He had had no formal schooling but early on developed an interest in learning and began copying manuscripts. Þorlákur Skúlason (1597–1656), the bishop of Hólar, employed him as a scribe and also had him write commentaries to accompany the texts. At this time each of the two bishoprics ran a seminary or cathedral school, primarily for the training of pastors and university students, and it was here that most organized scholarship took place. The schools constituted the only formal educational institutions in Iceland until the nineteenth century. Björn of Skarðsá recast *Landnámabók* (Book of settlements; see p. 80) and compiled a history of the so-called Turkish raid of 1627, discussed later in this chapter, that is based on a variety of sources. His most important work, however, is his annals, in particular *Skarðsárannáll*, which covers the period from 1400 to around 1640, when he appears to have stopped working on it.

Arngrímur the Learned's connection with Danish scholars resulted in a notable foreign correspondence, an exchange in which more and more Icelandic scholars gradually became involved. One of the most important participants in this exchange was the Danish polymath Ole Worm (1588–1675), one of whose interests was early Scandinavian history, in particular runology. He referred to himself as Arngrímur Jónsson's disciple and sent Jónsson a manuscript copy of his work the *Literatura runica* for comment. Another Icelander who was involved with Worm was Magnús Ólafsson of Laufás, whose reworking of Snorri's *Prose Edda*, known as *Laufás-Edda*, was printed in Copenhagen in 1665 (see earlier). Ólafsson, to some extent spurred on by Worm, also compiled the first Icelandic dictionary, which was published in 1650. It was thanks to Worm as well that Guðmundur Andrésson (1614–54) was released from the notorious Blue Tower prison in Copenhagen on the condition that he stay in Copenhagen and assist Worm with his study of Old Icelandic texts.

Revolt against Authority

Guðmundur Andrésson had wound up in the Blue Tower because of his *Discursus oppositivus*, a polemical work protesting the so-called Great Edict (Stóridómur), a series of laws that had come into force in 1564 and demanded harsh penalties for, in particular, "moral" offenses such as adultery and incest (broadly defined). Guðmundur Andrésson was of humble origins but had studied at the cathedral school at Hólar; he did not have the opportunity for further study abroad, however. Following the completion of his studies, he had one disappointment after another: he was unable to travel abroad; he was not ordained and was forced to leave the one position he did manage to secure himself, as deacon at Reynistaður, owing to (in his opinion) unjust and false accusations that had been made against him. In order to redress this he wrote the defamatory work *Þekktu sjálfan þig* (Know thyself), an attack chiefly on Bishop Þorlákur Skúlason, whom he believed had used the accusations made against him as a pretext to award another man the position. A short time later Guðmundur Andrésson had yet another misfortune: he fathered a child out of wedlock and had to pay a fine under the rules of the Great Edict. This made it virtually impossible for him to secure a position within the church, as first he would have had to receive a pardon from the religious authorities, which was unlikely in view of what had gone before.

It was probably around this time, 1647–48, that Guðmundur Andrésson wrote his *Discursus oppositivus*. The work takes the form of a logical disputation and contains a scathing attack on the Great Edict, which had taken moral authority away from the church by turning moral offenses into secular affairs, introducing the death penalty and, for lesser crimes, fines, whipping, and banishment. In his *Discursus* Andrésson argued that the Great Edict was contrary to the laws of God, supporting his argument with a wealth of biblical references, set forth with great dialectical skill. The work is most unusual for its time, challenging the rules of law and the freedom of opinion of the ruling power. It is fairly certain that the *Discursus* reflected the opinion of the general public in Iceland regarding the harsh legislation of the Great Edict. It is also probable that Guðmundur Andrésson had no intention of allowing the *Discursus* to become public. It was by coincidence that it fell into the hands of the authorities, and he was then prosecuted. The lawsuit was finally taken to Copenhagen, where he was imprisoned in the Blue Tower and forced to renounce the ideas and the arrogance of his writings. He was, as we have seen, also forbidden ever to return home to Iceland. He died in Copenhagen in 1654, only five years after his release. During these years he worked assiduously for Ole Worm.

Other works by Guðmundur Andrésson include an Icelandic-Latin dictionary, printed in Copenhagen in 1683. This was a remarkable achievement in Icelandic scholarship—and the first Icelandic dictionary to incorporate contemporary vocabulary. In 1665 Andrésson's critical edition in Icelandic and Latin of the Eddic poems "Hávamál" (Sayings of the High One) and "Völuspá" (The seeress's prophecy) (see pp. 10–12, 14–16) was published in Copenhagen by the Danish scholar P. H. Resen. Two of his poems saw print in Copenhagen in 1651, and, finally, a letter to Ole Worm, written from the Blue Tower in 1649, was published in *Bibliotheca Arnamagnæana*. Other poems by Guðmundur Andrésson—hymns and *rímur*—were preserved in manuscript but have never been published, except for his *Persíus rímur*, a set of *rímur* based on the Greek myth as related by Ovid that saw print in 1948 along with a set of *rímur* on Bellerophon that is thought likely to be Andrésson's work as well. Some bits and pieces of these were included in Þórarinn Eldjárn's 1996 novel *Brotahöfuð* (English trans.: *The Blue Tower* [1999]; see also p. 463), based on biographical sources and the fate of Guðmundur Andrésson.

Apocalypse Now
Other sixteenth- and seventeenth-century poetry in Iceland, and, indeed, generally in Europe, was inspired by the idea that doomsday was imminent. The poems of the Reverend Ólafur Einarsson of Kirkjubær are an example of this. He was the only son of Einar Sigurðsson of Eydalir, mentioned earlier. Like his father, Ólafur Einarsson was a good poet, but one who will always stand in the shadow of his son, Stefán Ólafsson, who, with Hallgrímur Pétursson, was one of the most noteworthy poets of the seventeenth century (more about both is offered below). Ólafur Einarsson was, as we have seen, born ca. 1573 and early on felt the powerful influence of the literary movement inspired by the recent Lutheran reforms. His position in the movement was unusual in that he recognized the value of foreign poetry, something that was not commonplace at the time. Earlier than others he brought to Iceland influences, both cultural and in terms of subject matter, from Denmark and Germany as well as other countries. He was, for

instance, familiar with the work of the famous Scottish poet and polemist George Buchanan (1506–82) and translated some of the *Psalms of David* that Buchanan had written in Latin. Einarsson also used foreign meters more often than did his contemporaries, and many assert that he was the first Icelandic poet to compose fully Icelandic hymns on a foreign foundation. This assertion is based on the fact that his were no longer mere imitations of foreign poems but displayed greater confidence in the use of language and style and greater independence with regard to his models, referring, for instance, to contemporary Icelandic events.

In Einarsson's own day, his poem "Árgali" (Herald) was well-known, although it did not appear in print until 1748, long after his death. The poem contained a most impressive description of Iceland and its people. The land, in the beginning, is described as a good vine that God himself had planted and consecrated. God then sent the land a good king and excellent teachers. But the people failed him, and now judgment threatened: omens were revealed in the air, on land, and in the sea. These ideas correspond fully to the worldview of the age. According to the poet, nature was full of messages to man. All deviations from the natural and normal were signs from God that men must try to interpret correctly. "Árgali" is an illustration of the end of the world—the sun loses its brightness, summer is shorter than it was, frightful storms rage, killing men and beasts, strange creatures are caught at sea, it rains snakes, and Mount Hekla spits fire. The poem contains severe criticism of foreign power and domestic leadership, both secular and spiritual, because neither turns to Iceland's defense. At the end comes a most intimate prayer to God on behalf of the country and its people. In this fervent and sincere prayer, the poet gives good advice to God himself: first, he wonders whether God might not spare and give relief to the East Fjords, where the ravages of the plague have killed so many during the previous three-quarters of the century; second, he prays that God might direct his punishment to heathen lands; and, third, he humbly suggests that there will be no one left to praise or thank God if all lie dead: "Your name no one worships or thanks from the dust of death" (*Ein lijtil psalma*, F12r, st. 46).

SUMMARY

The most distinctive features of Icelandic literature in the second half of the sixteenth century are the extraordinary influences from abroad, on the one hand, and the strict regulation of literature and culture by the church authorities, on the other. These directed what kind of new subject matter could be brought to the country in the wake of religious change and also caused traditional Icelandic literary genres to be subjected to a profound revaluation. Despite the very determined propagandizing of Christian devotional literature, which can be seen most clearly in the work of Bishop Guðbrandur Þorláksson, other currents may be discerned, for example, criticism of the new morals and teachings. At the same time it is clear that the stream of foreign devotional writing was accompanied by other literary influences: that of Continental poetic practices such as secular love lyrics and occasional verse. The subject matter of German and Danish popular literature was beginning to find its way into the *rímur* and other genres. From abroad, and especially from Denmark, the spirit of humanism was beginning to make itself felt, which would prove to have a comprehensive influence on Icelandic literature and culture.

THE SEVENTEENTH CENTURY AND THE AGE OF LEARNING

In sixteenth- and seventeenth-century Europe royal power steadily increased, eventually culminating in the establishment of absolute monarchies in the course of the seventeenth century. Denmark was no exception, and Iceland, too, felt the effects. The most severe cause of discontent was the trade monopoly with Denmark imposed by the mercantilist King Christian IV in 1602, which limited the Iceland trade to certain Danish citizens or companies and excluded competition, turning Iceland into a zone of fisheries and a source of income that only the Danes could exploit. At the time the Icelanders had no oceangoing ships and were, thus, dependent on foreigners for transportation to and from the country. They also depended on the importation of various essentials, including wheat, iron, and wood. Iceland was divided into trading districts, and official trading centers were established at the main harbors around the country; dealing with merchants from another district was strictly prohibited. Since merchants were not allowed to stay, this system prevented any economic development beyond farming and fishing. Instead, it continued to serve the small, conservative upper stratum largely made up of Icelandic officials. Thus, modernity and urbanization, which elsewhere characterized the period, were held at bay, and the country was to remain almost exclusively rural for centuries. Reykjavík was still only a large farm with a church and outlying crofts and did not develop into an urban center until the second half of the eighteenth century.

In spite of these severe restrictions, however, the Icelanders continued to conduct a lively — if illegal — trade with the English and the Dutch, particularly during the years 1630–90, and small centers developed around the country's main trading harbors, such as Eyrarbakki on the southern coast. At the same time the two bishoprics, Skálholt and Hólar, remained the main cultural centers, providing formal education, and supporting scholarship.

During the seventeenth century Iceland had about fifty-five thousand inhabitants, with an unusually low proportion of married people, and a corresponding high rate of illegitimacy, owing to social strictures dictating that only those running a farm could marry. Nearly the entire population was involved full-time in farming, with fishing as a sideline. The large majority of farmers were tenants; only 5 percent were landowners. Officials, of whom there were only about three hundred, often came from these landowning families, who thus formed the ruling class of Iceland. Families no longer capable of supporting themselves became reliant on the parish of their district of birth; they were separated and put to work on local farms, including children, who worked from as early as age six or seven. These parish paupers, who were rather numerous at this time in Icelandic history, often traveled around, finding work here and there. The standard of living in Iceland had declined since the Middle Ages, largely owing to climate change: colder temperatures contributed to economic relapse, and the end of the century in particular saw bad years and famine.

In spite of what has often been claimed, Iceland was not an egalitarian society as far as status and access to opportunities were concerned. In contrast to many other European societies, however, class divisions in Iceland were otherwise relatively minor, and social mobility was possible. This, in addition to geographic mobility, explains the relative homogeneity of Icelandic culture. Although formal education was limited to the male upper class, it is estimated that, by midcentury, a quarter of the population was literate, with literacy being less common among women and poor crofters. For Icelandic literature this meant that the distinction between high and low was not as clear-cut as elsewhere, at least until the nineteenth century. With the one printing press in the ownership of the church, the Icelandic literary canon continued to be religious, while literary production was mostly in the hands of learned writers. The fact that these writers composed in so many different genres, including popular ones, and translated so many works into Icelandic would seem to indicate, however, that this literature was intended for a wider audience than the educated elite alone. The tradition of evening entertainment (*kvöldvaka*), where everyone gathered in the main room to listen to sermons, stories, and poetry, ensured that, while only a few had the benefit of a formal education, everyone had access to literature (see Gíslason, 7–8). It is, nevertheless, quite clear that the popular preference in

Iceland was for romances, sagas, and *rímur* as well as other popular poetry and folktales, and their production and dissemination thrived.

In 1627 the so-called Turkish raid (Tyrkjarán) on the Vestmannaeyjar by North African pirates took place, in which many people were killed and over three hundred abducted. The raid left many stunned in the small Icelandic community. At the same time it brought home to Icelanders that they were part of the greater world and that the intellectual and religious conflicts that took place elsewhere in Europe affected them as well.

During the seventeenth century, superstition and a fear of damnation had increased across Northern Europe, and, as in the rest of Europe, there were those in Iceland during this time who considered it necessary to "rid" society of witchcraft by having suspects arraigned and burned. By the middle of the seventeenth century the witchcraft hysteria reached its peak in Iceland: twenty-one men and four women were burned. While in other countries the vast majority of victims were women, in Iceland it was men. The reason for this may lie in the fact that witchcraft charges in Iceland were often related to runic inscriptions and written texts. Women were less likely to be literate during the period and had less access to education. The burnings in Iceland were mainly concentrated in specific areas, especially the West Fjords, and can, in many cases, even be related to specific officials prone to witch-hunting. Prosecutions were directed against particular individuals. It seems safe to say that the hysteria passed more rapidly in Iceland than in other countries, and certainly fewer lost their lives there than elsewhere, although the numbers were high considering the small population.

On the political front, the king of Denmark declared himself the absolute monarch of the Danish realm in 1660. In 1662 representatives of Iceland were summoned to Bessastaðir, the official residence of the governor of Iceland, to swear allegiance and acknowledge the absolute sovereignty of the Danish king. Any Icelandic protest was limited as Icelanders were totally dependent on Denmark for trade and transport. Furthermore, the interests of the king and the Icelandic officials were closely tied.

Study and entertainment, however, bloomed as never before. Humanism had a profound impact on scholar and nonscholar alike: old poems were transcribed and commented on, and new poems were composed using both old and new meters. The amount of both printed and handwritten material increased during the century.

The Collection of Manuscripts and the Publication of Old Icelandic Literature
The systematic collection of Icelandic manuscripts began in the seventeenth century under the influence of Renaissance humanism: the climate of learning and the renewed interest in Greco-Roman classical texts and sources in

Northern Europe led to an increased interest in Scandinavian antiquity. In the wake of these developments sixteenth- and seventeenth-century scholars in Denmark focused their attention on the ancient history of the Nordic countries and began searching for sources and writing about the history of the Nordic peoples. They soon discovered that, in Iceland, a wealth of source material had been preserved in the form of manuscripts and, more important, that Icelanders could read these with relatively little effort.

The effects of this discovery soon made themselves felt in Iceland. In addition to Arngrímur Jónsson the Learned (whose work was discussed earlier), Brynjólfur Sveinsson, the bishop of Skálholt, and Þorlákur Skúlason, the bishop of Hólar, actively contributed to the recording and preservation of Old Icelandic lore. They had scribes working in the countryside surrounding their bishoprics. The introduction of paper in Iceland in the sixteenth century greatly contributed to the number of manuscripts and, thereby, to the preservation of the works they contained. The material of the ancient vellum manuscripts was transcribed onto paper, as a result of which important texts have been preserved from vellums that have since perished. This is true, for instance, of *Íslendingabók* (The book of Icelanders) by Ari Þorgilsson the Wise (see pp. 64–65, 76–80), which Jón Erlendsson, the pastor in Villingaholt, transcribed twice in the seventeenth century for Bishop Brynjólfur after an old manuscript that scholars presume was from around 1200 (not old enough to be Ari's own writing, however). This ancient manuscript is thought to have perished not long after Erlendsson transcribed it, for Árni Magnússon could not find any traces of it when he began his collection several decades later.

Árni Magnússon (1663–1730) went to Denmark to study at an early age and was in the service of the respected Danish scholar Thomas Bartholin (1616–80), who was working on a history of the Danish people. Magnússon collected and transcribed manuscripts for Bartholin as well as translating them into Latin. His encounter with Bartholin probably had an effect on his interest in manuscripts, but he had also been raised by a good scribe in Iceland, his maternal grandfather, Ketill Jörundarson. In any case Magnússon began collecting manuscripts early on and remained devoted to the task for the rest of his life. Most of his manuscripts he got in Iceland, but he also bought Icelandic manuscripts that he discovered abroad and collected Norwegian, Danish, and Swedish manuscripts as well as printed books. By the time of his death he was the owner of the most extensive and important collection of Icelandic manuscripts in the world. And he did not stop at collecting manuscripts, for he was also keen to get as much accurate information about their origin, age, and history as he could. He then wrote such information on slips of paper, many of which exist in his manuscript collection and have proved extremely useful for later scholars.

Although part of Árni Magnússon's precious collection was lost during the Copenhagen fire of 1728, most of the vellum manuscripts were saved. He bequeathed the collection to the University of Copenhagen.

POETRY DURING THE AGE OF LEARNING

To Master Nature

Jón Guðmundsson the Learned (1574–1658), like Guðmundur Andrésson, was a peculiar sort of rebel who often found himself in trouble because of his individualist behavior. "Fjölmóður" (Sandpiper [alternatively: Man of many moods]) is the title of a poem he wrote in his mideighties about his life, in the tradition of Einar Sigurðsson of Eydalir and others. In the poem, as elsewhere, his fundamental feeling for Catholicism surfaces, as does his sense that the Reformation had brought many negative things; in "Fjölmóður" he compares the change of religion to the apocalyptic battle of Ragnarök. Interestingly, he does this in a poem that he dedicated and sent to Bishop Brynjólfur Sveinsson, who seems partly to have shared this conviction, as can be seen in a Latin poem the bishop himself dedicated to the Virgin Mary entitled "Ad Beatam Virginem."

Jón Guðmundsson was born and grew up in the West Fjords (Strandir) but was driven away by the conflicts ignited by the so-called Spanish Killings (see above). These events were widely debated. Guðmundsson wrote an essay about the killings, *Sönn frásaga af spanskra manna skipbrotum og slagi* (The true history of the Spaniards' shipwreck and fight), published in Copenhagen in 1950 as *Spánverjavígin 1615*. In it Guðmundsson sides with the foreigners against the barbaric treatment that they received at the hands of the Icelanders. The essay was not popular with the powerful men who had been in the area during the events. After this Guðmundsson wandered around the country and abroad, sometimes on the run, and not always at liberty.

The life and writings of Jón Guðmundsson reflect his unusual and multifaceted lifestyle; he was entirely self-taught, thirsty for knowledge, and came into contact with the many sides of people's lives. He was a good writer who worked in a variety of genres. He practiced medicine and was said to have been knowledgeable about runes. Magnús Ólafsson of Laufás claimed that he was a master of this art, the cleverest reader of runes of his day. This might well have contributed to the rumors that began to circulate that Jón Guðmundsson was dabbling in witchcraft.

There is certainly no doubt about the fact that Guðmundsson wrote his "Snjáfjallavísur" (Snowy mountain verses) for the purpose of exorcising a ghost, or ghosts, in the West Fjords. In Iceland it was believed that a so-called *kraftaskáld* (magic poet) could work for good or evil with his verse, among other things banishing ghosts, trolls, and ogres (*óvættir*). The first part of the poem is called "Fjandafæla" (Devil-scare), but the story goes that it was not very effective, so he wrote a sequel, "Snjáfjallavísur hinar síðari" (Snowy mountain verses part two). This appeared to be so effective and phenomenal that he found himself driven to write "Umbót eða Friðar-huggan" (Reform, or the consolation of tranquillity). These verses are very Christian and full of humility, as it was thought that "magic poets" needed to exercise their powers with great delicacy. These poems increased both Guðmundsson's fame and his unpopularity. In 1627 Guðmundur Einarsson wrote "Hugrás (um svik og vélræði djöfulsins)" (Some thoughts [on the devil's deceit and treachery]), dealing with witchcraft in general, in which he attacked Jón Guðmundsson and his "Fjandafæla" directly. These accusations led to Guðmundsson's impeachment for crime at the Althing and, finally, to his conviction in 1631 for "a magic poem" that he had written.

In the summer of 1636 Jón Guðmundsson the Learned traveled to Copenhagen under investigation for the charges made against him. A trial was held a year later. The interrogation was conducted by Ole Worm, the rector of the University of Copenhagen at the time. It was decided that the case should be retried in Iceland as the original verdict there had not been reached under satisfactory circumstances. The case was taken up again at the Althing, which confirmed the original verdict of outlawry. When push came to shove, nobody wanted to take on the task of escorting Jón Guðmundsson out of the country, however. It was finally agreed that he should be allowed to settle in the eastern part of Iceland. His days as a fugitive from justice were over after his arrival there. When Brynjólfur Sveinsson became the bishop of Skálholt in 1639, Guðmundsson came under his protective wing. During the following years he worked very productively as a scribe for Bishop Brynjólfur. The bishop was planning to write about the ancient Nordic religion, and it seems likely that much of Guðmundsson's writing was in preparation for that work. Recent research suggests that Jón Guð-mundsson enjoyed greater prestige among scholars of his day than has previously been thought. He is believed to have transcribed a manuscript of the *Prose Edda* in Copenhagen during the winter of 1636–37. That manuscript is now preserved at Oxford.

Jón Guðmundsson the Learned is best known for his works *Um Íslands aðskiljanlegar náttúrur* (On the diversity of Icelandic nature) and *Tíðfordríf*

(Pastime). The latter, written at the behest of the bishop in 1644, is about the supernatural qualities of elves, stones, and plants. Naturalists today consider Guðmundsson to be their first important ancestor because of his book on Icelandic nature, which was based on his own observations. In it he speculates about geothermal heat, beach growth, the gender of whales, and metals, among other matters. It can be said that this book is the first Icelandic narrative of nature and a great innovation at the time. Guðmundsson also wrote books on botany and on medicine. He was a fine stylist and, at the same time, transcribed ancient, secular texts.

Seventeenth-Century Baroque: Lyric and Pastoral Poetry

It has been a subject of debate whether it is appropriate and relevant to apply the concept *baroque* to seventeenth- and eighteenth-century Nordic literature in the way that is done in relation to other European literatures. There is a consensus, however, that at that time the courts of Copenhagen and Stockholm were heavily influenced by Continental baroque literature. Some literary critics adhere to the idea of a distinctive baroque period in Icelandic literary history, while others will only go so far as to identify individual texts as exhibiting baroque influences, to distinguish them from those derived from older traditions. Baroque styles are characterized by the use of elaborate and excessive imagery, allegory, wordplay, contrast, and artificiality and extremes of expression. They flourish with the rise of absolute monarchy and an increasingly powerful church, their highly structured nature reflecting the underlying idea of a fixed, supreme order governing all aspects of life. Baroque genres include panegyrics on exalted individuals, hymns, and much occasional poetry.

In Iceland one example of direct influence of the fashionable new baroque is the poem "Lúkidor og Krysillis," translated from the Danish by Stefán Ólafsson (ca. 1619–88). It is a pastoral poem about the shepherd Lucidor and the beautiful shepherdess Chrysillis. In the poem Lucidor and Chrysillis flirt and kiss, surrounded by their grazing flock, while streams flow through the meadow. The poem was first published in a poetry anthology by the Dane Søren Terkelsen (d. 1656/57), who was a pioneer in introducing various foreign innovations into Danish poetic culture. His *Astræ Sjunge-Kor* (Astrea's song choir) was published in 1648, that is, around the time when Stefán Ólafsson returned home after his studies in Copenhagen. The pastoral mode was a great novelty in Denmark and cannot have been missed by the Icelander. Previously, pastoral poems had been written in Latin; Terkelsen's real innovation was to compose them in Danish.

The pastoral tradition could, of course, not be further removed from the daily experiences of Icelandic farming society in the seventeenth century. Pastoral poetry describes carefree lives in temperate country settings — an attitude imagined in city cultures. Life in Iceland, on the other hand, was a struggle, and nature there was harsh. Nonetheless, Ólafsson's poem has been preserved both in manuscript and in oral tradition. Throughout the nineteenth century there were people who were familiar with it and were used to hearing it sung, which is a good indication of its popularity. As a pastoral poem it is unique in seventeenth-century Icelandic; no others are recorded or remembered.

Stefán Ólafsson was born at Kirkjubær in the East Fjords in 1618 or 1619 and studied at Skálholt. It is thought that he graduated in 1642 and was writing for Bishop Brynjólfur Sveinsson the following winter. He then sailed to Copenhagen, where he studied from 1643 to 1648. His private tutor was Ole Worm, for whom he worked on, among other things, the translation of the *Prose Edda* into Latin. He was invited to Paris by Cardinal Mazarin to explain Nordic lore and especially the *Edda*, but the plan was never realized. He returned to Iceland and became a pastor in Vallanes in 1649. He has been described as a man of high spirits, troublesome in his early years, a great horseman, a fancy dresser, and always gallant. He wrote his autobiographical poem "Svanasöngur" (Swan song; see below) in his later years. He also wrote poems in praise of horses and poetry, ale, and tobacco.

Two other lyric poems by Stefán Ólafsson have been preserved: "Meyjar-missir" (Loss of a maiden) and "Raunakvæði" (Lament). Like the poems of Páll Jónsson of Staðarhóll discussed earlier, these poems show the clear influence of Danish and German love poetry; they are much simpler in form and style than was common in Icelandic poetry. In these poems the poet's emotions are the central concern. The girl's appearance is treated with precision, and descriptions of nature are used to evoke a state of mind. "Meyjarmissir" begins "Maiden bright and pure / my only love / in Ice-cold land" (*Kvæði*, 2:38) and goes on to describe the sorrow of the bereaved. "Raunakvæði" also deals with a ladylove who may not be approached. It describes her beautiful hands, tiny feet, radiant eyes, and fair skin. The structure of the poem is systematic. Classical rhetorical devices like metaphor and hyperbole are in evidence, and each verse ends with a variation of the same sentence.

Not much other seventeenth-century love poetry has been preserved. Lyric qualities are most commonly found in poems by anonymous authors, for example, in the "Vísur Fiðlu-Bjarnar" (Poems by Fiddle-Bjarni), and in carols (*vikivakakvæði*), poems on impermanence (*hverfulleikakvæði*), and *mansöngvar* in *rímur* (see above).

Neo-Latin Poetry in Iceland

In Iceland, as elsewhere in Europe, it was fairly common for scholars and poets to compose in Latin. This kind of poetry, of course, had, in terms of meter, imagery, and rhetorical devices, its models in the classical literature of the Greeks and Romans. During and after the Reformation the dominant view throughout Europe was that Latin poetry was superior in artistic value and potential to that composed in the vernacular. At the same time, however, there was an awakening interest in poetry in the mother tongue, with the aim to try to aspire to the sublimity of Latin poetry. It has been shown that both classical and neo-Latin poetry exercised an enormous influence on the poetry of the baroque period, in Germany as well as in the Nordic countries. In Iceland the circumstances were different in some respects, for there was a long tradition for composing in Icelandic. It is important, nevertheless, to remember that, in earlier centuries, all educated Icelandic men learned, not only Latin, but also classical poetics, which included being taught how to construct verses in Latin. The literature and poetry that they read were a part of their Latin studies and modeled on the classics. It was also quite common to compose occasional poetry in Latin, especially for weddings and funerals.

The Latin compositions of Arngrímur Jónsson and Magnús Ólafsson of Laufás have been mentioned. One of Iceland's most accomplished Latin poets in the seventeenth and eighteenth centuries was the Reverend Jón Þorkelsson Vídalín (1666–1720), the bishop of Skálholt, who wrote, for example, *Calliopes respublica* (Calliope's republic), which he recited himself at Skálholt in 1692 (see also below). At the time it was customary for scholars to gather there and conduct disputations, in the manner of foreign scholars. Vídalín's poem is in praise (*laudatio*) of the glory of Svada Skalholtlina, that is, the personification of oratory as it appeared in Skálholt. The author demonstrates his profound classical learning, both in the imagery used and in the rhetorical structure of the poem. Jón Vídalín composed a great number of poems in Latin, mostly occasional poetry.

Stefán Ólafsson also composed in Latin, including a small poem about the Danish island Samsø. He translated poems by Horace ("Rectius vives") and Virgil ("Útmálun hins vænsta reiðhests" [Description of the best riding horse] from the *Georgics*) into Icelandic in addition to imitating poems by Boethius (see also below).

Works about Nature and Creation

The period's shift in focus from the divine and the afterlife to the wonders of God's creation on earth, with man at the center of it all, had led to many discoveries in the areas of physics, astronomy, global navigation, and natural science. This is reflected in European literature of the time, much of which deals with nature and creation, as well as descriptions of countries and the landscape. The dominant view, which was based on the belief that an almighty God inspired everything with meaning and purpose, was that everything in creation was governed by a supreme order, that every object had its fixed purpose and role, and that natural phenomena had a symbolic meaning from which mankind might learn. Natural descriptions of the period are, therefore, mainly in praise of the creator. This applies to the work *Guds werk och hwila* (God's work and rest) by the Swedish poet Haquin Spegel (1645–1714) and *Hexaëmeron Rhytmico-Danicum. Det er: Verdens første Uges sex Dages prægtige og mægtige Gierninge* (The six-day work) by the Danish poet Anders Arrebo, which itself is a translation of *La première semaine* (1578), the important historical poem by Du Bartas that was translated into many languages in the sixteenth and seventeenth centuries.

Hallgrímur Pétursson (1614–74) wrote two such works. One is called *Diarium Christianum*, or "The Daily Practice of All the Lord's Day's Works with Comparison to the Ten Commandments of God to the Creation, and Memory of the Name of Jesus." It is thought to have been written in 1660, but it was first printed at Hólar in 1680. The *Diarium* is a meditation, where God's creation on each day of the week is linked with the day's name and one or two of the Ten Commandments. The Danish scholar Arne Møller has called it a sketch of the little *Hexaëmeron*. The work makes it clear that the world has a natural order. The workings of the celestial spheres, for instance, suggest reasons for our own obedience to authority. The poet uses a variety of classical rhetorical devices and quotes several other learned authors. When discussing the creation of the birds, for example, he applies metaphors linked to birds and flying to people's lives: "My Lord Jesus, make my heart fly up from earthly vanity to you in heaven. . . . Do not let me become a disgusting carrion bird in your sight, nor have the bird of prey's nature or the raven's disposition toward my neighbor" (*Sálmar og hugvekjur*, 182). Works like these were intended to help people interpret God's message in nature.

The same underlying thought appears in the poem by Bjarni Gissurarson (1621–1712) entitled "Um samlíking sólarinnar og Um gagn og nytsemi sólarinnar" (On the sun as metaphor; on the serviceability and usefulness of the sun). The poem begins with a series of beautiful natural images that demonstrate how the sun brings everything to life: "All nature broadly beams / with tender outstretched arms" (Gissurarson, *Sólarsýn*, ed. Samsonarson, 8). But nature, of course, also has symbolic meaning. The sun is like a God-fearing and virtuous woman, and the poet goes on to describe such a good woman. She is a wife and mother who, with her love and care, brightens up the croft. She is, he concludes, worth more than gold. A later poem begins with praise of the sun but then compares it to the Savior Jesus. Both poems are in carol meter, which was widely popular at the time (see also below).

Nature was dear to Bjarni Gissurarson; among other works he wrote "Þakklætisvísa fyrir blítt veður og gróða jarðar" (A poem in gratitude for mild weather and fruitful earth). He also wrote two works that can be considered topographical. The first is "Um góða landsins kosti" (On the benefits of the soil), which begins with praise and gratitude for a good summer but then becomes a comparison of Iceland with other, distant countries. Its purpose seems to be to encourage Icelanders and make them realize that their lot is not worse than that of others. Icelandic nature is generous; the animals have enough to eat; there are fish aplenty; there are woolen clothes and milk. Finally, there are merchants constantly on the move to bring the inhabitants the goods they need. The poet admits that the winters are hard, but he observes that Icelanders do not have to suffer the wars that are going on in other parts of the world. The second poem is "Vísa um Mjóafjarðarkosti" (A poem on the advantages of Mjóifjörður) which describes a small bay in the East Fjords. The poem imagines a journey to the bay and describes the landscape and its many advantages. The structure of the poem is such that it might have been the first section of a long topographical poem on the East Fjords.

Gissurarson in fact wrote a poem called "Austfjarðaóður" (Poem on the East Fjords) that has never been printed but survives in an autograph (Thott 473 4to, pp. 139–40). This is not a poem of praise, however, but the opposite: a poem lamenting the deterioration of the East Fjords. The poet begins by describing some good years when animals prospered, fish were abundant, whales drifted ashore, and merchants brought a variety of exciting merchandise. Now, however, everything has changed, and the poet is certain that God is punishing the people for bad behavior. He demonstrates how life has grown worse in every way and finally asks for God's mercy for the people and the country.

Occasional poetry and topographical poetry, which continued to be extremely popular during the baroque era, were often concerned with nature and the weather. Þorrakvæði (poems on winter; Þorri in ancient times was the January–February midwinter season) are a uniquely Icelandic variety of a genre that remained popular throughout the seventeenth and eighteenth centuries. It is likely that Bjarni Gissurarson is the pioneer of such poetry.

He personifies the winter months, Þorri and Góa, describes their appearances, has them visit farms in the countryside, and relates amusing attendant anecdotes. His example was followed by many later poets.

Poems on Historical Topics

In the post-Reformation era it became popular to put a variety of information into verse. Magnús Ólafsson of Laufás composed the fresh and amusing "Kvennadans" (Dance of women) in praise of the fair sex. In it he lists women, first from the Bible, then from the history of mankind. The poet enumerates their virtues and, at the same time, defends them from traditional accusations, such as their responsibility for the emergence of sin. "Einvaldsóður" (Poem on monarchy) by Guðmundur Erlendsson of Fell is a recapitulation of the history of mankind from the Flood to the Reformation. Its six episodes are composed in *fornyrðislag* meter (see p. 4). This extremely popular work contains fierce criticism of the pope and the Catholic Church (see Cook, "Chronica Carionis"). Also very learned is Guðmundur Bergþórsson's poem "Heimspekingaskóli" (School of philosophers) in *rímur* style. The subject matter is largely derived from a translation of a Danish work, *Collegium philosophorum* by Hans Hanssen Skonning, published in 1636. Guðmundur Bergþórsson (1657–1705) became mostly known as a *rímur* poet, with no less than 256 *rímur* to his name.

Seventeenth-Century Humor

The Reformation and the social and cultural revolution that followed in its wake found expression in literature through an abundance of satire, burlesque, and nonsense writing. Exaggeration and parody enjoyed great popularity in seventeenth-century poetry, and so-called topsy-turvy poems flourished. Bjarni Jónsson's topsy-turvy poetry has been mentioned.

In the drinking poems of the Reverend Ólafur Einarsson of Kirkjubær, some bizarre moments of drinking parties are captured, for instance, in "Ölkvæði" (Drinking song) with the Latin refrain *inter pocula* (in their cups). Einarsson's son Stefán Ólafsson took particular pleasure in creating comic images of people. Of course it is difficult now to approach the satiric reality of such poetry. Individuals are often mentioned by name, but it is as likely that such names are real as that they are fictions. In these poems the people are excessively ridiculed; fun is made of their appearance, sloth, vanity, and love affairs. Much of the amusement lies in the rhymes, original wording, wordplay, and pictorial descriptions. One such poem, called "Hornfirðingakvæði" (On the people of Hornafjörður), describes a group of peasants that hear of a wedding in another district. The poem is a hilarious report about their appearance, clumsiness, and troubles as they attempt to get to the reception, where their main interest is in the alcohol on offer. In the poem "Hrakfallabálkur" (Accident-prone) by Bjarni Gissurarson there is an exaggerated and playful description of all possible accidents that could plausibly befall a traveler in the East Fjords. It was also popular to make fun of those who overvalue themselves and overlook their status in society (e.g., the workingman who dresses like a gentleman in "Ásmundur hefðarhósti" [Ásmundur's aristocratic cough] by Stefán Ólafsson) or show affectation in their clothing or follow other new trends. In Hallgrímur Pétursson's "Oflátungalýsing" (Description of a dandy) a man is described dressed in all the latest fashions. He wears floral gloves, four pairs of trousers, an open-neck shirt with a Danish silk scarf, and Spanish boots and spurs. His whole attitude is arrogant, but, when spoken to, he reveals his stupidity and ignorance.

Occasional Poetry in the Seventeenth Century
Many occasional poems in Icelandic have been preserved from the seventeenth century. Scholarly interest in this kind of poetry has always been rather limited in Iceland, although it has increased somewhat in recent years as a result of the growing interest among scholars in noncanonical material and international influences on Icelandic literature.

Among wedding poetry there is Stefán Ólafsson's poem "Brúðkaupsvísur til Jörgens Kem" (Wedding verses for Jörgen Kem), written for a Danish merchant. The poem is written in the ancient *dróttkvætt* meter, garnished with old poetic language, and was, thus, undoubtedly difficult to understand, even for those having Icelandic as their mother tongue. It contains some beautiful natural imagery, but its main purpose is well-wishing. To the same man Ólafsson wrote the *propemptikon* (farewell poem) "Leiðarljóð" (Travel poem), also in *dróttkvætt* meter, on the occasion of the departure of the merchant from Iceland, in which there is, of course, the wish for a safe journey. Wedding poems appear to increase in the eighteenth century, for there are many extant examples, although these have not yet been studied.

Funeral elegies were extremely widespread after the Reformation. As are other occasional poems, they are shaped by classical oratory and Christian ideas of virtue and salvation. Their purpose was to transform grief into celebration and help people come to terms with the loss of a loved one or of an important member of society. In the construction of funeral elegies there are specific elements: praise of the dead; a description of his or her virtues and manner of life; and a description of the moment of death. There is then a declaration of grief over the loss of the deceased, followed by an expression of consolation and, finally, a prayer for those he or she left behind. Authors of funeral elegies in seventeenth-century Iceland include Guðmundur Erlendsson of Fell (ca. 1595–1670), Bjarni Gissurarson, and Hallgrímur Pétursson. Funeral elegies were written almost solely for members of the upper class — pastors, bishops, magistrates, and lawmen and their daughters, wives, and mothers.

Hallgrímur Pétursson lost his daughter, Steinunn, when she was only three and a half years old. He wrote two funeral elegies for her that are among the most beautiful funeral poems in Icelandic. The initial letters of the second of these form the words *Steinunn mín litla hvílist nú* (my little Steinunn is resting now). Bright and beautiful images are drawn of the saved, who celebrate and sing in heaven, free of all grief and suffering, and the poet consoles himself with the thought of his child being there now. Although she was only three when she died, she is described as having been "sensitive, bright and sweet tempered" (*Ljóðmæli*, 2:160). Her illness is also described, and, although that illness was brief, the reader still feels the profound pain of a parent who watches over his dying child and cannot save her.

Lullabies and Nursery Rhymes
There are several examples of occasional poetry being composed for children in Iceland. Guðríður Gísladóttir was wellborn, the daughter of the magistrate Gísli Magnússon, and, later, the wife of the bishop of Skálholt. She was just two years old when Stefán Ólafsson wrote "Nýársgjöf til Guðríðar litlu Gísladóttur" (A New Year's gift to little Guðríður Gísladóttir) for her. It is a poem of maxims, forty-six verses in the *fornyrðislag* meter, or *ljúflingslag* ("tender" meter), as it was often called. *Fornyrðislag* was often used in storytelling and maxim poetry as it is simple and flexible. The author says that he is going to give the girl, not gold and emeralds, but a little poem. The maxims are varied and reveal the virtues then considered most desirable in a woman, for example: "If you look in a mirror and are very pleased with what you see, beware that bad behaviour does not spoil the good looks. But if you are dissatisfied with your face and feel other women are much more beautiful, be superior to them in Christian behaviour and let your way of life compensate for your looks" (*Kvæði*, 2:195–96). Bjarni Gissurarson, Stefán Ólafsson's nephew, also wrote a maxim poem to the same girl, "Vögguvísur Guðríðar Gísladóttur" (A lullaby for Guðríður Gísladóttir).

Also extant by Bjarni Gissurarson is "Vöggukvæði Einars Marteinssonar" (A lullaby for Einar Marteinsson). As is the maxim poem for

Guðríður, it is composed in *fornyrðislag*. Sailing is the main motif of this allegorical poem. The first example is the sailing that began in the womb when all was sweet and comfortable. Now the baby lies in another boat, which is the cradle. It is not nearly as comfortable as the womb was, and now many strange things catch the eye, like curious people peeping in. Little by little it becomes clear that the baby is present in yet another ship, which is the church, and further ahead is the great sea journey, which is the boy's life. Now one comparison follows another. The ship carries the "merry sailors of Christ" (*Sólarsýn*, 36) and a quite considerable cargo of a spiritual nature. The Holy Spirit manages the sails of religion, and the captain is, of course, Jesus himself. On this fine ship the boy can be sure that he will eventually arrive in the safe harbor of heaven.

Such poems might also be categorized as *barnagælur* or "lullabies," poems that are hummed, sung, or chanted to a child to keep it busy or to calm it and put it to sleep. Until 1600, examples of such poems are rare in Icelandic manuscripts, but in manuscripts from the seventeenth century we find the poem "Ljúflingsljóð" (Tender poem). It is by an unknown author and seems to have been transmitted orally. A story is attached to the poem of an elfin man (a *ljúflingur*) who chanted it outside the window of a restless baby, which he had had with a human woman. In the beginning there is an enumeration of animals that sleep on land and in the sea, and just like those animals the baby is supposed to go to sleep.

Grýlukvæði (Ogress poems) were also meant for children. They were popular in the seventeenth and eighteenth centuries. Some are by known authors such as Stefán Ólafsson. They were passed on orally and were sung to children. The characters in these poems, Grýla and her husband, Leppalúði, come from Icelandic folklore. Grýla is a terrible and ugly troll woman who travels around the countryside with a sack on her back, in which she gathers unruly children. In "Leppalúðakvæði," which is attributed to Hallgrímur Pétursson, Leppalúði has come (because Grýla is sick and cannot come herself) to abduct some of the poet's children, three of which are named: Eyjólfur; Guðmundur; and Steinunn. When Leppalúði shows up, Hallgrímur is in the church. He tries to protest, but Leppalúði begins to enumerate various things that the children have done wrong: being noisy and causing a commotion; not bothering with reading and studying. Finally, Leppalúði prepares to attack Hallgrímur. The poet then puts on his pastor's cassock, which saves him from this evil creature.

Poems on Life's Wisdom and Life's Pleasures
During the baroque period the governing view was that poetry was meant to educate, encourage, teach, and admonish. Maxim poems and poems on the

virtues and vices are, therefore, very common. The *Vísnabók* of 1612 contains maxim poems by the Reverend Jón Bjarnason (d. 1634) bearing the title "Heilræðavísur" (Poems of sound advice), covering four human virtues (fear of God, justice, courage, and thrift or moderation), written in *dróttkvætt* meter. The Reverend Jón Magnússon of Laufás (1601–75) is the author of the poem "Hústafla" (House chart). In this poem, people from various classes are advised about good behavior and shown the virtues that are proper for each person according to his or her class and position, for example, the duties of married couples, parents and children, authority figures and dependents, pastors and parishioners. The poem was printed three times. Many maxim poems are attributed to Hallgrímur Pétursson. Some of them have endured well and are still used in primary schools in Iceland.

Despite this emphasis on moral instruction, poets did not ignore the lighter side of life in their works, as is evidenced by the many poems preserved on the various pleasures of life, such as alcohol and tobacco. Ólafur Jónsson of Sandar wrote in praise of "hinn góði bjór" (good beer). It is horses that are among the delights that Stefán Ólafsson extols. Benedikt Jónsson (d. 1744) suggests that the most precious moments in life are when riding a good horse, listening to an articulate pastor, and enjoying the pleasure of a woman. In these poems there is often a certain tension between morality and true relish, as when describing the influence of alcohol and tobacco. The value of moderation in drinking is the subject matter of Hallgrímur Pétursson's poem "Nú er ég glaður á góðri stund" (Now I am merry at a delightful moment). His poem "Leirkarlsvísur" (Wine jug verses) compares a man's destiny to a jug of wine. The poem is cheerful but, nonetheless, bears religious and philosophical thoughts and conclusions. Poems such as these are often composed in the meters of occasional verses, *rímur* and *dróttkvætt*.

Polemical Poetry

The line between humor and polemic in poetry is not always clear. In "Ómennskukvæði" (On the sloth of the age) Stefán Ólafsson creates a fantastic picture of lazy, cocky common people in a rhetorical fashion with quite ingenious rhyming. The poem begins with a comparison of old times and new. In the old days, of course, the men were heroes and highly accomplished. Today the spotlight is on working people who try to run independent farms; however, they are so lazy, stupid, and selfish that everything goes wrong. The humor is sometimes grotesque, even vulgar, as, for instance, when a man about to be married runs off "with swollen groin" to find himself lodgings.

The poem "Aldarháttur" (Ways of the present world) by Hallgrímur Pétursson is also a contemporary polemic in which the poet compares his own times to those of the Commonwealth, that is, the period before Icelanders were ruled by a king. In those days people were valiant, appreciated their freedom more than gold, and did not submit to oppression by threat. Here, Iceland's medieval past is for the first time glamorized in Icelandic poetry. The poet criticizes his own era for laziness, lack of solidarity, cowardice, and an unjust legal system. With a degree of certainty the poem can be dated to 1663, a year after Icelanders had pledged an oath to the king of Denmark as absolute monarch, and this event probably inspired the poem. Hallgrímur Pétursson himself was present at the Althing at the time of the oath. It became a nationalist commonplace that Icelanders never stooped lower than when sacrificing their freedom to a foreign power even if, in Iceland, it was a formality that changed nothing for them. On the other hand, Icelandic representatives had been forced to sign a document in which they renounced their former freedom and the laws of the land that were deemed to go against the authority of the king. The Icelanders had difficulty accepting this clause. Bishop Brynjólfur Sveinsson tried to protest, but the Danish governor of Iceland pointed toward the heavily armed Danish troops, and, finally, under duress, everyone agreed and signed the document.

"Aldarháttur" is written in a classical hexameter, a variation on leonic meter, the first example of its kind in Icelandic. In Germany and the Nordic countries poets were learning to use precisely this and other classical meters like the alexandrine. At the same time it is interesting that Hallgrímur Pétursson directly imitates the poetic language of the *dróttkvætt* verses from *Ólafs saga Tryggvasonar hin mesta* (The longest saga of Ólafur Tryggvason; see p. 163). The poem is, thus, remarkable in the way it is constructed equally from the classical traditions of Europe and the indigenous traditions of Iceland. Another of Pétursson's polemics is "Flærðarsenna" (Perfidy). The subject is at once classical and contemporary as the poem describes the perfidy of the world. The poet presents one example after another in verses of great originality and rich pictorial imagery.

It is sometimes hard for readers of a later period to know what in old poems is historical reality and what is literary convention. In the poem "Um þá fyrri og þessa öld" (Of the past and the present century), Stefán Ólafsson creates a picture of an ideal past when people were happy and peaceful in a beautiful, unspoiled natural setting. Present times, on the other hand, are characterized by disruption and greed. However, even though the poem mentions Hekla's lava flows and ash, it does not have a lot to do with

Icelandic reality because it is really an imitation of a poem by Boethius (verse 5 of *De consolatione philosophiae*). Where Boethius talks about Etna, Ólafsson describes Hekla; where the Latin poet talks about silk, the Icelander describes wool.

Vanitas *and* Memento Mori

After the Reformation one of the most common themes in European literature became transience, futility, and the instability of worldly possessions. The subject has a long tradition, but it appealed especially to poets of the baroque era. The oldest of such poems in Icelandic, dating back to Catholic times, is probably "Heimsósómi Skáld-Sveins" (Skáld-Sveinn's wicked ways of the world) by an otherwise unknown poet (see also p. 55). It is preserved in a vellum manuscript from the first half of the sixteenth century and is printed in Bishop Guðbrandur's *Vísnabók* of 1612. The poem begins with the traditional descriptions of the mutability of all things: the world stumbles on, and the wheel of fortune turns. There is a long description of bad times, greed, warfare, and betrayal and a reminder of death's inevitability followed by a final, Christian resolution.

There are certain images and metaphors particular to this form of poetry. Thus, Hallgrímur Pétursson compares the prosperity of the world to transient phenomena like glass, smoke, and a water bubble in "Um veraldarinnar velsemd" (On the prosperity of the world). Stefán Ólafsson in his "Svanasöngur" (see also above) says that all happiness is

> . . . like dust
> a moment
> an unsteady wheel
> a windblown bubble
> wave, stream or the moon.
> (*Kvæði*, 2:226)

All these images are known from foreign *vanitas* poetry. Hallgrímur Pétursson's poem "Fegurð veraldar mun hverfa" (The beauty of the world will fade) is an allegory or extended metaphor on transience. The beauty of nature is described at the beginning; then autumn arrives, and everything fades and decays. This evokes memories of the poem "Eikarlundurinn" by Páll Jónsson of Staðarhóll (see above), in which weather descriptions play a key role. In Hallgrímur Pétursson's poem the changing weather is a symbol for how everything in the world is subject to decay. The poem's subject matter and imagery of fruitful trees suggest foreign influence. The entire first part of the poem describes the beauty of nature in bloom with reference to the senses of sight, smell, and hearing. The structure is symmetrical; in addition to opening and closing verses, there are four verses on nature in bloom and four on autumn, wind, cold, and destruction, a metaphor intended to demonstrate human destiny in a nutshell.

Closely related to the poems on transience and mutability are the so-called *ellikvæði* (poems on old age), which were fairly widespread. Here, evanescence and decay are the main subject matter, and youth is compared to old age, often both in a realistic and in a highly metaphoric manner.

Contemplating death is another related subject in the period. Many of Hallgrímur Pétursson's poems are written as preparations for death. The poems contain metaphors that are commonplace in the baroque age: death with a scythe, with a bow and arrows, as a skeleton, as a half-decayed body, or as a dance. Probably on his deathbed Pétursson wrote the so-called "Andlátssálmar" (Hymns on the hour of death), in which he describes his illness and prepares for his end. The hymn suggests the contemporary fascination with the decay of the body and the termination of the physical being. However, there are also beautiful religious metaphors, as when death is compared to birth, with God himself as midwife helping the dying man get through the difficult passage toward life and light.

Hallgrímur Pétursson
Hallgrímur Pétursson's background is unusual in many ways. He studied at the cathedral school at Hólar. After that it would have been easy for him to get further education; bright young men of the official classes who received financial support usually went to the University of Copenhagen to continue their studies in the hope of getting good positions, as officials or clergymen, when they returned to Iceland. For reasons not entirely clear Hallgrímur Pétursson was forced to leave Hólar and went abroad. It seems that foreign seamen granted him passage, and he was next heard from in Glückstadt (north Germany), where he was employed by a blacksmith who treated him badly. It is said that Brynjólfur Sveinsson, later the bishop of Skálholt, had, by sheer coincidence, been passing by the smithy and heard someone denouncing his employer in a vigorous and not very pretty Icelandic. Brynjólfur found that the lad was good with words, although what he had heard was pretty crude, and, after talking to him, decided that he was very talented. He arranged for him to attend the Vor Frue Skole, or Copenhagen Cathedral School. There, a new chapter in the life of Hallgrímur Pétursson began. He quickly achieved good results and was soon among the best students.

Pétursson was around twenty-two years old when dramatic events occurred. A group of Icelanders, who had been abducted by North African pirates some ten years earlier, arrived in Copenhagen, having finally been ransomed by the Danish king. Pétursson was hired to remind them of Christian teachings. A member of the group was Guðríður Símonardóttir, a wife and mother from the Vestmannaeyjar who had been separated from her husband and child in the raid. The two fell in love, and soon she was pregnant with his child. Guðríður was thirty-eight at the time, so there was a sixteen-year age difference.

Hallgrímur Pétursson thus had to drop his studies for the second time, and the two traveled to Iceland. They learned then that her husband had died. They were married, and Pétursson provided for his family by means of hard manual labor. Times were difficult for the couple; they were poor and lost several young children. Again, however, radical changes happened in Pétursson's life and circumstances. For the second time Brynjólfur Sveinsson, now the bishop of Skálholt, intervened; he ordered Pétursson to take holy orders in 1644 and arranged a living for him. Pétursson's early years as a pastor cannot have been easy for him; some people could not forget that he had been a poor laborer. An old source says that people found it peculiar for the bishop to have ordained this poor fellow, but they changed their minds after having heard him preach. Only one of his sermons, a funeral oration, has been preserved, but it is known that he was considered a splendid preacher. Another indication of growing admiration for him is that, when the much richer living in Saurbær (north of Reykjavík) became available in 1651, he was appointed to it.

The next decade was a fruitful one for Pétursson as a writer. His greatest work is from this period, all of it religious. There were two books of hymns: *Samúelssálmar* (Hymns of Samuel) from the Old Testament Book of Samuel and the *Passíusálmar* (Passion hymns). There were also his two books on religious practice: the earlier-mentioned *Diarium Christianum* and *Sjö guðrækilegar umþenkingar* (Seven pious thoughts). In 1662 the farm at Saurbær burned. This was a tremendous shock, although plans were immediately made to rebuild. After this Pétursson's health began to deteriorate. He was diagnosed with leprosy, from which he died in 1674 at age sixty.

Hallgrímur Pétursson is best known for his *Passíusálmar* and the hymn "Allt eins og blómstrið eina" (Like the blooming flower), which in the author's manuscript bears the title "Um dauðans óvissa tíma" (On the uncertain hour of death). "Allt eins og blómstrið eina" is a reflection on death and begins with a quotation from the Psalms of David suggesting that the days of man are like the grass in the fields. In the first stanzas of the poem the image of vegetation and the personification of death as a grim reaper depict the transience of human life. In the second part, however, the belief in Christ brings light and hope to the poem, which concludes with a beautiful and effective confession that, with faith, man has nothing to be afraid of, not even death, and can, thus, welcome the arrival of death at any time. It has since become a tradition to sing this hymn at Icelandic funerals.

Reflections on the Passion Story

Hallgrímur Pétursson's *Passíusálmar* is the best-known work of Icelandic poetry of the seventeenth century. The Passion — the suffering and death of Jesus — is a major subject of Christianity and the pivot of Luther's theology, and it became a popular practice to reflect on the Passion story. Around forty such reflections exist in print in German, Danish, and Swedish from the seventeenth and eighteenth centuries. Besides Pétursson's work, others were composed in Icelandic as well, including *Píslarsaltari* (Book of Passion hymns) by the Reverend Jón Magnússon of Laufás, consisting of seven hymns about Christ's suffering, and the *Passíusálmar* of the Reverend Guð-mundur Erlendsson of Fell, also containing seven hymns. Erlendsson's later hymns were published in the first edition of Hallgrímur Pétursson's *Passíusálmar* in 1666.

A comparison of Jón Magnússon's and Guðmundur Erlendsson's hymns with Hallgrímur Pétursson's in terms of presentation, treatment, narrative method, and point of view is telling. Magnússon's, for example, are all in the form of an address; the poet talks directly to Jesus. There is, consequently, never any sense of dramatic staging, and, thus, Magnússon's mode of storytelling is not as effective as Pétursson's. There is also in Magnússon's hymns no emphasis placed on "seeing and viewing," which later became a principal characteristic of the Passion story in verse. Guðmundur Erlendsson's hymns, too, are mostly direct recapitulation without commentary.

Hallgrímur Pétursson produced fifty hymns altogether, one to be sung each day during Lent, with a conclusion during Holy Week. The title of the collection is *Historia pínunnar og dauðans Drottin vors Jesú Kristí, með hennar sérlegustu lærdóms-, áminningar-, og huggunargreinum, ásamt bænum og þak-kargjörðum, í sálmum og söngvísum með ýmsum tónum samsett og skrifuð anno 1659* (History of the suffering and death of Our Lord Jesus Christ, with special instruction, admonishment and consolation together with prayer and thanksgiving, in hymns and songs in various moods assembled and written in the year 1659). The structure of each hymn perfectly reflects this subtitle: each can be divided into history, which is a distinct part of the text of the story of the martyrdom, and commentary, which is threefold: commentary for instruction, for admonition, and for consolation. Such a four-fold division of a poem has a long tradition in Christian thought (consider Dante's description of his allegorical method in the *Convivio*), in which a text has, in order, a historic, an allegorical, a moral, and an anagogic level of significance, the latter bringing everything into eternal correlation and, thus, giving consolation.

The outer form of the hymns is, in fact, simple. Pétursson does not use internal rhyme, as he does in his other work. Nor does he use the ancient poetic language and other kinds of complex imagery. Everything is clear and lucid. There is, nevertheless, clear evidence of his knowledge and use of classical rhetoric. The opening verse, for example, is a typical *invocatio*, an invocation to the whole body to take part in the following meditation:

O, Saviour, let Thy Spirit guide
That none but Thee be glorified.
Let every word and thought expressed
To every one that reads be blessed
(Pétursson, *Hymns of the Passion*, trans. Gook, hymn 1, st. 8)

Reflection and preaching both aim to narrow the gap between contemporary times and the times of the Gospels, to make the events come to life and seem recent, rather than far in the past. The rhetorical method of *evidentia* is used the achieve this. The objective is to combine the two worlds and times and transfigure the distance between the readers and the events. There are many examples of this in Pétursson's *Passíusálmar*. Consider, for instance, the following: "Beneath Thy cross I take my stand, / The floods of scorn ignoring." Also, when the women are gathered by Jesus's grave: "Sit thou, my soul, with them awhile / Some thoughtful moments there beguile (Pétursson, *Hymns of the Passion*, trans. Gook, hymn 38, st. 12, and hymn 49, st. 8).

In his discourse Pétursson sometimes focuses on worldly and spiritual authority. It has often been observed that he was very critical of the Icelandic authorities, although he also admonishes the public. Studies of similar poems from Sweden reveal that the emphasis there is often on Jesus' submission, whereas pride and harshness characterize the deputies of spiritual and worldly power. Thus, passion poems generally can be directed pointedly at injustice in contemporary society.

As early as the eighteenth century Hallgrímur Pétursson was being referred to as a national poet of Iceland; in the opinion of many he remains the greatest Icelandic religious poet. The *Passíusálmar* has been reprinted many times and translated into a number of languages. His hymns have been sung during Lent for centuries. As this tradition was about to die because of radical social changes in the twentieth century, the advent of radio came to the rescue. Today, famous individuals and recognized performers read the poems on the air during Lent.

Religious Poetry

The amount of religious poetry that has survived from the seventeenth century is vast since that poetry played an important role in society. To perform or sing morning and evening hymns was a part of daily life: there were hymns related to daily chores, traveling, fishing, celebrations, and the seasons (New Year hymns, e.g., and hymns for the arrival of spring). Then there were hymns composed to suit specific situations, for example, when people faced troubles and sorrow. Hymns also had educational value, especially in teaching people about the contents of the Bible and religious doctrine. In Iceland, it was common to recite biblical stories in verse; that way, people enjoyed the stories more and remembered them more easily.

While Hallgrímur Pétursson was the most prolific hymnist in the seventeenth century, all prominent poets of the period wrote hymns. These include Stefán Ólafsson, who also translated hymns by the famous baroque Danish poet Thomas Kingo (1634–1703) and Sigurður Jónsson of Presthólar (d. 1661), a respected Icelandic poet. Ólafsson transformed the *Meditationes sacrae* (Religious reflections) of the German theologian Johann Gerhard (1582–1637; see also below) into hymns, first printed in 1652, which enjoyed huge popularity. Jónsson also composed a hymn cycle called *Dagleg iðkun guðrækninnar* (The daily practice of devotion) based on another of Gerhard's books, the *Exercitium pietatis quotidianum quadripartitum*. There is also preserved a peculiar religious poem by a woman who in the sources is called Sigga skálda. Her real name is thought to be Sigríður Jónsdóttir (d. 1707). It is said that she was a pauper for a while and at other times a vagrant. She is believed to have composed a religious poem called "Geðfró" (A comfort to the mind) consisting of seventy-three verses spoken by a woman.

PROSE DURING THE AGE OF LEARNING

Memoirs from the Seventeenth Century

As was mentioned previously, North African pirates attacked the Vestmannaeyjar in the summer of 1627 and abducted three hundred people, whom they sold as slaves in Africa. This event sparked a large literature about the outrage among Icelanders, and many of the poems and stories about the so-called Turkish Raid are preserved. Some poems gave a narrative account of the event, while others expressed sorrow or denigrated the "Turks" (by which was meant Muslims generally). There were also attempts to use the magic power of poetry to prevent further raids; stories were told of eighteen (or, in another case, thirty) "Turkish" ships being sunk by the power of poetry.

In 1643 Björn Jónsson of Skarðsá wrote a history of the events called *Tyrkjaránssaga* (History of the Turkish Raid) based partly on the *Reisubók* (Travel book) of the Reverend Ólafur Egilsson (1564–1639) of the Vestmannaeyjar, where Egilsson was a colleague of the hymnist Jón Þorsteinsson (see earlier). The reverend, his wife, and their two children were among the hostages—a third child was born during the passage. He returned to Iceland a year later, after a long journey from Africa to Denmark traveling via Italy and then from France to Holland by sea. He was released so quickly because his age and status suggested to his captors that he might be able to raise the appropriate ransom money. Because of his high expenditure on recent wars, however, the Danish king felt unable to help. Ólafur Egilsson's wife was not freed from slavery until 1637, when, finally, enough money had been raised to free a large proportion of the surviving prisoners who wished to return to Iceland. Egilsson's three children never returned. A large number of the prisoners had died shortly after their arrival in Africa; others elected to stay and adopted the culture and religion of the natives. This hostage taking was not unprecedented during the era. In the seventeenth century North African pirates were brash and daring and a real threat in the Atlantic. It is estimated that there were twenty-five thousand Christian slaves in Algeria in 1640, three thousand of them from the British Isles.

The *Reisubók* was written when the author had just come home after a long and difficult journey, at the end of which he had endured the tremendous disappointment of being denied ransom money for his family and the other prisoners. These extraordinary events were fresh in his mind. His account is remarkable because Ólafur Egilsson was keenly perceptive during his foreign sojourn and described in detail the appearance, clothing, food, and occupations of the people in the countries he had visited. At the same time his narrative provides a remarkable insight into his own personality and outlook on life. His is a story of suffering, one in which he compares himself to the anguished Job in the Old Testament. The Danish princess Leonora Christina used the same metaphor in a systematic way in her memoirs about her imprisonment in the notorious Blue Tower in 1663 (*Jammers Minde* [Memory of woe]; the manuscript was discovered and published in 1869). A certain conflict between the course of events and the authors' desired framework for their stories is shared by the two works. In both the Bible acts as a subtext, reflecting both personae and events, and putting the two stories in a much larger context, one of history and salvation. The central role of the Bible and its interpretation in European literature at this time explains why such different individuals as Ólafur Egilsson of the Vestmannaeyjar and Princess Leonora Christina would both choose the anguished Job as a parallel in their memoirs.

The story of the *Reisubók* covers only one year in Ólafur Egilsson's life and might, thus, be called an autobiographical fragment. Although the author focuses on his readers and addresses their curiosity about foreign lands, there is at the same time clearly an inner need for him to work through his catastrophic experiences. His main emphasis is that everything is God's will, which man must accept. Egilsson's religious conviction and attitude toward life allow him to accept his fate with stoicism and without bitterness. More remarkable, perhaps, is the fact that he preserves his balance in the narrative and in his description of the hated "Turks." Admittedly, he calls them thugs and miscreants, but he also records that they were good with their children and treated the prisoners well (with the exception of Egilsson himself, who alone was beaten at the time of the raid). The *Reisubók* is available in numerous copies, but the original manuscript is lost. The work has been published twice in Danish, first in 1741, and several times in Icelandic.

The Adventures of Jón Ólafsson Indíafari (India-traveler)

Another well-traveled seventeenth-century Icelander who published an autobiographical account was Jón Ólafsson (1593–1679), whose nickname India-traveler derives from the fact that he traveled as far as India. His autobiography, entitled *Reisubók Jóns Ólafssonar Indíafara* (The life of Jón Ólafsson, traveler to India; English trans.: Ólafsson, *The Life of the Icelander Jón Ólafsson, Traveller to India* [1923–32]), was written around 1660. The first section is mostly about the author's career in the navy of King Christian IV and sailing in Nordic seas. The second section deals with his trip to India, where Denmark had recently established a colony. The final section of the book was written after his death by his son and describes Ólafsson's life after he had stopped traveling and settled in Iceland.

The autobiography is as entertaining to read as it is important as source material. It contains, for instance, a priceless description of Copenhagen in the 1620s and of the dealings of the Nordic people in India at the time. To aid the reader, the author included material from the Danish geography book *Compendium cosmographiæ* by Hans Nansen. Jón Ólafsson's report is illuminated by his sheer joy of storytelling and his acute perceptions. The style is colorful and variegated, with original imagery. Ólafsson describes himself as a brave and successful adventurer who has had extraordinary experiences and who has learned many things that his readers might never have seen or heard about before. Since the account was written after Ólafsson's return to Iceland, the events are observed from a certain distance. The autobiography has always remained popular. It is preserved in many manuscripts, has been published in both Danish and English, and in 1992 was published in a new Icelandic edition.

Witch Fires and Paranoia

Píslarsaga Jóns Magnússonar (The martyrdom of Jón Magnússon) constitutes a defense against an indictment in criminal court of the author, the Reverend Jón Magnússon (ca. 1610–96). The whole episode began when the pastor fell ill in 1655. He assumed that a father and son, who were members of his congregation, were purposely causing his sickness by sorcery, and he prosecuted them publicly. A year later they were burned for witchcraft. Despite this, the sickness did not subside, so Magnússon turned the accusations against the daughter/sister of the burned men. She managed to clear herself, then turned the tables and prosecuted the pastor for causing her great damage and for unbecoming conduct. It was at this time (1658–59) that Jón Magnússon wrote his martyrdom to justify himself before public opinion.

The story was written during the time when a fear of witchcraft and the power of the devil prevailed, and it was, of course, colored by this. It is obvious, however, that the author was mentally disturbed, and this needs to be borne in mind when reading the work. The book should not be taken as documentation of the general attitude and mentality of the period. The author clearly had oratorical training as he uses several classical rhetorical devices and arguments. The narrative is highly subjective and the style florid. The imagery is flamboyant, often far-fetched, and, in some ways, typically baroque. Jón Magnússon's work is preserved in only one manuscript, which was forgotten for a long time. It was published for the first time in Copenhagen in 1912–14 and has been published three times since, most recently in 2001 in Matthías Viðar Sæmundsson's edition.

Ólafur Egilsson's *Reisubók*, Jón India-traveler's *Reisubók*, and the *Píslarsaga* of Jón Magnússon are all historical narratives. However, unlike, for instance, the report on the Spanish killings by Jón Guðmundsson the Learned, which is fairly objective, these works describe, not merely events and circumstances, but also the authors' own feelings and what they themselves experienced. The style therefore becomes more personal and subjective than had been the case in previous narratives. All these works can, therefore, be considered, at least in part, autobiography. The authors were all gifted orators, although they used this skill in very different ways.

Oratory and the Baroque

Sermon books for devotional reading in the home (*húslestrabækur*) and postils (commentaries on Scripture) were aimed at educating people in the basics of the Lutheran faith. From the time of the Reformation translated postils were common in Iceland; the theological works (*hugvekjur*; lit. "thought provokers") by the German Johann Gerhard, for instance, enjoyed popularity. Later, Icelanders began to write their own postils. Without doubt the postil collection known as *Vídalínspostilla* was the most important and most accomplished of these works in Iceland at the time. It was first printed at Hólar between 1718 and 1720 and was the central text in the home through the entire eighteenth century and beyond. The author was Jón Þorkelsson Vídalín, the bishop of Skálholt, both a preacher and a scholar (see also above). Vídalín studied theology at the University of Copenhagen, then returned and assumed the duties of teacher and parson at the Skálholt church. At the time cultural life in Skálholt was vibrant: disputations were held on various occasions, and poems were written in Latin.

Vídalín's postil was intended for use by the general public, but Vídalín himself was a highly educated man. Not only was he well versed in the art of oratory, but he had also studied English preachers and learned much from them. He introduced new ideas gleaned from his reading into Icelandic preaching. His two most important sources were the *Harmonia evangelica* by the German theologians Martin Chemnitz, Polykarp Leyser, and Johann Gerhard and *The Practice of Christian Graces, or the Whole Duty of Man* by Richard Allestree (1619–81), which Vídalín translated from the Danish into Icelandic. The innovation here was in adapting the gospel of the day to fit peoples' daily lives and, thus, to direct them in their daily behavior. The style is florid and powerful. Vídalín avoids using the same word twice but, rather, finds a variety of synonyms, thus creating a vast vocabulary. In addition he employs various devices, like antitheses and parallels, and revitalizes many old proverbs. In contrast to that in much writing of the time, Vídalín's diction is clear and purely Icelandic, devoid of foreign influence.

Jón Vídalín's near contemporary Þorleifur Halldórsson (ca. 1683–1713) composed the satire *Lof lyginnar* (In praise of lies). The work was originally written in Latin under the title *Mendacii encomium*, and the author himself translated it into Icelandic in 1711. Its prototype, of course, is Erasmus of Rotterdam's *Moriae encomium* (In praise of folly). Þorleifur Halldórsson was an erudite man who wrote most of his poems in Latin. His style is florid and employs classical rhetorical devices prominently. Both *Lof lyginnar* and the *Vídalínspostilla* are fine examples of the high-flown baroque style in Icelandic literature.

Jón Ólafsson of Grunnavík and Páll Vídalín

Jón Ólafsson of Grunnavík (1705–79) worked as amanuensis for Árni Magnússon for a couple of years and lived in Copenhagen for most of his life. His writings are extensive and varied. Ólafsson was a true polymath, writing about most of the subjects of intellectual interest of his time. He translated (as *Nikulás Klím*) the novel *Niels Klims Reise under Jorden* (The journey of Niels Klim to the underground), sometimes known as *Nicolai Klimii iter subterraneum*, by Ludvig Holberg in 1745, only four years after its original publication. The new ideas about society in the Enlightenment era made their appearance in literature in the form of stories about imagined cultures in distant lands, cultures that were both very different from and morally superior to those with which readers were familiar. These stories often took the form of imaginary journeys. In the seventeenth and eighteenth centuries many utopian traveler's tales were influenced by Thomas More's *Utopia* (1516), the most famous of them undoubtedly *Gulliver's Travels* (1726) by Jonathan Swift. *Niels Klim* belongs to this genre as well but at the same time parodies it. Holberg's aim was to make fun of all these exaggerated stories of faraway places and at the same time to satirize his own society, criticizing its superficiality, ostentation, formality, and fanatical pietism. *Niels Klim* was popular in Iceland and influenced Eiríkur Laxdal when he composed his *Saga Ólafs Þórhallasonar* (see below).

Jón Ólafsson's book *Hagþenkir* (Practical thoughts) concerns upbringing and education and contains guidelines to what is most useful for each individual to know in relation to his position in society. Ólafsson also collected and transcribed occasional poems by Páll Vídalín (1667–1727). Páll Vídalín was, along with Árni Magnússon, sent to Iceland to conduct a census and make a list of landowners in Iceland. He and Magnússon traveled around the country during the years 1702–12. Their *Jarðabók* (Estate book), along with the census, is a unique document for its time and one of the most important sources for Icelandic economic and cultural history.

Páll Vídalín was initially the rector at Skálholt but then moved on to become a magistrate and lawman. He was highly educated and wrote prose and verse in Latin. His books cover issues of country and people, law, the

Icelandic language, and Icelandic literature. His *Deo, regi, patriae* concerns Iceland's economy and its regeneration. His *Skýringar yfir fornyrði lögbókar* (Explanations of the ancient words in the law book [the so-called *Jónsbók*]) demonstrates his wide knowledge of old Icelandic law and literature. He also composed lists of poets and writers collectively called *Recensus poetarum et scriptorum Islandorum*, a work that was not printed until 1985. Of his poetry the occasional poems are the most significant; Vídalín is by far the most brilliant versifier of the Age of Learning. He is both witty and funny, and he has the ability to describe an occurrence so that it comes to life and leaves an impression. His material is extremely varied, including entertainment poems, love poems, scolding and mocking poems, and maxims.

POPULAR LITERATURE

Entertainment: Romances in Verse and Prose
Romances, usually based on extant material, constituted the most popular literary genre in Iceland from the late Middle Ages until the early twentieth century, both in prose form (the Legendary and Knights' Sagas, adventure and folktales, translated chapbook material) and in verse (in the form of the *rímur*). Since only religious material was printed in Iceland until the church lost its printing monopoly in 1773, this literature circulated orally and in manuscript. The Icelandic public was no exception in its predilection for romance: on the European continent publishers were enjoying a roaring trade in chapbooks featuring tales based on medieval chivalric romances. Where Iceland was unique, however, was in the continuing popularity of its own, native form of the metrical romance. The *rímur* are uniquely Icelandic, remaining unchanged in form and structure for centuries, and were "far and away the most important secular poetic genre of post-classical Iceland" (Driscoll, 10). They were widely enjoyed, and they were composed by poets from all levels of society, unschooled as well as learned, including such widely acclaimed ones as Hallgrímur Pétursson, Guðmundur Bergþórsson, and Sigurður Breiðfjörð (1798–1846), although this would change in the course of the eighteenth century. While the subject matter was most commonly a romance, a few *rímur* were also based on the Sagas of Icelanders and on stories from the Bible.

Although single *rímur* exist, the majority consisted of extended cycles, called *rímnaflokkar*. Often these cycles were so long that their recital lasted many evenings in a row and they became serials of sorts, to be continued the next evening. While *rímur* cycles were composed from full-length stories, single ones had a slighter content, often comedy or satire. An example is the *Fjósaríma* (Cowshed *ríma*) by Þórður Magnússon of Strjúgur, who lived in the sixteenth century. It tells the tale of a creditor and his debtor who meet up in a cowshed and fight there. They are compared mockingly to ancient warriors who fought many a battle, but never in a cowshed!

It had long been assumed that *rímur* were composed solely by men, but it has recently come to light that the *Landrésrímur* (*Rímur* of Landrés) from the fifteenth century must have been composed by a woman. These *rímur* concern Queen Ólíf, who is wrongly accused of being unfaithful to her husband. She is bricked up inside a stone building and kept there for years until she is freed by her son, Landrés. Two *rímur* by Steinunn Finnsdóttir of Höfn (1641–1710) are also extant. She is the first woman known by name in Icelandic literary history, and many of her poems have been preserved. She composed *Hyndlurímur* (*Rímur* of Hyndla) and *Snækóngsrímur* (*Rímur* of the Snow King), the material of which comes from adventure tales and poetry based on folktales (see below).

The *rímur* were among the most favored choices during the *kvöldvaka*, when people on farms gathered together in the main room during the winter months to perform indoor tasks, primarily working wool, after dusk had set in (and also in fishing stations during spring fishing). Stories and *rímur* provided entertainment to keep people awake and alert. It was common for the head of the household to borrow sufficient material to last the winter. A chosen reader would read out, and it seems that the listeners played an active role during the reading, making comments, and asking questions. *Rímur* were not read but recited or chanted, with each of the *rímur* meters having a melody appropriate to it (see Hughes, "Report on *Rímur* 1980"). Itinerant "chanters" (*kvæðamenn*) and storytellers made a living traveling across the counties and offering their services at farms. They were by all accounts always very welcome guests (see Driscoll, 38–45).

Other Popular Poetry

Popular foreign tales also found their way into a simpler kind of poetry known as *ævintýrakvæði* (adventure poems). These poems are generally much shorter than the *rímur*, they lack their complex language and imagery, and the meters are simpler and more supple. The subject matter is derived from foreign parables, fabliaux, and adventure tales. An example is "Barbírskvæði" (Infidel poem), which is preserved in a manuscript from the sixteenth century. The story was known in many European countries, occurring, for instance, in French fabliaux and also in the English poem known as "A Mery Iest of Dane Hew Munk of Leicestre." While it is not known what model the Icelandic poem is based on, the fact that the action largely takes place in England would indicate links with the English version. It is the account of a monk who fancies the wife of an infidel and is killed by him. To avoid suspicion the infidel then disguises the body in such a way as to make it seem alive and up to no good, thieving and generally being in the way. Someone else then "kills" the body and tries the same trick, and so the story goes on, with the body being "killed" over and over again. Another example is "Vinaspegill" (Mirror of friendship), based on a chapter from *Sjö meistara saga* (Story of the seven masters), a widely known and popular medieval tale based on the Persian Sinbad stories.

Another, similar type of popular poetry, the so-called *sagnakvæði*, was based in folktales. First collected and recorded in the seventeenth century, these poems had almost certainly been preserved through oral transmission, and the oldest ones probably date from a period before the Reformation. Their form is remarkable in that they are composed in *fornyrðislag*, one of the Eddic meters. The authors of these poems are not mentioned by name. One of the most famous examples is "Kötludraumur" (Katla's dream), concerning a married woman who has a baby with an elfin man (*huldumaður*) and how she finds a solution for her predicament of having a child out of wedlock.

Icelandic carols are characterized by their specific form, consisting of a refrain, with strict rhyme patterns, joined to each stanza. In some cases the refrain is very old and a story has been composed around it. Usually, carols begin with an introductory verse, and the refrain is one of the lines of that introductory verse. It is possible to add new refrains and intertwine them into the poem in a variety of ways. The subject matter can vary: there are both religious and secular, lyric and epic carols. Well-known poets like Bjarni Gissurarson used the carol meter, but most carols have been preserved anonymously. The Icelandic name for carols, *vikivakakvæði*, is derived from a particular dance step, the *vikivaki*, but its exact meaning is uncertain and has been the subject of much speculation.

SUMMARY

The seventeenth century is a lively period in Icelandic literary history. Religious poetry was blooming, and concomitant personal expression and lyricism became more common in Icelandic poetry from then on. We see the beginnings of a style of prose writing that includes the author himself and his experiences. Classical rhetoric undoubtedly had more influence on Icelandic literature than was believed until recently, its influences evident in one of the monuments of the period, the *Vídalínspostilla*, as well as in the various occasional poems. While learned poetry dominated the official canon, *rímur* and other romance material, both native and foreign, also enjoyed great popularity, as did other types of popular poetry, all of which was preserved either in manuscripts or by word-of-mouth.

In the first part of the eighteenth century, on the other hand, not much new happened in Icelandic literature. By the middle of the eighteenth century, however, it is obvious that a new era had arrived.

THE ENLIGHTENMENT IN ICELANDIC LITERATURE: 1750–1830

The Age of Enlightenment is generally associated with the spirit of classicism, rationalism, and empiricism unsettling the old verities of theology and with the ideals of economic liberalism, progress, and reform to be achieved through education. Like other cultural innovations, Enlightenment ideas arrived in Iceland with Icelandic scholars who had studied in Denmark. The Enlightenment in Denmark was, in turn, strongly influenced by that in Germany, where much emphasis was placed on progress, usefulness, and ethics. The German-Danish Enlightenment was more conservative than the French Enlightenment, which was characterized by mockery and satire directed at the regime and establishment culture. Among the most prominent Scandinavian authors of the period were the Norwegians Ludvig Holberg (1684–1754) and Johan Herman Wessel (1742–85). The work of the English poet Alexander Pope (1688–1744) was particularly influential in Northern Europe during this time, both his didactic poetry (e.g., the *Essay on Man*) and his topographical poetry (e.g., "Windsor Forest") serving as models.

While these foreign influences reached Iceland, certain premises were missing there for the seeds of the Enlightenment to take firm root. The bourgeois novel, for example, did not get under way in Iceland until much later. While in much of eighteenth-century Europe an emergent bourgeois class offered a ready market for novels, no such market was to be found in the largely static Icelandic farming society. Still, a few novels were written, although none ever saw print. The romance, on the other hand, continued to lead a healthy life in Iceland in the eighteenth and nineteenth centuries; many romances were transcribed and the manuscripts passed on from one farm to another. The great number of surviving manuscripts shows that the art of storytelling was blooming in the country. Recent research indicates that romances and folktales had a tremendous effect on the evolution of the novel in Iceland. It was not until a press was established in Hrappsey in 1773 that Icelanders began printing secular material.

With the establishment of the Hrappsey press, the printing monopoly at Hólar was finally at an end. The initiative came from a young Icelander who had studied in Copenhagen, Ólafur Ólafsson (1741–88), who called himself by the Latin name Olavius. During these years there were fresh winds of change in Europe, and new ideas were emerging. A press was starting to develop where issues and events were hotly debated in popular form, and censorship was abolished in Denmark in 1770, although this freedom lasted for only three years. And, while it cannot be claimed that the freedom of the press had a direct influence on Icelandic book publishing per se, it is certain that Olavius had been touched by these developments. He obtained permission to establish a press, on the condition that the press at Hólar had a prerogative in publishing religious books. This was a hard condition, for Christian material was the best-selling. The press at Hrappsey closed in 1794 and eventually merged with the Hólar press after it was moved to Leirárgarðar in 1799.

Although several secular texts were printed in Iceland in the late eighteenth century, including *rímur*, agricultural manuals, law books, and textbooks for the public, it was considered unnecessary to publish romances or other entertainment material, which in the view of the authorities was undesirable, even dangerous; such works were considered to promote superstition and bad taste. In accordance with the cultural climate of the day, the educated classes had come to regard the edification of the people and the improvement of literary taste as their duty, and it was during this time that a significant gap developed in Iceland between high and low literature.

The Enlightenment era was one of optimism and reform, and in this respect not even Iceland remained unaffected. Despite the inertia and conservatism of the agrarian Icelandic society at the time, it can be said that modernity in Iceland had its roots in the eighteenth century. Along with Enlightenment ideas came a progressive frame of mind and the spirit of change, which marked a sea change in Iceland thinking, even if the influence on Icelandic poetry was minimal. The effects can be seen in the establishment of the Lærdómslistafélag (the Society for the Art of Learning), which was established by twelve Icelandic students in Copenhagen in 1779 and published the first ever magazine written in Icelandic, *Rit þess konunglega íslenska lærdómslistafélags* (Journal of the Royal Icelandic Society for the Art of Learning). The magazine ran during the years 1781–98; its aim was to share pragmatic knowledge with the public and expand cultural consciousness, for example, by translating contemporary foreign literature.

Opinions have long differed as to the point at which the Age of Learning ended and the Age of Enlightenment began. Sometimes the early 1770s (the years that saw the establishment of the press at Hrappsey) have been seen as marking this transition, but it has also been convincingly argued that the Enlightenment actually reached Iceland shortly before 1750. Ludvig Harboe's mission to Iceland in 1741–46 certainly had a profound effect. Harboe was a pastor and, later, a bishop in the Danish Lutheran Church, but his ideas were closely related to the Danish fundamentalist movement known as pietism, to which King Christian VII (1730–46) adhered. Pietists sought to bring individual devotion to God back into religious life, rejecting the cold bureaucracy that Lutheranism had, they felt, become. They sought to achieve this particularly through education. Harboe was sent to investigate the state of church and school matters in Iceland and make suggestions for improvement. His mission caused great turmoil among the Icelandic pastors as everything was subject to review. Harboe gathered a vast number of documents and issued many decrees, which later became law in Iceland. It is safe to say that many of Harboe's changes were for the good, for instance, the requirement that everyone learn to read: while literacy was at the time fairly widespread in Iceland, many — especially women and the poor — were still illiterate. On the other hand, Harboe was, like the church hierarchy, of the opinion that people should read only religious literature. Under his influence, the production and consumption of all forms of secular literature became a crime, and the battle waged by the authorities against popular storytelling reached its peak.

Such restrictions seem particularly harsh in view of the ravages of nature from which Icelanders suffered during the eighteenth century. These were some of the most difficult times in the entire history of Iceland. The bad harvests and famine with which Iceland entered the new century were followed by a smallpox epidemic in 1707 that killed over 25 percent of the population, bringing it down to the all-time low of thirty-seven thousand. Weather conditions continued to get worse, resulting in several more years of famine. To top it all off, some of the worse volcanic eruptions in Icelandic history occurred at midcentury, starting with the Katla eruption in 1755, and culminating in the Skaftá eruption of 1783–84, which produced unprecedented lava flows and poisonous ash, killing both livestock and people. Yet another famine followed the Skaftá eruption — the so-called Famine of the Mist (see below) — and many more died as a result. The year 1784 also saw a number of earthquakes, and, during the following two years, another epidemic hit Iceland.

It is hardly surprising, then, that those who had come in contact with the ideals of reform and progress became interested in ways to implement such change in order to improve the situation in Iceland. Foremost among such pioneers was the enterprising Skúli Magnússon (1711–94), who, in the 1750s, succeeded in obtaining enough funding to build a water mill and establish a series of small factory workshops at Reykjavík, the goal being to set up a local industry along modern lines that would regenerate Icelandic agriculture, fishing, and wool processing. It was called the *Innréttingar* (New Enterprises). The effort turned out a complete failure, however, although it did prove to be the beginning of an urban nucleus that was to become the country's capital.

One consequence of the natural disasters in the eighteenth century was the bankruptcy of the bishopric of Skálholt, as a result of which the bishop's residence and the school were moved to Reykjavík. When the bishopric at Hólar was abolished a few years later, in 1801, the two cathedral schools merged to become the Latin school in Reykjavík, although it was operated at Bessastaðir during the period 1805–46.

When in 1786 the Iceland trade was opened to all Danish citizens, more than one trader was allowed to set up shop in a district, and, by the end of the century, there were several trading posts to serve the three hundred people living in Reykjavík. With the abolition in 1800 of the Althing as the national court of appeal, the only function left to it by that time, the new High Court (Landsyfirréttur) was established in Reykjavík by royal decree. Gradually, Reykjavík was beginning to replace Bessastaðir as the country's administrative center.

Other leaders of the Enlightenment in Iceland include Bishop Hannes Finnsson of Skálholt (1739–96) and Magnús Stephensen (1762–1833), a lawman with great ambitions to effect progress and introduce reforms in Iceland, largely through improved education. Stephensen was in charge of the old Hrappsey printing press, now at Leirárgarðar, for nearly forty years, which he used rather conspicuously to publish his own works. Not everyone shared his vision, many found him dogmatic, and his writings have not enjoyed great popularity or esteem.

A New Attitude toward Nature
Eggert Ólafsson (1726–68) was the most able innovator of the Enlightenment era in Iceland. He and Bjarni Pálsson, a fellow student, began their research on Icelandic nature around the middle of the eighteenth century. In the years 1752–57 they traveled all around Iceland, gathering information concerning natural phenomena, resources, geology, and the culture of the people. The comrades climbed Hekla, which was considered quite a daring act in those days. This trip was important because it was a sign

of a new attitude toward the natural landscape. Ólafsson and Pálsson supported the modern view that natural phenomena have natural causes, not religious or metaphysical ones, that is, that nature was not controlled by supernatural powers. Phenomena such as volcanic eruptions, for example, had a natural explanation and were not signs of the wrath of God. Ólafsson and Pálsson's findings were published in 1772 in the *Reise igiennem Island* (known in Icelandic translation as *Ferðabók*; English trans: *Travels in Iceland* [1805]).

A New Attitude toward Icelandic Culture

The infrastructure necessary to support a flourishing publishing enterprise or novel writing was still lacking in eighteenth-century Iceland, although a vigorous literary tradition lived on. Sagas were copied and circulated among the people. They were read out loud during the *kvöldvaka*, as Eggert Ólafsson and Bjarni Pálsson described in detail in their *Ferðabók*. Ólafsson and Pálsson also described the *rímur* that were chanted during the evening's entertainment. This popular literary activity was frowned on, not only by the church, but also by advocates of the Enlightenment. Both Magnús Stephensen and Hannes Finnsson reckoned that the nation had a duty to seek something more constructive and useful than *lygisögur* (tall tales; lit. "lying sagas"), a term used for the Knights' Sagas and the Legendary Sagas (see pp. 139–51) and the *rímur* based on them (see also Driscoll).

Many found Magnús Stephensen overly doctrinaire in his literary taste. He disliked Old Icelandic literature, at least some of it, which was unusual in Iceland, even in his day. Bishop Hannes Finnsson agreed with many of Stephensen's views on *lygisögur* and *rímur*, which he thought exacerbated stupidity and stood in the way of progress. Finnsson's and Stephensen's views are in many ways typical of the studious Enlightenment man who wanted the public to practice only what was wholesome and decent. The dominant preference was for an edifying literature of clarity and taste, one adhering to the rules of French classicism, accompanied by a profound disapproval of literature where the imagination had free reign, that of the exaggerated and fantastic. Stephensen also disliked *rímur* chanting, but his reasons were aesthetic: he was educated in music and considered the chanting in bad musical taste.

Many men of the Icelandic Enlightenment, like Eggert Ólafsson, saw Old Icelandic literature as an inspiration and a model, however. Ólafsson in fact consciously tried to make his language look ancient, an attempt to emphasize that Old Icelandic was alive and understandable in the eighteenth century.

The Past as a Model

Because of his use of examples from classical poetry (Greek, Roman, and Old Icelandic) a large part of Eggert Ólafsson's poetry is elusive and inaccessible to us today, although he helpfully explains many of his kennings in footnotes. In the introduction to his poetry collection Ólafsson frequently quotes Roman poets and says that he is "doing it their way." Interestingly, at the same time he names medieval Icelandic authors, like Snorri Sturluson and Ólafur Þórðarson (see pp. 29 and 71) and believes that there is much to be learned from them as well. He was evidently highly impressed by skaldic poetry and was very familiar with the poetics of the *Prose Edda* (see pp. 151–58). This is apparent in his poems, many of which use the meter, language, and rhyme of skaldic verse. Eggert Ólafsson was brought up on classicism and the conviction that classical poetry should be the model for every poet. At the same time he idealized Nordic mythology and looked for its relations to Greek mythology. Thus, he often uses Lofn, a Nordic goddess, as a parallel to Venus is his poems.

A Poetry That Instructs, Admonishes, and Edifies

Eggert Ólafsson's poem "Búnaðarbálkur" (Poem on farming) had the aim of educating and enlightening Icelanders about how to use the land and conduct farming in Iceland in a more profitable manner. The poem is both critical and didactic, with the main emphasis on the practical. And, in accordance with contemporary poetic practice, nature is used as an example from which humanity can learn. The cohabitation of married couples, for example, is seen from a pragmatic point of view: they bear fruit just like the land. Furthermore, it is a benefit to the country for a couple to have as many children as possible; indeed, it is a couple's duty, to the fatherland and to God, to conceive children and bring them up. Ólafsson also puts great emphasis on educating his countrymen on the usefulness of and opportunities for growing various grasses and potherbs. "Búnaðarbálkur" is divided into three parts: "Eymdaróður" (Poem on wretchedness) and "Náttúrulist" (Natural art), which comprise sixty verses together, and "Munaðardæla" (Luxury), which comprises one hundred. Eggert Ólafsson is clearly well versed in botany and gives much advice to his fellow countrymen, explaining the healing power of many herbs in a thorough manner. In some places it is undeniable that the didactic value comes before poetic considerations, but that doesn't really matter, for the message of the poet and his power of conviction carry the reader along.

"Búnaðarbálkur" is a legitimate offspring of the Enlightenment and one of the most important poems composed in Iceland during that period. Its kinship with classicism is evident. First, the presentation is lucid and to the point; it employs few Old Icelandic words and no recondite kennings and is distinct from Ólafsson's other poems in that respect. Second, it is clear that Ólafsson knew his Virgil (as well as many other Roman poets) and admired his bucolic poems as well as his rural idylls. In one place Ólafsson refers to the Greek and Roman cultivation of vegetables and wants Icelanders to learn from that. Eggert Ólafsson was the only poet of the Enlightenment to praise the quality of the land in Iceland, and Icelanders in the eighteenth century certainly had need of the encouragement at that particular time in Icelandic history.

Eggert Ólafsson's criticism is expressed in a mild way. He creates oppositions in his work, drawing a picture in "Eymdaróður" of a couple who are ignorant of proper farming methods. The perfect couple in "Munaðardæla," on the other hand, does everything properly and is exemplary in every way. In the introduction to his collection the poet says that poetry should be "a happy mix of the instantly useful and tasteful" (*Íslensk kvæðabók*, 7). Ólafsson here is quoting the Englishman William Temple (1628–99) but makes the words his own.

Criticism is a prominent feature of the poem "Ísland" (Iceland), in which satire on the world is widespread and more general. The female narrator tells the story of her life from a time before settlement to Ólafsson's time in the mid-eighteenth century. The poem is, in fact, an allegory, tracing the history of Iceland in a symbolic way. Before settlement the woman sat "dressed in gold and finery," awaiting suitors, until she was married to a prominent settler. The story is traced, recapturing every century and the reasons for decline, especially in the seventeenth century. The last four sections cover modern times, that is, the eighteenth century. The comparison to the splendid ancient era is very much to the disadvantage of modern times. The poet criticizes many characteristics of his own day, like poor management, dishonesty, lack of manners, and uneconomical trade with foreign countries.

Despite this, Eggert Ólafsson sometimes also praises Iceland in his poems. "Íslandssæla" (Iceland the blessed) is written in the same spirit as "Búnaðarbálkur," and the productivity of the land and the sea, the profusion of wholesome food, is celebrated. The subtitle leaves no doubt about the message of the poem: "how much better and healthier it is for Icelanders — most of them — to stay in their country, rather than go abroad." Many of the verses describe the idyllic qualities of Icelandic nature in the manner of pastoral poetry. The poem bears witness to the author's nationalism. Ólafsson believed in Icelandic agriculture and created beautiful images of life in the countryside. The Lærdómslistafélag later picked up his views on protecting the language, after which the Danish grammarian Rasmus Rask (1787–1834) made his famous comment that Icelandic would become extinct if nothing were done (see also p. 256). In the poem "Sótt og dauði íslenskunnar" (The illness and death of the Icelandic language) Ólafsson makes a metaphor out of a woman on her deathbed. She does not get enough healthy nourishment, being purely Icelandic, and, therefore, she has a stomachache. Finally, the Icelandic woman dies, and her sons stand over her body in the end while the poet contemplates and evaluates the damage that has been done.

Gunnar Pálsson (1714–91), pastor in Hjarðarholt in western Iceland, was of the same opinion. He was a distinguished poet and a great scholar of his time. He considers the Icelandic language invaluable and wants to preserve it at all cost. In the poem "Lítið ávarp til þess sem tjáist að fjörráð vilji brugga íslenskunni" (A little address to the one who says he wants to plot the decline of Icelandic) he points to the value of Icelandic, not only in itself, but also as a key to all the ancient literature of the Nordic countries.

Poetry Translations

The Age of Enlightenment saw an awakening interest in the translation of poems by foreign authors into Icelandic. The first attempt was made at the new press at Hrappsey. Olavius brought with him from Denmark poetry by the hugely popular Norwegian poet Christan Br. Tullin (1728–65), famous for his pastoral poems. He got the young and promising poet Jón Þorláksson of Bægisá (1744–1819) to translate some of them, and the result was published in 1774, along with four of Þorláksson's own poems, under the title *Nokkur, þess alþekkta danska skálds sáluga herra Christ. Br. Tullins kvæði með litlum viðbætir annars efnis á ísl. snúin af Jóni Þorlákssyni* (A few poems by the renowned poet, the late Mr. Chr. Br. Tullin, with a short appendix on a different subject, translated by Jón Þorláksson). This grand title belies the actual size of the book, which contained only ten poems, but it enjoyed great success and appears to have sold out. It was a novelty in Iceland for a young poet to see his poems in print. In 1783 a book with yet more translated poetry and original poems, thirty-two in all, was published by Jón Þorláksson. It is obvious that Þorláksson's reputation as a poet was boosted by this publication: the front page describes him as "the honourable and talented poet." Of his translations it can be said that precision and a remarkable range of vocabulary characterized most of them. All the same, some of them are clearly translations, for they are unaccommodating and, viewed through the eyes of nineteenth- and twentieth-century linguistic purism, contain quite a few Danishisms. These two attempts at translation spurred Jón Þorláksson on to subsequent endeavors. They were also good practice for his future encounters with larger and more extensive works.

During his years of study in Copenhagen (1786–91), Benedikt Gröndal Sr. translated "The Temple of Fame" (1711) by Alexander Pope, one of the most renowned poets of the European Enlightenment. His translation, "Musteri mannorðsins," which comprised a total of 190 verses using the Eddic *fornyrðislag* meter, was published in the yearbook of the Lærdóms-listafélag in 1790. Gröndal preferred a simple presentation and wanted to move poetic language in a direction away from *rímur* and *dróttkvætt*. His translation of "The Temple of Fame" was supposedly based on a German translation, but one faithful to the original text. It has to be borne in mind that a knowledge of English was rare in Iceland at the time, and it is uncertain whether Gröndal could have read the work in the original English. Similarly, Jón Þorláksson understood little, if any, English and had probably not seen the original texts of the English works he translated.

Around the same time, or a little earlier, Jón Þorláksson obtained *Tilraun um manninn* (1798), a Danish translation of Pope's classic *Essay on Man* (1733/34), a philosophical poem in four parts concerning the position of man in the universe. Þorláksson's own Icelandic translation of the *Essay* is marred by its reliance on a bad Danish translation by C. C. Lous, one that is inaccurate, too verbose, and takes no account of the fact that the original is composed in rhymed couplets. Þorláksson's own choice of meter for his translation turned out to be significant for Icelandic literature, for he continued the use of *fornyrðislag*. It can, moreover, be assumed that Bjarni Thorarensen and Jónas Hallgrímsson were influenced by these translations as they also used the Eddic meter in their poems in a masterful way (see chapter 3).

Certainly, the choice of meter in these first Icelandic poetic translations of Pope's poetry was not ideal. Pope's form, the rhymed couplet, a novelty at the time, had the potential for powerful, gnomic expression. Gröndal chose instead an unrhymed form, and a very casual one at that, one that is not far from prose. Þorláksson, on the other hand, followed Lous's translation, which changed Pope's rhyming couplets into four-line stanzas rhyming *abab*, without, however, adopting either Lous's or Pope's form.

Shortly after 1790, Jón Þorláksson embarked on *Paradísarmissir* (1828), his translation of Milton's great epic poem *Paradise Lost*, after he received the new Danish translation by J. H. Schönheyder from an old friend, Halldór Hjálmarsson, the vice-rector in Hólar. The work must have charmed him, as he was a man of God and he adored the inspiration and muse of John Milton (1608–74). Milton uses blank verse, and the Danish translator follows in his footsteps. Þorláksson must have shrunk from that as blank verse was unknown in Iceland and did not suit Icelandic metrics, lacking both end rhyme and alliteration. Instead, he decided to follow Benedikt Gröndal's example once more and used *fornyrðislag*, which is quite a flexible meter, without rhyme, but with alliteration. There is general agreement that the meter is well suited for an epic poem like *Paradise Lost*, even if it is very different from English blank verse; the poem gets a real Icelandic flavor this way. Most agree that *Paradísarmissir* is the most important of Þorláksson's translations. There also exists a humorous poem by him, called "Hamförin" (To hell and back), composed in 1805, right after the translation of Milton. In it Þorláksson describes a scene in which Milton uses him as a horse and rides him through the worlds of heaven, chaos, and hell. After this ride the translator is lame in one foot!

Þorláksson conducted his translation activity under very difficult circumstances. He was the only major Icelandic poet of the eighteenth century who was not widely traveled, and he was also so poor that he could not always afford to buy paper. Although he did not read English, he could read German, and his translation of *Paradise Lost*, for example, changed much for the better after he received a precise German translation of the work. By then he had, in fact, already translated the first three books, of which two had been published in the yearbooks of the Lærdómslistafélag (1794 and 1796). Þorláksson allegedly revised the text of the third book of his translation before it was published in 1798; unfortunately, that copy was not distributed to members of the society as it had ceased operating.

It did not take long for Þorláksson to take on another huge task: his *Messías* (1834, 1838), a translation of *Der Messias* (1749) by the German poet Friedrich Gottlieb Klopstock (1724–1803). *Der Messias* is an enormous piece of twenty books or songs in total, about twice the size of *Paradise Lost*. Its materials are divided into two parts. The first part covers the Crucifixion; the second deals with the Resurrection. *Der Messias* is not an epic poem like *Paradise Lost*. The main emphasis is on interpreting the Crucifixion and its significance for the poet's salvation. Klopstock was a pioneer of early romanticism and the new style of German literature, characterized by sincerity and religious passion. The material can be viewed as a continuation of *Paradise Lost*, however, and perhaps this affected Þorláksson's choice in taking it on. The material suited Þorláksson temperamentally. The meter of the German poem is a variation on the classical hexameter. Þorláksson again chose to use *fornyrðislag*, which had served him so well before. Whether the result is successful is certainly debatable. At first sight, the Eddic meter, with its very short lines, does not seem to suit the lengthy sentences of the original. However, Þorláksson somehow manages to make it work by using sentences that run over many lines, thus creating a coherent narrative. The end result is that the translation is handled well, in spite of the obvious difficulties involved. At the end of the day *Paradísarmissir* has enjoyed more popularity than *Messías* in Icelandic. The intangible, impassioned lyricism of Klopstock tries the patience of the reader. Klopstock's shorter poems have been more popular.

When one considers that, when he began translating Klopstock, Þorláksson was in his seventies and his health had started to fail, his achievement is remarkable. He finished the translation in 1818, a year before he died. Both his great translations had to wait another few years before being published. It was Hið íslenska bókmenntafélag (the Icelandic Literature Society) that published *Paradísarmissir* in 1828, after an English scholar, John Heath, put up the money for the project. *Messías* was published in two parts in 1834 and 1838. Both *Paradísarmissir* and *Messías* are mentioned occasionally as having been read during the *kvöldvaka* (see Driscoll, 44).

Jón Þorláksson was a pioneer in the translation of poetry. He translated the works of twenty-nine poets, most of them from his own era, but also Latin poets like Ovid and Horace. He was a skillful poet and had a way with words, to say the least. Some of the leading families of the time proved generous to him and supplied him with books so that the nation might enjoy his poetic talent. Þorláksson did not receive any pay for his writing until just before he died, when the king of Denmark granted him an annual stipend of forty rigsdalers. Þorláksson is thought to have been the only Icelandic poet to receive support from the king of Denmark.

Humor and Life's Pleasures in the Eighteenth Century

Humor is common in poems from the Enlightenment era. The subjects are varied and often quite everyday, like hard luck in relations with the opposite sex. One of the foremost humorous poets of the eighteenth century is undoubtedly our translator Jón Þorláksson. During his school years Þorláksson wrote "Píknaklögun" (Wench's complaint), written in the voice of a woman complaining about how she can't get a man: "Oh, oh, oh! / At students I never get a go!" (*Kvæði*, 136–38). Poems like this seem to have been popular among schoolboys and were a trend in the eighteenth century. Erotic poems on the communication between the sexes are also found in some of Eggert Ólafsson's work, although there are not many. One of them is "Píkuskrækur"

(Wench's shriek), in which Ólafsson talks about "human faults and the improbable behavior of men and women in matters of love" (*Íslensk kvæða-bók*, 150). To heighten the impact of the poem Eggert has a monk and a nun exchanging words. The monk tries to get the nun under his spell, and she resists at first, but in the end she surrenders to his importunings.

Drinking poems were also popular at the time, as is apparent in the songs of the Swedish poet Bellman (1740–95) and those of other students. Eggert Ólafsson was among those who wrote about Bacchus, his poems being longer and more formal than Bellman's. "Vínleikabragur" (Drinking parties poem) is written on the celebrations that were held in honor of Bacchus in ancient Greece every third year, the so-called Bacchanalia. Eggert Ólafsson mentions that these celebrations were held at night by women and men in most countries, not least in Iceland. He encourages all Icelanders to awake and join the celebrations of the Greek gods. But he also worries that Bacchus "holds one up for too long and the drinking gets out of hand" (*Íslensk kvæðabók*, 142–44), and in the two final verses Bacchus is asked to leave the country, for the nonsense has gone too far and the countrymen have grown used to the taste. Other of Ólafsson's poems in which he elaborates his ethics of drinking express similar sentiments. Ólafsson was a restrained man when it came to wine and knew both its advantages and its disadvantages. In his poem "Flösku-kveðjur" (Bottle greetings) he likens the bottle to a woman and the wine to the milk in her breasts. The poet loves the bottle more than his fiancée, and all is well. In the latter half of the poem the poet realizes that in the beginning one should anticipate the end. The repercussions of drinking are bad: vomiting; a bad head and stomach; and an inability to keep any food down. The view of the bottle is now completely changed; instead of a lovely woman, it is a vicious and revolting whore.

The Rímur *Withstand Foreign Attacks*

The *rímur* tradition remained vigorous in Iceland throughout the period, although it was strongly opposed by men of education and leaders of the Enlightenment. Árni Böðvarsson (1713–76), a farmer from Akrar in western Iceland, was a famous *rímur* poet in the latter half of the eighteenth century and a highly productive one. Snorri Björnsson (1710–1803), a pastor who was also from the west, was very famous as well. Their *rímur* were published by the press in Hrappsey during their lifetimes: Böðvarsson's *Úlfarsrímur* (Wolf-*rímur*) in 1775 and Björnsson's *Rímur af Sigurði snarfara* (*Rímur* of Sigurður the Fast One) in 1779.

The magistrate Sigurður Pétursson's (1759–1827) *Stellurímur* (*Rímur* of Stella) were unique. Presumably, they were composed in the winter of

1791–92. The subject matter is from the Norwegian poet and playwright Johan Herman Wessel's poem "Stella" (1785), a grotesque parody of Goethe's play *Stella, ein Schauspiel für Liebende* (1776; Stella, a play for lovers). In his poem, Wessel parodies Goethe's smooth emotions and easy manner. This must have appealed to Pétursson as his work resembles Wessel's in many ways and he is comfortably at home with humor and gentle satire. The form of the *rímur* makes it possible for the poet to display his gifts. He creates many peculiar and amusing kennings and enjoys stretching out his speech in long-winded fashion, as was done in the *rímur*. There can be little doubt that Pétursson is having some fun at the expense of the *rímur*. On the other hand it is questionable whether *Stellurímur* should be interpreted as a critique of the rhetorical devices of the genre in general. It seems more likely that humor is the deciding factor, as well as harmless comedy, rather than a deliberate criticism as such. In one place the poet criticizes the exaggerated descriptions of battles in *rímur*, which he feels are blown out of all proportion. Pétursson's *Stellurímur* are quite well composed: they are written in diverse and highly complex and ornate meters and show the poet's great skill and inspiration.

Toward the end of the era Sigurður Breiðfjörð was the most famous *rímur* poet. Breiðfjörð learned the art of cooperage in Copenhagen at an early age and later worked in that field, both in Iceland and in Greenland. He thus had a wider viewpoint than most other Icelandic folk poets. A large number of his *rímur* are extant, totaling thirty-one *rímur* cycles. At the beginning of his career his poetry was similar to that of his contemporaries. However, after he left for Greenland in 1831 his talent matured, and during the following two years he composed what is probably his most famous work, the *Rímur af Núma kóngi Pompólassyni* (*Rímur* of King Numa Pompilius), based on the novel *Numa Pompilius, second roi de Rome* by the French author J. P. C. de Florian (1755–94), first published in Paris in 1786, and enormously popular across Europe. Other of his *rímur* include the *Rímur af Tristrani og Indíönu* (*Rímur* of Tristan and Indiana) of 1831, about which Jónas Hallgrímsson wrote his famous article in *Fjölnir* in 1837 (see p. 285), and the *Rímur af Svoldarbardaga* (*Rímur* of the battle of Svold) of 1833, but the so-called *Númarímur* are considered among Breiðfjörð's best. His *mansöngvar* are considered the most outstanding feature of his poetry, because they are highly lyric and, at the same time, highly personal. The *mansöngur* of the third section of the *Númarímur* is a declaration of love for his country and anticipates the patriotic poetry of the romantic period.

In his introduction to *Númarímur* the poet expresses the view that the form of the *rímur* has become stiff and that many of the Eddic kennings are now degenerate and garbled, their subject matter mostly inconsequential, often dealing with tall tales or old adventure stories. Breiðfjörð was, thus, clearly aware of the generic problems, but he could not see a solution. In fact, while he was an extremely able craftsman, he was not a particularly original poet, especially when it came to subject matter. In the end, his poetry gets stuck in the rut of the *rímur* tradition, with all the accompanying strengths and weaknesses.

From around 1400 *rímur* had had a solid place in Icelandic literature, and their popularity and production had increased steadily until 1800. By then they had come under attack by proponents of the Enlightenment and, later, by the romantic poets, although for different reasons. Still, they remained popular throughout the nineteenth century. *Rímur* belong to the type of popular literature that we associate with leisure: they provided entertainment after a hard day's work, and good *rímur* poets were in high demand. Certainly, the value of the *rímur* for Icelandic culture is beyond question. Knowledge of Eddic poetry characterized good poets, and the kennings of skaldic verse were kept alive among the people, serving as a source of innovation among the more original poets. The rigidly complex forms of the *rímur* also helped preserve the language; in fact, the study of the history of the Icelandic language often uses *rímur* as a source for language changes. The *rímur* meters are many and varied; indeed, one poetic challenge of the genre was inventing new meters. The *rímur* were first and foremost metrical and formal exercises. By 1800, however, stagnation had begun to creep into the genre. Sigurður Breiðfjörð is the last of the great *rímur* poets. His poetry might be viewed as the genre's mighty swan song.

Religious Poetry during the Age of Rationalism
Hymns and spiritual poems had enjoyed total dominance in publishing for a long time, and a large number of hymn manuscripts have been preserved from the eighteenth century, which proves that hymns were still popular among the public. They were copied, read, and sung. Many of the leading poets of the eighteenth century wrote hymns, including Jón Þorláksson of Bægisá, the Reverend Jón Oddsson Hjaltalín (see below), Árni Böðvarsson, and, last but not least, Magnús Stephensen. At the same time, Hallgrímur Pétursson's popularity was never greater than during the eighteenth century. The *Passíusálmar* were printed many times, and, in 1755, the first edition of *Hallgrímskver* (Hallgrímur's book of poetry) came out, a work that included the hymns and other poems. Like the *rímur*, hymns are a feature of literature that remained popular throughout the eighteenth century and beyond, despite new cultural currents.

The Enlightenment had a widespread effect on Christianity and the church in Iceland. The key emphasis in the hymns of the period is on proper behavior and a virtuous lifestyle and on trust in God, or Providence, as it was common to say at that time. The followers of the Enlightenment did not want to change Christian doctrine, in spite of everything; rather, they wanted to express their belief in a new way with new words. In their hymns there is little urgency about Christian doctrine, very unlike the period of orthodoxy, when matters of proper doctrine were paramount.

A good example is the publication of a new hymnal, known as *Aldamótabók* (Turn-of-the-century book) in 1801, in which hymns had been updated and new ones added that were more in line with the spirit of rationalism. Advocates of the Enlightenment fought against any kind of superstition and fear of the supernatural and regarded a belief in the existence of the devil and hell as a sign of ignorance and an unhealthy imagination. Consequently, all references of this kind were expunged from the new hymnal. This did not go down very well, especially because the publisher, Magnús Stephensen, dared to change texts by contemporary poets without asking for their approval. This led to a renowned, and heated, dispute, which began with "Rustasneið" (Crusts of the loaf), a vilification poem by Jón Þorláksson that refers to the *Aldamótabók* as "bad verse." It has since been observed that the changes made by Magnús Stephensen were in no way without precedent; on the contrary, it had long been the practice of publishers to change texts as they pleased. The time had now come, however, when authors considered themselves to have a right to have their poetry published in its original form.

The most successful hymnist during the Enlightenment was the Reverend Þorvaldur Böðvarsson (1758–1836), who was nicknamed the "Court Poet" of the Enlightenment advocates. The *Aldamótabók* includes sixty-one of his hymns.

PROSE IN THE AGE OF ENLIGHTENMENT

A New Type of Storytelling
The eighteenth century was an age of innovation in the literature of many European countries. The novel emerged in England and France and spread to Germany and the Nordic countries, although it did not come to Iceland until much later. However, there were in Iceland important experiments in storytelling during the latter half of the century. The most interesting attempt was *Saga Ólafs Þórhallasonar* (The Saga of Ólafur Þórhallason) by Eiríkur Laxdal (1743–1816), considered by many to be the first Icelandic

novel. But more fictional narratives were written during the period, all of which have been considered romances because of their structure. Both Jón Bjarnason (1721–85) and Jón Oddsson Hjaltalín (1749–1835) wrote noteworthy works that show a certain evolution in the direction of the novel. At the same time there were developments in other genres of prose literature. Several travel books and autobiographies were written in the period, the origins of which can be traced to the seventeenth century, as we saw earlier. Plays also began to be written during the Enlightenment in Iceland. One thing all written prose literature of the period has in common is that much of it was not published until later, if at all.

Travel Literature
There are two noteworthy travel narratives from the latter half of the eighteenth century, both by Icelandic travelers who became famous for sailing as far as China. These are *Journal eður víðferlissaga* (Journal or the traveler's saga) by Eiríkur Björnsson (1733–91), written in 1768, and *Ferðasaga* (Travel story) by Árni Magnússon of Geitastekkur (1726–1801?), in all likelihood written around 1795. Árni Magnússon's travel account was published in Reykjavík in 1945. The *Víðferlissaga*, on the other hand, was not published until 2000. These two works are of particular interest from the point of view of cultural history. The authors both traveled to distant foreign countries and had many fascinating stories to tell.

There are also important travel diaries by two leaders of the Enlightenment. Bishop Hannes Finnsson wrote his *Stokkhólmsrella* (Memoirs from Stockholm) about his journey around Sweden in the summer of 1772. He accompanied the Danish lawyer Peder Kofod-Ancher; the purpose of the trip was to collect ancient Nordic law. Bishop Hannes kept a diary, in which he describes his reading and the transcriptions of ancient Icelandic manuscripts found in Swedish repositories. Of particular interest is his description of his and Kofod-Ancher's visit to the famous botanist Carl von Linnaeus (1707–78).

Magnús Stephensen also kept an important diary during his trip around Denmark in the winter of 1825–26, a work that he called *Ferðarolla* (Travel scroll). His goal was to get his edition of the *Jónsbók*, the Icelandic law book from 1281, which he had finished in Copenhagen, published. Although the trip did not bear this fruit, Stephensen's diary is an entertaining source about contemporary people, issues, and daily activity. In it Stephensen kept a daily record in which he describes such details as the weather, food, and table manners. *Ferðarolla* is, thus, a valuable source of information about the life of the wealthy, their clothing, customs, and traditions.

The Autobiography of Jón Steingrímsson the Fire-pastor
The most important autobiography of the eighteenth century is without a doubt *Ævisaga séra Jóns Steingrímssonar* (The autobiography of the Reverend Jón Steingrímsson; English trans.: Steingrímsson, *"A Very Present Help in Trouble"* [2002]). Steingrímsson's story has an intimate connection to the most horrifying natural catastrophe in Icelandic history, but it is remarkable in many other respects as well. Everyone in Iceland knows the story about the *eldklerkur* (fire-pastor) who with his words and prayers managed to halt the lava flow approaching the settlement.

The catastrophic Skaftá eruptions in southern Iceland began in 1783 and marked the first of several years of hardship known as the Móðuharðindi, the Famine of the Mist, which lasted until 1785. These eruptions are among the largest in recorded human history. Several islands were formed in the sea as a result, and there were eruptions under the glaciers. Southwest of the Vatnajökull glacier an eleven-kilometer fissure opened up called Lakagígar. Lava covered approximately 580 square kilometers of the country, and poison ash fell almost everywhere in Iceland. The erupting fissures polluted the air all the way to Siberia. In Scotland there was a failure of the harvest, and in many places in Europe there was a destruction of growth. Unusually cold weather, crop failures, and earthquakes followed these eruptions. In the latter part of the eighteenth century there were so many calamities and such suffering in Iceland that the authorities began to despair about the possibility of continuing to inhabit the country.

Jón Steingrímsson (1728–91) came to the cathedral school at Hólar at the age of sixteen and graduated from there in 1750. He became a deacon at Reynisstaður in Skagafjörður, in northern Iceland, where Jón Vigfússon was in charge of the monastery. Not long after, Vigfússon died suddenly, and Steingrímsson took up with his widow, Þórunn Hannesdóttir. Þórunn had a daughter "rather too early," and Jón lost his post as deacon. Vicious rumors spread that Steingrímsson had murdered Vigfússon, although there was nothing to substantiate these accusations. The couple were badly affected by this and had to move from farm to farm until Jón was ordained as a pastor and finally became dean to the entire Skaftafell district in southeast Iceland in 1779.

The year 1784 was a momentous one in Jón Steingrímsson's life. His wife died in the autumn, and he started writing his autobiography the following winter. He continued writing over the next few years and finished the work in 1791; he died the same year. His goals in writing the autobiography were twofold. First, he wanted to tell the bald truth about his life and to avoid exaggeration. Second, he wanted to thank God and praise his glory and guidance through good times and bad. He largely achieved his ambitions. The style is simple and straightforward, and there is much joy in the story-telling. The pastor's sincerity is unprecedented—he is extremely open and honest. In this respect his story reminds one of the *Confessions* of Saint Augustine, who, like Steingrímsson, struggled with various temptations of the flesh in his younger years. Steingrímsson believed in God's provi-dence—he sees himself and his suffering as a martyrdom, a testing of him by God. Such unflinching faith marks his story from beginning to end. He also tries to clear his name in the autobiography and to answer accusations brought against him.

Nothing is omitted in the autobiography, or so it seems. There are descriptions of various temptations and acts of disobedience, such as his participation in witchcraft mumbo jumbo with his schoolmates at Hólar and his relations with women, which caused him guilty unease. He even-tually managed to shake off all temptations but one: he did impregnate his wife-to-be too soon.

The highlight of Jón Steingrímsson's life is the famous fire-mass in the summer of 1783, shortly after the eruptions began. Most people fled from the lava flow, but the pastor stayed put with his congregation. The miracle happened during mass, when the flood of lava stopped just short of the church and the congregation was spared. The Reverend Jón did not doubt that this was the will of God and that the eruption was a punishment for an ungodly lifestyle. Two farms were destroyed in the eruption, and, according to Steingrímsson, there had been much discord there. The fire-mass con-vinced him that he was chosen to lead his congregation out of acute distress. These tragedies did not leave the fire-pastor untouched. A year later he was accused of having distributed money (support from the Danish authorities) to his parishioners without permission. But the greatest blow was the death of his wife the following summer. Depression engulfed him, and he nearly succumbed to thoughts of suicide in 1786, by which time he was sick with various illnesses, including urinary disease and hemorrhoids. He recovered from his depression with the help of faith and married again, to Margrét Sigurðardóttir, daughter of the pastor at Stafholt. Steingrímsson never fully recuperated after the disaster, and he died in 1791 at the age of sixty-three.

Jón Steingrímsson's autobiography is one of the most remarkable pieces of literature in the eighteenth century, and it points the way ahead to new times. His honesty and passion for the truth lift the piece above the ordi-nary autobiographies of his contemporaries. In the popular mind Jón Steingrímsson became the fire-pastor, the man who stopped the lava flow with the word of God as his weapon in the most terrible natural disaster that had occurred in the country since settlement. His reliance and toughness became symbolic of the struggle for survival of the Icelandic people, who had to endure such disasters.

Publishing at Hólar

Around 1760, important secular books began to be published at the press at Hólar owing to the influence of Björn Markússon (1716–91), who was a magistrate and land agent at Hólar at the time and the supervisor of the press. Gísli Magnússon (1712–79) had just been appointed a bishop, and he supported a publishing policy that aimed to increase the earnings for the bishopric. At first, the two men published two volumes of old Icelandic sagas: *Nokkrir margfróðir söguþættir Íslendinga* (Several learned Icelandic short sagas) and *Ágætar fornmannasögur* (Splendid sagas of old). These were pioneer publications, although some among the clergy were not favorably disposed toward the project as they felt that the publications contravened Harboe's earlier decrees.

The same year two fictional narratives were published together in one volume, narratives that were to be of some influence: *Þess engelska Bertholds fábreytilegar Robinsons eður lífs og ævi sögur* (The life stories of the unfortunate Robinson, the Englishman Berthold) and *Þess svenska Gustav Landkrons* (Of the Swedish Gustav Landkron). The former had been published in Denmark in 1740 and the latter in 1743. The Reverend Þorsteinn Ketilsson (1687–1754), the dean in Vaðlaþing, had translated them from the Danish. Both were most likely translated originally from the German and among the many imitations of Daniel Defoe's *Robinson Crusoe* (1714). Björn Markússon's introduction is revolutionary in its praise of the value of contemporary novels, which had not been printed in Icelandic before, and which he calls both entertaining and edifying. It seems as though Markússon here decided to ignore pietism and open the door to fictional stories of a more contemporary kind. It was partly thanks to these Robinson stories that the Icelandic romance was now finally on its way to becoming the novel, although the novel did not secure its place in Icelandic literature until the beginning of the twentieth century. However, many experiments were conducted with the novel form in the latter part of the eighteenth century, romances influenced by *Gustav Landkron* and *Berthold*: Eiríkur Laxdal's *Ólandssaga* (Saga of no such land) and *Saga Ólafs Þórhallasonar* stand out. In the latter in particular there is a plausible attempt to write a novel. The inheritance from the folktale is dealt with in an original way, and the development of the hero toward maturity is similar to that in other eighteenth-century novels.

Romances

Although fiction was vigorously opposed by the authorities, the many surviving manuscripts show its resilience. From the period after the Reformation some two hundred stories, written on paper, have been preserved. This
collection of manuscripts illustrates that this kind of storytelling flourished
throughout the seventeenth, eighteenth, and nineteenth centuries, until the
novel finally took over from the romance at the beginning of the twentieth
century.

The romances have always been in the shadow of the Sagas of Icelanders
and have, until recent decades, enjoyed little respect or attention from the
literary establishment. This "shadow growth" of Icelandic literature has
now, however, been drawn into the light, especially by foreign scholars, and
has begun to receive the attention it deserves. Nevertheless, there is still
much work to be done and many questions to be answered about the
origins of these stories, such as which are original compositions and which
translations. Interestingly, the Sagas of Icelanders had very little influence
on eighteenth-century romances. The literary heritage on which the romances relied included the *rímur*, fairy tales, folktales, the Knights' Sagas,
and the Legendary sagas as well as travel stories, the plot of the latter being
often reminiscent of romances and foreign novels. Indeed, the influence
from abroad is greater in the eighteenth century than previously thought;
clearly, the country was not as isolated then as has been assumed.

An Icelandic Version of Robinson Crusoe

Sagan af Parmes Loðinbirni (1756–75; The saga of Parmes Furry-bear) is
thought to have been written in response to the Berthold story mentioned
above. There is, for example, a detailed account of the shipwreck of Parmes
and his mate, Nilles. However, the hero, Parmes, is more like Robinson
Crusoe than Berthold. The author of the story is assumed to be Jón Bjarnason, the pastor at Balará, who is known for his fascination with Greenland
and even went so far as to fight for Icelanders to be allowed to form a colony
there.

The importance of *Sagan af Parmes Loðinbirni* lies in the ways in which it
attempts to incorporate realistic descriptions into its romantic framework,
adapting the imaginary to the worlds of experience; it is among the first
works of fiction in Icelandic to do so. While it is a traditional romance in
many respects, with an adventure plot, the realistic description of the barbarian land is reminiscent of a travel story. The life of the natives and the
landscape are described in a very realistic fashion, which makes the narrative
lively and memorable. The wonder world of romances and fairy tales is

retreating, and travel descriptions are closer to the present time of the story. Parmes is described less as an exaggerated superhero and more as a human being of flesh and blood. Foresters in the Alps manage to capture him and take him prisoner in the beginning of the story. Parmes's role is to turn the natives into ethical human beings, using kindness, like Robinson Crusoe, rather than using force, like Berthold.

Sagan af Parmes Loðinbirni thus has many of the characteristics of the novel. The author's emphatic tendency to invoke Christianity and ethical concerns can in some respects be traced to Robinson Crusoe. Mildly humanist viewpoints of the Enlightenment are visible in the description of the barbarian land. The work is much more realistic than traditional romances in its settings and descriptions of people. Jón Bjarnason's interest in education and the conversion of barbarians to Christianity colors the story and points to the time it was written, rather than the timelessness of the romance.

The Romances of Jón Oddsson Hjaltalín

One of the most important romance authors of the Enlightenment is certainly the Reverend Jón Oddsson Hjaltalín. Hjaltalín was well-read and had at least some familiarity with the work of the most respectable authors of his time, including Voltaire, Rousseau, Fielding, and Holberg, even translating works by some of them, including *Saga of Zadig*, a translation of Voltaire's 1747 philosophical adventure *Zadig*, and *Sagan af Thomas Jones*, a summary of Fielding's 1749 *Tom Jones* (both based on Danish versions of the texts in question, they date to ca. 1792–93 and are preserved in one manuscript). He was also interested in philosophy, and in his manuscripts it is common for him to mention various contemporary philosophers.

Jón Hjaltalín was a productive writer. In Deacon Hallgrímur Jónsson's (1780–1836) list of authors ten original stories are attributed to him, said to have been written between 1780 and 1820. Apart from one (*Sagan af Mána fróða* [The saga of Máni the learned]), all these stories have been preserved. Around sixty manuscripts of Hjaltalín's stories exist. *Sagan af Marroni sterka* (The saga of Marron the Strong) has been the most popular if the number of surviving copies is any indication: nineteen in all, plus one from around 1800 in the author's own hand that is defective but the only preserved original manuscript of his fiction. These stories are romances, and the relationship with the Knights' Sagas and the Legendary Sagas is hard to deny. *Sagan af Marroni sterka* is a typical romance. The plotline is made up of action and adventure, with the search of the hero for a wife as the main theme. Descriptions of battles also get a lot of attention. It is notable that a devout Lutheran pastor should write such a tall tale, one that went against the dictates of the leaders of the Enlightenment like Magnús Stephensen. It is also curious that the manuscripts do not mention an author. This supports the theory of the living storytelling tradition as "shadow growth," passed on from one reader to another in transcription.

Not all Jón Hjaltalín's stories were action packed and far-fetched. Two of them stand out: *Fimmbræðra saga* (The saga of the five brothers) and *Sagan af Hinrik heilráða* (The saga of Henry the Counsellor). These are not typical adventure romances. In them one can detect new emphases and ideas akin to Enlightenment ideals. They demonstrate that Hjaltalín was familiar with the literature of the period. The search for a bride is not as important as the adventure, and the travels of the heroes have a different purpose than they do in his earlier romances. In *Hinriks saga* the hero tries to attain fame and popularity by using wit and persuasion rather than weapons and is successful beyond all his dreams. In *Fimmbræðra saga* the quest is for the best religion in the world, something that is unnecessary in the world of the romance, where Christianity was the only true creed. There is a new tone in these stories; contemporary ideas peek in, evidenced by signs of critical thinking and a broadening of views in the radical spirit of the Enlightenment. These works thus share an attempt to stretch the form of the romance.

The Beginnings of the Novel

Eiríkur Laxdal composed both *rímur* and hymns but is now best known for writing two fictional works that mark the beginnings of novel writing in Iceland. Laxdal led a rather unruly life at first. He got a position as a deacon but lost it because he fathered an illegitimate child. After that he sailed abroad and began studies at the University of Copenhagen in 1769. He quit after two years because he lost his accommodation allowance, or *garðsstyrkur* (a grant for Icelandic students that provided free accommodation during their years of study at the university). He then worked as an ordinary seaman in the Danish navy until the autumn of 1774, when it is said that Sophie Hendrica, princess of Mecklenborg, helped toward his release. Laxdal stayed in Copenhagen during that winter but returned to Iceland in the spring of 1775. After his arrival, he first went home to his parents in Hof, where he fished, composed *rímur*, and wrote *Ólandssaga*. Not much else is known about his life and writings after his homecoming. It is thought that *Ólandssaga* was written mostly in Iceland, but it is conceivable that he had started writing it in Denmark. Clearly, his time in Copenhagen molded Laxdal as a writer and widened his horizons. He arrived in Copenhagen during the years of the influence of Struensee, the doctor and adviser of the mentally ill King Christian VII. Struensee's brief period of influence was characterized by a liberal point of view, the doctor having the public good as his guiding light. His reforms were unpopular with the establishment, however, and he was arrested in a court intrigue and executed in 1772.

Laxdal almost certainly knew the work of Holberg, especially his *Niels Klim*. He was very fond of natural history and science, and this interest is obvious in his *Ólafssaga*. He also knew Latin and German as well as Danish. There were clearly two sides to his nature. He is described as having been a good poet, bright, and adept at languages; on the other hand, he was eccentric and unlucky in worldly matters. He got into trouble time and again and repeatedly lost situations. He had a quick temper and found it difficult to conform to the rules and customs of society.

Ólandssaga *and* Saga Ólafs Þórhallasonar

Ólandssaga is preserved in one copy from the first half of the nineteenth century. The story is large-scale, running to 504 pages in manuscript. It is a romance, interwoven in a systematic way. It is in many ways like *Ólafssaga*, except that in the latter the author uses elf stories and other Icelandic folktales as the basis of his historic world. *Ólandssaga* is more of a utopia or dreamworld as the adventures are set in neither time nor place. The frame of the adventure, furthermore, is like the method used in the *Thousand and One Nights*, where one story merges into another (one person tells a story, and a person from that story tells the next).

Ólafssaga is a much more seamless piece. Various folktales are used and intertwined into a whole, so the story is more coherent. *Ólafssaga* is preserved in the author's own collection of manuscripts. The first four chapters are actually missing there, but they exist in a copy. *Ólafssaga* was most likely written around 1800.

The main character of the story is Ólafur Þórhallason. He is fifteen years old when the story begins and is called *eldseti* (sitting by the fire) because he lies about in the room where the fire was kept. The author here uses the *kolbítur* or "coal-biter" motif of the lazy, inauspicious problem youth, well known in Icelandic traditional lore, and also mentions Grettir Ásmundarson (another famous problem youth) and his stay on Drangey. After a warning from his father, Ólafur rises from his sloth and starts to look for the money his father needs. And here begins then "the great elf story," as it has been called. Ólafur gets to know many elfin ladies, who control his destiny from that moment on. Ólafur moves between the two worlds throughout the story. On one side, there is the world of the enlightened elves, which is underground, and, on the other, there is the world of men up above. But

Eiríkur Laxdal's stories are no ordinary folktales. The society of elves is carefully described. Their appearance, customs, agricultural methods, laws, and knowledge of science are all much more sophisticated than those of mankind. There is a very memorable and detailed description of the elf world during the underground travels of Ólafur and Eiríkur, the pastor in Vogósar. Álfbjörg in Krísuvíkurbjarg teaches them about elves and their settlements, then follows with a lengthy lecture on natural science and physics. Laxdal is known to have had a translation of a manuscript of *Physico-Theology* by the Englishman William Derham (1658–1735), published in London in 1716, and obviously used by Laxdal when he wrote *Ólafssaga*. In the story there is a description of a utopian society, the kind of which Enlightenment proponents dreamed. Knowledge is used to cultivate the land, and the society is characterized by humility and proper behavior of the workers. The world of men in the eighteenth century is severely lacking by comparison.

Ólafssaga is partly a coming-of-age story. Ólafur's path is filled with great obstacles, but there are also many detours in this complicated and eventful tale. In the course of the story it becomes clear that the diverse folktale material used obeys the laws of the narrative, in which the hero shapes his environment and is molded by it in return. Unlike the romances, the story describes real places and times. The elf world of the story is not merely a dreamworld but has the reality of an enlightened society, or at least a dream of that kind of world. When the definition of the novel is considered (and that definition is very wide today), it is clear that *Ólafssaga* deserves recognition as the first Icelandic novel.

It is hardly surprising that *Ólafssaga* has confused people. Laxdal was an original writer and far ahead of his time. He describes the emotions of his characters with great sensitivity and does not simplify, so the characters become fully rounded. The emotions of the characters are formed by strife, struggle, and contradiction. Laxdal describes women in a highly unusual way. They are the doers in the story — Ólafur wanders between them and learns from them at the same time. According to the story, the women are wise, and in the elf world they have the authority of judges. Gender equality therefore existed in the dreamworld long before the real public debate began. Of particular interest is the creation of Álfgerður's personality. She is Ólafur's counterpart and extremely influential in his life. In the beginning, and for a long time, she is represented as an evil creature who bewitches Ólafur and seduces him. By the end of the story there has been a sea change, when Álfgerður reveals her true self. She then behaves like an altruistic wife with an unselfish love for Ólafur. He marries her in the elf world, but she rejects him when he is seized by homesickness. Ólafur returns to the world of men and marries Ólöf. Ólafur still has a lot to learn, but by the end there is finally hope for him to control his unfaithfulness. Álfgerður is far above Ólafur as the elves are more mature intellectual beings than men. Ólafur learns that what he thought was a spell was, indeed, his own inner turmoil—the road to maturity is self-knowledge, which Ólafur attains after bitter experiences, distress, and humiliation. Ólafur's character is like that of characters in modern or postmodern literature. His is a divided and inconsistent personality. The truth is fluid, things are not always as they seem, and the characters are multifaceted. All this has helped in bringing the story to the attention of scholars at the end of the twentieth century, where it finally has received the credit it deserves.

SUMMARY

The eighteenth century was a time of varied upheaval and movement in Icelandic literary history. New ideas in the spirit of the Enlightenment and pietism arrived from abroad, giving rise to new views. The most radical changes occurred in publishing. Material that would never have been published before was printed; new literary genres and new magazines emerged; and contemporary foreign material was translated into Icelandic. There was also an obvious conflict between public literature, that which the church and civil authorities considered best for the public, and popular literature, a "shadow growth," which flourished despite various attempts to suppress it and formed the foundation of Icelandic novel writing.

Translated by Joe Allard

From Romanticism to Realism

Þórir Óskarsson

3

ROMANTICISM IN ICELAND

In the patriotic and nature poetry of Bjarni Thorarensen (1786–1841), written at the very beginning of the nineteenth century, we see the first firm indication of the influence of the romantic movement on Icelandic literature. Thorarensen's works demonstrate that he had at an early age been captivated by the waves engulfing European culture during this period: nationalism; idealism; and aesthetic relativism. Indeed, he is commonly considered to be the first and best representative of romantic thought in Icelandic, and some critics have even maintained that he is the only Icelandic poet who can with any accuracy be called a genuine romantic poet. At the same time his poems can clearly be read as a revolt against contemporary Icelandic writing, which consisted mainly of popular *rímur* (metrical romances), hymns and postils (sermons and commentaries on Scripture), and educational texts by the followers of the Enlightenment movement (see chapter 2).

Thorarensen's earliest poems were probably written around 1807, but it was only after 1818 that some of his works began to appear in Icelandic papers and journals on an incidental basis. Despite the fact that they constituted a radical innovation, they seem not to have inspired any immediate discussion or debate, nor were they imitated by other poets. It is largely because of this that most literary historians have maintained that Thorarensen did not pioneer a new movement or era in literature. The romantic movement in Icelandic literature is not even considered to have begun until

Unless a specific English-language source is given, all translations from the Icelandic are the author's.

either 1830, when intellectuals began insisting that Iceland was a separate nation with a right to a degree of autonomy, or 1835, when this political nationalism gained a literary mouthpiece in the form of the annual journal *Fjölnir* (1835–39, 1843–47). Its decline is, on the other hand, linked either to the year 1874, when Icelanders commemorated the millennium of settlement and received their own constitution, or to the year 1882, when the proponents of literary naturalism and social realism published the first and only issue of the journal *Verðandi*, influenced by the theories of the Danish critic Georg Brandes.

This demarcation of the romantic movement creates certain problems as it goes against the general views held on the development of Icelandic literature. Not only is it unquestionable that almost all Bjarni Thorarensen's romantic poetry was written before 1830, but critics have also had great problems connecting the writers of the period 1830–82 to European romanticism as it is generally defined. The work of Iceland's most acclaimed poet of the 1830s and 1840s, Jónas Hallgrímsson (1807–45), has, for instance, been considered surprisingly realistic, moderate, and classical compared to that of Bjarni Thorarensen and other European romantic poets. At the same time, other, still younger Icelandic poets, such as Grímur Thomsen (1820–96) and Matthías Jochumsson (1835–1920), have been regarded as homegrown poets, quite independent of all fashionable currents in literature. Consequently, the term *romanticism* has not loomed large in critical discussions on specific nineteenth-century poets and texts, and some critics have even claimed that Icelandic romanticism barely deserves its name.

No nineteenth-century Icelandic writers are known to have applied the term *romantic* to their own writing. The term first appears in an Icelandic work from 1839 describing a picturesque and varied landscape where the fertile Icelandic countryside meets the glacier-topped high mountains. Several years later the term appears in its literary-historical meaning, referring to literature that takes its subject from the European Middle Ages or forms an antithesis to classical or symbolic literature. It was, however, seldom applied to Icelandic literature, although the aesthete and poet Grímur Thomsen spoke of "pagan romanticism" when describing the characteristics of Icelandic medieval literature in an 1846 article. Most people seem to have limited their usage of the term *romanticism* to German literature from the beginning of the century and the literature directly influenced by it. Matthías Jochumsson, for instance, did so in an 1866 article ("Ávarp til lesendanna") in which he pointed out the special position of nineteenth-century Scandinavian literature, which was, he claimed, undeniably truer, healthier, and more robust than much of the so-called romantic literature. The realist writer Gestur Pálsson (1852–91), too, probably had literature of German origin in mind when he maintained in 1891 that the romantic movement had never reached Iceland in its purest form ("Ávarp 'Suðra,'" 435). Around the same time, however, a few historians started using the term *romantic* to describe a specific period in Icelandic literature. They nevertheless maintained that most Icelandic writers were independent and Icelandic in spirit, and some would even have it that there never had been a romantic school in Iceland.

In the discussion below an attempt will be made to unravel the development of Icelandic literature from 1807 until 1882, not only by considering German and German-based romanticism, but also by drawing attention to other movements that later influenced European literature. This change in approach is based on the view that Icelandic writers were relatively well acquainted with the literature of other countries and emulated it in many respects. By taking into account the writers' aesthetics, their choice of subject matter, and their attitude toward that subject matter, the aforementioned epoch will be divided into four shorter periods: romanticism (1807–30); national romanticism and poetic realism (1830–43); *romantisme* (1843–48); and political engagement and (critical) idealism (1848–82).

As is the case with all literary-historical classifications, this division relies on a certain degree of generalization and largely serves as an indication of when certain tendencies became apparent in Icelandic literature, rather than suggesting a complete transformation of any kind or a decisive turning point in literary history. Moreover, it should not obscure the many romantic links between the various writers during the entire period, such as their patriotism, their idealization of Icelandic nature and the Middle Ages, and their interest in purifying and protecting the Icelandic language from outside influences. It is also vital to emphasize that the following discussion is in no way a complete description of Icelandic literature from 1807 to 1882. It focuses first and foremost on those writers who sought out new paths in literature and is, therefore, less concerned with others who based themselves in older traditions. This explains, for instance, the amount of space allocated to Bjarni Thorarensen and Jónas Hallgrímsson.

LITERARY TRANSFORMATIONS

The nineteenth century is undoubtedly a period of great change in Icelandic literature. Wherever one looks, significant innovation and transformation of what had gone before were taking place. Of great importance was the flourishing of book publishing, especially in the latter half of the century. In particular, the publication of belles lettres and popular literature increased and started to threaten the thereto unquestioned reign of religious and educational literature. In the wake of this development followed an increased diversity in the writing available to the larger reading public. Alongside innovative poetry novels and plays by Icelanders gained in importance, while great emphasis was also placed on translating a variety of foreign fiction into Icelandic. At the same time folktales and folk poetry gained in respect as a form of literature that people could enjoy privately instead of in the company of others. Other factors also contributed to making the enjoyment of literature an individual experience rather than a social one: texts of a more introspective and personal nature grew in popularity, and social circumstances were changing as well by the end of the century. Homes were populated by fewer people, and *kvöldvökur* (communal evening readings and entertainment) lost the cultural role they once enjoyed (see also p. 000).

As the types of printed literature available became more diverse, the range of literary subject matter broadened and also received more varied treatments. This, in turn, influenced the general perception of what was considered literature, what role literature played, and how it should be approached and valued. This meant a certain shift within the literary system itself, with earlier traditions losing some of their influence or being interpreted in a new light. These changes affected specific formal aspects of literature: meter and rhyme; use of language and expression; which genres were considered to be of value. Overall, the emphasis now lay on the poetic imagination and poetic insight as well as on clear, poetic language. This negatively affected popular literature, especially the *rímur*, which had been a favorite genre across the centuries but, by the end of the nineteenth century, had few advocates left. *Rímur* poets were at best considered craftsmen; their main role as storytellers had now been taken over by novelists. Another popular national genre, the folktale, held in low regard by intellectuals at the beginning of the century, was, on the other hand, reshaped, and in part rewritten, to suit new literary tastes and gradually even came to be cherished as a national treasure.

These and other changes took their time, for Icelandic society and culture were ill prepared for them. There was no literary infrastructure to speak of. None of the writers mentioned in this chapter, for instance, had writing as their main profession. They all had to earn a living by other means, some as civil servants, others with the help of badly paid part-time work or scholarships. Their writing was mostly done during rare moments of spare time and often sparked by specific occasions, for instance, in reaction to certain events or for performance at public or private functions. There was also hardly any public forum for literary discussion, given the lack of media and educational institutions, not to mention the critics and teachers capable of generating debate. This kind of literary "institution" was, in fact, not formed until the turn of the twentieth century. As a result it remains unclear exactly how contemporaries viewed the changes that took place in the wake of the literary innovations of the nineteenth century.

HISTORY AND SOCIETY

With only forty-seven thousand inhabitants at the beginning of the nineteenth century, Iceland had not been so sparsely populated since the Middle Ages. Tremendous natural catastrophes, earthquakes, volcanic eruptions, bad weather conditions, and plagues during the previous century had taken their toll on people and livestock and continued to do so into the first decade of the nineteenth century. It is believed that 450 people starved to death in 1803, and many more walked around "pink and fleshless as ghosts," to quote Bishop Geir Vídalín's (1761–1823) description from 1807 (*Geir biskup*, ed. Sigmundsson, 72). Until the middle of the century the vast majority of the people (80–90 percent) in this poor dependency of Denmark lived in sparsely populated areas and survived on agriculture, especially sheep farming. Villages and towns were both few and small. At the beginning of the century only 0.5 percent of the people worked in the fishing industry; around 1880 this proportion had reached 12 percent. Industry was similarly almost nonexistent and had even deteriorated from the latter half of the eighteenth century. Transport was in a deplorable state, both within the country and between Iceland and other countries. Some years no foreign merchant ships arrived, which resulted in shortages of goods and news.

The country's main town, Reykjavík, was not especially remarkable at the beginning of the nineteenth century. It had approximately three hundred inhabitants, and its biggest and finest building was the prison, now Government House, built in 1770. There was, nevertheless, some indication of urban development. The only higher education establishment in the country, the Latin School (Lærði skólinn), had been moved to Reykjavík in 1786, and the town was, from 1801 on, also home to the bishop's residence and the High Court (Landsyfirréttur). The High Court replaced the old Althing at Þingvellir, which had been abolished in 1800, to the great disappointment of many. Besides the civil servants who worked for these institutions, merchants were the most prominent urban class. Most of them, as well as some of the civil servants, were Danish, which influenced the town's atmosphere. It was common for women to dress in Danish costume, and the men's coats were in accordance with the latest fashion among the higher classes in Copenhagen. In this half-Danish market town, Danish was the official language, not only among the civil servants and merchants, but also among the higher classes. The general public got by with some kind of mixture of Danish and Icelandic. This bastardized dialect became so insidious that the Danish linguist and Iceland aficionado Rasmus Christian Rask (1787–1834) predicted that the Icelandic language would soon become extinct. In a letter from 1813 he wrote that, if this development was not stopped and strong defenses put up, hardly anyone in Reykjavík would understand Icelandic in a hundred years' time and hardly anyone in other parts of the country in another two hundred years (*Breve Rask*, ed. Hjelmslev, 1:164).

Rask himself played a prominent role in the effort to save the Icelandic language, for instance, by founding in 1816 the Icelandic Literary Society (Hið íslenska bókmenntafélag), whose main goal was to protect and strengthen the Icelandic language and Icelandic literature and, with it, national education. The society also placed great emphasis on increasing people's knowledge of their country's history. It was active both in Reykjavík and in Copenhagen and soon became Iceland's most powerful educational and publishing society. Its annual journal, *Skírnir*, appeared for the first time in 1827 and is still published today.

It was not only the Danish-influenced language of Reykjavík's inhabitants that was considered suspect. During much of the century the streets of this capital in the making were unlit, and the town could boast neither a strong nor a varied cultural life. Alcohol consumption, on the other hand, was excessive. For these reasons many of the civil servants lived on the outskirts. In 1804 the Latin School was moved out of town because of housing problems. With it the mainstay of Reykjavík's cultural life and Icelandic theater disappeared. What was left was a small club of merchants and civil servants that mainly held dances, card-playing nights, and dinner parties. Among the club's members from 1830–32 was the poet Jónas Hallgrímsson, who recited a few society verses there, most of them in Danish. From this perspective not many things had changed since Rask stayed in Reykjavík in 1813. "The place wants to be Danish and never Icelandic, and that is why it will be a bastard forever," as the poet Bjarni Thorarensen characterized the scene in 1840 (Thorarensen, *Ljóðmæli*, 1:xlvi), and the theologian Tómas Sæmundsson (1807–41), the century's foremost thinker, agreed. In an 1835 essay Sæmundsson did, however, allow himself to dream of Reykjavík as a well-planned political and cultural center with broad and straight streets, pretty squares, and imposing buildings and monuments.

Sæmundsson's dream was based on his memories of the European cities where he studied between 1827 and 1834. The cultural awakening that took place in Iceland during the century also originated on the European continent, where Copenhagen occupied a special place as the real capital of Iceland at the time. Nearly all the most important Icelandic writers and intellectuals stayed there for long or short periods of time to study and work, and some stayed there almost all their working lives. From Copenhagen one also had easy access to other countries. In 1832, after his studies, Sæmundsson traveled around Europe for two years and visited all the main European cities — Berlin, Prague, Vienna, Rome, Athens, Paris, and London. He attended lectures at many universities, especially in theology and philosophy, visited art galleries, and acquainted himself with the traditions and customs of other nations, their literature, their political structures, and their industrial innovations such as factory production. All this he describes with much admiration in his *Ferðabók* (1834–35; Travel journal). Sailing to Iceland at the end of his trip to become a country vicar roused more mixed emotions. "Sometimes it occurred to me that I was now saying good-bye to the world and all its merriments, and this almost inspired feelings of dismay," he wrote shortly after he returned home (Sæmundsson, "Úr bréfi frá Íslandi," 49). Sæmundsson was, nevertheless, one of the era's most fervent nationalists and never tired of pointing out to his countrymen the beauty and other good qualities of the mother country. "It is not the country's fault, but rather your own, if you are less successful and happy at home than any other nation," he and his companions wrote in their introduction to the first issue of *Fjölnir* (1 [1835]: 3). Here, they also pointed out the value of old Icelandic literature for the nation in keeping the Icelandic language alive and kindling a burning love of the mother country.

Initially, the journals constituted the main outlet for innovative literature as well as being a meeting point for Icelandic and foreign culture. Here, educated men who were familiar with foreign cities talked to uneducated farmers in the scattered farms of the country, encouraged them to fight for progress along with the foremost among nations, and also emphasized shared national values: the mother country; its history; the Icelandic language and Icelandic culture. This involved some glaring paradoxes, as becomes apparent in the ideas of progress that are linked to urban life: business; industry; modern science; and international education. The farmers were, thus, in fact encouraged to rise against themselves to form the basis of a new society and new culture, which was supposed to be Icelandic and at the same time modern and highly developed. It is hardly surprising that the majority of the population understood little of this message, and some of the more radical journals, especially *Fjölnir*, always struggled, although they were later to attain an almost mythical status in Icelandic cultural history.

The progressive ideas current among Icelandic intellectuals sprang from the national ideals of the century, with the 1830 July Revolution in Paris as the main turning point. "The entire world is in an uproar, and great events seem to be near. The freedom spirit of man awakens and demands its rights from kings and dictators," as the law student Baldvin Einarsson (1801–33) described the turmoil of revolution (*Hafnarstúdentar skrifa heim*, ed. Sigmundsson, 56). With his writings in the journal *Ármann á Alþingi* (1829–32; Guardian at the Althing) Einarsson became a forerunner of those who wanted to awaken the spirit of the Icelandic nation and promote education and progress in the country. When, in 1831, Frederik VI, the king of Denmark, reacted to his subjects' demands for increased citizens' rights by founding four Consultative Assemblies for each of the four regions of the Danish state (Holstein, Schleswig, Jutland, and the islands [i.e., Zealand and other islands, Iceland among them]), Einarsson thought it right and proper that Icelanders should get a Consultative Assembly of their own, to which they themselves would elect representatives. He suggested, in fact, that the ancient symbol of national unity, the Althing at Þingvellir, should be reestablished.

The Icelandic fight for a national parliament continued into the 1840s. In 1843 Christian VIII decreed that an Icelandic Consultative Assembly should be founded, and in the summer of 1845 the new Althing met for the first time. Reykjavík was chosen as its location instead of Þingvellir, which created a great rift between those who wanted to build on the ancient tradition of parliament and those who wanted a more modern structure. The poets generally made up the former group; the leading proponent of the latter viewpoint was the historian and philologist Jón Sigurðsson (1811–79), the main political leader of the century and the strongest advocate of Icelandic self-governance. Sigurðsson first laid out his demands in one of the most influential political essays in Icelandic history, "A Homily to Icelanders," in the annual journal *Ný félagsrit* (1841–73; New society papers) in the revolutionary year 1848. The essay was written on the occasion of the Danish king's renunciation of absolute power and the introduction of a new and more liberal system of government.

The next few years were marked by great turbulence in Icelandic society, accompanied by protest meetings, petitions to the king, and a rousing of the national spirit. A public meeting in 1848 went so far as to claim that

Icelanders constituted "a nation apart with full nationality and national rights and a free country linked to Denmark but not part of it" (*Undirbúningsblað*, 1:3). For this reason Icelanders were entitled to a national parliament that would decide on national matters. This political fight influenced the era's literature in many ways; indeed, poets played a significant role in rousing the patriotic feelings of their countrymen. The turbulence reached its peak at the National Assembly in the summer of 1851 when the Danish government tried to contain Iceland permanently within the Danish state, with fervent opposition from the popularly elected Icelandic representatives, who demanded self-government in personal union with Denmark. This meeting — at which the representatives' final words were, "We all protest!" — constitutes a turning point in Icelandic political history, when the demand for Icelandic sovereignty was first made. Icelanders reached an important stage when they celebrated the millennium of settlement in 1874. That year they were granted their own constitution and were guaranteed legislative and budgetary powers in internal affairs. In the same year a special ministry for Iceland was founded in Copenhagen.

With the reestablishment of the Althing in Reykjavík in 1845, urban life began to come into its own. At around the same time the only printing press in the country, Landsprentsmiðjan (the National Printing Works) was established in Reykjavík (1844), the Latin School was moved back to town (1846), and the seminary, the first step toward an Icelandic university, was founded there (1847). During these years the number of inhabitants also increased, owing largely to the growing numbers of fishermen and craftsmen: in 1850 there were 1,150 people living in Reykjavík and in 1880 2,600, compared to a national population of 72,500. With this continuing population increase new life was breathed into Reykjavík's cultural and intellectual life. After the return of the Latin School, theater performances began anew, and Reykjavík even had its own poets from among the ranks of teachers and schoolboys. And this time it was considered right and proper to write in Icelandic rather than Danish.

National cultural societies also developed. Of special importance were the Reykjavík department of the Icelandic Literary Society, which started publishing books, and a closed debating society called the Evening Society, consisting of selected intellectuals and merchants, that operated from 1861 to 1874 and had as its main aim to encourage Icelandic cultural life, especially literature and the fine arts. Among its members were the poets Matthías Jochumsson, Kristján Jónsson Fjallaskáld (1842–69), and Steingrímur Thorsteinsson (1831–1913), the painter Sigurður Guðmundsson (1833–74), the folklorist Jón Árnason (1819–88), and the composer Sveinbjörn

Sveinbjörnsson (1847–1927), who were all prominent contributors to Icelandic cultural life during the latter half of the century. The society held regular debates where members read from their own works and discussed literature and the issues of the day, both national and foreign: general education; an Icelandic university; the death penalty; Darwin's theories; women's rights; religious freedom; nihilism; and communism. The society also supported its members' publications, theater life, and playwriting. Although things were moving slowly, the dreams of Tómas Sæmundsson about the city of Reykjavík began to assume an increasingly realistic form.

ROMANTICISM: 1807–1830

Up to the middle of the nineteenth century progressive Icelandic poets looked to German and Danish literature for inspiration. Through Danish and German translations they also came into contact with the literatures of other countries. The type of writing in these countries, often referred to by literary historians as *Frühromantik* (early romanticism) or *Universalromantik* (universal romanticism), has few equivalents in contemporary Icelandic literature, however. The only poet who seems to have been at all aware of these tendencies was Bjarni Thorarensen, who studied law in Copenhagen from 1802 to 1811. In general these were fertile and exciting years in Danish culture, not least in literature. Already in the autumn of 1802, only a few weeks after Thorarensen's arrival in Copenhagen, an important event took place: the German-educated philosopher and natural scientist Henrich Steffens (1773–1845) began his series of lectures on natural philosophy and German romantic ideas on art and the genius. Parts of these lectures were published a year later under the title *Indledning til philosophiske Forelæsninger* (1803; Introduction to philosophical lectures). In his lectures Steffens sharply criticized the rationalism of the Enlightenment and its tendency to view individual phenomena without connecting them to a larger whole. Instead, he encouraged people to look at life in its entirety, with its infinite variety and its paradoxes, as a biological and spiritual unity, the symbol of an eternal and divine original idea. The one who clearly sensed this unity and could interpret it for others was the poet-genius, a spark of godliness itself.

Steffens's lectures and his connection with Danish poets are generally regarded as the beginning of Danish romanticism, but it is more difficult to trace his influence on Icelandic literature. Only one Icelander is known for certain to have attended the lectures regularly: the theologian Steingrímur Jónsson (1769–1845), later the bishop of Iceland. He was very attracted to

Steffens's theories and mentions them regularly in his diaries. Although it is at times claimed that Bjarni Thorarensen attended the lectures, there is, in fact, no proof for this. By his own account Thorarensen did not start writing with any seriousness until after he passed his bar exam in 1807, a year sometimes considered to mark the beginning of the national romanticism (*Nationalromantik*) that colors Danish literature during the next three decades. Among the events that sparked this Danish patriotism was the armed conflict between Denmark and England after the Napoleonic wars, which reached its historical height when the English navy attacked Copenhagen on 4 and 5 September 1807 and forced the Danes to surrender their fleet. Like many other students, Thorarensen took a direct part in the defense of the city, and he alludes to this clash in one of his very earliest poems, "Kveðja til Árna Helgasonar" (1808; A greeting to Árni Helgason), one of the first indications of national romanticism in Icelandic literature. While the poet expresses his undying love for his mother country and describes its beauty and dignity, he denounces the Danes for cowardice, which he blames on city life and a gentle landscape and climate.

In Bjarni Thorarensen's poetry one can, nevertheless, detect signs of the unity-of-life idea that Steffens advocated in his lectures and that is also widely apparent in the works of Adam Oehlenschläger (1779–1850), the Danish poet Bjarni Thorarensen admired the most. This idea finds its clearest expression in one of Thorarensen's earliest poems, "Skóggangan" (ca. 1808; The walk in the wood), which is in some respects reminiscent of Oehlenschläger's poetic drama "Sanct Hansaften-Spil" (1803; Midsummer night's play). In Thorarensen's poem the speaker describes in a distinctly exalted and poetic manner the bloom, fragrance, and song of a Danish wood at dawn and the transformation that the sun causes as it rises — in the form of a young and beautiful woman the speaker immediately embraces in boundless desire. And in between these two worlds, heavenly and earthly, spiritual and physical, holy and human, he senses the beauty of the whole of creation in the girl's milk-white bosom.

Thorarensen describes such convergence between man and nature in several other poems as well. "Skóggangan" is, nevertheless, unique among his poetry because of the exalted descriptions of the mild and fertile nature of the Continent. In other nature poems where the poet makes this environment his subject he rejects it utterly despite its beauty, as in his view it is related to the corruption and weaknesses of Western civilization and bourgeois society. Here, Danish nature first and foremost serves to sharpen the image that the poet develops of Iceland's barren but magnificent nature and to bolster his description of the priceless meaning that the country has for its inhabitants. In this way Thorarensen's nature poems usually have a national reference. They aim to emphasize and idealize that which characterizes Iceland and differentiates it from other countries. Most Icelandic poets followed his example up to the final decades of the century.

These common features do not alter the fact that Thorarensen stood quite apart from other Icelandic poets in his subject treatment because of his radical revolt against bourgeois attitudes and contemporary rational and utilitarian views. His attention was first and foremost directed at the unusual, the mysterious, and even the threatening, and he appeals to readers' emotions rather than their logical thought processes. In this respect he had much in common with German late romanticists. In his first published work, the patriotic and nature poems "Ísland" (1818; English trans.: "Iceland," in *Icelandic Lyrics*, ed. Beck) and "Íslands minni" (1819; English trans.: "National Anthem," in *North American Book of Icelandic Verse*, ed. Kirkconnell), for instance, he mainly considered the uninhabited and uncultivated side of nature and praised the wild and magnificent powers that had threatened his countrymen the most: glaciers; volcanoes; and the ocean. The poet describes these natural forces as guardian angels who protect the nation from the weaknesses of more southerly countries and form the main features of the rough-hewn but beautiful Fjallkona (Mountain Woman), the personification of Iceland and the country's unifying symbol. This view is clearly expressed in "Ísland":

Thou wonderful medley of frost and fire
Where fell-peaks and plains, scree and oceanwaves meet,
How fair to view art thou and wondrously dire
When flames from glaciers flow at thy feet!

Thy flames grant us vigour, thy frosts strength afford us,
Thy fells show us arduous blessings to reach;
Thy silver-hued sea, like a seraph with sword, us
E'er sever from faintness and fortitude teach.
(trans. Skuli Johnson in *Icelandic Lyrics*, ed. Beck, 29)

These early patriotic poems of Thorarensen's quickly found their place in the national consciousness, and until the turn of the century "Íslands minni" was the unofficial national anthem of Iceland. Despite this the poet's view of nature was far from conforming to that of the common people of Iceland, who usually based their aesthetic judgment of nature on how fertile it looked, as, for instance, in the verse of the popular poet Látra-Björg (Björg Einarsdóttir; 1716–84), whose appreciation of the Icelandic places she knew depended on how mild the weather was, how rich the vegetation was, and how inviting the areas were to hunting and fishing. It is, therefore, not certain whether the nature poetry of Bjarni Thorarensen had any national basis. More likely it echoes the popular theories of the seventeenth-century philosophers Montesquieu (1689–1755) and Johan Gottfried von Herder (1744–1803) that geographic position, landscape, and climate exercise a decisive influence on peoples and societies and give them their characteristics (see Guðnason): the cold makes men stronger and fortifies both body and mind, while warmth deprives them of strength and courage. With these ideas in mind the poet made a sharp distinction between Iceland and Denmark and maintained that it was exactly the calm and summer warmth that had turned the Danes into cowardly weaklings. In the poem "Ísland" he also compares the Icelandic landscape with the Danish and claims that the flat Denmark is a boringly bland country, almost like a face without a nose and eyes. All this was, of course, intended to establish Icelanders' belief and trust in their own country, and to prove to them that it was not inferior to others even if its natural fertility was considerably less. The rationalization that "Iceland has never spoiled its children" would resound throughout the fight for independence during the century and was often related to a certain nostalgia, especially when evoking the memory of the heroic feats recounted in the Icelandic sagas.

Many of Thorarensen's patriotic poems reflect this type of connection between Icelandic nature and history. This is especially noticeable in one of his better-known poems, "Veturinn" (1823; English trans.: "Winter," in *Icelandic Lyrics*, ed. Beck), which the poet claimed to have written because he had read so many tedious spring poems (Thorarensen, *Ljóðmæli*, 2:129). This poem, like so many of Thorarensen's other poems, clearly shows the influence of the language and imagery found in Eddic poetry. Winter is personified as a dazzling and imposing saga hero who rides across the sky with a shield of ice on his shoulder and a helmet adorned with a sprinkling of aurora borealis. And here, as in his early nature poems, Thorarensen turns conventional ideas about the seasons upside down. In his eyes winter does not become an image of hardship and death; rather, it is described as a good, if slightly strict, father and mentor. It is he who rocks tired and weak earth children to sleep and spawns new and stronger progeny with Mother Earth. In this way he holds the world in his hands. He sustains life and strengthens it while at the same time settling the differences between opposite sides of existence. Here, as in much of Thorarensen's poetry, dualism is the ruling philosophy.

Dualism is also much apparent in Thorarensen's love poems, which are in many ways unique in nineteenth-century Icelandic poetry, both because of the daring descriptions and because of how closely love and beauty are related to disease, horror, and death. Here, everyday common sense loses out to burning passion and a desire to explode all boundaries that the body and earthly life set man. In the poem "Kysstu mig hin mjúka mær" (ca. 1820–33; English trans.: "Kiss Me," in *Icelandic Lyrics*, ed. Beck) the speaker whispers to his desperately ill beloved that he would gladly drink death from her lips because they are so beautiful: "Even death I gladly sip / From a rose, / For the beaker is so pure" (trans. Vilhjalmur Stefansson in *Icelandic Lyrics*, ed. Beck, 39).

This highly romantic desire of love and death is made even more obvious in "Sigrúnarljóð" (ca. 1820; English trans.: "Lines to Sigrún," in *North American Book of Icelandic Verse*, ed. Kirkconnell). It has been pointed out that this poem is in part modeled on examples from contemporary European literature, for instance, on Oehlenschläger's tragedy "Axel and Valborg" (1819), but the idea for the subject is from an Eddic lay, "Helga kviða Hundingsbana" II (The second lay of Helgi Hunding's killer; see p. 18). Here, the speaker tries to convince his beloved that his love will never fade even if she dies and her lips and cheeks lose their color. Or does not the sun kiss equally the white snow on a winter's day and the red summer roses? Thus, he asks his beloved to come to him by night if she dies before him so that he can still enjoy her love in death:

So when my ardor answers
And I open my arms and hold you,
Cast then your cold white bosom
Quickly upon my heart, dear!
Press on my pulses closely,
Press till your passion shall losen
My soul from the flesh and its fetters
To follow you upward forever.
(trans. Watson Kirkconnell in *North American Book of Icelandic Verse*, ed.
 Kirkconnell, 125)

Thorarensen's revolt against bourgeois ideology and lifestyle is also clearly apparent in the elegies he wrote about some of his talented contemporaries who went their own ways and were, therefore, outcasts in society, scorned and hounded. In these poems the poet investigates the inner life of these rightly named *individuals* who never wavered despite the odds and uses daring and grandiose metaphors to analyze and explain the paradoxes that marked their lives: for instance, their rich spiritual lives and their poor circumstances. As well as drawing clear images of these unique men, Thorarensen makes of them obvious symbols of the romantic genius, the one who renounces the life of the masses and creates instead his own utopia of freedom and beauty. They are like the salmon that strive upstream despite waterfalls and rapids.

Bjarni Thorarensen was neither a prolific writer nor especially concerned with getting his poetry into print. Consequently, his influence on Icelandic literature was limited in the early years, although he was respected as a poet and many of his poems became well-known. After he moved from Copenhagen to Iceland in 1811 and became one of the country's most powerful civil servants, first as a judge at the High Court and then as the regional governor (*amtmaður*) in the northeastern region, he became isolated from contemporary cultural movements. His only allies were the teachers in the Latin School at Bessastaðir, Sveinbjörn Egilsson (1791–1852), the poet and translator of Homer, and Hallgrímur Scheving (1781–1861), also a translator. Thorarensen's poetry was first discussed publicly in 1832 when Tómas Sæmundsson wrote a pamphlet in Danish, *Island fra den intellectuelle Side betragtet* (Iceland seen from an intellectual viewpoint), in which he encouraged Thorarensen to tend to his poetic muse as Iceland had never had a greater poetic genius (*et Digtergenie*): "Does he not understand that poets, like Molière, Milton and Klopstock, Holberg and Evald, have done more for their mother countries and the world than the Napoléons, more for ethics and religion than a thousand spiritual men. Not to use and develop such a talent is to refuse one of the most brilliant of God's gifts and is also to reject Poetry's holy spirit!" (13). These words describe well Sæmundsson's ideas on the importance of poets for their nation and, in fact, for the whole of humanity, religion, and ethics. With words alone they do more good than the spiritual and earthly authorities put together. The usefulness of literature and other arts depends, not on serving the powers that be, but on maintaining independence from them. Sæmundsson discussed these issues at length in his *Ferðabók*, maintaining Immanuel Kant's view that all proper art is an "autonomous play of the imagination": "It is free, it follows the law it sets itself" (333). Thorarensen probably found such ideas attractive. With the journal *Fjölnir*, which Sæmundsson edited together with the lawyer Brynjólfur Pétursson (1810–51), the poet and natural scientist Jónas Hallgrímsson and the philologist Konráð Gíslason (1808–91), innovative authors like Thorarensen finally found a proper outlet for their writings, and Thorarensen's influence on Icelandic literature grew.

It was, however, not until six years after Thorarensen's death that his anthology *Kvæði* (1847; Poems) was first published and received plaudits from younger poets. One of them, the impressionable Gísli Brynjúlfsson (1827–88), even maintained in his diary of 1848 that Thorarensen was "the greatest poet in the world" because his best works were more magnificent than any other writing (*Dagbók í Höfn*, 96). In an 1845 article another young poet, Grímur Thomsen, had placed Thorarensen among "the great poetic minds, who have in common that their wondrous imagination and depth of feeling at times overcome taste and intellect": "[Thorarensen] is one of the giants in the kingdom of poetry, on whom pedantic aesthetics cannot set rules: they break all bounds. With their superior strength of genius they even turn every breaking of a rule into beauty and originality" ("Bjarni Thorarensen," 196). Gísli Brynjúlfsson's and Grímur Thomsen's comments are clear indications of the adoration of the genius in the nineteenth century as well as of the understanding of literature that was in the making among Icelandic intellectuals around the middle of the century. In their view readers should identify with a work and try to understand the independent reality portrayed there, rather than judge it from a prepared set of rules or models.

NATIONAL ROMANTICISM AND POETIC REALISM: 1830–1843

The revolutionary year 1830 marks a turning point in Icelandic history and culture because of the nationalist ideas that then began to occupy people's minds. As usual Copenhagen was the ideological center. Initially, the law student Baldvin Einarsson played a significant role in strengthening national ambitions and in forming Icelanders' thinking on economic and political matters, but, after his sudden death in 1833, the editors of *Fjölnir* took up the fight. They, too, participated eagerly in the political debate of the time, and one of them, the lawyer Brynjólfur Pétursson, became in 1848 the first director of a separate Department of Icelandic Affairs in Copenhagen. At the same time the editors tried to draw their readers' attention to the poor state of affairs in Icelandic society and culture. In their opinion not only were Icelanders far behind other Europeans in this regard, but they were even more backward than their ancestors. They suffered from dullness of mind, lack of will, lethargy, and ignorance. It was essential to remove this dam to allow the nation's lifeblood to flow freely. The editors of *Fjölnir* especially pointed out three areas that could improve the nation's ability, awaken patriotism within Icelanders, and encourage general progress: the reestablishment of the Althing at Þingvellir as a national assembly; a better knowledge of the old sagas and the language that they preserved; and a careful examination of Icelandic nature. They also emphasized strongly that Icelanders should learn from other nations and use the progress that had already been made there to their own advantage.

Fjölnir was the first Icelandic journal largely dedicated to literature, one of its main objectives being the education of the nation in aesthetic matters, that is, to "awaken the feeling for beauty, which some consider to be a bit slow with us Icelanders" (*Fjölnir* 1 [1835]: 12). This attempt was closely related to the general idealistic ambitions of the editors. Like the German poet Friedrich von Schiller (1759–1805) and the Danish aesthete Johan Ludvig Heiberg (1791–1860), they considered beauty, not an isolated phenomenon, but closely related to all other aspects concerning man. It would, for instance, strengthen people's moral fiber and love of truth because it would not stand for brutishness or lies. The fine arts also had, then, a practical value as they would encourage people to consider their daily environment and lifestyle and to perform their daily tasks well in every way.

There is no doubt that the editors of *Fjölnir* provoked a strong response with their subject matter and manner of expression as they were both radicals and propagandists who neither strove for popularity nor worried whether the public liked the material on offer, be it fiction or general articles. Many resented this "revolutionary pamphlet" that sharply criticized most things Icelanders had been used to from childhood, from the general demeanor of the common people, their sense of dress, and their housing, to language, fiction, and, not least, political and economic issues. Most obvious was the opposition among the older generation of civil servants and intellectuals, who strongly objected to the apparent lack of respect and also to the criticism that the young men directed against other people's views. Conventional authors of the old school also rose to the defense of their tradition, which was now under attack. The young generation, on the other hand, applauded the journal, which played an important role in forming their ideas about the future of Icelandic culture.

Fjölnir's main poet was the natural scientist Jónas Hallgrímsson. Like Bjarni Thorarensen, Hallgrímsson developed his artistic talent in Copenhagen, where he stayed more or less from 1832 until the day he died in 1845. Initially, he was greatly influenced by European national romanticism, particularly the adoration of the past and nature. In many cases the love of nature and the love of the past converge in Hallgrímsson's work and form a clear antithesis to contemporary life, which, in his view, bore many signs of decadence. His poems thus have an ethical as well as a political message. This is most obviously demonstrated in the groundbreaking poem "Ísland" (1835; English trans.: "Iceland," in Ringler, *Bard of Iceland*), which was published in the first issue of *Fjölnir*. It is a tragic poem in elegiac form about the settlement of Iceland and the Commonwealth period, a time that was, according to the poet, characterized by freedom, beauty, and prosperity. This was the time when heroes populated the country and decorated ships sailed to bring back valuable cargo. The symbol of this fertile time, and the national spirit that it inspired, was the Althing at Þingvellir. There the splendid leaders of the sagas assembled, passed laws, and governed their own affairs, among them the chieftain Snorri goði Þorgrímsson (see pp. 92, 132, 136). The present situation was the complete opposite. The Althing was gone, and the nation's memories of its ancestors were forgotten:

> Snorri's old shed is a sheep pen: The Law Rock is hidden in heather,
> blue with the berries that yield boys and the ravens a feast.
> O you children of Iceland, old men and young men together!
> See how your forefathers' fame faltered and passed from the earth!
> (trans. Dick Ringler in his *Bard of Iceland*, 101)

In many of his later poems, Hallgrímsson reiterated and sharpened this contrast between the golden age now past and the downfall and humiliation of the nation in later times. This is especially apparent in "Gunnarshólmi" (1838; English trans.: "Gunnar's Holm," in Ringler, *Bard of Iceland*), where one of the best-known and bravest heroes of the sagas, Gunnar of Hlíðarendi (see p. 133), becomes patriotism personified as well as converging with the land itself and protecting it from destruction. Here, as in Hallgrímsson's "Ísland," the everlasting beauty and grandeur of nature serve to remind readers of the noble example set by their ancestors, their patriotism, nobility, and heroic feats, and give the nation hope of a brighter future in spite of being down at heel and living in poor conditions. In this way the poet urges his contemporaries to do well while criticizing them at the same time. The poet's sharp criticism of his spiritless contemporaries seems to have got through to his readers, for some sprang to the defense. In 1836 a considerable critique of the romantic adoration of the past, as championed by *Fjölnir*, was published in the journal *Sunnanpósturinn*, and the poem "Ísland" was said to be "an epitaph proper over Iceland" (Sverrisson, 28).

Despite such criticism, Hallgrímsson did not waver from his convictions. The poems "Alþing hið nýja" (1841; The new Althing) and "Annað kvæði um alþing" (1843; Another poem on the Althing) both constitute a direct contribution to the political discussion of the time. In the first poem the poet celebrates King Christian VIII's suggestion from 1840 to start the preparation for an Icelandic representative parliament and describes it as a gift of freedom to the nation. He also praises the perseverance and hard work of the nation and encourages it to even greater feats. In the latter poem, on the other hand, he pokes relentless fun at the ideas that the king put forth in 1843 about the working practices and location of this assembly, which, instead of a general democratic assembly, was now to become a gathering of a few civil servants, clergymen, and landowners. Worse, it was to be held in the half-Danish town of Reykjavík and not at Þingvellir, the place blessed by both nature and God during the settlement period.

Apart from national romanticism, the bourgeois literary movements in Denmark and Germany of the 1820s and 1830s, Biedermeier and the literary sensibility called poetic realism (*poetisk realisme, Poetischer Realismus*), influenced Hallgrímsson's poetry. Poetic realism involved a revolt against the initial idealism of romanticism and advocated a more pronounced rationalism than before as well as a will to strengthen ties to the times, everyday reality, society, and the immediate environment. It also involved a demand that poetry be beautiful and unified in its ideas and form and that it not offend general moral and classical taste. This of course presumed that a certain "selection" be made from reality, emphasizing common and superficial matters rather than the individual or psychological, while only the beautiful and the ethical were deemed proper.

It is not least these connections with poetic realism that separate the patriotic and nature poetry of Jónas Hallgrímsson from the antihumanitarian poetry of Bjarni Thorarensen, in which an uninhibited imagination and depth of feeling sometimes prevailed over fine form and taste. Hallgrímsson usually directs his attention to the knowable reality of this world, and often his descriptions are strictly tied to well-known Icelandic places, persons, and details from everyday life. Also apparent is a profound interest in the issues of the day, science, education, politics, and general working life at sea and on the farm. "Icelandic means of survival were for [Hallgrímsson] so clearly felt, with a deep lyricism, that in his most beautiful poems he could talk about the cod and the cow," wrote Halldór Laxness in 1929 (Laxness, *Alþýðubókin*, 60).

In general, Hallgrímsson supported liberal ideas and emphasized democratic reform and progress as molded by contemporary liberal views. He also had many things in common with the radical poets of Das junge Deutschland, however, although his political views were certainly more moderate in the works that were intended for publication. In his private letters and the poetry contained within them, however, he could at times be very direct, sarcastic, and crude. Usually, Hallgrímsson took the side of the masses, especially the farming classes, whose hard work was never-ending. In his mind the farmer was the pillar of society and the farm a pillar of the country, while, on the other hand, there existed a certain suspicion, even coldness, between him and the small class of Icelandic civil servants. Accordingly, his language is usually of the common colloquial variety. It is certainly more polished and more refined than everyday speech, but markedly more simple and easier to understand than had been the norm in Icelandic literature.

Owing to these characteristics the works of Hallgrímsson have never been considered especially romantic but have, rather, been tied to the Enlightenment or classicism. His nostalgia and his adoration of his native country are, however, clearly of the romantic persuasion, and the same can be said of his religious attitude toward nature. Here, he seems to have had views similar to those of Tómas Sæmundsson, who adhered to the views of the German theologian and philosopher Friedrich Schleiermacher (1768–1834) and maintained that religious belief should be based on "the natural inclination of each and every one to be connected to something higher and divine" (Sæmundsson, *Ferðabók*, 143). This neo-orthodoxy (*Supernaturalismus*), with its emphasis on the individual, his insight and feelings, led Jónas Hallgrímsson at times to a degree of pantheism where nature became a symbol of God. Similar views were also presented in the Danish pious text *Betragtninger over de christelige Troeslærdomme* (1833; Thoughts on Christian religious education) by Jakob P. Mynster, the bishop of Zealand, which Hallgrímsson helped translate into Icelandic, the translation appearing in 1839. This translation soon became very popular, decreasing, thereby, the influence of the religious writing of the Enlightenment.

In his nature poems Hallgrímsson was first and foremost the poet of vegetation, summer, and sunshine. In this way his poetry also differed markedly from that of the poet of mountains and winter, Bjarni Thorarensen. Hallgrímsson always focused closely on individual natural phenomena, writing especially about small creatures: bluebells; the bumblebee; the mouse; and the thrush. As a natural scientist he traveled across almost all the country as he intended later to write a detailed description of Iceland. Many of his poems are related to his travels in one way or another, for instance, "Fjallið Skjaldbreiður" (1841; English trans.: "Mount Broadshield," in Ringler, *Bard of Iceland*). This poem is one of the few where the harsher elements of nature are emphasized as it partly describes the creation of the momentous landscape of Þingvellir as a result of enormous volcanic activity:

Broadshield's icecap opened! Brawling
earthquakes wrenched and tore the land,
stunned as if the stars were falling,

strewn to Earth by heaven's hand;
spitting like a spray of midges
sparks went hissing through the air;
lava, spewed from rents and ridges,
wreaked destruction everywhere.
(trans. Dick Ringler in his *Bard of Iceland*, 192)

In most of Hallgrímsson's poems, however, the land is gentle and fertile, and it is interesting how often nature is given human features or appears as a supernatural being with a human face. In many of his poems Hallgrímsson creates images of green valleys where herds of cattle graze, lakes are full of fish, and pink fields abound. At the same time the beautiful and nonpractical vegetation, "the red rose," or at least the dandelion and buttercup, always has a safe place. As such the poems have a direct correlation in classical pastoral poetry. A good example of this is the following lines from "Gunnarshólmi": "Never before has Iceland seemed so fair, / the field so golden, roses in such glory, / such crowds of sheep and cattle everywhere!" (trans. Dick Ringler in his *Bard of Iceland*, 137). Only during the last years of his life did Hallgrímsson write increasingly about the bare and dangerous aspects of Icelandic nature, although not with the admiration that we find in Bjarni Thorarensen's work, but rather with suspicion and fear. By then his view of life and poetic style had also markedly changed.

ROMANTISME: 1843–1848

From the beginning an echo of loss and grief could be heard in the poetry of Jónas Hallgrímsson. This echo became increasingly louder during the last years of his life (1843–45), and the poetry became more inward looking and personal than before. The poet's close connection to his environment and the issues of the day was cut; he even started complaining that time would not tie itself to him. Instead in the late work we find oppressive loneliness, depression, and pessimism. These feelings were at least partly due to personal circumstances, such as the poet's illness and dire straits (he never obtained a permanent position), the death of close friends, and the loss of the many ideals that he had cherished, such as the establishment of the Althing at Þingvellir, the journal *Fjölnir*, and a text that he had worked on for a long time on the nature of Iceland. At the same time, however, the poet's pessimism had an obvious parallel in the European culture of the day: godlessness; nihilism; and weltschmerz. These marked Danish literature from the 1830s and 1840s to a large extent. Now, the individual was at the center of the poetry, and sentimentalism, fear, and ennui were the ruling sensibilities.

Hallgrímsson's ties to Danish literature are evident in that at the end of his life he translated poetry by two of its most important writers, the poet Frederik Paludan-Müller (1809–76) and the critic Peter Ludvig Møller (1814–65). Both were great admirers of George Gordon, Lord Byron (1788–1824). An obvious echo from his work ("The Tear," 1806) can be heard in Hallgrímsson's poems "Kveðja til Þorgeirs Guðmundssonar" (1839; A greeting to Þorgeir Guðmundsson) and "Einbúinn" (1845; English trans.: "The Solitary," in Ringler, *Bard of Iceland*). In "Einbúinn" the speaker describes his lonesome wanderings through nature in search of a secure place of his own. His search is fruitless, however: "Now I dwell all alone / in a home of my own / where the howling inferno is red" (trans. Dick Ringler in his *Bard of Iceland*, 350). These last-mentioned poems are among the first instances of Byron's influence on Icelandic literature.

Hallgrímsson's greatest example, however, was Heinrich Heine (1797–1856). Not only did Hallgrímsson translate much of Heine's poetry, but he also adjusted his own writing to Heine's style. This is most clearly exemplified in the group of poems entitled "Annes og eyjar" (English trans.: "Capes and Islands," in Ringler, *Bard of Iceland*), which Hallgrímsson wrote in the last year of his life. These are what might be termed *travel pictures* from Iceland, composed in the well-known Heine form, where nature is always in the foreground. The attention is, however, directed, not at nature's beauty, fertility, and goodness, as in the patriotic poems "Ísland" and "Gunnarshólmi," but at the deserted and alien, which provide neither comfort nor rest. The poems are characterized by mystery, fear, and death, and nature is the symbol of neither the nation nor the national spirit as before. Rather, it mirrors the personal feelings of the speaker and his thoughts about life and death. Life is usually in a losing position, and, although some beauty still persists in these poems, cynicism always has the last word and leaves the reader with an oppressive uncertainty and doubt. Another change in these later poems is that, instead of direct references to known facts, the emphasis is now placed on the unique and on personal perceptions and references. As a result many of the poems are quite obscure, as the poet himself pointed out in a note to one of them: "Here explanation is necessary if anyone is to understand" (Hallgrímsson, *Ritsafn*, 4:224). In this way he departed for the most part from poetic realism.

"Annes og eyjar" is among Hallgrímsson's most pessimistic poetry. In most of his other poems from the last years of his life the speaker is able to turn away from pessimism by referring to divine intervention or an existentialist outlook, where the individual becomes responsible for his own life and must give it meaning through his own actions and thoughts. For, despite everything, he still has thoughts and feelings, and it is better at least to "feel and live" than lie dead in one's grave. Here, a connection may be detected with the existential philosophy of one of Hallgrímsson's Danish contemporaries in Copenhagen, Søren Kierkegaard (1813–55), whose main emphasis was on the individual himself shaping his existence with his own decisions and actions. As a result of this outlook the desperation was never as bleak as that expressed in a letter from one of Hallgrímsson's best friends, Konráð Gíslason, who wrote him in 1844: "And the sun is not as bright and the weather not as warm and the world not as beautiful as in 1834. For God's sake, comfort me, Jónas! I have lost the whole world. Give me back the world, dear Jónas! and I will never ask you again" (Gíslason, 69–70).

In the 1840s a few poems by three young writers who were later to gain in influence were published in *Fjölnir*. These poets were Grímur Thomsen, Benedikt Gröndal (1826–1907), and Jón Thoroddsen (1818–68), all of them then university students in Copenhagen and very much influenced by the individualism and the sentimentality of their time. Grímur Thomsen was in many ways the forerunner of these writers as he was both precocious and greatly interested in the latest European literature and philosophy. In 1845 Thomsen stayed in Iceland for one year and taught French to the schoolboys at the Latin School as well as sharing his knowledge of contemporary philosophy and literature. In his autobiography, *Dægradvöl* (Passing the time), Benedikt Gröndal says that the young Grímur had been "the 'herald' of a new time" (Gröndal, *Ritsafn*, 4:345), heading the changes in the ideas of the younger generation. Among the works that Thomsen introduced to the students was *Die Leiden des jungen Werthers* (1774) by Johann Wolfgang von Goethe (1747–1832), and many became entranced by it. During these years Thomsen was, however, mainly interested in English and French contemporary literature, on which he wrote extensively in Danish: *Om den ny franske Poesi* (1843; On new French poetry) and *Om Lord Byron* (1845; On Lord Byron). He also took an active part in Danish literary debates and wrote a considerable amount for Danish papers. All these writings bear witness to his burning interest in the philosophy of Wilhelm Friedrich Hegel (1770–1831) and Kierkegaard, but it is also clear that he was well-read in contemporary literary theory, which increasingly interpreted writings in the light of the personality of the author and his times, inheritance, and environment.

With "Ólund" (1844; Ennui) and "Hafið" (1844), his translation, or rather imitation, of part of "Ocean" from Byron's *Childe Harold's Pil-*

grimage, Thomsen also introduced the new tone of weltschmerz into Icelandic literature. In "Ólund" the speaker's strongest desire is to rest his bones at the bottom of the ocean, stare "sad and broken-eyed" at the cold, horrific, tragic play of drowned men, and listen to the ocean's heavy moans of sadness. The same tone of weltschmerz, loneliness, and death also sets its mark on his other poems from this time, such as "Haustvísa" (1845; Autumn verse).

Soon, however, the weather changed. In an essay from 1846 on Icelandic literature old and new Thomsen attacked the "useless pessimism and feminine sentimentality that the elegies of the literature of our time bring forth" ("Den islandske Literaturs Charakteristik," 203). The main targets of his criticism were the poets of the "neo-German weakness," Heinrich Heine and Georg Herwegh (1817–75), although Ossian and Jónas Hallgrímsson were mentioned in the same breath. Against their poetry Grímur Thomsen placed the "courageous and profound patriotic poetry" of Bjarni Thorarensen, which he regarded as representative of "pagan romanticism" in nineteenth-century Icelandic literature, a term that applies equally well to Grímur Thomsen's later writing. Like Thorarensen, Thomsen finds his subject matter in medieval Icelandic literature, history, and nature. In his view literature had to carry certain national characteristics to be worthy of its name. Unlike other Icelandic writers, Thomsen was an advocate of the Scandinavianism of the time, which colored his poetry and his views on Icelandic nationality to some extent. Many of his poems are about ancient heroes of the Nordic countries or men who accomplished their feats outside Iceland. Thus, specifically Icelandic viewpoints are balanced considerably with a pan-Nordic sensibility.

Benedikt Gröndal has also been considered a revolutionary in Icelandic literature, and his innovative lyric forms influenced other poets, among them Matthías Jochumsson and Kristján Jónsson Fjallaskáld. Gröndal's earliest poems, from 1847, are, however, written in a style similar to that in Jónas Hallgrímsson's poetic cycle "Annes og eyjar" or, by extension, Heine's poetry. Their subject is the dreamlike and ghostly night, lit by a deathly pale moon or draped in grey fog, and the battle of life and death where land and ocean meet. Men kill themselves by walking into the sea, mermaids seduce them, or they are sold to bloodthirsty monsters from the depths of the ocean. All this is colored by a dualism in such a way that reality and dream converge. A good example of this is the poem "Nótt" (1847; English trans.: "Night," in *Icelandic Lyrics*, ed. Beck).

Many have considered Gröndal the most romantic of Icelandic writers because of his limitless imagination and his powerful and lyric language. In light of literary history, however, he appears as one of the best representatives of late romantic thought, a meditative explorer who, in many of his poems, battles with the ultimate existential questions and constantly swings between extremes. The unity between mind and matter, which characterizes most of Bjarni Thorarensen's and Jónas Hallgrímsson's works, is nowhere to be found. Between these two poles there rather exists a constant tension that it is not always possible to dissolve. At times the speaker is a misunderstood lone figure who does not have anything in common with his contemporaries, or he is a holy genius who sails the heavens or dives down into the blossom of the smallest of flowers in search of some understanding of reality. This speaker is not dissimilar from the poet himself, who was certainly highly educated in the natural sciences and Nordic studies as well as a talented draftsman and calligraphist, but who still had problems settling down in bourgeois society. During the latter half of the nineteenth century he was, nevertheless, quite popular and respected as a writer and was often considered to be one of the main national poets of his day. In the early twentieth century, however, other poets such as Grímur Thomsen who were considered to be more "Icelandic," that is, more masculine and moderate, overshadowed him. Gröndal's philosophical poems, which undoubtedly are among his most ambitious works, have never found favor among critics.

At the end of the 1840s several more noteworthy writers appeared who have since been mostly forgotten. Among them was Gísli Brynjúlfsson, one of the publishers of the journal *Norðurfari* (1848–49). Among the original writing in the journal there were two elegies written in the style of Lord Byron that aroused much attention: "Faraldur" (1848; Plague) and "Grátur Jakobs yfir Rakel" (1848; Jakob's lament for Rachel). These poems contain the life stories and tears of grief of men who have lost everything they valued — their country, their beloveds, and their friends — and are now awaiting death or wandering aimlessly in foreign countries bereft of hope. The tone of the poems is characterized by sentimentality, melancholy, and a complete lack of interest in practical matters or other people as everything in the world is considered to be empty, bare, and worthless. Similar views characterize most of Brynjúlfsson's other poems of these years. "In vain have I lived" he writes, only twenty years old, in the poem "Nú eru liðin tvisvar tíu" (1847; Now two times ten have passed).

This ennui is equally apparent in Brynjúlfsson's diary from 1848, *Dagbók í Höfn* (Diary in Copenhagen), the piece of Icelandic writing most marked by European *romantisme*. Here, the writer swings between extremes, caught in either the ecstasy of adoration or the depths of pessimism. Brynjúlfsson clearly defines himself as different from other people and lives completely immersed in the lyric and melancholy world of young Werther and Byron's heroes: "What is steady, unmoveable, and eternal? I do not know, but I would nevertheless give everything for the knowledge that something were steady, that something would be left when everything else topples and is destroyed, because now I am hapless, so completely without hope and support, and I find nothing that I can aim for with complete trust or conviction" (*Dagbók í Höfn*, 271). *Dagbók í Höfn* did not reach its readers until a century after it was written and is, therefore, first and foremost of documentary value for its depiction of the world of ideas inhabited by the author around the middle of the nineteenth century. Brynjúlfsson's poems mentioned above were, however, for a while very popular in Iceland among the younger generation and influenced other writers, for instance, the popular poet Hjálmar Jónsson of Bóla (1796–1875) and the eulogist Kristján Jónsson Fjallaskáld. After 1848 political activity and idealism grew in strength, in part a response to the preceding pessimism, although without doing away with it completely.

Weltschmerz was the most prominent feature in the poems of the sensitive and rootless writer Kristján Jónsson, who became nationally known in 1861 for his poem "Dettifoss" (English trans.: "The Cataract," in *Icelandic Lyrics*, ed. Beck) when he was only nineteen years of age. This poem is greatly influenced by the melancholy poetry of Byron, Benedikt Gröndal, and Grímur Thomsen. The speaker asks that the ancient and gigantic waterfall (Dettifoss) become his burial place and that its maniacal laughter replace the traditional sounds of grief of bereft friends and relatives. The poems that followed all describe the same ennui, desperation, and doubt about the meaningless struggle of life. In some of these poems, for instance, "Gröfin" (1868; English trans.: "The Grave," in *Icelandic Lyrics*, ed. Beck), the speaker calls for death and the oblivion that follows it and describes the dark and silent grave as the only resting place for the sorrowful man. In other poems, such as "Tárið" (1866; English trans.: "The Tear," in *Icelandic Lyrics*, ed. Beck), the speaker looks for trust in God and in the hope of the better world that he promises mankind while he sings the praises of "the world's sweet soothing lake," the silvery tear, and prays that it never dries on his cheeks. The life of the poet, marked by poverty, mood swings, and excessive drinking, in many respects echoed his poetry. Jónsson did not live long, only twenty-seven years, yet one of his friends, Matthías Jochumsson, thought that he had died long before he breathed his last.

POLITICAL ENGAGEMENT AND (CRITICAL) IDEALISM:
1848–1882

The February 1848 Revolution in Paris and the freedom movement that
grew in its wake across Europe constituted a considerable antidote to the
existential crises of the preceding years, and many Icelandic writers awoke
to political thought and activism. As Gísli Brynjúlfsson wrote in his diary
on 5 July 1848: "Farewell, then, thought and lyricism! I want to run blind in
the whirlpool of the times. But terrible what has been happening in Paris.
Had I been there, I would have dipped my pen in human blood on the
streets and written news such as this" (*Dagbók í Höfn*, 236). Brynjúlfsson
wrote long articles about the political events in the journal *Norðurfari* in
1848 and 1849, and they are thought to have had some political influence in
Iceland and played their part in giving the Icelandic fight for independence
new impetus. Brynjúlfsson himself took, without hesitation, the side of the
revolutionaries and considered their bloody fight a necessary step in the
progress of mankind to a new and better social structure: "A new era has
begun for mankind. Now everything is in turmoil, so it is no use to look for
shelter or peace. . . . Much of the old has to die so that the new can be born;
and it may well be that everything that has gone on is nothing but the
beginning of the mighty revolutions that will be before the nations can rise
again from their ruins more beautiful and better" ("Frá Norðurálfunni,"
73). Brynjúlfsson also wrote a number of poems about contemporary revolutionary attempts that are unique in nineteenth-century Icelandic literature. Their influence at the time was, however, less than it should have been
as only a few of them were published until his anthology, *Ljóðmæli* (1891;
Lyric verses), appeared. Two of the poems were published in the 1850s and
1860s: "Fall Ungara" (1852; Fall of the Hungarians) and "Bjarkamál hin
nýju" (1860; The new lay of Bjarki). The former poem is about the revolt
and fight of the Hungarians against the might of the Russians, the poet
taking the side of the revolutionaries, while in the latter poem Brynjúlfsson
writes about the struggle for freedom waged by many nations around the
world. In these poems a completely different view becomes apparent from
that expressed in his aforementioned elegies. Here, he rises against sentimentality with hero and battle worship as people are encouraged to revolt
against their oppressors and temper their swords in their blood. A similar
development took place among many other writers who initially had been
influenced by weltschmerz. Benedikt Gröndal wrote about both mythical
heroes like the revolutionary Prometheus ("Prometheus" [1860]) and the
contemporary hero Napoleon ("Napóleon" [1860]), and, when Grímur

*From Romanticism to Realism*277

Thomsen started publishing poetry again toward the end of 1860s, he, too, was preoccupied with the ancient heroic world.

With the exception of only a few poems that are colored by internationalism or refer to foreign events, the political engagement among writers mostly manifested itself in the Icelandic fight for independence. Here, they followed in part in the footsteps of Bjarni Thorarensen and Jónas Hallgrímsson, making people aware of the riches that the Icelandic "holy trinity" of country, history, and language had to offer. Indeed, this trinity remained a beloved subject of Icelandic poets until well into the middle of the twentieth century. At the same time the fight for independence in the 1840s and 1850s gained a new momentum under the influence of contemporary realism and the cold rationalism that Jón Sigurðsson followed in his politics. One of Sigurðsson's "court poets" in *Ný félagsrit* was Steingrímur Thorsteinsson, primarily a nature poet searching for respite in sacred solitude, although he also wrote a few poems that carried a political message. Unlike Jónas Hallgrímsson's poetry, however, Thorsteinsson's was mostly cheerful battle calls and uplifting poems calling for increased freedom, rather than elegies. In Thorsteinsson's poems the worship of the past is not as overriding as it is in Jónas Hallgrímsson's works; rather, Thorsteinsson looks to the nation's time of humiliation in later centuries and to the future, which can be influenced through action. Of his patriotic battle poems the most notable are "Vorhvöt" (1870; Spring cry), "Þúsund ára sólhvörf" (1874; Thousand-year solstice) and "Þingvallasöngur" (1885; Song of Þingvellir).

Steingrímur Thorsteinsson's "Þúsund ára sólhvörf" was one of many poems written for the national millennial celebrations in 1874. Among other poems published on this particular occasion "Lofsöngur" (English trans.: "The Millennial Hymn of Iceland," in *Icelandic Lyrics*, ed. Beck), the lofty patriotic hymn by the Reverend Matthías Jochumsson, deserves mention as it later became the Icelandic national anthem. The speaker views the thousand-year history of the nation from the eternal vantage point of God and interprets these years as "Eternity's flow'r, with its homage of tears / That reverently passes away" (trans. Jakobina Johnson in *Icelandic Lyrics*, ed. Beck, 101). This poem has been interpreted as the "pained cry of a nation in distress," and the poet was certainly not blind to the terrible catastrophes that nature had inflicted on the country and its people. In a letter from 1871 he claims that he cannot and does not want to romanticize Iceland any longer: "I still see the setting sun kiss the mountains and silver threads in the fields, but the sun is no longer golden nor the dew bejeweled: death's grip has long since extinguished the sun's kiss and the silver thread of the heart" (Jochumsson, *Bréf*, 82). In the poem "Volaða land" (1888; Desolate country), Jochumsson even goes so far as to suggest that this barren land of drift ice is hardly suitable for human habitation, with people fleeing it in droves: "Would you not be better for ravens?" In another poem, "Hafísinn" (1888; English trans.: "Drift Ice," in *North American Book of Icelandic Verse*, ed. Kirkconnell), he revolts against Bjarni Thorarensen's idea that the cold makes the nation stronger and more courageous. In Jochumsson's eyes the drift ice becomes "our country's ancient foeman," the image of famine and death and everything that stifles the spirit, and serves only to strengthen cruelty and harshness. Jochumsson himself sees no divine purpose in the catastrophes that have been inflicted on the nation. On the other hand, he does ask people to believe and hope that death will eventually turn into its opposite.

Matthías Jochumsson was one of those who attended the university lectures of Georg Brandes on European contemporary literature in Copenhagen in the winter of 1871–72, later published as *Hovedstrømninger i det 19de Aarhundredes Literatur* (1872–90; Main currents in nineteenth-century literature), and later he became personally acquainted with this radical literary critic and scholar who launched the concepts of realism and naturalism in Scandinavia and, thus, brought about the naturalistic breakthrough in the early 1870s (see p. 312). Jochumsson always had great problems combining Brandes's materialism and atheism with his own passionate religious beliefs. In this respect he had much more in common with the influential Danish clergyman, poet, historian, and educationalist Nikolaj F. S. Grundtvig (1783–1872), who emphasized the Christian concepts of faith, hope, and charity in his hymns, some of which Jochumsson translated into Icelandic. Nevertheless, the liberal ideas of realism, humanitarianism, and critical thought found an immediate place in Jochumsson's heart. This is brought out, not only by his descriptions of Icelandic nature, where the country's gigantic elemental forces are powerless against the few tears of a young child, but also in his radical revolt against the century's uncritical admiration of its past. Unlike Jónas Hallgrímsson, Jochumsson felt that the world was on a steady trajectory of progress in most areas and that people were always bound to consider the demands of their own time. The ancient past could never, therefore, be a timeless model or an example of unsurpassed beauty and fame that people simply had to rekindle.

Other poets also revolted against national romanticism in one way or another during the latter half of the nineteenth century. Among them was the subsistence farmer Hjálmar Jónsson of Bóla, who presented a rather bleak picture of Icelandic nature and history in many of his poems. This poor, unschooled poet had in part assimilated the aestheticism of the educated poets, but he adjusted it to his own realistic and critical view of life. In his patriotic poems "Þjóðfundarsöngur" (1851; A song for the National Assembly) and "Ísland fagnar konungi sínum" (1874; Iceland welcomes its king) he turned against both the relentless admiration that Bjarni Thorarensen had for the country's harsh nature and the poetic realism of Jónas Hallgrímsson. Instead, he gave a frank description of how terribly centuries past had treated the Lady of the Mountains, sucked her blood, scraped the flesh off her bones, and left her for dead. In his view only the people and God could save Iceland from complete destruction. The country itself had no defenses left.

Such descriptions were a rarity in Icelandic literature at a time when idealism formed the most defining characteristic of national poetry, represented most clearly by Benedikt Gröndal, Steingrímur Thorsteinsson, and Matthías Jochumsson. They were all essentially Christian idealists who viewed nature and its individual phenomena as the manifestation of a divine reality. "You say: glacier is glacier, / but I say: God's sacred temple," says Jochumsson in his poem "Ferð upp í Fljótsdalshérað 1900" (1900; A trip to Fljótsdalur in 1900) in response to the ideas of contemporary materialism. This convergence of the national and the divine receives its most detailed expression in some of Steingrímur Thorsteinsson's poems, where the whole of nature is viewed as a "universal church," with the sky a "vaulted ceiling," the mountains a "high altar," rivers the "organ," and the sun "God's image." Clearly, this image has its basis in Plato's ideas; nature is considered the ideal to which men should adjust their imperfect lives. This view is also apparent in the following comments made by Thorsteinsson in 1873: "If life in our country was worthy of nature, if spiritual life was its embellished reflection and physical life would get its color from this reflection, then things would be as they should, but now it is in most areas awry and askew" (qtd. in Pétursson, *Steingrímur Thorsteinsson*, 212). As this quotation shows, idealism was often colored by social criticism. And, while attempting to realize ideals, the poets attacked hypocrisy in ethical and religious matters, along with pretense, corruption, and the love of material goods. They turned their wrath especially toward the "haute bourgeoisie" and Western civilization, "where a pretty veil of deceit hides many a disgusting and soiled thing," to quote Benedikt Gröndal (*Ritsafn*, 4:510). In this respect they had many things in common with the Danish poets who were influenced by "critical idealism" (*kritisk idealisme*, 1845–55).

One of the most radical was Gísli Brynjúlfsson, who writes in his diary: "In general I dislike mankind. I want to go out into dead but magnificent nature; in it there is no deceit or cruelty. . . . I have from childhood despised ministers and their kind, who pretend to be a holy godsend; they should, as the man said, be hanged by the gut of the last king" (*Dagbók í Höfn*, 136, 198). Other radical writers of this era include the painter Sigurður Guðmundsson, the journalist Jón Ólafsson (1850–1916), and Kristján Jónsson Fjallaskáld as well as Hjálmar Jónsson of Bóla. In their writings the authority of both worldly and spiritual leaders was cast in doubt. In 1870 the twenty-year-old Ólafsson was even sued for his poem "Íslendingabragur" (1870; A song of Icelanders), a violent attack on the Danes and Danish authority, written in the same meter as the revolutionary anthem of the French republicans, "La Marseillaise." He chose to leave the country for a while and later became one of the forerunners of the realistic movement in Icelandic literature. Other writers turned against men of the church for preaching "blind faith" and keeping people tied in a web of deceit. Against this Sigurður Guðmundsson proffered — in his play *Smalastúlkan* (The shepherdess), written in 1872 — a dream of a society in which there was freedom, beauty, and love. Here, reality was put on a pedestal, along with a "noble form of deception," to use the words of Steingrímur Thorsteinsson in a letter of 1883: "Many a thing in our times I find disturbing, especially the general and uncomforting understanding of the fate of man. But even if the pessimism of today were right many times over, I would rather live for a noble form of deception than for an unworthy truth" (qtd. in Pétursson, *Steingrímur Thorsteinsson*, 244).

Although some might dream about a unity of ideal and reality, of spirit and form, doubts were never far away. They often took the form of romantic irony, where the poets suddenly ruptured the beautiful web of deception that they had woven in their works and rose against their own words, as Jónas Hallgrímsson had consistently done in "Annes og eyjar." A good example is Steingrímur Thorsteinsson's poem "Efra og neðra" (before 1881; Higher and lower). Despite a "golden hue of sunlight" the hidden dangers of the world underneath the calm ocean can be spotted: a sunken ship and a deathly gray shark crunching a pink corpse. Even the main religious poet of the century, the minister Matthías Jochumsson, occasionally voiced doubts about the purpose of life. As an idealist he was constantly searching for a religious view that could oppose the materialism of the century, but he also realized that "truth in these heavenly matters is hardly the gift one receives in this world and hardly — with hands of hope and belief" (Jochumsson, *Bréf*, 575). Many of Jochumsson's poems are centered on his search for values he might rely on, a search in which blind desperation and a sincere belief in God compete. "God, dear God, I cry out /

through black darkness,— / as if from an oven / the burned heart shouts," he says in the poem "Guð, minn Guð, ég hrópa" (1898; God, dear God, I cry out). Faith customarily won this fight, and usually the poems end in a perfect harmony where the speaker commends himself to God.

Art was the other significant way in which poets harmonized ideal and reality. In Benedikt Gröndal's poem "Hugfró" (1858; Mind rest), the artist is represented as analogous to God and art as "God's mirror." In art the poet finds the essence of individual phenomena and intuits the relations between other seemingly unrelated phenomena. In this way art is man's route to higher knowledge as well as affording him rest in a turbulent world. On the basis of this reasoning the poet justified idealism in a lecture from 1888: "The idealistic view of life does not distance us from life or from reality; rather, the idealists are, quite to the contrary, true men of reality; they are always busy making the ideal into reality or realizing the ideal" (Gröndal, *Ritsafn*, 4:221). It was exactly these kinds of views on literature and reality that realism rose against and that in the 1880s became the main disputed issue in the debate between older and younger generations of Icelandic poets.

This debate has usually been considered to mark a certain break in Icelandic literary history: the end of national and aesthetic romanticism and the beginning of literary nationalism and social realism, focusing on such social problems as the relationship between the sexes and the rights of the individual. This does not at all mean, however, that the older poets were silenced or disappeared from the scene. On the contrary some of them were even more prolific during the last two decades of the century. These years were, for instance, the most fertile for Grímur Thomsen and Matthías Jochumsson. In the late 1870s Jón Ólafsson's older brother, the self-educated farmer Páll Ólafsson (1827–1905), became one of the most popular poets in Iceland for his humorous love and nature songs, written in a mixture of the traditional popular poetry of Sigurður Breiðfjörð (1798–1846) and the poetical realism of Jónas Hallgrímsson.

In the 1870s and 1880s it also became more common that poets had their works printed, although many still had to rely on journals, newspapers, or anthologies such as the popular selection of Icelandic poetry entitled *Snót* (1850, 1865, 1877; Lass). During the 1870s the selected poetry of Jón Thoroddsen, Kristján Jónsson Fjallaskáld, and Hjálmar Jónsson was published posthumously: Jón Thoroddsen's *Kvæði* (1871; Poems); Kristján Jónsson's *Ljóðmæli* (1872; Lyric verses); and Hjálmar Jónsson's *Ljóðmæli* (1879). In 1880 the first collection of Grímur Thomsen's poetry appeared under the title *Ljóðmæli* (1880), and a second enlarged edition followed in

1895. Steingrímur Thorsteinsson published a selection of his original poetry in 1881 (*Ljóðmæli*), three years later Matthías Jochumson's *Ljóðmæli* (1884) appeared in print, and it was not until 1891 that, as we have seen, Gísli Brynjúlfsson's poetry was collected and published under the same title. For the first time many of the most interesting poems from the second half of the nineteenth century became accessible to the public. In 1883–84 the anthologies of Bjarni Thorarensen and Jónas Hallgrímsson were also reissued; and, remarkably perhaps, those who edited the poems and wrote the poets' biographies were the self-declared realists Einar H. Kvaran (1859–1938) and Hannes Hafstein (1861–1922). As paradoxical as this may sound the era of realism in Icelandic literature saw a great blossoming of the very literature that the realists sought to replace.

AESTHETICS AND IDEAS ON LITERATURE

Icelandic writers of the nineteenth century did not publish much on aesthetics or on the nature of literature. Bjarni Thorarensen's ideas on the matter are, for instance, demonstrated only in his private letters. There, however, it becomes apparent that he was a follower of the romantic ideas of the period. He considered literature to be an independent phenomenon, to be valued according to its originality and the inspiration of the writer. With such criteria in mind he criticized the literature of the Enlightenment as too pedestrian and prosaic and the popular *rímur* poets as base and tasteless. He also claimed that a view of artistic beauty is utterly independent from any consideration of "practicality" or "goodness." "It is not always aesthetically ugly, that which can damage — the sea has done away with many but still is one of the majestic elements, like thunder and lightning," he wrote in 1822, presenting his ideas on the sublime. All this was in utter contrast to the ideas that were prevalent in Icelandic literature at the start of the century, ideas that Thorarensen did not rate highly: "It is laughable that participants [in literature] here have no understanding of the being and nature of poetry and have in this not gone forward with the times," he wrote in a letter from 1819 (*Ljóðmæli*, 2:127, 322). These words were probably directed at the main leader of the Icelandic Enlightenment, Magnús Stephensen (1762–1833), who at that time was almost solely in charge of book publication in Iceland. His main aim was to educate and entertain the public, and it is clear that the value he placed on literature depended on how realistic, practical, and civilizing it was (see also pp. 229–30). At the beginning of the 1820s, however, Stephensen's views changed, and he began to emphasize aesthetic perfection and the imagination, like Bjarni Thorarensen and the generation following him (Senner, "Magnús Stephensen").

Even though Bjarni Thorarensen and Magnús Stephensen were certainly acquainted with some of the new ideas about the nature and value of literature, the editors of *Fjölnir* were the first to put forward theoretical views on the subject. The most detailed and philosophical among them was Tómas Sæmundsson in his *Ferðabók* from 1834–35, but Jónas Hallgrímsson contributed most toward realizing these ideas in his original writing, translations, and literary criticism. Sæmundsson and Hallgrímsson essentially followed the same line, although they based their thought on different tenets. While Sæmundsson mostly sought his examples in the works of Immanuel Kant (1724–1804) and German romantics like Friedrich Schelling (1775–1854), Hallgrímsson was more influenced by Danish and German writers of the 1830s and 1840s.

In Tómas Sæmundsson's view the gift of writing was truly the "daughter of heaven," "the descendent of the creative imagination" given to man. This gift certainly takes as its reference the rules of the intellect as to what constitutes beauty, but it is in other matters free, "follows the law that it lays down itself, satisfies only itself, has value in itself." Its main objective is to heighten everything it touches "to an idealistic image of beauty." Here, emphasis is placed on the imagination as the fountain of literature as well as its independent and idealistic aim. Sæmundsson's claim that "real artists" were absolutely unknown in Iceland shows how radical his views were at the time: "Hardly anyone among us has even heard about such persons" (Sæmundsson, *Ferðabók*, 329–37). To his mind, traditional Icelandic art had become a type of sport or handicraft, made of thoughtless habit, and shaped by its practical use in everyday life or in an effort to educate, entertain, and enchant the public. Thus, Icelandic "art theory" of former centuries was rejected and the foundations for a new one laid.

Sæmundsson was also the main author of the introduction to the inaugural issue of *Fjölnir* (1835), where the journal's aims and subjects were introduced. There, he specifically defined four related areas that he called the editors' "guide": utility; beauty; truth; and the good or moral. All this had a close parallel in the bourgeois literary practices of the era, for instance, in the writings of the Danish critic Johan Ludvig Heiberg, who tried to fuse romantic ideas and moderate and realistic views. The trinity of beauty, truth, and goodness is, of course, well-known from Greek and later German classicism, and many spokesmen of romanticism, such as Schelling, also made it the essence of their aesthetics. Utility has, on the other hand, often been considered one of the clearest indications of the inheritance of the Enlightenment to the ideas of *Fjölnir*'s editors. They interpreted it rather differently than before, however. Spiritual utility became of much greater significance than material, and the deciding factor in the evaluation of literary works was considered to be, not subject matter, but, rather, form and beauty: "If the superficial shape does not answer the demands of beauty, one can never be pleased with the most useful, the best work," writes Sæmundsson (*Ferðabók*, 331). As the editors also maintained in the inaugural issue, beauty is "so splendid, that all men crave it for itself" (*Fjölnir* 1 [1835]: 11).

In 1837 Jónas Hallgrímsson expressed a similar view in a review of the *Rímur af Tistrani og Indíönu* (1831; *Rímur* of Tristran and Indiana) by Sigurður Breiðfjörð. This was one of the most relentless reevaluations of Icelandic literary tradition that took place in the nineteenth century. Hallgrímsson now claimed that *rímur*, for centuries the most popular literary genre, had played a great part in "destroying and spoiling all feeling for what is beautiful and poetic and worthy of good poetry" (18). Many critics have even concluded that the review played a considerable role in the decline of *rímur* in the latter half of the century, although that view cannot be sustained. This literary genre simply lost its function with the introduction and development of new genres that better answered the needs of the modern reader. The novel offered more room for characterization and environmental and social descriptions, while lyric poetry was more suitable for singing. Hallgrímsson's review did, however, exercise a transforming influence on the literary ideas of the generation growing up at the time.

Although the *Rímur af Tistrani og Indíönu* were the first published works of Sigurður Breiðfjörð, this prolific *rímur* poet had long been popular among the larger public because of his considerable skill in versification and his firm grip on the fixed *rímur* form, where the most convoluted types of meter, rhyme, and kenning were the most highly valued (see also pp. 237–39). Breiðfjörð was unique, however, among *rímur* poets of the period because of his knowledge of foreign contemporary literature, specifically the poetry of the Danish poet Jens Baggesen (1764–1826). Breiðfjörð even wrote some patriotic and nature poems in which one can detect the influence of the current literary ideas of romanticism. At least one of them, "Fjöllin á Fróni" (1833; Iceland's mountains), left its mark on Jónas Hallgrímsson's poetry.

Hallgrímsson's critique of Breiðfjörð's *rímur* was twofold. On the one hand, it was directed against the *rímur* poet's unreflecting retelling of a story that Hallgrímsson regarded as, not only stupidly vile, badly written, and uninformative, but also an offense to the general sensibility. Hallgrímsson himself emphasized intuition and the imagination of the poet, who could change the original story in many ways, create interesting events, show the inner life of the persons who were worth knowing, and then express all this in a beautiful and unified image. Literature should be independent of possible models; imagination should be used to lift the subject over the coarseness and chaos of everyday reality. Thus, the author should connect beauty, truth, and morality.

On the other hand, Hallgrímsson criticized Breiðfjörð for his mechanical and thoughtless use of language characterized by clichés, formulas, and words that did not add to the meaning but were chosen merely to suit the form. He also aimed his criticism at the use of Danish words, incomprehensible poetic language, and an unbecoming or crude use of words that could even give the loftiest of ideas and phenomena a distasteful hue. The form of the literature should be perfect and the language clear, meaningful, and beautiful, befitting the ideas it expressed. In light of all this Hallgrímsson pointed out how far from the truth it really was to apply the term *literature* to Breiðfjörð's *rímur* and encouraged people to rise against it. As earlier in Tómas Sæmundsson's *Ferðabók*, here were drawn clear and uncompromising divisions between literature and other writing, high culture and low, divisions that had not existed up to then in Icelandic writing.

As a continuation of his review, Hallgrímsson showed in practice how poets should deal with their subject matter and what they should avoid in the poem "Móðurást" (1837; A mother's love), published in *Fjölnir* with an accompanying explanatory note. These texts were squarely directed at a poetry translation published in the journal *Sunnanpósturinn* in 1835 about a destitute traveling woman who died of exposure in a snowstorm but saved her two children by wrapping them in her clothes. In his explanatory note Hallgrímsson claims that this event obviously constituted a sound subject for a poet to write about. But, as he pointed out, the translator "had not watched out for what was horrible and would offend the aesthetic sensibilities of all those who had any such sensibility when he described the woman, how bone-thin she is and tramplike and how she sits and pulls off her rags one by one, until she is stark naked before the reader's eyes" (Hallgrímsson, "Grikkur," 30).

In Hallgrímsson's poem based on the same story, his ideas on "poetic realism" crystallize. There, Hallgrímsson avoids all specifics of the original story, such as the woman's poverty, nudity, and hardship, as such things could diminish her dignity and offend the aesthetic sensibilities and morality of the reader. Instead, he focuses on general aspects, such as motherly love and Christian faith. At the same time all is promptly stylized, colored by idealistic and emotional beauty. The woman is said to be "beautiful in tears" as she struggles along through the blizzard, and, when she is found dead the next morning, she "sleeps" with a "pure white veil of snow" covering her. Her infant son who had slept "calmly" during the storm now "smiles" to the "merciful sun." In this way the tragic story is lifted to a higher level and harmonized with bourgeois values.

On these idealistic tenets rested the aesthetic views of most of the poets who published their first works around the middle of the century, as evidenced in Steingrímur Thorsteinsson's poem "Baldursbráin" (ca. 1900; Mayweed), where it says: "Beauty, goodness, and truth are one." The poets often voice a desire to "view life in a higher and more dignified light than the everyday offers," as Benedikt Gröndal pointed out in his lecture "Um skáldskap" (1888; On fiction), where he defended his ideas on literature (Gröndal, *Ritsafn*, 4:218). Here, he emphasized among other things the opposition between ideal and reality and pointed to the need for poets to resolve the tension between the two in their works, for so, in his view, the best poets had always done. The poets who followed only ideal or only reality would soon find themselves in trouble. To prove this Gröndal referred to Schelling's ideas on literature. The essay "Nokkrar greinir um skáldskap" (1853; A few articles on poetry) is, however, the best indication of Gröndal's views on beauty, art, and poetry and demonstrates at the same time his wide-ranging knowledge of the history of aesthetics, from Plato and Aristotle to the nineteenth century. In this first comprehensive essay on aesthetics to be published in Icelandic Gröndal tries to find a compromise between classical ideas of absolute beauty and contemporary ideas of relative beauty, claiming that all art depends at the same time on harmonic proportions and on the individual's perception and ideas of beauty, where, for instance, education and nationality play an important role.

The literary criticism of Grímur Thomsen is to some extent a different matter as it was mostly directed at Danish readers. However, it is of interest here because of its direct relation to his own writing. Around the middle of the 1840s, after authoring several essays and books on contemporary French, English, and Danish literature, Thomsen started to focus on Icelandic medieval literature. His writings on the subject were influenced by the nationalist ideas of Herder as well as by contemporary Scandinavianism. He demanded, for instance, that Icelandic literature should have "special national characteristics" that differentiated it from the literature of other nations, thus rejecting "world literature" as a model, and pointing Icelandic writers toward their own literary heritage instead. This constituted a revolt against classical literary views, which, in Thomsen's opinion, were directly contrary to Nordic views. In Nordic literature one would not find the harmony of spirit and form or the harmony of tragic and comic elements as in classical literature; instead, the spirit would always reign supreme, while the tragic and comic were separated and exaggerated. In this way Nordic literature had all the hallmarks of "romantic literature" as defined by Hegel or, in Thomsen's own terminology, "pagan romanticism." Of later Icelandic poets Thomsen considered Bjarni Thorarensen to be the best representative of this literary view. Jónas Hallgrímsson, on the other hand, he regarded as slightly suspicious because of his close connection to the sentimental poets of contemporary Europe, especially the advocates of the "new-German debility" ("Den islandske Literaturs Charakteristik," 205).

POETRY

Poetry was the main literary genre in Iceland in the nineteenth century. Its primary mode was lyric, which constituted a major change from the *rímur*, where the story was the most important aspect. Now, emphasis was placed on the expression of emotions or on descriptions of a personal and poetic sense of reality. Poetry therefore became much more inward looking and more reliant on the use of imagery than before, and the works concentrated on relatively concise subject matter. In many poems the subject was of a historical nature, but usually the events themselves were only links in a larger chain of symbols. The poets only referred to the events without describing them in detail or telling the story around them. Thus, the epic became part of the lyric. One of the clearest examples of this was Jónas Hallgrímsson's poem "Gunnarshólmi," where the fate of one of the most remarkable Icelandic saga heroes is fused with a grand, symbolic, and poetic description of Icelandic nature. In this way the poet points to the hero's constant presence in Icelandic reality, and his patriotism becomes an example for the present.

This effort to throw light on the past is also evident in Matthías Jochumsson's elegy "Hallgrímur Pétursson" (1874; see also chapter 2), written to commemorate the bicentennial of the death of Hallgrímur Pétursson (1614–74). Here, this legendary leper and the nation's greatest hymn writer is described as Christlike. With his beloved hymns on the passion and death of Christ, Pétursson brightened the dark that surrounded the Icelandic people for centuries and eased their suffering; he himself then took the crown of thorns when his work was done and spent the last years of his life in a dark and dilapidated house, lonely, blind, and leprous. Thus, as this instance demonstrates, Jochumsson took a little licence when writing on well-known historical events and explained the characters involved with poetic insight.

Other nineteenth-century poets also took part in rejuvenating epic poetry in Icelandic. Bjarni Thorarensen, for instance, experimented with introducing the ballad into Icelandic literature with the poem "Kötlukvísl" (1824; The Katla confluent), about a contemporary tragedy, written in a well-known meter borrowed from Schiller's "Des Mädchens Klage" (1798). The poet's continuing attempts to get the poem in print were futile, even though the editor of the Icelandic journal to whom he submitted it liked it. He may have had doubts similar to those of the poet himself that the public would not appreciate this new form. In any event, the ballad form established itself only in the latter half of the century, largely thanks to the translations of Grímur Thomsen, Steingrímur Thorsteinsson, and Matthías Jochumsson, including Thomsen's translation of Goethe's "Der Fischer" (1808; The fisherman) as "Fiskimaðurinn" (1844), Thorsteinsson's translations of Schiller's "Der Taucher" (1797; The diver) as "Kafarinn" (1877), and Jochumsson's translation of J. Ludwig Uhland's "Des Sängers Fluch" (1814; The singer's curse) as "Ákvæðaskáldið" (1877). The Icelandic poet who was most prolific in his use of the ballad form was Thomsen, who looked to Icelandic folklore, the sagas, or events from world history for his subject matter. Most of his poems are built around character descriptions with a philosophical bent to them. He especially attempts to interpret the life and actions of strong individuals who trod uncommon paths or struggled in difficult circumstances but never wavered from their course or gave up despite the odds. Among Thomsen's best-known poems of this kind are "Arnljótur gellini" (1880–95; Arnljotur gellini) and "Hákon jarl" (1880–95; Earl Hakon).

Around the middle of the century Icelanders also started to write historical poetry proper. Benedikt Gröndal led the way with his "Drápa um Örvar-Odd" (1851; A poetic tribute to Arrow-Oddur), a lengthy poem about one of the warriors from ancient Nordic times (see p. 148), written in ottava rima like Byron's *Don Juan* (1821). True to the genre, the narrative is treated freely, the story itself subordinated to other elements such as nature descriptions, emotional expression, and philosophical ideas. The same was also true of Matthías Jochumsson's "Grettisljóð" (1897; Grettir's poem) and Grímur Thomsen's "Rímur af Búa Andríðssyni og Fríði Dofradóttur" (1906; The *Rímur* of Búi Andríðsson and Fríður Dofradóttir"). Another innovation in the area of lyric writing is "Ragnarökkur" (1868; Ragnarök), a lyric play by Gröndal relating the fate of the Nordic gods, but it was not followed up on.

Almost all lyric literature at the time was based on alliteration, rhyme, and rhythm, characteristics that were strongly imbedded in the Icelandic poetic tradition. Bjarni Thorarensen once claimed that Icelanders simply "could not imagine poetry that could not be sung or was not rhymed" (*Ljóðmæli*, 2:323). One of the first and most remarkable exceptions to this is the translation (by an unknown hand) of the lyric prose of "Paroles d'un croyant" (1834; Words of a believer) by the French priest Felicité Robert de Lamennais (1782–1854) as "Orð hins trúaða," which appeared in *Fjölnir* in 1835, in many respects pointing forward to Sigurður Nordal's (1886–1974) revolutionary work "Hel" (1919; Hell). Here, repetition and imagery move the text forward and give it a lyric quality. Between 1851 and 1860 Steingrímur Thorsteinsson also wrote some prose poems, or *uncomposed poetry*, as it was also called. These "soul soliloquies" are refined and rich in imagery, using symbolic and often allegorical metaphors, and nothing seems to prevent the texts from working on their own. Nevertheless, it shows just how strong the metrical tradition was that none of these were published until their inclusion in the poet's biography in 1964. Thorsteinsson did, however, rework some of them into "real" poems. As late as 1888 Benedikt Gröndal still maintained that, if meter and rhyme were abandoned, "then the poetic form is disbanded, then there is no literature" (*Ritsafn*, 4:219). As a result poetic translations from other languages were often more metrical than the originals were.

Although few would have considered abandoning meter and rhyme altogether, their importance was decreasing nevertheless as writers no longer stuck quite as firmly to their rules. Rather than remaining the central aspect around which all poetry revolved, they became just one among many aspects of a text. More than before poets used simpler meters where rhyme played only a minor role, and alliteration and rhythm were put to more liberal use than in the old *rímur* meters. In this respect they followed in the footsteps of the turn-of-the-century poets Benedikt Jónsson Gröndal (1760–1825) and Jón Þorláksson (1744–1819), who did not want to "suffocate meaning and inspiration in gothic klingklang of samesounding accented syllables" (Gröndal, "Musteri mannordsins af Alexander Pope," xvi). Here, the more flexible poetic heritage of the Eddic poems played a crucial role. On its foundation many of Bjarni Thorarensen's more mature poems rested, for instance, his elegies on Sæmundur Hólm (1749–1821) and Oddur Hjaltalín (1782–1840), as well as some of the most famous poems of Jónas Hallgrímsson, for instance, "Alþing hið nýja" and the love poem "Ferðalok" (1845; English trans.: "Journey's End," in Ringler, *Bard of Iceland*). Of the younger poets, Gísli Brynjúlfsson and Matthías Jochumsson were thought to use these ancient meters with the most artistry.

From Romanticism to Realism

Bjarni Thorarensen and Jónas Hallgrímsson also introduced Icelanders to a variety of foreign meters. Hallgrímsson played the larger role in this, and his poetry covers a broad metrical spectrum. Along with the simple meters of Heine and other contemporary European poets, Hallgrímsson was also attracted to complex and highly formal meters. Like the Danish and German poets of classicism and romanticism, he looked to the Italian and Spanish Renaissance. He was the first among Icelanders to adopt such forms as terza rima and ottava rima ("Gunnarshólmi"), the sonnet ("Ég bið að heilsa" [1844; English trans.: "I Send Greetings," in Ringler, *Bard of Iceland*]), the redondilla ("Eftir Tómas Sæmundsson" [1844; English trans.: "In Memory of Tómas Sæmundsson," in Ringler, *Bard of Iceland*]), and the triolet ("Dalvísa" [1844; English trans.: "Valley Song," in Ringler, *Bard of Iceland*]). He also introduced into Icelandic poetry the elegiac distich ("Ísland"). Few of these foreign meters were used to any extent by later Icelandic poets, except perhaps the sonnet and some versions of ottava rima.

It has been said of Bjarni Thorarensen that he placed most emphasis on the subject or ideas underlying his poems and in that way was more a poet of inspiration and emotion rather than of formal refinement. In his use of poetic language, he obviously stood at a turning point in Icelandic poetry. A connection to earlier times is most evident in his use of old language and an often stiff and forced choice of words. At the same time he also pointed to the future with his use of poetic imagery, symbols, and mythology, a practice that carries some of his poems, making them meaningful and broad in resonance. The main source for this imagery was Nordic literature, as, for instance, in the aforementioned "Veturinn," where the poet uses the ancient heroic world to draw a dramatic and much more positive image of winter than readers had known before. In other poems the country itself assumes the face of known ancient heroes and bears witness to the battle of good and evil of which ancient sagas tell. From such use of imagery it is a small step to the poet's well-known personification of Iceland as the beautiful Lady of the Mountains, where snowcapped peaks become an elegant headdress and foaming glacial streams form a precious ceremonial dress.

This use of imagery became more pronounced in the poetry of Jónas Hallgrímsson and the poets who followed. Hallgrímsson forged the path with the emphasis that he placed on the formal construction of poetry, at times following to the letter the rules of classical rhetoric on the planning and ordering of subject matter. While polishing and perfecting the lyric language, he attempted at the same time to turn it toward daily speech. In this way he linked everyday speech and formal poetic language, giving his poems at once simplicity and refinement. Among the nineteenth-century poets Hallgrímsson played without a doubt the greatest role in renewing Icelandic poetic form and in giving it classical overtones. His style is concise and pointed, and emotional expression is usually kept to a minimum. On the foundation that he built many of the most well-known poets of later times have based their writing. This development can be traced from Steingrímur Thorsteinsson, Grímur Thomsen, and Páll Ólafsson to the poets who have been considered the most artistic in the twentieth century, Jón Helgason (1899–1986), Snorri Hjartarson (1906–86), and Ólafur Jóhann Sigurðsson (1918–88).

A number of influential poets who appeared in the latter half of the century developed their poetry in quite a different manner, using an expansive and tense baroque style where imagination, uninhibited expression of emotion, and powerful wording were of the essence. Among them were Benedikt Gröndal, Matthías Jochumsson, and Kristján Jónsson Fjallaskáld. In their poetry one does not find the same polish and harmony as in the poetry of Jónas Hallgrímsson and Steingrímur Thorsteinsson. In a letter from 1914 Matthías Jochumsson pointed this out himself while attempting to explain: "I have never been but a part, a part of an intellectual child, had good moments and even seen visions, but not been able to handle them or had enough peace and quiet to find a form for them" (Jochumsson, *Bréf*, 694). For this these poets sometimes suffered criticism.

PROSE

The first Icelandic attempts at novel writing can be traced to the middle of the eighteenth century. Around the same time Icelanders also started to publish Icelandic sagas and translate stories into Icelandic, with the aim of entertaining as well as teaching a moral lesson. All these attempts were incidental, unfocused, and minor in scope, and only a small portion of the stories were published. For this reason the nineteenth century is usually considered to have seen the true birth of the modern novel. Crucial to this development were the increase in paper and book production in the country as well as Icelanders' growing knowledge of foreign prose writing. Most noteworthy among the earliest works of prose literature in the nineteenth century are translations, especially Sveinbjörn Egilsson's translations of Homer's odes (1829–55) and the translations by *Fjölnir*'s editors of several significant contemporary prose texts. In these texts we see a gradual renewal of Icelandic narrative and prose style, where idealistic and poetic elements gain in importance while the language becomes clearer and simpler than before.

As far as original prose works are concerned, people have often looked to

Jónas Hallgrímsson's short stories, anecdotes, and art tales published in *Fjölnir* in 1847. Among them is "Grasaferð" (English trans.: "Gathering Highland Moss," in Ringler, *Bard of Iceland*), probably written around 1836, and considered by many to be the first modern Icelandic short story. "Grasaferð" is at once a remarkable description of Icelandic country life and part bildungsroman about the first encounter of two young people with the world outside their home, a trip to the mountain, which seduces them with its distant innocent beauty but turns out to offer more mystery and threat as it draws closer. Here, Hallgrímsson draws on the well-known outlaw theme from folklore, which was to be used time and again in later Icelandic stories and plays. The point of view is that of a thirteen-year-old boy who thinks he is ready for anything but at times must look for support his cousin, who is two years older. This creates considerable irony. In the story landscape descriptions are prominent, but great emphasis is also placed on describing the young people's inner worlds of thought and imagination as well as how they view themselves. Both are on their way to becoming poets, and the descriptions are, therefore, very lyric at times, mixing poetry and prose.

Hallgrímsson's "Grasaferð" has sometimes been classified as a children's story, and as such it provides an excellent insight into nineteenth-century views of children. There is, for instance, never any attempt to smuggle in a formative message, as in the literature of the Enlightenment. Rather, childhood is described as a separate world where the characters themselves are allowed to discover their environment and tackle the problems that face them. Closer to the genre of the fable are two artistic fairy tales (*Kunstmärchen*) that Hallgrímsson wrote in the style of Hans Christian Andersen's tales and romantic gothic adventures: "Fífill og hunangsfluga" (1847; English trans.: "The Dandelion and the Bee," in Ringler, *Bard of Iceland*) and "Stúlkan í turninum" (1847; English trans.: "The Girl in the Tower," in Ringler, *Bard of Iceland*). The former story is characterized by poetic beauty and mild humor. It tells the life story of a dandelion from when it blossoms full of love of life and daydreams until it has become an emotionless blowbell that lives only to be able in some way to thank an elderly bumblebee for saving its life. The story thus displays the same philosophical stance as many of Hallgrímsson's poems: despite everything life is worth living. In "Stúlkan í turninum" the writer's viewpoint is also clear. It tells of a fight between the representatives of life and death, a young and beautiful girl and a horrible owl that wants to teach the girl to love the night better than the day. At the end of the story there is a terrific battle between these opposing powers from which the girl emerges victorious, and her courage and steadfastness are richly rewarded.

In a very different vein are a few short stories that Hallgrímsson wove into his letters, especially those written during his travels. Many of these letters are similar to Heine's "Reisebilder" (1827). Their form is open and allows a combination of poetry and prose, travel and nature descriptions, personal matters, general ruminations on politics, history and natural science, anecdotes, and jokes. The style is in part simple and realistic but also sincere, lyric, humorous, and grotesque in turn. Unlike Heine's "Reisebilder" these letters were not meant for publication and are in many places obscure because of references to Hallgrímsson's close-knit group of friends. Two of the stories were published in *Fjölnir* in 1847. One of them, "Úr gamanbréfi" (1843; English trans.: "The Queen Goes Visiting," in Ringler, *Bard of Iceland*), is a satiric account based on the grandiose reporting by Danish newspapers of Queen Victoria's state visit to King Louis Philippe of France in the autumn of 1843, while the other, "Brot úr bréfi skrifuðu 13. júlí 1841" (Part of a letter written on 13 July 1841), is a grotesque travel description of Þingvellir where the Icelandic nation appears in the guise of tethered cows and donkeys with empty skulls. The former story has all the characteristics of the carnivalesque. Every aspect is exaggerated and distorted. Royalty and courtiers are referred to as if they were ordinary farmers in the Icelandic countryside, yet they are dressed in glittering adventure costumes and act in a refined court manner. The latter story uses a more grotesque humor and is most obviously viewed as a bitter attack on Icelanders for their ignorance and lack of interest in the reestablishment of the Althing, a matter considered by the *Fjölnir* group to be of the utmost importance for Icelandic society.

Around and after the middle of the century more authors started writing stories, some of which were first published in papers and journals. Of these authors Jón Thoroddsen and Benedikt Gröndal wrote the pieces that have held up the best. Although one could argue that they followed in the footsteps of Jónas Hallgrímsson, it is also clear that they carved out a position of their own. Thoroddsen mostly favored historical and poetic realism, whereas Gröndal wrote first and foremost comic fantasies. Both these authors achieved considerable popularity, and they were to constitute a powerful opposition to the storytelling tradition of the *rímur*. The same can be said of the many translated stories from this time, especially Steingrímur Thorsteinsson's translation of *The Thousand and One Nights* (as *Þúsund og ein nótt* [1857–64]). These early stories also had a formative influence on later authors. Thoroddsen's novels were especially influential and became the main model for Icelandic novelists of the nineteenth century and the early part of the twentieth.

Jón Thoroddsen only wrote two novels, *Piltur og stúlka* (1850; English trans.: *Lad and Lass* [1890]) and the posthumous *Maður og kona* (1876; Man and woman). The former is the first novel published in Icelandic, and it is interesting to note that, in its first edition, in the tradition of Icelandic folktales and romances, the author is nowhere mentioned. Icelanders probably did not make a sharp distinction between these three genres in the middle of the nineteenth century. They were all fictional tales told to entertain. Both of Thoroddsen's novels are "romantic" rural love stories, partly influenced by eighteenth- and nineteenth-century English novels, both sentimental novels such as Samuel Richardson's *Clarissa* and the historical novels of Walter Scott. There are also connections with Icelandic sagas and folklore, especially in *Maður og kona*, which remains Thoroddsen's main work, although he never quite completed it. This novel was also meant to be a type of folktale in the sense that it depicts Icelandic folk, society, culture, traditions, and religion in all their variety. This attempt lends the story a realistic and specifically Icelandic feel, which counterbalances the idealization of the protagonists and the story's connection to foreign literature. It was probably on account of these aspects that the realist Gestur Pálsson claimed in 1889 that in the literature of the nineteenth century the "extremes of the realistic movement" were most notable in Jón Thoroddsen's work ("Nýi skáldskapurinn").

Thoroddsen's novels are otherwise similar in subject and form. They are concerned with matters of the heart and the emotional life of innocent and virtuous lovers whose relationship is prevented by their corrupt parents or relatives who have other marriage plans in mind for them. After various complications and troubles the lovers are united, and the stories end happily with the lovers' wedding. In this way they triumph over family power and parental social control and make their dream of love and freedom come true. This pattern was very popular in Icelandic novels in the latter half of the nineteenth century (Sæmundsson, *Ást og útlegð*) and clearly informs, for instance, Jón Mýrdal's (1825–99) successful novel *Mannamunur* (1872; Difference between men). But it was neither this pattern, nor Thoroddsen's blameless characters, but his comic and at times grotesque "antiheroes" and minor characters that earned him his popularity. It is in the broad descriptions of people and their individual mannerisms that Thoroddsen's narrative art becomes most apparent and provides an outlet for his boisterous humor. Some of these characters had their direct models in Thoroddsen's contemporaries, but in his stories they are mainly living personifications of human characteristics, particularly human flaws. One of the most important characters is the representative of slander, Gróa á Leiti, who still survives in the Icelandic language.

The Icelandic language has received more from Thoroddsen than Gróa á

Leiti alone, for he played an important role in revitalizing Icelandic prose in the nineteenth century. His language is, overall, simple but clear and polished and bears the marks of his close encounters with Icelandic common people. Thoroddsen was well versed in the art of putting himself in different roles, and his style can, therefore, be quite diverse. The largest divergence from everyday language is where he aims for comic effect and exaggerates and distorts the Danish-influenced language of Reykjavík or the speech of ignorant country folk who constantly make at times inappropriate and laughable references to the Bible or the sagas. Similarly, high is made to meet low, as Thoroddsen describes everyday, even lowly matters or events in the refined and lofty style of classical texts, Icelandic and foreign. His irony is sometimes sharp, yet all is kept within the boundaries of good taste.

The masterworks of grotesque and fantastic humor were Benedikt Gröndal's *Sagan af Heljarslóðarorrustu* (1861; The battle on hell's fields) and *Þórðar saga Geirmundssonar* (1891; The saga of Þórður Geirmundsson). Among the Icelandic authors of the century Gröndal was without doubt the black sheep as he cared neither for tradition in literature nor for public opinion and good taste. People's reactions to his stories were also quite diverse. Many welcomed them with open arms and read them as hilarious but harmless comic tales, but some were offended by his uninhibited imagination and coarse lack of solemnity. Few managed to explain the stories well or place them in a common context. In his review of *Sagan af Heljarslóðarorrustu* Sveinn Skúlason remarked: "We are not so clever that we know which genre this text belongs to as we know not and have not seen as far as we remember anything like it in the literature of any nation." The publisher was also sharply reprimanded for having the work printed: "He should know, that he degrades himself by issuing such material" (Skúlason, "Bókafregn," 93).

Of Gröndal's stories *Sagan af Heljarslóðarorrustu* has always been the most highly valued. It was written in Belgium in the autumn of 1859 and tells of a European contemporary event, the bloody battle of the French and Austrians at Solferino in Italy on 24 June 1859. From this very serious and tragic subject matter Gröndal crafted a boisterous comic tale where historical facts are mostly retained but put in new and surprising contexts. The story is written in the style of Icelandic chivalric tales but parodies them at the same time. In this way it is reminiscent of Cervantes's *Don Quixote*, although it is hardly a direct criticism of the romance tradition. It is, rather, a collection of the most popular character types and subjects of these heroic tales, which are then exaggerated as much as possible, distorted or refined. The heads of the two armies, the Emperors Napoléon III and Franz Josef, are made into medieval knights who lead a hoard of gigantic berserks, devils, and magicians from adventure stories as well as countless contemporary European politicians and writers, who use their well-known works as dangerous weapons and trusty defenses. On top of this Gröndal adds a few well-known Icelanders to the mix. In this way he blends past and present, Icelandic and foreign, in a manner similar to Jónas Hallgrímsson in his absurd-comic "Úr gamanbréfi."

All this is viewed in Gröndal's distorted mirror. The two emperors are at once stately national leaders, coarse medieval heroes, and nineteenth-century Icelandic farmers. They are as much at home mingling at refined parties as fighting ghosts and monsters, but equally worried about everyday trivia. To add to the humor everything is turned on its head in a way reminiscent of the French writer François Rabelais (1494–1553). Everyday and often lowly details are exaggerated and described in an expansive poetic manner, while unusual and great events become just another minor detail. The result is a certain mismatch between form and subject. This boisterous and carnivalesque style of Benedikt Gröndal exercised a considerable influence on the development of Icelandic prose; indeed, it has been said that no other author so influenced Icelandic humorous and parodic writing, in particular that of two of the main authors of the twentieth century, Þórbergur Þórðarson (1888–1974) and Halldór Laxness (1902–98).

FOLK- AND FAIRY TALES

From time immemorial folk- and fairy tales formed the mainstay of Icelandic narrative art. Up to the nineteenth century these stories survived, however, as a type of underground literature of the people, not least among women and children. They were completely disregarded among servants of the church and other intellectuals who wished to enlighten the public and do away with any type of superstition. According to the domestic discipline from 1746, one could be put in stocks if caught reciting stories or dancing, and in 1796 Hannes Finnsson (1739–96), the bishop of Skálholt, wrote: "I have often suffered from the knowledge that on many farms troll stories and fairy tales filled with vulgarities and superstitions are read" (*Kvöldvökurnar*, xxi). Even though some folklore was collected beginning in the late seventeenth century, especially by the famous manuscript collector Árni Magnússon (1663–1730), this material was not published until the middle of the twentieth century as *Munnmælasögur 17. aldar* (1955; Oral tales from the seventeenth century). It was only with the rise of nationalism in the nineteenth century that folk- and fairy tales gained in acceptance and began to be collected and published. By then Icelandic collectors of folklore found it hard to gain the full trust of the storytellers, who doubted both that the stories were important enough to be collected and the real motives of the collectors. Some even thought that they intended to "get superstitions and rubbish out of people and then belittle it or burn it afterward" (Vigfússon, "Formáli," xxviii).

The first folktale to reach Icelandic book readers was the story "Maríubarnið," a translation of "Marienkind" (Mary's child) from the German collection of the brothers Jakob and Wilhelm Grimm, *Kinder- und Hausmärchen* (1812–15), published in Icelandic by the law student Jóhann Halldórsson (1809–43) in his *Nýjársgjöf handa börnum* (1841; A New Year's gift for children). Halldórsson was in many ways a pioneer in the publication of children's stories in Icelandic. As had happened elsewhere, the Grimm brothers' collection served as an encouragement and example to those who collected and published Icelandic folklore. Jón Árnason and Magnús Grímsson (1825–60) were the forerunners in this field. In 1845 they started gathering tales, verses, rhymes, and riddles, and the first collection was published as *Íslenzk ævintýri* (1852; Icelandic fairy tales). In spite of its name this book contains no genuine fairy tales, only folktales and a few verses. This can be explained by people's suspicion of fairy tales, as was clearly demonstrated when the supposed "old wive's tale" "Der blonde Eckbert" by Ludwig Tieck (1773–1853) was translated and printed in *Fjölnir* in 1835 as "Ævintýri af Eggerti glóa" (see also below). And, indeed, Árnason and Grímsson found it necessary to defend such stories in their preface to *Íslenzk ævintýri*. Not only did they point out the value of the stories as the "literature of the people" and a "latter-day Edda," but they also emphasized the great respect in which similar stories were held in many other countries. This they mentioned "so that our countrymen will not be offended even though we have collected these stories and printed them. They are a credit to the nation rather than a disgrace" (Grímsson and Árnason, "Formáli," iii–vi).

Although *Íslenzk ævintýri* is a good example of Icelandic folklore, its reception was rather muted. Some thought that the stories lacked literary pretensions, while others worried that they encouraged people's belief in elves and trolls. This could be the reason that the collecting activities of Árnason and Grímsson were essentially put on hold for several years after *Íslenzk ævintýri* appeared. In 1858, however, the German scientist Konrad Maurer traveled the country and collected stories and other folk material that he then translated into German and published under the title *Isländische Volkssagen der Gegenwart* (1860). After being encouraged by Maurer Árnason again took up collecting folklore and soon obtained large quantities of material. Part of this collection was published in *Íslenzkar þjóðsögur og ævintýri I–II* (1862–64; Icelandic folk- and fairy tales), still a basic text in Icelandic ethnology. Another part was later printed in Jón Árnason and Ólafur Davíðsson's (1862–1903) *Íslenzkar gátur, skemmtanir, vikivakar og þulur I–IV* (1887–1903; Icelandic riddles, entertainments, dancing songs, and nursery rhymes).

In *Íslenzkar þjóðsögur og ævintýri I–II* fairy tales finally took their place as one of the main types of narrative among stories of outlaws, trolls, elves, ghosts, and magic. The work quickly gained a wide distribution and was very well received. In this context it was significant that the Icelandic Literary Society bought eight hundred copies of the work and distributed them free to its members, but it is also clear that the close cooperation between Jón Árnason and some of the nation's most influential intellectuals, not least ministers, had its part to play. This time everyone made an effort, both the public and the intellectuals. Certainly, Árnason's editorial work and that of his coworkers, especially Guðbrandur Vigfússon (1827–89), who among other things wrote a preface to the work, was an important contributing factor in earning the folktales the goodwill of the people and in linking their material and style to the rising patriotism of the times.

Árnason's methods were in many ways different from the general working practices in folklore publications at the time. Instead of traveling around the country himself and writing down the stories people told him, Árnason established a great network of informants all across the country, made up of representatives of all classes of society, and asked them to send him oral tales as they were told among the people. Thus, he was able to ensure both diversity in narrative mode and a close connection to the tales' origin. Then, when publishing the stories, he followed the rule of printing them "for the most part" unaltered from their written versions and without mixing different versions. The work is, therefore, considered to give a rather clear picture of Icelandic folktales as they were traditionally recited.

When Árnason's edition is compared with the original sources, printed in *Íslenskar þjóðsögur og ævintýri I–VI* (1954–61), however, it becomes apparent that this scientific method was not followed consistently. The stories were to a certain extent harmonized and polished in language and style, following the example of those writers Árnason considered the best, more often than not ministers and other intellectuals. The stories told by uneducated people were generally edited and censored where they were considered tasteless or coarse and, thus, an offense to good taste. There is no doubt that this editing must have played a part in the favorable reception that the collection received as well as influencing the oral storytelling tradition and later collections of folklore.

Publication meant that Icelandic folktales changed considerably in nature. Now they were no longer confined to common oral culture, mostly preserved by older, illiterate women who told them to children for entertainment. Instead, they had become polished literature that the public, along with the educated, could enjoy in private. Soon, they were given a place in the canon of Icelandic literature and, thereby, began to influence other forms of writing as well as people's views of literature. This becomes evident from the novels and plays written in the nineteenth century, which often use elements from folktales or folk belief, for instance, Matthías Jochumsson's play *Útilegumennirnir* (1862; The outlaws) and Indriði Einarsson's (1851–1939) *Nýjársnótt* (1871; New Year's Eve), which find their basis in Árnason's fairy tales (see also chapter 9). The influence from folklore made itself felt to a considerably lesser extent in poetry, until the arrival of late nineteenth-century neoromanticism (Scandinavian symbolism; see also chapter 4). Until then folklore elements are most apparent in Gísli Brynjúlfsson's and Grímur Thomsen's poetry, for instance, in Thomsen's famous poem "Á Sprengisandi" (1861; English trans.: "On the Desert," trans. A. H. Palmi, in *Songs of Iceland*, ed. Hall). This poem describes farmers herding sheep over the desertlike highland of Iceland and the many dangers that the area hides, for instance, unfriendly elves and outlaws who appear when darkness descends. Another poet who also frequently used folktales in the 1870s was Jón Ólafsson. His poem "Máninn hátt á himni skín" (1871; The moon shines high in the sky), written for a torchlight procession in Reykjavík on New Year's Eve 1871, is still part of the New Year's Eve tradition in Iceland.

TRANSLATIONS

During the nineteenth century translations proliferated and had an important role in revitalizing Icelandic literature and in changing people's perception of it. This literary activity started initially with the poets who inhabited the borderline between Enlightenment and Romanticism, Jón Þorláksson, Benedikt Jónsson Gröndal, and Sveinbjörn Egilsson. The publication of their translations coincided with the advent of new tendencies in Icelandic literature (see also pp. 233–36). Worth mentioning in this respect are Benedikt J. Gröndal's translation of Alexander Pope's *The Temple of Fame* (as "Musteri mannorðsins" [1790]) and Jón Þorláksson's translations of John Milton's *Paradise Lost* (as "Paradísar missir" [1794–96]), Pope's *Essay on Man* (as "Tilraun um manninn" [1798]), and Friedrich Gottlieb Klopstock's *Der Messias* (as "Messías" [1834–38]). As was the case with the first printed poems by Bjarni Thorarensen, these translations did not elicit much response among the public at first, and there are few indications that they gained any popularity. They were, however, very important examples for writers who were in search of new forms of literary expression as they gradually moved away from a literary heritage based on complex meter, rhythm, and rhyme. Instead, the emphasis now lay on introducing ideas in a clear and easily comprehensible manner, using the simple meter of the Eddic poems, especially *fornyrðislag* (see pp. 4–5). The literary language also became more independent and played a larger role than it had done before. Sveinbjörn Egilsson's prose translations of Homer's *Odyssey* (as *Odysseifskviða* [1829–40]) and *Iliad* (as *Ilíonskviða* [1855]) marked a turning point in Icelandic prose style. Here, Egilsson looked to medieval Icelandic literature for models that were at once national and literary.

Through the journal *Fjölnir* Icelanders became acquainted with the romantic literature of other nations. As early as the first issue (1835) those translations appeared that were the most groundbreaking in the journal's history, those of Tieck's "Der blonde Eckbert" and Lamennais's "Paroles d'un croyant," as we have seen, and a translation of the last part of Heine's "Reisebilder" (as "Frá Hæni"). Alongside these were introductions in which the authors' desire for freedom, inspiration, and formal innovation was emphasized, especially the interweaving of tender and loving emotional expressions with revolt and passion. This material constituted an obvious attempt to give a fairly broad overview of the latest trends in contemporary European literature, including a fantasy with a psychological strand, a lyric prose text describing a romantic outlaw and national repression, and a satiric attack on the "fool's" loyalty to the authorities that were toppled in the revolutions of the period.

With these translations a new tone was introduced into Icelandic literature, and in light of readers' response one can tell that many had difficulty harmonizing these narrative methods with their ideas of literature and grasping the full meaning of the texts in question. In a letter to the editors in the second issue of *Fjölnir* (1836), one of the country's most literary ministers considers "Der blonde Eckbert" and other such stories of little use to Icelanders: "They have hardly much sense of and even less use for them. At least I have heard many criticize and dislike this kind of untrue story that they do not know the meaning of. Pretty verses, believable stories, and such like I believe to be much more to the public's taste and of more use" (Indriðason, "Úr brjefi af Austfjörðum," 40). One of the editors, Tómas Sæmundsson, told of similar responses in a letter to his friends: "The story of Eggert ["Der blonde Eckbert"] I find unusually enchanting. Many say nevertheless that it is like our old wives' tales, others that it is ugly (because it ends badly!)" (Sæmundsson, *Bréf*, 161).

This shows the traditional responses of those who looked more to the subject and the message of literature and judged it according to how realistic and useful it was rather than according to the art or beauty of the writing. The translated fragment of Heine's "Reisebilder" was criticized mainly because of the political views expressed there, which were mostly directed against absolute monarchy. "Although nonsense floats on top, underneath is hidden a dangerous spirit of liberty and opposition to legal authority," wrote one reader (Sverrisson, "Sendibréf," 188). *Fjölnir*'s editors tried to counter this criticism in an editorial (*Fjölnir* 4 [1838]: 3–19). They rejected the validity of judging the translations from such viewpoints; instead, they pointed out their literary merit and the authors' attempts to strengthen morality and mediate common truths. It seems clear, however, that the editors did not find it possible to continue their work: translations were at least mostly discontinued in the journal until 1843. By then a considerable change had taken place in the choice of material, so considerable that, instead of symbolic or political fantasies, "pretty verses" and academic articles had become the main components. In the last issue (1847) a few translated adventures appeared, but they were considerably more innocuous than "Der blonde Eckbert."

At this time Jónas Hallgrímsson was virtually the only translator working with *Fjölnir*, whether the subject matter was literature or science. He found his material mostly from among nineteenth-century German and Danish writers. Of the literary works that he translated, most were by Heine, despite the fact that from 1836 there was a ban in Denmark on translating Heine and other Das junge Deutschland writers. Alongside this favorite poet Hallgrímsson also tackled Schiller, Adelbert von Chamisso, Oehlenschläger, Carsten Hauch, P. L. Møller, and F. Paludan-Müller as well as Tieck, Johann Peter Hebel, H. C. Andersen, and the Grimm brothers. Of all Hallgrímsson's translations, the twelve Heine poems have been the most important for Icelandic literary history. Before the end of the century Heine had become one of the most popular foreign poets in Iceland, and it has even been suggested that no other foreign poet has left such a lasting impression on Icelandic literature. Many of the most popular poets in the latter half of the nineteenth century and the first decades of the twentieth attempted at least some translations of his works. Among the most prolific was Steingrímur Thorsteinsson, who translated eight poems. One of the main writers of Icelandic realism, Hannes Hafstein, however, outdid Thorsteinsson by far, translating forty-three of Heine's poems, more than any translator before or since.

In Jónas Hallgrímsson's Heine translations lyric love poetry and nature poetry are most in evidence. Here, the unique irony of Heine is clearly apparent, without becoming bitter or critical. In subject matter most of the translations stay true to the original, but it is interesting to see how often Hallgrímsson employs a different meter. He frequently uses Eddic meters, for example, as Benedikt Jónsson Gröndal and Jón Þorláksson did in many translations. Occasionally, he can even be said to have created new Icelandic poems, as he stuck only to the main idea and spirit of the original, feeling free to change all other aspects. Sometimes, what appears is almost like a dialogue between the German poet and his translator, something we also find in Hallgrímsson's original poetry, where he often uses Heine's meters. The translations, therefore, shed light on Hallgrímsson's struggle with form and his attempt to harmonize national and foreign traditions of form. At the same time his method reflects one of his main literary ideas: the emphasis that he placed on a work's independence from its models.

Even though the *Fjölnir* group played a large role in introducing Icelanders to literature from other countries, it was not until the latter half of the nineteenth century that Icelandic translations really began to flourish. The reason for this is twofold: first, increased book and paper publication and, second, people's open-mindedness toward new literature. Many of these translations were also considered to be of high quality. Much of the source material was still in the German and the Scandinavian languages, but from the 1840s on Icelanders turned with increasing interest to English-language authors, especially Scott and Byron, but also Robert Burns and Percy Bysshe Shelley. Grímur Thomsen, for instance, translated three poems by Byron and Gísli Brynjúlfsson another six. In his youth Steingrímur Thorsteinsson immersed himself in Burns's poetry and translated at least five of his poems. Some translations were also made of English prose texts. In 1848 the journal *Norðurfari* published Benedikt Gröndal's translation of one of Washington Irving's *Tales of the Alhambra* (1832), along with a short introduction by the translator, and in 1860 Gröndal's translation of Irving's short story "The Spectre Bridegroom" (1820) was published in the journal *Ný sumargjöf* (1859–65; New summer gift) as "Brúðardraugurinn." Translations of a few short stories by Charles Dickens were published in the journal *Íslendingur* in 1860–61, along with an introduction to Dickens, who was praised for, among other things, his realistic and clear-sighted descriptions of the spirit of the age and the conditions that that spirit had created, his humanity, and his attempts to improve social malaise.

During the latter half of the nineteenth century, the poets Steingrímur Thorsteinsson and Matthías Jochumsson were by far the country's most prolific translators. They did not limit themselves to poetry and short stories but also tried their hand at some of the great works of playwriting and fiction. Among Thorsteinsson's main translations, besides the afore-mentioned *Thousand and One Nights*, are *Axel* by Esaias Tegnér (as *Axel* [1857]), one of Washington Irving's *Tales of the Alhambra* (as *Pílagrímur ástarinnar* [1860]), *Undine* by Friedrich de la Motte-Foque (as *Úndína* [1861]), *The Prisoner of Chillon* and "The Dream" by Byron (as *Bandinginn í Chillon og Draumurinn* [1866]), Shakespeare's *King Lear* (as *Lear kon-ungur* [1878]), *The Recognition of Sakuntala* by Kalidasa (as *Sakúntala* [1879]), and *Eventyr og historier* by H. C. Andersen (as *Ævintýri og sögur* [1904–8]). Among Jochumsson's translations are *Frithiofs saga* by Tegnér (as *Friðþjófs saga* [1866]), *Manfred* by Byron (as *Manfred* [1875]), *Brand* by Henrik Ibsen (as *Brandur* [1898]), and the following Shakespeare plays: *Macbeth* (as *Macbeth* [1874]), *Hamlet* (as *Hamlet* [1878]), *Othello* (as *Ótelló* [1882]), and *Romeo and Juliet* (as *Rómeó og Júlía* [1887]). None of these plays were, however, performed any more than Thorsteinsson's Shakespeare translation. Together, Thorsteinsson and Jochumsson pub-lished a diverse anthology of poetry from many countries, *Svanhvít* (1877; Swan white). It contained poems by many of the main poets of the eigh-teenth and nineteenth centuries, such as Goethe, Schiller, Uhland, Heine, Friedrich Hölderlin, Grundtvig, Johan Ludvig Runeberg, Bernhard Sev-erin Ingemann, Bjørnstjerne Bjørnson, Byron, Shelley, and Burns.

As this sampling demonstrates the translations included a mixture of older and more recent works. Some writers, such as Grímur Thomsen, Steingrímur Thorsteinsson, and Benedikt Gröndal also attempted to emu-late Sveinbjörn Egilsson and introduce classical authors like Homer, Sap-pho, Pindar, Anacreon, Euripides, Aeschylus, Plato, and Sophocles. These translations were in some part an attempt to defend the decreasing classical emphasis in the Icelandic education system, but they were also meant as an example to young Icelandic writers. With this considerable translation effort Icelanders now had available to them in their own language many of the main works of world literature, many of which have since become classics in Icelandic literature.

PUBLISHING AND READING

Up to the middle of the nineteenth century book publishing in Iceland was at a minimum. Between ten and fifteen works were printed annually, count-ing religious texts, educational books, and all types of official reports. Al-though it was quite rare for authors to have their literary works printed, a considerable amount of literary material circulated in manuscript form. In the 1830s it became more common for *rímur* poets to publish their works, as this type of poetry had a large and reliable readership. The most prolific and most popular *rímur* poet of the century, Sigurður Breiðfjörð, published nine *rímur* cycles in all from 1831 to 1843. Literary innovations had a more difficult time of it: the anthologies of Bjarni Thorarensen's and Jónas Hallgrímsson's poems, for instance, were published only posthumously in 1847. Journals constituted the main forum for these poets, but, because space was limited, they could publish only short texts. It is not unlikely that restrictions like these played a part in directing literature toward concise poetry and short stories, the characteristic genres of the first half of the century.

At the start of the century the hub of Icelandic book publishing was in Copenhagen, where there usually lived a large group of Icelandic intellectuals who were in a position to attend to publishing. Among publishing firms the Copenhagen division of the Icelandic Literary Society (1816–) was the largest and the most powerful. Along with its news and educational journals, *Íslensk sagnablöð* (1816–26) and *Skírnir* (1827–), the society published Bjarni Thorarensen's *Kvæði*, Jónas Hallgrímsson's *Ljóðmæli* (1847; Lyric verses), Jón Thoroddsen's *Kvæði*, and later Thoroddsen's novel *Maður og kona*. It also supported the publishers of *Íslenzkar þjóðsögur og æfintýri I–II* (1862–64), and it took part in the publication of medieval Icelandic literature and other works concerning the history of Iceland, among them *Sturlunga saga* (1817–20; Saga of the Sturlungar), *Biskupa sögur* (1858–78; Biographies of bishops), *Íslands árbækur* (1821–55; Icelandic almanacs) by Jón Espólín, and *Safn til sögu Íslands og íslenskra bókmennta* (1856–1939; Collection towards a history of Iceland and Icelandic literature). The Icelandic Literary Society had for the most part the widespread support of the Icelandic people. In 1859, for instance, 780 people from all classes of society paid membership fees.

Among other publishing societies in Copenhagen to which Icelandic authors and intellectuals were linked is the Royal Society of Old Norse Studies (1824; Hið konunglega norræna fornfræðafélag). As its name suggests, the society concentrated on the research and publication of medieval Nordic literature, and its first subject was the publication of the Kings' Sagas: *Fornmanna sögur* (1825–37). Many Icelanders worked on the publication, which was well received by Icelandic readers: Of all the subscribers to the third volume of *Fornmanna sögur* (1827), 770, or 75 percent, were from Iceland. More than half the Icelandic subscribers were farmers and workers, a fact that bears witness to the public's interest in reading and in medieval literature. Also popular were the books published by Páll Sveinsson (1818–74), a bookbinder in Copenhagen, in the latter half of the nineteenth century, among them the annual journal *Ný sumargjöf*, which Steingrímur Thorsteinsson edited and which was the first illustrated magazine in Icelandic, the anthology *Svava* (1860), many translations by Steingrímur Thorsteinsson, such as Tegnér's *Axel* and *Þúsund og ein nótt*, and Benedikt Gröndal's *Sagan af Heljarslóðarorrustu*.

After the middle of the century book and journal publication in Iceland increased to a certain extent. In 1848 the first proper news and political paper, *Þjóðólfur*, appeared. It was published in Reykjavík from 1848 to 1912, first biweekly, and later weekly, and enjoyed a wide circulation. Fiction, poetry, and stories regularly appeared in *Þjóðólfur* and other papers as many of the editors were well-known poets, among them Matthías Jochumsson and Steingrímur Thorsteinsson. Among the literary innovations introduced by the papers were serials, translated and original, often printed at the bottom of the page. It was not least love stories and thrillers that became popular reading material, and they soon started to compete with the *rímur* for the interest of readers. The first Icelandic serial was *Böðvar og Ásta* (Böðvar and Ásta) by Magnús Grímsson, the collector of folklore, which was published in *Lanztíðindi* in 1851. Occasionally, young poets became nationally famous overnight with poems that were published in the newspapers' pages. One of the best examples of this is Kristján Jónsson Fjallaskáld. It is also worth mentioning that most of the papers published comments or reviews on new books, the first, albeit modest, sign of a national literary criticism.

Another important event in the history of Icelandic publishing was the founding of a printing press in Akureyri in 1852. This meant that there were now two printing presses in the country, which gave more authors the opportunity to see their works in print. Some writers were very prolific. In the years from 1851 to 1861 Benedikt Gröndal, for example, published three original books of poetry, one play, one novel, and three translations of fiction as well as publishing a variety of works in journals and anthologies. Other authors followed suit, although few could match Gröndal's output. Not even Gröndal was able to live off writing alone, however, and grants to authors were unknown until the end of the century, while royalties were low or nonexistent. "It is common with Icelanders that they say, 'You should write, mate,' but then they don't remember that, if one is to write, one has to have something to eat," as Gröndal put it in 1870 (*Ritsafn*, 3:140), intimating that it was in itself a proper job to work as a writer; occasional free time was simply not enough.

When discussing the poor circumstances of Icelandic writers, one should not forget that, up to the end of the nineteenth century, book publishing was in the hands of individuals or societies, mostly without capital, who sold their publications mainly to subscribers or through intermediaries all over the country. Sometimes payment for books appeared late or never, and then the publishers themselves had to pay. The first bookshop in Iceland was not opened until 1874, and until 1886 printers had to obtain a royal license to establish a printing press. Both can be seen as an indication of the difficulties faced by Icelandic publishers in the nineteenth century, although this era also saw the main transformations in bookmaking and the distribution of printed material.

FINAL WORD

Variety is what first catches the eye when viewing Icelandic literature of the nineteenth century, not only because so many, and so many different, poets appeared during this time, but also because of the sheer diversity of their work. It is, therefore, counterproductive to claim that they all belong to one and the same movement (romanticism), as is often done, or to consider the poets who appeared around the middle of the century merely as the followers of Bjarni Thorarensen and Jónas Hallgrímsson. If each and every poet, and every generation, of this revolutionary century is to be heard, the different tendencies evident in their works all need to be examined in their own right, even if, in some cases, they appear only in a very few works by one or two poets. Often, these tendencies are clearly reactions to contemporary local or international events or the movements that swept Europe. Indeed, it is important to note the close relation between Icelandic literature and the literature of other countries. While the works produced in Iceland during this era were obviously fewer in number and smaller in scope than those produced in larger nations, many of them have, nevertheless, left their mark on the Icelandic consciousness and have for some time now been considered among the most treasured by the Icelandic people.

Translated by Gunnþórunn Guðmundsdóttir

From Realism to Neoromanticism

Guðni Elísson

4

Although the dates 1874–1918 have no specific literary-historical signifi-
cance, they have, nevertheless, often been used to demarcate a period in
Icelandic literary history. Neoromanticism did not draw to a close in 1918,
as is highlighted by the fact that two of its main proponents, Stefán frá
Hvítadal (1887–1933; Stefán of Hvítadalur) and Davíð Stefánsson (1895–
1964), did not publish their first works until 1918 and 1919, respectively.
Similarly, the first part of this period is hardly dominated by realism alone.
Icelandic romanticism remained, as it had been before 1874, nearly all-
embracing, and three of its most significant poets — Grímur Thomsen
(1820–96), Steingrímur Thorsteinsson (1831–1913), and Matthías Jochumsson (1835–1920) — published their first collections during the years
1880–84, although by then their poems were already well-known to the
Icelandic public from journals, magazines, and anthologies.

The reasons behind the demarcation are, rather, historical; they are reflected in two important dates in the Icelandic struggle for independence.
In 1874 King Christian IX issued a new constitution for Iceland that
granted the Althing legislative power. In 1918 Icelanders gained their independence from Denmark while continuing to share a Danish monarch. The
most significant stage between these two milestones was the establishment
of a national government in 1904. Hannes Hafstein (1861–1922), a poet

The author wishes to thank Gunnþórunn Guðmundsdóttir and Rory McTurk for their
assistance with translation and Daisy Neijmann and Joseph Brown for their helpful comments,
from which the final version of this chapter has benefited.

Unless specified otherwise, all translations from the Icelandic are the translator's.

and politician and one of the most significant proponents of realism, became the first secretary of state for Iceland.

This is not to say, however, that the dates 1874–1918 are completely arbitrary from a literary perspective. The Icelandic realist movement was born in the 1870s, and the appearance of the single issue of the journal *Verðandi* in 1882 has long been considered to mark its inception. Along the same lines neoromanticism had lost much of its freshness when Jóhannes úr Kötlum (1899–1972; Jóhannes of Katlar) published his first books of poetry: *Bí bí og blaka* (1926; Lullaby) and *Álftirnar kvaka* (1929; Swan song), which must be considered part of that literary movement. From then on the epic social-realist novels of Halldór Laxness (1902–98) became the frame of reference for Icelandic literature.

During the nineteenth century Iceland became increasingly isolated from other European nations. While in Europe this had been the century of progress and innovation, characterized by radical changes in industry and society, in Iceland hardly any changes had taken place, life there remaining much as it had been for centuries, generations coming and going without any signs of progress. Árni Pálsson maintains that, as a result, a certain pessimism can be detected in the generation of Icelanders growing up during the latter half of the nineteenth century: "The truth is that the idea that Iceland was in fact a doomed country—doomed to huddle outside European culture, the nation, like an outlaw, incapable of taking part in the work of progress of other nations—had taken root like a poison in the minds of most Icelanders" (*Á víð og dreif*, 333–34). Small wonder, then, that the generation to whom the Danes handed over the country in 1874 was not particularly optimistic: it held out few hopes, given the bleak outlook for the country's future. Pálsson even goes so far as to claim that, by 1874, the Danes had finally lost their faith in the country's potential and that this lack of faith was their only legacy to the Icelanders in 1874.

Adding to the general sense of hopelessness were the similarly bleak climatic conditions at the time. The weather had been exceptionally severe in 1880, and there was drift ice along the shores north and east of the country that brought harsh winters. Mount Askja erupted in 1875 in what was the century's worst natural disaster, and many farms in the northeast and east of the country had to be abandoned after being covered by a thick layer of ash. This was followed by a powerful earthquake in the south in 1896. In his memoirs, published posthumously in the collection *Samtíningur* (1920; Compilation), the writer Jón Trausti (the pen name of Guðmundur Magnússon [1873–1918]) described the situation as follows:

I was only nine years old, but I will never forget the hardships suffered by the people on Melrakkaslétta. The peninsula was surrounded by ice as far as the eye could see. The ground was covered with ice. What the sun melted during the day — when it shone — froze during the night. But the sun seldom shone. Even in clear skies, there was a freezing mist over the ground and over the ice, which weakened the rays. The rain never came, warmth never came. At times a thick fog descended. But it wasn't the mild, warm spring fog that collects the sun's rays and melts the snow so that the ice disappears. No, this fog was full of sharp ice needles that hurt the skin. . . . The poor lost their livelihood in droves. Whole families became dependent on the local authorities or took to the road — which in fact was the same thing. I remember when these wretched souls dragged themselves from farm to farm, blue in the face from starvation and weakness, with scurvy in their gums and arthritis in their knees — until they lay down at some farm and couldn't get any farther. There they had to die or get better. Most of them got better and — were sent to America in the summer. (*Ritsafn*, 1:308–9)

In the 1870s, emigration to North America had started in earnest. The first groups left for Canada in 1873–74, although 1876 was the first year of extensive emigration as 1,190 Icelanders boarded ship and headed west. A large percentage of these people had been forced to leave their farms because of the Askja eruption and had nowhere else to go. It is estimated that up to 15,000 Icelanders emigrated to America in 1870–1914, most of them from the northeastern part of the country — a great loss for a nation that in 1900 counted only 78,000 people. It was a particularly savage bloodletting as the emigrants were mostly young people: over 80 percent had not yet reached thirty.

But changes were at long last afoot in Icelandic society. In 1874–1900 the first discernible steps toward progress were made, although it is mostly after 1900 that significant breakthroughs occur. The Icelandic National Bank was established in 1885, the Bank of Iceland in 1904, an agricultural college in Ólafsdalur (western Iceland) in 1880, and a naval college in Reykjavík in 1881, and in 1906 telegraph communication was established between Iceland and other countries, finally breaking the country's centuries of isolation. But the most groundbreaking and important revolution occurred in the nation's fishing industry. From the time of settlement Icelanders had gone fishing in open rowboats and continued to do so up to 1870. By this time the number of open boats had decreased and the age of decked vessels was under way. For example, during the period 1881–1905 — the *skútuöld*, the "golden age of decked vessels" — the share of fish in Icelandic exports grew from just under 60 percent to 77 percent. The peak was reached in 1906, but then the dominance of the decked vessels slowly receded as trawlers and motorboats began to appear on the scene. In the wake of these changes farmers and country folk flocked to the coastal towns. This is most evident in the fact that, at the turn of the century, 80 percent of the nation's population lived in rural areas and 20 percent in towns, while, in 1920, those numbers had become 57 and 43 percent, respectively.

At the same time as the motorization of the fishing fleet was revolutionizing Icelandic industry, similarly revolutionary changes were occurring in Icelandic society. These changes can in large part be explained by the changed attitudes and increased optimism of the generation then in power. The ambitions of that generation are portrayed in the poetry of Einar Benediktsson (1864–1940), who, shortly before the turn of the century, wrote in "Íslandsljóð" (A poem on Iceland) on the helplessness of the Icelandic fisherman, who, because of poor conditions, cannot venture far from shore and, therefore, loses his share to the Frenchman, who can stay much further out on better fishing grounds:

> How long will you lads
> Fish by jigging a line,
> Indolent by the shore?
> (Benediktsson, *Ljóðmæli*, 1:66 [trans. Guðni Elísson])

Realist and neoromantic writers tackled the problems facing Icelandic society during the last decades of the nineteenth century, each in their own way. Their solutions varied, even though their goal was the same. The realists wanted to cure social ills by making their countrymen aware of their circumstances through sharp social criticism. The neoromantic message of progress was characterized by an increased optimism in relation to social issues, influenced by the "superman" ideal propounded by the German philosopher Friedrich Nietzsche (1844–1900) at the end of the century.

Realism heralded a new golden age in Icelandic prose writing, but it did not influence poetry to any great extent. It began to attract Icelandic students in Copenhagen at the end of the 1860s and forged its path in the Icelandic literary world. In their revolt against romantic values, the realist writers demanded that literature describe reality in a true and objective manner, concealing nothing.

The rise of realist literature in Scandinavia can primarily be linked to one man: the Dane Georg Brandes (1842–1927). In the autumn of 1871 Brandes embarked on a lecture series that was eventually published as *Hovedstrømninger i det nittende Aarhundredes litteratur* (1872–90; Main currents in nineteenth-century literature). In those lectures he advocated the idea that research in literature and aesthetics was dependent on the same principles as was research in other sciences. At first Brandes was greatly influenced by the German philosopher Hegel and his disciples, also known as the left-wing Hegelians. He viewed the drive of progress as a repeated battle between two opposites, revolution and reaction. Reaction is not negative in itself but imposes the necessary restrictions on the revolution, examines its most valuable assets, assimilates them, and lays the foundation for further progress.

Brandes followed the ideas of the left-wing Hegelians, who maintained that scientists should be not just objective observers but active shapers of their environment and that they should rebel against reaction wherever necessary. The introduction to *Hovedstrømninger*, where Brandes announces his manifesto, bears witness to this: "Literature in our time lives because it puts problems under debate. Accordingly, George Sand debates marriage, Voltaire, Byron, and Feuerbach debate religion, Proudhon private property, Alexander Dumas *fils* the relationship between the sexes, and Emile Augier social customs. Literature that debates nothing will . . . lose all meaning" (Brandes, *Emigrantlitteraturen*, 15–16). Brandes encouraged Scandinavian authors to become — like Honoré de Balzac (1799–1850), who called himself *docteur des sciences sociales*, "a doctor of social sciences" — the healers of society. Brandes's ideas soon caught on in Iceland. The poet Matthías Jochumsson, for instance, listened to his lectures in the autumn of 1871 in Copenhagen and was attracted to his message of justice and individual rights.[1] The editor Jón Ólafsson (1850–1916) also played a role in the realist movement in Iceland: in 1879 he published a translation of a short chapter from the second volume of *Hovedstrømninger* in his newspaper *Skuld*, and, in the spirit of Georg Brandes, he also translated John Stuart Mill's (1806–73) *On Liberty* (1859), the translation being published in Icelandic in 1886.[2]

In the spring of 1882 the journal *Verðandi* was published, an event that, as we have seen, has traditionally been considered to mark the beginning of the realist movement in Iceland. Behind the project were four students in Copenhagen, Gestur Pálsson (1852–91), Hannes Hafstein, Bertel E. Ó. Þorleifsson (1857–90), and Einar Hjörleifsson Kvaran (1859–1938). The journal published short stories by Pálsson and Kvaran and poems by Hafstein and Þorleifsson. Even though only one issue was ever published and that issue did not include a manifesto, Hafstein and Pálsson stated their views in speech and in print in the course of the coming years and were faithful to Brandes's ideas about subjecting problems to debate in their efforts to improve Icelandic society. A year after the publication of *Verðandi*, Pálsson became the editor of the Reykjavík newspaper *Suðri*, and there he published a manifesto to which, he claimed, *Suðri* would adhere:

> The realist movement presumes that something has no beauty (i.e., has no place in art or literature) unless it is true (i.e., occurs in human society or nature). . . . We claim that writers should themselves go into battle, they should find their subject matter in human society and sacrifice everything to obtain correct knowledge and unswerving views on individuals, on the order of society, on the relationship between individual and society, and they should base their writing on the results of their research. They should look into the hearts and souls of men, learn to know them, write about them. Only in this way do we believe literature to be truly useful to human society. ("Úr ávarpsorðum," 120–21)

Pálsson emphasized social analysis in literature and the importance of exposing the vulgar truth of social conventions. In his lecture "Hnignun íslensks skáldskapar" (The decline of Icelandic literature), Hannes Hafstein emphasized the importance of social progress, in which, he believed, writers could directly take part: "Our time is the time of investigating wounds and of healing, in both a spiritual and a physical sense. The call of the times is for the life of the individual, not a glorification of the derived idea of 'nation.' Our time is the time of industrial progress, steam and electricity, the proud time of research." As Jón Karl Helgason ("Tímans heróp," 115, 121) has pointed out, this is reminiscent of Georg Brandes's ideas on the new Faust who rises up against the earth spirit, takes over its land, and conquers it with steam and electricity, with scientific research.

The call for the necessity of research and critical study was taken up in the work of the poet and social democrat Þorsteinn Erlingsson (1858–1914), for instance, in the poem "Skilmálarnir" (1897; The terms), where he emphasizes that an open mind is the only path to social progress:

> And if you wish the secret lore of nature to read,
> Approaching it in meekness, like a child in its need,
> Accepting nothing twisted through another man's view,
> — Then humbly I'll begin at the beginning with you.
> (trans. Jakobína Johnson in *Icelandic Lyrics*, ed. Beck, 129–31)

Gestur Pálsson, like Hannes Hafstein and Þorsteinn Erlingsson, criticized the stagnation of Icelandic literature and cultural life. He gave three lectures in Reykjavík in 1888–89. In one of them, "Menntunarástandið á Íslandi" (The state of education in Iceland), he takes up Brandes's ideas on revolution and reaction, which he believes to be the source of all progress. Pálsson describes education in Iceland thus: "No spiritual criticism, no spiritual battles anywhere — the reason being that there is not an idea in the country that any living soul would fight for; no one sacrifices anything for a single thing because no one believes in anything they would suffer for. No new thought awakens anywhere. All that individuals have are old thoughts and redundant ideas, nothing but ghosts. One could become fearful of the dark from thinking about the spiritual life in Iceland" (Pálsson, *Ritsafn*, 2:111). Pálsson's and Hafstein's lectures aroused some debate, and, in the essay "Um skáldskap" (On literature) from 1888, Benedikt Gröndal (1826–1907) defended the ideas of the romantic generation of writers (see also p. 287). Many critics found the attempt to effect progress by the *Verðandi* group somewhat limited, claiming that it stood in no relation to the state of society and that the group ignored the specific nature of Icelandic circumstances. Einar Benediktsson, for instance, subjected them to an unfair attack in "Gestur Pálsson," an 1896 article in *Dagskrá*, in which he claimed that the realists were not patriotic enough. In addition he did not support the movement's material outlook and view of life.

Pálsson's and especially Hafstein's ideas were influenced by the French literary theorists Charles-Augustin Sainte-Beuve (1804–69) and Hippolyte Taine (1828–93) and their belief in the power of science, as advocated by Brandes. In Hafstein's work one also finds the worship of the genius that characterizes Brandes's work throughout. Indeed, Brandes was later to abandon the realist movement; he became the first to introduce Friedrich Nietzsche's philosophy in Scandinavia. The worship of masculinity and unfettered energy is, thus, not limited to the neoromantic poets. Similar ideas appear quite early in, for instance, Hannes Hafstein's poems "Stormur" (1882; The storm) and "Undir Kaldadal" (1882; Nearing Cold-Dale), which first appeared in the journal *Verðandi*. In fact, both these poems could easily be regarded as examples of neoromantic poetry in their praise of the empowering and cleansing energy that wipes out anything weak and ill. The first and last stanzas of "Undir Kaldadal" are as follows:

I wish for rain — and I wish for snow,
As on through Cold-Dale our horses glide;
And that a bracing wind may blow

Down from the glacial mountain-side.
. . .
To brave the tempest with might and main
Lends steel to courage and spurs to pride.
— I hope there will be a rush of rain
Or an Iceland storm — on our Cold-Dale ride.
(trans. Jakobina Johnson in *Icelandic Lyrics*, ed. Beck, 155)

Hannes Hafstein appeared to his countrymen as a manly warrior, and he gained the public's admiration for poetry such as this. "Undir Kaldadal" and similar works seem far removed, however, from the subjecting of problems to debate that he and other realists proclaimed, showing how difficult it was to alter the romantic lyric tradition that for so long had held Icelandic literature in its grip. Hafstein's poems are powerful, imbued with a solid rhythm, for instance, "Skarphéðinn í brennunni" (1882; Skarphéðinn in the fire), which is written almost exclusively in dactylic tetrameter. Still, even though his poems do not bear witness to the traditional belief in patriotism and a golden age that so often characterized the works of his romantic contemporaries, and even though his language is more colloquial than that of the preceding generation, Hafstein does not paint a realistic picture of society in his poetry.

It could, in fact, be maintained that, despite his call for realism, Hafstein himself is not a realist poet at all. Thus, he ignores ordinary situations involving average characters, makes use of romantic images and metaphors, and in no way attempts to reproduce actual speech or natural prose rhythms. Although Gestur Pálsson will hardly be remembered for his poetry, his poem "Betlikerling" (1882; The beggar woman) does, by contrast, exemplify realist poetry, as the first stanza demonstrates:

She cringed and stooped nigh steps
    when the winter frost controlled;
She huddled herself together
    and to a snail-shape rolled;
With her gnarled hands she groped e'er,
    atrembling, to and fro,
And at her tatters clutched she
    that they might warmth bestow.
(trans. Skuli Johnson in *Icelandic Lyrics*, ed. Beck, 123)

It must be emphasized, however, that Hafstein's poetry incorporates many of Brandes's main ideas on the cultural revolution that he advocated in Denmark, a view supported by Sveinn Skorri Höskuldsson (*Gestur Páls-son*, 2:567), who has pointed out that, in Icelandic literature, realism did not represent the same novelty as it did in many other European countries, thanks to the sagas and the fact that a strong realist tendency also character-izes the romantic generation of writers. Gestur Pálsson himself had ques-tioned the strict borderline between realism and romanticism in foreign as well as Icelandic literature in his essay "Nýi skáldskapurinn" (The new literature): "I want to make it clear from the start that in Iceland realism and idealism are more or less inseparable for most writers of this century, so it would hardly be possible to divide them into two groups and say: this writer is an idealist and this writer a realist. This is quite natural as these terms and the characteristics, or rules, of these movements did not reach Iceland until a few years ago" (Pálsson, *Ritsafn*, 2:73).

Pálsson's critique of romantic poetry was specifically directed against the patriotism and the nostalgia prevalent among older poets and, indeed, the whole nation, the two ingredients with which romanticism had most pow-erfully influenced the national consciousness. While this nostalgia had cer-tainly helped make Icelanders aware of their nationality and awakened their sense of independence, it had also, according to Pálsson, filled them with an unfounded sense of national pride and led them astray. As a result positive influences from other countries were less apparent than they might have been, and in this way nostalgia had hindered true progress. Furthermore, in Pálsson's view, and as Brandes maintained in his lectures, this nostalgia was also based on falsehoods, on myth rather than truth. Jón Karl Helgason observes in this connection: "In accordance with the belief of the educa-tional role of literature, Gestur [Pálsson] sees nostalgia, especially the read-ing of the sagas, reflected in the restlessness and brutish behavior that, according to him, characterize life in most rural areas" ("Tímans heróp," 132). Pálsson believes that, in contemporary literature, humanity should be valued above nostalgia, and his and Einar Kvaran's stories bear witness to this conviction. In the spirit of Brandes, their writing, and that of the realists who followed, aimed to heal social ills by discussing them critically.

In his lecture "Um skáldskap," mentioned above, Benedikt Gröndal counters the realists' critique with full force, especially as he believes their vi-sion of progress to be naive. He pays little heed to the idea that the "nation has no will." The will of the nation is simply that "people want something to eat." He then traces in detail the problems plaguing nineteenth-century Iceland, political and financial poverty, general apathy, and pessimism: "It is therefore appropriate that one hardly sees anything now but epithets and elegies, but it is wrong to blame individuals for that; it is rather the fault of the times and circumstances, as I have shown" (Gröndal, *Rit*, 2:183, 185).

According to Gröndal, a starving nation hardly cares about literature, whether it is aligned with romanticism or realism.

Gröndal is doubtless correct in his judgment that the Icelandic public showed little interest in the works of the romantic poets. But, here, realist literature faced an even thornier problem than its predecessors had done. Abroad, increasing financial wealth had created a loyal readership for realist and naturalist literature among the ever-growing middle classes. Not only did that literature reflect a middle-class lifestyle and middle-class values; it also brought within the ken of the bourgeoisie the alien world of the lower classes, where hunger, hardship, and repression were daily realities. In Iceland, however, social circumstances were quite different. The nation was suffering after years of hardship and preferred romantic escape rather than a realist reminder of life in all its dreadfulness, which was already available in abundance.

ICELANDIC REALIST LITERATURE

The realist movement had limited influence on the development of Icelandic poetry, the roots of which were too firmly planted in the romantic spirit of the century for it to be changed to any extent. Þorsteinn Erlingsson published his first book of poetry, *Þyrnar* (Thorns), in 1897. Soon after the poet Einar Benediktsson claimed in a review: "His poetry is light and delightful, written in the style of the older poets who relied on human emotions such as happiness, sorrow, love, hate — rather than the passion for criticizing the bugs and bacteria in human society that characterizes the objectively dim school" ("Þorsteinn Erlingsson," 280–81). This view of *Þyrnar* is correct in that Erlingsson's patriotism was very much influenced by older poets, in particular, Steingrímur Thorsteinsson. His nature poetry is in the romantic spirit, full of patriotic feeling, and with a strong sense of beauty.

Nevertheless, Erlingsson had also undoubtedly been influenced by the realist movement. He arrived in Copenhagen the year after the publication of *Verðandi* and stayed there for the next thirteen years, until 1896. He was quick to appropriate Brandes's theories and became a social democrat. In the spirit of the realist movement he harshly criticized the state and the church authorities and declared his loathing of capitalism and of blind religious fervor. His book *Þyrnar* was, thus, aimed at the thorns in the side of society. In religious matters he was in many ways reminiscent of the English poet George Gordon, Lord Byron, whom Erlingsson revered. Both were rebels who refused to accept the idea of an unjust God of suffering and inequality.

The poem "Eiðurinn" (1913; The oath) is a historical epic based on a well-known event in the life of Ragnheiður, the daughter of Bishop Brynj-ólfur at Skálholt, in seventeenth-century Iceland. It is in ottava rima, the verse form that made Byron famous in the English-speaking world with his epic poem *Don Juan*. The bishop's daughter publicly avowed that she had never been with a man but then gave birth to a son forty weeks later. In addition to the scandal she was, thus, also suspected of perjury. This event has inspired many writers. The novelist Torfhildur Hólm (1845–1918) devoted a novel to it, *Brynjólfur Sveinsson biskup* (1882; Bishop Brynjólfur Sveinsson), and Guðmundur Jónsson Kamban (1888–1945) based his best-known work, *Skálholt*, on it (see below).

Erlingsson employed simple and accessible verse forms, such as the four-line stanza, which he used extensively and refined to perfection. He wanted to write in simple language to make matters clear and unambiguous, to the extent that even children would be able to understand what he was saying.

Another polemical poet is the Icelandic-Canadian Stephan G. Stephansson (1853–1927), who moved to Wisconsin when he was only twenty years old. He lived for a while in North Dakota before settling in Alberta, Canada. Stephansson had no formal schooling and was a farmer all his life. His first collections of poetry are called *Úti á víðavangi* (1894; Out in the open) and *Á ferð og flugi* (1900; Traveling far and wide; English trans.: "En Route" [1987]). The latter is an epic poem on the life of Icelanders in North America (see also pp. 623–24). In the spirit of the Icelandic realists he criticized free enterprise and the clergy, both of which, he believed, threatened the well-being of Icelanders in North America. Like Erlingsson, Stephansson quickly turned against conservatism and became, in addition, a declared atheist. Late in his career he published the collection *Vígslóði* (1920; Battlefield), a fierce polemic against war in which the horrors of the First World War and the leaders who lead their children to slaughter are condemned. As before, his message was a humanitarian one.

From 1909 on, Stephansson published six books of poetry under the title *Andvökur* (Wakeful nights), the last one posthumously in 1938. The title refers to the fact that Stephansson usually wrote during the evening and at night, after working all day. Stephansson described how his poems came into being in the poem "Við verkalok" (1883; When day is done):

When sunlight fades and shadows wrap the hillsides
by summer night
and hovering, as if hung unto the branches,
a half-moon bright
when cool nocturnal breeze befriends my forehead

all flushed with sweat
and weary toilers know the rest of nighttime
is nearing yet —

when in the meadows metal bells are tinkling
among the herd
and evening songs are warbled in the woods by
a wistful bird,
the gentle zephyr tooting in return its
antistrophe
and shrieks of children playing by the brooklet
are borne to me —

while, as if spots of moonlight, grain fields glimmer,
the ground all blue,
and glutted with a gauzy mist the hollows
light gray of hue,
and golden stars like distant tapers twinkle
between the trees,
I sit and rest outside my house enjoying
the sundown's peace.
(Stephansson, "When Day Is Done," trans. Hallmundsson, 117)

Stephansson had read the sagas in his youth and sought inspiration in them, portraying ancient heroes as examples for modern times in such works as "Illugadrápa" (Ode to Illugi), "Hergilseyjarbóndinn" (The farmer in Hergilsey), and "Ástríður Ólafsdóttir Svíakonungs" (Astrid princess of Sweden).

Like other followers of the realist movement Stephansson often wrote on the lot of the down-and-out. His best-known poem of this type is based on the folktale of Jón hrak (Worthless Jón). Jón is born out of wedlock and is, thus, from the start the victim of social prejudice. He is an eccentric child of nature and a poet who has problems accepting the Christian message. Jón lives on the margins of society and finally dies of hypothermia in a terrible frost. And even in death he is a misfit, for, when his body is to be laid to rest, the ground is frozen solid, and he must be buried north to south, that is, with his body placed in such a way that, in the event of his resurrection, he would find himself facing north rather than east. Because of this break in burial tradition, Jón returns from the dead and stalks the living. The poem concludes with a general critique of the shame of a society that treats its most underprivileged in this way.

In Iceland realism was most influential in the area of prose writing, where Jón Thoroddsen's (1818–68) novels *Piltur og stúlka* (1850; Lad and lass) and *Maður og kona* (1876; Man and woman) had in many ways been the only Icelandic prose narratives since the time of the sagas (see also pp. 294–96). During the period 1880–1920 prose writing changed dramatically under the influence of foreign novels and, more important, was shaped by the ideas of the realist movement. As a result it became for the first time a recognized literary genre in Iceland. It is, thus, primarily in the prose works of the realists that we see a clear break with the romantic tradition in Icelandic literature.

In the journal *Verðandi* the prose writers Gestur Pálsson and Einar Hjörleifsson Kvaran published their first stories, loyal to the cause of "debating problems" in an effort to transform Icelandic society through art. Verðandi was one of the three mythological Fates, the one who controlled the present. In choosing to use her name as the title of its journal the *Verðandi* group wanted to emphasize the status of Icelanders in the present and to distance themselves from the past so admired by the romantic poets. Pálsson's and Kvaran's stories criticize in no uncertain terms the hypocrisy of Icelandic society with regard to the relations of the sexes, religion, and the individual's relationship to society. They often contain ironic social descriptions, speaking on behalf of the members of the lower classes, such as workers, water carriers, misfits, and thieves.

Pálsson's story "Kærleiksheimilið" (1882; The house of love) was published in *Verðandi* and is his first realist narrative. It describes the love between Jón, a young farmer's son, and Anna, a poor but beautiful farmhand at Jón's mother's home. Blinded by love, Jón asks for Anna's hand in marriage, but his mother forbids the union. When she finds out that Anna is pregnant, she throws her out and finds another bride for Jón, the daughter of the local vicar. Overcome with despair and sorrow Anna drowns herself on the wedding night. Jón is, of course, shocked by the news and regrets having allowed his mother to control his actions. But, when his mother offers to pay for Anna's funeral and the vicar gives a heartfelt speech over her grave, he feels a certain peace, even absolution:

> How could Jón doubt anymore? And he did not doubt. It was as if a large rock had been lifted off his chest. All his suffering was no more than a figment of his imagination; he looked for a moment to his future: he was a pillar of his community, a shelter for people in need, a supporter of all good activities. . . . When he carried the coffin down the aisle, he felt new life streaming through his veins, as if new vigor

and strength had been born in his chest. He shoveled the earth quickly into the grave; he was so lighthearted, he wanted to exercise all his tasks diligently and conscientiously. Then it was all over. Anna from Hraun rested in her grave, for the grace of "true Christian charity," which had followed her beyond the grave." (Pálsson, *Ritsafn*, 2:77–78)

Pálsson's verdict on Icelandic society was harsh, and many thought him guilty of immorality and blasphemy. The social realism of the story exposes a lack of integrity as well as Christian hypocrisy and oppression of the poor by the elite. As in many other realist stories the individual comes up against a society that crushes her. The love of Jón and Anna threatens the ruling order of society as they do not honor the rules of marriage, class difference, and the blessing of the church with their relationship. When Jón chooses to surrender to his mother's tyranny, he is rewarded with security and moves up the social ladder, but at the same time his lack of integrity means that he has given up the freedom that his love for Anna could have given him, even though he would have been forced to leave refined society behind.

A similar message can be found in Pálsson's story "Vordraumur" (1888; Spring dream), in which a young theology student accepts a well-paying living acquired through deception when it is made clear to him that otherwise his career will be compromised. Other well-known stories by Pálsson are "Hans Vöggur" (1883), about a water carrier and misfit in Reykjavík, and "Tilhugalíf" (1888; Courtship), about a carpenter in Reykjavík who steals food to alleviate his hunger and is ostracized from society as a result.

Pálsson's colleague Einar Hjörleifsson Kvaran published his first stories in the early 1870s, but it was not until the story "Vonir" (1890; Hopes) that he made his mark on Icelandic literature. Kvaran wrote the story in Canada, where until his return to Iceland in 1895 he lived in the large Icelandic community in Winnipeg and edited the emigrant journals *Heimskringla* and *Lögberg*. The story tells of the hopes and disappointments of the thousands of Icelanders who moved to North America during the last decades of the nineteenth century. Icelanders were indifferent to "Vonir" until Georg Brandes wrote a review of it in 1900, just after it had been translated into Danish, claiming that it was "a true pearl": "The narration is without fault, the description masterly. Everything is in fact concentrated in a single scene, but it is unforgettable. . . . It is, all in all, as well crafted as it possibly could be" (*Politiken*, 19 November 1900). Soon after Kvaran published the short story collection *Vestan hafs og austan* (1901; West and East), where "Vonir" was published alongside two new stories.

Kvaran's next collection was entitled *Smælingjar* (1908; The poor). A considerable change had occurred in Kvaran's message as he had left behind the social criticism of the realist movement and adopted a Christian humanitarian approach, one based on the message of the New Testament. In the story "Fyrirgefning" (Forgiveness) Kvaran describes a little orphan girl who has been fostered and is very badly treated by the lady of the house. At the start of the story, the lady has recently passed away, and the body has been laid out in a coffin in the living room. The story is told from the point of view of the little girl and follows her thoughts, from her relief at being free from beatings and cruelty, to her worries for the lady's soul. The child's forgiveness becomes complete when she crawls out of her bed in the middle of the night and places a book of hymns on the body to guarantee the lady a place in heaven. Steingrímur J. Þorsteinsson had the following to say about "Fyrirgefning":

> Einar [Kvaran]'s fiction influenced Icelandic readers in two ways in particular, and both of these appear in this story: in their attitude toward the doctrine of eternal damnation and toward the traditional methods of child rearing. During the first decades of the century Einar played a large part in assuaging the nation's fear of hell and in loosening the tighter bonds of orthodoxy—and his stories had a much greater impact than any pedagogue's teachings in lessening the harshness prevalent in child rearing, in making it more humane and gentle. (Þorsteinsson, "Einar H. Kvaran," 13)

By the time *Smælingjar* was published Kvaran had turned his attention almost exclusively to the writing of novels. *Ofurefli* (1908; Superior forces) and its sequel, *Gull* (1911; Gold), describe life in Reykjavík in the first decade of the twentieth century. They tell of a young vicar's battles against a merchant's power and corruption. With his theory of forgiveness and charity, the vicar finally gains the upper hand, and the merchant dies repentant. Friðrik J. Bergmann had the following to say about *Ofurefli*: "This is in fact the first time in our literature that an Icelandic vicar is described with love and care, in any real sense. He is, in this novel, made to be an exemplary man, as a vicar should always be. It has been a regular fashion to include at least one farcical story of a priest in every novel and make him the lowliest and most shameful character in the story" (review of *Ofurefli*, 88–89).

During the following years Kvaran published the novels *Sálin vaknar* (1916; The soul awakens), *Sambýli* (1918; Communal living), and *Sögur Rannveigar* I–II (1919 and 1922; Rannveig's tales). At the same time his interest in spiritualism grew, and in 1918 he became the president of the

Icelandic Society for Psychical Research. This was to inform his fiction, where the dead make an appearance and his characters hear voices, with spiritual powers having a direct impact on their development and behavior. To this group of works belongs *Sögur Rannveigar*, Kvaran's most accomplished novel (see also p. 364). Also influenced by spiritualism, the novel form in *Sögur Rannveigar* has been linked to "symbolic realism" (Sæmundsson, *Ást og útlegð*, 189).

Kvaran also wrote the plays *Lénharður fógeti* (1913; Bailiff Leonard), a historical play, and *Syndir annarra* (1915; Other people's sins), set in contemporary Reykjavík. Presumably, Kvaran wanted to follow in the footsteps of Jóhann Sigurjónsson (1880–1919), whose play *Fjalla-Eyvindur* (1912; English trans.: *Eyvind of the Hills* [1916]), had been received very favorably in Copenhagen, but Kvaran's plays did not meet with great success (see also p. 557).

During the last decade of the century three authors from the northern district of Þingeyrar appeared on the Icelandic literary scene, Þorgils gjallandi (Jón Stefánsson, 1851–1915), Jón Trausti, and Guðmundur Friðjónsson (1869–1944). They were part of a local cultural movement that reached its peak during the period 1880–90. Originally, the movement was characterized by nationalism, but it soon developed a more cultural focus and actively encouraged the study of foreign books, mainly works from Scandinavia. Its members were, thus, influenced early on by realist ideas and naturalist literature.

Ten years after *Verðandi*, Þorgils gjallandi published the short-story collection *Ofan úr sveitum* (1892; From the country). It met with a harsh reception and was felt to be highly blasphemous in that it aimed primarily to speak ill of the clergy and church doctrine. Þorgils gjallandi gained popularity later, mainly for the animal stories that he started writing during this period, among them "Fölskvi" (1890; Ash) and "Móa-Móra" (1891; Mountain-Móra). Both tell of the ill treatment of horses. For a while he collaborated with Þorsteinn Erlingsson, who was also well-known for his animal stories. Þorgils gjallandi continued to write animal stories for the rest of his life. The best known of his later stories is without a doubt "Heimþrá" (1909; Homesickness), about the horse Stjarna (Star). All his animal stories were collected in *Dýrasögur* (1910; Animal stories), his last work.

Þorgils gjallandi's only novel, *Upp við fossa* (1902; By the waterfalls), has often been considered the first naturalistic novel in Iceland, and it remains one of the most hotly debated works in the history of Icelandic prose writing. The first part of the story tells of the love affair between the young farmer's son, Geirmundur, and Gróa, a married woman. Geirmundur and Gróa meet in secret, but their relationship ends when Gróa does not dare divorce her husband. She chooses a safe income over love and is not strong enough to rebel and follow her feelings. The latter half of the novel describes the friendship and love between Geirmundur and Þuríður, the vicar's daughter. Þuríður is portrayed as Gróa's opposite: Gróa is descended from poor people, while Þuríður is both educated and strong willed. She is ready to rebel against parental authority and the class system and to follow Geirmundur, until she finds out that they are half siblings, as the old vicar fathered them both. This revelation comes a little too late, however, as they have by then already slept together. Geirmundur does not want to hide behind lies, and, thus, it turns out that clandestine love affairs can have unforeseen consequences—in this case a young couple unknowingly commits incest. Love then becomes a moral crime because society teaches its children hypocrisy and deceit instead of courage and love of truth.

  Upp við fossa caused an uproar in Icelandic cultural society. The author's attitude toward the church and its clergy was considered scandalous, the descriptions of lovemaking were too revealing, and the subject of incest was new to Icelandic literature. The author Guðmundur Friðjónsson described the book's reception as follows: "Housewives especially have slated the book. I have seen intelligent women and good housewives jump from their seats at the mention of this story. And they were most angry with the author" ("Þorgils gjallandi," 101). The reviews were similarly harsh. Friðrik J. Bergmann wrote in the journal *Aldamót*: "[The novel] becomes vulgar and almost disgusting because of the author's manifest tendency to describe the most repulsive aspects of people's behavior and drag into the story what does not belong in any literature at all. As a result the description becomes false, and the risk is that the book will be viewed as sacrilegious because Icelandic rural life is not as sick and repugnant as it is in the author's description" (review of *Upp við fossa*, 164–65). Þorgils gjallandi mainly based *Upp við fossa* on foreign works, and it constitutes a significant milestone in Icelandic literature. He was already forty years old when he embarked on his writing career, and he was, therefore, not very prolific, although it should be noted that he was a farmer all his life and wrote only in his spare time.

  Guðmundur Friðjónsson published his first book of poetry, *Úr heimahögum* (From home), in 1902. It received bad reviews, and almost a quarter of a century passed until his next book, *Kvæði* (1925; Poems), appeared. It contains some of his best-known poems, such as "Ekkjan við ána" (The widow by the river) which describes the endurance of the Icelandic country woman in a harsh land, someone who accepts everything that happens with silence and patience, unlike many of her countrymen, who flee the country when life becomes difficult. In his poems and stories Friðjónsson praises the ancient virtues of the old farming society. He held a dim view of the migration from the country to the villages and towns and was not very impressed by people's increasing demands for comfort. He also criticized the new education law of 1907, which introduced compulsory school attendance for children aged ten to fourteen. In the lecture "Skólamenning — listagildi — lífsgildi — manngildi" (School education — artistic values — life values — human values) he claims: "Marriage is without a doubt the foundation of society. If it is correct, as I believe, that schools undermine the foundation of society, then serious-minded people who value country life and progress should feel threatened by these schools. Schooling influences many people in such a way that they become uprooted from the grounding of the everyday and become like daffodils and buttercups in a jar of water. Such vegetation bears no fruit; it becomes short-lived during hard times" (Friðjónsson, *Ritsafn*, 7:42–43).

Friðjónsson published quite a few short story collections, for instance, *Einir* (1902; Juniper), *Undir beru lofti* (1904; In the open air), *Tólf sögur* (1915; Twelve stories), *Úr öllum áttum* (1919; From all directions), and *Héðan og handan* (1925; From here and there). Many of his stories provide detailed descriptions of traditional Icelandic rural life and now-abandoned farming methods. His animal stories also remain among his best work and resemble the animal stories by Þorgils gjallandi and Þorsteinn Erlingsson. Friðjónsson's only novel, *Ólöf í Ási* (1907; Ólöf from Ás), was rather ill received. Like earlier realist fiction, the novel is concerned with social criticism and preaches increased personal freedom, for instance, in choice of partner. Friðjónsson does not take this idea as far as he might, however, because, as Matthías Viðar Sæmundsson puts it: "His stories contain the idea that love is the original situation of man and, at the same time, that oppression and repression are a necessity" (*Ást og útlegð*, 210). Friðjónsson advocates measured progress, but he was no revolutionary. Like Þorgils gjallandi, he was a mostly self-educated farmer who wrote in his spare time.

The most prolific novelist during the first decades of the twentieth century was Jón Trausti. Trausti began his writing career with *Heima og erlendis* (1899; Home and abroad) and *Íslandsvísur* (1903; Verses on Iceland). It was not until the publication of his novel *Halla* (1906), however, that he received full recognition among his countrymen. This popular novel was followed by *Heiðarbýlið* (1908–11; The farm on the moor), a four-volume sequel to *Halla*. The story takes place in the area where Trausti grew up during the 1860s and 1870s and concludes in the Great Frost Winter of 1881–82.

Halla is a poor but graceful young girl who is seduced by a married vicar and bears his child. Despite the vicar having kept his marriage a secret from her Halla decides to protect his reputation and moves to a barren moor farm with a farmhand whom she claims is the father of her child. Halla's story is broken up in the third and fourth volumes by the story of the lovers Þorsteinn and Jóhanna and the siblings Borghildur and Pétur from Kross. In both accounts the individual's rebellion against society and the class system is evident. As in "Kærleiksheimilið" by Gestur Pálsson, a farmer's son, in this case Þorsteinn, falls in love with a farmworker, in this case Jóhanna. Þorsteinn's mother, Borghildur, tries to prevent the marriage, but, unlike Jón in "Kærleiksheimilið," Þorsteinn rebels and moves his lover to Heiðarhvammur, Halla's farm. There she dies in childbirth. The last part of the story tells of the difficulties that Halla and her children face in a terrible frost on the moor. Halla fights her way to town in a storm while the children sit at home by their father's body. The story concludes with Halla moving to town.

After the novels about Halla and the farm on the moor, Trausti turned to writing historical novels. *Sögur frá Skaftáreldi* (Tales from the Skaftár fires) was published in 1912–13 and is, in part, based on the autobiography of the "fire-pastor" Jón Steingrímsson (1728–91; see also pp. 242–44). It describes the natural disaster when the eruption in Lakagígar created one of the biggest lava fields on earth (five to six hundred square kilometers). The novel *Anna frá Stóruborg* (1914; Anna from Stóraborg) is set in the sixteenth century and is based on an old folktale. It tells of doomed love but breaks with tradition in that the lovers do come together in the end.

Jón Trausti was a very prolific author, but his style is highly varied. He was, for instance, accused of careless treatment of language and subject matter by many followers of the neoromantic movement, among them Einar Benediktsson and Sigurður Sigurðsson of Arnarholt (1879–1939), who advocated new aesthetic tastes that emphasized the treatment of subject matter and "art for art's sake." Jón Trausti died of Spanish influenza in 1918.

In accordance with Brandes's ideas, Icelandic realist authors clearly did not shun the demand to debate society's problems. Gestur Pálsson and Einar Kvaran criticized the oppression of the workers, outcasts, and children. Þorgils gjallandi propounded an open debate on marriage and love between the sexes as well as trying to improve the lot of animals with his stories, as did Þorsteinn Erlingsson and Guðmundur Friðjónsson. Despite this the subject matter of Icelandic prose during the period 1880–1918 was rather monotonous and at times formulaic. Gestur Pálsson's criticism of religion and especially of the Icelandic clergy, repeated in one story after another, became bland as time passed. In his earlier-mentioned review of Kvaran's novel *Ofurefli*, Friðrik J. Bergmann complained about the lack of ideas among Icelandic authors. Matthías Viðar Sæmundsson, who has written in detail on the inception and origin of the Icelandic novel, addresses this main problem in early Icelandic prose writing: "Many [of these works] were tales rather than fiction and don't hold together well in the way that is necessary for a text to become a work of art. Artistic consciousness and realism are also seriously wanting, as the main aim is to entertain, . . . but the act of *writing* itself gives them a place of honor in Icelandic literary and cultural history. The works of those authors [i.e., the first Icelandic novelists] are also important sources on the formation of a literary genre" (*Ást og útlegð*, 9).

Alongside the development of realism a new literary movement appeared during the last decade of the nineteenth century, one known as neoromanticism. This new movement was shaped by an increased optimism in Icelandic politics and romantic ideas of progress. The new century was a symbol of new times. The belief in man's powers grew, as did the belief that by will alone people could rid themselves of the torpor of the past. The spirit of progress appears to have been widespread as the poet Sigurjón Friðjónsson (1867–1950), Guðmundur Friðjónsson's brother, pointed out in an article in *Norðri* in 1906 on the new generation of writers. He claims no single author as the leader of the new movement: "Rather, one could say that the national spirit and especially the sense of a national spring is unconsciously forging itself a path in two directions at once. . . . It is possible that this points to the fact that we Icelanders have now reached the same stage in our national development as the main educated nations of the continent reached during the first part of the last century, when 'romanticism' began to flourish there" (Friðjónsson, "Hið nýja skáldakyn," 33). Icelandic neoromanticism grew from the same roots as European romanticism had and involves a natural convergence of literature and progress as well as innovation in technology and industry. The only difference is that, in Iceland, all this happened a century later.

SYMBOLISM AND NEOROMANTICISM

In the above-mentioned *Norðri* article, "Hið nýja skáldakyn" (The new poets), Sigurjón Friðjónsson stressed the great shift that had occurred in

Icelandic poetry, brought about mainly by two forces: an increased emphasis on artistic form and a changed aesthetic perspective. According to Friðjónsson, the new poets are refined in their poetic taste, while their subject matter is seldom grand in scope, and there is little indication that they dive deep into life's waves.

While Friðjónsson's view is, in many ways, perceptive, it shows a certain misunderstanding on his part. The neoromantic poets in Iceland are a very diverse group, but most of them look inward; their interests lie in the soul's hidden depths. They emphasize insight and poetic sensitivity, rather than attempting to solve man's social or ethical problems, with Einar Benediktsson as the only exception. The new poets' disregard for contemporary problems is different from the progressive poetry of the previous decades. In addition, under the influence of symbolism, their poems become more concentrated, and direct descriptions are replaced by indirect ones. According to the French poet Stéphane Mallarmé (1842–98), one of the main characteristics of the symbolist movement was the art of evoking an object little by little so as to reveal a mood. Along the same lines the neoromantic poets believed that inner life could not be expressed directly, that only images or symbolic anecdotes would evoke in the reader a sense of what lay behind things. This was not always sufficient, however; at times one would have to symbolize inner reality primarily with sound or the rhythm of the meter. The formal revolution introduced by the neoromantic poets can, thus, be directly attributed to the symbolist movement.

Vilhjálmur Jónsson wrote an article in *Eimreiðin* in 1895 on the "youngest Danish poets," who had taken up a new direction in poetry. These poets were

influenced by French poets and have begun a new trend that they call *symbolisme*, a trend characterized by all the elusive *symbols that the eye, ear, or mind grasp at the moment of seeing, hearing, or thinking*; the poet tells us only what flashes before his eyes, ears, or soul — the rest one has to tell oneself, or, in other words, one must understand a half-told story; the reader must create or solve the mysterious language. These poets are medieval in their attitude, and the writing of many of them is tinged with a certain mystical or ghostlike hue. They often become as dreamlike and ambiguous as Heine; their language is often biblical; it is arch and full of similes and adjectives, original in the context in which they are used, for instance, in the descriptions of colors or color nuances. . . . They care less for rhyme than subject matter and often work in prose. (Jónsson, "Yngstu skáld Dana," 140)

Among the neoromantic poets in Iceland, not only was the move from realism apparent in a fresh view of life, but it also permeated poetic form as the poets attempted to create a structure for their poems as far removed from prosaic reality as possible. In his well-known introduction to the works of four neoromantic poets, the modernist poet Hannes Pétursson (1931–) strongly emphasized these aspects of neoromantic poetry: "The vision of neoromantic poets confirms a deep chasm between art and life; art is a world unto its own, with its own laws; the poet exists in this world of art and, therefore, stands outside the world of the masses. Just as poets are not ordinary citizens, their art is not the expression of the masses but an interpretation of the personal perception of unique individuals" (Introduction, ix).

Neoromanticism therefore brings about both ideological and formal changes. The emphasis is placed on creating poetry in a form that is most likely to evoke the nuances of a dreamlike reality. Poets focus on writing in a simple and direct language and try to avoid artificial words and phrases, and the demand for a formal aesthetic becomes more pressing. Jónas Hallgrímsson's battle against poetic licence is taken up again (see also p. 286) and, with it, the strict demand that form should be perfect. This caused a decisive change in the handling of poetic language (Pétursson, xiv) and had a positive influence on poetic form in Iceland, where poetry was still very much dominated by exceedingly strict formal rules and archaic diction.

Icelandic poets now increasingly looked to folk verse for models, with regard to both form and subject matter. One of the many models adopted was the Heine form that Jónas Hallgrímsson had introduced into the Icelandic lyric tradition with "Annes og eyjar" (see pp. 272–73). Most of the neoromantic poets wrote something in this particular form; best known among these works are probably Jóhann Sigurjónsson's poems "Heimþrá" (Homesickness) and "Ódysseifur hinn nýi" (The new Odysseus), first published in the journal *Skírnir* in 1910 (see also below). Women poets made their mark with *þulur* (sg. *þula*, a kind of nursery rhyme in traditional folk meter) adapted to contemporary taste. Hulda (Unnur Benediktsdóttir Bjarklind [1881–1946]) published her first *þulur* in 1905, reissued in her collection *Kvæði* (1909; Poems). Theodora Thoroddsen (1863–1954) also deserves mention in this connection; her *þulur* were first published in the journal *Skírnir* in 1914 and were reissued in her collection *Þulur* (1916). Prose poetry, too, made its appearance, most significantly *Hel* (1919; Hell [in Norse mythology also the goddess of death]) by Sigurður Nordal (1886–1974) and *Myndir* (1924; Vignettes) by Hulda. Finally, there is Jóhann Sigurjónsson's poem "Sorg" (Sorrow), first published in the journal *Vaka* in 1927, eight years after his death. It is now generally agreed that it was written in 1908–9, and it is considered by most to be the first modern poem in Icelandic literature. The poem gets its imagery from the Book of Revelation and begins:

Woe, woe, unto the fallen city!
Where are thy streets,
Thy towers,
And thy sea of lights, the joy of night?
Like a coral in the bosom of the ocean
Thou dwelt beneath the blue sky.
Like a brooch of purest silver
Thou rested on the breasts of earth.
Woe, woe!
Down in dark wells poisonous snakes are crawling,
But the night takes pity on thy ruins.
(trans. Magnús Á. Árnason in *Icelandic Lyrics*, ed. Beck, 191–93)

It is clear that form became freer in neoromantic poetry. More was written in unrhymed meters, and more influence from Icelandic folk verse was evident. Folk meters were traditionally simpler and freer in rhyme and alliteration. With their potential for unusually clear and direct poetic expression, they quickly won the hearts of the young poets.

ICELANDIC NEOROMANTICISM AND THE SUPERMAN

As was mentioned earlier, Georg Brandes was one of the main contributors to the neoromantic movement in Scandinavia in that, after having gradually turned his back on his earlier ideas, he became in 1887 the first in Scandinavia to draw attention to the German philosopher Friedrich Nietzsche. In the concluding part of his article on Nietzsche, "Aristokratisk Radikalisme" (1889; On aristocratic radicalism), Brandes bemoaned the status of Scandinavian literature. He had come to believe that the ideas that he had earlier introduced on the importance of the author's attempts to transform society through art were, in fact, redundant. He defended his new opinions as follows:

People are still busy with the same doctrines, certain theories of heredity, a little Darwinism, a little emancipation of woman, a little morality of happiness, a little free-thought, a little worship of democracy, etc. . . . Soon, I believe, we shall once more receive a lively impression that art cannot rest content with ideas and ideals for the average mediocrity. . . . Great art demands intellects that stand on a level with the most individual personalities of contemporary thought, in exceptionality, in independence, in defiance, and in aristocratic self-supremacy. (Brandes, *Essay on Aristocratic Radicalism*, 55–56)

Icelanders were, of course, familiar with Danish symbolist poetry and its most important forum, the journal *Taarnet*; Viggo Stuckenberg's poetry, for instance, was translated into Icelandic by the poets Sigurður Sigurðsson of Arnarholt and Jónas Guðlaugsson (see below). It was primarily Nietzsche's ideas on the superman, however, that turned out to be seminal for Scandinavian neoromanticism, and, once they had been introduced in Iceland, those ideas found fertile ground, even though each generation interpreted them in its own way. Most of the poets focused on invoking the heroic in man, the importance of triumphing over mediocrity and being bound by no authority. The older poets' love of the past, criticized by the realists, now returned, but with the main emphasis on the strong Nordic spirit and a certain distortion of Darwin's ideas on natural selection and the "survival of the fittest." The poets thought that they could detect an evolutionary purpose in the creation of Nietzsche's superman. The main focus is now the solitary male, shaped by his own will and the hardship of Nordic nature. The type of Darwinism that Hannes Hafstein had previously envisioned in his poem "Stormur" (The Storm) became much more common during these years, although the emphasis is now placed on the strengthening effects of the Icelandic winter.

Winter was always a particularly difficult time in Iceland, draining the nation of all energy. It should, thus, come as no surprise that Icelanders were not in the habit of glorifying this terrible foe, which tended to bring poverty and famine. It simply hit too close to home. Bjarni Thorarensen's (1786–1841) poems "Veturinn" (Winter) and especially "Ísland" (Iceland; see also pp. 262–63) were rare exceptions in Icelandic poetry until neoromanticism took up the theme and made it its own. Many neoromantic poets linked the cold to strength and asked themselves the question that Nietzsche put forward in *The Gay Science*: "Whether a tree that is supposed to grow to a proud height can dispense with bad weather and storms; whether misfortune and external resistance, some kinds of hatred, jealousy, stubbornness, mistrust, hardness, avarice, and violence do not belong among the *favorable* conditions without which any great growth, even of virtue, is scarcely possible" (91–92). Winter now became the touchstone of masculinity, a cleansing power that destroys all that is sick and weak so that only what is strong and healthy survives. This is also apparent in the worship of the "healthy Icelandic race," as, for instance, in Einar Benediktsson's poem "Hafís" (Ocean ice):

But ice in our world has gifts to bestow,
There's light on the hardened brow of our foe.
For ills of the flesh and the earth that are grim
The cold is our northern leech supernal.
It streams to our strands with a rush infernal,
And strengthens each force to the utmost rim, —
And everything lacking in vigor and vim
It freezes to death and sends to sleep eternal.

Thus strong our northern character grows,
Toughness the neighbor of death possesses.
In frost's hard school our nakedness dresses.
Thick is the armor necessity knows.
(Benediktsson, *Harp of the North*, ed. and trans. Wood, 55)

In Nietzsche's view, the strong must suffer adversity in order to attain their full potential. These ideas appear in many of Benediktsson's works, for example, "Stökur" (Stanzas; from his first collection, *Kvæði* [1897; Poems]): "Hate aims upward." The article "Kyngæði og kynspilling" (Racial values and racial corruption), published in the journal *Eimreiðin* in 1925, gives us a good idea of a similar attitude. The author praises the Nordic stock of the settlers of Iceland who for centuries suffered harsh Norwegian winters. He believes it to be the Icelanders' good luck to be descended from such a strong race as the settlers' strength is an integral part of them and makes them almost immortal (see Lárusson, 17). Such questions concerning racial purity are, of course, disturbing from a postwar perspective, but it is important to remember that the so-called science of eugenics had a worldwide appeal during the first part of the twentieth century, when no one could have foreseen the devastating turn that these ideas would take in Nazi Germany during the 1930s and 1940s.

Montesquieu's (1689–1755) climate theory (set out in *De l'esprit des lois* [1748]), which had earlier inspired romantic poets like Bjarni Thorarensen, now appeared in a slightly changed guise. The influence of these ideas quickly subsided, however, and did not extend beyond the first generation of neoromantic poets, where they occur, for instance, in Einar Benediktsson's poems "Egill Skallagrímsson" and "Ólafs ríma Grænlendings" (The ballad of Olaf the Greenlander), Jónas Guðlaugsson's (1887–1916) poem "Andri," and Jón Trausti's poems "Vetur" (Winter), "Veturinn kemur" (Winter is coming), and "Norðri" (The north). Other forms of the superman theory — not least comparisons with the bird of prey and the figure of the viking — became, however, deeply rooted in the lyric language and imagery of the time.

It should come as no surprise that the viking became a popular topic among the neoromantic poets. The heroes of the Sagas of Icelanders had, of course, occupied an important place in romantic poetry, but there was now something of a change of emphasis. Not only was the love of the past meant to wake the nation from its sleep; it also glorified the poet. Hannes Pétursson maintains: "The solitary male is the main character for the neoromantic poets, the outlaw in the figurative sense of the word. In his adoration the poet swings between cold hero worship and softhearted sentimentalism. He is himself an outlaw because his ideas are full of dreams and images unknown to the masses" (Introduction, xx). The neoromantic viking may have appeared in different guises, but he unites all the main characteristics of the superman. He is a Nordic hero, the image of masculinity as raw and untamed power. He has the freedom to enjoy without pressure; he is his own master, a traveler who settles new countries and satisfies his need for freedom (see also below). In his poem "Víkingar" (Vikings) Jóhann Sigurjónsson praises the Dionysian powers of the vikings along with their *Herrenmoral* (ethics of the master race). Sigurjónsson says in the third stanza:

They did not love many, but prized them a lot,
For the common man's life they cared not a jot,
For crying with slaves was then not the mode.
And if the gods deigned not to come to their aid,
Unlike Christian suitors they were not afraid,
But toppled them from their abode.
(*Ritsafn*, 3:87 [trans. Guðni Elísson])

From the neoromantic point of view, the vikings rejected Christian ideas of humility, and their gods served them, rather than vice versa. This contrast between Christianity and paganism appears in many places, for instance, in Einar Benediktsson's poem "Haugaeldur" (Grave mound fire), where it says of the religiosity of the vikings: "They respected their gods, / But loved them not" (*Ljóðmæli*, 2:36 [trans. Guðni Elísson]).

Guðmundur Finnbogason's (1873–1944) 1905 article on the viking and poet Egill Skallagrímsson was instrumental in introducing some of the more important ideas on which many poets relied when they wrote on the Varangians of old, warriors who left their homes in the North in the hope of finding adventure, conquest, and great riches. The Viking Age was referred to as the "age of cosmic power, free and searching for a subject," the "age of the unfettered law of the strongest." Finnbogason sees the life of the vikings as a fight, where the whole of existence is the battlefield and each man has to "fight without mercy for victory and power." In other words, power constitutes the highest and only authority in all matters. The viking is, in Finnbogason's view, a "hammer with life and soul who despises the anvil. He is self-defense in flesh and blood." But the viking temperament has a deeper significance for Finnbogason. Certainly, the vikings burned and killed, with sharp and bloody weapons, but their spirit conquered countries, and it is primarily the viking's cultural world that is in the foreground. He was "influenced by the world, he had the power of youth, which could dress opinions and experience in words that remain undiminished in their power across the centuries. They were *poets*" (Finnbogason, "Egill Skallagrímsson," 9, 11). This was the monument that Einar Benediktsson built for the Icelandic viking with his poem "Egill Skallagrímsson," where the emphasis is placed on the love of freedom, the superman, and the poet:

> He honored and loved the rule of dower,
> As strength of his arms, as his sword's sharp power,
> As goal of his life that beckoned ahead
> And joined all things both living and dead.
> His mind so clear saw in radiance shining:
> The magnate's [*sic*] created by men liberated,
> And thousands the wealth of one have fed,
> As jewels need years for refining.
> (Benediktsson, *Harp of the North*, ed. and trans. Wood, 51)

Power, wanderlust, master-race ethics, and poetic imagination all merged into one in the figure of the viking. The idea of the nature of the viking was integral to the ideas of the time and was one of the main characteristics of the superman theory in Iceland.[3]

To the neoromantic poets, the bird of prey represented the attitude of the superman. The bird of prey was a force of nature, and, like the wind, it could be destructive, but never immoral. In the eyes of the neoromantic poets it symbolized the freedom of the loner, the awoken life-bringing power. Its predatory nature made it the "viking of the air," as Þorsteinn Gíslason (1867–1938) put it in his poem "Örninn" (1920; The eagle). The best-known neoromantic poem of this nature is "Haukaberg" (1912; Hawks' cliff) by Sigurður Sigurðsson of Arnarholt, dedicated to the memory of Friedrich Nietzsche. For this reason Sigurðsson is the only Icelander whom Harald Beyer mentions in his large compendium *Nietzsche og Norden* (1962; Nietzsche and the North). This is the first stanza of the poem:

> In rugged height,
> In rugged height,

A hawk is perched, he does not shelter seek,
Nor grows he giddy on the craggy peak.
  Knows no fright,
  Knows no fright!
His is the nature of the solitaire —
Free, cold, and soaring, on the world to stare.
(*Ljóðasafn*, 35 [trans. Guðni Elísson])

As Hannes Pétursson has pointed out, one can clearly see here the neo-romantic poet's admiration for "individuals who pave their own way": "Brave, free, and independent of the masses, they find nothing more pathetic than the masses, and this antipathy is often close to contempt for humanity. The superman is far above the crowds and is supposed to be a symbol for them; he lays down his own laws" (Introduction, xix). The neoromantic poets had a strong tendency to compare their place in society to the place of the bird of prey in the animal kingdom. He flies higher than all birds, is literally above them.[4] Consequently, Jónas Guðlaugsson was admonished for his arrogance as expressed in *Dagsbrún* (1909; Dawn). One of its reviewers said of the poet: "He flies like the eagle, alone and proud, high above the crowds, and would so much like to pull the whole nation up with him, up to where the air is clear" (M.J., review of *Dagsbrún*).

The Nietzschean theory of will was surprisingly common and unusually varied in Icelandic poetry. In Sigurjón Friðjónsson's review of Einar Benediktsson's collection *Hafblik* (1906; Ocean view), a solid understanding of this aspect of Icelandic poetry is voiced: "In Einar Benediktsson's work this idea takes on a new meaning, very much related to the German philosopher Fr. Nietzsche. Benediktsson raises the question whether the spirit's 'power,' that is, the powers that have tamed nature to the will of man, can replace Christian humility and self-sacrifice in relation to God. Einar Benediktsson's temperament is here very apparent: the intellect and the will demand the throne on which the Christian author places feeling, sympathy, or love" (Friðjónsson, review of *Hafblik*). The Icelandic poets saw in Nietzsche the bearer of new ideas and ideals that made it possible for them to look to the future. In his book *Nítjánda öldin* (1906; The nineteenth century), the philosopher Ágúst H. Bjarnason pondered the character of Nietzsche's superman, what its nature and aims would be. His discussion and conclusion reflect the ideas of a whole generation: "We hardly yet know what he will become. One thing is certain, however: he will be much more and far nobler than the man now living. He is the dawn of the great day when humanity begins to near its perfection" (*Nítjánda öldin*, 378).

There are no clear lines of distinction between the nationalist poetry of the realists and that of the generation of neoromantics that followed; the pioneers of neoromanticism preached the gospel of progress and sacrifice just as the realists had done in the previous decade. Their dreams of large-scale industrialization appeared early on in the words of Hannes Hafstein: "Our time is the time of industrial progress, steam and electricity, the proud time of research" ("Hnignun íslensks skáldskapar"). And those dreams became the driving force in the life and works of Einar Benediktsson. Benediktsson is the main poet of neoromantic nationalism, and his poetry describes dreams of grand projects, national wealth obtained from the bottomless natural resources of country and ocean. Thus, he fought, for instance, for the establishment of a telegram station, even though it lasted only a short while until the telegraph took over. He supported the founding of a bank to allow foreign investment into the country. He also set up limited companies with the help of foreign investment in order to establish hydroelectric plants and factories because he envisaged large-scale industry for Iceland, based on the hydroelectric power from the country's waterfalls, that could compete with those of nations rich in coal. In his poem "Dettifoss" (Dettifoss is Iceland's largest waterfall), first published in *Hafblik*, these ideas are much in evidence:

> Our land and folk in wealth could surely grow
> By setting shafts of strength upon thy bow,
> And at the summit all thy power treating,
> So that increased would be thy waters' flow,
> And air creative drawn to flower and tree,
> Yes, garments of the glaciers used for heating.
> Here life enclosed in death might be set free
> And light within thy darkness kindled be,
> Where in magnetic nerves thy heart is beating.
> (Benediktsson, *Harp of the North*, ed. and trans. Wood, 15)

That same year Þorsteinn Erlingsson published his poem "Við fossinn" (By the waterfall) as a protest against Benediktsson's ideas. Erlingsson emphasizes instead the beauty that a hydroelectric plant would spoil and the danger that heavy industry can pose. He claims that Benediktsson's only motivation is greed (Þorsteinsson, "Æviágrip Einars Benediktssonar," 640–47). Stephan G. Stephansson, too, became involved in the debate with his poem "Fossa-föll" (1910; Waterfalls), in which he tried to mediate and bring together the opposing points of view.

Benediktsson's life was always shrouded in the mystique of the cosmopolitan who had experienced everything and seen it all. This is very apparent in reviews by his contemporaries. Guðmundur Finnbogason says in a review of the collection *Hrannir* (1913; Billows): "Einar Benediktsson is a Varangian among Icelandic poets. He has traveled further, seen and heard more than any of our poets, and he has on his travels made inroads into foreign subjects" (*Skírnir* 87 [1913]: 372). Einar Benediktsson lived abroad for many years, in Edinburgh, Oslo, Copenhagen, and London, where he attempted to realize his dreams of the industrialization of Iceland. He founded many companies, not only to establish hydroelectric plants, but also to build harbors and piers in the western part of the capital and to introduce gold mining in Mosfellssveit, north of Reykjavík. He was also the first and last Icelandic imperialist: Greenland, he felt, ought to be an Icelandic colony. Sigurður Nordal, poet and scholar, says of Benediktsson's idea: "Primarily, this was an extension of the Icelandic fight for independence, the rights of Icelanders to a lost colony" (*Einar Benediktsson*, 52). Benediktsson appealed to Western countries — Britain and the United States — to support this preposterous cause. Even though none of his ideas came to fruition, they very much describe the man and inform much of his poetry.

Despite Benediktsson's emphasis on the importance of foreign investment for industrial development, he was also a fervent nationalist who praised "ancient national values, the worth of Icelandic culture, the nobility of the Icelandic language, and the role of the Icelandic race" (Þorsteinsson, "Æviágrip Einars Benediktssonar," 597). His poetry shows plainly that the work of the individual should benefit Icelandic society. If people traveled abroad, they should broaden their horizons and deepen their spirit — and be of use to their country on its way to progress. Their one duty was to let the nation reap the rewards of their work. Benediktsson says in his poem "Væringjar" (1921; Varangians):

Though the isle may give birth to the wing that flies,
It needs must return to that land;
For no one can sever the ancient ties
Of the child to its dear mother's hand.
Though our countryman's dreams take him far, far away,
To the land of the cradle his dues he must pay,
And there must his monument stand.
(trans. Rory McTurk)

Benediktsson's patriotism is spurred by the will to progress because only in this way is it possible to export Icelandic culture to foreign countries. Benediktsson's dreams of progress are, therefore, based on his sincere but unfounded belief in the spiritual leadership role of Icelanders in matters concerning the entire world.

A significant number of fin de siècle poems were written in the spirit of the Nietzschean belief in the will to power explained earlier, and this was obviously beneficial when the faith of Icelanders in themselves and in their country needed strengthening. Much of the poetry celebrating progress during this time is, therefore, greatly preoccupied with the will and strength of the individual since all that was needed was to go decisively to work. The vision of progress, however, often turns into a message of sacrifice and at times resembles the sacrificial ideas that were later to be found widely in national socialist literature: people should not run away from the difficulties facing them but instead be determined to overcome them and achieve their original aim, which is above all to serve the motherland. One of the best examples from contemporary Nordic literature is undoubtedly Isac the farmer in Knut Hamsun's (1859–1952) *Markens Grøde* (1917). Isac works the soil without the help of others and turns a deserted heath into fertile soil; he is the independent man of neoromantic nationalism that Halldór Laxness later attacked so vehemently in his novel *Sjálfstætt fólk* (1934–35; English trans.: *Independent People* [1945/46]; see also chapter 5).

Einar Benediktsson voices this sacrificial ideal in his poem "Á Njálsbúð" (At Njal's stead), from *Hafblik*, in which he says that Icelanders need to practice self-sacrifice if the nation is to survive. He elevates patriotism above individualism and adds that a nation that forgets its patriotic duties is doomed. People like Benediktsson found it a matter of great concern if the individual placed himself above his duties. These ideas are very apparent in the opposition of many Icelanders to the move from the country to towns and villages during this time, a trend that had been growing steadily more marked from the first decades of the century; this development, like the migration of Icelanders to America, was considered dangerous to Icelandic rural culture. Jón Trausti's poem "Bendingar í hendingum" (1900; Counsels in stanzas) consists, as the title suggests, of pieces of advice to emigrants and those planning to move to America. Trausti claims it to be the duty of all Icelanders to improve their country, and improvement in the name of patriotism has its own rewards. Those who leave their country are, on the other hand, traitors. The emigrants are making a mistake; they do not understand that cultivating the land costs blood, sweat, and tears. Iceland has a future, but only if its children are loyal to it and work for it. Of course, those who were vikings in spirit were encouraged by the period's poets to go abroad and gain knowledge of the ways of the world and to perform great and good deeds. But they always had to serve the interests of the mother country. Or, as Benediktsson put it in the conclusion to "Væring-jar": "And there must his monument stand."

Shortly after the turn of the century a new generation of neoromantic poets appeared on the scene, and with it came a change of emphasis. The same worship of power is present, but power was no longer to be used for the benefit of society; rather, poets should make use of it themselves, for their own benefit. Hannes Pétursson (Introduction, vii) emphasizes this when he points out that these poets withdrew from daily worries, for the most part did not take part in politics, and had a great antipathy toward all social problems. As there was no urban culture in Iceland, many of the main poets at this time traveled abroad and started writing in foreign languages. The poet no longer served his country, which did not live up to his expectations. The glorification of poets, on the other hand, blossomed, and the poet is more often than not seen as an irresponsible bohemian. Poetry of pleasure quickly gained ground, as the poet now had duties only to himself, and a rebellion against existing values commenced. Árni Pálsson (*Á víð og dreif*, 48) describes the poet Jóhann Sigurjónsson, for instance, thus: "He was not secretive and never hid his plans, and they were neither few nor small. . . . First and foremost he was going to be a poet, *a great poet!* . . . The man was filled with battle spirit and determined to let the world know of his existence and preferably bring it all within his power, if there was any chance. This he told anyone who would listen, and he was probably much more serious in this than most suspected at first." Most neoromantic poets were convinced of their talents, as Stefán frá Hvítadal himself admitted when he said in retrospect: "One could not think of anything less than world fame in those days" (Orgland, 218; see also chapter 5).

This period in Icelandic literature has been described in different ways at different times, and the most varied pictures have been drawn of its poets. Usually, the basic tenet is the same, however: the image of the young poet-genius who is above all that smacks of the mediocre, who is imbued with boundless life and with excited emotions, and who is intelligent but lacks good fortune. In his book *Íslenskur aðall* (1938; Icelandic aristocracy), which tackles this generation in its own ironic way, the writer Þórbergur Þórðarson (1889–1974) put it thus: "This was the genius. Its nobility had been formed in young men's consciousness during the first two decades of the century as follows: he is highly intelligent, different from all others, perfectly poor, torn by the pessimism of a luckless life" (10; see also p. 390).

This was consistent with the spirit of romanticism as it appeared, for instance, in English literature. The poets were at once geniuses like Lord Byron and as luckless as Thomas Chatterton and John Keats. Such an attitude also looked back to Icelandic romanticism, where Jónas Hallgrímsson often became the main model, and ideas that originally appeared, for example, in the poetry of Kristján Jónsson Fjallaskáld were taken up again. The solitary hero was resurrected once more. The main poets of this generation are without a doubt Jóhann Sigurjónsson, Sigurður Sigurðsson of Arnarholt, Jóhann Gunnar Sigurðsson (1882–1906), and Jónas Guðlaugsson.

Also of note here are certain other aspects that contributed significantly to the formation of the temperament of the neoromantic poet. Nietzsche wanted man to set free the wild, uninhibited forces within him so that he could live and experience pleasure unbound by bourgeois morality. The writer Gunnar Gunnarsson (1889–1974) emphasizes primarily these elements in the temperament of the artist in his discussion of his friend and colleague Jóhann Sigurjónsson. In Gunnarsson's descriptions the poet has distanced himself from the message of sacrifice in which he should serve the common good and be the pillar of society. The new image of the poet involves a rebellion against the moral and economic demands of contemporary society; genius is dependent only on its own will, which can often be quite startling. Gunnarsson explains:

> When Jóhann [Sigurjónsson] was growing up, bohemian tastes and bohemian demands ruled supreme. Especially as an artist, one had no status without being full of contradictions and clashes in temperament and lifestyle; the more obvious the contradictions, the better the artist. Artists who did not drink or turn night into day were bourgeois, and a bourgeois could never become an artist. . . . What was most important were the contradictions: depressed on the one hand, joyful on the other; gentle today, cruel tomorrow; chaste in desire, lustful in reality; humility and pride; humanism and thirst for power; heroic one day, humble the next. ("Einn sit ég yfir drykkju," xiv–xv)

Árni Pálsson and Sigurður Nordal agree with Gunnarsson's portrayal of Sigurjónsson: they all describe the poet as a man imbued with wild forces and willpower, a man who seems to have been a living legend because of his excitable temperament and immense intellect. In his world of ideas, originally at least, there are only exaggerated contradictions to be found. He can choose between becoming a superman or becoming a worm; his will controls which path he chooses. To wait is the solution of mediocrity; in his eyes the superman is a bright flame, burning quickly through his short life. Even though this image appears in fragmented form in Sigurjónsson's youthful poetry, one can, nevertheless, detect the whole picture. Patience is not a virtue; Sigurjónsson does everything with the fervor of mad ambition, as reflected in many of his poems written around the turn of the century, including "Allt sem þú gjörir það gjör þú skjótt" (Everything you do you should do quickly) and "Strax eða aldrei" (Now or never), in which he says:

> Like a falcon I want to fly through the air,
> For the worm in the dust I do not care,
> My fulfillment never came from the soil.
> (*Ritsafn*, 3:88 [trans. Guðni Elísson])

But Sigurjónsson did not enjoy the youthful dream of the superman for long. His doubts about power grew, his depression increased, and he steadily became more bitter in his writing. In a letter he wrote to his wife, Ib, dated 4 August 1911, he says: "Not much should be expected of me, a weak man with insufficient talents" (*Ritsafn*, 3:217). This thought is far away from "the might of the creative will" that he wrote about in the poem "Strax eða aldrei." This change in attitude toward life was to mark the latter half of Sigurjónsson's writing career, and one can even say that it constituted a reappraisal of the neoromantic period as a whole (Sæmundsson, "Jóhann Sigurjónsson og módernisminn," 324). From these later years date some of his best-known poems, such as "Bikarinn" (1910; The cup) and "Heimþrá." Sæmundsson believes these poems to be characterized by modernist nihilism, where all that is left "is only a certainty of the lack of meaning and purpose of it all" ("Jóhann Sigurjónsson og módernisminn," 337).

Sigurjónsson's poem "Ódysseifur hinn nýi" (1910; The new Odysseus) shows this development clearly, as Sigurjónsson finds new forms for old motifs. The traveler, the new Odysseus, who can be seen as a Greek viking, was fooled by his youthful dreams and now circles the oceans forever without a destination.[5] He searched for a dream that never existed and in his search became alienated from his origins and the attributes of youthful vigor. The final stanza of the poem establishes a clear opposition with the homecoming in Homer's *Odyssey*, where eventually the battle ends and reconciliation is achieved:

> The palace is now in ruins,
> The throne is covered in sand. —
> No one knew the bones that were
> Washed by the wave on land.
> (*Ritsafn*, 3:96 [trans. Guðni Elísson])

Sæmundsson ("Jóhann Sigurjónsson og módernisminn," 325) rightly emphasizes the need of neoromantic poets to overcome their limitations and how such an effort is bound to be doomed sooner or later. When this occurs, the works of Sigurjónsson "revolve around man's powerlessness in life and the sense of meaninglessness that follows from the consciousness of death." In a letter that Sigurjónsson wrote to his brother during the initial phase of his career, this danger is already very apparent: "I am so strange at times, this uncontrollable desire to do something great, something big, seldom leaves me alone. Imagine standing on a loose bridge of ice and having to jump across a deep, wide chasm or otherwise be carried with the quick flowing water over the blue cold rocks and then disappear like a weak-winged duckling into the whirlpool of emptiness, having to jump while doubting one's strength" (12 June 1900, qtd. in Sigurjónsson, *Ritsafn*, 3:188).

Even though traces of nihilism occur in the writing of Sigurjónsson's contemporaries as well, it is of a different nature and usually not as profound. In the spirit of the contradictions mentioned by Gunnar Gunnarsson, Sigurður Sigurðsson of Arnarholt emphasizes the uncertainty of existence but remains within the limits of romantic hero worship. In the poem "Í dag" (1912; Today) the hero sits alone and abandoned, shorn of power and the will to live, but has nevertheless had a full life. Similar ideas are also very apparent in the final stanza of Sigurðsson's "Haukaberg."

In the work of Jóhann Gunnar Sigurðsson, who died of consumption at only twenty-four years of age, hopelessness cuts deeper for obvious reasons: he wrote most of his poems, including "Í val" (1909; Among the fallen) and "Ég elskaði" (1909; I loved), in the shadow of death. Even his hedonistic poetry is marked by the knowledge of death and is, therefore, often more restrained than the works of his contemporaries. This is clear in the poem "Fossinn heima" (1909; The waterfall at home) where he says:

If you dream of foreign sights,
Some distant shore that's bathed in light,
You should not dare to hope for the best.
(*Kvæði og sögur*, 78 [trans. Guðni Elísson])

When Sigurðsson desires dreamlands, it is because of the sadness of his condition, not because all reality is in itself unpleasant (Pétursson, xxxvii). In its most critical form the desire for other worlds (imaginary or real) appears in descriptions of a narrow Icelandic reality where the countryside becomes the symbol of imprisonment and the deep valleys are represented as forces of spiritual repression where ignorance reigns. Such ideas are also apparent in the works of many other neoromantic poets, for instance, in Sigurðsson's poems "Ævisaga" (1909; Life story), "Svanasöngvar" (1909; Swan songs), "Samtal" (1909; Conversation), and "Stef" (1909; Refrain), but nowhere are they as clearly expressed as in the poetry of Jónas Guðlaugsson, where they become a central theme.

Among the neoromantic poets Guðlaugsson was the foremost opponent of apathy, and few poets were as preoccupied with their role, status, and future aims. Even at the early age of seventeen or eighteen Guðlaugsson was already filled with despair over the indifference with which his countrymen responded to his poetic gift, and his suffering finds expression in his first book, *Vorblóm* (Spring flowers), published in 1905. In the poem "Snjótittlingur" (Snow bunting) he complains angrily about his lot and threatens to commit suicide as his work is no use to "a stupid crowd." A year later he published the collection *Tvístirnið* (Twin stars) in cooperation with Sigurður Sigurðsson of Arnarholt. His last book in Icelandic, *Dagsbrún*, was published in 1909. In these books he continues to scold his compatriots harshly. In the poems "Dalbúar" (Dwellers in the valleys) and "Þjóðskáldið" (The poet laureate) he turns on his countrymen's bad taste in poetry, and in the poems "Þið spyrjið" (You ask) and "Til kunningjanna" (To my friends) he considers the masses who in their despicable mediocrity want to drag him down to their level. Finally of note is his poem "Hos Jónas Hallgrímsson" (With Jónas Hallgrímsson) published in Danish in his book *Viddernes Poesi* (1912; Wilderness poetry). There, he clearly identifies with the national poet and describes how Icelanders are always worst to their best sons.

Many were offended by Guðlaugsson's conceited attitude toward his countrymen and thought him full of poetic arrogance. In a contemporary review of *Dagsbrún* that appeared in the paper *Ingólfur*, Guðlaugsson is reproached in the following manner:

> The author complains constantly over disappointment and a harsh life. He flies like the eagle, lonely and proud, high above the public. . . . But the nation is stubborn like sheep and stupid like a bull and makes fun of all his noble efforts. . . . In a young man this whinging is only laughable. He sees himself as a Byron or a Heine or an Ibsen, hounded and ignored by his compatriots, standing alone, shouting over the crowds. (M.J., review of *Dagsbrún*)

This generation's poetry was colored by the idea of the genius who is above the masses, and many tried to imitate this image of the poet-genius. And, as social circumstances in Iceland at the beginning of the century were such that it was impossible to live by writing (grants for writers were scarce and the reading population small), poets had to go abroad in the hope of gaining the fame and reward they desired. The question was no longer what one could do for one's country but what one's country could do for one. In "Sönglok" (The end of the song), Jónas Guðlaugsson provides an answer:

In pain and pleasure, my deepest lay,
I to my country gave,
O, land that does the poet pay,
With flowers for his grave!
(*Dagsbrún*, 104 [trans. Guðni Elísson])

Guðlaugsson was only twenty-two years old when his last book in Icelandic was published. It contains one of his best-known poems, "Mig langar" (I want), which well reflects the neoromantic movement in Iceland in general. The poem describes "an aching desire for attractive beauty far removed from reality, a thirst for powerful changes in temperament and rebellion against one's surroundings. The poet wants to attack and 'sever the hereditary links'; existence should be renewed; emotions should be free and strong" (Pétursson, xliv). This last sentiment stands in noteworthy contrast to Benediktsson's lines from "Væringjar," quoted earlier, that "there must his monument stand," that is, in the land of the cradle, and reflects the gap between these two generations of poets. As Pétursson has pointed out, probably "no other poet in the country—who touches literary history in any significant way—disappeared so young from the field of Icelandic poetry" (xliv). Like so many of his contemporaries, Guðlaugsson thought his future lay abroad.

Before moving on to the poets who left Iceland and wrote in languages other than Icelandic, it is only right to look at the one woman who made her mark in the large group of turn-of-the-century poets: Hulda. Hulda's poems were to a large extent inspired by contemporary issues and are at the same time among the best examples we have from this time of the influence of a female consciousness on literary creation (see also chapter 8). Her first book, *Kvæði*, was published in 1909, and Jónas Guðlaugsson wrote a review of it in the paper *Lögrétta*, in which he says: "Emotions and dreams are the main issues of the poetess; weak, ever-moving female desires and dreams that will, for the most part, not be fully understood by men" (review of *Kvæði*, 194). Considering that Guðlaugsson was himself a poet of the generation that most emphasized "emotions and dreams," this seems a peculiar assessment. Hulda's sorrow was linked to wanderlust, as was the case for most male poets, yet one can definitely detect a difference between her writing and that of her male contemporaries, a difference that can be attributed to a different self-consciousness that is in many ways a response to the male tradition. Accordingly, in reviews of her poetry Hulda is constantly likened to nature or feminine virtues. Einar Benediktsson wrote a famous eulogy to her, "Til Huldu" (1913; To Hulda), containing the following lines: "You rejoice in accordance with your heart / And you sing with a nature-child's voice" (*Ljóðmæli*, 2:237).

The male tradition reminds Hulda of her social duties and prevents her from stepping out of her role as a wife, mother, and housewife, and it requires that she accept her lot. This is echoed in the works of the poet Ólöf Sigurðardóttir of Hlaðir (1857–1933), who concludes one of her poems, "Jeg uni mér ekki" (1913; I am not appeased), with the words: "I must not complain" (*Nokkur smákvæði*, 68; see also pp. 521–23). In Hulda's poem "Sumarnótt við hafið" (Summer night by the sea), from her first book of poetry, the neoromantic dreams of freedom and the virtues of hard work and wage earning battle it out. At the beginning of the poem the narrator says: "I want to fight for victory / In the turmoil of life" (*Kvæði*, 78 [trans. Guðni Elísson]). The poem then follows the inner struggle of the narrator, who does her best to ignore her dreams and accept life in the narrow valley instead of traveling in the wide world. Even though the desire for travel is stronger than all other desires, she decides to smother it and thinks that this is most easily done close to home. In the concluding lines of the poem she says of her home district:

> The waterfall sings, the mountains summon,
> The leveled fields stretch out their arms.
> There we shall heal all winter harms,
> In the headlands work the common!
> (*Kvæði*, 78 [trans. Guðni Elísson])

This reflects the ideas of the older neoromantic poets, but one could also read this conclusion in feminist terms. Hulda's solution is to work her garden because "work is life's shelter," as she says at the end of her writing career (*Kvæði*, 78 [trans. Guðni Elísson]). Ragnhildur Richter ("'Ljóðafugl lítinn ég geymi,'" 330–33) has rightly pointed out that in the last book Hulda completed, *Söngur starfsins* (1946; The song of work), the message appears that women should be content with their lot, as virtue, duty, and isolation alone are worth striving for.

Hulda differs also from her male colleagues in that her self-consciousness keeps her from taking up contemporary motifs and themes linked to the worship of the superman. In the poem "Haukurinn" (1909; The hawk) she glorifies the power of the bird of prey and envies it its freedom. But in the last two stanzas she breaks with convention by identifying with the small bird, in direct opposition to what the male poets did:

I keep a small songbird —
It wants to fly
Far into light and day
And sing of the joy of life.
(*Kvæði*, 51 [trans. Guðni Elísson])

The poem concludes that, if her bird is not allowed to follow the hawk, it will soon die. As Ellen Moers, who has discussed gendered metaphors in romantic poetry, explains: "The eagle and the dove are the most familiar pair of bird contrasts . . . the contrast . . . between ailing, feminine, mystical saintliness and aggressive, domineering, organizational accomplishment" (246). Hulda's poetic birds are, therefore, always small.

Hulda also runs into difficulties when confronted with the viking motif, which causes obvious problems as she clearly cannot identify with a viking of ancient times. She can at most search for a model among the formidable women characters in the Sagas of Icelanders, a kind of neoromantic Bergþóra who follows her man even unto death (see p. 135). This thought is clearly voiced in the poem "Ef að þú víkingur væri" (If you were a viking) published in *Kvæði* (1909), but even this idea critics viewed askance, as is clear from the following review by Karl Finnbogason:

But why does she say *if* and not *though*? Did she want her lover to be a viking? . . . No, a viking does not suit Hulda or her like. Battle dress would ill suit her. Her breasts could not take the armor. They are too sensitive and motherly for that. . . . Other things suit her: to recite verses at the cradle of good and clever children — young and old, as this she does better than any man or woman who yet has recited *þulur* [folk verses]. ("Bækur," 162)

As mentioned earlier, Hulda introduced many formal innovations into Icelandic poetry. She has, for instance, the honor of reinventing the *þula*, an old folk-verse meter that had survived in oral tradition. Hulda's first *þulur*, published in 1905, were not written in the old meter, however, but were adjusted to contemporary tastes. As Guðrún Bjartmarsdóttir and Ragnhildur Richter have pointed out, Hulda has an obvious tendency to free herself from the strictures of rhyme in her first three books: a little under "half of the poems in *Kvæði* and *Segðu mér að sunnan* [1920] are either written in unrhymed meter, Nordic or classical, or traditional rhyme is abandoned in one way or another" (40). This formal development, which is quite a revolutionary one when one keeps in mind the long Icelandic poetic tradition dominated by strict meter and rhyme, is most apparent in *Myndir*, which is characterized by lyric descriptions resembling those found in prose poetry.

Hulda also published many short stories and fairy tales. *Æskuástir* (1914; First loves) and *Æskuástir II* (1919) are romantic stories that describe everything good that Icelandic rural culture has to offer. The same goes for the novel *Dalafólk* (People of the valley), published in two parts in 1936 and 1939 (see also pp. 338, 525). *Dalafólk* was in many ways planned as a challenge to Halldór Laxness's *Sjálfstætt fólk*, published earlier in the decade, as his descriptions were thought to be both untrue and denigrating. Bjartmarsdóttir and Richter call *Dalafólk* an interesting "attempt at creating a female character who has many characteristics of the neoromantic artist and describing her development and painful assimilation to the demands of society and tradition" (83). As a description of society the novel has, however, little to say to modern readers; the national romanticism is idealized, as is the old Icelandic aristocracy. Bjartmarsdóttir and Richter claim: "[*Dalafólk*] describes great social changes, the battle of old and new culture, the foundation of workers' unions and the blurring of rural class distinctions where a type of educated demagoguery had reigned" (89).

In her works Hulda often describes the responsibility and duties with which women are burdened, but in few places is there a clearer image of the sacrificial role of women than in her poem "Bera drottning" (Queen Bera), published in the collection *Myndir*: "Not a single moment in life may die barren, vanish for no reason. Women must be thousandfold and still more solid than the roots of the rocks of the earth, all-capable, all-loving. Suns bringing spring and summer to all worlds, so that while in one there is warmth and daylight, others dream by starlight. Ceaseless springs water other people's lands — all lands — forgetting where they came from and where they are going — for else all will die of drought" (*Myndir*, 152–53).

VARANGIANS

Many reasons lay behind the emigration of poets at the start of the twentieth century. First of all, there was the emphasis that neoromanticism placed on the viking temperament, which they regarded as the assimilation of power, master-race ethics, and poetic imagination. Not only did they desire to gain recognition abroad; it also tempted them to gather "hold of the distant," as the poet Jakob Jóhannesson Smári put it. In his article

"Norræn sál" (Nordic soul), he discusses the nature of, and difference between, races and maintains: "The main characteristic of the Nordic soul is the desire to travel, . . . which is physically apparent in its great migrations (the Indo-Germanic migration, Germanic migration, Nordic Viking migration, emigration to America) while modes of transport were very poor and travel, therefore, difficult. . . . The celebration of the characteristic Nordic desire for struggle does not involve an achieved victory but lies in the striving for victory while it is still within reach" (328–30).[6] This ideology had become fundamental in the minds of a whole generation of poets. They had learned to identify with the poetic image of the viking and were not prepared to limit this ideology to poetic creations alone.

But there were certainly other reasons for the emigration of Icelandic poets as well. Helga Kress emphasizes the social background: "The nation was poor and few in number, and it lacked both the social and the cultural basis to provide its poets, who wanted to dedicate themselves to writing, with the necessary support, understanding, and maturity. . . . It was well nigh impossible to get Icelandic works translated into any world language, and for the ambitious poet this particular route was, thus, unavailable. Hard-up poets fought hard for their livelihood and wrote only in their spare time" (*Guðmundur Kamban*, 9–10). One by one the poets left — first Jóhann Sigurjónsson (in 1899), then Gunnar Gunnarsson (in 1907), and, finally, Jónas Guðlaugsson and Guðmundur Kamban (in 1910). They were followed by Kristmann Guðmundsson (1901–89) and Jón Björnsson (1907–94), who moved away in the 1910s and 1920s. Even the poet Snorri Hjartarson (1906–86) wrote his first book in Norwegian, the novel *Høit flyver ravnen* (1934; The raven flies high). These emigré poets left for Denmark or Norway and wrote both in Danish or Norwegian and in Icelandic. Guðmundur Kamban even planned to become a writer in the English language.

A man as ambitious as Jóhann Sigurjónsson realized early on how difficult it would be to realize any of his dreams at home in Iceland, where his genius would be "dependent on the results of harsh living conditions," as Halldór Laxness put it many years later when discussing the poet Stefán frá Hvítadal (52). This is very apparent in a letter Sigurjónsson wrote to his brother from Copenhagen (14 January 1902), where he says about his possible future in Iceland: "I believe that for a man with needs and will it must be like Napoléon's stay on Saint Helena, yet one still cares for the old reef" (Sigurjónsson, *Ritsafn*, 3:196).

And Sigurjónsson's success was quick to materialize. In 1905 his play *Dr Rung* was published at the urging of the Norwegian writer Björnstjerne

Björnsson (1832–1910). It was, however, not until 1912 that Sigurjónsson attracted considerable attention in Denmark. That year his play *Fjalla-Eyvindur* premiered in Copenhagen, a work based on an Icelandic folktale (see also pp. 557–58). It was performed all over Scandinavia, in Germany, and in London, where William Butler Yeats watched it, awestruck (Toldberg, 11). *Fjalla-Eyvindur* was also the first Icelandic work to be filmed, by the Swedish director Victor Sjöstrom in 1917. The plays that followed — *Bóndinn á Hrauni* (1908; English trans.: *The Hraun Farm* [1916]; performed in Reykjavík 1908–9), *Galdra-Loftur* (1915; in Danish *Ønsket* [The wish]), based on an Icelandic folktale, and *Mörður Valgarðsson* (1917; in Danish *Løgneren* [The liar]), based on material from *Njáls saga* — did not live up to the expectations set by *Fjalla-Eyvindur*, and during the First World War Sigurjónsson's career drew to a halt.

Much has been written on Sigurjónsson's plays. Many have pointed out the strong influences of Nietzsche, as in *Dr Rung* and in *Galdra-Loftur*, and critics have often seen Loftur as a mixture of Goethe's Faust and Nietzsche's superman. It is now more commonly believed that both works are tragedies about failed attempts at turning the superman into a reality; seen from that angle Loftur's fate is the author's confrontation with the superman ideal, that is, his rejection of it. With his plays Sigurjónsson turned his back on the ideology of his early poetry. In a letter, probably written in the autumn of 1908, he says: "Nietzsche writes beautiful German and is a great poet, but the main thought in all his works on the superman and the unlimited rights of the individual is and will be wrong" (*Ritsafn* 3:212). Dagný Kristjánsdóttir ("Loftur á 'hinu leiksviðinu'") has developed Helge Toldberg's idea (133–34) that Dostoyevsky's murderous student Raskolnikov is to be preferred as a parallel to Loftur; indeed, Sigurjónsson wrote the name in the pages of his first draft of the play.

In 1912, the same year that *Fjalla-Eyvindur* was performed in Copenhagen, Gunnar Gunnarsson became well-known in Scandinavia for his novel *Ormarr Örlygsson*, the first part of *Saga Borgarættarinnar* (1912–14; English trans.: *Guest the One-Eyed* [1920]; see also p. 359). This Icelandic rural story was fused with a strong belief in life and purpose, hope and balance, but this belief was short-lived as the war in Europe destroyed Gunnarsson's romantic outlook. In the books that followed — *Ströndin* (1915; The coast of life), *Vargur í véum* (1917; Wolf in the temple), and *Sælir eru einfaldir* (1920; English trans.: *Seven Days' Darkness* [1930]) — a modernist outlook had taken its place. Matthías Viðar Sæmundsson, who has closely examined this period in Gunnarsson's works, argues that Gunnarsson's characters are products of modernity: "Their Achilles' heel is that they are conscious of fatality and terminality. The growth of this painful consciousness causes a rift within them and contradicts their emotional needs. They are destroyed because their manic search for roots and truth involves a merciless exposure of the values that could possibly have reconciled them to life" (*Mynd nútímamannsins*, 21).

After Jónas Guðlaugsson left for Norway in 1910, he published his first collection of poetry in a foreign language, *Sange fra Nordhavet* (1911; Songs from a northern sea). It is in the main a translation of poems that had appeared in the Icelandic collection *Dagsbrún*. From Norway Guðlaugsson went to Denmark, where he published the collections *Viddernes Poesi* (1912) and *Sange fra de blaa bjerge* (1914; Songs from the blue mountains), in many ways reminiscent of his earlier work. He also wrote some prose in his later years. In 1913 the novel *Solrún og hendes bejlere* (Solrún and her suitors) was published, one year later *Monika*, and, finally, the short story collection *Bredefjordsfolk* (1915; People of Breiðafjörður). Guðlaugsson's poems were quite well received in Denmark, but he did not live long enough to follow up on his success as he died in April 1916 at only twenty-eight years of age. *Solrún* and *Bredefjordsfolk* were published in Icelandic translations by the writer Guðmundur G. Hagalín (1898–1985) shortly after Guðlaugsson's death.

Guðmundur Jónsson Kamban followed up Jóhann Sigurjónsson's success in the theater with *Hadda Padda* (English trans.: *Hadda Padda* [1917]), a play in neoromantic style that is set among the Icelandic bourgeoisie. The play was performed in the Danish Royal Theatre in Copenhagen in 1914, a year after Georg Brandes had brought it to people's attention. It was performed for four months to good audiences and was considered a great success for the author. The play was published in English translation in 1917 with a foreword by Brandes. In the summer of 1923 Kamban directed a film based on the play.

In 1915 Kamban moved to the United States, where he apparently planned to become a writer in English. His stay in America was shorter than expected as he had problems adjusting to life there. He returned to Copenhagen after two years in New York. As Helga Kress points out, however, the "trip was not for nothing because one could maintain that it was only in the United States that Kamban matured as a writer" (*Guðmundur Kamban*, 55). Kamban's next four works are all set in New York and contain mostly social-realist criticism. Unlike his earlier works they are not limited to Icelandic society but directed at the inhumane penal laws in the United States. The play *Marmari* (1918; Marble) is strongly influenced by Oscar Wilde's *De profundis* (1905) and Ibsen's *En folkefiende* (1881; An enemy of the people). Here, Kamban introduces "the idealist who is up against an old and thoroughly corrupt society" (Einarsson, 15). In 1920 appeared Kamban's most accomplished work, *Vi mordere* (We murderers), a play about the couple Ernest and Norma McIntyre. Ernest believes his wife to be unfaithful and leaves her after having sold an invention for a large amount of money and giving her the proceeds. She looks for him and tries to get him back. She admits, after some denial, to infidelity but then withdraws the confession and claims that it was a test of his love. This infuriates Ernest, and he deals Norma a fatal blow to the head with a paperweight. In an epilogue that has never been performed four gamblers sit and discuss the crime and McIntyre's death sentence. Helga Kress has shown the links between Kamban's work and Tolstoy's *Kreutzer Sonata* (1889). The performance of the work was Kamban's greatest theatrical success, but the works that followed were not very well received, and he turned increasingly to writing novels.

Kamban's first novel, *Ragnar Finnsson* (1922), is, like the plays that came before it, a work on crime and punishment. A young Icelander sails to Copenhagen to pursue a degree course, drops out of college, and decides after a few years' stay to seek his fortune in the United States. He ends up stealing food, is arrested and tried, and receives a ten-year sentence. He comes out of prison a hardened criminal. He rapes and murders a young girl and dies trying to escape from the police. Kamban's next novel, which appeared first in Denmark as *Skaalholt* in 1930–32 and then in Icelandic as *Skálholt* in 1930–35 (English trans.: *The Virgin of Skalholt* [1936]), is also his best-known work. As was mentioned earlier, it deals with the life and fate of the seventeenth-century bishop's daughter Ragnheiður Brynjólfs-dóttur, which had long enjoyed popularity as a literary topic in Iceland. Kamban's description of Ragnheiður is considered a particularly great achievement (see also p. 376). Finally of note is the historical novel *Jeg ser et stort skønt land* (1936; English trans.: *I See a Wondrous Land* [1938]), about the discovery and settlement of Greenland and Vinland by Icelanders around the year 1000. It was published simultaneously in Germany and Denmark and was dedicated to the "Nordic spirit."

Kamban's connections in Germany after Hitler's rise to power and during the Second World War later made him unpopular in Denmark. In 1945 he was killed by Danish patriots who incorrectly believed him to be a Nazi sympathizer.

ICELANDIC DECADENCE

The main proponents of the movement that was named after the fin de siècle in Europe made themselves heard in Iceland in the 1910s. This is the final phase of Icelandic neoromanticism, and it completed the progression from the Apollonian theory of will, characteristic of the reformist poets, to the Dionysian pleasure theory. The poet heroes of the time found no higher purpose than pleasure in their lives, either in serving their country or in taking on the world. Unlike the bohemian poets, they had mostly lost the belief in power and strength. The decadent poet is more depressed than his predecessor, often full of melancholy and despair, a victim of his own desires, a self-elected wanderer abandoned by God and man. Perhaps one could consider him the exaggerated heir of the dreamer who was driven by wanderlust, although it is certainly doubtful whether this poetic hero is searching for anything in particular. His motto could be taken from Jónas Guðlaugsson's Danish poem "Den gamle historie" (1914; The old story): "I was born to find my peace / In being lost" (*Sange fra de blaa Bjærge*, 105). But Nietzsche also saw in the soul of the tragic poet the need to perfect oneself in an endless joy of becoming, a need that harbored the desire for destruction. This temperament, a self-consciousness that understands itself through destructive needs, becomes more important, and one could say that here, for the first time, after one hundred years of Icelandic romanticism, the Icelandic antihero emerges complete.

Even though Sigurður Nordal and Davíð Stefánsson did not publish their first books until 1919, mention of them in this chapter cannot be avoided as their writing careers are so closely linked to Icelandic neoromanticism. The third writer of this generation is Stefán frá Hvítadal, whose first book, *Söngvar förumannsins* (Songs of the vagabond), was published in 1918. Stefán frá Hvítadal's poems are, however, not quite in the same vein, although the figure of the traveler does appear there and the joy of the moment is praised. It is primarily Álfur of Vindhæli, the main character in Nordal's *Hel* who stands out as the best representative of the desire for destruction in late Icelandic neoromanticism. His behavior is entirely governed by Dionysian longings. Álfur is driven by his own nature and a profound nihilism, or, as he says himself: "The fall rests within you" (Nordal, "Hel," 121). Álfur's hedonism makes him terrifying. He drinks from the sickness of life and cares little for the scolding of those around him. His main goal in life is to subjugate everything to his will, yet there is no meaning to his actions. He says: "We shattered family ties and marriages and destroyed profound plans. And when we tired of spoiling and were sick of ourselves, we drank, not wine, but poison and potions" (139). Álfur's love is the alienated love of pain, inextricably linked to death. He associates with "fallen women," women who know how to love but carry death and destruction in their embrace, and he is sickened by them. Nevertheless, he is always bound to destroy innocence, to spoil its beauty and abuse the love of those who truly love him:

She was the soul of nature. Because of her the sky was bluer, the sea brighter and the rocks were like my brothers . . . why couldn't I . . . bow to her. . . . You will marry a man who has slept with prostitutes, violated all his emotions, and only loves you as a female animal. He will make you coarse and physical, kindle unimaginable lust in you, blow out the godly fire in your eyes and the brightness of your forehead. You will be convulsed with pain giving birth, your breasts will be sucked dry, you will gape over pots, fade, wilt, and shrivel. (116–17 [trans. Guðni Elísson])

Libertinism now becomes a significant force in Icelandic poetry. Stefán frá Hvítadal wrote about it in "Förumannsóður" (Vagabond song), as did Davíð Stefánsson, for instance, in the poems "Komdu—" (Come—), "Brúður söngvarans" (The singer's bride), and "Allar vildu meyjarnar—" (All did the maidens—), published in his first collection, *Svartar fjaðrir* (1919; Black feathers). Freedom in love plays a large role in Stefánsson's poetry, along with love and forgiveness. In the poem "Komdu—" he describes the desire of the ill-treated woman who is ready to sacrifice everything, give everything, if she only could reclaim her lover's love. The woman says:

I will live off the bones
That fall by your chair,
And your house I will sweep
With a lock from my hair.

The sound of my shoes,
Shall not bother you much;
The tiles of your house,
Barefoot I'll touch.
(*Að norðan*, 1:6–7 [trans. Guðni Elísson])

Sigurður Nordal once mentioned the great effect that the image in the first stanza quoted above had on him when he heard Stefánsson recite the poem in 1916, from which we may deduce that Nordal was in his writings fascinated by the figure of the cruel man who leaves such a deep mark on Stefánsson's poetry and whom he himself re-created in the character Álfur of Vindhæli. Álfur says when he parts with Dísa: "Let the women complain over broken promises and lost love. I complain over hopes that came true, loves that were given and kept too long" ("Hel," 110).

There is often little difference between love and dark hatred. A good example of the latter is the poem "Sagan af Tótu" (The story of Tóta) by Davíð Stefánsson, where the frivolous woman is murdered for her behavior, and "Hefnd vitfirringsins" (The revenge of the madman) from *Drottningin í Algeirsborg* (1917; The queen from Algiers) by Sigfús Blöndal (1874–1950), who is otherwise much better known for his Icelandic-Danish dictionary. In the latter poem the hero is a crazed madman who murders the one who betrayed him and her lover in a disgusting manner. But the decline of the superman ideology did not involve only the afore-mentioned aspects. Now, poetic heroes increasingly associate with spiritual beings, ghosts, and monsters.

Of course, much had been written on ghosts previously in neoromantic Icelandic literature, for instance, Einar Benediktsson's "Hvarf séra Odds frá Miklabæ" (1897; Reverend Oddur's disappearance from Miklibær) and "Martröð" (1921; Nightmare), Sigurður Sigurðsson of Arnarholt's "Nóttin langa" (1906; The long night), Jóhann Gunnar Sigurðsson's "Kveðið í gljúfr-um" (1904 1906; Canyon song), and Jónas Guðlaugsson's "Á draugsrifi" (1905; On ghost reef) and "Hrafninn" (1909; The raven). Ghost poems like these were now quite numerous, however, and horror-romanticism became a large part of Icelandic poetry, for instance, in the works of Davíð Stefáns-son. But the status of the narrator also changed. In the previous examples he had usually been an innocent bystander, but now he often became a partici-pant, for instance, in "Aðsóknir" (Hauntings), "Kuldahlátur" (Cold laugh-ter), and "Abba-labba-lá," all from Stefánsson's *Svartar fjaðrir*. And Stefáns-son seems to have identified with his dark poetic characters, at least in part. On the evening that he saw *Galdra-Loftur*, Jóhann Sigurjónsson's play, performed, he wrote: "I am excited. I am both sane and mad. I love no one — and am loveless. But he whom no one loves, he is a monster. Perhaps I have never loved any one" (qtd. in Nordal, "Litið í gömul bréf," 136).

Other poems in a similar vein are, for instance, "Seiðkonan" (The sor-ceress) and "Vofur" (Phantoms) from Sigfús Blöndal's book *Drottningin í Algeirsborg* and many poems by Sveinn Jónsson (1892–1942), such as "Draugagil" (Ravine of ghosts) and "Einn í myrkrinu" (Alone in the dark). Jónsson is not considered an important poet, any more than Blöndal, and is now chiefly known for his poem "Eitur" (Poison), where pleasure is linked to death through a mad, crazed dance. The refrain explains all:

Poison! More poison!
Warm will I dance and wanton.
Poison! Poison! Poison!
(*Sveinn Framtíðarskáld*, 96 [trans. Guðni Elísson])

Davíð Stefánsson also writes about the drinking of poison and wild danc-ing. Dance, here, becomes a symbolic phenomenon, as in Nietzsche's *Thus*

Spoke Zarathustra, where we read: "You Higher Men, the worst about you is: none of you has learned to dance as a man ought to dance — to dance beyond yourselves!" (306). In the poem "Kuldahlátur" demons dance a wild dance. In the poem "Sódóma" (Sodom) it is the wild and lustful dance of those who have no morals. In "Eldur í öskunni leynist" (Fire hides in the ashes) the narrator greets death by drinking poison in his depression.

There is no doubt that Davíð Stefánsson learned much from the Swedish poet Gustav Fröding (1860–1911); few poets were so clearly influenced by Nietzsche. In *Nietzsche og Norden* Harald Beyer discusses the role of the dance in Fröding's poems and its links to Nietzsche's ideas on the dancing god:

> In *Also spr. Z.* the dance not only symbolizes strength, flexibility, the erotic, the rhythm of life. It also belongs to the intellect of Higher Men. And here is also one aspect of religious ritual. Zarathustra calls himself "der Tänzer," "der Wahrsager," "der Wahrlacher," and he only wants to believe in a god who can dance. (188)

Stefánsson emphasizes most of these aspects in his poem "Óráð" (Delirium), in which we find the betrayal, the queen's violated body, the horror, and the mad drinking. The poem is blasphemous but derives much of its power from that. The narrator betrays the queen by giving her a "Judas kiss," in the "name of Jesus," and smears her breast with a sign of the cross made from his own blood. But the contradictions and lies manifested in this "marriage ritual" seem to have further meaning in the hellish world of the poem, for in the dance there is also strength, passion, and a search for life's purpose, a purpose in the madness of the moment. The poem concludes thus:

> Then we'll keep on dancing
> And drink poisonous wine.
> . . . I'll be the king of the devils,
> and the queen will be mine.
> (*Að norðan*, 1:34 [trans. Guðni Elísson])

The rejection of social values by bohemian poets had now become a mainstay. The antihero was symbolic of youth's rebellion, a rebellion that demanded utter freedom from the demands of duty and sacrifice in order to obey the call of the emotions. Álfur of Vindhæli puts it most succinctly when he criticizes Dísa: "Young girls your age rebel against relatives and rules and the whole world to follow the fire rod of their emotions, even though they know that it leads them off the gaping precipice" (Nordal, "Hel," 106).

Even though the poetry of Davíð Stefánsson and Stefán frá Hvítadal developed and saw certain changes, both wrote in the spirit of neoromanticism all their lives. In the year that *Svartar fjaðrir* came out Halldór Laxness published his first novel, *Barn náttúrunnar* (1919, The child of nature), which is also in the spirit of the neoromantic poetic imagination, but he left the movement as early as the second decade of the century. Dionysian hedonism and decadence were now slowly replaced with the social-realist fiction of Halldór Laxness, where the message of social responsibility was the guiding light.

Translated by Gunnþórunn Guðmundsdóttir

NOTES

1. See, e.g., Kristjánsson, "Lífsviðhorf," 17–18. Jochumsson got to know Brandes personally in 1885, and their friendship lasted from then on.

2. The most detailed discussions of Brandes's influence on Icelandic realist literature are to be found in Höskuldsson's *Gestur Pálsson* and Helgason's "Tímans heróp."

3. Other poems on the subject are Jónas Guðlaugsson's "Víkingarnir" (The vikings; *Dagsbrún* [1909]) and "Eric den røde" (Eric the Red; *Viddernes poesi* [Wilderness poetry] [1912]); Guðmundur Friðjónsson's "Eiríkur víðförli leitar Ódáinsakurs" (Eiríkur the Wide Traveler's search for the pastures of immortality) and "Leifur heppni" (Leif the Lucky; Sigurður Sigurðsson of Arnarholt wrote a poem with the same title); Jakob Jóhannesson Smári's "Norrænir víkingar" (Norse vikings; *Handan storms og strauma* [1936]); and many examples from Einar Benediktsson's writings, such as "Væringjar" (The Varangians), "Vínland," and "Arfi Þorvalds" (Thorvald's legacy).

4. Other poems on the bird of prey from this period are Jakob Thorarensen's (1886–1972) "Valurinn" (The falcon); Jónas Guðlaugsson's "Örninn" (1909; The eagle) and "Flyvende ørn" (1914; The flying eagle); Jóhann Sigurjónsson's "Örninn" and "Strax eða aldrei" (Now or never); Hulda's "Haukurinn" (The hawk; *Kvæði* [1909; Poems]); and Jakob Jóhannesson Smári's "Valur" (Falcon) and "Munur" (Desire; *Kaldavermsl* [1920; Warm spring]).

5. The same motif can be found in Jóhann Gunnar Sigurðsson's poem "Ókunna landið" (The unknown country) and Jónas Guðlaugsson's "Bak við hafið" (Beyond the ocean).

6. This article is Jóhannesson's interpretation of the book *Die nordische Seele: Artung, Prägung, Ausdruk* (1923), by L. F. Clausz.

Realism and Revolt: Between the World Wars

Jón Yngvi Jóhannsson

5

THE BIRTH OF A NATION — THE BEGINNING OF MODERNITY?

The year 1914 marks a decisive break in European history. The beginning of the First World War and the unknown horrors it brought on the Continent shattered the old social order and put a definite end to what Stefan Zweig in his memoirs later termed *the world of yesterday*: the European ideal of a civilized and refined culture to which the idea of a protracted and brutal war was unthinkable. The historian Eric Hobsbawm, in his three-volume history of modern times, puts the beginning of what he calls *the short twentieth century* down to this awakening of Europe to an "age of extremes."

On the western periphery of Europe, however, the beginning of this short twentieth century has traditionally been located at a different date. In most Icelandic accounts of literary history at least it makes its entrance at the end of the Great War, not at the beginning; to be more precise, on 1 December 1918, the day when Iceland became a sovereign state in personal union with the Danish king, according to the treaty signed a few months earlier. As a result, the beginning of the twentieth century in Iceland bears, not the character of Armageddon, as it does in Hobsbawm's and Zweig's accounts, but rather that of a fresh start. The birth of Iceland as an independent nation also marks a new beginning in its literature, a period viewed as the new golden age that the romantics had dreamed of. This view relies, of course, on a deeply felt nationalistic interpretation of Icelandic history that

The author wishes to thank Hagþenkir, the association of Icelandic nonfiction writers, for financial support in the writing of this chapter.

Unless a specific English-language source is given, all translations from the Icelandic are the author's.

can sometimes be difficult to substantiate with examples from literature itself. One of the pioneers of this periodization, Kristinn E. Andrésson, writes in his *Íslenskar nútímabókmenntir, 1918–48* (1949; Modern Icelandic literature, 1918–48):

> None of the literary currents that emerged and flourished in Europe during and after the war reached us at home. Surrealism, expressionism, *Neue Sachlichkeit*, etc. are known to us only from foreign literature. In Iceland we find no *postwar literature* worthy of the name.
>
> Nonetheless, a natural change of epochs takes place in Icelandic literature at the end of the First World War. In 1918 a certain phase in the evolution of Icelandic political history comes to an end. After a hundred years of uninterrupted struggle for independence, the nation at last had its sovereignty acknowledged. This struggle had given the nation as a whole a goal to strife for and had put its mark on all aspects of life. Now victory had been achieved, earlier even than the Icelanders had anticipated, and with less effort. The nation therefore directed its intellectual and material powers to new challenges at home, but it needed time to absorb what had happened and to gather strength for a new struggle. It is this turning point in national history that also brings on a new epoch in literature. (11)

If we are to accept this transference of political history into literary history, we must look past some of the most influential writers and poets of the first two decades of the twentieth century proper, both the more traditional and established novelists such as Einar H. Kvaran, who was active until the 1920s, and the major figures among the younger generation such as the novelist Gunnar Gunnarsson and the poet and playwright Jóhann Sigurjónsson, both of whom wrote their works primarily in Danish.

We might also note that the generation gap, which played an important part in the beginnings of a modern literature as Andrésson and others after him saw it, does not actually occur in prose writing until well into the 1920s, while in the realm of poetry one must go to at least the mid-1930s to find a radical break with the ruling tradition born out of nineteenth-century national romanticism.

GUNNAR GUNNARSSON AND THE COLLAPSE OF EUROPEAN CULTURE

Although Gunnar Gunnarsson (1889–1975) wrote the bulk of his oeuvre in Danish and lived in Denmark from 1907 to 1939, he should be considered part of Icelandic literary history as well as Danish. All his novels draw on Icelandic material, and their backdrop is Icelandic society, which is often the main topic as well. Until 1922 his works were published in Iceland almost simultaneously with their Danish editions. The first three novels were translated by Gunnarsson himself, but as he became increasingly successful abroad others took over the task of translating.

Gunnarsson made his breakthrough in 1912–14 with the four-volume *Af Borgslægtens Historie* (The history of the Borg family; English trans.: *Guest the One-Eyed* [1920]; see also p. 349). It is a very eventful, at times melodramatic novel, its themes and conflicts played out in a highly expressive and very serious mode. Its structure is often loose, and in later editions the last volume is left out as it takes place after all conflicts have been resolved.

The main character of the first volume is a young Icelander by the name of Ormarr Ørlygsson, the son of the wealthy farmer at Borg. Ormarr travels to Denmark driven by his passion for music, but neither that nor his success in business can satisfy his need for new conquests. He is also torn between his ambition in the outside world, on the one hand, and his duties to his father and his father's estate, on the other. It is only after his brother, Ketill, has betrayed the family and seduced a young protégée of their father's that Ormarr returns to Iceland. Then his combativeness and the love for his country can be combined in his mission to save the family's future. Ormarr marries the girl and supports his father in fighting off Ketill's slander. Ketill, on the other hand, tries to turn the neighbors against the Borg family, which results in a dramatic confrontation between father and son, after which Ketill wanders into the wilderness, to return in the third volume as a holy man, Guest the One-Eyed, to become reconciled with his family. *Af Borgslægtens Historie* thus plays out conflicts between the old and the new, loyalty to the father and the fatherland, on the one hand, and passion for art and the outside world, on the other.

One of the faults that contemporary critics found with *Af Borgslægtens Historie* was the author's lack of familiarity with the genre of the novel: Gunnarsson used dramatic events as the main and perhaps only driving force of his narrative. This criticism is not entirely groundless: the book does have many qualities that link it to the romance rather than the modern novel, such as the abundance of adventurous events and the simplified psychology of the characters. It is based, not on continuity or logical evolution, but rather on impulses and sudden dramatic leaps of character or motives. The events propelling the story forward are often completely unexpected and their descriptions brief. A large part of the text is instead made up of long meditations and reflections, either the narrator's or the characters'. In the first half of the novel these are mainly centered on art and the conflict that arises from Ormarr's experience of cultural borders, being an Icelander in Copenhagen as well as a farm boy in artistic and musical circles. His art and his family tradition seem irreconcilable, and his feelings toward his home are a mixture of love and hate. It is even implied that Ormarr's split nature and his ambitions are at the root of the family's tragedy. His father decides to have another son, contrary to the family doctor's advice, to secure himself an heir since Ormarr seems to be more interested in his music than in farming. This decision brings about the death of his wife as well as the birth of the evil brother, Ketill.

The conflicts are resolved on the surface as Ormarr manages to turn the continuity of the Borg family into his final struggle and eventually becomes reconciled with his brother. Nevertheless, he is still a split personality, and this manifests itself in his occasional musical outbursts. The split in his character and his desire to achieve a wholeness of self and identity were to return in Gunnarsson's more mature works.

Af Borgslægtens Historie — especially the third volume, *Gæst den enøjede* (Guest the one-Eyed), which bears a certain likeness to a saint's life — was exceptionally well received in Denmark by readers and critics alike. The last two volumes and the first edition of the complete work in 1915 sold tens of thousands of copies, and the novel was soon translated, in whole or in part, into Swedish (1915), Dutch (1915–19), and English (1920). Most critics agreed that the primary quality of Gunnarsson's work lay in his portrayal of Iceland as a unique, organic society where the connection between man, history, and nature had been preserved, undisturbed by modern civilization and its alienation. Gunnarsson was also linked to Iceland's literary heritage, and reading his work could, in some critics' opinion, become a way of connecting to a common Scandinavian heritage. Gunnarsson's image of Iceland thus became a refuge for the modern Danish city dweller, or, as one critic remarked about *Ormarr Ørlygsson* (the first volume): "This book should be read because in it one gets to know the nature and characteristics of the Icelandic people, and this is something we Danes need" (*Dansk Folketidende* 25 November 1912).

The reception of *Af Borgslægtens Historie* in many ways fashioned that of Gunnarsson's later works. No matter what their subject matter or attempt at artistic innovation, they could and would always be read as a representation of Iceland, or a certain version of Iceland, and the symbolic value that it had acquired in Danish literary circles. More than any other Icelandic works of fiction his next novels bear witness to the collapse of values and the devaluation of optimism that followed the First World War, yet they were persistently read as portraits of Icelandic character traits rather than as the existential realism that the author strove for and that mainly accounts for their importance in Icelandic literary history.

In an epilogue to the second Icelandic edition of *Livets Strand* (*Ströndin*, 1945; The coast of life), the first of these following novels, Gunnarsson described his reactions to the First World War: "I did not bleed on the outside; neither cuts nor bruises could be found on my body. . . . No, the insane frenzy of war inflicted wounds of another nature on me. My soul resembled burned soil, defiled with foul heaps of corpses; each emptied field reminded me of ground ploughed with gunfire, polluted by freshly mutilated human bodies. I bleed on the inside" ("Fyrsta glíma," 349–50). These so-called crisis novels are an attempt to come to terms with a world treated so foully and with a civilization that has turned on itself in this manner. Centered on religion, they all come to a rather pessimistic conclusion: God is dead, and what little hope there is left resides only in human compassion. Thus, the protagonists of *Livets Strand* (1915) and *Varg i Veum* (1917; Wolf in the temple) both perish in the end: the priest Sturla in *Livets Strand* becomes insane, while the young lawyer Úlfur Ljótsson in *Varg i Veum* drowns in his attempt to begin a new life as a sailor. Both are split or dispersed personalities, unable to attain wholeness in either faith or love.

The third novel, *Salige er de enfoldige* (1920; Blessed are the simple; English trans.: *Seven Days Darkness* [1930]) has enjoyed a longer life and more popularity than the other crisis novels and has been translated into ten languages. *Salige er de enfoldige* is a tightly structured narrative, told by a narrator who is a friend of the two protagonists and who witnesses the events set in Reykjavík. The setting is incredibly somber and dark. On the horizon a volcanic eruption sends a pillar of fire and ash into the air, and in the town itself a plague rages; large parts of the population are either dead or dying, while many are too sick to offer any help to those worse off than themselves. This would sound like an exaggerated expressionistic cityscape were it not for the fact that in the autumn of 1918 the Spanish influenza arrived in Reykjavík, only a week after an eruption had begun in Mount Katla that was well visible from the capital and sent up into the air large amounts of ash, which the wind carried over Reykjavík.

The story that unfolds in this setting is that of a genesis reversed, where the world of the eminent doctor Grímur Elliðagrímur collapses bit by bit in the course of seven days until he is left insane in a psychiatric ward. His fall is triggered by a battle of wits and beliefs with an old acquaintance, the nihilist philosopher Páll Einarsson. Páll has lost faith in good and evil and has substituted for these concepts those of the strong and the weak. The weak are those who have faith in something, be it God, morality, or simply the goodness of others. Their faith, according to Páll, makes them dependant on something other than themselves, and, when that is taken away from them, their weakness reveals itself, a philosophical stance quite obviously based on the contemporary reading of Nietzsche and his theories of the superman.

Grímur Elliðagrímur's faith, on the other hand, is anchored in his marriage and his absolute trust in his wife. When this trust is undermined by Páll at the same time as Grímur suffers from the stress of being one of only a handful of doctors fighting the plague, Grímur collapses and loses his mind. His good friend Jón Oddsson, the narrator, stands by, unable to help. His conclusion after witnessing the events is as simple as it is desperate: "Be kind to one another" (*Sælir eru einfaldir*, 258). *Salige er de enfoldige* thus confirms the collapse of moral as well as religious values but offers no solution and does not explore any of the consequences of this conclusion. The narrator's only answer is a humanitarianism based on the love of one individual for another, although he himself realizes exactly how fragile a fundament this is.

Salige er de enfoldige was to be the last of Gunnarsson's existential novels. The year 1918 saw the first of a series of historical novels that Gunnarsson continued in the 1930s, while he devoted the 1920s to writing his magnum opus, a semiautobiographical novel in five volumes describing the childhood and early adult life of his alter ego, Uggi Greipsson, in Iceland and Denmark. It is Gunnarsson's crisis novels, however, especially *Salige er de enfoldige*, that have been classified among the pioneering works of modernism in Icelandic literature, on the grounds that they introduce a new character type into Icelandic literature: the split and bewildered modern man (Sæmundsson, *Mynd nútímamannsins*). Their narrative form, however, is too anchored in traditional prose writing to justify such a claim. The existential crisis is never manifested in the form of Gunnarsson's novels or in their language. *Salige er de enfoldige* is, in fact, quite the opposite of a modernist novel, its form bordering on the schematic. One might even see Gunnarsson's use of form as a counterpart to his existential conclusion. Despite, or perhaps because of, the collapse of forms and values, the realistic narrative and traditional modes of communication are a fort worth defending.

THE LAST NOVELS OF EINAR H. KVARAN AND JÓN TRAUSTI

The two "grand old men" of Icelandic fiction, Jón Trausti (the pen name of Guðmundur Magnússon; 1873–1918) and Einar H. Kvaran (1859–1938), were still active in the years after 1914. However, their glory days were over, and their last works do not equal those written between 1906 and 1914. Jón Trausti wrote only one novel during this period, *Bessi gamli* (Old Bessi), which was published in 1918, the same year the author died from the Spanish influenza.

Bessi gamli is a polemical novel, written from a sternly reactionary point of view. It describes a young man, fresh out of school, who becomes the editor of the social democratic newspaper in Reykjavík but who, through his acquaintance with the scientist and businessman Bessi, changes his ways and takes up the older man's views, including a belief in an organic society without class conflict, a distrust of democracy, and a dislike of liberalism and women's rights. The story ends with old Bessi's funeral, where he is mourned by the entire town. The novel has been called Jón Trausti's literary will and testament. It manifests an almost fanatic conservatism without a trace of irony or ambivalence. Trausti's best works describe the old agricultural society in Iceland, its conflicts and hardship. Almost all his qualities as a writer are absent from this last novel, however, although it could be seen as ironic that some of old Bessi's views resurfaced during the 1920s and 1930s in the ideas of young intellectuals who relished the old society; some of them even took up Trausti's critique of democracy as the rule of the unenlightened masses.

Einar H. Kvaran wrote three novels in the years 1916–22, during which time he was the leading novelist in Icelandic literature written in Icelandic. His novels were initially well received and quite popular, but later they became an obvious target for a new generation of critics and writers who rebelled against Kvaran, both his aesthetics and his politics. *Sambýli* (1918; Neighbors) and *Sálin vaknar* (1916; The soul awakens) both show Kvaran's growing interest in spiritualism and in his own form of Christianity, one centered on forgiveness and mercy, but they are at the same time bourgeois and heavily influenced by a Protestant ethic. Kvaran's characters are richly rewarded for their piety with material wealth. They are guilty either of negligence or of outright crimes, but they are forgiven by their adversaries, leading eventually to a better life for both those who trespass and those who are trespassed against. Kvaran's characters thus possess a saint-like quality, which sets them apart. Their position in society is ambiguous, for, by obeying the laws of Christianity that society claims to follow, they pit themselves against that same society's norms. This, for example, is the lot of Eggert Sölvason, the main character of *Sálin vaknar*, who solves a crime mystery with the help of his clairvoyance and then chooses to go to jail for smuggling the murderer out of the country. By creating sympathy for the murderer's motives and his poor situation in life, Kvaran justifies Eggert's actions even though the law condemns them. There are, however, those who symphathize with Eggert, and toward the end of the novel his hopes of a good marriage and a career in politics seem bright. The nobility and piety of Kvaran's characters thus do not go unrewarded in this life; the rich and successful are always those who follow Christ's example of forgiveness and self sacrifice. It is tempting to read Kvaran's novels from this period as Protestant hagiography, where good deeds are the path, not only to salvation, but to riches as well.

Kvaran's *Sögur Rannveigar* (Rannveig's tales), published in two volumes in 1919–22, carries the same philosophy of forgiveness as *Sambýli* and *Sálin vaknar*. The novel is composed of six fragments from the life of Rannveig, who at the time when she narrates her story is the wife of a wealthy Icelandic businessman in Copenhagen. The first fragment introduces Rannveig, her father, and her future husband, who is the son of her father's greatest enemy. The story then unfolds through a series of events where Rannveig either settles old grievances and convinces the parties to forgive each other and obtain peace with God or is tested herself and forgives others who trespass against her. As in Kvaran's two previous novels the protagonist in this one, Rannveig, is very well off. Her father remarks early in the novel that his wealth is blessed and multiplied by God, and material wealth and money are among the novel's main preoccupations. Money is the measure of value and status as well as the reward for a good and God-fearing life.

Kvaran's last novels are the best and perhaps only examples of a purely bourgeois literature in Icelandic literary history. The synthesis of the material and the spiritual adds to their fantastic and unreal character and made them an obvious target for the iconoclasts of the 1920s.

THE 1920S: THE REVOLT OF THE YOUNG AND THE RESTLESS

Einar H. Kvaran was by far the most influential novelist in Iceland during the first two decades of the twentieth century, but during the 1920s a new generation of writers and intellectuals arrived on the small Icelandic literary scene and broke his hegemony, both by writing radical experimental prose and by directly attacking him as a representative of an older generation and its values.

The University of Iceland was established in 1911 and, along with other new cultural and academic institutions, made it possible for a growing number of intellectuals to pursue academic careers and devote themselves to research and cultural criticism and commentary. During the first three decades of the century a number of young Icelanders returned from the Continent with doctorates in literature, history, psychology, and philosophy. Many of them became prominent figures in the country's intellectual life. The most prominent figure on the literary scene was Sigurður Nordal (1886–1974), who became a professor of literature at the University of Iceland in 1918. Nordal and other intellectuals of his generation were visible in most spheres of Icelandic culture from 1920 on. Guðmundur Finnbogason (1873–1944) introduced new ideas in the areas of education and labor policies; Guðmundur Hannesson (1866–1946), a professor of medicine, wrote articles on housing and sanitation; Ágúst H. Bjarnason (1875–1952) paved the way for the teaching and study of philosophy; while the state architect Guðjón Samúelsson (1887–1950) was instrumental in shaping the new Reykjavík with his buildings. Although not sharing many of the views of these intellectuals, Björg Þorláksson (1874–1934) was the first Icelandic woman to receive a doctorate. She defended her thesis on neuropsychology at the Sorbonne in 1926 and published articles in Icelandic journals during the 1920s on, among other things, psychoanalysis.

The foreign influences that these young intellectuals brought with them were, of course, diverse, and not everything they had learned in Europe seemed fitting for their own country. They considered it necessary to fashion a new cultural politics. Most of them found a common denominator in a nationalism inspired by the idea of the golden age of Icelandic culture as manifested in the sagas as well as by neoromantic currents, mainly from Scandinavia.

This nationalism took many forms. The most paradoxical one is what might be labeled *ruralism* or *pastoralism*. Even though intellectuals such as Sigurður Nordal had themselves been educated in Europe and were quite familiar with the advances of European culture and societies, they did not think that the same evolution could take place in Iceland or, indeed, that it was desirable. Their goal was to moderate the effects of modernity on Icelandic society and to build a new modern Icelandic culture on the values and customs of the old agricultural society. In order to progress and at the same time retain the organic nature of Icelandic society, according to Nordal, a return to the past was necessary, one based on the culture of the traditional, rural Icelandic society, a culture that had not severed its ties with nature or with its cultural heritage. It was in particular the Norwegian novelist Knut Hamsun (1859–1952) who influenced Icelandic intellectual thinking on nation and country in this respect, to such a large degree, in fact, that scholars refer to this stance as *Hamsunism* (see Sigurjónsson, *Laxness og þjóðlífið*; and Guðmundsson, *"Loksins, loksins"*).

This pastoralism, with its opposition to modernity and urbanization, occasionally took forms that, in retrospect, seem absurd. Sigurður Nordal, for instance, opposed general schooling on the grounds that the home education traditionally provided in the countryside should be the model for Icelandic education. The nationalism among intellectuals also manifested itself in their interest in medieval Icelandic literature. As a professor of Icelandic literature at the University of Iceland Nordal himself was a prolific and original scholar. He was one of the pioneers of what has been termed the *Icelandic school* in saga studies, an approach that emphasizes the literary nature of the Icelandic sagas, considering them the work of true authors rather than of collectors or scribes who wrote down material already formed in an oral tradition. This school of thought had a decidedly nationalistic side to it, drawing attention away from the events related in the sagas and their historical value toward the achievements of the authors and the medieval Icelandic culture that molded them. Thus, the heroes of Nordal's cultural history are, not the vikings and fighters of the ninth and tenth centuries, but the learned people of the thirteenth and fourteenth centuries who wrote the sagas. This in turn transforms the golden age of Icelandic history from a barbaric but noble society of vikings into a society of learning and literary geniuses, more fitting as predecessors to a civilized and educated nation at the beginning of the twentieth century.

In one of Nordal's more famous polemics he turned against the novels of Einar H. Kvaran. In 1924 an interview with Nordal was published in a Swedish magazine where he comments on the rumors that Kvaran was among the candidates for the Nobel Prize in 1923. Nordal is quoted as saying the he found it unthinkable that such a prize should be awarded to an author who represented his country as badly as Kvaran did. Even though Nordal claimed to have been misquoted, he added that the interviewer's intuition obviously led her to attribute to him a viewpoint not too far removed from his own. He then published an article on Kvaran in the journal *Skírnir* (1925) where he criticizes both the artistic merits of Kvaran's later works and his philosophy. It was in particular Kvaran's exaggerated compassion and outdated humanitarianism that Nordal opposed. He reduces Kvaran's later works to one concept alone: "If one should describe the message of Einar H. Kvaran's later books in one word, that word would without a doubt be *forgiveness*" (*List og lífsskoðun*, 306).

This Christian dictum of forgiveness is, in Nordal's view, worthless as it has no limits and tolerates everything. As an alternative to Kvaran's piety Nordal refers to the Germanic tradition of blood feud, which in his opinion was a harsh philosophy, but also one that forced men to claim their right and fight for it. This combative spirit, to some extent inspired by the common understanding of Nietzsche at that time, Nordal saw as a way of fighting the sense of a split or dissolved identity and achieving wholeness again. His critique is, thus, directed, not only at Kvaran, but also at the era that molded him: "I said before that I disagreed with Einar H. Kvaran on matters that regarded most men. The truth is that ours is more a disagreement between two generations than between two men." Nordal's article provoked a response from Kvaran, and their dispute evolved into a literary debate that lasted for more than two years. As a consequence of the generational disagreement Nordal, in his final reply to Kvaran, calls for a new literature, a new romanticism that must oppose Kvaran's realism and the Christian morality that comes with it: "Einar H. Kvaran hates romanticism. And no wonder. A new romanticism will blow away his worldview. Thus it has always been. When literature has turned human psychology into a soulless flatland of bourgeois leisure, the abyss opens up, and the storms clear the mountaintops from fog" (*List og lífsskoðun*, 309).

The storms that Nordal predicted were already detectable in Icelandic prose fiction. But whether or not they can be labeled *romantic* is a totally different matter. Nordal's own writing undoubtedly bears the mark of a new romanticism, but others that were to attempt changes in Icelandic prose writing were more subversive and did not share his romantic view of the national or of the virtues of the old society as a source of redemption.

In Halldór Laxness (1902–98) and Þórbergur Þórðarson (1888–1974) we find the proponents of urbanization: their knowledge of European culture and civilization led them to a different conclusion than that of the nationalist intellectuals. In the 1920s both writers emerged as prophets of innovation—in cultural as well as material matters. They were also the authors of revolutionary works of prose writing, different from anything the Icelandic reading public had ever known.

But the first of the three prose works that challenged Kvaran and his traditional approach to novel writing and morality was Sigurður Nordal's own *Hel* (Hell [in Norse mythology also the goddess of death]), a poetic narrative or long prose poem published in 1919. The fragmented nature of the text is reflected in the protagonist's character and fate. Álfur of Vindhæli is a rootless man who travels the world in pursuit of short-term happiness, and his outlook on life resembles that of Ormarr Ørlygsson in Gunnar Gunnarsson's *Af Borgslægtens Historie*: the struggle for happiness is everything, its reward nothing. Thus, Álfur betrays the women he seduces to pursue new adventures. Toward the end of his travels, in a chapter entitled "The Day of Judgment," he meets two representatives of a different path in life: a scientist who has spent his whole life on one discovery and a man happily married to one of his old loves. The contrast between these two ways of living — the wanderings of the adventurer, on the one hand, and the purposeful but uneventful life of everyday people devoted to a single goal, on the other — is the main philosophical concern of *Hel*. Nordal himself addressed a similar problem in a series of philosophical lectures published in 1918–19 where he discusses the two ways of living as fundamental opposites.

Hel — with its sense of split self and uprootedness and its fragmented metaphoric language — is one of the first attempts to move toward modernism in Icelandic literature. Even though its mythological landscape has a rural, often desolate setting, one could easily link Álfur to Baudelaire's flaneur; his wanderings have no purpose other than what they are: wanderings and the search for adventure or challenge. As Nordal himself later stated, *Hel* was not the beginning of a literary career but a farewell to old sins. At the time of its publication he had already turned his attention to researching old Icelandic literature. He did not, however, disappear from the literary scene, remaining one of Iceland's most eminent critics and cultural commentators for decades to come.

A LETTER TO LAURA

Þórbergur Þórðarson is one of the main figures in twentieth-century Icelandic literary history, but unlike Halldór Laxness and Gunnar Gunnarsson, he never made a reputation beyond Iceland. Together with Halldór Laxness Þórðarson was the front man of the revolt against the bourgeois realism of Einar H. Kvaran and the romanticism of younger poets as well as against the nationalism and pastoralism that saw the past as a path to a new society. His own evolution in this direction remains a bit of a mystery. He did not leave Iceland until after the publication of his first major work in 1924, and his education is no match for Laxness's autodidactic cosmopolitanism.

Þórðarson's first publications were two slim collections of poetry: *Hálfir skósólar* (1914; Half soles of shoes) and *Spaks manns spjarir* (1915; Wise man's clothing). The 1922 *Hvítir hrafnar* (White ravens) collected the poems published in the two earlier volumes. Its title is a parody of Davíð Stefánsson's 1919 *Svartar fjaðrir* (Black feathers) (see below). According to Þórðarson, he published these collections himself and sold them on the street in order to raise the money to buy decent clothes for Christmas. The poems contained in them were satirical, many of them parodies based on contemporary neoromantic poetry, which Þórðarson found sentimental and hollow. Among the poems are some that he called *futuristic*, although it is not likely that he had any knowledge of either the Russian or the Italian futurists. These literary pranks proved to be the beginning of a long and prosperous literary career. Þórðarson did, however, always maintain a certain distance from the traditional genres of poetry and novel writing, finding himself more at home among the more peripheral genres or, indeed, outside them in his own hybrid inventions.

His first major work is an example of his originality. In 1924 Þórðarson published a book under the title *Bréf til Láru* (A letter to Laura). It begins with an address to the author's esteemed lady friend Laura. Personal letters were one of his favorite genres. They were often written for a wider public than the recipient alone: Þórðarson was well aware that his letters were read aloud at homes and parties. But the letter to Laura soon grew beyond the framework of an ordinary letter into a unique writing project. In its published form it contains political satire and polemic as well as critical essays on Christianity, especially Catholicism, which Þórðarson had taken a serious disliking to. It also includes descriptions of the author's travels around Iceland and his fantastic childhood memories, travesties of Icelandic nature and culture, dream descriptions, and a few gothic short stories somewhat in the style of Edgar Allan Poe, Þórðarson having translated a few of his stories into Icelandic.

The book created a scandal, provoking responses from clergymen and intellectuals alike, and causing Þórðarson to be dismissed from his teaching jobs at two of Reykjavík's secondary schools. The outrage that followed *Bréf til Láru* was not due to the author's political beliefs or his attacks on Christianity alone. One of the aspects of the text that stirred up the Icelandic literary world was his candidness when it came to bodily functions and sexuality. The text has been called *carnivalesque* in its use of the body in a subversive manner, the most infamous clause being the following, where he turns an idyllic scene in Icelandic nature into a profane attack on the traditional peasant culture of Iceland:

The world is wonderful. This mellow tranquillity that reigns over land and sea, the smell of green grass and leaves. Where am I? Have I come to Italy? Is this the sky-blue Mediterranean about which Davíð Stefánsson composed a meager poem? Or is this the summerland where Raymond drank heavenly wines and smoked the cigars of sanctified tobacco merchants? I sat down in a bush and shat. When sitting down in this way one enters a spiritual harmony with nature. — What the devil! Behind me a raven with its belly full crows about handicrafts and death from starvation. "Icelandic peasant culture," I mumbled and pulled up my pants in anger. (*Bréf til Láru*, 23).

The grotesque imagery of *Bréf til Láru* can be divided into at least three kinds. First, the carnivalesque, where the material shape of the body and its ruptured form, for example, in defecation, is used to mock or ridicule traditional values or hierarchical structures. In Þórðarson's text, however, it is not always the joyous deconstructive laughter that results from this blend of the high and the low, or, as in the case of his shitting in the bush, of the spiritual and the material, but a more direct political attack, as the authorial voice of the text is a dedicated socialist and, indeed, a preacher of a certain subversive kind.

Another form of the grotesque manifests itself in the gothic parts of the letter. This is a more negative experience of the body, a penetrating body angst where sexuality is a prominent feature. One of the narrator's many phobias is his fear of eels. One of his horror dreams plays out this phobia:

> It was four years ago. I dreamed I was walking south along the eastern bank of the Reykjavík pond. It was a beautiful night in spring, clear skies, the sun setting in the west. . . . Then, before I know it, an electric eel jumps from the pond, bites my member, and hangs on to it. I shall not attempt to describe the terror that possessed every nerve in my body. I stood as if frozen on the bank of the pond, like a fossil from the Ice Age, and watched the blasted beast do its tricks. After what seemed an eternity I finally managed to shake the enemy off me. I ran in a frenzy up to Laufásvegur. By no means would I let the bastard get to me again. In that moment I woke up and praised God for my salvation. From that day I have felt no desire toward women. Nobody but me could have dreamed such a dream since the days of Edgar Allan Poe. (*Bréf til Láru*, 71)

In the gothic sections of *Bréf til Láru*, all borders between life and death, the body and the world surrounding it, are transgressed. The narrator is murdered and tries desperately to reenter his body, or he becomes pregnant at a young age. Thus, the traditional roles of the sexes are put into play, as are the borders separating life and death. On the one hand, the narrator is a firm believer in strict "external forms that transform people" (34), but, on the other hand, he has extreme difficulties conforming to the forms and structures that constitute reality and deconstructs them one after the other. Although the text is narrated in one very characteristic, personal voice, the narrator's self becomes a channel for a multitude of discourses, voices, and tales as well as political and religious propaganda. *Bréf til Láru* is a work that is open at both ends and resists all categorization, to the extent that it eludes characterization as even the open and hybrid modern novel.

Þórðarson was always reluctant to look on himself as a literary writer, even though he never doubted his own stylistic genius. During the nine years following *Bréf til Láru* he did not publish any literary works but concentrated on the study of Esperanto, on which he wrote a book in 1933, and on the collection of folktales published together with Sigurður Nordal in 1928–36. In 1933 he published a work even more ambiguous in form than *Bréf til Láru*: *Pistilinn skrifaði . . . I* (This epistle was written by . . . I), a collection of diverse articles and letters collected into one book. According to the preface, his intention was to publish one such collection every year, where everything he wrote would be compiled, with no organizing principle other than the calender year and no limits to the number of volumes but his own life span. In the end only one volume was published, but that one volume stands as a manifestation of his opposition to traditional forms and his polyphonic and transgressive writing, mixing genres, styles, and discourses.

After *Pistilinn skrifaði . . . I*, Þórðarson did not publish any work of fiction until the end of the 1940s, when he took up one of the threads from *Bréf til Láru*, that of autobiography.

THE GREAT WEAVER

The cacophonic monomania that characterizes *Bréf til Láru* manifests itself in a different manner in Halldór Laxness's *Vefarinn mikli frá Kasmír* (1927; The great weaver from Kashmir). Laxness had published his first novel, *Barn náttúrunnar* (Child of nature), in 1919 at the age of seventeen and his second, *Undir Helgahnúk* (Under the holy mountain), in 1924. After publishing his first novel he traveled around Europe, first to Denmark in 1919–20, then to Germany and Austria in 1921. All this time he submerged himself in European culture, literature, and philosophy, reading Freud, Nietzsche, and the sexology of Otto Weininger as well as all the latest in avant-garde literature. In November 1922 Laxness arrived at the Benedictine monastery of Saint Maurice de Clervaux in Luxembourg, where he spent a year studying Catholicism and living among monks. He converted to Catholicism and received the lowest ordination of a Benedictine monk before returning to Iceland. His intentions at the time were to study theology and achieve full monastic status. But literature also held his attention, and the struggle between religion and art, as well as that between religion and life, is an important theme played out in *Vefarinn mikli frá Kasmír*.

Bréf til Láru and *Vefarinn mikli frá Kasmír* show many similarities. Not only was Þórðarson the only Icelandic author who can be said to have had some stylistic influence on Halldór Laxness, but the turmoil of the 1920s left its mark on both texts, and they share a common goal of breaking down conventional forms and genres. In an afterword to the second edition, Laxness described *Vefarinn mikli frá Kasmír* as follows:

> Actually, there are several viewpoints at large in my work, especially artistic ones. I wished to explore my talents in as many fields of so-called fine literature as possible, and the Weaver is, thus, an experiment in various forms. It is an attempt at composing a novel approximately according to the realistic method of the nineteenth century, but in several places surrealism as it was emerging in French literature at the time is woven into the text — I was fascinated by André Breton's theories in *Manifeste du surréalisme* (1923) as well as Guillaume Appollinaire's poetry. Essays bordering on philosophy can be found in the book as well as four short stories . . . , a few children's tales, poetry, attempts at translation in verse and prose, Christian mysticism in prayer book style adapted from the *Imitatio Christi*, sketches of homily style and hagiography, as well as further literary exercises. ("Hvernig Vefarinn varð til," 382)

The plot of the novel, which Laxness himself classes as nineteenth-century realism, revolves around a young Icelander, the poet and genius Steinn Elliði. Brought up in wealth with the whole of Europe as his playground, Steinn is totally at one with modernity and its turmoils, fluent in the major European languages, and extremely well-read in literature, philosophy, and religion. The main conflict experienced by Steinn is that between religion and life, or, more directly, between a life devoted to God and the profanity of earthly love. This struggle also obtains between devotion, celibacy, and asceticism, on the one hand, and art and literature, on the other, as Steinn is torn between his dreams of greatness as a poet and the salvation of total devotion to God in a monastery. The other main character of the novel is Diljá, his childhood friend and admirer who competes with religion for his love. On his last visit to Iceland before taking his vows as a monk, Steinn starts a love affair with Diljá, who consequently burns all her bridges and follows him to Rome. There, he makes his final decision, abandoning her in order to enter the church, while she is left outside the Vatican, having abandoned everything for her own ideal of love. Thus, the two extremes of the text, religion and earthly love, encapsulate the two protagonists at the end. Steinn gives up his own self for the solitude of the church, while Diljá has sacrificed everything for love.

This brief account of the plot, however, does not give a full picture of the text with its feverish roller-coaster ride from one extreme to the other. Steinn's multisplintered self is a channel through which every thinkable discourse—holy, profane, subversive, or strictly moral—flows in a polyphonic stream. Apart from all its stylistic innovation the work also introduces the Icelander as a cosmopolitan in literature and, thus, confirms the break with the Icelandic narrative tradition already visible in *Bréf til Láru*.

Vefarinn mikli frá Kasmír became the subject of two of the most famous reviews written on Icelandic literature. The two reviews were published simultaneously in the literary journal *Vaka*. One was written by Kristján Albertsson, a young conservative critic who later became a lecturer at the University of Berlin and a diplomat in the Icelandic foreign service, the other by Guðmundur Finnbogason, the director of the national library and a former professor of psychology at the University of Iceland. Albertsson began his review with these words: "At last, at last, a magnificent work of literature, one that rises like a mighty cliff from the flatland of Icelandic poetry and prose of the last years! Iceland has gained a new literary genius—it is simply our duty to acknowledge this and to rejoice!" (Albertsson and Finnbogason, "Tveir ritdómar," 306). Finnbogason, on the other hand, restricted his review to two words, words that are not easily translated: "Vjelstrokkað tilberasmjör" (Albertsson and Finnbogason, "Tveir ritdómar," 316). The word *tilberasmjör* refers to butter stolen by a ghost conjured up by women for that particular purpose, and in Finnbogason's formulation it is butter fabricated by a machine (*vjelstrokkað*). The two words together therefore connote theft, black magic, and an allusion to the nonorganic nature of the work; *Vefarinn mikli frá Kasmír* is, in other words, a modern mechanical monstrosity.

Scholars have disagreed on whether these radical works from the middle of the 1920s can be seen as the beginning of modernism or a "modern literature" in Iceland. In *"Loksins, loksins,"* a study of *Vefarinn mikli frá Kasmír* published in 1987, Halldór Guðmundsson defended the theory that this work marks a definite break in Icelandic literary history and the arrival of a thoroughly modern literature even more radical than the "half-blooded" modernism of Sigurður Nordal, Gunnar Gunnarsson, and Þórbergur Þórðarson. Guðmundsson's theory was opposed by Ástráður Eysteinsson, who in his "Fyrsta nútímaskáldsagan og módernisminn" claimed that, even though the experimental works of the 1920s struck a new tone in Icelandic literature, they did not have a lasting impact on its development. No wave of modernism followed in their wake; instead, the paradigm of realism grew even stronger in the 1930s with Halldór Laxness's rise to stardom through the renovation of realistic narrative. The conclusion of the dispute depends perhaps on the vantage point. Modernism as such certainly did not emerge as a paradigm in Icelandic literature in the 1920s or the 1930s. But the pioneering works of Halldór Laxness and Þórbergur Þórðarson had a lasting impact in making Icelandic literature and Icelandic literary life more modern and in bringing it more in sync with the rest of the world.

Although Þórðarson and Laxness dominate what has been written about Icelandic prose in the 1920s, they were not quite alone on the scene. The tradition of the rural novel as it had evolved from Jón Thoroddsen through Jón Trausti was still strong among authors such as Guðmundur Friðjónsson (1869–1944; see p. 324), who was a prolific author of short stories and poetry deeply rooted in the traditional society, which he views with a sympathetic eye even though he is critical of some of its aspects. Friðjónsson was inspired in part by the naturalist movement of the late nineteenth century, and his short stories are often highly political, putting problems up for debate, in accordance with Brandes's dictum.

Another writer of traditional Icelandic novels at the time is Kristín Sigfúsdóttir (1876–1953; see also p. 526). Her novel *Gömul saga* (1927–28; An old tale) is reminiscent of nineteenth-century realism in many ways, particularly in its emphasis on morality and the hypocrisy of its guardians.

Political literature was also emerging with authors such as Jón Björnsson, who wrote a novel called *Jafnaðarmaðurinn* (1924; The socialist) that focuses on contemporary Reykjavík politics. The characters are mostly channels for different political views, and the novel has an obvious bias as the class struggle and strike actions of the militant socialists have dire consequences for the poor. Sigurjón Jónsson (1888–1980) came from the opposite political front. His novels *Silkikjólar og vaðmálsbuxur* (1922; Silk dresses and wadmal trousers) and *Glæsimennska* (1924; Elegance) share some of Þórðarson's radical ideas and socialist critique. It has also been argued that their style and narrative technique foreshadow that of Þórðarson and Laxness and that they should be considered as a part of the renewal of narrative form during the turbulent 1920s (see Sigurjónsson, "Nútímaleg skáldsagnagerð").

ICELANDIC WRITERS ABROAD IN THE 1920S AND 1930S

In Norway Kristmann Guðmundsson (1901–83) became a best-selling author with his *Islandsk Kærlighed* (1926; Icelandic love) and *Brudekjolen* (1927; English trans.: *The Bridal Gown* [1931]), a short story collection and a novel, respectively, both romantic, bordering on the erotic. During the years until 1939, when he returned to Iceland, Guðmundsson published

Realism and Revolt

a further ten novels in Norwegian. His writing was notorious in its day for its candid expression of eroticism and love, but it has since been completely forgotten in Norway. Guðmundsson's work in Norwegian falls into two categories. On the one hand, there are two large historical novels, *Det hellige fjell* (1932; The holy mountain), which takes its material from the settlement of Iceland, and *Gudinnen og oksen* (1938; The goddess and the ox; English trans.: *Winged Citadel* [1940]), which goes back to Crete in the year 1000 BC. These novels are best described as psychohistorical as they attempt to tackle modern psychological problems, most notably the relationship between mothers and sons. In *Det hellige fjell* this relationship takes on almost mythological dimensions, resulting in the killing of the father, while in *Gudinnen og oksen* the absence of the mother is the force driving the protagonist.

Many of Guðmundsson's other novels share a similar, almost repetitive story line as they tell of men who, in middle age, after rising from rags to riches, seek out their childhood homes and their old girlfriends. Often, the protagonist's life has led him abroad so that the return to childhood love is also a return to Iceland. This course of events has a certain affinity with Guðmundsson's own relationship with Iceland as he always considered himself misunderstood and even hated in Icelandic literary circles. These novels could, therefore, be read as a postcolonial adventure where conflicts between the old Icelandic society and the longing for art or freedom are played out, not unlike Gunnarsson's *Af Borgslægtens Historie*. Guðmundsson returns to this theme in his four-volume autobiography, published in 1959–62, which may yet turn out to be his most significant work.

In Denmark, meanwhile, Gunnar Gunnarsson and Guðmundur Kamban produced their best work during this period: Gunnarsson with *Kirken paa Bjerget* (1923–28; The church on the mountain; English trans.: *Ships in the Sky* [1938] and *The Night and the Dream* [1938]) and Kamban with his historical novel *Skaalholt* (1930–32; English trans.: *The Virgin of Skálholt* [1936]). Kamban's novel was published in Icelandic in 1930–35 as *Skálholt*, but *Kirken paa Bjerget* did not appear in Icelandic until 1941–43 in Halldór Laxness's translation. At first glance both these works seem far removed from what was going on in Icelandic literature at the time. *Skálholt* describes the life and times of Bishop Brynjólfur Sveinsson (1605–75) and his daughter, Ragnheiður Brynjólfsdóttir (1641–63; see also p. 351). The main object of the novel was, according to Kamban, to "attempt a psychohistorical explanation of Ragnheiður's fate" (*Skálholt*, 5). Her story had long been famous in Iceland, and Torfhildur Hólm had written a historical novel about Bishop Brynjólfur in 1882. Ragnheiður gave birth to an illegitimate child only nine months after having sworn to the congregation at Skálholt cathedral that she was a virgin. Her father, the bishop, sent her away and expelled her lover, a young priest named Daði Halldórsson, from Skálholt. Ragnheiður died only two years later, and her son, whom the old bishop later adopted, also died at the age of twelve, leaving Brynjólfur without any descendant or heir. Kamban's interpretation of events is that Ragnheiður was innocent of perjury but that she slept with Daði the very same night she took the oath, to spite her father and in revenge for the humiliation that she had been made to suffer. In Kamban's novel Ragnheiður comes across as a thoroughly modern woman, living according to principles of freedom and autonomy well ahead of her time. Kamban's psychological approach is, thus, based on empathy rather than on an attempt to historicize the events and trying to understand them in terms of their own time.

Kamban's novel does not end with Ragnheiður's death but continues to describe Brynjólfur's life in two more volumes. The same outlook on history is evident in the later volumes, where events of great importance in Icelandic history are explained on a personal, psychological level. Accordingly, Brynjólfur's two most critical decisions — to sign an oath of allegiance to the Danish king as the absolute sovereign of Iceland and to present the Codex Regius (see p. 7) to the Danish king a few years later — are explained in light of his personal life. At the time when he signed the oath of allegiance he had applied to the king for absolution for his daughter and could not, therefore, go against his will. Kamban's *Skálholt* thus touches on some of the key events in Icelandic history in its nationalist interpretation, the loss of rights following Danish absolutism, and how some of the nation's most valuable manuscripts ended up in the possession of the Danish authorities.

Gunnarsson's *Kirken paa Bjerget* received favorable reviews in Denmark, but, as one volume followed another for five years, sales dwindled, even though many critics considered the later volumes among the best of Gunnarsson's writing. In Denmark this most ambitious of Gunnarsson's works never reached the same status as his *Af Borgslægtens Historie* or his historical novels. In Iceland, however, *Kirken paa Bjerget* is considered his main work, in particular its first two volumes, which describe the youth of Uggi Greipsson, Gunnarsson's alter ego, in eastern Iceland toward the end of the nineteenth century. The first half of *Kirken paa Bjerget* is probably the most idyllic and lyric account of old Icelandic society ever written and by far the most captivating portrayal of childhood in Icelandic letters. The point of view is that of a child, but the voice belongs to the grown-up narrator who depicts the child's perception of the world as a lost paradise of innocence.

The first sentences, often quoted, give an impression of the mood that characterizes the first two volumes:

> Gone are the years when I was young and still innocent except for original sin . . . the years when adventures brought me experience without bitterness . . . the years when my sympathy with all things living was uncritical and intense . . . when God seemed to me a generous, friendly grandfather, the Devil a rather dangerous and moody but, on the whole, essentially stupid and harmless godfather . . . the years when light was triumphant indeed, and all evil, all fear, could be turned aside by an *Our father* or the sign of the Cross . . . the years when in the morning I could but dimly foresee the evening and sat safely in the shelter of a wall of sod playing with straw . . . these indeed are the years that will never return. (*The Night and the Dream*, trans. Ramsden, 1)

This idyllic world is shattered at the end of the second volume by the death of Uggi's mother. The remaining volumes describe his struggles to educate himself and to realize his dream of becoming a writer. Although his sensitivity is the same, his unconditional trust in God and men is gone, and his character changes, becoming more stern and determined. Like the author, Uggi moves to Denmark to study at a folk high school and pursue his dream of becoming a writer in Danish.

The last two volumes of *Kirken paa Bjerget* are overshadowed by the first volumes with their lyric and sensitive prose. This is not entirely justified, however, as they possess other merits often overlooked, such as the vivid description of the life of young Nordic writers in Copenhagen at the beginning of the twentieth century, a time when the Nordic literatures circulated in what was more or less one market. They also describe Uggi's struggle to become a writer in a foreign language and to gain acceptance in a foreign culture, all the while forging his identity to match that of his calling.

In the 1930s Gunnarsson started another series of novels, this time a sequence of what were to be twelve novels in all, portraying the history of Iceland from settlement to the present. The first volume, *Edbrødre* (English trans.: *The Sworn Brothers* [1920]), appeared in 1918, and in the 1930s Gunnarsson published four more: *Jón Arason* (1930); *Jord* (1933; Earth); *Hvide Krist* (1934; White-Christ); and *Graamand* (1936; Grey man). Halla Kjartansdóttir considers the last three of these novels a religious historical trilogy as they deal with the establishment of the pagan commonwealth state (*Jord*), the acceptance of Christianity (*Hvide-Krist*), and the violent Age of the Sturlungar (*Graamand*) (see her *Trú í sögum*). These novels are a rewriting of medieval Icelandic literature, both the Sagas of Icelanders and contemporary sagas such as *Þorgils saga og Hafliða* (The saga of Þorgils and Hafliði; see p. 74). This rewriting bears the mark of Gunnarsson's religious and political interests. It has been interpreted as an attempt at synchronizing Christianity and the pagan religion of Iceland's settlers. The historical novels also have a national-historical dimension to them as they describe the unification of the Icelanders into one nation, which Gunnarsson saw as a model for the unification of the Nordic countries into one state. Gunnarsson was an ardent follower of pan-Scandinavianism, a political movement dating back to the nineteenth century whose goal was to unify the different Nordic states into one. The series of historical novels came to a stop after *Graamand* in 1936. The historical optimism and national romanticism that are inherent in Gunnarsson's grand plan to write the nation's history in fiction had no place in the Europe of the 1930s.

In Iceland the historical novels have never been rated among Gunnarsson's best work, although they were quite popular in Denmark and even more so in Germany. Scholarly interest in them has grown in the last few years but has mainly focused on their political and religious aspects. Still, aesthetically, they do not rank among Gunnarsson's finest achievements. Three works written during the same period not belonging to the settlement series, however, do: *Svartfugl* (1929; English trans.: *The Black Cliffs* [1967]); *Vikivaki* (1932; Folk dance); and *Advent* (1937; English trans.: *The Good Shepherd* [1940]).

Svartfugl has been considered the first Icelandic crime novel, although it has little or no relation to detective stories or suspense literature as known today. It is based on a notorious murder case that took place in Iceland at the beginning of the nineteenth century, when Bjarni Bjarnason and Steinunn Sveinsdóttir, both living on the small farm Sjöundá in western Iceland, were sentenced to death for killing their spouses. Gunnarsson used the case files and court transcripts from the case as building material for his novel. The third main character of *Svartfugl* is the parish chaplain, Eiúlfur Kolbeinsson, who is also the narrator of the novel. Written in a somewhat archaic, but by no means saga-like, style, *Svartfugl* deals with the problem of shared human responsibility. Eiúlfur is a witness to the events at the trials and is closer to the two murderers than anyone else. But he is also an actor in their story, coercing them into confessing to their crimes. His narration takes the form of a confession, where he ponders over his role in the trials and his responsibility for the fate of Steinunn and Bjarni.

Eiúlfur's conclusion is, as most scholars have agreed, that the fates of all men are entwined and that he is in part responsible for the fate of the murderers as well as for their actions. This conclusion can, however, be interpreted in more than one way. Early critics and scholars agreed that it was in accordance with the novel's direct message, which was one of shared human responsibility that could not be avoided. A Marxist analysis by Dagný Kristjánsdóttir (see her "Synd er ekki nema fyrir þræla") takes a different view, arguing instead that, as a representative of the ruling class, Eiúlfur uses the notion of humanity to look past his responsibility and to justify oppression based on class and economic power. Most recently Jón Yngvi Jóhannsson argues (in his introduction to *Svartfugl*) for a reading of the novel as a negative bildungsroman, one that describes Eiúlfur's growth into his role as a man of power, thus unmasking the way power relations mold the identity and fate, not only of those oppressed, but also of the oppressor, as Eiúlfur himself becomes an executioner in the process of bringing the guilty to justice.

Gunnarsson's two nonsettlement novels from the 1930s suffered quite a different fate in their contemporary reception. *Vikivaki* was met with almost unanimous bafflement by Danish critics, while *Advent* was hailed both in Denmark and abroad and became Gunnarsson's biggest success, appearing in the United States, for instance, as a Book-of-the-Month Club selection in 1940.

Vikivaki is Gunnarsson's most modernistic work, a novel that puts the very art of narration on trial. In it a group of dead people are woken by a sound they think is the trumpets of doomsday but is, in fact, a radio playing in the home of the writer Jake Sonarsson in his hypermodern villa far up in the Icelandic highlands. The characters of the past thus seek out Jake, forcing him to reconsider his life and his writing.

The title of a characteristic review of *Vikivaki* was "??? [*sic*]." The reviewer remarks: "Halfway through reading these mystic papers one despairs and asks what the point is — and when one has read the latter half one still hasn't found out" (*Nakskov Tidende* 11 January 1933). Other critics were more subtle and found some merit in Gunnarsson's descriptions of Icelandic nature or the individual tales of the ghosts' past lives. Nobody, however, attempted to understand the author's motives or purpose in writing the novel, which, according to one critic, should have come with "directions for use" (*Berlingske Tidende* 22 November 1932). While these directions are still wanting, recent scholars have been able to make more sense of *Vikivaki*. It has, for instance, been read as a book that defies all norms of realist narration, rationality, and bourgeois morals (Óskarsson, "Bók án borgaralegs öryggis").

The novel also stands in stark contrast to Gunnarsson's own work, not least his historical novels, which were quite traditional in method and use of form. The fantasy and the reflexivity of *Vikivaki*'s narration also clashed with Gunnarsson's image in Danish literature as being first and foremost a portrayer of Iceland, its history and nature. The confusion surrounding the novel is, therefore, understandable.

Advent is of a totally different nature. An allegorical tale filled with religious symbolism, it tells of a shepherd's journey into the Icelandic highlands around Christmas, where Icelandic nature at its fiercest plays a major part. The story of the shepherd Benedikt and his loyal companions, the dog Leo and the ram Gnarly, not only shows obvious affinities with the story of Christ, but also indicates a new direction in Gunnarsson's philosophy, stressing virtues such as tolerance, humility, and self-sufficiency. This is also evident in Gunnarsson's last novels, *Brandur paa Bjarg* (1940; Elegy for the highlands), *Sálumessa* (1952; Requiem), and *Brimhenda* (1954; Sonata by the sea), written after he returned to Iceland in 1939.

THE 1930S: THE POLITICIZATION OF LITERATURE

If the 1920s were marked by experiments and uproar in Icelandic literature, one could say that the 1930s were a period during which experimentation was laid to rest and the radical currents of the preceding decade found new channels. During and after the Great Depression, Icelandic literature became more overtly political, and cultural criticism and debate in magazines and newspapers followed suit. New political movements that had begun to surface in the years following 1918 now became dominant as the political struggle in Iceland had gradually changed from revolving around different means to the common end of national liberation into class politics. The situation in Iceland was beginning to resemble the political landscape in other countries in Northern Europe. A social democratic party had been established in 1916 as well as a farmers' party, the Progressive Party, and a conservative/liberal party came into being in 1929, when two older parties merged into one. In 1930 the Icelandic four-party system was completed with the foundation of a Communist party, which became a socialist party in 1938 when it merged with a faction of the social democrats.

The institutionalization of class politics also affected literary life. In 1933 a society of revolutionary writers called the Red Pens was formed by some of the country's leading young writers and intellectuals. In 1935–38 this society published an influential journal or yearbook entitled *Rauðu pennarnir* (The Red Pens). Among its contributors was Halldór Laxness, who was well on his way to becoming a leading figure in Icelandic literature and the main socialist writer whom leaders pinned their hopes on.

Laxness enjoys a unique position in Icelandic literary history and in Icelandic literary life as a whole. Indeed, it is not an overstatement to call him a literary institution in his own right. His name and his works have functioned as a paradigm for the writing of the history of literature as well as the standard against which other authors are measured. In the 1930s Laxness published three voluminous realistic novels that for many critics and readers have become the nucleus of his life's work. These works also provided the basis for his rise to power in Icelandic literature from the 1940s on. Laxness's stature in Icelandic literature does not rely solely on the merits of his novels or the support of his fellow socialists and others who appreciated his works, however. His importance lies no less in his position as the favorite adversary of right-wing intellectuals and politicians. He became, not only the champion, but the epitome of the new literary movement and, thus, the focus of opposition attacks.

The first of Laxness's social-realist novels, *Salka Valka* (English trans.: *Salka Valka* [1936]), was published in two volumes in 1930 and 1931. Laxness had spent the years between the publication of *Vefarinn mikli frá Kasmír* and *Salka Valka* in the United States, among other places, where he had converted to socialism, publishing the highly critical *Alþýðubókin* (The people's book) in 1930. *Alþýðubókin* is a collection of essays on matters that concerned, or, in the author's opinion, should concern, the general public in Iceland. Its criticism is fierce, attacking anything from the state of housing and public sanitation to what Laxness calls the *bourgeois novel* and American movies — all but Chaplin's. The diverse essays occasionally contradict each other, but what most of them have in common is an optimism that technological solutions to social problems can be found and a faith in a scientific socialism or Marxism (see Sigurjónsson, *Den politiska Laxness*).

Salka Valka follows in the wake of *Alþýðubókin* and constitutes Laxness's first attempt at writing a novel where Icelandic society is analyzed in terms of class struggle and where a modern sociohistorical approach is in evidence. Originally written as a screenplay for Metro-Goldwyn-Mayer under the title "Woman in Pants," *Salka Valka* is set in a small fishing village in the west of Iceland. It describes the youth and young adult years of the girl Salka Valka and her relationship with her mother, Sigurlína, with her mother's lover, Steinþór, and with her childhood friend Arnaldur.

The novel's two volumes describe Salka Valka's personal growth from being a poor child to becoming a grown woman, a worker, and a boat owner, in fact, one of the more influential figures in the small coastal town of Óseyri. However, it also describes the social evolution of the small community during some of the most turbulent times Icelandic society has known. When Salka and her mother arrive at Óseyri, the society is static, locked in what might be termed *feudal capitalism*. The whole village is owned by one man, Jóhannes Bogesen, who controls all fishing, the production of salt fish for export, and trade with groceries, clothing, and equipment for fishing as well as alcohol and tobacco. The economy of the village lies entirely in his hands. Money is not used in small trades among the inhabitants; when valuables exchange hands, the appropriate sum is simply subtracted from one account in Bogesen's shop and added to another. The only other power in the village is the Salvation Army, which runs a hostel and functions as a religious community as well as a social center and network, but without ever threatening Bogesen's power. Salka's mother enters the Salvation Army and does, indeed, find her salvation there, while Salka herself soon becomes a worker and a part of Bogesen's economy in her own right.

The main conflict of the first volume, however, is psychological: Salka's mother becomes engaged to Steinþór, a local fisherman, drunkard, and megalomaniac who soon turns his attentions toward Salka. At the end of the first half of the first volume he tries to rape Salka and then disappears abroad. On his return he renews his betrothal to Sigurlína, but, when Sigurlína discovers his continued interest in Salka, he disappears again, and Sigurlína drowns herself on Good Friday, to be discovered on Easter morning.

The staging of Sigurlína's death demonstrates that religious motives are not absent from *Salka Valka*. Indeed, the two volumes of the novel can also be read in an exegetic manner as the events of the first volume are in many ways repeated with variations in the second. There, the love-hate triangle of Salka-Sigurlína-Steinþór is, for instance, replaced by a new triangle where Arnaldur, Salka's childhood friend, becomes her lover and, by extension, Steinþór's competitor. Arnaldur returns to Óseyri in order to mobilize the workers against Bogesen and the new boat owners, including Salka.

Arnaldur shares many of the views that Laxness himself proclaimed in *Alþýðubókin*. He is well versed in Marxism and has great plans for improving the living standards of the people through such endeavors as the foundation of fishing and trade cooperatives and municipally owned dairy farms and improved housing and schools. On these grounds Arnaldur has traditionally been interpreted as the author's voice in *Salka Valka* (see Sigurjónsson, "Hugmyndafræði Alþýðubókarinnar"; and Markey, "*Salka Valka*"). He is an ideologue and an idealist and manages to persuade the workers to go on strike. His efforts fail, however, and the revolution at Óseyri leads only to the rise of Steinþór as the new town king, taking Bogesen's place. Arnaldur's love affair with Salka ends with her helping him out of the country to America. Arnaldur's socialism thus proves unsuccessful, and Salka is left behind, although it could be argued that she is the stronger for it, strong enough to send him away and to continue her life in Óseyri, and that she is, in a sense, also liberated after her sexual — and possibly political — awakening with Arnaldur.

Interpreting Arnaldur as a representative of Laxness's full-fledged commitment to socialism, however, eliminates other ways of reading *Salka Valka*. Clearly, his systematic and ideological approach to life in a small fishing village fails. Instead, what emerges triumphant is Salka's down-to-earth mentality and humane socialism. Her words to Arnaldur are crucial: "Arnaldur, you are filled with the world's theories. But I am just who I am" (*Salka Valka* [1959], 313). On the basis of this statement it is possible to read *Salka Valka* as a novel where all systematized ideologies fail. In the first volume we see this reflected in Sigurlína as her ideals anchored in the religion of the Salvation Army crumble when they collide with everyday reality. In the second volume Arnaldur's character can be seen as analogous to Sigurlína's, his Marxism the analogy of her religion. What prevails in the novel are the values of Salka Valka, a down-to-earth compassion and individualism coupled with sympathy for the poor and a certain willingness to make sacrifices. Salka can, thus, be seen as a hero who combines the best of both worlds in a life unencumbered by grand theories and ideologies, which makes it possible for her to survive in the harsh world described in the novel.

Read in this way, *Salka Valka* becomes more ambivalent in its social realism and can be seen instead as a work that embodies the transition from the religious conflicts of *Vefarinn mikli frá Kasmír* to the more determined socialism of Laxness's next realist work, the two-volume *Sjálfstætt fólk* (1934–35; English trans.: *Independent People* [1945]). This reading also brings Laxness closer to the "Hamsunism" described earlier. Hamsun's greatest work, *Markens Grøde* (1917; Growth of the soil), is a strong subtext of *Sjálfstætt fólk*, to such a degree that *Sjálfstætt fólk* can be read as a complete negation of Hamsun's work (see Guðmundsson, "Glíman við Hamsun").

Salka Valka was every bit as controversial in Iceland as *Vefarinn mikli frá Kasmír*. The conflicts surrounding it were, however, more political, and in many ways its appearance marks the split of the literary community into two opposed fronts. On the one hand, there were the left-wing intellectuals and writers, who were gaining ground in Iceland in the 1930s and soon chose Laxness as their leader, while, on the other hand, there were the more conservative politicians and intellectuals, who attacked Laxness for his "misrepresentations" of life in Iceland and his militant socialism. *Salka Valka* also became Laxness's first novel to gain popularity outside Iceland. It was translated by Gunnar Gunnarsson into Danish in 1934 and appeared in an English translation in 1936.

Even though Laxness's politics were emphasized in the contemporary reception of *Salka Valka* and, indeed, have been ever since, it should be noted that the novel's appearance also marks a change in Laxness's aesthetics and constitutes a groundbreaking work in the evolution of realism as the main genre of Icelandic prose writing. Laxness's realist turn is not a return to the realism that had dominated Icelandic literature for decades; rather, it is an attempt to bring that tradition of Icelandic prose into a dialogue with the European novel. Laxness achieves this, for instance, through his variations in style and point of view. The narrator of *Salka Valka* is omniscient. Laxness uses this freedom in many ways, sometimes describing events from above and outside as if seen through a camera lens, at other times using various characters as focus points. This role is not limited to human characters as even animals provide the narrator with their point of view. The narrator's tone swings between sincerity and blatant, even grotesque irony, the latter used sometimes to describe highly serious and even tragic events.

In Laxness's next novel, *Sjálfstætt fólk*, his realist narrative technique reaches its peak. As in *Salka Valka*, in *Sjálfstætt fólk* the narrator is omniscient, interfering, and on the surface highly ironic. *Sjálfstætt fólk* tells a story similar to that in, for instance, Hamsun's *Markens Grøde*: the protagonist, Bjartur, a farmhand for eighteen years, realizes his lifelong dream of becoming his own man, an independent farmer on a desolate farm close to the edge of the highlands that has been in ruins for decades. Just as the actual economic history of Icelandic coastal towns provided the basis for *Salka Valka*, *Sjálfstætt fólk* had its origins in recent events. Icelandic politicians had at the beginning of the twentieth century encouraged the building of new farms in places where farming had not been attempted for decades or even centuries. The reasons for this were both demographic and political. When farmland became scarce owing to an increase in the country's population, some political forces saw the building of new farms as a means to preserve agriculture as the foundation of Icelandic society and to slow down the growth of towns and cities.

The first part of the novel carries the title *The Settler of Iceland*. It contains some powerful discourses, for instance, that of a certain frontier mentality often romanticized by Icelandic historians and politicians where the origins of Icelanders as settlers in an unknown country, free from any higher authority, were seen as the very basis of the nation's existence. Another discourse conspicuously present in Bjartur's tale is that of the independent farmer who, by taming nature and making it subordinate to himself, reaps riches from the land. These two ideas are combined in Bjartur's stern individualism, which puts independence above everything else, even his family and his own health. Whereas Laxness's ironic descriptions of individual characters and events can at times be almost crude and can hardly be missed, the underlying irony of the whole novel, at which level these discourses are undermined, is much more subtle, so subtle, in fact, that Laxness's political adversaries were able to read the first volume as advocating individualism and the type of freedom that Bjartur desires.

Bjartur's life is a constant struggle against forces bigger than himself— nature, his old master and debtor Jón, banks, merchants and the swings in the international economy as a result of the First World War, not to mention ghosts and demons. Bjartur never acknowledges the power of these phenomena or succumbs to them. His belief in his own strength and his right to independence is always greater. He suffers one loss after another, although there are times when he seems to succeed in building a decent life for himself. But gradually he loses everything: his two wives; his children, who either die or emigrate to America; and eventually his most prized possession, his farm.

Toward the end of the novel Bjartur encounters socialist workers in a town close to his farm. Contrary to his former beliefs, he joins them in a meal of stolen bread and leaves his son with them to join them in their struggle. This, it can be argued, is the political conclusion of *Sjálfstætt fólk*: when all his hopes have crumbled, Bjartur shows his solidarity with the workers even though it is too late for him to join them.

Like *Salka Valka*, *Sjálfstætt fólk* has mainly been studied with regard to its politics, while less attention has been paid to its aesthetic merits. More than any other modern narrative in Icelandic the story of the farmer Bjartur has over the years assumed the role of a national epic. Bjartur has become a stock character, a proverbial reference, in everyday life as well as in various discourses, to the perceived nature of Icelandic nationality and individuality. This holds true for other characters from Laxness's novels as well. They have assumed the guise of living or historical persons rather than fictional creations. Herein lies a peculiarity of literary debate in Iceland, where realism has been the dominant mode for the best part of modernity: literature is often read as a direct reflection of reality. This explains the power of Laxness's novels as well as the controversy that they provoked by describing the darker sides of Icelandic life at the beginning of the twentieth century.

Laxness's novels are, however, not entirely imprisoned by their role in Icelandic cultural history: *Sjálfstætt fólk*, for example, has also been read as a complex, psychological novel, not least for the relationship between Bjartur and his daughter Ásta Sóllilja (who is probably not his child), and even a deconstructive reading, with the old grandmother Hallbera as a key figure, has been suggested recently (Jakobsson, "'Hinn blindi sjáandi'"). Not least, the novel can be viewed as a polyphonic, modern novel, not only because of its irony and multitude of voices and points of view, but also because of its intertextual use of poetry, politics, and folklore and its dialogic relation to other texts.

Sjálfstætt fólk was even more controversial than *Salka Valka* and confirmed the battlefronts in Icelandic cultural life formed by the latter's reception. *Salka Valka* takes place in a fishing village, a relatively new social venue in Iceland. *Sjálfstætt fólk*, on the other hand, deals with the life of a small farmer and, thus, addresses issues that for many were at the very heart of what was considered Icelandic: farming, life in the countryside, was, to politicians and many intellectuals, the very essence of Icelandic nationality.

Until the early twentieth century, Icelandic society was completely agricultural, and its transformation into a modernized urban society was taking place at an astonishing rate. The controversy surrounding *Sjálfstætt fólk* thus revolved around the representation of that society, the way the country's most recent history was written and interpreted. Laxness's realism provoked various responses. One of them, harsh but in many ways typical, was a pamphlet published by the farmer and writer Guðmundur Friðjónsson under the title "Sveitaómenningin í skugga skáldsins frá Laxnesi" (1937; The cultureless countryside as seen through the prism of the poet from Laxnes). Friðjónsson blames Laxness for misrepresenting life in the countryside since the people portrayed in Laxness's novels are caricatures of Icelanders, especially Icelandic farmers. Moreover, since Laxness's novels have been translated into foreign languages, this defamation also sullies the Icelandic nation's reputation abroad. In other words, Laxness had made the lice and fleas on the backs of poor Icelandic farmers an export product in order to promote himself in the world.

The third and last of Laxness's social-realist novels, *Heimsljós* (English trans.: *World Light* [1969]), was published in four volumes in 1937–40. If we take the three realist novels together, one could say that *Salka Valka* deals with the worker, *Sjálfstætt fólk* with the farmer, and *Heimsljós* with the third pillar of Icelandic society and culture: the poet.

Based on the journals of a real-life poet named Magnús Hj. Magnússon, who lived his entire life in poverty without ever publishing a single book, *Heimsljós* is perhaps the most lyric of Laxness's novels. The poet Ólafur Kárason Ljósvíkingur, the novel's protagonist, is a sensitive being who dreams of poetry and beauty. His situation in life is in stark contrast to his dreams as he is an orphan who has been brought up by people who mistreat him and misunderstand him. Once he is grown he is trapped in poverty as he is barely able to sustain himself or his family by ordinary work. The use of irony is more subtle in *Heimsljós* than in Laxness's other novels, and the descriptions of both Ólafur Kárason's rich inner life and his view of the world, not least of nature, sometimes border on the romantic. *Heimsljós* points in many ways toward Laxness's next great achievement, *Íslandsklukk-an* (English trans.: *Iceland's Bell* [2003]; see also p. 405), where Icelandic history and the Icelandic narrative tradition are combined in a profoundly national historical novel.

THE COUNTRY AND THE CITY

Although Laxness now stands as the main portrayer of the old agricultural society and the changes that it underwent at the beginning of the twentieth century, he was by no means the only one in the 1930s, and his status was far from being as undisputed then as it came to be later. In fact, the bulk of Icelandic novel writing during this period deals with this topic in one way or another and uses almost without exception the form of the realist epic novel. Many of these novels were read in direct opposition to Laxness's version of Icelandic society and history. Fictionalizing the country's imme-diate past thus became a battlefield of opinions and interpretations no less than the more traditional venue of essays and polemics. In many ways Icelandic novel writing and Icelandic literary criticism of the period, which was practiced not just by professional critics but to no lesser extent by poli-ticians, provide a textbook example of the political nature of representation.

The most obvious and famous case in point is that of Guðmundur G. Hagalín's (1898–1985) *Sturla í Vogum* I–II (1938; Sturla of Vogar), a voluminous novel about the farmer Sturla. Hagalín had written three nov-els before *Sturla í Vogum* and had engaged in polemics about the aesthetics of the novel with Halldór Laxness in which he defended Knut Hamsun and his descriptions of the organic life of the farmer. Hagalín's best-known novel before *Sturla í Vogum* was *Kristrún í Hamravík* (1933; Kristrún of Hamravík), a short novel mainly centered on the character description of old Kristrún, an elderly woman in the most isolated part of Iceland, the Hornstrandir. This region was, according to Hagalín, the last refuge of the traditional old society, a place where the people were still robust and hum-ble. Robustness and virility are Sturla's dominant characteristics. His story is the heroic epic of a man who faces impossible odds, in the form of a harsh natural environment and the animosity and envy of his neighbors. His situation as a poor farmer who has risen from being a farmhand to being his own man mirrors that of Bjartur in Laxness's *Sjálfstætt fólk*, with the slight difference that Sturla succeeds in every one of his endeavors and that the discourses of freedom and independence, which are highly ironic in Laxness's novel, are the driving force of Hagalín's narrative. Sturla's story ends with his conclusion that he is not alone in the world and that his future lies in cooperating with others of his class. Although there was some harsh dissent, Hagalín's novel was soon hailed as a masterpiece by the conservative press and readership, some making favorable comparisons to Laxness's work. This in turn spurred reactions by socialist critics such as Kristinn E. Andrésson and Gunnar Benediktsson, who attacked the book for being reactionary and individualistic, the perfect weapon for conservative forces in their war against Halldór Laxness and other socialist writers.

Another novel overtly written as a response to *Sjálfstætt fólk* is *Dalafólk* (1936–39; People of the valley) by the renowned neoromantic poet Hulda (the penname of Unnur Benediktsdóttir Bjarklind, 1881–1946; see also pp. 344–47 and 523–26). Best described as utopian realism, the novel portrays a model society in the Icelandic countryside, one seen from the point of view of Ísól, the daughter of a wealthy farmer. Ísól overcomes all obstacles, both external and internal, caused by her own desires, to become what society expects of her: a respectable housewife at the family farm. All around her, the country blossoms as one generation follows in the footsteps of the one before to carry on the traditions of the old society. What is most interesting in Hulda's novel today, however, is, not the utopian image of the agricultural society, or her differences with Halldór Laxness, but the obvious difficulties and conflicts invested in the construction of this image. Again and again Ísól is tempted to seek her happiness elsewhere, but, through either good fortune or self-sacrifice and self-repression, she returns to her home and to a childhood friend whom she eventually marries. Even though the novel was written as a programmatic appraisal of the old agricultural society, it stands at the same time as one of the best descriptions of its patriarchal structures and their role in the development of Icelandic cultural identity well into the twentieth century.

Even though the mainstream of Icelandic prose in the 1920s and 1930s deals in one way or another with traditional rural life and its demise, new subjects also emerged. It has often been said that, with the exception of *Vefarinn mikli frá Kasmír*, Reykjavík did not become the subject of Icelandic fiction until the 1960s. However, such a generalization overlooks several works, some written by women, others considered inferior on the grounds of genre or aesthetic merit. Among these are the works of Sigurjón Jónsson and Jón Björnsson from the 1920s, Guðmundur Kamban's *30th Generation* (1933), and Þórunn Elfa Magnúsdóttir's novels and short stories.

Þórunn Elfa Magnúsdóttir (1910–95) has been excluded from most Icelandic literary histories and textbooks. She made her debut in 1933 and remained active as a writer until the 1980s. Her earliest work deserves more attention than it has received, for it is innovative and stands apart from the main currents of Icelandic prose at the time, for instance, in its descriptions of Icelandic society and its point of view. In the three-volume *Dætur Reykjavíkur* (1933–38; Daughters of Reykjavík) she lends a voice to the young generation of Reykjavík's upper middle class: carefree and joyful, on the one hand, and in revolt against the traditional roles of the sexes, on the other. The heroine of the last two volumes, Svala Egilsson, is a young woman from a good family whose ambitions turn toward writing. Her struggles against family, friends, and not least her lover to become free to pursue her ambitions are the main focus of the novel, although the millennial celebration of the Althing in 1930 described in the story also leaves room for patriotic outbursts. Svala's is a completely modern writing project as she shuns the tradition of saga writing and language cultivation, instead claiming her right to describe modern life in the modern language of the city. This also applies to the novel itself; its language is a far cry from the literary and at times conservative style employed by most Icelandic novelists at the time as it introduces, for instance, slang into Icelandic prose. Many of Magnúsdóttir's later works are more akin to the trivial, and perhaps their reputation has overshadowed the merits of her earlier work. It is, however, also tempting to see in Magnúsdóttir a classic example of a woman writer not accepted on an equal footing with her male contemporaries.

Although Guðmundur Kamban (1888–1945) lived in Denmark and Germany during the 1920s and 1930s, his presence in Icelandic literary and cultural life was significant. He came to Iceland in 1927 to direct his own plays for a local theater company and again in 1935 — together with a suspect German named Dr. Paul Burkert who later turned out to be a member of the SS and a friend of Heinrich Himmler's — to make a documentary film on Icelandic fish exportation. Kamban was adamant about modernizing Iceland and the Icelanders in both material and cultural matters. His novel *30th Generation* is, perhaps, more a contribution to the cultural political debate than an ambitious novel. It might also be considered a modern novel of manners as its protagonists share and discuss many of Kamban's own views on such diverse subjects as modern literature, the building of large-scale harbors, and women's fashion. In the context of the Danish-Icelandic literature of which it was a part (it was originally published in Danish in 1933) it stands apart as being the only Danish-Icelandic novel dealing directly with modern Iceland and making a case for a general modernization of the country. It did not appear in Icelandic, however, until Kamban's collected works were published in 1969.

The politicization of literature in the 1930s, together with Halldór Laxness's achievements in his realist fiction, led to a general rise of the novel as a dominant genre in Icelandic literature and as a venue for the exchange of political views. This hegemony of the realist novel was not seriously threatened until the late 1960s. Another genre, however, also materialized during this period, one that acquired a large popular readership. Biography, often written in close cooperation with the subject, and sometimes even taking the form of interviews, first emerged in Guðmundur G. Hagalín's pioneering works: *Virkir dagar: Saga Sæmundar Sæmundssonar skipstjóra skráð eftir sögn hans sjálfs* (1936–38; The life and times of Captain Sæmundur Sæmundsson based on his own account) and *Saga Eldeyjar Hjalta. Skráð eftir sögn hans sjálfs* (1939; The life and times of Eldeyjar Hjalti. Based on his own account). Others followed in Hagalín's footsteps, among them Þórbergur Þórðarson, who published a multivolume biography of the Reverend Árni Þórarinsson in the 1940s.

Þórðarson embraced biography and various forms of autobiography; indeed, they became the core of his writing. Toward the end of the 1940s he published two works of an autobiographical nature, *Íslenskur Aðall* (1938; Icelandic nobility; English trans.: *In Search of My Beloved* [1961]) and *Ofvitinn* I–II (1940–41; The mastermind). These texts describe the society of aspiring poets in Reykjavík at the beginning of the twentieth century, emphasizing the protagonist's painstaking attempts to manifest himself as the poetic genius and lover he longs to be. Highly ironic, and at times grotesquely comic, these works share many of the qualities of *Bréf til Láru*. What sets them apart, however, is their attempt at constructing a self among the ruins of a world where everything has become uncertain. Whereas *Bréf til Láru* is highly deconstructive, these autobiographical works are centered on how a man is made through his own construction of himself and through his interactions with others. This construction of the self differs from traditional autobiography in that it is never complete: even though the more mature narrator of the text seems to rest securely in his own self and identity, the transformations of the protagonist never lead to a complete realization of the self. This thread in Þórðarson's writing becomes his main obsession in later works, including the biographies he wrote of others and his veiled autobiography *Sálmurinn um blómið* (1954; The hymn of the flower). Þórðarson's works in the 1930s and 1940s can, thus, be read as experiments with the limits of autobiography. Ever since his early works his writing avoided the dominant literary genre of the novel. His aesthetics are, in fact, marked by a resistance to the epic novel and constitute perhaps the only aesthetic alternative to the hegemony of Halldór Laxness and the realist novel.

FORERUNNERS OF MODERNISM IN POETRY

If the idea that the year 1918 marks a new epoch in Icelandic literature holds true for any genre, that genre would be poetry, even if the new currents in Icelandic verse that emerged in 1918–19 should be seen as the peak of the new romanticism that had prevailed since the turn of the century rather than as a break with it.

It is primarily the publication of two particular books of poetry that stands out in this respect. These works, both debuts, received unprecedented attention and admiration from critics and the general public alike. Stefán frá Hvítadal (Stefán of Hvítadalur) published his *Söngvar föru-mannsins* (The wanderer's songs) in 1918 and Davíð Stefánsson his *Svartar fjaðrir* in 1919. Both poets captured especially the younger generation, who learned their poems by heart, composers setting them to music, and aspiring poets imitating them. Poetry became fashionable as never before: Tómas Guðmundsson, in a poem published in 1933, remembers sixteen poets in his grammar school class.

Stefán of Hvítadalur (1887–1933) enjoyed a short but intense period of popularity, although his influence on Icelandic meter and poetic language secured him a long life in Icelandic literary history. When *Söngvar föru-mannsins* was published, he had recently returned from a four-year stay in Norway. When he arrived in Reykjavík, he soon became something of a mystery, and his reputation as a free poet and lover who traveled the world, singing its praises, fully lived up to the title of his book. He also bore with him a certain air of melancholy. Having been infected at an early age by tuberculosis, his health was poor, and he had lost his foot to the disease and used an artificial leg.

After publishing *Söngvar förumannsins*, Stefán converted to Catholicism and settled as a farmer in the west of Iceland with his wife. He published his second book, *Óður einyrkjans* (The farmer's ode), in 1921, and already by then his poetry had changed considerably; instead of the jovial and carefree hedonism of the first book, one finds a questioning of the small farmer's lot and his relationship with nature. Stefán makes attempts at reconciling himself with this role in life, but memories from his wandering years are also prominent, and the tension between the quiet life of the family man and the longings of the free poet are obvious. The meters are more traditional and the language less original. Stefán's third volume of poetry, *Heilög kirkja* (Holy church), published in 1924, is a long poem in *drápa* form (see p. 30) written to the Roman Catholic Church. *Helsingjar* (Barnacle geese) from 1927 was his last publication, evenly divided between religious and secular poems. Although Stefán was active throughout the 1920s, he will first and foremost be remembered for his first book of poems and the new spirit and language that it brought to Icelandic poetry.

In contrast to Stefán of Hvítadalur, Davíð Stefánsson (1895–1964) went on to become the most celebrated poet of his time and published five volumes of poetry during the years 1920–40. In many ways he became the last "national poet," his status sometimes resembling that of the great late romantics of the nineteenth century. His first books, however, stand as his most original contribution to Icelandic poetry. This does not least hold true for those works that deal with sexuality and death. In many of Stefánsson's poems sexuality and death are intrinsically linked, even to the extremes of cannibalism, as in "Abbalabbalá" (1919), which describes the savage and sensual creature called Abbalabbalá. These poems, which play on the themes of sex, death, and destruction, such as "Óráð" (1919; Fever), also often have an ironic side to them. Stefánsson's poetry is also characterized by a great intensity of emotion, and many poems have a woman as the narrator, usually a woman betrayed, bitter, even vindictive. These aspects have received growing critical attention during the last few years (see Albertsdóttir, "'Ég verð konungur djöflanna'").

The new romanticism of Davíð Stefánsson and Stefán of Hvítadalur became a model for young poets, and, during the first years of the 1920s, some followed in their footsteps with poetry in light meters, celebrating love and death, filled with melancholy and longing. Many of them published only one book of poetry and were soon forgotten; others only later found their own voice and developed their own style to become poets of merit in their own right. Among the disciples of the new romanticism was Sigurður Grímsson (1896–1975), who published his only volume of poetry, *Við langelda* (By the hearths), in 1922. Grímsson's poems were in no way different from those of many of his contemporaries, but one line from the poem "Gestur" (Guest) has secured him a place in literary history: "Mér fannst ég finna til," or "I thought I felt something" (*Við langelda*, 52). This line became a symbol for the poetry of his generation, sentimental and vague, and for the poets' posed and constructed descriptions of feelings and experiences based on poetic clichés and formulas rather than actual experience. The line became famous because of a 1922 review entitled "Við lang-

elda" in which Kristján Albertsson expressed the wish that Icelandic literature would rid itself of this "sentimental, whinging poetry, this false
sporting of emotion, all this I-thought-I-felt-something poetry" (170).
Among the young poets of this kind were two who went on to develop in
completely different poetic directions: Jóhannes úr Kötlum (1899–1972;
Jóhannes of Katlar), who published his first volumes of poetry in 1926 and
1929, and Tómas Guðmundsson (1901–1983), who published his first
book, *Við sundin blá* (By the blue channel), in 1925.

Not all poetry from the 1920s can be categorized as neoromantic imitation, however. Poets of the older generation were still active and carried on
the tradition of the nineteenth-century romantics, including Jakob Jóhannesson Smári (1889–1972) and Jón Þorkelsson (1859–1924), a literary historian and archivist who in 1923 published a voluminous book of poetry
mostly written in late medieval meters under the pseudonym Fornólfur
(the Ancient One). Others sought new forms in poetry or, like Þórbergur
Þórðarson, mocked the ruling neoromanticism.

Two more original poets who died at a young age should be mentioned as
the first potential modernists in Icelandic poetry. In 1922, Jón Thoroddsen
(1898–1924) published his only book, a slim volume of short prose pieces
that he called *Flugur* (Flies). Thoroddsen refrained from calling his texts
poems, although scholars have since not hesitated to call them *prose poems*.
Apart from Sigurður Nordal's *Hel* and a few other instances, for example, by
Thoroddsen's mother, Theodora Thoroddsen (1863–1954; see pp. 506,
525–26), prose poems were rare in Icelandic literature. Those published
before Thoroddsen's *Flugur* were mostly of a philosophical or religious
nature, their style accordingly formal and solemn. Although some pieces in
Thoroddsen's *Flugur* were also of a philosophical nature, others were more
unconventional in their use of everyday rhythms and subject matter. The
author's hesitation to call his texts *poems* is reflected in their seeming simplicity and lack of seriousness, but, nonetheless, the texts are ambitious, complex
under the surface, for instance, "Eftir dansleik" (After the dance):

Does he love me? she asked, and fixed her hair.
Does he love me? she asked, and hastily powdered her face.
Does he love me? she asked.
The mirror smiled.
Yes, said the mirror, and smiled. (*Flugur*, 35)

Love is Thoroddsen's most frequent subject, although in his poetry it is
always narcissistic, as in "Eftir dansleik": instead of the romantic love between two people comes a more modern notion of love for love's sake.
Modern man's preoccupation with love and sexuality is described in an

ironic fashion as love of oneself, rather than as a connecting force between people: "You do not love me, I said. You only love my love, but it only loves itself" ("Lauslæti" [Promiscuity]). Thoroddsen's irony also permeates his form and mode of expression. The poems in *Flugur* are more reflexive than most Icelandic poetry at the time, even metatextual, for instance, "Pan," which starts off thus: "The poem begins with the treetops nodding as if to acknowledge something that I don't understand" (*Flugur*, 72). Thoroddsen's poetry can be regarded as an instance of modernism that did not acquire its significance until long after his death, when in the 1950s the battle about form really began and modernism finally arrived in Iceland as a force to be reckoned with.

The same could be said about the work of Jóhann Jónsson (1896–1932), another forerunner of modernism in Icelandic literature, even though his poetry is radically different from that of Thoroddsen. His influence during his lifetime was no greater than Thoroddsen's, perhaps even less since he did not publish any of his poems in book form. (They were published posthumously by Halldór Laxness in 1952.) Despite this, he was well-known among writers and intellectuals and was considered the most promising poet of his generation. His fame is almost entirely based on one poem, "Söknuður" (Regret), which was published in the literary journal *Vaka* in 1928. "Söknuður" is a poem in free verse, rhetorical, and rich in imagery. Its beginning is striking, and is among the most famous lines of lyric poetry in Icelandic:

> Where have the days of your life lost their colour?
> And the poems which surged through your veins from dream to dream
> Where did they become the prey of weathers, oh child, who thought
>   yourself
> Born with wonderment's own
> Bottomless well in your breast.
> Where . . . ?
>
> At strange words like these, which some voice utters
> Upon our road — or as it seems,
> The wind blows through the streets,
> From us, the sleepwalkers of habit.
> (trans. Magnús Á. Árnason in Benedikz, ed., *Anthology of Icelandic
>   Poetry*, 120)

The poem was written in Germany in or around 1926, when German expressionism was in its final phase. Ingi Bogi Bogason finds several expressionistic features in the poem, such as its dynamic vocabulary, neologisms, and words used in unusual contexts as well as the speaker's longing for a new awakening for the "sleepwalkers of habit," whose days whither away in their alienated and mundane everyday lives (see Bogason, "Expressjónískir drættir í Söknuði").

On the whole one can say that, in Iceland, changes were slower to occur in poetry than in prose writing, at least until the 1940s and 1950s. This is partly due to the strong Icelandic tradition of alliteration and rhyme, which was not seriously challenged until Steinn Steinarr (Aðalsteinn Kristmundsson; 1908–58) arrived on the scene in the late 1930s. This is not to say that the currents that swept through Europe did not influence Icelandic poets, just that they did not emerge in modernized form in Icelandic poetry until later. One of the most prominent figures of Icelandic poetry during this period was Magnús Ásgeirsson (1901–55). He only ever published one volume of original poetry, *Síðkvöld* (Late evening), in 1923. The rest of his career he devoted to the translation of poetry, publishing his translations in six volumes in 1928–41. Modern Scandinavian poets such as Gustaf Fröding, Viktor Rydberg, and Pär Lagerkvist are most prominent here, but he also translated poems by Heine, Goethe, Tolstoy, Tennyson, and García Lorca, one of his most treasured translations being, in fact, of Lorca's "Lullaby."

The works of the high priests of modernism, such as Eliot and Pound, are rarely found among his translations, however. Indeed, Eliot's *The Waste Land* (1922) is one of the poems that Ásgeirsson gave up on. And, although Ásgeirsson was responsible for introducing Iceland to contemporary foreign poetry and was a great influence on and mentor to many poets of the younger generation, he may at the same time have played a part in delaying the arrival of modernism in Icelandic poetry. His methods of translation are dubious at times, not least his strict adherence to traditional form. Even poems that were originally written in free verse appear in the Icelandic as fully rhymed and alliterated stanzas in known meters. Thus, foreign poetry was familiarized in Ásgeirsson's translations, and, while this probably made it more readily accessible to the general reading public, it also stripped it of its more radical innovations, reinforcing instead the impression that the nature of poetry as such lay in its formal features, at least in Icelandic. Ásgeirsson himself defended his method in a note on his translation of a poem by Tolstoy in the first volume of his translations: "The poem is translated from a German translation by Fiedler. That translation uses the original meter, which is without rhyme, but, because Icelandic readers — luckily — do not appreciate that form of poetry, I choose to use rhyme in my translation" (Ásgeirsson, *Þýdd ljóð*, 90).

Although Ásgeirsson later used looser forms, he never abandoned the traditional form entirely. His justification for translating instead of writing original poetry was that it brought foreign poetry to young and aspiring poets, perhaps inspiring them to seek new modes of expression. His position was borne out when some of the poets who in the 1940s and 1950s revolutionized Icelandic poetry and even some of his contemporaries acknowledged their debt to his work. Nevertheless, Ásgeirsson's translations also had the reverse effect of confirming and strengthening the stronghold of the very tradition that these revolutionary poets fought against.

Magnús Ásgeirsson's translation project stands as an example of just how strong this tradition was. Differences of opinion on modernism or free verse in general are, of course, part of the literary history of most European countries in the twentieth century. However, as was the case with most cultural conflicts in twentieth-century Iceland, it is the added ingredient of nationalism that gives the poetic tradition its unusual strength and prolonged life span. In addition verse — not necessarily poetry — was traditionally not limited to literature as such but was a living part of everyday life and language in Iceland until well into the twentieth century.

Halldór Laxness published his one and only book of poetry in 1930 under the title *Kvæðakver* (Poems). It contained poems in diverse styles, traditional as well as ironic poems on nature and love, and poems inspired by surrealism and expressionism. Laxness's poems, like those of Jón Thoroddsen and Jóhann Jónsson, must be seen as isolated events in Icelandic literary history, experiments that, of course, were noted, and sometimes opposed, but that did not have a lasting impact on the evolution of poetry or poetic form as such. Some of the poems had been incorporated into Laxness's novels (e.g., *Vefarinn mikli frá Kasmír* and *Undir Helgahnúk*), and, indeed, the bulk of his poetry after 1930 springs from his novels and is written as the poetry and expression of the individual characters in them.

Laxness's poetic style is characterized by its mixture of high and low, somber lyric expressions alongside slang and everyday speech. Many of his poems have a novelistic quality to them. They form a part of the polyphony of voices that give scope and depth to his novels. The more experimental poems in *Kvæðakver*, such as "Rhodymenia Palmata" (the Latin name for Iceland moss), also share this quality. With the exception of "Unglíngurinn í skóginum" (The youth in the forest) all the poems in *Kvæðakver* are written in accordance with the Icelandic poetic tradition even though the meters are irregular. The subject matter and, in particular, the language, however, set these poems apart. The material symbols of modern life — motor cars, trains, and steamships — are the venues of Laxness's poems, even those that deal with traditionally nationalist topics such as Þingvellir (see his "Alþingishátíðin" [Celebration of the Althing]).

Two men stand side by side as the most influential poets of the 1930s, Tómas Guðmundsson, one of the last representatives of the old tradition of Icelandic poetry and a phenomenally popular poet, and Steinn Steinarr, the pioneer of modernism in Icelandic poetry and the godfather of the "atom poets" movement, which rose to prominence in the 1950s (see chapter 7). Politically as well as poetically, the two were opposites. Steinn Steinarr belonged to the new movement of socialist writers in the 1930s, although he was never active in the direct political struggle, while Guðmundsson was a moderate conservative whose poetry was almost completely apolitical. Despite this Guðmundsson and Steinn Steinarr also have a lot in common. In fact, Steinn Steinarr gave Guðmundsson a copy of *Rauður loginn brann*, his first book of poems, inscribed "thank you for the loan," implying that the style of his more traditional poems owed a lot to Guðmundsson's poetry (Karlsson, "Formáli," x).

As mentioned earlier Guðmundsson's first book of poetry belonged to a wave of poetry imitating that of Davíð Stefánsson and Stefán of Hvítadalur. It raised no hopes for the poet's future, and nothing suggested that his fate would be different from that of his young contemporaries, who published only a single book of poetry in their youth. This fate did not, however, await Guðmundsson, although the generation of poets who made their debut in the 1920s played a large part in his development. Instead of following the same path, he chose to make their fate and their short-lived careers as poets the subject of his poetry.

In 1933 Guðmundsson published his second book, *Fagra veröld* (Beauteous world), which contained thirty-six new poems. *Fagra veröld* marks a complete break with the sentimentalism of his first book and demonstrates that he had found a voice distinctly his own. Instead of the neoromanticism of his first book comes a new tone of lightness and nostalgic irony, as he describes his youth in Reykjavík and looks back on his and his friends' first attempts at living up to the image of being great poets and lovers. While the language of the poems in *Við sundin blá* resembled that of Guðmundsson's fellow poets at the time, high-strung and serious, the poems in *Fagra veröld* are written in a language closer to common, if very refined, speech. Kristján Karlsson considers Guðmundsson's main innovation in poetic language to be the importation of daily conservative speech into the realm of poetry while at the same time adapting romantic poetic language to the tone of spoken Icelandic (Karlsson, "Inngangur," xxxiii). Guðmundsson thus took the refinement of the traditional poetic form employed by the neoromantics one step further, using it to describe everyday phenomena in a lyric and crisp language, more adaptable to irony and sarcasm than their lofty speech and symbolism. Guðmundsson's poetry is humorous, paradox being his favorite trope. The use of irony, humor, and paradox often deepens the seemingly simple poems and saves Guðmundsson's nostalgic poems from sentimentality.

The attention to everyday life and detail is one of the hallmarks of Guðmundsson's poetry. The poet of *Fagra veröld* opens his eyes to his nearest surroundings, the streets of the city of Reykjavík, the harbor, and the newly built houses. He thus became the first Icelandic poet to sing the praises of the city. In the poems of *Fagra veröld* the city comes to life as a place of youthful exuberance and growth rather than a place of corruption and degradation, as had often been the case in earlier Icelandic literature. The lyricism and humor of the poems in *Fagra veröld* brought Guðmundsson instant success, and the book sold out and was reprinted twice in the year following its first edition, which was exceptional for a volume of poetry in Iceland. It was not least Guðmundsson's discovery of Reykjavík as a poetic space that secured him a large audience, not to mention praise from critics and the public alike. Guðmundsson was hailed as the poet of Reykjavík, and the municipal authorities awarded him a travel grant in order to make it possible for him to travel throughout Europe.

But, although Guðmundsson deserves to be considered the first poet of the young city of Reykjavík, his poetry is in no sense urban. Its dominant mode is one of nostalgia. The poems eulogize the days of youth and idleness, young love and comradeship among schoolboys. The city in Guðmundsson's poetry thus takes on an almost pastoral character, and the poet's praise of its streets and houses resembles descriptions by other poets of a lost innocence belonging to the countryside rather than to the modern city. The imagery does not belong to the modern city of asphalt, steel, glass, and concrete; it is organic and describes the city as a living being or a part of nature. From a strictly realistic point of view one could, of course, claim that Reykjavík was neither countryside nor modern city: its streets were muddy, its low houses were scattered, and it lacked anything resembling a plan. Therefore, like many a romantic poet before him, Guðmundsson looks past the city itself and reinvents it as a place of beauty past, surpassing even that of exotic palaces belonging to the emperor of China ("Í Vesturbænum" [In the West End]). The poems in *Fagra veröld* can be seen as a transference of nature to the city. In the poem called "Höfnin" (The harbor) we read: "The blood in your veins here surges most briskly, / O city, growing and young" (trans. Magnús Á. Árnason in Benedikz, ed., *Anthol-*

ogy of Icelandic Poetry, 124–25). Thus, Guðmundsson's praise of the city is not at the same time a praise of modernity, as was, for example, the case in European futurism or, indeed, in poetry in other Scandinavian literatures, such as the poems of Tom Kristensen and Emil Bønnelycke in Denmark.

Those critical of Guðmundsson's poetry, both at the time of the publication of *Fagra veröld* and later in his career, often deride him for his escapism, for not paying attention to his immediate surroundings but seeking refuge in the past instead. The socialist critic Kristinn E. Andrésson said, for instance, about Guðmundsson that his art was "distinctively unmodern, freed from serious morality or humanity, the unconditional worship of an unrealistic, even mystic poetic beauty" (Andrésson, "Tómas Guðmundsson," 195). Critique of this kind is, perhaps, not surprising when it is kept in mind that *Fagra veröld* was published in 1933, when the Depression had already hit Iceland and literature was turning more political. In 1930 Sigurður Einarsson (1898–1967) had published a volume of poetry called *Hamar og sigð* (Hammer and sickle), and another poet of Guðmundsson's generation, Jóhannes of Katlar, had abandoned the refined neoromanticism of his earlier books to emerge as a socialist poet and preacher during the early 1930s.

The other major figure in Icelandic poetry in the 1930s and 1940s also reacted to the Depression and to the demand for a political literature in a manner different from Guðmundsson — and perhaps not unexpectedly so considering the different backgrounds of the two. Tómas Guðmundsson came from a well-to-do family of farmers in the south of Iceland. He studied law, opened his own law firm for a few years, and after that held a secure job at the state Statistical Bureau. Steinn Steinarr, on the other hand, was of working-class origins from the west of Iceland. He moved to Reykjavík at the beginning of the 1930s and felt the Depression as harshly as other workers, possibly even more so. One of his arms was disabled, and he therefore had difficulty with manual labor, which was the only occupation open to him as he had received no formal education.

Steinn Steinarr published his first book of poetry, *Rauður loginn brann* (The red flame), in 1934. The title indicates the poems' political nature, and the atmosphere of the Depression and the turbulent times in Icelandic politics left their mark on the book. The bulk of the poems were politically radical in nature. The book begins with a salute to the proletarian youth and contains poems on the poor conditions of workers as well as lighter verse in the style of Tómas Guðmundsson on everyday events as well as short poems in praise of women. But, even though Steinn Steinarr acknowledged his debt to Guðmundsson, it was not these poems, or, indeed, the inspired political poems, that were to mark him as the most influential poet of the 1930s and 1940s. *Rauður loginn brann* also contained some poems in free verse with a symbolic and existential dimension, making them most unusual for the time. This turn in Steinn Steinarr's poetry seems even more radical and unexpected if one keeps in mind that in the 1930s his fellow socialists had become very conservative in their poetic tastes even though the discovery of new forms and new modes of expression had been on their agenda only a few years earlier (Ólafsson, *Rauðu pennarnir*, 119–29). Even the leaders of the modernist experiments of the 1920s had abandoned modernism as it did not contribute anything to the struggle at hand.

An example of this is a review written by Halldór Laxness about a book of poetry by Guðmundur Böðvarsson (1904–74), a poet and farmer who participated in the movement of the Red Pens and had received much praise for his first book of poetry, the 1936 *Kyssti mig sól* (The sun kissed me). In his first two books Böðvarsson experimented with the poetic form and the existentialism that later were to dominate Steinn Steinarr's poetry. Laxness's review is of Böðvarsson's second book, *Hin hvítu skip* (1939; The white ships):

> Good poetry has never been written in Icelandic except in an exact form; any deviations or surrender of the strict form results in its dissolving and corruption. Lesser poets who did not master alliteration have done much to confuse the Icelandic poetic sensibility, both with the kind of ridiculous prose they call *free verse*, or the irregular use of verse feet and rhymes (corresponding lines in the same stanza of unequal length or an unequal number of lines in the stanzas of the same poem and such), and especially with the special invention of putting a dash in the middle of a poem when they have lost the thread and no longer know where they are going or what they were about to say. ("Stuttar ádrepur," 30–32)

Laxness's views were shared by many, conservatives and socialists alike, and they seem to have had the desired effect, for Böðvarsson did not attempt any similar formal experiments until decades later.

This reactionary view of poetry did not, however, stop Steinn Steinarr. In his second book, *Ljóð* (Poems), published in 1937, modernist, existentialist poetry dominates, and Steinn Steinarr emerges as a poet with his own peculiar and highly personal style. Before Steinn Steinarr, experiments in free verse had been few and had left no lasting impact on other poets or on the very definition of poetry in Iceland. It would be only a slight simplification to say that in the minds of many Icelanders during the first half of the twentieth century—and this applies to parts of the intelligentsia as well as to the general public—poetry was still synonymous with strict poetic form, rhyme, and alliteration. Steinn Steinarr's deviations from this tradition are, therefore, more radical than may seem to be the case from a twenty-first-century point of view. Although some poets had experimented with free verse, none had published a book of poetry where the majority of the poems were written in free form or took certain liberties with the rules of Icelandic meter. The title of Steinn Steinarr's second book of poetry could, therefore, be read as a provocation: unlike Jón Thoroddsen, who hesitated to call the texts in his *Flugur poems*, with the title *Ljóð* Steinn Steinarr unabashedly claims the right for these texts to be called *poetry*, no matter what their form.

As radical as Steinn Steinarr's use of form may have been, however, it was to no lesser extent the content of the poems and his methodology that set him apart from other Icelandic poets at the time. The label *philosophical poet* soon stuck to Steinn Steinarr, but critics and scholars have had a hard time defining his philosophy, or, indeed, comprehending it. Kristján Karlsson even claimed: "Steinn Steinarr became a philosophical poet, and his originality and his genius can be attributed to the philosophy of his poetry. Having said that does not mean that this philosophy is good or right; when we attempt to decipher it with logic, it turns out to be simple statements: when we want to open the shell of the poems to get to the philosophical core, it turns out to be the shell itself" ("Formáli," xii).

This commentary is a paradox worthy of Steinn Steinarr himself: the philosophy is at the core of his writing, while this core is nothing but the writing itself. Karlsson's comment could be read as an allusion to the conclusion of many of Steinn Steinarr's poems, for instance, "Ekkert" (Nothing) from *Ljóð*:

You stare into the darkness
And whisper:
Who are you?
And a hollow voice answers:
Nothing, nothing. (*Kvæðasafn og greinar*, 50)

Steinn Steinarr's contemporaries called his philosophical stance nihilistic (Aðalsteinsdóttir 1981), and Karlsson comes to the conclusion that it is "apathy, yes, but first and foremost a form of homemade self-centrism" ("Steinn Steinarr," 80). Scholars have since argued for Steinn Steinarr's close ties to existentialism, ties that Karlsson rules out, along with ties to other established philosophies, on the grounds of the poet's lack of formal education.

Steinn Steinarr is the first Icelandic poet to voice the anxiety and uncertainty often associated with European modernity, where the very existence of the self is subject to doubt. This finds expression in the poem "Svartlist" (Black art), published in *Spor í sandi* (Traces in the sand) from 1940: "And did you know, that you do not exist, / and what you see, are shadows of the past" (*Kvæðasafn og greinar*, 104). The sense of nothingness and the anxiety that follows from it become the very essence of many of Steinn Steinarr's poems, to the extent that the anxiety and the alienation that the poet feels become one with life itself. Like Tómas Guðmundsson, Steinn Steinarr used paradox to great effect, but to a more philosophical end. His paradoxes depict life and being in the world as an almost entirely futile and impossible project: "See! I bring you, loyal and faithful / nothingness: Life itself" ("Vöggugjöf," in *Kvæðasafn og greinar*, 77). Thus, life itself is without meaning, and man must either accept it or perish. He must himself create his life and his being. This is the freedom that he is doomed to, as the high priest of twentieth-century existentialism, Jean-Paul Sartre, put it: to create his life in a world without meaning. However, even this project at times seems hopeless in Steinn Steinarr's poetry.

CONCLUSION

In the period from the end of the First World War to the beginning of the Second, Icelandic literature underwent certain drastic changes, and its traditions and conventions came to be seriously challenged. In older accounts of literary history the first part of the period is referred to as a melting pot or even as a time characterized, as Andrésson put it, mainly by "a total lack of form, a complete chaos" (*Íslenskar nútímabókmenntir*, 33). Andrésson's evaluation of the period is marked by his own cultural politics, which sees the 1930s as a new beginning, the emergence of a socialist literature, mainly in the works of Halldór Laxness, but also in the poetry of Jóhannes of Katlar and Steinn Steinarr.

But what Andrésson saw as a period marked by lack of form and chaos has since become the most debated and significant decade of twentieth-century Icelandic literature, a period when the first attempts at creating a thoroughly modern literature made themselves felt. The first modernist works of Halldór Laxness, Þórbergur Þórðarson, and others did not, however, trigger a modernist tradition in Iceland immediately or establish a paradigm of modernism strong enough to challenge the reigning mode of realism and socially engaged literature. In particular Laxness's works of the 1930s had, in fact, the reverse effect, establishing the realist novel as the primary literary genre in Iceland, yet at the same time renewing its premises, both ideological and aesthetic. The one thread connecting his experimental uproar in the 1920s with his great realist works in the 1930s is that of the dialogue that he establishes between native tradition and history, on the one hand, and the tradition of European culture and the European novel in particular, on the other. Seen from this perspective the "cultural revolution" of the 1920s was, indeed, the beginning of the modernization of Icelandic literature.

It has been argued here that the 1930s mark the beginning of the institutionalization of Halldór Laxness and his works in Icelandic cultural and literary life. The political polarization of the literary community in the 1930s was to become the basis of Icelandic cultural life for decades and would be intensified during the cold war years following the Second World War.

It is an established cliché in Icelandic literature that a whole generation of writers after this period lived and wrote in Laxness's shadow. To some degree this holds true, and the dominance of Halldór Laxness in Icelandic literary life is not merely a fabrication and simplification of later literary historians and other literary gatekeepers. It plays a significant role in the self-understanding of critics and writers of the period, as well as in our understanding of the premises they wrote from.

In poetry the period witnessed some of the high points of the native tradition, which had remained fundamentally unchanged for centuries, incorporating new modes of expression and poetic styles into the strict forms of Icelandic meter. But it also witnessed the first signs of innovation, which indicated a coming revolution in Icelandic poetry and caused a serious split in the literary community that would manifest itself in the controversy surrounding poetic form of the 1940s and 1950s.

Icelandic Prose Literature, 1940–2000

Ástráður Eysteinsson and Úlfhildur Dagsdóttir

6

Icelandic Prose Literature, 1940–1980: *Ástráður Eysteinsson*

THE BELLS OF LAXNESS

In terms of the historical development of formal and generic qualities, Icelandic prose literature underwent no paradigmatic shift in the 1940s. Realism remained the dominant mode of representation in both the novel and the short story, often with a strong but rationalized neoromantic undercurrent.

This is not to say that Icelandic fiction as a whole had become stagnant. For one thing history itself provided it with no stable ground on which to foster such complacency. If one had to choose a single most dramatic day in the history of Iceland in the twentieth century, it would, in fact, be a day on the eve of this decade. On 10 May 1940 the British armed forces landed in Reykjavík in order to occupy, first, the capital and, later, the whole country to prevent it from being seized by Nazi Germany. In 1941 the Americans replaced the British.

The presence of a major foreign power in Iceland had enormous consequences for a nation that numbered roughly 120,000 inhabitants and had been going through a decade of dire economic straits and unemployment. Within a very few years Iceland experienced a veritable boom. War brought economic prosperity to the country, and tremendous changes either started taking place or were greatly accelerated in terms of technology, urbanization, and culture, in both the public and the private sphere. After a gradual modernization in the first decades of the century, Iceland now ineluctably entered the modern age with what seemed to be a single leap. These changes were most obvious in Reykjavík, which rapidly grew from a provincial town into a (small) city that had to serve the ever more widely reaching functions of a capital and a vital cultural and economic center. There was large-scale migration of both individuals and families from the rural areas to Reykjavík.

The war also accelerated the final severance of Iceland from the Danish crown, and the nation's independence was officially declared and celebrated at Þingvellir, the ancient site of the Althing (the parliament), on 17 June 1944, while Denmark was still under German control. But, while the nation had become independent, the country was still occupied by a foreign army, and the whole question of Iceland's authenticity and integrity as a nation among other nations was to be a vital issue for years to come. It was a question with strong ties to the past: to the consolidation of Icelandic national identity around the ancient literary heritage and to the nineteenth-century struggle for independence, which, in turn, seemed inextricably bound to the rural community that had preserved the nation's language and literature. So, while Icelandic culture and society had suddenly and anxiously arrived at a crossroads, it is hardly surprising that its writers should seek to come to terms with Icelandic history and tradition.

This is amply illustrated in Halldór Kiljan Laxness's three-volume *Íslandsklukkan* (1943–46; English trans.: *Iceland's Bell* [2003]), which is probably the most significant novel of the 1940s. It is a historical novel, set in the late seventeenth century, intricately stitched together with threads that link together three main characters: a poor peasant who is sentenced to death for killing the king's henchman; his protector, one Arnas Arnæus, a figure based on the great Icelandic philologist and manuscript collector Árni Magnússon (see p. 198); and the woman whose love Arnas betrays in order to devote himself to saving the manuscripts of the Old Norse sagas, poetry, and mythology. For Arnas, the only role of his bereaved nation is "að leggja sína sögu á minnið til betri tíða" (being mindful of one's history until better times; Laxness, *Íslandsklukkan*, 362). With the web formed by the life of these three people Laxness richly portrays the predicament of a class-divided society under ruthless Danish post-Reformation usurpation. He explores its search for meaning, both through its literary heritage and through its elusive struggle for justice and for justification of Iceland's existence as a nation in its own right. The novel itself constitutes a historical quest, aiming to prove that "being mindful of one's history" is a crucial element in bringing about "better times," for the novel has a not-so-hidden message for its contemporary readers, who had just achieved independence from Denmark but now had to cope with the presence of a world super-power on the island.

In this respect, Laxness was still very much a political writer and the preeminent author of the Red Pens (Rauðu pennarnir; see also p. 380), a group that remained the most important center of literary activity and debate in Iceland and effected a literary continuity from the 1930s into the 1940s. Even though the writers who formed the group were by no means engaged in a uniform sociorealist aesthetics, they were a major force in Iceland's literary life at the time, for instance, in consolidating around the Mál og menning (Language and culture) publishing company, headed by the literary scholar Kristinn E. Andrésson.

By the mid-1940s, however, Laxness had become, not only one of Iceland's most prolific writers, but also, to some extent, an institution in his own right. He attained this centrality most obviously through his career as a novelist — which, in retrospect, may seem to form a master narrative in the history of the Icelandic novel from the 1920s into the 1960s, reaching its epitome with his being awarded the Nobel Prize in 1955. But it also rests on his other activities: his numerous essays and articles on literature, culture, and politics; his translations; and his pioneer editions of five Old Icelandic sagas with modernized spelling, a populist endeavor that caused great uproar among those who wanted to preserve the "purity" of the ancient texts, which the Icelandic public was expected to understand and revere as they had been handed down. For Laxness, however, this was a significant part of a crusade that aimed to revitalize a nation's sensitivity to its tradition, identity, and a historical destiny that had been articulated and preserved in its literary heritage.

As a result Laxness became more than the "head" of the Icelandic novel. In the decades to come he grew to be a champion of a national epic identity circumscribed by history and by a vigorous realist narrative, which had to stave off the influence of modernist tendencies, such as were to be found in Laxness's own first major novel, *Vefarinn mikli frá Kasmír* (1927; The great weaver of Kashmir; see pp. 371–74). The prose writers of Iceland had long been living in the shadow of the saga tradition — now they had to face a literary craftsman who managed to draw energy from this tradition, in fact thrive on it, while re-creating realist narrative on his own terms. And for many of them there was nothing for it but to live in the shadow of Laxness.

Laxness's success in revitalizing epic realism stems not only from the way in which he taps energy from the saga tradition, however. He is also extremely versatile in adapting and reworking a broad stylistic and historical spectrum of the Icelandic language. *Íslandsklukkan* is, in part, a work in the romantic vein, especially in its depiction of Icelandic nature, which is magnificently woven into the narrative and the characterization. Laxness was striving to become a "poet of the Icelandic consciousness" ("Um Jónas

Hallgrímsson," 57), as he himself once said about the nineteenth-century romantic poet Jónas Hallgrímsson.

This consciousness — which, strictly speaking, may not exist in any unified form — and the language used to express it were steeped in a long history of rural existence close to nature. This historical continuity was an obvious source of material and human experience for the Icelandic novelist as the genre developed from its modest early days in the nineteenth century and into the twentieth. Even the changes brought about by the Second World War did not immediately disrupt this continuity. Laxness's main contribution to it was perhaps his translation of Gunnar Gunnarsson's *Fjallkirkjan* (1941–43; The church on the mountain; see also pp. 375–77), a five-volume autobiographical novel written in Danish in the 1920s. Even though some of his other novels had already been translated into Icelandic, the translation of *Fjallkirkjan* claimed for Gunnarsson a place as a major novelist in the Icelandic language. At the same time the Icelandic version confirms and elaborates the manifestations of Icelandic national identity in a prose discourse that often combines realistic and (neo)romantic features in its portrayal of Icelandic nature and Icelandic rural communities.

RURAL FICTION, REALISM, AND TRANSLATION

Among somewhat younger writers the two most committed to the depiction of the early twentieth-century rural community both grew up in the countryside of southern Iceland. In an entire sequence of novels, the best known of which is *Á bökkum Bolafljóts* (1940; On the banks of Bull River), Guðmundur Daníelsson (1910–90) describes affairs and entanglements on the farms and in the villages of the southern lowlands. He paints a brisk picture of the landscape, the changing seasons, and the often limited environment that his characters move through and sometimes outgrow. The realistic layout of his novels often barely contains their romantic disposition, which in itself is somewhat contradictory, swinging as it does from a raw primitivism, for instance, in sexual relations, to sentimental and melodramatic attitudes. The emotional life of his novels is acted out at a level that sometimes relates only weakly to their social context, even though private life is shown to clash with public opinion and love affairs with local aggregation of power. The reason may be that the author is injecting the somewhat bewildered moral perspectives of the age into the classical realism of rural narrative. This becomes more apparent in some of his later work, for instance, in the novel *Blindingsleikur* (1955; Blindman's buff), when he seeks to embed existential symbolism in his traditional narrative.

Hence, despite its narrative exuberance his work may be seen to signal a crisis in the rural novel, which is finding it ever more difficult to resign itself to its former space. The genre's inclination to cultural exploration is, perhaps, hampered by traditional perceptions of rural life.

This crisis also resides in the novels of the other "southern" writer, Ólafur Jóhann Sigurðsson (1918–88), even though it is tempered by his finely balanced and polished prose style. In the novel *Fjallið og draumurinn* (1944; The mountain and the dream) and its sequel, *Vorköld jörð* (1950; Spring-cold earth), Sigurðsson describes the struggles and dreams of a peasant family in the early decades of the century. His nuanced and lyric language is perfectly in tune with the closeness to the soil and to nature that characterize this life. But, while this world is very much the source of the moral and social values that guide the author's pen here and for the rest of his career, there is also a sense that the honest struggle for existence is in vain. It seems that, if the family in *Vorköld jörð* is to survive on the farm, the farmer must suppress all his dreams and, significantly, his poetic inclination. Hence, while Sigurðsson re-creates a world of the past, painting it in nostalgic colors, he resists the urge to present it as an idealized way of life. The main alternative, however, appears to be the debased society of the town where the farmers trade, a "fallen" place in terms of life and language. It is interesting to note, in this context, that, in what was becoming a central concern of the Icelandic novel, the sociocultural opposition between urban and rural life, with the farmstead and Reykjavík as the ultimate polar opposites, the smaller towns and villages can fall on either side of the structural dichotomy. This is partly because this dualism could be historically traced to the cultural issues of the struggle for independence, in which the farms and the countryside had been instrumental in preserving the Icelandic language and an "authentic" way of life, as opposed to the towns and trade centers, which were "contaminated" by a Danish presence.

It is testimony to the fact that literature is never an immediate reflection of society that, while fishing had become increasingly vital to Icelandic society, few novelists sought to capture on a broad scale the life of the fishing villages. A noteworthy exception to this are four novels by Vilhjálmur S. Vilhjálmsson (1903–66), published 1945–51, later reissued in one volume entitled *Brimar við Bölklett* (1963; The surf at Calamity Cliff), a broad epic realistically describing the life and class struggles in a seaside village. It is one of the clearest Icelandic examples of proletarian or working-class literature.

The 1940s were the last decade to see an uninhibited flourishing of the realist narrative in Icelandic prose fiction. There were as yet few signs of its interaction with the tradition of the European novel, which may partly

explain why its epic and historical mentality and its plot were rarely thick-
ened by psychological complexity, even though such narrative layering may
emerge through the imagery used in portraying nature. In fact, psychological depth is a more significant feature in the short story, in which authors
like Halldór Stefánsson (1892–1979) had shown that it was not incompat-
ible with a realist story line. This is further demonstrated in the 1940s by
Ólafur Jóhann Sigurðsson's short stories, which, while modest on the surface, explore less charted regions than his novels.

But it would seem, at least from one perspective, that by the 1940s
Icelandic fiction could no longer avoid intercourse with the European or
the American novel. What has been emphasized so far is the prevalent
supremacy of realism and the rural novel and the distinctive canonization of
Halldór Laxness (1902–98), although this was, of course, not fully established until somewhat later. In retrospect it may seem that Laxness is *the*
shaping force of this period in Icelandic fiction, but we are bound to shift
our focus if we inquire into the book market of the time: what was being
read? The first answer that publication figures give us is translations of
European and American novels.

Translated fiction had, in fact, been the largest component of Icelandic
book production throughout the early part of the century. But, when the
book market suddenly expanded with the economic boom of the war years,
the increase was most obvious in the area of translation. In the 1940s more
than 700 translated novels and short story volumes were published in Iceland (almost three times more than in the 1930s), as opposed to roughly
240 "original" volumes of prose fiction. A large part of this translation
output consists of popular literature — thrillers, romances, adventure stories. It is a characteristic of modern literary life in Iceland that, aside from a
tradition of rural romance novels, its popular needs in the realm of fiction
have been predominantly catered to by translations. Until late into the
twentieth century it was an exception to see, for instance, a thriller or a
detective novel written by a native author, while the occasional contemporary Icelandic (urban) romance novel lives very much in the shadow of its
translated cousin.

However, the translation boom of the 1940s also included Icelandic
versions of numerous works by leading fiction writers on both sides of the
Atlantic. Readers now had access to important nineteenth-century writers
in Icelandic, such as Victor Hugo, Leo Tolstoy, Mark Twain, Charles Dickens, and the Brontë sisters. Of twentieth-century authors, aside from individual cases like Erich Maria Remarque and Romain Rolland, two categories are conspicuous: American novelists, in particular John Steinbeck,
Ernest Hemingway, Pearl S. Buck, and Jack London; and the major Scan-

dinavian novelists of the early twentieth century, Alexander Kielland, F. E. Sillanpää, Selma Lagerlöf, Sigrid Undset, Martin Andersen Nexø, Hans Kirk, Knut Hamsun, and, last but not least, Gunnar Gunnarsson.

It is impossible to present in a nutshell any kind of coherent picture of the Icelandic translators involved in this linguistic and cultural transfer. Some were well-known novelists, for instance Halldór Laxness and Guðmundur G. Hagalín (1898–1985). Magnús Ásgeirsson (1901–55) is renowned as Iceland's leading poetry translator of the midcentury, but he was also a significant translator of prose. Some received primary recognition, against all odds, as translators of novels, in particular, Jón Sigurðsson of Kaldaðarnes (1886–1957), who translated five novels by Hamsun; Stefán Bjarman (1894–1974), who translated Hemingway and Steinbeck; and Karl Ísfeld (1906–60), who translated Émile Zola, Hemingway, and Jaroslav Hasek.

What can be deduced, however, is that, while this translation activity introduced several important prose writers to an Icelandic readership, it did not promote any radical shift in the relation between fiction, language, and the reader in Iceland. In an expanding book market it served, rather, to anchor realist discourse in the various branches of fiction at a time when Iceland was coming into ever closer contact with the rest of the Western world. This is not to say that translation was limited to a servile position — since there were, within existing boundaries, unoccupied areas that were, perhaps, "defined" by, for instance, translations of Hamsun or Steinbeck — but its function in the world of fiction consisted very much of securing and nourishing the discourse of realism. An outside observer can hardly fail to notice the conspicuous absence of the modernist novel, which earlier in the century had unsettled existing correlations in American and European fiction. Hemingway's novels are about the closest we get to modernism, and Hemingway has, in fact, been judged the chief source of foreign influence on some Icelandic writers — but significantly only writers who continued working in the realist mode. And, while Flaubert's *Madame Bovary* (1857) — which many see as a nineteenth-century precursor to the modernist novel — was translated into Icelandic in 1947, it was stripped of some of the passages that "obstruct" its narrative unfolding of events; the abridged Icelandic version from 1947 is, therefore, very much a realist translation.

URBAN FICTION, BIOGRAPHICAL WRITINGS, COUNTRYSIDE

It seems likely that one of the reasons for the late arrival of modernism in Iceland (aside from individual experiments during the first half of the century) is the absence of the modern urban experience so often associated with modernist literature and art. This is not to say that there was no urban fiction. Reykjavík life had been the source of Einar Kvaran's novels in the early years of the century, while in several novels from the 1930s to the 1950s Þórunn Elfa Magnúsdóttir (1910–95) comes to terms with the social environment in Reykjavík during a transitional period, paying attention to class tensions, morals and manners, material and marital struggles, and the position of women. Her novel *Snorrabraut 7* (1947; 7 Snorri Street) reveals how the prosperity of the war years involved its share of misery: housing problems; shortages of various goods; economic anxieties; corruption; and the upheaval of traditional values.

It was Halldór Laxness, however, who in the following year brought out what many readers and critics gradually came to think of as the exemplary Reykjavík novel. Ugla, the protagonist of *Atómstöðin* (1948; English trans.: *The Atom Station* [1961]), is a farmer's daughter who views with fresh eyes the new bourgeois lifestyle in the city along with its political intrigues, in particular as regards Iceland's newly won independence as it relates to the emerging ties with the United States and the American military presence on the island. *Atómstöðin* has been a hotly debated political work, but it is also a novel that in some respects deviates from the realism of Icelandic social fiction. There are absurdist traits in its characterization, especially when it moves into the strange, subcultural realm of an organist who becomes Ugla's Taoist mentor.

Against the background of a solidly realist discourse, unruffled by modernist aesthetics, Laxness's novel actually appears quite experimental, but its experiments are reigned in by the work's social outlook. The same holds true for another city novel that followed in the wake of *Atómstöðin*, Elías Mar's (b. 1924) *Vögguvísa* (1950; Lullaby), which renders teenage experiences in contemporary Reykjavík by registering its street life and its new slang and even by probing the thoughts of a character in a stream-of-consciousness fashion. But in this novel, as well as in the subsequent *Sóleyjarsaga* I–II (1954, 1959; Sóley's story), Elías Mar's method is largely traditional, driven by a desire to let Reykjavík life, and the life of his central characters, reflect the predicament of Icelandic social life in a new and hazardous world.

It is far more difficult for the reader to make such links in Jóhann Pétursson's (b. 1918) first and only novel, *Gresjur guðdómsins* (1948; Divine meadows). It is a Reykjavík novel, but one in which the locale is often like a mirage of the tormented narrator, whose emotional and intellectual life has drifted off its social moorings. In many ways it is very much in line with contemporary European existentialism, full of nausea, paranoia, hallucination, isolation, and a search for meaning, fleshed out in a loose, often untidy narrative that seems to be governed only by the narrator's states of mind. In postwar Iceland Pétursson's novel seems to have fallen into a void, and its groundbreaking aspects have never really been recognized. In some ways it appears as a "negative" signpost, showing us that Icelandic literary life was not yet ripe for such antirealist novels or for such a subversive portrayal of the urban experience.

Meanwhile, the traditional structure of the novel was being more successfully challenged by experiments in another genre. In the 1920s and 1930s Þórbergur Þórðarson (1888–1974) had written radical works that are difficult to place within any clear genres and that even seriously challenge the traditional boundaries of literature (see also pp. 368–71). His jubilant reception of Theodór Friðriksson's (1876–1948) *Í verum* (1941; Fishing station) bears testimony to his appreciation of the resources of conventional (auto)biography and its potential to serve as a chronicle of an individual's struggle with society and the elements. In its vision and expression of life, however, (auto)biography seemed inevitably to play second fiddle to the novel. This is what Þórðarson continues to repudiate in the 1940s and 1950s as he keeps radicalizing the genre and creating an extraordinary alternative to the novel in Icelandic prose literature. From 1945 to 1950 he recorded a massive six-volume biography of the contemporary but already legendary pastor Árni Þórarinsson that was published as *Æfisaga Árna prófasts Þórarinssonar* (The biography of Pastor Árni Þórarinsson). It is a remarkable collaboration between writer and subject, showing "life" to be more of an open form than a coherent narrative, taking the reader along all kinds of byways and eccentric detours. It is an uninhibited recital, ranging freely from the quirkily personal to the sublime, unabashedly incorporating gossip and fabulation as well as meticulous description of social affairs.

Þórðarson's next major work is also in a sense a collaborative biographical effort, even more unusual than the pastor's chronicle — indeed, a project that took most readers by complete surprise. *Sálmurinn um blómið* (1954–55; The hymn about the flower) is a two-volume account of a few years in the life of a little girl and of her friendship with the aging writer, who lives in the same apartment building and to some extent adapts her point of view as they discuss everything from everyday occurrences to the Korean War. This method gives Þórðarson the freedom to relate whatever musings or stories come his way and to re-view the world from the fresh perspective of childhood.

His interest in childhood next led Þórðarson to write the story of his own growing up on a farm in the southeast of Iceland. It is an imaginative portrayal of how a young mind comes to grips with the world around him, a world that is described in ethnographic and even scientific detail. The first three volumes appeared 1956–58, but the author, probably disheartened by their unenthusiastic reception, did not finish the fourth volume. It was published posthumously as part of the one-volume edition *Í Suðursveit* (1975; In Suðursveit District).

By the 1950s Þórðarson was already acknowledged as one of Iceland's major prose writers. But he was seen as a very special case; while highly regarded, his work did not serve as the defining center of a literary system in the way that Laxness's novels did. Even his herculean effort in the area of (auto)biography, demonstrating the innovative potential of the genre, had hardly any effect on mainstream writing in the field of biography and memoirs. This field was not void of talent — Guðmundur G. Hagalín and Vilhjálmur S. Vilhjálmsson wrote several biographies during the 1930s — but it was growing rapidly into the industry that it was to become from the 1960s on, few writers seeing it as a means of innovative expression.

In the 1950s biographies and memoirs were probably second only to the rural romance novel as a homegrown brand of popular literature in Iceland (as opposed to the translations already discussed). And there is a link between these genres. The biographical subject had almost invariably grown up in the countryside in turn-of-the-century Iceland. The narrative world, not least when observed through the mirror of childhood, tended to be pastoral in nature, and this would also determine its view of present society. Rural existence was a solidly coded way of life, and as such it continued to regulate socially symbolic narrative — even for those who by now were leading urban lives, for they had not accepted a new code in the domain of narrative representation. It is for this reason, and not just pure nostalgia, that the rural novel continued to thrive in the 1940s and 1950s and even into the 1960s. Its prominent authors were Elínborg Lárusdóttir (1891–1973), Jón Björnsson (1907–94), Guðmundur Friðfinnsson (1905–2004), and not least Guðrún of Lundur (1887–1973), whose *Dalalíf* I–V (1946–51; Life in the valleys) was one of the most popular novels in postwar Iceland (see p. 529). Also, several older rural novels were reissued during this period, such as those of Jón Mýrdal (1825–1899); in fact, a number of his unpublished manuscripts saw print for the first time in the late 1950s and early 1960s.

FROM COUNTRY TO CITY

However, the popularity of the rural novel should not obscure the fact that, insofar as Icelandic prose writers were engaged with contemporary issues, their preeminent concern was precisely the change from rural life to an urban existence, a change that was, moreover, strongly affected by the new foreign (American) presence. The move from the old family farm to city life in Reykjavík becomes a symbolic road in fiction, traveled by dozens of characters emerging from the countryside to face the modern world. This journey forms a pattern in several Reykjavík novels, such as Laxness's *Atóm-stöðin*, in which an inexperienced country girl is thrown into the turbulent action of city life, class tensions, and fateful political decisions. A broader picture of a girl growing up in the country and then going to live in Reykja-vík is presented in Ragnheiður Jónsdóttir's (1895–1967) novel quartet *Úr minnisblöðum Þóru frá Hvammi* (1954–64; From the notebooks of Þóra of Hvammur). This is a bildungsroman; in it the life of Þóra from childhood to middle age, often related with psychological nuances unusual in Icelandic realist novels, is also the story of how Icelandic society is changing, how it is affected by occupation by a foreign army, and how a woman struggles to acquire an education and a space for herself in a world of new opportunities and new threats.

More characteristically, however, these changes were reflected in the character of a young man, and some critics see them most clearly spelled out in the novels of Indriði G. Þorsteinsson (1926–2000). In *Land og synir* (1963; Land and sons) Þorsteinsson tells the story of a farmer's son who decides that it is not worthwhile to struggle on at the farm and leaves to find a new life for himself. Þorsteinsson's earlier novel, *79 af stöðinni* (1955; Taxi 79), had already demonstrated how hard it was for a country boy to form urban roots. Its protagonist's desperate attempt to return "home" results in what appears to be a fatal car crash. Interestingly enough, what is possibly Þorsteinsson's most successful work, *Þjófur í paradís* (1967; Thief in paradise), is a rural novella in which the paradise of the rural community is disrupted by the arrest and exposure of a thieving farmer. Here, the author's terse style is well balanced by the atmosphere and the irony of the whole affair. This is much less the case in *Norðan við stríð* (1971; English trans.: *North of War* [1981]), in which Þorsteinsson returns to the historical dislocations of midcentury, this time describing the occupation of an Icelandic town during the war. Much of the novel is concerned with the so-called *ástand* (situation), a term used to signify the relationships between foreign soldiers and local women (sometimes married ones). The foreign superpower is endowed with fabulous potency, leaving the Icelandic male sexually wounded and searching for substitute power in new commercial options. Seen from Þorsteinsson's perspective, the historical upheaval of midcentury is very much an unmanning of traditional Icelandic society.

In some sense this also holds true for Ólafur Jóhann Sigurðsson, who in the 1950s took leave of the rural novel and wrote *Gangvirkið* (1955; Clockwork), the first part of a trilogy depicting Reykjavík life in the 1940s (the other parts came much later: *Seiður og hélog* [Magic and will-o'-the-wisp] in 1977 and *Drekar og smáfuglar* [Dragons and small birds] in 1983). The young protagonist, a journalist by the name of Páll Jónsson, is in many ways the author's emissary, an innocent and honest man who was raised on his grandmother's rural wisdom in a distant and quiet part of the country. But he is also a strangely passive and colorless observer who is stunned by his urban experiences and can only store them for future ruminations, and as a character he hardly bears the great weight allotted him.

While Sigurðsson had shifted his focus from rural to urban Iceland, it is obvious that the values that continued to guide his writing—quiet dignity, reverence for tradition, simple integrity, and honest work—stem from the rural community, and he sees them as being undermined by urban modernity. This disposition, as we see in the novel *Hreiðrið* (1972; The nest), could even lead this modest humanist into shrill attacks on anything he saw as modern and corrupted, for instance, literary modernism. It is doubtful whether his characterization and his style—attuned to describing the contours of nature and the countryside—always managed to come to terms with the urban world; in many ways he continued writing within a rural discourse. So, while Sigurðsson remains a prominent literary chronicler of life in midcentury Reykjavík, his perspective is in some ways that of an outsider from the past.

However, we are hard-pressed to try and find a novelist who successfully explored the cultural dislocations from *inside* the urban world and recreated the city as a living organism within an urban discourse. Young novelists who had grown up with the city, especially Elías Mar, but also Agnar Þórðarson (1917–2006) and Jökull Jakobsson (1933–78), sought to come to terms with different facets of the modern experience, but their frame of reference and experience was often weak—perhaps because they could not fall back on a cultural tradition of city life. As a result, the city, as a realist background, would sometimes appear as a mistake, a fallen place where young people lose their way. Even in the works of younger writers life in the countryside often remained a positive and sometimes romantic antithesis to life in the city. And so, while Reykjavík was becoming more and more important as a political and cultural center of the nation as well as its point of contact with the outside world, the modern capital failed to become, as one might have expected, the central locus of the Icelandic novel. This remained the case until the 1970s and can be seen as one of the characteristics of the history of the novel in Iceland.

This is not to say that novelists who did not deal with life in the capital necessarily failed to meet the challenge of modernity. Jóhannes úr Kötlum (1899–1972; Jóhannes of Katlar), best known for his poetry, wrote a trilogy of novels — *Dauðsmannsey* (1949; Dead man's island), *Siglingin mikla* (1950; The great voyage), and *Frelsisálfan* (1951; The continent of freedom) — in which he describes the emigration of the farmer Ófeigur and his family to the United States. The trilogy has its historical base in the massive emigration of the late nineteenth century, but the author plays a temporal trick on the reader and moves the family across the ocean and into the heavily industrialized and alienated mass society of twentieth-century Chicago, thus boldly magnifying Iceland's recent jump into the modern, Americanized world. Ófeigur's son, Siggi, is at first very much a child of romanticism and the nineteenth-century Icelandic countryside, as we see in the following passage, which may serve as a key to Icelandic rural discourse, even as it emerges in the realist novel: "The boy closed his eyes and listened. And he heard the murmur of the brook, that clear silvery sound that was like a poem by Jónas Hallgrímsson, and he began to tremble all over as if he were himself flowing through the gravel and clay of the land — no, I'll never go to America" (*Dauðmannsey*, 196). But he does, and, while the American experience devastates his father, Siggi discards his background and is swallowed up by the American dream, which perhaps serves to show that losing a culture need take no longer than one generation.

The voyage across the ocean and through time into a different world lends *Dauðsmannsey* a strong underlying metaphor. But the reader's parallel voyage is hampered by the fact that the implied author is very much the boy in the above quotation. There is a sense in which the novel never goes to America: the horrors of industrial Chicago are related to us in a discourse that presents them as distant examples of the dark forces of modern capitalism rather than integral features of a distinctive place. This is, in turn, reflected in the rickety structure of the third novel. Hence, the trilogy is yet another example of the difficulties that Icelandic realism has had absorbing modern urban culture.

This was less of a problem for Stefán Jónsson (1905–66), a novelist who did not attempt a mimetic representation of the traumatic experience of the 1940s, the occupation and the *ástand* — a subject that in its overall execution led many novelists into dire straits — yet succeeds in portraying Iceland's anguished shift from a rural to an urban culture. His large epic novel *Vegurinn að brúnni* (1962; The road to the bridge) is, in fact, the most solidly constructed fictional rendition of this shift. Jónsson, also well-known as an author of children's books (see pp. 592–93), chose to place his story in the prewar years, demonstrating that the urban revolution was already under way, that the supremacy of the rural community was already dissolving, and that it is a mistake to believe that it was only the war that had thrown Iceland into the modern age. Thus, while Jónsson of course writes with the benefit of hindsight, he subtly approaches the experience of the midcentury shake-up from the other direction. The protagonist is a familiar type: yet another young man who has lost his rural roots without forming new ones in the city. But this time the familiar historical experience is underpinned by a carefully worked-out psychological drama that is woven into the novel's explorations of cultural and social dislocation.

WARRIORS, HAPPY AND UNHAPPY

Vegurinn að brúnni may well be the outstanding realist novel of the postwar era, for it is highly questionable whether one can place Laxness's big novel of that period under the rubric of realism. *Gerpla* (1952; English trans.: *The Happy Warriors* [1958]) is, in part, a historical novel, based on two major Old Icelandic sagas, *Fóstbræðra saga* (The saga of the sworn brothers) and *Ólafs saga helga* (Saint Olaf's saga). To a certain extent it is written in the language of these sagas — and the rural discourse of the Icelandic realist novel has strong links with the realism of saga narrative. In view of the popular conviction that modern Icelandic storytelling still exists in the same linguistic and narrative world as the medieval sagas, it is not surprising that some novelists have sought to restage the historical setting and the heroic realism of the sagas. But *Gerpla* is a great deal more complex than most such modern "sagas"; as a novel it is acutely aware of how recent history (modern warfare and the Nazi reverence for Nordic relics) has problematized the reception of the Icelandic literary heritage. Thus, it becomes a troubled inquiry into the literary tradition generally taken to be the foundation of Icelandic culture. Laxness resends the traditional saga heroes — the king, the warrior, and the poet — on their quests, but with a gruesome twist, turning heroic feats into acts of terror and senseless cruelty.

At the same time, *Gerpla* is a comic novel, portraying even the most terrifying moments of violence and death in an overblown, grotesque manner. While many of the grotesque elements are already present in *Fóstbræðra saga*, the prevailing perception of saga heroism was bound to make readers feel that Laxness was deliberately misreading or mistranslating the saga canon, and many were deeply upset by what they saw as a wholesale undermining of the values of the saga age, values that had given the nation strength throughout the centuries and had been a mainstay in its struggle for independence. Others saw Laxness's subversion of "innocent" involvement with these classical texts as a vital element in his engaged inquiry into the whole meaning of the saga tradition — by which means he reaffirms the relevance of that tradition for our age, for instance, with regard to questions of power, loyalty, heroism, freedom, and the role of literature. There were, indeed, many who saw *Gerpla* as securing Laxness's status as a one-man renaissance of Icelandic epic literature — a view that played no small role in bringing him the Nobel Prize three years after the publication of *Gerpla*.

While *Gerpla* may appear to have reaffirmed Laxness's place at the heart of Icelandic narrative aesthetics and historical identity, it also curiously distances him from all the writers who seemed to share his concerns, although this may not have been apparent at the time. It was a prevalent view that the role and value of the novel as a genre were based on a mimetic rendering of reality, and Laxness himself was an adamant spokesman for this premise. Yet, in spite of this, *Gerpla* is an experiment in language, an intertextual and metafictional adventure that defies the laws of realism. Its language is neither that of the sagas nor that of the modern realist novel; in its amalgamation of different language styles it constitutes a striking idiolect, achieved through a linguistic freedom that the contemporary practice of the novel could hardly account for.

But, while Laxness may have been quite radical in his textual experiments, *Gerpla* did not at the time appear as a revolt against classical realist narrative. Its preoccupation with the saga tradition and its epic dimension precluded any surmise that Laxness was seriously questioning the boundaries of realism. There was no doubt, however, that a young writer who published his first work in 1950, following it up with two more in 1954 and 1957, did transgress these boundaries in an idiolect that sounded quite alien to many readers. *Maðurinn er alltaf einn* (Man is always alone), *Dagar mannsins* (The days of man), and *Andlit í spegli dropans* (English trans.: *Faces Reflected in a Drop* [1966]) by Thor Vilhjálmsson (b. 1925) are all volumes of short prose pieces. Some of these pieces could be considered short stories, but many are better described as sketches, often verging on poetry; indeed, the first book includes a few poems. All these pieces depict moments snatched from a context of which the reader is only dimly aware, but one drawn with a painter's precision in terms of contours and colors. Many of them appear to be glimpses of Europe after the war, its cities and its experiential deserts. From his travels in Europe, and perhaps especially from his extended stay in Paris, Vilhjálmsson introduced landscapes and mindscapes with which the Icelandic literary sensibility was unfamiliar but that it was certain to encounter sooner or later. We see characters bound on romantic, if often bleak, existential quests, but we see them only momentarily, as they pass through moments of love, passion, leave-taking, intense pain, or solitude, or as they face death. Moreover, their often dreamlike quests also take them into dimensions of consciousness that subvert any reliable encounters with concrete reality. This was an inward turn unparalleled in Icelandic literature, mediated in a poetic language that purports to be prose while often rebelling against the very notion of narrativity.

While Vilhjálmsson's prose collections were a radical modernist turn away from realism in the short story, a more gradual transformation of the genre during the 1950s is manifested in the short stories of Ásta Sigurðardóttir (1930–72) and Geir Kristjánsson (1923–91). Some of their stories resemble those of Halldór Stefánsson in their realistic portrayal of people displaced or marginalized by their community. In other stories, however, the relation of such characters with their environment eludes rational apprehension, assuming bizarre or strangely symbolic guises, as in the title story of Kristjánsson's collection *Stofnunin* (1956; The institution). Ásta Sigurðardóttir wrote a number of groundbreaking short stories in the 1950s, when she was still in her twenties. Most of them were collected in *Sunnudagskvöld til mánudagsmorguns* (1961; Sunday evening to Monday morning). (An expanded collection, *Sögur og ljóð* [Stories and poems], appeared in 1985.) Sigurðardóttir was one of the first writers to capture, from within a vernacular perspective, a truly urban discourse, growing out of the "raw" experience of the postwar era and a disillusioned view of its expanding bourgeois world. The energy of her stories emanates from a subcultural sphere of poverty and bohemianism, violated childhood, and wounded femininity (see p. 536). In some of her urban stories and in the stunning, antipastoral "Frostrigning" (Frost rain), she delves deeper than most other authors into dangerous topics, not the least of which is the psychopathology of family life, leaving the reader with haunting images of emotional as well as physical torment.

CROSSROADS: LAXNESS AND THE OTHER NOVELISTS

By the early 1950s a radical modernist breakthrough had taken place in Icelandic poetry, and the same period also saw, although to a lesser extent, the advent of modernism in the short story. It may appear as a striking literary-historical incongruence that a similar systemic shift did not occur in the novel at that time. This can be partly explained by the enduring predominance of what I have called *rural discourse*, and its ties with Icelandic national and social identity, woven into the broad narrative of the rural-realist novel. The status and stature of Halldór Laxness is also a key element. In the 1920s it was Laxness's *Vefarinn mikli frá Kasmír* (1927), together with Þórðarson's *Bréf til Láru* (1924; A letter to Laura), that had indicated that a modernist paradigm might be under construction in Icelandic prose literature, just as it was in some other Western countries at the time. In his subsequent works, however, Laxness turned decisively away from modernist aesthetics, becoming Iceland's preeminent novelist with his great realist novels of the 1930s. And it was Laxness more than anyone else who made the novel an important and respectable genre in Iceland, made its narrative potential measure up to that of the Icelandic saga in the minds of readers, critics, and other writers. He was the avatar of the epic-realist novel, and anyone who sought to subvert the genre was in a way challenging his dominating presence. Whatever the implications of his own maneuvers in *Gerpla*, he remained the guardian of the realist novel. Right to the end of the 1950s he vigorously defended its principles and was highly critical of any attempts to turn the novel into a more subjective, inward-looking medium. It was this stance, together with his central position in the house of fiction and the general awareness of his total achievement, that left a firm mark on the transition from the 1950s to the 1960s, more so than his actual novels of that period: *Brekkukotsannáll* (1957; English trans.: *The Fish Can Sing* [1966]) and *Paradísarheimt* (1960; English trans.: *Paradise Reclaimed* [1962]). While realistic in mode, they attest to Laxness's withdrawal from his previous politicized and aggressive wrestling with tradition and ideological issues. Tradition becomes more of a sanctuary in which he cultivates his composed and Taoist humanism. There are few overt references to contemporary affairs, but Laxness is unobtrusively discussing the nature of paradise and the question of values, addressing a nation that had slipped somewhat crudely into the modern world and was turning into a welfare state.

While they certainly bear the fruit of his brilliance, these novels saw Laxness relinquish his position as Iceland's foremost practicing novelist. He had for quite some time been the unquestioned center of the Icelandic novel, but his most recent work was no longer on the cutting edge of the genre. However, there was no one then on the Icelandic literary scene to take his place. The novel had gradually developed into a distinct and cardinal genre, and the other prose writer whose stylistic genius was beyond doubt, Þórbergur Þórðarson, was working outside its boundaries. The epic writers working within its boundaries were very much in Laxness's shadow, and no one seriously thought of taking the epic-realist novel further than he had already done. At the same time the genre still guarded itself against any major disruption, allowing little space for the sporadic attempts to incorporate signs of modernity into the very structure or narrative representation of the novel. The year 1958 was exceptional in that it saw the publication of three novels that were quite radically modernist in one respect or another: Jóhannes Helgi's (1926–2001) *Horft á hjarnið* (Looking at the snow crust), Loftur Guðmundsson's (1906–78) *Gangrimlahjólið* (The wagon wheel), and Steinar Sigurjónsson's (1928–92) *Ástarsaga* (Love story). But such endeavors had precious little impact on the foundation of the genre; there was a strong resistance to the adoption of the new premises needed to receive and discuss such works *as novels*.

It seems, in retrospect at least, that the transition from the 1950s to the 1960s landed the novel in a vacuum, a kind of black hole, that swallowed up, not only any attempt at modernist innovation, but in a sense also individual achievements in the prevalent mode, like Jónsson's *Vegurinn að brúnni* or the first novel of the promising young writer Guðbergur Bergsson (b. 1932), *Músin sem læðist* (1961; Mouse on the prowl). A genre that has stagnated not only fends off any threatening "otherness"; it also becomes almost incapable of registering differences within its accepted boundaries. Moreover, it seems almost inevitable that some writers would be "lost" in trying to make their mark on the novel in this vacuum. Making the point even more broadly, Guðbergur Bergsson was later to say that, between those born around the turn of the century (e.g., Laxness) and his own generation, there was a "whole generation of authors lost inside the walls of Icelandic culture" (*Tómas Jónsson metsölubók*, 6).

But even the talented prose writers of Bergsson's generation found it no easy task to enter the arena of the novel. Ásta Sigurðardóttir never wrote a novel, and neither did Geir Kristjánsson. Thor Vilhjálmsson also delayed his entrance, working in the meantime in an alternative prose genre. *Undir gervitungli* (1959; Under an artificial moon), *Regn á rykið* (1960; Rain on the dust), and *Svipir dagsins, og nótt* (1961; Daytime apparitions and night) are travel books in which the author registers his impressions of Europe. The textual manipulation of the traveler, the narrative devices, and the language facilities used, however, often challenge the boundaries separating this form from fiction, and these books constitute an important stage in Vilhjálmsson's career.

Vilhjálmsson was also one of the editors of *Birtingur* (1955–68), a journal that probably constituted the single most concentrated and sustained attempt during the period to revitalize Icelandic literature and culture. Between its covers, as well as in various other cultural activities with which it was affiliated, there were a number of signs indicating a space waiting to be explored by a radicalized form of the novel. Criticism of contemporary literature was becoming more pointed and serious, and critics who had accepted the formal revolution in poetry began calling attention to the dormant state of the novel. As for Halldór Laxness, in the early 1960s he had begun writing plays that seemed more related to the theater of the absurd than to the realism of his earlier novels (see p. 566).

But, while there may have been considerable unrest under the surface, there was still no consensus as to which direction the novel would take. There were those who believed that it might still embark anew on a realist-political crusade, a view that called considerable attention to two novels published in 1965, Jóhannes Helgi's *Svört messa* (Black mass) and Ingimar Erlendur Sigurðsson's (b. 1933) *Borgarlíf* (City life). Both angrily portray contemporary society as a place of capitalist corruption, governed by people who have sold their souls to foreign forces and have betrayed the spirit and the culture of the nation. Both are weighed down by their urgent message, especially *Borgarlíf*, while *Svört messa* is an ambitious attempt to re-create Icelandic society, in miniature, on a small island on which there is both a town and a foreign military base. But both novels lack shape and structure, and neither is saved by the omnipresent central character, in both cases a conceited young man who indignantly observes and condemns the atrocities around him.

A structurally more successful novel, published in the same year, and one that really sought a new form within the realist mode, was Jakobína Sigurðardóttir's (1918–94) *Dægurvísa* (1965; A ditty). It was unusual in not concentrating on one or two protagonists, dealing instead with a day in the lives of a number of people who share a house of flats in Reykjavík but seem to have little else in common. The novel thus approaches contemporary society through the everyday affairs of people from different social circles.

That the novel of 1965 was eagerly searching for new modes of expression is even more apparent in *Orgelsmiðjan* (The organ factory) by Jón of Pálmholt (b. 1930). Here, as in *Svört messa*, the protagonist is a writer facing the disarray of modern life. The hero is arrested and put in jail, but his mind takes off on a wild journey, racing through history and all across the world, from one hallucinatory and apocalyptic scene to another. This is a daring antinarrative novel, but, like some of the earlier modernist experiments in the novel, it is naive in its attempts to create an extensive vision of a modernity that is out of control. Its censure of all that has gone wrong with the world is simplistic and based in a traditional moral and political point of view.

The eventual modernist breakthough was to come in the following year, with the publication of Guðbergur Bergsson's *Tómas Jónsson metsölubók* (1966; Tómas Jónsson bestseller), a work that for many readers has come to represent the paradigmatic modernist revolt in the novel lasting the rest of the decade and into the 1970s. But, while *Tómas Jónsson metsölubók* remains a landmark in Icelandic fiction, a work that still poses a challenge to Icelandic writers and readers today, it would be misleading to view it as a precursor in terms of influence. Rather, it helped unleash a wave that had been swelling up and was to leave the landscape of the Icelandic novel much altered. This revolution blew up the existing epic horizon of the novel, opened its form and structure, leaving no laws of tradition unquestioned. It is important to note that while there are certain links between the writers concerned—Guðbergur Bergsson, Steinar Sigurjónsson, Thor Vilhjálmsson, Svava Jakobsdóttir (1930–2004), Þorsteinn frá Hamri (b. 1938; Þorsteinn of Hamar), Jakobína Sigurðardóttir, and a few others—they draw on very diversified modes of modernist writing and do not constitute a unified group, with the result that they can be considered to constitute a movement only in the very broadest of senses. It may be noted, however, that most of their works were brought out by the same publisher, Helgafell, whose director was a well-known patron of the arts, Ragnar Jónsson of Smári.

The protagonist of *Tómas Jónsson metsölubók*, a retired and senile Reykjavík bank clerk who is confined to his basement apartment, is writing his memoirs, but also partly recording his present circumstances. The novel is written at a time when biography had become the foremost brand of popular (best-seller) literature written in Iceland. It radically parodies and subverts the genre and its inflated and often conceited claims on behalf of the authentic subject or the sovereign individual. Tómas Jónsson does not manage to package his overblown ego in the prevailing fashion, instead dispersing it all over his strange and unruly chronicle. At the same time his contradictory identity is still a force that lends the work an integrity that most previous modernist novels had lacked.

Tómas Jónsson is a member of that much-discussed and often-eulogized generation, born around the turn of the century, that savored the old, heroic values of rural Iceland, and wanted to be guided by them in regaining the island's independence and glory, but then had the task torn from its hands in the war and had to run to keep up with the times and to enjoy at least the material benefits of the new age. It was this generation, more than any other, that consolidated the emerging Icelandic bourgeois identity. Tómas Jónsson represents this generation, but through his senility Bergsson makes him a signifier whose referent becomes ever more amorphous as his values are satirically emptied of their traditional meaning and shown to be linked with very mundane desires. The grand narrative of his life is constantly interrupted by the weirdest of diversions, in which precision and confusion go hand in hand. Many readers were shocked and dismayed by the carnivalesque attention paid to bodily functions, which are sometimes the ultimate object of Tómas's spiritual quests. Others were frustrated by the chaos that readers are made to face by entering his flow of thoughts, undergoing bewildering temporal shifts, and being exposed to a profusion of texts, voices, fantasies, and observations. While he feels he is becoming one with his apartment ("I am a basement apartment" [*Tómas Jónsson met-sölubók*, 125]), he cannot properly tell apart his tenant-relatives, one of whom, Katrín, or "Annakatrín" (for at one point she merges with another female character, Anna), he takes to be his soul and his muse as well as a symbol of his nation.

There is a certain parallel between Tómas and Bergsson, for Bergsson was himself to become a chronicler of his nation, presenting in several novels and short stories the most sustained critical view in Icelandic literature of the postwar era. It would be tempting to refer to this effort as a condition-of-Iceland portrayal if this did not bring to mind the very mimetic approach that Bergsson does so much to subvert. Never claiming to show the "truth of the matter," he explodes mythic notions that Icelanders have regarding their identity, culture, and independence, often by building into the discourse of his novels what he takes to be the essence of the message sent out by a nation that was not able to withstand the pressure of suddenly becoming an "independent" welfare state: carping (*nöldur*, also used as the title of a story in his short story collection *Leikföng leiðans* [1964; The toys of boredom]). Carping becomes the cultural medium of a people who have been housed and fed and do not know where to go from there.

Tómas Jónsson metsölubók was followed by *Ástir samlyndra hjóna* (1967; The love life of a harmonious couple), structurally an even more radical novel since it almost breaks up into twelve episodes or short stories, tied together only by dialogic interludes and certain leitmotifs, not the least of which is a funeral, as well as by an emphasis on family affairs. The novel forms a bridge from *Tómas Jónsson* to a whole cycle of stories of Tómas's relatives who live in the village of Tangi in southwest Iceland. The Tangi cycle consists of the novels *Anna* (1969), *Það sefur í djúpinu* (1973; It sleeps in the deep), *Hermann og Dídí* (1974; Hermann and Dídí), and *Það rís úr djúpinu* (1976; It rises from the deep) as well as the short story collection *Hvað er eldi guðs?* (1970; What is God's food?). The setting and some of the characters had, in fact, already been introduced in *Leikföng leiðans*. In this cycle Bergsson burrows deep into, and severely fractures, two prevailing myths inherited from the rural community, both of which are also instrumental in Icelandic notions of nationhood: the myth of the family as the ideal social unit and the myth of the home as a sanctuary. These myths are examined with a view to the nearby presence of the contentious American army base, which produces both the livelihood of and the popular culture consumed by many people in the area. This means that Bergsson was dealing with what was for a long time the hottest political issue in Iceland, but he does so with a total disregard for political rhetoric of any sort. He does not condemn the American presence in any simplistic way, instead inquiring relentlessly into its meaning for Icelandic culture.

Readers may be able to see Samuel Beckett's Malone somewhere behind Tómas Jónsson, but Bergsson's total effort, his depiction of the family, whose internal relations we can never fully straighten out, and his creation of the mythic but very Icelandic village of Tangi, is Faulknerian in character. And, like Faulkner, Bergsson unveils the ruthless realism that characterizes much human intercourse, however idealistic it may seem on the surface; and rudely realistic and macabre scenes are woven into a modernist text that is disjointed in its occasional employment of the stream-of-consciousness technique and its sometimes absurdist dialogues and descriptions. Some readers are taken aback by what they see as Bergsson's lack of positive characters and values and his irreverent revolt against any sign of consolation, not least when it is sought in the past. There appears to be no respect for tradition, and Bergsson shies away from nothing, for, significantly, *Tómas Jónsson metsölubók* parodies even the prose style of Halldór Laxness, who by that time had become a father figure to Icelandic novelists.

The value of Bergsson's works, however, lies precisely in their negativity, not least in the toppling of male images and patriarchal viewpoints. In dislodging the stable identities of his male "heroes" Bergsson shows them as circumscribed by the family and by women capable of extracting sense, however vulgar, from the family chaos. In this Bergsson's creative urge appears to be feminine — in fact, he gives us more than one hint that Annakatrín, the tenant and muse of Tómas Jónsson, is after all also his own muse, for often she seems to be the one composing the text. This, in turn, may serve as an example of the self-reflexive nature of the text, for, if the characters sometimes seem to be leading a senseless and degrading existence, some of them are also aware of the fictional nature of that existence, aware of being thrown into the narrative that is culture and that they take part in writing themselves. It would be hard to deny that these characters are very much alive and that they contain a real spark of creativity. Also, the satire aimed at the characters, and at society and its morals, is shot through with proverbial and circumstantial humor.

MODERNISM: SHADOWS AND BIRDS

Tómas Jónsson metsölubók not only cleared the way for other experimental works; it also helped make sense of what Steinar Sigurjónsson had been doing earlier, in particular in *Ástarsaga* (1958), whose relevance became apparent as a new paradigm emerged in the novel. In fact, Sigurjónsson's *Blandað í svartan dauðann* (1967; Mixed with gin) is in many ways a re-worked version of *Ástarsaga*. Both novels take place in the same fishing village, where the heroes play their dismal roles as fishermen and husbands who, when ashore, are torn between their families and the bottle. Their drinking is amply reflected in the flow of uncultivated, vernacular language, in which it is sometimes hard to distinguish dialogue from internal speech or one character's thoughts from those of another. Here, as often also in Bergsson's novels, the reader faces "low life" and seemingly futile attempts to transcend the monotony of everyday existence and the workaday world. But both writers find in their communities, and manage to bring into their texts, a brutal life force, an unrefined bodily exultation, mixed with real anxiety, and this is mediated in a language of raw lyricism that acquires its own mythic qualities even as it is being deromanticized. Gradually, it dawns on the reader that, in these subcultural realms, the writers may have brought to the fore some essence or hinterland of the dominant bourgeois way of life while also finding, in these dominions of disgrace, a source of unstifled life and art.

In some of his other novels Sigurjónsson does, in fact, concern himself with the contradictions of art and the bourgeois way of life, with its emphasis on decency, rationality, and material values. In *Farðu burt skuggi* (1971; Go away, shadow) a musician's search for an apartment turns into aimless drifting, and what he ultimately finds is, perhaps, the source of his art: pain and shadow. In *Skipin sigla* (1966; The ships are leaving), a novel in which even the outer design of the text is partially fragmented, a young poet and his friend commit arson for a businessman who plans to collect the insurance money. This act turns into a terrifying "artwork" that plunges the poet into "the deep"; his visions are carried across in terrifying and strong imagery, some of which is characteristically risky, but sustained by genuine power.

Sigurjónsson came to draw increasingly on his fascination with the ocean and its depths. *Djúpið* (1974; The deep) is his most revolutionary and obscure work—and, in fact, one of the most radically experimental of all Icelandic novels. It describes how a young boy leaves the wreck of a sunken ship and starts roaming the ocean depths and socializing with its monsters. Liberated from social constraints, he gives himself up to the rhythm of the ocean, and the text is saturated with music; indeed, it is as if the boy's mind is turned into a musical instrument of language. "The deep" of the novel's title refers, of course, also to the depths of the mind, the subconscious, which the author, paradoxically and sometimes brilliantly, pulls to the surface of his text. All in all, *Djúpið* is a unique work in Icelandic literature, although it has a younger and, perhaps, more accessible cousin in Guðbergur Bergsson's *Froskmaðurinn* (1985; The diver), published under the pseudonym of Hermann Másson (who happens to be a character in the Tangi cycle), in which a diver comes to feel more at home underwater than in his natural element.

In Sigurjónsson's autobiographical novel *Sigling* (1978; Sailing) the ship does not sink but takes its author far away, to the south of India. While marred by the lengthy metaphysical and speculative ramblings that weaken some of his later books, it contains passages that strikingly blend the rough and the sensitive, the hard and the tender. In doing so it unveils the romantic streak in Sigurjónsson; intertwined with his pursuit of intellectual and artistic freedom — which, significantly, leads him away from Icelandic society — *Sigling* is a very serious inquiry into love.

In these respects Sigurjónsson resembles Thor Vilhjálmsson, who, in his novels of the 1960s and 1970s, continued the European journeys of his travel books. His first novel, *Fljótt fljótt sagði fuglinn* (1968; English trans.: *Quick Quick Said the Bird* [1987]), has come to stand next to *Tómas Jónsson metsölubók* as a work that anchored the modernist paradigm in the Icelandic novel. Vilhjálmsson's career is remarkable for his ex-centric or centrifugal way of participating in contemporary Icelandic culture, constantly searching abroad, on his own terms, for new experiences and bringing them into his language, patiently waiting for them to become an integral part of the culture. This is not to say that the travelers in his *Fljótt fljótt sagði fuglinn*, *Óp bjöllunnar* (1970; Cry of the beetle), and *Mánasigð* (1976; Moon sickle) are methodical tourists, seeking to map a certain piece of foreign soil. They are restless and often anguished explorers of both inner and outer regions — and it is often hard to tell when we cross the border between the two. Whether they are walking down city streets or mysterious hallways, wandering in forests, sitting in the midst of bohemian parties, talking to a group of friends, or lying in bed with someone, the reader must follow them through mesmerizing transformations. For, even when they are motionless, their minds are never at rest, and the present may be engulfed by a powerful memory or the imagined perspective of another, a lover or a stranger.

In order to allow for the full metamorphic force involved when the life of the mind is set free on a level with other narrative elements, Vilhjálmsson usually discards a reliable narrator's voice, and, while the narrator is a shape-shifter who can be placed wherever the author chooses, the reader is offered very limited guidance. It is, indeed, often difficult to keep track as we glide from one narrative or temporal level to another. But such shifts are inherent in the author's aesthetic, resulting from the way in which his characters and narrators search for ways of expressing or captivating emotion. An image arises, a memory, a dream, or some detail or person in the environment catches the eye and becomes somehow linked with a character's state of mind, and this metamorphic level may come alive on its own terms, sometimes on a grand symphonic scale, sometimes with meticulous attention to detail. Vilhjálmsson resorts to a broad spectrum of techniques, often borrowing from the other arts: we follow the action through the camera lens, or a film may be superimposed on another scene; part of the environment may be suddenly transfigured in a surrealist manner; other scenes seem to be descriptions of paintings. Music is often important, particularly in *Óp bjöllunnar*, as is dance in *Fljótt fljótt sagði fuglinn*—many of Vilhjámsson's novels could, in fact, be described as an intricate ritualistic dance of men and women moving toward and away from one another, driven by passion and desire, frustrated by anxiety and pain.

It is no coincidence that Vilhjálmsson's major protagonists are anonymous—they are drifting subjects, and, just as their lives are in flux, so they flow in what is often best described as a river of text. While Vilhjálmsson frequently resorts to the other arts in mediating experiences, his text is more often than not obsessed with narrative itself and with storytelling—sometimes in an overtly metafictional manner—with how people fabricate one another's lives, as well as their own, seeking to understand things by creating a narrative for them or "reading" people into existing stories. Significantly, some characters are seen retracing the patterns of ancient myths.

It can be hard to tell whether these figures are searching for or escaping from something, except that, in their struggle toward self-discovery, they are caught in an intricate web of love and erotic involvements (the novels include some magnificent erotic scenes). There is, however, a counterforce that resists giving up one's identity to those who offer warmth, understanding, and salvation from loneliness. The sectarian group that plays a part in

Mánasigð can be seen as standing for the kind of threat to individuality that makes it crucial never to stop searching for oneself and also to be able to retreat into solitude, which is, if not the source of art, then the precarious ground of its creation.

In Vilhjálmsson's first two novels there are strong tragic undertones, a theme that echoes the title of his first book: man is always alone. Many readers first discovered his humorous side in *Folda* (1972; Native soil), a book containing parodies of three kinds of Icelandic travel stories, embodied in a relatively straightforward narrative, which also characterizes the farcical first part of *Fuglaskottís* (1975; Bird dance), a novel that gradually becomes deeper and more complex but never loses this light touch. The following two novels, too, contain stretches of very humorous prose in which Vilhjálmsson spins puns, rhymes, and plays on words into the text. But in *Mánasigð* (1976) he returns to the complex, multilayered structure of the earlier novels, with an enhanced emphasis on repetitions and variations of scenes and motifs, designed as a cyclic motion. The cycle is also an underlying form in *Turnleikhúsið* (1979; The Tower Theater), which is the author's first novel set in Iceland, or, to be more precise, in its national theater, a building that is transformed into an astounding labyrinth, providing for yet another odyssey.

Vilhjálmsson's own odyssey has taken him on an adventurous voyage through the Icelandic language. Calling his style *lyric* only tells part of the story, important as it is to acknowledge that his descriptive prose is almost without exception also poetry. No Icelandic novelist has such an extensive vocabulary at his command, and in calling on that resource Vilhjálmsson has also found extraordinary suppleness in a language that is heavily inflected. The Icelandic sentence will never be quite the same.

While Vilhjálmsson often incorporates mythological material into his novels, the most adamant mythographer in Icelandic fiction is another master of language, Þorsteinn frá Hamri. A leading contemporary poet, he was already the author of several volumes of poetry when he brought out his first novel, *Himinbjargarsaga eða Skógardraumur* (1969; The saga of Himinbjörg, or a forest dream). It opens with a description of a jar on which a mythological story in pictures spirals its way from top to bottom, except that the jar has been damaged and there are "gaps in the story."

The gap turns out to be a leitmotif, and it brings into relief the author's approach, which also characterizes his later novels: *Möttull konungur eða Caterpillar* (1974; King Möttull, or caterpillar) and *Haust í Skírisskógi* (1980; Autumn in Sherwood Forest). No level of history, and certainly not the present, exists as a single unbroken narrative. Stories of the past flow into the apertures of the present, and our epic desire seeks links between relevant episodes of time gone by. In the novels of Þorsteinn frá Hamri myths, heroic legends, fairy tales, anecdotal stories, and memories make up much of the narrative action, even though the present point of departure is never far off. The reader often makes surprising transitions from one story level to another, and sometimes these levels blend into each other, constantly uncovering new interfaces between the worlds involved. The author does the same with the language, bringing together discourses of past and present, which is also one of the striking features of his poetry.

Himinbjargarsaga is the most complex and ambitious of these novels. While some of its present-time action unmistakably occurs in Iceland, *Himinbjargarsaga* is, in fact, a quest story of universal proportions. Its hero is Sigurður (Siegfried), whom readers may know from medieval heroic literature. He sets out on a Grail-like crusade to free the maiden Himinbjörg, captive in the city of the forces of evil, who are also preparing an apocalyptic, "final solution." But there is much to delay our hero, many stories to go through, many outcasts of history to attend to, and so many things that can change us on the way; and Himinbjörg—whatever she signifies—may not exist, or, if she does, then only as "naked life" or a gap.

The other two novels are more rooted in an Icelandic context, even though the mythic base of *Haust í Skírisskógi* is the tale of Robin Hood and his companions—their modern counterparts being a group of Reykjavík cronies exchanging stories. These stories are in a sense their autumnal Sherwood Forest. The humor and playfulness that mark all the novels grow to a streak of comedy in *Haust í Skírisskógi*, whereas in *Möttull konungur* the historical and linguistic interchange of past and present merges into the hues and shapes of nature and the wilderness—which makes this novel the one closest to the author's poetry.

THE LODGER AND THE LOST EMISSARY

The modernist revolt in the late 1960s, especially as it appeared in the novels of Thor Vilhjálmsson, Steinar Sigurjónsson, and Guðbergur Bergsson, was not least a mutiny of excess. In their different ways these authors rebelled against the classical Icelandic principles of economy in narrative style by flooding the generic form, creating a textual abundance for the reader to cope with. Svava Jakobsdóttir's modernism and mastery of language are of a different order. At one level her style is impeccably classical and, in fact, very disciplined and polished. As such it appears at first to correspond to the regulated existence of her protagonists, almost always women (see pp. 539–

41). But, just as this existence crumbles, so the reader must renegotiate his or her understanding of the language.

It was her use of language as a veritable surface of experience, whose fragility (and sometimes outrage) is perceptible in the text itself, that made Jakobsdóttir Iceland's leading short story writer with *Tólf konur* (1965; Twelve women) and *Veizla undir grjótvegg* (1967; Party under a stone wall), a status reinforced when she collected her stories of the next decade and a half in *Gefið hvort öðru . . .* (1982; Give unto each other . . .). Some of her stories are fantasies in which the impossible or the improbable (and sometimes the horrifying) is concretized in a cool, balanced, and "realistic" narrative. The story "Gefið hvort öðru . . ." opens with a bride who, in giving her hand in marriage, actually cuts it off and gives it to her husband-to-be. Some of the fantasies are, at one level, feminist allegories, but Jakobsdóttir rarely presents us with a key to one, clear-cut interpretation of a story, and in the story of the bride the bodily imagery grows ever more complex, as biblical, sexual, and social elements interweave and merge.

In the majority of Jakobsdóttir's stories, however, the action is more inherently realistic and may seem more at ease with the finely tuned narrative voice. But this balance rests on a razor's edge. The reader suspects, and often discovers, that the grace of the language is only a fragile crust hiding painful and buried experiences in an internalized world. Absurdities may start creeping stealthily into dialogues or descriptions, and rigid idioms and other properties of language are brought to life, revealing how habituated perspectives are often deeply embedded in the language we use. Much of Jakobsdóttir's imagery involves metaphors for women's lives in which social safety and stability are often ironic forms of imprisonment or a state of split identity; the stories elaborate on mirrors, photographs, walls, and enclosed spaces, particularly homes and houses — the woman's traditional domain.

Leigjandinn (1969; English trans.: *The Lodger and Other Stories* [2000]), Jakobsdóttir's first novel, focuses on a married woman who feels unsafe in a rented apartment, impatiently waiting for her husband to finish building their own house. It comes as a strange sort of relief for them when a foreign stranger unexpectedly takes up residence in the hall. He also helps them finish their house and then as a matter of course moves with them into "their own" abode. The story grows more and more fantastic, and eventually the two men physically merge, forming a two-headed being. On one level the novel is an allegory of a nation that is about to acquire its much desired independence but is then occupied by a foreign power that shows no signs of leaving. This facet of the novel is one version of a story that other writers had told before, but it is complicated by its entanglement with the story of a woman desperately trying to find her place, her sanctuary, in a male-dominated world:

> She closed her eyes and experienced nothing but the touch of the house. She stood like this until she could no longer distinguish between her skin and the stone, but felt her nerves and veins run directly into the walls of this house and felt her heart pumping her own blood to where the concrete defined her space in existence. Blindly, she walked like this along all the walls of the sitting-room, assuring herself that the echo of tumbling walls had been her imagination. (*The Lodger and Other Stories*, trans. D'Arcy, 65)

Most of Jakobsdóttir's stories occur in an urban setting, and the above quotation seems to have brought us a long way from the rural discourse that dominated Icelandic fiction into the 1960s. But the values associated with the rural community still provided guiding lights for some writers, for instance, Jakobína Sigurðardóttir, who is deeply concerned with the urbanization of the Icelandic way of life. At the same time she seeks to meet new social conditions with structural innovations — not so much in her short stories, collected in *Púnktur á skökkum stað* (1964; A misplaced endmark) and *Sjö vindur gráar* (1970; Seven gray spools), as in her novels, as we saw in the case of *Dægurvísa*. Her second novel, *Snaran* (1968; The noose), is an unusual and imaginative text, one in which the entire narrative consists of a monologue, or half of a conversation between fellow workers in a factory run by foreigners. The novel's future vision is grim, and its method involves the reader in a moral and political exposure of the protagonist's class betrayal and social blindness. *Lifandi vatnið – – –* (1974; Living water . . .) also grapples with the consciousness of a worker in an alienated and reified urban society, his shattered inner world, rooted in the country, being portrayed in a heavily fragmented modernist text. The hero is a "lost" man in his new world, and one day he actually disappears, traveling back "home" on his own. While it is made clear that there is no turning back to origins, Sigurðardóttir has, here, not come fully to terms with urban existence as a basic way of life, and she fails to give rural experience a new literary and cultural meaning in an altered society.

This is what Halldór Laxness succeeds in doing in *Kristnihald undir Jökli* (1968; English trans.: *Christianity at Glacier* [1972]) and what, together with other aspects of the work, brings him back to the forefront of the contemporary novel. The rural community appears here, not as the self-sufficient world of old, but as a kind of estranging mirror held up to the outside world. Other writers were later to accomplish this in their own way, notably Jakobína Sigurðardóttir in *Í sama klefa* (1981; In the same cabin; see p. 541). Laxness actually reverses the traditional pattern: his young and inexperienced observer-hero comes from the city and loses his innocence in the mists of the countryside. He is sent by the bishop to look into and report on the (allegedly neglected) maintenance of Christianity in a parish at the foot of the Snæfells glacier, made world famous in Jules Verne's *Journey to the Center of the Earth* (1864).

The young emissary's journey takes him, in more than one sense, to the center of the earth, but also to the edge of his rational mind, whether it be in coping with unusual forms of religion or with the mysteries of the *Ewig-Weibliche* (the Eternal Feminine), which plays a significant role here, as it does in many of Laxness's novels. The narrator's bewildered attempts to document events and phenomena result in a narrative that involves a multiplicity of genres, making this one of the most innovative novels of the modernist period. The text is a report, but it is also in part a strange drama, with links to the author's plays of the 1960s, and the narrator fears that it may also be "a book of dreams." Laxness mixes his Taoism with a good deal of playful skepticism, if not anarchism, which, on a formal level, allows him to incorporate a mixed bag of ingredients, such as folktales and myths, ancient and modern, together with humorous but often deep inquiries into theology, philosophy, and the nature of language. A similarly flexible documentary or essayistic form characterizes his next two novels, *Innansveitarkronika* (1970; A county chronicle) and *Guðsgjafaþula* (1972; Recitation of God's gifts), involving maneuvers with the narrative frame and an ironic play with objectivity. Neither possesses the depth or the mystique of *Kristnihald undir Jökli*, however, nor do they lead the reader as brilliantly along the edges of mimesis and illusion. In *Kristnihald undir Jökli*, Laxness undermines the form of the novel while reaffirming its mission; we are given to understand that a novel is like a bird — we will never truly comprehend how it flies.

As we have seen, the form of the Icelandic novel underwent considerable change during the period stretching approximately from 1966 to 1976. This was a period marked by multitudinous modernist innovation, involving a breadth of talent previously unknown in the genre of the novel. It can, at least partly, be explained as a wave that had been building under the surface for some time — the Icelandic novel was in a way eagerly catching up with some forty years in the history of modernism in the West. The prose modernists discussed above certainly differ considerably from one another. What their works have in common, however, aligned with their varying revolts against the epic-realist tradition, is an erosion of the classic narrative self; the boundaries of the subject begin to flutter and disintegrate, and we are led to wonder whether a new subject is in the making or whether the individual will no longer serve as a mirror of social forces and values. This in itself is a radical social gesture at a time when the nation had acquired both independence and prosperity and should have been coming into its own, in political as well as cultural terms. But this also involved challenging the classic Icelandic reader, who had always been more interested in epic encounters of socially representative individuals than in the orchestration of ideas, motifs, or psychological insights.

A NEW REALISM AND REYKJAVÍK

It was, therefore, to be expected that many readers would welcome the reemergence of a solid narrative self and more easily definable social issues. In the 1970s, well before the modernist wave subsided, one can see the first signs of what came to be termed *neorealism*. It was heralded by Vésteinn Lúðvíksson (b. 1944), a young writer whose promising debut had been a short story collection with modernist traits, *Átta raddir úr pípulögn* (1968; Eight voices from the pipeline). In 1970 Lúðvíksson wrote a long essay expounding the theories of Georg Lukács, indirectly questioning the modernist experiments of the last few years. He went on to write *Gunnar og Kjartan* I–II (1971–2; Gunnar and Kjartan), a long, uneven novel in the classic realist mold, in which he seeks to paint a holistic picture of class society and capitalist corruption in contemporary Iceland. His second novel, *Eftirþankar Jóhönnu* (1975; Jóhanna's second thoughts), describing the social and personal struggles of a divorced mother of five children, is more representative of the neorealist novel as it took shape in the late 1970s. It is more limited in scope than *Gunnar og Kjartan* and focuses more directly on specific social issues in a contemporary urban environment.

Neorealism grew partly out of a social and political awakening among members of the '68 generation, many of whom had lived and studied in Scandinavia. This period saw a burgeoning interest in leftist ideology and feminism, linked to the rise of the social sciences within the universities. A variety of social discourses emphasized critical analysis of the various problems of the so-called welfare state. By 1978 this movement had gathered considerable momentum in Icelandic literature, and many novels published that year are all in one way or another representative of neorealism: Guð-laugur Arason's (b. 1950) *Víkursamfélagið* (The bay community) and *Eld-húsmellur* (Kitchen whores); Ólafur Haukur Símonarson's (b. 1947) *Vatn á myllu kölska* (Water for the devil's mill); Ása Sólveig's (b. 1945) *Einka-*

mál Stefaníu (Stefanía's private affairs); Ólafur Gunnarsson's (b. 1948) *Milljón prósent menn* (One million percent men), and Úlfar Þormóðsson's (b. 1944) *Átt þú heima hér?* (Do you live here?). (Both *Víkursamfélagið* and *Eldhúsmellur* won publisher's prizes, and *Einkamál Stefaníu* was awarded the Radio Literature Prize.)

The reception of these and other novels indicated that there was a considerable demand for straightforward narrative works on what was considered everyday reality, works in which the characters faced various "realistic" social and personal problems, supposedly leaving the reader free from any textual problems. The title of Auður Haralds's (b. 1947) spirited *Hvunndagshetjan* (1979; Everyday hero) is telling: the protagonists are, by and large, heroes of everyday life, sometimes women seeking to carve out their space in a male world. Many of these novels portray social corruption at various levels or other social ills relating to class conflicts, social and sexual inequality, injustice, and abuse of power.

These novels present a mimetic picture of contemporary life in urban Iceland. While some of them are located in typical seaside towns and villages, it is, nonetheless, during the period of neorealism that Reykjavík finally becomes the capital of Icelandic fiction, at a time when its metropolitan population had risen above the 100,000 mark, in a country whose total population was still under 250,000. And, while there was a demand for contemporary realism, there was in particular a lack of novels representing contemporary life in Reykjavík, as can be deduced from the initial popularity of Hafliði Vilhelmsson's (b. 1954) first novel, *Leið 12: Hlemmur-Fell* (1977; Route 12: Hlemmur-Fell). It may appear as a meager and rather trivial work today, but at the time it seemed to many refreshing proof that the lives of young people going through their everyday motions, their nightlife, their love affairs, in contemporary Reykjavík, was the kind of stuff worthy of a novel.

In spite of this development, Reykjavík rarely, if ever, comes alive as an organic environment, that vital additional or even major character in itself that many cities have been in modern European and American fiction. Often, it is little more than a dull backdrop of affairs and incidents common to contemporary urban society. It may be that Reykjavík lacked distinctiveness as a city; perhaps Icelanders were still searching for their "authentic" urban way of life, even if the rural community had been marginalized for some time; or perhaps urban Icelandic culture has not yet fully reached an internal city scale, remaining at the level of the smaller town or village — which may partly explain why Guðbergur Bergsson's Tangi cycle has remained such a vital record of recent and contemporary Icelandic society.

Reykjavík has, perhaps, been more of a distinctive urban setting in some children's fiction, in which the perspective of the child plays an important role (see chapter 10). This also holds true for novels portraying experiences of childhood and growing up, such as Pétur Gunnarsson's (b. 1947) novels about Andri Haraldsson, *Punktur punktur komma strik* (1976; Matchstick man) and *Ég um mig frá mér til mín* (1978; I me my mine). These bildungs-romans were continued in *Persónur og leikendur* (1982; Characters and actors) and *Sagan öll* (1985; The whole story). Gunnarsson is very much a member of the legendary '68 generation, but, while his novels take a critical stance toward nouveau riche bourgeois society, his status with regard to neorealism is ambivalent. The playful metaphoric quality of his writing, while shy of his modernist predecessors, went beyond the textual limits of his peers and served to make him the most celebrated novelist of his genera-tion during this period.

HISTORICAL FICTION AND AUTOBIOGRAPHY

When observing neorealism in retrospect, even if we accept its realist prem-ises, it seems that few, if any, epic masterpieces came out of this movement. Its most significant novel, excluding those of Pétur Gunnarsson, may, in fact, be Ólafur Haukur Símonarson's *Vík á milli vina* (1983; What separates friends), in which the author draws up a grim balance sheet for his own generation of '68 and its floundered ideals. In terms of actual output neo-realism was a pronounced force in fiction for only five or six years, ca. 1977–82. But, owing to the attention it attracted, in popular as well as critical circles — often attacked in the latter, yet its historical significance con-firmed — it has unduly overshadowed other important works within the wider boundaries of realism in the 1970s.

A case in point is Þorgeir Þorgeirson's (b. 1933) *Yfirvaldið* (1973; The authorities), a historical novel based on a nineteenth-century criminal case, and a psychologically acute study of the ramifications of power and crime, money and guilt. Another work that renegotiates the borders between his-tory and epic fiction was Björn Th. Björnsson's (b. 1922) *Haustskip* (1975; Autumn ships), an excellently composed account of the harsh punishments meted out to Icelanders at the time of the Danish trade monopoly during the seventeenth and eighteenth centuries. Some of the historical novels of the 1980s similarly dealt with the codes of social transgression and punish-ment in earlier ages, such as Njörður P. Njarðvík's (b. 1936) *Dauðamenn* (1982; Condemned men) and Úlfar Þormóðsson *Þrjár sólir svartar* (1988; Three black suns) — holding up a historical mirror quite different from the one Icelanders are used to when they celebrate their early literary achievements and cultural legacies.

However, this period also saw a flowering of a different kind of historical narrative and creative realism, one that makes it even harder to maintain that neorealism was all that dominating a current even in the late 1970s and into the 1980s: the autobiography with literary aspirations. Tryggvi Emilsson's (b. 1902) trilogy *Fátækt fólk* (1976; Poor people), *Baráttan um brauðið* (1977; The battle for bread) and *Fyrir sunnan* (1979; In the south) tells the story of yet another member of the turn-of-the-century generation (see also p. 599). But Emilsson is no Tómas Jónsson, and he can look back on a lifetime as a laborer, a participant in class struggles, and a keen observer of society when he finally taps his considerable literary talent in his autobiography. Sigurður A. Magnússon (b. 1928), one of Iceland's most versatile writers, wrote a five-volume autobiography (1979–86) of his early life in the form of the bildungsroman, the first two volumes, *Undir kalstjörnu* (1979; Under a cold star) and *Möskvar morgundagsins* (1981; Meshes of tomorrow) being an especially poignant portrayal of childhood and adolescence in midcentury Reykjavík. Halldór Laxness also told the story of his tender years in four autobiographical volumes that he termed *essay-novels*, thus entering the history of Icelandic prose literature at yet another stage: *Í túninu heima* (1975; The fields at home); *Úngur eg var* (1976; When I was young); *Sjömeistarasagan* (1978; The story of the seven masters); and *Grikklandsárið* (1980; The Greek year).

The interest in childhood (and its literary representation), evident in all these autobiographies, was to prevail in prose literature throughout the 1980s, and there have been signs that Þórbergur Þórðarson's childhood memoirs are now being (re)read and their significance appreciated. The only writer who can be compared to Þórðarson in terms of originality in autobiographical composition is Málfríður Einarsdóttir (see also pp. 542–43). She was born in 1899 (d. 1983), and her first books were the autobiographical volumes *Samastaður í tilverunni* (A place to be) and *Úr sálarkirnunni* (From the soul vessel), published in 1977 and 1978. Like Þórðarson, Einarsdóttir discards the notion of life as a solidly shaped entity or narrative. For her writing a life is more like traveling through it, often haphazardly, perhaps as one travels within the self; going back and forth, she registers various impressions and observations, sometimes in a grotesque or delightfully naive manner. At the same time she is a diligent, if eccentric, chronicler of her environment, of its social customs and traditions, including its oral traditions, and her work is interspersed with portraits of numerous individuals, whom she approaches in the same ironic and humorous way as she portrays herself. The total effect is one of collage rather than story. Her other autobiographical writings, *Bréf til Steinunnar* (1981; Letter to Steinunn) and the posthumously published *Rásir dægranna* (1986; The tracks of time), are in the same vein, and so are her novels, *Auðnuleysingi og Tötrughypja* (1979; Luckless and the shaggy lady) and *Tötra í Glettingi* (1983; Tötra at Gletting), although they take the reader on more radical flights of fancy and absurdity and are sometimes both funny and confusing in their mixture of quixotic and "folkish" naïveté and structural complexity. They may be said to constitute a most idiosyncratic extension of the modernist novel, written in a style that draws at once on classical resources and modern flexibility.

Icelandic Prose Literature, 1980–2000
Ástráður Eysteinsson and Úlfhildur Dagsdóttir

A period of contradictions and conundrums, the 1980s were defined by the advent of video, the popularity of poetry readings, and the influx of literature in translation. These were the years of the punk and the yuppie, where the leftover anarchism of the 1970s mingled and clashed with conservative cultural values, whether critical or affirmative, and with emergent ultraconservative currents in economic affairs and the social sphere. Iceland was marked by the increasing effects of market-driven capitalism and its encroachment on the cultural scene. At the same time books continued to hold an iconic value, popular as ever for presents, and avidly read and discussed, at least in some circles.

TRANSLATION, MODERNIST LEGACIES, GENDERED PLACES

The interplay of past and present in terms of style, language, and thematic concerns would seem to have been greatly facilitated in the postmodern era, if the term *postmodern* can be used to refer to developments in Icelandic prose literature after modernism had blown open its horizons. This flexibility and openness was buttressed by a new wave of prose translations, starting in the late 1970s, translations having been a marginal force for about a quarter of a century. Some of these translations encouraged a reevaluation of the nature of realism, especially Gabriel García Márquez's *One*

Hundred Years of Solitude (1967) in the 1978 translation of Guðbergur Bergsson (b. 1932); William Heinesen's *The Tower at the End of the World* (1976) in the 1977 translation of Þorgeir Þorgeirson (b. 1933), who went on to translate several other of Heinesen's works; and Mikhail Bulgakov's *The Master and Margarita* (1967), in the 1981 translation of Ingibjörg Haraldsdóttir (b. 1942).

The 1980s saw more concentrated and systematic efforts in the area of ambitious prose translation than ever before, and, while Iceland's preeminent translator of recent years, Helgi Hálfdanarson (b. 1911), devoted himself to poetry and drama (translating all Shakespeare's plays and the Greek tragedies as well as several volumes of poetry), prose translation also attracted significant talents, who worked on long-term projects. While Þorgeirson has focused his translation efforts on Heinesen, Haraldsdóttir has rendered Fyodor Dostoyevsky's novels into Icelandic, and Hjörtur Pálsson (b. 1941) has translated a number of Isaac Bashevis Singer's books. Several other translators have been doing important work, including Thor Vilhjálmsson (b. 1925), Kristján Árnason (b. 1934), and Sigurður A. Magnússon (b. 1928), who has translated works by James Joyce, including (in 1992–93) *Ulysses* (1922). Indeed, the recent translations of Joyce, Marcel Proust, and Franz Kafka into Icelandic manifest a certain (belated) anchoring of the modernist paradigm in Icelandic prose. The most prolific prose translator, however, has been Guðbergur Bergsson, who has translated not only (in 1981–84) *Don Quixote* (1604 and 1614) and a number of Márquez's novels but also several other Latin American and Spanish works.

Bergsson was also instrumental in diverting the Icelandic novel of contemporary life away from the path of neorealism and into what some have called *magical realism*, using the term generally associated with Latin American fiction. Bergsson's *Hjartað býr enn í helli sínum* (1982; The heart still resides in its cave) is a parody of neorealistic "problem literature," satirically turning one of its most popular themes, the women question, against dogmatic forms of feminism, tracing the nightmarish wanderings of a divorced man through the streets of Reykjavík. The author who, in his previous work, had so vehemently dislodged male ideologies (see p. 423) thus proved that he was ready to attack anything that had become dogma.

Vésteinn Lúðvíksson (b. 1944), having abandoned his realist agenda (see p. 434), and about to take his leave of fiction as he turned to Zen Buddhism, similarly wrote a dream-like novel, *Maður og haf* (1984; Man and sea), about a man drifting away from his social moorings, having experienced a tragic loss. This obscure quest, in turn, is reminiscent of Thor Vilhjálmsson's *Turnleikhúsið* (1979; The Tower Theater; see pp. 427–29), which, incidentally, features a good deal of debate about feminism. It would seem that, in the fiction of the early 1980s, men have lost their traditional roles and are looking for their place in a changed world, something also borne out in Ómar Þ. Halldórsson's (b. 1954) *Þetta var nú í fylleríi* (1982; Drunk as a skunk) as well as in Ólafur Gunnarsson's (b. 1948) *Gaga* (1984; English trans.: *Gaga* [1988]), in which the protagonist travels around Reykjavík at night, believing that he has been transported to the planet Mars. The most "deconstructed" male image, however, may have appeared in Þórarinn Eldjárn's (b. 1949) *Kyrr kjör* (1983; Still life), which is based on the life of the crippled eighteenth-century poet Guðmundur Bergþórsson. While magical realism is a more significant element in Eldjárn's second novel, *Skuggabox* (1988; Shadowbox), *Kyrr kjör* calls attention to a salient factor in some of the prominent novels of the 1980s: the renegotiation of tradition and history.

Jakobína Sigurðardóttir's (1918–94) *Í sama klefa* (1981; In the same cabin), Thor Vilhjálmsson's *Grámosinn glóir* (1986; English trans.: *Justice Undone* [1998]), and Svava Jakobsdóttir's (1930–2004) *Gunnlaðar saga* (1987; The saga of Gunnlod) all involve the reader in an innovative dialogue with the past while problematizing its narrative mediation. In *Í sama klefa* the old rural community, as experienced at an isolated farm, and contemporary urban life are made to hold a mirror up to one another. The refractions are re-created in a multiple narrative frame, conveying the lives of two women from different social worlds who are accidental fellow travelers sharing a ship's cabin. The novel is also a metafictional inquiry into what it means to turn human experience into a work of literature and art. Vilhjálmsson's *Grámosinn glóir* (for which the author received the Nordic Literature Prize in 1988) takes us back to a criminal case at the turn of the century, involving an incestuous love affair at a farm. The magistrate in charge — who is also a poet — is shown losing his sense of social power as he faces the fate of the people involved, and this connects with his absorption of the landscape that he travels though, the natural scenery being brilliantly delivered in the text. *Gunnlaðar saga* takes readers into the more distant past of Old Norse mythology, in the company of a girl who "relives" the experiences of the goddess Gunnlöð, from whom the god Odin stole the sacred chalice of poetry while also misusing his power to initiate the Iron Age and the ruthless violation of mother earth (see p. 541). Addressing mythic sources of meaning, and making myth speak to the present, Jakobsdóttir shows us how the heroine and her mother seek to reclaim the chalice, a symbol of women's mediating role between the earth and male power, an act that also implies unearthing their experience as women.

In these and a number of other novels of the 1980s the legacy of modernism has been evident as the genre seemed again to be moving away from classic realism (as it had done in the late 1960s). Even where these works make use of realistic narrative, this is counterbalanced by an intricately structured text as regards motifs, ideas, or temporal shifts. Several novels of this period evince how the genre was moving into more lyric and romantic territory, but in a radical, nonsentimental sense; it adopted a variety of confessional modes that break traditional boundaries of recounting personal experiences. If, in some of the novels of the early 1980s, men were searching for their role in society, the decade also saw the creation of challenging female characters, in texts that delve into raw emotional life, involving provocative and often painful searches for love, for a place in the family, in society, indeed, in life itself. Particularly important among these novels, beside *Í sama klefa* and *Gunnlaðar saga*, are Steinunn Sigurðardóttir's (b. 1950) *Tímaþjófurinn* (1986; Thief of time), Álfrún Gunnlaugsdóttir's (b. 1938) *Hringsól* (1987; Circling), Vigdís Grímsdóttir's (b. 1953) *Ég heiti Ísbjörg, ég er ljón* (1989; My name is Ísbjörg, I am a Leo), and Fríða Sigurðardóttir's (b. 1940) *Meðan nóttin líður* (1990; English trans.: *Night Watch* [1995]).

These works differ significantly from one another, however, in their formal approaches. *Tímaþjófurinn* is structurally the most radical, frequently breaking up the narrative and veering into poetry as the heroine seeks to come to terms with her life, past and present, after a love affair that has unsettled her fixed notions of existence and modern femininity. It is probably the most hotly debated Icelandic novel of recent years, partly because it threads salient issues, such as modern women's educated liberation and recapture by the male gaze, into the life of a female character, with whom the reader is bound to have an uneasy relationship. This character, Alda (the name means "wave"), is both a spoiled brat and someone who is flooded by poetic images that run the whole gamut from facile egocentricism to deep internal injury.

The young woman who is at the center of *Ég heiti Ísbjörg, ég er ljón* also poses a challenge for traditional readerly sympathies. Ísbjörg has ended up in prison after a tumultuous life that has pushed her literally to the margins of society. Her way of opposing her sea of troubles has only isolated her more and led to desperate acts. This theme is not treated in conventional moral terms, however. In fact, Ísbjörg possesses a dignity and willpower of a Nietzschean kind, which attracts her defense attorney, but which he cannot comprehend. Something can be created out of what seems to be sheer loss and destruction, even if that something is an illusion that constitutes a hidden space inside oneself, a space alternately bright and dark, cold and fiery. Ísbjörg is the tough female counterpart to the gentle boy in Grímsdótt-ir's first novel, *Kaldaljós* (1987; Cold light), who grows into an artist after escaping an unspeakable catastrophe. Young Grímur is an unusual boy living with his family in a coastal settlement. He befriends a strange old woman whom he believes to be a witch, having seen her flying through the air on a broomstick. One night, when Grímur is sent on an errand to a nearby village, an avalance falls on his homestead, killing everyone. Grímur is adopted by the family he was visiting at the time but grows up a troubled youth. In the second half of the novel he has moved to Reykjavík and aspires to become an artist. The novel is partly fantastic in tone, the fantasy focusing around Grímur's relationship with the old woman and his art. Grímsdóttir, who made her debut with the short story collections *Tíu myndir úr lífi þínu* (1983; Ten images from your life) and *Eldur og regn* (1985; Fire and rain), would continue to explore in her writing the intertwined themes of the outsider and the artist and the vision of those who step beyond generally accepted social borders. Two of her novels, *Ég heiti Ísbjörg, ég er ljón* and *Grandavegur 7* (1994; 7 Grandi Road), were adapted for the stage, to general acclaim, and *Kaldaljós* was filmed in 2004.

Álfrún Gunnlaugsdóttir, a professor of comparative literature at the University of Iceland, brought out her first book of fiction in 1982, the finely crafted short story collection *Af manna völdum* (By human design). In *Hringsól*, her second novel, an elderly widow looks back on her life. Her various memories, along with the dialogue that she conducts with her deceased husband, are woven into her present. Such temporal and narrative weaving has been a characteristic of Gunnlaugsdóttir's fiction. She allows strands of her narrative to cross and play off each other. The strands stem from different periods in an individual's life, but they may also originate in different historical periods with which the present comes into existential alignment, as in her third novel, *Hvatt að rúnum* (1993; Tête-à-tête). Many of the memories in *Hringsól* are painful — and since *hringsól* means "going around in circles," this seems to imply that we are stuck with the pain of our past. At least we certainly are in this author's world; there is nothing for it but to face our former selves and find the courage to confront our memories in the present moment. Yet this also means that we are able to move the weight of the past; it does not have to pull us down.

The past as a world that one has run away from but that revisits us in one way or another, often as part of a crisis that is looming in our midst, is a prime motivation of Fríða Sigurðardóttir's writing. In *Meðan nóttin líður*, which won her the Nordic Literature Prize in 1992, a woman is sitting at her dying mother's bedside and gradually becomes entangled in the story of the women in her family, going back several generations. She is, in a way, claimed by the lives of these women who faced harsh rural surroundings, apparently so different from her own urban life. The built-in historical dialogue reminds us that the author, like her older sister, Jakobína (see above), has family roots in what used to be one of the most isolated districts of Iceland, Hornstrandir, a rural area depopulated by the mid-twentieth century. In the following two novels by Sigurðardóttir, *Í luktum heimi* (1994; In a sealed world) and *Maríuglugginn* (1998; The virgin window), the historical-biographical span is that of individuals in a modern urban setting who have, as it were, run ahead of themselves and are left to cope with moral and ethical questions without any guidance from an earlier era. These later novels are ambitiously designed to capture the alienating effects of modern life in a country marked by an urgency to adapt to the speed and urban patterns of Western modernity. The questions of what happens to love, compassion, and family commitments in such a world are eminently worthy, but the author does tend toward overdramatization of her characters' crises. Her ability to wield her topics in a more nuanced and subtle manner, however, is evident in her short story collection *Sumarblús* (2000; Summer blues).

URBANISM AND CHILDHOOD

It was perhaps inevitable that the generation of writers born and/or raised in Reykjavík during the postwar era would have a different view of urban culture than their older colleagues. For the younger writers the classic theme of migration from countryside to town was no longer a pressing one, and, as pointed out in part 1 of this chapter, Reykjavík finally became a central setting for fiction in the 1970s, in large part owing to neorealist concerns with contemporary social issues. One of the attractions of Pétur Gunnarsson's (b. 1947) novel quartet about Andri Haraldsson (see p. 436) was, indeed, the lively description of growing up in and with Iceland's only city. Gunnarsson's novels form a kind of bridge from neorealism to some of the fiction that was to draw much attention in the 1980s, especially novels that also portray boyhood in Reykjavík: Einar Már Guðmundsson's (b. 1954) *Riddarar hringstigans* (1982; Knights of the round staircase) and *Vængjasláttur í þakrennum* (1983; Wingbeats in the drainage), and Einar Kárason's (b. 1955) *Þar sem djöflaeyjan rís* (1983; English trans.: *Devils' Island* [2000]) and *Gulleyjan* (1985; Treasure island). In these novels Reykjavík is approached, not only through childhood, but also by creating demarcated fictional worlds based on particular neighborhoods that are either emerging or have already disappeared. No sooner had Reykjavík materialized as a modern urban setting than it acquired a historical dimension, one that also allowed for mythic and nostalgic dimensions. At the same time these novels register the signs and rhythms of Anglo-American popular culture as it makes its way into the youthful consciousness of this new urban scene, although this cultural influx had, in fact, been prominent since the wartime occupation of Iceland.

It remains an open question how far these books can be seen as exemplifying a reconstructed male (or boy-turning-into-man) image in the context of Icelandic urbanity. Childhood in the city was a new Icelandic experience, and in fiction it was one that, initially at least, was primarily explored in terms of boyhood. However, a more thorough fictional exploration of the dynamics of childhood would soon take place in the prose works of Gyrðir Elíasson (b. 1961), who is also a leading poet of his generation. Elíasson's writing defies the logical development of Icelandic writing into urban settings, for he leads his readers back to the villages, farms, and open spaces that tend to be forgotten in recent paradigms of Icelandic culture, geared as they are toward Reykjavík as both the cultural center and the gateway to foreign parts. But Elíasson discovers the foreign in the Icelandic hinterland, a realm by no means always found on regular maps, for the author is, as he has put it himself, a "mystical ruralist."

Elíasson's first novel was *Gangandi íkorni* (1987; Walking squirrel); it was followed by the four interconnected stories of *Bréfbátarigningin* (1988; Paper boat rain) and the novel *Svefnhjólið* (1990; Sleepcycling), along with several books of poetry and six volumes of short fiction, the most recent being *Gula húsið* (2000; The yellow house) and the novel *Næturluktin* (2001; The night lantern), a sequel to *Gangandi íkorni*. The elements of Elíasson's poetry and prose, varied as they are, have gradually created an entire world, unmistakably bearing the mark of its author and his quiet mastery of style, even though many fragments stem from folk- and fairy tales, from the oral traditions of rural Iceland, or from various foreign literary sources. His characters, usually strangely sensitive and quirky, sometimes drowsy wanderers, slip from one narrative space into another, sometimes with ease, at other times through a violent occurrence. The everyday and the fabulous, danger and serenity, are in close proximity. Everything around us is potentially meaningful and, thus, carries within it a mirror that is also a boundary of our self. Many of Elíassson's works focus on such boundaries, on walls, windows, enclosures, demarcations, and on the rupturing of such divisions. Some of those are ever present in our lives but do not divulge their secret, such as the line between life and death or the one separating childhood from adult life. "When I open the refrigeration door, I am met by a bright light, and my mind is filled with the aura of a children's book read a long time ago" (*Heykvísl og gúmmískór*, 49). This sentence, from one of Elíasson's many short stories, is an indication of what could be called his *labyrinth of lucidity*.

Childhood is a world that Elíasson has probed in greater depth than most other Icelandic writers. We find out that the bridges connecting the child with the adult self are not always where we think they are; they travel elusively within us. As in the works of Kafka, albeit differently, in Elíasson writing the child is intimately linked with the creative mind, or the artist, and the figure that completes the triangle is the animal. The group of three should, perhaps, be supplemented with the ghost, a figure guarding the border between life and death, belonging to neither, and also linking the humorous with the horrible. Elíasson's literary field abounds with eccentric characters, children, old people, animals, and ghosts, all of them belonging to cultural margins, but as such they illuminate the outlines and otherness of society. In this respect his writing borders on the oeuvre of Vigdís Grímsdóttir, although the emotional intensity and expansiveness of her texts seem a far cry from the deceptively fine vibrations of Elíasson's limpid and disciplined style.

Grímsdóttir's novel *Grandavegur 7* is narrated by the girl Einfríður (Fríða), who is quite a match for the boys in the novels of contemporary writers. Endowed with second sight, she slowly travels, in the company of the dead, toward a place among the living, each belonging to the house of meaning that Fríða is constructing as she looks back to her childhood. The novel is heavily metafictional, not only because of the text's foregrounded and sometimes playful awareness of a story in the making, but also in the more urgent sense of people belonging to us as elements of a narrative or network that we piece together. The border between these people as individuals and as parts of our "design" is unclear, and even death, notoriously, does not clarify it. This is an existential question in everyone's life, but it looms especially large for writers and artists, who find the lifeblood of their creation in their environment, in texts and art around them, and not least in people they encounter. Grímsdóttir had already studied this question in her previous novel, *Stúlkan í skóginum* (1992; The girl in the woods), where a woman artist who specialized in dollmaking becomes obsessed with the figure and existence of a disfigured bag lady, who, in turn, is an unlikely collector of books, parts of which she learns by heart, while also carrying within her a forest of the mind, where a whole different life is taking place.

The artist does not stop until she has imprisoned this social outcast and taken over her body. In the novel *Þögnin* (2000; The silence), Grímsdóttir takes even further this theme of how people live on art and art thrives on people and the ways in which this corresponds to how people live on one another to the point of taking over the lives of others.

In her fiction Grímsdóttir has traveled widely in the terrain of woman's sexuality—one more aspect of which is the lesbian relationship so poignantly depicted in the novel *Z—ástarsaga* (1996; English trans.: *Z—a Love Story* [1997]). The challenging ways in which she has thrown light, and darkness, on the delights, risks, and vulnerabilities of the awakening female psyche, and on the girl within the woman, have made their mark on Icelandic fiction, at a time when childhood and gender issues have been of central importance. Perhaps *girl within the culture* is a more apt formulation, as one may gather from Guðbergur Bergsson's *Svanurinn* (1991; English trans.: *The Swan* [1998]), a novel that took many Icelanders by surprise, brought its author new readers, and has been translated into several languages. Through the character of a nine-year-old girl who is sent to stay on a farm as punishment for a minor misdemeanor, Bergsson finds a way back to the countryside, whose symbolic images of birth, fertility, and death, along with the significance of mountains, clouds, and unpaved ground, are eerily, lovingly, humorously conveyed through the girl's consciousness.

MINIMALISM AND FANTASY

The 1980s may not have achieved breakthroughs in the novel to the extent that the late 1960s and early 1970s did, but the decade did yield a greater variety, a more pluralistic spectrum of Icelandic prose literature than had ever been in evidence before. While the novel remained the literary genre most appealing to the general readership and most discussed by critics, a number of writers are clearly skeptical of its prevalent format, the unfolding of a consistent plot and course of dramatic action. As a result, minimalism has thrived in different forms, from the growing quietude of Elíasson's fiction, through various experiments in microfiction (e.g., the very short stories of Elísabet Jökulsdóttir [b. 1958], in which the playful parody of storytelling throws light on situations normally overshadowed in grander narratives), to the recent novels of "inaction" by Bragi Ólafsson (b. 1962), *Hvíldardagar* (1999; Days of repose) and *Gæludýrin* (2001; The pets). Ólafsson had made his name as a poet before he turned to fiction, and these novels are in certain ways like blown-up poetic images of young men who get themselves into situations where they become immobilized. They are stuck, frozen stiff in positions from which they can only observe, listen to, or imagine the life going on "out there." The limited and delayed action of these works, sometimes reminiscent of both Kafka and Paul Auster, may be understood as an antithesis to the apparent energy and mobility of novelty-crazed Icelandic society, in which so many of Ólafsson's contemporaries have quickly moved up (and down) the ladders of economic and social life. But such connections are only latent in the texts.

In the meantime, other writers had found different alternatives to traditional, epic storytelling. In 1993 the artist Ragna Sigurðardóttir (b. 1962) published her first novel, *Borg* (City). Sigurðardóttir is one of several artists who turned to writing in the 1980s, and, by the time *Borg* appeared, she had already published three books containing texts that straddled the borderline between prose and poetry. *Borg* is a highly unusual novel in the Icelandic literary landscape; it is in many ways a conceptual work, a reflection on the nature and function of the city while simultaneously mapping out various theoretical issues relating to city life and the cityscape. The city is personified as a living entity, and this personification is further stressed by aligning one of the persons of the novel with the city. Úlla is a city creature; the city is a part of her body; she speaks its language and knows its rhythm and flow intimately, moving along its streets with utter confidence. Like her friend Logi she is obsessed with the consumerist aspect of city life; quoting ads and pop songs, she treats the city as a text. Vaka, the third person in the triangle, is a country girl who does not know the city as well as Úlla and Logi. She is a linguist and a translator and uses her talent to understand the cityscape around her, translating the map of the city into a book that she reads from one sentence to another street, comparing the arteries of one city to those of another.

While this city, and the country surrounding it, bears a clear resemblance to Reykjavík and the southern part of Iceland, this is not Reykjavík as we knew it then or, indeed, as we know it today. *Borg* is partly futuristic and aligns itself with fantasy rather than realism, detailing a society and cityscape that could be Reykjavík in one possible future or an alternative version of Reykjavík today.

Three novels of the late 1980s concern themselves with catastrophic and futuristic images of cities similar to *Borg*, and all these cityscapes are recognizably derived from Reykjavík: *Stálnótt* (1987; Night of steel) by Sjón (Sigurjón B. Sigurðsson; b. 1962); *Miðnætursólborgin* (1988; Midnight sun city) by Jón Gnarr (b. 1967); and *Byggingin* (1988; The building) by Jóhamar (Jóhannes Óskarsson; b. 1963). In the rather long and winding literary tradition of contrasting city and country, the urban and the rural, the novelty of these works is striking, and while two of them (*Miðnætursólborgin* and *Byggingin*) are underground texts, their influence on *Borg* is indisputable. Furthermore, the fantastic-futuristic content of the works gives them a certain international aura that is seldom found in Icelandic novels.

This international aura is partly due to the strange position of fantasy in Icelandic fiction. Realism has been the dominant mode in prose literature, and, while modernist writers such as Svava Jakobsdóttir, Guðbergur Bergsson, Steinar Sigurjónsson (1928–92), and Thor Vilhjálmsson all employed fantasy to a considerable extent, it functioned as a part of the modernist aesthetic. Fantasy has, of course, been the subject of many sundry definitions, ranging from Tzvetan Todorov's theory of the nonresolution between realistic and supernatural explanations to Rosemary Jackson's theory of the subversive potentials of the mode. In popular discourse fantasy is usually simply seen as either a wholly separate world, as in J. R. R. Tolkien's *The Lord of the Rings* (1953), or a certain tendency away from realism, as in the magical realism of some Latin American fiction. While the latter type of fantasy was occasionally seen in Icelandic fiction, the former type was practically nonexistent, and, where it did appear, it was clearly positioned within the boundaries of children's literature. In the 1990s, however, there was a considerable surge of fantastic literature, its authors including Ragna Sigurðardóttir, Sjón, Ísak Harðarson (b. 1956), Bjarni Bjarnason (b. 1965), Vigdís Grímsdóttir, and Kristín Ómarsdóttir (b. 1962). In Grímsdóttir's and Ómarsdóttir's works fantasy appears mostly as a tendency or a theme, placed within an ostensibly realistic frame. With Grímsdóttir the fantastic element is often linked with art and artistic expression, for instance, in *Kaldaljós*, *Grandavegur 7*, and *Þögnin*, where the worlds of fantasy and art collide through painting, writing, and music.

Kristín Ómarsdóttir has published both poetry and prose fiction, including the novels *Svartir brúðarkjólar* (1992; Black wedding dresses), *Dyrnar þröngu* (1995; The Narrow doors), and *Elskan mín ég dey* (1997; My love, I die), and two books of short stories, *Í ferðalagi hjá þér* (1989; Traveling with you) and *Einu sinni sögur* (1991; Once upon a time stories). She has also written several plays. All her works contain elements of fantasy as well as a consistent exploration of sex and gender, sexuality and love. *Dyrnar þröngu* is arguably her most fantastic work to date, drawing on themes from Lewis Carroll's *Alice's Adventures in Wonderland* (1865), and containing a large number of grotesque elements, a certain hallmark of her work, while also bearing a distinct resemblance to the work of Guðbergur Bergsson, as illustrated in her novel from 2001, *Hamingjan hjálpi mér I og II* (Gracious me! I and II).

While *Dyrnar þröngu* is as opaque as its title suggests, *Elskan mín ég dey* is considerably more accessible and more competently crafted. It tells the story of a small fishing village somewhere on the Icelandic coast, describing a family of five children and their father. The mother and the oldest sister died some years previously, and at the start of the novel the second sister is brought home dead, leaving only the boys in the house. The three women keep watch from one of the many halls of heaven and participate in the story by discussing their fates as the number of family members continues to dwindle. The narrator is Högni, the third son, who has just turned seventeen. The style is playful, sometimes moving into dark horror. The story is both realistic and fantastic, providing a dialogue and a tension between the two, and maintaining a delicate balance between wistfulness and comedy. The family household is the realist anchor, full of minute details about everyday life. However, these minute details, while appearing realistic, continually slip into the realm of the fantastic, simply being too minute. Similarly, the marvelous realm of heaven is all too realistic, depicting heaven as a kind of coffeehouse, with white-gloved angels in the role of servants. Thus, the style refutes any clear distinction between the space of the fantastic and the realistic setting, adding the writerly dimension of a scribbling angel and his manuscript and the presence of Hemingway and Leonardo da Vinci. The novel, furthermore, is full of stark sexuality and smooth sensuality, adding another level to this textual game of death, dead bodies, and teenage boys. Stories of fishing villages are a standard in Icelandic literature, but in her novel Ómarsdóttir offers a completely fresh approach to a traditional and worn formula. From the start Kristín Ómarsdóttir has challenged the boundaries of literary genres, fusing drama into novel, poetry into narrative, and connecting short stories into a thematic whole. This has resulted in a highly successful dialogue between form and content, while her language and style similarly refute clear demarcations between fantasy and realism. Her texts offer a comprehensive challenge to traditional ideas of gender and sexuality, where the interrogation of traditional form mirrors the interrogation of sex and gender.

Other writers, such as Gyrðir Elíasson, whose first novel, *Gangandi íkorni*, is partly a fantasy, continued working with the fantastic in their prose fiction. This wave of fantasy also happened in children's literature. The artist Þorvaldur Þorsteinsson (b. 1960) published two critically acclaimed books about the winged character Blíðfinnur, paving the way for Andri Snær Magnason's (b. 1973) illustrated story *Sagan af bláa hnettinum* (1999; The story of the blue planet) to become the first children's book to receive the Icelandic Literary Prize. *Sagan af bláa hnettinum* is notable for its design and illustration; indeed, the artist Áslaug Jónsdóttir no doubt contributes considerably to the story's success among both children and grown-ups. A perfect salesman, Gleði-Glaumur (Noisy-Joy), visits a children's world on a blue planet. Little by little he manages to sell foibles to the children in return for their eternal youth, and it is not until one of the children is ready to make the ultimate sacrifice that they realize what they are losing. In many ways a cruel and demanding story, and pointedly critical of consumer society, *Sagan af bláa hnettinum* is very different from, yet in some ways similar to, Þorvaldur Þorsteinsson's two books of Blíðfinnur. While the world of Blíðfinnur is different from the children's planet, the stories are similarly demanding, neither offering the comfortable escapist route of fantastic adventures or, indeed, a wholly comforting solution. The first book, *Ég heiti Blíðfinnur en þú mátt kalla mig Bóbó* (1998; My name is Betterby, but you can call me Bobo), establishes the world of the small winged creature Blíðfinnur and his friend Smælkið (Tiny). Despite their friendship Blíðfinnur is a little lonely and so becomes very happy when he finds a child in his garden one morning. After a few days of fun and bliss the child disappears, and Blíðfinnur, desperate, starts a perilous journey to reclaim his lost friend. On their quest Smælkið falls victim to the "academons," who feed on the creative energy of passersby. When he finally reaches home again, the child is back in his garden, now looking completely different: it has grown old and in its senility has returned to its childhood world of Blíðfinnur's fantasy, where it dies happy. In *Heitir þú Blíðfinnur, ég er með mikilvæg skilaboð* (2000; Are you Betterby? I have an important message) Blíðfinnur is making new friends again. When he is kidnapped by evil "bluffers," his newly found friends embark on a search-and-rescue mission. Meanwhile, Blíðfinnur has to face the shadows within himself.

All three books appealed to adult readers as well as to children, as have English and American works of fantasy so prominent in the late 1990s, J. K. Rowling's Harry Potter novels and the films based on them, the renewed interest in Tolkien's *Lord of the Rings*, and Philip Pullman's trilogy of dæmons and dust, *His Dark Materials* (1996–2000). The popularity of fantasy is also apparent in other culture products, such as films, comics, computer and role-playing games, all bridging generation gaps. The enthusiastic reception of these works would seem to indicate the stronger position of fantasy in an international context, which has undoubtedly influenced and abetted the success of Magnason's and Þorsteinsson's children's books and aided the reception of other fantastic works.

The city continued to feature prominently within Icelandic fantasy, particularly in the work of Bjarni Bjarnason and Ísak Harðarson. While Bjarnason had produced a varied body of work, all self-published, he did not attract much attention as a writer until his novel *Endurkoma Maríu* (The return of Mary) appeared in 1996. The novel is a fantastic tale of an unusually talented young woman and an unusual young man who loves her from afar. It takes place in several cities that show distinct similarities to certain European cities but are clearly illusory spaces. Bjarnason continued exploring this image of the city in his two novels *Borgin bakvið orðin* (1998; The city behind the words) and *Næturvörður kyrrðarinnar* (1999; The night watchman of silence). Time is an important element in all his novels; their imagery is influenced by ancient myths and invested with a fairy tale atmosphere while simultaneously referring to modern phenomena. Harðarson's novel *Mannveiðihandbókin* (1999; Manhunting manual) similarly conflates past and present, or, rather, the future. *Mannveiðihandbókin* starts out realistically enough, describing a small fishing village on the Icelandic coast. Soon, however, futuristic fantasy enters the story as a young girl, desirous of adventure, moves to the city, where she starts working in a large shopping center. In the city she discovers machines (hoovers) that seem to have a life of their own, and the shopping center turns out to be a kind of cybernetic system, powered by angels singing the glory of consumerism. While Bjarnason's novels stage the act of storytelling and, thus, invite the reader to reflect on language, in particular poetic language and the idea of fictionality, Harðarson's novel conveys a rather conventional critique of consumer society.

Consumerism certainly is an important theme in *Stálnótt* by Sjón, which conjures up one of the slipstream cityscapes that appeared in the late 1980s. Like Ísak Harðarson's and Ragna Sigurðardóttir's novels, Sjón's *Stálnótt* is a futuristic story, describing a city reminiscent of Reykjavík that is besieged by four demons. The novel has its roots in cyberpunk as well as Enid Blyton's children's books: indeed, the four people attacked by the demons carry the names of the young protagonists in her *Adventure* series. At the time Sjón was mainly known as a poet and a member of the surrealistic group Medusa, young poets, visual artists, and musicians who organized various events such as poetry readings, theatrical performances, and exhibitions. In 1989 Sjón published a second novel, *Engill, pípuhattur og jarðarber* (Angel, top hat, and strawberry) that is also a fantasy, describing the collision of two worlds, one a small tourist village by a beach, the other a dark world of shadows running underneath and at the margins of the village.

Sjón's *Augu þín sáu mig* (Thine eyes did see me) appeared in 1994, to considerable critical acclaim. The novel is an ambitious collage of texts and textual references, all gathered together to form a new being, a baby made of clay. This seemingly fragmented approach is tightly woven, and a clear narrative is always present; the story is told by the creature himself, describing the sudden appearance of one Leó Löwe, who is on the run with a hatbox. He finds himself in a small German village being taken care of by Marie-Sophie, a young maid at the local guesthouse. They become friends, and together they form a baby boy out of the mass of clay that Leó carries in his hatbox. Another main thread revolves around the angel Gabriel and his attempt to end the world by blowing his doomsday horn, an attempt that is blocked by the tricks of the devil and eventually results in Gabriel's discovery of his true sex, which is female. This biblical reference supports the novel's main frame of reference, the Jewish myth of the creation of the golem, a man of clay. The work thus revolves around the theme of creation, a theme that is reiterated in the numerous creation stories that appear in the collage of texts, as dreams, anecdotes, or intertextual references to other novels and films. The creation plot is, then, further explored through the postmodern trope of self-conscious literary creation, where the author/ storyteller is present in his own work, reflecting on the relationship between author and work, reality and fiction. A sequel, *Með titrandi tár: Glæpasaga* (With a trembling tear: A crime story), appeared in 2001, also to critical acclaim.

In many respects, Sjón's oeuvre constitutes a novelty in Icelandic literature. The way in which Sjón employs international culture, myth, literature, and popular culture is unique, as is the breadth of his scope of reference. The narratives are enriched by light and humorous touches, which allow him to work pliably with what would otherwise seem obscure matters.

SEXUALITY AND FAMILY

While fantasy has been gaining ground in Icelandic literature, it is still a marginal practice, and authors such as Ragna Sigurðardóttir, Kristín Ómarsdóttir, and Sjón still occupy an aesthetic position slightly off-center. Significantly, intimations of fantasy can also be traced in the work of other writers outside the mainstream of Icelandic literature. One such writer is Sigfús Bjartmarsson (b. 1955). His work on the wilderness of Icelandic nature is ultrarealistic, but his powerful and idiosyncratic prose at times takes the narrative into the world of fantasy. *Mýrarenglarnir falla* (1990; The swamp angels are falling) is a compilation of loosely connected stories, told variously from the point of view of a young boy and a grown-up who has returned to the countryside of his youth. Even though the story takes place in the not-so-distant past of the mid-twentieth-century, modernity is far away, and the language emphasizes the feeling of an archaic world and worldview, far removed from the bourgeois household: the earthy prose spells out the rough edges of a hunter's primordial mind-set. The same atmosphere permeates Bjartmarsson's most impressive work to date, *Vargatal* (1998; A dictionary of predators). Similarly archaic in tone, this collection of stories on scavengers and carnivores in Icelandic nature conjures up a whole new wilderness world within Iceland's fauna. The text is a mixture of natural history, personal impressions, folklore, and fiction, and the conflation of these elements invokes a distinctly mythological tone, adding to the powerful reading experience.

Similarly challenging in the culturescape, but entirely different in content, are Didda's (b. 1964) two novels to date, *Erta* (1997; Erta) and *Gullið í höfðinu* (1999; The gold in her head). They are, in fact, highly realistic, but their style and structure are so ruptured that they appear fantastic at times. Didda is a writer rooted in the punk movement, and in her writings she focuses on the margins of Icelandic society, or, perhaps, the wilderness of Icelandic urban culture. *Erta* is a reflection on the diary form. Written in the first person, it describes the inner life of a girl who is a complete outsider, focusing on her sexual fantasies. Also emphasizing sexuality, *Gullið í höfðinu* is the story of a young girl residing in a mental institution. She has done terrible damage to her genitals, and she is mute, refusing to speak. The root of her problems is located in the disappearance of a girl at her school. Both novels map the underbelly of the city of Reykjavík, a world of violence, drugs, and destitution.

This side of Reykjavík also appears in the work of another young writer, Mikael Torfason (b. 1974). Much like Didda's work, his three novels— *Falskur fugl* (1997; Fake bird), *Saga af stúlku* (1998; A girl's story), and *Heimsins heimskasti pabbi* (2000; The world's stupidest dad)—caused a stir on the literary scene. The first novel is the most noteworthy of the three. Taking place in the rapidly growing suburb of Grafarvogur, it is a tale of youth gangs and drug trafficking, considerably influenced by gritty British and American films of the mid-1990s. The story is told by a fifteen-year-old boy whose family suffers a horrible tragedy when the older brother commits suicide by setting himself on fire in the bathtub. The novel is most remarkable for its thorough mapping of Icelandic suburbia, invoking a compelling feeling for space. Graphic sex scenes are recurrent and continue to mar the sensationalist *Saga af stúlku*, the story of a pubescent girl who experiences great difficulties with her self-image owing to the fact that she had been born a boy. Torfason returns to family life in *Heimsins heimskasti pabbi*, about a young stoma patient and his troubled marriage. The work is placed within a distinctly contemporary setting, with references to specific people and events, and is partly a reflection on the status of masculinity in contemporary society.

Sexuality and the archaeology of gender play an even larger role in Rúnar Helgi Vignisson's (b. 1959) fiction. His novel *Nautnastuldur* (1990; Indulgence denied) probes daringly into a male complex of sex drive and personal insecurity. The protagonist, whose name, Egill Grímsson, is, ironically, almost but not quite identical to that of one of the Icelandic saga heroes, Egill Skallagrímsson, is baffled by a gay foreigner who befriends him and also deeply worried about not being man enough for the young woman he loves. In the novel *Ástfóstur* (1997; Love fetus) Vignisson continues his excavation of male identities that do not have a tight grip on patriarchal structures and are constantly looking for assurance and comfort in the female embrace. Here, however, female identity, too, is in turmoil. The opening sentence is: "I was never born." The narrator is an aborted fetus whose sex remains undisclosed and whose paternity is in considerable doubt. Like many of Vignisson's other texts, this novel is written in a self-conscious, ironic, yet ambivalent tone, one that readers often find grating and discomforting. Vignisson is also an accomplished author of short stories and has produced several translations, including novels by William Faulkner, Philip Roth, Amy Tan, and J. M. Coetzee.

Sexual destabilization is a common feature in the work of the younger writers working with fantasy who were discussed earlier, such as Kristín Ómarsdóttir, Sjón, and Vigdís Grímsdóttir, but it is also a prominent element in the work of older writers such as Guðbergur Bergsson. Fantasy has long been a playground for sexual disruption, where the traditional definitions of sex and gender are undermined. Ómarsdóttir, Grímsdóttir, and Bergsson all have written novels that could be defined as queer writing, and queer elements also appear in Sjón's work, particularly *Stálnótt*, but also *Augu þín sáu mig*. The sexual flux characterizing Ómarsdóttir's novels refutes any clear demarcations between heterosexuality and homosexuality, while both Grímsdóttir and Bergsson have written homosexual love stories, Grímsdóttir in *Z — ástarsaga*, and Guðbergur Bergsson in *Sú kvalda ást sem hugarfylgsnin geyma* (1993; Tormented love in the recesses of the mind), where the boundaries crossed in a secret homosexual love affair turn out to coincide with, or perhaps cross, other significant borders in our culture, borders that mark the limits of beauty, faith, and the very notion of an inner life. This is one of Bergsson's most challenging novels and certainly his most philosophical one.

Difficult and complex family issues are a recurring theme in the work of

Vigdís Grímsdóttir, for example, in *Ég heiti Ísbjörg, ég er ljón* and *Granda-vegur 7*, both discussed earlier, as well as in *Þögnin* and *Frá ljósi til ljóss* (2001; From light to light), always revolving around intense emotions and various, often unusual, forms of love. Complex family issues also abound in Steinunn Sigurðardóttir's fiction. Like Grímsdóttir, Sigurðardóttir first stepped onto the scene of fiction in the early 1980s with a short story collection, *Sögur til næsta bæjar* (1981; Something to write home about), soon to be followed by another, *Skáldsögur* (1983; Novels), both collections containing stories of strange family relationships. Sigurðardóttir started out as a poet, publishing three books of poetry in 1969, 1971, and 1979 (see p. 489), and, in her 1986 novel *Tímaþjófurinn* (discussed earlier), she successfully merged poetry with prose. Her novella *Ástin fiskanna* (1993; The love of the fishes), somewhat like *Tímaþjófurinn*, details a rather unusual love affair where a young woman falls in love under fairy tale circumstances but finds out that fairy tales do not always end happily. The love story in the otherwise powerful *Hjartastaður* (1995; Place of the heart) is so muted as to be practically invisible. In this expansive road novel Sigurðardóttir returns to the theme of complicated family relationships. Harpa, a single mother, takes her recalcitrant daughter on a trip across the country, intending to place her daughter in the care of her relations living on a quiet farmstead as she is well on her way to becoming a juvenile delinquent. Accompanying them on their journey are Harpa's friend Heiður, who is the driver, and Harpa's deceased mother—yet another Icelandic ghost character—continually arguing posthumously with her daughter, chastising her for her upbringing of the child. Sigurðardóttir's highly ironic tone is in many ways characteristic of women's writing in Iceland, although none can match her perfectly tuned blend of bubbly humor and breathtaking emotional impact.

While Gerður Kristný (b. 1970) most often cites Svava Jakobsdóttir as her main influence, the marks of Steinunn Sigurðardóttir can also be discerned in her work, for instance, in the way she uses cool humor and independent female characters. Thus, an influence can be traced through three generations of women writers, indicating the strong position that women have gained in the cultural landscape. This positioning is stressed in the premise of Gerður Kristný's first novel, *Regnbogi í póstinum* (1996; Rainbow in the mail). This work was partly meant as a female response to the "boys' school of writing," made popular in the 1980s by writers like Einar Kárason, Einar Már Guðmundsson, and Pétur Gunnarsson. Partly parodically, Gerður Kristný has her young heroine follow in the footsteps of generations of young men who sailed to Copenhagen—Iceland's former capital city—in search of experience, education, and poetic inspiration, among them the Nobel laureate Halldór Laxness (1902–98). The cool girl heroine has just finished secondary school and is at something of a loss at this important milestone in her life. She goes to France as an au pair but swiftly finds out that child care and other household chores do not really suit her. She therefore decides to head for the classic Icelandic destination, Copenhagen. A bildungsroman featuring a young woman, the story was something of a novelty and without a doubt exercised considerable influence on the contemporary novel in Iceland.

Gerður Kristný's next work was a short story collection, *Eitruð epli* (1998; Poisoned apples), a significantly more aggressive take on women's experiences in Icelandic society. Clearly influenced by Svava Jakobsdóttir's work, Gerður Kristný moves toward the grotesque in these stories, particularly in the loosely connected tales of the *saumaklúbbur* (lit. "sewing club," a traditional way for Icelandic women to get together and chat, usually under the pretext of doing some handicraft together, such as sewing or knitting) and in "Mengele var misskilinn húmoristi" (Mengele was a misunderstood humorist), an uncanny story about a strained relationship between mother and daughter. Gerður Kristný's prose works are highly ironic; her text is self-consciously nonsentimental, demonstrating a tough approach to writing and women's place within the literary arena. This is also apparent in her extraliterary work. Hers is a powerful voice in contemporary Icelandic society: she worked for several years as the editor of one of Iceland's most popular magazines, and both there and elsewhere she has been unafraid to be outspoken about feminist issues concerning family values, women's rights, violence against women, and women in the media. As such, she has become a highly controversial figure.

POPULAR APPEAL

Together, as well as individually, women writers have made considerable changes in the Icelandic literary landscape, providing women's voices and women's issues with a more prominent place, and offering fresh insights into the cultural milieu, indicating new ways of coping with a changing society and refashioning the cultural heritage.

While women writers have not been as preoccupied with the tradition of "realistic" storytelling as have some of their male contemporaries, they have, like Einar Kárason and Einar Már Guðmundsson, bridged the gap between readerships of different cultural groups. The works of Vigdís Grímsdóttir, Steinunn Sigurðardóttir, and Gerður Kristný enjoy both popular appeal and critical acclaim, and each of these writers is unafraid of tackling emotionally charged issues concerning love, family values, and the continual search for a (female) identity in tumultuous times. Kristín Marja Baldursdóttir's (b. 1949) work has also been important in breaking down the borders between elite and popular culture. Her first novel, *Mávahlátur* (1995; The seagull's laughter), takes place in the years after the Second World War, telling the story of the unexpected return of Freyja (named after the Nordic goddess of love and war), who had married an American soldier. Freyja's sophisticated appearance causes a considerable stir in the small village community, and the novel illustrates issues of changing femininity, the influence of American values, and the subsequent changes in the Icelandic cultural landscape. Baldursdóttir's later novels continue this concern with women's issues in contemporary urban society.

In some ways Baldursdóttir's highly popular works should be viewed in the context of the so-called *kerlingabækur*, popular fiction from the 1950s, 1960s, and 1970s whose authors were mainly women — hence the (derogatory) name, literally meaning "old wives' tales" (see also p. 538). Written by middle-aged women like Guðrún of Lundur (1887–1973) and Ingibjörg Sigurðardóttir (b. 1925), these novels were rural romances, offering a much-desired nostalgia during a time of rapid urbanization. These changes affected, not only society, but also letters as modernism made its mark on Icelandic arts, absorbing a significant part of the literary critical debate while never really becoming the ruling discourse of the actual fiction, which continued to be dominantly realistic. However, the hold that modernism had on the critical discourse alongside traditional male-oriented social realism offered little space for fruitful discussion of popular, romantic rural realism, which met with an almost exclusively negative critical response — not least, of course, because it was popular — as the epithet *old wives' tales* indicates.

The current poor state of Icelandic popular fiction is, in fact, something of a puzzle. While critical response has been unanimously negative, it is unlikely that this would, in and of itself, have stifled the urge for the production of light entertainment in the literary field to this extent. One explanation might be the fact that this kind of reading material has been amply supplied in the form of translations of international popular fiction: romances, thrillers, and detective stories (fantasy, science fiction and horror are as yet a negligible part of the output). And, much to the consternation of critics, these titles until recently tended to dominate every best-seller list (by the 1990s translated popular fiction had been largely eclipsed by popular visual culture such as television and video). Alistair MacLean, Sidney

Sheldon, and Danielle Steel sold very well in Iceland even though their novels appeared in expensive hardcover editions (paperbacks did not become a large part of Icelandic book production until the 1990s).

Iceland's best-selling author of recent years, however, has been, not a foreign writer of thrillers or romances, but an Icelander who has lived abroad for many years and who tends toward protagonists who have left Iceland but remain tied to it via their families, friendships, or memories. Even though Ólafur Jóhann Ólafsson (b. 1962; marketed abroad as Olaf Olafson), son of the writer Ólafur Jóhann Sigurðsson (1918–88; see p. 408), has had a successful business career in the United States, he has found time to write several novels in his native Icelandic that have been translated into a number of foreign languages. His novels—from *Fyrirgefning synd- anna* (1991; English trans.: *Absolution* [1994]), through *Slóð fiðrildanna* (1999; English trans.: *The Journey Home* [2000]), to *Höll minninganna* (2001; Castle of memories)—are realist in narrative scope, and his traditional style is a little ceremonious, sometimes to the point of being affected. The attraction of his books largely stems from a well-crafted narrative, combined with the alluring theme of Icelandic destinies abroad and the melodramatic depiction of his characters' inner agitations and longings.

Birgitta H. Halldórsdóttir (b. 1959) is one of the few contemporary writers who has continued the tradition of popular fiction. She is, perhaps, the most prolific writer of the past two decades, having published a book a year since 1983, but she is as yet more or less absent from the critical discourse. Her books are a mixture of the romance and the thriller/crime genres, often interspersed with gothic elements, and always featuring a young, independent heroine with an investigative spirit.

Popular genres such as crime fiction have no tradition in Iceland, and it was not until recently that Birgitta Halldórsdóttir's efforts found an echo in the fictional milieu, when a handful of writers devoted their talents to writing detective stories. In 1997 the journalist and film critic Arnaldur Indriðason (b. 1961) published a detective novel entitled *Synir duftsins* (Sons of earth). That same year *Morðið í Stjórnarráðinu* (Murder at Government Hall) appeared under the pseudonym Stella Blómkvist, featuring an eponymous heroine. Indriðason followed his first novel with *Dauðarósir* (1998; Silent kill) during the same year that Árni Þórarinsson (b. 1950) made his debut with *Nóttin hefur þúsund augu* (The night has a thousand eyes) and Viktor Arnar Ingólfsson (b. 1955) published *Engin spor* (No trace). While highly uneven in quality, this sudden surge seemed to confirm that Icelandic crime fiction was here to stay. Indriðason, Þórarinsson, and Blómkvist have all since continued to publish new novels, and the genre's status now seems to be assured. The crime novels deal mostly with contemporary issues, often making room for social analysis and commentary. This is a welcome addition since much Icelandic literature has tended to focus on the past and has, apparently, not attended to the nuances of modern society. This tendency has been criticized by those who feel that historical fiction is not confronting the rapidly changing cultural scene of the present, shying away from such provocative issues as the impact of technology, globalization, and cultural diversity. While several works of fiction are, in fact, attempting to come to terms with these new and continually altering cultural conditions, it can also be argued that historical fiction is, in part, directed against the cultural amnesia often seen as a characteristic of the 1990s and the new century.

URBAN EPICS AND THE HINTERLAND

Realism is a dominant feature of crime fiction, and it continues to have a strong hold on Icelandic fiction in general, often assuming an epic dimension. The novels of Einar Kárason, Einar Már Guðmundsson, and Ólafur Gunnarsson can all be termed *urban epics*. Einar Kárason's popular "island" novels, *Þar sem djöflaeyjan rís*, *Gulleyjan*, and *Fyrirheitna landið* (1989; The promised land), were adapted for film in 1996, renewing their popularity. The novels are set in Reykjavík in the years during and after the Second World War and describe the life of the poor, usually homeless, people who moved into the barracks left by the American army. Owing to the occupation by the British and American armies, these years constitute a very important period in the history of Iceland, particularly in Reykjavík. The island trope is central to the structure of the novels, where Iceland serves as a frame surrounding an even smaller island that is the camp of barracks, while the camp, in turn, frames the smallest island unit, the family, including the main characters. Given this historical staging, the story of the camp becomes also a story of Reykjavík, its emergence as a capital city, and, eventually, reflects on the development of the entire country from a backward, barely industrial community into a treasure island of fishing industry and urban growth. Reference is made to the sagas, and Kárason has, indeed, been praised for injecting new blood into the ancient Icelandic tradition of epic storytelling. In his novels *Heimskra manna ráð* (1993; The council of fools) and *Kvikasilfur* (1995; Quicksilver) Kárason attempted to create another such epic setting, this time turning his attention to the 1960s, but continuing to map Reykjavík's expansion and transformation with his special flair for exaggeration and swaggering masculinity. Most recently, he has turned to the historical novel with *Norðurljós* (1999; Northern lights) and *Óvinafagnaður* (2001; To please the enemy).

While Kárason's trilogy is clearly epic in character, this is not quite so clear in the case of Einar Már Guðmundsson's trilogy, *Riddarar hringstigans*, *Vængjasláttur í þakrennum*, and *Eftirmáli regndropanna* (1986; English trans.: *Epilogue of the Raindrops* [1994]). Things start out realistically enough: the first novel is a highly nostalgic story of a few young boys growing up in one of the new suburbs of Reykjavík. The same characters appear in the much more fantastic *Vængjasláttur í þakrennum* and again in the even more fantastic *Eftirmáli regndropanna*, where the main concern has shifted from the characters to the neighborhood itself. Like Einar Kárason's fiction, the novels all document the growth of Reykjavík, illustrating the emergence of an urban reality that was about to change Icelandic society dramatically and irrevocably. Today, Guðmundsson is best known for his novel *Englar alheimsins* (1993; English trans.: *Angels of the Universe* [1995]), a semifictional biography of his schizophrenic brother told in the first person by the dead biographical subject. Emotionally charged, but skirting sentimentalism, the story describes the lives of the mentally disturbed and socially inept, the underground, or downside, of Reykjavík's urban growth. The text is highly poetic but also humorous, and the narrative is fragmentary. Fragmentation is also a feature in Guðmundsson's historical novels, *Fótspor á himnum* (1997; Footprints in heaven) and *Draumar á jörðu* (2000; Dreams on earth). In these family sagas he continues to use the history of Reykjavík as a basis, focusing on the first few formative decades of the twentieth century. Highly popular, the novels are characterized by a mixture of traditional storytelling and postmodern fragmentation, creating an effective form for emotional descriptions of poverty and struggle.

Ólafur Gunnarsson's trilogy, *Tröllakirkjan* (1992; English trans.: *Troll's Cathedral* [1996]), *Blóðakur* (1996; English trans.: *Potter's Field* [1999]), and *Vetrarferðin* (1999; Winter's journey), consists of three separate novels connected through style, form, and social concerns. All three novels illustrate a return to highly realist and epic narrative. This traditional structure is clearly exemplified in *Tröllakirkjan*, a family saga taking as its starting point a difficult situation that, however, swiftly improves. From there the rise is steep, followed, after a brief moment at the top, by a fast fall. The novel's form is self-consciously used, but without becoming strictly parodic. Before the success of *Tröllakirkjan*, Gunnarsson had written a number of novels and short story collections. Like the trilogies of Guðmundsson and Kárason, *Tröllakirkjan* describes the period of progress and prosperity in Reykjavík during the early 1950s. At this time Reykjavík is literally in the process of being built, most prominently by the state architect Guðjón Samúelsson. This is, thus, not only a family saga, but also a history of city architecture and a history of Reykjavík and its modernization. Gunnarsson uses the slow building of Hallgrímskirkja cathedral as a major symbol of this urbanization and portrays the church spire as a personal symbol for the ambitions of the main protagonist, the architect Sigurbjörn. Sigurbjörn dreams of building his own version of a towering church on Skólavörðuholt, but, when this is not to be, he settles for the design and construction of the first shopping center in Reykjavík. Large, glamorous, and bright, it changes the city permanently, moving it into the modern era, erasing its village identity and replacing it with an urban spirit — a spirit that turns out to have its dark side as well.

While many writers have been preoccupied with urban development in recent years, there always remain those who turn back to the country in one way or another. This is not only because so much of Iceland's history is resolutely rural but also because this is a country that has a great deal of space to be observed as a background to the urban culture that has become paradigmatic.

Perhaps one of the more unexpected returns to the country is constituted by the narratives of the young urban writer Jón Kalman Stefánsson (b. 1963): *Skurðir í rigningu* (1996; Ditches in the rain), *Sumarið bakvið brekkuna* (1997; The summer behind the hill), and *Birtan á fjöllunum* (1999; Light in the mountains). These playful narratives, balancing irony and nostalgia, evoke to some degree the rural community of old, but they depict its way of life as modern, a setting, in fact, that crystallizes certain cultural aspects of modernity and its entrepreneurial spirit. In this they may remind the reader of Laxness's *Kristnihald undir Jökli* (1968; Under the glacier), although in Stefánsson's novels the actual business of agriculture is still going on and we witness a more traditional, lyric view of Icelandic nature.

In her novel *Gunnlaðar saga* Svava Jakobsdóttir had in a sense staged a return to nature, to the origins of its technological usurpation. In her masterful collection of short stories *Undir eldfjalli* (1989; Under a volcano) it becomes even clearer how she is turning toward nature, to the hinterland that Icelanders will resettle in one way or another, whether by harnessing the natural forces of their island — sometimes at considerable environmental cost — or by finding a plot of land to cultivate, as does the couple in the title story, even though they know it may be destroyed by a volcanic eruption at any time. A particularly noteworthy aspect of these stories is how the increasing attention to the nonurban in its relation to modernity interacts with movements between Iceland and the outside world, evident in some of the other stories. There is a sense in which nature, as well as the rural sphere with all its history, is becoming a foreign world. It may be as hard to find a language to cross this border as it is for the girl in the story "Fyrnist yfir allt" (Everything fades into oblivion), who finds herself between languages when moving from Iceland to Canada.

HISTORICAL FICTION

One of the motivations of historical novels is, of course, the urge, not only to preserve the past from oblivion, but also to unearth and dramatize traditions, sign systems, narratives of earlier ages that speak to, or even clash with, modern life. Given the significance of Iceland's medieval literary output, it is no wonder that historical novels often go back to the Middle Ages, even to the mists of its mythological accounts, as does Jakobsdóttir's *Gunnlaðar saga*. It is also noteworthy how often historical novels — certainly one of the most prominent categories of Icelandic fiction during the past twenty years — cross an interest in the past with an awareness of Iceland's connections with the outside world, a double movement similar to that found in Jakobsdóttir's recent work. Such novels seem to refute the insularity that is sometimes seen as an integral part of Icelandic history and its preservation of language and literary traditions, emphasizing instead how Icelandic identities are partly marked by routes between the island and other shores.

In 1994 the writer and cultural journalist Árni Bergmann (b. 1935) made his most significant mark as a novelist with *Þorvaldur víðförli* (1994; Thorvaldur the traveler), a historical novel that traces the turbulent life and travels of a man who participated in the Christianization of Iceland around the year 1000 but would later travel widely on the roads of religion, royalty, war, solitude, and, finally, love. It gradually comes to light that the search for identity is not as exclusively modern an affair as we sometimes like to think. We may learn a similar lesson in another striking historical novel, *Morgunþula í stráum* (1998; The tune of the morning grass) by Thor Vilhjálmsson, who, having reaffirmed the modernism of his earlier work in *Tvílýsi* (1994; Twilight), a musical sequence of scenes and prose pieces that form a whole that may or may not be a novel, now turned his attention to the thirteenth century. This was the golden age of medieval learning and literacy in Iceland, when many of the sagas were committed to vellum, but it was also a time of civil strife that would end in the collapse of the free confederacy. *Morgunþula í stráum* relates the story of one of the leading chieftains of this period, Sturla Sighvatsson, focusing on his journey to

Rome to obtain absolution for his sins at home (see pp. 85–88). As he travels through war-torn areas, Sturla is strengthened in his peaceful intentions, but these are all too easily forgotten when he is sucked back into the power play and the violence on his native soil. At the same time the novel contains deep echoes of European wars of more recent times, indeed, of present-day violence.

The author that has most consistently worked within the realm of the historical novel is Björn Th. Björnsson (b. 1922). While some of Björnsson's novels use fictional elements to tie together parts of the documented history of unusual Icelanders of recent times, his most celebrated works go further back to key periods in Iceland's long colonial history. While *Haustskip* (1975; Autumn ships), mentioned in part 1 of this chapter, may be seen more as a historical document than as a novel, *Falsarinn* (1993; The counterfeiter) falls on the other side of this elusive line. It is a documentary novel that pieces together the history of a family descended from an eighteenth-century Icelander who was first sentenced to death and later to life imprisonment for counterfeiting a single banknote. He was eventually pardoned, and his grandsons became members of high society in nineteenth-century Denmark, but their family history had to be kept secret. Some of the family members settled in Chile, a thread is spun between the three countries, and the book's narrative force thus stems from our travels between centuries as well as between continents. Björnsson knows the art of molding and peppering his language in accordance with the historical twists and turns that he makes in his novels, and he also knows, perhaps better than anyone else, how to draw on and manipulate the Danish elements that have seeped into the Icelandic language through the centuries.

Another, more parodic master of historical language use is Þórarinn Eldjárn, who in 1996 brought out one of the most significant novels of this genre, *Brotahöfuð* (English trans.: *The Blue Tower* [1999]). In many of his short stories, and in the intricate patchwork of the novel *Skuggabox*, Eldjárn had repeatedly turned playfully to history, sometimes in a mock-folkloric tone, and his first novel, the already mentioned *Kyrr kjör*, draws on historical material. *Brotahöfuð* is set in seventeenth-century Iceland. The literal meaning of the title is "fractured head" or "fractured skull," but the noun *brotahöfuð* brings to mind the Icelandic idiom equivalent to *racking one's brains*, which is what the narrator, the peasant son Guðmundur Andrésson, does a good deal more than the authorities are ready to accept. Most of the novel's tale is told by Guðmundur while he is imprisoned in the infamous Blue Tower in Copenhagen, a prison that is, ironically, elevated above the adjacent royal residence. The only personal belonging he has, apart from his ragged clothes, is a copy of Apuleius's *Metamorphosis* (or *Golden Ass*), which he finds solace in consulting as he reminisces about the course of events that has led to his imprisonment.

Guðmundur was born into a poor peasant family and seemed destined to a lifelong struggle for basic survival in a society characterized by social rigidity and plagued by the hardships of nature, disease, and colonization. But it was also an age of spiritual and intellectual turbulence, which eventually leads to our hero's "metamorphosis" into one of the most idiosyncratic luminaries to emerge from a dark century. His birthplace may be a humble farm, but it is no ordinary place: Bjarg in Miðfjörður (literally "Rock in Central Fjord" — Guðmundur comments on the symbolic irony of the very name) was also the farm that, centuries before, had fostered Grettir Ásmundarson, one of the heroes of Old Iceland, about whom one of the most famous sagas was written. Grettir's head is said to be buried in a little hillock near the farm, and our hero speculates quite a bit on it, wanting to dig it up, but is discouraged by an old farmhand, a defrocked priest who is instrumental in directing the hero's curiosity toward the Old Icelandic literary heritage as well as the pursuit of knowledge and education.

Tortuous as the historical Guðmundur's own struggle for glory was, as a character in this novel he is a success. He comes across, simply put, as a wonderfully flawed human being. It was said of Grettir that great gifts did not ensure him good fortune. A man imbued with immense strength and physical prowess as well as valor, he ended up as an adversary of social rule. Guðmundur is differently gifted; he is a man of meager physical stature but shares Grettir's guts and fiery temperament — and, for the longest time, his bad luck. In his passionate desire for education and the pursuit of knowledge Guðmundur may remind the reader of Thomas Hardy's Jude in *Jude the Obscure* (1895). But, instead of the melodramatic qualities of Hardy's novel, *Brotahöfuð* is full of grotesque elements and crackling humor. And this is where Apuleius's work assumes significance as a subtext in the novel. Guðmundur's attempts to move out of his class, break through social boundaries, lead to his metamorphosis into, well perhaps not an ass, but certainly a kind of creature that does not fit into the frame of his time.

One aspect of Icelandic history that has fascinated many but also used to carry a certain stigma was the massive emigration to North America during the last quarter of the nineteenth century. This issue is taken up in what may be the most popular historical novels of recent times, Böðvar Guðmundsson's (b. 1939) *Híbýli vindanna* (1995; English trans.: *Where The Winds Dwell* [2000]) and its sequel, *Lífsins tré* (1996; Tree of life). The novels map out the history of Ólafur fíólín (violin) and his family, starting with the course of events in Iceland leading up to emigration, and then beginning a new life in Canada. The finality of leave-taking is poignantly expressed and echoes throughout the work. The emigrants knew that they were leaving their old lives for good and would probably never again see those who stayed behind, usually parents, children, and siblings. Ólafur fíólin, an able workman and musician, nicknamed after his instrument, is one of the few who does return, only to emigrate a second time, thus underlining the fragmented lives of first-generation settlers. It is also touch-and-go with his children: they die or stay behind in Iceland, become "successful" in Winnipeg, turn into restless adventurers or even circus clowns who portray the "typical" Icelander onstage as a weird, exotic creature. The novels are narrated in the form of letters that the grandson of the son who stayed behind in Iceland writes to his daughter, on the premise that the double heritage of the family must not be neglected and forgotten.

Women writers have also been active in the domain of historical fiction, which can effectively reflect the changes — or lack thereof — in the conditions faced by women. Vilborg Davíðsdóttir (b. 1965) brought out four historical novels in the 1990s. The first two are young adult novels, *Við Urðarbrunn* (1993; At Urður's well) and *Nornadómur* (1994; Witches' fate), describing Viking society during the period of settlement. The other two, *Eldfórnin* (1997; Sacrifice by fire) and *Galdur* (2000; Witchery), are romances taking place during the fifteenth and sixteenth centuries, respectively. All feature young female heroines trying to find their own place in a patriarchal culture.

Þórunn Valdimarsdóttir's (b. 1954) *Stúlka með fingur* (1999; Girl with a finger) is similarly concerned with the situation of independent young heroines in a patriarchal society. Using elements from the rural romance, *Stúlka með fingur* is partly an urban novel that, like Einar Már Guðmundsson's two historical works, focuses on Reykjavík at the turn of the twentieth century. One of the fresh and innovative female voices of the 1990s, Valdimarsdóttir made her debut with a fantasy novel, *Júlía*, in 1992, followed by *Höfuðskepnur* (1994; Elements), an epistolary novel detailing strange and uncomfortable events in the life of a young woman who becomes the unexpected victim of a bogus sex survey. *Alveg nóg* (1997; Enough is enough) uses *Laxdæla saga* as a blueprint for a modern setting, a historical undertone that was fully realized in *Stúlka með fingur*, unquestionably her most interesting work of fiction to date. Valdimarsdóttir is a historian by education and could be said to have migrated into fiction from history, for in her well-known historical study *Snorri á Húsafelli* (1989; Snorri at Húsafell), about a legendary eighteenth-century priest, she supplemented her documented material with a touch of fictional imagination, a move disapproved of by some historians even though Valdimarsdóttir is not the only historian ever to have done so, a recent Icelandic example being Guðjón Friðriksson (b. 1945) in his popular three-volume biography (1997–2000) of the poet Einar Benediktsson.

CONTEMPORARY ISSUES

While several authors have performed the art of positioning the mirrors of history and the present in relation to one another, others have concentrated on contemporary reality, shuffling through the scene of a society that appears to rapidly embrace ever more colorful forms of culture. Hallgrímur Helgason (b. 1959) became well-known as the author of the novels *Þetta er allt að koma* (1994; We're getting there) and especially *101 Reykjavík* (1996; English trans.: *101 Reykjavík* [2002]), which was turned into a film and is seen by many as a key statement about the nightlife of Reykjavík's inner city. Loose and baggy in their undisciplined structure, these novels are irreverent and satiric in their postmodern mix of ingredients, not the least of which is a host of jokes and word games, some of them clever and sharp, some facile and silly, and this spectrum is perhaps in line with the cultural vision of these works. A different, more lyric strain is apparent in the author's first novel, *Hella* (1990; The village of Hella), about a girl growing up in a southern village, and in the descriptions of nature in *Höfundur Íslands* (2001; The author of Iceland), which relates how an author, who resembles Halldór Laxness, dies and wakes up in the countryside of one of his own novels.

The novel *Dís* (Dís) cowritten by three young women, Birna Anna Björnsdóttir (b. 1975), Oddný Sturludóttir (b. 1976), and Silja Hauksdóttir (b. 1976), was an unexpected hit in 2000. Somewhat in the style of the extremely popular *Bridget Jones's Diary* (1997) by Helen Fielding, this story of one summer in a young girl's life in Reykjavík is quite a successful attempt at tackling the contemporary. While contemporary novels by men seem to garner more attention, there have actually been more attempts on the part of women to take on modern society with its rapidly changing worldview. Auður Jónsdóttir (b. 1973) wrote a remarkable story of a young girl living with her single mother on a farmstead close to a little fishing village. The novel, called *Stjörnlaus lukka* (1998; Fortune gone wild), demonstrates the growing generation gap between a mother, an old flower child with set political and personal opinions, and her daughter, who has just finished secondary school and is at loss what to do with her life, much like the eponymous heroine of *Dís*. In her next novel, *Annað líf* (2000; Another life), Jónsdóttir took on the hotly debated issue of the import of Asian women into Iceland for marriage purposes.

While Guðrún Eva Mínervudóttir's (b. 1976) novels do not as squarely devote themselves to contemporary issues, they can also be seen as part of this movement. The short story collection *Á meðan hann horfir á þig ertu María mey* (1998; While he is looking at you, you are the Virgin Mary) was a fine debut, with strikingly perceptive depictions of both calm and unruly emotions, while the novel *Ljúlí ljúlí* (1999; Ljúlí ljúlí), describing the unusual life of a girl just out of secondary school, was not so successful a follow-up. Mínervudóttir returns to form with her third book, the novel *Fyrirlestur um hamingjuna* (2000; A lecture on happiness). Juggling three generations, the story is an intriguing reflection on the changes in Icelandic society during the latter half of the twentieth century, moving slightly into the future of the twenty-first. Mínervudóttir makes clever use of Icelandic idiosyncracies such as the tradition of personal names and creates a remarkable feeling of circular continuity within the generational time span of the novel.

Hallgrímsson's *101 Reykjavík* is an ultraurban novel whose protagonist hardly ever leaves the capital's downtown area. When the novel is viewed from a certain perspective, the author has captured one essence of contemporary life in Iceland. When it is viewed from another, he has narrowed down a focus that we also find in Guðmundur Andri Thorsson's (b. 1957) *Íslenski draumurinn* (1991; The Icelandic dream), a novel describing how the Icelandic dream of the independent fate and the possibilities of the new and sovereign nation is trickling down the drain of self-serving, materialist pursuits. But the critical perspective built into this novel may be on the wane, and there are signs that consumer culture is not something that young writers try to wish away. At the same time, however, there are indications that Icelandic urbanism, with its short history, will not suffice to explain cultural or geopolitical identities in Iceland and that this calls for a broader perspective. Thorsson went on to write *Íslandsförin* (1996; The journey to Iceland), in which he goes back to the nineteenth century and has a young English gentleman visit Iceland, where he hopes to sort out a personal dilemma as he travels through this land of sagas and untouched nature. Huldar Breiðfjörð (b. 1976) tried a more direct method: he bought an old four-wheel drive, packed his sleeping bag, and traveled around Iceland in midwinter. His story, as told in *Góðir Íslendingar* (1998; Fellow

Icelanders), humorously portrays him as an urban idiot who is often clue-less out in the wild and is constantly acting out the various roles of the visitor or the would-be travel writer/ethnographer.

Thus, we see once more the inclination to go back to the country, an urge that weaves its way through the history of Icelandic fiction like a leitmotif, even as it becomes increasingly urban and more oriented toward the Reykjavík metropolitan area, which by now houses more than half the nation's population. This tendency toward a more holistic, as well as a more historical, understanding of the condition of Iceland is even more promi-nent in Pétur Gunnarsson's recent novel *Myndin af heiminum* (2000; Pic-turing the world). This novel, the first in a planned cycle of novels, begins with nothing less than a universal historical overview, which gradually nar-rows down to Iceland, creating, as it progresses, intertextual links with *Njáls saga*, often seen as the key medieval work reflecting Icelandic national identity. It remains to be seen whether Gunnarsson can successfully carry out this ambitious plan within the scope of three books.

The conflation of autobiography and fiction, practiced earlier by writers such as Þórbergur Þórðarson (1888–1974) and Málfríður Einarsdóttir (1899–1983), is another tendency that can be detected in Breiðfjörð's *Góðir Íslendingar* and, in a much more detailed and nuanced manner, in Guðberg-ur Bergsson's *Faðir og móðir og dulmagn bernskunnar* (1997; Father, mother, and the mysticism of childhood) and *Eins og steinn sem hafið fágar* (1998; Like a stone polished by the ocean). The Icelandic concept for such writing was, in fact, invented by Bergsson and stands as the subtitle of these two massive books about his childhood: *skáldævisaga*, where he merges the terms *skáldsaga* (novel) and *ævisaga* (biography) while also echoing the concept of *sjálfsævisaga* (autobiography). This biofictional framework — one more cre-ative turnaround in the career of this prolific and versatile writer — allows him, not only to relate his childhood memories, but also to invent memories for his parents and to make readers, who may have thought that they knew this seaside village from Bergsson's earlier novels, see it all over again as a whole universe of meaning.

FINALLY: THE ICELANDIC LITERARY SEASON

Icelandic literary publication centers around Christmas, and the great major-ity of books — fiction and nonfiction — appear during the autumn months, generally from mid-October and often well into December. This creates a unique and often-uncomfortable setting for literary criticism. On the one hand, it can be said that this condensed publication period makes it easier to read each year along clear critical lines and that the dense output also secures a lively literary discussion — for about two months a year. The limitations of this state of affairs are also obvious. With the literary debate — at least within the popular forum of newspapers and other media — staying largely silent for the remaining ten months a year, the annual literary discussion tends toward uniformity and repetition. There is scant continuous dialogue, so each season appears to start from scratch, sometimes with well-rehearsed critical comments about this very situation. This concentrated publication period also obscures the connection between Icelandic literature and the international context it exists in since the cultural gaze tends to turn inward during the hectic literary season.

It has been said, however, that Icelanders should be thankful that books still receive so much attention, especially in the weeks before Christmas, the book still being a Christmas present favored by a large number of people. Only quite recently have there been signs that the book is running into difficulties as a market commodity. While poetry still seems to be a widespread cultural practice in Iceland, as evinced by the large numbers of people participating in poetry competitions, books of poetry are generally not selling well at all. But this is not a recent phenomenon, nor is it unique to Iceland. More worrisome is probably the recent drop in the sales of translated world literature. One reason may be that, as globabization facilitates easy access to a great deal of foreign — mainly American — popular culture, the field of literature becomes increasingly an area of local and national concerns, readers wanting to see how Icelandic life is reflected and mediated in the art of language.

But life in Iceland possesses an increasingly global character, so it is also a question of how successful a small, economically prosperous nation is in keeping its language in tune with new cultural settings. This is, in itself, a matter of translation, and it is interesting to note how well the reading public is receiving the new wave of crime fiction written in Icelandic. It has added a new string to the instrument of the Icelandic novel, although this may not be enough to assuage the criticism that the seasonal literary discussion in Iceland revolves around the novel in too limited a fashion.

Another threat — that of uniformity — seemed, however, to loom even larger on the horizon at the turn of the twenty-first century. The two largest publishing houses of Iceland merged in 2000, forming the conglomerate Edda (now divided into a number of publishing groups), which is in control of a large part of the book market. Competition, as far as literature is concerned, comes mainly from two much smaller publishing houses that manage to bring out a surprising number of books with limited staff and minimal overhead: JPV-Publishing and Bjartur. JPV is a market-savvy company, bringing out a wide array of books, including fiction, while Bjartur focuses mainly on fiction and has published several books by young authors who have experimented with literary discourses, often setting up a dialogue of the novel with other genres. But all three publishing venues have, in fact, recently brought out books that illustrate how the novel, having apparently swallowed up all other discourses, also seems on the verge of splitting up into numerous, as yet unidentifiable genres.

Icelandic Poetry since 1940

Eysteinn Þorvaldsson

7

TOWARD A NEW POETRY

The beginning of the 1940s marked a turning point in Icelandic poetry. Young writers began experimenting with a more innovative poetry, one that in form and thought differed from the existing norm and the long-standing lyric tradition characterized by alliteration, a regular rhythm and rhyme, and a regularity and conformity in line and stanza length. During this period, however, there were also a few poets whose command of traditional form and lyricism was unrivaled: Davíð Stefánsson (1895–1964), Jóhannes úr Kötlum (1899–1972; Jóhannes of Katlar), Tómas Guðmundsson (1901–83), and Guðmundur Böðvarsson (1904–74). Magnús Ásgeirsson (1901–55), a prolific translator of poetry, was at his peak during this period and introduced significant foreign works of poetry into Icelandic. In all his translations, however, he employed a traditional Icelandic structure, as other translators of poetry had done before him, adding alliteration, rhythm, and even rhyme words, so the end result was usually far removed from its original version. This Icelandic translation method clearly shows the strength of the lyric tradition: even those who knew foreign modern poetry well could not imagine poetry in Icelandic without alliteration and rhyme.

Soon after the Second World War, however, the Icelandic poetic tradition was gradually abandoned without reservation and the road paved for a more modernist poetry. The reasons for these changes were varied. One of the underlying causes was the change in perspective caused by the great social changes introduced during the war years. But also playing their part

Unless a specific English-language source is given, all translations from the Icelandic are Gunnþórunn Guðmundsdóttir's.

were influences from foreign modernist poetry and clear signs of crisis in the rigid Icelandic poetic structure and modes of expression, which had remained unchanged for so long. And, last but not least, works began to appear by a new generation of poets who, together, challenged conventional strictures and began writing poetry that broke with tradition.

Two poets led the way in this respect, each in his own way. Steinn Steinarr (the pen name of Aðalsteinn Kristmundsson; 1908–58) was already a rather well-known poet by 1940, the year in which he published his third collection of poems, but his poetry had received little recognition so far (see pp. 399–402). While many of Steinn Steinarr's poems are traditional in form, using alliteration and rhyme, others are in free verse, and in many respects their structure was alien to Icelandic readers. Steinn Steinarr broke with tradition in wording and imagery, but it was especially the outlook on life that was expressed in his poetry that shocked many, so entirely contrary to the progressive optimism that had characterized traditional poetry. Steinn Steinarr painted a picture of desolation, loneliness, and life without purpose in an existential manner, made light of commonly held values, and challenged taboos.

Another pioneer of modernist poetry, Jón of Vör (1917–2000), chose a different path. He, too, rebelled against traditional poetic structure and formal poetic language, but his views and imagery were not as novel as Steinn Steinarr's. The rigid and monotonous formal strictures offered limited expressive modes and had led to a certain staleness in Icelandic poetry. Jón of Vör broke away from those narrow strictures, most notably with his most innovative work, the collection Þorpið (The village) from 1946. It consists exclusively of poetry in free verse that has as its subject matter the simple childhood memories of poverty in an Icelandic fishing village. Both Steinn Steinarr and Jón of Vör began their careers in the 1930s. They were to become colleagues and comrades of the next generation of poets and in many respects became role models for the young poets after the war who wrote nontraditional poetry and fought for the recognition of experimental poetry in Icelandic literature.

Others also joined this group. Snorri Hjartarson's (1906–86) first book of poetry appeared in 1944 when he was already thirty-eight years old, and he published only four books of poetry in all. In the course of time he came to be regarded as one of the most aesthetically gifted poets of the twentieth century. He initially wrote in traditional meter but at the same time began to force traditional form onto the path of freer expression, developing a concise style rich in imagery. His language is polished, and the words echo perfectly the content and atmosphere of the poems. He turned increasingly to modernist methods and eventually wrote consistently modernist verse.

His work broke new ground in Icelandic poetry in being the first to demonstrate the ways in which one could artfully link modernism and the Icelandic lyric tradition.

Hjartarson's early books contain some poems where he puts his weight behind the struggle against foreign military bases in Iceland, but he also concentrates to a large extent on nature and history in a broad sense; he occasionally touches on love and loss and at times death. In 1981 Hjartarson received the Nordic Literature Prize for his last book of poetry. Throughout his career Snorri Hjartarson wrote poetry rich in imagery and with a characteristically inward-looking expression, using carefully placed in-rhymes, assonances, and alliteration that give each poem its unique rhythm even though they do not adhere to traditional rules of form. He also composed many poems in free verse without any traditional features at all. All his poetry is characterized by his precise use of imagery, however. His style became an example to many younger poets.

Jóhannes of Katlar was one of the main poets of the social-realist movement during the 1930s and had published ten books of traditional poetry when he completely transformed his style and started writing modernist poems in the mid-1940s. No other Icelandic poet transformed his poetics and poetic expression as radically as Jóhannes of Katlar. For ten years he published his poetry under the pseudonym Anonymus (*sic*), which he also used for the publication of his poetry translations. No one knew who the poet behind the pseudonym was until the book *Sjödægra* (Seven days' mountain) was published in 1955. He never became a radical modernist, nor was that his aim, but he learned much from modernist approaches and techniques as he searched for innovations, convinced that he needed new modes of expression in his poetry. He succeeded in imbuing his poems with new images and similes, showing a particular partiality for modernist metaphors in his work. His use of language did not alter radically; it remained rather elevated and romantic, although it did at times approach polished daily speech. However, he used his poetic language in new ways, avoided clichés and platitudes, and controlled the rhetoric—and the result was a fresh style. Jóhannes of Katlar's poetic renewal also made itself felt in his poetry translations from many languages, among them modernist works, all translated in free verse.

Although some poets broke entirely with the rules of traditional form, others continued to use alliteration and rhyme. Among them was Þorsteinn Valdimarsson (1918–77), who wrote in free verse but whose poems were otherwise mostly traditional, some of them intricate meter riddles. Valdimarsson's nature poetry is rich in imagery and emotion and shows a rare insight into nature. Valdimarsson was educated in music, and sounds and rhythm characterize many of his poems. He translated many foreign song lyrics along with a few librettos. "Poetry and song are two inseperable parallels; neither can survive without the other," he said in an interview ("Ljóð er söngur," 43). Valdimarsson made the limerick popular in Icelandic poetry with the publication of his book *Limrur* (1965; Limericks), which was very well received. Ever since, the limerick has been a popular and common form of occasional verse in Iceland, along with the quatrain.

Two poets of the same age also wrote mostly in traditional form, but with some exceptions. One was Kristján frá Djúpalæk (1918–94; Kristján of Djúpalækur). Along with common subject matter he enriched entertainment culture in Iceland with his fine song lyrics. The other was Ólafur Jóhann Sigurðsson (1918–88), who mostly focused his efforts on the novel and claimed to write poetry only as a hobby. Despite this he received the Nordic Literature Prize in 1976 for his poetry. Sigurðsson's poems are for the most part traditional, with a polished and clear use of language. The basis for many of his poems was Icelandic nature, which he used to express thoughts and views on life and culture. At times his poems are critical of technology and the emptiness of urban life.

THE ATOM POETS

The period of modernism has been demarcated differently in different countries, for its influence did not make itself felt everywhere simultaneously. According to Frank Kermode's *Continuities*, the modernist period in British literature lasted approximately from 1910 until 1925. In Iceland, on the other hand, modernist influences remained few and minor during the first decades of the twentieth century. While this has often caused people to claim that in Iceland modernism arrived exceptionally late, it appeared, in fact, no later than in the rest of Scandinavia, that is, during and after the Second World War; the only exception was Sweden, which was slightly ahead in this respect (Brøndsted, ed., *Nordens litteratur efter 1860*, 2:427). Since then Icelandic poetry has followed the main trends in Western literature.

The generation of poets who made their appearance in the 1940s and 1950s quickly came to be known as the *atom poets* and have been called this ever since. The name was coined by Halldór Laxness (1902–98) in his novel *Atómsstöðin* (1948; English trans.: *The Atom Station* [1961]), and it was quickly taken up and used initially as a pejorative name for young modernists; the atom poet in the novel is a bad poet and a less than sympathetic character. The demarcation of this group is not entirely clear-cut, but the nucleus of the atom poets consists of the following five: Stefán Hörður

Grímsson (1919–2002), Einar Bragi (1921–2005), Jón Óskar (1921–98), Hannes Sigfússon (1922–97), and Sigfús Daðason (1928–96). These poets, along with several others, played a part in forging a place for modernism in Icelandic poetry, and the phrase *atom poet* has since been applied to all poets who wrote in a nontraditional manner, either entirely or in part. Their works consequently became known in Icelandic as *atom poems*. The innovations introduced by these poets have often been called a *structural revolution*, although the changes have affected more than poetic form alone.

Although the atom poets do not appear in Icelandic literature as a united group, they have many things in common: they start writing around the same time, they are of a similar age, their social background is in many ways comparable, and they have a similar outlook on life, society, and writing. The "atom generation" grew up during the Depression, when the tenacious lyric tradition was still dominant, and they were still young when the Republic was founded in 1944. During the period when these young poets started to write, they felt that a certain staleness had settled in the traditional school of lyricism and began experimenting individually. They did not form a society and did not have a manifesto, although later on some of them joined the editorial board of the magazine *Birtingur*, the main forum for Icelandic modernists, which was first published in 1953 under the editorship of Einar Bragi, who was the life and soul of the magazine during the fifteen years of its publication.

At an early age Einar Bragi wrote extensively on the necessity of poetic renewal and often had to defend the atom poets and their works. He proved a dedicated radical who emphasized that one could not gauge the quality of poetry by its formal characteristics; instead, he claimed, modern poetry was different from earlier poetry mainly in its inner workings; new times demanded innovation in art, and those who criticized modernism were stuck in the past and in methods that had become obsolete.

These young experimental poets faced fierce opposition and prejudice when they began publishing their poetry in the 1940s and 1950s, and the same hostility was also directed at experimentation in painting. These art forms were up against the dominant traditional outlook and had to struggle for their right to exist. Their opponents included the cultural and political establishment, which wanted to protect and preserve conventional forms at the expense of newer and more liberal forms. The attacks on modern artists began in 1940 and continued almost without respite up until 1960, when they gradually subsided. Modern artists were berated for abandoning figurative painting and for distorting reality. Inward-looking poems were alien to many, as was modernist imagery. Many did not want to accept any poetry if it did not contain both alliteration and rhyme, as it had done for centuries. It is important to note, however, that, for all their innovations, the atom poets all borrowed freely from traditional poetry when they saw fit. They were, in fact, from the start very much linked to Icelandic reality and history and to the cultural traditions reflecting these. Those who opposed modernist poetry seldom mentioned what probably offended them the most: the outlook and opinions of the new poets. They were felt to fail national ambition, and their poems were perceived as wanting in power, optimism, and ideals. They did not encourage progress and a fighting spirit, expectations that had been intrinsic to traditional poetry from the early days of romanticism and the Icelandic struggle for independence — poets were still expected to inspire the nation with courage.

The atom poets published relatively few poems during their writing careers, and their publications are neither many nor large. This generation ensured the success of modernism, however, and it has influenced Icelandic poetry ever since. The individual poets show differences in style, but they all experimented in innovative ways with form and expression, and they all experimented with prose poetry, which had been rare until then. They were painstaking in their use of the Icelandic language, something that had, in fact, characterized Icelandic literature since the nineteenth century. They explored the various attributes of the language and its signifying powers more profoundly and radically than earlier poets and examined the language's fresh expressive possibilities. The poets urgently felt the need to expunge meaningless rhetoric and empty phrases of false idealism and give the language a new lease on life, new meaning, new truth. The world had changed almost overnight, and old methods of expression were no longer relevant. To express the new worldview it was necessary to add new dimensions to the poetic language and its imagery.

Stefán Hörður Grímsson, who was a fisherman in his youth, soon developed a personal style, one that was concise and peculiarly modest on the surface but full of temper underneath, fueled by powerful emotions and, at times, sharp criticism. His metaphors were drawn in a few clear strokes, at times obscure, but always highly compelling. His use of language is polished and precise, and his neologisms often shed new light on the subject.

Nature and the protection of nature are important subjects in Grímsson's poetry. His presentation of man's relation to nature is impressive. Grímsson is fiercely critical of greed and exploitation and of those who waste natural resources. As a counterpoint to such destruction he creates powerful images of earthly beauty. Many of his poems deal with the subject of love. They are both quiet and full of emotion and do not contain commitments or declarations of love but, rather, focus on a love that is transient yet valuable and desirable. In poems where he reveals his outlook he criticizes greed and exploitation.

Einar Bragi has always concentrated on imagery, with a growing emphasis on metaphor. He uses highly varied forms, often with alliteration, rhythm, and rhyme, but he also writes free verse and prose poetry. Some of his poems are concise, while others use a longer format resembling the traditional *þula* or Icelandic nursery rhyme (see pp. 346, 525); all his poems are informed by a strong sense of unity, however. The language is polished and rich but never obscure.

Love and nature are joined together in Einar Bragi's works and are often accompanied by a praise of fertility and a fresh sense of beauty, for instance, in the poem "Mansöng" (1957; Love song; originally titled "Con Amore"):

> I love a woman naked
> with nightingales in her eyes
> a newly awakened fragrant lily
> bathed in the morning sun,
> a young woman and pregnant
> with button-red blossoms
> on pale knolls
> seething with desire. . . .
> (*Postwar Poetry*, trans. Magnússon, 74)

Einar Bragi has also written on human fate, social experience, daily tasks, and the everyday and is critical of social injustice, military violence, and political hypocrisy. His criticism is expressed either through sarcasm or with the help of nature images and is completely free of the sermonizing so commonly found in political poetry.

Hannes Sigfússon's style is characterized by a powerful and imaginative use of language and imposing imagery, particularly metaphors. His command of language comes to the fore when he describe great events, the arms race, and war. He was one of the first to write on technological innovations, for instance, space travel. He tends to focus on contemporary issues, social and world politics, and sharply criticizes injustice and oppression. The focus is frequently on man's destructive tendencies, which appear, not only in the genocides of world wars, but in their factual symbol, the atom bomb, which had become humanity's companion, a threat impossible to be rid of. His poem "Líf meðfærilegt eins og vindlakveikjarar" (1961; Life manageable like cigarette lighters) begins thus:

The day of tomorrow lies heavy on my mind. . . .
They have woven for themselves nests of fear
and laid their fragile eggs on the edges of precipices
on the very edges

Everywhere they nest, even in our midst
and their eggs are more numerous
than the days of all men
of all times

For how multiple a future have they laid their eggs?

At last we have our lives in a nutshell
manageable like cigarette lighters
with walls of steel. . . .
(*Postwar Poetry*, trans. Magnússon, 93)

Thor Vilhjálmsson (b. 1925) also belongs to the atom generation and is one of the most purely modernist of Icelandic writers. Although his main works are in prose, and a very lyric prose at that (see also p. 427), Vilhjálmsson has always written poetry as well. He has published a few books of poetry that are highly distinct and artistic in subject matter and presentation. He collaborated with artists in most of them, in fact, combining poetry and painting. His latest book of poetry is called *Snöggfærðar sýnir* (1995; Quick visions); his first book of poetry in English, *The Deep Blue See, Pardon the Ocean*, was published in the United States in 1981.

While Jónas Svafár (1925–2005) is of this generation too, his poetic innovations are of a different kind: he uses absurd imagery akin to that of surrealism and attempts to achieve unexpected effects by linking unrelated words and concepts. He also uses slang and loanwords, something that had not been done in Icelandic poetry before. Svafár illustrates most of his books of poetry with his own drawings, which are no less unusual than the poems. Some poems he has published more than once, with changes, and under different titles.

Elías Mar's (b. 1924) book of poetry, *Ljóð á trylltri öld* (1951; Poems in a frenzied age), consists of modernist poems written during the years 1946–51, after which period there was a long interval where he wrote predominantly in prose.

The world had changed radically in a very short time, and these new human experiences inevitably demanded poetic attention and a reevaluation of what went before. Rhyme and defined narrative were no longer deemed suitable, and neither were explicit messages or sermonizing. Instead, the emphasis was on imagery, much more so than had previously been the case. Lyric images became a poem's main components. Poetry was now inward looking, its attention focused primarily on man's inner life and soul rather than on outer reality, and, when it turned to scrutinizing the mind of modern man, it quickly became apparent that doubts and uncertainty had disrupted the old worldview, where everything was solid, clear, and unified and had its proper place. The revolutionary achievements of the Icelandic experimental poets of this era thus consisted of the following: the introduction of a fresh poetic form that increased the expressive possibilities of the language; a radical shift in focus toward an inward-looking expression; and a much greater emphasis on imagery.

Although the atom poets shared much of their subject matter with older poets, especially with the romantics and neoromantics, they handled it very differently. Nature, for instance, is a prominent theme for many atom poets, although it is no longer primarily praised for its beauty and magnificence. Instead, nature enjoys poetic consideration because it forms the basis of existence; it is interwoven with human life, and all lives should be respected. Nature is, thus, not just a symbolic medium for moods and emotions; it is strongly linked to society, even becoming a participant in political developments, and serves as a kind of crystal ball revealing the fate of humanity and society. Many of Einar Bragi's poems bear witness to this, while Stefán Hörður Grímsson's poems severely criticize man's exploitation of nature. Hannes Sigfússon's nature poetry is rich in imagery, often musical, and his sense of nature is honest and colorful and possesses an unusual insight.

Jón Óskar's poem "Vorkvæði um Ísland" (1958; Spring poem about Iceland) deals at the same time with Icelandic nature and with politics. It was composed on the occasion of the foundation of the Republic of Iceland in 1944 and concludes thus:

The day when rain was streaming
and the rain was your own mirror
and the rain was your own sunlight
on your shoulders and your eyelids
the day your white-clad country
grew free in the rainy embrace
and joy gave you a handshake
in the sunny arms of showers

One day when rain is falling
my people will come to me
one day when rain is falling.
(*Postwar Poetry*, trans. Magnússon)

Jón Óskar was a musician, and this influenced his poetry: some of his poems feature a particular rhythm or the repetition of a motif, as evidenced in the poem quoted above. Love in all its various forms is one of his favorite themes — as well as all sorts of subjects taken from daily life.

Environmental description in traditional poetry originated almost exclusively in the countryside or the mountains, formed as it was by the ideas of romanticism and fostered by centuries of rural life. It is not until the works of Steinn Steinarr and the atom poems that modern city life is represented for the first time in Icelandic poetry in its own right. This urban poetry bears witness to a new sensibility and a new interpretation of the life of modern man, who is surrounded by cement and cars, asphalt and noise. The city molds man's fate. Its appearance is sometimes empty and bare, sometimes frightening, but at times it is also the setting for human relationships. During this period the city finally becomes a significant theme in Icelandic poetry.

Atom poetry displays a keen social awareness, handled and represented in a completely different fashion than had been the norm: the horizon is wider, and international issues are also on the agenda. Almost all poets during the so-called golden age of modernism, 1940–55, show an interest in social and political developments in the world and at home. They voice their disgust with the arms race, the cold war, and Iceland's membership in NATO, which the country joined in 1949 after much national debate, conflict, and controversy. No less aversion was shown to the arrival of the U.S. military in Iceland in 1951 and the establishment of a military base in the country. The poets felt that Iceland's newly achieved independence was being eroded only a few years after the foundation of the Republic. Worry about the fate and future of the nation and mankind is apparent in their poetry, an increasing worry as the cold war continued.

This becomes immediately apparent in the poetry of Sigfús Daðason, where social critique and historical reference go hand in hand. Daðason wrote many political poems on contemporary imperialism. Many of his poems consist of existential meditations that advocate resignation to one's fate, although, as he got older, his works began to display a censorious tone and an impatience with people and unappealing times. Judging by his poetry, nature leaves the author cold, and love does not feature extensively either. Daðason's style is usually eloquent, with grand statements, at times sarcastic. The poems are seldom obscure, although some of his imagery demands close consideration. Many feature literary references, often classical.

One of the reasons for the rejuvenation of Icelandic poetry around the middle of the twentieth century was the growing acquaintance among Icelandic poets with contemporary foreign poetry, in particular, modernist poetry from Scandinavia, France, Britain, and the United States. Many atom poets translated a considerable amount of contemporary poetry from around the world. Sigfús Daðason and Jón Óskar mainly concentrated on French poetry and in their early years at times combined their efforts. Einar Bragi and Hannes Sigfússon have mainly translated Scandinavian poets, although not exclusively. Einar Bragi's translations of poetry from small nations in marginal areas, in particular, Sami poetry and poetry from Greenland, deserve mention as well. During these years and after, many more, in fact, worked at translations than at writing original poetry. Helgi Hálfdanarson (b. 1911) is particularly worthy of mention. Even though he is best known for his Shakespeare translations, he has also translated with great skill a considerable amount of poetry from many continents, in particular, poetry from centuries past, but also poetry by the pioneers of modernism. The translation and publication of modern foreign poetry in those years meant that Icelandic poets now had much better access to contemporary writing from other countries.

Despite the antagonism that the guardians of tradition showed toward the first modernists, modernism gained a foothold in Icelandic poetry in a relatively short space of time. With the passing of time, society came to accept modernist poetry, and most have now forgotten the hatred and prejudice that such innovative work initially had to suffer. In time the revolution of the atom poets came to be regarded as quite moderate, as is usually the case with cultural innovations that achieve their goal. But the effects and influence of these changes are undeniable and are still felt today: since the atom poets forged the path of modernism, Icelandic poets have mostly written in free verse and adopted many other modernist stylistic conventions, although some used traditional formal aspects as well, just as their forerunners had. As a result, Icelandic poetry became much more diverse after 1940 than it had been previously. As Einar Bragi said when the fight was at its peak: "In art there is no way back" ("Í listum liggur engin leið til baka," 25). The direction had to be forward. Poems express a similar view, e.g., Daðason's "I" (1951):

We left an old dwelling place behind
— like newspapers in the wastebasket —
let us now continue and never look back.

Or did we suddenly break the glass heavens
over our old days?
That is why we set off.

These lines from Daðason's first book of poetry describe a young poet's view in times of radical literary change.

The period 1945–55 is often named after the atom poets because their generation, along with their forerunners and older colleagues, managed during these years to open Icelandic poetry to modernism and make modernist methods a permanent creative force in Icelandic literature.

A NEW GENERATION

But what comes on the heels of such a transformative period? What would be the new generation's attitude toward the recent innovations — and toward the tradition of Icelandic poetry with its long and unusual history? The atom generation continued, of course, to write and to develop its own brand of modernism, and the same can be said for the older modernists. But still also active were many poets of different ages who wrote in the traditional style, although they were becoming ever fewer.

Around the middle of the 1950s a new generation of poets made itself heard, the first after the atom poets. By then the noisiest debates about the legitimacy of innovation in poetry had subsided. The work of these new poets, most of them born in the 1930s, is, in the main, a logical and natural continuation of that of the atom poets. There was no return to traditional expression, to its regulated form and rhetoric. Instead, the period 1955–70 is characterized by the stabilization of modernism in Icelandic poetry. The renewal and expansion of poetic form became an encouragement to younger poets and released new forces in poetry. During this period several books of poetry by older poets who had adopted a modernist style also appeared. Of these writers two in particular are worth mentioning: Þorgeir Sveinbjarnarson (1905–71) and Arnfríður Jónatansdóttir (b. 1923), whose book Þröskuldur hússins er þjöl (1958; The house's threshold is a file) is the first modernist book of poetry by an Icelandic woman. Jónatansdóttir's poems are peculiar, often featuring strong and unusual imagery and a sharp use of words. They express loneliness, sadness, and pain, but also resignation.

New generations during the 1950s and 1960s continued in various ways the transformation of language and form initiated by the structural revolutionaries of the atom period. It is clear that traditional form did not fulfill their needs any more than it had the atom poets' in the examination of their times and the expression of their thoughts and conclusions. Many poets referred to this in their works and wrote about the problems and role of poetry in the age of technology. The outer form of the poems varies, and the style is diverse, although they share an interest in breaking with most aspects of tradition.

Three of the main poets of this later period of modernism made use of traditional methods more than others: Hannes Pétursson (b. 1931); Þorsteinn frá Hamri (b. 1938; Þorsteinn of Hamar); and Matthías Johannessen (b. 1930). They have all written both traditional poetry and free verse, and their traditional works show the different ways of deviating from the strict formal rules. While they use alliteration, rhythm, and rhyme in some of their poems, they do not adhere to the strict traditional rules and manage to achieve new nuances and fresh expression as a result. This is a method similar to the one found in the works of Snorri Hjartarson, discussed above, and Einar Bragi was quite fond of it as well. Modernist poetry with varied alliteration is a uniquely Icelandic phenomenon.

Hannes Pétursson uses alliteration in most of his poetry but seldom rhyme. The outlook expressed in his poetry is in many ways similar to that found in romantic nature poetry and nationalism, but the view of human existence and its ultimate fate is different, and its expression has found a different mode and sound than it had during the romantic era. The poetry of Þorsteinn frá Hamri is similar, but Þorsteinn's poems are more inward looking and symbolic. Both poets have their roots in rural society but moved to the city when they were young, and their attitude is molded by these different spheres of existence and their experiences of them. Matthías Johannessen, on the other hand, was born and raised in Reykjavík and writes about the city as his childhood home. The poetry of these three writers is more closely connected to Icelandic history and the nation's cultural heritage than is the poetry of the atom poets, not to mention the poetry of younger generations. It often refers to events from ancient literature, folklore, and myth and makes use of ancient motifs, often in poems concerning contemporary issues. In this way it links modernism with the Icelandic cultural heritage.

Þorsteinn frá Hamri's style is characterized by a polished use of language that is always to the point and never noisy. His poems are concise, and, with his exact choice of words and the emphasis that those words receive, Þorsteinn often manages to increase the tension and power of his poems. His poetry is critical, modest on the surface, but with a serious undertone and condemns warmongering, corruption, and dishonesty. His poems generally consider the circumstances of modern man, his position and behavior, and contain meditations on time and the value and difficulty of literature, but some of his poems express a more personal experience, one that at the same time carries a wider resonance. His poems often encourage vigilance and warn against apathy in the face of the chaos of the times; they suggest that it is better to search for real values. He often uses images from nature to express his views: varied phenomena in the landscape, the weather, the seasons, or changes in the light. His nature imagery reflects experience, emotions, moods, and thoughts. Not only is Þorsteinn frá Hamri a prolific poet, but he has also authored three modernist novels and translated some foreign poetry and many prose works, among them children's books.

Hannes Pétursson writes a multifaceted nature poetry that is rich in imagery. Some of his poems have their roots in the rural life of his youth, marked as they are by its lively society and his myriad memories. Others are tied to a limited sphere of nature, interwoven with meditations on opinions and issues of the times. As mentioned above, Pétursson uses motifs from ancient lore and Norse mythology and also takes his subjects from folktales, which he transforms to shed new light on familiar subject matter. Sweeping metaphors characterize many of his nature poems; the four seasons, a varied landscape, and the ever-changing Icelandic weather inform his work, as do images from abroad. At the same time his poems voice dismay at militarism and doubts about technological innovations that do not seem to be a blessing for humanity. He often tackles the subject of death, in the process proving himself a skeptic. His outlook finds clear expression in the cycle "Söngvar til jarðarinnar" (Songs to the earth) in the book Í sumardölum (1959; In summer valleys). Pétursson's love poetry is beautiful, emotive, and usually nostalgic.

Matthías Johannessen has published many books of poetry; he has a great command of imagery and language. Life in the city and the landscape surrounding it is a common theme; the city of Reykjavík has grown up with the poet. Icelandic nature also makes its appearance and is often connected to man's mental state; this is evident, for instance, in one of Johannessen's later books, Árstíðaferð um innri mann (1992; A seasonal journey of the inner man).

Jóhann Hjálmarsson (b. 1939) is a prolific poet and translator who has written many poems in a simple, straightforward style on the everyday and the immediate environment. Occasionally, he has made use of surrealist imagery as well. He seldom takes a political stance in his poetry; his subjects are derived from ancient stories and carry a resonance far beyond their original sphere.

Many eloquent writers appeared during this period whose work showed the many ways in which it was possible to harness the language and increase its influence by disrupting and challenging accepted usage, thereby discovering fresh possibilities for expression. This method is often linked with the concentration of language associated with most modernist poetry. The uses of language, imagery, and expression in both early and late modernist Icelandic poetry share many important characteristics, and the lyric style in the works of nearly all poets who appeared between 1940 and 1970 is, all in all, quite similar. This time frame may, thus, be considered as a single period, that of modernism in Icelandic poetry.

The introduction of modernism sparked an increased interest in writing poetry. For many writing poetry provided a welcome opportunity for freedom of artistic expression. Many more poets started writing between 1955 and 1970 than during all the preceding fifteen years, and, although there is greater diversity of outlook among them than among previous generations of poets, they share many main points of emphasis. The classic subjects that come from personal experience, everyday life, and human relationships are, of course, apparent in poetry from this period, but at this time everything is colored by fear and menace owing to the threat of a nuclear holocaust. In the poem "Ráðið" (1960; The advice), Vilborg Dagbjartsdóttir (b. 1930) puts it this way:

They sit round the table
alien players
and throw dice for my life
our lives.
Tonight I was surprised
that they were also children
as he who lies in the cradle
and fills the room with his breathing.

While there were no women among the atom poets who wrote in free verse, a few women writers who made their appearance during the period 1955– 70 composed noteworthy poetry, indicating that the introduction of free verse into Icelandic poetry was attractive as a mode of expression for women as well as for men. Vilborg Dagbjartsdóttir has not only criticized the arms race and called for peace, as in the poem quoted above. She is also concerned with the status of women in society and with social inequality in general. Two young women writers made themselves heard in her wake: Þuríður Guðmundsdóttir (b. 1939) and Nína Björk Árnadóttir (1941– 2000). They are both very close to Icelandic nature, and their poetry is often concerned with individual experience and interprets not least everyday life and the experience of women in a richly emotional way (see also pp. 545–46).

The view of most of these young modernist poets of nature resembles that of the older modernists. Indeed, this strong sense of nature, found in the works of most modernist poets, characterizes Icelandic lyric modernism and remains a characterizing feature all the way to the transformation of the 1970s. Most of these poets grew up in the countryside and moved to the capital only later in life. The countryside, the landscape, and the memories associated with it exercise a strong hold over them, but at the same time there is a growing awareness that the roots of rural culture are losing their hold, which causes a certain nostalgia or even tension, as is apparent in some of the poems. Baldur Óskarsson (b. 1932) introduces many different subjects using sharply drawn and colorful nature imagery.

Matthías Johannessen and Dagur Sigurðarson (1937–94) are the only urbanites among this generation of poets, and they have a markedly different perspective on their environment. Sigurðarson treats bourgeois values with sarcasm and voices criticism in several directions, often in raw and shocking colloquial language. The city is a rather desolate setting for human life in his poetry. In Johannessen's poetry, on the other hand, Reykjavík is a friendly place; the city's environment is, at times, joined with Icelandic nature, and life in the city is shown to be no less appealing than life elsewhere.

Late modernist poetry shows that poets had become even more introspective, weighing their options carefully, and expressing in their poems the fear generated by the nuclear arms race, the tension and lack of security in world affairs, and doubts about the politics of the superpowers as well as about the talent and will of those in power to work toward peace and equality. But, despite such skepticism, poets are determined to stick to the view that peace and cooperation among the world's inhabitants should be the ultimate goal for everyone.

Much modernist poetry, by both young and old, makes reference to world affairs, particularly during the first decades after the Second World War, thus breaking the traditionally insular nature of Icelandic poetry. These were eventful times in history. Third World countries gained their independence from the old colonial powers only to encounter new difficulties. Despite economic growth in the West, wars were fought, and hunger, injustice, and violence ruled in many places around the world. The works by poets at this time display an aversion to the oppression and violence that dominated many areas across the globe and side with those who are denied freedom. They also describe the sense of guilt suffered by those who, in fact, have no part in these events, for they are far away, so that their empathy becomes useless and borders on pretension. The cold war marches on, the nuclear arms race speeds up, and a war of total destruction looms.

Not surprisingly, many poems are colored by pessimism and convey an atmosphere of impending doom. They interpret the alienation of man, his disjunctive existence, his weariness, and the tension between hope and fear. Yet, although the poetry of this generation often describes disappointment over various social issues, there is one part of human nature that is undeniably trustworthy: love. Love never fails and becomes a welcome lifeline in an unpredictable world and a shelter from the storms of the time. This generation of poets wrote many beautiful poems on the subject of love, and in them the way in which feelings and the expression of love are represented is, in fact, not unlike the role that love plays in many atom poems.

The poets who burst onto the scene in the 1950s and 1960s translated much contemporary poetry and in that way enriched the Icelandic lyric tradition, as the atom poets and Jóhannes of Katlar did before them. These were poems, not only from Europe, but also from other continents, especially North and South America and Africa. Jóhann Hjálmarsson has been the most prolific translator and has published several books of poetry translations, although many others have also tried their hands at this, including Hannes Pétursson and Sigurður A. Magnússon (b. 1928), who has also translated Icelandic poetry into English. Hallberg Hallmundsson (b. 1930), who resided in the United States for a long time, has translated many works of Icelandic literature into English, including many modern poems. He has also translated many foreign poems into Icelandic and published collections of original Icelandic poems.

FROM MODERNISM TO POSTMODERNISM

Despite certain similarities in the poetry of the last two decades of the twentieth century, no clear united front or characteristic emphases are apparent. Instead, we find the coexistence of various ideas and styles. When trying to view poetry after 1970, that is, in the postmodern period, as a whole, the picture becomes even more fragmented. A merging of different styles and the reevaluation of earlier values characterize many poems in this period as nearly all methods and modes of expression are experimented with. Some consider this to be exactly one of the main defining characteristics of postmodernism in various art forms, with literature placing the emphasis on the reworking of former elements, weaving them into the experience of the present, sometimes from a critical perspective.

The postmodern period in contemporary Icelandic poetry as viewed in this chapter can be roughly divided into two periods that produced very different writing: on the one hand, the so-called neorealist period, which flourished in the 1970s, and, on the other hand, a more inward-looking poetry that has gained prominence from the 1980s on.

THE 1970S: NEOREALISM

Around 1970 another transformation occurred in Icelandic poetry. A new generation of poets, generally known as the '68 generation, came forward with its own distinctive views and a style that was markedly different from what had gone before. The year 1968 has acquired a certain resonance, and myths have formed surrounding the events linked to it. No anarchist student revolt took place in Iceland, but the tendencies and views among the politically awakening young people of the time nevertheless reached the country. Their influence on the literature of young Icelandic writers manifests itself in their increased social awareness, in their political messages, and in their at times outspoken criticism expressed in innovative ways.

Neorealism is the term generally used to describe Icelandic literature during the 1970s, and it is associated with two features in particular: on the one hand, an increased political awareness and social criticism and, on the other hand, an innovative use of language and the renewal of lyricism. The result is a realist poetry that emphasizes external, social issues, making it radically different from the introspection of modernist poetry. This poetry is polemical in nature, directing its sharp social criticism primarily against capitalism and warmongering. It often depicts the dark side of consumer society: the exploitation of workers; materialism; alienation; insecurity; the inhumanity of institutions; the power of advertising and the media; injustice; and pollution. While these constitute an inescapable reality, we also occasionally find the expression of a longing to get away from "the hell of the consumer duty / the apathy of the cliché / the poison of the paper soup / . . . / from the fat sentimentalism of those who do not doubt," as it says in the poem "Á hringvegi ljóðsins I" (1980; On the poem's ring road I) by Sigurður Pálsson (b. 1948).

The neorealist political stance is usually harshly expressed and at times combative in spirit. Einar Ólafsson (b. 1949) says in a foreword to his collection *Ljóð* (Poems) from 1971 that some people do not have the opportunity to listen to birdsong and be happy because of oppression or hunger or "because the welfare state has killed all birds and all flowers." Then the young poet asks: "Do these people not concern us; should we not fight for them and dedicate to them some of our poetry and songs?" His poems answer this question in the affirmative, obviously, and many other poets took a similar stance. Poets increasingly turned their attention toward the work environment in all its rawness and wrote from the viewpoint of laborers, the workers at sea, and those in the fish factories. In accordance with these efforts the style and presentation of this poetry is simpler and more accessible than before as poetry was now expected to contribute to pressing social discourses and work political change.

Even though political persuasion and social tendencies markedly shaped poetry during the heyday of neorealism, there were also poets who sought inspiration elsewhere. Among them are three of the most talented poets of the period, Steinunn Sigurðardóttir (b. 1950), Þórarinn Eldjárn (b. 1949), and the aforementioned Sigurður Pálsson. While their poems are clearly marked by the realism of the times with regard to form and concerned with everyday life and feelings, sometimes in a playful manner, political polemics are largely absent.

Steinunn Sigurðardóttir has written both poetry and prose (see chapter 6). Her poems frequently revolve around love and other forms of human interaction, focusing on places and events, on travels abroad and at home. The tone is often frivolous, ironic, even cheeky, and the language is without lofty pretensions and approaches the colloquial. Her style imbues the poems with a fast-paced and cheerful atmosphere.

The changes around 1970 are so transformative that they can be seen as signaling the end of the modernist era in Icelandic poetry and the beginning of postmodernism, although earlier literary conventions survive. By the time neorealism made its influence felt, modernism had gained a solid foothold in Iceland and had been a creative force in poetry for a quarter of a century. And, although the time had now come for different poetic experiments, modernists continued to write on their preferred subjects and in their usual style, and they continued to gain respect. They were, in fact, joined by several new poets who made a late debut during the 1970s. Of particular note in this respect is Kristján Karlsson (b. 1922); his poems are concise, featuring a quick rhythm and unusual images of people and their environment, both at home and abroad. Karlsson's poetry is crowded with people, some of whom are mentioned by name and appear in more than one book of poetry. *New York* (1983), for instance, is a collection of poems on New Yorkers going about their everyday business; Karlsson lived in the United States for many years. The poet Þóra Jónsdóttir (b. 1925) has written on people's position toward past and present and on the search for lasting values in chaotic times.

The voices of the older, traditional poets had for the most part become silent. Instead, it was now the modernists who adopted certain aspects of the traditional lyric style. The neorealist poets, on the other hand, wrote nearly always in free verse, although two of them have proved fond of traditional forms: Þórarinn Eldjárn and Ragnar Ingi Aðalsteinsson (b. 1944). Both write ironic poems on their times, often with reference to ancient lore. Eldjárn is proficient in many lyric styles as well as being a well-known prose writer (see also chapter 6). He is also the only living poet who has written poetry specifically for children, which has been very well received (see p. 606). Eldjárn achieved immediate and great popularity with his first collection, *Kvæði* (1974; Poems). These are all epic poems written in traditional form, that is, using alliteration and rhyme in the traditional way, and in this Eldjárn is unique among his generation. But, whether he writes in traditional meters or free verse, his popularity as a poet is not least due to his unique sense of humor, which finds expression in his use of the burlesque, making the serious comic and vice versa, and playing with all kinds of mismatches between form and content. Eldjárn mixes traditional poetic language, old words with contemporary colloquialisms, and slang and wordplay; he uses modern language to deal with ancient themes and antiquated language for contemporary matters. Familiar historical or fictional characters often appear in a surprising light in his work.

Although the lyric styles of the neorealists are, in fact, diverse, rhetoric and narrative make a prominent reappearance, and there is not nearly as much of a tendency to look inward or to be concise in the use of language as was so prominently the case in the works of the modernists. Instead, the language becomes more colloquial and transparent. Both the poetry and the fiction of the neorealist period develop, in fact, in direct opposition to modernist literature, which many considered inaccessible and barely comprehensible, except to the chosen few. This is a development similar to that which took place in neighboring countries and has often been interpreted as a reappraisal of modernism and its inward-looking modes of expression. Now poetry had to be open, an accessible medium for ideological messages.

As music was one of the main political weapons, many lyrics were written, and many troubadours were active during this period, some of whom are still writing and singing today. One of the more singular among them was Megas (Magnús Þór Jónsson; b. 1945). His texts are often coarse, like his voice; his subjects are either historical events or an ironic view of the times. His language is crude, his expression a reflection of a bohemian culture that posits itself in opposition to public opinion.

Icelandic neorealist poetry was, however, not always as simple, as without artifice, or as colloquial as contemporary poetry in other Western countries during this period. Some of the Icelandic poets used, in fact, quite intricate metaphors and other conceits in their poetry. Birgir Svan Símonar-son (b. 1951), for instance, adeptly uses powerful words and images in his depiction of reality. His *Gjalddagar* (1977; Due dates) consists of a single poem that concentrates on the destruction of natural resources, the arms race, and the robotization of man and environment, as, for instance, in the following stanzas:

> In the smirking rearview mirror
> highways with foul breath stretch
> cars tear with heartbeat
> from newly wakened suburbs
>
> . . .
>
> in the waking hours hellstorms rage
> gigantic cities rise
> stakes of scorn woven with blazing alphabet
> skyscrapers on steel feet
> light green ocean valleys
> greedy fire burns
> laborers work shifts
> in the suffocating metallic fog.

Símonarson has written many poems of note on the lives of contemporary working people; they depict in realistic fashion the situation and condition of laborers, for instance, fishermen, and they are often polemical in nature.

Although modernism had caused a substantial transformation of Icelandic poetry around the middle of the twentieth century, it still fostered, on its own terms, two time-honored aspects of the lyric tradition: a close attention to language and a nature poetry connected to patriotism. By 1970, however, younger poets began to fight off these two final influences. They launched an attack on the accepted use of language, including the deep-rooted convention of using elevated diction in poetry. Instead of attempting a refined language, they used slang, coarse colloquialisms, and foreign loanwords, attempting to raise their status in poetry. They created innovative imagery that gets its references from contemporary consumer society, thereby making it more recognizable and accessible to the larger public. This imagery often creates an ironic effect, one that points to the restlessness and consumerism of contemporary society. Poets frequently used wordplay to explore the expressive possibilities of the language and coax hidden meanings and new energy from it. Words and set phrases were broken up and various language components linked in innovative ways. Established lyric language was now perceived to be an obstacle, a hindrance to further "poetry roadwork," the name of a poem and a poetry collection by Sigurður Pálsson (b. 1948). As Pálsson says in "Ljóðvegagerð IV" (1982; Poetry Roadwork IV): "Words are stuck / between you and the world." Innovation in language is necessary in a world of swift change:

Sentences
and sentence structure

Syntax
stands between you
and the world
armed to the teeth
Sad on burning sand concludes
swiftly with brusqueness
that words are chains.
(*Ljóð vega menn*, 7)

Sigurður Pálsson is a poet who has concentrated on giving poetic language a fresh resonance and on sharpening the meaning of words by freeing them from the shackles of habit. His poems are often rich in imagery, humor, and wordplay. The opinions expressed in his work are, however, quite different from the openly political poetry of the neorealists. Many of his poems have a foreign setting, while others tell of travels and places at home and abroad. Pálsson is one of the most important poets of the last decades and has also written novels and plays.

Patriotism, not to mention nationalism, gave way to internationalism and ideals of peace during these years. The neorealists cynically turned their backs on the surviving romantic legacy of patriotism and love of nature in Icelandic poetry. The surroundings of rural life had until 1970 been a common feature in poetry, but, by now, significantly fewer people were dependent on nature or had a close connection with it through their daily lives and work. Most people lived out their everyday lives in cities or towns, and their existence was increasingly marked by this fact. The 1970s see the first generation of poets who can be collectively and fully considered urban, and they are eager to express this in their poetry. Yet, despite such declarations of love for the city, the image of the alienated urbanite who has lost all connection with nature is drawn with considerable irony as well.

Einar Már Guðmundsson (b. 1954), better known for his fiction, began his writing career as a poet and has published five poetry collections. His poetry has many of the characteristics of neorealism. He attempts to illuminate young people's lives in the here and now in a fresh and surprising manner, for instance, with a risky use of language and unusual similes often linked to images derived from entertainment and popular culture. His analysis of contemporary life involves a reckoning with social opinion, establishment poetry, and even his own work and views.

Love, the loyal companion of poetry, receives cold treatment from the neorealists. They do not consider it appropriate to talk about love in a sentimental fashion. Love is transient, part of an alienated world, and not to be trusted. It is objectified like everything else and is valued only in relation to material goods. The treatment of love and sentiment is rare and often cynical, but, when it is treated, it is spoken of openly and without prudishness.

The common goal for many around the world during this period was to call for peace and for an end to the arms race, to relieve suffering in the Third World, to improve archaic and inhumane educational establishments, and to unsettle the power system in the Western world in general. At the same time there was strong opposition to the behavior of the superpowers, U.S. warfare in Vietnam, and the Soviet invasion of Czechoslovakia. Empathy with other countries was clearly apparent in Icelandic writing, as it was in that of other countries. The student protests of 1968 were the clearest and most dramatic example of the political changes and the demands of young people at the time. But things eventually turned back to the way they were before. The student uprising, which had been one of the main bases of neorealism, came to nothing. Poems were written on the disappointment that followed, such as "París '68" (1973) by Ólafur Haukur Símonarson (b. 1947):

> this morning as I woke
> I saw a red rose had grown
> out of my navel.
> it smiled like a child.
>
> I hurried out to fetch it water.
>
> but when I returned it was gone
> and you said you never saw
> any flower
> oh Paris!
> (*Postwar Poetry*, trans. Magnússon, 218)

The women's liberation movement, which rose to prominence during this period, brought with it new views and an increased interest in and understanding of the status of women in society. This is also apparent in the poetry of the time; the poems by young women (and some men as well) firmly drew attention to the social circumstances of women and encouraged the fight against women's oppression. The strength of this poetry by women lies not least in the frank descriptions of women's reality, descriptions based on their experience and viewpoints, both in the private and in the social sphere. Such poetry aims to sharpen the social views of young people and to encourage political thought. The poems by Ingibjörg Haraldsdóttir (b. 1942) are the clearest examples of this; they handle in a straightforward way the daily life of women, motherhood, and social circumstances while at the same time making effective use of rich imagery. Haraldsdóttir's style is characterized by a simple and straightforward use of words and a lyric honesty that gives the poems a soft nuance devoid of sentimentality. Haraldsdóttir is also a prolific translator of poetry and prose, in particular, from Russian and Spanish.

By the end of the 1970s and after, doubts start to creep into poetry as to the good fight. We find expressions of disappointment and fatigue, the poems are increasingly further removed from social issues, and the value of political engagement is cast in doubt and even treated with cynicism.

FIN DE SIÈCLE: POSTMODERNISM

Neorealism exercised little influence on the writing of the modernists, who carried on their own work regardless, although they kept rather quiet during the 1970s. After 1980, however, they made a comeback and published a considerable amount of poetry. In fact, all the main atom poets remained active in the field of literary creation during the last decades of the century. A notable exception is Einar Bragi, who has, however, made a significant contribution in the form of his many translations, as mentioned earlier. Two collections by Stefán Hörður Grímsson appeared in the 1980s, and for the latter, *Yfir heiðan morgun* (1989; On a bright morning), he received the Icelandic Literary Prize in 1989, the first time it was awarded. This honor could be regarded as symbolic of the extent to which modernism had achieved a reputable standing in Icelandic literature. Hannes Sigfússon moved back to Iceland in 1988 after having lived in Norway for several decades and published three collections in the years before his death. Jón Óskar and Sigfús Daðason also published books and were prolific in translating poetry from French. These later works are without a doubt among their best, and, indeed, the same can be said about younger modernists such as Þorsteinn frá Hamri and Matthías Johannessen, who have been quite prolific since 1980. Þorsteinn's style has become even more polished, the use of language both powerful and modest in his concise portrayals of human existence. Johannessen writes on society in its widest sense as before and is also a passionate nature poet, linking natural treasures with human thought and feeling.

Some of the poets associated with neorealism have also remained prolific, for instance, Birgir Svan Símonarson and Sigurður Pálsson as well as Ingibjörg Haraldsdóttir. Others have turned first and foremost to prose but have also continued on occasion to write poetry, among them Þórarinn Eldjárn, Einar Már Guðmundsson, and Steinunn Sigurðardóttir, although a few have turned exclusively to novel and play writing. Pétur Gunnarsson (b. 1947), who started his writing career as a forerunner of the neorealists with the collection *Splúnkunýr dagur* (1973; A brand new day), has written only prose since. Ólafur Haukur Símonarson has gone down a similar route and published several novels and, more recently, popular plays (see also chapter 9).

After 1980 new voices also appeared in Icelandic literature that clearly did not go along with the methods and views of the preceding generation of poets. This is, for instance, quite obvious in the first collections by Gyrðir Elíasson (b. 1961) and Ísak Harðarson (b. 1956), published in 1982 and 1983, respectively. Elíasson and Harðarson have both been prolific in poetry as well as prose and been honored for their work. Harðarson has published eight collections of poetry in all and Elíasson ten. Although their poetry is quite different, they both write inventively on the human environment in a modern technological world.

While these new poets may have left neorealism behind, in particular, the descriptions of a superficial reality combined with a strong and aggressively expressed social message, they did not automatically dismiss their entire literary heritage along with it. In fact, it is quite evident that many of them have much in common with the atom poets in particular. Once again we see a turn inward, the use of intricate imagery, and an avoidance of direct polemics. Poetry is still written about everyday life, as was the case in the 1970s, but this time the raw surface is missing. Rather, the focus is on the fear that everyday life harbors and the threat that it can pose to people's peace of mind. Many poets turn their attention to the individual experience but also to the existence of contemporary people in a technological world, where the individual is at the mercy of propaganda, authority, the media, and objectification. The gaze is once again on an inner world.

In his early works Gyrðir Elíasson writes on the anxiety and loneliness that has increased with the expansion of the Information Age. In his poetry known phenomena from popular culture appear time and again as he investigates all kinds of objects from everyday life, at times including their brand names, in his poetry. The language is usually simple and accessible, and sometimes English words are used to add to the flavor of the poem. In Elíasson's poetry the environment is often full of fear and under a spell of menace. The atmosphere is heavy with terror, fear of death, and desperation, as, for instance, in the following lines from the collection *Blindfugl/svartflug* (1986; Blindbird/blackflight):

A mixture of dream and reality,
light standing on stalks and
flickering, eyes painted on tautly stretched
canvas look at me incessantly,
isolation sharpens the eye contact,
a tape ripped off the mouth, an inkwell
turns over, on the table stands a clay
bottle of Dutch gin
emptied long ago, an old telefunken
and a box from glassware guard
me, I'm kept under the microscope
of things day and night, nowhere
a shelter to be found, a candle staring
at the foot of the bed, a moon peeks
through lace curtains, shadows link up
with radiators.
(trans. Hallberg Hallmundsson)

Horrors such as these have been replaced in Elíasson's later works with poems on human relationships and on man in nature. These poems are characterized by a sensitive insight into the human soul and show people's actions, their strange behavior, or their peculiar experiences, usually in everyday circumstances, but often simultaneously viewed in a fantastic light. There are frequently curious beings afoot as well as ghosts and animals in all kinds of roles. His lyric style and imagery are also simpler than before; the use of language is always meticulous and contains magical powers under its humble surface, for instance, in the poem about the worm that climbs up the hill and not down because "it is on its way / to the library / where the thought grass grows / . . . / The most durable of all grass" ("Þekkingarleit" [Search for knowledge], from *Hugarfjallið* [1999; Mind mountain]).

Ísak Harðarson's lyricism is never overly formal. Harðarson uses many kinds of speech, sometimes foreign words and slang, or children's language and naivisms. He has experimented with language, creating surprising word links and humorous wordplay. In this way, and using original settings, he is able to describe our times and environment ironically and draw attention to the absurdities in society while at the same time drawing attention to the more desirable values governing our lives. Occasionally, sharp criticism is voiced in his poetry, but there is also evidence of a religious bent and a search for security in life, and in this respect Harðarson occupies a unique position in Icelandic poetry. Like Gyrðir Elíasson, Harðarson has also tried his hand at writing concrete poetry.

Surrealism rose out of the ashes of the First World War but did not at the time become influential in Icelandic poetry. Surrealist methods have, however, become more apparent in the works of turn-of-the-century poets in Iceland, especially in the use of imagery and allowing the imagination free reign. Sjón (Sigurjón Sigurðsson; b. 1962) in particular has been prominent in this respect, for instance, in his descriptions of pressing contemporary phenomena such as mass culture, but also when he deals with eroticism or describes his own thoughts and ideas. Sjón soon became associated with punk art and rock bands, for instance, the Sugarcubes. Since the demise of the band, he has, for instance, collaborated with Björk Guðmundsdóttir on song lyrics.

In the final decades of the twentieth century women's voices have been heard more prominently than in any earlier period in Icelandic poetry. Women's participation in Icelandic poetry has always been relatively minimal. It is interesting to note that it increased significantly during the neorealist period, but, even then, only just over 10 percent of published collections by new poets were by women. In many poems by women we find a new, socially based interpretation of women's experience and situation. Since the last two decades of the century young women poets have not played as great a part in Icelandic literature as in the 1970s, although some quite noteworthy work has appeared. While the polemical stance and the fight for equality are almost gone from women's poetry, the articulation of women's experiences and views remains a significant feature in women's work. One of the most unique among recent women poets is Kristín Ómarsdóttir (b. 1962; see also p. 448). Most of her poetry handles close encounters and a search for identity: "Does the moon have an address or not. / It is punctual, it is always in the same place. / But it is also like my lips on a long trip" ("Lokaðu augunum og hugsaðu um mig" [1998; Close your eyes and think of me], in *Lokaðu augunum og hugsaðu um mig*, 17). The attempt of the lyric "I" to define the body and analyze people often leads to bizarre images in Ómarsdóttir's poems: "The watermelon does not leave your lips / when you eat and neither do I" ("Vatnsmelónan og ég" [1998; Watermelon and I], in *Lokaðu augunum og hugsaðu um mig*, 18).

As mentioned above, the poem again became an independent world of sensations and imagination in the 1980s, obeying its own rules without necessarily making an accurate reference to outer reality. Poets significantly shifted their focus from that of the neorealists: continuous sensations and social messages did not agree with their view of the world. This development has since continued, with poets exploring their feelings instead and trying to achieve a positioning of their own existence, which is, in most cases, loaded with considerable fear. The hope that was once the hallmark of the '68 generation is long gone, as is the radical fighting spirit that characterized neorealism. In recent poetry pressing views and issues remain, such as the confrontation with an unstable political situation, dislike and sometimes criticism of an inhumane environment, and also the hope for a happy life. But the dream of peace and equality has been left behind, and no one puts any faith in ideological solutions anymore. Instead of rebellion there is a certain dissolution. Poetry is handling an uncertain world without any vision of a future and without belief in a new spring. Contemporary reality still has a role to play for poets, but optimism is rare, and many poets write with irony about the various injustices, the systematic oppression, and the horror in our existence. The fear of total destruction, on the other hand, once among the main fears of the cold war poets, no longer has a place in recent poetry, whether written by young or older poets.

As a result, direct social criticism and a more international approach have disappeared from poetry. Many poems derive their subject matter from other countries, different corners of the world, as poets describe their own travel experiences, for instance, Bragi Ólafsson (b. 1962), Sigurbjörg Þrastardóttir (b. 1973), and Jónas Þorbjarnarson (b. 1960) as well as Sigfús Bjartmarsson (b. 1955), who began his writing career during the neorealist era and has written both poetry and prose, and whose work reflects the fact that he has traveled widely. Þrastardóttir calls one of her books *Hnattflug* (2000; Global flight); it depicts a kind of poetic journey around the world and features poems on many different cities. Bragi Ólafsson's lyric style is always simple and colloquial, and the characters that appear in his poems are often ordinary and strange at the same time, displaying surprising behavior. Nature and the environment at times take over his poetry and become an alien force as he directs his attention toward man's alienation from nature. Ólafsson has written several intriguing novels that in the treatment of subject matter share many characteristics with his poetry (see p. 446).

Poets become once again concerned with the self and engage in a search for themselves and an examination of the private, which they link with shared human struggles such as alienation and social problems. *Njósnir um eigið líf* (Spying on my own life) is the revealing subtitle of one of the most interesting poetry collections from recent years entitled *Harði kjarninn* (1999; The hard core) by Sindri Freysson (b. 1970). Freysson's poems contain a delightful and sometimes cynical self-examination amid the pressing issues of a technological society.

Many recent poems focus on individual feelings and emotional relationships with others and are often self-referential with a narrow perspective but expressed objectively and without sentimentality. This is, for instance, the case in the poetry of Margrét Lóa Jónsdóttir (b. 1967) and Linda Vilhjálmsdóttir (b. 1958) as well as Gerður Kristný (b. 1970), whose poems are inward looking and rich in imagery, with alliteration and rhyme forming a peculiar rhythm all their own.

Throughout history there are poets who start publishing later in life and are older than most of their counterparts. One recent example is Ágústína Jónsdóttir (b. 1949), whose first book of poetry was published in 1994 and who has published quite a few since. Her poetry is full of emotion and rich in imagery, sometimes oblique, and demonstrates an admirable command of lyric language. Jónsdóttir's poetry centers on love, life experiences of all kinds, and the exploration of the self from a woman's point of view.

In the poetry of recent years, love is no longer treated in an offhand way or with cynicism, as in the days of the neorealists, but neither is there any romantic passionate love to be found, although there is certainly passion and human relationships and emotional connections are considered valuable and desirable. As before, however, it is not happy love that forms the main focus but, rather, the instability and disappointment of love, as in "Þessi ást, þessi ást" (1994; This love, this love) by Gerður Kristný:

The sheen on the water is gone
it is back

back in the coldest place
seawet with long hair
and turns on

a smile fall and fate
and follows the smoke.

In contemporary nature poetry, after its absence in the neorealist period nature is not so much praised as it has become an attractive place to be. It does not seem to matter that urban poets are in the majority; the country's impressive natural landscape has once again become a pressing topic for many poets, most often used as a setting for people's lives and a companion to thought rather than as scenery watched from a distance. Most powerful is the natural sphere in the poetry of Gyrðir Elíasson, which is rich in imagery and at times takes on mystical and fantastic overtones. Another vantage point can be found in Sigurbjörg Þrastardóttir's poetry. Þrastardóttir looks at nature more as a spectator and a tourist, although she does connect with the places she observes. Jónas Þorbjarnarson is also noteworthy for his nature poetry; his poems exhibit a close proximity to the landscape.

Life is now lived mostly in the city, however. And for many poets life in the city is not always unpleasant, although at times everyday things become uncanny and their proximity tiresome, even threatening. People find themselves at the mercy of the media, speed and technology, impersonal and alien phenomena, and unfeeling objects. Others, however, delight in their city environment.

Poets after 1980 often show an acute sensibility to imagery and subject matter, which is often taken from new fields in a society increasingly dominated by technology, itself sometimes imbued with a frightening atmosphere. The language tends to be more polished, colloquialisms and slang having lost some of their previous attraction, although instances of these can occasionally still be glimpsed as part of the continuing search for new modes of expression. While this type of language exploration has been universal, it is not possible to gauge a unified style.

The latest poets to have burst onto the Icelandic scene have grown up in a rich society where comfort, financial gain, and profit take precedence over ideals. Their society is characterized by advanced technology, increased speed, and the rude aggression of the media, much more than has ever been the case before. There is no apparent criticism of social issues in their poetry, and the threat of militarism and war, a staple of postwar poetry for decades, is now significantly less acute.

Mass culture and the media, globalization, materialism, and consumerism, on the other hand, play a prominent part in many poems and are more important than tradition or lessons from the past. Television is the medium that has most notoriously increased its role as the most influential tool in the spread of capitalism and global culture, while computers have become a powerful medium for information and entertainment. These magical tools of technology have become pressing matters and are not infrequently portrayed as inhuman, but they appear at the same time as positive images and metaphors, being part of the general experience of poets today, part of their upbringing, and even an indispensable everyday companion. In fact, it would seem that poetry has to some extent become more amenable to technology and directs its attention to the convenience that technology provides rather than the dangers inherent in it. Poets are ambiguous when expressing their view of this unavoidable reality, and sometimes it is hard to gather whether there is a sense of passivity or cynicism in their work. Some poetry would seem to indicate that a generation is growing up that considers itself happy in this world of technology and riches, wants to enjoy the best that this world has to offer, and not let other things worry it, as in the following example:

Once my life was a black-and-white television
and on a good day
a certain contrast was sharpened in the greyness
but nothing more

then you came

Now life is 40 inches
in color and 3D
the birds sing in surround sound.

This poem, called "Fyrir þig" (1995; For you), is by the poet who has attracted the most attention of late, Andri Snær Magnason (b. 1973). Magnason has published poems, short stories, and a play, and he received the Icelandic Literary Prize in 2000 for a children's book (see pp. 449, 606). The poem could certainly be interpreted as a critique of machines and the worship of technology: the criteria for human and emotional values are now measured by consumer goods and their technological value. Poets from the neorealist era used a similar approach, for instance, Birgir Svan Símonarson and Einar Már Guðmundsson, but their perspective was usually an ironic one.

As the end of the century drew closer, poetry became more varied in form and expression. This diversity in poetry during the short period of postmodernism in Icelandic poetry shows that postmodernism does not constitute a literary movement in itself in that it is not characterized by one perspective but is, rather, a melting pot where the old and the new are thrown together.

CONCLUSION

Since 1940 Icelandic poetry has seen many transformations. It has become more international in form, and its perspective has widened. The old, traditional verse form has consistently lost in importance and influence, although certain elements still play a part in some of the best Icelandic poetry.

Social views have changed radically over time, as has the view of life overall, reflecting the drastic changes that Icelandic society and culture have undergone in the course of the twentieth century. Patriotism is no longer a chief element of Icelandic poetry, as it was in the days of the struggle for independence and the Republic. The most serious issues are no longer tied to one nation alone but are shared by all of humanity across the globe. Yet patriotism remains an inherent part of the nature and art of small nations that know that their fight for independence continues, not least in the cultural sphere.

While innovation and freshness are necessary to poetry, the poetry of each nation, of each language, has to have its own cultural characteristics. Not only have Icelanders created literature continuously from the start of their history; they have also preserved old stories, verses, and myths that once were part of a larger, ancient European verse and storytelling tradition. This literary heritage has provided Icelandic poets with a rich source of materials, motifs, and styles across the centuries. It has informed the Icelandic consciousness, not least thanks to poetry, and the Icelandic poetic tradition is still nourished by it today, if to a lesser extent.

Translated by Gunnþórunn Guðmundsdóttir

Searching for Herself: Female Experience and Female Tradition in Icelandic Literature

Helga Kress

8

"I AM A WOMAN"

"When I made the decision to become a writer—that is, with publishing in mind—I reckoned squarely with the fact that I am a woman," wrote Svava Jakobsdóttir in a 1979 essay on women's poetics entitled "Experience and Reality: Some Reflections of a Woman Writer." "That is, I was painfully aware that I lacked the experiences in life that seemed to be the fabric of literature. Sometimes I felt that I had not experienced anything that was suitable for fiction." At the same time she was equally convinced that, to achieve even the minimum results in creating art, she would have to observe the fundamental responsibility of being true to herself and her own experience. She would have to write about what she knew. She places this problem in a cultural context, showing that what is at issue is a difficulty, not just for her, but for all women writers:

> Female experience is, for the most part, concealed beneath the surface of our culture. Any woman who begins to write, and with the intention of trying to heed her responsibility as an author to be faithful to her own experience and adhere to the truth, quickly discovers a wide gap between her world of experience—which is hidden and, above all, closed—and the dominant, official culture. If she searches for herself and her experience in the prevailing literary tradition, she soon realizes that only one-tenth of this experience is visible; the other nine-tenths are hidden. ("Reynsla og raunveruleiki," 226–27)

The role of the woman writer is to give this nine-tenths a language or, as Svava Jakobsdóttir puts it, "to bring these undercurrents to the surface" ("Reynsla og raunveruleiki," 227). This presents various difficulties, but for the woman writer there are two in particular: on the one hand, her social position as a woman and, on the other, her position within the literary establishment and the dominant literary tradition.

Men have shaped the dominant literary tradition and controlled the literary establishment of each era, as seen in both the subject and style of the official canon. Here only a few women are visible, and those who do appear are merely stereotypes unsupported by the actual experiences of women. When women writers aim to depict women and their lives, they encounter this tradition, which they cannot build upon. Some try to adapt to the tradition, others break new ground. Speaking of the position of women writers in this regard, Svava Jakobsdóttir uses the metaphor of a woman who ventures out on the street after dark: "The street of literary tradition that she walks along is well trodden and paved by men. A woman writer always runs a risk of being seduced with elegant symbols and beautiful metaphors which originate in a perspective toward the subject that is totally different from hers, and which lead to a perspective that the woman writer, in the end, has only appropriated for herself but not experienced. Thus the female experience has not been conveyed" (224). To be able to write, women must break away from the tradition and rework both subject and language in a way different from what is instilled by this tradition.

"SHE HAD A DESK, IN FACT"

A notable aspect of Icelandic literary history is how few women writers there are. Of all the practicing Icelandic writers in the year 1984, only one in five was a woman, and in previous years there were proportionally fewer (Kress, "Listsköpun kvenna," 194–96).

Icelandic literary history is filled with the "silences" of women writers. Twenty-six years elapsed between the first two books of poems of Sigríður Einars, nineteen years between the books of poems of Halldóra B. Björnsson, and a similar period between the most recent books of poems of Vilborg Dagbjartsdóttir. Also typical for women is how late in life they begin to write, to tackle substantive material. Jakobína Sigurðardóttir saw the publication of her first novel when she was over forty years old, and the same is true of her sister, Fríða Sigurðardóttir. Ragnheiður Jónsdóttir was in her late forties when she published her first novel, Guðrún Árnadóttir of Lundur began to write in her fifties, and Málfríður Einarsdóttir was almost eighty when her first book was published.

Some women have tried to write at night; others use every free moment. An article in a 1924 issue of the women's periodical *19. júní* recounts a visit to the farmstead of the writer Kristín Sigfúsdóttir and describes her writing facilities:

> Next to the sitting room was her kitchen. There stood a table with writing materials. We asked in fun whether this was her desk, and she told us that she had no time for writing except at night, but that, whenever she was working around the house and something good occurred to her, she would jot it down as a reminder, and that was why she kept her writing materials handy. Back in the sitting room was a little bookshelf; here were several works in various Scandinavian languages and other classics. The only thing Kristín complained about was how much trouble she had getting books and how little time she had for reading, for books were her passion; that was obvious. (Sigurðardóttir, "Kristín Sigfúsdóttir," 73–74)

The work habits of Unnur Benediktsdóttir Bjarklind, who wrote under the penname Hulda, are described by her son in this way: "She had a desk, in fact, although I hardly ever remember seeing her sitting at it. But I remember many a morning when I awoke to see her sitting up in bed writing. She went to bed very early but got up at the crack of dawn, when she would eagerly take up her pen and devote all her energy to writing — before the long workday of the housewife began" (Bjarklind, "Ljósklædd birtist hún mér," 153).

Other women have been able to shut themselves off from their surroundings, not allowing disturbances to bother them. In an interview on her eightieth birthday Elínborg Lárusdóttir said: "What helped me most was that I got used to writing even when I didn't have the peace and quiet for it. I concentrated on the writing and didn't hear what was going on around me. If I hadn't managed to do so, I would never have written anything" (Lárusdóttir, "Dag skal að kveldi lofa," 834). And Ása Sólveig, who is half a century younger, made a similar comment when asked whether she needed privacy to be able to think and write: "You see, then I would never have written a word. . . . I've trained myself to work in noise" (Ása Sólveig, " 'Ég hefði aldrei skrifað orð,' " 36).

"THE TASK WAS MINE"

The writings of Icelandic women contain many statements that show a keen awareness of their situation. In a handwritten bulletin from 1913, circulated among the members of the Women's Reading Club of Reykjavík, Theodora Thoroddsen (1863–1954) wrote: "The way it is with poetic talent, as with most other intellectual abilities, is that we women are generally second fiddle to men. It shall be left here unsaid whether the cause of this is that our brain is lighter on the scales than theirs, as claimed by some, or whether it is rooted in the intellectual and physical oppression of many centuries" (Thoroddsen, *Ritsafn*, 111). Theodora Thoroddsen, who had thirteen children and many mouths to feed, never fully achieved her potential as a writer. She often mentions this, and not always without anguish, in the few but fine works that she produced. Her well-known poem "Mitt var starfið" (The task was mine) from *Ritsafn* (1960; Collected writings) begins this way: "In this world the task was mine / on days both hot and cold / to wipe kids' bottoms and comb their hair / and toil to darn the holes." The poem's five verses all end on the word *staga* (darn), which the poet underlined in the manuscript. Like so many women writers of her generation, she tries to pin her hopes on another world, but even there she is accompanied by her darning: "If Death should come with her paring knife / and cut short my days as they unfold / I think it will prove to be my lot / in Hell to darn more holes" (*Ritsafn*, 123–24). In his introduction to Theodora Thoroddsen's collected works, the influential literary scholar Sigurður Nordal calls these verses "words of impatience" and concludes that they were "composed on behalf of many mothers" ("Theodora Thoroddsen," 28).

A poem in Halldóra B. Björnsson's (1907–68) collection *Við sanda* (1968; At sands) is reminiscent of Theodora Thoroddsen's verses. Entitled "Og þá rigndi blómum" (And then it rained flowers), it is written in the words of a deceased poet who is honored with flowers for her casket but who was never nurtured during her lifetime and given the chance to realize her potential. She accepts her death but feels that "the greatest ill is how often I was dead / while I subsisted." Her few poems either were lost or "ended up with trolls," and her time was spent "in the baking and churning chores / for an urgent question / was on everyone's lips: / Don't you have any coffee / or bread — or some mended socks in the drawer?" Now that she is dead, people have begun to search for these few poems of hers: "Every scrap of paper is devoured, / but mention has been suspended / of those countless cooking days / and the overwhelming multitude / of rags I have mended" (*Við sanda*, 76–77).

In the poem "Heimsókn gyðjunnar" (The muse's visit) from *Kvæði* (1960; Poems), Jakobína Sigurðardóttir (1918–94) describes a similar conflict. The muse visits the poet as she is washing the cellar steps. Before she has time to attend to the muse, she must finish the task, and then she has to boil the fish and set the table. These obligations are described in everyday language and with an urgent rhythm: "Now, out goes the dirty water from the pail in a hurry! / Then I fling the plates on the table fast." But there is still more to do; the chores are endless, and the poet has to dismiss the muse: "Indeed, Muse, you give me a look of reproach, / but awaiting me now is the laundry. / I send you my thoughts, though I turned my back / when you kindly sought my company" (*Kvæði*, 70, 72).

"HANDICRAFT RATHER THAN LITERATURE"

"Housecleaning, laundry, factory work, / would that be the stuff of poetry?" (*Kvæði*, 23), asked Jakobína Sigurðardóttir at the beginning of her writing career in the poem "Náttmál" (Bedtime). The question is the same as the one that Svava Jakobsdóttir asked herself when she began to write, feeling that she had not experienced anything that would be appropriate for fiction. The question is answered negatively by the literary establishment: female experience is not the stuff of literature.

The attitude of the literary establishment toward women's literature is manifested in various ways. But, generally, there has been a tacit agreement in all discussions of Icelandic literature and literary history to bypass literary works by women as if they did not exist. Until quite recently it was an exception whenever literature by women was mentioned in literary histories. In her pioneering work on early women poets Guðrún P. Helgadóttir asserts that, over the ages, considerably more women's poetry has been lost than men's. There is little account of women's poetry in manuscripts from the eighteenth and nineteenth centuries, and women are not mentioned in rosters of authors. Sometimes, their names are written in the margins, and in one entry the scribe apologized for counting women among the poets (Helgadóttir, *Skáldkonur fyrri alda*, 2:16). Nor is their lot much better in the twentieth century. For example, the literary survey *Nordens litteratur* (1972), which covers Scandinavian literature from its inception until approximately 1960 (the most recent book discussed in the survey was published in 1970), a total of 101 Icelandic authors are mentioned. Of these, one is a woman.

Poetry written by women has not been taken seriously, as clearly seen in the reviews and various comments about works by women, and seldom has work by women been discussed without reference to the sex of the author. If women writers are included in literary histories, they are most often treated as a group — discussed as women and relegated to a section at the very end. Furthermore, critics often have difficulty distinguishing between the woman and the work being discussed. Adjectives such as *little, pretty, tasteful, neat*, and *feminine* characterize many of these reviews. Terms like *long-winded, common,* and *ordinary* are also much used. In his history of Icelandic fiction during the period 1940–70 Erlendur Jónsson has this to say about the works of Jakobína Sigurðardóttir: "Her best stories are stories about ordinary people in ordinary circumstances. Their problems are also ordinary. Consistent with such subjects, the stories are told in an ordinary way" (*Íslensk skáldsagnaritun,* 166). Some critics are fond of jesting about women's literature, comparing it to handicraft. A 1953 reviewer in the literary magazine *Helgafell* offered this evaluation of the novel *Í biðsal hjóna-bandsins* (1949; In the waiting room of matrimony) by Þórunn Elfa Magn-úsdóttir: "The author takes great pleasure in describing landscape and households, domestic practices, and all sorts of trivial pursuits, and does it fairly well, but she carries this to extremes so that it becomes tedious. What also emerges here is a great interest in needlework and handicraft of various kinds, and, in fact, the book must be regarded more as handicraft rather than literature" (Crassus, "Nokkrar nýjar bækur," 114).

Another prevalent attitude is that the creativity of women is not at all conscious but, rather, unintentional. Speaking of the poets and twin sisters Herdís Andrésdóttir and Ólína Andrésdóttir, Sigurður Nordal writes in a 1925 issue of the journal *Iðunn*: "The sisters have composed poetry along with their daily chores, as the bird sings, without realizing that they were creating works of art" ("Ritsjá," 73). Such an attitude toward the literature of women has an inevitable influence on women writers, many of whom begin to doubt their abilities and what they are writing. Hulda called the drawer where she kept drafts of her poems her "drivel drawer" (*Úr min-ningablöðum,* 106), and for Ólöf Sigurðardóttir of Hlaðir the finished manuscripts of her poems were "stuff" (Kress, "Um konur og bókmenntir," 17). There are many instances of women burning their manuscripts with-out showing them to anyone.

THE ORIGINS OF ICELANDIC WOMEN'S LITERATURE

Icelandic women writers belong to an ancient and rich oral literary tradition rooted in Old Norse culture. The oral tradition in poetry can be traced to women's culture, particularly to such activities as healing and prophesying. The poetic genres were mainly visions (*spár*) and incantations (*seiðr*) as well as laments, dreams, work songs, and poems of healing.

The greatest part of Old Icelandic literature is anonymous, and any named authors are almost exclusively men. No prose work is attributed to a woman, and of the surviving 250 poems by known authors only a few are attributed to women. The author of *Jóns saga helga* (The life of Saint Jón of

Hólar) describes the scholastic life at the bishopric of Hólar in the twelfth century and mentions, in particular, that one woman is among the pupils. Although she is apparently not being taught to read or write, she is said to be competent "in book arts" (*Jóns saga helga*, 43), which she teaches to the other pupils while she embroiders.

The most important remnants of the Old Icelandic oral tradition are the Eddic poems (see chapter 1). *Edda* means "great-grandmother" and may be etymologically related to *óðr*, or "ode" (see also p. 153). This loose collection of poetry, composed before the eleventh century and preserved in a manuscript dating from ca. 1270, has come down to us in more or less distorted forms through many channels of the written male culture. Many of the Eddic poems are characterized by a woman's point of view and such female experiences as giving birth, embroidering, and doing laundry. They describe feelings of love, betrayal, mourning, and abandonment. Some are women's monologues, whereas others are dialogues between women. In "Sigrdrífumál" (The lay of Sigrdrífa) a woman is teaching a man healing verses. "Guðrúnarkviða forna" (The old lay of Guðrún) is about a woman who is trying to cry over her husband's corpse. "Oddrúnargrátr" (Oddrún's lament) is a dialogue between a woman in labor and a midwife who shares her own sorrows. In "Grottasöngr" (The song of Grotti) two slave women are singing as they work at an enormous millstone called Grotti, grinding out death and destruction to their oppressors. "Skírnismál" (The lay of Skírni) is a poem about male desire and sexual violence toward a beautiful giantess. "Völuspá" (The sybil's prophecy), the most celebrated poem of Old Icelandic literature, has traditionally been interpreted as a poem about the apocalypse of the pagan culture—or the end of the world in general. However, the powerful image of the sibyl sinking into the earth, after relinquishing all her knowledge to Odin, symbolizes a more specific apocalypse: that of women's culture (see also Kress, "The Apocalypse of a Culture," and "'Hvad en kvinde kvæder'").

A similar story of appropriation can be seen in the myth in which Odin steals the mead of poetic inspiration from the giantess Gunnlöð by tricking her. The story appears in Snorri Sturluson's *Edda*, known in English as the *Prose Edda* (ca. 1240), a textbook of poetics compiled to encourage young men to learn the metaphors of the ancient oral tradition for use in their courtly verses (see p. 151). This work culminated a process, beginning with the coming of Christianity and then literacy, by which poetry was taken out of the realm of women's culture and transferred to what became the first Icelandic literary establishment: the schools; the scribes; and the monasteries. At the same time the thirteenth century marks the rise of the Icelandic sagas, an anonymous but overtly masculine genre emphasizing feuds and battles based on old tales and chronicles. Of special interest is the famous *Laxdæla saga* (The saga of the Laxdælir) because of its female antagonist and its emphasis on women's activities. A curious female perspective runs through the entire story, frequently suppressed by the genre's demand for masculine adventures and exploits (see also Kress, "'You Will Find It All Rather Monotonous'"). The same kind of structure, although not quite so obvious, can be seen in several other sagas, such as *Gunnlaugs saga* (The saga of Gunnlaugr), *Eiríks saga rauða* (The saga of Eirik the Red), *Svarfdæla saga* (The saga of the Svarfdælir), and *Bárðar saga Snæfellsáss* (The saga of Bárðr), all of which attempt to put a woman in the role of the main character.

Laxdæla saga contains the symbolic narrative of the Irish princess and slave Melkorka, who rebels against her enslavement by pretending to be mute. One day Melkorka's master, hearing voices, discovers his son with his mother: "He realized then that she was not speechless at all, for she was talking busily to the child" (*Laxdæla saga*, trans. Magnusson and Pálsson, 68). This image of the mother secretly breaking her silence in order to pass on to her son the knowledge of her native language has been interpreted as an illustration of women's great cultural influence. Because women held a strong position in the native oral tradition, a tradition that they passed on to their learned sons, the literature was written in the vernacular rather than in Latin, the official language elsewhere in Europe (Kellogg, "Sex and the Vernacular in Medieval Iceland").

ANONYMOUS LITERATURE: BALLADS AND FOLKTALES

For centuries women's literature survived in oral form alongside the dominant and learned canon of men. These genres were the more flexible ones: ballads; lyrics; quatrains; folk songs; and folktales. When women attempted a genre with strict metrical rules, they tended to parody it. Ballads (see also pp. 60–63) in particular were recited and preserved by women. Conversely, those who collected the poems and wrote them down were almost always men (Ólason, "Inngangur," 82). Ballads were sung, and it has been pointed out that the melodies stem directly from the realm of women's work, capturing the rhythms of, say, rocking a child or spinning (Elíasson, "Eru sagnadansar kvennatónlist?"). The ballads are mainly concerned with women's lives, and women play a major role in these stories. Common themes are violence against women, forbidden love, rape and incest, and concealed childbirth and infanticide as well as women's solidarity and friendship, their concern for their children, and their revenge against evildoers. In "Margrétar kvæði" (The ballad of Margaret) Margrét is first raped and impregnated by her brother, then burned alive, as punishment, by her father, the king. "Tófu kvæði" (The ballad of Tófa) describes the internal conflict of a young woman who must decide whether the child she has delivered in secret will live or die: "She dared not nurture / because of her brothers. / She dared not dispatch in front of her god" (*Íslensk fornkvæði*, 80). In "Ebbadætra kvæði" (The ballad of Ebbi's daughters) women avenge themselves on their rapists by beheading them. Other ballads belittle men by making fun of them. "Skeggkarls kvæði" (The ballad of Beard-man) is about a man with such a great long beard that five men are needed to carry it. When the man wants to kiss the girls, the beard gets in the way; when he tries to walk, he trips over it.

The church strongly opposed ballads and managed to suppress them. To counteract their influence Guðbrandur Þorláksson, the bishop at Hólar, supervised the publication of *Vísnabók* (1612; Book of verses) and commissioned recognized poets to compose secular poetry for the book (see also p. 180). No woman was among them, but the most beautiful and enduring poems in the book imitate the ballads and make use of their free meter.

One of Iceland's oldest fairy tales in manuscript, *Brjáms saga* (The tale of Brjám), was recorded about 1700 from a woman's narrative, and over the centuries women have played a major role in the creation and preservation of folk- and fairy tales. Guðbrandur Vigfússon (preface, xxxviii) has observed that, although women have not written as many books as men, they are primarily responsible for the preservation of folktales and folk poems. Either the stories were told to scribes by women, or they were passed on by other storytellers who had heard them in childhood from their mothers or other women. A great many folktales are about women's lives and experiences, such as secret love, backbreaking labor, forced marriages, and childbirth. In particular fairy tales and outlaw stories depicting the utopian life outside society can be traced to women. Several ghost stories have also been recorded from women's narratives, including the best known of all, "Djákninn á Myrká" (The deacon at Myrká). This is the story of a dead man who comes to a farmhouse to take his sweetheart to a dance, although, in fact, he intends to take her with him into the grave. The description of their moonlit journey on horseback over the frozen landscape is poetic yet filled with horror. The young woman gradually realizes where the journey will end and manages to save herself at the last minute by grabbing the bellpull at the graveyard gate. The deacon plunges into the grave, and the woman goes mad, for now she can no more return to society than he can. Another famous but brief story, "Móðir mín í kví, kví" (Mother mine in the sheep-fold, sheepfold), tells of an unwed mother who has given birth to her child in secret and then put it out to die of exposure. The story makes it clear that she would otherwise have faced severe punishment and even death. The dead child comes back to haunt her, following her to the sheepfold where she is milking and feeling sorry for herself because she has no fine clothes to wear to an upcoming dance. The child recites a rhyme, offering the mother its swaddling cloth as a dance frock. The shock drives the woman mad.

"EVEN THOUGH THE SWAN SINGS BETTER"

Rímur (metrical romances; lit. "rhymes") are epic poems with fixed forms and complicated meters, their narratives drawing on accounts of heroic feats found in ancient tales (see also previous chapters). *Rímur* formed the dominant genre in Icelandic literature from the sixteenth century until well into the nineteenth. Unlike ballads, *rímur* constitute a male genre in which authors are identified by name and women are largely tangential.

Legend has it that Rannveig, the daughter of the sixteenth-century poet Þórður of Strjúgur, composed a section of her father's *Rollantsrímur* (The *rímur* of Rollant) while stirring a pot of porridge. When her father had finished the first part of the poem, he became ill and took to his bed. His daughter, thinking that he was going to die, took up the poem where he had left off and added to it. The father recovered, however, and, when he discovered what she had done and realized that her verses were better than his, he became so angry that he slapped her (Þorkelsson, *Om Digtningen på Island*, 343).

One of the few women among the numerous poets of this genre was Steinunn Finnsdóttir (1641–1710), the first Icelandic woman whose po-etry has survived in some quantity. She freed up the genre's strict form by connecting it with the folk poetry and rhymes of oral tradition. The subjects of her metrical romances are drawn from fairy tales and Icelandic ballads, which makes them unique among the metrical romances. Whereas the male poets address an audience primarily made up of women and, thus, write so-called love songs (*mansöngvar*, sg. *mansöngur*; see pp. 57, 182) to them, Steinunn Finnsdóttir addresses either young girls or children. At many points in her metrical romances she apologizes for her poetry. In *Snækóngs-rímur* (The *rímur* of the Snow King) she compares herself to the ptar-migan, which conceals itself in eiderdown but keeps up its spirits even though the swan sings better. The voices of both are God given but dif-ferent, and she expresses her thanks "for the little / that is lent to me." She makes frequent use of conditional clauses, which came to typify the discourse of Icelandic women poets. In *Hyndlurímur* (The *rímur* of Hyndla) she blesses those who do not condemn her poetry even though it is not praiseworthy, and she ends by asking the "good" poets to correct what she has composed (Finnsdóttir, *Hyndlu rímur og Snækóngs rímur*, 97, 34).

Steinunn Finnsdóttir also composed *vikivakar* (sg. *vikivaki*), a particular kind of ballad with lyric refrains (see also pp. 224–25). In "Kappakvæði" (Poem of champions) she writes about the male heroes of the Icelandic sagas. The refrain is provocative and ambiguous, drawn from traditional *vikivaki*: "They want an audience with me" (Finnsdóttir, *Hyndlu rímur og Snækóngs rímur*, 115). The heroes depend on her to write poems about them, and they all want their chance. Thus, she is often playful in her poetry. She makes fun of the masculine tradition and inverts its heroic discourse by placing events in ordinary surroundings.

Another dominant genre in Icelandic literature at this time was the hymn, which, unlike the *rímur*, was an officially recognized form of poetry. Significantly, no woman was among Iceland's best-known hymnists. Yet the first work to appear in print by an Icelandic woman was a hymn, "Daglegt andvarp guðhræddar sálar" (The daily sigh of a god-fearing soul). Composed by Guðný Guðmundsdóttir (b. 1660) and printed in a 1772 hymnal at Hólar, the hymn makes use of physical, almost erotic imagery in describing a yearning for the embrace of Jesus, who is depicted as the ideal lover. In other hymns by women God in heaven becomes the ideal father, unlike the cruel fathers on earth.

The first book published by an Icelandic woman is the cookbook *Einfalt matreiðsluvasakver fyrir heldri manna húsfreyjur* (A simple pocket pamphlet of cookery for gentlemen's housewives), which was printed in 1800. Although Marta Stephensen is listed on the title page as the author, the book has commonly been attributed to her brother-in-law, Magnús Stephensen, one of the major exponents of the Enlightenment in Iceland. In the introduction Marta's husband says that "for understandable reasons" he has had to correct this and that for his wife before the pages were sent to the printer. Yet the cooking instructions reveal that only a woman could have compiled the book, whether she wrote it herself or dictated it.

POEMS IN MANUSCRIPT

Until the eighteenth century specific women poets are mentioned only sporadically in literary sources, and the few surviving poems by women are fragmentary. Their main mode of expression was the quatrain (*lausavísa*), a four-line metrical fragment from everyday life that describes personal experiences, daily events, and reflections on nature (see also pp. 27, 42, 178).

During the nineteenth century poems were circulated in manuscript, and some of these manuscripts contained poems by women. A section of one such manuscript, archived in the National Library of Iceland, bears the heading "Kvennaljóðmæli" (Women's poetry; collected by Páll Pálsson, Lbs 167 4to) and contains poems written exclusively by women, so the concept was not unknown during that period. This manuscript includes poems by eighteen women poets of the eighteenth and nineteenth centuries. The works of some of these poets, such as Látra-Björg and Vatnsenda-Rósa, were later published.

The legendary Látra-Björg (Björg Einarsdóttir; 1716–84) lived in the country's most remote settlement in the northern fjords. She was unmarried, fished the open sea, did other kinds of men's work, and was considered odd and unfeminine. She dissolved her household, became a drifter, and died a beggar. Some of her poetry has survived. She avoids convention, writing neither hymns nor *rímur* but, rather, occasional verses about her surroundings and the present moment. She writes about nature and the weather, the horizon, and place-names of reefs and cliffs. In her poems she often situates herself at the boundary between land and sea, on the beach or up in the surrounding mountains and cliffs. She is fascinated by the surf that pounds the shore, and her descriptions abound in vivid imagery and onomatopoeia: "Breakers roar over boulders / Steeds of the surf smash, / bluffs tremble on the brink / many stones wail." One of Látra-Björg's best-known poems is "Fagurt er í Fjörðum" ('Tis fair in the fjords), in which her native district becomes a metaphor for the whole world. Here, life is good when the weather is fair and there is enough to eat, but in the harsh winter there can be no worse district: "People and animals then die" (Helgadóttir, *Skáldkonur fyrri alda*, 2:65, 76). Some of her verses are very grotesque. She lampoons her neighbors, especially men, and in this respect shares the female tradition.

Vatnsenda-Rósa (Rósa Guðmundsdóttir; 1795–1855) also became a legend, but, unlike the masculine Látra-Björg, she is known in literary history as a femme fatale, with many scandalous love affairs to her credit. Very little of her poetry has survived — only two epistolary poems and some quatrains. She is one of the few Icelandic women poets who wrote love poems, some of which quickly became classics: "Your eye and my eye, / oh lovely orbs that gleam / mine is yours, and yours is mine, / you know what I mean." Most of her lyrics stem from abandonment and are less concerned with love per se than with grief and longing, disappointment and betrayal.

The vanished lover is put on a pedestal and compared with other men, who never measure up. He is a dream vision and exists only in the distance: "It was long ago that I saw him / truly handsome and proud. / A man graced by all gifts, / he stood out from the crowd" (Helgadóttir, *Skáldkonur fyrri alda*, 155). In this personal poetry of pathos are glimpses of the emerging romantic movement in Icelandic literature.

THE SISTER OF ROMANTICISM

"Grasaferð" (Moss gathering) by Jónas Hallgrímsson, which was published in the journal *Fjölnir* (1846) and is considered the first modern-day Icelandic short story (see p. 293), contains a notable section on women and poetry. The young narrator, who is a poet despite his age, and his cousin, whom he calls his "sister," begin to discuss poetry and translations while they are out gathering moss. The girl is as knowledgeable about these subjects as he is, if not more so, and a translation of a Schiller poem is attributed to her in the story. She has been hiding her poetry, but the narrator discovers one of her poems on the wrapper of some prunes that she has given him. Having been found out, she blushes with shame and anger and asks him not to show anyone: "I wouldn't want it to get around that I'm engaged in this sort of thing, for it has never been regarded as becoming to womenfolk." He tells her not to worry and then becomes so chivalrous that he offers to take whatever she writes off her hands. But she sees no need for this: "I write hardly enough for my poetry to cause us problems" ("Grasaferð," 20). The girl's statement about the inappropriateness of women writing poetry has become proverbial in Icelandic literary history and has also made an impression on Icelandic women poets, who have taken this conversation literally instead of recognizing that Jónas Hallgrímsson was criticizing society for this opinion (see also Kress, "'Sáuð þið hana systur mína?'").

It is interesting to compare the girl in "Grasaferð" with an actual woman poet who lived during the same period. Guðný Jónsdóttir of Klömbur (1804–36) was born in the same district as Jónas Hallgrímsson and was also close to his age. Yet their lives were very different. She married a man with a seminary education and bore four children, who either died or were taken away from her. Her husband left her, reportedly because she was more intelligent and articulate than he was. She went to live with her sister in a place she never liked and died there in her early thirties, supposedly of grief. In 1837, the year after her death, *Fjölnir* printed one of her best-known poems, "Endurminningin er svo glögg" (The memory is so vivid), along with her obituary. This is the first secular poem by an Icelandic woman to appear in print. Although the story of Guðný Jónsdóttir's life made a lasting impression on Icelanders, her poems were not published until 1951: as *Guðnýjarkver* (Guðný's chapbook).

The subjects of Guðný Jónsdóttir's poems are drawn from her own life and its painful experiences. Most of them are laments over her separation from her husband and children. "Á heimleið" (Returning home) was composed after Guðný Jónsdóttir had to take her daughter, only several months old, to another farm to place the infant in foster care:

> 'Tis dark from dread,
> the girl-child fair
> they took from me.
> The world is bare,
> the cosmos empty,
> many a backward look.
> But I must not forget,
> the son at home
> who gives me joy.
> The eye weeps quietly,
> there is a balm for every pain
> if only it could be found.

She weeps the poem forth, trying to come to terms with her grief, but to no avail. In her last poem, "Saknaðarstef" (Lament), she writes about the separation from her husband: "I sit and mourn the missing / the friend I yearn for sorely." Her sorrow is so great that it overshadows everything else: "I bitterly wept and bid you good-bye, / I will grieve for you until I die" (*Guðnýjarkver*, 91, 103–4). Abandoned, she reacts to the experience as banishment and sees no way out except death.

"A LITTLE MAID GREETS HER COMPATRIOTS"

The first literary work published by an Icelandic woman is a book of poems, *Stúlka* (1876; A lass), by Júlíana Jónsdóttir (1838–1917), who worked as a maid in western Iceland. Júlíana Jónsdóttir was born into the male tradition of romanticism in Icelandic literature, and her poetry shows that she was very fascinated by the poets who formed its literary canon and the tradition that they represented. She cites them in her poems and even sets up a dialogue with them. The consciousness of gender reflected in the very title of her book is immediately striking. With the name *Stúlka* she is apparently referring to the title of Jón Thoroddsen's famous novel *Piltur og stúlka* (1850; English trans.: *Lad and Lass* [1890]), which is regarded as the first Icelandic novel (see pp. 294–95). Júlíana Jónsdóttir's *stúlka* is independent and alone, a lass without a lad. The title can also be seen as a response to *Snót* (Maiden), the title of a popular anthology of Icelandic poems that was published in 1850 and then reprinted in 1865. *Snót* is a poetic word for "girl," an idealized term for the more ordinary *stúlka*, which not only refers to a girl but connotes a working girl as well. This ironic and teasing mode of expression is a distinctive characteristic in many of her poems and is especially obvious when she deals with gender and the traditional metaphors for men and women. It should be noted that Júlíana Jónsdóttir's emphasis on gender is manifested not only in her poetry but also in her play *Víg Kjartans Ólafssonar* (The slaying of Kjartan Ólafsson), based on the ill-fated love affair of Kjartan and Guðrún Ósvifursdóttir in *Laxdæla saga*. Despite its title, the tragedy is first and foremost about Guðrún's psychological torments, conveyed for the most part through the character's monologue. Performed at Stykkishólmur in 1879, it is Iceland's oldest extant play by a woman and the first Icelandic historical play as well (see Kress, "'Sökum þess ég er kona'").

Júlíana Jónsdóttir's epigraph for *Stúlka* is a short poem that establishes a significant analogy: "A little maid greets / her compatriots, / young and unlearned / but not shy, / seeking hospitality / of good men, / a fatherless child / of a poor mother" (*Stúlka*, ii). The poem can be read simply as an autobiographical description, Júlíana Jónsdóttir being the child of a single mother who was poor. But it can also be seen as a personification of the book itself, parallel to the "lass" in the title — that is, the book is the daughter of a single mother, the woman poet with no tradition behind her.

In many of her poems Júlíana Jónsdóttir writes about women, especially their laborious lives and powerlessness, and often connects these subjects with metaphors of imprisonment. In one of her best poems, "Við dúnhreinsun" (Cleaning eiderdown), from *Stúlka*, she sees herself as literally imprisoned: "It is dark in the prison / of down and haze." From this confined space she expresses "the laments / of a silent mind" (*Stúlka*, 10–11). The protest in her poems is most fully expressed in her use of grotesque imagery, with which she often succeeds in deconstructing masculinity as well as masculine discourse. Thus, some of her poems are inversions of traditional love poems. Her "love poems" are from the perspective of the lover, who is a feeble old man chasing young women and promising them all kinds of gifts, but the sole outcome is that they laugh at him.

The very first word in this first book of poetry by an Icelandic woman is *little.* This metaphor of littleness is very common in Júlíana Jónsdóttir's poetry, expressing a feeling of both cultural and social inferiority. In her greeting the little maid is almost humbly asking for a kind response from the literary establishment. But, in fact, she received none. The book went completely unnoticed and has also been totally ignored in literary histories, as has the name of the poet. Júlíana Jónsdóttir emigrated to America, and she never came back. One year prior to her death she published her second book of poems, *Hagalagðar* (1916; Fleece sheddings), in which she is disillusioned and has given up the search for originality.

Júlíana Jónsdóttir was quite literally seeking a place when she left Iceland. Unlike the male poets of romanticism, who all longed to return home to Iceland, she wanted to get away and, for a poet of the period, wrote surprisingly few patriotic poems. Her poem "Ísland" (Iceland), in *Stúlka*, even goes so far as to parody Bjarni Thorarensen's "Íslands minni" (To Iceland), which was Iceland's national anthem for many years (see p. 262). With this poem Bjarni Thorarensen created the metaphor of the Fjallkona (lit. "Mountain Woman"), a personification of the country. The poem is a hymn to this woman from her Icelandic sons, who are in Denmark longing to return to her: "Ancient motherland of ice / beloved nurturing soil, / mountain woman so fair" (Thorarensen, *Ljóðmæli,* 27). Júlíana Jónsdóttir turns her poem into a parody and a protest: "Ancient motherland of ice, / infertile is your soil, / wind-blown and barren" (*Stúlka,* 8).

The emphasis on gender, which runs through the whole book, is interesting in the context of Icelandic romanticism in that the identity of its male poets was strongly connected with nationalism. Júlíana Jónsdóttir's identity, however, concerns gender. Júlíana Jónsdóttir is not so much an Icelander as she is a woman. This strong awareness of being a woman in a patriarchal world is typical of Icelandic women writers up to the present day.

THE FIRST WOMEN AUTHORS

The advent of the suffrage movement in the nineteenth century marked a turning point in the history of women and Icelandic women's literature. One of the major pioneers in the movement in Iceland was Bríet Bjarnhéðinsdóttir (1856–1940). In 1885 she published an article in the newspaper *Fjallkonan* concerning the education and rights of women, the first article to appear in print by an Icelandic woman, and two years later she delivered Iceland's first public lecture by a woman. In 1894 the Icelandic Women's Society was established, the first women's organization dedicated to equal rights between the sexes. In 1895 two women's magazines were launched, *Kvennablaðið* (The women's journal) in Reykjavík and *Framsókn* (Progress) in Seyðisfjörður. The Icelandic Federation for Women's Rights was founded in 1907 and the first women's trade union in 1914. On 19 June 1915 Icelandic women were granted limited suffrage; the constitution of 1918 awarded them full suffrage with the right to vote and run for office.

Torfhildur Hólm (1845–1918), another pioneer of the suffrage movement in Iceland, is the first woman in Iceland who can be termed a professional writer as well as the first Icelander to make a career of writing. Her first novel, *Brynjólfur Sveinsson biskup* (1882; Bishop Brynjólfur Sveinsson), is not only the first Icelandic novel by a woman but also the first historical novel in modern Icelandic literature. Unlike their counterparts in many other countries, early women writers in Iceland generally did not attempt fiction, perhaps because of the strong male tradition of the sagas.

Torfhildur Hólm's writing career began during the years she lived in Canada, where she compiled folktales and other lore from interviews with fellow immigrants. She wrote six long novels in all as well as short stories for children and adults, and she was the founder and editor of three periodicals: *Draupnir* (1891–1908; Odin's ring); a magazine for children, *Tíbrá* (1892–93; Mirage); and *Dvöl* (1901–17; Sojourn).

All Torfhildur Hólm's novels are about recognized historical subjects. In *Elding* (1889; Lightning) she deals with Iceland's conversion to Christianity, and, in addition to her novel about Bishop Brynjólfur, she wrote novels about the country's two other famous bishops, *Jón biskup Vídalín* (1891–92) and *Jón biskup Arason* (1896–1902). *Kjartan og Guðrún* (1886; Kjartan and Guðrún) is based on the female perspective of *Laxdæla saga*, much like Júlíana Jóndóttir's drama *Víg Kjartans Ólafssonar*. Torfhildur Hólm's novels are overburdened with historical information, which she seems to use to justify her writings. But this feature in particular came to characterize much of the literature written by Icelandic women, especially memoirs and autobiographies.

The struggle for women's rights during this period was primarily aimed at increasing educational opportunities, and this subject preoccupied the earliest women writers. In her short stories, published in *Sögur og ævintýri* (1884; Stories and fairy tales), Torfhildur Hólm often addresses the issue of women's education and their position in marriage. The stories are often told from the viewpoint of men, who are sometimes envious of women's education, until they comprehend the issues and start to advocate women's liberation, or are sometimes made laughable with grotesque humor. In the story "Týndu Hringarnir" (The lost rings) a young woman's education results in a broken engagement because her university-educated fiancé cannot tolerate the fact that she is more knowledgeable than he is.

Torfhildur Hólm was a young widow with no children, which explains her prolific output as a writer and the opportunity that she had for pursuing pioneering work. At any rate there is an unequivocal correlation between the literary pursuits of women during this period and their marital state. Júlíana Jónsdóttir was unmarried, as was Guðbjörg Árnadóttir (1826–1911), whose *Nokkur ljóðmæli* (1879; A few poems) was the second collection of poems to be published by an Icelandic woman. Nor did Torfhildur Hólm escape the consequences of a tendency to mix her role as a writer with her role as a woman. The stipend given to her by the Icelandic parliament for writing and for being the first woman to pursue such work aroused much opposition, both in parliament and in the press; as a result, the amount of the stipend was reduced and changed to a widow's pension. Torfhildur Hólm commented on this in a letter written around the turn of the century: "I was the first that nature condemned to harvest those bitter fruits of the antiquated, deeply rooted prejudice against literary ladies" (Gíslason, "Torfhildur Þorsteinsdóttir Holm," viii).

The women's magazines played an important role in women's literature during this period. They printed anonymous short stories that were probably by Icelandic women, and in 1901 Hulda's first poems appeared in *Framsókn*. In 1911 the Women's Reading Club of Reykjavík was founded, and for twenty years it collected women's original and translated works and circulated them among its members as a handwritten bulletin called *Mánaðarrit* (1912–31; Monthly). The periodical *19. júní*, established in 1917 and named for the day on which Icelandic women gained the vote, printed a great deal of women's literature. The magazine *Dropar* (1927, 1929; Drops) printed poetry and sketches exclusively by women.

Many of the earliest stories by women concern the mistreatment of women and children, often caused by a man's drinking, and they advocate temperance and Christianity. The first contemporary novel by an Icelandic woman, *Kaupstaðarferðir* (1888; Trips to town) by Ingibjörg Skaftadóttir (1867–1945), deals with a farmer's drinking and its consequences for his family and home. A Christian message is the underpinning of the works of Guðrún Lárusdóttir (1880–1938), who not only wrote numerous novels and short stories for both children and adults but also translated Harriet Beecher Stowe's *Uncle Tom's Cabin*, which was published as *Tómas frændi* in 1901. Like many other works by women in this period, Guðrún Lárusdóttir's stories are about single mothers, children, and the poor and underprivileged in society.

María Jóhannsdóttir (1886–1924) published short stories and poems in magazines. Her only novel, *Systurnar frá Grænadal* (1906; The sisters from Grænadal), concerns the dissimilar destinies of two sisters—one lives for love, is jilted, and flees to North America; the other finds satisfaction in staying home and devoting herself to the needy. The narrative is fragmented and in parts epistolary, a characteristic of many stories by women during this period, which suggests that letters provided an inspiration for women's writing.

Ólafía Jóhannsdóttir (1863–1924) spent much of her life in Norway, where she cared for indigent women in hospitals and prisons. Her short stories, collected in *De ulykkeligste: Livsskildringer fra Kristiania* (1916) and published in Icelandic as *Aumastar allra* (1923; Most wretched of all), are based on this experience and are unique in Icelandic literature. They deal with prostitutes, female offenders, and women with syphilis—all taboo subjects. Ólafía Jóhannsdóttir is also the author of the first full-length autobiography published by an Icelandic woman, *Frá myrkri til ljóss* (1925; From darkness to light), which tells of her decision to devote her life to religion. But it also contains revealing glimpses of life in Reykjavík during her childhood. She is especially concerned with women's lives, which she frequently sees as a reflection of her own. In the following sketch the woman reading becomes a kind of warning sign for the author: "I was sent on some errands to a house in town. First I knocked on the front door, but no one answered. Then I opened the kitchen door. There everything was chaos, heaped on tables, benches, the hearth, wherever I looked. I walked to the parlor door, which stood ajar. The same confusion was over everything, no matter what, but in the midst of the heap sat a woman, half-dressed and absorbed in a storybook, completely out of her senses" (*Frá myrkri til ljóss*, 26–27).

"EVERYTHING I EVER HAD WAS INADEQUATE"

Ólöf Sigurðardóttir of Hlaðir (1857–1933) is one of the most distinctive poets in Icelandic literature around the turn of the century. She published two books of poetry with the same title, *Nokkur smákvæði* (1888; Some little verses) and *Nokkur smákvæði* (1913). A selection of her poems, short stories, and sketches appeared in *Ritsafn* (1945; Collected works). Ólöf of Hlaðir spent most of her life in the country on a small farm in Eyjafjörður. At an early age she contracted tuberculosis, which left her disabled. For a time she worked as a midwife but never had children of her own. In her poetry she often personifies her poems as children, as in "Til hinna ófæddu" (To the unborn), in *Ritsafn*, in which she calls her poems her "thought-children." The poem is her autobiography in a nutshell. Like her other poems, it is characterized by pathos, negation, and metaphors of littleness: "But never was I created bonny or fair / . . . / I was born little and utterly wretched" (*Ritsafn*, 61, 62). In her poems she scrutinizes her self-image, defining herself as a poet and someone who is different from other women. In the poem "Ó, gæti hún þó dáið" (Oh, if but only it could die), in *Nokkur smákvæði* (1913), which deals with futile, undefined desire, she says: "When the damsels attend to the latest fashion, / and men have their minds on the crop, / and the women cook and care for their brood, / I sit with the poems that I begot" (16). She writes panegyrics to established male poets whom she admires and with whom she compares herself. In "Óðulin mín" (My estate), also in *Nokkur smákvæði*, she says that she has inherited "a grain of sand / in the ode masters' land" (51). She wants to sail to this land, but, not knowing how to navigate, she loses her way and runs aground.

Ólöf's poems are highly personal and deal mainly with the poet herself as she contemplates being a woman and a poet. They are the products of want and intense longing, describing rebellion and strong conflict as well as disappointment, defeat, and surrender, often lamenting what never was. "Everything I ever had was inadequate" (*Ritsafn*, 161), she says in "Þreyta" (Fatigue). Ólöf's poems contain various innovations in Icelandic poetics. They deal with daily life, are more realistic and colloquial than was customary, and are often very ironic.

Like other women at this time, Ólöf of Hlaðir drew on the oral tradition of women and wrote fairy tales. But, here, she also used her own life as literary material, and the sketch "Bernskuheimili mitt" (My childhood home), which appeared in 1906 in the journal *Eimreiðin*, was the first printed autobiographical piece by an Icelandic woman. Her realistic, unadorned descriptions of rural life clashed with the image that Icelanders had of themselves and created a great uproar. In her descriptions of her environment and the details of daily life — including clothing, bed linens, and bad food — everything is characterized by want, poverty, squalor, and ignorance. In this respect they anticipate Málfríður Einarsdóttir's much later descriptions of her childhood.

Ólöf of Hlaðir is the first Icelandic author to attempt to tell a story from an inside point of view. This technique is used in the fragment "Hjálpin" (The saving grace), which she apparently began shortly after her marriage in 1887. The point of view is directly connected to a state of mind that had not previously been treated in Icelandic literature. "She was afraid, terribly, terribly afraid, on the day they married," the story begins, and the narration unfolds within the anguished and apprehensive thoughts of a young woman as she is getting dressed in her wedding gown (*Ritsafn*, 165).

In the short story "Móðir snillingsins" (Mother of the genius) Ólöf goes against society's ideology concerning the proper behavior of women. The story is about an unmarried woman who decides to have a child as she wants to "become the mother of a fine man." She succeeds, but she never recovers from the strain, goes mad, and dies. The stated purpose of the story is to give readers a glimpse "into the psyche of women" (*Ritsafn*, 229, 249), and it contains various notable features that were later to occur more regularly in women's literature. It is told largely through a series of letters, with some dialogue, as an older woman corresponds with a younger one about the fate of a third. The story, which reveals a woman's secrets, is narrated in confidence and based largely on gossip. It revolves mostly around illness and death, and it is the first to contain the theme of the madwoman whose mental state is the direct consequence of her revolt against the female role. The ideal man, the object of the desire expressed in the story, is no ordinary man but an artist.

"LEND ME WINGS"

Around the turn of the century a group of women writers emerged who developed a new form of *þulur* (sg. *þula*; see also pp. 346, 477), an old genre of oral litany characterized by fantasy, rhapsodic structure, and fragments of nursery rhymes and other kinds of folk poetry. The most prominent figure in this group was Unnur Benediktsdóttir Bjarklind (1881–1946), who chose to hide her identity with the pseudonym Hulda, meaning "fairy" or "hidden one." In addition to her contribution to the *þulur* genre, Hulda became one of the main proponents of symbolism. Praised but misinterpreted in her own time, she had an enormous literary output that included seven volumes of poetry, nine short story collections, and one novel.

In her memoirs Hulda tells about her first attempts at writing poetry and how she was found out. She hides in anguish and shame, recalling the passage in "Grasaferð" concerning the propriety of women writing poetry: "It was as if I stood utterly naked for all the world to see. It was ghastly. 'Writing poetry,' as it says in Jónas [Hallgrímsson]'s 'Grasaferð,' 'has never been regarded as becoming to womenfolk'" (Hulda, *Úr minningablöðum*, 49). In her poetry Hulda deals with her position as a woman and a poet, and one can argue that her struggle for a place in a literary tradition dominated by men towers over other aspects of her poetry (Richter, "'Ljóðafugl lítinn jeg geymi'"). In "Haukurinn" (The hawk), which appeared in her first book of poetry, *Kvæði* (1909; Poems), she likens herself to a songbird that yearns for the freedom of the great, powerful hawk: "A little poem-bird I keep — / it longs to take flight / far out in the radiant day / and sing, filled with delight" (*Kvæði*, 53). If the little bird is not allowed to fly, "soon it shall die."

With her *þulur*, which appeared first in the magazine *Ingólfur* in 1905 and then in *Kvæði*, Hulda frees herself from traditional formal constraints and revives the oral tradition of folk poetry. The language is simple, there are no stanza breaks, the line length is variable, the rhythm is irregular, and rhyme and alliteration are handled freely. At the same time there is a great deal of repetition, and allusions to other poems are common. Thus, the *þula* "Ljáðu mér vængi" (Lend me wings) begins with a fragment from an old *þula* for children that is then further developed: "'Mother Gray Goose! Lend me wings' / so I might soar / south over seas." The poem displays the intense — and always unfulfilled — longing that is so characteristic of the poems of Icelandic women. The bird flies away and leaves the poet behind on the cold shore: "For me she did not linger — / beyond the cliff high and sheer / I saw her glide and glide / into blue space far and wide, / the uncharted space blue and clear" (*Kvæði*, 23).

In drawing on oral tradition, Hulda also sympathetically reinterprets famous female characters. In the poem "Brynhildur Buðladóttir" she gives this femme fatale of the heroic Eddic poems psychological depth, explaining her as a woman who would not "tolerate treachery and compromise / sorrow and disgrace / in a lean pantry" (*Kvæði*, 103–5) (see also p. 21).

Hulda also played a major role in the revival of prose, and her lyric story "Síðsumarskvöld" (A late summer evening), in volume 2 of *Æskuástir* (1919; Young loves), is no less innovative than Sigurður Nordal's "Hel" (Death; in Norse mythology also the goddess of death, in *Fornar ástir*), which was published in the same year and hailed as a milestone in Icelandic literature (see pp. 329, 367). Hulda's story is a letter written by a woman confiding to another woman, her close friend. She sits at the window in the evening and reminisces about her secret trysts with her lover, a poet who has gone away. In her memories she moves back and forth in time and space, talking with the lover as she does with the friend, and sometimes the narrative dissolves into his poetry. In *Myndir* (1924; Vignettes), a collection of lyric prose texts representing a completely new genre, Hulda continues to develop these techniques — the setting is a foreign country, the form fragmented, and the distinction between myth, dream, and reality blurred.

In Hulda's works the longings of the female protagonists constantly clash with society's norms. The women take refuge in nature, where they either are alone or have a secret lover. The conflict between woman's role and freedom, between confinement and the desire to go out into the world, between duty and the creative urge, is the impetus in her poetry. Under the polished surface mysticism and horror prevail, and images of birds, wings, and flight are predominant.

With time Hulda's literary career begins to show signs of reconciliation, a pattern that is seen in the careers of many Icelandic women authors. The novel *Dalafólk* (1936–39; Valley people) is a bildungsroman about a young woman who is possessed by a strong desire for freedom and ventures out into the world. But she comes around and returns home, where her fiancé is waiting for her. She decides to accept the narrow horizon of her community, work for charity, and preserve the nation's cultural heritage (see also pp. 347, 388).

With her *þulur* Hulda transformed Icelandic poetry. Her poems were very well received, and Hulda is one of the few Icelandic women writers to win recognition from the literary establishment. Much was written about her *þulur* in the press, where she was praised either for her agreeable disposition, for the childlike innocence and beauty of her poems, or for "thinking as logically and forcefully as men" (Erlingsson, "Annar pistill til Þjóðviljans," 11). One critic was pleased with the form of her poetry but not its content, which he called "weak, wavering female hankerings and dreams, which most men cannot make heads or tails of anyhow" (Guðlaugsson, "Bókafregn," 194).

Women poets found in the *þula* an outlet for their emotions and yearnings. Theodora Thoroddsen's *Þulur* (1916) consisted exclusively of poems in this form, and Ólína Andrésdóttir (1858–1935) collected her popular *þulur* in *Ljóðmæli* (1924; Poems), which she published with her twin sister, Herdís (1858–1939). In her second book of poetry Ólöf of Hlaðir published a *þula* that sparked the first formal dispute in Iceland over women's literature. In a review of the book in a 1914 issue of *Skírnir* Guðmundur Finnbogason connected the *þula* to femininity, thus personifying it as a woman. Calling the *þula* a "feminine meter," he claimed that the genre is "not bound to any law" and is, thus, "frivolous, ever-changing, and capricious" ("Ólöf Sigurðardóttir," 101–2). Theodora Thoroddsen challenged this notion in her preface to her earliest *þulur*, which she published that same year in the next issue of *Skírnir*. She offers another explanation, one based on her own experience: women compose *þulur* to keep children occupied; they are a last resort for getting the peace and quiet to mend clothes and darn socks. Theodora Thoroddsen often addresses children in her *þulur*, as Steinunn Finnsdóttir did in her *rímur* two centuries before. Herdís Andrésdóttir's autobiographical poem "Kveðið við spuna" (Composed while spinning), in *Ljóðmæli*, in which spinning, composing and chanting poetry, and caring for children all take place at the same time, is likewise addressed to children.

Theodora Thoroddsen also wrote quatrains and published poetic essays in which she attributes her verses to various anonymous women. Her short stories in *Eins og gengur* (1920; As things go) usually deal with something she has heard or been told and, thus, border on autobiography and fiction. In "Sniglarnir mínir" (My snails) she depicts an event from her life as a housewife. At the same time the story deals with her desire to write and her silence as a writer. After finding snails in the soil of some imported potatoes and putting them in a pot plant on the window sill, she fantasizes about their journey across the ocean and then their escape when she opens the balcony door during housecleaning. She imagines how their story would have been in Hans Christian Andersen's telling of it and ends the story by silencing herself: "I have even wanted to try writing their story, as eventful and magnificent as it seems to me. But I won't be so bold as to write a fairy tale. In my opinion that would require more than I have at my disposal" (*Ritsafn*, 279).

"I SHALL BECOME A WRITER"

The period from 1920 to 1950 saw the development of the novel at the hands of several women writers who were among the most prolific of the twentieth century. Kristín Sigfúsdóttir (1876–1953), a farmer's wife in Eyjafjörður, began to write after her oldest children were grown. She wrote her first story, "Digra Gudda" (Tubby Gudda), for a handwritten bulletin produced by youngsters in the district. She went on to write more stories for the bulletin, and these became the core of her short story collection *Sögur úr sveitinni* (1924; Stories from the country). Her first published work was the play *Tengdamamma* (1923; Mother-in-law), the first play published in Iceland by a woman (see p. 561). The novel *Gestir* (1925; Guests) was followed by the two-volume *Gömul saga* (1927–28; Old story). Kristín Sigfúsdóttir's collected works appeared in three volumes as *Rit* (1949–51; Writings). At first her stories were well received by the critics, who were impressed that the author was a poor, uneducated farmer's wife. The reviews gradually became harsher, and in 1927 one reviewer said that he was "afraid that Kristín Sigfúsdóttir has started writing too much" (Sigurðsson, "Bækur," 185). She took him at his word and stopped writing. Thus, her literary career spanned only five years.

Kristín Sigfúsdóttir's stories are in the spirit of social realism. She writes a great deal about women's hard lives—the drudgery, exploitation, forced marriages, illness, disillusionment, madness, and death. Frequently, the women in her stories are fleeing from one settlement to another in search of a better place, where they end up either in a degrading marriage or on a remote farm on the heath, isolated or even mad. The narration is driven by gossip or rumor centering on an enigmatic female figure who is not what she seems but is, nevertheless, different from others, usually a stranger and an outsider who harbors a secret sorrow in her mysterious past. The narrator is often an onlooker, witnessing the action instead of participating in it. The short story "Þeim var ek verst" (I was worst to the one—), which appeared in a 1929 issue of *19. júní*, borrows Guðrún's famous words in *Laxdæla saga*, "I was worst to the one I loved the most" (*Laxdæla saga*, trans. Magnusson and Pálsson, 238), to explore the psychology of a woman named Þórey, who has long been an enigma in the district. The narrator is a younger woman who accompanies Þórey as the two make their way home from a trip to the village for provisions. Along the way Þórey, who has been drinking, reveals the incident of betrayal and loss in her youth that has destroyed her and left her bitter, withdrawn, and filled with self-recrimination. The main scene typifies many of Kristín Sigfúsdóttir's stories, in which older, more experienced women share their experiences with younger women, advocating self-sacrifice and the surrender of one's dreams. Thus, her works often end on a note of reconciliation that belies their rebellious content.

Elínborg Lárusdóttir (1891–1973) wrote a number of novels, short stories, biographies, and tracts on spiritualism and other subjects. Her first novel, *Anna frá Heiðarkoti* (1936; Anna of Heiðarkot), deals with an innocent country girl who is debauched in the city, a subject very much pondered by women writers at this time. One of Elínborg Lárusdóttir's most ambitious works is the trilogy *Förumenn* (1939–40; Tramps), a historical novel about vagabonds of bygone days who wandered from one farm to another, begging for food and shelter. In her various short stories, especially the later ones, Elínborg Lárusdóttir treats gender roles and male behavior in a comic fashion. "Mikill maður" (Great man), collected in *Svipmyndir* (1965; Snapshots), is about a husband whose greatest fear is that his wife is superior to him. "Einn dagur" (One day), in *Leikur örlaganna* (1958; Game of fate), describes a wife who carries out her domestic duties with silence and forbearance until one evening when she rebels and attends a meeting on women's rights, leaving the men of the house in the dark.

Oddný Guðmundsdóttir (1908–85) published five novels as well as short stories that appeared in magazines like *Melkorka* (1944–62), a journal of women's politics and culture. Her protagonists are often strong, independent women who are fighting public opinion. The novel *Veltiár* (1946; Years of plenty) takes place during the war and tells about a young woman who has had a child with a British soldier. Like many other novels of the period it criticizes the foreign occupation of Iceland. Yet it sympathetically adopts the perspective of a woman *í ástandinu* (lit. "in the situation") — a euphemism for women's fraternizing with soldiers, which was severely castigated in men's novels as wanton and treasonous behavior (see also p. 414). In the story "Stefnuvottar" (Constables), published in *Melkorka* in 1958, men are portrayed as obtuse in matters concerning women's lives and literature. The narrator, a woman in her seventies, gets the idea to tell about her life experiences, however insignificant they may be. But as she is, by her own estimate, "barely able to write" and does not know how to put her thoughts into "poetic dress," she asks her grandson — a writer, as it happens — to write down what she says. The grandson and his friend, who is also an author, do not find what the old woman has to say about her long life very remarkable and want to improve on her account by editing it. She gives up, breaks off her story, and never again speaks about literature "with a single soul" (Kress, ed., *Draumur um veruleika*, 116–22).

Ragnheiður Jónsdóttir (1895–1967) is best known as an author of children's books, but she has also written notable works of fiction for adults, significant in their use of ambiguity to expose the deceptive surfaces of daily life. In all her novels women are the protagonists and often narrators as well. They must contend with much conflict and anguish, either because of love affairs or because of a desire to make something of themselves as artists, writers, or educated women. Her plots, as in *Arfur* (1941; Inheritance) and *Villieldur* (1967; Wildfire), often conceal gruesome events — violence, treachery, murder, or the contemplation of murder — beneath an innocent surface. The quartet *Ég á gull að gjalda* (1954; I have gold to give), *Aðgát skal höfð* (1955; Have heed), *Sárt brenna gómarnir* (1958; Burned fingers), and *Og enn spretta laukar* (1964; The lilies still grow) is a bildungsroman that traces the story of Þóra from her childhood in the country until she is a mature married woman in Reykjavík. Þóra has a strong desire for an education and also longs to be a writer, but at the same time she suffers from a sense of guilt toward her daughter and family. The story is Þóra's autobiography, as indicated by the subtitle, *Úr minnisblöðum Þóru frá Hvammi* (From the notes of Þóra of Hvammur), and is told in the first person and the present tense. But there is no mention in the story that she is writing it, thus suppressing the woman writer.

The earliest works by Þórunn Elfa Magnúsdóttir (1910–95) — the short story collection *Dætur Reykjavíkur* (1933; Daughters of Reykjavík) and the novel *Vorið hlær* (1934, 1938; The spring laughs), both in the three-volume collection *Dætur Reykjavíkur* — concern the lives of young women in Reykjavík during this period. The protagonist and narrator in *Vorið hlær* is Svala, and the novel begins with her oath on her twenty-first birthday: "I, Svala Egilson, hereby swear, I shall become a writer, and I invoke all good spirits in the fulfillment of this resolution!" (*Dætur Reykjavíkur*, 2:5). The story then describes the difficulties that she encounters, such as the discouraging response of publishers and several tempting offers of marriage.

The style of *Vorið hlær* is generally playful and makes extensive use of colloquialisms and slang, which at that time were novelties in Icelandic literature. Early in the novel Svala announces her poetics in a conversation with her mother, who is of the old school: "Mother dear, nobody writes a modern novel from Reykjavík in one-thousand-year-old Norwegian. We write in Icelandic, which is still in the making, and if need be, in the language we speak in Reykjavík, . . . even if those words would not tip the scales of the classics" (*Dætur Reykjavíkur*, 2:50). Svala's dreams of becoming a writer are not pursued further, and they evaporate as the novel shifts to a love story. Þórunn Elfa Magnúsdóttir's subsequent fiction is in the vein of social realism and the style more traditional. In these works Þórunn Elfa Magnúsdóttir is concerned with the condition of women, especially in marriage, and the common conflict between career and family. In the novel *Dísa Mjöll* (1953), subtitled *Scenes from the Life of a Woman Artist*, the conflict between domestic duty and art becomes so intense that it leads to a suicide attempt. The novels *Snorrabraut 7* (1947) and *Sambýlisfólk* (1954; Neighbors) depict young married couples and their ordeals when building a house, a subject that would appear later in the stories of Svava Jakobsdóttir.

The enormously prolific Guðrún Árnadóttir of Lundur (1887–1973) wrote period romances about family clans and rural life. Her bestsellers established a genre that continues to attract numerous women writers up to the present day. She began writing at an early age, but on her marriage she burned everything she had written. In her early fifties she took up writing again and quickly became Iceland's most productive and most-read author. Her first novel, and her best-known, is *Dalalíf* (1946–51; Valley life), published in five volumes. The novel is a broad description of rural life, with repressed emotions and forbidden love. It tells the story of a great farmer — powerful, passionate, tender — with whom all the women are smitten. As in her other novels passion is the force that drives the plot forward, but the women experience love only as secret longings that are never fulfilled. In the end they must accept their lot and content themselves with their romantic dreams.

Guðrún Finnsdóttir (1884–1946) emigrated west across the Atlantic at the age of twenty and settled in Winnipeg, Canada. Early on, she had dreamed of "writing poems and stories — especially stories — but the opportunity did not come until late, after the children were grown up" (Einarsson, "Vestur-íslensk skáldkona," 144). She published two collections of short stories, *Hillingalönd* (1938; Enchanted lands) and *Dagshríðar spor* (1946; Tracks of the day's struggle), but some of her stories had appeared previously in periodicals. Her narrators are often elderly people who reflect on the past. "Traustir máttarviðir" (Sturdy timbers) tells the story of an old woman who had long ago "dreamt childish dreams of poetry." She is described as two women — one old and Canadian, the other young and Icelandic. The Icelandic woman belongs to poetry that the old woman tries to suppress, convinced that in a happy home life she has found the fulfillment of her dreams: "At times, though, in moments of solitude, the young Icelandic girl entered her thoughts, looking at Þórhildur with accusing eyes that said: 'You have failed me, buried me alive at the bottom of a chest with yellowed sheets of paper.'" After much internal conflict the old woman finally comes to terms with her life, and the story ends with acceptance. She looks out over the land and realizes that, "with the bright eyes of the little girl who tried to write poetry such a long time ago, she saw the beauty around her." She envisions her children disappearing into the flow of human life to do their part: "They were her poems, imbued with life and soul" (*Dagshríðar spor*, 27–28).

Iceland — its national character, culture, and landscape — is, likewise, a utopia in the poetry of Jakobína Johnson (1883–1977). As a child she emigrated with her family to America, where she lived mainly in Seattle. In spite of a large family and many household responsibilities, she took an active role in the cultural life of the Icelandic emigrants. Many of her poems appeared in periodicals before they were collected in *Kertaljós* (1938; Candlelight); later, she published a book of verse for children, *Sá ég svani* (1942; Swans I saw). In addition she translated many works of Icelandic literature into English. She also worked tirelessly to promote her native country, traveling widely, and delivering lectures about Iceland. In the introduction to the complete collection of her poetry, *Kertaljós* (1955), the editor marvels at her output, saying: "She developed the effective habit of having paper, a pencil, and a book handy on the ledge of the cookstove. In a brief moment — while the food was cooking . . . she could read a short poem or a page in a textbook, or jot down a good word or a line of verse that came to mind" (Friðriksson, "Um höfundinn," ix). This recalls the description of Kristín Sigfúsdóttir quoted above. Although one woman is in Iceland and the other in America, their situation as writers is the same.

In many ways, the stories of Arnrún of Fell, the pen name of Guðrún Tómasdóttir (1886–1972), are pioneering works. They appeared in periodicals in North America, where she emigrated at the age of forty. Her first story, "Fiskur í alla mata" (Fish at every meal), was printed in *Tímarit Þjóðræknisfélags Íslendinga í Vesturheimi* (Journal of the Icelandic National League in North America) in 1922; her only book, the short story collection *Margs verða hjúin vís* (The servants know many things), was published in Reykjavík in 1956. Her stories, which are set in Reykjavík, are about the city's young women, who are much like those portrayed in the early stories of Þórunn Elfa Magnúsdóttir. The narrative voice is playful, the style light and fluid, and the idiom contemporary, incorporating many of the colloquialisms and slangy terms of city life. In Arnrún's stories a new image of woman emerges in Icelandic literature. Like so many women's stories they portray the conflict between the generations, but they reject the past and side with the modern woman.

SILENT POETS

Overshadowed during this period by fiction, poetry had several practitioners. Many women composed traditional poems with a moral or religious message, such as Margrét Jónsdóttir (1893–1971), Erla (Guðfinna Þorsteinsdóttir; 1891–1972), and Hugrún (Filippía Kristjánsdóttir; 1905–96), and they all wrote a great deal for children as well.

Guðfinna Jónsdóttir of Hamrar (1899–1946) published her first poems in her early forties, only a few years before her death. Her works consist of *Ljóð* (1941; Poems), *Ný ljóð* (1945; New poems), and the posthumous *Ljóðabók* (1972; A book of poems), which included some previously unpublished poems. Her training in music is reflected throughout her poems, which show a preoccupation with sounds, often those that arise from a deep silence. Significant too in this regard are the titles of her poems, such as "Rokkhljóð" (Hum of the spinning wheel), "Undirspil" (Accompaniment), and "Þagnargull" (Golden silence). The inspiration for the poems is nature, the earth itself, which she invokes as her muse in "Yrkisföng" (Poetry-trove), in *Ný ljóð*: "Be lavish, Earth, / with your poetry-trove, / while the spring / stirs in me song, / for short is my life, / but art is long" (*Ný ljóð*, 64). Her perception of nature is physical and, as in "Heiðakyrrð" (Heath stillness), in *Ljóð*, almost erotic: "I walked around Víðihlíð one spring day / and slipped off my shoe with care / and felt the warm, alluring joy, / as the birches struck my ankle bare" (*Ljóð*, 71). Often, the imagery of nature is associated with concealment, privacy, and stealth, in dialogue with unfulfilled longing. In "Dynskógur" (Whistling woods), in *Ný ljóð*, the poet identifies with the destruction of the land, especially the woods that have been cut down, at the same time that she gives the silence a voice: "The whistling woods call me / vanished, felled, burned" (*Ný ljóð*, 34). In one of her last poems, "Mig dreymir enn" (Still I dream), in *Ljóðabók*, nature has disappeared into the world of the mind: "Still I dream and dream. / The dreamlands are mine. / I traversed them with fire / that no one could see. / I hide in foliage / while life passes by" (*Ljóðabók*, 131).

Sigríður Einars of Munaðarnes (1893–1973) published her first book, *Kveður í runni* (Chants from a thicket), in 1930; it includes translations of poems by the Norwegian poet Sigbjørn Obstfelder as well as two original prose poems, "Nótt" (Night) and "Dauðinn" (Death). Other poems in the volume are traditional in form, but there is more to them than meets the eye, for they parody themselves with the inversion of accepted ideas and a glaring discrepancy between subject and style. This is especially true of the love poems, in which the poet makes fun of her own romantic feelings — the sleepness nights and the obsessed thoughts of *him*. In "Tragískur ástaróður" (Tragic ode of love), a hymn about a pale, wretched lover, the tone conveys pathos, but the imagery is grotesque. In choosing to be herself instead of submitting to the burdens of marriage, the poet turns the tables on the love poems of tradition and makes fun of them. In her next book, *Milli lækjar og ár* (1956; Between brook and river), she bridges the gap between modern and traditional poetry and becomes one of the main forerunners of modernism in Icelandic poetry, although she was greatly underrated (see Birgisdóttir, "Brúarsmiður — atómskáld — módernisti"). Many of her poems depict the horrors of war, a dominant theme in the poetry of women in this period. She wrote numerous prose poems about nature, filled with images of autumn and dying vegetation. A few of the poems tell stories based on remembrances from her own life, and these narrative poems are also a characteristic of her last books, *Laufþytur* (1970; Rustle of leaves) and *Í svölu rjóðri* (1971; In a cool clearing).

A number of women poets of this generation who have disappeared beneath the surface of literary history have one thing in common: they published only one book, either at their own expense or through patronage, and their poetry went unnoticed when it appeared in print. All of them composed a kind of lament in which duty always stands in opposition to hope and desire. Their poems examine life in retrospect, a life that they regard as lost. In the darkness and shadows that assault them they look to art — the poem — *to which* and *about which* they write, often seeing it as their sole comfort, purpose, and friend. Thus, their poems are frequently meta-texts, poems about the act of composition.

Among this group is María Bjarnadóttir (1896–1976), whose book of poetry *Haustlitir* (1964; Autumn colors) was not sold in bookstores and was never reviewed. Her poems are very sincere, as if she is confiding in the reader, with a distinctive subtle rhythm. In "Ljóðið" (The poem) she writes about her poems welling up from the silence. She takes refuge in the solitude and silence of her own soul, and "out of the stillness words began / to flow at last / and the soliloquy of my mind became / a little poem." But the poem, which "was born to quiet / my restless heart," never "produced a pitch that would reach / the ears of others, / only a prayer whispering out into / the long night" (*Haustlitir*, 118).

The poems of Þuríður Bjarnadóttir (1899–1973) were published posthumously under the title *Brotasilfur* (1985; Scrap silver). As the introduction aptly states, the book "belongs to the silent poets" (Steingrímsdóttir, "Formálsorð," 7). Although Þuríður Bjarnadóttir was known as someone who could put together a quatrain, it was not until after her death that a notebook with the poems was discovered. "I write poetry from an inner need / and only for myself," she says in the poem "Greinargerð" (Statement). In another, "Töðugjöldin" (Harvest home), she says that she "kneads her poetic fancy into her bread." In "Til Braga" (To Bragi) she composes a love poem to the god of poetry, but he does not return her love: "I begged and beseeched you for your bounty and love, / thus with the chosen I might consort, / but your answer was this, no more and no less, / that silence was fitting for my sort" (*Brotasilfur*, 17, 36, 39).

Later in life Guðrún Árnadóttir of Oddsstaðir (1900–1965) published the book of poems *Gengin spor* (1949; Trodden trails). In one of his autobiographical works the author Kristmann Guðmundsson (see pp. 374–75) describes a trip to Oddsstaðir to see his cousin Guðrún in 1910, when he was eight years old and she was ten and "knew how to play the harmonica." They hiked to a waterfall across from the farm, where she confided to him that she intended to be a poet: "'If I dare,' she added. I still remember these words because I didn't understand them. 'I'm going to be a poet, too,' I said, and in fact I had made that decision a long time ago. But the difference was that, for me, there was no lurking doubt that I both dared to do it and could do it" (Guðmundsson, *Ísóld hin svarta*, 66–67, 72–73).

Gengin spor is very innovative for women's literature of its time. The poems alternate between women's traditional laments over unfulfilled desires and a life that has run out and, on the other hand, direct, critical anger. They often reveal a fear of imminent attack, a common theme in women's literature. "Lítil dís" (Little nymph) conveys menace in the form of a nursery rhyme:

Now, behave yourself,
little nymph of cheer.
The man in the dark,
he is capable of anything.
The man in the dark,
he has his eye on you,
if ever he gets you,
he'll never let you go.

In "Ekkert svar" (No reply) the poet accuses Duty of killing her soul, but there is no reply except endless demands: "Is the porridge steaming, / is the mending complete, / are the shoes all brushed at last? / Are the floors gleaming, / is the bread fit to eat, / and the loose button sewn fast?" In "Litla ljóðið" (The little poem) she refers to her poetry as "chopping pain into words." Existing solely for her, the poem is silent and "has nothing to convey to anyone else" (*Gengin spor*, 88, 32, 14).

THE FIRST SIGNS OF MODERNISM

Around 1950 important changes began to occur in women's literature. The first signs of modernism emerge in poems and short stories, which seem to be the forms that have best suited Icelandic women writers through the ages.

Halldóra B. Björnsson is a pioneer in Icelandic literature who is generally unappreciated and whose contributions to Icelandic literary history are, thus, largely unknown. Her published works include three volumes of poetry — *Ljóð* (1949; Poems), *Við sanda* (already discussed), and the posthumous *Jarðljóð* (1968; Earth poems) — in addition to *Trumban og lútan* (1959; The tambour and the lute), containing translations of poetry from Greenland, Africa, and China, and her translation of the Old English poem *Beowulf, Bjólfskviða* (1983).

In the 1950s and 1960s Halldóra B. Björnsson was very active in the struggle of Icelandic women for culture and peace. She was the editor of *19. júní* and published *Pennaslóðir* (1959; Pen paths), an anthology of short stories by Icelandic women. At that time the women's movement was focused on the foreign military presence in Iceland, the subject of her posthumous collection of tracts in *Jörð í álögum* (1969; Spellbound earth). Her memoirs, *Eitt er það land* (1955; There is a land), are among the most original in Icelandic literature. They are told from the perspective of the child who creates a land of make-believe, a utopia where adults are excluded. The tone is humorous and playful, and everything contrary to real-world society can take place.

Parallels between earth, women, and children in contrast to a society of militarism, class struggle, racism, and patriarchy are dominant in Halldóra B. Björnsson's work, which is characterized by irony and pointed satire modulated by a subtle lyricism that echoes the refrains and rhythms of Icelandic folk verse. Halldóra B. Björnsson writes extensively about women — their position in society, their emotional life, and their hardships, often resulting from betrayal at the hands of men. Many of her poems portray women's common situations and experiences, which are often connected to their search for a place to be. In *Jarðljóð* she writes about Valentina Tereshkova, the first woman to orbit the earth in a spacecraft, and asks "the women of earth" to go outdoors with candles and lights, for "somewhere up there / is Valentina Tereskova / traveling alone / in dark space" (*Jarðljóð*, 49). Like Sigríður Einars, Halldóra B. Björnsson wrote narrative poems based on events in her own life. "Í skjóli Skarðsheiðar" (In the shelter of Skarðsheiði) tells the story of women who, during the war, take their children to the country to be safe from attacks, only to find a bomb in the field where the children are playing.

Like other Icelandic women poets, Halldóra B. Björnsson turns to women of the past. She greatly admired folk poetry and translated Jóhann Sigurjónsson's classic poem "Þjóðvísa" (Ballad), composed in Danish, about a young woman who loses her heart to a cavalier passing through. In her own "Þjóðvísur," in *Við sanda*, a woman sits at the window embroidering and watching life go by. In "Á þjóðminjasafninu" (At the national museum), in *Ljóð*, she tries to decipher the life of a long-departed woman on the basis of the embroidery on a displayed garment, the only remaining evidence of her existence. She questions the woman but receives no replies. The poem bears the characteristics that have since become common in women's poetry — the questioning voice, the mystery to be puzzled out, the silence.

Halldóra B. Björnsson's few but highly original short stories have appeared only in periodicals. They often depict women in a kind of no-man's-land, at the boundary between life and death. "Faðmlag dauðans" (1955; English trans.: "Death's Embrace," in *Scandinavian Women Writers*, ed. Claréus [1989]), which originally appeared in the journal *Birtingur*, is a detective story told from the perspective of a woman whose husband is strangling her in their bed. Another brief story, "Það vissi það enginn" (1956; Nobody knew), which also appeared in *Birtingur*, is a fantasy, one of the first in Icelandic literature. The story is told from the viewpoint of a woman who has committed suicide, yet she does not know why—and never finds out because she had told no one.

Arnfríður Jónatansdóttir (b. 1923) published her first poem, "Barn vildi byggja" (A child wanted to build), in *Embla*, a women's literary journal that was issued during the period 1942–45. Her book of poetry *Þröskuldur hússins er þjöl* (1958; The threshold of the house is a file) appeared at the height of the modernist revolution in Icelandic poetry but is nowhere mentioned in literary history or in studies of that subject. Her poems are surrealistic, with unexpected syntax and enigmatic metaphors, often drawn from the tradition of folk poetry and fairy tales. Many of them are satires of war and patriarchy, but the problem of poetic creation is also a conspicuous theme. In "Þú vitjar mín" (You visit me), which is about the tradition within which her poems are written, Arnfríður Jónatansdóttir compares this tradition to a high cliff and the poem to a shadow that is threading its way along a narrow trail and must hurry to keep up with the "master" in the lead: "The shadow of my primitive poem threads its way along a narrow trail." In "Þrá" (Yearning), which evokes the descriptions of women in heroic Eddic poetry, the poet is both shackled and concealed: "On a wide sound-sea / a wind-spread sail. / Image-life of song and saga. / A maiden wakes. / Fettered in willow withes, / Hidden in flickering flames" (*Þröskuldur*, 11, 17).

The short stories of Ásta Sigurðardóttir (1930–71) mark the breakthrough of modernism not just in women's prose but Icelandic prose in general. Ásta Sigurðardóttir's first stories, "Sunnudagskvöld til mánudagsmorguns" (Sunday evening to Monday morning) and "Gatan í rigningu" (The street in rain), appeared in 1951 in the periodical *Líf og list* (Life and art), followed by *Draumurinn* (1952; The dream), a short story printed as a chapbook. The short story collection *Sunnudagskvöld til mánudagsmorguns* was published in 1961 with illustrations by the author, then reprinted in *Sögur og ljóð* (1985; Stories and poems) along with poems and additional stories.

Ásta Sigurðardóttir's short stories, with their shocking subject matter and bold descriptions, caused a stir when they were first published. In a new literary style they portray the outcasts of middle-class society, especially women, and their utter alienation. Many of them focus on experiences that are specific to women—rape, abortion, motherhood. Through colloquial language and domestic images they describe traumatic experiences, including assault and other acts of physical violence. The point of view is often naive or surprised, the narrators lost in their fantasies, numbed by alcohol, or gripped by an obsession. "Í hvaða vagni?" (1953; English trans.: "In What Carriage?" in *Scandinavian Women Writers*, ed. Claréus [1989]) is told from the perspective of a young girl who wanders the streets in search of her child, fathered by an American soldier and then taken away from her. On the constant lookout for baby carriages she waits for her chance to peek inside them at those moments when the mothers leave them unattended. She tries to make herself as invisible as possible, a fugitive from a society that shoos her away. The carriages are described with sensuous detail. They are of all models and classes, with different sorts of wheels, brakes, hoods and aprons, bedding, diapers, baby bottles, rattles, and the smells of baby powder and sour milk. The narration is fragmented as well as fluid, and the story has the effect of an endless loop.

Another of Ásta Sigurðardóttir's short stories, "Frostrigning" (Freezing rain), unfolds in the mind of a man standing at his wife's grave after driving her insane with suppression and violence and then killing her. Pervaded by horror, silence, and a sense of unease, the story is told in fragments and flashbacks. It describes a life of misery on a remote farm and the difficult journey of the man and his horse as they haul the woman's coffin to the graveyard. The man is unable to tear himself away from the grave, as if he has not entirely finished her off and she will return to haunt him.

WOMEN'S RIGHTS AND OLD WIVES' TALES

In the late 1960s the second wave of the feminist movement reached Iceland, and the Red Stockings movement was founded in 1970. Consciousness-raising was its main emphasis, encouraging women to share their experiences and recognize common issues. The movement spread widely, and its influence clearly explains why an unprecedented number of new women writers emerged in the next few years and why much of their work deals with the condition of women. In this group were older women — some of whom had engaged in literary activities previously but now turned to the vigorous pursuit of a writing career — such as Líney Jóhannesdóttir (1913–2002) and Málfríður Einarsdóttir (1899–1983). The sister of the famous sculptor Einar Jónsson, Guðný Jónsdóttir of Galtafell (1886–1978), published two books at the age of ninety, *Bernskuminningar* (1976; Childhood memories) and the novel *Brynhildur* (1978). Others used their final years for writing, such as Unnur Eiríksdóttir (1921–76), who published the novel *Villibirta*

(1969; Will-o'-the-wisp), the book of poems *Í skjóli háskans* (1971; Under danger's protection), and the short story collection *Hvítmánuður* (1974; White month). Drífa Viðar (1920–71), who had previously written feminist literary criticism for the periodical *Melkorka* as well as several short stories that appeared there, published the novel *Fjalldalslilja* (1967; Mountain lily) and the short story collection *Dagar við vatnið* (1971; Days at the lake).

Young authors emerged with stories that used the techniques of social realism to explore the role and position of women. Auður Haralds's (b. 1947) autobiographical novel *Hvunndagshetjan* (1979; The everyday hero) aroused a great deal of attention and controversy. With frankness as well as humor it depicts a single mother with three children, her conflicts with the children's fathers, and society's prejudices (see also p. 435). Ása Sólveig (b. 1945) published *Einkamál Stefaníu* (1978; Stefania's private affairs), which is about suburban life in Reykjavík and various women's issues — pregnancy, sexuality, psychological abuse in marriage. Her objective was to write about "what men do not know and women have kept silent about" (Ása Sólveig, "'Það sem karlmenn þekkja ekki og konur þegja um,'" 11).

It is worth noting that literature tends to precede public political discourse, blazing the trail, as it were. Between 1961 and 1965 so many novels by women were published that men reacted as if they were being threatened. The year 1964 saw the publication of twelve novels by women, compared with nine by men (Kress, "Listsköpun kvenna"). The same year marked the appearance of the label *kerlingabækur* (old wives' tales, superstitions), which over the next decade became the literary establishment's slogan equating women's literature with "old ladies' yarns" and, ultimately, their "scribblings." The notion can be traced to a 1964 article by the author Sigurður A. Magnússon entitled "Engu að kvíða — kerlingarnar bjarga þessu" (Never fear — the old ladies are coming to the rescue). Here, Sigurður Magnússon discusses what he sees as the dim future of Icelandic literature, which is "in the hands of roughly eight or ten old ladies who are barely even literate in Icelandic." Their books sell "like hotcakes," he says, whereas the public "hardly acknowledges" the nation's promising young poets (Magnússon, *Sáð í vindinn*, 140). In an article the following year he refers to "the famous '*kerlingabækur*' of recent years," which shows that the term had become entrenched (*Sáð í vindinn*, 64).

As a pun that played on the word's literal sense, *kerlingabækur* was considered clever, especially since many women who were publishing books at this time were, in fact, old. For example, the best-selling author Guðrún of Lundur published her nineteenth volume in 1964, when she was in her late seventies. While the term *kerlingabækur* was a big hit in some circles, it gave rise to an intense and often bitter debate about literature written by women. In a 1965 issue of *Skírnir*, in a review of Jakobína Sigurðardóttir's first short story collection, *Púnktur á skökkum stað* (1964; A period in the wrong place), the reviewer says that he firmly believes that "in this country too many women feel the urge to write." Granted, one might frequently "smile at our women's literature," but more commonly it is "irritation that gets the upper hand." In this regard the reviewer is pleased with Jakobína Sigurðardóttir's book, which he hopes will become, not only "an incentive for additional efforts" on the part of the author herself, but also "a lesson for some of her sisters to be more professional in their methods or else entrust their output to the fire" (Sveinsson, "Jakobína Sigurðardóttir," 218–19).

In *Íslendíngaspjall* (1967; Icelanders' chat) Halldór Laxness challenges this attitude toward women's literature and discerns in the novels of Guðrún of Lundur and her peers a native and unbroken narrative tradition. Laxness views the popularity of these "distinctive storytellers" as unique in European culture. Furthermore, not only do they write better than academics by and large, but they are "storytellers in a direct line from our old fairy tale women" and are "resurrected in a new land, a transformed society, another world" (88–90). In a 1972 article Oddný Guðmundsdóttir linked the debate to the escalating women's movement by commenting: "Those learned men who are hired for their expertise in everything written can do something more useful than take out their frustrations on so-called *kerlingabækur*." But somehow, she adds, "the masters have to get even with those shrews who demand the same pay for the same work" ("Lærðir og leikir," 11). For her first novel Líney Jóhannesdóttir pointedly chose the title *Kerlingarslóðir* (1976; An old lady's paths), teasing the literary establishment's penchant for using the word *kerling* as an insult and discounting women's daily lives as valid literary material.

IN SEARCH OF IDENTITY

The novels, short stories, and plays of Svava Jakobsdóttir (1930–2004) are some of the most revolutionary works in contemporary Icelandic literature. With her first two volumes of short stories, *Tólf konur* (1965; Twelve women) and *Veizla undir grjótvegg* (1967; Party under a stone wall), she not only introduced the new women's liberation movement but also became the most influential exponent of modernism in Icelandic literary prose. Svava Jakobsdóttir describes women's experiences first and foremost as inner experience. She rejects objective realism, which, in her view, reflects and promotes a traditional perception of the world. Instead, she looks beyond the dominant tradition to the narrative mode of fairy tales, with their mixture of fantasy and daily life. The women in her stories are usually middle-class housewives who, confined by their houses and domestic roles, suffer from a negative self-image. The stories reflect the women's search for identity as ordinary reality is transformed through grotesque and surreal metaphors of fantasy and horror. Houses, stone, concrete, walls, pictures, photographs, mirrors, clothes, postures, and masquerades occur frequently in the stories. Often they describe rites of passage, a wedding, a journey, or a move into a new house. In "Verkamaðurinn" (The laborer), in *Tólf konur*, the author describes the mental state of a housewife whose new awareness of her position leads her to experience her housework as a nightmare:

> Dishes numbering in the thousands, cups, glasses, mugs, brooms, bowls, all came hopping, tumbled in, piled up, attacked her, commanding, powerful; and her boy's sweater with the hole in the elbow sat down in her arms, and she began darning and darning but she never got anywhere with the hole, and she had gotten old and the thread was all gone, and she began to pull gray hairs out of her head to darn with, and then her son was a grown man and had outgrown the sweater. Then she knew that it was things which had lived, but not she. (*Tólf konur*, 65)

Thus, the most ordinary objects are magnified and animated or the most shocking incidents related as if they were commonplace, often with a tragicomical effect. In "Saga handa börnum" (A story for children), which appeared in *Veizla undir grjótvegg*, the children cut out the brain of their self-sacrificing mother while she prepares a meal because they want to know what a brain looks like. They throw the brain in the trash can, but the mother continues with her work as if there has been no intrusion. The father comes home and scolds the children, not for maiming their mother, but, rather, for acting up at mealtime. Attacks and amputations figure prominently in the stories, often in connection with bodily metamorphoses. The title story of the collection *Gefið hvort öðru* (1979; English trans.: "Give unto Each Other," in Jakobsdóttir, *The Lodger and Other Stories*, trans. D'Arcy and Hill [2000]) describes a marriage ceremony at the altar as if it were a stage, with the bridal couple portrayed as the actors and the wedding guests the audience. The bride takes the minister's words literally, amputating her hand and giving it to the groom. The novel *Leigjandinn* (1969; English trans.: *The Lodger*, in Jakobsdóttir, *The Lodger and Other Stories*, trans. D'Arcy and Hill [2000]) is about a woman who searches for her identity in the safety and isolation of her house, with which she ultimately merges: "She closed her eyes and experienced nothing but the touch of the house. She stood like this until she could no longer distinguish between her skin and the stone, but felt her nerves and veins run directly into the walls of this house and felt her heart pumping her own blood to where the concrete defined her space in existence" (Jakobsdóttir, *The Lodger and Other Stories*, 110).

Svava Jakobsdóttir's last collection of short stories, *Undir eldfjalli* (1989; Under a volcano), displays a shift from the grotesque to the more ecological, with an interest in wilderness and nature (Eysteinsson, "At Home and Abroad"; see also p. 431). In the lyric novel *Gunnlaðar saga* (1986; The saga of Gunnlöð) she reworks the old myth of the giantess Gunnlöð, blending contemporary and ancient times, myth and reality, to create a utopia in which nature, woman, and poetry are linked together.

A PLACE TO BE

Houses and other kinds of dwellings are important symbols in women's novels of recent decades. Jakobína Sigurðardóttir's first novel, *Dægurvísa* (1965; A twelve-hour verse), employs several points of view to tell the story of the residents of a house in Reykjavík. Her futuristic novel *Snaran* (1968; The snare) takes place entirely within a factory and consists of a worker's soliloquy to a silent interlocutor. *Í sama klefa* (1981; A shared cabin) describes the problematic connection of reality and text in the relationship of two women who end up in the same cabin on a ship. One is a writer from the city, and the other, a woman from the country, is her elusive subject. The parallel relationship between two women is also at the center of a novel by Vigdís Grímsdóttur (b. 1953), *Stúlkan í skóginum* (1992; The girl in the grove). One woman is physically and emotionally handicapped, trapped inside the house of the other, who is a dollmaker bordering on madness and in need of material for her art. Grímsdóttir's novel *Ég heiti Ísbjörg, ég er ljón* (1989; My name is Ísbjörg, I am a Leo) tells the story of a girl in prison, a victim of sexual abuse and incest. The first novel of Gréta Sigfúsdóttir (1910–91), *Bak við byrgða glugga* (1966; Behind curtained windows), takes place in Norway during the war and portrays a woman who breaks society's rules by having an affair with a German soldier. Expelled from society, she withdraws to the confines of her house, where she lives in seclusion.

The houses in these works are often located on the outskirts of town, as in the stories of Svava Jakobsdóttir, or along the shore, as in *Tímaþjófurinn* (1986; The thief of time) by Steinunn Sigurðardóttir (b. 1950) as well as

Eins og hafið (1986; Like the sea) by Fríða Sigurðardóttir (b. 1940). The latter's novel *Meðan nóttin líður* (1990; English trans.: *Night Watch* [1995]), which weaves together the lives of many generations of women, takes place in the mind of a woman who spends a night at the hospital sitting at the bedside of her dying mother. The story by Unnur Eiríksdóttir entitled "Hvítmánuður" (White month), in the short story collection of the same name, depicts the interaction of two women — an artist living in a tent at the edge of the hay field, the other woman inside the farmhouse. Líney Jóhannesdóttir's novel *Kerlingarslóðir*, mentioned earlier, describes the life of a middle-aged married woman with a full-time job who lives, significantly, in a half-finished house on the coast. Conversely, the central image in Líney Jóhannesdóttir's other novel, *Aumingja Jens* (1980; Poor Jens), is a group of old houses at the city limits that are being razed. Both of Líney Jóhannesdóttir's novels are filled with violence and oppression, especially against powerless people — women, children, the elderly and the isolated, the sick and the poor. These individuals are described as the counterparts of nature and animal life, subjugated by modern technological society.

Violence in some form is highly visible in contemporary fiction by Icelandic women. Fear of violence is a driving force in many of Fríða Sigurðardóttir's short stories in *Þetta er ekkert alvarlegt* (1980; It's nothing serious) and *Við gluggann* (1984; At the window), stories that also deal with the difficulties of relationships, especially communication problems. Many of the novels and short stories of Álfrún Gunnlaugsdóttir (b. 1938) feature women fleeing from a threatening environment, and it becomes the central theme in Álfrún Gunnlaugsdóttir's first book of short stories, *Af manna völdum* (1982; By human design), many of the stories in which depict various rites of passage. For example, the first story in the volume concerns the pain of becoming an adult, initiated into the male society of violence. It takes place during the war and is narrated in fragments, reiterations, and flashbacks from a child's point of view — that of a little girl who lives in a summerhouse with her mother on the outskirts of Reykjavík. Into their harmonious female world a soldier intrudes, carrying a rifle, and they flee. The mother drags the girl on and through a barbed-wire fence in a metaphor of birth. On the other side of the fence the girl stands bloodied by the sharp wire, injured physically and emotionally. It is here that the story both begins and ends, forming a circle, a narrative device that characterizes other short stories by Álfrún Gunnlaugsdóttir as well as her two novels, *Þel* (1984; Sympathy) and *Hringsól* (1987; Circling).

One of the most original writers of the last decades of the twentieth century is Málfríður Einarsdóttir. Her fragmented memoirs and novels,

not published until she was in her late seventies, mix stream of consciousness, philosophy, lyricism, fantasy, grotesque imagery, and irony to create a strange and unreliable world. Among her six books are the novels
Auðnuleysingi og Tötrughypja (1979; Luckless and the shaggy lady) and
Tötra í Glettingi (1983; Tötra at Gletting), which are two of the most
original novels about artists in Icelandic literature, as well as four autobiographical works, including the posthumous *Rásir dægranna* (1986; Tracks
of time). The central metaphor in her work is the search for a place that she
never finds, for it ultimately exists only in the vanished house of her childhood, a touchstone for all other houses that she encounters. Yet she "never
needed to be nowhere" (*Samastaður*, 46), as she says in her first book,
Samastaður í tilverunni (1977; A place to be), in one of her typically paradoxical statements. Málfríður Einarsdóttir frequently writes about language, and her work is full of allusions to Icelandic and world literature that
she turns upside down and reinterprets.

A similar mixture of genres and inversions of language characterizes the
poetry and fiction of Steinunn Sigurðardóttir, as seen in the playful titles of
her two collections of short stories, *Sögur til næsta bæjar* (1981; Tales worth
telling) and *Skáldsögur* (1983; Fictions). The nonchalant tone with which
Steinunn Sigurðardóttir juxtaposes lofty themes and ordinary phenomena
like sexual relationships results in farcical but incisive statements about life.
Her extremely ironical style, which is built on colloquial language, can
become morbid in its overall effect. Like Málfríður Einarsdóttir, she reworks material from older texts, and some of her most noted themes and
metaphors are based on intertextual relations. The novel *Tímaþjófurinn*,
which verges on poetry, describes a woman's desperate search for love and a
place in society; at the same time the woman sees herself through the eyes of
others and objectifies herself as a fictional character (Kress, "'Dæmd til að
hrekjast'"). In the novel *Síðasta orðið* (1990; The last word) she parodies
the obituaries of the daily press, which are a popular and uniquely Icelandic
genre.

Steinunn Sigurðardóttir's poems often deal with the act of composing
poetry and the struggle of the woman poet against the male tradition.
"Fyrir þína hönd" (On your behalf), in *Verksummerki* (1979; Traces), is a
poem that speaks for a young woman in a fish factory who is trying to
describe her life and, thus, gives a voice to the otherwise silent worker. As is
so common in women's poetry, it repudiates the traditional picture of
happy family life: "At home, Mama is sickly and my daddy in a rage / Little
Maja is cross-eyed and beaten like a fish." Through the image of the poet
and the factory worker the poem explores the problem of writing and

expressing oneself as the connection between poet and subject is made concrete:

There's nothing, nothing I can do. Hardly even cut fillets.
. . .
And me, I just want to sing. There's nothing quite like hearing me sing.
They tell me to shut my mouth.
. . .
I'm so stupid / that I can't even write this.
That's done by a woman in town. But what does she know?
(*Verksummerki*, 51–52)

In the poem "Skírlífi" (Chastity), in *Verksummerki*, Steinunn Sigurðardóttir personifies the various isms of literary tradition as rapists breaking in on the woman poet lying in her bed. To avoid violence she has no alternative but to let them in and submit.

"AND I THOUGHT I WAS A POET"

The real breakthrough in women's poetry occurred with Vilborg Dagbjartsdóttir's (b. 1930) first two volumes of poetry, *Laufið á trjánum* (1965; The leaf on the trees) and *Dvergliljur* (1968; Crocuses), a breakthrough solidified in her *Kyndilmessa* (1971; Candlemas). *Ljóð*, a complete collection of her poetry, including poems from periodicals and her translations of poems, appeared in 1981, followed by *Klukkan í turninum* (1992; The bell in the tower). The innovations in her poetry spring from an overtly feminist point of view, consisting of colloquial language and images of daily life and familiar surroundings. These features, along with the blending of fantasy and ordinary reality as well as the use of unexpected points of view, characterize much of contemporary women's poetry.

A childlike perspective and metaphors of littleness are characteristic of many of Vilborg Dagbjartsdóttir's poems, along with twists of convention whereby the little becomes big and the big little or inanimate objects — the traditional symbols for technology and alienation — are brought to life. In the poem "Á fjórðu hæð við umferðargötu" (Fourth floor on a busy street), in *Kyndilmessa*, automobiles cower in a parking lot like frightened animals, and the child viewing them from an upstairs window wants to go down and pet them. In Vilborg Dagbjartsdóttir's many political poems against war and the U.S. military's presence in Iceland, the child is seen as analogous to poetry, and both are placed in contrast to the warfare of males.

Many of Vilborg Dagbjartsdóttir's poems are concerned with women's liberation and the position of women, topics examined by a voice that ranges from questioning to innocently puzzled to sarcastic and angry. The woman in "Óður til mánans" (Ode to the moon), in *Ljóð*, vows to go out on the balcony and shake her scrub brush in the moon's face when she finishes her endless housework, for that is one place where "no woman has / been sent with / THE DISHRAG / not yet" (*Ljóð*, 124). The poet thus reworks the romantic imagery of literary convention by turning it around and linking it with daily life and the perspective of women. Vilborg Dagbjartsdóttir frequently alludes to literary classics and reinterprets the major characters of world literature, such as Ibsen's Hedda Gabler and Nora Helmer and Tolstoy's Anna Karenina. The subject of the prose poem "Draumur" (Dream), in *Ljóð*, is the position of the woman poet vis-à-vis tradition, represented by Odin, the god of poetry in Old Norse mythology. She dreams that she is walking along a narrow trail, with the sea on one side and sheer cliffs on the other, where she meets a man with a hat pulled down over his face. She recognizes him as the god of poetry and calls out to him, for "I thought we had a lot to talk about." But, when he looks at her, beneath the brim of his hat she sees the glint in his eye, burning with lust: "Then I realized that even Odin himself had only one thing in mind when it came to women. And I thought I was a poet" (*Ljóð*, 107). Vilborg Dagbjartsdóttir experiences the woman poet's oppression as physical violence — impending rape — as do Steinunn Sigurðardóttir in "Skírlífi" and Svava Jakobsdóttir in "Experience and Reality," in which the woman risks going out on the street of literary tradition. In Vilborg Dagbjartsdóttir's poem what saves the protagonist is that she manages to shake off sleep and escapes by waking up, but "in my soul I burned with anger" (*Ljóð*, 107).

The child is a prevalent figure in all six volumes of poetry of Þuríður Guðmundsdóttir (b. 1939), the first of which, *Aðeins eitt blóm* (Only one flower), appeared in 1969. In the beginning the child is at one with the environment, full of hope and trust in life, with a strong connection to budding nature, spring, and play. In "Barn vorsins" (Child of spring), from *Og það var vor* (1980; And it was spring), the smallness of the child undergoes symbolic expansion in the image of a little girl skipping rope. In "Og það var vor," from the same volume, life is personified as a girl who goes outside to play, tears her dress, picks flowers, and then brings them home that evening, wilted. Þuríður Guðmundsdóttir's poems are short and lyric, revolving around a central image. The subjects of her poems are taken from nature, memories, and daily life, often capturing feelings of pain and sorrow, loneliness and abandonment. "Eitt lítið ástarljóð" (One little love poem), in *Það sagði mér haustið* (1985; The autumn told me so), is about the difficulties of human relationships, especially communication, and the fear of being abandoned with so many words still to be uttered: "Sometimes / I'm afraid / that you'll go away / and leave me all by myself / with all my unspoken words / that were meant for you" (*Það sagði mér haustið*, 72). Thus, many of Þuríður Guðmundsdóttir's poems deal with the fear of being unable to express oneself, or, rather, the fear of being silenced.

The poems of Nína Björk Árnadóttir (1941–2000) deal with people who are outsiders in society, and the innocent surface of the language conceals violence, horror, and madness. Her first book of poems, *Ung ljóð* (1965; Young poems), was published the same year as Vilborg Dagbjartsdóttir's first book, and it was followed by six books of poetry and a novel, *Móðir, kona, meyja* (1987; Mother, woman, maiden). Nína Björk Árnadóttir also wrote plays, both for stage and for television. Her poems are often very dramatic—for example, monologues in which the speakers directly address an absent listener and try to describe themselves, struggling to achieve self-knowledge. The emphasis of the poems is usually identity and relationships, with the speakers seeking to understand themselves, both through language and in society, with frequent use of repetition, negations, unfinished sentences, and metaphors of concealment, escape, and silence. "Þú spurðir" (You asked), in *Undarlegt er að spyrja mennina* (1968; It's strange to ask people), alludes to Icelandic folktales about the fairy in the rock, which becomes a metaphor for woman as outsider, excluded from society, and enclosed in silence and darkness:

> You asked where I was to be found
> I haven't hidden myself,
> but I live inside a blue rock
> deep inside a dark blue rock
> that turns black sometimes.
> And without a doubt you would find
> it strange in there. (*Undarlegt*, 71)

Nína Björk Árnadóttir's poems are often tragicomic, as seen in "Doddi," from *Svartur hestur í myrkrinu* (1982; Black horse in the dark), a poem that is not only a study of the connection between reality, perception, and words but also a highly original love poem: "I can't believe I did that / did I really beat her / did I beat her / I can't believe / I did that / I love her" (*Svartur hestur*, 45). Women with a poor self-image, offering their endless litanies of apologies and excuses, are central figures in Nína Björk Árnadóttir's poems. In "Anna," also in *Svartur hestur í myrkrinu*, a woman makes repeated efforts to find words to explain herself in relation to others but finally gives up, and the poem dissolves in ellipses: "Please forgive me / that I should / that I have / for being / for being so / as / if / I / . . ." (*Svartur hestur*, 46). A similar disintegration of language occurs in a number of Nína Björk Árna-dóttir's short prose pieces, such as the short story "Og síðan hef ég verið hérna hjá ykkur" (And I've been here with you ever since), which blends dramatic, lyric, and fantastic modes to describe the struggle of a young secretary and single mother against an authoritarian male boss, resulting in the fragmented and stressed discourse of a woman who is going mad. The style is characterized by exclamations, unfinished sentences, and semiotic language that verges on being unintelligible. She expresses her frustrations by parodying the phone conversations of her boss — "Yes. Yes, yes, yes, yes. . . . Yes, we have blah blah blah blah blah" — or consoles herself by reciting the poems of her poet lover (*Draumur um veruleika*, ed. Kress, 179). The story ends when she makes her exit from society by stepping out of a tenth-floor window, and it is from this vantage point that she speaks.

The use of startling viewpoints is also apparent in the surrealistic and often philosophical epigrams of Þóra Jónsdóttir (b. 1925), who by 1995 had published a total of seven books of poetry. Her search for identity and a place to be pervades her poems, as indicated by the title of her first book, *Leit að tjaldstæði* (1973; Search for a campsite). The poems frequently de-scribe difficult journeys whose terminus is either an impassible road or the margins of a settled area. These journeys are undertaken sometimes on foot and at other times by such unpoetic means as the automobile, which is typical of Þóra Jónsdóttir's distinctive figurative language. In "Stæði í miðborginni" (A parking place downtown), in *Leiðin heim* (1975; The way home), the search symbolizes a personal quest and, at the same time, the human condition: "It's hard / to find a parking place downtown / some early birds / have parked their vehicles there / though one or two might open up / parking is hard / because vehicles / are never allowed to touch" (*Leiðin heim*, 12). In Þóra Jónsdóttir's later poems the journeys tend to take place solely in the mind.

Unlike the majority of Iceland's women poets, Ingibjörg Haraldsdóttir (b. 1941) lived abroad for many years, and in her first book of poetry, *Þangað vil ég fljúga* (1974; There I want to fly), Iceland is the place that inspires nostalgia. Her next book, *Orðspor daganna* (1983; Rumors of the days), deals with homecoming and disappointment. Ingibjörg Haraldsdótt-ir composes political poems opposing corruption and warfare as well as poems about the immediate surroundings of daily life, often mixed with a mourning for vanished ideals and lost childhood, when anything was possi-ble. In many of her poems, especially those concerning women, their isolation in their roles, and their search for identity, she counteracts daily reality with fantasy. The poem "Angist" (Agony), in *Orðspor daganna*, describes a woman's split identity as a result of traditional housework. Agony gnaws slowly but persistently at her "root" deep in the soil until one day "it gnaws me in two / and a part of me rushes off, without restraint / into the blue / disappears out of the kitchen window / . . . / the other stays behind / and finishes the dishes" (*Orðspor*, 37).

The poems of the youngest generation of Icelandic women poets offer strong words of encouragement to their sisters to hold their own in the battle. This message is apparent in "Ef sverð þitt er of stutt" (If your sword is too short), a poem by Elísabet Þorgeirsdóttir (b. 1956) in her *Salt og rjómi* (1983; Salt and cream):

As if it's nothing
you zip through the dish washing
. . .
you scrub, wash, vacuum
. . .
Look straight ahead
with feminine dignity
. . .
stand on both feet
wherever you are
be an even greater woman.
(*Salt og rjómi*, 51)

Even more irony can be seen in the poem by Berglind Gunnarsdóttir (b. 1953) entitled "Súper súper . . ." in her first book of poetry, *Ljóð fyrir lífi* (1983; Poems for life): "Be brave / be strong / be realistic / . . . / no emotional giddiness / no groping / no shilly-shallying / . . . / leniency accomplishes nothing in the battle" (*Ljóð fyrir lífi*, 19). The title of her next book of poetry, *Ljóðsótt* (1986; Poetry pangs), contains a pun that likens the act of writing poetry to that of giving birth, with the poet in the role of the delivering mother. Þórdís Richardsdóttir (b. 1951) creates a similar image in the title of her first book of poetry, *Ljóð í lausaleik* (1976; Poems out of wedlock), and its opening poem, an image that is reminiscent of the epigraph to Júlíana Jónsdóttir's book of poems precisely a century earlier: "My illegitimate poems / are footloose and fancy-free / unfathered / without support payments / neither adopted / nor in foster care / merely born." The association between the birth of a child and the creation of a poem is developed in the poem's various sections. In the end the mother/poet takes the child in her arms and looks at it: "I see that you are a girl" (*Ljóð í lausaleik*, 7, 19).

"FOR ONE THOUSAND YEARS"

The most distinctive feature of literature by Icelandic women is its critical stance toward the literary tradition. Images are reversed or inverted, and ordinary women are turned into protagonists. But women bring to literature, not only new subject matter, but also new forms and a new style. The search for form is simultaneously a search for identity, a female identity that women can accept, and experiments with form seem to be most compelling among those writers who seek to portray the emotional life, thoughts, and experiences of women. It is striking that so many Icelandic women writers, both early and contemporary, have looked outside the dominant literary tradition for an expressive form that they viewed as capable of interpreting women's experience. Many avail themselves of the rich legacy of folk poetry, folktales, and fairy tales to shape their work, thus connecting with the female tradition that preceded them.

From early times to the present day one of the main characteristics of women's literature in Iceland is the use of fantasy. In modern works this element is often combined with the realism of everyday life and grotesque imagery, as best seen in the stories of Svava Jakobsdóttir. Here, the connections between female experience and literary form emerge clearly in the use of narrative point of view. A very prominent feature of women's fiction is an effort to describe the inner life of the female characters from their own perspective. Women see the world from the inside. This type of inside point of view appears first in Icelandic literature with Ólöf of Hlaðir, and it has been prevalent in women's prose up to the present day.

The first book of poetry by an Icelandic woman began with the word *little*. Metaphors of littleness characterize much of Icelandic women's literature, reflecting women's sense of being subjugated in their lives and culture by a larger social power. Women readily identify with that which is small and powerless. Flowers, birds, butterflies, little objects, and children are very common in the figurative language of Icelandic women writers. In one poem after another the women describe themselves as little. Nowhere is this more apparent than in the work of Ólöf of Hlaðir, who titled both her books of poetry *Some Little Verses*. In the poem "Lítil" she equates her physical stature with her stature as a writer: "A little might lifted me up / but little did I achieve. / Little I came and little I am, / little I'll take my leave." To Ólöf, her body is "small-limbed" and her mind "of little value."

She fully realizes the social causes of her smallness, for she compares society to a "wasteland" where nothing can grow, and at the end of the poem she speculates that she might grow taller in the afterlife, where "conditions will be a little bit better" (*Ritsafn*, 73).

In their search for identity, not only do women resort to the older female tradition, an inside point of view, and metaphors of littleness, but they also transform and reinterpret the conventions of the dominant tradition, presenting them in a different light. These iconoclasms of women's literature, based on inversions and oppositions, are patently directed at exposing ideologies about the position of women and the relationship between the sexes. A good example of this kind of protest is Vilborg Dagbjartsdóttir's "Skassið á háskastund" (The shrew at the moment of danger), in *Kyndilmessa*. The poem inverts the famous passage in *Njáls saga* in which Hallgerður, one of the most notorious female characters in Icelandic literature, refuses to give Gunnar two locks of her hair for his bow, which would save his life:

Slaps to my cheek and bitter words
all is forgotten
oh, my dear
here is my braid
twist you a bowstring
I'll whet the pantry knife
and fight as well
no house of mine will they
ever burn down
damn their hide.
(*Kyndilmessa*, 33)

Vilborg Dagbjartsdóttir's Hallgerður is a woman who hands her husband, not just locks of hair, but her entire braid, takes responsibility for defending her home, and fights with the womanly weapons that are available to her.

Many of the iconoclasms of women's literature are aimed at tearing down the concept of masculinity, often in a highly grotesque way. This is how Málfríður Einarsdóttir begins the chapter "Umkomuleysi kvenfólks á Íslandi" (The vulnerability of women in Iceland) in *Samastaður í tilverunni*: "For one thousand years we Icelandic women have huddled shivering here in this disagreeable country without any school to go to and few things to enjoy unless it would be the men, and a plenty entertaining lot they mostly were, drunk as skunks, palsied, bloated from schnapps, black below the nose from tobacco, getting no pleasure out of anything at all" (*Samastaður*,

134). One might observe that this passage is the history of Iceland in a nutshell from the perspective of women. Men's heroic ideas of themselves are upended, along with their idealization of the country and its people.

All these qualities connect to women's search for identity at the same time as they violate the norms of a tradition that prevailed when women made their first appearance in print. In this way, Icelandic women writers have consistently turned to innovations that the literary tradition has then appropriated and integrated.

Translated by Alison Tartt

Icelandic Theater

*Árni Ibsen
and Hávar Sigurjónsson*

9

Icelandic Theater, 1790–1975: *Árni Ibsen*

BEGINNINGS

Playwriting presupposes an urban society with an audience to fill a theater, however small. Being an essentially rural society until well into the twentieth century, Iceland therefore has a relatively short theater history proper; it did not produce playwrights of any note until the first two decades of the twentieth century, when Reykjavík had assumed the role of a growing capital. Whatever merit can be attributed to nineteenth-century playwriting in Iceland, its achievements are purely incidental, and the early promise of playwrights like Matthías Jochumsson and Indriði Einarsson did not provide them with the conditions or the means to pursue their craft seriously. Their example and the enormous popularity of their main plays can, however, be considered the cornerstone of Icelandic drama.

Without taking into account the theoretical possibility that the texts of the Eddic poems may be scripts of dramatic dialogue, a persistent contention that has yet to be proved, we can justifiably claim that the seeds of Icelandic playwriting were sown during the last decade of the eighteenth century with Sigurður Pétursson (1759–1827), who wrote two short but excellent satiric comedies for school productions in Reykjavík, after the fashion of Ludvig Holberg and Molière. Pétursson's first play was *Slaður og trúgirni* (1796; Gossip and gullibility), probably inspired by Molière's *L'avare* (1668; The miser) and often called *Hrólfur* after one of the main characters, followed in 1799 by *Narfi, eður sá narraktugi biðill* (Narfi, or the foolish suitor), an excellently crafted satiric comedy inspired by Holberg's *Jean de France* (1723). Unfortunately, this second play fell prey to the 1799–1820 ban on theater activity instituted by the Danish king's Icelandic officials, who feared that such activity in itself might, when prompted by Enlightenment ideals, incite rebellion. The ban was not lifted until 1820, but by that time Pétursson was old and sick and totally disillusioned with the world. His comedies, especially *Narfi*, remained popular during the nineteenth century and greatly influenced later Icelandic comic writing, such as the novels of Jón Thoroddsen (see pp. 294–96), and comedic playwriting in particular, where his influence can be discerned well into the twentieth century.

It was not until romanticism had become a fixed part of the country's literary life, and contemporaneous with the publication of Jón Árnason's momentous collection of folktales *Íslenzkar þjóðsögur og ævintýri* (1862–64; Icelandic folk- and fairy tales; see pp. 297–300), that serious playwriting came into existence, although, again, only for a brief period since there were no regular theater activities in Reykjavík at the time. By the 1850s any effort at theater in Reykjavík was predominantly of Danish origin. These were amateur productions put on for the most part by Danish merchants and performed in Danish. The artist Sigurður Guðmundsson (1837–74; see also p. 281) became the mentor of Icelandic theater and playwriting on his return from studies in Copenhagen, where he had frequented the Royal Danish Theater, which was among the most important theaters in Europe at the time, and seen outstanding productions of plays by Shakespeare, Molière, Holberg, and J. L. Heiberg. During the 1860s Guðmundsson had a leading hand in organizing theater activities. He also painted the scenery, for the most part romantic Icelandic landscape representations, and created tableaux, which, for many, justifies the claim that he was, in effect, the first Icelandic stage director.

Guðmundsson envisioned an Icelandic drama that would draw its raw material from the wealth of the nation's folklore as well as from saga literature and history, drama that would be written in Icelandic for a "national stage," specifically aimed at an Icelandic audience in order to confront people with a mirror in which they would be enlightened about their national identity and cultural heritage. He encouraged young, potential writers, prompting them to learn their trade by studying and translating "the greatest playwrights," meaning Shakespeare especially, but also Schiller, Molière, and the Greek tragedians. Guðmundsson's energetic idealism bore fruit in two young disciples, Matthías Jochumsson (1835–1920) and Indriði Einarsson (1851–1939), who both wrote plays based on Icelandic folklore and later tried their hand at histories modeled on Shakespeare. Both were later to translate several works by Shakespeare, although the bard's plays were not actually staged in Iceland until after 1920.

Jochumsson's first play, and by far his best, was the romantic *Útilegumenn-irnir* (1862; The outlaws), which, after extensive revisions, eventually came to be known simply as *Skugga-Sveinn* (Shadow-Sveinn), after the leading character, the belligerent chief of the outlaws whose fearful, larger-than-life presence made him the archenemy of law and order. *Skugga-Sveinn* remains the most frequently performed play in Iceland and has remained in the popular repertory until this day. Likewise, Einarsson's first play, *Nýársnóttin* (1872; New Year's Eve), has enjoyed lasting popularity, although it has been rarely performed after 1970. It became the model for a tradition of plays about the supernatural, which evolved into a tradition of playwriting for children.

Inspired by the dramaturgy of Shakespeare and Schiller's *Die Räuber* (1788; The robbers), Jochumsson's *Skugga-Sveinn* is the prototypical Icelandic play since its lasting popularity made it a model for generations of young Icelanders of what theater was all about. The plot is a simple tale of a conflict between outlaws and country folk, interspersed with songs set to well-worn tunes by the Danish romantic composer Frederik Kuhlau, and brimming with popular ingredients such as superstition and magic, and interwoven with various folk customs as well as the chase and capture of criminals, mistaken identities, and forbidden love. Among the gallery of its colorful cast of characters is a silly sheriff who, in spite of all his blunders, manages to do his job and eventually catches the outlaws. Another memorable character is Ketill skrækur (screech), one of the outlaws, who has some of the animal-like qualities of a Caliban, although he is traditionally played as a comic character. There is also a *Romeo and Juliet* aspect to the play in the forbidden love between a farmer's young and innocent daughter and an equally young and innocent outlaw boy supposedly born in the mountains. The love affair is happily resolved in the end, however, as the boy turns out to be the legitimate son of a wealthy neighboring farmer who was abducted in infancy. The plot evolves through episodes set alternatively in the mountains and at a couple of farms below them.

Of greatest significance in light of later developments in Icelandic playwriting is Jochumsson's fine observation in *Skugga-Sveinn* of detail in local speech and odd behaviorial patterns in characters who have spent their lives in the seclusion of the countryside. The text is elegant and eloquent throughout, with several lines having found their way into everyday speech and become popular sayings. The play's characters are larger-than-life portrayals, frequently verging on the grotesque. In Skugga-Sveinn himself Jochumsson created a character destined to become the outstanding model for subsequent playwrights to live up to, a gigantic theatrical figure of mythical proportions. Characteristically, Skugga-Sveinn escapes from his captors in the end and throws himself into one of the country's biggest waterfalls to become, as he himself claims, "part of the nation's mythology."

In spite of the very limited theater possibilities Jochumsson remained devoted to playwriting for at least four decades after the appearance of *Útilegumennirnir*, penning inspired yet flawed translations of four Shakespeare tragedies, and writing a handful of short plays in addition to one historical drama on a grand scale, the potentially impressive *Jón Arason* (1900; The last bishop), set in the sixteenth century, about the tragic fate of the last Catholic bishop in Iceland and his two sons, a work that remained unstaged until the ambitious 1974 National Theater production.

Einarsson's *Nýársnóttin* is a fairy tale, naive in tone, portraying simple country folk and their dealings with supernatural beings such as elves, who live in a rock near the farm, as well as "little devils," who are representatives of the darker forces. Essentially melodramatic, the play contains some fine, often comic observations of the simple, everyday existence of a typical farming family in the harsh landscape of rural Iceland, but it never rises to the level of grandeur that characterizes the language and characters of *Skugga-Sveinn*. Unabashedly modeled on the Danish playwright J. L. Heiberg's *Elverhöj* (1828; Elfin hill) and, to a lesser degree, on Shakespeare's *A Midsummer Night's Dream*, its juxtaposition of harsh realities and a gentle fairy tale quality, as well as the eternal struggle between good and evil, spoke directly to the Icelandic imagination and prompted a host of other, lesser writers to try their hand at fairy tale plays, but with less success. The most popular of these was possibly *Sigríður Eyjafjarðarsól* (1879) by Ari Jónsson (1833–1907).

Einarsson wrote several plays in addition to *Nýársnóttin*, although none of them were as successful or have yet proved to have the lasting value of his first play. The historical dramas *Hellismenn* (1897; The cave dwellers), a blank verse tragedy with echoes of *Richard III*, and *Sverð og bagall* (1899; Sword and crozier) possibly show Einarsson's greatest ambition in the theatrical field; the latter undeservedly remains unperformed since its scope was far too large for the intimate Iðnó Theater, where the Reykjavík Theater Company put on its productions. His next effort was an early attempt at writing a contemporary and realistic Ibsenian play in Icelandic, *Skipið sekkur* (1902; The ship is sinking). His last plays are the highly theatrical and Faustian *Dansinn í Hruna* (1925; The dance at Hruni), based on folklore and written in blank verse, and the historic but slight *Síðasti víkingurinn* (1936; The last viking), which is the first in a curious line of Icelandic plays about Jörgen Jörgensen (1780–1841), a Danish-born rebel captain in the

Royal British Navy, who during the summer of 1809 proclaimed himself "king of Iceland" and subsequently "reigned" as a popular and enlightened ruler during the brief summer months until his arrest and deportation to Australia, where he died an outlaw.

Einarsson is the first Icelandic writer to devote his writing efforts to play-writing. He remained devoted to the theater and specifically to Sigurður Guðmundsson's ideal of an Icelandic national theater, putting in great personal effort to help realize this dream, which earned him the name "Father of the National Theater." Accordingly, when the National Theater opened in 1950, it did so with a lavish, albeit traditional production of *Nýársnóttin*.

During the last decades of the nineteenth century amateur theater activities became quite common in Reykjavík as well as in the various villages around the coast of the country and not least in the farming communities, although none of the companies were long-lived. Many villages saw productions of plays by local playwrights, and theater became an important communal activity as well as the most popular form of entertainment, a status that it has retained to this day. These playwrights were all amateurs, however, and did not pursue or develop their craft any further. The amateur activities outside Reykjavík are without precedent and can be seen as a direct result of Guðmundsson's idealism. People had come to realize that, in Jochumsson's words, "acting out the life of our nation" was a meaningful way of creating an awareness of a national identity.

EARLY FLOURISH

Important for the further development of playwriting was the formation in 1897 of the Reykjavík Theater Company, which aimed at raising the level of production and furthering the cause of Icelandic drama. Indriði Einarsson was one of the active company members during its formative years, directing a number of the early productions. In 1907 the company produced his *Nýársnóttin* in a much revised version, a production that became the standard for all subsequent productions of the play. In 1908 the same happened with Jochumsson's *Skugga-Sveinn*. These two productions can be said to mark the beginning of the first proper and unbroken "period" in the history of Icelandic playwriting since, during the next decade or so, there were first productions of a number of outstanding plays and at least three new, important playwrights came into prominence: Einar H. Kvaran (1859–1938), who has a greater reputation as a novelist than as a playwright (see p. 321); Jóhann Sigurjónsson (1880–1919; see pp. 348–49); and Guðmundur Kamban (1888–1945; see pp. 350–51).

Einar H. Kvaran, the oldest of the three, stands in the shadow of his two younger contemporaries. A lesser playwright, he is still one who consistently displayed a mastery of dramatic form, despite the fact that his playwriting efforts were incidental. Like Indriði Einarsson, he was actively involved during the formative years of the Reykjavík Theater Company, directing plays, and giving advice on repertory. When Kvaran wrote theater criticism, it was evident that he had worked in the theater and learned the ropes, which could hardly be said of reviewers before him. Kvaran's best-known play is *Lénharður fógeti* (1913; Bailiff Leonard), a historical drama, while his subsequent plays — *Syndir annarra* (1913; Other people's sins), *Hallsteinn og Dóra* (1931; Hallsteinn and Dora), and *Jósafat* (1932; Jo-saphat), a dramatization of one of his novels — all have a contemporary setting. *Hallsteinn og Dóra* is a finely wrought yet naive spiritualist drama that enjoyed great popularity. It is essentially realistic until the last act, which takes place in the afterlife, on a plane of existence where human shortcomings and sins are not only forgiven but also too petty to thrive.

Jóhann Sigurjónsson's debut play on the stage was *Bóndinn á Hrauni* (1908; English trans.: *The Hraun Farm* [1916]), a romantic drama set in the country. This he followed up with a romantic tragedy, *Fjalla-Eyvindur* (1911; English trans.: *Eyvind of the Hills* [1916]), his outstanding achievement, which was produced a year later at the prestigious Royal Theater in Copenhagen, the first Icelandic play to be thus exported, although Sigurjónsson had already had an unperformed play that had been published in Denmark — *Dr. Rung* (1905) — warmly received by none other than Georg Brandès. *Fjalla-Eyvindur* was subsequently seen in many cities in Scandinavia and on the continent of Europe as well as in New York in 1916, and it remains to date among the most frequently performed Icelandic plays abroad. Sigurjónsson followed this success with *Galdra-Loftur* (1914; The wish), known in Danish as *Ønsket*, a play that, at the time, seemed likely to meet with even more international success than *Fjalla-Eyvindur*, but the outbreak of the First World War aborted all plans for productions in various European cities outside Scandinavia. Sigurjónsson's last work was *Mörður Valgarðsson* (1917; The liar), known in Danish as *Løgneren*, an epic play about one of the main characters of *Njáls saga*, written on commission from the Royal Theater for a foreign audience supposedly unfamiliar with the source. It was not seen in Iceland until 1970, when, possibly, the time was at last felt to be right for dramatic treatment of this beloved saga. The play was long considered the only failure of a master playwright, but a 1980s radio production helped rectify that evaluation.

Like *Skugga-Sveinn*, *Fjalla-Eyvindur* is a play on outlawry. The story is drawn from orally preserved tales of real-life characters outlawed in the eighteenth century. The subject of the drama is the tragedy of individuals sacrificing wealth and social status — in fact, everything — for love. In four acts the play tells the story of Halla, a well-to-do farmer's widow, who hires Eyvindur as a farmhand without knowing that he is a wanted thief. Eyvindur stays at her farm one summer under an assumed name and proves to be both honest and resourceful. The two fall in love, and, when the neighboring farmers discover Eyvindur's true identity, he has no alternative but to escape to the mountains. Halla, whose many suitors are simply bothersome to her in their inferiority, has little sympathy with the envy and pettiness of her neighbors and decides to leave everything in order to go with him. She thus sacrifices worldly goods for love and freedom. The couple spend a happy time hunting in the mountains, where they eventually have a daughter. They are later joined by another outlaw, Arnes, whose love and respect for Halla makes his life a misery. Arnes decides to leave in order to try his luck on his own, but shortly afterward the sheriff's men approach, having discovered their hideout. Halla realizes that they will never be able to escape with the child, so she drowns her daughter by throwing her into a waterfall. Thus, a blissful summer scene is transformed into a horrifying tragedy. The last act is set in a makeshift hut somewhere in the mountains during a blizzard. There is no food, and the couple are freezing to death. Under these conditions love has become a burden and is about to turn into hate, and the audience wonders whether the couple will end up killing each other. There are two endings available to this play. In the original and normally used ending, the couple are separated in the blizzard, and nothing remains but death. In the formerly popular ending, which Sigurjónsson wrote in order to please a great Norwegian actress, a stray horse all of a sudden comes to the door of the hut, and, consequently, the couple's lives are miraculously saved by an abundance of horse meat.

The international reputation of the play in its time rested not simply on its being an exotic curiosity. It is an extremely well-crafted neoromantic tragedy whose characters remain intriguing and credible in the depth of their feelings, despite the beautiful, at times even heightened language. Furthermore, in the character of Halla, Sigurjónsson created a full-blooded neoromantic tragic heroine for his times.

Sigurjónsson's *Galdra-Loftur*, his other outstanding but lesser play, is also based on folklore. The protagonist here is Loftur, a character who, like the play itself, is indebted to Shakespeare's *Hamlet*. Loftur is a student at the Skálholt cathedral school who, driven by excessive ambition and by the social aspirations of his father, makes a pact with the devil in order to learn the greatest secrets hidden to other people. Thus, like Halla, Loftur is made of the right stuff for tragedy as he has become obsessed with his illogical yearning to rise above the common crowd. Here, Sigurjónsson wrote some of his finest poetic passages in prose, as, for instance, in the famous monologue when he has Loftur take the girl he supposedly loves on an imaginary flying carpet ride. The ending works effectively and has proved to be very powerful in production. Here, Loftur conjures up all the dead bishops buried under the cathedral but dies as he is reaching out to receive the all-important book from the last in the line of bishops.

Guðmundur Kamban became something of a myth during his lifetime and just after his death. He was an aspiring writer and a student in Copenhagen at the time of Sigurjónsson's 1912 success at the Royal Theater. His first play was *Hadda Padda* (1914; English trans.: *Hadda Padda* [1917]), a romantic portrayal of love in the Icelandic countryside, very reminiscent of Sigurjónsson's *Fjalla-Eyvindur*, with a tragic ending where the betrayed heroine throws herself over the edge of a cliff. The play was premiered at the Royal Theater to no less praise than *Fjalla-Eyvindur* had met with two years earlier. *Hadda Padda* was seen in Reykjavík a year later and then followed there by another romantic play, *Konungsglíman* (1918; Wrestling before the king), which had been turned down by the Royal Theater in 1915. *Konungsglíman* is a far inferior play, a crude mixture of melodrama and romanticism, brimming with primitive passion, set against a backdrop of erupting volcanoes, and clearly aimed at playing up to the romantic idealism with which foreign peoples often viewed a then-distant Iceland.

Kamban became disillusioned with the cultural life of Copenhagen, and in 1915 he settled in New York in the hope of finding a wider and more receptive audience there. Although he had no luck in America and returned virtually bankrupt to Copenhagen after only two years, his visit eventually became worth his while, as is evident in his next plays. *Marmari* (1918; Marble) is his first social satire, set among the bourgeoisie in a cosmopolitan city. It reflects the influence of American social realist writers on Kamban and his newly discovered interest in social issues, especially the legal system and prison reform. *Marmari* is an impressive yet deeply flawed play, centered around a single character who at times is rather undramatic in that he becomes a mouthpiece for the author's views. Kamban's next piece, *Vér morðingjar* (1920; English trans.: *We Murderers* [1970]), constitutes perhaps his greatest achievement in playwriting. Here, Kamban deals with an unhappy marriage and the circumstances leading to a blameless husband's murder of his wife. The play carries an echo of Henrik Ibsen's *A Doll's House* (1879), but, where Ibsen argues that the wife must inevitably leave her husband, Kamban argues the husband's case. Helga Kress says in her pioneering study of Kamban:

The play is also a satire on American society, with its adulation of the meretricious, amusement, and superficial values. The corruption of society is reflected in the characters themselves, their way of life, attitudes, and actions. . . . In this play Kamban sets out to destroy the deeply rooted concept of the born criminal — the criminal type. In [the husband's] place we could all have become criminals — no murder is horrible except that by the state, for it cannot be extenuated by passion. Of such a murder we all share the guilt — and in this respect we are all murderers. (*Gudmundur Kamban*, 114)

Kamban's subsequent output for the theater is varied and uneven. His satiric fantasy *Sendiherrann frá Júpíter* (1927; The ambassador from Jupiter) was a disaster when first produced in Copenhagen, while his late comedies, such as *Stórlæti* (1941; Grandezza) and *Vöf* (1941; Complexes), show a master playwright at ease with his material. His adaptation for the stage of his own historical novel *Skálholt* was popular with audiences (see pp. 351, 375–76).

After the flourishing of Icelandic playwriting during the years 1908–20, when both Jóhann Sigurjónsson and Guðmundur Kamban came of age and produced their best work, the genre declined and did not regain some of its former status until the 1960s and 1970s. The period effected no change in the writers' living conditions; both Sigurjónsson and Kamban had left the country already before the First World War in order to break away from the isolation of Icelandic letters and try their luck with a broader public in Copenhagen and on the continent of Europe. Kamban remained in Copenhagen for the most part, working as a writer and stage director, while Sigurjónsson, a celebrity lauded to the skies in Copenhagen and elsewhere, failed to follow up his two early successes of *Fjalla-Eyvindur*, which was seen in some twenty countries, and *Galdra-Loftur*, and his premature death in 1919, together with the first production of Kamban's *Vér morðingjar* in 1920, can be seen as marking the end of an era sometimes considered the golden age of Icelandic playwriting.

INCIDENTAL PLAYWRITING, 1920–1960

Partly owing to internal strife and financial difficulties, the Reykjavík Theater Company was no longer as well equipped to deal with new drama. As a result, the 1920s produced few noteworthy playwrights, with the possible exception of Steinn Sigurðsson (1872–1940), whose moral comedies and melodramas set in fishing villages, such as *Stormar* (1922; Storms), were frequently performed, and Kristín Sigfúsdóttir (1876–1953), whose debut was *Tengdamamma* (1924; Mother-in-law). Sigfúsdóttir is the first important woman playwright, but the early promise that she displayed in *Tengdamamma* remained unfulfilled in her subsequent plays in spite of considerable ambition (see also p. 526). Significantly, both playwrights were first produced outside Reykjavík, although both were eventually to grace the Iðnó stage. Other playwrights at the time were somewhat hampered by the still looming presence of Jóhann Sigurjónsson.

The 1930s saw a few moderately successful attempts at writing realistic dramas about fishermen and workers, most notably the somewhat impressionistic *Brimhljóð* (1939; The sound of breaking waves) by Loftur Guðmundsson (1906–78), who subsequently became a prolific writer of comedies for stage and radio, his best work in the genre evident in *Seðlaskipti og ástir* (1948; Money and love), while his knack for parody proved fruitful when he turned to screenwriting, as evidenced by his folkloristic *Síðasti bærinn í dalnum* (1950; The last farm in the valley). The decade produced two highly popular adaptations of novels by Jón Thoroddsen, inspired by the precedent set by the German *Volksstück* (lit. "folk piece"). *Piltur og stúlka* (1933; Lad and lass), adapted for the stage by Emil Thoroddsen, and *Maður og kona* (1934; Man and woman), adapted by Emil Thoroddsen and Indriði Waage, both stayed true to the Jochumsson tradition of larger-than-life character portrayal (on the novels themselves, see pp. 295–96). The year 1934 also saw Halldór Laxness's first play, the Strindberg-inspired *Straumrof* (Short circuit), which can justifiably be called the first *modern* play as regards subject matter and parodic style, although the author never placed any worth on this drama, claiming to have written it in just three days in order to relax while writing his epic novel *Sjálfstætt fólk* (1934–35; English trans.: *Independent People* [1945]; see p. 384). Expressionistic in tone while subtly satiric, this Laxness play provides the cue for a spate of expressionist one-act plays, most of which remain unperformed. The most prolific writer of these was the Icelandic Canadian Guttormur J. Guttormsson (see p. 624).

The 1940s produced two outstanding yet very different plays in the enormously popular *Gullna hliðið* (1941; English trans.: *The Golden Gate*, in *Fire and Ice* [1967]), by the poet Davið Stefánsson (1896–1964; see p. 391), and *Uppstigning* (1945, Ascension), the only play by the author and scholar Sigurður Nordal (1888–1972; see p. 365). The decade also produced several fine comedies, some of which have become minor classics, including *Leynimelur 13* (1943; 13 Hideaway), which was cowritten by three authors.

Gullna hliðið belatedly completed the romantic folklore tradition in playwriting and achieved immediate and lasting popularity. Based on a popular folktale, it warmly describes simple country folk on a fantastic journey to heaven. It tells the story of an old farmer's wife who has her heart set on getting the soul of her deceased husband into heaven. The farmer had been thoroughly dishonest during his lifetime, was continually brought up on charges of stealing, and hardly ever opened his mouth without a string of curses passing his lips. His soul, of course, is no better, and, although the wife keeps it in a small bag she carries with her, the farmer's voice keeps uttering foul language from within. It is a rough journey; there are steep mountains to climb, clouds to wade through, little devils to fend off, and, last but not least, the archenemy himself, who has come to claim the farmer's soul, his prized possession. The wife manages to trick the devil several times through her cunning resourcefulness and eventually reaches heaven's gate. She knocks on the door, and Saint Peter opens it. After consulting his register he says he is sorry but this particular farmer will have to go to the other place. The wife pleads with Saint Peter, trying to persuade him to make an exception, but he is adamant. Eventually, she pretends to give up and asks to be allowed a brief glimpse through the gate since she has come this far. Saint Peter sympathizes with the woman and opens the gate just a crack. The wife is overwhelmed by what she sees and asks Saint Peter to open the gate a little more. He complies, but then the wife quickly throws the bag containing her husband's soul inside and makes a run for home. She knows that whatever has entered through the Golden Gate will never be cast out. Stefánsson wrote three other plays, large-scale historical epics for big casts, but none of these were successful.

Nordal's very Pirandellian *Uppstigning* is a well-structured and sophisticated modern comedy about a young clergyman's identity crises and failed rebellion against small-town morals. His frustration with his role in life eventually leads him into a confrontation with the author as well as with the producer, who join hands in bringing him to his senses and literally drag him back into the action just in time for the conclusion. While Stefánsson's *Gullna hliðið* can be considered the last great play of the romantic tradition, Nordal's *Uppstigning* can be regarded as the first postwar play.

Apart from Nordal's *Uppstigning* and a handful of comedies, historical plays were prominent during the 1940s and 1950s, a late response, perhaps, to Sigurður Guðmundsson's call, but many of these are rather stilted literary works rather than suitable plays for performance.

Agnar Þórðarson (1917–2006) was the most prominent playwright on the scene during the 1950s. Inspired by the possibilities of the new National Theater, he began writing *Þeir koma í haust* (1955; Autumn return) as early as 1951, a historical drama based on myths about the fate of Nordic settlers in Greenland, but his real breakthrough came with a comedy, the enormously popular *Kjarnorka og kvenhylli* (1955; English trans.: *Atoms and Madams*, in *Fire and Ice* [1967]). Here, as well as in most of his subsequent plays, Þórðarson lightly satirizes the lifestyle of the bourgeoisie without ever becoming overtly critical. Þórðarson is at his best in his comedies, although these may eventually prove to be too slight to have any lasting value. He is also a pioneer in radio drama, the first Icelandic playwright to use this medium for serious dramatic writing, penning both single plays and several series that enjoyed enormous popularity. His early work for radio arguably makes Þórðarson's audience the largest any Icelandic playwright has ever had.

Another significant comic talent to emerge during the 1950s is that of Jónas Árnason (1923–98). Influenced by the revue genre, he penned several musical comedies with his brother, the jazz composer Jón Múli Árnason (1921–2002), including *Deleríum búbónis* (1959; Bubonic delirium), while his most significant work belongs to the 1960s and 1970s.

THE ABSURD AS SOCIAL SATIRE

The 1960s were characterized by profound social change, which, in turn, is reflected in significant changes in theatrical style and tastes, notably a heightened sense of values, together with a growing awareness among writers and theater artists of their social responsibility. By this time the postwar wealth and affluence had begun to expose the increasingly dominant signs of hollow materialism on all levels of society. It became evident to the socially conscious artists that the fast-growing population of the Reykjavík area and the numerous towns around the coasts would gradually lose touch with its rural origins and even its sense of history.

This changing awareness may explain in part the fact that Icelandic playwriting rose to prominence again during the 1960s and 1970s, although another important contributing factor was the new and passionate belief in the possibilities of playwriting, which coincided with fresh inspiration from the European theater of the absurd. The National Theater had failed during its first decade to make a difference to playwriting, but — with the Reykjavík Theater Company turning fully professional, the formation of fringe theater groups, and, to a lesser degree, television — playwrights were able to get their work produced more readily than before. Consequently, more writers were able to devote their energies to writing plays. The 1960s produced several playwrights who made a career of the theater, most of whom had pursued theater studies in Europe. These include Jökull Jakobsson (1933–78), Oddur Björnsson (b. 1932), Guðmundur Steinsson (1925–96), Erlingur E. Halldórsson (b. 1930), and the stage designer Birgir Engilberts (1946–98), while the end of the decade marked the playwriting debuts of two significant women writers, the novelist Svava Jakobsdóttir (1930–2004) and the poet Nína Björk Árnadóttir (1941–2000).

The impressionistic Jökull Jakobsson is often considered the leading playwright of the 1960s and 1970s, and he is certainly the most prolific. At the same time, the theater of the absurd was instrumental in the development of Icelandic playwriting during these years and served as a liberating factor for writers such as Oddur Björnsson, Erlingur E. Halldórsson, Birgir Engilberts, and Guðmundur Steinsson.

Jakobsson's second play, *Hart í bak* (1962; Hard-a-port), broke box office records and became instrumental in creating the new dedication to playwriting on the part of the theaters. Here was a writer with a fine ear for the local, everyday speech of common people, supplemented with an impressionistic lyricism and a nostalgic kind of tragicomedy. It is one of the chief hallmarks of Jakobsson as a writer that his characters speak in a living idiom, as opposed to the literary idiom of plays by earlier playwrights. It is a trait already apparent in his first play, the satiric comedy *Pókók* (1961). His stature as a major playwright was secured in subsequent plays, including *Sjóleiðin til Bagdad* (1965; English trans.: *The Seaway to Bagdad*, in *Modern Nordic Plays* [1973]), *Sumarið '37* (1968; The summer of '37), *Dómínó* (1972; Dominoes), *Kertaljós* (1973; Candlelight), *Klukkustrengir* (1973; Bell chords), *Herbergi 213* (1975; Room 213), and the posthumously produced *Sonur skóarans og dóttir bakarans* (1978; The shoemaker's son and the baker's daughter) and *Í öruggri borg* (1980; In a strong city). During his short playwriting career Jakobsson wrote some twenty plays for stage, radio, and television, making effective use of influences as seemingly disparate as Chekhov, Tennessee Williams, and Harold Pinter.

In the world of Jakobsson's plays there is usually a juxtaposition, and consequently a dramatic tension, between inside and outside, the here and now and the there and then, between Iceland, or a certain part of it, and the rest of the world. Thus, in his early plays there is usually a character who is about to leave the stale atmosphere of his surroundings in order to follow a dream, or escape one that will never be realized, in search of either adventure or simply a better life elsewhere, usually in another country. Jakobsson's later plays, on the other hand, often feature a character who has just returned from the outside world and who, with his mere presence, disrupts the apparent tranquillity of the world he has returned to. This calls to mind Tennessee Williams and even Eugene O'Neill and his treatment of pipe dreams.

Jakobsson frequently confronts us with a world that is doomed and characters who are conditioned by their surroundings. Thus *Hart í bak* presents a world that will simply be submerged by time, and at the end of the play most of the characters leave it, one to an old people's home, another to get married, and yet another to seek his fortune abroad, etc. The characters are faced with a choice, and in this play they are free to make a choice, which is rarely, if at all, the case in the later plays.

There are similar concerns in *Sjóleiðin til Bagdad*, which is a transitional play where the playwright is seen to be moving toward his mature style, as well as in *Sumarið '37*, where he moves his setting away from the slums and poverty of the earlier plays into the world of the affluent bourgeois. The gradual change in style through these two plays following *Hart í bak* is a move away from the outspoken, and even the eloquent, toward dramatizing inner conflict, making effective use of pauses and silences as an integral part of speech. This style is mastered in *Dómínó*, a realistic play on the surface but brimming with inner dramatic conflict underneath the veneer, expressed in a lyric text.

After *Dómínó* Jakobsson pursues even further the drama of inner conflict, yet complementing it with stylized satire, using clichés and even stereotypes as dramatic tools. This is evident in *Klukkustrengir*, which can be interpreted as something of a mystery play, in *Herbergi 213*, and in that powerful, modernly stylized *danse macabre* that is *Í öruggri borg*, while *Kertaljós* and *Sonur skóarans og dóttir bakarans* are in categories of their own. *Kertaljós* is a fairly explicit play, set in a mental asylum, and deals with characters who, for the sake of their sanity, are compelled to rebel against their conditioning. *Sonur skóarans og dóttir bakarans* is on a grander scale and more complex than Jakobsson's other plays. Here, a young man returns home from a distant war, upsetting the entire community, especially since he is followed by someone determined to bring him to court as a war criminal, and by Kap, his wealthy, mysterious boss, who can be seen as a personification of capitalism itself and promises to bring wealth and prosperity to the community by setting up an ammunition factory. Essentially a morality play about collective responsibility, and more than ten years in the making, *Sonur skóarans og dóttir bakarans* is Jakobsson's only attempt at writing large-scale drama.

Jónas Árnason in some respects resembles Jakobsson, at least in his concern with the disappearance, or even the prostitution, of older values. There is, furthermore, a resemblance detectable in his romantic tone, especially when Árnason is describing life as yet unspoiled by postwar materialism, although his style is more openly humorous than Jakobsson's. Árnason's plays are comedies in the traditional sense, mostly *pièce bien faite*, or well-crafted plays consciously aimed at a very general audience, although his moral comedies constitute his most outstanding achievement. Árnason began writing light, satiric plays with songs, including the popular *Deleríum búbonis*, but his best work is contained in his one-act plays such as *Koppalogn* (1967; God's blessed millpond) as well as in *Skjaldhamrar* (1975; Operation Shield Rock), a well-written play that has enjoyed lasting popularity both at home and abroad. Here, Árnason confronts the audience with a secluded and tranquil prewar world that is disrupted by the presence of British troops in search of an alleged German spy who turns out to be a blundering, young natural scientist missing his mother's cooking.

Although Halldór Laxness (1902–98) was primarily a novelist as well as a prolific essayist, he made the occasional foray into theater. *Straumrof*, his cynical 1934 play, is a well-shaped thriller, written in Strindberg fashion and expressionistic in tone, where highly strung bourgeois characters are locked in deadly combat with one another. His second play was *Silfurtúnglið* (1954; The silvery moon), which owes a great deal to Bertolt Brecht and is a biting satire or morality play about a young nation's loss of innocence and consequent fall from grace. For a period of several years during the early 1960s Laxness temporarily abandoned the novel in order to write three important plays for the stage, all of which are marked by his special brand of absurdist theater. *Strompleikurinn* (1961; The chimney play) is an excellent satiric comedy where nothing is real and the characters make a living from faking everything they are supposed to stand for; *Prjónastofan Sólin* (1966; Knitting workshop "The Sun") is an ambitious and complex, almost surreal allegory on the world situation; and, finally, the subtle Taoist comedy on values called *Dúfnaveislan* (1966; English trans.: *The Pigeon Banquet*, in *Modern Nordic Plays* [1973]) focuses on an old and humble presser of men's trousers who discovers the means to get rid of all his useless money by inviting the upper crust of society to a pigeon banquet.

From Laxness's plays, as well as those written by other Icelandic absurdists, we can deduce that Icelandic absurdism is satiric rather than metaphysical, closer in method to early Edward Albee and Arthur Kopit than to Samuel Beckett and other European absurdist playwrights. It has produced plays that deal with values or even a social situation, rather than with states of mind or the human condition in general. Erlingur E. Halldórsson, Odd-ur Björnsson, and Birgir Engilberts all wrote absurdist allegories during the 1960s.

Halldórsson, a disciple of Brecht and Jean Vilar, wrote political allegories such as *Reiknivélin* (1963; The calculator) and *Minkanir* (1974; English trans.: *Mink*, in *Modern Nordic Plays* [1973]), essentially about the presence of a foreign army base in Iceland, which was a major political issue during the cold war. Engilberts wrote satiric allegories about the destructive nature of materialism, set in highly concentrated situations in one-act plays, such as *Loftbólur* (1966; Bubbles), *Hversdagsdraumur* (1972; An everyday dream) and *Ósigur* (1972; Defeat). In *Loftbólur* three sleepless painters are busy painting an invisible wall. The painters' lives are empty and joyless, while the demands made on them by materialism will push them ever further away from themselves. In *Hversdagsdraumur* a married couple has shrunk and eventually disappears among their material possessions. Engilberts virtually stopped writing long before his untimely death.

Björnsson, an admirer of Beckett and Eugène Ionesco, is often considered the chief exponent of absurdist playwriting, even though his plays can hardly be considered purely absurdist, if such a judgment is valid at all. Apart from numerous early one-act absurdist plays, such as *Köngulóin* (1963; The spider), *Jóðlíf* (1964; English trans.: *Yolk-Life*, in *Modern Nordic Plays* [1973]), and *Tíu tilbrigði* (1968; English trans.: *Ten Variations*, in *Modern Nordic Plays* [1973]), some of which are characterized by satiric traits, Björnsson's product for the theater consists for the most part of satires and comedies, which frequently evolve into relentless dramatic games. He sees the theater, not as a frame around dramatic action, but as an expressive instrument in itself. Thus, his stage plays often present pure, non-Aristotelian theater forms that would be inconceivable in other mediums and are compositions of situations in theatrical time and space rather than storytelling.

Björnsson's greatest ambition is evident in three large-scale, "universal" plays. *Dansleikur* (1974; Dance play), based on material that he explored in at least two previous plays, is set at the court of Alexander Borgia during a feast and presents a world gone mad through passionate meaninglessness. In an orgy of cruelty and killings any humanistic effort at creating sense and peace is thwarted since words and ideals are meaningless. *Eftir konsertinn* (1983; After the concert) depicts another feast turned orgy and, under the veneer of a drawing-room comedy, evolves into an allegory about a world gone mad and the futility of revolution. His most ambitious piece, *13. krossferðin* (1993; The thirteenth crusade), is a dramatic poem on an epic scale and can even be seen as a coda to the playwright's oeuvre. The play is about three soldiers on a futile search for their war, if not *the* war. The three set off from a happy fiesta, a celebration of life in a Spanish village, travel through several layers of history as well as through myth without ever finding their war, yet manage to leave death and destruction in their path. As the action unfolds it becomes clear, not only that they have the same dreams and nightmares, but also that they are aspects of the same Freudian personality, an id, an ego, and a superego. This is evident, for example, in the recurrent anecdote that Stefán (the superego) tells Seppi (the id) every night before they go to sleep, where he tells him to observe that he is split in three and his enemies are within. Eventually, the superego kills the other two. The ego is killed after raping and plundering, while the killing of the id is akin to an act of mercy. On one level, the play can be read as an allegorical journey through life, a kind of bildungsroman, where the "hero" reaches maturity in the end.

While Björnsson's subject material is inspired by the Renaissance, his stance is inspired by the Enlightenment as well as by the new and progressive playwriting of the postwar period, and he found his models for composition in classical music. Indeed, his methods are reminiscent of composers' methods as he repeatedly uses threads, themes, routines, and refrains again and again, elaborating on them, or interweaving them differently. In *Dansleikur*, *Eftir konsertinn*, and *13. krossferðin* he holds up a mirror to a morally corrupt world in dissolution, one where human rationality and human endeavor are threatened by a savage irrationality. Björnsson can be considered a complex ironist who exposes a chaotic, amoral world where antisocial forces pose a threat to human sensibility.

Guðmundur Steinsson is one of the playwrights liberated by the apparent freedom of absurdism, although he was initially influenced by Brecht. He evolved a satiric style of his own during the 1970s and wrote several highly popular, albeit serious, satiric plays, if such a thing exists. Relatively late in life Steinsson was to become the contemporary Icelandic playwright most often performed in other countries. His best-known play is *Stundarfriður* (1979; A brief respite), which broke attendance records at the National Theater and was subsequently seen in various European countries as well as in Japan and America. The play is a satiric portrayal of a crumbling family in a mobile society moving quickly toward its doom, increasingly driven by the growing demands of individual careers and materialism. Under the veneer of the happy family the individual family members are seen to be essentially egocentric and apathetic. Steinsson's other popular successes include *Lúkas* (1975; Matthew), an allegory on greed, and *Sólarferð*

(1976; Viva España), a comedy about holidaymakers abroad who unwittingly display their lack of values as well as sides to their characters that are normally hidden within their own society. His satiric allegories from the 1980s about a human race sans values, sans faith, and, consequently, on the verge of global disaster were less successful in terms of the box office. These include the sparely written *Garðveisla* (1982; The garden party), which daringly juxtaposes biblical myth (ranging from Genesis to the Crucifixion) and the situation of an affluent, modern family giving a garden party, and *Brúðarmyndin* (1987; The wedding portrait). Steinsson used simple, even simplistic everyday speech and often made effective comic use of clichéd talk and thought.

Nína Björk Árnadóttir and Svava Jakobsdóttir, two important women playwrights, emerged around 1970. Already a celebrated poet, Árnadóttir graduated from acting school before trying her hand at playwriting. She had her theatrical debut with two one-act plays, jointly titled *Í súpunni* (1969; Trouble), and followed this with a full-length play, *Fótatak* (1972; Footfalls). Her most significant plays for the stage are *Hvað sögðu englarnir?* (1979; What did the angels say?), *Súkkulaði handa Silju* (1982; Hot chocolate for Silja), and *Fugl sem flaug á snúru* (1985; A bird caught on a wire). The world of Árnadóttir's plays is a harsh, cold, and unjust capitalist society where any rebellion is romantic, shortsighted, and doomed to failure; it is a world where, according to *Fugl sem flaug á snúru*, there are both "systems and isms" in place to exploit and, eventually, crush the individual. In *Súkkulaði handa Silju* a single, working-class mother struggles to build a future for her only daughter and gains nothing by it but further humiliation. In the end she takes her daughter's life for much the same reasons that George takes his brother Lenny's life in John Steinbeck's *Of Mice and Men* (1937). In *Fugl sem flaug á snúru* it is as if time and causality have been dissolved. The events flow freely back and forth in time and space and among the dead as well as among the living, most of the characters are naive and their discourse lyric more than anything else, and the form of the play is essentially circular — the "feminine" circle — where everything eventually folds back to the beginning and the audience has witnessed an unchangeable situation. Thus, unlike most plays written a few years previously, this one offers no solution to the problems of the world. On one level, Árnadóttir's plays address the problem of leaving childhood and adapting to the world of grown-ups, or, rather, adapting to the world of men, since it is masculinity that rules supreme while femininity is kept down and exploited.

The novelist Jakobsdóttir's debut play, *Hvað er í blýhólkunum?* (1971; What's in the cornerstone?), is written in the style of documentary drama and deals in essence with women's rights, the first Icelandic play to do so exclusively, providing a clearheaded look at women's position in society, underlining a woman's right to a career of her own and equal rights. At the time it was a refreshing approach to playwriting in Iceland. In her few subsequent plays, like *Æskuvinir* (1976; Childhood friends), Jakobsdóttir applied a different, allegorical style, although her concerns remained similar. Her most impressive play is *Lokaæfing* (1983; Dress rehearsal), set in a private fallout shelter that an engineer has built under his house. The affluent engineer and his wife decide to test their plan for nuclear disaster by shutting the world out and staying in the shelter for a whole month. The rehearsal, of course, ends in disaster as the couple's relationship begins to crumble during the early stages and rapidly deteriorates until, eventually, the deadlocked situation culminates when the engineer kills an unexpected intruder who turns out to be his wife's young piano student. The wife grimly concludes that the only thing that can save them is nuclear war. Within this realistic framework Jakobsdóttir uses allegory to reflect on the world situation as well as on the relationship between male and female.

CONCLUSION

In his monumental study *World Drama* Allardyce Nicoll claimed, with some justification, that "the Icelandic theatrical genius" fares best when dealing with "the fantastic, the mythical, and the historic" (738), to which should be added another feature, the almost grotesque portrayal of character. Without a doubt this trend can be traced to the important early influence of Sigurður Guðmundsson on his young contemporaries, such as Matthías Jochumsson, whose Skugga-Sveinn became a mythical figure. Prophetically, *Skugga-Sveinn* ends with Skugga-Sveinn taking his final place among the landscape to become part of the Icelandic consciousness and the country's lore. For several successive generations the play became a model for what theater was all about.

It is no surprise, then, that, until the 1960s, the main interest among playwrights lay in the creation of character, with less attention paid to intrigue and plot. A strong romantic trend runs parallel to this. Romanticism is a trait that runs through most Icelandic plays right up to Laxness's pieces, Jakobsson's *Hart í bak*, and Jónas Árnason's *Skjaldhamrar*, while absurdists like Oddur Björnsson and Birgir Engilberts were committed to creating an image of a world that would be credible on its own logical terms.

In *Hart í bak*, the pioneering play of postwar Icelandic drama, it is

almost as if Jakobsson is on one level attempting to deconstruct this character type in Jonathan the Shipwreck-captain. The old and blind Jonathan
stands for a different kind of society now gone and a set of values that have
run aground and become bankrupt. There is no such complication, however, in Árnason's protagonist, Kormákur the Lighthouse-keeper, in *Skjaldhamrar*. He continues to proudly stand guard over the old values as outside
military forces disrupt the peace and his world begins to crumble.

A predominant theme that characterizes most Icelandic plays after the
Second World War is a concern with values, and the plays in themselves
often tend to become idealistic warnings of the dangers inherent in the
corruption of traditional values and in replacing them with a false commer-
cialism. The persistence of this thematic concern may stem from Guðmundsson's idealistic, nineteenth-century vision of a theater of moral enlightenment. Too often, however, the serious, moralizing impulse has had a
constraining effect on plays. Moralist traits run through all Laxness's plays
as well as those of Jökull Jakobsson and Guðmundur Steinsson. They constitute a predominant feature of Agnar Þórðarson's plays as well and forms
the backbone of all Jónas Árnason's plays. We find similar concerns in Svava
Jakobsdóttir's allegorical plays of the 1970s and 1980s and in those of Nína
Björk Árnadóttir with their delicately woven texture of everyday realistic
drama juxtaposed with lyricism.

To this day there is still a tendency to rely on the epic tradition, perhaps
understandably as the epic seems to have provided writers with access to
audiences. There has always been a strong connection between the theater
and epic literature in Iceland. Thus, the plays that are based on either
folklore or historical themes have normally reached a broad, general public,
and the best plays in this tradition have had a secure place in the popular
repertory of the Icelandic theater. It was Laxness, himself the master storyteller, who always made a clear distinction between epic and drama and
succeeded in creating theatrical works that present the audience with an
image of a world contracted within the form of his plays.

Icelandic Theater since 1975: *Hávar Sigurjónsson*

Theater in Iceland has seen a number of significant changes during the last
quarter of the twentieth century. As the previous chapter has shown the

twenty-five years prior to that were the first years of professional theater activity in Iceland, with the opening of the National Theater in 1950 and the Reykjavík Theater Company turning fully professional in 1963. The Akureyri Theater Company turned professional in 1972 and, thus, became the first and, to date, the only professional theater company operating entirely outside the capital, Reykjavík. The Reykjavík Theater Company was founded in 1897, and its profile was semiprofessional in that the actors were amateurs to a degree: they were not professionally trained but had acquired their acting skills through practice. Their talent was second to none, as this was the only outlet available for those who had an ambition to pursue an acting career. Serious thespians in the capital area grouped together within the Reykjavík Theater Company.

During the 1930s and 1940s a number of young people sought acting training overseas, in England and Denmark mostly, and returned to form the core of the National Theater's ensemble in 1950, along with many of the older generation of actors and directors from the Reykjavík Theater Company. Contrary to the expectations of many, the Reykjavík Theater Company did not fold but entered into a vigorous competition with the National Theater, a situation that reached a new level when the Reykjavík Theater Company turned professional in 1963. During the 1960s a number of experimental theater groups were established; most were short-lived, but they had a strong impact on the established theaters as many of the group members became the establishment's leading actors and directors during the 1970s and 1980s. Many of these individuals remain among Iceland's most influential theater artists.

Owing to the smallness of the Icelandic theater community, the influence of individuals on various aspects of Icelandic theater is, perhaps, more apparent in Iceland than elsewhere, but another characteristic of Icelandic theater must also be kept in mind. Most of the theater practitioners in Iceland work across the board; that is, they may have established an experimental group, but they are at the same time working at the National Theater or the Reykjavík Theater Company, or even both. Thus, ideas and work methods quickly spread among the theater community, and never has there been a time when a particular method or style has been solely identified as that of a particular group or individual. One result of this situation is that the experimental groups have had neither the time nor the opportunity to develop their own method or recognizable style; another is that the so-called established theaters have followed closely the latest trends and developments on the sometimes hardly discernible Icelandic fringe.

In 1975 a new theater group came into being that pointed the way ahead in many respects as far as Icelandic theater practice is concerned. The People's Theater (Alþýðuleikhúsið) was the first professional company in the country to base its operation entirely on touring year-round with no permanent theater space as a home base or to perform in. During the late 1950s and 1960s a number of summer touring companies were operated, mainly on a commercial basis, but the advent of Icelandic state television in 1966 made a touring commercial summer theater a much riskier business than before. Accordingly, the People's Theater was founded with a very different aim in mind. It had a clearly defined socialist political agenda that it followed through in its productions, which were a far cry from the productions of the established theaters, both in style and in method. Another important aspect of the company that prevented comparison with its predecessors was that its members were all seasoned theater artists with years of diverse professional experience behind them, including acting, directing, writing, choreography, design, and music composition.

All these elements came together most successfully in two productions: *Krummagull* (1975; Raven's gold) and *Skollaleikur* (1976; Blindman's buff), both plays written by Böðvar Guðmundsson (b. 1939) and directed by Þórhildur Þorleifsdóttir (b. 1945). Although Guðmundsson has since written several plays and stage adaptations, his best work is in the field of historical narrative fiction, and as such he belongs to a long line of Icelandic writers who deal with historical subjects in a time-honored tradition. In *Skollaleikur*, which deals with events during Iceland's darkest period of history, the witch hunts of the seventeenth century, he successfully combined his Marxist view of history with real events of a period hitherto ignored by historical writers. The novelty of the play as a piece of writing rested in the author's choice of period, and the play was a long overdue departure from the usual adulation of a glorified literary past. Yet the two plays that he wrote for the People's Theater owed most of their success to a highly innovative and stylized production method, where commedia dell'arte, modern choreography, and music were used in a manner hitherto rarely encountered in Icelandic theater. *Skollaleikur* remains a landmark in Icelandic theatrical history and has rightly long since become a theatrical legend.

The People's Theater changed character in 1978 when it became based in Reykjavík and obtained a permanent performing space in Lindarbær and, later, in Hafnarbíó, a Second World War–era army barracks that had been used as a cinema for thirty years or so. At the same time it turned from being a small touring group to a large theater collective that embraced nearly all young and new actors for a period of five years, from 1978 to 1982. After that, the company changed character once again, this time becoming a producing company that hired artists on a onetime basis, and it continued to operate in this fashion until its final production in 1993.

The People's Theater received an annual grant from the parliament from 1982 until 1993, during which time it was very active, producing a variety of plays. When it closed down, it had certainly served an important role, first in setting the standard for independent theater work, and then in becoming a beacon for a whole generation of theater artists who today form the backbone of Icelandic theater.

RECENT DEVELOPMENTS

During the 1980s a number of new theater groups were established. Most were short-lived, formed as they were by young actors who were primarily creating work for themselves and were, consequently, lacking in long-term theatrical vision; they were quickly disbanded when other, more lucrative theater work became available. Financial and personal considerations had an impact too as most of these groups were operated on an amateur level with regard to salaries, although the members were all professionally trained. The most significant of these enterprises was the Theater Group Emilia, led by the director Guðjón Pedersen (b. 1957) and the dramaturge Hafliði Arngrímsson (b. 1951). Pedersen and Arngrímsson started the company in 1986, and it operated until 1995, receiving official support from the Ministry of Culture during its last two years. Emilia was the first independent company after the People's Theater to have its own permanent theater space, first in Skeifan (1988), a small locale, and later in Héðinshúsið (1993), a space that was later to become Loftkastalinn (see below).

The 1990s saw some significant changes in Icelandic theater groups. First, in 1990, the first children's theater company was established, Möguleikhúsið, a touring company that today, ten years later, is still operating and has twenty-three productions to its credit. Every year Möguleikhúsið visits nearly every preschool and grammar school in the country. While the company has received government support, the amount offered has been insufficient, especially considering Möguleikhúsið's dedication to its mission and its general popularity. The company has produced only new, original work and as such has contributed significantly to the body of Icelandic theater literature for children. It opened its permanent theater space in a building near Reykjavík's Hlemmur square in 1995, where it performs for the general public on weekends. Other groups have since appeared on the scene that tour productions for children and teenagers, in the capital area mostly. As a result the children and young people of the 1990s experienced more theater than any generation before them.

The Hafnarfjörður Theater Company is a professional company that has dedicated itself to the production of new Icelandic drama. To date it has produced nine new plays, nearly all of which have been both artistic and commercial successes, a rare combination indeed. In light of the fact that the company is based in Hafnarfjörður, on the outskirts of Reykjavík, and, thus, competes for its audiences with both the National Theater and the City Theater, its success is particularly significant. From 1996 on the company received an annual state grant as well as a grant from the Hafnarfjörður municipal authorities. In 2005 the Ministry of Culture, the Hafnarfjörður municipal council, and the Hafnarfjörður Theater Company signed a five-year contract, thus securing the financial side of the company for the first time.

In 1995 Icelandic theater saw another new development: the country's first independent commercial theater enterprise was launched. The producing company Flugfélagið Loftur opened with a production of the musical *Hair* (1967) and quickly followed this big success with a production of *The Rocky Horror Picture Show* (1973). It took over Héðinshúsið, turning it into Loftkastalinn, a four-hundred-seat theater space, and operated commercially for the next three years, a critical and popular, if not necessarily a financial, success. Flugfélagið Loftur wanted to make a statement—that it was possible to run a theater company in Iceland without financial support from the government—but at the same time it insisted that, owing to its critical and popular success, such support was its due. Problems escalated for the troubled theater company in May 2000, when it merged with another company to form the Icelandic Theater Company, with two theater buildings at its command, Loftkastalinn and Iðnó. The Reykjavík Cultural Committee signed a three-year contract with the new company that gave it a break on its lease of Iðnó and an annual grant, but despite this the company folded in the fall of 2001, heavily in dept, and unable to meet the terms of the contract.

The influence of Loftkastalinn and later the Icelandic Theater Company can be measured in several ways. Most important, perhaps, is that the young entrepreneurs who stepped into the arena of theater were of a kind not seen before in Icelandic theater. They were market and profit oriented, openly taking a position on the right of the Icelandic political spectrum, flaunting business ideas previously heard only in the corridors of stock exchanges and financial institutions. They intended to go public with the Icelandic Theater Company and turn it into a shareholding company with promises of profits for their investors. As it turned out nobody was interested in buying the offered shares, and the pipe dream of turning Icelandic theater into a business venture collapsed. The damage had, nevertheless, been done, leaving many convinced that a theater that cannot turn a profit is simply a badly run business. In the meantime, the intellectual debate and practical ramifications of theater politics, that is, the artistic direction of the various theater companies, and cultural policy, in the form of municipal and government support, were somewhat ignored during this period. Since the Icelandic Theater Company has ceased to operate, the atmosphere has gradually changed. There are signs that theater activity is becoming more serious again — serious both in approach and in purpose — and that more emphasis is being placed on content and artistic merit and less on instant popularity and profit margins. A further reason for optimism is that this shift is originating among the youngest generation of theater artists.

FRESH WINDS

The general feeling during the 1990s was that of growing theater activity, and, certainly, the number of productions available to the general public during the height of the season is proof of this. On any given weekend some twenty-five to thirty professional productions were on offer in the capital area, and some have, indeed, wondered how the companies managed to survive in a region with no more than 150,000 people, many of whom never go to the theater. Still, companies were selling 350,000–400,000 seats annually, a staggering figure considering that the total population of Iceland at the time numbered around 285,000. At the same time it must be said that the great number of productions on offer did not necessarily signify variety; the homogeneity of Icelandic theater has sometimes been a cause for worry. A greater diversity of style would certainly be desirable, while the public choice of theater on a given night is generally dictated by subject and not by the company as such.

There have been attempts to improve the situation. The National Theater's artistic director, Stefán Baldursson, injected new ideas into the theater scene when in 1992 he brought to the country a team of three from Lithuania — the director Rimas Tuminas, the designer Faustas Latenas, and the composer Vytautas Narbutas — to direct a production of Chekhov's *The*

Seagull (1898). Tuminas had an approch to directing that swept the National Theater's actors off their feet, and the team was to return two more times, staging Molière's *Don Juan* (1665) in 1994 and Chekhov's *Three Sisters* (1901) in 1997. Tuminas's ideas were taken up by two young directors who have dominated the scene for the last few years: Hilmar Jónsson (b. 1964), who founded and still runs the Hafnarfjörður Theater Company, and Baltasar Kormákur (b. 1966), who founded Loftkastalinn and directed its most significant productions but has now turned to filmmaking, with three films to his credit so far.

PLAYWRITING

The Icelandic playwrights who were active during the last twenty-five years of the twentieth century belong to three different generations. During the early 1970s established playwrights were few. Jökull Jakobsson had made a strong debut in 1961 and kept his central place until his untimely death in 1978. Along with other playwrights of his generation, notably Oddur Björnsson and Birgir Engilberts, he helped pave the way for the absurdist element in Icelandic playwriting. Of the same generation was also Guðmundur Steinsson, who wrote close to twenty plays, twelve of which were produced during his lifetime. Steinsson was a dedicated dramatist, totally committed to playwriting without ever paying heed to popular demands or taste. He struck up a working relationship with the National Theater during the 1970s, and, from 1977 to 1996, the year of his death, five of his plays were produced at the National, which, by Icelandic standards, is an exceptional dedication to one playwright.

Birgir Sigurðsson (b. 1937) was a strong newcomer in the early 1970s and had two contemporary social-realist dramas produced during that decade, *Pétur og Rúna* (1972; Peter and Runa) and *Selurinn hefur mannsaugu* (1975; Seals have human eyes). In 1977 he turned out a historical melodrama, *Skáld-Rósa* (Rosa the poet), which played to a large audience. His most notable success was with *Dagur vonar* (1986; Day of hope). It is arguably the most significant Icelandic play of the decade, a truly dramatic piece of writing, where a working-class family of two artistically inclined brothers living with a widowed overworked mother, her alcoholic lover, and an insane sister become the true representatives of the postwar generation.

Although Sigurðsson has often been called the *social-realist of Icelandic theater*, his best writing contains beautiful stage poetry in well-crafted dialogue. After the success of *Dagur vonar* he turned his attention to the writing of novels but returned to the theater in 1998 with a new play,

Óskastjarnan (Wishing star). The play is set in the 1980s on an Icelandic farm where two artistically talented sisters grew up together. One has since left for Hollywood and started a lucrative film career, while the other sacrificed her career to tend to their ailing parents and eventually takes over the farm. It is a play about love, sacrifice, and the true meaning of life, probing the question what makes for a quality life. While it is not Sigurðsson's best, it is certainly a well-constructed play by any standards. Sigurðsson's latest play, *Dynamite*, a philosophical piece about the relationship between Friedrich Nietzsche and his sister, was produced at the National Theater in 2005.

IRONY AND SATIRE

The playwright and director Kjartan Ragnarsson (b. 1945) has written several plays and adapted a number of novels, most of which have been enormously successful. During the 1980s Ragnarsson was the unofficial artistic champion of the Reykjavík Theater Company as his plays and adaptations, more than anything else, shaped the popular character of the company and the successive box office successes of his productions kept the company financially afloat; he was a golden goose indeed. Ragnarsson is at his best as a comic writer, although his serious work reveals a strong social conscience. His popularity as a playwright and adaptor of novels for the stage rests on his finely balanced sense of popular taste and theatrical craftmanship.

The poet and dramatist Sigurður Pálsson (b. 1948) wrote his first play, *Hlaupvídd 6* (Bore 6), in 1977. Since then he has written several plays, most of which have been produced by the Reykjavík Theater Company. A more recent play is *Einhver í dyrunum* (2000; Someone at the door). A once-grand actress has shut herself away from the world in her home and refuses to go out among people. Her husband, a bureaucrat who collects butterflies, has no luck in getting her back to reality. When a young admirer enters her life, she is forced to review the events that caused her to abandon her acting career. In this play of language, theater, and madness the actress is haunted by ghosts of the past until she breaks down and manages to translate her discomfort and pain into speech. Pálsson is in many ways a breed apart in Icelandic drama. His dramatic voice is finely tuned to the poetic possibilities of language, and his formal experiments have largely gone unnoticed. His is a quiet but probably a more lasting voice than that of many others in Icelandic drama of the 1980s and 1990s. Pálsson's latest piece for the theater, *Edit Piaf* (2005), a musical biography of the French singer, was a great success thanks in large part to the performance of Brynhildur Guðjónsdóttir in the title role.

Ólafur Haukur Símonarson (b. 1947) began his writing career in the late 1970s and has turned out to be the most prolific of all Icelandic playwrights. Starting out as a radical socialist with *Blómarósir* (Factory flowers), a play about the plight of women working in a canning factory produced by the People's Theater in 1978, he showed an unmistakable talent for dramatic writing in *Milli skinns og hörunds* (Under your skin), produced at the National Theater in 1982. This play is written in a style of modern stage realism, a style that Icelandic writers had not employed before. It is realistic in character portrayal, dialogue, and emotional motivation, but the narrative structure is epic, making use of cinematic technique in the juxtaposition of scenes. The play is grim and utterly devoid of socialist romanticism in its portrayal of a contemporary working-class family in the early 1980s. It is a political play in the sense that it is a disturbing analysis of people who have lost their social identity and, thus, seek status in material posessions and find emotional gratification in alcohol, violence, and sex — significantly, in that order.

In *Bílaverkstæði Badda* (1987; Baddi's garage) Símonarson turned his dramatic skills to create a psychothriller where the action centers around the return of an old friend to the family of a widowed mechanic, Baddi, and his three grown-up children. This story of murder and betrayal was later turned into a film entitled *Ryð* (1990; Rust), directed by Lárus Ýmir Óskarsson.

Símonarson next teamed up with the City Theater and moved to lighter fare with the musical *Á köldum klaka* (1990; On cold ice) and the play *Kjöt* (1991; Meat), both of which must be regarded as the buildup to his strongest play to date, *Hafið* (1992; English trans.: *The Sea*, in *Contemporary Icelandic Drama* [2001]), where all his best features as a dramatic writer are successfully combined: the dialogue is witty, the characterization is clear, and the two-act structure is a natural part of the dramatic fabric. The social comment is unmistakable but is cleverly integrated into action and situation. It is a play that tackles many important contemporary issues. At its center is a dying man, an old fishing magnate in a fishing town. Owing to the new fishing legislation passed in parliament in the mid-1980s the traditional fishing rights of the area are now his personal capital — a central political issue in Iceland ever since — and his family has gathered around his deathbed, all intent on securing their share of the fortune. The play deals skillfully with the issue of the ownership of the greatest national source of wealth, the fish in the sea. If the fishing rights are sold to a company in a different part of the country, the town will lose its means of survival. Thus, the play takes on another central political issue: the future of the rural townships around the country in the face of a growing centralization in the capital area of Reykjavík.

After *Hafið* Símonarson adapted one of his most popular novels, *Gaura-gangur* (1994; Hullabaloo), a production that was quickly followed by one of the greatest hits of the decade, the musical *Þrek og tár* (1995; Endurance and tears), set in Reykjavík in the 1960s to period music. Next came the social drama *Kennarar óskast* (1998; Teaching vacancies), after which the Hafnarfjörður Theater Company produced *Vitleysingarnir* (2000; The idiots), a social comedy about the 1960s generation now grown desperately middle-aged. The 2001–2 season saw two plays of his produced: *Borðorðin 9* (The nine commandments) at the City Theater, and *Viktoría og Georg* (Victoria and George), a play about the renowned love affair between the literary giant Georg Brandes and the Swedish poet Victoria Benedictsson. Símonarson's latest play is *Halldór í Hollywood* (2005; Halldor in Hollywood). Produced at the National Theater, it is a lighthearted comedy with music about the adventures of the young poet Halldór Laxness trying to become a screenwriter in 1920s Hollywood.

Árni Ibsen (b. 1948) made his debut with *Skjaldbakan kemst þangað líka* (1984; The turtle gets there too), a highly literary play that deals with the relationship between the two American poets Ezra Pound and William Carlos Williams. A fine poet himself, Ibsen next turned his efforts toward comedy and satire, and after two attempts at this dramatic genre in the form of the plays *Afsakið hlé* (1988; Excuse me, an interval) and *Fiskar á þurru landi* (1992; Fish out of water), he unexpectedly produced a highly dramatic piece, *Elín Helena* (1994), a serious inquiry into the possibilities of theatrical form where the dramatic tension is created by constant shifts in time, "real" time being no more important or more physical than historical time; onstage the mind is just as real as the body. The play revolves around the search of a young woman for the true story of her family history, which takes her to the United States, her father having been a soldier stationed in Iceland during his time in the military service. This play probes the search for the real identity of a people faced with half a century of "friendly spiritual occupation," in the author's own words.

Ibsen continued his experiments with dramatic form by combining his findings into his greatest success to date, *Himnaríki* (1995; English trans.: *Heaven*, in *Contemporary Icelandic Drama* [2001]), a marvelously sharp social comedy based on the original staging idea that simultaneous action is carried out for two sets of audiences, which change places during the interval. A group of young people get together at a summer cottage, planning to have the greatest weekend of their lives. But, for people who have the greatest weekend of their lives on a regular basis, the attempt is futile, and the play is a hilarious description of a generation of a well-provided-for superconsumers who have no greater ambition than to fulfill their own physical desires.

Ibsen has since written the farce *Ef ég væri gullfiskur* (1996; If I were a goldfish) and another madcap comedy, *Að eilífu* (1997; Forever). As a dramatist Ibsen has consistently explored the possibilities of theatrical form and the nature of the dramatic character, although his greatest achievement in the area of comedy has been the creation of a theatrical language for modern-day urban characters who are more or less unable to express themselves verbally. This has turned out to be something of a dilemma for the critics, some of whom have not been wholly convinced that it is his characters and not Ibsen himself who is lacking in command of the language.

The arrival of the group of dramatists mentioned above clearly signifies a certain change in tone and content in Icelandic theater. Comedy and satire, irony and wit, have taken over from social realism, on the one hand, and from the part-absurdist, part-symbolic drama, on the other. The most popular recent theater pieces have been adaptations of epic literature, both modern and classic, the latest of these being Kjartan Ragnarsson's monumental adaptation of Halldór Laxness's *Sjálfstætt fólk* (1998; Independent people) for the National Theater, a six-hour epic that was staged and performed in two separate productions.

WOMEN PLAYWRIGHTS

Women playwrights began making their mark during the 1970s and 1980s, the two pioneers being Svava Jakobsdóttir (1930–2004), with her first play *Hvað er í blýhólknum?* (1970; What's in the cornerstone?), and the poet and dramatist Nina Björk Árnadóttir (1941–2000), whose two most significant plays, *Fugl sem flaug á snúru* (1979; Bird caught on a wire) and *Súkkulaði handa Silju* (1982; Chocolate for Silja), discussed in part 1 of this chapter, combine poetry and realism.

Of the same generation are Steinunn Jóhannesdóttir (b. 1948) and Þórunn Sigurðardóttir (b. 1944) who have both written successful modern and historical plays. Jóhannesdóttir has written three plays for the stage. Her strongest piece, *Ferðir Guðríðar* (1996; Guðríður's travels), is a historical play based on the actual life of a seventeenth-century woman who was abducted into slavery by Algerian pirates but managed to return to Iceland, was married to the poet Hallgrímur Pétursson (see p. 214), and lived to a ripe old age. It is a play about religion, moral strength, and endurance. *Ferðalok* (1995; Journey's end) is a parable play about the nineteenth-century poet Jónas Hallgrímsson that is named after one of his poems (see p. 290).

Sigurðardóttir has written three plays for the stage as well as some pieces for radio. For her strongest play she too turned to a historical female figure. *Haustbrúður* (Autumn bride) revolves around a Danish lady who was brought to Iceland in the late eighteenth century only to endure the most horrific abuse by her fiancé, Niels Fuhrman, the Danish governor of Iceland at the time.

Hlín Agnarsdóttir (b. 1953) has written several plays for both stage and television. Her dramatic writing is best described as social comedy; she writes fast-paced and witty dialogue in a somewhat traditional formal sense. *Konur skelfa* (1996; Scary women) is her most significant play to date; set in a women's room at a discotheque, it unfolds the dreams and longings of a group of women who wander in one after the other.

Hrafnhildur Hagalín (b. 1965) made her remarkable debut in 1990 with the award-winning play *Ég er meistarinn* (I am the maestro). It is a study of the relation between natural talent and acquired artistic skill and the struggle that ensues. Two classical music students, guitarists, are living together; the woman has the talent and the man the ambition. The triangle of love, ambition, and art is completed when the maestro arrives on the scene to convince the girl of her responsibilities to her art. *Ég er meistarinn* received the Nordic Drama Prize in 1992.

Hagalín's second play, *Hægan Elektra* (2000; English trans.: *Easy Now, Electra*, in *Contemporary Icelandic Drama* [2001]), is a complete departure from her first piece. Here, Hagalín explores the relationship between two actresses — a mother and her daughter. The play starts off sometime after the two actresses have finished their first performance together, a show based on the art of improvisation. As it turns out, it was a show that they could not finish. Now they are locked inside a room, "imaginary or real," and here they continue their game of improvisation while a video recording of the fateful performance is projected onto a screen at regular intervals. We follow them onstage and onscreen as they gradually lose control of their situation and the disturbing truth about their relationship is unveiled. The third actor, a young man, plays the role of stage manager, guard, or even Orestes, omnipresent but silent. *Hægan Elektra* is a complex theatrical study of the nature of theater as a medium of truth, a study of time as a concrete theatrical device, and perhaps also a study of theatrical literary history as a living component of the relationship between the actor and his audience. Hagalín's latest play, *Norður*, produced at the National Theater in 2004, marks yet another departure for the playwright. It is a kind of dramatic "still life" set in a domestic airport waiting lounge whose diverse inhabitants are examined one after another to make up a complete mosaic of dramatic prose.

Kristín Ómarsdóttir (b. 1962) has produced four plays to date, although her main sphere has been that of short stories and novels (see pp. 448–49). Her piece *Ástarsaga 3* (1998; Love story 3) was the first Icelandic play to take homosexuality as its central theme. Her latest play, *Sjáðu* (Look), was produced at the City Theater and won the 2005 national drama prize, Griman, for best play. Bjarni Jónsson (b. 1966) has produced two plays for the professional stage, *Kaffi* (1998; Coffee) and *Vegurinn brennur* (2004; Down the burning road). *Kaffi* is about a family in a country town where soccer is the element unifying the inhabitants and at the same time a convenient excuse for not addressing the problems that have haunted the family for three generations. *Vegurinn brennur* is a play about contemporary Iceland — the new businessmen, drugs, young people lost in their search for identity, dysfunctional families; a large canvas indeed. *Ástarsaga 3* and *Kaffi* were nominated as the Icelandic candidates for the Nordic Drama Prize in the years 1998 and 2000, respectively.

NEW VOICES

Þorvaldur Þorsteinsson (b. 1960) has his artistic roots in the visual arts. He started out as a writer of short radio plays, which he performed himself in a style utterly devoid of dramatic expression. His cynical comic talent was quickly recognized, as was his sharp eye for the absurd and meaningless in normal everyday dialogue. He turned this to its best effect in *Maríusögur* (1996; English trans.: *Talespin*, in *Contemporary Icelandic Drama* [2001]), his first full-length drama for the stage. As a writer Þorsteinsson has gained a solid reputation as an author of children's books, two of which have gained international recognition for being among the best written in the genre during the 1990s: *Ég heiti Blíðfinnur, en þú mátt kalla mig Bóbó* (1998; My name is Betterby, but you can call me Bobo) and *Ert þú Blíðfinnur? Ég er með mikilvæg skilaboð* (2000; Are you Betterby, I have an important message; see p. 450). Both of these he adapted into a play for the City Theater under the title *Blíðfinnur* (2001; Betterby). Previously, he had written two original children's plays, *Skilaboðaskjóðan* (1996; The message bag), a grand-scale musical adventure full of magic, dwarfs, elves, and exotic characters, and *Ævintýrið um ástina* (1999; Love's fable), a simple adventure tale about the poor boy who wins the princess as result of a heroic deed. The play is written in rhymed verse, a refreshing novelty in Icelandic children's drama that, perhaps surprisingly, turned out to be part of the play's public appeal.

Þorsteinsson surprised his admirers somewhat with his next play, *Við feðgarnir* (1998; Me and my boy), a merciless portrayal of the relationship between an alcoholic father and his codependent son that is laced with comic irony. The dramatic pitch is turned up a notch when the past catches up with them in an unexpected way and their lives are exposed for what they really are. The strength of the play lies in the fact that the revelation of old truths is not likely to change the present situation in any way. Þorsteinsson has recently added three plays to his credit, two short plays for children, both based on Icelandic folklore, *Prumpuhóllinn* (Wind hole) and *Það var barn í dalnum* (There was a child in the valley), and *And Björk of course...*, which opened in March 2002 at the City Theater. Altogether, Þorvaldur Þorsteinsson has produced an impressive body of work that collectively suggests that his primary concern in his dramatic writing is with the visual power of theater as a place of magic and with language as a somewhat limited and misleading means of communication.

Hallgrímur Helgason (b. 1959) has written three plays to date and adapted several others. Most famous for his award-winning novel *101 Reykjavík* (1998; see p. 466), he has repeatedly declared his passion for dramatic writing. His play *Skáldanótt* (2000; The night of the poets) is a modern comedy based on the idea that one night a year certain nineteenth-century Icelandic poet laureates return from the grave to take part in a poetry competition that is conducted in much the same way as a boxing match. The verse, however, is poor, and the play stands as a brave but puerile attempt at turning cultural icons on their heads using satire and rap, the modern street poetry.

Hávar Sigurjónsson (b. 1958) authored three extensive serial plays for radio during the years 1995–2000, after having made his first appearance as a playwright with his much-discussed adaptation of Vigdís Grímsdóttir's novel *Ég heiti Ísbjörg ég er ljón* (1989; My name is Ísbjörg, I am a Leo; see also pp. 441–42) for the National Theater (1992). This piece deals with issues that recur in Sigurjónsson's first original composition for the stage, *Englabörn* (Angels), which had its premiere in the Hafnarfjörður Theater in the autumn of 2001. Incest, violence, and murder are put on display here in the form of a black comedy, yet the pain of the unbearable circumstances in which the characters are caught is always there as well. Sigurjónsson's next play, *Pabbastrákur* (Our boy), deals with the relationship between a prejudiced father and his gay son and the ramifications for the wife/mother and the son's lover. *Pabbastrákur* opened at the National Theater in the autumn of 2003. Sigurjónsson's latest play is *Grjótharðir* (2004; Slammer), a realistic play set in an Icelandic prison that describes the lives of five convicts, all of whom are incarcerated for different reasons but all of whose lives are connected, both in the past and in the present.

Jón Atli Jónasson is the youngest playwright whose work has attracted much attention in the last three years. Jónasson already has four plays to his credit: *Draugalest* (2002; Ghost train); *Brim* (2004; Surf); *Rambo 7* (2005; Rambo 7); and *Sokkabandið* (2006; Mindcamp). He has also cowritten a screenplay, *Strákarnir okkar* (2005; Eleven men out). Jónasson's style is somewhat difficult to pin down at this point in his career. His dialogue is realistic and his language everyday. In *Brim* he describes life aboard a fishing boat, the play's greatest strength lying in its strong portrayal of characters and a good sense of situation. Dramatic structure is Jónasson's weakness, but structure seems not to be his concern, as *Rambo 7* demonstrates. That work deconstructs completely all traditional ideas of dramatic construction. In this project he is supported by the director Egill Heiðar Anton Pálsson, who has directed Jónasson's last two plays and could even be considered the coauthor of *Sokkabandið*. Here the main concern is the inability of theater to be spontaneous; theater is depicted as being frozen in formalities and rules of performance that no longer have any reference to the experience of the audience. The real play is, thus, acted out in the changing rooms behind the stage, where the actors can talk and relax. This "play" is then projected onto screens for the audience, which sits in front of an empty stage for most of the play.

FINAL WORD

Also worthy of note is the development in recent years of improvisational theater. Although this cannot be called playwriting in its traditional sense, such material does, nevertheless, constitute a significant part of the fare currently offered to the public. The positive side of this is that, often, the productions have been more visual and theatrical, as the inspiration has, in many cases, been the imagination and the improvisational skill of the ensemble. At the same time one could argue that, in varying degrees, the productions are somewhat lacking in literary value. Some of these productions have been simple and naive concoctions, but they have enjoyed great popularity owing to their theatrical energy and visual force. In the best of cases such work has spawned new writing talent. Aspiring young writers have in the last few years been drawn to the theater, perhaps because they feel the energy and creative power emanating from it, and it is to be hoped that this trend will bring forth more productions created by the acting ensemble but strongly supported by scripts of lasting literary value.

Icelandic Children's Literature, 1780–2000

Silja Aðalsteinsdóttir

10

In my history of Icelandic children's books, *Íslenskar barnabækur, 1780–1979* (1981), I maintain that the first Icelandic publication for children came out in the year 1780. One must start somewhere, and this was perhaps said somewhat in jest because "Barnaljóð" (Poem for children) was not published in the way we now regard as "for children." On the contrary, the printed letters are tiny and the lines very close together, and there are no pictures in the book except for a small angel on the title page.

This long poem consisting of 106 verses was, nevertheless, specifically written for a child, the vicar Vigfús Jónsson's little girl, when she was born in 1739, much to her father's delight. And it makes an excellent start to a history of Icelandic children's literature because it stands out among the many didactic poems that children learned by heart during the eighteenth century. In his poem the vicar gives his baby daughter good advice, as befits a Christian father. He begins by hoping that she will not have to pay for his sins, that she will stay on the narrow path and keep her faith in the heavenly father. In spite of this solemn beginning, however, the poem is both worldly and optimistic. Perhaps this attitude comes with the meter, the old Eddic *fornyrðislag* (old epic meter), which turns the poem into a kind of children's "Hávamál" (Sayings of the High One; See p. 14), equally full of wisdom, and pragmatic and laconic in its approach to life.

"If you should meet a false man with a sweet tongue, as will often happen," the vicar says for instance, "be sure to accept his friendliness, but put a solid lock on your own tongue." The girl shall be careful of what she says, but she shall not be too quiet; she must choose her friends with care, but she shall love all men; she shall work well and serve God, but she must not be boring, and she must learn to amuse herself in a polite and befitting way. She must learn self-control and believe in herself. She shall be trusting — but as there are all kinds of people in this world she must also be wise, or, as it says in verse 41: "Be simple like a dove, but also cunning like a snake, because the world can be slippery, and he is lucky who keeps himself out of harm" (*Barna-Liood*, 11, 13). Nowhere is it specifically made clear that the poem is addressed to a girl rather than a boy. The vicar's humane, pedagogical policy is applicable to both sexes. He simply wants to bring up a healthy, independent individual.

"Barnaljóð" did not have any direct followers or spark a wave of other literature for children. The main reason for this was that no infrastructure was yet in place for children's literature. In the backward rural society of eighteenth- and nineteenth-century Iceland, children were still treated like small adults, living and working alongside their elders. They did not yet have any life of their own in nurseries and schools where books were being used. Literature was mostly used for reading aloud in the so-called *baðstofa*, the communal room, while people were working, and it was intended for everyone — women, men, and children, farmers and farmhands alike — although one may presume that children had their own favorites, such as folk- and fairy tales, for instance.

The first Icelandic writers and publishers of storybooks for children after "Barnaljóð" all had been educated and/or were living abroad, where they had observed how other nations produced books specifically for children, and they wanted Icelandic children to enjoy similar benefits. They were Enlightenment men, however, and were vehemently opposed to fantastic literature such as folktales, which they thought immoral, full of superstition, and entirely unfit for young ears. Their opposition was, thus, squarely directed at the very same material that in the twentieth century became a mainstay in literature for children and that the psychologist Bruno Bettelheim (1903–90) claimed is the very stuff that helps children in their development toward maturity. In *The Uses of Enchantment* (1976) Bettelheim argued that the struggles of the adventurous hero reflect the inner conflicts that all children must deal with while growing up and show them that these battles can be overcome and a bright future awaits ahead.

The first publications for children in Iceland were, thus, quite different, not only from "Barnaljóð," but also from what we nowadays think of as children's literature. Vigfús Jónsson never says, for instance, what will happen to his daughter if she does not heed his advice. There are no descriptions in the poem of naughty children. In most of the translated stories and adaptations that begin to appear in the late eighteenth century and the nineteenth, on the other hand, children are forced to learn obedience, by hook or by crook, and they are taught by way of prohibition. They are forbidden to tease, to demand, to refuse to eat, to lie, to be curious or ungrateful, and, if they disobey, they will live to regret it — if their disobedience does not prove fatal, that is. Playing children's games can prove fatal as well, as, for instance, in the story of the girl who participates in a game of the dangerous blindman's buff and breaks her head in two so that her brain is scattered all around. This story is included in the book *Sumargjöf handa börnum* (1795; A summer present for children), where we also come across sexist upbringing for the first time. Girls are not supposed to read and write, no matter how much they would like to. Instead, they must sew, knit, and cook, and, if they are reluctant, they are told horrific tales of no-good females who come to desperate ends.

The only nineteenth-century author of children's stories that are still readable today was a romantic. The poet Jónas Hallgrímsson (1807–45; see chapter 3) wrote and retold a number of fairy tales for children in the fashion of the famous Danish author H. C. Andersen (1805–75) that appeared in the magazine *Fjölnir* (1847), notably "Fífill og hunangsfluga" (English trans.: "The Dandelion and the Bee," in Ringler, *Bard of Iceland*) and "Leggur og skel" (English trans.: "Shankbone and Seashell," in Ringler, *Bard of Iceland*). He also wrote an enchanting short story, "Grasaferð" (1847; English trans.: "Gathering Highland Moss," in Ringler, *Bard of Iceland*), about a young boy and his elder cousin, a beautiful young girl, and their walking trip into the mountains to collect Iceland moss. The rich text of this story has long been a gold mine for literary studies (see also p. 293).

A few other Icelandic authors tried their hand at producing reading material for children, among them Torfhildur Hólm (see p. 519), but their efforts could not overcome the fact that, in Iceland, the time for children's literature had not yet arrived. It is not until the development of an urban, middle-class society where children go to school on a daily basis and live part of their lives outside the realm of their elders that the need for specific children's books — for stories that reflect their situation and experiences and prepare them for a society in which they, as children, are no longer direct participants — arises.

CHILDHOOD MEMOIRS

At the beginning of the twentieth century a migration from country to town took place in Iceland that would entirely transform Icelandic society and culture. As the number of people living in villages and towns grew, the number of schools increased, as did the number of children attending school on a regular basis, rather than participating in the daily struggle to feed the family. With this transformation came the need for educational and reading material specifically for children.

Sigurbjörn Sveinsson (1878–1950) was the son of poor farmhands in northern Iceland and was moved from farm to farm when he was a boy, most often with his mother. In his small volume entitled *Bernskan* (1907; Childhood), the first original Icelandic children's book, he tells thirty-five short tales, or anecdotes, of his childhood years from age five to age fifteen, when he is confirmed and leaves home. In spite of all the moving the stories describe a secure world filled with love and harmony. The children must work like everybody else in this unyielding land, but they are also allowed to play. Everybody is kind to them, and they feel secure enough to play tricks on the grown-ups—in all innocence, of course. Life continues to change outwardly, but God is a steady presence on his throne in heaven, and his representative on earth is the boy's mother, the only stable thing in his life.

It may surprise the modern reader to see how small a part the mother plays in nineteenth-century stories for children. The father seems to be the main authority figure and the one responsible for his children's welfare, both mental and physical. Sigurbjörn Sveinsson's works signal an abrupt change in this respect, as, indeed, they do in many others, and set a trend of mother worship in Icelandic children's literature that continued for quite some time. The descriptions of the bond between the boy Sigurbjörn and his mother are moving and influential; for decades this book served as a model for parent-child relationships.

The best among Sveinsson's stories are well written in an easy-flowing language that has withstood the passage of time. They are not overly moralistic; happiness matters much more than good manners in the author's eyes. Many writers of children's books modeled their works on Sveinsson's, and his works are still read today.

The next author to use his childhood memories as material for children's stories became even more famous than Sigurbjörn Sveinsson, even acquiring international fame, his books being translated into many languages, including English and Japanese. Jón Sveinsson (1857–1944), better known as Nonni, left his beloved town of Akureyri in northern Iceland as a twelve-year-old boy to study in France and returned to Iceland only as a visitor after that. He later became a Jesuit priest and worked both in Germany and in Denmark. All his books were written in German or Danish and were translated into Icelandic.

Nonni wrote his childhood memoirs, *Nonni* (1922; English trans.: Sveinsson, *At Skipalón* [2002]), forty years after he left Iceland, and they are consequently pure nostalgia. According to his books, in Akureyri and the surrounding Eyjafjörður area, the land of his youth, children enjoy complete freedom; boys travel unhindered through the wild and beautiful countryside, on foot or on horseback if they want to, for horses are everywhere to be had, as long as they are returned to the same place. Children are absolutely free to roam wherever they like on land and at sea, and everyone they meet is eager to assist and amuse them. In short what we find described here is the kind of youth that everyone wishes he had had, and Nonni himself is an ideal kind of child — upright, honest, intelligent and God-loving. Little wonder, then, that Nonni's tales were a great success right from the start, with the first publication in German, and have continued to be so. Although no complete edition has yet appeared, several editions and translations of individual tales have been published since 2002 (see, e.g., Sveinsson, *At Skipalón*) and have also done extremely well in the form of a 1988 television series.

The stories written by Sigurbjörn Sveinsson and Nonni proved an endless source of ideas and inspiration for other Icelandic authors, and, as a result, entertaining stories about resourceful and happy children abounded. Together, these two authors created the myth of Iceland as a children's paradise, a place where everyone is free and equality reigns, a myth that has proved particularly long-lived outside Iceland. Their works inspired many others to write entertaining adventures for children — prankster stories mostly about young boys in search of adventure — that became very popular in the 1950s. Stories about the contemporary lives and adventures of children in the growing city also began to appear in their wake: in 1910, Hallgrímur Jónsson (1875–1961) published his *Barnasögur* (Children's stories), the first children's book to focus primarily on children in Reykjavík.

The popularity of Sigurbjörn Sveinsson and Nonni may in part explain why childhood memoirs make up such an important part of Icelandic children's literature, in contrast to the early children's literature of many other European countries, which either was didactic and moralistic or consisted of romantic stories like H. C. Andersen's fairy tales in Denmark (after 1835) or Walter Scott's novels in Britain (after 1814). One could just as easily argue, however, that Sveinsson and Nonni themselves are part of a larger tradition in Icelandic literature that has tended to favor "true" stories over fiction and that delights in biographical writing, a tradition going as far back as the Sagas of the Icelanders and the Kings' Sagas (see part 2 of chapter 1).

Until the 1930s, all Icelandic children's books consisted of stories of one kind or another, including memoirs, fairy tales, moralistic tales, and didactic stories. It was not until after 1930 that the juvenile novel finally reached Icelandic children, quite possibly in the wake of the coming-of-age of the Icelandic novel for adults with the works of authors like Halldór Laxness and Gunnar Gunnarsson (see chapter 5).

Most of the writers of these juvenile novels were teachers at the same school in Reykjavík, Austurbæjarskólinn, in the eastern part of the old town, which was established in 1930 and introduced many new teaching methods. The Swiss-educated headmaster was himself an accomplished writer called Sigurður Thorlacius (1900–1945) who seems to have actively encouraged his schoolteachers to produce reading material for their students, and they proved both eager and capable of writing serious literary works for children.

Reykjavík was at the time a fast-growing town, very dirty and uncultured on the whole. The new inhabitants came from the country, many driven away from their farms by the economic crisis of the 1930s. These people did not know how to live in a city themselves, much less how to teach their children to live in a city. They still believed that they could let their children out in the mornings and back into the house at night, as was customary in the countryside, where children had plenty of work to do all day. In the city, however, children ran wild and received precious little education, even during the few hours they spent at school each day during the winter. These were the children of urban pioneers, settlers in a new land, and Sigurður Thorlacius's teachers at Austurbæjarskólinn set out to explain the new society to them and teach them how to survive, and, perhaps, even live happily ever after, in it. The works that they produced were mostly bildungsromans about a young hero's development from uncouth youth into a mature young individual or about the road from self-illusion to self-knowledge. At the same time these authors also wanted to develop their readers' literary taste, and some of them succeeded in writing some of the finest juvenile novels of the twentieth century.

An additional factor contributing to the development of literature for young people in Iceland was the fact that a gap had been opening up between adult and children's literature as a result of contemporaneous developments in Icelandic fiction. Novels had begun to appear that were considered revolutionary, if not downright scandalous, and quite unfit for children's ears at a time when most reading still occurred out loud in a communal or family context (see Hughes, "Children's Literature"; see also p. 196).

First to write an entire juvenile novel, and in two volumes at that, was Gunnar M. Magnúss (1898–1988). The first volume, entitled *Börnin frá Víðigerði* (1933; The children from Víðigerði), takes place in the late nineteenth century and is about an orphaned boy in Reykjavík who is sent to a foster home in the country. His new family then decides to move to America, where the wild boy from Reykjavík immediately feels more at home than the others. Magnúss's other novels also deal with poor young people and describe how they struggle and overcome their circumstances and eventually become — if not rich, then at least sure of what they want in life.

Even more realistic in their approach, in a social and psychological sense, were the authors Stefán Jónsson and Ragnheiður Jónsdóttir, both of whom wrote novels for adults as well as for children. They found exciting ways in which to relate what it was like to grow up in a society about which parents knew so little and how children and teenagers had to find their own ways and devise their own rules in order to achieve their goal, which is always the same: to become an upright member of society. What is particularly unusual about their works is the fact that they bring out the complexity of their fictional world. In most children's books everything is simple and straightforward, particularly where morality is concerned: parents are always right and must be obeyed, and the adult world is a haven, comfortable and safe. Here, we find for the first time children's texts that are multilayered and intended for the development of their readers, who are encouraged to try out, think, and decide for themselves and evaluate what grownups tell them rather than just take them at their word. This is children's literature that encourages independence.

Stefán Jónsson (1905–66) was the son of poor farmhands in western Iceland and worked as a schoolteacher all his life. He wrote many books about children in Reykjavík, creating characters based on the people he taught at school, difficult children, but also very charming. Possibly his best novel is *Börn eru besta fólk* (1961; Children are the best people). His stories are well structured, his characters alive, their surroundings vividly described, his style witty and to the point. He describes his characters' development in relation to both inner and outer events, and no author has provided deeper insights into life in both rural and urban Iceland during the twentieth century. In all Jónsson wrote twelve novels for children and young people and two collections of short stories, all worthy of description in more detail, but, here, his best-known work, a trilogy about the boy Hjalti, who was a contemporary of the author himself and probably a close relative, must suffice.

The first book, *Sagan hans Hjalta litla* (1948; The story of little Hjalti), starts when Hjalti is nine years old and is parted from his mother for the first time. She is a farm laborer and a single mother with two children; she is allowed to bring only one of them with her to the farm where she will be working, and, since Hjalti is the eldest, he is sent to another farm on his own. Hjalti misses his mother desperately, but the year covered in the first book is an eventful one, and he learns much about human nature. In the next volume, *Mamma skilur allt* (1950; Mummy understands everything), Hjalti's little sister is dead, and Hjalti is allowed to be with his mother in yet a new place of service. He loves his mother deeply, she can do no wrong, and he is very happy in the wealthy household of a member of parliament — until his mother tells him that she is going to get married. Hjalti feels that she has forsaken him and at the beginning of the last volume, *Hjalti kemur heim* (1951; Hjalti comes home), is full of wild thoughts of revenge. Hjalti hates his mother's husband, but eventually, by working beside him on the little farm they rent and by battling poverty and his mother's illness with him, Hjalti gains a solid foothold in life and a proper home at last. Hjalti is a charming boy, good-looking, bright, and sensitive. The Hjalti books became very popular, and their influence can be seen in many later novels for young adults.

Not surprisingly, the school is the scene for many events in Jónsson's books, and teachers, both good and bad, are among his most memorable characters; although he was a schoolteacher himself, Jónsson was quite critical of schools and the influence of teachers over children. And he is even more critical of the family. Whether in the countryside or in the towns, the nuclear family, with all its dark secrets and strange ways of shaping the individual, is the underlying theme in many of Jónsson's works, where parents can be incredibly stupid and unfeeling in dealing with their children. It is a main characteristic of Jónsson as a writer that he is unafraid of tackling difficult subjects — something unusual among writers of children's novels. For instance, he deals with the death of parents or other close relatives in five of his books, and some of these descriptions are extremely vivid and moving, like the tragic death of the mother in *Hanna Dóra* (1956). Today, his books are considered too intense for children of the same age as his protagonists, although they are without a doubt classic literature for all age groups.

Some of Jónsson's most interesting characters are strong, upright, intelligent women who are much more capable of bringing up their children than their menfolk are. Ragnheiður Jónsdóttir (1895–1967) was even more interested in the woman question, and, accordingly, her books deal mostly with girls. It is said that she started writing *Dóra* (1945), the first entry in her first popular novel series about the rich girl Dóra and her poor friend Vala, as an Icelandic answer to the American series about Beverly Gray written by Clair Blank, which her husband was translating at that time. Although Jónsdóttir and Jónsson wrote contemporaneously, her books seem more modern. Most of them take place in Reykjavík and incorporate current events and even political issues, something that Jónsson avoids. Jónsdóttir writes, for example, about the effects that the British and American occupation armies have on the lives of her heroines during the Second World War.

Jónsdóttir likes to play with opposites. Dóra is a typical heroine in a girls' series, an only child, beautiful and rich, everybody's living doll. Her friend Vala, on the other hand, is the daughter of an unemployed worker; she has many brothers and sisters and lives in utter poverty. She is the more intelligent one of the two friends, however, and helps Dóra with her studies, while Dóra, much to her own surprise, feels more relaxed in Vala's home than in her parents' posh villa. The story moves between their two worlds and creates vivid pictures of each, in Jónsdóttir's free and entertaining style of writing. In the last book of the series, *Dóra í dag* (1954; Dora today), Dóra marries Vala's brother, whom she has loved since she was a teenager, but we are given to understand that the marriage will not be an easy one. Jónsdóttir devoted two separate books to Vala—*Vala* (1948) and *Vala og Dóra* (1956; Vala and Dora) —retelling the events in the Dóra series from Vala's perspective, something unprecedented in Icelandic children's narrative at the time.

Jónsdóttir's last series revolves around Katla, a teenage girl in Reykjavík during the late 1950s and early 1960s. Her parents are divorced, and Katla lives with her mother, a bitter woman and not too intelligent. She has forbidden Katla to see her father, who has remarried, and Katla eventually collapses under the strain. In the first book, *Katla gerir uppreisn* (1959; Katla rebels), Katla decides to disobey her mother and goes to see her father on a regular basis. This proves extremely painful for both mother and daughter, but gradually they find a way out of their emotional jail. The Katla books are not as funny as the ones about Dóra and Vala, but they became surprisingly popular, perhaps because they dealt with subject matter that concerned more and more children in modern Icelandic society.

ADVENTURE STORIES

While Ragnheiður Jónsdóttir and Stefán Jónsson were writing serious bildungsromans for and about young Icelanders, publishers were thriving on translated trivia, mainly from England and the United States. During the war years book publication in Iceland skyrocketed. The war brought an increase in wealth for many, and, in the years during and after the war, books were in such great demand that Icelandic authors could hardly keep up. Translations gradually took over, particularly in the area of popular literature: love stories; thrillers; and detective novels (see p. 409). The number of translated children's books, which had always roughly equaled that of original Icelandic works, doubled, if not more. Enid Blyton's (1897–1968) *Adventure* series in particular became extremely popular in Iceland, as, indeed, it did in other countries, and sold like hotcakes. Not surprisingly, Icelandic authors wanted a piece of the action, and some began to compete by creating Icelandic versions of these popular genres, while others wrote what later became Icelandic children's classics. Among the authors were many who had already made their mark in the area of literature for adults. The postwar years were rather uneventful in Icelandic fiction, while the modernist revolution in Icelandic poetry spelled doom and gloom, which may explain why so many authors wanted to try their hand at writing for children instead. This period, which lasted until around 1960, could be considered the golden age of Icelandic children's literature.

Novelists such as Stefán Jónsson and Ragnheiður Jónsdóttir had tried to explore Icelandic society, past and present, in their works, how it had developed, how it worked, what was wrong with it, and even how it might be changed for the better. The trivial literature that took over during the 1950s and 1960s, on the other hand, was not interested in views. It took one slice of human existence — love, crime, adventure, competition — and blew it up out of all proportion so as to outweigh everything else. While these books may have rested the mind and entertained the reader, they also made life smaller and less significant.

Nevertheless, there are a few excellent storytellers among Icelandic authors of adventure stories and other light reading for youngsters. One of the most prolific, Ármann Kr. Einarsson (1915–99), wrote a large variety of children's literature: moralistic tales; adventure stories; literary fairy tales; short stories about preschool children; light detective novels; and so on. His characters tend to be drawn in black-and-white, and his descriptions of events and surroundings are usually weak, but he spins a good yarn, and his stories have been popular with children.

The first writer to write childhood memoirs from the city was Hendrik Ottósson (1897–1966). Ottósson's books about Gvendur Jóns and his friends — the first of which, *Gvendur Jóns og ég* . . . (Gvendur Jóns and I . . .), appeared in 1949 — are set in Reykjavík at the turn of the century and paint a lively picture of the imaginative world of city children at that time and how they experience their environment.

Many authors tried their hand at the detective novel for children and young people during the 1960s and early 1970s. The most talented of these is Guðjón Sveinsson (b. 1937), who has written other types of children's books as well, including picture books and stories inspired by his own children about everyday life in a small village. Sveinsson became best known, however, for his series of detective novels dealing with the adventures of three boys and two girls in the Icelandic countryside, including *Njósnir að næturþeli* (1967; Spying by night) and *Leyndardómur Lundeyja* (1969–70; The secret of Lund Island). His yarns are formulaic but tightly spun and exciting, his criminals really dangerous, and the setting recognizably Icelandic in its realism.

One particular brand of trivial literature for children, and a prolific one, deals with the supposed bliss of rural life in the old days, when almost everyone lived in the country. In these nostalgic tales, nobody is unhappy, at least not for long. Children work only when they want to and spend the rest of their time playing and teaching stupid, sometimes even immoral, town children a thing or two. Many a child from Reykjavík is saved from neglect and corruption by being sent to a farm in the country. At a time when half the country's population lived in towns, it must be considered a dubious practice to tell children how morally wrong it is to live there. This anachronism can, perhaps, be partly explained as nostalgia on the part of the authors themselves, almost all of whom were brought up in the country, at a time of profound change in Icelandic society. They possibly found city life insignificant, even depraved, and preferred to continue the myth of another, more child-friendly and generous society.

Just after 1970, however, Icelandic authors stopped writing both detective stories and sweet nostalgia for young people. New waves in the realm of children's literature broke on Iceland's shores and inspired an altogether different kind of writing.

THE SCANDINAVIAN WAVE

The new fashion in children's literature that reached Iceland from the Scandinavian countries demanded that children's books deal with everyday life in the present. No more unrealistic fantasies set in the past or the future — or in the countryside for that matter. In these stories we find that the daily environment is Reykjavík, or another town or larger village, and children spend their days in day-care centers and take part in everyday activities: they go to a birthday party, take a trip to the swimming pool; they start school, go to the doctor, and so on. Many of these stories introduce problems to be discussed between parent and child, although bigger issues remain once removed from the main characters: they are something "other" people have to deal with.

These changes constituted a fresh wind and were very necessary in deconstructing the myth of the careless, free childhood presented in earlier books. They inspired the poet Vilborg Dagbjartsdóttir (b. 1930), for instance, to write a charming book entitled *Labbi pabbakútur* (1971; Labbi daddy's lad) which successfully expresses the feelings of a little boy who feels caged, not allowed to play outside because of all the cars and at the day-care center all day because his mother needs to work. His desire for freedom is effectively reflected in his love of cars and his dream of driving one himself one day.

In many instances, however, the results were less fortunate, leading to rather boring narratives. The focus on an outer realism frequently was achieved at the cost of an inner reality. The characters are cut from cardboard, the style is flat, and the problems tend to be unliterary: they remain isolated and are not connected to children's existence and the larger environment as a whole. The intended realism rarely went beyond the surface and was neither artistic nor psychological. Worse, these books awoke neither curiosity nor wonder in their young readers, while the slightest spark of rebellion was suppressed.

This neorealist current did, however, bring to the fore the most popular Icelandic author of children's books in recent times: Guðrún Helgadóttir (b. 1935). The everyday adventures of her delightful twins, Jón Oddur and Jón Bjarni, take place in Reykjavík and in the present and constituted a small revolution in Icelandic children's literature. The surrroundings are lively, the characters many sided and true to life, and the style fresh and very funny. Helgadóttir has written three books about the twins in total, starting with *Jón Oddur and Jón Bjarni* (1974), as well as many others, including picture books for the very young and novels for older children, one of which, *Undan illgresinu* (1990; From under the weed), won her the Nordic Children's Book Award.

Helgadóttir's most ambitious work to date is a trilogy based on her own childhood in Hafnarfjörður, a neighboring town of Reykjavík. The titles of the books form the second half of a traditional evening prayer that all Icelandic children used to know: *Sitji guðs englar* (1983; May God's angels sit), *Saman í hring* (1986; Together in a circle), *Sænginni yfir minni* (1987; Above my bed). The stories take place during and after the Second World

War. The fishing village is occupied by the American army, while the people live in constant fear of losing their two trawlers at sea (Iceland lost proportionally more men, mostly fishermen, during the war than did the United States). But the three sisters who are the main protagonists, each in her own third of the trilogy, are more worried about life in grandmother and grandfather's little house, where mother is always producing more babies and father does not always bring home enough money from the fisheries. The main thing, however, is that father stays alive, as they discover after one of the trawlers is sunk by the Germans and sixty-five children in the village lose their fathers. The description of the fishing village, cowering on the coast in the icy winds after so much loss of life, is marvellously written.

Iceland's loss during the war was not just men to the sea, however. Many British and American soldiers took their Icelandic girlfriends abroad with them when they returned home. And in the trilogy Helgadóttir is the first Icelandic children's author to deal with this fact. The situation becomes almost comic when one of the sisters counts off more and more of the village girls who are gone or going away and finally asks her grandmother: "Is there a shortage of girls in America, granny?" (Helgadóttir, *Saman í hring*, 30). Instead of the girls, the sisters would have preferred the soldiers to take home with them the small black rats that they brought into the country, so different from the gray Icelandic rat that never went into human dwellings.

One of the main concerns in the trilogy is the clear and accurate depiction of the profound changes taking place in Iceland at that time and the ways in which Icelandic society was developing, seen from the perspective of three different children in a small village. Helgadóttir successfully blended old and new, comedy and tragedy, and in the process created what have become classics in Icelandic children's literature.

THE RETURN OF THE MEMOIRS

Guðrún Helgadóttir's trilogy about the large family in Hafnarfjörður is one in a line of books that, inspired by developments in adult literature, revived the childhood memoir in children's books. The neorealist wave in Icelandic literature coincided with changes in Icelandic life writing: instead of detailed descriptions of outer events, a deep emotional undercurrent now made itself felt in these texts, an undercurrent that greatly appealed to readers. Many of these works contained moving descriptions of childhood poignantly showing that children are neither oblivious nor immune to what happens around them; their world is not an isolated one, untouched by the suffering of others. Two works were particularly influential in this respect, one by the laborer Tryggvi Emilsson, called *Fátækt fólk* (1976; Poor people), and the other by the journalist and writer Sigurður A. Magnússon, entitled *Undir kalstjörnu* (1979; Under a frozen star; see also p. 437). While Magnússon describes the effects of the Depression years in Reykjavík on children as well as adults, Emilsson exposed the darker side of growing up in the Icelandic countryside. These works exploded the myth of childhood innocence and bliss, demonstrating that childhood can be marked by cruelty as well as beauty. Sooner or later, this development had to find its way into children's literature.

The first noteworthy new children's story of this kind was written by an old hand in the field of Icelandic children's literature, Hreiðar Stefánsson (1918–95), who, together with his wife, Jenna Jensdóttir (b. 1918), had for almost forty years been producing stories for children and youngsters. His novel *Grösin í glugghúsinu* (1980; Grass growing in the window) takes place in northern Iceland during the late 1920s. The boy Garðar is the son of laborers in Akureyri. There is unemployment and poverty among the workers, and Garðar's large family does not have enough to eat. The summer he turns eleven he is sent to a farm to be properly fed, and the story describes the events of his long and colorful summer there.

What makes this story so different from most other country tales since Stefán Jónsson's Hjalti books is a strong, unsentimental love for the unusual people Garðar meets, an unexpected depth in character, and a rich feeling for the environment. It is a bold story, not least in the art of storytelling, as the entire book is written in the second person, as if the storyteller were directly addressing his character. The opening lines are as follows: "Your name is Garðar. You are a ten-year-old boy from town, small and skinny, with dark hair and blue eyes. Today your biggest dream has come true — a dream you share with most of your playmates — they're just not as lucky as you are. You have been hired as a farmhand" (Stefánsson, *Grösin*, 5). This had the effect of bringing the reader really close to the story's main character.

Hreiðar Stefánsson's *Grösin í glugghúsinu* was published in 1980, the first volume of Guðrún Helgadóttir's trilogy in 1983. Helgadóttir is much younger than Stefánsson, and her youth was spent in a fishing village rather than the countryside. Younger still was Guðni Kolbeinsson (b. 1946), who in the unusually funny *Mömmustrákur* (1982; Mummy's boy) relates the events of a summer long ago when his mother decided to get married to a man who is not his father. The story starts in the country, moves to Reykjavík for a short while, and ends in a seaside village, the boy's future home.

Guðlaug Richter (b. 1953) was born in Reykjavík and paints a vivid picture of children's lives there in her *Þetta er nú einum of* (1985; This is too much). The difference here is that she is herself a minor character in the story, one of the many sisters in the house. The main protagonist is her older brother, who has to take on the role of the man around the house while his father is at sea and take care of the younger children while his mother is busy.

These more recent memoirs share a certain tone that is not easily described. They are nostalgic and sentimental yet at the same time quite harsh in their realism. The hero is more like an antihero, a thoughtful child rather than the outwardly active and happy child of the traditional childhood memoirs. This development gradually made its way into other children's books set in the present, for instance, in the quartet about little Tobías (1982–87) by Magnea of Kleifar (the pen name of Magnea Magnúsdóttir; b. 1930). Tobías is lame, a sensitive, gifted little boy, ill matched with his stressed, ambitious parents. Without being consciously aware of it, his parents dislike him because he is not "as boys should be," happy, noisy, pushy. The boy lives in a large block of flats, and one day he decides to take the lift all the way to the top and pay a visit to God, who, he believes, lives there, to discuss his problems with him. As it happens, a happy-go-lucky painter lives on the top floor; he welcomes Tobías with open arms and becomes a god-like figure to the boy. The four books are a study of the boy's inner life and his immediate surroundings; they are humorous while at the same time effectively pulling at readers' heartstrings, and they have attracted many readers.

Probably the most famous work in this vein is *Benjamín dúfa* (1992; Benjamin Dove) by Friðrik Erlingsson, which describes one summer in the lives of three boys around 1970. Particularly remarkable about the story is that it takes place on two different levels — aside from the symbolic subtext, which forms a third. On the surface it is the description of three active, lovable boys who turn on the neighborhood bully for killing old Guðlaug's cat and who collect money on behalf of the old lady when she loses everything she owns in a fire. Below the surface of this happy children's world, however, another story takes place about which the grown-ups know nothing, one in which cruelty and fear, cowardice and bravery, battle it out. Symbolically, the book tells the archetypal tale of the creation of the world, its development and destruction, and the eventual birth of a new one once an innocent has paid with his life for the crimes of man. This is an exceptionally accomplished children's book, lively, action-packed, and full of excitement, with an added emotional and intellectual depth, and remarkable for its references to Nordic mythology and Christian morality. It won the Icelandic Children's Literature Prize in 1992 and was successfully made into a 1996 film of the same name by Gísli Snær Erlingsson.

The feature that particularly characterizes these books is that they take their protagonists — and, by extension, their readers — seriously. The more trivial literature always relied on some deus ex machina solution to all problems, while neorealism either solved problems through discussion or left them unsolved altogether — because that is, after all, the way life is. These more recent books, many of them with roots in their authors' own childhoods, try to let children solve their own problems through open conflict and inner struggle, while the nuclear family comes under scrutiny from the child's point of view. The authors often make their passionate protagonists a counterpart to the cold indifference of a market-driven society toward its children. Feelings run both high and deep in these characters and clearly aim toward the emotional and moral development of the readers in a harsh, uncaring world. To this day childhood memoirs produce some of the best children's books in Iceland, just as they did a century ago.

TEENAGE NOVELS

Although it mainly made its influence felt in books for preschool children, the Scandinavian neorealism of the 1970s also brought about a new type of teenage novel, introducing a trend that has been a great hit on the market since the late 1970s. The work to set the trend was *Búrið* (1977; The cage) by Olga Guðrún Árnadóttir (b. 1953), a well-written novel about a young girl's rebellion against the two institutions that govern her life: the family and the school. This was a radical novel that was widely discussed for a long time and can still spark anger today, especially among schoolteachers. The story revolves around the fifteen-year-old Ilmur, who is very unhappy both at home, where her mother hangs listless about the house, and in school, where tyrannical teachers determine the fate of their students. Ilmur tries to rebel, but her friends let her down, so she runs away from school and finds herself a job in a cannery. While traditional bildungsromans for youngsters end in the reconciliation between youth and adult, Ilmur finds her own solution independent of those in charge, as had the most rebellious characters in Stefán Jónsson's works.

In *Búrið* Árnadóttir attacks many of the myths common to children's literature: the mother who understands everything; a happy family life; fun at school; the teacher who makes a difference. The way in which she launched her attack pulled no punches and left the pillars of society reeling and complaining. Whether despite or because of this, the novel sold well, and the teenager now became a best-selling hero, although with a difference: Ilmur's rebellious nature completely went out of the teenage hero of the bestsellers. The typical protagonist in these popular novels is a mild character, a bit shy perhaps, or maybe hiding a little secret or an inferiority complex. Some of these books are funny, while others can be quite realistic, in a superficial sort of way. The protagonists are usually fourteen to sixteen years old, but, as the books do not describe any conflicts, they do not satisfy readers of that age who are truly curious about what awaits them in the future. In fact there is no future in these books, just the present with its minor problems that are easily solved. The main readership for these books therefore consists mostly of teenagers who are a few years younger and who can view the events in the stories as a possible future.

These are of course generalizations. Auður Haralds's (b. 1947) *Baneitrað samband á Njálsgötunni* (1985; Poisonous relationship in Njal's Street), for instance, is a happy exception: it provides a wonderfully funny and thought-provoking description of the relationship between a single mother and her teenage son who fight in an uncommonly intelligent way about pocket money, school, housework, and the nuclear bomb. It also broke through the isolated view of teenagers' lives as being somehow entirely unconnected to those of other people.

The authors of teenage novels have had a difficult time finding ways in which to describe convincingly the pains involved in growing up. Adult literature of the late 1970s and the 1980s exercised a positive influence on children's literature, with a growing number of novels portraying experiences of childhood and growing up, notably Pétur Gunnarsson's (b. 1947) novels about Andri Haraldsson, *Punktur punktur komma strik* (1976; Matchstick man) and *Ég um mig frá mér til mín* (1978; I me my mine), which inspired authors of children's books to be even more aware of the many and various aspects of childhood (see also p. 436). Nevertheless, many Icelandic teenage novels long continued to suffer from an exaggerated focus on either love or action or both, with plot overtaking many other concerns, such as character development, and insufficient attention paid to narrative detail and technique.

One of the most popular authors of teenage novels who has succeeded better in this genre than most is Andrés Indriðason (b. 1941), also a television producer. His first two books revolved around younger protagonists and are quite serious stories about the children of irresponsible parents who think more about houses and furniture than they do about their children's happiness. In 1982 he published *Viltu byrja með mér?* (Do you want to go out with me?), which set the trend for a large number of books to come: boy meets girl, both of whom are in their early teens, and a playful, innocent courtship begins, interwoven with funny, or not so funny, events at home and in school. All Indriðason's books are lively, well constructed, and often exciting — but absolutely without a sting.

In Jónína Leósdóttir's (b. 1954) *Sundur og saman* (1993; Apart and together) the protagonist, Birna, and her younger brother are suddenly forced to move to Reykjavík with their father when he finds out that their mother is in love with one of his younger colleagues. Birna finds it difficult to deal with her parents' shenanigans and childish behavior but learns to understand them better when she herself gets to experience how difficult it is to control one's emotions and love the person one is supposed to love.

Despite the focus on budding love, teenage sexuality long remained invisible in Icelandic children's literature. While the characters happily pursued criminals through mountains and fjords, kissing apparently never occurred to them. Eðvarð Ingólfsson's (b. 1960) *Fimmtán ára á föstu* (1984; Fifteen and going steady) constituted a watershed in this respect. Its main protagonist becomes pregnant, and, in the next book, *Sextán ára í sambúð* (1985; Sixteen and living together), she moves in with her boyfriend. Although the stories do not dig very deep, they became extremely popular, especially among ten- to thirteen-year-olds. Since then several authors have attempted to deal with teenage sexual experiences more openly in their works, but without much success; the descriptions tend to be forced and clumsy.

More successful have been the various attempts of recent authors to bring the past closer to the world of teenagers today. Guðlaug Richter has written two remarkable novels that deal with the age of the sagas. In *Jóra og ég* (1988; Jóra and I) the life and fate of a present-day teenage girl is juxtaposed to that of a twelfth-century girl of the same age in a strikingly original way. Both their fates are connected to Mount Hekla, which erupted in the year 1104 and destroyed prosperous settlements in southern Iceland. Novels like these make the world of the Sagas of the Icelanders more accessible to young people. Vilborg Davíðsdóttir (b. 1965) has also made use of a medieval setting in her two adventure novels about the slave girl Korka, *Við Urðarbrunn* (1993; By Urður's well) and *Nornadómur* (1994; Witches' judgment). The novels are set in Iceland, Scandinavia, and the British Isles, and, although they lack the historical and social depth of Richter's books, they are well-crafted action novels that show that not all that much has changed in human, and particularly women's, existence during the last thousand years.

During the 1980s and 1990s, fantasy began to play an ever greater role in Icelandic children's literature, as, indeed, it did in literature for adults during this time, both in Iceland and in a larger international context, with the books and films of J. K. Rowling's Harry Potter, Philip Pullman's *His Dark Materials* (1996–2000), and the renewed interest in J. R. R. Tolkien's *The Lord of the Rings* (1953), all of which have enjoyed an avid Icelandic readership (see also p. 448). It may well be that the neorealism in children's literature, which many claimed inhibited the imagination, had its role to play in this development as well. Generally, these fantasy books can be divided into two kinds: those that are set entirely in a fantasy world and those that have a realistic setting in which something fantastic occurs. The works that have tended to be most successful in this genre are those that use classic or folkloric motifs in a new, often contemporary, context.

In works aimed at younger readers fantasy replaced the realistic preschool story in ever bigger and brighter picture books for children. It has always been very expensive to print books in full color for the tiny Icelandic market, and, although some books with color pictures had been produced over the years, most of the picture books came from abroad. In the 1980s this changed owing to lowered printing costs, and a few pictures books began to be published every year. In these new books just about anything can happen: one meets giants and elves, dwarfs and trolls, who either live in their own world or among us here in ours. In *Ástarsaga úr fjöllunum* (1981; English trans.: *A Giant Love Story* [1999]), the story of Flumbra the giantess, Guðrún Helgadóttir "explains" various natural phenomena to a little boy by referring to the life and history of Flumbra. Earthquakes happen when the giants make love. The small white-foaming riverlets running down the steep mountains are the milk from Flumbra's breasts after the birth of her young. And strange rock formations are really the fossilized bodies of giants who were too late to hide before sunrise. This story has been translated and published in many countries with excellent illustrations by Brian Pilkington.

In these new picture books there are also exciting old people to be found, grandfathers and grandmothers who play around and do marvelous things. In *Blómin á þakinu* (1985; Flowers on the roof) by Ingibjörg Sigurðardóttir and Brian Pilkington, old Gunnjóna has to move from her turf cottage in the country into a modern block of flats in Reykjavík. She befriends a little boy next door, who tries to entertain her by showing her the city, but she gets bored all the same. To relieve her boredom she gradually moves the country into the city: first the cat, then vegetables, then hens, until finally she puts turf onto the roof of the block of flats, as there was on her old cottage. The last picture in the book shows sheep grazing on the turf roof, and the story ends with old Gunnjóna wondering whether she will be able to get the cow into the lift.

Fantastic elements can also be found in a number of stories for older children. Vésteinn Lúðvíksson (b. 1944) wrote two books about the girl Sólarblíðan (1981 and 1982) — the name translates as "Sunshine" — who does not shrink from using black magic when required in her constant fights with pushy grown-ups. Ármann Kr. Einarsson wrote *Mamma í upp-sveiflu* (1979; Mummy's mania), a lively story about a group of imaginative kids who decide to open a children's theater. Interestingly, sometime later a group of children in Reykjavík did just that and managed quite well for a number of years.

In Andrés Indriðason's *Elsku Barn!* (1985; Darling child!) seven-year-old Ólafía is the daughter of a fireman and an opera singer. Both her parents work long hours and are much too tired to give their daughter the attention she needs. She is a lonely child with a rich inner life, and in her desperate need for a friend she creates one in her imagination. He is Tobbi, a famous clown in a circus she once saw, and together Ólafía and Tobbi can do anything. Although he is a figment of her imagination, Tobbi helps Ólafía through a difficult period in her life, and, when she no longer needs him, she is ready to admit that he is no miracle worker; he too is just a man.

Kristín Steinsdóttir (b. 1946) wrote two contemporary ghost stories, *Draugar vilja ekki dósagos* (1992; Ghosts don't care for cola) and *Draugur í sjöunda himni* (1994; Ghost on cloud nine). The ghost in these stories is not of the white-sheet variety but more like a traditional Icelandic *móri*, or family ghost, in this case a young wretch who died in an epidemic during the nineteenth century and whose body was unceremoniously buried in a hay field. He cannot find peace until he is laid to rest in hallowed ground. This narrative informs children of the Icelandic past and old Icelandic lore in an original way that is relevant to children today.

Vigdís Grímsdóttir (b. 1953), better known for her novels and poetry for adults (see pp. 445–46), published her first children's book, *Gauti vinur minn* (Gauti my friend), in 1996. It is a lyrical story about a little boy and a mature girl who abandon their everyday reality and disappear to adventurous places with the help of an eye that Gauti finds on his birthday. There, they meet all kinds of fantastic creatures who possess remarkable secrets and great wisdom.

Þorgrímur Þráinsson's (b. 1959) prizewinning novel *Margt býr í myrkr-*

inu (1997; What hides in the dark) relates the experiences of fourteen-year-old Gabriel, who travels west to the Snæfellsnes peninsula between Christmas and New Year's to stay with his grandfather. On the way the coach driver tells him the story of Axlar-Björn, the infamous serial killer who lived on the farm next to his grandfather's four hundred years ago. When Gabriel arrives, events begin to take place that seem to indicate that the killer's ghost is on the loose, although in the end it turns out that the ghost is made of flesh and blood after all.

Much deeper is the pain in *Silfurkrossinn* (1996; The silver cross) by Illugi Jökulsson (b. 1960). The siblings Gunnsi and Magga are moving with their parents into a new house in a new neighborhood. Although the house is newly built and the family its first inhabitants, the children quickly become aware of something unsavory, which soon manifests itself as a shadow. With the help of a clairvoyant schoolmate they find out that the shadow is that of a thousand-year-old Irish monk who was murdered by vikings in the early days of Iceland's settlement. He now wants to chase them away because the house is built on his grave; the diggers have disturbed his grave and misplaced the silver cross with which he was buried. The parents gradually become more and more unhappy in the house, but the children cannot tell their parents about the monk, until they finally find a solution.

While children's literature tends to be limited almost exclusively to fiction, one author has published pioneering works in the field of poetry for children. Þórarinn Eldjárn (b. 1949), also well-known for his poetry for grown-ups and his fiction (see pp. 463, 490), has created playful experiments with language and absurdist images in several poetry collections for children — including *Óðfluga* (1991; Speedy), *Heimskringla* (1992; Globe), and *Halastjarna* (1997; Comet) — which work like a powerful trigger to the imagination. The illustrations of Sigrún Eldjárn (1954), the author's sister, remain completely true to the fantastic world created by the poems.

The most recent success in the realm of children's literature is Andri Snær Magnason's (b. 1973) illustrated story *Sagan af bláa hnettinum* (1999; The story of the blue planet), the first children's book to receive the Icelandic Literary Prize (see p. 449).

CONCLUSION

According to a survey conducted in 1986, Icelandic children were avid readers. It was a matter of pride for them to have read books, and they would pretend to have read more rather than fewer. The majority found it necessary to read the best-selling teenage novels to be able to take part in conversations with their peers, although they tended to know more about popular heroes in foreign books in translation than about books by Icelandic authors.

A recent, much larger survey showed that, in Iceland, as in most neighboring countries, children are reading less and less, especially boys. Many parents, teachers, librarians, and other friends of literature are trying to fight this trend, and Icelandic authors of children's books have joined the fight. In fact, Icelandic children's books have, on the whole, never been better than they are now.

One characteristic of Icelandic children's literature is that, throughout the twentieth century, many well-known writers of adult literature have also published one or two books for children. In a small market it is, of course, always wise not to limit oneself to one genre alone. The number of authors currently writing children's books, that is to say, who have been publishing with some regularity, is around forty, while original Icelandic children's books have numbered thirty to forty per year on average in recent years.

Characters in children's books are people we get to know when we are young, and they never leave us. It is vitally important that new generations get to know the same characters as their parents and grandparents so that they can share their experiences and opinions of them, discuss them, argue about them, and use them for comparison with other fictional characters as well as people in real life. Much has been done in Iceland to keep the best work of previous generations in circulation; all of Stefán Jónsson's and many of Ragnheiður Jónsdóttir's works have been republished with new illustrations, for instance. In 1992 an anthology of Icelandic children's literature was published. Called *Sögustund* (1992; Story time), it includes 750 pages of stories, folktales, and verse for three- to eight-year-olds, and among those pages we find Sigurbjörn Sveinsson, his older contemporary Nonni, and even Jónas Hallgrímsson as well as other writers mentioned here. Publications like these will, it is hoped, keep alive the memory of the many fictional friends that Icelandic children have had over the decades and help preserve the continuity in Icelandic children's literature.

Icelandic Canadian Literature

Daisy Neijmann

11

Romantic-nationalist definitions of culture have long tended to limit our understanding and recognition of cultural contributions that do not conform to the traditional requirements of language and place. In Iceland the so-called holy trinity of land, language, and people has been a particularly strong influence in the way *Icelandicness* has been defined and perceived (see also chapter 3). This probably holds true for Icelandic literature more than any other form of Icelandic culture, both because of the dominant part that literature has had in Icelandic cultural history and, by extension, self-perception and because of the prominent political role that literature played in the struggle for independence from Denmark as a tool both to promote national pride and to advance the idea of Iceland as a separate nation with its own exclusive culture. The Icelandic literary canon was to a large extent constructed by the author and scholar Sigurður Nordal during the 1920s and 1930s and long bore the marks of its original nationalist role: it officially established Old Icelandic literature as the matrix of the Icelandic language and of Icelandic culture and identity and emphasized cultural continuity, verisimilitude, and the role of the Icelandic landscape as the "natural" environment for and reflection of its people.

It has been only during the last number of years and the current postnationalist climate that Icelandic nationalism and, by extension, the Icelandic canon and its exclusions have come under critical scrutiny. And it can hardly be a coincidence that, after decades of neglect, the literature created by Icelandic emigrants to the New World and their descendants has been the subject of renewed attention in Iceland, among both academics and the larger public. The very fact of the continued existence of an Icelandic community that had preserved the Icelandic language and culture in North America gave rise to great enthusiasm among nationalist scholars like Sigurður Nordal and Guðmundur Finnbogason (see also pp. 365–66). They promoted the idea of the organic community and took great interest in the state and fate of Icelandic culture beyond Iceland's shores, which they embraced as part of a larger Icelandic family and culture, witnessed by the Icelandic name for the immigrants, *Western Icelanders* (Vestur Íslendingar). They acknowledged that certain changes in outlook and custom, resulting from life in a different country, were inevitable, but they tirelessly supported the ideal of cultural preservation and a "little Iceland" away from Iceland. With the inevitable loss of the Icelandic language as the primary medium of communication and literary creation, however, and the continuing development of an Icelandic Canadian culture, Icelanders were less and less able to recognize their overseas cousins as *Icelandic* by the traditional definition. All that remained was genealogy.

As Iceland has started to turn its critical gaze inward, however, and examine the changes that have occurred in Icelandic society, culture, and identity, perceptions of Icelandic Canadian literature are gradually changing as well. Rather than being seen as a "bastardization" or even an entirely alien form of literature, it seems that Icelandic Canadian literature is speaking to Icelanders today, its experimentations with the expression of cultural identity containing vital clues to the survival of minority, or "small," cultures in a global and dominantly English-speaking world. And, along with the renewed recognition of older Icelandic literature written in Latin and based on foreign models, it seems that room is now opening up for difference, for other forms of Icelandic literature, written first in Icelandic, and later in English, challenging traditional definitions of what constitutes *Icelandic* and *Icelandic literature*.

HISTORY AND BACKGROUND

At the start of the nineteenth century Icelandic society was to a large extent isolated from the rest of Europe. The disasters of the previous century had reduced the population to fewer than fifty thousand, and the rush of industrialization and modernization that characterized so many other European countries largely passed Iceland by at this time. In the course of the century, however, slowly but surely changes began to take place. Good years and fairly stable climatic conditions led to a substantial increase in population, and Reykjavík gradually began to come into its own as the country's main cultural center.

The initial ramifications of these developments began to be felt early in the 1850s. Icelandic society had remained largely unchanged for centuries and could ill accommodate the sudden increase in population. Its almost exclusively rural nature, sheep farming being the mainstay of the economy, meant that those who could not find work as farmhands hardly had any other recourse. The urban areas that tended to absorb any surplus population in other countries barely existed, and it was at this time still forbidden to make a living exclusively from fishing or to work as a free laborer. Adults who did not run a farm of their own were expected to serve as farmworkers or domestic servants or to try to eke out a living as cottars.

At the same time Icelandic culture was flourishing. Initiatives set in motion during the Enlightenment era—the printing and circulation of newspapers and magazines and the foundation of cultural societies—meant that the scattered Icelandic population could now receive information about recent events and developments that were effecting radical changes elsewhere in the world. Icelandic literature was being infused with new forms and ideas, while on the political front Icelandic intellectuals were challenging Iceland's subordinate status within the Danish realm. There was a ruling spirit of optimism and a growing belief in the possibility of effecting change. Northern Iceland, in particular the district of Þingeyrar, was at the forefront of these developments, being home to a cultural movement that encouraged its members to read and debate foreign books, nurturing a spirit of radical thinking. It was here that emigration was first discussed as a serious possibility for Icelanders, and it was from here that the first emigrants left.

People had been emigrating to the New World en masse since the Napoleonic wars, and mainland Scandinavia was no exception. Norway in particular had seen large numbers of its people leave to start a new life in North America from as early as 1830. In Iceland, however, transportation was an obstacle, restricted as it was to small vessels sailing back and forth from Copenhagen during limited times of the year. Emigration to the New World from Denmark started later and had less impact than in Norway and Sweden, which may also partly explain why Iceland was slow to catch on to the possibility. This began to change in the course of the 1850s, when the idea of emigration started to strike a chord in Iceland as well. In 1855, a small number of Icelanders who had converted to the Mormon faith emigrated to Utah. While this group left for very different reasons than later emigrants, the very occurrence of their emigration must have had an influence on those interested in the possibility. And this possibility gained in attraction in 1859 when Iceland was hit by a scab epidemic that killed large numbers of sheep and climatic conditions deteriorated severely, just at the time when the generation of people reaching adulthood was exceptionally large owing to the population increase in the 1830s and 1840s. The situation brought fears to many that another wave of bad years might once again nip in the bud all hopes of progress and a better life.

Emigration offered a solution for the population surplus, and the idea of personal freedom and individual opportunity must have seemed attractive to those whom a static Icelandic society had little to offer. Newspapers began to carry translated articles about Scandinavian settlements in America and reported on the growing interest among Icelanders elicited by the possibility of emigration. A number of influential, interested parties from Þingeyrar began to pursue the matter more seriously.

In the meantime a practical solution for the transport problem announced itself, in the form of a Reykjavík merchant who became an agent for the Canadian Allen Line in 1873, organizing transportation by steamship from Iceland to Scotland and on to North America. And so it was that, in that same year, a group of around 165 people left northern Iceland for North America. The event marked the beginning of an exodus from Iceland, with people leaving the country virtually every year until 1914. Emigration peaked after 1875, when a large volcanic eruption in Mount Askja, in eastern Iceland, destroyed the lands and possessions of many, and again during the 1880s. It is estimated that, in total, approximately fifteen thousand people, about one-fifth of the total population, left the country never to return.

AN ICELANDIC IMMIGRANT COMMUNITY

The first substantial group of emigrants that left Iceland in 1873 was, like so many, bound for the United States, where Páll Þorláksson, a young man of the cloth who had gone ahead, had made arrangements for them. On arrival in Quebec, however, they were met by another Icelander, Sigtryggur Jónasson, who had traveled to the New World independently and had been employed by the Canadian government as an immigration agent. Canada needed people to settle and work the vast stretches of land west of the Great Lakes that it had recently bought from the Hudson Bay Company, and it offered the Icelanders temporary quarters and free land. Since the Icelanders did not have any emigration history in the United States and no such offers were forthcoming from there, the large majority were easily persuaded to stay, although a small group went on to the United States with Páll Þorláksson.

This unexpected change in direction would have important consequences for the history of Icelandic immigrants in North America. Unlike almost any other European country, Iceland saw the large majority of its emigrants settle in Canada rather than the United States. Within Canada they were among the first European immigrants not from the British Isles to settle western Canada and were granted a separate stretch of land, along the western shore of Lake Winnipeg in what later became the province of Manitoba, where they were allowed to establish an exclusively Icelandic colony and preserve their Icelandic heritage. These rather exceptional circumstances, together with the fact that emigration from Iceland occurred within a relatively short and limited period of time (there was virtually no influx of new arrivals from Iceland after 1914), meant that the larger cultural context for the immigrants and their descendants was the same; they were connected in place and time. This allowed for the preservation of the Icelandic language and culture to a remarkable degree and, in the longer term, for the development of a unique minority culture, one based on the community's Icelandic heritage, immigrant history, and experience as Canadians. The main form of expression for this culture was literature.

Icelandic immigrant history in North America is exceptionally well documented, and early records make it quite clear that, while most emigrants had left their country simply to make a better life for themselves and their children, their leaders were well versed in the romantic-nationalist rhetoric that dominated Iceland at the time, and their actions and intentions for the future of Icelanders in the New World were guided by nationalist politics. At a time when Iceland was still fighting for independence and the struggle appeared to be stagnating, settlement in the New World was seen as an alternative means to create an independent Iceland, so the tract of land along Lake Winnipeg that was to be an exclusively Icelandic colony was known as "New Iceland." A constitution was created, a colony newspaper called *Framfari* (Progress) was founded, various local councils and a central colony council were established, schools were set up, and arrangements were made for a community pastor to take up the religious care of the colony.

The exclusive nature of the colony was quickly challenged, however. First, it soon transpired that the Canadian authorities had given the Icelanders land that was not yet theirs to give and to which local Salteaux people laid claim. Religious factionalism between two would-be pastors, one who supported survival and acculturation, the other emphasizing the importance of religion as a means of cultural preservation, led to the exodus of part of the immigrant community. Finally, and most important, while nationalist fervor and cultural politics kept the leaders busy, the immigrants starved in their isolation and ignorance of how to survive in the new environment. Cultural decisions led to disaster: New Iceland was intended to become a rural farming community like Iceland, but it was heavily wooded, and the Icelanders, who had only been familiar with sheep farming, knew nothing about soil preparation or growing crops, nor were they familiar with lake or ice fishing. Gradually, as it became clear that survival in the new environment and cultural exclusivity did not go together, the immigrants began to disperse, and the leaders had to admit defeat as far as the ideal of a single, exclusive Icelandic colony was concerned. This was reinforced in practical terms when New Iceland was annexed by the province of Manitoba in 1881. Ukrainian and Polish settlers were allowed into the area and quickly outnumbered the Icelandic immigrants who had remained. As they did know how to work the soil, most of the Icelanders sold their land and went on to try their luck elsewhere, entered other occupations, and/or moved to Winnipeg.

Living among other cultural groups in rural or urban areas created very different conditions for cultural adaptation and survival, but it did not spell the death of the Icelandic cultural heritage in the New World, as the leaders had feared. It merely meant the end of the ideal of cultural purity and of re-creating an independent version of the motherland. At the very same time, emigration from Iceland was reaching its peak, and large numbers arrived every year, while, in Iceland, frustration was growing at the stagnation of the political ideal of independence and seeing such large numbers of people leaving. A vicious campaign against emigrants and emigration agents resulted, abuse was heaped on everyone who had left or was thinking of leaving, and letters from immigrants often did not reach their final destination. The Icelandic immigrants in Canada were well aware of these events as the immigrant newspapers regularly carried news from Iceland, and relations between the two communities cooled significantly. The result of these developments was twofold. On the one hand, some immigrants now felt less obligation to remain obsessively loyal to Iceland and its nationalist ideals, which created some room for experimentation and flexibility in the area of cultural adaptation and preservation. On the other hand, a defensiveness on the part of many immigrants ensued, expressing itself in rather forced efforts to prove their cultural loyalty.

Within this context it should not be forgotten that the immigrant experience is one of profound duality and that the immigrants were, in a sense, fighting a cultural war on two fronts. Not only were they engaged in efforts to prove their continuing *Icelandicness*, as it were, but they also had to counter prejudice and accusations on the part of a Canadian establishment that, in the face of increasing numbers of so-called foreign immigrants, considered everyone not of white, Anglo-Saxon, Protestant stock inherently inferior and suspect and demanded that all immigrants be assimilated into their dominant culture as quickly as possible.

A NEW LITERATURE

It is against this background that Icelandic immigrant literature develops. Poetry and fiction became the main vehicles for the expression and negotiation of the issues of acculturation, cultural preservation, and identity construction, providing an insight into the process of how Icelanders in Canada began to, and continued to, imagine themselves as a community, first as immigrant Icelanders, then as Icelandic Canadians.

Eli Mandel is among the writer/critics who has offered ideas as to what characterizes immigrant writing as literature. He has defined it as "a literature existing at an interface of two cultures, a form concerned with defining itself, its voice, the dialectic of self and other and the duplicities of self-creation, transformation and identities" ("The Ethnic Voice in Canadian Literature," 65). This definition exposes the quintessence of immigrant literatures, their dual nature. As we will see, much of Icelandic immigrant literature displays a deep concern with the polarities of culture and self and with the creation of a Canadian Icelandic social and cultural identity.

The first immigrant literature was written almost as soon as the Icelanders arrived in the New World and was published by the many immigrant papers that came and went. Within a short span of time poets and writers proliferated in the immigrant community, as *Vesturheimsprent* (1986), a compilation of all Icelandic works published in Icelandic in the New World until 1900, bears witness. The narrative impulse has been shown to be common to almost every immigrant group, but it was particularly strong among the Icelanders, who brought with them a strong popular tradition of literature that constituted a natural creative outlet in the midst of profound cultural shock and change. This context was neither understood nor appreciated in Iceland, where this initial proliferation of poetry quickly earned the Icelandic immigrant community a reputation as "Eldórado leirskáldanna" (the El Dorado of bad poets; Guttormsson, "Sigurður Júl. Jóhannesson," 159). It effectively sent out the message that any literary efforts overseas would be viewed exclusively on Icelandic terms, interpreted in an Icelandic rather than a Canadian immigrant context. Any definition of *Icelandicness* was still on national Icelandic terms, which left little room for experimentation: the first

Icelandic immigrant literature is, thus, by its very nature conservative. As in the ideal of New Iceland, the expression of transplantation was through the articulation in literary terms of a different natural and social landscape: the introduction of the wide-open prairie, the Rocky Mountains, agricultural crops, thunderstorms, cultural diversity, and urban frontier life. The immigrants found these easier to embrace in their literature, and they had the added advantage of finding a relatively easy and interested reception among Icelanders at home.

It is only in the works of writers born in Canada to Icelandic immigrant parents that we begin to see more profound changes and experimentation. It is also among this generation of writers that the most radical and traumatic watershed development takes place: the change of language. The fact that the Icelandic immigrant community had made it a matter of pride not only to preserve their cultural heritage, to be "the best Icelanders," but also to be "the best Canadians" and become acculturated as quickly as possible, together with the fact that emigration from Iceland stopped after 1914, meant that the change from Icelandic to English as the primary medium of literary expression happened much earlier among them than among many other of Canada's cultural minority groups. For many the loss of Icelandic signified the end of Icelandic culture in North America, and it should, therefore, come as no surprise that it caused great upset initially as the first literary experiments in English appeared. This was followed by decades of virtual silence on the literary front as an entire generation grew up almost exclusively English speaking and hardly any literary activity took place beyond what had already occurred.

It was left to later generations—those four or five times removed from the original immigrant generation and, in many cases, the products of one or more mixed marriages—and to a change in the cultural and political climate in Canada to create a literature that demonstrated through form and content the possibility of transcending traditional definitions of national cultures.

ICELANDIC IMMIGRANT WRITING

The early settlers regarded themselves as pioneers of a transplanted Iceland, a place where Icelandic culture could thrive in an environment that fed rather than starved its inhabitants. Indeed, the earliest poems submitted to the first immigrant newspaper, *Framfari*, use the romantic Fjallkona (lit. "Mountain Woman," or the "Mother Iceland" trope; see pp. 262, 518) to posit Iceland as the "bad" mother who starves her children and New Iceland or Canada as the "good" mother who feeds them. As pioneers, the settlers romantically likened themselves to the settlement heroes of early Iceland, creating a new golden age. Accordingly, as Viðar Hreinsson has pointed out, the earliest literature either expresses deep sorrow and loss, nostalgia for the old country and the past, or tries to deal with the immediate effects of the immigrant experience, either celebrating the achievements of the settlers as brave pioneering heroes of old or, in a very few cases, lamenting the fates of those who failed or fell victim to physical or social hardship (see Hreinsson, "Vestur-Íslenskar bókmenntir"). Failure and sorrow, however, quickly became taboo—originally perhaps as a means of survival, later on as a significant gap or silence in community memory. Instead, cultural defensiveness created an obsession with achievement. At this early stage it is not yet possible to speak of what Homi Bhabha has termed the manifestation of transformational change, a "hybrid moment," as yet made impossible by the notion of cultural purity that was such an important part of Icelandic nationalism and that still dominated Icelandic immigrant culture (see Bhabha, *The Location of Culture*).

This is not to say, however, that Icelandic immigrant literature was entirely lacking in innovation or failed completely to use to its advantage what the immigrant experience and the new environment had to offer. On the contrary it provides intriguing and revealing glimpses into the gradual and traumatic process whereby the immigrants learned to adapt to their new situation, became settled, and later rooted, in the New World, and negotiated an entirely new and unique identity for themselves, one that adequately reflected their situation. This identity was, in fact, largely constructed with the help of literature: despite an often-limiting and rigidly conservative framework, they wrote themselves into existence as Icelandic Canadians (Mandel, "The Ethnic Voice in Canadian Literature").

Poetry was the most practiced form of literature among Icelandic immigrant writers, for obvious reasons. Poetry had a long, popular history. The rigid formal strictures of the Icelandic poetic tradition provided a convenient outlet for the expression of profound emotional upheaval without demanding too much of the author. Finally, the composition of short verse required considerably less time of the settlers than plotting a complete work of fiction. Thanks to a vibrant community life that has been able to sustain a large variety of cultural societies as well as an immigrant press from the first days of settlement, with the founding of *Framfari* in 1877 to the continued publication of the weekly *Lögberg-Heimskringla* today, writers had a ready forum and readership for their work, so much so, in fact, that serious writers complained about the fact that the flood of writing prevented them from commanding their own exclusive audience (Guðmundsson, *Stephan G. Stephansson*, 42; Wolf, "Heroic Past — Heroic Present," 433). In addition many popular poems circulated in manuscript and by word of mouth. The folklorist Magnús Einarsson found that most Icelandic Canadian folklore is actually contained in verse (Einarsson, "Oral Tradition and Ethnic Boundaries").

Among the most common genres of poetry composed in the New World were occasional verses, which had a long tradition in Iceland and served a practical purpose in the immigrant community both as a ritual way of adding luster to public community occasions and as a time-honored way of encapsulating community anecdotes in a form that was easily remembered and transmitted orally, a kind of grassroots history through versified storytelling. It was mostly the formal occasional verse that was published, however, and that verse bears testimony to the public self-image of the community. It is usually overly stylized and formulaic, a clichéd litany of the community's trials and achievements, with only a very few exceptions.

Another very common strand of Icelandic immigrant poetry is romantic in mood and style, reflecting the duality and divided loyalties with which the immigrants struggled, and can roughly be divided into two kinds: one group sings the praises of the new environment, usually extolling the beauty and riches of the natural landscape that carry the hope for a glorious future, while the other is nostalgic and gives expression to feelings of homesickness, loss, and uprootedness. Most of this poetry is, again, conservative, conventional in its use of form and imagery, and lacking in true emotion and originality, although here, too, there are exceptions.

Finally, we do also find a more radical strain of immigrant poetry. Starting a new life in a different environment meant that certain Old World strictures and limitations were loosened, and a marked number of people allowed themselves to hope for radical social reforms that went beyond mere individual improvements in life. Not surprisingly, many immigrants who came from northern Iceland were among this group of polemicists who regarded the New World as an opportunity to see some of the more radical ideas that had been discussed in Iceland put into practice. And in the immigrant community these poets — often unschooled and a significant number of them women — were allowed a voice, even if they often gave rise to vigorous debate and, in some cases, bitter factionalism. In fact, as Kirsten Wolf notes, it is telling that the first woman to publish a book of poetry in Iceland, the first Icelandic woman novelist, and the first Icelandic woman to publish a play were all immigrants (*Writings by Western Icelandic Women*, ed. Wolf).

One woman who saw her poetry published after she emigrated to North America and whose work became quite popular was Helga Steinvör Baldvinsdóttir (1858–1941), who wrote under the pen name Undína. Undína's poems are romantic rather than polemic, but they struck a novel, personal tone in their simplicity and their expression of genuine and profound emotion. Although hardly exceptional in its use of imagery and form, Undína's poetry stands out among other immigrant poetry in its sincerity of feeling: it neither glorifies nor suppresses. Instead, it expresses with touching clarity, aptness, and beauty the alienation, confusion, duality, nostalgia, and loss that are such an important part of the immigrant experience.

While in many of her poems Undína describes her homesickness for Iceland and the people she left behind, in others she expresses grief and longing that stem from difficult personal circumstances, and in some instances she also expresses her frustration about her situation as a woman, lonely and restrained, unable to follow her ambitions and desires. Undína saw many of her poems published in immigrant newspapers during her lifetime, and her collected poetry was published posthumously under the name *Kvæði* in 1952.

The poetic response of Júlíana Jónsdóttir (1837–1917) to her disappointment over a hard life of poverty, drudgery, and loneliness is rather more bitter and defiant than that of Undína. Jónsdóttir had already published poetry before she came to North America; in fact, the collection *Stúlka* (1876) is the first published book of poetry by a woman in Iceland (see p. 516). Her second publication, *Hagalagðar* (1916; Fleece sheddings), deals exclusively with her testing experiences in North America. Although her poems too are expressive of alienation and loneliness, in them Jónsdóttir strikes back with force at a world that has dealt her such misery. She does not look back to her native country with nostalgia; instead, she often subverts traditional patriotic poetry. Although Jónsdóttir's poetic talent was limited by circumstance, it does form a healthy and refreshing antidote to the often screwed-up, excessively romanticized voice and image that we find in so many other immigrant poems.

Jónsdóttir's brutal honesty, her grotesque imagery, and her descriptions of how her poems are born while "mucking out the byre" are reminiscent of the poetry of K.N., the pen name of Kristján Níels Júlíus Jónsson (1860–1936). Both Jónsdóttir and K.N. were unschooled poets whose lives were marked by poverty and adversity and whose poetic creations are down-to-earth and often subversive, delighting in exposing hypocrisy and dishonesty and in taking the gloss off the glorified image of the mother country and the immigrant experience. What makes K.N.'s poetry different from Jónsdóttir's is the humor and the great artistry with which he turned a conventional form, the *lausavísa*, or epigram (see pp. 42, 178), into a sparkling vehicle of clever verbal manipulation that managed to capture in an unprecedented way the life and experience of Icelandic immigrants. In addition K.N.'s work provides the first instance of an attempt to translate the experience of cultural transplantation into language and form rather than subject matter alone.

K.N. was among the most widely popular poets in the Icelandic immigrant community, and in many ways his poetry can be regarded as a more literary form of Icelandic Canadian folk poetry, not only because of the extensive use that he made of the popular form of the epigram, but also because most of his poetry deals with the daily life and environment of the community in its widest sense. Many of his poems appeared in the immigrant newspapers, while others circulated orally and were written down only later. He saw only one book of his poetry published during his lifetime, *Kviðlingar* (1920); a collection of his work, entitled *Kviðlingar og kvæði* (1945), was published posthumously.

In his poetry K.N. celebrates the Icelandic Canadian immigrant language, often using it to good effect to create double voicing, ambiguity, and irony. He chastises the cultural purists no less than those who would deny their Icelandic background, focuses on those areas of immigrant culture that the nationalists considered a "blemish" and preferred to deny, relishes cultural diversity and, indeed, hybridity, and generally creates poetic glimpses of immigrant culture as it was lived rather than imagined and idealized. His immense popularity bears witness to the extent to which the immigrant community recognized itself in the mirror that his poetry held up to them.

K.N. delighted not only in humorous descriptions of Icelandic immigrant life but also in its verbal expressions: he often interlaced his Icelandic with English words and expressions and used many typically Icelandic Canadian words, usually English words adapted to Icelandic, such as *baslari*, from *bachelor* (in "Baslara-vísa" [1945; A bachelor's verse]; see K.N., *Kviðlingar og kvæði*, 242). A typical example of K.N.'s humor captured in an unexpected final twist and wordplay through the mixing of languages is the poem "Brúin" (The bridge), where he has Iceland and North America, in the form of a young man and lady, hold hands and connect the Icelanders on each side "með 'home'-brú" (*Kviðlingar og kvæði*, 141), playing with the pronunciation of the Icelandic word *brú*, which means "bridge" but sounds like English *brew*. Paul Sigurdsson, the Icelandic Canadian poet who translated some of K.N.'s poetry, shows an instance where K.N. managed to corrupt the English as well:

Hjartakær með hárið klippt
hjá mér situr frúin.
Ef hún væri ekki gift,
yrði "something duin."
("'Ef—'," *Kviðlingar og kvæði*, 251)

Warm of heart and coiffed in style
Close by me sits the *frúin* [lady]
Were she not a married gal,
There'd be "something duin."
("'Ef—'," trans. Sigurdson, 4)

The contemporary Icelandic American poet Bill Holm once described K.N.'s poetry as inimitable expressions and perceptions of "the inner life of the pickled-in-amber immigrant culture that persisted for a few generations in every ethnic group. It had amputated the old world but didn't have time enough in one life to grow the new one inside itself. K.N. Julius wrote Icelandic salted with English words, peppered with the malapropisms of immigrants who attached Icelandic inflections and phonemes to English words, and new world meanings to unsuspecting ancient Norse words" ("Kristjan Niels Julius," 2). Thus, by mixing the two languages, playing with sound and meaning, K.N. opens up virgin territory that allows him to explore aspects of transplantation, the uneasy suspension between two cultures that each claim the immigrant's loyalty. Stefán Einarsson once called K.N. "the only humourous poet in Icelandic literary history" (*Íslensk Bókmenntasaga*, 460) and suggested that this was the influence of his North American environment. Perhaps it was the very fact that he felt less burdened by the weight of literary tradition within his genre that made him feel free to experiment.

But it was not all harmless fun. K.N. frequently used his humor as a tool for sharp social criticism and often aimed his arrows at hypocrisy and social injustice. Equally frank are his poetic expressions of sexual desire and his love of the bottle. His poem "Æfintýri á gönguför" (1930; English trans.: "Tale of the Wayside," in *Icelandic Lyrics*, ed. Beck) gained great popularity in Iceland as a drinking song but offended many in the Icelandic Canadian community who had been influenced by North American Puritan values and mores, as, indeed, did the following:

Fairest of all maidens and handsome in design;
Graced with women's virtue and excellently fine.
She lounged upon a sofa, a warming eye on me —
"Just help yourself, dear fellow, and God will then help thee."
("Sweet She Was," trans. Sigurdson, 3)

As Matthías Johannessen (1958) observes, K.N. was also the first poet who played with and subverted one of the most famous scenes in *Njáls saga*, the one where the hero Gunnar defies his sentence of exile because he does not want to leave his country. The nineteenth-century romantic poet Jónas Hallgrímsson made this scene the topic of his poem "Gunnarshólmi" (1838; see p. 268), in which Gunnar is patriotism personified as he becomes part of the land itself as well as an example of ancestral nobility and heroic feats. K.N. turns this image completely on its head, which at that time virtually amounted to a form of literary sacrilege. In his poem "Gunnar would rather go to hell / than stay at home on native shores," where he walked around as one of the living dead, although he does not fare much better when he arrives in North America ("Gunnars-saga hin nýja" [1945; The new saga of Gunnar]; *Kviðlingar og kvæði*, 272–73). In K.N.'s poetry we thus have the first indications of what Homi Bhabha called the *hybrid moment*, the attempt to create something truly new, beyond, or besides, the one or the other.

One of the difficulties that writers from minority cultures are faced with is the fact that, belonging to and drawing their inspiration from two (or more) literary traditions, they often end up in a literary no-man's-land. The poet Stephan G. Stephansson (1853–1927) is a notable exception in this respect. Not only was he included in the Icelandic literary canon early on, but he is also recognized, if not exactly canonized, in Canada, which may be considered quite an achievement, bearing in mind that he wrote exclusively in Icelandic and that there exists a history of dissatisfaction with the quality of the various translations made of his work.

His great appeal in Iceland seems to have been the way in which Stephansson managed to perfect the combination of Old World culture and New World landscape. He succeeded in stretching the Icelandic language and poetic tradition to its limits by infusing it with new concepts and ideas, thereby taking both to new heights. A self-taught man who left Iceland at seventeen and settled land three times over, Stephansson achieved a mastery of the long-standing Icelandic popular poetic tradition, in language and form, and skillfully used it in original ways to describe his new environment as a pioneer farmer in the Albertan foothills of the Rocky Mountains.

Stephansson's works inevitably show the change in outlook that his transplantation has effected: his concerns are international, his social criticism is largely based in Canadian situations, and there is evidence of the diverse cultures among which he lived. His poems about Icelandic history focus mainly on pioneers, in the broadest sense of the word, celebrating their vision and achievement.

Stephansson hailed from northern Iceland, and his work bears clear witness to his radical thinking, which grew to fruition under the influence of American transcendentalism, the freethinkers' movement, and Marxism, for he read widely and extensively. He was a humanitarian and a pacifist, and his poetry has a very wide scope, dealing with international issues that range from the Bolshevik Revolution to the Boer War, and shifting perspective from the local to the universal and from past to present. "The whole world is my district," he once claimed (*Andvökur*, 2:73). Indeed, this is probably what has earned him a measure of recognition in Canada, which, at the time of Stephansson's writing, could not boast of much local writing that displayed this kind of universal outlook and modern sensibility.

However, despite the originality and broad scope of his work, there is, in the end, no real cultural transformation that occurs in Stephansson's works, only a sensibility of cultural displacement. "I have acquired somehow no fatherland" ("Útlaginn" [1891; English trans.: "The Exile," in *Stephan G. Stephansson: Selected Prose and Poetry*]) and "Though you wide-journeying place / every country underfoot, / your mind and heart bear / your homeland's resemblance" ("Úr Íslendingadagsræðu" [1904; English trans.: "From an Islendingadagur Address," in *Stephan G. Stephansson: Selected Prose and Poetry*]) are lines from two of his most celebrated poems (Stephansson, *Selected Prose and Poetry*, 75, 53). Stephansson acknowledged that, culturally, he would always remain an Icelander living abroad. He was twenty years of age when he left Iceland and recognized himself that he was by then "already formed and unable to yield to outside pressure," as he put it in his autobiographical fragment (*Selected Prose and Poetry*, 20).

Stephansson's position, then, can be seen at the same time as one of international exposure and of exile and displacement, particularly so because he was at frequent points of his writing life an exile in his own community. His radical views often caused antagonism, particularly his atheism and his pacifist views. His collection of fierce antiwar poems, *Vígslóði* (1920; Battlefield), which expresses his deeply felt opposition to the First World War and the participation in it of Canada, and Icelandic Canadians in particular, caused deep and painful divisions within the community, divisions that were very slow to heal. The poems in *Vígslóði* are virtually unique in both Icelandic and Canadian literature in the way in which they deal with modern warfare and its effects on the common people from a profoundly modern sensibility: Stephansson posits the soldiers as brothers set against each other, the pawns of imperialist forces of greed. In "Vopna-hlé" (1915; Ceasefire) the soldiers talk to each other across the trenches during a cease-fire, knowing that they will have to kill each other as soon as the call to arms comes. In "Sláturtíðin" (1916; Slaughter time; English trans.: "In Wartime," in Kirkconnell, ed. and trans., *Canadian Overtones*) Stephansson portrays Europe as a slaughterhouse, killing its own people to feed the fleshpots:

> In Europe's reeking slaughter-pen
> They mince the flesh of murdered men,
> While swinish merchants, snout in trough,
> Drink all the bloody profits off!
> (Kirkconnell, ed. and trans., *Canadian Overtones*, 22)

The original contains a particularly gory image of Britain stirring a pot of blood that the Canadian translator left out of his translation. Indeed, many of the arrows of Stephansson's pacifist poetry are directed at British imperialist politics, a fact that led some to prepare charges of treason against him (Gudsteins, "Rediscovering Icelandic Canadian Pacifism").

The long narrative poem *Á ferð og flugi* (1900; English trans.: "En Route," in *Selected Translations from Andvökur*) was a departure from the poet's more traditional narrative poems based in the Icelandic past. Here, Stephansson paints a lively picture of the prairies in pioneer times as well as of his fellow Icelandic pioneers, adapting form, language, and imagery to convey the atmosphere and the landscape in a vivid, accurate way. The poem is written in light, smoothly flowing lines that, although they do contain the inevitable Icelandic alliterative patterns, are especially suited to Canadian subject matter: they convey the speed of the train as it is rolling through the flat prairie landscape, the rush of the people who are out to gain a fortune quickly in the mining town of Golden and are just as quickly brought down, and the rootlessness and superficiality of the crowds who have shaken off their past to live in a present of materialism and appearances. In the following example this is effectively contrasted with the intransience of the surrounding natural landscape:

> On through the vastness and darkness the train
>   Kept ever its shadowy way,
> With no halt in the heat of its thunderous haste,

No hesitant falter nor stay.
Far out in the infinite vault of the sky,
    The stars in their courses look'd on
To mock the machine and its stertorous breath
    With flames that for eons had shone.
But the prairies flowed by like an ebony sea
    Of boundless and billowless black,
Where our train, a long Doomship, with belly of fire,
    Sought Asgard with death in its track.
    (trans. Watson Kirkconnell, in *Selected Translations from Andvökur*, 9)

The poem's main theme is one that echoes through much Icelandic immigrant literature: that of the innocent Icelandic girl who loses her moorings in a frontier city, becomes separated from her culture and compatriots, and ends up going to the dogs. Rather than painting a conventional black-and-white picture that firmly lays the blame at the door of either the girl or the "English" and the city, however, Stephansson criticizes the hypocrisy of the Icelandic immigrants, particularly the servants of the church, who rejected those who fell by the wayside in the struggle to "make it" in the New World, condemning them as a shame to the Icelandic nation. In *Á ferð og flugi*, the real gold is to be found in the heart of the poem's disreputable heroine, Ragnheiður.

Stephansson's poetry was collected and published in six volumes under the title *Andvökur* (1909–38), referring to the "waking nights" during which Stephansson wrote his poems, after working as a farmer during the day. In many ways his work constitutes the realization of a nationalist ideal, the transplantation of a national Icelandic culture, its preservation in a different place, widening the scope of Icelandic literature, yet fully recognizable as Icelandic, and uncontaminated at its core.

The peak of this ideal was realized in the work of another farmer poet, also a playwright, Guttormur J. Guttormsson (1878–1966), who was born to Icelandic immigrants and lived in the New Iceland area all his life. He never saw Iceland until 1938, when he was invited to visit by the Icelandic government in recognition of his cultural achievements. These "cultural achievements" were his poetry and plays, which were written exclusively in Icelandic. Guttormsson frequently described phenomena unknown in Iceland and Icelandic, but he succeeded in doing so without admitting Canadian English–language influences into his own poetic language. Instead, he modeled his work largely on traditional Icelandic poetic diction and imagery, coining new words where necessary, as had his predecessor Stephansson. Unlike Stephansson, however, Guttormsson used more international influences in his choice of form.

Guttormsson belonged to the generation that was born and brought up in Canada, and we can discern a more historical perspective in his works. He looks back at the achievements of the pioneer generation with awe and pays tribute to it in his poetry to make sure that its sacrifices are not forgotten. His most successful tribute is also his most famous poem, "Sandy Bar" (1920; English trans. in *Aurora/Áróra*), which is concerned directly with the loss and tragedy involved in the pioneer experience. The poem is named after a graveyard in New Iceland where victims of the smallpox epidemic that struck the immigrant community in 1876 were buried. In the poem the narrator visits this graveyard, where atmosphere, nature, and lingering ghosts mingle into what becomes an apocalyptic vision of the pioneer experience. The poem is written in the form used by Edgar Allan Poe in "The Raven" (1845), which adds to its haunting atmosphere, while its poetic diction is based in the Icelandic tradition, as are its literary images. The natural scenery, however, with its towering trees and wild thunderstorm, is Canadian.

In "Sandy Bar" the uneven bargain of the pioneers is poignantly described through images of broken hearts and broken strength as the pioneers built the road to the future with the breath of death on their necks and the haunting fear of not being able to finish their work. As lightning lights up the graves, the narrator realizes that the pioneers awaited no gratitude or glory, not even the satisfaction of a job finished, only a grave and a forgotten name. As, in the climactic last stanzas, the natural surroundings seem to reenact the tragedy of those pioneers, the elements suddenly blend together to form a vision that links the pioneers to the deeds and glory of the ancient saga heroes through literary allusion. In the last stanza the sky suddenly breaks open and shows a star-ridden arch of heaven, and the narrator realizes that the eventual pioneer settlement is achieved and enjoyed in heaven rather than on earth.

Like his fellow poets Stephansson and K.N., Guttormsson could be highly polemical, and his more critical poems are quite strikingly grim and black, often using satire as a vehicle for his social critique. A dramatic example is the poem "Indíána hátíð" (1930; English trans.: "Indian Festival," in Kirkconnell, "A Skald in Canada"), modeled on Henry Wadsworth Longfellow's *Song of Hiawatha* (1855). The poem is a scathing invective against Canada's treatment of its native peoples, as the final stanzas show:

Such are our Indians: tattered wrecks,
In exile from life's busy strand;
Held in this limbo by law's checks
That will not let them roam the land —
Land, where their fathers used to play,
Land, that is theirs no longer now,
Land, that at best they may survey
With silent grief and gloomy brow.

A roasting-stake above the fire
Is bending, spitted through a cur
(Shot with an arrow when desire
For dinner smote the reveller).
Low on their haunches they devour
The reeking fragments, loath to wait;
This white dog over which they glower
Stands for the White Man, whom they hate.
(trans. W. Kirkconnell, in *Aurora/Áróra*, 121)

Guttormsson, who grew up in close proximity to Salteaux settlements, was all too aware of the plight of the Salteaux and the fact that the Icelandic settlement in this area had meant their displacement. He was one among only a very few Icelandic immigrant authors who included native Canadians in his writing, and his descriptions stand out for their realism, tainted neither by hostility nor by a romantic idealism.

Guttormsson's most original contribution to Icelandic Canadian poetry is probably his use of symbolism and imagery. He created some outstanding images in which he combined elements from his native Canadian environment with his ancestral literary heritage in highly original ways, such as his delicate, lyric portrayal in "Á víð og dreif" (1944; Far and wide) of Indian summer as a native Canadian maiden with the shiny hue of the stars on dark winter nights in her hair and wearing a dress of rainbow-colored leaves, her complexion carrying the copper glow of wheat fields under the autumn sun, who suddenly, on the arrival of winter, pulls on her polar bear fur cloak and disappears. At the same time it is clear that Guttormsson stopped short of the kind of poetic experiments that one might have expected of someone in his unique position and with his obvious talent. In this he was quite clearly held back by the filial duty he felt toward his Icelandic immigrant heritage. The one notable exception is his popular poem "Winnipeg Icelander" (1920), in which he follows in K.N.'s footsteps and writes in the Icelandic-English mixture that was the everyday language of many immigrants, although for Guttormsson this is clearly a one-off joke, whereas for K.N. it was a regular feature of his poetry.

Guttormsson published six volumes of poetry in total. His work was generally well received and popular among Icelandic Canadians, but, ultimately, beyond his own community, his position as a poet was an isolated one. His work never reached a larger Canadian readership, while the Icelandic recognition of his writing was largely symbolic and had very little to do with his actual poetry.

ICELANDIC IMMIGRANT FICTION

At the time of emigration the modern novel or short story hardly existed in Iceland. For immigrant writers this proved to be both an obstacle and an advantage. On the one hand, it meant that native fictional models were lacking. We see this reflected in the fact that much Icelandic immigrant fiction is marred by amateurism and clumsiness, the stories weighed down by their moral message, a lack of natural character development, and an obvious stiltedness. On the other hand, it meant that fiction writers had more freedom to experiment than did poets, who worked in a time-honored tradition and were under severe pressure to preserve this heritage with their work. In the hands of the most capable writers Icelandic immigrant fiction becomes an intriguing experiment in creating a literary vehicle for the negotiation and construction of an appropriate New World identity that encompassed both the Old and the New.

Immigrant fiction is importantly shaped by a documentary impulse, recording the settlement experience and how to survive it, as well as providing psychological support through the reexamination and redefinition of an old value system to suit the new context. At the same time it is pervaded by a profoundly romantic strain — and inevitably so, for, as the Canadian author and critic Robert Kroetsch has pointed out, it is a literature born not just from nostalgia but, more important, from rebirth and regeneration (Kroetsch, "The Grammar of Silence"). Immigrant narrative is constructed out of binary patterns, the immigrant being caught in between opposites until he or she eventually reaches a point of silence, followed by the creation of a new self and a new life. The garden myth thus assumes special importance in the literary context of emigration to the New World, the promised land. In Icelandic immigrant fiction, this promised land becomes the home of an Icelandic hero figure, who embodies the best of the old and successfully applies it in the new. This heroic image embodies the dual aspirations of the Icelandic pioneers: to become successful in their new environment against all odds yet remain loyal to their ancestral culture.

However, like poetry, fiction, too, became a battleground for contesting ideas regarding the morals and ideals that were to become the foundation for a new culture and identity. The budding Icelandic realist movement in literature provided a suitable literary framework in this context, particularly while some of its most talented proponents, the authors Einar H. Kvaran (1859–1938) and Gestur Pálsson (1852–91), both discussed in an earlier chapter, stayed in Canada and became newpaper editors for a time. Kvaran's short story "Vonir" (1890; Hopes), which deals with the immigrant experience, is, in fact, considered to be among his best work. Later, Kvaran edited, along with Guðmundur Finnbogason, an anthology of immigrant writing in Icelandic entitled *Vestan um haf* (1930; From across the Atlantic).

PIONEERING NARRATIVES

It is probably because of both a lack of models and adverse conditions during the early pioneer years that Icelandic immigrant fiction was considerably slower to develop than poetry, which was literally composed from the very day the first group of emigrants left Iceland.

Although Torfhildur Þorsteinsdóttir Hólm (1845–1918) is not generally classified as belonging to the Icelandic Canadian literary tradition because her works do not deal with the emigration to and settlement in the New World, she must still be regarded as a pioneer in more than one way, as Kirsten Wolf shows in her study of immigrant women writers (Wolf, *Writings by Western Icelandic Women*; see also p. 519). Hólm was widowed young, only a year after her marriage, which gave her a certain independence. During the first years after her arrival in the New World in 1876 she lived with her sister and brother-in-law, Sigtryggur Jónasson, a leader (as we have seen) in the immigrant community and better established than most immigrants at that time. Thus, she was in a better position than most to devote herself to literary activities, and she certainly lost no time. During the first two years, she collected oral tales among the Icelandic immigrants, four of which were published in *Draupnir* in 1897, one of the magazines she edited after her return to Iceland. Several of her short stories appeared in the immigrant papers, the first one, "Tárablómið" (The flower of tears), in *Framfari* in 1879.

While many of Hólm's stories resemble fables or moral allegories, others depict daily life in Iceland. The importance of women's education as a means toward their liberation is a prominent theme in her work. Hólm is, however, no real polemicist or radical thinker, preferring to communicate her message in ways that are the least likely to alienate more conservative readers, and trying to persuade through gentle logic instead. It was also during her years in New Iceland that her first novels were published, *Brynjólfur Sveinsson biskup* (1882; Bishop Brynjolfur Sveinsson) and *Kjartan og Guðrún* (1886; Kjartan and Gudrun), as well as two collections of short stories, *Smásögur og æfintýri* (1884; Short stories and fairy tales) and *Smásögur handa börnum* (1886; Short stories for children). Hólm returned to Iceland in 1889.

Hólm's early example was followed up somewhat later by Margrjet Jónsdóttir Benedictsson (1866–1956), who has become primarily known as a women's rights activist and as the editor of the suffragette and literary journal *Freyja* (1898–1910), and whose writing has rather undeservedly been overlooked. Although Benedictsson wrote in many genres, including poetry, her short stories, some of which are, in fact, more like sketches, are particularly worthy of closer study. Like Hólm's, they are highly symbolic, sometimes bordering on the impressionistic, and carry a clear moral message, but Benedictsson's stories are both more original in their symbolism and much more radical and outspoken in their social criticism. Although the condition of women is a frequent theme, Benedictsson is concerned with the downtrodden in general: her writings no less than her activism reveal her profound commitment to the ideal of a new and better world in Canada for everyone. In her social polemicism and the satiric vein in some of her stories she has, in fact, much in common with her contemporaries Stephan G. Stephansson and K.N., with whom she kept in touch, and there are clear influences of the realist movement in her writing. Most of her published work appeared under various pen names in *Freyja*, which, in fact, provided an opportunity for publication for other women writers such as Undína and Jakobína Johnson (see p. 530).

IMMIGRANT HEROES

The author Jóhann Magnús Bjarnason (1866–1945) contributed to virtually all genres of Icelandic immigrant writing and was among the very first to see his work published in book form, including *Sögur og kvæði* (1892; Stories and poems) and *Ljóðmæli* (1898; Collection of poetry). While the social criticism in his early stories upset many in the community, his poems were quick to achieve popularity, particularly his sensitive, lyric depictions of immigrant sacrifices and victims, for instance, that in "Íslenskur sögunarkarl í Vesturheimi" (1898; An Icelandic sawyer in North America). Bjarnason continued this softer, more lyric strain in his later prose, in his best work using it to good effect to expose the "other side" of the immigrant experience, the plight of the socially and economically disenfranchised. His sympathy and concern always rested with the unfortunate and downtrodden in life, and his works are a clear attempt to give them a voice and make them heard. As a result, his work introduces for the first time into Icelandic literature the ethnic mosaic that was developing in Canada and, along with it, an awareness of the "muted" position of the socially excluded in general and the immigrant in particular. In his fiction this situation is turned on its head as the immigrant becomes a hero who struggles and emerges victorious against all odds. This heroism represents not only a re-creation but, more important, also a validation of the immigrant experience. While Bjarnason's heroes are frequently Icelandic, they are by no means exclusively so. On the contrary, his work features a remarkable gallery of cultures and nationalities, all of whom get along and respect each other. The dominant dialectic in Bjarnason's fiction is, in fact, that of multicultural self versus Anglo-Canadian other. In this respect Bjarnason's work is an extraordinarily early example of a feature that has since come to be regarded as a commonality of Canadian minority literatures: the awareness of a multidimensional self that is extended to the social and geographic environment (Padolsky, "Canadian Minority Writing").

Bjarnason's best-known and most popular work is undoubtedly *Eiríkur Hansson*, initially serialized (1899–1903), and later published in Iceland (1949–50). Largely autobiographical, *Eiríkur Hansson* represents in many ways the archetypal immigrant novel, featuring the characteristic structure of home idyll, reasons for emigration, journey across the Atlantic, settlement, hardships in the New World, symbolic death, and, finally, rebirth followed by prosperity. The novel is told from the point of view of a young boy, Eiríkur, who is seven years old at the time of emigration. His naive perspective is very effective as it reinforces the immigrant experience: in a strange new environment, unable to speak the language, and cut loose from all social and cultural securities, the immigrant's situation resembles that of a child in many ways. In addition Eiríkur's last name, Hansson (lit. "his son"), makes him into a kind of immigrant Everyman.

As well as introducing new subject matter *Eiríkur Hansson* struck a new tone in Icelandic literature. Bjarnason was a great admirer of Charles Dickens, and the influence of *David Copperfield* (1850) is widely apparent in the novel. This led some to complain about the verbosity and mawkishness that occasionally mar the work and, in fact, some of Bjarnason's fiction in general. On the whole, however, *Eiríkur Hansson* successfully achieves its aims as an immigrant novel. Among the best and most memorable descriptions in the book are those of the physical and psychological cost of emigration and of the deaths of Eiríkur's grandfather and, later, his grandmother, who raised the orphaned Eiríkur. Both were physically broken as well as heartbroken by the experience. Another moving passage relates Eiríkur's feelings as he returns to the Icelandic settlement in the Nova Scotian Mosquodoboit Valley, which had to be abandoned because the soil was unfit for crops. As Eiríkur sits down in the ghost settlement he sees a squirrel that becomes the personification of the ghostly, haunted atmosphere that the place conjures up in his mind:

> It was in high spirits. It moved about restlessly with glee and turned the nut around to all sides, looking at me at times, screeching. It was like it was telling me that now everybody was gone. "Everybody gone, — everybody gone, everybody, — everybody — everybody!" I thought I heard it say. "And why don't you go — you go — you go?" Then it finally got the kernel out of the nut and dropped the shell. It ran from branch to branch up and down the birch tree and screeched continually. It was like its screeching carried irony. "I can manage," I thought it said, "and *I* can live here well enough, but *they* couldn't — they couldn't — they couldn't — ar-r-r-r!" (Bjarnason, *Eiríkur Hansson*, 179–80)

Among Bjarnason's other work, his fantasy and fairy tales, later collected under the title *Gimsteinaborgin* (1977; City of jewels), are noteworthy as experiments in "translating" Icelandic folklore and mythology into something uniquely Icelandic Canadian. In the detective novel *Í Rauðárdalnum* (1914–22; English trans.: *In the Red River Valley* [1988–94]), Bjarnason approached the matter from the opposite end and attempted to give the Icelandic immigrants a place in local, particularly native, folklore. Both are remarkable literary instances of cultural transplantation, although Bjarnason was obviously not prepared to make the final, definitive step: his works ultimately still confirm the possibility of being an Icelander in Canada, without challenging or changing in any significant way the definition of *Icelander*, as Karl, the child protagonist in his story "Karl litli — saga frá Draumamörk" (1935; Little Karl — a story from dream forest), confirms when he visits Iceland and tells the children there: "I am an Icelander just like you. I live in Manitoba in Canada. I will live there all my life, and yet I always want to remain an Icelander" (Bjarnason, *Gimsteinaborgin*, 141).

In the fiction of Gunnsteinn Eyjólfsson (1866–1910) we find a much darker, satiric tone. Eyjólfsson's first publication, the novella *Elenóra* (1894), which was inspired by an obituary in the immigrant press, is a pastoral-realist work. It seems to aim toward a subversion of the New World comedy, the garden myth, where the informing opposition is that between country and city. Elenóra, an innocent country girl from New Iceland, departs for the city and becomes the sacrificial victim, offered up as the price of success in the New World. The story ends in death without regeneration; the twins to which she gives birth just before her death are stillborn. However, Eyjólfsson lays the blame, not on Canada or the "other" world outside the Icelandic community, but on the Icelandic immigrants who are willing to offer up everything for material success, a willingness that, in Eyjólfsson's view, can result in nothing but spiritual and moral death.

Eyjólfsson's second story, "Amerísk gestrisni" (1895; American hospitality), is again a scathing attack on social inequality and moral degeneration. This time, however, it is set in an Anglo-Canadian context, and the oppositions of rich versus poor and morality versus immorality are played out through a pastor and his wife, on the one hand, and, on the other, a lost, starving Irish boy who is victimized by a legal system that works only for the wealthy Anglo-Canadian level of society.

In the three stories about the Icelandic immigrant farmer Jón of Strympa, probably his best-known pieces, Eyjólfsson changed from the tragic to the satiric. These stories are highly carnivalesque, subverting every possible polarity and way of acculturation and success in the New World. New Iceland is here no longer paradise but the site of Jón of Strympa's battles with the community's morals and values, as symbolized by the local board. This Icelandic Canadian antihero, whose motto for success in the New World is "own nothing and do nothing" (*Western Icelandic Short Stories*, ed. and trans. Wolf and Hjaltadóttir, 47), sets out to rewrite Icelandic Canadian history with his account of "Hvernig ég yfirbugaði sveitaráðið" (1897–8; English trans.: "How I Defeated the Local Board," in *Western Icelandic Short Stories*) after he has been unnamed in local history. Jón's fascination with renaming and creating an identity is introduced early in the story, where he relates his obsession with collecting his name in print on the labels of the immigrant paper *Lögberg*. He tells his story to create his own legend, subverting the patterns used by Icelandic immigrant writers such as Bjarnason to mythically locate Icelanders in Canada through the creation of Icelandic Canadian culture heroes.

The satire is continued in "Járnbrautarnefndin" (1901; The railroad committee; originally called "Íslenzk þröngsýni" [Icelandic narrow-mindedness]), where Jón is elected by the local board to represent the New Icelanders' petition for a railroad. Again, a New Icelander goes to the city, and a clash between community self and outside other takes place, but this time the clash is depicted in much more subtle and effective ways, for instance, in the following scene where Eyjólfsson works out the polarities between success and failure, city and country, as Jón watches the bedbugs on the walls of his hotel room:

> And these were tidy creatures. He thought he could discern some difference between them and their sisters that crawled the walls of Strympa and hardly had a drop of blood in them. There was of course quite a difference in the type of life they led. Up north they had lived with starvation and misery for twenty years, and had had nothing else to feed on but lethargic and run-down old people, while the others had grown up and lived in affluence and indulgence with wealthy Icelanders and maidens in the city. It was hardly surprising that they were plump and happy-looking. (Eyjólfsson, *Jón á Strympu og fleiri sögur*, 39)

The Jón of Strympa stories, as well as the story "Góðar taugar" (1898; Good at heart), are also examples of how Eyjólfsson uses writing as a process of revelation or exposure, beginning to tell the untold stories of the Icelandic immigrants in Canada. "Góðar taugar" is the tale of an Icelandic pauper who descends into alcoholism and violence and almost commits suicide. Instead, he emigrates to Canada to begin a new life and finds a way to atone for his past sins. In this story Canada is the site of reconciliation and new life. Unsurprisingly, Eyjólfsson's stories rubbed many in the community the wrong way and were largely ignored or dismissed as being too dark. It is largely thanks to the efforts of the poet, printer, and publisher Gísli Jónsson, who recognized Eyjólfsson's talent and original voice and published his collected stories under the title *Jón á strympu og fleiri sögur* (1952; Jón of Strympa and other stories), that his work has not been entirely lost to later generations of readers.

Gísli Jónsson was also the one to recognize and encourage the writing talent of his wife, Guðrún Helga Finnsdóttir (1884–1946), who published two collections of short stories, *Hillingalönd* (1938; Mirages) and *Dagshríðar spor* (1946; Tracks of the day's struggle), and one collection of essays, *Ferðalok* (1950; Journey's end). Although she herself was an immigrant who came to Canada when she was twenty years old, Finnsdóttir emigrated relatively late, in 1904, and seriously embarked on her writing only once her children had grown up. As a result, her work largely reflects the perspective of the second generation, those who were born in Canada, and the conflict between their views and those of the original immigrants.

This is a common theme in later immigrant fiction, where matters can now be viewed in retrospect and cultural tensions often take the form of a clash between the hopes and aspirations of the generation born in the New World and the experiences and ideals of the original immigrants, which occurs as both try to come to grips with the acculturation process. Structurally, the historical perspective frequently appears as a flashback in Finnsdóttir's fiction, usually an older person reflecting on a certain event in her or his life.

We find this exemplified in Finnsdóttir's first story, "Landskuld" (Land debt), which was published in 1920. An elderly widow, Ingibjörg, has seen her adopted son Einar volunteer for service in the First World War and his engagement to his fiancée, Sigríður, end because of it; being fiercely opposed to the war, she broke with him when he told her he had signed up. On the news of Einar's death, Ingibjörg reflects on the deep and painful divisions that the war has caused within the community and, closer to home, between loved ones. She herself bitterly resented and rebuked Sigríður at the time, feeling that the Icelanders were obliged to Canada for having offered them a new life and new opportunities. On reflection, however, she feels only loss and regret, concluding that there are no winners in war and that factionalism has only made things worse. This story clearly demonstrates the historical perspective in the way it deals from a distance in time with an issue that was so deeply controversial and split the Icelandic immigrant community. Sigríður's convictions echo Stephansson's views as expressed in his antiwar poetry, while Ingibjörg's represent those of many others who felt indebted to Canada. The story's conclusion is one that echoes throughout Finnsdóttir's work: that of the reunion of polarized selves.

The reconciliation between polarities also features prominently in the two-part story "Fýkur í sporin" (1921; Wind blowing in the tracks), where many binary patterns interact: old versus new; self versus other; city versus country; integration versus separation; cultural versus material values; inferiority versus superiority. All these binaries are worked out through the marriage of the Icelandic immigrant daughter Ragnhildur to an Anglo-Canadian. In the first part we get the viewpoint of Ingólfur, Ragnhildur's father, on his daughter's wedding day. Ingólfur must come to terms with the fact that his daughter is not marrying someone of Icelandic descent. For him this event has major implications. Like all pioneers, he had to pay a high price for his success as a farmer in Canada. He lost his wife during the pioneer years, and now he is losing his daughter too, the object of his hopes and future dreams, as she leaves him for an "Englishman." In his view she is as good as lost, for she will disappear in the "ocean of English." However, as Ingólfur sits and watches over his land, he comes to the realization that the future brings a new generation that will have its own history and experience. The story ends affirmatively as Ingólfur takes the final step toward his psychological root taking in Canada: "The life's wages of the immigrant are usually meager, and always the same: He is given land, it is true, but in return he gives his life, his health, and all his workpower. Yes, the land absorbs him, body and soul, and his children in flocks of thousands" (Finnsdóttir, *Dagshríðar spor*, 205). In spite of its elegiac tone, this is New World comedy, ending with the affirmation of life, marriage, and regeneration, in the peace and affluence of Ingólfur's prairie garden.

The second part of the story is told from Ragnhildur's point of view as she looks back to the first years of her marriage. She is introduced in the story as the New World child of spring and hope who gradually withers in the city's chilling social climate. Ragnhildur's parents-in-law are wealthy social snobs who strongly object to their only son's marriage to a "foreign" farmer's daughter. Caught between two worlds, the marriage descends into silence. Their daughter brings the matter to a head when she speaks Icelandic to the "wrong" grandfather. As Ragnhildur's father-in-law threatens to disinherit the little girl if she is taught any more "foreign talk," Ragnhildur flees back to her father's farm and the Icelandic community. There, like her father before her, she regains her balance and comes to realize that, by polarizing, she only helps aggravate the situation instead of changing it. She opts for her marriage and her daughter, for integration rather than separation, and comes to terms with the fact that her nationality as well as everyone else's will be absorbed by Canada in return for new life in a new country.

Finnsdóttir's fiction is largely introspective and focuses primarily on the female perspective and women's experience of immigration and acculturation. The ultimate optimism in her stories stems from a belief in ancestral continuity, where women usually act as a vehicle for the community's collective memory and are the ones who pass on cultural values, wisdom, and lore. No character is so widely present in her work as the older, storytelling woman rich in worldly wisdom. Thus, women in Finnsdóttir's fiction embody the future of the community and its culture in the New World. That Finnsdóttir's portrayal of women as culture bearers should not be confused with the nationalist objectification of woman as the "mother of Iceland" and the guardian of the country's purity, however, is demonstrated in the stories "Á vegamótum" (At crossroads) and "Enginn lifir sjálfum sér" (No man is an island), both in *Hillingalönd*. Here, Finnsdóttir attacks the community's and the church's double standards toward women in the form of Steinunn, a district nurse who leaves her alcoholic and adulterous husband and becomes an outcast in the community.

At the time of Finnsdóttir's writing, the Icelandic language was quickly losing ground, and Canadian values, viewpoints, and loyalties were taking over. While Finnsdóttir sympathized with the original immigrants' concerns about the future of the Icelandic heritage, she also understood the younger generation who had never seen Iceland. Her stories often revolve around this painful reality, but they also express hope, for as she says in "Dyr hjartans" (Door of the heart): "Heredity follows the generations. . . . The generations hold hands, whatever people say" (Finnsdóttir, *Dagshríðar spor*, 118–19).

For Finnsdóttir the only way forward in the New World was through mutual understanding and respect. While her stories break no new ground in any way, they are well written and quietly effective in their depiction of the slow acculturation process and their expression of the psychological consequences of immigration, consequences that lingered long after the initial pioneer struggles were won.

ICELANDIC LITERATURE IN ENGLISH

Traditionally, the "end" of Icelandic immigrant literature as a part of Icelandic literature has been marked by the change in language, both by Icelanders in Iceland and by North American Icelanders. Although from a national-literary perspective this is as sensible a demarcation as can be expected when dealing with something that is inherently and inevitably artificial, it does create certain problems. The change to English did not automatically signify the end of the Icelandic immigrant imagination in literature or its concerns with the preservation of the Icelandic heritage, nor did it mean the automatic transformation from an "Icelandic" to a "Canadian" literature. This becomes abundantly clear when we consider the work of Laura Goodman Salverson (1890–1970), who, like Guttormsson, was born in Canada to Icelandic immigrant parents, and who, like Finnsdóttir, published her first works in the early 1920s. Salverson was brought up in an Icelandic-speaking environment, learning English only when she was ten years old, and her father was an active participant in the Icelandic community. An important part of Salverson's work deals with the immigrant experience in Canada. In fact, the similarities between her work and that of her colleagues writing in Icelandic are striking, and one can hardly escape the conclusion that Salverson's work forms in many ways a natural continuation of and even an internal dialogue with Icelandic immigrant literature. All these significant facts, however, are lost when Salverson is regarded only as a Canadian writer, as, indeed, she has been; lost also is much of the significance of her work.

Salverson was very much an author of two worlds who tried to straddle both by transgressing the boundaries between them; as a result, her writing is informed by duality and ambiguity, and her attempts at translating Icelandic culture and the immigrant experience in Canada as she knew it into English Canadian fiction were often misinterpreted and/or misunderstood. More recently, however, her authorship and her contribution to both Icelandic and Canadian literature have come to be reevaluated on both sides of the Atlantic.

Salverson had lived in many of North America's urban immigrant slums before she reached adulthood, including the culturally diverse urban landscape of Winnipeg. She was brought up a fierce Icelandic nationalist by her father, but she was also immensely proud of being Canadian. She made it her driving ambition to write her ancestral culture into the literature of her native country, Canada. At the time Canadian literature was still the domain of a small cultural elite: the general interest in Canadian literature, or any literature, for that matter, was minimal, and what literature had been written about the Canadian pioneer experience reflected the cultural bias of the Anglo-Canadian establishment, which regarded all "foreigners" as culturally inferior. Salverson aimed to change the dominant perception with her writing by drawing attention to the contributions of all of Canada's pioneers whose sacrifices had earned them the right to be considered Canadians and whose cultures enriched the cultural mosaic that was developing in Canada. While Canadian models for such a project were wanting, Salverson had at her fingertips an abundance of Icelandic models and a literary tradition to base herself on, taking these examples one step further by writing in English.

Salverson was soon to find out that what might have seemed a simple choice of language would have unforeseen ramifications and become a highly complex matter. The contribution of a writer of Icelandic descent to Canadian literature in English had been a long-anticipated and much-debated event in the Icelandic immigrant community. Ideologically, literature was the field where Icelandic Canadians wanted to make their most important contribution to Canadian culture, and it was an extremely contentious issue. Ideally, this envisaged masterpiece had both to carry over the Icelandic literary tradition into Canadian culture and to gain recognition among Canadians; in other words, it had to succeed on Icelandic as well as on Canadian terms. The large amount of Icelandic immigrant writing had generated disdain and ridicule in Iceland, and the Icelanders in Canada were, therefore, highly sensitive to the quality of their literature. They were eager to prove their excellence in the field of literature to their Canadian compatriots, and expectations were very high indeed.

After having had several poems published and won a prize for the short story "Hidden Fire" (1923), Salverson brought out her debut novel, *The Viking Heart* (1923). It tells the story of the Icelandic emigration to Canada, focusing on the character of Borga, and follows the archetypal patterns of exodus, settlement, pioneer hardships and sacrifice, symbolic death, and rebirth. However, it is not only the pattern that the novel has in common with other Icelandic immigrant fiction, particularly that of Bjarnason. Although it aims toward an epic scope, it is at the same time quite clearly a romance, a New World comedy set in the prairie garden of western Canada that ends in the affirmation of life, as Borga is finally reborn as a Canadian and rejoices in the birth of her grandchild as the embodiment of her hopes for the future. At the same time the novel contains fierce social criticism, exposing the social and economic injustice, discrimination, inequality, and grinding poverty that blighted the "promised land."

Polarities and their resolution inform the novel's structure to a large extent, echoing Finnsdóttir's fiction: Salverson's characters are poised between the binaries of inner and outer values, cultural separation and assimilation, as well as good and evil. These polarities must be resolved through tolerance, mutual understanding, and respect and, more important, through the acceptance of totality and the collapse of opposites, what Gudrún Gudsteins calls "the constructive potential of impurity: good within evil . . . past within present" (Gudsteins, "Wake-Pick Weavers," 142). Within the context of an immigrant culture this is a powerful statement: it challenges the ideal of cultural purity and authenticity, thereby making room for new definitions of cultural identity. And Salverson made no attempts to sweeten her message: her challenge is partly contained in a symbolic subtext that posits the war controversy in the community as one between separatism and assimilation, both of which cause alienation in *The Viking Heart* (Gudsteins, "Rediscovering Icelandic Canadian Pacifism"). In Salverson's fiction it is integration that holds the key to a better future.

The Viking Heart became an instant success in Canada. It was hailed for breaking new ground in its sympathetic depiction of a non-English immigrant group's experiences settling in Canada, the first Canadian novel to do so. Opinion in the Icelandic community, however, was divided, to say the least. Some praised her for the way in which she had portrayed the Icelandic contribution to Canada and translated the Icelandic way of speaking into English, as, for instance, in the following passage:

"Well, and isn't that the truth! You that made that coffee that day and me to forget. Picture it! What a dullness!" . . .
"Good evening, friend. It's sorry I am not to remember where I met you. But you know how it is in this world — so much to think of and me with a head so queer-like." (Salverson, *The Viking Heart*, 190)

Many others, however, criticized her for her "inaccurate" descriptions of Icelandic customs and character traits and for misrepresenting Icelandic geography in the opening chapter. Salverson had meant the initial chapter to be symbolic, condensing the various, complex, and profoundly emotional experiences of leaving the native country into one apocalyptic image of a volcanic eruption that literally drives people into boats and into the ocean. The Icelandic community did not recognize the symbolism and accused Salverson of having "shrunk" Iceland.

Clearly, the community's main interest in the novel lay in the way Salverson had presented the Icelandic people to the larger Canadian public, a way with which many took issue. This reaction likely stems from a combination of alienation as a result of reading and seeing themselves in the language of the "other" and a clash between "transformed memory" and historicism (Gunnars, "Translation as Appropriation"). As a "cultural translator" Salverson had, with her fiction, appropriated her personal memory and interpretation of the community and tried to find commonalities to make the inevitable untranslatabilities in Icelandic culture understandable in a foreign context, thus changing the accepted definition of Icelandic cultural identity in Canada. She had, in other words, taken part of the community's innermost concerns beyond its cultural boundaries and the linguistic safety of Icelandic and exposed them to an outside readership. In addition the reception of Salverson's novel indicates a growing dichotomy between those who had been born in the "old country," and still had a sense of an "authentic," or national, culture that they had left behind, and those born in the New World, like Salverson, for whom the inherited culture is a reconstruction, a symbol open to negotiation and reinterpretation to make it applicable in the larger Canadian context.

Salverson's other main work is her autobiography, *Confessions of an Immigrant's Daughter* (1939). This work, even more than *The Viking Heart*, exposes the dualities informing Salverson's life, both on a personal and on a professional level. In addition it addresses the problems inherent in being both a woman and an immigrant, a "double jeopardy," and in being an immigrant woman author. It is as much bildungsroman as autobiography as well as a literary apologia and an attempt at creating an identity that would unify her fragmented sense of self. The contemporary Icelandic Canadian author Kristjana Gunnars has even analyzed it as being both a New World comedy, ending with the author's successful debut and the realization of her dreams, and an Old World tragedy that ends with Salverson's sense of having failed in spite of her success, of having had her intentions so misunderstood, of not being recognized, and sometimes of not even being heard at all (Gunnars, "Laura Goodman Salverson's Confessions").

The merits of *Confessions* lie not only in its exposition of the complexities involved in being a woman, an immigrant, and a writer, however. With its astute and lively descriptions of daily life "on the wrong side of the tracks" and among the various Icelandic immigrant groups across the North American continent during the region's formative years as a multicultural society, it also has great documentary value. It is probably for this reason that *Confessions* is the only work by Salverson still in print today, although she has many others to her credit, among them a romance about Leif Eiriksson entitled *Lord of the Silver Dragon* (1927), a novel set in seventeenth-century Iceland and Algeria following the fates of the kidnapped victims of the pirate raids called *The Dove* (1933), and another immigrant epic, *The Dark Weaver* (1937), which won her the Governor General's Award, the highest literary recognition in Canada. *Confessions* is the only one of Salverson's works to have been translated into Icelandic, and that only as recently as 1994.

THE ICELANDIC HERITAGE IN CANADIAN LITERATURE

While Laura Salverson is in many respects a borderline figure, with one foot in Icelandic and one foot in Canadian literature, more recent authors of Icelandic descent firmly define themselves as Canadian authors, albeit with a difference. The best known among them have successfully experimented with different ways of articulating minority identity and cultural heritage, including Icelandic ancestry and an immigrant past, and still derive both encouragement and inspiration from their Icelandic heritage. While the Icelandic element is increasingly hybrid and symbolic and the Icelandic language largely lost and replaced with a symbolic language, it is no less influential or powerful for it, even if it is not always easily accessible to outsiders (nor, indeed, is it always meant to be).

The work of W. D. Valgardson (b. 1939), who was born and grew up in the area that used to be New Iceland, deals with the inheritance of a minority culture and an immigrant past. Being "three-eighths Icelandic" ("Myth of Homogeneity," 210), Valgardson explores issues concerned with cultural hybridity and cultural perceptions. His second novel, *The Girl with the Botticelli Face* (1992), as well as a children's book called *Thor* (1994) and several of his short stories have been translated into Icelandic and raised intriguing questions in Iceland about traditional definitions of *Icelandicness* and what it means to be an Icelander. In the two short stories — "The Man from Snaefellsness" and "The Man from Snaefellsness: Part Two" — a Canadian of Icelandic descent is invited to Iceland, where he has to deal with issues long repressed regarding his Icelandic ancestry: he inherited a deep resentment from his great-grandfather Ketill, who was on poor relief and practically forced to emigrate so that the district could save money. And, further, ostracized as a child for inadvertently interspersing his English with Icelandic words. Not only did the subject matter itself cause interest in Iceland, however, but the translation did as well. Like Salverson before him, Valgardson uses Icelandic as it has survived in North America and spells it as English speakers hear it. To Icelanders in Iceland, however, this appears as a "bastardization" that breaks the rules governing the language and protecting it from foreign influences. Thus, it challenges traditional ideas on linguistic as well as cultural purity.

Other authors include David Arnason (b. 1940), also from the former New Iceland area, and the highly original Icelandic American author Bill Holm (b. 1943), who has immortalized the tiny Icelandic settlement of Minneota, Minnesota, in his works, which include *The Music of Failure* (1985) and *The Heart Can Be Filled Anywhere on Earth* (1996), parts of which have been translated into Icelandic. Kristjana Gunnars (b. 1948) was born in Iceland to an Icelandic father and a Danish mother and emigrated to North America in her teens. She has established herself as a highly successful writer in Canada whose innovative works deal with the diasporic experience and the meaning of cultural identity and cultural heritage. She also wrote several works about the Icelandic immigrant experience in Canada, notably *Settlement Poems 1 and 2* (1980) and *The Axe's Edge* (1983), even though her own experience is quite radically different. Among her works dealing with her Icelandic heritage are *The Nightworkers of Ragnarok* (1985) and *The Prowler* (1990).

FINAL WORD

Although Icelandic literature in North America followed a rather different course from that originally imagined by the nationalist immigrant leaders, it could be argued that it has done more to challenge traditional definitions of Icelandic identity and Icelandic literature in its 130-year history than any other external influence. At the height of Icelandic nationalism, when it was still firmly considered a part of the Icelandic tradition, it introduced new subject matter, new perceptions, and new experiences into Icelandic literature and experimented with the language so that it could accommodate these. Initially, the innovations were conservative ones, but, as time passed and the North American Icelanders settled, the transformations gradually became more radical. The language changed, followed by more profound changes in culture and identity, which were also reflected in the literature. These changes initially created alienation as the culture and literature were no longer recognized as being Icelandic. In recent years, however, Icelanders have been gradually rediscovering Icelandic Canadian literature, a rediscovery to which a flood of recent publications bears witness, including a two-volume collection of Icelandic immigrant letters edited by Böðvar Guðmundsson entitled *Bréf Vestur-Íslendinga* (2001–2) and a chapter on Icelandic Canadian literature by Viðar Hreinsson ("Vestur-Íslenskar bókmenntir") in the latest Icelandic literary history, *Íslensk Bókmenntasaga* (1992–2006).

The value of Icelandic Canadian literature as a part of Icelandic literary history in our day lies not only in the fact that it has provided fascinating insights into how Icelandic culture and identity have responded to a new life in a completely different environment. Perhaps more important, as part of the global village Iceland currently faces unprecedented challenges in the area of cultural and linguistic survival; Icelandic Canadian experiences and literary experiments in this particular area, based on a more flexible interpretation of culture and identity in the midst of cultural diversity, provide some valuable lessons as to how Icelandic identity and Icelandic literature can survive in a way that is relevant in today's world.

Bibliography

General

HISTORIES OF ICELANDIC LITERATURE
Beck, Richard. *History of Icelandic Poets, 1800–1940*. Islandica 34. Ithaca NY: Cornell University Press, 1950.
Brøndsted, Mogens, ed. *Nordens litteratur*. 2 vols. Copenhagen: Gyldendal, 1972. Translated into German by Hans-Kurt Mueller as *Nordische Literaturgeschichte* (Munich: Fink, 1984).
Einarsson, Stefán. *History of Icelandic Prose Writers, 1800–1940*. Islandica 32–33. Ithaca NY: Cornell University Press, 1948.
———. *A History of Icelandic Literature*. New York: Johns Hopkins University Press, for the American-Scandinavian Society, 1957.
Íslensk bókmenntasaga. Vols. 1–2, ed. Vésteinn Ólason. Vols. 3–5, ed. Halldór Guðmundsson. Reykjavík: Mál og menning, 1992–93, 1996–2006.
Íslenzk fornrit. 23 vols. to date. Reykjavík: Hið íslenzka fornritafélag, 1933–.
Rossel, Sven Hakon. *A History of Scandinavian Literature, 1870–1980*. Translated by Anne C. Ulmer. Minneapolis: University of Minnesota Press, 1982.

ANTHOLOGIES IN ENGLISH
Icelandic Lyrics: Originals and Translations. Edited by Richard Beck. Reykjavík: Þórhallur Bjarnarson, 1930.
The North American Book of Icelandic Verse. Edited by Watson Kirkconnell. New York and Montreal: Louis Carrier & Alan Isles, 1930.

HISTORY AND CIVILIZATION
Karlsson, Gunnar. *The History of Iceland*. London: Hurst; Minneapolis: University of Minnesota Press, 2000.

Nordal, Sigurður. *Icelandic Culture*. 1942. Translated by Vilhjálmur T. Bjarnar. Ithaca NY: Cornell University Press, 1990.

Chapter Bibliographies

CHAPTER 1: OLD ICELANDIC POETRY

GENERAL

Clunies Ross, Margaret. *Prolonged Echoes: Old Norse Myths in Medieval Northern Society*. 2 vols. Odense: Odense University Press, 1994–98.

——. *A History of Old Norse Poetry and Poetics*. Cambridge: D. S. Brewer, 2005.

Dictionary of the Middle Ages. Edited by Joseph R. Strayer. 13 vols. New York: Scribner's, 1982–89.

Eliot, T. S. *Selected Essays: New Edition*. New York: Harcourt, Brace, 1950.

Foley, John Miles. *The Theory of Oral Composition: History and Methodology*. Bloomington: Indiana University Press, 1988.

Foote, Peter. *Aurvandilstá: Norse Studies*. Odense: Odense University Press, 1984.

Glendinning, Robert J., and Haraldur Bessason, eds. *Edda: A Collection of Essays*. Winnipeg: University of Manitoba Press, 1983.

Íslensk bókmenntasaga. Vols. 1–2, ed. Vésteinn Ólason. Reykjavík: Mál og menning, 1992–93.

Ker, W. P. *Epic and Romance: Essays on Medieval Literature*. London, 1896. 2nd ed., London: Macmillan, 1908. Reprint, New York: Dover, 1957.

Kindlers neues Literaturlexikon. Edited by Rudolf Radler. 22 vols. Munich: Kindler, 1988–92. A revised edition of the 20-volume *Kindlers Literaturlexikon* (1970–74).

Kristjánsson, Jónas. *Eddas and Sagas: Iceland's Medieval Literature*. Translated by Peter Foote. Reykjavík: Hið íslenska bókmenntafélag, 1988.

Kulturhistorisk leksikon for nordisk middelalder fra vikingetid til reformationstid. 22 vols. Copenhagen: Rosenkilde & Bagger, 1956–78.

Medieval Scandinavia: An Encyclopedia. Edited by Phillip Pulsiano. New York: Garland, 1993.

Nordal, Sigurður. *Icelandic Culture*. 1942. Translated by Vilhjálmur T. Bjarnar. Ithaca NY: Cornell University Press, 1990.

Old Norse–Icelandic Literature: A Critical Guide. Edited by Carol J. Clover and John Lindow. Islandica 45. Ithaca NY: Cornell University Press, 1985.

See, Klaus von. *Edda, Saga, Skaldendichtung: Aufsätze zur skandinavischen Literatur des Mittelalters*. Heidelberg: C. Winter, 1981.

Sigurðsson, Gísli. *Gaelic Influence in Iceland: Historical and Literary Contacts*. Studia Islandica 46. Reykjavík: Bókaútgáfa Menningarsjóðs, 1988. Reprint, Reykjavík: Háskólaútgáfan, 2001.

Sveinsson, Einar Ól. *Íslenzkar bókmenntir í fornöld*. Reykjavík: Almenna Bóka-félagið, 1962.

Turville-Petre, E. O. Gabriel. *Origins of Icelandic Literature*. Oxford: Clarendon, 1953.

———. *Myth and Religion of the North: The Religion of Ancient Scandinavia*. London: Weidenfeld & Nicholson, 1964.

Vries, Jan de. *Altnordische Literaturgeschichte*. 1941–42. 2 vols. Grundriss der germanischen Philologie, 15–16. 2nd, rev. ed., Berlin: Walter de Gruyter, 1964–67.

ANTHOLOGIZED SOURCES

Eddic Poetry

Edda: Die Lieder des Codex Regius nebst verwandten Denkmälern. Edited by Gustav Neckel. Revised by Hans Kuhn. Heidelberg: C. Winter, 1962.

Eddica minora: Dichtungen eddischer Art aus den Fornaldarsögur und anderen Prosa-werken. Edited and with an introduction by Andreas Heusler and Wilhelm Ranisch. Dortmund: Fr. Wilh. Ruhfus, 1903.

Eddukvæði. Edited by Gísli Sigurðsson. Reykjavík: Mál og menning, 1998.

Konungsbók eddukvæða: Codex regius. Manuscripta islandica medii aevi 3. Edited by Vésteinn Ólason and Guðvarður Már Gunnlaugsson. Reykjavík: Lögberg / Edda — miðlun og útgáfa, 2001. A facsimile edition with a diplomatic transcrip-tion and a transcription in Modern Icelandic spelling as well as an introduction in Icelandic and English.

Skaldic Poetry

Good texts of much skaldic verse with commentary are found in the saga editions in the series Íslenzk fornrit (23 vols. to date [Reykjavík: Hið íslenzka fornritafélag, 1933–]).

Den norsk-islandske skjaldedigtning A–B. 4 vols. Edited by Finnur Jónsson. Copen-hagen: Villadsen & Christensen, 1912–15.

Religious and Lyric Poetry from the Late Middle Ages

Íslenzk miðaldakvæði: Islandske digte fra senmiddelalderen. Edited by Jón Helgason. 2 vols. Copenhagen: Munksgaard, 1936–1938. Vol. 1 is incomplete.

Kvæðasafn eptir íslenzka menn frá miðöldum og síðari öldum. Edited by Jón Þorkelsson. Reykjavík: Hið íslenska bókmenntafélag, 1922–27.

Rímur and Ballads

Íslenzk fornkvæði: Islandske folkeviser. Edited by Jón Helgason. 8 vols. Editiones Ar-namagnæanæ, ser. B, vols. 10–17. Copenhagen, 1962–81.

Rímnasafn: Samling af de ældste islandske rimer. Edited by Finnur Jónsson. 2 vols. Copenhagen: Samfund til udgivelse af gammel nordisk litteratur, 1905–22.

Sagnadansar. Edited by Vésteinn Ólason. *Supplement: Lög við íslenska sagnadansa*, ed. Hreinn Steingrímsson. Reykjavík: Bókaútgáfa Menningarsjóðs, 1979.

Eddic Poetry

Hávamál. Edited by David A. H. Evans. Viking Society for Northern Research Text Series, vol. 7. London: Viking Society for Northern Research, University College London, 1986.

The Poetic Edda. Translated and edited by Ursula Dronke. 2 vols. Oxford: Clarendon, 1969–97.

The Poetic Edda. Translated by Carolyne Larrington. Oxford: Oxford University Press, 1996.

The Saga of the Volsungs. Edited and translated by R. G. Finch. London and Edinburgh: Nelson, 1965.

Völuspá. Edited by Sigurður Nordal. 1923. Translated by B. S. Benedikz and John McKinnell. Durham and St. Andrews Medieval Texts 1. Durham: University of Durham, 1978.

Völuspá: The Sibyl's Prophecy. Edited by Hermann Pálsson. Edinburgh: Lockharton, 1996.

Skaldic Poetry

Sturluson, Snorri. *Edda: Prologue and Gylfaginning*. Edited by Anthony Faulkes. 1982. Reprint, London: Viking Society for Northern Research, University College London, 1988.

——. *Edda: Skáldskaparmál*. Edited by Anthony Faulkes. 2 vols. London: Viking Society for Northern Research, University College London, 1998.

——. *Edda: Háttatal*. Edited by Anthony Faulkes. 1991. Reprint, with addenda and corrigenda, London: Viking Society for Northern Research, University College London, 1999.

——. *Edda*. Translated by Anthony Faulkes. Oxford: Clarendon, 1982. Reprint, London: Dent, 1987.

Monographs and Articles

Árnason, Kristján. *The Rhythms of Dróttkvætt and Other Old Icelandic Metres*. Reykjavík: Institute of Linguistics, University of Iceland, 1991.

Fidjestøl, Bjarne. *Det norrøne fyrstediktet*. Øvre Ervik: Alvheim & Eide, 1982.

——. *Selected Papers*. Edited by Odd Einar Haugen and Else Mundal. Odense: Odense University Press, 1997.

——. *The Dating of Eddic Poetry: A Historical Survey and Methodological Investigation*. Bibliotheca Arnamagnæana, vol. 41. Copenhagen: Reitzel, 1999.

Frank, Roberta. *Old Norse Court Poetry: The Dróttkvætt Stanza*. Ithaca NY: Cornell University Press, 1985.

Gade, Kari Ellen. *The Structure of Old Norse Dróttkvætt Poetry*. Islandica 49. Ithaca NY: Cornell University Press, 1995.

Gunnell, Terry. *The Origins of Drama in Scandinavia*. London: D. S. Brewer, 1995.

Hallberg, Peter. *Old Icelandic Poetry: Eddic Lay and Skaldic Verse*. 1962. Translated by

Paul Schach and Sonja Lindgrenson. Lincoln: University of Nebraska Press, 1974.

Heusler, Andreas. *Die altgermanische Dichtung.* 2nd ed., Potsdam: Athenaion, 1941.

Krag, Claus. *Ynglingatal og Ynglingesaga: En studie i historiske kilder.* Oslo: Universitetsforlaget, 1991.

Lange, Wolfgang. *Studien zur christlichen Dichtung der Nordgermanen, 1000–1200.* Palaestra 222. Göttingen: Vandenhoeck & Ruprecht, 1958.

Lie, Hallvard. *Om sagakunst og skaldskap: Utvalgte avhandlinger.* Øvre Ervik: Alvheim & Eide, 1982.

Marold, Edith. *Kenningkunst: Ein Beitrag zu einer Poetik der Skaldendichtung.* Berlin: Walter de Gruyter, 1983.

Meletinsky, Eleazar M. *The Elder Edda and Early Forms of the Epic.* 1968. Translated by Kenneth H. Ober. Trieste: Parnason, 1998.

Mitchell, Stephen. *Heroic Sagas and Ballads.* Ithaca NY: Cornell University Press, 1991.

Nordal, Guðrún. *Tools of Literacy: The Role of Skaldic Verse in Icelandic Textual Culture of the Twelfth and Thirteenth Centuries.* Toronto: University of Toronto Press, 2001.

Ólason, Vésteinn. *The Traditional Ballads of Iceland: Historical Studies.* Reykjavík: Stofnun Árna Magnússonar, 1982.

Paasche, Frederik. *Kristendom og kvad: En studie i norrøn middelalder.* Oslo: Aschehoug, 1914. Reprinted in Frederik Paasche, *Hedenskap og kristendom* (Oslo: Aschehoug, 1948), 25–218.

Poole, R. G. *Viking Poems on War and Peace: A Study in Skaldic Narrative.* Toronto: University of Toronto Press, 1991.

Sävborg, Daniel. *Sorg och elegi i Eddans hjältediktning.* Stockholm: Almqvist & Wiksell, 1997.

Schottmann, Hans. *Die isländische Mariendichtung: Untersuchungen zur volkssprachigen Mariendichtung des Mittelalters.* Munich: Fink, 1973.

See, Klaus von, Beatrice La Farge, Eve Picard, and Katja Schulz. *Kommentar zu den Liedern der Edda.* Vol. 2, *Skírnismál, Hárbarðsljóð, Hymiskviða, Lokasenna, Prymskviða.* Vol. 3, *Völundarakviða, Alvíssmál, Baldrs draumar, Rígspula, Hyndluljóð, Grottasöngr.* Vol. 4, *Helgakviða hundingsbana I, Helgakviða Hjørvarðssonar, Helgakviða hundingsbana II.* Heidelberg: C. Winter, 1997–2004.

Sprenger, Ulrike. *Die altnordische heroische Elegie.* Berlin: Walter de Gruyter, 1992.

Turville-Petre, E. O. Gabriel. *Scaldic Poetry.* Oxford: Clarendon, 1976.

Wolf, Alois. "Mythisch-heroische Überlieferungen und literarische Bestrebungen im alten Island: Überlegungen zur Edda." *Litteraturwissenschaftliches Jahrbuch* 40 (1999): 9–72.

Þórólfsson, Björn K. *Rímur fyrir, 1600.* Copenhagen: Hið íslenska fræðafjelag, 1934.

CHAPTER 1: OLD ICELANDIC PROSE
This is a selected bibliography only.

GENERAL REFERENCE AND LITERARY HISTORY

Byock, J. L. *Medieval Iceland: Society, Sagas, and Power*. Berkeley and Los Angeles: University of California Press, 1988.

Clover, C., and J. Lindow, eds. *Old Norse–Icelandic Literature: A Critical Guide*. Islandica 45. Ithaca NY: Cornell University Press, 1985.

Einarsson, Stefán. *A History of Icelandic Literature*. Baltimore: Johns Hopkins University Press, 1957.

Foote, P. G., and D. M. Wilson. *The Viking Achievement*. London: Sidwick & Jackson, 1970.

Hallberg, P. *The Icelandic Saga*. Lincoln: University of Nebraska Press, 1962.

Íslensk bókmenntasaga. Vols. 1–2, ed. Vésteinn Ólason. Reykjavík: Mál og menning, 1992–93.

Jónsson, Finnur. *Den oldnorske og oldislandske litteraturs historie*. 3 vols. 2nd ed. Copenhagen: G. E. C. Gads, 1920–24.

Kristjánsson, Jónas. *Eddas and Sagas: Iceland's Medieval Literature*. Reykjavík: Hið íslenska bókmenntafélag, 1988.

Medieval Scandinavia: An Encyclopedia. Edited by P. Pulsiano. New York: Garland, 1993.

Pálsson, Hermann, and Rudolf Simek, eds. *Lexikon der altnordischen Literatur*. Stuttgart: Alfred Kröner, 1987.

Schier, K. *Sagaliteratur*. Stuttgart: J. B. Metzlersche, 1970.

Sigurðsson, Jón Viðar. *Chieftains and Power in the Icelandic Commonwealth*. Odense: Odense University Press, 1999.

Sørensen, M. P. *Saga and Society: An Introduction to Old Norse Literature*. Odense: Odense University Press, 1993.

Turville-Petre, G. *Origins of Icelandic Literature*. Oxford: Clarendon, 1953.

Vries, Jan de. *Altnordische Literaturgeschichte*. 2 vols. Grundriss der germanischen Philologie, 15–16. 2nd, rev. ed., Berlin: Walter de Gruyter, 1964–67.

EDITIONS AND ANTHOLOGIES

Alfræði íslenzk. Edited by N. Beckman and K. Kålund. 3 vols. Samfund til Udgivelse af gammel nordisk litteratur, vols. 37, 41, 45. Copenhagen, 1908–18.

Biskupa sögur. Edited by Sigurgeir Steingrímsson et al. 2 vols. Íslenzk fornrit, vol. 15. Reykjavík: Hið íslenzka fornritafélag, 2003.

Biskupa sögur. [Edited by Guðbrandur Vigfússon and Jón Sigurðsson]. 2 vols. Copenhagen, 1858–78.

Bósa saga og Herrauðs. Edited by Sverrir Tómasson. Reykjavík: Mál og menning, 1996.

Bretasögur. See *Hauksbók*.

Danakonunga sögur. Edited by Bjarni Guðnason. Íslenzk fornrit, vol. 35. Reykjavík: Hið íslenzka fornritafélag, 1982.

Drei Lygisögur. Edited by Å. Lagerholm. Altnordische Saga-Bibliothek 17. Halle: Max Niemeyer, 1927.

Edda: Háttatal. By Snorri Sturluson. Edited by Anthony Faulkes. Oxford: Clarendon, 1991.

Edda: Prologue and Gylfaginning. By Snorri Sturluson. Edited by Anthony Faulkes. Oxford: Clarendon, 1982.

Edda: Skáldskaparmál. By Snorri Sturluson. Edited by Anthony Faulkes. 2 vols. London: Viking Society for Northern Research, University College London, 1998.

Eiríks saga víðförla. Edited by H. Jensen. Editiones Arnamagnæanæ, ser. B, vol. 29. Copenhagen, 1983.

Elucidarius in Old Norse Translation. Edited by E. S. Firkow et al. Rit Stofnunar Árna Magnússonar á Íslandi, vol. 36. Reykjavík: Stofnun Árna Magnússonar, 1989.

Fagrskinna, Nóregs konunga tal. Edited by Bjarni Einarsson. Íslenzk fornrit, vol. 29. Reykjavík: Hið íslenzka fornritafélag, 1985.

Fornaldar sögur Nordrlanda. Edited by C. C. Rafn. 3 vols. Copenhagen, 1829–30.

Fornsögur Suðrlanda. Edited by G. Cederschiöld. Lund, 1884.

Grágás. Edited by Vilhjálmur Finsen. 3 vols. Copenhagen, 1852–83.

Guðmundar sögur biskups. Vol. 1, *Ævi Guðmundar biskups, Guðmundar saga A*. Edited by Stefán Karlsson. Editiones Arnamagnæanæ, ser. B, vol. 6. Copenhagen, 1983.

Hákonar saga [Hákonarsonar] and a Fragment of Magnús saga [Hákonarsonar]. Edited by Guðbrandur Vigfússon. London, 1887.

Hauksbók. Edited by Eiríkur Jónsson and Finnur Jónsson. 1 vol. Copenhagen, 1892–96.

Heilagra manna søgur. Edited by C. R. Unger. 2 vols. Christiania, 1877.

Heimskringla. By Snorri Sturluson. Edited by Bjarni Aðalbjarnarson. Íslenzk fornrit, vols. 26–28. Reykjavík: Hið íslenzka fornritafélag, 1941–51.

Heimskringla: Lykilbók. Vol. 3 of *Heimskringla*, ed. Bergljót Kristjánsdóttir et al. Reykjavík: Mál og menning, 1991.

Hrafns saga Sveinbjarnarsonar. Edited by Guðrún P. Helgadóttir. Oxford: Clarendon, 1987.

Islandske Annaler indtil 1578. Edited by G. Storm. Christiania, 1875.

Íslendinga sögur og þættir. Edited by Bragi Halldórsson et al. 3 vols. Reykjavík: Svart á hvítu, 1987.

Íslendingabók. By Ari Þorgilsson. In *Íslendingabók; Landnámabók* (Íslenzk fornrit, vol. 1), ed. Jakob Benediktsson. Reykjavík: Hið íslenzka fornritafélag, 1968.

Islendzk Ævintyri: Isländische Legenden Novellen und Märchen. Edited by H. Gering. 2 vols. Halle: Waisenhauses, 1882–83.

Konungs skuggsiá. Edited by L. Holm-Olsen. Oslo: Kjeldskriftfondet, 1945.

Landnámabók. In *Íslendingabók; Landnámabók* (Íslenzk fornrit, vol. 1), ed. Jakob Benediktsson. Reykjavík: Hið íslenzka fornritafélag, 1968.

Late Medieval Icelandic Romances. Edited by Agnethe Loth. 5 vols. Editiones Arnamagnæanæ, ser. B, vols. 20–24. Copenhagen, 1962–65.

Laurentius saga biskups. Edited by Árni Björnsson. Reykjavík: Handritastofnun Íslands, 1969.

Lárentíus saga biskups. Edited by Guðrún Ása Grímsdóttir. Vol. 3 of *Biskupa sögur*. Íslenzk fornrit, vol. 17. Reykjavík: Hið íslenzka fornritafélag, 1998.

Morkinskinna. Edited by Finnur Jónsson. Samfund til Udgivelse af gammel nordisk litteratur, vols. 53. Copenhagen, 1932.

Óláfs saga helga. See *Heilagra manna søgur*, vol. 2.

Olafs saga hins helga. Edited by O. A. Johnsen. Christiania: Jacob Dybwad, 1922.

Óláfs saga Tryggvasonar en mesta. Edited by Ólafur Halldórsson. 3 vols. Editiones Arnamagnæanæ, ser. A, vols. 1–3. Copenhagen, 1958–2000.

Orkneyinga saga. Edited by Finnbogi Guðmundsson. Íslenzk fornrit, vol. 34. Reykjavík: Hið íslenzka fornritafélag, 1965.

Otte brudstykker af den ældste saga om Olav den hellige. Edited by G. Storm. Christiania: Grøndahl & Søns, 1893.

Postola sögur. Edited by C. R. Unger. Christiania, 1874.

Reykjahólabók. Edited by Agnethe Loth. 2 vols. Editiones Arnamagnæanæ, ser. A, vols. 15–16. Copenhagen, 1969–70.

Rómveriasaga. Edited by R. Meissner. Palaestra 88. Berlin, 1910.

Saga Óláfs konungs hins helga. By Snorri Sturluson. Edited by Jón Helgason. 2 vols. Oslo: Kjeldeskriftfondet, 1941.

Saga Óláfs Tryggvasonar. By Oddur Snorrason. Edited by Finnur Jónsson. Copenhagen: G. E. C. Gads, 1932.

Samsons saga fagra. Edited by J. Wilson. Samfund til Udgivelse af gammel nordisk litteratur, vol. 65. Copenhagen, 1953.

Stjórn. Edited by C. R. Unger. Christiania, 1862.

Strengleikar: An Old Norse Translation of Twenty-One Old French Lais. Edited and translated by R. Cook and M. Tveitane. Oslo: Kjeldeskriftfondet, 1979.

Sturlunga saga. Skýringar og fræði. Edited by Örnólfur Thorsson et al. 3 vols. Reykjavík: Svart á hvítu, 1988.

Sverris saga. Edited by G. Indrebø. Oslo: Norske Historiske Kildeskriftkommission, 1927.

Thómas saga erkibyskups. Edited by Eiríkur Magnússon. 2 vols. London, 1875–83.

Trójumanna saga. Edited by J. Louis-Jensen. Editiones Arnamagnæanæ, ser. A, vol. 8. Copenhagen, 1963.

Trójumanna saga: The Dares Phrygius Version. Edited by J. Louis-Jensen. Editiones Arnamagnæanæ, ser. A, vol. 9. Copenhagen, 1981.

Vitae patrum. See *Heilagra manna søgur*, vol. 2.

Þiðriks saga af Bern. Edited by H. Bertelsen. Samfund til Udgivelse af gammel nordisk litteratur, vols. 34. Copenhagen, 1905–11.

Örvar-Odds saga. Edited by R. C. Boer. Altnordische Saga-Bibliothek 2. Halle, 1892.

LITERATURE IN ENGLISH TRANSLATION

Ágrip af Nóregskonungasögum: A Twelfth-Century Synoptic History of the Kings of Norway. Edited and translated by M. J. Driscoll. London: Viking Society for Northern Research, University College London, 1995.

The Book of Settlements: Landnámabók. Translated by Hermann Pálsson and Paul Edwards. Winnipeg: University of Manitoba Press, 1972.

"The Book of the Icelanders." By Ari Thorgilsson. Translated by Gwyn Jones. In *The Norse Atlantic Saga*, by Gwyn Jones, 101–13. London: Oxford University Press, 1964.

The Complete Sagas of Icelanders. Edited by Viðar Hreinsson. 5 vols. Reykjavík: Leifur Eiríksson, 1997.

Edda. By Snorri Sturluson. Translated by A. Faulkes. London: Dent, 1987.

The First Grammatical Treatise. Edited and translated by Hreinn Benediktsson. Reykjavík: Institute of Nordic Lingustics, 1972.

Gautrek's Saga and Other Medieval Tales. Translated by Hermann Pálsson and Paul Edwards. London: University of London Press, 1968.

Göngu-Hrolfs Saga. Translated by Hermann Pálsson and Paul Edwards. Edinburgh: Canongate, 1980.

Heimskringla. By Snorri Sturluson. Translated by L. Hollander. Austin: University of Texas Press, 1964.

A History of Norway and the Passion and Miracles of the Blessed Óláfr. Edited and translated by C. Phelpstead and D. Kunin. London: Viking Society of Northern Research, University College London, 2001.

Laws of Early Iceland: Grágás. Translated by A. Dennis, P. Foote, and R. Perkins. 2 vols. Winnipeg: University of Manitoba Press, 1980–2000.

Morkinskinna: The Earliest Icelandic Chronicle of the Norwegian Kings (1030–1157). Translated by T. M. Andersson and K. E. Gade. Islandica 51. Ithaca NY: Cornell University Press, 2000.

Norse Romance. Edited by M. E. Kalinke. 3 vols. Arthurian Archives, vols. 3–5. Cambridge: D. S. Brewer, 1999.

Orkneyinga Saga: The History of the Earls of Orkney. Translated by Hermann Pálsson and Paul Edwards. London: Hogarth, 1978.

The Saga of Tristram and Ísönd. Translated by P. Schach. Lincoln: University of Nebraska Press, 1973.

Seven Viking Romances. Translated by Hermann Pálsson and Paul Edwards. Harmondsworth: Penguin, 1985.

Sturlunga Saga. Translated by J. H. McGrew and R. G. Thomas. 2 vols. New York: Twayne, 1970–74.

Sverrissaga: The Saga of King Sverri of Norway. Translated by J. Sephton. London: David Nutt, 1899.

Theodoricus Monachus. *Historia de antiquitate regum Norwagiensium: An Account of the Ancient History of the Norwegian Kings*. Translated by D. McDougall and I. McDougall. London: Viking Society for Northern Research, University College London, 1998.

MONOGRAPHS AND ARTICLES

Introduction

Bekker-Nielsen, H. "The Victorines and Their Influence on Old Norse Literature." In *The Fifth Viking Congress*, ed. Bjarni Niclasen, 32–36. Tórshavn: Føroya Fródskaparfelag, 1968. Proceedings.

Benediktsson, Hreinn. *Early Icelandic Script*. Reykjavík: Manuscript Institute of Iceland, 1965.

Foote, P. *Aurvandilstá: Norse Studies*. Odense: Odense University Press, 1984.

———. *1117 in Iceland and England*. Dorothea Coke Memorial Lecture in Northern Studies Delivered at University College London, 14 March 2002. London: Viking Society for Northern Research, University College London, 2003.

Halldórsson, Ólafur. *Helgafellsbækur fornar*. Studia Islandica 24. Reykjavík: Bókaútgáfa Menningarsjóðs, 1966.

Harris, J. "Genre and Narrative Structure in Some Íslendinga þættir." *Scandinavian Studies* 44 (1972): 1–27.

———. "Genre in the Saga Literature: A Squib." *Scandinavian Studies* 47 (1975): 427–36.

Karlsson, Stefán. *Stafkrókar*. Rit Stofnunar Árna Magnússonar á Íslandi, vol. 49. Reykjavík: Stofnun Árna Magnússonar, 2000.

Kirby, I. J. *Bible Translations in Old Norse*. Geneva: Droz, 1986.

Lönnroth, L. "The Concept of Genre in Saga Literature." *Scandinavian Studies* 47 (1975): 419–26.

Pálsson, Hermann. *Sagnaskemmtun Íslendinga*. Reykjavík: Mál og menning, 1962.

Springborg, P. "Weltbild mit Löwe: Die Imago mundi von Honorius Augustodunensis in der Altwestnordischen Textüberlieferung." In *Cultura classica e cultura germanica settrionale*, ed. P. Janni et al., 167–219. Rome: Herder, 1988.

Sørensen, P. M. *Fortælling og ære: Studier i islændingesagaerne*. Aarhus: Aarhus Universitetsforlag, 1993.

Tómasson, Sverrir. *Formálar íslenskra sagnaritara á miðöldum: Rannsókn bókmenntahefðar*. Rit Stofnunar Árna Magnússonar á Íslandi, vol. 33. Reykjavík: Stofnun Árna Magnússonar, 1988.

———. "The History of Old Nordic Manuscripts I: Old Icelandic." In *The Nordic Languages: An International Handbook of the History of the North Germanic Languages*, ed. O. Bandle et al., 793–801. Berlin: Walter de Gruyter, 2002.

National Histories

Aðalsteinsson, Jón Hnefill. *Under the Cloak. The Acceptance of Christianity in Iceland with Particular Reference to the Religious Attitudes Prevailing at the Time*. Studia Ethnologica Uppsaliensia 4. Uppsala: Acta Universitatis Upsaliensis, 1978.

Bragason, Úlfar. "On the Poetics of Sturlunga." PhD diss., University of California, Berkeley, 1986.

———. "The Structure and Meaning of Hrafns saga Sveinbjarnarsonar." *Scandinavian Studies* 60 (1988): 267–92.

Brenner, O. *Über die Kristni-Saga: Kritische Beiträge zur altnordischen Literaturgeschichte*. Munich: C. Kaiser, 1878.

Ellehøj, S. *Studier over den ældste norrøne historieskrivning*. Bibliotheca Arnamagnæana, vol. 26. Copenhagen: Munksgaard, 1965.

Glendinning, R. J. *Träume und Vorbedeutung in der Islendinga saga Sturla Thordarsons: Eine Form- und Stiluntersuchung*. Kanadische Studien zur deutschen Sprache und Literatur 8. Bern: Herbert Lang, 1974.

Grímsdóttir, Guðrún Ása. "Sturla Þórðarson." In *Sturlustefna* (Rit Stofnunar Árna Magnússonar á Íslandi, vol. 32), ed. Guðrún Ása Grímsdóttir and Jónas Kristjánsson, 9–36. Reykjavík: Stofnun Árna Magnússonar, 1988.

———. "Um sárafar í Íslendinga sögu Sturlu Þórðarsonar." In *Sturlustefna* (Rit Stofnunar Árna Magnússonar á Íslandi, vol. 32), ed. Guðrún Ása Grímsdóttir and Jónas Kristjánsson, 184–203. Reykjavík: Stofnun Árna Magnússonar, 1988.

Jóhannesson, Jón. *Gerðir Landnámabókar*. Reykjavík: Hið íslenska bókmenntafélag, 1941.

Líndal, Sigurður. "Sendiför Úlfljóts." *Skírnir* 143 (1969): 5–26.

Nordal, Guðrún. *Ethics and Action in Thirteenth-Century Iceland*. Odense: Odense University Press, 1998.

Perkins, Richard. *Flóamanna saga, Gaulverjabær and Haukr Erlendsson*. Studia Islandica 36. Reykjavík: Bókaútgáfa Menningarsjóðs, 1978.

Rafnsson, Sveinbjörn. *Studier i Landnámabók: Kritiska bidrag till den isländska fristatstiden historia*. Bibliotheca Historica Lundensis 31. Lund: CWK Gleerup, 1974.

Tómasson, Sverrir. "Helgisögur, mælskufræði og forn frásagnarlist." *Skírnir* 157 (1983): 130–62.

Tranter, S. N. *Sturlunga Saga: The Rôle of the Creative Compiler*. Frankfurt: Peter Lang, 1987.

Pseudohistorical Works: Universal Histories and Annals

Eysteinsson, Sölvi. "The Relationship of Merlínússpá and Geoffrey of Monmouth Historia." *Saga-Book* 14 (1953–55): 95–112.

Helgadóttir, Þorbjörg. "On the Sallust Translation in Rómverja Saga." *Saga-Book* 22 (1987–88): 263–77.

Kristjánsson, Jónas. "Annálar og Íslendingasögur." *Gripla* 4 (1980): 295–319.

Óskarsdóttir, Svanhildur. "Universal History in Fourteenth-Century Iceland: Studies in AM 764 4to." PhD diss., University College London, 2000.

Pálsson, Hermann. *Eftir þjóðveldið: Heimildir annála um íslenzka sögu, 1263–98*. Reykjavík: Heimskringla, 1965.

———. *Tólfta öldin: Þættir um menn og málefni*. Reykjavík: Prentsmiðja Jóns Helgasonar, 1970.

Wolf, K. "Gyðinga Saga, Alexanders Saga and Bishop Brandr Jónsson." *Scandinavian Studies* 60 (1988): 371–400.

Würth, S. *Der "Antikenroman" in der isländischen Literatur des Mittelalters: Eine Untersuchung zur Übersetzung und Rezeption lateinischer Literatur im Norden*. Basel: Helbing & Lichtenhahn, 1998.

Kings' Sagas

Ciklamini, M. *Snorri Sturluson*. New York: Twayne, 1978.

Clunies Ross, Margaret. *Skáldskaparmál: Snorri Sturluson's Ars Poetica and Medieval Theories of Language*. Odense: Odense University Press, 1987.

Dronke, P., and U. Dronke. "The Prologue of the Prose Edda: Exploration of a

Latin Background." In *Sjötíu ritgerðir helgaðar Jakobi Benediktssyni 20. júlí 1977* (Rit Stofnunar Árna Magnússonar á Íslandi, vol. 12), ed. Einar G. Pétursson et al., 153–76. Reykjavík: Stofnun Árna Magnússonar, 1977.

Faulkes, A. "Pagan Sympathy: Attitudes to heathendom in the Prologue of 'Snorra Edda.'" In *Edda: A Collection of Essays*, ed. R. J. Glendinning, 283–314. Winnipeg: University of Manitoba Press, 1983.

———. "The Sources of *Skáldskaparmál*: Snorri's Intellectual Background." In *Snorri Sturluson: Kolloquium anläßlich der 750. Wiederkehr seines Todestages*, ed. A. Wolf, 59–76. Tübingen: Gunter Narr, 1993.

Guðnason, Bjarni. *Um Skjöldungasögu*. Reykjavík: Bókaútgáfa Menningarsjóðs, 1963.

———. *Fyrsta sagan*. Studia Islandica 37. Reykjavík: Bókaútgáfa Menningarsjóðs, 1978.

Halldórsson, Ólafur. "Sagnaritun Snorra Sturlusonar." In *Snorri átta alda minning*, ed. Helgi Þorláksson, 113–38. Reykjavík: Sögufélag, 1979.

———. *Grettisfærsla*. Stofnun Árna Magnússonar Rit 38. Reykjavík: Stofnun Árna Magnússonar, 1990.

Jakobsson, Ármann. *Í leit að konungi: Konungsmynd íslenskra konungasagna*. Reykjavík: Háskólaútgáfan, 1997.

———. *Staður í nýjum heimi: Konungasagan Morkinskinna*. Reykjavík: Háskólaútgáfan, 2002.

Kalinke, M. E. "Sigurðar saga Jórsalafara: The Fictionalization of Fact in Morkinskinna." *Scandinavian Studies* 56 (1984): 152–67.

Knirk, J. E. *Oratory in the Kings' Sagas*. Oslo: Universitetsforlaget, 1981.

Louis-Jensen, J. *Kongesagastudier: Kompilationen Hulda-Hrokkinskinna*. Bibliotheca Arnamagnæana, vol. 32. Copenhagen: Reitzel, 1977.

Nordal, Sigurður. *Snorri Sturluson*. Reykjavík: Þórarinn B. Þorláksson, 1920.

Tómasson, Sverrir. "The Hagiography of Snorri Sturluson Especially in the Great Saga of St Olaf." In *Saints and Sagas: A Symposium*, ed. H. Bekker-Nielsen et al., 49–72. Odense: Odense University Press, 1994.

Weber, G. W. "Intellegere historiam: Typological Perspectives of Nordic Prehistory (in Snorri, Saxo Widukind and Others)." In *Tradition og historieskrivning*, ed. K. Hastrup and P. M. Sørensen, 95–141. Acta Jutlandica 63:2, Humanistisk Serie 61. Aarhus: Aarhus Universitetsforlag, 1987.

Würth, S. *Elemente des Erzählens: Die þættir der Flateyjarbók*. Basel: Helbing & Lichtenhahn, 1991.

Sagas of Icelanders

Allen, R. F. *Fire and Iron: Critical Approaches to Njáls saga*. Pittsburg: University of Pittsburg Press, 1971.

Andersson, T. M. *The Problem of Icelandic Saga Origins: A Historical Survey*. New Haven CT: Yale University Press, 1964.

———. *The Icelandic Family Saga: An Analytic Reading*. Cambridge MA: Harvard University Press, 1967.

———. "Some Ambiguities in Gísla Saga: A Balance Sheet." In *Bibliography of Old Norse–Icelandic Studies*, ed. H. Bekker-Nielsen, 7–42. Copenhagen: Royal Library, 1969.

Byock, J. L. *Feud in the Icelandic Saga*. Berkeley and Los Angeles: University of California Press, 1982.

Clover, C. *The Medieval Saga*. Ithaca NY: Cornell University Press, 1982.

Dronke, U. *The Role of Sexual Themes in Njáls Saga*. Dorothea Coke Memorial Lecture in Northern Studies Delivered at University College London, 27 May 1980. London: Viking Society for Northern Research, University College London, 1981.

Einarsson, Bjarni. "On the Rôle of Verse in Saga-Literature." *Mediaeval Scandinavia* 7 (1974): 118–25.

Foote, P. "An Essay on the Saga of Gisli and Its Icelandic Background." In *The Saga of Gísli*, trans. G. Johnston, 93–134. London: Dent, 1963.

Kristjánsson, Jónas. "Learned Style or Saga Style?" In *Specvlvm norroenvm: Norse Studies in Memory of Gabriel Turville-Petre*, ed. U. Dronke et al., 260–92. Odense: Odense University Press, 1983.

Lönnroth, L. "Kroppen som själens spegel—ett motiv i de isländska sagorna." *Lychnos* 1963–64: 24–61.

———. *European Sources of Icelandic Saga Writing: An Essay Based on Previous Studies*. Stockholm: n.p., 1965.

———. "The Noble Heathen: A Theme in the Sagas." *Scandinavian Studies* 41 (1969): 1–29.

———. *Njáls Saga: A Critical Introduction*. Berkeley and Los Angeles: University of California Press, 1976.

Madelung, M. A. *The Laxdæla Saga: Its Structural Patterns*. Chapel Hill: University of North Carolina Press, 1972.

Nordal, Sigurður. "Sagalitteraturen." In *Norge og Island* (Nordisk Kultur, vol. 8B), ed. Sigurður Nordal, 180–273. Stockholm: Bonniers, 1952.

Ólason, Vésteinn. "Nokkrar athugasemdir um Eyrbyggja sögu." *Skírnir* 145 (1971): 5–25.

———. *Dialogues with the Viking Age: Narration and Representation in the Sagas of the Icelanders*. Reykjavík: Heimskringla, 1998.

Pálsson, Hermann. *Art and Ethics in Hrafnkels Saga*. Copenhagen: Munksgaard, 1971.

———. "Death in Autumn: Tragic Elements in Early Icelandic Fiction." In *Bibliography of Old-Norse Icelandic Studies, 1973*, ed. H. Bekker-Nielsen, 7–39. Copenhagen: Royal Library, 1974.

Schach, P. "Some Forms of Writer Intrusion in the Íslendingasögur." *Scandinavian Studies* 42 (1970): 128–56.

Tómasson Sverrir. "Bandamanna saga og áheyrendur á 14. og 15. öld." *Skírnir* 151 (1977): 97–117.

———. "Skorið í fornsögu." In *Sagnaþing helgað Jónasi Kristjánssyni sjötugum 10 apríl*

1994, ed. Gísli Sigurðsson et al., 787–99. Reykjavík: Hið íslenska bókmenntafélag, 1994.

———. " 'Ei skal haltr ganga': Um Gunnlaugs sögu Ormstungu." *Gripla* 10 (1998):
7–22.

Romances

Bandle, O. *Schriften zur nordischen Philologie.* Edited by J. Glauser et al. Tübingen: A.
Francke, 2001.

Bibire, P. "From Riddarasaga to Lygisaga: The Norse Response to Romance." In *Les
sagas de chevaliers (Riddarasögur): Actes de la Ve* Conférence Internationale sur les
Sagas, ed. R. Boyer, 55–74. Paris: Presses de l'Université Paris Sorbonne, 1985.

Glauser, J. *Isländische Märchensagas: Studien zur Prosaliteratur im spätmittelalterlichen
Island.* Basel: Helbing & Lichtenhahn, 1983.

Gottzman, C. L. "Völsungasaga: Legendary History and Textual Analysis." Paper
presented at the Fourth International Saga Conference, Munich, 1979.

Hallberg, P. "Is There a 'Tristram-Group' of the Riddarasögur?" *Scandinavian Studies* 47 (1975): 1–17.

———. "Some Aspects of the Fornaldarsögur as a Corpus." *Arkiv för Nordisk Filologi*
97 (1982): 1–35.

Kalinke, M. E. *King Arthur, North by Northwest: The Matière de Bretagne in Old
Norse–Icelandic Romances.* Bibliotheca Arnamagnæana, vol. 37. Copenhagen:
Reitzel, 1981.

———. *Bridal-Quest Romance in Medieval Iceland.* Islandica 46. Ithaca NY: Cornell
University Press, 1990.

Kalinke, M. E., and P. M. Mitchell. *Bibliography of Old Norce–Icelandic Romances.*
Islandica 44. Ithaca NY: Cornell University Press, 1990.

Kretschmer, B. *Höfische und altwestnordische Erzähltradition in den Riddarasögur:
Studien zur Rezeption der altfranzösischen Artusepik am Beispiel der Erex saga, Ívens
saga und Parcevalsaga.* Hattingen: Bernd Kretschmer, 1982.

Lönnroth, L. "The Double Scene of Arrow-Odd's Drinking Contest." In *Medieval
Narrative: A Symposium*, ed. H. Bekker-Nielsen, 94–109. Odense: Odense University Press, 1979.

Nahl, A. van. *Originale Riddarasögur als Teil altnordischer Sagaliteratur.* Frankfurt:
Peter Lang, 1981.

Tómasson, Sverrir. "Hvenær var Tristrams sögu snúið?" *Gripla* 2 (1977): 47–78.

———. "The 'Fræðisaga of Adonias.' " In *Structure and Meaning in Old Norse Literature*, ed. John Lindow et al., 378–93. Odense: Odense University Press, 1986.

Tulinius, Torfi H. *The Matter of the North: The Rise of Literary Fiction in Thirteenth-
Century Iceland.* Odense: Odense University Press, 2002.

Mythology and Poetics

Foote, Peter. "Latin Rhetoric and Icelandic Poetry: Some Contacts." In *Aurvandilstá: Norse Studies*, 249–70. Odense: Odense University Press, 1984.

Nordal, Guðrún. *Tools of Literacy: The Role of Skaldic Verse in Icelandic Textual Culture of the Twelfth and Thirteenth Centuries.* Toronto: University of Toronto Press, 2001.

Nordal, Sigurður. *Snorri Sturluson.* Reykjavík: Þórarinn B. Þorláksson, 1920.

Schier, K. "Zur Mythologie der Snorra Edda: Einige Quellenprobleme." In *Specvlvm norroenvm: Norse Studies in Memory of Gabriel Turville-Petre*, ed. U. Dronke et al., 405–20. Odense: Odense University Press, 1981.

Religious Literature

Gad, Tue. *Legenden i dansk middlealder.* Copenhagen: Dansk Videnskabs Forlag, 1961.

Hallberg P. *Stilsignalement och författarskap i norrön sagalitteratur: Synpunkter och exempel.* Nordistica Gothoburgensia 3. Göteborg: Acta Universitatis Gothoburgensis, Göteborg University, 1968.

Kalinke, M. E. *The Book of Reykjahólar: The Last of the Great Medieval Legendaries.* Toronto: University of Toronto Press, 1996.

Lönnroth, Lars. "Studier i Olaf Tryggvasons saga." *Samlaren* 84 (1963): 54–94.

Tómasson, Sverrir. "The Icelandic Lives of St Nicholas." In *Helgastaðabók* (Íslensk miðaldahandrit 2), ed. Jónas Kristjánsson, 147–76. Reykjavík: Lögberg/Sverrir Kristinsson, 1982.

Tveitane, Mattias. *En norrøn versjon av Visio Pauli.* Humanistik Serie 1964:3. Bergen and Oslo: Årbok for Universitetet i Bergen, 1965.

CHAPTER 2: FROM REFORMATION TO ENLIGHTENMENT

GENERAL

Hermannsson, Halldór. *Icelandic Books of the Sixteenth Century (1534–1600).* Islandica 9. Ithaca NY: Cornell University Library, 1916.

———. *Icelandic Books of the Seventeenth Century.* Islandica 14. Ithaca NY: Cornell University Library, 1922.

LITERATURE IN ENGLISH TRANSLATION

Benediktsson, Jakob, ed. *Ole Worm's Correspondence with Icelanders.* Bibliotheca Arnamagnæana, vol. 7. Copenhagen: Munksgaard, 1948.

Bishop Guðbrand's Vísnabók, 1612. With an introduction in English by Sigurður Nordal. Monumenta Typographica Islandica, vol. 5. Facsimile ed., Copenhagen: Levin & Munksgaard, 1937.

Icelandic Christian Classics. Edited and translated and with an introduction by Charles Venn Pilcher. Melbourne: Geoffrey Cumberlege; Oxford: Oxford University Press, 1950.

Ólafsson, Eggert, and Bjarni Pálsson. *Travels in Iceland by Eggert Ólafsson and Bjarni Pálsson Performed 1752–57.* London: Richard Phillips, 1805. 2nd ed., Reykjavík: Örn og Orlygur, 1975.

Ólafsson, Jón. *The Life of the Icelander Jón Ólafsson, Traveller to India: Written by Himself and Completed about 1661 A.D. with a Continuation, by Another Hand, up to*

His Death in 1679. Translated by Bertha Phillpotts. London: Hakluyt Society, 1923–32.

Pétursson, Hallgrímur. *Hymns of the Passion: Meditations on the Passion of Christ.* Translated by Arthur Charles Gook. Reykjavík: Hallgrímskirkja 1966. Reprint, Reykjavík: Hallgrímskirkja, 1978.

Steingrímsson, Jón. *"A Very Present Help in Trouble": The Autobiography of the Fire-Priest.* Translated by Michael Fell. New York: Peter Lang, 2002.

Vídalínspostilla: Whom Wind and Waves Obey: Selected Sermons of Bishop Jón Vídalín. Translated and with an introduction by Michael Fell. New York: Peter Lang, 1998.

COLLECTED WORKS, MONOGRAPHS, AND ARTICLES

Popular Literature
Driscoll, Matthew J. *The Unwashed Children of Eve: The Production, Dissemination and Reception of Popular Literature in Post-Reformation Iceland.* London: Hisarlik, 1997.

Ólafur Egilsson
Egilsson, Ólafur. *Reisubók séra Ólafs Egilssonar.* Edited by Sverrir Kristjánsson. Reykjavík: Almenna Bókafélagið, 1969.

Oddur Einarsson
[Einarsson, Oddur]. *Qualiscunque descriptio Islandiae.* Edited by Fritz Burg. Hamburg: n.p., 1928.

———. *Íslandslýsing.* Translated by Sveinn Pálsson. With an introduction by Jakob Benediktsson. Reykjavík: Bókaútgáfa Menningarsjóðs, 1971.

Ólafur Einarsson of Kirkjubær
Einarsson, Ólafur. *Ein lijtil psalma og visna book.* Hólar, 1757.

Bjarni Gissurarson
Gissurarson, Bjarni. *Sólarsýn: Kvæði.* Edited by Jón M. Samsonarson. Reykjavík: Almenna Bókafélagið, 1964.

Þorleifur Halldórsson
Halldórsson, Þorleifur. *Mendacii encomium: Lof lyginnar.* Edited by Halldór Hermannsson. Islandica 8. Ithaca NY: Cornell University Library, 1915.

Arngrímur Jónsson the Learned
Arngrimi Jonae opera latine conscripta. Edited by Jakob Benediktsson. 4 vols. Bibliotheca Arnamagnæana, vols. 9–12. Copenhagen: Munksgaard, 1950–57.

Benediktsson, Jakob. *Arngrímur Jónsson and His Works.* Copenhagen: Munksgaard, 1957. Also published as the introduction to vol. 4 of Jakob Benediktsson, ed., *Arngrimi Jonae opera latine conscripta,* 4 vols., Bibliotheca Arnamagnæana, vols. 9–12 (Copenhagen: Munksgaard, 1950–57).

Bjarni Jónsson

Íslenskt ljóðasafn: Fornöld, miðaldir, siðskiptaöld. Edited by Kristján Karlsson. Reykjavík: Almennabókafélagið, 1976.

Ólafur Jónsson of Sandar

Íslenskt ljóðasafn: Fornöld, miðaldir, siðskiptaöld. Edited by Kristján Karlsson. Reykjavík: Almennabókafélagið, 1976.

Jón Magnússon

Magnússon, Jón. *Píslarsaga séra Jóns Magnússonar.* Edited by Matthías Viðar Sæmundsson. Reykjavík: Mál og menning, 2001.

Eggert Ólafsson

Hermannsson, Halldór. *Eggert Ólafsson: A Biographical Sketch.* Islandica 16. Ithaca NY: Cornell University Library, 1925.

Ólafsson, Eggert. *Reise igiennem Island.* Sorøe: Jonas Lindgrens Enke, 1772.

———. *Íslensk kvæðabók.* Copenhagen: S. L. Möller, 1832.

Jón Ólafsson

Ólafsson, Jón. *Reisubók Jóns Ólafssonar Indíafara, samin af honum sjálfum.* Edited by Völundur Óskarsson. Reykjavík: Mál og menning, 1992.

Magnús Ólafsson

Faulkes, Anthony, ed. *Magnúsarkver: The Writings of Magnús Ólafsson of Laufás.* Reykjavík: Stofnun Árna Magnússonar, 1993.

Stefán Ólafsson

Ólafsson, Stefán. *Kvæði.* Edited by Jón Þorkelsson. 2 vols. Copenhagen: Hið íslenska bókmenntafélag, 1885–86.

Hallgrímur Pétursson

Møller, Arne. *Hallgrímur Péturssons Passionssalmer: En studie over islandsk salmedigtning fra det 16. og 17. aarhundrede.* Copenhagen: Gyldendalske Boghandel, 1922.

Pétursson, Hallgrímur. *Sálmar og kvæði.* Edited by Grímur Thomsen. 2 vols. Reykjavík: Sigurður Kristjánsson, 1887–90.

———. *Ljóðmæli.* 3 vols. Vol. 1 ed. Margrét Eggertsdóttir. Vols. 2–3 ed. Margrét Eggertsdóttir, Kristján Eiríksson, and Svanhildur Óskarsdóttir. Reykjavík: Stofnun Árna Magnússonar, 2000–2005.

Jón Steingrímsson

Steingrímsson, Jón. *Æfisaga Jóns prófasts Steingrímssonar.* Edited by Jón Þorkelsson. Reykjavík: Sögufélag, 1913–16. Reprint, ed. Guðbrandur Jónsson, Reykjavík: Skaftfellingafélagið, 1945.

Jón Vídalín

Pétursson, Sigurður. "Jonas Widalinus Thorkilli Filius: Calliopes Respublica." In

Acta Conventus Neo-Latini Hafniensis: Proceedings of the Eighth International Congress of Neo-Latin Studies, Copenhagen, 12 August to 17 August 1991 (Medieval and Renaissance Texts and Studies 120), ed. Rhoda Schnur, 807–15. Binghamton NY: Medieval and Renaissance Texts and Studies, 1994.

Páll Vídalín

Vídalín, Páll. *Recensus poetarum et scriptorum Islandorum hujus et superioris seculi*. With an appendix by Þorsteinn Pétursson. Edited by Jón Samsonarson. Reykjavík: Stofnun Árna Magnússonar, 1985.

Jón Þorláksson

Beck, Richard. "Jón Þorláksson — Icelandic Translator of Pope and Milton." *Journal of English and Germanic Philology* 34 (1935): [73]–100.
———. "Alexander Pope and Icelandic Literature." *Scandinavian Studies* 25 (1953): 37–45.
———. *Jón Þorláksson, Icelandic Translator of Pope and Milton*. Studia Islandica 16. Reykjavík: Heimspekideild Háskóla Íslands, 1957.
Cook, Robert. "Pope Joan in Iceland." In *Sjötíu ritgerðir helgaðar Jakobi Benediktssyni 20. júlí 1977*, ed. Einar G. Pétursson and Jónas Kristjánsson, 138–46. Reykjavík: Stofnun Árna Magnússonar, 1977.
Þorláksson, Jón. *Kvæði, frumort og þýdd: Úrval*. Edited by Heimir Pálsson. Reykjavík: Rannsóknastofnun í bókmenntafræði/Bókaútgáfa Menningarsjóðs, 1976.

OTHER REFERENCES

Benediktsson, Jakob. "Den vågnende interesse for sagalitteraturen på Island i 1600-tallet." In *Lærdómslistir*, 227–41. Reykjavík: Mál og menning/Stofnun Árna Magnússonar, 1987.
Cook, Robert. "The Chronica Carionis in Iceland." In *Opuscula* (vol. 8, Bibliotheca Arnamagnæana 38), 226–63. Copenhagen, 1985.
Eggertsdóttir, Margrét. "Eddulist og barokk í íslenskum kveðskap á 17. öld." In *Guðamjöður og arnarleir: Safn ritgerða um eddulist*, ed. Sverrir Tómasson, 91–116. Reykjavík: Stofnun Árna Magnússonar, 1996.
———. "Nye strømninger og gammel tradition i islandsk barokdigtning." In *Om barocken i Norden*, ed. Kristina Malmio, 81–105. Helsingfors: Avdelningen för Nordisk Litteratur, Helsingfors Universitet, 1999.
Faulkes, Anthony, ed. *Two Versions of Snorra Edda from the Seventeenth Century*. 2 vols. Reykjavík: Stofnun Árna Magnússonar, 1977–79.
Friese, Wilhelm. *Nordische Barockdichtung: Eine Darstellung und Deutung Skandinavischer Dichtung zwischen Reformation und Aufklärung*. Munich: Francke, 1968.
———. "Ein ewiger Bestseller: Hallgrímur Pétursson's 'Passíusálmar.'" In ". . . Am Ende der Welt": Zur skandinavischen Literatur der frühen Neuzeit, 161–73. Leverkusen: Literaturverlag Norden, 1989.
Gíslason, Magnús. *Kvällsvaka*. Studia Ethnologica Upsaliensis 2. Uppsala: Acta Universitatis Upsaliensis, 1977.
Guðmundsson, Böðvar. "Nýir siðir og nýir lærdómar — bókmenntir, 1550–1750." In

Íslensk bókmenntasaga, vol. 2, ed. Vésteinn Ólason, 379–519. Reykjavík: Mál og menning, 1993.

Halldórsson, Óskar. *Bókmenntir á lærdómsöld*. Reykjavík: Hið íslenska bókmenntafélag, 1996.

Hermannsson, Halldór. *Two Cartographers: Guðbrandur Thorláksson and Thórður Thorláksson*. Islandica 17. Ithaca NY: Cornell University Library, 1926.

Hughes, Shaun F. D. "Report on *Rímur* 1980." *Journal of English and Germanic Philology* 79 (1980): 477–98.

———. "Rímur." In *Dictionary of the Middle Ages*, ed. Joseph R. Strayer, 10:401–7. New York: Scribner's, 1988.

———. "The Re-Emergence of Women's Voices in Icelandic Literature, 1500–1800." In *Cold Counsel: Women in Old Norse Literature and Mythology*, ed. Sarah M. Anderson and Karen Swenson, 93–128. New York: Routledge, 2002.

Kress, Helga, ed. *Stúlka: Ljóð eftir íslenskar konur*. Reykjavík: Bókmenntafræðistofnun Háskóla Íslands, 1997.

Ólason, Vésteinn. *The Traditional Ballads of Iceland*. Reykjavík: Stofnun Árna Magnússonar, 1982.

Pétursson, Sigurður. "Iceland." In *A History of Nordic Neo-Latin Literature*, ed. Minna Skafte Jensen, 96–128. Odense: Odense University Press, 1995.

———. "Latin Teaching in Iceland after the Reformation." In *Reformation and Latin Literature in Northern Europe*, ed. Inger Ekrem, Minna Skafte Jensen, and Egil Kraggerud, 106–22. Oslo: Scandinavian University Press, 1996.

Ringler, Richard. "Fyrirmynd kvæðisins 'Um þá fyrri öld og þessa' eftir Stefán Ólafsson." *Mímir* 5, no. 1 (1966): 20–22.

Samsonarson, Jón. "The Icelandic Horse-Epigram." In *Sagnaskemmtun: Studies in Honour of Hermann Pálsson on His 65th Birthday, 26th May 1986*, ed. Rudolf Simek, Jónas Kristjánsson, and Hans Bekker-Nielsen, 159–82. Vienna: Böhlau, 1986.

Seelow, Hubert. *Die isländischen Übersetzungen der deutschen Volksbücher*. Reykjavík: Stofnun Árna Magnússonar, 1989.

———. "Vier Gedichte für eine Hochzeit im Jahre 1738." *Gripla* 7 (1990): 131–67.

Sigurðardóttir, Þórunn. "Erfiljóð: Lærð bókmenntagrein á 17. öld." *Gripla* 11 (2000): 125–80.

Tómasson, Sverrir. "Eikarlundurinn: Athuganir á tveimur kvæðum Páls Jónssonar á Staðarhóli." *Mímir* 6, no. 1 (1967): 13–21.

———. " 'Suptungs mjöðurinn sjaldan verður sætur fundinn': Laufás Edda og áhrif hennar." In *Guðamjöður og arnarleir: Safn ritgerða um eddulist*, ed. Sverrir Tómasson, 65–89. Reykjavík: Stofnun Árna Magnússonar, 1996.

·CHAPTER 3: FROM ROMANTICISM TO REALISM

GENERAL

Beck, Richard. "Icelandic Literature." In *The History of Scandinavian Literatures*, ed. Frederika Blankner, 231–80. New York: Dial, 1938. Rev. ed., New York: Kennikat, 1966.

Egilsson, Sveinn Yngvi. *Arfur og umbylting*. Reykjavík: Hið íslenska bókmennta-félag, 1999.

Íslensk bókmenntasaga. Vol. 3, ed. Halldór Guðmundsson. Reykjavík: Mál og menning, 1996.

Íslensk stílfræði. By Þorleifur Hauksson and Þórir Óskarsson. Edited by Þorleifur Hauksson. Reykjavík: Styrktarsjóður Þorbergs Þórðarsonar & Margrétar Jónsdóttur, 1994.

Senner, W. M. *The Reception of German Literature in Iceland, 1775–1850*. Amsterdamer Publikationen zur Sprache und Literatur 62. Amsterdam: Rodopi, 1985.

Sæmundsson, Matthías Viðar. *Ást og útlegð: Form og hugmyndafræði í íslenskri sagnagerð, 1850–1920*. Studia Islandica 44. Reykjavík: Bókaútgáfa Menningarsjóðs, 1986. With an English summary (pp. 284–92).

LITERATURE IN ENGLISH TRANSLATION

An Anthology of Icelandic Poetry. Edited by Eiríkur Benedikz. Reykjavík: Ministry of Education, 1969.

Icelandic Lyrics: Originals and Translations. Edited by Richard Beck. Reykjavík: Þórhallur Bjarnarson, 1930.

Icelandic Poems and Stories: Translations from Modern Icelandic Literature. Edited by Richard Beck. Princeton NJ: Princeton University Press, for the American-Scandinavian Foundation, 1943.

The North American Book of Icelandic Verse. Edited by Watson Kirkconnell. New York and Montreal: Louis Carrier & Alan Isles, 1930.

Ringler, Dick. *Bard of Iceland: Jónas Hallgrímsson, Poet and Scientist*. Madison: University of Wisconsin Press, 2002. Contains sixty-eight translations.

Songs of Iceland: With English Texts. Edited by Steingrímur K. Hall. Toronto: J. H. Peel, 1954.

Thoroddsen, Jón. *Lad and Lass*. Translated by Arthur M. Reeves. London: Sampson Low, Marston, Searle & Rivington, 1890. A translation of *Piltur og stúlka* (1850).

COLLECTED WORKS, MONOGRAPHS, AND ARTICLES

Folk- and Fairy Tales

The Folk-Stories of Iceland. Translated by Benedikt Benedikz. Edited by Anthony Faulkes. Revised by Einar G. Pétursson. Viking Society for Northern Research Text Series, vol. 16. London: Viking Society for Northern Research, University College London, 2003.

Icelandic Legends. Collected by Jón Árnason. Translated by George E. J. Powell and Eiríkur Magnússon. London: Richard Bentley, 1864–66.

Íslenzk ævintýri. Edited by Magnús Grímsson and Jón Árnason. Reykjavík: E. Þórðarson, 1852.

Íslenzkar þjóðsögur og ævintýri. Edited by Jón Árnason. 2 vols. Leipzig: J. C. Hinrichs, 1862–64.

Íslenskar þjóðsögur og ævintýri: Ný útgáfa. Edited by Árni Böðvarsson and Bjarni Vilhjálmsson. 6 vols. Reykjavík: Bókaútgáfan Þjóðsaga, 1954–61.

Munnmælasögur 17. aldar. Edited by Bjarni Einarsson. Íslenzk rit síðari alda, vol. 6. Reykjavík: Hið íslenska fræðafélag, 1955.

Gísli Brynjúlfsson

Beck, Richard. "Gísli Brynjúlfsson—an Icelandic Imitator of *Childe Harold's Pilgrimage*." *Journal of English and German Philology* 28 (1929): 220–37.

Brynjúlfsson, Gísli. "Frá Norðurálfunni." In *Norðurfari*, ed. Gísli Brynjúlfsson and Jón Árnason, 1:50–77. Copenhagen: Útgefendur, 1848.

——. *Ljóðmæli Gísla Brynjúlfssonar.* Copenhagen: J. H. Schultz, 1891.

——. *Dagbók í Höfn.* Edited by Eiríkur Finnbogason. Reykjavík: Heimskringla, 1952.

Benedikt Gröndal

Einarsson, Stefán. "Benedikt Gröndal and Heljarslóðarorrusta." *Journal of English and German Philology* 36 (1937): 307–25, 543–50.

Gröndal, Benedikt. *Ritsafn.* Edited by Gils Guðmundsson. 5 vols. Reykjavík: Ísafoldarprentsmiðja, 1948–54.

Óskarsson, Þórir. *Undarleg tákn á tímans bárum: Ljóð og fagurfræði Benedikts Gröndals.* Studia Islandica 45. Reykjavík: Bókaútgáfa Menningarsjóðs, 1987. With an English summary (pp. 157–64).

Jónas Hallgrímsson

Hallgrímsson, Jónas. "Um rímur af Tistrani og Indíönu." *Fjölnir* 3 (1837): 18–29.

——. "Grikkur (Úr bréfi.)" *Fjölnir* 3 (1837): 29–32.

——. *Ritsafn.* Edited by Haukur Hannesson, Páll Valsson, and Sveinn Yngvi Egilsson. 4 vols. Reykjavík: Svart á Hvítu, 1989.

Ringler, Dick. *Bard of Iceland: Jónas Hallgrímsson, Poet and Scientist.* Madison: University of Wisconsin Press, 2002.

Valsson, Páll. *Jónas Hallgrímsson: Ævisaga.* Reykjavík: Mál og menning, 1999.

Matthías Jochumsson

Beck, Richard. "Matthías Jochumsson." *Scandinavian Studies and Notes* 13 (1934–35): 111–24.

Jochumsson, Matthías. "Ávarp til lesendanna og formáli fyrir Friðþjófssögu." In *Esaias Tegnér: Friðþjóssaga: Norræn söguljóð í 24 kvæðum*, vii–xxiv. Reykjavík: Einar Þórðarson, 1866.

——. *Bréf Matthíasar Jochumssonar.* Edited by Steingrímur Matthíasson. Akureyri: Bókadeild Menningarsjóðs, 1935.

——. *Ljóðmæli.* Edited by Árni Kristjánsson. 2 vols. Reykjavík: Ísafoldarprentsmiðja, 1956–58.

Hjálmar Jónsson

Jónsson, Hjálmar. *Ritsafn.* Edited by Finnur Sigmundsson. 6 vols. Reykjavík: Ísafoldarprentsmiðja, 1949–60.

Kristján Jónsson
Jónsson, Kristján. *Ljóðmæli*. Edited by Matthías V. Sæmundsson. Reykjavík: Almenna Bókafélagið, 1986.

Páll Ólafsson
Ólafsson, Páll. *Ljóðmæli*. 2 vols. Reykjavík: Jón Ólafsson, 1899–1900.

Tómas Sæmundsson
Senner, W. M. "Tómas Sæmundsson's *Ferðabók*." *Seminar* 13 (1977): 125–35.
Sæmundsson, Tómas. *Island fra den intellectuelle Side betragtet*. Copenhagen: C. Græbe & Søn, 1832.
——. "Úr bréfi frá Íslandi." *Fjölnir* 1 (1835): 48–94.
——. *Bréf Tómasar Sæmundssonar*. Edited by Jón Helgason. Reykjavík: Sigurður Kristjánsson, 1907.
——. *Ferðabók Tómasar Sæmundssonar*. Edited by Jakob Benediktsson. Reykjavík: Hið íslenska bókmenntafélag, 1947.

Grímur Thomsen
Beck, Richard. "Grímur Thomsen: A Pioneer Byron Student." *Journal of English and Germanic Philology* 27 (1928): 170–82.
Thomsen, Grímur. "Bjarni Thorarensen: En Skizze." In *Gæa, æsthetik Aarbog*, 187–203. Copenhagen: Berlingske Bogtrykkeri, 1845.
——. "Den islandske Literaturs Charakteristik." *Nordisk Literatur-Tidende* 22 (1846): 169–72; 23 (1846): 177–81; 25 (1846): 193–97; 26 (1846): 201–3.
——. *Ljóðmæli*. Edited by Sigurður Nordal. Reykjavík: Mál og menning, 1969.
——. *On the Character of the Old Northern Poetry*. Studia Islandica 31. Reykjavík: Bókaútgáfa Menningarsjóðs, 1972.
——. *Íslenzkar bókmenntir og heimsskoðun*. Edited by Andrés Björnsson. Reykjavík: Bókaútgáfa Menningarsjóðs, 1975.

Bjarni Thorarensen
Beck, Richard. "Bjarni Thorarensen — Iceland's Pioneer Romanticist." *Scandinavian Studies and Notes* 15 (1938): 71–80.
Guðnason, Bjarni. "Bjarni Thorarensen og Montesquieu." In *Afmælisrit Jóns Helgasonar*, ed. Jakob Benediktsson et al., 34–47. Reykjavík: Heimskringla, 1969.
Hauksson, Þorleifur. *Endurteknar myndir í kveðskap Bjarna Thorarensens*. Studia Islandica 27. Reykjavík: Bókaútgáfa Menningarsjóðs, 1968. With an English summary (pp. 91–94).
Thorarensen, Bjarni. *Ljóðmæli*. Edited by Jón Helgason. 2 vols. Copenhagen: Hið íslenska fræðafélag, 1935.

Jón Thoroddsen
Thoroddsen, Jón. *Skáldsögur Jóns Thoroddsens*. Edited by Steingrímur J. Þorsteinsson. 2 vols. Reykjavík: Helgafell, 1942.
Þorsteinsson, Steingrímur J. *Jón Thoroddsen og skáldsögur hans*. 2 vols. Reykjavík: Helgafell, 1943.

Steingrímur Thorsteinsson

Beck, Richard. "Steingrímur Thorsteinsson — Lyric Poet and Master Translator." *Scandinavian Studies and Notes* 20 (1948): 82–91.

Pétursson, Hannes. *Steingrímur Thorsteinsson: Líf hans og list.* Reykjavík: Bókaútgáfa Menningarsjóðs, 1964.

Thorsteinsson, Steingrímur. *Ljóðmæli frumkveðin og þýdd.* Edited by Hannes Pétursson. Reykjavík: Helgafell, 1973.

OTHER REFERENCES

Brandes, Georg. *Hovedstrømninger i det 19de Aarhundredes Litteratur.* Copenhagen: Gyldendal, 1872–90

Breiðfjörð, Sigurður. *Númarímur.* 1835. Reprinted in *Rímnasafn,* ed. Sveinbjörn Beinteinsson, 4:3–208. Reykjavík: Ísafoldarprentsmiðja, 1963.

Breve fra og til Rasmus Rask. Edited by Louis Hjelmslev. 2 vols. Copenhagen: Munksgaard, 1941.

Finnsson, Hannes. *Kvöldvökurnar, 1794.* Leirárgörðum, 1796.

Fjölnir: Árs-rit handa Íslendíngum. Edited by Brynjólfur Pétursson, Jónas Hallgrímsson, Konráð Gíslason, and Tómas Sæmundsson. 11 vols. Copenhagen: Prentað hjá J. D. Kvisti, 1835–47. A periodical.

Geir biskup góði í vinarbréfum, 1790–1823. Edited by Finnur Sigmundsson. Reykjavík: Bókfellsútgáfan, 1966.

Gíslason, Konráð. *Bréf Konráðs Gíslasonar.* Edited by Aðalgeir Kristjánsson. Reykjavík: Stofnun Árna Magnússonar, 1984.

Grímsson, Magnús, and Jón Árnason. "Formáli." Preface to *Íslenzk ævintýri,* ed. Magnús Grímsson and Jón Árnason, iii–iv. Reykjavík: E. Þórðarson, 1852.

Gröndal, Benedikt J. "Musteri mannordsins af Alexander Pope, snúit á Islenzku af B Grøndahl: Formáli þýdandans." In *Rit þess konunglega íslenzka Lærdómslistafélags,* 10:285–87. Copenhagen, 1790.

Hafnarstúdentar skrifa heim. Edited by Finnur Sigmundsson. Reykjavík: Bókfellsútgáfan, 1963.

Indriðason, Ólafur. "Úr brjefi af Austfjörðum." *Fjölnir* 2 (1836): 38–48.

Laxness, Halldór. *Alþýðubókin.* 1929. Reprint, Reykjavík: Helgafell, 1956.

Norðurfari. Edited by Gísli Brynjúlfsson and Jón Árnason. 2 vols. Copenhagen: Útgefendur, 1848–49.

Pálsson, Gestur. "Ávarp 'Suðra.'" In *Ritsafn: Sögur, kvæði, fyrirlestrar, blaðagreinar,* ed. Þorsteinn Gíslason, 433–38. Reykjavík: Þorsteinn Gíslason, 1927.

———. "Nýi skáldskapurinn." In *Ritsafn: Sögur, kvæði, fyrirlestrar, blaðagreinar,* ed. Þorsteinn Gíslason, 373–402. Reykjavík: Þorsteinn Gíslason, 1927.

Senner, W. M. "Magnús Stephensen: Precursor of the 'Fjölnismenn' and Icelandic Romanticism." *Scandinavian Studies* 72, no. 4 (2000): 411–30.

Skúlason, Sveinn. "Bókafregn." *Norðri.* Akureyri, 15 November 1861.

Steffens, Henrich. *Indledning til philosophiske Forelæsninger.* Copenhagen: Gyldendals Trane-Klassikere, 1968.

Sunnanpósturinn. Viðey, 1835–38.

Sverrisson, Eiríkur. "Sendibréf eins Borgfyrðíngs." *Sunnanpósturinn* 2 (1836): 4–9, 23–28, 62–64, 89–96, 155–60, 170–75, 185–89.

Undirbúningsblað undir þjóðfundinn að sumri 1851. Reykjavík and Copenhagen, 1850–51.

Vigfússon, Guðbrandur. "Formáli." Preface to *Íslenzkar þjóðsögur og æfintýri,* 1:v–xxxiii. Leipzig: J. C. Hinrichs, 1862.

Þjóðólfur. Reykjavík, 1848–1912.

CHAPTER 4: FROM REALISM TO NEOROMANTICISM

GENERAL

Pétursson, Hannes. Introduction to *Fjögur ljóðskáld,* ed. Hannes Pétursson, 7–51. Reykjavík: Bókaútgáfa Menningarsjóðs, 1957. 2nd rev. ed., Reykjavík: Mál og menning, 2000.

Princeton Encyclopedia of Poetry and Poetics. Edited by Alex Preminger. Princeton NJ: Princeton University Press, 1977.

LITERATURE IN ENGLISH TRANSLATION

Benediktsson, Einar. *Harp of the North: Poems by Einar Benediktsson.* Edited and translated by Frederic T. Wood. Charlottesville: University of Virginia Press, 1955.

Gunnarsson, Gunnar. *Guest the One-Eyed.* Translated by W. W. Worster. London: Gyldendal, 1920; New York: Knopf, 1922.

——. *Seven Days' Darkness.* Translated by Roberts Tapley. New York: Macmillan, 1930; London: Allen and Unwin, 1931.

Icelandic Lyrics: Originals and Translations. Edited by Richard Beck. Reykjavík: Þórhallur Bjarnarson, 1930.

Kamban, Guðmundur. *Hadda Padda.* Translated by Sadie Luise Peller. With an introduction by Georg Brandes. New York: Knopf, 1917. A translation of *Hadda Padda* (1914).

—— *The Virgin of Skalholt.* Translated by Evelyn Ramsden. Boston: Little Brown; London: Ivor Nocholson & Watson, 1936. A translation of *Skaalholt* (1930–32).

——. *I See a Wondrous Land.* Translated by Evelyn Ramsden. New York: Putnam, 1938. A translation of *Jeg ser et stort skønt land* (1936).

Laxness, Halldór. *Independent People: An Epic.* Translated by J. A. Thompson. London: Allen & Unwin, 1945; New York: Knopf, 1946. Reprint, New York: Vintage International, 1997; London: Harvill, 1999. A translation of *Sjálfstætt fólk* (1934–35).

Sigurjónsson, Jóhann. *Eyvind of the Hills and The Hraun Farm.* Translated by Henninge Krohn Schanche. Scandinavian Classics 4. New York: American-Scandinavian Foundation, 1916. A translation of *Bjærg Ejvind og hans Hustru* (1917) and *Gaarden Hraun* (1912).

Stephansson, Stephan G. "En Route." Translated by Watson Kirkconnell. In *Ste-*

phan G. Stephansson: Selected Translations from "Andvökur," 8–10. Edmonton: Stephan G. Stephansson Homestead Restoration Committee, 1987. A translation of selected stanzas of Á ferð og flugi (1900).

———. "When Day Is Done." Translated by Hallberg Hallmundsson. Jón á Bægisá 8 (2004): 117–18.

COLLECTED WORKS, MONOGRAPHS, AND ARTICLES

Einar Benediktsson

Benediktsson, Einar. *Ljóðmæli.* 3 vols. Reykjavík: Ísafoldarprentsmiðja, 1945.

———. "Gestur Pálsson." In *Laust mál*, 1:274–75. Reykjavík: Ísafoldarprentsmiðja, 1952.

———. "Þorsteinn Erlingsson." In *Laust mál*, 1:280–88. Reykjavík: Ísafoldarprentsmiðja, 1952.

Bjarnason, Loftur L. "'Harp of the North': Poems by Einar Benediktsson." *Scandinavian Studies* 29, no. 1 (1957): 24–28.

Friðjónsson, Sigurjón. Review of *Hafblik* by Einar Benediktsson. *Norðri* 2, no. 10 (1907).

Friðriksson, Guðjón. *Einar Benediktsson: Ævisaga.* 3 vols. Reykjavík: Iðunn, 1997–2000.

Kristjánsdóttir, Bergljót, and Haukur Ingvarsson. "'Líkami þinn er rafmagnaður' eða Einar Benediktsson og vísindin." In *Engill tímans: Til minningar um Matthías Viðar Sæmundsson*, ed. Eiríkur Guðmundsson and Þröstur Helgason, 87–96. Reykjavík: JPV Útgáfa, 2004.

Kristjánsdóttir, Dagný. "'Sár Sólveigar.'" In *Undirstraumar: Greinar og fyrirlestrar*, by Dagný Kristjánsdóttir, 77–85. Reykjavík: Háskólaútgáfan, 1999.

Nordal, Sigurður. *Einar Benediktsson.* Reykjavík: Helgafell, 1971.

Sæmundsson, Matthías Viðar. "Villusýn beinu línunnar: Um Einar Benediktsson." In *Myndir á sandi: Greinar um bókmenntir og menningarástand*, 149–65. Reykjavík: Bókmenntafræðistofnun Háskóla Íslands, 1991.

———. "Nætursýnin og beygurinn mikli: Út af kvæði eftir Einar Benediktsson." In *Skorrdæla*, ed. Bergljót Kristjánsdóttir and Matthías Viðar Sæmundsson, 119–33. Reykjavík: Háskólaútgáfan, 2003.

Þorsteinsson, Steingrímur J. "Æviágrip Einars Benediktssonar." In *Einar Benediktsson Laust mál*, 2:525–752. Reykjavík: Ísafoldarprentsmiðja, 1952.

Sigfús Blöndal

Blöndal, Sigfús. *Drotningin í Algeirsborg og önnur kvæði.* Reykjavík: Þorsteinn Gíslason, 1917.

Þorsteinn Erlingsson

Erlingsson, Þorsteinn. *Rit.* 3 vols. Reykjavík: Ísafoldarprentsmiðja, 1958.

Erlingsson, Þorsteinn, and Ólöf of Hlaðir. *Orð af eldi: Bréfasamband Ólafar Sigurðardóttur á Hlöðum og Þorsteins Erlingssonar á árunum 1883–1914.* Edited by Erna Sverrisdóttir. Reykjavík: Háskólaútgáfan, 2000.

Richer, Ragnhildur. "Í ómildra höndum? Um bréfasamband Ólafar á Hlöðum og Þorsteins Erlingssonar." *Andvari* 125 (2000): 170–76.

Guðmundur Friðjónsson

Friðjónsson, Guðmundur. *Ritsafn.* 7 vols. Akureyri: Prentverk Odds Björnssonar, 1955–56.

Guðmundsson, Þóroddur. *Guðmundur Friðjónsson: Ævi og störf.* Reykjavík: Ísafoldarprentsmiðja, 1950.

Þorsteinn Gíslason

Beck, Richard. "Skáldið Þorsteinn Gíslason." *Tímarit Þjóðræknisfélags Íslendinga í Vesturheimi* 28 (1947): 39–48.

Gíslason, Þorsteinn. *Ljóðmæli.* Reykjavík: Þorsteinn Gíslason, 1920.

Benedikt Gröndal

Gröndal, Benedikt. *Rit.* 3 vols. Hafnarfjörður: Skuggsjá, 1982.

Jónas Guðlaugsson

Gíslason, Vilhjálmur Þ. "Jónas Guðlaugsson skáld." *Andvari* 21 (1979): 54–61.

Guðlaugsson, Jónas. *Vorblóm.* Reykjavík: Aldarprentsmiðja, 1905.

——. *Tvístirnið.* Reykjavík: Prentsmiðjan Gutenberg, 1906.

——. *Dagsbrún: Söngvar og kvæði.* Reykjavík: Kostnaðarmaður Sigurður Kristjánsson, 1909.

——. Review of *Kvæði* by Hulda. *Lögrétta* 4 (1909): 194.

——. *Sange fra nordhavet: Islandske dikte.* Christiania and Copenhagen: Gyldendalske Boghandel, Nordisk Forlag. 1911.

——. *Viddernes poesi.* Christiania and Copenhagen: Gyldendalske Boghandel, Nordisk Forlag, 1912.

——. *Solrún og hendes Bejlere: Fortelling fra Island.* Christiania and Copenhagen: Gyldendalske Boghandel, Nordisk Forlag, 1913.

——. *Monika: Islandsk Bondefortælling.* Christiania and Copenhagen: Gyldendalske Boghandel, Nordisk Forlag, 1914.

——. *Sange fra de blaa Bjærge.* Christiania and Copenhagen: Gyldendalske Boghandel, Nordisk Forlag, 1914.

——. *Bredefjordsfolk.* Christiania and Copenhagen: Gyldendalske Boghandel, Nordisk Forlag, 1915.

——. *Bak við hafið: Úrval úr ljóðum Jónasar Guðlaugssonar.* Reykjavík: Flugur / Mál og menning, 1990.

M.J. Review of *Dagsbrún* by Jónas Guðlaugsson. *Ingólfur* 7, no. 43 (1909).

Stefánsson, Gunnar. "Að árroðans strönd og aftur heim: Þrjár nýjar bækur um nýrómantísk skáld." *Andvari* 33 (1991): 155–66.

Søiberg, Harry. "Jónas Guðlaugsson." *Andvari* 29 (1987): 165–71.

Guðmundur Guðmundsson

Guðmundsson, Guðmundur. *Ljóðmæli.* 1900. Reprinted in *Ljóðasafn*, ed. Steingerður Guðmundsdóttir. 2 vols. Reykjavík: Ísafoldarprentsmiðja, 1954.

———. *Ljóðasafn*. Edited by Steingerður Guðmundsdóttir. 2 vols. Reykjavík: Ísafoldarprentsmiðja, 1954.

Gunnar Gunnarsson

Björnsson, Sigurjón. *Leiðin til skáldskapar: Hugleiðingar um upptök og þróun skáldhneigðar Gunnars Gunnarssonar*. Reykjavík: Bókaútgáfa Menningarsjóðs, 1964.

———. "Hugleiðing um *Brimhendu* Gunnars Gunnarssonar." In *Skorrdæla*, ed. Bergljót Kristjánsdóttir and Matthías Viðar Sæmundsson, 149–54. Reykjavík: Háskólaútgáfan, 2003.

Gunnarsson, Gunnar. *Skáldverk*. 8 vols. Reykjavík: Almenna Bókafélagið / Helgafell, 1960–63.

Huldudóttir, Silja Björk, and Þorkell Ágúst Óttarsson. "Sviðsetning á ævi Krists: Biblíulegar vísanir í *Aðventu* Gunnars Gunnarssonar." *Andvari* 43 (2001): 99–112.

———. "Sálarvoði í óbyggðum: Um heimsmynd Gunnars Gunnarssonar." In *Myndir á sandi: Greinar um bókmenntir og menningarástand*, 260–74. Reykjavík: Bókmenntafræðistofnun Háskóla Íslands, 1991.

Hannes Hafstein

Albertsson, Kristján. *Hannes Hafstein: Æfisaga*. Reykjavík: Almenna Bókafélagið, 1961–64. 2nd ed., Reykjavík: Almenna Bókafélagið, 1985.

Hafstein, Hannes. "Hnignun íslensks skáldskapar." *Fjallkonan*, 2nd ed., 18 January 1888.

———. *Ljóð og laust mál*. Reykjavík: Helgafell, 1968.

Helgason, Jón Karl. "Tímans heróp: Lestur á inngangi Georgs Brandesar að meginstraumum og á textum eftir Hannes Hafstein og Gest Pálsson." *Skírnir* 163 (spring 1989): 111–45.

Hulda (Unnur Benediktsdóttir Bjarklind)

Bjartmarsdóttir, Guðrún, and Ragnhildur Richter. Introduction to *Ljóð og laust mál: Úrval*, by Hulda, ed. Guðrún Bjartmarsdóttir and Ragnhildur Richter, 11–98. Reykjavík: Bókmenntafræðistofnun Háskóla Íslands / Bókaútgáfa Menningarsjóðs, 1990.

Elísson, Guðni. "Líf er að vaka en ekki að dreyma: Hulda og hin nýrómantíska skáldmynd." *Skírnir* 161 (spring 1987): 59–87.

Finnbogason, Karl. "Bækur." *Norðurland* 9, no. 45 (1909): 162.

Hulda. *Kvæði*. Reykjavík: Sigurður Kristjánsson, 1909.

———. *Syngi syngi svanir mínir*. Reykjavík: Bókaverzlun Arinbj. Sveinbjarnarsonar, 1916.

———. *Segðu mjer að sunnan: Kvæði*. Reykjavík: Þorsteinn Gíslason, 1920.

———. *Myndir*. Akureyri: Prentsm. Odds Björnssonar, 1924.

———. *Við ysta haf*. Akureyri: Bókaverzlun Þorsteins M. Jónssonar, 1926.

———. *Ljóð og laust mál: Úrval*. Edited by Guðrún Bjartmarsdóttir and Ragnhildur Richter. Reykjavík: Bókmenntafræðistofnun Háskóla Íslands / Bókaútgáfa Menningarsjóðs, 1990.

Richter, Ragnhildur. "'Ljóðafugl lítinn ég geymi." *Tímarit Máls og Menningar* 3 (1985): 330–33.

Yershova, Yelena. "Hinn nýi 'gamli' kveðskapur: Þululjóð 20. aldar og síðmiðaldaþulur." *Andvari* 45 (2003): 123–51.

Jóhannes úr Kötlum (Jóhannes of Katlar)
Jóhannes úr Kötlum. *Ljóðasafn*. 9 vols. Reykjavík: Heimskringla, 1972.

Sveinn Jónsson
Jónsson, Sveinn. *Sveinn Framtíðarskáld*. Edited by Björn O. Björnsson. Reykjavík: Almenna Bókafélagið, 1971.

Guðmundur Jónsson Kamban
Einarsson, Stefán. "Guðmundur Kamban." *Tímarit Þjóðræknisfélagsins Íslendinga í Vesturheimi* 14 (1932): 7–29.

Kress, Helga. *Guðmundur Kamban: Æskuverk og ádeilur*. Studia Islandica 29. Reykjavík: Bókaútgáfa Menningarsjóðs, 1970. With an English summary.

Einar H. Kvaran
Bergmann, Friðrik J. Review of *Ofurefli* by Einar Hjörleifsson Kvaran. *Breiðablik*, November 1907, 88–89.

Brandes, Georg. Review of *Vonir* by Einar Hjörleifsson Kvaran. *Politiken*, 19 November 1900. For an Icelandic translation, see *Bjarka*, 25 January 1901.

Höskuldsson, Sveinn Skorri. "Hinn langi og skæri hljómur: Um höfundarverk Einars H. Kvarans." *Andvari* 38 (1996): 78–97.

Kristjánsdóttir, Bergljót. "Hjarta með hjarta ef hjarta er til: Um Marjas eftir Einar H. Kvaran." *Tímarit Máls og Menningar* 52, no. 2 (1991): 57–63.

Kvaran, Einar H. *Ritsafn*. 6 vols. Reykjavík: Leiftur, 1944.

Þorsteinsson, Steingrímur J. "Einar H. Kvaran: Aldarminning." *Andvari* 2 (1960): 3–23.

Sigurður Nordal
Nordal, Sigurður. "Hel." In *Fornar ástir*. Reykjavík: Þór. B. Þorláksson, 1919. 2nd ed., Reykjavík: Helgafell, 1949.

Sæmundsson, Matthías Viðar. "Að vera eða ekki: Um sögur eftir Gest Pálsson og Sigurð Nordal." *Skírnir* 157 (spring 1983): 5–35. Reprinted in Matthías Viðar Sæmundsson, *Myndir á sandi: Greinar um bókmenntir og menningarástand* (Reykjavík: Bókmenntafræðistofnun Háskóla Íslands, 1991), 216–45.

Gestur Pálsson
Helgason, Jón Karl. "Tímans heróp: Lestur á inngangi Georgs Brandesar að meginstraumum og á textum eftir Hannes Hafstein og Gest Pálsson." *Skírnir* 163 (spring 1989): 111–45.

Höskuldsson, Sveinn Skorri. *Gestur Pálsson*. 2 vols. Reykjavík: Bókaútgáfa Menningarsjóðs, 1965.

Pálsson, Gestur. "Úr ávarpsorðum Suðra." In *Ritsafn*, 2:120–21. Reykjavík: Ísafoldarprentsmiðja, 1945.

————. *Sögur og kvæði*. Reykjavík: H. F. Leiftur, 1949.
————. *Ritsafn*. 2 vols. Reykjavík: Menningar- og fræðslusamband Alþýðu, 1952.
Sæmundsson, Matthías Viðar. "Að vera eða ekki: Um sögur eftir Gest Pálsson og Sigurð Nordal." *Skírnir* 157 (spring 1983): 5–35. Reprinted in Matthías Viðar Sæmundsson, *Myndir á sandi: Greinar um bókmenntir og menningarástand* (Reykjavík: Bókmenntafræðistofnun Háskóla Íslands, 1991), 216–45.

Ólöf Sigurðardóttir of Hlaðir
Sigurðardóttir frá Hlöðum, Ólöf. *Nokkur smákvæði*. Akureyri: Bókaverzlun Odds Björnssonar, 1913.

Jóhann Gunnar Sigurðsson
Sigurðsson, Jóhann Gunnar. *Kvæði og sögur*. Edited by Helgi Sæmundsson. 2nd ed., Reykjavík: Bókaútgáfa Guðjóns Ó. Guðjónssonar, 1943.
Stefánsson, Gunnar. "Ég elskaði lífið og ljósið og ylinn: Aldarminning Jóhanns Gunnars Sigurðssonar skalds." *Samvinnan* 76, no. 3 (1982): 22–25.

Sigurður Sigurðsson of Arnarholt
Sigurðsson, Sigurður. *Ljóðasafn*. Reykjavík: Helgafell, 1978.

Stefán frá Hvítadal (Stefán of Hvítadalur)
Laxness, Halldór. "Stefán frá Hvítadal." In *Af skáldum*. Reykjavík: Bókaútgáfa Menningarsjóðs, 1972.
Orgland, Ivar. *Stefán frá Hvítadal*. Reykjavík: Bókaútgáfa Menningarsjóðs, 1962.
Stefán frá Hvítadal. *Ljóðmæli*. Reykjavík: Helgafell, 1970.

Jóhann Sigurjónsson
Gunnarsson, Gunnar. "Einn sit ég yfir drykkju." Introduction to *Rit eftir Jóhann Sigurjónsson*, 1:xiii–xlviii. Reykjavík: Mál og menning, 1940–42.
Jónsson, Jón Viðar. "Loftur á leiksviðinu." *Skírnir* 154 (1980): 24–76.
Kristjánsdóttir, Dagný. "Loftur á 'hinu leiksviðinu.'" *Tímarit Máls og Menningar* 46, no. 3 (1985): 287–307.
Sigurjónsson, Jóhann. *Ritsafn*. 3 vols. Reykjavík: Mál og menning, 1980.
Sæmundsson, Matthías Viðar. "Jóhann Sigurjónsson og módernisminn." *Tímarit Máls og Menningar* 40, no. 3 (1979): 322–37.
————. "Hlátur og helgríma: Um *Rung lækni* og andlega útþurrkun." In *Myndir á sandi: Greinar um bókmenntir og menningarástand*, 166–86. Reykjavík: Bókmenntafræðistofnun Háskóla Íslands, 1991.
Toldberg, Helge. *Jóhann Sigurjónsson*. Reykjavík: Heimskringla, 1966.

Jakob Jóhannesson Smári
Smári, Jakob Jóhannesson. "Norræn sál." *Eimreiðin* 31 (1925): 328–29.
————. *Kaldavermsl*. 1920. 2nd ed., Reykjavík: Bókaútgáfa Menningarsjóðs, 1960.
————. *Handan storms og strauma*. 1935. 2nd ed., Reykjavík: Bókaútgáfa Menningarsjóðs, 1960.

Davíð Stefánsson

Höskuldsson, Sveinn Skorri. "Söngvari lífsfögnuðarins: Hugleiðing um skáldskap Davíðs Stefánssonar á aldarafmæli hans." *Tímarit Máls og Menningar* 56, no. 2 (1995): 36–53.

Nordal, Sigurður. "Litið í gömul bréf." In *Skáldið frá Fagraskógi*, 134–41. Reykjavík: Kvöldvökuútgáfan, 1965.

Skáldið frá Fagraskógi: Endurminningar samferðamanna um Davíð Stefánsson. Edited by Árni Kristjánsson and Andrés Björnsson. Reykjavík: Kvöldvökuútgáfan, 1965.

Stefánsson, Davíð. *Að norðan*. 2 vols. Reykjavík: Helgafell, 1952.

———. *Ljóð: Úrval*. Edited by Ólafur Briem. Reykjavík: Rannsóknastofnun í bókmenntafræði/Bókaútgáfa Menningarsjóðs, 1977.

———. *Ljóðasafn*. 4 vols. Reykjavík: Vaka-Helgafell, 1995.

Stephan G. Stephansson

Hreinsson, Viðar. *Ævisaga Stephans G. Stephanssonar*. Vol. 1, *Landneminn mikli*. Vol. 2, *Andvökuskáld*. Reykjavík: Bjartur, 2002–3.

Kristjánsson, Kristján. "Að kasta ekki mannshamnum: Um heimspekina í ljóðum Stephans G. Stephanssonar." *Tímarit Máls og Menningar* 56, no. 4 (1995): 18–30.

Nordal, Sigurður. *Stephan G. Stephansson: Maðurinn og skáldið*. Reykjavík: Helgafell, 1959.

Stephansson, Stephan G. *Andvökur*. 4 vols. Reykjavík: Bókaútgáfa Menningarsjóðs, 1953–58.

Jón Trausti (Guðmundur Magnússon)

Trausti, Jón. *Ritsafn*. 8 vols. Reykjavík: Bókaútgáfa Guðjóns Ó. Guðjónssonar, 1960.

Þorgils gjallandi (Jón Stefánsson)

Þorgils gjallandi. *Sögur: Úrval*. Edited by Þórður Helgason. Reykjavík: Rannsóknastofnun í bókmenntafræði/Bókaútgáfa Menningarsjóðs, 1978.

———. *Ritsafn*. Edited by Jóhann Hauksdóttir and Þórður Helgason. 3 vols. Hafnarfjörður: Skuggsjá, 1982–84.

OTHER REFERENCES

Beyer, Harald. *Nietzsche og Norden*. Vol. 2. Bergen: Årbok, Universitetet i Bergen, 1958.

Bergmann, Friðrik J. Review of *Upp við fossa* by Þorgils gjallandi. *Aldamót* 12 (1902): 164–65.

Bjarnason, Ágúst H. *Nítjánda öldin*. Reykjavík: Bókaverzlun Guðm. Gamalíelssonar 1906.

Brandes, Georg. *Emigrantlitteraturen*. 1872. Reprint, Copenhagen: Gyldendal, 1971.

———. *An Essay on Aristocratic Radicalism*. Translated by A. G. Chater. London: William Heinemann, 1914.

Chadwick, Charles. *Symbolism*. London: Methuen, 1971.

Finnbogason, Guðmundur. "Þorgils gjallandi." *Eimreiðin* 15 (1909): 101.

———. "Egill Skallagrímsson." In *Huganir*. Reykjavík: Ísafoldarprentsmiðja, 1943.

Friðjónsson, Sigurjón. "Hið nýja skáldakyn." *Norðri* 1, no. 33 (1906): 33.

Jónsson, Vilhjálmur. "Yngstu skáld Dana." *Eimreiðin* 1 (1895): 140–41.

Kristjánsson, Gunnar. "Lífsviðhorf Síra Matthíasar." *Skírnir* 161 (spring 1987): 17–18.

Kristjánsson, Sverrir, and Tómas Guðmundsson. *Minnisverðir menn*. Reykjavík: Forni, 1968.

Lárusson, Ól. Ó. "Kyngæði og kynspilling." *Eimreiðin* 31 (1925): 16–21.

Moers, Ellen. "Metaphors: A Postlude." In *Literary Women*. New York: Doubleday, 1976.

Nietzsche, Friedrich. *The Gay Science*. Vol. 1. New York: Vintage, 1974.

———. "Of the Higher Men." Sec. 20 of *Thus Spoke Zarathustra*, trans. R. J. Hollingdal, 306. Harmondsworth: Penguin, 1985.

Pálsson, Árni. *Á við og dreif*. Reykjavík: Helgafell, 1947.

Sæmundsson, Matthías Viðar. *Mynd nútímamannsins: Um tilvistarleg viðhorf í sögum Gunnars Gunnarssonar*. Studia Islandica 41. Reykjavík: Bókaútgáfa Menningarsjóðs, 1982.

———. *Ást og útlegð*. Reykjavík: Bókaútgáfa Menningarsjóðs, 1986.

Þórðarson, Þórbergur. *Íslenskur aðall*. 1938. Reprint, Reykjavík: Mál og menning, 1971.

CHAPTER 5: REALISM AND REVOLT: BETWEEN THE WORLD WARS

GENERAL

Andrésson, Kristinn E. *Íslenskar nútímabókmenntir, 1918–1948*. Reykjavík: Mál og menning, 1949.

Carleton, Peter. "Tradition and Innovation in Twentieth-Century Icelandic Poetry." PhD diss., University of California, Berkeley, 1967. Reprint, Ann Arbor: UMI, 1974.

Einarsson, Stefán. "Two Novels about Iceland." *Scandinavian Studies and Notes* 13 (1934): 67–68.

Guðmundsson, Halldór. "Det modernes forsinkede gennembrud/The Belated Breakthrough of Modernism." *Nordisk litteratur/Nordic Literature* 2000: 49–51, 80–82.

Jóhannsson, Jón Yngvi. "Islandske forfattere p det danske parnas/Icelandic Writers on the Danish Literary Scene." *Nordisk litteratur/Nordic Literature* 2000: 42–45.

———. "Scandinavian Orientalism: The Reception of Danish-Icelandic Literature, 1905–50." In *Nordisk litteratur og mentalitet* (Annales Societatis Scientarium Færoensis Supplementum 25), ed. Malan Marnersdottir and Jens Cramer, 254–61. Tórshavn: Fróðskaparsetur Færeyja, 2000.

———. " 'Jøklens Storm svalede den kulturtætte Danmarks Pande': Um fyrstu viðtökur dansk-íslenskra bókmennta í Danmörku." *Skírnir* 175 (spring 2001): 33–66. With an English summary.

Ólafsson, Örn. *Rauðu pennarnir: Bókmenntahreyfing á 2. fjórðungi 20. aldar.* Reykjavík: Mál og menning, 1990.

SELECTED WORKS IN ENGLISH TRANSLATION

Anthologies

Allwood, Martin, ed. and trans. *Modern Scandinavian Poetry: The Panorama of Poetry, 1900–1975.* Mullsjö: Anglo-American Centre, 1982.

Benedikz, Eiríkur, ed. *An Anthology of Icelandic Poetry.* Reykjavík: Ministry of Education, 1969.

Boucher, Alan, ed. and trans. *Poems of Today from Twenty-Five Icelandic Poets.* Reykjavík: Iceland Review, 1971.

Brement, Marshall, ed. and trans. *Three Modern Icelandic Poets: Selected Poems of Steinn Steinarr, Jón úr Vör and Matthías Johannessen.* Reykjavík : Iceland Review, 1985.

Kristmann Guðmundsson

The Bridal Gown: A Novel of Iceland. Translated by O. F. Theis. New York: Cosmopolitan, 1931. A translation of *Brudekjolen* (1932).

The Morning of Life. Translated by Elizabeth Sprigge and Claude Napier. London: Heinemann; New York: Doubleday, Doran, 1936. A translation of *Livets morgen* (1929).

Winged Citadel. Translated by Barrows Mussey. New York: Henry Holt, 1940. A translation of *Gudinnen og oksen* (1938).

Gunnar Gunnarsson

Advent. Translated by Evelyn C. Ramsden. London: Jarrolds, 1939. A British translation of *Advent* (1937).

The Black Cliffs. Translated by Cecil Woods. Madison: University of Wisconsin Press, 1967. A translation of *Svartfugl* (1929).

The Good Shepherd. Translated by Kenneth C. Kaufman. New York: Bobbs-Merrill, 1940. An American translation of *Advent* (1937).

Guest the One-Eyed. Translated by W. Worster. London: Gyldendal, 1920. A translation of *Af Borgslægtens Historie* (1912–14).

The Night and the Dream. Translated by Evelyn Ramsden. New York: Bobbs-Merrill; London: Jarrolds, 1938. A translation of the second half of *Kirken paa Bjerget* (1923–28).

Seven Days' Darkness. Translated by Robert Tapley. New York: Macmillan, 1930; London: Allen & Unwin, 1931. A translation of *Salige er de enfoldige* (1920).

Ships in the Sky: Compiled from Uggi Greipsson's Notes. Translated by Evelyn C. Ramsden. New York: Bobbs-Merrill; London: Jarrolds, 1938. A translation of the first half of *Kirken paa Bjerget* (1923–28).

The Sworn Brothers: A Tale of the Early Days of Iceland. Translated by C. Field. London: Gyldendal, 1920; New York: Knopf, 1921. A translation of *Edbrødre* (1918).

Trylle and Other Small Fry. Translated by Evelyn C. Ramsden. London: Hutchinson, 1947. A translation of *Trylle og andet Smaakram* (1939).

Guðmundur Kamban
Hadda Padda: A Drama in Four Acts. Translated by Sadie Luise Peller. New York: Knopf, 1917. A translation of *Hadda Padda* (1914).
The Virgin of Skalholt. Translated by Evelyn Ramsden. Boston: Little Brown; London: Ivor Nocholson & Watson, 1936. A translation of *Skaalholt* (1930–32).
I See a Wondrous Land. Translated by Evelyn Ramsden. New York: Putnam, 1938. A translation of *Jeg ser et stort skønt land* (1936).
We Murderers. Translated by Einar Haugen. Madison: University of Wisconsin Press, 1970. A translation of *Vi Mordere* (1920).

Halldór Laxness
Iceland's Bell. Translated by Philip Roughton. New York: Vintage, 2003. A translation of *Íslandsklukkan* (1943–46).
Independent People: An Epic. Translated by J. A. Thompson. London: Allen & Unwin, 1945; New York: Knopf, 1946. Reprint, New York: Vintage International, 1997; London: Harvill, 1999. A translation of *Sjálfstætt fólk* (1934–35).
Salka Valka. Translated by F. H. Lyon. 1936. Reprint, London: Allen & Unwin, 1973. A translation of *Salka Valka* (1930–31).
World Light. Translated by Magnus Magnusson. 1969. Reprint, New York: Vintage International, 2002. A translation of *Heimsljós* (1937–40).

Jóhann Sigurjónsson
Eyvindur of the Mountains: A Play in Four Acts. Translated by Francis P. Magoun Jr. Reykjavík: Helgafell, 1961. A translation of *Bjærg Ejvind og hans Hustru* (1917)
Loft's Wish. Translated by Jakobina Johnson. Boston: Poet Lore, 1940. A translation of *Ønsket* (1915).
Loftur: A Play. Translated by Jean Young and Eleanor Arkwright. Reading: University of Reading, 1939. A translation of *Ønsket* (1915).
Modern Icelandic Plays: Eyvind of the Hills, The Hraun Farm. Translated by Henninge Krohn Schanche. New York: American-Scandinavian Foundation, 1916. Translations of *Bjærg Ejvind og hans Hustru* (1917) and *Gaarden Hraun* (1912).

Þórbergur Þórðarson
In Search of My Beloved. Translated by Kenneth Chapman. Reykjavík: Helgafell, 1961. Reprint, New York: Twayne / American Scandinavian Foundation, 1967. A translation of *Íslenskur aðall* (1938).

COLLECTED WORKS, MONOGRAPHS, AND ARTICLES

Sigurður Grímsson
Grímsson, Sigurður. *Við langelda.* Reykjavík, 1922.

Tómas Guðmundsson
Andrésson, Kristinn E. "Tómas Guðmundsson: Stjörnur vorsins." *Tímarit Máls og Menningar* 3, no. 2 (1941): 195.

Karlsson, Kristján. "Inngangur." Introduction to *Ljóðasafn*, by Tómas Guðmundsson, vii–xlv. Reykjavík: Helgafell, 1961.

Gunnar Gunnarsson

Arvidsson, Stellan. *Gunnar Gunnarsson: Islänningen*. Stockholm: LT, 1960.

Bessason, Haraldur. "Gunnarsson, Gunnar: The Black Cliffs." *Scandinavian Studies* 41, no. 3 (1969): 276–77.

Gunnarsson, Gunnar. *Sælir eru einfaldir*. 1920. 4th ed. Reykjavík: Almenna bókafélagið, 1982.

Jóhannsson, Jón Yngvi. "Formáli." Introduction to *Svartfugl*, by Gunnar Gunnarsson, v–xxiii. Reykjavík: Íslensku bókaklubbarnir, 2001.

———. "Fyrsta glíma við engilinn." In *Ströndin*, 347–60. Reykjavík: Landnáma, 1945.

Kjartansdóttir, Halla. *Trú í sögum: Um heiðni og kristni í sögum og samtíma Gunnars Gunnarssonar*. Studia Islandica 56. Reykjavík: Bókmenntafræðistofnun Háskóla Íslands, 1999. With an English summary.

Kristjánsdóttir, Dagný. "Synd er ekki nema fyrir þræla: Um þema og hneigð í Svartfugli eftir Gunnar Gunnarsson." *Skírnir* 152 (1978): 78–106.

Óskarsson, Þórir. "Bók án borgaralegs öryggis." *Skírnir* 163 (1989): 315–29.

Sæmundsson, Matthías Viðar. *Mynd nútímamannsins: Um tilvistarleg viðhorf í sögum Gunnars Gunnarssonar*. Studia Islandica 41. Reykjavík: Bókaútgáfa Menningarsjóðs, 1982. With an English summary.

Hulda

Birgisdóttir, Soffía Auður. "Hin norræna móðir og svanurinn: Andstæðusýn og togstreita í Dalafólki I eftir Huldu." *Mímir* 26, no. 1 (1987): 67–77.

Jóhann Jónsson

Bogason, Ingi Bogi. "Að mála yfir litleysi daganna. Söknuður: Um ljóðið, skáldið og expressjónisma." *Skírnir* 165 (spring 1991): 11–45

———. "Expressjónískir drættir í Söknuði: Á aldarafmæli Jóhanns Jónssonar." *Mímir* 35, no. 1 (1996): 44–48.

Sigurjón Jónsson

Sigurjónsson, Árni. "Nútímaleg skáldsagnagerð: Um æskuverk Sigurjóns Jónssonar rithöfundar." *Andvari* 38 (1996): 98–110.

Guðmundur Kamban

Kamban, Guðmundur. "Forord." Preface to *Jomfru Ragnheiður* (vol. 1 of *Skálholt*), 1:5–9. Copenhagen: Haseselbach, 1930.

———. *Skálholt*. Reykjavík: Ísafoldarprentsmiðja, 1930.

Halldór Laxness

Albertsson, Kristján, and Guðmundur Finnbogason. "Tveir ritdómar." *Vaka* 1, no. 3 (1927): 306–16.

Bessason, Haraldur. "Halldór Laxness." In *European Writers—the Twentieth Century*, ed. William T. H. Jackson, vol. 12, ed. George Stade, 2457–78. New York: Scribner's, 1990.

Birgisdóttir, Soffía Auður. "'Hvað er kona af konu fædd? Getur hún aldrei orðið frjáls?': Um samband móður og dóttur í Sölku Völku." *Tímarit Máls og Menningar* 53, no. 3 (1992): 9–19.

Bjarnason, Loftur L. "Halldor Kiljan Laxness, World Light." *Scandinavian Studies* 42, no. 2 (1970): 214–17.

Eysteinsson, Ástráður. "Fyrsta nútímaskáldsagan og módernisminn: Loksins hvað?" *Skírnir* 162 (fall 1988): 273–316.

Guðmundsson, Halldór. *"Loksins, loksins": Vefarinn mikli og upphaf íslenskra nútímabókmennta*. Reykjavík: Mál og menning, 1987.

———. "Glíman við Hamsun: Sjálfstætt fólk og Gróður jarðar." *Tímarit Máls og Menningar* 57, no. 3 (1996): 66–82.

Hallberg, Peter. *Den store vävaren: En studie i Laxness' ungdomsdiktning*. Stockholm: Rabén & Sjögren, 1954.

———. *Skaldens hus: Laxness' diktning från Salka Valka till Gerpla*. Stockholm: Rabén & Sjögren, 1956.

———. *Halldór Laxness*. Translated by Rory McTurk. New York: Twayne, 1971.

Jakobsson, Ármann. "'Hinn blindi sjáandi': Hallbera í Urðarseli og Halldór Laxness." *Skírnir* 170 (fall 1996): 325–39.

Laxness, Halldór. "Hvernig Vefarinn varð til." In *Vefarinn mikli frá Kasmír*, 381–83. 1927. 2nd ed., Reykjavík: Helgafell, 1948.

———. *Salka Valka*. 1930–31. 3rd ed. Reykjavík: Helgafell, 1959.

Markey, Thomas L. "*Salka Valka*: A Study in Social Realism." *Scandinavica* 11, no. 1, suppl. (May 1972): 63–70.

Nedelyaeva-Steponavichiene, Svetlana. "On the Style of Laxness' Tetralogy 'World Light.'" *Scandinavica* 11, no. 1, suppl. (May 1972): 71–88.

Ólason, Vésteinn. "Halldór Laxness og íslensk hetjudýrkun." *Tímarit Máls og Menningar* 53, no. 3 (1992): 31–41

Sigurjónsson, Árni. "Hugmyndafræði Alþýðubókarinnar." *Tímarit Máls og Menningar* 63, no. 1 (1982): 38–63.

———. *Den politiska Laxness: Den ideologiska och estetiska bakgrunden till Salka Valka och Fria män*. Stockholm: n.p., 1984. With an English summary.

———. *Laxness og þjóðlífið: Bókmenntir og bókmenntakenningar á árunum milli stríða*. Reykjavík: Vaka-Helgafell, 1986.

Sønderholm, Erik. *Halldór Laxness: En monografi*. Gyldendal: Copenhagen, 1981.

Þorvaldsson, Eysteinn. "Ljóðagerð sagnaskálds: Um ljóð Halldórs Laxness." In *Halldórsstefna 12.–14. júní 1992*, ed. Elín Bára Magnúsdóttir and Úlfar Bragason, 124–38. Reykjavík: Stofnun Sigurðar Nordals, 1993.

Davíð Stefánsson

Albertsdóttir, Sigríður. "'Ég verð konungur djöflanna': Ást og óhugnaður í ljóðum Davíðs Stefánssonar." *Skírnir* 170 (autumn 1996): 303–23.

Steinn Steinarr

Aðalsteinsdóttir, Silja. "Þú og ég sem urðum aldrei til: Existensíalismi í verkum Steins Steinarrs." *Skírnir* 155 (1981): 29–51.

Karlsson, Kristján. "Steinn Steinnar." *Nýtt Helgafell* 2 (1958): 79–82.

——. "Formáli." Introduction to *Kvæðasafn og greinar*, by Steinn Steinarr, vii–xxvii. Reykjavík: Helgafell, 1964.

Steinn Steinarr. *Kvæðasafn og greinar*. Reykjavík: Helgafell, 1964.

Jón Thoroddsen

Thoroddsen, Jón. *Flugur*. Reykjavík, 1922.

Þórbergur Þórðarson

Bessason, Haraldur. "Thordarson, Thorbergur: In Search of My Beloved." *Scandinavian Studies* 40, no. 2 (May 1968): 173–75.

Einarsson, Stefán. "Thórbergur Thórdarson, Humorist: A Note." *Scandinavian Studies* 35, no. 1 (February 1963): 59–63.

Rögnvaldsdóttir, Sigríður. "Brotin heimsmynd: Um sýnd og reynd í Íslenskum Aðli og Ofvitanum." *Tímarit Máls og Menningar* 50, no. 3 (1989): 291–306.

Þórðarson, Þórbergur. *Bréf til Láru*. 1924. 6th ed. Reykjavík: Mál og menning, 1974.

OTHER REFERENCES

Albertsson, Kristján. "Við langelda: Ljóð Sigurðar Grímssonar." *Eimreiðin* 20 (1922): 168–72.

Ásgeirsson, Magnús. *Þýdd ljóð*. Vol. 1. Reykjavík: Bókaútgáfa Menningarsjóðs, 1928.

Eysteinsson, Ástráður. "Á tali: Til varnar málefnalegri gagnrýni." *Tímarit Máls og Menningar* 50, no. 3 (1989): 267–82.

Friðjónsson, Guðmundur. *Sveitaómenningin í skugga skáldsins frá Laxnesi*. Reykjavík: n.p., 1937.

Guðmundsson, Halldór. "Orðin og efinn: Til varnar bókmenntasögu." *Tímarit Máls og Menningar* 50, no. 2 (1989): 191–204.

Hobsbawm, Eric. *Age of Extremes: The Short Twentieth Century*. London: Michael Joseph, 1994.

Laxness, Halldór. "Stuttar ádrepur: Hin hvítu skip Guðmundar Böðvarssonar." *Tímarit Máls og Menningar* 2, no. 2 (1939): 30–32.

Nordal, Sigurður. *List og lífsskoðun*. Vol. 2, ed. Jóhannes Nordal et al. Reykjavík: Almenna Bókafélagið, 1987.

Williams, Raymond. *The Country and the City*. London: Chatto & Windus, 1973.

Zweig, Stefan. *The World of Yesterday: An Autobiography*. London: Cassell, 1943.

CHAPTER 6: ICELANDIC PROSE LITERATURE, 1940–1980

GENERAL

Brøndsted, Mogens, ed. *Nordens litteratur efter 1860*. Vol. 2 of *Nordens litteratur*. 2 vols. Copenhagen: Gyldendal, 1972.

Eysteinsson, Ástráður, and Eysteinn Þorvaldsson. "Modern Literature." In *Iceland: The Republic*, ed. Jóhannes Nordal and Valdimar Kristinsson, 264–86. Reykjavík: Central Bank of Iceland, 1996.

Pálsson, Heimir. *Straumar og stefnur í íslenskum bókmenntum frá 1550*. 3rd ed., Reykjavík: Iðunn, 1987.

———. *Sögur, ljóð og líf: Íslenskar bókmenntir á 20. öld*. Reykjavík: Vaka-Helgafell, 1998.

LITERATURE IN ENGLISH TRANSLATION

Anthologies

Short Stories of Today, by Twelve Modern Icelandic Authors. Translated and edited by Alan Boucher. Reykjavík: Iceland Review, 1972.

Svava Jakobsdóttir

The Lodger and Other Stories. Translated by Julian Meldon D'Arcy et al. Reykjavík: University of Iceland Press, 2000.

Halldór Laxness

The Atom Station. Translated by Magnus Magnusson. 1961. Reprint, London: Harvill, 2003. A translation of *Atómstöðin* (1948).

Christianity at Glacier. Translated by Magnús Magnússon. Reykjavík: Helgafell, 1972. Reprinted as *Under the Glacier* (Reykjavík: Vaka-Helgafell, 1996). A translation of *Kristnihald undir Jökli* (1968).

The Fish Can Sing. Translated by Magnús Magnússon. 1966. Reprint, London: Harvill, 2000. A translation of *Brekkukotsannáll* (1957).

The Happy Warriors. Translated by Katherine John. London: Methuen, 1958. A translation of *Gerpla* (1952).

Iceland's Bell. Translated by Philip Roughton. New York: Vintage, 2003. A translation of *Íslandsklukkan* (1943–46).

Paradise Reclaimed. Translated by Magnus Magnusson. 1962. Reprint, New York: Knopf, 2002. A translation of *Paradísarheimt* (1960).

Thor Vilhjálmsson

Faces Reflected in a Drop. Translated by Kenneth G. Chapman. Reykjavík: Helgafell, 1966. A translation of *Andlit í spegli dropans* (1957).

Quick Quick Said the Bird. Translated by John O'Kane. Kapuskasing ON: Penumbra/Unesco, 1987. A translation of *Fljótt fljótt sagði fuglinn* (1968).

Agnar Þórðarson

The Sword. Translated by Paul Schach. New York: Twayne/American-Scandinavian · Foundation, 1970. A translation of *Ef sverð þitt er stutt* (1953).

Indriði G. Þorsteinsson

North of War. Translated by May Hallmundsson and Hallberg Hallmundsson. Reykjavík: Iceland Review, 1981. A translation of *Norðan við stríð* (1971).

COLLECTED WORKS, MONOGRAPHS, AND ARTICLES

Birgisdóttir, Soffía Auður, ed. *Sögur íslenskra kvenna, 1879–1960*. Reykjavík: Mál og menning, 1987.

Kress, Helga. *Speglanir: Konur í íslenskri bókmenntahefð og bókmenntasögu*. Reykjavík: Rannsóknastofa í kvennafræðum við Háskóla Íslands, 2000.

Guðbergur Bergsson

Bergsson, Guðbergur. *Tómas Jónsson metsölubók*. 2nd ed. Reykjavík: Forlagið, 1987.

Bjarnadóttir, Birna. *Holdið hemur andann: Um fagurfræði í skáldskap Guðbergs Bergssonar*. Reykjavík: Háskólaútgáfan, 2003.

Jóhannes úr Kötlum (Jóhannes of Katlar)

Jóhannes úr Kötlum. *Dauðmannsey*. Reykjavík: Heimskringla, 1949.

Halldór Laxness

"Ekkert orð er skrípi ef það stendur á réttum stað": Um ævi og verk Halldórs Laxness. Edited by Jón Ólafsson. Reykjavík: Hugvísindastofnun Háskóla Íslands, 2002.

Eysteinsson, Ástráður. "Er Halldór Laxness höfundur Fóstbræðasögu? Um höfundargildi, textatengsl og þýðingu í sambandi Laxness við fornsögurnar." *Skáldskaparmál* 1 (1990): 171–88.

Guðmundsdóttir, Gunnþórunn, and Daisy Neijmann, eds. "'The Silent Music of the Clouds': 100 Years with Halldór Laxness." Special issue, *Scandinavica*, vol. 42, no. 1 (May 2003).

Guðmundsson, Halldór. *Halldór Laxness: Leben und Werke*. Göttingen: Steidl, 2002.

Hallberg, Peter. *Halldór Laxness*. Translated by Rory McTurk. New York: Twayne, 1971.

Höskuldsson, Sveinn Skorri, ed. "Special Issue Devoted to the Works of Halldór Laxness." *Scandinavica*, vol. 11, no. 1, suppl. (May 1972).

Laxness, Halldór. "Um Jónas Hallgrímsson." In *Alþýðubókin*. 5th ed. Reykjavík: Helgafell, 1956.

———. *Íslandsklukkan*. 3rd ed. Reykjavík: Helgafell, 1969.

Magnúsdóttir, Elín Bára, and Úlfar Bragason, eds. *Halldórsstefna: 12.–14. júní 1992*. Reykjavík: Stofnun Sigurðar Nordals, 1993.

Sønderholm, Erik. *Halldór Laxness: En monografie*. Copenhagen: Gyldendal, 1981.

Thor Vilhjálmsson

Kress, Helga, ed. *Fuglar á ferð: Tíu erindi um Thor Vilhjálmsson*. Reykjavík: Bókmenntafræðistofnun Háskóla Íslands/Háskólaútgáfan, 1995.

Þórbergur Þórðarson

Þórðarson, Þórbergur. *Æfisaga Árna prófasts Þórarinssonar*. 6 vols. Reykjavík: Helgafell, 1945–50.

OTHER REFERENCES

Daðason, Sigfús. *Ritgerðir og pistlar*. Edited by Þorsteinn Þorsteinsson. Reykjavík: Forlagið, 2000.

Eysteinsson, Ástráður. *Tvímæli: Þýðingar og bókmenntir*. Reykjavík: Bókmennta-fræðistofnun Háskóla Íslands/Háskólaútgáfan, 1999.

———. *Umbrot: Bókmenntir og nútími*. Reykjavík: Háskólaútgáfan, 1999.

Jónsson, Ólafur. *Líka líf: Greinar um samtímabókmenntir*. Reykjavík: Iðunn, 1979.

Kristjánsdóttir, Dagný. *Kona verður til: Um skáldsögur Ragnheiðar Jónsdóttur fyrir fullorðna*. Reykjavík: Háskólaútgáfan, 1996.

———. *Undirstraumar: Greinar og fyrirlestrar*. Reykjavík: Háskólaútgáfan, 1999.

Magnússon, Sigurður A. *Sáð í vindinn: Greinar og fyrirlestrar*. Reykjavík: Helgafell, 1968.

———. *Iceland Crucible: A Modern Artistic Renaissance*. Reykjavík: Vaka, 1985.

Sæmundsson, Matthías Viðar. *Myndir á sandi: Greinar um bókmenntir og menningarástand*. Reykjavík: Bókmenntafræðistofnun Háskóla Íslands, 1991.

CHAPTER 6: ICELANDIC PROSE LITERATURE, 1980–2000

GENERAL

Eysteinsson, Ástráður, and Eysteinn Þorvaldsson. "Modern Literature." In *Iceland: The Republic*, ed. Jóhannes Nordal and Valdimar Kristinsson, 264–86. Reykjavík: Central Bank of Iceland, 1996.

Icelandic Literature. Reykjavík: Reykjavík City Library, n.d. http://www.bokmenntir .is (in Icelandic); http://www.literature.is (in English). Articles in Icelandic and English, and some in Danish, on contemporary Icelandic authors.

Nordisk litteratur/Nordic Literature. Copenhagen: NORDBOK/Nordic Council of Ministers, 1993–. Articles, in Danish and English, on contemporary Nordic literature, including Icelandic.

LITERATURE IN ENGLISH TRANSLATION

Guðbergur Bergsson
The Swan. Translated by Bernard Scudder. London: Mare's Nest/Shad Thames, 1998. A translation of *Svanurinn* (1991).

Þórarinn Eldjárn
The Blue Tower. Translated by Bernard Scudder. London: Mare's Nest, 1999. A translation of *Brotahöfuð* (1996).

Vigdís Grímsdóttir
Z — a Love Story. Translated by Anna Jeeves. London: Mare's Nest, 1997. A translation of *Z — ástarsaga* (1996).

Böðvar Guðmundsson
Where the Winds Dwell. Translated by Keneva Kunz. Winnipeg MB: Turnstone, 2000. A translation of *Híbýli vindanna* (1995).

Einar Már Guðmundsson
Angels of the Universe. Translated by Bernard Scudder. London: Mare's Nest, 1995. A translation of *Englar alheimsins* (1993).
Epilogue of the Raindrops. Translated by Bernard Scudder. London: Mare's Nest, 1994. A translation of *Eftirmáli regndropanna* (1986).

Ólafur Gunnarsson
Gaga. Translated by David McDuff. Moonbeam ON: Penumbra, 1988. A translation of *Gaga* (1984).
Potter's Field. Translated by Ólafur Gunnarsson and Jill Burrows. London: Mare's Nest, 1999. A translation of *Blóðakur* (1996).
Troll's Cathedral. Translated by David McDuff and Jill Burrows. London: Mare's Nest, 1996. A translation of *Tröllakirkjan* (1992).

Hallgrímur Helgason
101 Reykjavík. Translated by Brian FitzGibbon. London: Faber & Faber, 2002. A translation of *101 Reykjavík* (1996).

Arnaldur Indriðason
Jar City. Translated by Bernard Scudder. London: Harvill, 2004. Reissued as *Tainted Blood* (London: Vintage, 2005). A translation of *Mýrin* (2000).
Silence of the Grave. Translated by Bernard Scudder. London: Harvill, 2005. A translation of *Grafarþögn* (2001).

Svava Jakobsdóttir
The Lodger and Other Stories. Translated by Julian Meldon D'Arcy et al. Reykjavík: University of Iceland Press, 2000.

Einar Kárason
Devils' Island. Translated by David McDuff and Magnus Magnusson. Edinburgh: Canongate, 2000. A translation of *Þar sem djöflaeyjan rís* (1983).

Ólafur Jóhann Ólafsson (Olaf Olafsson)
Absolution. New York: Pantheon, 1994. A translation of *Fyrirgefning syndanna* (1991).
The Journey Home. New York: Pantheon, 2000. A translation of *Slóð fiðrildanna* (1999).
Walking into the Night. London: Faber & Faber, 2004. A translation of *Höll minninganna* (2001).

Fríða Á. Sigurðardóttir
Night Watch. Translated by Katjana Edwards. London: Mare's Nest, 1995. A translation of *Meðan nóttin líður* (1990).

Thor Vilhjálmsson
Justice Undone. Translated by Bernard Scudder. London: Mare's Nest, 1998. A translation of *Grámosinn glóir* (1986).

COLLECTED WORKS, MONOGRAPHS, AND ARTICLES

Elíasson, Gyrðir. *Heykvísl og gúmmískór*. Reykjavík: Mál og menning, 1991.

Eysteinsson, Ástráður. *Umbrot: Bókmenntir og nútími*. Reykjavík: Háskólaútgáfan, 1999.

———, ed. *Heimur skáldsögunnar*. Reykjavík: Bókmenntafræðistofnun Háskóla Íslands, 2001.

Magnússon, Sigurður A. *Iceland Crucible: A Modern Artistic Renaissance*. Reykjavík: Vaka, 1985.

Sæmundsson, Matthías Viðar. *Myndir á sandi: Greinar um bókmenntir og menningarástand*. Reykjavík: Bókmenntafræðistofnun Háskóla Íslands, 1991.

CHAPTER 7: ICELANDIC POETRY SINCE 1940

GENERAL

Brøndsted, Mogens, ed. *Nordens litteratur efter 1860*. Vol. 2 of *Nordens litteratur*. 2 vols. Copenhagen: Gyldendal, 1972.

Eysteinsson, Ástráður, and Eysteinn Þorvaldsson. "Modern Literature." In *Iceland: The Republic*, ed. Jóhannes Nordal and Valdimar Kristinsson, 264–86. Reykjavík: Central Bank of Iceland, 1996.

Pálsson, Heimir. *Straumar og stefnur í íslenskum bókmenntum frá 1950*. 3rd ed., Reykjavík: Iðunn, 1987.

———. *Sögur, ljóð og líf: Íslenskar bókmenntir á 20. öld*. Reykjavík: Vaka-Helgafell, 1998.

Rossel, Sven Hakon. *A History of Scandinavian Literature, 1870–1980*. Translated by Anne C. Ulmer. Minneapolis: University of Minnesota Press, 1982.

LITERATURE IN ENGLISH TRANSLATION

Brushstrokes of Blue: The Young Poets of Iceland. Translated by Bernard Scudder, David McDuff, and Sigurður A. Magnússon. Edited by Páll Valsson. London: Shad Thames/Greyhound, 1994.

Icelandic Writing Today. Translated by Bernard Scudder, Kristjana Gunnars, Sigurður A. Magnússon, and Sverrir Hólmarsson. Edited by Sigurður A. Magnússon and Kristjana Gunnars. Reykjavík: Menntamálaráðuneytið, 1982.

Johannessen, Matthías, and Kristján Karlsson. *Voices from across the Water*. Translated by Bernard Scudder and Joe Allard. London: Greyhound, 1997.

Kristján frá Djúpalæk. *The Song of the Stone*. Translated by Hallberg Hallmundsson. Akureyri: Háhóll, 1977.

Laxness, Halldór. *The Atom Station*. Translated by Magnus Magnusson. 1961. Reprint, London: Harvill, 2003. A translation of *Atómstöðin* (1948).

Magnússon, Sigurður A., trans. "Icelandic Issue." Special issue, *Modern Poetry in Translation*, no. 30 (1977).

Northern Voices: Five Contemporary Icelandic Poets. Translated by Alan Boucher. Edited by Konrad Hopkins and Ronald van Roekel. Paislet: Wilfion, 1984.

Poems of Today: From Twenty-five Modern Icelandic Poets. Edited and translated by Alan Boucher. Reykjavík: Iceland Review, 1971.

The Postwar Poetry of Iceland. Translated by Sigurður A. Magnússon. Iowa City: University of Iowa Press, 1982.

Three Modern Icelandic Poets: Selected Poems of Steinn Steinarr, Jón úr Vör and Matthías Johannessen. Translated by Marshall Brement. Reykjavík: Iceland Review, 1985.

Treasures of Icelandic Verse. Edited by Árni Sigurjónsson. Reykjavík: Mál og menning, 1996.

COLLECTED WORKS, MONOGRAPHS, AND ARTICLES

Andrésson, Kristinn E. *Um íslenskar bókmenntir*. Vol. 2. Reykjavík: Mál og menning, 1979.

Benediktsson frá Hofteigi, Bjarni. *Bókmenntagreinar*. Edited by Einar Bragi. Reykjavík: Heimskringla, 1971.

Carleton, Peter. "Tradition and Innovation in Twentieth-Century Icelandic Poetry." PhD diss., University of California, Berkeley, 1967. Reprint, Ann Arbor: UMI, 1974.

Daðason, Sigfús. *Ritgerðir og pistlar*. Edited by Þorsteinn Þorsteinsson. Reykjavík: Forlagið, 2000.

Einar Bragi. "Í listum liggur engin leið til baka." *Birtingur* 1 (1955): 25.

Elíasson, Gyrðir. *Hugarfjallið*. Reykjavík: Mál og menning, 1999.

Eysteinsson, Ástráður. *Tvímæli: Þýðingar og bókmenntir*. Reykjavík: Bókmenntafræðistofnun Háskóla Íslands / Háskólaútgáfan, 1996.

——. *Umbrot: Bókmenntir og nútími*. Reykjavík: Háskólaútgáfan, 1999.

Hjálmarsson, Jóhann. *Íslensk nútímaljóðlist*. Reykjavík: Almenna Bókafélagið, 1971.

Höskuldsson, Sveinn Skorri. *Að yrkja á atómöld*. Reykjavík: Helgafell, 1970.

Johannessen, Matthías. *Bókmenntaþættir*. Reykjavík: Almenna Bókafélagið, 1985.

Jónsson, Ólafur. *Líka líf: Greinar um samtímabókmenntir*. Reykjavík: Iðunn, 1979.

Kermode, Frank. *Continuities*. London: Routledge & Kegan Paul, 1968.

Ljóðaárbók, 1989. Edited by Berglind Gunnarsdóttir, Jóhann Hjálmarsson, and Kjartan Árnason. Reykjavík: Almenna Bókafélagið, 1989.

Magnússon, Sigurður A. *Sáð í vindinn: Greinar og fyrirlestrar*. Reykjavík: Helgafell, 1968.

——. *Iceland Crucible: A Modern Renaissance*. Reykjavík: Vaka, 1985.

Ólafsson, Einar. *Ljóð*. Reykjavík, 1971.

Ómarsdóttir, Kristín. *Lokaðu augunum og hugsaðu um mig*. Reykjavík: Mál og menning, 1998.

Pálsson, Sigurður. *Ljóð vega menn*. Reykjavík: Mál og menning, 1980.

Valdimarsson, Þorsteinn. "Ljóð er söngur." *Samvinnan* 9–10 (1976): 43.

Þorvaldsson, Eysteinn. *Atómskáldin: Aðdragandi og upphaf módernisma íslenskri ljóðagerð*. Reykjavík: Institute of Literature, University of Iceland / Hið íslenska bókmenntafélag, 1980.

——. *Ljóðaþing: Um íslenska ljóðagerð á 20. öld*. Reykjavík: Ormstunga, 2002.

CHAPTER 8: SEARCHING FOR HERSELF: FEMALE EXPERIENCE AND
FEMALE TRADITION IN ICELANDIC LITERATURE

GENERAL
Helgadóttir, Guðrún P. *Skáldkonur fyrri alda*. 2 vols. Akureyri: Kvöldvökuútgáfan, 1961–63.
Jónsson, Erlendur. *Íslenzk skáldsagnaritun, 1940–1970*. Reykjavík: Ísafoldarprent-smiðja, 1971.
Kress, Helga. "Um konur og bókmenntir." Introduction to *Draumur um veruleika: Sögur um og eftir íslenskar konur*, ed. Helga Kress, 11–35. Reykjavík: Mál og menning, 1977. Reprinted in Helga Kress, *Speglanir: Konur í íslenskri bókmennta-hefð og bókmenntasögu* (Reykjavík: Rannsóknastofa í kvennafræðum við Háskóla Íslands, 2000), 55–83.
———. "'Hvad en kvinde kvæder': Kultur og køn på Island i den norrøne mid-delalder." In *Nordisk kvindelitteraturhistorie*, ed. Elisabeth Møller Jensen, 1:22–81. Copenhagen: Rosinante, 1993.
———. *Máttugar meyjar: Íslensk fornbókmenntasaga*. Reykjavík: Háskólaútgáfan, 1993.
———. "Kona og skáld." Introduction to *Stúlka: Ljóð eftir íslenskar konur*, ed. Helga Kress, 11–102. Reykjavík: Bókmenntafræðistofnun Háskóla Íslands, 1997.
———. *Speglanir: Konur í íslenskri bókmenntahefð og bókmenntasögu*. Reykjavík: Rannsóknastofa í kvennafræðum við Háskóla Íslands, 2000.
Nordens litteratur. Edited by Mogens Brøndsted. 2 vols. Copenhagen: Gyldendal, 1972.
Þorkelsson, Jón. *Om Digtningen på Island i det 15. og 16. Århundrede*. Copenhagen: Høst, 1888.

ANTHOLOGIZED SOURCES
Draumur um veruleika: Íslenskar sögur um og eftir konur. Edited by Helga Kress. Reykjavík: Mál og menning, 1977. Translated into Norwegian by Helga Kress et al. as *Drøm om virkelighet: Noveller om og av islandske kvinner* (Oslo: Tiden, 1979).
Íslensk fornkvæði. Vol. 5. Edited by Jón Helgason. Editiones Arnamagnæanæ, ser. B, 14. Copenhagen: Munksgaard, 1965.
Íslenskar þjóðsögur og ævintýri. Vol. 2. Edited by Árni Böðvarsson and Bjarni Vil-hjálmsson. Reykjavík: Þjóðsaga, 1961.
Sagnadansar. Edited by Vésteinn Ólason. Reykjavík: Rannsóknastofnun í bók-menntafræði/Bókaútgáfa Menningarsjóðs, 1979.
Stúlka: Ljóð eftir íslenskar konur. Edited by Helga Kress. Reykjavík: Bókmennta-fræðistofnun Háskóla Íslands, 1997.

LITERATURE IN ENGLISH TRANSLATION
Jakobsdóttir, Svava. *The Lodger and Other Stories*. Translated by Julian Meldon D'Arcy and Dennis Hill. Reykjavík: University of Iceland Press, 2000.

Laxdæla Saga. Translated by Magnus Magnusson and Hermann Pálsson. London: Penguin, 1969.

Scandinavian Women Writers. Edited by Ingrid Claréus. New York: Greenwood, 1989.

Sigurðardóttir, Fríða. *Night Watch*. Translated by Katjana Edwardsen. London: Mare's Nest, 1995. A translation of *Meðan nóttin líður* (1990).

Thoroddsen, Jón. *Lad and Lass*. Translated by Arthur M. Reeves. London: Sampson Low, Marston, Searle & Rivington, 1890. A translation of *Piltur og stúlka* (1850).

Writings by Western Icelandic Women. Edited and translated and with an introduction by Kirsten Wolf. Winnipeg: University of Manitoba Press, 1996.

COLLECTED WORKS, MONOGRAPHS, AND ARTICLES

Ólína Andrésdóttir and Herdís Andrésdóttir
Andrésdóttir, Ólína, and Herdís Andrésdóttir. *Ljóðmæli*. 3rd, expanded ed. Reykjavík: Jón Thoroddsen, 1976.

Guðrún Árnadóttir of Oddstaðir
Árnadóttir, Guðrún. *Gengin spor*. Reykjavík: Minningarsjóður Hlöðvers Arnar Bjarnasonar, 1949.

Nína Björk Árnadóttir
Árnadóttir, Nína Björk. *Undarlegt er að spyrja mennina*. Reykjavík: Almenna bókafélagið, 1968.
———. *Svartur hestur í myrkrinu*. Reykjavík: Mál og menning, 1982.

Ása Sólveig
Ása Sólveig. "'Eg hefði aldrei skrifað orð, ef ég þyrfti næði til þess.'" *Vikan* 20 (1973): 28–29, 34–36. Interview.
———. "'Það sem karlmenn þekkja ekki og konur þegja um.'" *Dagblaðið*, 26 February 1979, 10–11. Interview.

María Bjarnadóttir
Bjarnadóttir, María. *Haustlitir*. Reykjavík, 1964.

Þuríður Bjarnadóttir
Steingrímsdóttir, Jóhanna Álfheiður. "Formálsorð." Introduction to *Brotasilfur*, by Þuríður Bjarnadóttir, 7–16. Akureyri: Bókaforlag Odds Björnssonar, 1985.
Bjarnadóttir, Þuríður. *Brotasilfur*. Akureyri: Bókaforlag Odds Björnssonar, 1985.

Halldóra B. Björnsson
Björnsson, Halldóra B. *Jarðljóð*. Reykjavík: Helgafell, 1968.
———. *Við sanda*. Reykjavík: Helgafell, 1968.

Vilborg Dagbjartsdóttir
Dagbjartsdóttir, Vilborg. *Kyndilmessa*. Reykjavík: Helgafell, 1971.
———. *Ljóð*. Reykjavík: Mál og menning, 1981.

Málfríður Einarsdóttir
Einarsdóttir, Málfríður. *Samastaður í tilverunni.* Reykjavík: Ljóðhús, 1977.

Guðrún Finnsdóttir
Einarsson, Stefán. "Vestur-íslensk skáldkona." In *Ferðalok*, by Guðrún Finnsdóttir, 139–58. Winnipeg: Gísli Jónsson, 1950.
Finnsdóttir, Guðrún. *Dagshríðar spor.* Akureyri: Árni Bjarnason, 1946.

Steinunn Finnsdóttir
Hyndlu rímur og Snækóngs rímur. Edited by Bjarni Vilhjálmsson. Rit Rímnafélagsins 3. Reykjavík: Rímnafélagið, 1950.

Oddný Guðmundsdóttir
"Lærðir og leikir." *Þjóðviljinn*, 17 June 1972, 11.

Þuríður Guðmundsdóttir
Guðmundsdóttir, Þuríður. *Það sagði mér haustið.* Reykjavík: Skákprent, 1985.

Berglind Gunnarsdóttir
Gunnarsdóttir, Berglind. *Ljóð fyrir lífi.* Reykjavík, 1983.

Ingibjörg Haraldsdóttir
Haraldsdóttir, Ingibjörg. *Orðspor daganna.* Reykjavík: Mál og menning, 1983.

Hulda (Unnur Benediktsdóttir Bjarklind)
Bjarklind, Benedikt S. "Ljósklædd birtist hún mér." In *Móðir mín: Nýtt safn*, ed. Pétur Ólafsson, 141–56. Reykjavík: Bókfellsútgáfan, 1958.
Bjartmarsdóttir, Guðrún, and Ragnhildur Richter. Introduction to *Ljóð og laust mál: Úrval*, by Hulda, ed. Guðrún Bjartmarsdóttir and Ragnhildur Richter, 11–98. Reykjavík: Bókmenntafræðistofnun Háskóla Íslands / Bókaútgáfa Menningarsjóðs, 1990.
Erlingsson, Þorsteinn. "Annar pistill til Þjóðviljans (Huldupistill)." *Þjóðviljinn*, 15 June 1905, 98–99.
Guðlaugsson, Jónas. "Bókafregn." *Lögrétta*, 20 November 1909, 194–95.
Hulda. *Kvæði.* Reykjavík: Sigurður Kristjánsson, 1909.
———. *Úr minningablöðum.* Reykjavík: Helgafell, 1965.
———. *Ljóð og laust mál: Úrval.* Edited by Guðrún Bjartmarsdóttir and Ragnhildur Richter. Reykjavík: Bókmenntafræðistofnun Háskóla Íslands / Bókaútgáfa Menningarsjóðs, 1990.
Richter, Ragnhildur. " 'Ljóðafugl lítinn jeg geymi — hann langar að fljúga': Athugun á stöðu skáldkonu gagnvart bókmenntahefð." *Tímarit Máls og Menningar* 3 (1986): 324–34.

Torfhildur Þorsteinsdóttir Hólm
Gíslason, Vilhjálmur Þ. "Torfhildur Þorsteinsdóttir Holm." In *Ritsafn*, by Torfhildur Hólm, ed. Brynjólfur Sveinsson, 1:v–xii. Akureyri: Norðri, 1949.

Bibliography

Svava Jakobsdóttir

Eysteinsson, Ástráður. "At Home and Abroad: Reflections on Svava Jakobsdóttir's Fiction." In *The Lodger and Other Stories*, by Svava Jakobsdóttir, trans. Julian Meldon D'Arcy and Dennis Hill, 5–12. Reykjavík: University of Iceland Press, 2000.

Jakobsdóttir, Svava. *Tólf konur*. Reykjavík: Almenna bókafélagið, 1965.

———. "Reynsla og raunveruleiki: Nokkrir þankar kvenrithöfundar." In *Konur skrifa til heiðurs Önnu Sigurðardóttur*, ed. Valborg Bentsdóttir, Guðrún Gísladóttir, and Svanlaug Baldursdóttir, 221–30. Reykjavík: Sögufélag, 1980.

Kress, Helga. "Kvinnebevissthet og skrivemåte: Om Svava Jakobsdóttir og den litterære institusjonen på Island." *Norsk litterær Årbok*, 1979, 151–66. Reprinted in Helga Kress, *Speglanir: Konur í íslenskri bókmenntahefð og bókmenntasögu* (Reykjavík: Rannsóknastofa í kvennafræðum við Háskóla Íslands, 2000), 121–38.

Ólafía Jóhannsdóttir

Jóhannsdóttir, Ólafía. *Frá myrkri til ljóss*. Akureyri: Arthur Cook, 1925.

Jakobína Johnson

Friðriksson, Friðrik. "Um höfundinn." In *Kertaljós*, by Jakobína Johnson, ix–xxvii. Reykjavík: Leiftur, 1955.

Arnfríður Jónatansdóttir

Jónatansdóttir, Arnfríður. *Þröskuldur hússins er þjöl*. Reykjavík: Heimskringla, 1958.

Guðfinna Jónsdóttir of Hamrar

Jónsdóttir, Guðfinna. *Ljóð*. Reykjavík: Ísafoldarprentsmiðja, 1941.

———. *Ný ljóð*. Reykjavík: Helgafell, 1945.

———. *Ljóðabók*. Edited by Kristján Karlsson. Reykjavík: Almenna bókafélagið, 1972.

Guðný Jónsdóttir

Jónsdóttir, Guðný. *Guðnýjarkver*. Edited by Helga Kristjánsdóttir. Reykjavík: Helgafell, 1951.

Júlíana Jónsdóttir

Jónsdóttir, Júlíana. *Stúlka*. Akureyri, 1876.

Kress, Helga. "'Sökum þess ég er kona': Víg Kjartans Ólafssonar og upphaf leikritunar íslenskra kvenna." Introduction to *Víg Kjartans Ólafssonar: Sorgarleikur í einum þætti*, by Júlíana Jónsdóttir, ed. Helga Kress, 7–33. Hafnarfjörður: Söguspekingastifti, 2001.

Þóra Jónsdóttir

Jónsdóttir, Þóra. *Leiðin heim*. Reykjavík: Almenna bókafélagið, 1975.

Elinborg Lárusdóttir

"Dag skal að kveldi lofa." *Sunnudagsblað Tímans*, 7 November 1971, 832–34. Interview.

Þórunn Elfa Magnúsdóttir
Crassus. "Nokkrar nýjar bækur." *Helgafell* 5 (May 1953): 86–121.
Magnúsdóttir, Þórunn Elfa. *Dætur Reykjavíkur*. 3 vols. Reykjavík, 1933–38.

Þórdís Richardsdóttir
Richardsdóttir, Þórdís. *Ljóð í lausaleik*. Reykjavík, 1976.

Kristín Sigfúsdóttir
Sigurðardóttir, Aðalbjörg. "Kristín Sigfúsdóttir." *19. Júní* 11 (1924): 73–74.
Sigurðsson, Steindór. "Bækur." *Nýjar kvöldvökur* 1–6 (January–July 1927): 184–86.

Jakobína Sigurðardóttir
Sigurðardóttir, Jakobína. *Kvæði*. Reykjavík: Mál og menning, 1960.
Sveinsson, Gunnar. "Jakobína Sigurðardóttir: Púnktur á skökkum stað." *Skírnir* 139 (1965): 218–19.

Ólöf Sigurðardóttir of Hlaðir
Finnbogason, Guðmundur. "Ólöf Sigurðardóttir: Nokkur smákvæði." *Skírnir* 88 (1914): 99–102.
Sigurðardóttir, Ólöf. *Nokkur smákvæði*. Akureyri: Prentsmiðja Odds Björnssonar, 1913.
———. *Ritsafn*. Edited by Jón Auðuns. Reykjavík: Helgafell, 1945.

Steinunn Sigurðardóttir
Kress, Helga. "'Dæmd til að hrekjast': Um ástina, karlveldið og kvenlega sjálfsmynd í Tímaþjófnum eftir Steinunni Sigurðardóttir." *Tímarit máls og Menningar* 49, no. 1 (1988): 55–93.
Sigurðardóttir, Steinunn. *Verksummerki*. Reykjavík: Helgafell, 1979.

Theodora Thoroddsen
Nordal, Sigurður. "Theodora Thoroddsen." Introduction to *Ritsafn*, by Theodora Thoroddsen, ed. Sigurður Nordal, 9–41. Reykjavík: Bókaútgáfa Menningarsjóðs, 1960.
Thoroddsen, Theodora. *Ritsafn*. Edited by Sigurður Nordal. Reykjavík: Bókaútgáfa Menningarsjóðs, 1960.

Elísabet Þorgeirsdóttir
Þorgeirsdóttir, Elísabet. *Salt og rjómi*. Reykjavík: Iðunn, 1983.

OTHER REFERENCES
Birgisdóttir, Soffía Auður. "Brúarsmiður — atómskáld — módernisti: Þrjár nýsköpunarkonur í íslenskri ljóðagerð." In *Ljóðaárbók, 1989*, ed. Berglind Gunnarsdóttir, Jóhann Hjálmarsson, and Kjartan Árnason, 50–65. Reykjavík: Almenna Bókafélagið, 1989.
Elíasson, Nína Björk. "Eru sagnadansar kvennatónlist?" In *Konur skrifa til heiðurs Önnu Sigurðardóttur*, ed. Valborg Bentsdóttir, Guðrún Gísladóttir, and Svanlaug Baldursdóttir, 143–54. Reykjavík: Sögufélag, 1980.

Guðmundsson, Kristmann. *Ísóld hin svarta*. Reykjavík: Bókafellsútgáfan, 1959.

Hallgrímsson, Jónas. "Grasaferð." *Fjölnir* 9 (1846).

Jóns saga helga. In *Biskupasögur*. Vol. 2. Edited by Guðni Jónsson. Reykjavík: Íslendingasagnaútgáfan, 1953.

Kellogg, Robert. "Sex and the Vernacular in Medieval Iceland." In *Proceedings of the First International Saga Conference: University of Edinburgh, 1971*, ed. Peter Foote, Hermann Pálsson, and Desmond Slay, 244–58. London: University College London, 1973.

Kress, Helga, ed. *Draumur um veruleika: Sögur um og eftir íslenskar konur*. Reykjavík: Mál og Menning, 1977.

——. "Bækur og 'kellingabækur': Þáttur í íslenskri bókmenntasögu." *Tímarit Máls og Menningar* 4 (1978): 369–95. Reprinted in Helga Kress, *Speglanir: Konur í íslenskri bókmenntahefð og bókmenntasögu* (Reykjavík: Rannsóknastofa í kvennafræðum við Háskóla Íslands, 2000), 85–119.

——. "Listsköpun kvenna: Bókmenntir." In *Konur, hvað nú? Staða íslenskra kvenna í kjölfar kvennaárs og kvennaáratugar Sameinuðu þjóðanna, 1975–1985*, 193–212, ed. Jónína Margrét Guðnadóttir. Reykjavík: Jafnréttisráð, 1985.

——. "'You Will Find It All Rather Monotonous': On Literary Tradition and the Feminine Experience in Laxdæla Saga." In *The Nordic Mind: Current Trends in Scandinavian Literary Criticism*, ed. F. E. Andersen and J. Weinstock, 181–93. Lanham MD: University Press of America, 1986.

——. "'Sáuð þið hana systur mína?' Grasaferð Jónasar Hallgrímssonar og upphaf íslenskrar sagnagerðar." *Skírnir* 2 (autumn 1989): 261–92. Reprinted in Helga Kress, *Speglanir: Konur í íslenskri bókmenntahefð og bókmenntasögu* (Reykjavík: Rannsóknastofa í kvennafræðum við Háskóla Íslands, 2000), 315–349.

——. "The Apocalypse of a Culture: Völuspá and the Myth of the Sources/Sorceress in Old Icelandic Literature." In *Poetry in the Scandinavian Middle Ages: Proceedings of the Seventh International Saga Conference, Spoleto, 4–10 September 1988*, ed. Teresa Paroli, 279–302. Spoleto: Presso la Sede del Centro Studi, 1990.

Laxness, Halldór. *Íslendíngaspjall*. Reykjavík: Helgafell, 1967.

Magnússon, Sigurður A. *Sáð í vindinn*. Reykjavík: Helgafell, 1968.

Nordal, Sigurður. "Ritsjá." *Iðunn* 1 (1925): 73–76.

Ólason, Vésteinn. "Inngangur." Introduction to *Sagnadansar*, ed. Vésteinn Ólason, 7–86. Reykjavík: Rannsóknastofnun í bókmenntafræði/Bókaútgáfa Menningarsjóðs, 1979.

Sigurðsson, Steindór. "Bækur." *Nýjar kvöldvökur* 1–6 (January–July 1927): 184–86.

Thorarensen, Bjarni. *Ljóðmæli*. Edited by Jón Helgason. Vol. 1. Copenhagen: Hið íslenska fræðafélag, 1935.

Vigfússon, Guðbrandur. "Formáli." Preface to *Íslenzkar þjóðsögur og æfintýri*. In *Íslenskar þjóðsögur og ævintýri*, ed. Árni Böðvarsson and Bjarni Vilhjálmsson, 2:x–xxxviii. Reykjavík: Bókaútgáfan Þjóðsaga, 1961.

GENERAL

Einarsson, Sveinn. "Isländsk teater." *Garðar* 4 (1973): 6–16. With an English summary.

——. *Íslensk leiklist.* Reykjavík: Bókaútgáfa Menningarsjóðs, 1991. Reykjavík: Hið íslenska bókmenntafélag, 1996.

Magnússon, Sigurður A. Introduction to *Modern Nordic Plays: Iceland* (Scandia Books 14), 7–20. Oslo: Universitetsforlaget, 1973.

Nicoll, Allardyce. *World Drama from Aeschylus to Anouilh.* London: Harrap, 1949.

Sigurjónsson, Hávar. "The People's Theatre in Iceland." BA thesis, Manchester University, Department of Drama, 1982.

Theatre in Iceland: 1975–2002. Edited by Hávar Sigurjónsson. Reykjavík: Icelandic Theatre Association and the Ministry of Culture and Education. Published biannually.

The World of Theatre: 1994–1996. 5th ed., Paris: International Theatre Institute, Unesco, 1996.

The World of Theatre: 1996–1998. 6th ed., Paris: International Theatre Institute, Unesco, 1998.

LITERATURE IN ENGLISH TRANSLATION

Contemporary Icelandic Drama: Five Icelandic Playwrights. With an introduction by Hávar Sigurjónsson. Reykjavík: Consulate General of Iceland, 2001. Includes Hrafnhildur Hagalín Guðmundsdóttir's *Easy Now, Electra*, Árni Ibsen's *Heaven: A Schizophrenic Comedy*, Olafur Olafsson's *A Feast of Snails*, Ólafur Haukur Símonarsson's *The Sea*, and Þorvaldur Þorsteinsson's *Talespin: A Tragedy in 9 Acts*.

Fire and Ice: Three Icelandic Plays. Nordic Translation Series. Madison: University of Wisconsin Press, 1967. Includes Davíð Stefánsson's *The Golden Gate* (trans. G. M. Gathorne-Hardy), Jóhann Sigurjónsson's *The Wish* (trans. Einar Haugen), and Arnar Þórðarson's *Atoms and Madams* (trans. Einar Haugen).

Five Modern Scandinavian Plays. Edited and translated by Carl Erik Soya et al. Library of Scandinavian Literature, vol. 11. New York: Twayne/American Scandinavian Foundation, 1971. Includes Davíð Stefánsson's "The Golden Gate."

Hadda Padda: A Drama in Four Acts. Translated by Sadie Luise Peller. New York: Knopf, 1917. A translation of *Hadda Padda* (1914).

Independent People: An Epic. Translated by J. A. Thompson. London: Allen & Unwin, 1945; New York: Knopf, 1946. Reprint, New York: Vintage International, 1997; London: Harvill, 1999. A translation of *Sjálfstætt fólk* (1934–35).

Modern Icelandic Plays: Eyvind of the Hills, The Hraun Farm. Translated by Henninge Krohn Schanche. New York: American-Scandinavian Foundation, 1916. Translations of *Bjærg Ejvind og hans Hustru* (1917) and *Gaarden Hraun* (1912).

Modern Nordic Plays: Iceland. Edited and with an introduction by Sigurður A. Magnússon. Scandia Books 14. Oslo: Universitetsforlaget, 1973. Includes Halldór Laxness's *The Pigeon Banquet* (trans. Alan Boucher), Jökull Jakobsson's *The Sea-*

way to Baghdad (trans. Alan Boucher), Erlingur E. Halldórsson's *Mink* (trans. Alan Boucher), and Oddur Björnsson's *Ten Variations* and *Yolk-Life* (trans. Guðrún Tómasdóttir).

We Murderers. Translated by Einar Haugen. Madison: University of Wisconsin Press, 1970. A translation of *Vi Mordere* (1920).

MONOGRAPHS AND ARTICLES

Björnsson, Oddur. *13. krossferðin: Drama þor episodius*. Reykjavík: Vaka-Helgafell, 1993.

Einarsson, Sveinn. "Vorið geingur í lið með kálfum: Um Laxness og leiklistina." *Ritmennt: Ársrit Landsbókasafns Íslands og Háskólabókasafns* 7 (2002): 23–49.

Kress, Helga. *Gudmundur Kamban: Æskuverk og ádeilur*. Studia Islandica 29. Reykjavík: Bókaútgáfa Menningarsjóðs, 1970. With an English summary.

Sigurðardóttir, Fríða A. *Leikrit Jökuls Jakobssonar*. Studia Islandica 38. Reykjavík: Bókaútgáfa Menningarsjóðs, 1980.

Þorsteinsson, Steingrímur J. *Um leikrit Matthías Jochumssonar*. Reykjavík: n.p., 1961.

CHAPTER 10: ICELANDIC CHILDREN'S LITERATURE, 1780–2000

GENERAL

Aðalsteinsdóttir, Silja. *Íslenskar barnabækur, 1780–1979*. Reykjavík: Mál og menning, 1981.

Barna-Liood ordt af Sal: Sira Vigfusa Johnssyni. Copenhagen, 1780.

Helgadóttir, Guðrún. *Saman í hring*. Reykjavík: Iðunn, 1986.

Raddir barnabókanna. Edited by Silja Aðalsteinsdóttir. Reykjavík: Mál og menning, 1999.

Stefánsson, Hreiðar. *Grösin í glugghúsinu: Saga*. Reykjavík: Iðunn, 1980.

ANTHOLOGIES

Sögustund: 365 valdir kaflar úr íslenskum barnabókmenntum. Edited by Silja Aðalsteinsdóttir. Reykjavík: Mál og menning, 1992.

LITERATURE IN ENGLISH TRANSLATION

Helgadóttir, Guðrún. *A Giant Love Story*. Translated by Christopher Sanders. Reykjavík: Vaka-Helgafell, 1999. (First published as *Flumbra: An Icelandic Folktale* [Minneapolis: Carolrhoda, 1981; Calton: T. & A. D. Poyser, 1984]).

Icelandic Literature for Children and Young People. Edited by Bernard Scudder. Reykjavík: Bókmenntakynningarsjóður, 2000.

Ringler, Dick. *Bard of Iceland: Jónas Hallgrímsson, Poet and Scientist*. Madison: University of Wisconsin Press, 2002.

Sigurðardóttir, Ingibjörg. *Flowers on the Roof*. Translated by Julian Meldon d'Arcy. Reykjavík: Mál og menning, 1993.

Steinsdóttir, Kristín. *Armann and Gentle*. Translated by Louise Heite. N.P.: Suttering Foundation of America, 1997.

Sveinsson, Jón. *At Skipalón: Adventures of an Icelandic Boy in the Mid-Nineteenth Century*. Translated from the German by Francis de Sales. Kearney NE: Morris, 2002.

Thorsteinsson, Guðmundur. *The Story of Dimmalimm*. Reykjavík: Vaka-Helgafell, 1999.

OTHER REFERENCES

Aðalsteinsdóttir, Silja. *Þjóðfélagsmynd íslenskra barnabóka: Athugun á barnabókum íslenskra höfunda á árunum 1960–1970*. Studia Islandica 35. Reykjavík: Bókaútgáfa Menningarsjóðs, 1976.

———. "Trú og siðferði í íslenskum barnabókum." *Studia theologica Islandica* 9 (1994): 231–54.

Bettelheim, Bruno. *The Uses of Enchantment: The Meaning and Importance of Fairy Tales*. London: Thames & Hudson, 1976.

Children's Literature: The Development of Criticism. Edited by Peter Hunt. London: Routledge, 1990.

Guttormsson, Loftur. *Bernska, ungdómur og uppeldi á einveldisöld: tilraun til félagslegrar og lýðfræðilegrar greiningar*. Ritsafn sagnfræðistofnunar 10. Reykjavík: Institute for Historical Studies, University of Iceland / Sögufélagið, 1983.

Hughes, Felicity A. "Children's Literature: Theory and Practice." *ELH: English Literary History* 45 (1978): 542–61.

Jóhannsdóttir, Þuríður. "Úr búrinu í meiri gauragang: Um íslenskar unglingabækur." *Tímarit Máls og Menningar* 53, no. 1 (1992): 3–18.

Lurie, Alison. *Don't Tell the Grown-Ups: Subversive Children's Literature*. London: Bloomsbury, 1990.

Pálsdóttir, Anna Heiða. "Rolling Hills and Rocky Crags: The Role of Landscape in English and Icelandic Literature for Children." In *Text, Culture and National Identity in Children's Literature*, ed. Jean Webb, 65–76. Helsinki: NORDINFO, 2000.

CHAPTER 11: ICELANDIC CANADIAN LITERATURE

GENERAL

Einarsson, Stefán. *Íslensk Bókmenntasaga, 874–1960*. Reykjavík: Snæbjörn Jónsson, 1961.

Hreinsson, Viðar. "Vestur-Íslenskar bókmenntir." In *Íslensk Bókmenntasaga*, vol. 3, ed. Halldór Guðmundsson, 723–66. Reykjavík: Mál og menning, 1996.

———. "Western Icelandic Literature, 1870–1900." *Scandinavian-Canadian Studies* 6 (1993): 1–14.

Íslensk bókmenntasaga. Vols. 1–2, ed. Vésteinn Ólason. Vols. 3–5, ed. Halldór Guðmundsson. Reykjavík: Mál og menning, 1992–93, 1996–2006.

Kirkconnell, Watson. "Four Decades of Icelandic Poetry in Canada, 1922–62." *Icelandic Canadian* 22, no. 2 (1963): 17–27.

Neijmann, Daisy L. *The Icelandic Voice in Canadian Letters: The Contribution of*

Icelandic-Canadian Writers to Canadian Literature. Ottawa ON: Carleton University Press, 1997.

———. "In Search of the Canadian Icelander: Writing an Icelandic-Canadian Identity into Canadian Literature." *Canadian Ethnic Studies* 29, no. 3 (1997): 64–74.

Vesturheimsprent: Skrá um rit á íslensku prentuð vestan hafs og austan af Vestur-Íslendingum eða varðandi þá: A Bibliography of Publications in Icelandic Printed in North America or Elsewhere by or Relating to the Icelandic Settlers in the West. Compiled by Ólafur F. Hjartar. Reykjavík: Landsbókasafn, 1986.

Wolf, Kirsten. "Western Icelandic Women Writers: Their Contribution to the Literary Canon." *Scandinavian Studies* 66 (1994): 154–203.

ANTHOLOGIES

Unexpected Fictions: New Icelandic Canadian Writing. Edited by Kristjana Gunnars. Winnipeg MB: Turnstone, 1989.

Vestan um haf. Edited by Einar H. Kvaran and Guðmundur Finnbogason. Reykjavík: Bókadeild Menningarsjóðs, 1930.

LITERATURE IN ENGLISH (TRANSLATION)

Anthologies

Bjarnason, Paul. *Odes and Echoes*. Vancouver: privately printed, 1954.

Icelandic Lyrics: Originals and Translations. Edited by Richard Beck. Reykjavík: Þórhallur Bjarnason, 1930.

Kirkconnell, Watson, ed. and trans. *Canadian Overtones*. Winnipeg MB: Columbia, 1935.

Western Icelandic Short Stories. Edited and translated by Kirsten Wolf and Arný Hjaltadóttir. Winnipeg: University of Manitoba Press, 1992.

Writings by Western Icelandic Women. Edited and translated and with an introduction by Kirsten Wolf. Winnipeg: University of Manitoba Press, 1996.

Jóhann Magnús Bjarnason

In the Red River Valley. Translated by Thelma Whale. *The Icelandic-Canadian Magazine* 46, no. 3 (1988); 46, no. 4 (1988): 19–22; 47, no. 2 (1988): 28–34; 47, no. 3 (1989): 45–55; 48, no. 2 (1989): 48–56; 48, no. 3 (1990): 21–29; 48, no. 4 (1990): 36–46; 49, no. 2 (1990): 36–42; 49, no. 3 (1991): 27–46; 50, no. 1 (1991): 34–42; 50, no. 3 (1992): 161–66; 51, no. 1 (1992): 44–54; 51, no. 2 (1992): 121–31; 51, no. 4 (1993): 213–26; 52, no. 1 (1993): 35–42; 52, no. 2 (1993): 86–92; 52, no. 4 (1994): 215–21. The translation remains incomplete.

Guttormur J. Guttormsson

Aurora/Áróra: English Translations of Icelandic Poems by Guttormur J. Guttormsson. Edited by Heather Alda Ireland. Vancouver: privately printed, 1993.

K.N. (Kristján Níels Júlíus Jónsson)

Selected translations of K.N.'s poems by Paul Sigurdson appeared in the *Lögberg-Heimskringla* from October 1990 to October 1991, among them:

"Sweet She Was." Translated by Paul Sigurdson *Lögberg-Heimskringla*, 8 February 1991, 3.

"'Ef—.'" Translated by Paul Sigurdson. *Lögberg-Heimskringla*, 18 January 1991, 4.

Stephan G. Stephansson
Selected Translations from Andvökur. Edmonton AB: Stephan G. Stephansson Homestead Restoration Committee, 1987.
Stephan G. Stephansson: Selected Prose and Poetry. Translated by Kristjana Gunnars. Red Deer AB: Red Deer College Press, 1988.

COLLECTED WORKS, MONOGRAPHS AND ARTICLES

Margrjet J. Benedictsson
Wolf, Kirsten. "Til varnar mannúð og jafnrétti: Margrjet J. Benedictsson og *Freyja*." *Skírnir* 175 (spring 2001): 119–39.

Jóhann Magnús Bjarnason
Beck, Richard. "Jóhann Magnús Bjarnason." In *Gimsteinaborgin*, by Jóhann Magnús Bjarnason, v–xxvii. Akureyri and Reykjavík: Bókaútgáfa Edda, 1977.
Bjarnason, Jóhann Magnús. *Eiríkur Hansson: Skáldsaga frá Nýja Skotlandi.* Vol. 4 of *Jóhann Magnús Bjarnason: Ritsafn.* Akureyri: Bókaútgáfan Edda, 1973. Originally serialized over the period 1899–1903.
———. *Í Rauðárdalnum.* Vol. 2 of *Jóhann Magnús Bjarnason: Ritsafn.* Akureyri: Bókaútgáfan Edda, 1976. Originally serialized over the period 1914–22.
———. *Gimsteinaborgin.* Vol. 1 of *Jóhann Magnús Bjarnason: Ritsafn.* Akureyri: Bókaútgáfan Edda, 1977. Included are *Karl litli: Saga frá Draumamörk*, which first appeared in 1935 from the Reykjavík publisher E. P. Briem, and the collected *Ævintýri*, which first appeared in 1946 from the Reykjavík publisher Fjallkonaútgáfan.

Gunnsteinn Eyjólfsson
Eyjólfsson, Gunnsteinn. *Jón á Strympu og fleiri sögur.* Reykjavík: privately published, 1952.
Jónsson, Gísli. "Gunnsteinn Eyjólfsson." *Eimreiðin* 19 (1913): 44–50.

Guðrún Helga Finnsdóttir
Birgisdóttir, Soffía Auður. "Guðrún Helga Finnsdóttir." In *Sögur íslenskra kvenna, 1879–1960*, ed. Soffía Auður Birgisdóttir, 911–71. Reykjavík: Mál og menning, 1987.
Einarsson, Stefán. "Vestur-íslensk skáldkona." *Eimreiðin* 53 (1947): 10–26.
Finnsdóttir, Guðrún Helga. *Hillingalönd.* Reykjavík: Félagsprentsmiðjan, 1938.
———. *Dagshríðar spor.* Akureyri: Árni Bjarnarson, 1946.

Guttormur J. Guttormsson
Beck, Richard. *Guttormur J. Guttormsson, skáld.* Winnipeg MB: Columbia, 1949.
Gunnlaugsdóttir, Sigfríður. "'Þótt greini oss mál, oss sameinar sál': Cultural Hybridity in the Poetry of Guttormur J. Gutttormsson." In *Rediscovering Canadian*

Difference (Nordic Association for Canadian Studies Text Series 17), ed. Gudrun Björk Gudsteins, 68–73. Reykjavík: NACS/VFI, 2001.

Guttormsson, Guttormur J. *Kvæðasafn*. Edited by Arnór Sigurjónsson. Reykjavík: Iðunn, 1947.

Kirkconnell, Watson. "A Skald in Canada." *Transactions of the Royal Society of Canada*, 3rd ser., sec. 2, 33 (1939): 107–21.

Sigurjónsson, Arnór. "Guttormur J. Guttormsson og kvæði hans." In *Kvæðasafn*, ed. Arnór Sigurjónsson, 5–36. Reykjavík: Iðunn, 1947.

K.N.

Beck, Richard. "Kristján N. Júlíus (K.N.)." In *Kviðlingar og Kvæði*, by K. N. Júlíus, ed. Richard Beck, xi–xxii. Reykjavík: Bókfellsútgáfan, 1945.

Holm, Bill. "Kristjan Niels Julius (K.N.): A Four-Part Project." *Lögberg-Heimskringla*, 7 December 1990, 2.

K.N. *Kviðlingar og kvæði*. Edited by Richard Beck. Reykjavík: Bókfellsútgáfan, 1945.

Sigurdson, Paul. "Insights into the Humourous Poetry of K.N." *Lögberg-Heimskringla*, 26 October 1990, 4.

Laura Goodman Salverson

Gudsteins, Gudrun Björk. "Wake-Pick Weavers: Laura G. Salverson and Kristjana Gunnars." *Dolphin* 25 (1995): 142–63.

——. "Rediscovering Icelandic Canadian Pacifism." In *Rediscovering Canadian Difference* (Nordic Association for Canadian Studies Text Series 17), ed. Gudrun Björk Gudsteins, 50–60. Reykjavík: NACS/VFI, 2001.

Gunnars, Kristjana. "Laura Goodman Salverson's Confessions of a Divided Self." In *A Mazing Space: Writing Canadian Women Writing*, ed. Shirley Newman and Smaro Kamboureli, 148–53. Edmonton AB: Longspoon/NeWest, 1986.

Neijmann, Daisy L. "Damned with Faint Praise: The Reception of Laura Goodman Salverson's Works by the Icelandic-Canadian Community." *Scandinavian-Canadian Studies* 12 (1999): 40–62.

——. "Laura 'Lárusdóttir' Salverson: Walking in the Narrative Ways of the Father." In *Rediscovering Canadian Difference* (Nordic Association for Canadian Studies Text Series 17), ed. Gudrun Björk Gudsteins, 153–64. Reykjavík: NACS/VFI, 2001.

Salverson, Laura Goodman. "Hidden Fire." *MacLean's* 36, no. 1 (15 February 1923): 14, 50–51.

——. *The Viking Heart*. 1923. New Canadian Library 116. Toronto: McClelland & Stewart, 1975.

——. *Lord of the Silver Dragon: A Romance of Lief the Lucky*. Toronto: McClelland & Stewart, 1927.

——. *The Dove of El-Djezaire*. Toronto: Ryerson, [1933].

——. *The Dark Weaver*. Toronto: Ryerson, 1937.

——. *Confessions of an Immigrant's Daughter*. 1939. Social History of Canada 24. Toronto: University of Toronto Press, 1981.

Stephan G. Stephansson

Beck, Richard. "Stephan G. Stephansson." *American-Scandinavian Review* 44, no. 2 (1956): 151–56.

Guðmundsson, Finnbogi. *Stephan G. Stephansson in Retrospect: Seven Essays*. Reykjavík: Icelandic Cultural Fund, 1982.

Guðsteinsdóttir, Guðrún Björk. "'Ameríku-Stephán': 'Reiðfantur á ótemju' tungunnar." *Skírnir* 170 (autumn 1996): 389–412.

Hreinsson, Viðar. *Ævisaga Stephans G. Stephanssonar*. Vol. 1, *Landneminn mikli*. Vol. 2, *Andvökuskáld*. Reykjavík: Bjartur, 2002–3.

Kirkconnell, Watson. "Canada's Leading Poet: Stephan G. Stephansson (1853–1927)." *University of Toronto Quarterly* 5, no. 2 (1936): 263–77.

Stanton Cawley, F. "The Greatest Poet of the Western World." *Scandinavian Studies* 14 (1942): 99–106.

Stephansson, Stephan G. *Andvökur*. 6 vols. Reykjavík: Nokkrir Íslendingar í Vesturheimi, 1909–38.

Tvær ritgerðir um kveðskap Stephans G. Stephanssonar. Edited by Steingrímur J. Þorsteinsson. Studia Islandica 19. Reykjavík: Leiftur, 1961.

Undína (Helga Steinvör Baldvinsdóttir)
Kvæði. Reykjavík: Ísafoldarprentsmiðja, 1952.

OTHER REFERENCES

Bhabha, Homi. *The Location of Culture*. London: Routledge, 1994.

Bréf Vestur-Íslendinga. Edited by Böðvar Guðmundsson. 2 vols. Reykjavík: Mál og menning.

Einarsson, Magnus. "Oral Tradition and Ethnic Boundaries: 'West' Icelandic Verses and Anecdotes." *Canadian Ethnic Studies* 7, no. 2 (1975): 19–32.

Gunnars, Kristjana. "Translation as Appropriation." In *Rediscovering Canadian Difference* (Nordic Association for Canadian Studies Text Series 17), ed. Gudrun Björk Gudsteins, 61–67. Reykjavík: NACS/VFI, 2001.

Guttormsson, Guttormur J. "Sigurður Júl. Jóhannesson og íslenzka hagyrðingafélagið." *Eimreiðin* 72 (1966): 152–60.

Houser, George J. *Pioneer Icelandic Pastor: The Life of the Rev. Paul Thorlaksson*. Edited by Paul A. Sigurdson. Winnipeg: Manitoba Historical Society, 1990.

Johannessen, Matthías. *Njála í íslenzkum skáldskap*. Reykjavík: Hið íslenska bókmenntafélag, 1958.

Kroetsch, Robert. "The Grammar of Silence: Narrative Patterns in Ethnic Writing." *Canadian Literature* 106 (fall 1985): 65–74.

Mandel, Eli. "The Ethnic Voice in Canadian Literature." In *Identities: The Impact of Ethnicity on Canadian Society*, ed. Wsevolod Isajiw, 57–68. Toronto: Peter Martin, 1977.

Padolsky, Enoch. "Canadian Minority Writing and Acculturation Options." In *Literatures of Lesser Diffusion*, ed. Joseph Pivato, 46–64. Edmonton AB: Research Institute for Comparative Literature, University of Alberta, 1990.

Valgardson, W. D. *Stúlkan með Botticelli andlitið*. Translated by Gunnar Gunnarsson and Hildur Finnsdóttir. Seltjarnarnes: Ormstunga, 1995.

———. *Thor*. Translated by Guðrún B. Guðsteinsdóttir. Seltjarnarnes: Ormstunga, 1995.

———. "The Myth of Homogeneity — or Deconstructing Amma." In *Rediscovering Canadian Difference* (Nordic Association for Canadian Studies Text Series 17), ed. Gudrun Björk Gudsteins, 209–13. Reykjavík: NACS/VFI, 2001.

Wolf, Kirsten. "Heroic Past — Heroic Present: Western Icelandic Literature." *Scandinavian Studies* 63 (1991): 432–52.

The Contributors

Silja Aðalsteinsdóttir holds an MA in Icelandic literature from the University of Iceland. She is the editor of the literary magazine *Tímarit Máls og menningar* and is the author of *Íslenskar barnabækur, 1780–1979* (1981) as well as several textbooks and biographies. She received the Icelandic Literary Prize for her biography of the poet Guðmundur Böðvarsson, *Skáldið sem sólin kyssti* (1994).

Úlfhildur Dagsdóttir holds an MA in comparative literature from the University of Iceland and is a part-time lecturer at the Iceland Academy of the Arts and a part-time librarian at the Reykjavík City Library. She also works as a freelance scholar and literary critic and has written extensively on contemporary Icelandic literature and culture, film genres (particularly horror films and fiction), and cyborg studies.

Margrét Eggertsdóttir is an associate professor at the Árni Magnússon Institute in Reykjavík. She is one of the editors of the complete edition of Hallgrímur Pétursson's works and has written extensively on seventeenth-century Icelandic literature, including *Barokkmeistarinn: List og lærdómur í verkum Hallgríms Péturssonar* (2005).

Guðni Elísson is an associate professor in the Department of Literature and Linguistics at the University of Iceland. He holds an MA in Icelandic literature from the University of Iceland and a PhD in English from the University of Texas, Austin. He has edited numerous books in the field of literature, cultural studies, and film theory.

Ástráður Eysteinsson is a professor of comparative literature at the University of Iceland. He has worked in the areas of modern literary theory, modernist and postmodern studies, twentieth-century literature (English, German, Icelandic), and translation studies. His publications include *The Concept of Modernism* (1990), *Tvímæli* (on translation and literature; 1996), and *Umbrot* (on literature and modernity; 1999).

Árni Ibsen is a poet and playwright. He studied drama and English literature at the University of Exeter and has lectured in dramaturgy and playwriting both in Iceland and abroad. He has worked as a director, actor, and translator and is the author of nine produced plays, including *Heaven — a Schizophrenic Comedy* (1996), *For Ever* (1997), and *Man Alive* (1999). His plays have been performed in various countries as well as in Iceland, where his work has been performed by all the major theater companies.

Jón Yngvi Jóhannsson holds an MA in Icelandic literature from the University of Iceland. He is the director of Hagthenkir (the union of Icelandic nonfiction writers) and also works as a freelance critic and as a part-time lecturer at the University of Iceland. He has published widely on twentieth-century Icelandic literature and is the coauthor of *Íslensk bókmenntasaga IV–V* (forthcoming).

Helga Kress is a professor of comparative literature at the University of Iceland, Reykjavík. She has published widely on women and gender in Icelandic literary history, especially medieval literature, including *Máttugar meyjar* (1993), *Fyrir dyrum fóstru* (1996), and *Speglanir* (2000). For further information, see www.hi.is/~helga.

Daisy Neijmann is the Halldór Laxness Lecturer in Modern Icelandic Language and Literature at University College London. She has worked in the areas of Icelandic Canadian studies and contemporary Icelandic fiction. Her publications include *The Icelandic Voice in Canadian Letters* (1997) and *Colloquial Icelandic* (2000).

Vésteinn Ólason is the director of the Árni Magnússon Institute and a professor of Icelandic literature at the University of Iceland. Besides editions of sagas and ballads and numerous articles on Icelandic literature and folklore, his major publications are *The Traditional Ballads of Iceland* (1982) and *Dialogues with the Viking Age: Narration and Representation in the Sagas of the Icelanders* (1998).

Þórir Óskarsson is an editor at the Icelandic National Audit Office and an independent scholar. He has previously taught at the Universities of Kiel and Oslo. His publications include *Undarleg tákn á tímans bárum: Ljóð og fagurfræði Benedikts Gröndals* (1987) and (with Þorleifur Hauksson) *Íslensk stílfræði* (1994). His main fields of research are stylistics, literary historiography, and nineteenth-century Icelandic literature.

Hávar Sigurjónsson authored three extensive serial plays for radio during the years 1995–2000, after having made his first appearance as a playwright with his adaptation of Vigdís Grímsdóttir's novel *Ég heiti Ísbjörg ég er ljón* for the National Theater (1992). His first original composition for the stage, *Englabörn*, had its premiere in the Hafnarfjörður Theater in 2001. His most recent play, *Pabbastrákur*, opened at the National in 2003.

Sverrir Tómasson is a professor at the Árni Magnússon Institute in Reykjavík. He has taught at universities in Germany, England, and the United States as well as at the University of Iceland and has published widely in the area of Old Icelandic literature. He is among the authors of *Íslensk bókmenntasaga I–II* (1992–93) and is one of the editors of *Gripla*. His publications include editions of *Íslendinga sögur* (1985–87) and *Sturlunga saga* (1988).

Eysteinn Þorvaldsson is professor emeritus of Icelandic literature at the University College of Education, Iceland. His fields of specialty include modern Icelandic literature and Nordic mythology. He has written extensively on Icelandic poetry, with an emphasis on modernist poetry, and has also researched the pedagogical mediation of poetry. His books include *Atómskáldin* (1982), *Ljóðalærdómur* (1988), and an edition of the poetry of Þorsteinn Valdimarsson (1998).

Index

Authors from the medieval period are listed under given names followed by the patronymic (e.g., Snorri Sturluson). Authors from later periods are listed, usually, under a last patronymic unless another name is used more frequently (e.g., Jakobsdóttir, Svava). Accented letters (Á, Í, É, Ó, Ö, Ú, Ý) are interfiled with non-accented equivalents. Letters with no equivalents in English (Þ, æ) appear at the end of the index.

À bökkum Bolafljóts, 407
Absolution. See Fyrirgefning syndanna
absurdism: in fiction, 410, 425; in theater, 563–70, 577, 581, 606
acculturation of Icelandic Canadians, 612, 614, 632, 634–36
Aðalsteinsson, Ragnar Ingi, 490
Adam of Bremen, 68
Aðeins eitt blóm, 545
Aðgát skal höfð, 528
Adónías saga, 145
Advent, 378–79, 380
adventure poems (ævintýrakvæði), 224–25
adventure stories: children, 594–96; in rímur, 239; rural fiction, 409
aetates mundi. See universal histories
Af Borgslægtens Historie, 359–60, 367, 375–76
Á ferð og flugi, 318, 623–24
Af manna völdum, 542
afmorskvæði (poems of love), 55
Agnarsdóttir, Hlín, 582
Ágrip, 100–101

Albee, Edward, 566
Albertsson, Kristján, 364
Alcuin, 72
aldartala. See universal histories
Alexander Villa-Dei, 69
Alexandreis (Alexanders saga), 96, 97–98
Alice in Wonderland, 448
alliteration: ballads, 61; Eddic poetry 3–4; in folk poetry, 330, 524; and Icelandic poetic tradition, 290, 395, 400–401, 471; in late medieval secular poetry, 53; in poetry translations, 235, 471; post-1940, 472–73, 476–77, 483, 490, 499; and post-Reformation religious poetry, 179–80; in saga prose, 129
"Allt eins og blómstrið eina," 214
alphabet, Icelandic, xi, 65
Althing (general assembly), 2, 66, 77, 128, 229, 255, 258–59, 266, 271, 308, 405; in literature, 77–78, 268, 294, 389, 396
"Alvíssmál" (in Codex Regius), 9, 10, 13
Alþýðubókin, 269, 381

Alþýðuleikhúsið. See People's Theater
Anatome Blefkeniana, 269, 381
Andersen, Hans Christian, 293, 302, 304, 526, 588, 590
Andrésdóttir, Herdís, 508, 525, 526
Andrésdóttir, Ólína, 508, 525
Andrésson, Guðmundur, 192–93, 199, 463
Andrésson, Kristinn E., 358, 388, 402, 406
Andvökur, 318, 622, 624
Angels of the Universe. See Englar alheimsins
animal stories, 323, 325
Anna frá Heiðarkoti, 527
annals, 72, 85, 88, 90, 93–95, 191
Annálsbrot úr Skálholti, 94
Anonymus (Jóhannes of Katlar), 473
antiheroes: decadence, 352, 355; nineteenth-century, 295; post–World War I, 362; Sagas of Icelanders, 138
Apostles' Sagas. See *postula sögur*
Apuleius, 464
Arason, Guðlaugur, 434
Arason, Guðmundur, 56
Arason, Jón, bishop: in Reformation, 177–79; religious poetry, 52; secular poetry, 54–55; in *Vísnabók,* 181
Arfur, 528
"Árgali," 194
"Arinbjarnarkviða," 40–41
aristocracy: chivalric literature, 141, 142, 143, 145; Eddic poetry, 23, 27; and lineage, 99; neoromanticism, 347; Sagas of Icelanders, 122; and written records, 66
Ari Þorgilsson the Wise, 65, 75, 76–80, 100
Árnadóttir, Guðbjörg, 520
Árnadóttir, Guðrún of Lundur, 504, 529, 538–39
Árnadóttir, Guðrún of Oddsstaðir, 533–34
Árnadóttir, Nína Björk, 546–47
Árnadóttir, Olga Guðrún, 601
Árna saga biskups, 85, 90–91, 93
Árna saga Þorlákssonar, 88, 90
Arnason, David, 641
Árnason, Jón, 259, 298–99
Árnason, Jónas, 563, 566
Árnason, Jón Muli, 563
Árnason, Kristján, 439
Arngrímur the Learned. *See* Jónsson, Arngrímur the Learned

Arnór Þórðarson *jarlaskáld,* 37–38
Áróns saga, 92–93
Arrebo, Anders, 184, 204
Árstíðaferð um innri mann, 484
Ása Sólveig, 434, 505, 538
Ásbirnigar family, 67
Ásbjarnar þáttur Selsbana, 105, 109
Ásgeirsson, Magnús, 395–96, 410, 471
Ásmundar saga kappabana, 26
"Á Sprengisandi," 300
ástandið ("the situation"), 414, 416, 528
Ástarsaga, 421, 426
Ástarsaga 3 (play), 583
Ástarsaga úr fjöllunum, 604
Ástfóstur, 454
Ástin fiskanna, 455
Ástir samlyndra hjóna, 424
"Atlakviða" (in Codex Regius), 23–24
"Atlamál in grænlensku" (in Codex Regius), 22, 23, 24
"Atom" poets, 397, 474–82, 485, 494
The Atom Station. See Atómstöðin
Atómstöðin, 411, 414, 474
Auðnuleysingi og Tötrughypja, 543
Auðunar þáttur, 112
Augu þín sáu mig, 451, 454
Aumastar allra, 521
Aumingja Jens, 542
Auster, Paul, 447
"Austrfararvísur," 36
autobiographical poems (*ævikvæði*), 183, 202
autobiographies: Enlightenment, 241–44; by Icelandic Canadians, 630, 639–40; nineteenth-century, 273; seventeenth-century, 219–21; twentieth-century, 362, 371, 375, 390–91, 407, 427, 436–38, 468; by women, 517, 519, 521, 522, 526, 535, 538. *See also* memoirs

Bak við byrgða glugga, 541
"Baldrs draumar," 12
Baldursdóttir, Kristín Marja, 457
Baldvinsdóttir, Helga Steinvör. *See* Undína (Helga Steinvör Baldvinsdóttir)
ballads: middle ages, 60–63, 153; post-Reformation, 178; and *rímur,* 56–57; and sagas, 151; by women, 510–12, 513. See also *vikivakar*

Bandamanna saga (Sagas of Icelanders),
126, 127, 138
Baneitrað samband á Njálsgötunni, 602
Bárðar saga, 126
Bárðar saga Snæfellsáss, 510
"Barnaljóð," 586
Barn náttúrunnar, 371
baroque: influence of, 175, 184, 203, 217;
poetry, 201–2, 205, 209, 212, 213, 292;
prose, 220, 221–22
Bartholin, Thomas, 198
Baudelaire, Charles, 368
Beckett, Samuel, 425, 566, 567
Bede (Venerable), 79, 82, 110, 171
Bellum Jugurthinum, 70, 94
Benedictsson, Gunnar, 388
Benedictsson, Margrjet Jónsdóttir, 629
Benediktsson, Einar: decadence, 354; neoro-
manticism, 331–39, 344, 345; realism,
311, 314, 317, 326; symbolism, 328
Benjamín dúfa, 600
Beowulf, 3, 534
Bergmann, Árni, 462
Bergsson, Guðbergur: contemporary issues,
468; minimalism, 448, 454; modernism,
423–26, 430; neorealism, 435; rural dis-
course, 421; translations, 439
Bergur Sokkason, abbot, 121, 165, 166, 168,
170
Bergþórsson, Guðmundur, 206, 223
Bernskan, 589
"Bernskuheimili mitt," 522
Bernskuminningar, 537
"Bersöglisvísur," 36, 37
Bessi gamli, 363
"Betlikerling," 315
Bible translations, 97, 160, 178, 179. *See also*
religious poetry and literature
bildungsroman: absurdist theater, 568; children's literature, 591, 601; in English,
640; neorealism, 436–37; rural to urban
change, 414; by women, 525, 529
biographies: Bishops' sagas, 88–92; King's
biographies, 116–22; leaders, 92–93;
post–World War II, 410–13. *See also*
autobiographies; memoirs
Birtingur journal, 535, 536

Birtingur magazine, 421, 475, 535, 536
Bishops' Sagas (*biskupasögur*), 29, 88–92
"Bjarkamál," 26
Bjarklind, Unnur Benediktsdóttir. *See* Hulda
(Unnur Benediktsdóttir Bjarklind)
Bjarnadóttir, María, 533
Bjarnadóttir, Þuríður, 533
Bjarnason, Ágúst H., 335, 365
Bjarnason, Bjarni, 378, 448, 450–51
Bjarnason, Jóhann Magnús, 629–31, 638
Bjarnason, Jón (1721–85), 241, 245–46
Bjarnason, Jón (ca. 1560–1634), 181, 210
Bjarnhéðinsdóttir, Bríet, 518–19
Bjarni Jónsson *Borgfirðingarskáld* (*skáldi*).
See Jónsson, Bjarni *Borgfirðingaskáld*
(*skáldi*)
Bjartmarsson, Sigfús, 452–543, 498
Bjólfskviða (translation of Beowulf), 534
Björnsson, Björnstjerne, 348, 436, 463
Björnsson, Björn Th., 241
Björnsson, Eiríkur, 257
Björnsson, Halldóra B., 504, 506, 534–35
Björnsson, Jón, 348, 374, 389, 413
Björnsson, Oddur, 564, 567–68, 570, 577
Blandað í svartan dauðann, 426
Blíðfinnur (play), 583
Blíðfinnur series, 449–50
Blómarósir, 579
Blómin á þakinu, 604
Blómkvist, Stella, 458
Blöndal, Sigfús, 354
The Blue Tower. See *Brotahöfuð*
Blyton, Enid, 451, 595
Boccaccio, Giovanni, 112
Böðvarsson, Guðmundur, 400, 470
Boethius, 203, 212
Böglunga sögur, 99, 119–20
bohemianism, 339–47
Bóndinn á Hrauni, 349, 557
Book of Icelanders. See *Íslendingabók*
Book of Settlements. See *Landnámabók*
book prose (*bókfesta*), 124
Borg, 447–48
Borgarlíf, 422
Borgfirðingaskáld (*skáldi*). *See* Jónsson,
Bjarni *Borgfirðingaskáld* (*skáldi*)
Bósa saga og Herrauðs, 150–51

bourgeois literature, 364

Bragi Boddason the Old, 13, 25, 28, 29, 32

Brandes, Georg: realism, 312, 314, 316, 321; romanticism, 252; symbolism, 330; theater, 557, 580; Varangians, 350

Brandsson, Arngrímur, 168–69, 170–72

Brands þáttur örva, 112–13

Brandur Jónsson, abbot (d. 1264), 97–98

Brecht, Bertolt, 566, 567, 568

Bréf til Láru, 369–71, 372, 373, 390, 420

Breiðfjörð, Huldar, 467, 468

Breiðfjörð, Sigurður: aesthetics, 285–86; political engagement, 282; popular literature, 223; publication, 305; *rímur*, 238–39

Brekkukotsannáll, 420

Brendan, Saint, 127

Breta sögur (*Historia regum Britanniae*), 96, 143, 144

Breton, André, 372

Brevis commentarius de Islandia, 188

Bridget Jones's Diary, 466

Brimhljóð, 561

Brjáms saga, 511

"Brot af Sigurðarkviðu" (in Codex Regius), 21

Brotahöfuð, 193, 463, 464

Brotasilfur, 533

Brother Eysteinn. *See* Eysteinn (Brother)

Brudekjolen, 374

brunakvæði (passionate poems), 55

Brynhildur, 537

Brynjólfsdóttir, Ragnheiður (daughter of Bishop Brynjólfur Sveinsson), 318, 351, 375–76

Brynjólfsson, Gísli: folktales, 300; poetry, 290; political engagement, 277, 280–81, 283; romanticism, 266; romantisme, 275; translations, 303

Brynjólfur Sveinsson biskup, 519

Buchanan, George, 194

Bulgakov, Mikhail, 439

"Búnaðarbálkur," 231–32

Búrið, 601–2

burlesque, 206, 480. *See also* humor

Burns, Robert, 303, 304

Byggingin, 447, 448

Byron, George Gordon, Lord, 272, 273, 275–76, 289, 303, 304, 312, 317–18, 340, 343

Calf the poet, 58

Calliopes Respublica, 203

Canadian-Icelandic literature. *See* Icelandic Canadian literature

canon: folktales, 300; and Icelandic Canadian literature, 608; Icelandic Canadians, 621; rural to urban change, 417; seventeenth-century, 196, 226; women's writing, 504, 516

carnivalesque writing: Icelandic Canadian writing, 632; nineteenth-century, 294, 297; twentieth-century, 369, 370, 424. *See also* grotesque

carol (meter). *See* *vikivakakvæði* (carols or dance poems)

Catholic Church, 199, 369, 371, 391

Celtic influences, 6, 14, 17–18, 30

chansons de geste, 143, 151

chapbooks, German, 188, 223

Chekhov, Anton, 564, 576–77

childhood, 443–46

children's literature, 449–50, 586–607; beginnings, 586–94; folktales, 297; nineteenth-century, 293; poetry, 530; writers for, 531

Chinese literature, translations from, 534

chivalric literature, influence of: ballads, 60–61; Eddic poetry, 22; histories, 97; Knights' sagas, 141–44; Legendary sagas, 151; nineteenth-century novels, 296–97; popular literature, 223; skaldic poetry, 54

Chrétien de Troyes, translations of, 142–43, 144

Christianity: conversion to, 1–2, 83–84; influence on literature, 2; influence on mythological poetry, 12; in *Íslendingabók*, 78–79; twelfth-century, 66, 68. *See also* religious poetry and literature

chronicles, 65, 122, 510

City Theater, 575, 579, 580, 583, 584

classical literature, 70, 96, 141, 158, 185, 203

classicism, 231, 232, 270, 284, 291

class struggle, 374, 381, 408, 437, 535

Codex Regius manuscript, 7–27. See also
  Poetic Edda (Sæmundar Edda)
Cold War, 403, 480, 486, 498, 567
colloquialisms and slang: middle ages, 92;
  modernism, 396, 536; poetic realism,
  270; postmodernism, 496, 498, 500;
  post–World War II, 411, 478, 486, 490,
  491; realism, 315, 389; Sagas of Icelanders, 130; women's writings, 522, 529,
  531, 543, 544
comedy: in children's literature, 598; in emigrant literature, 632, 635, 638, 640; in
  medieval literature, 13; in *rímur*, 223,
  238; in theater, 552–53, 560–63, 566–67,
  569, 580–82, 584; in twentieth-century
  literature, 430, 449
comics and fantasy, 450
commedia dell'arte, 573
commemorative verse, 178
computer games and fantasy, 450
concrete poetry, 497
Confessions (St Augustine), 243
Confessions of an Immigrant's Daughter, 639–
  40
consumerism: contemporary issues, 467; fantasy, 450, 451; minimalism, 447; neorealism, 488, 491; postmodernism, 500, 501
cookbooks, 513
Copenhagen: as cultural center for Iceland,
  x, 179, 199, 201, 257, 266, 273, 279, 305,
  553; and Icelandic writers, 190–93, 200–
  202, 213–14, 219, 221–22, 227, 241, 247,
  256, 257, 260, 267, 273, 275, 311–12,
  323, 337, 349, 350, 360, 364, 377, 455–
  56, 553, 559, 560
court poetry, 27–39
crime and detective fiction: children, 595,
  596; Icelandic Canadians, 621; literary
  season, 469; modernism, 536; popular
  literature, 457, 458–59; post–World War
  I, 363, 378; rural fiction, 409
Crymogæa, 121, 189–90
cultural centers: Enlightenment, 230; middle ages, 66–67, 71–72
cultural diversity, 459, 615, 619, 642. *See also*
  multiculturalism
cultural politics, 365, 402, 613

Daðason, Sigfús, 475, 480, 481, 494
Dagar við vatnið, 538
Dagbjartsdóttir, Vilborg, 504, 544–45, 550
Dagbók í Höfn, 266, 275, 276
"Daglegt andvarp guðhræddar sálar," 513
Dagshríðar spor, 530
Dagur vonar, 577
Dalafólk, 388, 525
Dalalíf, 529
"Dánaróðr Hildibrands," 26
"Dánaróðr Hjálmars," 26
Daníelsson, Guðmundur, 407
Dansleikur, 567, 568
Dante Alighieri, 46, 216
Dares Phrygius, translations of, 94, 96
The Dark Weaver, 640
Darwinism, 260, 331
Dauðamenn, 436
Dauðsmannsey, 416
Davíðsdóttir, Vilborg, 465
De antiquitate regum Norwagiensium, 72, 100
decadence, 267, 351–56, 494
The Deep Blue Sea, Pardon the Ocean, 478
Denmark: ballads from, 60; emigrant writers
  in, 359–62; influence on late medieval
  Iceland, 54; national histories, 114–16;
  trade monopoly, 195, 436
Depression of 1930s, 380, 399, 475
detective fiction. *See* crime and detective
  fiction
"Dettifoss" (Einar Benediktsson), 335
"Dettifoss" (Kristján Jónsson Fjallaskáld),
  276
De ulykkeligste, 521
Devil's Island. See Þar sem djöflaeyjan rís
devotional reading, 221–22. *See also* religious
  poetry and literature
Dialogues (Gregory), 155, 169, 172
Diarium Christianum, 204, 214
Dickens, Charles, 303, 409, 630
didactic poetry: middle ages, 14–16;
  seventeenth-century, 209–10
Didda, 453
Dís, 406
Dísa Mjöll, 529
Disciplina clericalis, 169, 172
Discursus oppositivus, 192–93

displacement, 622, 626
"Djákninn á Myrká," 511–12
Djúpalækur, Kristján of, 474
Djúpið, 427
documentary: drama, 569; film, 389; writing, 276, 433, 463, 627, 640
A Doll's House, 559
Dómínó, 564, 565
Donatus, 69, 70
Don Quixote, 296, 439
Dóra series, 593–94
Dostoyevsky, Fyodor Mikhailovich, 349, 439
The Dove, 640
drama. *See* playwriting; theater
drápur (praise poems), 30, 34, 44, 47–48
Draugar vilja ekki dósagos, 605
Draupnir journal, 519
dream visions, 86, 104
Drífa Viðar, 538
Dropar journal, 520
dróttkvætt (court meter), 6, 29, 30, 34, 36, 38, 41, 44, 122, 157, 185; influence on later poets, 207, 210–11, 234. *See also* skaldic poetry
Dúfnaveislan, 566
Dvergliljur, 544
Dvöl journal, 519
Dyrnar þröngu, 448–49
Dægurvísa, 541
Dætur Reykjavíkur, 389, 528–29

"Ebbadætra kvæði," 62, 511
Eberhard of Bethune, 69
Edda (Snorri Sturluson), 151–58; compilation of, 103; and grammar, 69–70; Legendary Sagas in, 26; skaldic poetry in, 28, 29, 32–33, 34; women's culture, 509
Eddic poetry, 7–27, 509
education: Enlightenment, 226–29; in literature: 141, 156, 217, 222, 246, 251, 254, 270, 287, 304, 316, 414, 456, 464, 528, 628; middle ages, 2, 54, 67–72, 92, 94, 102, 119, 166; nineteenth-century, 255–58, 260, 267, 304–5, 314; post-Reformation, 175, 191, 196, 213; twentieth-century, 325, 365–66, 589, 591; of women, 197, 414, 518–19

Edward, Saint, 161
Eftir konsertinn, 567–68
Eftirmáli regndropanna, 460
Eftirþankar Jóhönnu, 434
Ég er meistarinn, 582
Ég heiti Ísbjörg, ég er ljón, 541
Egill Skallagrímsson, 34, 39–41, 42
Egils saga, 34, 39
Egilsson, Ólafur, 218–19
Egilsson, Sveinbjörn, 265, 300–301
Ég um mig frá mér til mín, 436, 602
"Eikarlundurinn," 188
Eilífur Guðrúnarson, 33, 43
Eimreiðin journal, 522
Einar Bragi, 475, 477, 481, 483, 494
Einar Gilsson, 56
Einar Haflíðason, 88, 91
Einarsdóttir, Björg. *See* Látra-Björg
Einarsdóttir, Málfríður, 504, 537, 542–43, 550
Einar *skálaglamm*, 34, 39
Einar Skúlason, 44, 162
Einars of Munaðarnes, Sigríður, 504, 532
Einarsson, Ármann Kr., 595, 605
Einarsson, Baldvin, 258
Einarsson, Gissur, 177, 178, 179
Einarsson, Guðmundur, 200
Einarsson, Indriði, 300, 552, 553, 554–56
Einarsson, Magnús, 617
Einarsson, Marteinn, 179
Einarsson, Oddur, 183, 190–91
Einarsson, Ólafur of Kirkjubær, 181–86, 193–94, 206
Einarsson, Sigurður, 399
Einarsson, Stefán, ix
Einfalt matreiðsluvasakver fyrir heldri manna húsfreyjur, 513
Einhver í dyrunum, 578
Einkamál Stefaníu, 435, 538
Eins og gengur, 526
Eins og hafið, 542
Eins og steinn sem hafið fágar, 468
Eiríksdóttir, Unnur, 537, 542
Eiríks saga rauða, 127, 135, 510
Eiríks saga víðförla, 127, 172
Eiríkur Hansson, 630–31
Eiríkur Oddsson, 99

Eitruð epli, 456
Eitt er það land, 535
"Eitur," 354
"Ekkjan við ána," 324–25
Elding, 519
Eldjárn, Þórarinn: children's fantasy, 606; historical fiction, 463; neorealism, 489, 490; postmodernism, 440, 495; on post-Reformation period, 193
elegiac lays (in Codex Regius), 21–22
Elenóra, 631–32
Elías Mar, 415
Elíasson, Gyrðir, 444–45, 449, 495, 500
Eliot, T.S., 31, 395
"Ellikvæði," 55
ellikvæði (old age poetry), 55, 213
Elskan mín ég dey, 448–49
Elsku Barn!, 605
Elucidarius, 70, 102, 155
elves: ballads, 62; children's literature, 604; folktales, 299, 300; nature poetry, 201; theater, 555, 583. *See also* supernatural motifs
emigrant writers: in Denmark, 359–62; neoromanticism, 347–51; 1920s, 374–75; women, 530–31, 617. *See also* Icelandic Canadian literature
emigration from Iceland. *See* Icelandic Canadian literature
end rhyme: Christian poetry, 7, 45, 48, 50, 52; secular poetry, 55; skaldic poetry, 34; sources of, 63–64
Endurkoma Maríu, 451
Engilberts, Birgir, 564, 567, 570
Engill, pípuhattur og jarðarber, 451
Englabörn, 584
Englar alheimsins, 460
English influence on late medieval Iceland, 54, 68
English language literature, 636–40
Enlightenment, 226–30
entertainments, 56. See also *kvöldvaka* (evening reading/entertainment)
"Erfidrápa," 35, 162
Erla (Guðfinna Þorsteinsdóttir), 531
Erlendsson, Guðmundur of Fell, 206, 208, 215

Erlingsson, Friðrik, 600
Erlingsson, Þorsteinn, 313–14, 317, 323, 325, 326, 336
Erta (Didda), 453
Eustace, Saint, 44
exempla, 46, 88, 111, 112, 173
existentialism, 400, 401, 411
expressionism, 358, 361, 394, 396, 561, 566
Eyjólfsson, Gunnsteinn, 631–32
Eyrbyggja saga: biography in, 93; categories, 126, 127; characters, 135, 136; narrative mode, 131; skaldic poetry, 42; structure, 132; worldview, 138
Eysteinn (Brother), 48–51, 53, 158
Eysteinn Ásgrímsson, 48
Eyvindur *skáldaspillir*, 28, 107

fables, 12, 293
fabliau, 112, 143, 150–51
Faðir og móðir og dulmagn bernskunnar, 468
"Faðmlag dauðans," 535–36
"Fáfnismál" (in Codex Regius), 20
Fagra veröld, 397–99
Fagurskinna, 100–101
"Fagurt er í Fjörðum," 514
fairy tales. *See* folk and fairy tales
Falsarinn, 463
Falskur fugl, 453
fantasy fiction: for children, 604–6; contemporary, 446–56; in women's literature, 549
Farðu burt skuggi, 426
Fátækt fólk, 437, 599
Faulkner, William, 425, 454
Fell, Arnrún of (Guðrún Tómasdóttir), 531
Ferðabók (Eggert Ólafsson), 230
Ferðabók (Tómas Sæmundsson), 257, 281, 284
Ferðalok (Guðrún Finnsdottir), 633
"Ferðalok" (Jónas Hallgrímsson), 290
Ferðalok (play; Steinunn Jóhannesdottir), 581
Ferðarolla, 241
Ferðasaga (Árni Magnússon), 241
Ferðir Guðríðar, 581
fiction: contemporary issues, 466–68; fantasy, 446–56, 549, 604–6; historical fic-

fiction (*continued*)
   tion, 436–38, 462–66; introduction of,
   226; 1980–2000, 438–70; nineteenth-
   century, 292–97; origins of, 248–49;
   post–World War II, 404–38; science fic-
   tion, 457; urban fiction, 410–13. *See also*
   crime and detective fiction
Fielding, Henry, 246
Fimmbræðra saga, 247
Fimmtán ára á föstu, 603
fin de siècle periods. *See* decadence;
   postmodernism
Finnbogason, Guðmundur, 365, 525
Finnsdóttir, Guðrún Helga, 530
Finnsdóttir, Steinunn, 512–13
Finnsson, Hannes, bishop, 229, 230, 241,
   297
The First Grammatical Treatise. See *Fyrsta
   málfræðiritgerðin*
The Fish Can Sing. See *Brekkukotsannáll*
Fjalla-Eyvindur, 323, 349, 557–58, 560
Fjallaskáld, Kristján Jónsson. *See* Jónsson,
   Kristján Fjallaskáld
Fjalldalslilja, 538
Fjallið og draumurinn, 408
Fjallkirkjan. See *Kirken paa Bjerget*
Fjallkona ("Mountain Woman"), 262, 518,
   615
Fjallkonan newspaper, 518
Fjölnir journal, 294, 515
Flateyjarbókarannáll, 94
Flateyjarbók manuscript, 55–59, 118–19,
   121, 139, 147, 163
Flaubert, Gustav, 410
Fljótt fljótt sagði fuglinn, 427–28
flokkar (praise poems), 30
Flóres saga, 140
Flugur, 393–94, 401
flyting, (*senna*), 13, 18
folk and fairy tales: in Eddic poetry, 27;
   nineteenth-century, 297–300; women,
   510–12, 522, 535, 538–39, 549. See also
   lygisögur ('lying sagas')
folk poetry, 27, 188, 225, 254, 511–12, 523–
   24, 536, 619
foreign influences: Enlightenment period,
   226; histories, 79, 107–8; middle ages,

   67–70, 72; 1920s, 364–65; post-
   Reformation period, 187–88; Prose
   Edda, 103
fornaldarsögur. *See* Legendary Sagas
Fornar ástir ("Hel"), 329, 352, 367–68, 524
Forni annáll, 94
fornyrðislag (old epic meter), 4–5; in chil-
   dren's literature, 586; in folk poetry, 208,
   225; in post-Reformation poetry, 208; in
   Romantic poetry, 234, 301; in Snorri
   Sturluson's *Edda*, 157; in translations,
   143, 234–36
Förumenn, 527
Fóstbræðra saga, 126, 129, 139, 417
Framfari (newspaper), 612, 615, 616, 628
Framsókn journal, 519, 520
Frá myrkri til ljóss, 521
free prose (*sagnfesta*), 124
free verse, 394–96, 400–01, 472–73, 477,
   481, 483, 485, 490
Freud, Sigmund, 371, 568
Freyja (journal), 629
Freyja (Norse goddess), 14, 35, 43, 59, 78,
   457
Freysson, Sindri, 499
Friðjónsson, Guðmundur, 323–24, 326, 374,
   386, 413
fringe theater, 563, 572
Fröding, Gustav, 355
Froskmaðurinn, 427
Fugl sem flaug á snúru, 569, 581
futurism, 369, 399, 447–48, 451
"Fýkur í sporin," 634–35
"Fyrirgefning," 322
Fyrirgefning syndanna, 458
Fyrirlestur um hamingjuna, 467
Fyrsta málfræðiritgerðin, 65, 160
Færeyinga saga (Sagas of Icelanders), 124

Gaga, 440
Galdra-Loftur, 349, 354, 557, 558, 560
Gamli, 44–45
Gangandi íkorni, 444, 449
Gangvirkið, 415
García Lorca, Frederico, 395
García Márquez, Gabriel, 439, 448
Garðveisla, 569

"Gátur Gestumblinda," 27
Gauti vinur minn, 605
Gefið hvort öðru, 431, 540
Geirmundar þáttur, 84
"Geisli," 44
genealogy, 33, 65–66, 99
Gengin spor, 533–34
Geoffrey of Monmouth, 73, 96, 97, 143
Gerður Kristný, 455–56, 499
Gerhard, Johann, 217, 221
Germanic elements: in Eddic poetry, 16; heroic poetry, 18, 23, 25, 26; late medieval, 54; middle ages, 3; skaldic poetry, 28
Gerpla, 417–18, 420
Gesta Danorum, 146
Gestir, 526
ghost stories, 511–12
Gimsteinaborgin, 631
Gísla saga, 126, 127, 132, 134, 135
Gíslason, Konráð, 265, 273
Gíslason, Þorsteinn, 334
Gissurarson, Bjarni, 204–5, 207, 208, 225
Gjalddagar, 491
gjallandi, Þorgils (Jón Stefánsson), 323–24, 326
globalisation, 459, 500
"Glymdrápa," 34
"Glælognskviða," 162
Glæsimennska, 374
Gnarr, Jón, 447
Góðir Íslendingar, 467, 468
Goethe, Johann Wolfgang von, 238, 273, 289, 304, 349, 395
Gömul saga, 374, 526
Göngu-Hrólfs saga, 149, 150
gossip, 412, 523, 527
Gottskálksannáll, 94
Gottskálksson, Oddur, 177–78, 179
Grágás: battlefield laws, 85; education of priests, 69; as laws, 66–67
Grámosinn glóir, 440
Grandavegur 7, 442, 445, 448, 455
"Grasaferð," 293, 515, 523, 588
Great Migration, 147, 151
Greek literature. *See* classical literature
Greenlandic verse, 24–25

Gresjur guðdómsins, 411
Grettis saga, 126
Grimm, Jacob and Wilhelm, 298, 302
"Grímnismál" (in Codex Regius), 10, 13
Grímsdóttir, Vigdís, 446, 454, 541
Grímsson, Magnús, 298, 306
Grímsson, Sigurður, 392
Grímsson, Stefán Hörður, 474–76, 494
"Grípisspá" (in Codex Regius), 19–20
Gröndal, Benedikt (1826–1907): aesthetics, 287; nineteenth-century, 296; poetry, 289, 292; political engagement, 277, 280, 282; publication, 306; realism, 314, 316; romantisme, 273–74, 276; stories, 294; translations, 303, 304
Gröndal, Benedikt, Sr., 234, 235
Grösin í glugghúsinu, 599
grotesque: nineteenth-century, 290, 293, 294, 296; 1920s, 369, 370; popular fiction, 458
"Grottasöngr" (in Codex Regius), 17, 509
Guðbrandur, Þorláksson. *See* Þorláksson, Guðbrandur, bishop
Gudinnen og oksen, 375
Guðlaugsson, Jónas: decadence, 352, 354; neoromanticism, 331, 332, 335, 340, 343–44; Varangians, 348, 350
"Guðmundar drápa," 51
Guðmundar saga, 90, 93, 169, 170, 172
Guðmundar saga dýra, 84
Guðmundsdóttir, Guðný, 513
Guðmundsdóttir, Oddný, 527–28, 539
Guðmundsdóttir, Rósa. *See* Vatnsenda-Rósa
Guðmundsdóttir, Þuríður, 545–46
Guðmundsson, Böðvar, 464, 573, 642
Guðmundsson, Einar Már: poetry, 492–93; popular literature, 459; postmodernism, 443, 495, 501; sexuality, 455, 456; urban epics, 460–65; in world literature, x
Guðmundsson, Jón the Learned, 199–201
Guðmundsson, Kristmann, 348, 374–75, 533
Guðmundsson, Loftur, 421, 561
Guðmundsson, Sigfús, 181
Guðmundsson, Sigurður, 281, 553, 556, 562, 570, 571
Guðmundsson, Tómas, 391, 393, 397–98, 399, 471

Guðmundur, Saint, 158, 160, 169, 170

Guðnýjarkver, 516

"Guðrúnarhvöt" (in Codex Regius), 22, 25

"Guðrúnarkviða" (in Codex Regius), 22

"Guðrúnarkviða forna," 509

Guðrún of Lundur. *See* Árnadóttir, Guðrún of Lundur

Guds Werk occh Hwila, 204

Gulleyjan, 443, 459

Gullið í höfðinu, 453

Gullna hliðið, 561–62

Gunnar og Kjartan, 434

Gunnars, Kristjana, 640, 641

Gunnarsdóttir, Berglind, 548

"Gunnarshólmi," 268, 271–72, 288, 291, 621

"Gunnars-saga hin nýja," 621

Gunnarsson, Gunnar, 358–62; neoromanticism, 340; 1930s, 384; rural fiction, 410; translations, 407; Varangians, 348, 349; writers abroad, 375, 380

Gunnarsson, Ólafur, 435, 440, 459

Gunnarsson, Pétur: children, 602; postmodernism, 468, 495; sexuality, 455; urbanism, 436, 443, 460

Gunni Hallsson, 53

Gunnlaðarsaga, 540

Gunnlaugsdóttir, Álfrún, 441, 442, 542

Gunnlaugs saga, 42, 126, 131, 137, 144, 510

Gunnlaugur Leifsson, 97, 159, 163, 166, 168

Guttormsson, Guttormur J., 561, 624–27

Gvendur Jóns og ég . . . , 595

Gyðinga saga, 97–98

Gylfaginning (Prose Edda), 154, 155–57

Gæst den enøjede, 360

Hadda Padda, 350, 559

"Hafið" (Grímur Thomsen), 273

Hafið (Ólafur Haukur Simonarson), 580

Hafnarfjörður Theater Company, 575, 577, 580, 584

Hafstein, Hannes, 283, 302, 308–9, 312–15, 330, 336

Hagalagðar, 518

Hagalín, Guðmundur G., 350, 387–88, 390, 410, 413

Hagalín, Hrafnhildur, 582

Hair (play), 575

"Hákonardrápa," 34

Hákonar saga Hákonarsonar, 74, 87, 99, 120–21

"Háleygjatal," 107

Hálfdanarson, Helgi, 439, 481

Hálfir skósólar, 368

Halla, 325–26

Halldórsdóttir, Birgitta H., 458

Halldórsson, Erlingur E., 564, 567

Halldórsson, Jóhann, 298

Halldórsson, Ómar Þ., 440

Halldórsson, Þorleifur, 221–22

Hallfreðar saga, 126, 133–34

Hallfreður Óttarsson *vandræðaskáld*, 34, 35–36

Hallgrímsson, Jónas, 293–94, 515, 523

Hallmundsson, Hallberg, 487

Hallson, Jón, 55

Hallsteinn og Dóra, 557

Hallur Ögmundsson, 51, 52, 53

Hallur Þorarinsson, 38

Hamar og sigð, 399

"Hamðismál" (in Codex Regius), 23, 25

Hamlet, 304, 558

Hamsun, Knut, 365, 383, 387, 410

Hannesson, Guðmundur, 365

Haralds, Auður, 538

Haraldsdóttir, Ingibjörg, 547–48

Haraldur Fairhair: court poets of, 24, 28, 29, 34; dynasty of, 33

Haraldur Hard-ruler, 37, 100, 112

"Hárbarðsljóð" (in Codex Regius), 10, 13

Harboe, Ludvig, 228, 244

Harðarson, Ísak, 448, 450, 495, 496

Harði kjarninn, 499

Hardy, Thomas, 464

"Harmsól" (Gamli), 44–45

Harry Potter, 450, 604

Hart í bak (Jökull Jakobsson), 564, 565, 570–71

Háttalykill (catalog of meters), 38

Háttatal (Prose Edda), 38, 102, 119, 152, 154, 157

Haukadalur, 69, 71

Haukdæla þáttur, 84

Haukdælir family, 67, 68, 71, 78, 99, 121

Hauksbók, 80, 81, 82–83, 84, 96, 97

Haukur Erlendsson, 80, 81, 82
"Haukurinn," 345, 356n4, 523
Haukur Valdísarson, 38
Haustbrúður, 582
Haust í Skírisskógi, 429, 430
Haustlitir, 533
"Haustlöng," 32
Haustskip, 436, 463
"Hávamál" (in Codex Regius): composition
    of, 27; as didactic poetry, 14–16; Eddic
    poetry, 9; influence of, 46; as mythologi-
    cal poetry, 10
healing poems, 508, 509
hedonism, 352, 356, 391
Hegelianism, 312
Heiberg, Johan Ludvig, 267, 284, 553, 555
Heiðarvíga saga, 125, 130, 133
Heiðreks saga, 26
"Heilags anda vísur," 45
heimsaldrar. See universal histories
    (veraldarsögur)
Heimsins heimskasti pabbi, 453
Heimskra manna ráð, 459
Heimskringla (emigrant newspaper), 321
Heimskringla (Snorri Sturluson): Danish
    national histories, 114–15; genres, 75;
    history, 76; national histories, 100, 101,
    102–3, 105–11; skaldic poetry in, 28
Heimskringla (Þórarinn Eldjárn), 606
Heimsljós, 386–87
"Heimsókn gyðjunnar," 506
"Heimsósómi" (Skáld-Sveinn), 55
Heinesen, William, 439
heiti: Christian poetry, 43; in late medieval
    secular poetry, 53, 57; in old Icelandic
    poetry, 6; in Prose Edda, 157; in skaldic
    poetry, 31
"Hel," 329, 352, 367–68, 524
"Helga kviða Hjörvarðssonar" (in Codex
    Regius), 18–19
"Helga kviða Hundingsbana" (in Codex
    Regius), 18–19
Helgason, Hallgrímur, x, 466, 584
Helgisagan um Ólaf digra Haraldsson, 161–
    62
Det hellige fjell, 375
"Helreið Brynhildar" (in Codex Regius), 22

Hemingway, Ernest, 409, 410
von Herder, Johan Gottfried, 263, 287
heroic poetry, 18–26, 58–59
Hexaëmeron Rhytmico-Danicum, 204
Híbýli vindanna, 464
Hildebrandslied, 3–4, 26
Hillingalönd, 530, 633, 635
Himinbjargarsaga eða Skógardraumur, 429–
    30
Himnaríki, 580
Hin hvítu skip, 400
His Dark Materials, 450, 604
Historia de antiquitate regum Norwagiensium,
    72, 100
Historia ecclesiastica gentis Anglorum, 79, 110
Historia eremitica, 159
Historia monachorum in ægypto, 159
Historia Norvegiæ, 100, 107–8
Historia regnum Britanniae, 107. See also
    Geoffrey of Monmouth; Breta sögur
Historia scholastica, 98
historical fiction: 1960s–, 436–38; 1980–
    2000, 462–66
historical poetry, 206
historiography, 73, 75–98
Hjálmarsson, Jóhann, 484, 487
Hjaltalín, Jón Oddsson, 239, 241, 246–47
Hjaltalín, Oddur, 290
Hjartað býr enn í helli sínum, 439
Hjartarson, Snorri, 292, 348, 473, 483
Hjartastaður, 455
"Hlöðskviða" (Legendary Saga), 23, 26
Hofgarða-Refur, 41–42
"Höfuðlausn," 34, 41, 46, 130
Höfundur Íslands, 466
Hólar (diocese), 71
Holberg, Ludvig, 22, 226, 246, 248
Holm, Bill, 620, 641
Hólm, Torfhildur Þorsteinsdóttir, 318, 375,
    519–20, 588, 628
Homer, 150, 265, 304
homosexuality, 454, 583, 584
Honorius Augustodunensis, translations of,
    70, 102
Horace, 203, 236
Høyersannáll, 94
Hrafnkels saga (Sagas of Icelanders), 125,
    126, 133, 135

"Hrafnsmál," 101

Hrafns saga Sveinbjarnarsonar, 84, 90, 92, 93

Hreiðars þáttur heimska, 112, 113

Hringsól, 441, 442, 542

Hrólfs saga kraka, 146, 147–48, 150, 157

Hryggjarstykki, 99, 116

Hugh of Saint Victor, 72

Hugrún (Filippía Kristjánsdóttir), 531

Hulda, 113

Hulda (Unnur Benediktsdóttir Bjarklind): neoromanticism, 344–47; publishing, 505; rural settings, 388; symbolism, 329; women, 508, 520; *þulur*, 523–25

humanism, 174, 189, 195, 197, 420

humor: eighteenth-century, 236–37; *rímur*, 59; seventeenth-century, 206–7; skaldic poetry, 33, 36

Hungurvaka, 88, 89, 93

"Hússdrápa," 6, 32, 33

Hversdagsdraumur, 567

Hvíldardagar, 446

Hvítadalur, Stefán of: decadence, 352–53, 356; influence of, 392, 397; modernism, 391; nationalism, 339; neoromanticism, 308; urbanism, 446; Varangians, 348

Hvítir hrafnar, 368

Hvítmánuður, 538, 542

Hvunndagshetjan, 435, 538

"Hymiskviða" (in Codex Regius), 13

hymns: Christian poetry, 43; Passion hymns, 57, 215–17; post-Reformation period, 182–84; and women poets, 513

Hyndlurímur, 513

Hægan Elektra, 582

Íbiðsal hjónabandsins, 508

Ibsen, Árni, 580–81

Ibsen, Henrik, 350, 403

Iceland: Age of Learning, 185–95; 1874–1918, x, 308–9, 357; Enlightenment, 195–250; and European culture, ix–x; middle ages, 1–3, 54, 66–67, 71–72; Migration period, 18; nineteenth-century, 255–60; post-Reformation period, 179–95; Reformation 1550–1627, 176–78; Settlement Period, 80–84

Icelandic Canadian literature, 608–42; early

literature, 614–15; in English, 636–40; fiction, 627–28; first immigrant community, 611–14; history and background, 609–11; pioneer narratives, 628–30; poetry, 615–27

Icelandic Federation for Women's Rights, 519

Icelandic Literary Society, 256, 259, 299, 305

Icelandicness, 608, 613–14, 641

Icelandic School in saga studies, 365

Icelandic Theater Company, 575–76

Icelandic Women's Society, 518–19

Iceland's Bell. See *Íslandsklukkan*

iconoclasm, 364, 549–50

Ilias Latina (*Trójumanna sögur*), 70, 94, 96–97, 144, 150

Í luktum heimi, 443

image of Iceland, 360, 386, 387, 404, 413, 421

Imago mundi, 72, 155

"Indíána hátíð," 625

Independent People. See *Sjálfstætt fólk*

Indriðason, Andrés, 602–3, 605

Indriðason, Arnaldur, 458

information age, 495

Ingólfsson, Eðvarð, 603

Ingólfsson, Viktor Arnar, 458

Ingólfur journal, 343, 524

Ionesco, Eugène, 567

Í Rauðárdalnum, 631

Irish influences. See Celtic influences

Í sama klefa, 433, 440–41, 541

Isidore of Seville, 72, 155, 169

Í skjóli háskans, 538

"Ísland" (Bjarni Thorarensen), 262–63, 331

"Ísland" (Eggert Ólafsson), 232

"Ísland" (Jónas Hallgrímsson), 267–68, 272, 291

"Ísland" (Júlíana Jónsdóttir), 518

Íslandsförin, 467

Islandsk Kærlighed, 374

Íslandsklukkan, 387, 405

"Íslands minni," 518

Ísleifs þáttur Gissurarsonar, 88

Íslendingabók, 64–65, 75, 76–80, 198

"Íslendingadrápa," 38

Íslendinga saga (Sturla Þórðarson): and

annals, 95; manuscripts of, 84, 90; on Snorri, 102; and Sturlunga saga, 85–87
Íslendingasögur. See Sagas of Icelanders (*Íslendingasögur*)
Íslendín gaspjall, 539
Íslendingaþættir, 137
Íslensk bókmenntasaga, x
Íslenski draumurinn, 467
Íslenskur aðall, 390
Íslenzkar þjóðsögur og æfintýri, 298–99, 553
Í svölu rjóði, 531
Ívars þáttur Ingimundarsonar, 112

Jafnaðarmaðurinn, 374
Jakobsdóttir, Svava, 430–32, 503–4, 539–41, 545, 549
Jakobsson, Jökull, 415, 564–66, 570, 571, 577
Jammers Minde, 218
Jarðabók, 222
Jarðljóð, 534, 535
Jarteinabók Guðmundar Arasonar, 85
Jensdóttir, Jenna, 599
Jochumsson, Matthías: aesthetics, 288; folktales, 300; nineteenth-century culture, 259; plays, 552, 553, 554–56, 561, 570; poetry, 289, 290, 292; political engagement, 278, 279, 280, 281–82; publication, 306; realism, 312; romanticism, 252, 308; romantisme, 274; translations, 303, 304
Jóhamar (Jóhannes Óskarsson), 447
Jóhannesdóttir, Líney, 537, 539, 542
Jóhannesdóttir, Steinunn, 581
Jóhannes Helgi, 421, 422
Johannessen, Matthías, 483, 484, 486, 494
Jóhannes úr Kötlum. *See* Katlar, Jóhannes of
Jóhannsdóttir, María, 521
Jóhannsdóttir, Ólafía, 521
Johnson, Jakobína, 530–31
Jökulsdóttir, Elísabet, 446
Jökulsson, Illugi, 606
Jómsvíkinga saga, 37, 38, 114
Jón Arason (Gunnar Gunnarson), 377
Jón Arason (Matthías Jochumsson), 555
Jón á Strympu stories, 632–33
Jónatansdóttir, Arnfríður, 536

Jón biskup Arason, 519
Jón biskup Vídalín, 519
Jón Loftsson, 99, 102
Jón Oddur og Jón Bjarni, 567
Jón Óskar, 475, 479–81, 494
Jónsbók, 223, 241
Jónsdóttir, Ágústína, 499
Jónsdóttir, Áslaug, 450
Jónsdóttir, Auður, 466–67
Jónsdóttir, Guðfinna of Hamrar, 531–32
Jónsdóttir, Guðný of Galtafell, 537
Jónsdóttir, Guðný of Klömbur, 515–16
Jónsdóttir, Júlíana, 516–18, 520, 618
Jónsdóttir, Margrét (1893–1971), 531
Jónsdóttir, Margrét Lóa (b. 1967), 499
Jónsdóttir, Ragnheiður, 414, 504, 528, 592, 593–94, 595, 607
Jónsdóttir, Sigríður (Sigga *skálda*), 217
Jónsdóttir, Þóra, 489, 547
Jóns saga baptista, 146, 168
Jóns saga helga, 166, 168–69, 508–9
Jónsson, Ari, 555
Jónsson, Arngrímur the Learned, 114, 181, 188–89
Jónsson, Benedikt, 210
Jónsson, Bjarni (b. 1966), 583
Jónsson, Bjarni *Borgfirðingaskáld* (*skáldi*), 184–85, 206
Jónsson, Björn of Skarðsá, 191, 218
Jónsson, Erlendur, 508
Jónsson, Gisli (1513–87), 177, 179
Jónsson, Gisli (Canadian publisher), 633
Jónsson, Hallgrímur, 590
Jónsson, Hilmar, 577
Jónsson, Hjálmar of Bóla, 276, 279, 281, 282
Jónsson, Jóhann, 394, 396
Jónsson, Kristján Fjallaskáld: neoromanticism, 340; nineteenth-century culture, 259; poetry, 292; political engagement, 281, 282; publication, 306; romantisme, 274, 276
Jónsson, Magnús prúði, 158, 181
Jónsson, Ólafur of Sandar, 182–83, 186, 210
Jónsson, Páll of Staðarhóll. *See* Staðarhóls-Páll
Jónsson, Sigurður, 217
Jónsson, Sigurjón, 374, 389

Jónsson, Stefán, 416–17, 592–94, 595
Jónsson, Sveinn, 354
Jóns þáttur Halldórssonar, 88
Jóra og ég, 786
Jörð í álögum, 535
Journal eður víðferlissaga, 241
Joyce, James, 439
Justice Undone. See *Grámosinn glóir*

Kaffi, 583
Kafka, Franz, 439, 445, 447
Kaldaljós, 442, 448
Kamban, Guðmundur Jónsson, 318, 350–51, 375–76, 389–90, 559–60
Kant, Immanuel, 284
"Kappakvæði," 513
Kárason, Einar, 443, 455, 456, 459–60
Karlamagnús saga (The Saga of Charlemagne), 58, 143, 169
Karl Jónsson, abbot, 71, 116–17
Karlsson, Kristján, 397, 401–2, 489
Katla gerir uppreisn, 594
Katlar, Jóhannes of, 309, 393, 399, 402, 416, 471, 473, 487
Kaupstaðarferðir, 520
kennings: Christian, 43; in *kviðuháttur* poems, 34–35; in late medieval secular poetry, 53, 57–58; skaldic poetry, 7, 31, 32, 40
kerlingabækur, 538–39
Kerlingarslóðir, 539, 542
Kertaljós, 530
Kertaljós (play), 564–65
Kielland, Alexander, 410
Kierkegaard, Søren, 273
Kings' Sagas (*kon ungasögur*), 29, 56, 75, 98–122
Kirk, Hans, 410
Kirken paa Bjerget, 375–77
Kjarnorka og kvenhylli, 563
Kjartan og Guðrún, 434, 519, 629
Klemens saga (Sagas of Icelanders), 122, 159
Klopstock, Friedrich Gottlieb, 235–36, 300
Klukkan í turninum, 544
K.N. (Kristján Níels Júlíus Jónsson), 618–21, 627
Knights' Sagas (*riddarasögur*), 56, 58, 75, 139–45

"Knúts drápa," 36
Knýtlinga saga, 114–15
Kolbeinn Tumason, 45–46
Kolbeinsson, Guðni, 378, 599
"Komdu—," 353
kon ungasögur. See Kings' Sagas
Konungsannáll, 90, 94, 95
Konungs skuggsjá, 112, 141
Konur skelfa, 582
Kormáks saga (Sagas of Icelanders), 42, 126
Kormákur, Baltasar, 577
"Kötludraumur," 172, 225
Kristjánsdóttir, Filippía. See Hugrún (Filippía Kristjánsdóttir)
Kristjánsson, Geir, 419, 421
Kristnihald undir Jökli, 432–33, 461
Kristni saga, 75, 83–84
Kristrún í Hamravík, 387
Króka-Refs saga (Sagas of Icelanders), 126, 137
Króksfjarðarbók manuscript, 84
Kvaran, Einar Hjörleifsson: in Canada, 628; plays, 556, 557; political engagement, 283; post–World War I, 362–64, 366–68; realism, 312, 316, 320–23, 326–27; urban fiction, 411
Kveður í runni, 531
Kvennablaðið journal, 519
"Kvennaljóðmæli" (poetry manuscript), 514
Kvikasilfur, 459
kvöldvaka (evening reading/entertainment), 175, 196, 224, 230
"Kvæði af Knúti í Borg," 62
"Kvæði af kóng Símoni," 62
Kvæði journal, 524
Kyndilmessa, 544, 550
Kyrr kjör, 440, 463
Kyssti mig sól, 400

Labbi pabbakútur, 597
Lagerkvist, Per, 395
Lagerlöf, Selma, 410
Lais (Marie de France), 142, 143
Lamennais, Félicité Robert de, 290, 301
Landnámabók (Book of Settlements), 75, 80–83, 191
Land og synir, 414

Landrésrímur, 224
"Landskuld," 634
Lárusdóttir, Elínborg, 505, 527
Lárusdóttir, Guðrún, 520
Latin American writing, 439, 448
Latin language, 68–70, 95. *See also* classical
   literature
Latin poetry, 45
Látra-Björg (Björg Einarsdóttir), 514
Laufás-Edda, 181, 191
Laufið á trjánum, 544
Laufþytur, 531
Laurentius saga, 88, 89, 90–92, 93, 95
lausavísur (occasional stanzas or epigrams):
   in personal poetry, 27; religious poetry,
   44; skaldic poetry, 39, 41, 42; by women,
   513–14
law codes, 65–66, 66–67, 87
Laxdal, Eiríkur, 240, 244, 247–50
Laxdæla saga, 75, 257, 510, 517, 519
Laxness, Halldór: absurdist theater, 566;
   decadence, 356; early works, 371–74;
   historical fiction, 437, 466; influences on,
   297; modernism, 391, 396, 425; modernist revolt, 432, 433; nationalism, 338;
   1940s, 405–6; 1930s, 380–82, 383–84,
   386, 387, 400, 402, 403; 1920s, 367, 368;
   plays, 561, 571; poetry, 474; realism, 309;
   responses to, 388; rural discourse, 420,
   422; sexuality, 456; Varangians, 348;
   women's writing, 539; in world litera-
   ture, x
Legenda aurea, 98, 159
Legendary Sagas (*fornaldarsögur*): Eddic
   verse in, 26–27; as genre, 75; men's ele-
   gies in, 22; and *rímur*, 56, 58
Leið 12: Hlemmur-Fell, 435
"Leiðarvísan," 44, 45
Leiðin heim, 547
Leifur örlaganna, 527
Leigjandinn, 431, 540
Leit að tjaldstæði, 547
Lénharður fógeti, 323, 557
Leósdóttir, Jónína, 603
Leynimelur 13, 562
Lifandi vatnið – – –, 432
Líf og list journal, 536

"Líknarbraut," 45
"Lilja" (Brother Eysteinn), 48–51
limericks, 474
literacy: early women's writing, 509;
   Enlightenment period, 228; historical fic-
   tion, 462; late middle ages, 54; Reforma-
   tion, 175; seventeenth-century, 196;
   twelfth-century, 38
literary genres: middle ages, 75–76
literary season, 468–70
Lives (*vitae*). *See* Bishops' sagas
   (*biskupasögur*); saints' lives
Livets Strand, 361
"Ljáðu mér vængi," 524
Ljóð á trylltri öld, 478
Ljóð fyrir lífi, 548
Ljóð í lausaleik, 548
Ljóðsótt, 548
"Ljómur," 51–52
Loftbólur, 567
Loftur Guttormsson, 54
Lögberg (emigrant newspaper), 321, 632
Lögberg-Heimskringla (Icelandic Canadian
   newspaper), 616
Lögmannsannáll, 91, 94, 95
"Lokasenna" (in Codex Regius), 10, 12–13
Lokaæfing, 570
Lokrur, 58
Lorca, García, 395
The Lord of the Rings, 448, 450, 604
Lord of the Silver Dragon, 640
low style. *See sermo humilis*
Lucan, translations of, 70, 96
Lúðvíksson, Vésteinn, 434, 439, 605
lullabies, 208–9
Lundur, Guðrún of. *See* Árnadóttir, Guðrún
   of Lundur
lygisögur ('lying sagas'), 145–46, 230
lyric poetry: in late medieval period, 54–55;
   seventeenth-century, 201–2; skaldic
   poetry, 5–6

Maðurinn er alltaf einn, 418
Maður og haf, 439
Maður og kona, 295, 305, 320, 561
magical realism, 439, 440, 448
Magnason, Andri Snær, 449–50, 501, 606

Magnus, Saint, 116, 158, 161, 165
Magnúsar saga lagabætis, 87, 99, 116, 120–21
Magnúsdóttir, Magnea of Kleifar, 600
Magnúsdóttir, Þórunn Elfa, 389, 411, 508, 528–29, 531
Magnúss, Gunnar M., 592
Magnús saga Eyjajarls, 161
Magnússon, Árni, 123, 153, 198, 222, 297, 405
Magnússon, Árni of Geitastekkur, 241
Magnússon, Gisli, 244
Magnússon, Guðmundur, 309, 362
Magnússon, Jón of Laufás, rev., 210, 215, 220
Magnússon, Magnús Hj., 386
Magnússon, Sigurður A., 437, 439, 487, 538, 559
Magnússon, Skúli, 229
Magnússon, Þórður of Strjúgur, 224, 512
Mallarmé, Stéphane, 328
Málskrúðsfræði, 29
Mánaðarrit (journal), 520
Mánasigð, 427, 429
Mannveiðihandbókin, 451
mansöngur (lyrical introduction in *rímur*), 57, 59, 132, 238, 512
manuscript collection during Enlightenment, 197–99
"Margrétar kvæði," 511
Margs verða hjúin vís, 531
Margt býr í myrkrinu, 605–6
Marian: miracles, 160, 169; poems, 52, 183
Marie de France, 142
Maríuglugginn, 443
Maríu saga, 52
Marmari, 350, 550
Marxism, 282, 379, 381, 573, 622
Mary, Virgin, 48, 49, 50–51, 52
masculinity: absurdist theater, 569; neoromanticism, 331, 333; popular literature, 459; realism, 314; sexuality, 454; women's writing, 517, 550
materialism: absurdist theater, 566, 567, 568; Icelandic Canadians, 623; 1970s, 488; political engagement, 279, 280, 281; postmodernism, 500; theater, 563
Maurer, Konrad, 124, 298

Mávahlátur, 457
Meðan nóttin líður, 441, 442–43, 542
media, 456, 469, 488, 495, 500
Megas (Magnús Þór Jónsson), 490
Melabók, 80–82
Melkorka journal, 527, 528, 538
memoirs: children, 598–601; children's literature, 588–90; seventeenth-century, 217–19. *See also* autobiographies; biographies
Merlínusspá. See *Prophetiae Merlini*
metaphor: in Eddic poetry, 7; in Legendary sagas, 150; in nineteenth-century literature, 264, 290, 346; in post-Reformation literature, 188, 202, 204, 212, 213; in *rímur*, 59; in Sagas of Icelanders, 122, 129–30; in skaldic poetry, 31, 33, 34–35, 40; in twentieth-century literature, 368, 431, 436, 473, 477, 491, 500; in women's literature, 346, 431, 504, 517, 518, 536, 540, 543, 544, 546, 549–50
metatexts: historical fiction, 418; modernism, 394, 428; plays, 553; postmodernism, 440; urbanism, 445
meters, 3–7; *dróttkvætt*, 30, 41; *ferskeytt*, 56; *fornyrðislag*, 4–5; *hrynhent*, 37–38, 43, 48, 51; *kviðuháttur*, 33; *Liljulag*, 51; *ljóðaháttur*, 4, 13, 46; *málaháttur*, 24; *runhent*, 34, 45–46; *stafhent*, 56; *stuðlar* in, 4; *töglag*, 36; *vikivaki*, 180. *See also* Eddic poetry
meters, catalog of. See *Háttalykill*
"Meyjarmissir," 202
middle class: children's literature, 588; modernism, 536; realism, 317; urbanism, 389; women, 540
Miðnætursólborgin, 447–48
Migration period, 18
Milli lækjar og ár, 531
Milli skinns og hörunds, 579
Milton, John, 234–35, 300
Mínervudóttir, Guðrún Eva, 467
Mírmanns saga, 139, 145
missionary work, 83
"Mitt var starfið," 506
modernism, 426–30; forerunners to, 391–96; historical fiction, 419; and Laxness,

373–74; 1960s, 423–26; 1930s, 397, 400, 402; 1920s, 368; post–World War I, 362; rural fiction, 410; rural to urban change, 415; in women's writing, 534–37, 539

modernist revolt, 430–34

Móðir, kona, meyja, 546

"Móðir mín í kví, kví," 512

"Móðurást," 286

Molière, 265, 552, 553, 577

Møller, Peter Ludvig, 272

monasteries: annal writing, 95; centers of learning, 44, 48, 68, 70, 71; Reformation, 178; saints' lives, 160, 165–66, 170

Montesquieu, Charles de, climate theory of, 263, 332

Morðið í Stjórnarráðinu, 458

Mörður Valgarðsson (play), 349

Morgunþula í stráum, 462

Morkinskinna, 99–100, 111–13, 124, 162

Möttuls saga, 142, 143, 145

multiculturalism, 630, 640. *See also* cultural diversity

Munka-Þverá, 71

Músin sem læðist, 421

Myndin af heiminum, 468

Myndir, 329, 347, 524

Mýrarenglarnir falla, 452

Mýrdal, Jón, 413

mythological elements: in heroic poetry, 20; Prose Edda, 151–58; in skaldic poetry, 31, 32

mythological poetry, 10–14

"Náð," 51, 52

Narfi, eður sá narraktugi biðill, 552–53

narrative poetry: late medieval period, 55–59; middle ages, 55–59. See also *rímur*

national identity, 405–7, 468, 553, 556

nationalism, xi, 336–39; in Icelandic Canadian settlements, 612; 1920s, 365

National Theater: absurdist theater, 568; beginnings, 555, 556; modernism, 429; new playwrights, 579, 580, 581, 584; 1920–1960, 563; since 1975, 572, 575, 576, 577, 578; women playwrights, 582–83

naturalist literature, 278, 317, 323, 374

nature poetry: Age of Learning, 199–201; Atom poets, 479; national romanticism, 269; neorealism, 491; poetry since 1940, 484; postmodernism, 499, 500; realism, 317; since 1940, 473; translations, 303. *See also* pastoral poetry

nature writing: Enlightenment, 229–30; seventeenth-century, 203–6

Nautnastuldur, 454

neo-Latin poetry, 203

neorealism: modernist revolt, 430–34; 1960s, 434–36; poetry since 1940, 488–94; postmodernism, 495; teenage novels, 601, 604

neoromanticism: late nineteenth-century, 330–39; in poetry, 339–47

New Iceland colony, 612–13, 615

New York, 489

Nexø, Martin Anderson, 410

Nibelungenlied, 3

Niðurstigningar saga, 52, 53

"Niðurstigningarvísur," 52, 53

Nietzsche, Friedrich: decadence, 352, 354–55; and Laxness, 371; nationalism, 338; neoromanticism, 331–32, 334, 335; 1920s, 367; postmodernism, 441; post–World War I, 362; realism movement, 314; "superman" ideal, 311, 330–35, 340–41, 345, 349, 354, 362; symbolism, 330; Varangians, 349

Night Watch. See *Meðan nóttin líður*

nihilism, 260, 271, 341, 342, 352

Nikulás Bengsson of Munka-Þverá, 68

Nikulás Klím, 222

Nikulás saga erkibiskups, 160, 169

19. júní magazine, 504, 520, 527, 534

Njáls saga, 125, 126, 127; characters, 130, 134, 135, 136; chivalric literature, 144; contemporary issues, 468; as genre, 75; Icelandic Canadians, 621; narrative mode, 130, 131; structure, 133; theater, 557; women's writing, 550; worldview, 138

Njarðvík, Njörður P., 436

Njósnir að næturþeli, 596

Nonni, 590

Nonni (Jón Sveinsson), 589–90, 607

Nordal, Sigurður: on Danish national histories, 115; decadence, 352–53; Icelandic Canadian writing, 608, 609; and Laxness, 371, 373; nationalism, 337; neoromanticism, 340; ruralism, 365, 366–68; symbolism, 329; theater, 561, 562; on women, 506, 508, 524

Norðan við stríð, 414

"Noregskonungatal," 33, 99

Nornadómur, 465, 603

Nóttin hefur þúsund augu, 458

novels. *See* fiction

Númarímur, 238

nursery rhymes, 208–9, 329, 477, 534.

Nýársnóttin, 554–56

Nýjársnótt(in), 300, 554–56

Næturluktin, 444

Obstfelder, Sigbjørn, 531

occasional poetry, 185–87, 203, 205, 207–8, 617

Oddaverjaannáll, 94

Oddaverjar family, 33, 67, 68, 71, 99, 102, 121

Oddaverja þáttur, 167

Oddi, 68, 69, 71

"Oddrúnargrátr" (in Codex Regius), 22, 509

Oddur Snorrason, 106, 146, 159, 161, 163

Odin: in early Christian poetry, 43; in Eddic poetry, 6, 10, 14, 15, 509; in Legendary Sagas 139, 147, 150–51; in modern Icelandic literature, 440, 545; in Norse pantheon, 13–14, 30; in Old Icelandic historiography, 65, 114; in the Prose Edda, 155, 509; in *rímur*, 59; in Sagas of Icelanders, 136; in skaldic poetry, 33–35, 40

Óður einyrkjans, 391

"Ódysseifur hinn nýi," 329, 341

Oehlenschläger, Adam, 261, 264

öfugmælavísur (topsy-turvy poems), 185, 206

Og enn spretta laukar, 528

Og það var vor, 545

Olaf, St.: ballads about, 62–63; Kings' sagas, 99; poems about, 44, 53, 56, 58; and Snorri Sturluson, 104–5

Ólafs ríma Haraldssonar, 56, 58

Olafssaga (Saga Ólafs Þórhallasonar), 240, 244, 248–49

Ólafs saga helga: historical works, 104; national histories, 103; rural to urban change, 417; and Snorri Sturluson, 108, 110; sources, 58

Ólafs saga helga hin sérstaka: history, 106; national histories, 101, 103, 115; and Snorri Sturluson, 105, 110–11

Ólafs saga Tryggvasonar, 105–6

Ólafs saga Tryggvasonar hin mesta, 102, 121. See also *Saga Óláfs Tryggvasonar* (Oddur Snorrason)

Ólafsson, Bragi, 446–47, 498

Ólafsson, Eggert, 229, 230–33, 236–37

Ólafsson, Einar, 488

Ólafsson, Jón (1850–1916), 281, 300, 312

Ólafsson, Jón (Indíafari), 219–20

Ólafsson, Jón of Grunnavík (1705–79), 222

Ólafsson, Magnús of Laufás, 153–54, 181, 185–86, 191–92

Ólafsson, Ólafur (Olavius) (1741–88), 223, 227

Ólafsson, Ólafur Jóhann (Olaf Olafsson) (b. 1962), 458

Ólafsson, Páll, 282, 292

Ólafsson, Stefán: and baroque poetry, 201–2; historiography, 193; humor, 207; lullabies and nursery rhymes, 208, 209; poems on pleasures, 210; polemical poems, 210, 211–12; religious poetry, 217

"Óláfs vísur" (Gunni Hallsson), 53

Ólafur Haraldsson (Saint Olaf). *See* Olaf, St.

Ólafur Þórðarson *hvítaskáld*, 29, 38, 39, 71, 93

Ólandssaga, 244, 247, 249–50

old age poetry (*ellikvæði*), 55, 213

"Ólund," 273–74

Ómarsdóttir, Kristín, 448–49, 452, 454, 497, 583

101 Reykjavík, 466, 467

Óp bjöllunnar, 427–28

"Óráð," 355, 392

Orðspor daganna, 547–48

Orgelsmiðjan, 422
Orkneyinga saga, 108, 115–16
Ormarr ørlygsson, 349
Örvar-Odds saga, 27, 148–49
Óskarsson, Baldur, 486
Óskastjarnan, 578
Ottósson, Hendrik, 595–96
Ovid, 70, 141, 142, 236

Pabbastrákur, 584
Páll Jónsson, 68, 167
Pálmholt, Jón of, 422
Páls saga, 88, 89, 90, 93, 166
Pálsson, Bjarni, 229–30
Pálsson, Gestur, 253, 295, 312–16, 320
Pálsson, Gunnar, 233
Pálsson, Ögmundur, 177
Pálsson, Sigurður, 488, 489, 492, 495, 578
Paludan-Müller, Frederik, 272, 302
panegyrics, 158, 163, 201, 522. See also praise
    poetry
Paradísarheimt, 420
Paradise Lost in Icelandic translation, 234–
    35, 300
Paradise Reclaimed. See Paradísarheimt
paradoxes (topsy-turvy poems), 185, 206
"París '68," 493
parody, 206, 510, 518, 532, 561
Passion hymns, 57, 215–17
Passions. See píslarsögur
Passíusálmar (Guðmundur Erlendsson), 215
Passíusálmar (Hallgrímur Pétursson), 214–
    16, 239
pastoral poetry, 201–2. See also nature poetry
Pennaslóðir, 534
People's Theater, 573–74, 579
Peter Comestor, 72, 95
Pétursson, Brynjólfur, 265, 266
Pétursson, Hallgrímur, 213–17; didactic
    poems, 210; humor, 207; nature poetry,
    204; nineteenth-century poetry, 288;
    nursery rhymes, 209; occasional poetry,
    208; polemical poems, 211; popular liter-
    ature, 223; post-Reformation period,
    184; vanitas poems, 212
Pétursson, Hannes: nationalism, 339; neoro-
    manticism, 333, 335, 344; poetry since
    1940, 483–84, 487; symbolism, 329

Pétursson, Jóhann, 411–12
Pétursson, Sigurður, 237–38, 239, 552–53
Pharsalia, 70, 96
Physiologus, 70
pietist movement, 222, 228, 244
Pilkington, Brian, 604
Piltur og stúlka, 294, 320
Piltur og stúlka (play), 561
Pinter, Harold, 564
pioneers (emigrants), 623, 625, 627–30, 637
Píslarsaga Jóns Magnússonar, 220–21
píslarsögur (Passions), 159
Pistillinn skrifaði . . . I, 371
"Plácítusdrápa," 44
Plácítus saga, 44
playwriting: new playwrights, 583–85; since
    1975, 577–78. See also theater
pleasures, poetry about: Bohemianism, 339–
    40; decadence, 352, 354; eighteenth-
    century, 236–37; middle ages, 150;
    Reformation, 178; seventeenth-century,
    208, 210
Poetic Edda (Sæmundar Edda), 7–27, 8, 64,
    147. See also Codex Regius manuscript
poetic realism, 266–71
poetry: Enlightenment period, 231–40; Ice-
    landic Canadian, 615–27; Middle Ages
    period, 1–64; 1930s, 391–403; secular,
    medieval, 53–63; seventeenth-century,
    199–217; since 1940, 471–502; sixteenth-
    century, 185–89; women poets, 504. See
    also baroque: poetry; concrete poetry;
    court poetry; didactic poetry; Eddic
    poetry; heroic poetry; historical poetry;
    lyric poetry; mythological poetry; narra-
    tive poetry; nature poetry; neo-Latin
    poetry; occasional poetry; old age poetry
    (ellikvæði); pleasures, poetry about;
    polemical poetry; praise poetry; religious
    poetry and literature; Sami poetry; sat-
    ire: in poetry; secular poetry; skaldic
    poetry; topographical poetry; vanitas
    poetry
polemical poetry, 210–12, 318, 363
politicization of literature, 380–87
Pontus rímur, 188
Pope, Alexander, translations of, 226, 234,
    300

popular literature: ballads as, 60–63; biographies as, 390, 413, 423; and children's fiction, 595; Eddic poetry as, 9; Enlightenment, 230; 1980–2000, 456–59; nineteenth-century, 254, 306; post–medieval romances, 176, 188, 246–50; post-Reformation, 196–97, 223–25; post-war, 409, 413; *rímur* as, 57, 223–24, 239, 283, 285

postmodernism, 439–43, 487–88, 494–501

postula sögur (Apostles' Sagas), 159

Pound, Ezra, 395

praise poetry, 5, 28, 30, 34. *See also* panegyrics

Prestssaga Guðmundar góða Arasonar, 84, 90

printing presses: introduction of, 176–79, 196; nineteenth-century, 259, 306–7. *See also* publishing

Priscian, 69

Prjónastofan Sólin, 566

proletarian literature, 408

Prophetiae Merlini, 97, 107, 143

Prose Edda. See Edda

prose poetry, 329, 347, 476–77

Prosper's Epigrams, 70

Proust, Marcel, 439

pseudohistories, 75, 93, 96, 123, 144

Pseudo-Turpin Chronicle, 143

publishing: Christmas season, 469–70; Enlightenment, 227, 230, 244; nineteenth-century, 254, 256, 304–7; post–World War II, 406; religious literature, 239; women writers, 504–5. *See also* printing presses

Pullman, Philip, 450, 604

punk movement, 453, 497

Punktur á skökkum stað, 432, 439

Punktur punktur komma strik, 436, 602

queer writing. *See* homosexuality

Rabelais, François, 297

Ragnarök, 10, 12, 199

Ragnarökkur (play), 289

"Ragnarsdrápa," 25, 28, 32

Ragnars saga loðbrókar, 147

Ragnarsson, Kjartan, 578

Ragnheiður Brynjólfsdóttir (daughter of Bishop Brynjólfur Sveinsson). *See* Brynjólfsdóttir, Ragnheiður

Rásir dægranna, 438, 543

rationalism, 239–40. *See also* Enlightenment

Rauðu pennarnir (Red Pens), 380, 406

Rauður loginn brann, 399–400

realism: late nineteenth-century, 309–29; poetic realism, 266–71; women's writing, 537–39. *See also* social realism

Red Stockings movement, 537. *See also* women's rights movement

Reformation, 174–84

"Reginsmál" (in Codex Regius), 20

Regnboginn í póstinum, 455

Reisubók (Ólafur Egilsson), 218–19, 220

Reisubók Jóns Ólafssonar Indíafara, 219–20

religious poetry and literature: devotional reading, 221–22; eighteenth-century, 239–40; influence on elegiac lays, 22; middle ages, 43–53; and skaldic poetry, 31, 35–36

Resensannáll, 94, 95

Reykholt, 102, 104

Reykjarfjarðarbók manuscript, 84, 85, 170

Reykjavík: in children's fiction, 591–92, 594, 596, 600, 604; as cultural centre, 228–29, 255–59, 365, 404, 459, 552, 579, 609; and journalism, 306, 312; in literature, 320–21, 323, 361–62, 373, 388–90, 397–98, 408, 411, 413–16, 421, 434–36, 437, 443–46, 447, 451, 453, 459–61, 465–67, 483–84, 486, 521, 529, 531, 538, 541, 599; migration to, 405, 413–16, 563; and theater, 552–53, 556, 563, 573, 580

Reykjavík Theater Company, 555, 556–57, 560, 563, 572, 578

rhetoric, classical, 70, 72–73

Richard of Saint Victor, 72

Richardsdóttir, Þórdís, 548–49

Richardson, Samuel, 395

Richter, Guðlaug, 600, 603

Riddarar hringstigans, 443, 460

riddarasögur. See Knights' Sagas

riddles, 27, 130, 298

"Rígsþula" (in Codex Regius), 10, 14

rímur: eighteenth-century, 237–39; late middle ages, 55–59; nineteenth-century, 254; and women, 512–13. *See also* popular literature

Rímur af Núma kóngi Pompólassyni, 238

Rímur af Svoldarbardaga, 238

Rímur af Tristrani og Indiönu, 237, 238, 285

Rit þess konunglega íslenska lærdómslistafélags (Journal of the Icelandic Society for the Art of Learning), 227

Rocky Horror Picture Show, 575

Rögnvaldur kali, 38, 116

Rollantsrímur, 512

romances: Enlightenment, 245–47. *See also* Knights' Sagas (*riddarasögur*); Legendary Sagas (*fornaldarsögur*); popular literature; *rímur*

Roman literature. *See* Classical literature; Latin language

romanticism: late nineteenth-century, 308; nineteenth-century, 251–55, 260–67; 1920s, 367; women's writing, 515–18

romantisme, 271–76

Romeo and Juliet, 304, 554

Rómverja saga, 70, 96

"Rósa," 51

Rousseau, Jean Jacques, 246

runes: in magic, 16, 197, 199; runic script, 65; runology, 191

rural fiction, 295, 347, 349, 374, 388, 407–10, 413–417, 419, 432, 435, 440, 444, 457, 461–62, 465, 480, 484, 486, 522, 529, 579, 592, 596

rural idyll, 232

ruralism, 338, 365–67, 374, 388, 444

rural to urban change, 404, 413–17

Rydberg, Viktor, 395

Sá ég svani, 530

Saga af stúlku, 453

Saga Borgarættarinnar, 349. See also *Af Borgslægtens Historie*

Saga Eldeyjar Hjalta, 290

Saga Haralds harðráða, 112–13

Sagan af bláa hnettinum, 449–50, 606

Sagan af Heljarslóðarorrustu, 296, 306

Sagan af Hinrik heilráða, 247

Sagan af Mána fróða, 246

Sagan af Marroni sterka, 246

Sagan af Parmes Loðinbirni, 245–46

Sagan af Thomas Jones, 246

Sagan hans Hjalta litla, 593

Sagan öll, 436

Saga of the Confederates. See *Bandamanna saga* (Sagas of Icelanders)

Saga Óláfs Tryggvasonar (Oddur Snorrason), 146, 161, 163–65. See also *Ólafs saga Tryggvasonar hin mesta*

Saga Óláfs Þórhallasonar (*Olafssaga*), 240, 244, 248–49

Sagas of Icelanders (*Íslendingasögur*), 122–39; as genre, 75–76; law codes in, 66–67; personal poetry in, 29; in settlement narratives, 82, 83; skaldic poetry, 41; sources for *rímur*, 58

sagnadansar. See ballads

sagnakvæði. See folk poetry

saints' lives, 73, 75, 160, 165–67

Salige er de enfoldige, 361–62

Sálin vaknar, 322, 363

Salka Valka, 381–84, 386

Sallust, translations of, 70, 72, 94, 96

Sálmurinn um blómið, 390, 412

Salt og rjómi, 548

Salverson, Laura Goodman, 636–40

Samastaður í tilverunni, 437, 543, 550

Sambýli, 322, 363, 364

Sambýlisfólk, 529

Sami poetry, 481

Samsons saga fagra, 140, 145

Samúelsson, Guðjón, 365, 461

"Sandy Bar," 625

Sárt brenna gómarnir, 528

Sartre, Jean-Paul, 402

satire: in emigrant literature, 625, 629, 631–32; in poetry, 12–13, 54–55, 178, 180, 206, 221–22, 223, 232, 238, 368; in prose literature, 134, 148, 221–22, 294, 301, 369, 424, 426, 439, 466; in theater, 552, 559–60, 563–70, 578–81, 584; in women's literature, 535, 536

Saxo Grammaticus, 26, 146

Scandinavianism, 274, 287, 378

Schiller, Friedrich von, translations of, 289, 553, 554

science fiction, 457
Scott, Walter, Sir, 295, 303, 590
scriptoria, 71, 160. *See also* monasteries
secular poetry: in middle ages, 53–63; sixteenth-century, 185–88, 193–94
secular writing at centers of learning, 71
senna (flyting), 13, 18
sermo humilis (low style), 98, 110, 129
sermons, 55, 158, 214, 221–22, 251
sexuality, 33, 369–70, 392–93, 446, 449, 452–56, 538, 603
Shakespeare, William, 304, 439, 481, 553, 555, 558
short stories: for children, 595; immigrant fiction, 627–29, 632–33; middle ages, 82, 112; minimalism, 446, 448–49; modernism, 419, 424–25, 431–32; neorealism, 434, 442–43; neoromanticism, 347; 1980s, 455–56, 461, 463; nineteenth-century, 293–94, 303, 305; realism, 312, 321, 323–25, 372, 374, 409, 418; realist revolt, 369; rural to urban change, 389; Varangians, 350; women, 515, 519–21, 523, 526–28, 531, 534, 536–37, 539, 542. *See also* fiction
Síðasta orðið, 543
Síðasti bærinn í dalnum, 561
Síðasti víkingurinn, 555
"Síðsumarskvöld," 524
Sigfúsdóttir, Gréta, 541
Sigfúsdóttir, Kristín, 374, 505, 526–27, 561
Sigfússon, Hannes, 475, 477, 479, 481, 494
Sigga *skálda*. *See* Jónsdóttir, Sigríður
Sighvatur Þórðarson, 36–37, 37, 162
Sigling, 427
Siglingin mikla, 416
"Sigrdrífumál" (in Codex Regius), 20, 509
Sigríður Eyjafjarðarsól, 555
Sigurðardóttir, Ásta, 419, 421, 536–37
Sigurðardóttir, Fríða Á., 441, 442–43, 504, 542
Sigurðardóttir, Ingibjörg, 457
Sigurðardóttir, Jakobína, 539–41; modernism, 423; modernist revolt, 432, 433; postmodernism, 440; publishing patterns, 504; rural discourse, 422; and women, 506–7, 508

Sigurðardóttir, Ólöf of Hlaðir, 345, 508, 521–23, 525, 549–50
Sigurðardóttir, Ragna, 447, 448, 451, 452
Sigurðardóttir, Steinunn: neorealism, 489; postmodernism, 441, 495; sexuality, 455–56; women's writing, 541, 543–44, 545
Sigurðardóttir, Þórunn, 581–82, 604
"Sigurðarkviða skamma" (in Codex Regius), 21, 22
Sigurðarson, Dagur, 486
Sigurðsson, Birgir, 577–78
Sigurðsson, Einar of Eydalir: historiography, 191; occasional poems, 186; post-Reformation period, 183; in *Vísnabók*, 181
Sigurðsson, Ingimar Erlendur, 422
Sigurðsson, Jóhann Gunnar, 340, 342, 354
Sigurðsson, Jón, 258, 278, 410
Sigurðsson, Jón of Kaldaðarnes, 410
Sigurðsson, Ólafur Jóhann, 414–15, 458, 474
Sigurðsson, Sigurður of Arnarholt: decadence, 354; modernism, 426; modernist revolt, 434; neoromanticism, 331, 334, 340, 342; realism, 326; rural discourse, 421
Sigurður the Blind of Fagradalur, 51, 53
Sigurjónsson, Hávar, 584
Sigurjónsson, Jóhann: decadence, 354; modernism, 535; nationalism, 339; neoromanticism, 333, 340–42; plays, 556–57, 558, 559, 560; realism, 323; Varangians, 348–49
Sigurjónsson, Steinar: minimalism, 448; modernism, 423, 426, 427, 430; rural discourse, 421
Silfurkrossinn, 606
Silfurtúnglið, 566
Silkikjólar og vaðmálsbuxur, 374
Sillanpää, F.E., 410
Símonarson, Birgir Svan, 491, 495, 501
Símonarson, Ólafur Haukur, 434, 436, 493, 495, 579–80
Sjálfstætt fólk, 338, 383–85, 388, 581
Sjödægra, 473
Sjón (Sigurjón B. Sigurðsson), 447, 448, 451–52, 454, 497

Skaalholt, 375. See also *Skálholt*
Skaftadóttir, Ingibjörg, 520
Skafti Þoroddsson, 43–44
skald (court poet), 5, 28
Skáldanótt, 584
Skáldatal, 28
Skald-Helga *rímur*, 58
skaldic poetry, 27–43, 122; audience of, 31–32, 38; characteristics of, 5–7, 29–31; in Christian poetry, 44, 45; diction of, 54, 55; influence on later poets, 185, 231; in Prose Edda, 153, 157; relation to Eddic poetry, 9; and *rímur*, 56, 57–59, 239. See also *dróttkvætt* (court meter)
Skáldskaparmál (Prose Edda), 152–54, 157
Skáld-Sveinn, 55, 212
Skálholt, 318, 351, 375–76, 560
Skálholt (diocese): Bishops' sagas, 89–90; center of learning, 68, 71, 175; eighteenth-century, 229; historical writing, 77, 94; post-Reformation period, 183, 191; Reformation, 177–79; saints' lives, 166; seventeenth-century, 196, 198
Skálholtsannáll, 94
Skarðsárannáll, 191
Skarðsárbók, 80
Skaufhalabálkr, 59
"Skeggkarls kvæði," 511
Skíðaríma, 59, 172
Skikkju saga. See *Möttuls saga*
Skipin sigla, 426
Skírnir journal, 256, 305, 329, 339, 366, 525, 538
"Skírnismál" (in Codex Regius), 10, 14, 509
Skjaldbakan kemst þangað líka, 580
Skjaldhamrar, 566, 570, 571
Skjöldunga saga, 97, 114
Skollaleikur, 573
Skugga-Sveinn (play), 554–55, 556, 570
Skúlason, Þorlákur, bishop, 191, 198
Skurðir í rigningu, 461
Slaður og trúgirni, 552
slang. See colloquialisms and slang
Snaran, 432, 540
"Snjáfjallavísur," 200
Snorrabraut 7, 411, 529
Snorri á Húsafelli, 465

Snorri *goði* (the Chieftain) Þorgrímsson, 136, 268
Snorri Markússon, 80
Snorri Sturluson: center of learning, 71; early women's writing, 509; education at, 68; in Enlightenment, 231; genres, 75; handbook on poetics, 69–70; histories, 73, 76, 100, 101–11, 114–16; kings' biographies, 120, 121; Kings' sagas, 99; Legendary Sagas, 26; Sagas of Icelanders, 124, 132; skaldic poetry, 28, 38, 39; as source, 58; sources, 10, 33, 57; in *Sturlunga Saga*, 85; translations of pseudohistorical works, 96; in *Vísnabók*, 181. See also *Edda* (Snorri Sturluson); *Heimskringla* (Snorri Sturluson)
Snót, 282, 517
Snækóngsrímur, 224, 512
social criticism: Icelandic Canadian literature, 620, 622, 629, 638; 1970s poetry, 488; political engagement, 280; postmodernism, 498; realism, 311, 322, 325
social democracy, 313, 317, 363, 380
social realism: decadence, 356; 1930s, 381, 383, 386; poetry since 1940, 473; political engagement, 281, 282; popular literature, 457; realism, 309, 321; theater, 577; women's writing, 527, 529, 538
Sögur Rannveigar, 322, 323, 364
Sögur til næsta bæjar, 455, 543
Sögur úr sveitinni, 526
Sólarblíðan books, 605
Sólarferð, 568–69
"Sólarljóð," 46–47, 172
Sóleyjarsaga, 411
"Sonatorrek," 40
Söngvar förumannsins, 352, 391
"Söngvar til jarðarinnar," 484
Sonur skóarans og dóttir bakarans, 564–65
"Sorg," 329–30
Spaks manns spjarir, 368
"Spanish" killings (*Spánverjavíg*), 187, 199
spelling and orthography, Icelandic, xi, 65
spiritualism, 322–23, 363, 527, 556
Spor í sandi, 535
Staðarhóls-Páll (Páll Jónsson), 187–88, 202, 212

Stálnott, 447, 451, 454

Stefánsson, Davíð: modernism, 391–92; neoromanticism, 308, 352–56; 1930s poetry, 397; plays, 561–62

Stefánsson, Halldór, 409, 419

Stefánsson, Hreiðar, 599

Stefánsson, Jón Kalman, 461

Steingrímsson, Jón, rev., 242–44, 326

Steinn Steinarr (Aðalsteinn Kristmundsson), 395, 397, 399–402, 472, 480

Steinsdóttir, Kristín, 605

Steinsson, Guðmundur, 524, 568–69, 577

Steinunn Refsdottir, 41–42

Stellurímur, 237–38

Stephansson, Stephan G., 318–19, 336, 621–25

Stephensen, Magnús: aesthetics, 283–84; Enlightenment, 229; Icelandic culture, 230; religious poetry, 239–40; and women's writing, 513

Stephensen, Marta, 513

Stjórn I, 72, 161

Stjórn II, 161

Stjórn III, 72, 97, 161

Stjórnlaus lukka, 466

Stofnunin, 419

Stokkhólmsrella, 241

"Stormur," 314, 331

storytelling: in children's literature, 599; in emigrant literature, 617, 635; Enlightenment, 226, 228, 240–41; and folktales, 299; influence on eighteenth-century literature, 243, 245, 247; influence on medieval romances, 139; influence on post–medieval poetry, 208, 215, 220, 294; influence on Sagas of Icelanders, 125, 129; in men's literature, 459–60; middle ages, 73–75; in twentieth-century literature, 417, 428, 446, 451, 502; in women's literature, 456, 635

Straumrof, 561–66

stream of consciousness technique, 425, 543

Strengleikar, 142–43

Strindberg, August, 561, 566

Strompleikurinn, 566

Ströndin. See *Livets Strand*

Stúlka, 516–18, 618

Stúlka með fingur, 465

Stúlkan í skóginum, 445, 541

Stundarfriður, 568

Sturla í Vogum, 387

Sturla Þórðarson: annals, 95; Bishops' sagas, 90; as historian, 7; Kings' sagas, 116, 120–21; Knights' sagas, 141; *Kristni saga*, 84–87; saints' lives, 170; settlement narrative, 80–83; skaldic poetry, 28, 38; on Snorri, 102, 109, 152; storytelling, 74. See also *Íslendinga saga*

Sturlubók, 80, 82, 84

Sturlungar family: annals of, 95; center of learning, 71; family history, 71; nationalism, 337; power of, 67; and Prose Edda, 152; writings of, 38

Sturlunga saga, 75, 84–88, 90

Sturlu saga, 84–85, 167

Sturlu þáttur, 74, 84, 120

Styrmir Kárason, 81, 118–19, 163

Styrmisbók, 81, 82

sublime, 283, 412

Súkkulaði handa Silju, 569, 581

Sú kvalda ást sem hugarfylgsnin geyma, 454

Sumargjöf handa börnum, 588

Sundur og saman, 603

Sunnudagskvöld til mánudagsmorguns, 419, 536

superman. See Nietzsche, Friedrich

supernatural motifs: ballads, 61, 62; Eddic poetry, 18, 20; Enlightenment, 240; fantasy fiction, 448; national histories, 104; nature writing, 201, 230; poetic realism, 271; romances, 139; Sagas of Icelanders, 131; theater, 554, 555

surrealism, 358, 372, 396, 428, 451, 478, 484, 497, 536, 547

Svafár, Jónas, 478

Svanurinn, 446

Svarfdæla saga, 126, 510

Svartar fjaðrir, 353–54, 391

Svartfugl, 378–79

Svartur hestur í myrkrinu, 546–47

Svefnhjólið, 444

Sveinbjarnarson, Þorgeir, 482

Sveinsson, Brynjólfur, bishop: and Hallgrímur Pétursson, 213, 214; and Jón

Guðmundsson, 199, 200; manuscript collection, 198
Sveinsson, Guðjón, 576
Sveinsson, Jón. *See* Nonni
Sveinsson, Sigurbjörn, 589, 590, 607
Sverris saga, 99, 116–19, 153
Svínfellingar family, 67, 127
Svínfellinga saga, 84–85
"Svipdagsmál," 17–18
Svipmyndir, 527
Svört messa, 422
symbolism movement, 300, 327–28, 331, 523
Systurnar frá Grænadal, 521
Sælir eru einfaldir, 349, 362. See also *Salige er de enfoldige*
Sæmundsson, Tómas, 256–57, 265, 284–85, 301
Sæmundur Sigfússon the Wise, 68, 100

Tangi cycle, 424–25, 427, 435
Taoism, 411, 420, 433, 566
teenage novels, 601–4
television: children's literature, 590; popular literature, 457; postmodernism, 500; teenage novels, 602; theater, 563–64, 573, 582; women's writing, 546
"Temple of Fame," 234, 300
Tengdamamma, 526, 561
Tennyson, Alfred, Lord, 395
Terkelsen, Søren, 201
theater, 552–85: absurdist theater, 563–70; beginnings, 552–56; early twentieth-century, 556–60; 1920–1960, 560–63; postmodernism, 581; since 1975, 571–85
Theodoricus the Monk: foreign influence, 72; influence of, 68; Norwegian national histories, 100; St. Olaf, 162, 164
13. krossferðin, 567–68
30th Generation, 389
Thomas Becket of Canterbury, Saint, 169
Thomsen, Grímur: folk tales, 300; poetry, 289, 292; romanticism, 308; translations, 303, 304
Thorarensen, Bjarni: aesthetics, 283–84, 288; nineteenth-century culture, 256; poetic realism, 269, 270, 271; poetry,

289; realism, 326; romanticism, 251–53, 260–67; romantisme, 274, 275; translations, 234; women's writing, 518
Thoroddsen, Jón (1818–1868): fiction, 294–95; political engagement, 282; realism, 320; romantisme, 273; ruralism, 374; women's writing, 517
Thoroddsen, Jón (1898–1924), 393, 394, 553, 561
Thoroddsen, Theodora, 329, 393, 505–6, 525–26
Thorsson, Guðmundur Andri, 467
Thorsteinsson, Steingrímur: aesthetics, 287; nineteenth-century culture, 259; poetry, 289–90, 292; political engagement, 278, 280, 281, 283; publication, 306; realism, 317; romanticism, 308; stories, 294; translations, 302–4
thrillers, 306, 409, 457, 458, 566, 579, 594
Tíbrá journal, 519
Tieck, Ludwig, 298, 301, 302
"Til hinna ófæddu," 521–22
Tímarit þjóðræknisfélags Íslendinga í Vesturheimi (journal), 531
Tímaþjófurinn, 441, 455, 541, 543
"Tófu kvæði," 511
Tólf konur, 431, 539–40
Tolkien, J.R.R., 448, 450, 604
Tolstoy, Leo, 351, 395, 409, 544
Tómasdóttir, Guðrún. *See* Fell, Arnrún of (Guðrún Tómasdóttir)
Tómas frændi, 520
Tómas Jónsson metsölubók, 423–26, 427
Tómas saga erkibiskups, 169, 171
Tómas Þórarinsson, 92
topographical poetry, 185–86, 205
topsy-turvy poems (*öfugmælavísur*), 185, 206
Torfason, Mikael, 453–54
Tötra í Glettingi, 438, 543
translations: classic literature, 70, 72, 94, 96; Enlightenment authors, 226, 233–36, 241, 256; 1980–2000, 438–43, 454; nineteenth-century, 300–304, 320; post–World War II, 409–10
Trausti, Jón (Guðmundur Magnússon), 309, 323, 325–26, 338, 362–63

travel literature: Enlightenment, 241;
eighteenth-century, 240–41; nineteenth-
century, 257, 272, 294; seventeenth-
century, 219–20; twentieth-century, 421,
427, 429, 467–68, 489, 492, 498
"Tristrams kvæði," 63
Tristrams saga og Isöndar, 141, 144, 158
Trójumanna sögur (*Ilias Latina*), 70, 94, 96–
97, 144, 150
Tröllakirkjan, 460
Troll's Cathedral. See *Tröllakirkjan*
Trumban og lútan, 534
Tullin, Christian Br., 233
"Turkish" raid (*Tyrkjarán*), 191, 197, 217,
218
Turnleikhúsið, 429, 439
Twain, Mark, 409
"Týndu hringarnir," 519–20
Tyrkjaránssaga, 218

Úlfs þáttur, 112
Úlfur Uggason, 6, 32
"Um hrörnun Íslands," 186–87
Um Íslands aðskiljanlegar náttúrur, 200
Uncle Tom's Cabin, 520
Undan illgresinu, 597
Undarlegt er að spyrja mennina, 546
Under the Glacier. See *Kristnihald undir Jökli*
Undína (Helga Steinvör Baldvinsdóttir),
618, 629
Undir beru lofti, 325
Undir eldfjalli, 461, 541
Undir gervitungli, 421
Undir Helgahnúk, 371, 396
"Undir Kaldadal," 314–15
Undir kalstjörnu, 437, 599
Undset, Sigrid, 410
"Unglíngurinn í skóginum," 396
Ung ljóð, 546
universal histories (*veraldarsögur*), 93–95
University of Iceland, 364
Uppstigning, 561–62
Upp við fossa, 323–24
urbanism, 367, 443–46; in fiction, 410–13;
urban epics, 459–62. See also Reykjavík
Úr minnisblöðum Þóru frá Hvammi, 414, 528
Útilegumennirnir, 300, 554. See also *Skugga-
Sveinn* (play)

"Vafþrúðnismál" (in Codex Regius), 10, 12,
13, 155
Vaka journal, 373, 394
Vala books, 594
Valdimarsdóttir, Þórunn, 465–66
Valdimarsson, Þorsteinn, 473–74
Valgardson, W. D., 640–41
valkyries: in Eddic poetry, 18, 20, 30; influ-
ence on Sagas of Icelanders, 135
vanitas poetry, 212–13
Varangians, 347–51
Vargatal, 453
Varg í Veum, 361
Vatn á myllu kölska, 434
Vatnsdæla saga, 126
Vatnsenda-Rósa (Rósa Guðmundsdóttir),
514–15
Vefarinn mikli frá Kasmír, 371–74, 383, 388,
396, 406, 420
Vegurinn að brúnni, 416, 417, 421
Vegurinn brennur, 583
Veizla undir grjótvegg, 431, 539, 540
"Vellekla," 34
Veltiár, 528
Veraldar saga, 93–94, 96
veraldarsögur. See universal histories
Verðandi journal, 252, 309
Verksummerki, 543, 544
Vér morðingjar. See *Vi mordere*
vernacular: early women's writing, 510; as
entertainment, 73; foreign influences,
69; historical fiction, 419; late medieval
period, 65; modernism, 426; occasional
poetry, 185; post-Reformation period,
180; saints' lives, 160; *vs.* neo-Latin
poetry, 203
Verne, Jules, 433
Vestur Íslendingar, 609
"Veturinn" (Bjarni Thorarensen), 263, 291,
331
Vídalín, Jón Þorkelsson, bishop, 203, 221
Vídalín, Páll, 222–23
Vídalínspostilla, 221, 222, 225
video: in popular culture, 438, 457; in theatrical productions, 582
Við feðgarnir, 583
Við gluggann, 542

Við langelda, 392
Við sanda, 506, 534, 535
Við sundin blá, 392
Við Urðarbrunn, 465, 603
Vigfússon, Guðbrandur, 90, 299, 511
Víg Kjartans Ólafssonar (play), 517
Vignisson, Rúnar Helgi, 454
Vígslóði, 318, 622–23
Vík á milli vina, 436
Viking Age (c. 800–1066), 9
The Viking Heart, 638–39
vikivakakvæði (carols or dance poems), 63,
    202, 225
vikivakar (dancing songs/steps; sg. *vikivaki*),
    225, 299, 513
Vikivaki (Gunnar Gunnarsson), 378–80
vikivaki meter (carol meter), 180
Vilhelmsson, Hafliði, 435
Vilhjálmsdóttir, Linda, 499
Vilhjálmsson, Thor: Atom poets, 478; his-
    torical fiction, 418–19, 462; minimalism,
    448; modernism, 423, 427–30; post-
    modernism, 439, 440; rural discourse,
    421–22
Vilhjálmsson, Vilhjálmur S., 408, 413
Villibirta, 537–38
Villieldur, 528
Viltu byrja með mér?, 602
Vi mordere (*Vér morðingjar*), 351, 559, 560
Vincent of Beauvais, 95
Vínland saga, 124
Virgil, 203, 232
Vísnabók, 511
Vögguvísa, 411
Völsapáttr, 27
Völsunga saga, 18, 20, 146, 147, 157
Völsungs rímur, 58
Voltaire, François-Marie Arouet, 246, 312
"Völundarkviða" (in Codex Regius), 16–17
"Völuspá" (in Codex Regius), 8, 9, 10–12,
    27, 509
Vopnfirðinga saga, 126, 136
Vör, Jón of, 472
"Vordraumur," 321
Vorið hlær, 529
Vorköld jörð, 408
Vængjasláttur í þakrennum, 443, 460

Walter of Châtillon, translations of, 96, 98
wanderlust: Bohemians, 339; decadence,
    352; neoromanticism, 339–47, 344; Vik-
    ings, 334
Weltschmerz: political engagement, 277;
    romantisme, 271, 274, 276
Wessel, Johan Herman, 226, 238
Western Icelanders. *See* Vestur Íslendingar
Wilde, Oscar, 350
Williams, Tennessee, 564–65
Williams, William Carlos, 580
"Winnipeg Icelander," 626–27
witch burnings, 197, 220
witchcraft, 199, 200, 243
women's literature, 503–51; ballads and
    folktales, 62, 297, 510–12; eighteenth-
    century, 513–15; emigrant writers, 530–
    31, 617; middle ages, 21–22; modern-
    ism, 534–37; origins, 508–10, 516–18;
    playwrights, 581–83; poetry, 507, 512–
    17, 521–23, 531–34, 544–49; realism,
    537–39; respect for, 507–8; restrictions
    on, 504–7, 521–23; *rímur*, 512–13;
    romanticism, 515–18; twentieth-century,
    526–29, 531–34; *þulur*, 523–26
women's magazines, 520
Women's Reading Club of Reykjavik, 505, 520
women's rights movement, 518–20, 534. *See
    also* Red Stockings movement
working class, 408
World Light. *See Heimsljós*
worldview: Atom poets, 476, 479; Christian
    poetry, 43, 47; Eddic poetry, 9; historical
    fiction, 466; literary season, 469; middle
    ages, 49; mythological poetry, 12; Refor-
    mation, 194; Sagas of Icelanders, 137–38
Worm, Ole, 181, 191–92, 193, 200, 202

Yfir heiðan morgun, 494
Yfirvaldið, 436
Ynglinga saga, 33, 105, 114, 124, 157
"Ynglingatal," 33, 107
Yngvars saga víðförla, 127
young adult novels, 601–4

Z-Ástarsaga, 446, 454
Zola, Émile, 410

Það sagði mér haustið, 545, 546
Þangað vil ég fljúga, 547
Þar sem djöflaeyjan rís, 443, 459
þáttur. See þættir (tales)
Þel, 542
Þess engelska Bertholds fábreytilegar Robinsons
    eður lífs og ævi sögur (Berthold), 244
Þetta er ekkert alvarlegt, 542
Þetta var nú í fyllerí, 440
Þiðriks saga, 58, 75, 139, 143, 147, 151
Þjóðolfur of Hvinir, 32, 33, 107
Þjófur í paradís, 414
Þögnin, 446, 448, 455
Þóra frá Hvammi. See Úr minnisblöðum Þóru
    frá Hvammi
Þórarinn loftunga (Praise-tongue), 44, 162
Þórarinsson, Árni (b. 1950), 458
Þórarinsson, Árni (pastor), 390, 412
Þorbjarnarson, Jónas, 498, 500
Þorbjörn hornklofi, 34
Þórðarbók, 80, 81, 82, 99
Þórðar saga kakala, 84
Þórðarson, Agnar, 415, 563, 571
Þórðarson, Þórbergur: biographies, 412–13;
    contemporary issues, 468; historical fic-
    tion, 437; influences on, 297; modern-
    ism, 390–91, 393; nationalism, 339;
    1930s, 402; 1920s, 367, 368–71; rural dis-
    course, 420
Þórður Jónsson, 80
Þórður of Strjúgur, 512. See Magnússon,
    Þórður of Strjúgur
Þorgeirsdóttir, Elísabet, 548
Þorgeirson, Þorgeir, 436, 439
Þorgeirs rímur, 62
Þorgils saga og Hafliða, 74–75, 84, 145

Þorgils saga skarða, 85
Þorláks saga, 166–67, 168
Þorláksson (of Bægisá), Jón, 233–36, 239,
    240, 290, 300, 303
Þorláksson, Björg, 365
Þorláksson, Guðbrandur, bishop, 179, 183,
    186, 195, 511
Þorlákur Þórhallsson, St., 68, 158, 160, 165–
    67
Þormóðsson, Úlfar, 435, 436
Þormóður Kolbrúnarskáld, 41
Þormóður Ólafsson, 93
Þorpið, 472
Þorrakvæði, 205
"Þórsdrápa," 33
Þorsteinn frá Hamri, 423, 429–30, 483, 484,
    494
Þorsteinsdóttir, Guðfinna. See Erla
    (Guðfinna Þorsteinsdóttir)
Þorsteinsson, Indriði G., 414
Þorsteinsson, Jón, 184, 218
Þorsteinsson, Þorvaldur, 449, 450, 583–84
Þorvaldur víðförli, 462
Þráinsson, Þorgrímur, 605–6
Þrastardóttir, Sigurbjörg, 498, 500
Þrjár sólir svartar, 436
Þröskuldur hússins er þjöl, 482, 536
Þrymlur, 58
"Þrymskviða" (in Codex Regius), 10, 13, 58
þulur (sg. þula), 523–26
þættir (tales), 111–12

æskuástir, 524
ættartölur, 84
ævisaga séra Jóns Steingrímssonar, 242–43
ævi Snorra goða, 93

In the *Histories of Scandinavian Literature* series

Volume 1
A History of Danish Literature
Edited by Sven H. Rossel

Volume 2
A History of Norwegian Literature
Edited by Harald S. Naess

Volume 3
A History of Swedish Literature
Edited by Lars G. Warme

Volume 4
A History of Finland's Literature
Edited by George C. Schoolfield

Volume 5
A History of Icelandic Literature
Edited by Daisy Neijmann